MAGRUDER'S

American Government
INTERACTIVE

SAVVAS
LEARNING COMPANY

Social Studies Reimagined

 To start, download the free **BouncePages** app on your smartphone or tablet. Simply search for the BouncePages app in your mobile app store. The app is available for Android and IOS (iPhone®/iPad®).

Make your book come alive! Activate your digital interactivities directly from the page.

To activate myStory videos and lesson flipped videos look for the Bounce icons.

| BOUNCE to Activate My Story Video |
| BOUNCE to Activate Flipped Video |

1. **AIM** your camera over the image so it is easily viewable on your screen.
2. **TAP** the screen to scan the page.
3. **BOUNCE** the page to life by clicking the icon.

ISBN-13: 978-1-418-39161-4
ISBN-10:　　1-418-39161-1

5 2023

Authors, Consultants, Partners

Author

Daniel M. Shea

Daniel M. Shea is Professor and Chair of the Department of Government at Colby College, where he directed the Goldfarb Center for Public Affairs and Civic Engagement from 2012 to 2017. He earned his Ph.D. from the University of Albany, State University of New York. An award-winning teacher, Shea has spearheaded numerous initiatives at Colby and other institutions designed to help young Americans better appreciate their potential to effect democratic change. The author or editor of nearly twenty books and dozens of articles and chapters on the American political process, Shea's research focuses on campaigns and elections, political parties, the politics of scandal, and grassroots activism. His most recent book is *Why Vote? Essential Questions About the Future of Elections in America* (2019). His coauthored volume *The Fountain of Youth* (2007) garnered national attention for its findings on how local party organizations often neglect young citizens. His work on civility and compromise led to the publication of *Can We Talk? The Rise of Rude, Nasty, Stubborn Politics* (2012). Other recent works authored by Shea include *Let's Vote: The Essentials of the American Electoral Process* (2013) and the college text *Living Democracy* (2020). Shea has provided commentary and analysis for a number of media outlets, including *The New York Times, The Wall Street Journal,* FOX News, CNN, *The Washington Post, USA Today,* and Yahoo News.

Magruder's American Government, first published in 1917, is a testament to the authors' faith in American ideals and American institutions. Frank Abbott Magruder's life and work serve as an outstanding example of American patriotism. After Magruder's death in 1949, his student, Bill McClenaghan, authored the text for the next sixty years and poured his own passion for American government into his work. The torch has now been passed to a new author, but the legacies of the previous authors endure through the lives of the students they have taught and inspired.

Program Partner

Constitutional Rights Foundation is a nonprofit, nonpartisan organization focused on educating students about the importance of civic participation in a democratic society. Constitutional Rights Foundation is the lead contributor to the development of the Civic Discussion Topic Inquiries for this program.

Reviewers & Academic Consultants

Magruder's American Government was developed especially for you and your students. We launched our efforts to revise this program with a series of teacher roundtables that shaped our new approach, crafted to ensure your students' mastery of content and skills. A dedicated team, made up of Savvas authors, content experts, and social studies teachers, worked to bring our collective vision into reality.

Savvas would like to extend a special thank you to all of the teachers who helped guide the development of this program. We gratefully acknowledge your efforts to bring to fruition this new approach to teaching and learning American Government—an approach that will prepare American students for college, careers, and active citizenship.

Program Academic Consultants

Murali Balaji
Graduate Diversity Advisor and
    Professional Development
    Supervisor
University of Pennsylvania
Annenberg School for
    Communication
Philadelphia, Pennsylvania

Barbara Brown
Director of Outreach
College of Arts and Sciences
African Studies Center
Boston University
Boston, Massachusetts

William Childs
Professor of History Emeritus
The Ohio State University
Columbus, Ohio

Jennifer Giglielmo
Associate Professor of History
Smith College
Northhampton, Massachusetts

Joanne Connor Green
Professor, Department Chair
Political Science
Texas Christian University
Fort Worth, Texas

Ramdas Lamb, Ph.D.
Associate Professor of Religion
University of Hawaii at Manoa
Honolulu, Hawaii

Huping Ling
Changjiang Scholar Chair Professor
Professor of History
Truman State University
Kirksville, Missouri

Jeffery Long, Ph.D.
Professor of Religion and Asian Studies
Elizabethtown College
Elizabethtown, Pennsylvania

Gordon Newby
Professor of Islamic, Jewish
    and Comparative Studies
Department of Middle Eastern and
    South Asian Studies
Emory University
Atlanta, Georgia

Audrey Peterson
Associate Director of News and
    Information
Brooklyn College
Brooklyn, New York

Mark Peterson
Associate Professor
Department of Asian and Near
    Eastern Languages
Brigham Young University
Provo, Utah

William Pitts
Professor, Department of Religion
Baylor University
Waco, Texas

Benjamin Ravid
Professor Emeritus of Jewish History
Department of Near Eastern and
    Judaic Studies
Brandeis University
Waltham, Massachusetts

Harpreet Singh
College Fellow
Department of South Asian Studies
Harvard University
Cambridge, Massachusetts

Christopher E. Smith, J.D., Ph.D.
Professor
Michigan State University
MSU School of Criminal Justice
East Lansing, Michigan

John Voll
Professor of Islamic History
Georgetown University
Washington, D.C.

Michael R. Wolf
Associate Professor
Department of Political Science
Indiana University-Purdue University
    Fort Wayne
Fort Wayne, Indiana

Magruder's American Government Interactive

American Government is more than the study of the structure and function of government. It's the story of the people who forged that government and the public servants and ordinary citizens who have worked to uphold its principles ever since. See what's new in *Magruder's American Government Interactive.*

Welcome to *Magruder's American Government Interactive!*

Since 1917, *Magruder's American Government* has been the premier high school textbook for American Government classrooms. In this edition, *Magruder's American Government Interactive* becomes the first high school program designed to keep up with the times. With each election cycle and every passing year, *Magruder's American Government Interactive* will be updated with the latest information to show students how the daily changes of government affect their lives.

The Program Includes:

- Full of engaging photographs, infographics, and more, the **Student Edition** is available in both print and digital formats. Based on foundational principles and core concepts that never go out of date, it will become your "go-to" source to help students learn the principles of American Government.

- **Hook & Inspire: Connections to Today** digital teaching resources help educators show students how government is present in their everyday lives.

- **Case Study Connections** examine critical issues in today's world through a current event. Students will use primary sources to discover how key government concepts relate to issues they care about, as well as to other subjects they are studying. They'll learn how to form their own viewpoint and to take action based on those views.

- **Current Content Digital Activities** build citizenship skills while keeping your government program up-to-date! Students will complete quick-hit activities to learn more about the government today and to analyze current trends and data.

SAVVAS **realize.** ™

The digital course is on Realize! Go online to find digital resources.

Connect: Make Learning Personal

CONNECT! Students will begin *Magruder's American Government Interactive* by engaging in the Topic and connecting it to their own lives.

>> **Connections to Today** brings the past to the present. Students will be introduced to a Topic by seeing how government connects to today. Educators will find more resources on the Savvas Realize digital course.

>> Instruction begins with an **Essential Question**. These thought-provoking questions engage students and introduce the Topic.

Topic 2

The Beginnings of American Government

ESSENTIAL QUESTION How much power should a government have?

Painting of George Washington, the first President of the United States

Connections to Today

Government in the thirteen colonies was influenced by British ideas, laws, customs, documents, and institutions. Reaction to British policies and growing colonial unity led to a revolutionary war and ultimately to American independence in the late 1700s.

The government established under the Articles of Confederation had several weaknesses that seriously threatened the future of the new United States.

In 1787, State delegates wrote a new Constitution for the United States that

NBC LEARN

Learn about one of the most important political thinkers in U.S. history, James Madison.

BOUNCE to Activate My Story Video

43

ESSENTIAL QUESTION How much power should a government have?

>> Developed in partnership with NBCLearn, the **My Story** videos help students connect to the Topic content through personal and topical stories related to government.

QUEST!

Inquiry Center

Discover how to become a thoughtful and active citizen. Use the **Inquiry Center** to help students find a project idea, then use the inquiry-based project materials so they can turn their project into action!

INVESTIGATE! *Magruder's American Government Interactive* helps students investigate the Topic story through a number of engaging features as they learn the content.

>> The inviting **Student Edition** teaches core concepts that will never go out of date. Find **leveled lesson summaries** online in the Realize Reader eText.

>> Reinforce key content with **flipped lesson videos** on the Savvas Realize digital course.

>> Connect through Current Events! We've partnered with **Listenwise™** to bring you daily news updates to help bring what's happening outside your classroom into your daily instruction.

>> Feel like you're part of the story with interactive **3-D models, primary sources**, and more.

Synthesize: Practice Knowledge and Skills

SYNTHESIZE! Practice citizenship skills and keep students up-to-date with what's happening in their communities and in their world. Use current content to synthesize key concepts in government while practicing digital literacy skills.

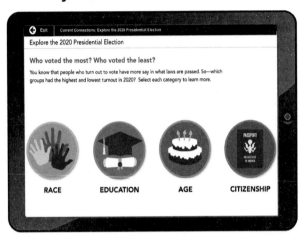

>> Find the latest information with **Current Connections** digital activities. Students will practice civic responsibility by researching the latest facts and trends about American Government with these compelling activities.

Demonstrate: Show Understanding

DEMONSTRATE! Ask students to demonstrate their knowledge of key concepts with various assessments, and use data to customize learning.

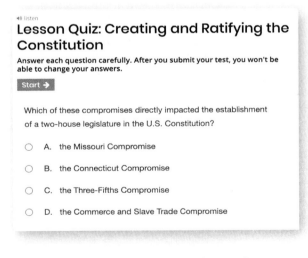

>> **Class and Data** features on Realize make it easy to use students' data to show if time is needed to re-teach.

>> **Assessment:** Demonstrate understanding through Lesson Quizzes, Topic Tests, and Quest Inquiry performance assessments.

Case Study Connections

Examine the principles of government through current issues and events. Case Study Connections are focused on items in the news and how they tie to government and students' everyday lives. Find new Case Study Connections every year on the Realize digital course.

Use a current issue to engage students

>> Take your instruction from the daily headlines. Engage with a **current event** and discover how it is related to students' lives and government.

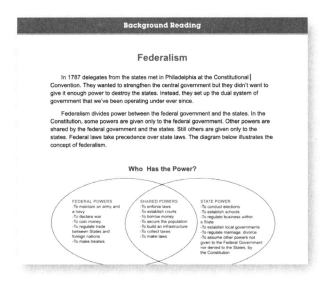

>> Use the **background reading** to establish foundational knowledge.

Create context for current issues with primary sources

>> Engaging **primary and secondary sources** will examine how the current issue connects with students' studies in other areas, including government, history, economics, and geography. Each primary source will provide greater context for students to see how the core concept has endured throughout time.

Develop students' perspectives

>> Take action and help students **develop an informed viewpoint** on current issues and to then take action based on what they've learned and their own views.

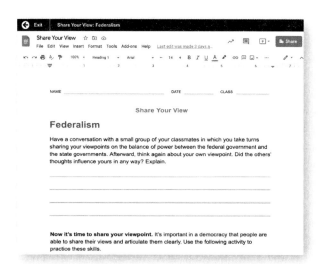

Table of Contents

Topic 1

Foundations of Government and Citizenship   **2**

NBC LEARN myStory Video: John Locke, Natural Rights

Quest Inquiry: Inquiry Center 5

1.1 Principles of Government 6

    Primary Sources: Early Theories on Government 14

1.2 Types of Government 16

1.3 Origins of the Modern Democratic State 23

    Primary Sources: Enlightenment Ideas 31

1.4 The Basics of Democracy 33

Review and Assessment 40

Topic 2

The Beginnings of American Government   **44**

NBC LEARN myStory Video: James Madison. The *Federalist Papers*

Quest Inquiry: Should the Constitution Be Ratified?
(Document-Based Question) 47

2.1 Origins of American Political Ideals 48

    Primary Sources: Groundbreaking English Documents 54

2.2 Independence 56

    Primary Sources: Voices of American Patriots 65

2.3 First Steps 67

2.4 Creating and Ratifying the Constitution 72

Review and Assessment 84

Topic 3 The Constitution   88

ﷺ**NBC LEARN** **myStory Video:** The Fight for Suffrage

Quest Inquiry: Inquiry Center 91

3.1 An Overview of the Constitution 92

3.2 Amending the Constitution 104

    Primary Sources: Virginia Declaration of Rights 113

3.3 Federalism: Powers Divided 115

3.4 The National Government and the States 125

Review and Assessment 138

Topic 4 The Legislative Branch   142

ﷺ**NBC LEARN** **myStory Video:** Loretta Sanchez, A Different Path to Office

Quest Inquiry: The Filibuster (Civic Discussion) 145

4.1 National Legislature Overview 146

4.2 The Two Houses 155

    Primary Sources Supreme Court Cases: *Wesberry* v. *Sanders*, 1964 165

4.3 The Expressed Powers 167

4.4 The Implied and Nonlegislative Powers 179

4.5 Congress at Work—Organization and Committees 190

4.6 Congress at Work—Making Laws 202

    Primary Sources Comparing Viewpoints: Passing the USA PATRIOT Act 216

Review and Assessment 218

Table of Contents

Topic 5

The Executive Branch: The Presidency and Vice Presidency — 222

🔴**NBC LEARN myStory Video:** Theodore Roosevelt and Ronald Reagan, Qualities of a President

Quest Inquiry: Inquiry Center 225

5.1 The Presidency—An Overview 226

5.2 The Vice President and the First Lady 233

5.3 The President's Domestic Powers 237

    Primary Sources Supreme Court Cases: *Youngstown Sheet & Tube Co.* v. *Sawyer,* 1952 250

5.4 The President's Foreign Affairs Powers 252

    Primary Sources Comparing Viewpoints: Desegregation of the Armed Forces 258

Review and Assessment 260

Topic 6

The Executive Branch at Work — 264

🔴**NBC LEARN myStory Video:** NASA, Independent Executive Agency

Quest Inquiry: Inquiry Center 267

6.1 The Federal Bureaucracy 268

6.2 The EOP and the Executive Departments 274

6.3 The Independent Agencies 283

6.4 Foreign Policy Overview 293

    Primary Sources: Presidents on American Foreign Policy 305

6.5 Diplomacy 307

6.6 National Security 318

Review and Assessment 326

Topic 7   The Judicial Branch   330

NBC LEARN myStory Video: Thurgood Marshall and
Brown v. Board of Education

Quest Inquiry: Inquiry Center 333

7.1 The National Judiciary 334

7.2 The Supreme Court 342

     Primary Sources: *Out of Order: Stories of the History of the
     Supreme Court,* Sandra Day O'Connor 349

7.3 The Inferior Courts and the Special Courts 351

Review and Assessment 358

Topic 8   Protecting Civil Liberties   362

NBC LEARN myStory Video: Surveillance and Security

Quest Inquiry: Inquiry Center 365

8.1 The Unalienable Rights 366

8.2 Freedom of Religion 373

8.3 Freedom of Speech and Press 380

8.4 Freedom of Assembly and Petition 390

8.5 Due Process of Law 395

     Primary Sources Supreme Court Cases: *In re Gault,* 1967 400

8.6 Freedom and Security of the Person 402

8.7 Rights of the Accused 414

Review and Assessment 428

Table of Contents

Topic 9 **Citizenship and Civil Rights** **432**

NBC LEARN myStory Video: Minniejean Brown-Trickey, A Sojourn to the Past

Quest Inquiry: Inquiry Center 435

9.1 American Citizenship 436

9.2 Diversity and Discrimination 444

    Primary Sources: The Middle Passage and a Demand for Equality 451

9.3 Equality Before the Law 453

    Primary Sources Supreme Court Cases: *Brown* v. *Board of Education:* Majority Opinion 460

9.4 Federal Civil Rights Laws 462

    Primary Sources: Outlawing Discrimination 468

Review and Assessment 470

Topic 10 **Government by the People** **474**

NBC LEARN myStory Video: Politics and the New Media

Quest Inquiry: Are Special Interests Good or Bad for Democracy? (Document-Based Question) 477

10.1 The History of Voting Rights 478

    Primary Sources: Civil Rights in the 1960s 486

10.2 Your Right to Vote 488

10.3 Voting Trends 496

10.4 The Voting Process 506

10.5 Public Opinion and Polling 514

10.6 Influencing Public Opinion: The Mass Media 527

    Primary Sources Comparing Viewpoints: The Media and the Vietnam War 536

10.7 Understanding Interest Groups 538

Review and Assessment 554

Topic 11   Elections   558

NBC LEARN myStory Video: Political Operatives and Spin Doctors

Quest Inquiry: The Electoral College (Civic Discussion) 561

11.1 Political Parties and What They Do 562

11.2 Nominations 578

11.3 Electing the President 588

Primary Sources Comparing Viewpoints: The Function of
Presidential Debates 605

11.4 Money and Elections 607

Primary Sources Supreme Court Cases: *Citizens United* v. *FEC*, 2010 617

Review and Assessment 620

Topic 12   Government and the Economy   624

NBC LEARN myStory Video: The United States Currency System

Quest Inquiry: Inquiry Center 627

12.1 Types of Economic Systems 628

12.2 Fiscal and Monetary Policy 639

12.3 Financing Government 646

Primary Sources Supreme Court Cases: *Pollock* v. *Farmers'
Loan and Trust Company*, 1895 655

12.4 Spending and Borrowing 657

12.5 The U.S. in a Global Economy 666

Review and Assessment 676

Table of Contents

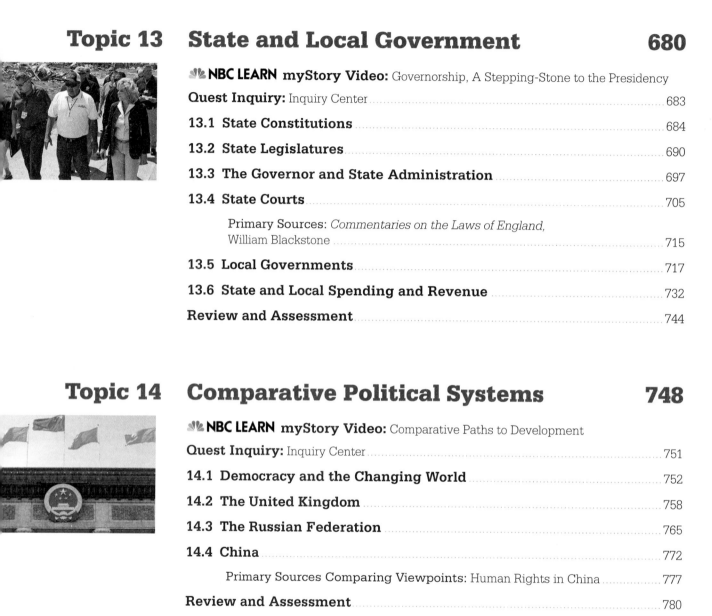

Topic 13 **State and Local Government** **680**

NBC LEARN myStory Video: Governorship, A Stepping-Stone to the Presidency

Quest Inquiry: Inquiry Center 683

13.1 State Constitutions 684

13.2 State Legislatures 690

13.3 The Governor and State Administration 697

13.4 State Courts 705

    Primary Sources: *Commentaries on the Laws of England,*
    William Blackstone 715

13.5 Local Governments 717

13.6 State and Local Spending and Revenue 732

Review and Assessment 744

Topic 14 **Comparative Political Systems** **748**

NBC LEARN myStory Video: Comparative Paths to Development

Quest Inquiry: Inquiry Center 751

14.1 Democracy and the Changing World 752

14.2 The United Kingdom 758

14.3 The Russian Federation 765

14.4 China 772

    Primary Sources Comparing Viewpoints: Human Rights in China 777

Review and Assessment 780

Reference Section   784

United States Constitution Quick Study Guide 784

Annotated United States Constitution 786

Declaration of Independence 808

Primary Sources 810

21st Century Skills 840

Glossary 872

Spanish Glossary 889

Index 910

Acknowledgments 948

Print Resources

Primary Source Excerpts

Declaration of Independence, 1776 .... CF
Aristotle, *Politics* 14
Jean-Jacques Rousseau, *The Social Contract,* 1762 15
Alexander Pope, *Essay on Man,* 1733 16
Baron de Montesquieu, *The Spirit of Laws,* 1748 31
John Locke, *Two Treatises of Government,* 1690 32
Abraham Lincoln, Message to Congress, 1861 36
Abraham Lincoln, Fragment on Government, 1840s 39
Aristotle, *Politics, Book Four, Part XI,* c. 350 B.C.E. 43
Plato, *Republic, Book VIII,* c. 360 B.C.E. 43
Old Oligarch, *The Constitution of the Athenians,* c. 424 B.C.E. 43
Petition of Right, 1628 50
English Bill of Rights, 1689 50
The Magna Carta, 1215 54–55
English Bill of Rights, 1689 55
The Declaration of Rights and Grievances, 1774 59–60
Richard Henry Lee, Resolution of June 7, 1776 61
The Unanimous Declaration of the Thirteen United States of America, 1776 62
Patrick Henry, "Give Me Liberty or Give Me Death," 1775 65
Thomas Paine, *Common Sense,* 1776 66
The United States in Congress Assembled, 1787 70
Edmund Randolph, Constitutional Convention, 1787 74
James Madison, *Notes of Debates in the Federal Convention of 1787* 79
James Madison, *Notes of Debates in the Federal Convention of 1787* 79–80
Constitution of the United States, Article VII, 1789 80
Amos Singletary, Massachusetts Ratifying Convention, 1788 81
Ebenezer Stevens, Quote on Boston Tea Party, 1773 87
Joshua Wyeth, Boston Tea Party, 1773 87
Thomas Hutchinson, Report to the East India Company, 1773 87
Samuel Cooper, 1773 87
United States Constitution, 1789 92
James Madison, *The Federalist* No. 51, 1788 95
U.S. Constitution, Article II, Section 1, 1789 95
James Madison, *Notes of Debates in the Federal Convention of 1787* 96
U.S. Constitution, Article III, Section 1 96
The Federalist No. 78, 1788 101–102
The Federalist No. 51, 1788 103
Virginia Declaration of Rights, 1776 113–114
U.S. Constitution, Article I, Section 8, Clause 18 118
U.S. Constitution, Article VI, Section 2 122
McCulloch v. *Maryland,* 1819 123
McCulloch v. *Maryland,* 1819 123–124
Justice Oliver Wendell Holmes, Collected Legal Papers 124
U.S. Constitution, Article IV, Section 4 126
U.S. Constitution, Article I, Section 8, Clause 1 131
U.S. Constitution, Article IV, Section 2, Clause 2 135
U.S. Constitution, Article IV, Section 2, Clause 1 136
George Mason, speech to the Virginia ratifying convention, 1788 141
Opinion of the Court, *Cohens* v. *Virginia,* 1821 141

Meredith Medoway, "Why the Federal Government, Not States, Should Regulate the Environment," Policy.Mic, 2012........... 141
James M. Burns, et al., *Government by the People* 147
Representative Luther Patrick, on the role of members of Congress 149–150
U.S. Constitution, 20th Amendment, Section 2 151
U.S. Constitution Article I, Section 5, Clause 4 152
U.S. Constitution, Article I, Section 4, Clause 1 159
Woodrow Wilson, Congressional Government 162
Justice Hugo Black, Majority Opinion, *Wesberry* v. *Sanders,* 1964 165
Justice John Marshall Harlan, Dissenting Opinion, *Wesberry* v. *Sanders,* 1964 166
Gibbons v. *Ogden,* 1824 169
U.S. Constitution, Article I, Section 8, Clause 1 170
U.S. Constitution, Article I, Section 9, Clause 4 171
U.S. Constitution, 16th Amendment 171
U.S. Constitution, Article I, Section 8, Clause 8 174
U.S. Constitution, Article I, Section 8, Clause 18 179–180
Fair Labor Standards Act, 1938... 183
Sherrod Brown, *Congress From the Inside* 190–191
U.S. Constitution, Article II, Section 3... 192
Senator Russ Feingold, Senate Floor Debate, 2001 216–217
Senator Orrin Hatch, Senate Floor Debate, 2001 217
Troubled Asset Relief Program (TARP), treasury.gov 221
Medea Benjamin and Arun Gupta, "Time for a Taxpayer Revolt," *The Nation* 221
Simon Johnson, "TARP, the Long Goodbye," *The New York Times*... 221
Robert P. Murphy, "Was TARP Good for the Taxpayers?" Ludwig Van Mises Institution, 2010 221
U.S. Constitution, 25th Amendment, Section 2 234
Theodore Roosevelt, *Theodore Roosevelt: An Autobiography,* 1913... 238
William Howard Taft, *Our Chief Magistrate and His Powers,* 1916 238
U.S. Constitution, Article II, Section 1, Clause 8 242
U.S. Constitution, Article II, Section 2, Clause 2 243
U.S. Constitution, Article II, Section 2, Clause 1 246
U.S. Constitution, Article II, Section 3... 247
Justice Hugo Black, Majority Opinion, *Youngstown Sheet & Tube Company* v. *Sawyer,* 1952........... 250
Chief Justice Fred Vinson, Dissenting Opinion, *Youngstown Sheet & Tube Company* v. *Sawyer,* 1952 251
Executive Order 9981, 1948... 258
General Omar Bradley, statement on military desegregation, 1949 259
Leó Szilárd, Petition to the President of the United States, 1945 263
Harry Truman, letter, 1953... 263
J. Samuel Walker, *Prompt and Utter Destruction* 263
James Madison, *The Federalist Papers,* No. 51, 1788.. 270
William Howard Taft, *Our Chief Magistrate and His Powers,* 1916 282
Speech by President James Monroe to Congress, 1823.. 295
Speech by President Harry S Truman to Congress, 1947 299
George Washington, Farewell Address.. 305–306
Ronald Reagan, "Tear Down This Wall"... 306
Charter of the United Nations, 1945 313
Senator Patrick Leahy (D., Vermont), "Cuts to Foreign Aid Cost the U.S. Globally," *US News,* 2011 329
Representative John Mica (R., Florida), mica.house.gov.. 329
Based on Budget of the United States Government, Fiscal Year 2015... 329
U.S. Constitution, Article III, Section 1.. 335
Sandra Day O'Connor, *Out of Order: Stories of the History of the Supreme Court, 2013* 349–350
Strom Thurmond, (R., South Carolina), Judiciary Committee hearings, 1981............................... 361

Print Resources

Joint Statement, Wayne LaPierre, NRA Executive Vice President, and Chris Cox, Executive Director,
NRA Institute for Legislative Action, 2010 361

Declaration of Independence 367

West Virginia Board of Education v. *Barnette*, 1943 368

Schenck v. *United States*, 1919 368

U.S. Constitution, 14th Amendment, Section 1 370

U.S. Constitution, 9th Amendment 372

U.S. Constitution, 1st Amendment 374

Justice Hugo L. Black, *Engel* v. *Vitale*, 1962 376

Justice Abe Fortas, *Epperson* v. *Arkansas*, 1968 377

Justice Robert H. Jackson, *West Virginia State Board of Education* v. *Barnette*, 1943 379

Chief Justice John Roberts, *Snyder* v. *Phelps*, 2011 381

Justice Oliver Wendell Holmes, *Schenck* v. United States, 1919 382

Justice William J. Brennan, Jr., Texas v. *Johnson*, 1989 384

Justice Felix Frankfurter, *Rochin* v. *California*, 1952 396–397

Justice Abe Fortas, Majority Opinion, *In re Gault*, 1967 400

Justice Potter Stewart, Dissenting Opinion, *In re Gault*, 1967 401

Civil Rights Act of 1866 403

Justice Potter Stewart, *Jones* v. *Mayer*, 1968 404

U.S. Constitution, 2nd Amendment 404

U.S. Constitution, 5th Amendment 416

U.S. Constitution, 6th Amendment 418

U.S. Constitution, 8th Amendment 422

Justice Potter Stewart, *Gregg* v. *Georgia*, 1976 424

William J. Brennan, former U.S. Supreme Court Justice, 1996 424

Chief Justice John Roberts, Opinion of the Court, *McCutcheon* v. *FEC*, 2014 431

Justice Stephen Breyer, Dissenting Opinion, *McCutcheon* v. *FEC*, 2014 431

Shaun McCutcheon, "The System Works—and Donald Trump Proves It," *The Daily Caller*, 2015 431

U.S. Constitution, 14th Amendment, Section 1 437

Thomas E. Patterson, *The American Democracy* 446

Declaration of Sentiments, 1848 449

Olaudah Equiano, *The Interesting Narrative of the Life of Olaudah Equiano*, 1789 451–452

Declaration of Sentiments and Resolutions, 1848 452

Chief Justice Earl Warren, *Brown* vs. *Board of Education*, 1954 455

Justice Joseph P. Bradley, Concurring Opinion, *Bradwell* v. *Illinois*, 1873 457–458

Chief Justice Earl Warren, Opinion of the Court, *Brown* v. *Board of Education*, 1954 460–461

Title IX of the 1972 Education Amendments 468

Americans with Disabilities Act, 1990 469

Federation for American Immigration Reform (FAIR), "Immigration, Labor Displacement and the American Worker" 473

U.S. Chamber of Commerce, "Immigration Myths and Facts" 473

Organizing for Action, "Comprehensive Immigration Reform" 473

Council on Foreign Relations, "The U.S. Immigration Debate" 473

Chief Justice John Roberts, Opinion of the Court, *Shelby* v. *Holder*, 2013 484

Martin Luther King, Jr., "I Have a Dream" 486

Civil Rights Act of 1964 487

U.S. Constitution, 26th Amendment 491

Justice William O. Douglas, Opinion of the Court, *Harper* v. *Virginia Board of Elections*, 1966 494

Benjamin Ginsberg, Theodore Lowi, and Margaret Weir, *We the People* 517

Thomas Jefferson, Letter to Colonel Edward Carrington, 1787 528

David Halberstam, *The Powers That Be* 529

Hanson W. Balwin, "Washington Feels Vietcong Offensive Failed Maximum Objective", 1968 536

Walter Cronkite, "We Are Mired in Stalemate", 1968..537
Alexis de Tocqueville, *Democracy in America*..541
John F. Kennedy 547
Ed Rollins..548
Pew Research Center, "Americans' Internet Access, 2000–2015"...557
WebRootsDemocracy.org...557
David Pogue, "When Will We Be Able to Vote Online?," *Scientific American,* February 1, 2016 557
Barack Obama, "President Obama: The Fast Company Interview," *Fast Company,* June 15, 2015 557
Charles Francis Adams (ed.), *The Works of John Adams,* 1856..580
R.M. Easley, "The Sine qua Non of Caucus Reform," *Review of Reviews,* 1897.....................582
President Jimmy Carter, Carter-Reagan Debate, 1980 605
Ronald Reagan, Carter-Reagan Debate, 1980...606
Justice Anthony M. Kennedy, Majority Opinion, *Citizens United* v. *FEC,* 2010...............617–618
Justice John Paul Stevens, Dissenting Opinion, *Citizens United* v. *FEC,* 2010.....................618
Herbert Hoover, Address at Madison Square Garden, October 31, 1932...................................623
CNN, "Winfrey tells Iowa crowd: 'Barack Obama is 'the one'," December 8, 2007 623
U.S. Constitution, Article I, Section 8, Clause 1 647
U.S. Constitution, Article I, Section 9, Clause 4 648
U.S. Constitution, 16th Amendment 649
Justice Stephen J. Field, Concurring Opinion, *Pollock* v. *Farmers' Loan and Trust Co.,* 1895............655–656
Justice Henry B. Brown, Dissenting Opinion, *Pollock* v. *Farmers' Loan and Trust Co.,* 1895................656
U.S. Constitution, Article I, Section 9, Clause 7 659
House Intelligence Committee Chairman Mike Rogers, October 4, 2011 679
Senator Bernie Sanders (I., Vermont), interview with Ezra Klein, Vox.com, July 28, 2015.......679
Second Continental Congress, 1776..685
Alan Ehrenhalt, "Clueless in Boise," *Governing* magazine 691
Retired New Hampshire Supreme Court Justice Joe Nadeau, on responsibilities of judges 712
William Blackstone, *Commentaries on the Laws of England*...715–716
Adam Smith, *Wealth of Nations,* 1776..737
Elizabeth Joh, "Yes, States and Local Governments Can Close Private Businesses and
   Restrict Your Movement," March 18, 2020 747
Ilya Shapiro, "State Police Powers and the Constitution," September 15, 2020.......................747
Office of the Governor, "New Emergency Public Health Order in Effect," October 16, 2020.......747
Joint Statement on Xinjiang, U.S. Department of State, March 22, 2021 777
Foreign Ministry Spokesperson's Remarks on the Statement by Friendly Countries in Support of China
   at the 47th Session of the Human Rights Council, June 22, 2021 778
Country Reports on Human Rights Practices for 2014, U.S. State Department 783
"Progress in China's Human Rights in 2014," Chinese State Council Information Office 783

Timelines

The Road to Independence 46
Bill of Rights...90
The Role of State and Federal Governments in Welfare Reform 117
The Growth of Presidential Power...224
The Executive Departments Over Time...279
The Evolution of the National Judiciary..332
Landmark Supreme Court Cases: Civil Liberties 364
Citizenship and Civil Rights..434
The Five Stages of Expanding Suffrage..476
Elections and Political Parties...560

Print Resources

Government and the Economy 626
Supreme Court Decisions 692
Germany's Path to Democracy..753

Maps

Sovereignty: A Characteristic of a State...9
Forms of Government Around the World 18
Spread of Christianity, 300–800 A.D...26
Triangular Trade Routes 29
Colonial America, 1775..51
Territorial Expansion..128
2020 Congressional Reapportionment...156
2020 Congressional Reapportionment...220
September 11, 2001...256
Examples of U.S. Military Interventions After World War II 262
Cold War Conflicts, 1947–1991..298
Middle East and North Africa Uprisings, 2010–2013..303
UN Founding Members 313
Federal Court Circuits and Districts...352
Electoral Votes by State..561
Electoral Votes by State..598
Dissolving the Soviet Union 636
Federal Reserve System..640
Major Native American Reservations...721
United Kingdom 759
Districts of the Russian Federation 766
China's Provinces..775

Charts, Graphs, and Tables

Direct and Indirect Democracy...17
Elements of a Democratic Government 41
Timeline of the Modern State 41
How States Arose..41
Who Can Participate in Government?...41
Basic Concepts of Government...49
British Colonial Policies, 1761–1774 57
Key Delegates to Second Continental Congress, 1775 60
Major Compromises of the Constitutional Convention...78
Ratification of the Constitution..81
The Articles of the Constitution...85
Types of Colonial Governments 85
Constitution: Key Facts 85
The Road to the Constitution...85
Ratification of the Constitution..86
Articles of the Constitution 93
Who has the Power?...102
The Bill of Rights 107
Examples of Powers Expressly Denied to the Federal Government 119
The Formal Amendment Process 139

The Bill of Rights 139
Basic Principles of the Constitution 139
Division of Power 139
The Bill of Rights 140
Roles of Members of Congress 148
Growth of Seats in Congress, Selected Years 161
The Delegated Powers 168
Historical Snapshot of Federal Taxes 171
Strict vs. Liberal Constructionists 181
Constitutional Limits on the Commerce Power 183
Examples of Senate Rejections of Cabinet Nominees 184
Congressional Influence 185
Congressional Committees 199
The Longest Filibusters 210
More Filibusters, More Cloture: Selected Congresses 211
Types of Bills and Resolutions 219
Congressional Leaders 219
Congressional Powers 219
Comparing the House and the Senate 219
Presidential Rankings 229
The Line of Succession 231
United States v. *Nixon,* 1974 243
Recess Appointments, Selected Presidents 244
Changing Roles 261
Foreign Policy Powers 261
The President's Domestic Powers 261
The Presidency 261
The Executive Branch 266
The Executive Branch 271
Staff and Line Agencies 272
The OMB and the Budget 276
Types of Independent Agencies 284
Government vs. Private Corporations 291
Selected 19th and 20th Century Revolutions 296
American Troops in Vietnam & Other Wars 300
The Nicaraguan Revolution, 1978–1979 301
Travel Documents 310
RSM Top Troop-Contributing Nations 312
UN Millennium Development Goals 316
Civilian Control of the Military 319
Prevent Terrorism or Protect Civil Liberties? 323
Structure of the Executive Branch 327
Key American Foreign Policies 327
National Security 327
Federal Civilian Employment by Branch 328
Types of Inferior Federal Courts 340
The Court of Appeals for the Federal Circuit 354
Which Cases do Federal Courts Hear? 359
How Cases Reach the Court 359
Structure of the Federal Courts 359
A Supreme Court Case 359

Print Resources

Federal District Courts..360
Senate Votes on Supreme Court Nominees...361
Provisions of the 14th Amendment's Due Process Clause..370
Supreme Court at a Glance..407
The Factors Lawyers Consider When Selecting a Jury..417
Incarcerated Persons in the U.S..423
First Amendment Freedoms..429
Protections of Freedom and Security..429
Rights of the Accused...429
The *Lemon* Test...430
Acquiring Citizenship at Birth..437
Steps to Naturalization...438
U.S. Immigration and the Immigration and Nationality Act of 1965......................................440
U.S. Population by Race...445
Population Increase, 2010–2020..447
Selected Supreme Court Decisions on Gender Discrimination...458
Two Views on Affirmative Action...464
Affirmative Action...471
Key Federal Civil Rights Laws..471
American Citizenship..471
Segregation in American Society...471
Immigration by Region (in Millions)..472
African American Elected Officials in the U.S..482
Why the Voting Rights Act Amendments Were Needed..483
Historic Events and Voter Turnout...497
Voting by Income and Gender, 2004...501
How Can a Small Sample Represent a Huge Population?...523
Questions to Ask About Polls..524
Examples of the Media as Watchdogs...533
Pivotal Events in the Recent History of the Media...534
Interest Groups v. Political Parties...539
Evaluating Interest Groups..543
U.S. Chamber of Commerce Lifetime Scores, Selected U.S. Representatives............................550
Conducting a Poll..555
Voter Qualifications...555
Influences on Public Opinion...555
Expansion of Voting Rights in the U.S..555
Voter Turnout, 1992–2012..556
Multiparty vs. Two-Party Systems...569
Minor Parties' Stands on the Issues...570
2000 Presidential Election Nader's Spoiler Effect...572
Strong Minor Party Efforts, 1924 –Present...573
1992 Presidential Primary Schedule and Results..586
1980 Presidential Election Results in Massachusetts..599
Different Possible Outcomes: 1960 Presidential Election...602
Hard and Soft Money Raised by National Party Committees, 2000–2021 (in Millions of Dollars)....611
Spending by Super PACs..615
Regulating Campaign Finance..621
Political Parties in the United States..621
The Electoral College...621
Two-Party System in American Government...621

Multiparty vs. Two-Party Systems 622
Propaganda Techniques 623
Supply and Demand 631
Marxist Economies 635
U.S. Free Enterprise System and Other Economic Systems 637
Main Tools Used by the Federal Government to Influence the Economy 644
How Do Indirect Taxes Work 648
The Effect of the Revenue Act of 1942 649
Social Security Program Revenue and Cost: Historical and Projected 652
Winners and Losers of International Trade 667
Manufacturing vs. Services in the U.S. Economy 673
Major Economic Institutions 677
Free Enterprise 677
Goals for the Economy 677
Government Revenue and Spending 677
Economic Systems 678
U.S. Trade Deficit with China 679
State Government Organization 682
Elements of State Constitutions 686
Examples of Constitutional Initiatives from Selected States 696
200 Years of Governors Who Became President 699
Examples of Special Sessions Called by Governors 702
The Use of Precedent 706
In the Courtroom 710
Duties of County Officials 719
Education Spending Per Student 733
AFDC and TANF, 1967–2006 734
State vs. Federal Government Revenues, 1930–1950 738
State Budget Process 741
State Government Organization 745
Revenues and Expenditures 745
Legal Terms 745
Local Government Responsibilities 745
Comparing United States and Russian Legislatures 770
Changes in China's Government 781
Russia's History 781
What Makes Democracy Succeed? 781
The United States and the United Kingdom 781
Comparing United States and Russian Legislatures 782
China's Human Rights Record 783
China and Social Media 783

Infographics

Roots of Democracy 4
Four Characteristics of a State 8
Historical Theories of the Origins of the State 10
Distribution of Power by Government Type 20
Structure of the Roman Government During the Republic 25
Monarchical Government During the Middle Ages 27
Roots of Democracy 28

Print Resources

U.S. Free Enterprise System......38
Social Contract Theory......42
State Constitutions and America's Founding Documents......63
Selected Framers of the Constitution......73
Highlights of the Virginia Plan......75
Highlights of the New Jersey Plan......76
Two Sides of Ratification......80
Representation in Congress......94
Checks and Balances......100
Amending the Constitution......105
Types of Federal Grants to States......131
The Capitol......144
Terms and Sessions of Congress......151
The Implied Powers of Congress......180
Electoral Duties of Congress Who Wins?......188
Vice-Presidential Vacancy......189
A Bill in the House......198
How a Bill Becomes a Law......212
The Power of the Veto......248
From The Office of National Drug Control Policy......277
NASA Technologies Government Research Benefits the Private Sector......286
The Iran Hostage Crisis......309
Which Court?......337
Who Gets the Job?......338
The Three Branches of Government......343
The Appellate Path of the Federal Courts......353
Due Process......396
Exceptions to the Exclusionary Rule......410
How Are Juries Selected?......419
Miranda Warning......421
Capital Punishment Debate......424
Capital Punishment Facts......425
Residence Requirements......490
Why are Mailed Ballots Often Failed Ballots?......512
Poll Results Depend Upon How You Ask the Question......525
What is Yellow Journalism?......532
Labor Union Membership......544
Lobbying in Action......547
Key Facts About Lobbyists......548
Major Propaganda Techniques......552
The American Political Spectrum......568
Common Local and State Party Organization......576
Winner-Take-All vs Proportional Representation......590
Factors of Production......629
Government Regulation and Private Enterprise......633
Progressive Taxes......651
The Executive Branch and the Budget......659
Congress and the Budget......660
Final Steps to Passing the Budget......661
Understanding the Economic Crisis of 2007–2008......663
Which Countries Own Part of the Federal Debt?......664

How Tariffs Work 669
How to Propose Changes to a State Constitution 688
Choosing Executive Officers 703
Criminal & Civil Law 707
Voices of Government 712
Typical County Government Structure 718
Mayor-Council Government: Strong Mayor Model 725
Commission Form of Government 726
Council-Manager Form of Government 727
Adam Smith's Four Principles of a Sound Tax System 737
What Makes Democracy Succeed? 750
What Makes Democracy Succeed? 755
The Government of the United Kingdom 760
Organization of Russian Federation Government 768
Government in the People's Republic of China 774

Political Cartoons

"Democracy Stew," Steve Artley....,..35
"The Right Of Way," Beaumont Fairban 39
"Join, or Die," Benjamin Franklin 58
The Federal Edifice, unknown 82
Government RC Car, Artley 97
"Sure, he's big . . . but WE hold the leash!" Artley 98
Power Bake Off, Artley 98
Checks and Balances, Artley 99
"What ta' ya mean 'Out of Bounds'?" Artley 101
"The Making of a Senator," Joseph Keppler, Jr. 106
"The Keepers at the Gate," Uto Keppler 121
"The 'rail splitter' at work repairing the union," Joseph E. Baker 126
"Sorry, but all my power's been turned back to the states" Lee Lorenz 129
"Take that you evil federal tyrant!" Bagley..141
"All in favor of our congressional pay raise," Ed Fischer 153
Gerrymander Salamander, unknown 157
"We all know the senator's position regarding term limits," Chris Wildt 163
"I Assure You Madam," Robert Weber 172
"Gibbons v. Ogden," Stu's Views...182
"Hey, Soldier . . . Mind Squeezing Over?" Trever 203
"Help the Bill Find Its Way to Becoming a Law," Ed Steed....................................206
"Hepburn Rate Bill," Clifford K. Berryman 213
"King Andrew the First", unknown 238
Teddy Roosevelt and Willie Taft, Flohri 239
"Do you have any 'Congratulations on Your Presidential Pardon' cards?" Gradisher 245
"The government wants to announce a target date," Fran Orford 269
"Left," F. Opper 287
"Unleashing the Dogs of Regulation," Matt Wuerker..290
"Foreign Aid Corruption," Kjell Nilsson-Maki...329
"Supreme Court Upholds Warrantless DNA Collection," Jeff Parker 356
"I checked several key qualifications," Gary McCoy 361
"The American River Ganges," Thomas Nast..371
"When the teacher says 'heaven help me', is that praying in school?" Martha Campbell.............376

Print Resources _____

"Free speech zones" 392

"Of course I ate the fish," Stu's Views 406

"Well, if you're going to wiretap your people you are going to hear things," Charles Barsotti 409

"What Privacy?" Hypojustice.com 411

"Change it to, 'not guilty by reason of personal health issues,'" Mike Baldwin 411

"Thanks again to the Supreme Court," Mike Keefe 431

"Anybody Home?" RJ Matson 443

"Another day, another eighty cents," Clay Bennett 449

"Voting Rights Act Shredded," Dave Granlund 484

"Voter Fraud," Jeff Parker 492

"The tests show it's a boy," Roy Delgado 500

Wooing Independent Voters, Paul Fell 505

"...and please bless and keep safe . . .," Mort Gerberg 508

"Callahan, Get Off My Coattails!" James Stevenson 508

"Darn it! I can't find a voting app," Ralph Hagen 513

"Get me some shares in public opinion," Grizelda 520

"A Nauseating Job, But It Must Be Done," unknown 529

"I get my news online...none of that fake stuff for me . . .," Paul Fell 535

The intricate mechanics of government, Wiley Miller 546

"Apparently the antelopes are lobbying . . .," Hagen 549

Pacs and Super Pacs, Matt Wuerker 551

The Next Thing in Order and The Off Year, Thomas Nast 567

"You bet it's a legitimate platform!" Milt Priggee 593

Big Sky Country, Matt Wuerker 610

"I'd love to give them my two cents' worth...," Jeff Stahler 613

"Some of it is soft and some of it is hard...," J. B. Handelsman 614

"Psst! Wanna Buy A Democracy?" Mike Flinn 617

"Great news!" Grizelda 642

"Gibbs, I subtracted your federal, state, and local...," Schwadron 653

Polly's chance to get some nice crackers, *Puck* 655

Chinese Takeout, Dave Granlund 679

"Look—if I'd had any idea...," Baloo 685

"Don't Worry. We are good at that." Jeff Parker 691

The California Recall Keeps on Truckin', Monte Wolverton 699

"He's big, all right, and he's definitely a wolf...," Michael Maslin 709

"My wife wouldn't like anything reversible...," Martha Campbell 711

"...and ten more years, because I'm running for re-election...," Bill Stormont 713

"It was a real bargain...," Mark Parisi 729

Great Urban Sprawl, Warren Miller 730

"Hi, I'm a tax man", Dmitri Bandura 739

"Thank you, Governor—We'll take it from here." Ed Fischer 746

Federal Gov't Virus Response, Steve Sack 747

Digital Resources

This course includes an online component that offers interactivities, biographies, primary sources, maps, and other resources to expand your study of American Government and bring the content to life.

Case Study Connections

See how a core concept plays out in the real world through a recent event. Then analyze a collection of primary sources associated with the core concept to learn how it can be seen in history, economics, geography, and government.

Current Connections

Learn about current events and apply key government ideas by interacting with data and other information, both within the course and online.

Interactivities

Interactive 3-D Models
- The Capitol: A Working Symbol of Representative Democracy, Topic 1 Lesson 2
- A Tour of the Capitol, Topic 4 Lesson 1
- The White House West Wing, Topic 6 Lesson 2

Interactive Cartoons
- Limited Government, Topic 3 Lesson 1
- Immigration Reform, Topic 9 Lesson 1
- Affirmative Action, Topic 9 Lesson 4

Interactive Charts and Graphs
- The Three Branches of Government, Topic 1 Lesson 1
- Choosing a Chief Executive, Topic 1 Lesson 2
- Duties and Responsibilities of Citizenship, Topic 1 Lesson 4
- The Government Created by the Articles, Topic 2 Lesson 3
- Articles of Confederation, Topic 2 Lesson 3
- The Connecticut Compromise, Topic 2 Lesson 4
- Checks and Balances, Topic 3 Lesson 1
- Division of Power, Topic 3 Lesson 3
- Reapportionment of Congressional Districts, Topic 4 Lesson 2
- The Expressed Powers of Congress, Topic 4 Lesson 3
- Forms of Legislation, Topic 4 Lesson 6
- Making Law: The Process in the House and Senate, Topic 4 Lesson 6
- Comparing Treaties and Executive Agreements, Topic 5 Lesson 4

- Constitutional and Special Courts, Topic 7 Lesson 1
- How a Case Reaches the Supreme Court, Topic 7 Lesson 2
- Civil and Criminal Cases, Topic 7 Lesson 3
- Understanding the Free Exercise Clause, Topic 8 Lesson 2
- The Limits of Free Speech and Press, Topic 8 Lesson 3
- Procedural and Substantive Due Process, Topic 8 Lesson 3
- Exceptions to the Exclusionary Rule, Topic 8 Lesson 6
- Protection of Individual Rights: Limits on Government, Topic 8 Lesson 7
- The Steps of Justice, Topic 8 Lesson 7
- Voter Behavior Key Terms, Topic 10 Lesson 3
- Interest Groups Lobby Congress, Topic 10 Lesson 7
- Outside Sources of Campaign Funding, Topic 11 Lesson 4
- Three Types of Economic Systems, Topic 12 Lesson 1
- Setting Interest Rates, Topic 12 Lesson 2
- Booms, Busts, and Fiscal and Monetary Policy, Topic 12 Lesson 2
- Comparing Federal Taxes, Topic, 12 Lesson 3
- Federal Spending Comparison, Topic 12 Lesson 4
- Demand-side and Supply-side Economics, Topic 12 Lesson 4
- State Constitutions Today, Topic 13 Lesson 1

Digital Resources

- Powers of the Governor, Topic 13 Lesson 3
- State Law, Topic 13 Lesson 4
- The State Courts, Topic 13 Lesson 4
- State and Local Spending, Topic 13 Lesson 6
- Comparing Governments: United States and United Kingdom, Topic 14 Lesson 2

Interactive Galleries

- The Beginning of Monarchy, Topic 1 Lesson 3
- Great Thinkers of the Enlightenment Age, Topic 1 Lesson 3
- Expanding Democratic Rights, Topic 1 Lesson 4
- Analyzing Political Cartoons Topic 2 Lesson 2
- Prohibition: The 18th and 21st Amendments, Topic 3 Lesson 2
- Powers Reserved to the States, Topic 3 Lesson 3
- A Case Study on Copyrights and Patents, Topic 4 Lesson 3
- The Implied Power of Congressional Investigation, Topic 4 Lesson 4
- Presidential Pay and Benefits, Topic 5 Lesson 1
- Balancing the Ticket, Topic 5 Lesson 2
- Expansions and Limitations of Presidential Powers, Topic 5 Lesson 3
- Women and Minorities in the Cabinet, Topic 6 Lesson 2
- Independent Agencies: A Closer Look, Topic 6 Lesson 3
- A Day at the Department of Homeland Security, Topic 6 Lesson 6
- U.S. Special Courts, Topic 7 Lesson 3
- The Founding of American Rights and Freedoms, Topic 8 Lesson 1
- Examples of the Incorporation of the Bill of Rights, Topic 8 Lesson 1
- Freedom of Speech in the U.S. and Around the World, Topic 8 Lesson 3
- Free Assembly in *Edwards* v. *South Carolina* (1963), Topic 8 Lesson 4
- Protecting the Public Through Police Power, Topic 8 Lesson 5
- Personal Privacy—Communication and the 4th Amendment, Topic 8 Lesson 6
- Women's Rights, Topic 9 Lesson 2

- Poll Taxes and the 24th Amendment, Topic 10 Lesson 1
- Voter ID Laws, Topic 10 Lesson 2
- *Bush* v. *Gore:* The Contested 2000 Election, Topic 10 Lesson 4
- The Politics of Public Opinion, Topic 10 Lesson 5
- The Transformation of the Mass Media, Topic 10 Lesson 6
- Political Appointees, Topic 11 Lesson 2
- Economic Sanctions: The Case of South Africa, Topic 12 Lesson 5
- State Constitutional Change, Topic 13 Lesson 1
- State Government Executive Officers, Topic 13 Lesson 3
- Special Districts, Topic 13 Lesson 5
- Comparing Rights and Freedoms in Russia, Topic 14 Lesson 3
- Analyzing Primary and Secondary Sources From China, Topic 14 Lesson 4

Interactive Illustrations

- What Does a Judge Do?, Topic 7 Lesson 1
- Social Media and the 2012 Election, Topic 10 Lesson 6
- Federal Tax Dollars at Work, Topic 12 Lesson 3
- State and Local Revenue, Topic 13 Lesson 6

Interactive Maps

- Four Characteristics of a State, Topic 1 Lesson 1
- Forms of Government Among Countries of the World, Topic 1 Lesson 2
- The Thirteen Colonies in 1775, Topic 2 Lesson 1
- Territorial Expansion of the U.S. 1787–1898, Topic 3 Lesson 4
- Gerrymandering: Redistricting Voters, Topic 4 Lesson 2
- Four Characteristics of a State, Topic 5 Lesson 1
- Examples of U.S. Military Interventions After World War II, Topic 5 Lesson 4
- U.S. Embassies Around the World, Topic 6 Lesson 5
- Examples of Types of Primaries, Topic 11 Lesson 2
- The Presidential Election, Topic 11 Lesson 3
- Comparing Governments Around the World, Topic 14 Lesson 1

Interactive Timelines

- Foundations of American Rights, Topic 2 Lesson 1
- The Road to Independence, Topic 2 Lesson 2
- The Bill of Rights, Topic 3 Lesson 2
- The Necessary and Proper Clause in Education, Topic 4 Lesson 4
- Isolationism to Internationalism, Topic 6 Lesson 4
- Protests That Made a Difference, Topic 8 Lesson 4
- Events in the History of Inequality, Topic 9 Lesson 3
- An Expanding Electorate, Topic 10 Lesson 1
- Counting Your Vote, Topic 10 Lesson 4
- History of the Two-Party System, Topic 11 Lesson 1
- The Race for the Presidency, Topic 11 Lesson 3

Core Concepts

Culture

- What Is Culture?
- Families and Societies
- Language
- Religion
- The Arts
- Cultural Diffusion and Change
- Science and Technology

Economics

- Economics Basics
- Economic Process
- Economic Systems
- Economic Development
- Trade
- Money Management

Geography

- The Study of Earth
- Geography's Five Themes
- Ways to Show Earth's Surface
- Understanding Maps
- Earth in Space

- Time and Earth's Rotation
- Forces on Earth's Surface
- Forces Inside Earth
- Climate and Weather
- Temperature
- Water and Climate
- Air Circulation and Precipitation
- Types of Climate
- Ecosystems
- Environment and Resources
- Land Use
- People's Impact on the Environment
- Population
- Migration
- Urbanization

Government and Civics

- Foundations of Government
- Political Systems
- Political Structures
- Conflict and Cooperation
- Citizenship

History

- How Do Historians Study History?
- Measuring Time
- Historical Sources
- Archaeology and Other Sources
- Historical Maps

Personal Finance

- Your Fiscal Fitness: An Introduction
- Budgeting
- Checking
- Investments
- Savings and Retirement
- Credit and Debt
- Risk Management
- Consumer Smarts
- After High School
- Taxes and Income

Digital Resources

Landmark Supreme Court Cases

- *Korematsu* v. *United States*
- *Marbury* v. *Madison*
- *McCulloch* v. *Maryland*
- *Gibbons* v. *Ogden*
- *Worcester* v. *Georgia*
- *Dred Scott* v. *Sandford*
- *Plessy* v. *Ferguson*
- *Schenck* v. *United States*
- *Brown* v. *Board of Education*
- *Engel* v. *Vitale*
- *Sweatt* v. *Painter*
- *Mapp* v. *Ohio*
- *Hernandez* v. *Texas*
- *Gideon* v. *Wainwright*
- *Wisconsin* v. *Yoder*
- *Miranda* v. *Arizona*
- *White* v. *Regester*
- *Tinker* v. *Des Moines School District*
- *Roe* v. *Wade*
- *Baker* v. *Carr*
- *Grutter* v. *Bollinger*
- *Edgewood* v. *Kirby*
- *Texas* v. *Johnson*
- *National Federation of Independent Businesses et al.* v. *Sebelius et al.*
- *Mendez* v. *Westminster* and *Delgado* v. *Bastrop*
- *Obergefell* v. *Hodges*
- *New York Times* v. *United States*
- *Shelby County* v. *Holder*
- *Katz* v. *United States*
- *District of Columbia* v. *Heller*
- *Burwell* v. *Hobby Lobby*
- *Massachusetts* v. *EPA*
- *New York Times* v. *Sullivan*

Selected Interactive Primary Sources

See the online course for a full list of Interactive Primary Sources.

- Code of Hammurabi
- *The Republic,* Plato
- Politics, Aristotle
- De re publica, Cicero
- Edicts, Asoka
- The Magna Carta
- *The Prince,* Niccolò Machiavelli
- Mayflower Compact
- English Petition of Right
- English Bill of Rights
- *Two Treatises of Government,* John Locke
- *The Spirit of Laws,* Baron de Montesquieu
- *The Social Contract,* Jean-Jacques Rousseau
- *The Interesting Narrative of the Life of Olaudah Equiano*
- "Give Me Liberty or Give Me Death," Patrick Henry
- "Remember the Ladies," Abigail Adams
- *Common Sense,* Thomas Paine
- *The Wealth of Nations,* Adam Smith
- Declaration of Independence
- Virginia Declaration of Rights
- Virginia Statute for Religious Freedom, Thomas Jefferson
- "To His Excellency, General Washington," Phillis Wheatley
- Articles of Confederation
- Anti-Federalist Papers
- The Federalist No. 10, James Madison
- The Federalist No. 39, James Madison
- The Federalist No. 51
- The Federalist No. 78, Alexander Hamilton
- Northwest Ordinance
- Iroquois Constitution
- Declaration of the Rights of Man and the Citizen
- Farewell Address, George Washington
- Debate Over Nullification, Webster and Calhoun
- *Democracy in America,* Alexis de Tocqueville
- 1836 Victory or Death Letter from the Alamo, Travis
- Texas Declaration of Independence
- Declaration of Sentiments and Resolutions
- The Communist Manifesto, Karl Marx and Friedrich Engels

- "Ain't I a Woman?," Sojourner Truth
- *Uncle Tom's Cabin,* Harriet Beecher Stowe
- "A House Divided," Abraham Lincoln
- First Inaugural Address, Abraham Lincoln
- Declaration of Causes: February 2, 1861
- Emancipation Proclamation, Abraham Lincoln
- Gettysburg Address, Abraham Lincoln
- Second Inaugural Address, Abraham Lincoln
- "I Will Fight No More Forever," Chief Joseph
- *How the Other Half Lives,* Jacob Riis
- The Pledge of Allegiance
- Preamble to the Platform of the Populist Party
- Atlanta Exposition Address, Booker T. Washington
- "The White Man's Burden," Rudyard Kipling
- *The Jungle,* Upton Sinclair
- Hind Swaraj, Mohandas Gandhi
- The Fourteen Points, Woodrow Wilson
- Four Freedoms, Franklin D. Roosevelt
- *The Diary of a Young Girl,* Anne Frank
- Charter of the United Nations
- "The Sinews of Peace," Winston Churchill
- Universal Declaration of Human Rights
- Inaugural Address, John F. Kennedy
- *Silent Spring,* Rachel Carson
- "I Have a Dream," Martin Luther King, Jr.
- "Letter From Birmingham Jail," Martin Luther King, Jr.
- State of the Union address, Lyndon Johnson
- State of the Union address, Gerald Ford
- "Tear Down This Wall," Ronald Reagan
- "A Thousand Points of Light," George H.W. Bush
- "Glory and Hope," Nelson Mandela
- State of the Union address, Bill Clinton
- State of the Union address, George W. Bush
- 16th Birthday Speech at the United Nations, Malala Yousafzai
- Speech at the United Nations, Greta Thunberg
- COVID-19 Briefing, Dr. Tedros Adhanom Ghebreyesus

Selected Biographies

See the online course for a full list of Biographies.

- Abigail Adams
- John Adams
- John Quincy Adams
- Samuel Adams
- Susan B. Anthony
- James Armistead
- Crispus Attucks
- Moses Austin
- Stephen F. Austin
- James A. Baker III
- Emily Greene Balch
- William Blackstone
- Simón Bolívar
- Napoleon Bonaparte
- Chief Bowles
- Omar Bradley
- John C. Calhoun
- Andrew Carnegie
- César Chávez
- Wentworth Cheswell
- George Childress
- Winston Churchill
- Henry Clay
- William Jefferson Clinton
- Jefferson Davis
- Martin De León
- Green DeWitt
- Dwight Eisenhower
- James Fannin
- James L. Farmer, Jr.
- Benjamin Franklin
- Betty Friedan
- Milton Friedman
- Bernardo de Gálvez
- Hector P. Garcia
- John Nance Garner
- King George III
- William Gladstone
- Henry B. González
- Raul A. Gonzalez, Jr.
- Mikhail Gorbachev
- William Goyens
- Ulysses S. Grant
- José Gutiérrez de Lara
- Alexander Hamilton
- Hammurabi
- Warren Harding
- Václav Havel
- Friedrich Hayek
- Jack Coffee Hays
- Patrick Henry
- Adolf Hitler
- Oveta Culp Hobby
- James Hogg
- Sam Houston
- Kay Bailey Hutchison
- Andrew Jackson
- John Jay
- Thomas Jefferson
- Lyndon B. Johnson
- Anson Jones
- Barbara Jordan
- Justinian I
- John F. Kennedy
- John Maynard Keynes
- Martin Luther King, Jr.
- Marquis de Lafayette
- Mirabeau B. Lamar
- Robert E. Lee
- Abraham Lincoln
- John Locke

Digital Resources

- Niccolò Machiavelli
- James Madison
- John Marshall
- George Marshall
- Karl Marx
- George Mason
- Mary Maverick
- Jane McCallum
- Joseph McCarthy
- James Monroe
- Charles de Montesquieu
- Dwight L. Moody
- Edwin W. Moore
- Gouverneur Morris
- Moses
- Lucretia Mott

- Benito Mussolini
- José Antonio Navarro
- Chester A. Nimitz
- Richard M. Nixon
- Barack Obama
- Sandra Day O'Connor
- Thomas Paine
- Quanah Parker
- Rosa Parks
- George Patton
- Pope John Paul II
- John J. Pershing
- Sam Rayburn
- Ronald Reagan
- Hiram Rhodes Revels
- John D. Rockefeller
- Franklin D. Roosevelt

- Theodore Roosevelt
- Lawrence Sullivan Ross
- Antonio Lopez de Santa Anna
- Phyllis Schlafly
- Erasmo Seguín
- Juan N. Seguín
- Roger Sherman
- Adam Smith
- Haym Soloman
- Alexander Solzhenitsyn
- Joseph Stalin
- Elizabeth Cady Stanton
- William Graham Sumner
- Billy Sunday
- Raymond L. Telles

- Margaret Thatcher
- Alexis de Tocqueville
- Hideki Tojo
- William B. Travis
- Harry Truman
- Lech Walesa
- Mercy Otis Warren
- George Washington
- Daniel Webster
- Lulu Belle Madison White
- William Wilberforce
- James Wilson
- Woodrow Wilson
- Lorenzo de Zavala
- Mao Zedong

21st Century Skills

- Identify Main Ideas and Details
- Set a Purpose for Reading
- Use Context Clues
- Analyze Cause and Effect
- Categorize
- Compare and Contrast
- Draw Conclusions
- Draw Inferences
- Generalize
- Make Decisions
- Make Predictions
- Sequence
- Solve Problems
- Summarize
- Analyze Media Content
- Analyze Primary and Secondary Sources
- Compare Viewpoints
- Distinguish Between Fact and Opinion
- Identify Bias
- Analyze Data and Models
- Analyze Images

- Analyze Political Cartoons
- Create Charts and Maps
- Create Databases
- Read Charts, Graphs, and Tables
- Read Physical Maps
- Read Political Maps
- Read Special-Purpose Maps
- Use Parts of a Map
- Ask Questions
- Avoid Plagiarism
- Create a Research Hypothesis
- Evaluate Web Sites
- Identify Evidence
- Identify Trends
- Interpret Sources
- Search for Information on the Internet
- Synthesize
- Take Effective Notes
- Develop a Clear Thesis
- Organize Your Ideas
- Support Ideas With Evidence

- Evaluate Existing Arguments
- Consider & Counter Opposing Arguments
- Give an Effective Presentation
- Participate in a Discussion or Debate
- Publish Your Work
- Write a Journal Entry
- Write an Essay
- Share Responsibility
- Compromise
- Develop Cultural Awareness
- Generate New Ideas
- Innovate
- Make a Difference
- Work in Teams
- Being an Informed Citizen
- Paying Taxes
- Political Participation
- Serving on a Jury
- Voting

Atlas

- United States: Political
- United States: Physical
- World Political
- World Physical
- World Climate
- World Ecosystems
- World Population Density
- World Land Use
- North Africa and Southwest Asia: Political
- North Africa and Southwest Asia: Physical
- Sub-Saharan Africa: Political
- Sub-Saharan Africa: Physical
- South Asia: Political
- South Asia: Physical
- East Asia: Political
- East Asia: Physical
- Southeast Asia: Political
- Southeast Asia: Physical
- Europe: Political
- Europe: Physical
- Russia, Central Asia, and the Caucasus: Political
- Russia, Central Asia, and the Caucasus: Physical
- North America: Political
- North America: Physical
- Central America and the Caribbean: Political
- Central America and the Caribbean: Physical
- South America: Political
- South America: Physical
- Australia and the Pacific: Political
- Australia and the Pacific: Physical

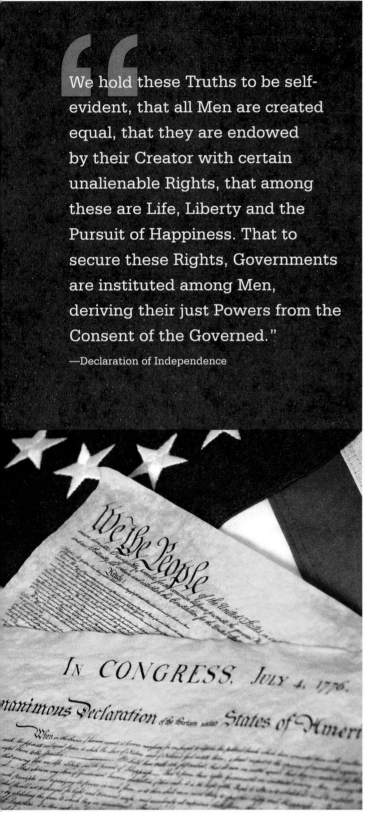

> "We hold these Truths to be self-evident, that all Men are created equal, that they are endowed by their Creator with certain unalienable Rights, that among these are Life, Liberty and the Pursuit of Happiness. That to secure these Rights, Governments are instituted among Men, deriving their just Powers from the Consent of the Governed."

—Declaration of Independence

Declaration of Independence

The Declaration of Independence, largely written by Thomas Jefferson, is one of the most important documents in the history of the world. It declares the independence of a colony from its mother country, thereby setting a precedent for other oppressed peoples to follow. It also establishes the first government in the world in which the people are the sole source of government power—in Abraham Lincoln's words, a "government of the people, by the people, for the people."

Jefferson makes this revolutionary assertion in the first section of the Declaration, the preamble. In it, he establishes the main principle underlying democracy—that government gets its power from the people. In this section, he also outlines the basic premise of liberal constitutionalism, which is that individuals are born with certain "unalienable" rights—rights that cannot be taken away.

The ideas of the Declaration had a profound effect on the world. You can see them at work in the causes that ignited the American Revolution, of course. They are also reflected in the ideas found in the U.S. Constitution (including the Bill of Rights), the movement to end slavery, women's struggle to win the right to vote, the fight for equality waged by Native Americans and other minority groups, and wars for independence fought in many countries.

Read the first paragraph of the Declaration of Independence, found in the Reference Section of this book. Consider its meaning and then answer the questions below.

☑ ASSESSMENT

1. **Identify Central Ideas** What do the words of the preamble (left) say about the fundamental principles and moral values of American democracy?

2. **Contrast** According to the preamble, how much power should a government have over citizens?

3. **Apply Information** The preamble lists "Life, Liberty and the Pursuit of Happiness" as some of the unalienable rights. What others can you list?

Constitution Day Assembly

September 17 is Constitution Day, and your school may hold an assembly or other celebration in honor of the day. As part of this celebration, your teacher may ask you to participate in planning and holding a Constitution Day assembly.

Organize As a class, create the basic plan for your assembly. Discuss the following:

1. When and where should the assembly take place?

2. How long should it take? Should you plan on a short program taking a single class period, or a longer program?

3. Who should be involved? Will other classes or other grades take part? Will you invite outsiders, such as parents or people from the community?

4. What activities might be included?

Plan After your discussion, divide the class into committees to complete jobs such as getting permission from the school administration, preparing a program, inviting any guests, advertising the plan beforehand, and blogging about it afterward.

Give thought to the types of activities that might be included in the assembly. You might invite a guest speaker from your community. You might run an essay contest among students and have the winners read their essays during the assembly. Some students might prepare a video presentation about the Bill of Rights. Others might write and perform a skit about what the Declaration of Independence or U.S. Constitution mean to them.

You might start your assembly by asking everyone to rise to say the Pledge of Allegiance to the United States flag. One student might give a brief speech about how the pledge reflects the ideas of the Declaration of Independence and the U.S. Constitution.

Encourage those who speak or perform at your assembly to address these questions: What rights and responsibilities does a citizen have in a democracy? When must the rights of the individual give way to the public good?

>> Your school may hold a Constitution Day assembly like the one shown here.

Communicate Present your Constitution Day assembly. After the assembly is over, discuss the event with the class. Ask yourselves questions such as these:

1. How well was the assembly planned and organized? What imporvements could we have made?

2. How would you rate each of the presentations or other activities of the assembly?

3. Was the audience engaged?

4. How effectively did the class work together?

Foundations of Government and Citizenship

ESSENTIAL QUESTION What Should Governments Do?

United States Capitol in
Washington, D.C.

Connections to Today

It is hard for all people to agree on all issues all the time. Think about a time when you strongly disagreed with a family member or friends. How did you handle it?

People in the United States sometimes disagree about national or local issues. In a democracy, the ability to compromise to settle these disagreements is critical. In this Topic, you'll learn how societies developed governments to make policies to regulate actions and resolve differences. How does the government help resolve differences among Americans today?

NBC LEARN

Learn about political philosopher John Locke and his theory of natural rights.

> BOUNCE to Activate My Story Video

Topic 1 Overview

In this Topic, you will learn about the roots of American Government and the different types of governments in the world today. Look at the lesson outline and explore the flow chart. As you study this Topic, you can work on your Quest Inquiry.

LESSON OUTLINE

1.1 Principles of Government

1.2 Types of Government

1.3 Origins of the Modern Democratic State

1.4 The Basics of Democracy

ROOTS OF DEMOCRACY

ATHENIAN DEMOCRACY
The Athenians introduced direct democracy. Citizens debated public questions and decided them by majority vote. Courts administered justice.

ROMAN REPUBLIC
The Roman Republic gave decision-making power to an elite Senate and consuls who could check each other and, in theory, represented the people. The laws of Rome were written for all to see.

FEUDALISM
In the Feudal Era, Europe's first parliaments emerged and began to limit the powers of kings. England provided for trial by a jury of one's peers.

SOVEREIGNTY
Sovereignty emerged in the 17th century, with states with fixed borders, a national identity, and a centralized government with broad authority.

DEMOCRACY
Signed on September 17, 1787, the U.S. Constitution established an American government based on Enlightenment philosophies. The Constitution limited the power of the Federal Government and separated it into three branches: executive, legislative, and judicial.

Inquiry Center

Want to become an active and effective citizen? Make a difference in your community and beyond by using the **Inquiry Center** on the digital course.

Connect with issues you're passionate about by using the **Interest Finder**.

Investigate public policies, get involved in your community, influence public opinion, and develop leadership skills.

Synthesize the work you've done and what you've learned along the way.

Demonstrate what you've learned once you've finished your project by sharing your work.

1.1

The Preamble to the Constitution spells out the purpose of the U.S. Constitution and identifies the values and principles of the government.

 BOUNCE to Activate Flipped Video

Objectives

Define government and the basic powers every government holds.

Describe the four defining characteristics of a state.

Identify the four theories that attempt to explain the origin of the state.

Understand the purpose of government in the United States and other countries.

Key Terms

government
public policies
legislative power
executive power
judicial power
dictatorship
democracy
Aristotle
state
sovereign
Thomas Hobbes
John Locke

Principles of Government

This is a course about government—and, more specifically, about government in the United States. The Preamble to the U.S. Constitution begins with the phrase, "We the People of the United States." As a citizen, you are an important member of the "We." For that reason alone, you should know as much as you possibly can about government. Government affects you in an uncountable number of very important ways. It does so today, it did so yesterday, and it will do so every day for the rest of your life.

Government–We the People

Think of the point in this light: What would your life be like *without* government? Who would protect you, and all of the rest of us, against attacks? Who would provide for education, guard the public's health, and protect the environment? Who would pave the streets, regulate traffic, punish criminals, and respond to fires and other human-made and natural disasters? Who would protect civil rights and care for the elderly, the poor, and those who cannot care for themselves? Who would protect consumers and property owners?

The Need for Government Government does all of these things, of course—and much more. In short, if government did not exist, we would have to invent it.

    Government is the institution through which a society makes and enforces its public policies. Government is made up of those people who exercise its powers, all those who have authority and control over people.

    The **public policies** of a government are, in short, all of those things a government decides to do. Public policies cover matters ranging from taxation, defense, education, crime, and healthcare to transportation, the environment, civil rights, and working conditions. Indeed, the list of public policy issues handled by government is nearly endless.

Basic Powers of Government Governments must have power in order to make and carry out public policies. Power is the ability to command or prevent action, the ability to achieve a desired end.

Every government has and exercises three basic kinds of power: (1) **legislative power**—the power to make laws and to frame public policies; (2) **executive power**—the power to execute, enforce, and administer laws; and (3) **judicial power**—the power to interpret laws, to determine their meaning, and to settle disputes that arise within the society. These powers of government are often outlined in a country's constitution. A constitution is the body of fundamental laws setting out the principles, structures, and processes of a government.

The ultimate responsibility for the exercise of these powers may be held by a single person or by a small group, as in a **dictatorship**. In this form of government, those who rule are not held responsible to the will of the people. The fundamental components that typically distinguish democracies from dictatorships include state control of the media, a lack of political and personal freedoms, corruption of public officials, a lack of governmental transparency, and the lack of any mechanisms through which citizens can change the government. In short, a dictatorship, unlike a democracy, does not rest on the consent of the governed.

When the responsibility for the exercise of these powers rests with a majority of the people, that form of government is known as a democracy. In a **democracy**, supreme authority rests with the people.

Government as Human Invention Government is among the oldest of all human inventions. It first appeared when human beings realized that they could not survive without some way to regulate their own actions, as well as those of their neighbors.

The appearance of major political ideas began early in history. The earliest known evidence of government dates from the ancient Babylonian Empire, Egypt, India and China, and as far back as 1700 BCE. More than 2,300 years ago, the Greek philosopher **Aristotle** observed that "man is by nature a political animal." When he wrote those words, Aristotle was only recording an observation that, even then, had been obvious for thousands of years.

What did Aristotle mean by "political"? That is to say, what is "politics"? Although people often equate the two, politics and government are very different

>> Many governments carry out their work through legislative bodies. Today in the U.S. Congress, legislators decide matters of public policy as they did in ancient Rome or Greece.

>> When the emerging Roman republic was threatened by war with neighboring Sabine tribes, the Roman senate appointed Lartius as a dictator to defeat the enemy.

things. Politics is a process, while government is an institution. More specifically, politics is the process by which a society decides how power and resources will be distributed within that society.

☑ **EXPLAIN** What are public policies?

The State

We often use the term **"state"** to mean any body of people, living in a defined territory, organized politically (that is, with a government), and with the power to make and enforce law without the consent of any higher authority.

Note that the word *state* describes a legal entity. In popular usage, a state is often called a "nation" or a "country." In a strict sense, however, the word *nation* is an ethnic term, referring to races or other large groups of people. The word *country* is a geographic term, referring to a particular place, region, or area of land.

There are nearly 200 states in the world today. They vary greatly in size, military power, natural resources, and economic importance. Still, each of them possesses all four of the characteristics of a state. That is, each of them has population, territory, sovereignty, and government.

Population Clearly, a state must have people—a population. The size of that population, however, has nothing directly to do with the existence of a state. One of the world's smallest states, in population terms, is San Marino. Bound on all sides by Italy, it has only some 30,000 people. The People's Republic of China is the world's most populous state, with more than 1 billion people. The more than 300 million people who live in the United States make it among the world's most populous states, after China and India.

The people who make up a state may or may not be homogeneous. The adjective *homogeneous* describes members of a group who share customs, a common language, and ethnic background. Today, the population of the United States includes people from a wide variety of backgrounds. Still, most Americans think of themselves as exactly that: Americans.

Territory Just as a state cannot exist without people, so must it have land—territory—with known and recognized boundaries. The states in today's world vary as widely in terms of territory as they do in population. Here, too, San Marino ranks among the world's smallest states. It covers less than 24 square miles, and so is smaller than thousands of cities and towns in the United States. The United States also recognizes the state of Vatican City,

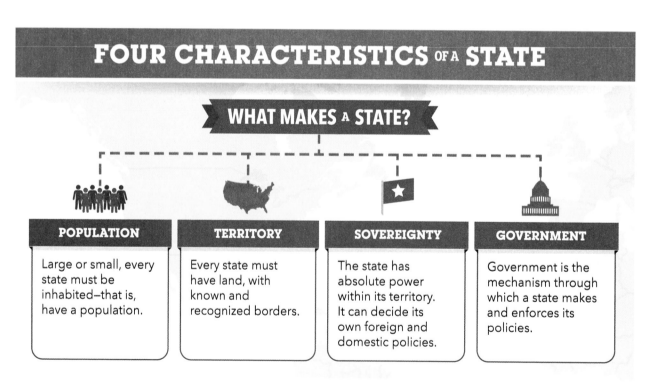

FOUR CHARACTERISTICS OF A STATE

WHAT MAKES A STATE?

POPULATION	TERRITORY	SOVEREIGNTY	GOVERNMENT
Large or small, every state must be inhabited—that is, have a population.	Every state must have land, with known and recognized borders.	The state has absolute power within its territory. It can decide its own foreign and domestic policies.	Government is the mechanism through which a state makes and enforces its policies.

>> Every state in the world has four characteristics. **Analyze Charts** How does the sovereignty of a State in the U.S. compare to the national sovereignty of the U.S. as a whole?

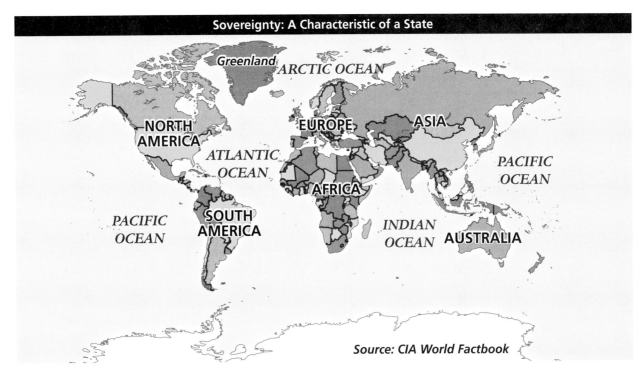

Source: CIA World Factbook

>> Sovereignty is one of the four characteristics possessed by every state in the world.
Analyze Maps How many sovereign states are in the United States?

which is completely surrounded by the city of Rome. It has a permanent population of less than 900 and an area of only about 109 acres.

Russia, the world's largest state, stretches across some 6.6 million square miles. The total area of the United States is about 3.8 million square miles.

Sovereignty Every state is **sovereign**—that is, it has supreme and absolute power within its own territory and can decide its own foreign and domestic policies. It is neither subordinate nor responsible to any other authority. Sovereignty is the one characteristic that distinguishes the state from all other, lesser political units in the world.

Thus, as a sovereign state, the United States can determine its form of government, frame its own economic system, and shape its own foreign policies. The States within the United States are not sovereign and so are not states in the international, legal sense. Each State is subordinate to the Constitution of the United States. At the United States' international borders, citizens observe the laws and serve the public good of countries on both sides of the border by showing passports and other identification in compliance with the rules of each state.

Government Every state is politically organized. That is, every state has a government. Recall, a government is the institution through which society makes and enforces its public policies and is the agency through which the state works to accomplish its goals. Government includes the machinery and the personnel by which the state is ruled.

Government is necessary to avoid what the English philosopher Thomas Hobbes (1588–1679) called "the war of every man against every man." Without government, people would live in what is called the state of nature. In this condition, wrote Hobbes, there would be "continual fear and danger of violent death and the life of man [would be] solitary, poor, nasty, brutish, and short." Indeed, in Lebanon, Bosnia, Somalia, and many other places over recent years, the world has seen a number of sobering examples of what happens when government disappears.

☑ **DESCRIBE** How would you describe the concept of sovereignty?

How States Arose

For centuries, historians, philosophers, and others have pondered the question of the origin of the state. What major political ideas in history resulted in the emergence of states?

Over time, many different answers have been offered, but history provides no conclusive evidence to support any of them. However, four theories have emerged as the most widely accepted explanations for the origin of the state.

The Force Theory Many scholars have long believed that the state was born of force. They hold that one person or a small group claimed control over an area and forced all within it to submit to that person's or group's rule. When that rule was established, all the basic elements of the state—population, territory, sovereignty, and government—were present.

The Evolutionary Theory Others claim that the state developed naturally out of the early family. They hold that the primitive family, of which one person was the head and thus the "government," was the first stage in political development. Over countless centuries, the original family became a network of related families, a clan. In time, the clan became a tribe. When the tribe first turned to agriculture and gave up its nomadic, wandering ways, tying itself to the land, the state was born.

The Divine Right of Kings Theory The theory of divine right of kings was widely accepted in much of the Western world from the fifteenth through the eighteenth centuries. It held that God created the state and that God had given those of royal birth a "divine right" to rule. The people were bound to obey their ruler as they would God; opposition to "the divine right of kings" was both treason and a mortal sin.

During the seventeenth century, philosophers began to question this theory. Much of the thought upon which present-day democracies rest began as a challenge to the theory of divine right of kings.

The notion of divine right of kings was not unique to European history. The rulers of many ancient civilizations, including the Chinese, Egyptian, Aztec, and Mayan civilizations, were held to be gods or to have been chosen by the gods. The Japanese emperor, the *mikado*, governed by divine right of kings until 1945.

The Social Contract Theory In terms of the American political system, the most significant of the major political theories on the origin of the state is that of the "social contract." Philosophers such as Thomas Hobbes, James Harrington (1611–1677), and **John Locke** (1632–1704) in England and Jean Jacques Rousseau (1712–1778) in France developed this theory in the seventeenth and eighteenth centuries. In fact, earlier versions had existed long before that time, including in the works of the ancient Indian philosopher Chanakya (c. 300 B.C.E.).

Hobbes wrote that in earliest history humans lived in unbridled freedom, that is in a "state of nature," in which no government existed and no person was subject to any superior power. That which people could take by force belonged to them. However, all people were similarly free in that state of nature. No authority existed to protect one person from the aggressive actions of another. Thus,

HISTORICAL THEORIES OF THE ORIGINS OF THE STATE

FORCE THEORY	DIVINE RIGHT OF KINGS THEORY	EVOLUTIONARY THEORY	SOCIAL CONTRACT THEORY
An individual or group claimed control over a territory and forced the population to submit. In this way, the state became sovereign, and those in control formed a government.	God created the state, making it sovereign. The government is made up of those chosen by God to rule a certain territory. The population must obey their ruler.	A population formed out of primitive families. The heads of these families became the government. When these families settled in one territory and claimed it as their own, they became a sovereign state.	A population in a given territory gave up as much power to a government as needed to promote the well-being of all. In doing so, they created a sovereign state.

>> There are four theories as to how the state came to be. **Analyze Charts** Which of the theories best describes the origins of the United States? Why?

individuals were only as secure as their own physical strength and intelligence could make them.

Human beings overcame their unpleasant condition, says the social contract theory, by agreeing with one another to create a state. By contract, people within a given area agreed to give up to the state as much power as was needed to promote the safety and well-being of all. In the contract (that is, through a constitution), the members of the state created a government to exercise the powers they had voluntarily given to the state.

People Agree to Form a State In short, the social contract theory argues that the state arose out of a voluntary act of free people. It holds that the state exists only to serve the will of the people, that they are the sole source of political power, and that they are free to give or to withhold that power as they choose. The great concepts that this theory promoted—popular sovereignty, limited government, and individual rights—were immensely important to the shaping of the American governmental system.

The Declaration of Independence justified its revolution through the social contract theory, arguing that King George III and his ministers had violated the contract. Thomas Jefferson called the document "pure Locke." In the Declaration of Independence, Jefferson also included justification based on the "laws of nature and nature's God," meaning that the colonists' right to have an equal voice in their government was given by God and could not be taken away by the king.

☑ **INFER** How does the divine right of kings theory relate to the Declaration of Independence?

What Government Does

What does government do? The answer to that question differs greatly depending on the type of government. In an authoritarian regime, government does only those things that preserve its power. In the American constitutional democracy, however, a very meaningful answer to that question can be found in the Preamble to the Constitution, which begins: "We the People of the United States, in Order to form a more perfect Union. . . ."

Form a More Perfect Union The United States, which had just won its independence from Great Britain, faced an altogether uncertain future in the postwar 1780s. In 1781, the Articles of Confederation, the nation's first constitution, created "a firm league of friendship" among the 13 States. That league soon

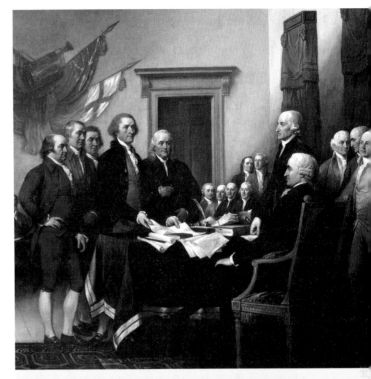

>> Locke believed that the powers of governments are based on the powers of the governed. The signers of the Declaration of Independence (shown here) embraced this idea as one of the self-evident truths.

proved to be neither very firm nor very friendly. The government created by the Articles was powerless to overcome the intense rivalries and jealousies among the States that marked the times.

The Constitution of today was written in 1787. The original States adopted it in order to link themselves, and the American people, more closely together. That Constitution was built in the belief that in union there is strength. A written constitution is important as an official record of governing principles.

Establish Justice To provide justice, said Thomas Jefferson, is "the most sacred of the duties of government." No purpose, no goal of public policy, can be of greater importance in a democracy.

But what is justice? The term, like truth, liberty, and fairness, is difficult to define. It, like the others, is a concept—an idea, an invention of the human mind.

As the concept of justice has developed over time in American thought and practice, it has come to mean this: The law, in both its content and its administration, must be reasonable, fair, and impartial. Those standards of justice have not always been met in this country. We have not attained our professed goal of "equal justice for all." However, this must be said: The history of this country can be told largely in terms of our continuing attempts to reach that goal.

>> The U.S. Coast Guard, part of the U.S. Department of Homeland Security, serves the public good by carrying out such functions as rescues at sea and patrolling the nation's coastlines.

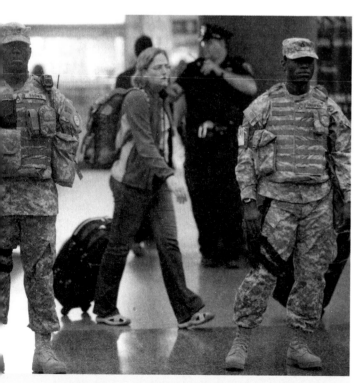

>> National Guard troops can be called upon to serve in military actions and in domestic emergencies such as patrolling Penn Station after 9/11.

"Injustice anywhere," said Martin Luther King, Jr., "is a threat to justice everywhere." You will encounter this idea again and again in this course.

Insure Domestic Tranquility Order is essential to the well-being of any society, and keeping the peace at home has always been a prime function of government. Most people can only imagine what it would be like to live in a state of anarchy—without government, law, or order. In fact, people do live that way in some parts of the world today. For years now, Somalia, located on the eastern tip of Africa, has not had a permanent functioning government; rival warlords control different parts of the country.

In *The Federalist* No. 51, James Madison observed: "If men were angels, no government would be necessary." Madison knew that most human beings fall far short of that standard.

Provide for the Common Defense Defending the nation against foreign enemies has always been one of government's major responsibilities. You can see its importance in the fact that defense is mentioned far more often in the Constitution than any of the other functions of government.

The nation's defense and its foreign policies are but two sides of the same coin: the security of the United States. To provide this security, the nation maintains an army, navy, air force, and coast guard. Departments such as the Department of Homeland Security keep watch for threats to the country and its people.

The United States has become the world's most powerful nation, but the world remains a dangerous place. This country must maintain its vigilance and its armed strength. Just a glance at today's newspapers or at one of this evening's television news programs will furnish abundant proof of that fact.

Promote the General Welfare Few people realize the extent to which democratic government acts as the servant of its citizens, yet examples are everywhere. Public schools are one illustration of government's work to promote the general welfare, as are its efforts to protect the quality of the air you breathe, the water you drink, and the food you eat.

In addition to these efforts to protect the environment, the government has also worked to combat climate change in recent years, through federal regulations such as one that controls the release of methane from oil and gas wells on public land. Yet another example of government serving citizens can be seen in the fight against monopolies during the Progressive Era, which the Federal Government addressed by passing the Sherman

Anti-Trust Act in 1890 and establishing the Anti-Trust Division of the Justice Department in 1933. The list of tasks government performs for your benefit goes on and on.

Some governmental functions that are common in other countries—operating steel mills, airlines, and coal mines, for example—are not carried out by government in this country. In general, the services that government provides in the United States are those that benefit all or most people. In those governments in which powerful leaders hold absolute authority over the people—authoritarian regimes—the general welfare of the people is not an underlying purpose of government. Thus, these governments, both past and present, do not concern themselves with tasks to promote that welfare unless there is some benefit to the ruling elite.

Secure the Blessings of Liberty
This nation was founded by those who loved liberty and prized it above all earthly possessions. They believed with Thomas Jefferson that "the God who gave us life gave us liberty at the same time." They subscribed to Benjamin Franklin's maxim: "They that can give up essential liberty to obtain a little temporary safety deserve neither liberty nor safety."

The American dedication to freedom for the individual recognizes that liberty cannot be absolute. It is, instead, a relative matter. Among the responsibilities, duties, and obligations of citizenship are observing the laws and serving the public good. No one can be free to do whatever he or she pleases, for that behavior would interfere with the freedoms of others. As Clarence Darrow, the great defense lawyer, once said: "You can only be free if I am free."

Both the Federal Constitution and the State constitutions set out many guarantees of rights and liberties for the individual in this country. That does not mean that those guarantees are so firmly established that they exist forever, however. To preserve and protect them, each generation must learn and understand them anew, and be willing to stand up for them when necessary.

For many people, the inspiration to protect our rights and liberties arises from deep feelings of patriotism. Patriotism is the love of one's country; the passion that drives one to serve one's country, either by defending it from invasion or by protecting its rights and maintaining its laws and institutions. Patriotism is the defining characteristic of a good citizen, the noblest passion that animates a man or a woman in the character of a citizen. As a good citizen, you, too, must agree with the belief that "eternal vigilance is the price of liberty."

Government in Citizens' Daily Lives
How does government affect your daily life at the local, State, and national levels?

Government at both the national and State levels protects your rights. On a day-to-day basis, this means you are free to do such things as write a letter to the editor criticizing the President or gather with others at a rally opposing the building of an oil pipeline.

If you woke this morning to the alarm on a cell phone, the time on the clock was set to official U.S. time, which is provided by the National Institute of Standards and Technology in the executive branch. If you rode to school on a school bus, the bus was paid for by taxes collected by your local government. Construction of the road on which the bus traveled was funded by either the State or local government.

Perhaps you work at the local grocery store after school. If so, your State sets the minimum wage that your employer must pay you—and that wage cannot be lower than the federal minimum wage for your age and student status. If you happened to stop by the bank to deposit your paycheck, that deposit is automatically insured against loss by the Federal Government.

These are just a few examples. As you can see from them, government at all levels in this country has a major effect on citizens' daily lives.

☑ **EXPLAIN** Why is it important to have a written constitution?

☑ ASSESSMENT

1. **Distinguish** Distinguish among the three basic types of power that many governments have.

2. **Infer** Explain why the phrase "the laws of nature and nature's God" was included in the Declaration of Independence.

3. **Summarize** Summarize the divine right of kings and the social contract theories.

4. **Make Generalizations** How can people demonstrate their understanding of the responsibilities, duties, and obligations of citizenship?

5. **Apply Concepts** How does the Federal Government serve the purposes set forth in the Preamble to the Constitution?

Early Theories on Government

The Greek philosopher Aristotle (384–322 B.C.) was suspicious of direct democracy, which he thought could lead to mob rule. Instead, Aristotle favored rule by a single strong and virtuous leader. In this excerpt from *Politics*, Aristotle outlines the forms of government and discusses the strengths and weaknesses of each. Some 2,000 years later, philosopher Jean-Jacques Rousseau (1712–1778) commented on government in his work *The Social Contract* (1762). In it, he says that the individual gives up some of his or her freedom in exchange for the protection and benefits offered by government.

>> Greek philosopher Aristotle

Politics: Aristotle

First, let us consider what is the purpose of a state, and how many forms of government there are by which human society is regulated. We have already said, in the first part of this treatise [written work on a particular topic], when discussing household management and the rule of a master, that man is by nature a political animal. And therefore, men, even when they do not require one another's help, desire to live together . . . and are also brought together by their common interests . . . well-being . . . is certainly the chief end, both of individuals and of states. . . .

☑ **DETERMINE CENTRAL IDEAS** According to Aristotle, what is the purpose of a state?

The conclusion is evident: that governments which have a regard to the common interest are constituted [made or composed of] in accordance with strict principles of justice, and are therefore true forms; but those which regard only the interest of the rulers are all defective and perverted forms, for they are despotic [characteristic of a tyrant or absolute ruler], whereas a state is a community of freemen. . . .

☑ **SUMMARIZE** What are the two types of government that Aristotle describes in this passage?

Of forms of government in which one rules, we call that which regards the common interests kingship or royalty; that in which more than one, but not many, rule, aristocracy; and it is so called, either because the rulers are the best men, or because they have at heart the best interests of the state and of the citizens. But when the citizens at large administer the state for the common interest, the government is called by the generic [general] name—a constitution. . . .

☑ **COMPARE AND CONTRAST** How does Aristotle define a constitutional government, as opposed to a royal government or an aristocracy?

Of the above-mentioned forms, the perversions are as follows: of royalty, tyranny; of aristocracy, oligarchy; of constitutional government, democracy. For tyranny is a kind of monarchy which has in view the interest of the monarch only; oligarchy has in view the interest of the wealthy; democracy, of the needy; none of them the common good of all.

Tyranny, as I was saying, is monarchy exercising the rule of a master over the political society; oligarchy is when men of property have the government in their hands; democracy, the opposite, when the indigent, and not the men of property, are the rulers.

☑ **DETERMINE AUTHOR'S POINT OF VIEW** What is Aristotle's view of democracy, and why?

The Social Contract: Jean-Jacques Rousseau

What we have just said confirms . . . that the depositaries [people who are entrusted with] of the executive power are not the people's masters, but its officers; that it can set them up and pull them down when it likes; that for them there is no question of contract, but of obedience and that in taking charge of the functions the State imposes on them they are doing no more than fulfilling their duty as citizens, without having the remotest right to argue about the conditions. . . .

It is true that ... the established government should never be touched except when it comes to be incompatible with the public good; but the circumspection [careful thought and judgment] this involves is a maxim [general truth or rule of conduct] of policy and not a rule of right, and the State is no more bound to leave civil authority in the hands of its rulers than military authority in the hands of its generals. . . .

The periodical assemblies of which I have already spoken are designed to prevent or postpone this calamity, above all when they need no formal summoning; for in that case, the prince cannot stop them without openly declaring himself a law-breaker and an enemy of the State.

The opening of these assemblies, whose sole object is the maintenance of the social treaty, should always take the form of putting two propositions that may not be suppressed, which should be voted on separately.

The first is: "Does it please the Sovereign to preserve the present form of government?"

The second is: "Does it please the people to leave its administration in the hands of those who are actually [currently] in charge of it?"

☑ **DETERMINE CENTRAL IDEAS** What is the central idea of this passage from *The Social Contract?*

☑ ASSESSMENT

1. **Define Meaning** What does Aristotle mean when he says, "man is by nature a political animal"?

2. **Identify Supporting Details** What details does Rousseau provide to support the central idea that you have identified?

3. **Summarize** Write an accurate summary that shows how the details you have identified support Rousseau's central idea.

1.2

The United Kingdom is a constitutional monarchy, in which a monarch acts as head of state guided by a constitution. In this photograph of Parliament, Queen Elizabeth and Prince Philip sit on thrones.

 BOUNCE to Activate Flipped Video

Objectives

Classify governments according to three sets of characteristics.

Define systems of government based on who can participate.

Identify ways that power can be distributed, geographically, within a state.

Describe a government by the distribution of power between the legislative branch and executive branch.

Key Terms

autocracy
oligarchy
theocracy
unitary government
federal government
division of powers
confederation
presidential
 government
parliamentary
 government
Alexander Pope
Abraham Lincoln

Types of Government

Does the form a government takes, the way in which it is structured, have any importance? Political scientists, historians, and other social commentators have long argued that question. The English poet Alexander Pope wrote a couplet about the issue in 1733:

> For Forms of Government let fools contest;
> Whate'er is best adminster'd is best. . . ."

—*Essay on Man*

Classifying Governments

Was Pope right? Does it matter what form a government takes? Pope thought not. You can form your own opinion as you read this section.

No two governments are, or ever have been, exactly alike, for governments are the products of human needs and experiences. All governments can be classified according to one or more of their basic features, however. Over time, political scientists have developed many bases upon which to classify (and so to describe, compare, and analyze) governments.

Three of those classifications are especially important and useful. These are classifications according to (1) who can participate in the governing process, (2) the geographic distribution of governmental power within the state, and (3) the relationship between the legislative (lawmaking) and the executive (law-executing) branches of the government.

☑ **SUMMARIZE** Restate in your own words the three most important characteristics that political scientists use to classify governments.

Who Can Participate?

To many people, the most meaningful of these classifications is the one that depends on the number of persons who can take part in the governing process. Here there are two basic forms to consider: democracies and dictatorships.

Democracy In a democracy, supreme political authority rests with the people. The people hold the sovereign power, and government is conducted only by and with the consent of the people.

Abraham Lincoln gave immortality to this definition of democracy in his Gettysburg Address in 1863: "government of the people, by the people, for the people." Nowhere is there a better, more concise statement of the American understanding of democracy.

A democracy can be either direct or indirect in form. A direct democracy, also called a pure democracy, exists where the will of the people is translated into public policy (law) directly by the people themselves, in mass meetings. Such was the case in Ancient Greece and Rome. Clearly, direct democracy can work only in small communities, where the citizenry can meet in a central place, and where the problems of government are few and relatively simple.

Direct Democracy and Indirect Democracy

Direct democracy does not exist at the national level anywhere in the world today. However, the New England town meeting and the *Landsgemeinde* in a few of the smaller Swiss cantons are excellent examples of direct democracy in action.

Americans are more familiar with the indirect form of democracy—that is, with a constitutional republic or representative democracy. In a representative democracy, a small group of persons, chosen by the people to act as their representatives, expresses the popular will. These agents of the people are responsible for carrying out the day-to-day conduct of government—the making and executing of laws and so on. They are held accountable to the people for that conduct, especially at periodic elections.

At these elections, the people have an opportunity to express their approval or disapproval of their representatives by casting ballots for or against them. To put it another way, representative democracy is government by popular consent— government with the consent of the governed.

Republic Some people insist that the United States is more properly called a republic rather than a democracy. They hold that in a republic the sovereign power is held by those eligible to vote, while the political power is exercised by representatives chosen by and held responsible to those citizens. For them, democracy can be defined only in terms of a direct democracy.

Many Americans use the terms *democracy, republic, representative democracy,* and *republican form of government* interchangeably, although they

Direct And Indirect Democracy

WHO GOVERNS?	
Direct Democracy	**Indirect Democracy**
• Also called pure democracy • The people themselves formulate public policy • Works only at a small, local level	• Also called representative democracy • A group of persons chosen by the people formulates public policy • Widely used at the national, State, and local levels

>> Democratic government derives its power from the people but can be either direct or indirect democracy. **Analyze Charts** Why might indirect democracy be better for a larger population?

are not the same. Whatever the term used, remember that in a democracy the people are in charge. They are the only source for any and all of government's power. In other words, the people rule.

Dictatorship Authoritarian forms of government such as a dictatorship exists where those who rule cannot be held responsible to the will of the people. The government is not accountable for its policies, nor for how they are carried out. Dictatorship is probably the oldest, and it is certainly the most common, form of government known to history.

Dictatorships are sometimes identified as either autocracies or oligarchies. An **autocracy** is a government in which a single person holds unlimited political power. An **oligarchy** is a government in which the power to rule is held by a small, usually self-appointed elite.

Modern Dictatorships All dictatorships are authoritarian; those in power hold absolute and unchallengeable authority over the people. Modern dictatorships have tended to be totalitarian, as well. That is, they exercise complete power over nearly every aspect of human affairs. Their power embraces all matters of human concern.

The leading examples of dictatorship in the modern era have been those in Fascist Italy (from 1922 to 1943), in Nazi Germany (from 1933 to 1945), in the Soviet Union (from 1917 until the late 1980s), and one that still exists in the People's Republic of China (where the present regime came to power in 1949).

Although they do exist, one-person dictatorships are not at all common today. A few close approaches to such a regime can be found in North Korea, led by Kim Jong-un (who succeeded his father, Kim Jong-il, in 2011), and in some European, Arab and African states.

Most present-day dictatorships are not nearly so absolutely controlled by a single person or by a small group as may appear to be the case. Outward appearances may hide the fact that several groups— the army, religious leaders, industrialists, and others—compete for power in the political system.

Dictatorships often present the outward appearance of control by the people. The people often vote in popular elections, but the vote is closely controlled, and ballots usually contain the names of candidates of only one political party. An elected legislative body often exists, but its only purpose is to rubber-stamp the policies of the dictatorship.

Forms of Government Around the World

KEY
- Constitution-based federal republic
- Constitutional monarchy
- Communist state
- Communist state one-man dictatorship
- Theocracy

>> There are different forms of government all over the world. People express their will differently in each. **Analyze Maps** How does each government's reaction differ to expressions of will?

Typically, dictatorial regimes are militaristic in character. They usually gain power by force. The military holds many of the major posts in the government. After crushing all effective opposition at home, these regimes may turn to foreign aggression to enhance the country's military power, political control, and prestige.

Theocracy A **theocracy** exists where the legal system of a state is based on religious law. Theocracies were more common in early civilizations, but have become rare in modern times. Iran is one example of a present-day theocracy, often referred to as a theocratic Islamic republic.

Iran's government resembles a parliamentary democracy, based upon their 1979 constitution, and holds elections to fill many of its governmental posts. However, most scholars agree that Iran is a theocracy because the Supreme Leader, who is appointed by an Islamic religious advisory board, is the highest state authority and has the final say in all matters. All laws passed by the government must also be compatible with Sharia, the moral code and religious law of Islam.

A Tribal Government and the Venetian Republic
The Vandals were one of many Germanic tribes in Europe during the Roman Empire. Their original leader was a central chief, a member of the royal clan, who was elected for life and held religious and military responsibilities. This type of military chieftainship was replaced when the Vandals established their kingdom in North Africa. Government officials replaced the old tribal aristocracy, and later, a monarchy was created that allowed only the royal family to succeed to the throne. This new kingdom helped to bring about the fall of the Roman Empire.

Another type of republic was the Venetian republic. Its capital was Venice, a center of industry, trade, and culture. The Venetian republic existed from the late 7th century to the late 18th century and was one of the most successful city-states. The republic was ruled by the Doge, elected by representatives of the rich and noble families, and the Great Council who managed the state's affairs. During its later years Venice began to lose its position as the center of trade to other empires surrounding the Mediterranean Sea, such as the Ottoman Empire. The state eventually came to an end with the outbreak of the French Revolution. Napoleon Bonaparte, a military reformer of the revolution, was determined to destroy the Venetian republic. Venice was without an ally in the conflict

>>North Korean dictator Kim Jong-un observes a military procession. Kim has the same "military first" policy as his father, the previous dictator.

and was forced to depose its last Doge and become a part of the state of Austria.

☑ **IDENTIFY MAIN IDEAS** What is the most important feature of a democracy?

Geographic Distribution of Power

In every system of government, the power to govern is located in one or more places geographically. From this standpoint, three basic forms of government exist: unitary, federal, and confederate.

Centralized Government A **unitary government** is often described as a centralized government. All powers held by the government belong to a single, central agency. The central (national) government creates local units of government for its own convenience. Those local governments have only those powers that the central government chooses to give them.

Great Britain Most governments in the world are unitary in form. Great Britain is a classic illustration.

DISTRIBUTION OF POWER BY GOVERNMENT TYPE

UNITARY GOVERNMENT	FEDERAL GOVERNMENT	CONFEDERATE GOVERNMENT
ADVANTAGE	**ADVANTAGE**	**ADVANTAGE**
One **central government** means greater uniformity and efficiency.	The **national government** and the **states** are coequal partners.	Most power belongs to the **local (regional) governments.**
DISADVANTAGE	**DISADVANTAGE**	**DISADVANTAGE**
Distant **central government** may not understand citizens' needs.	Conflicts inevitably arise between the two levels of government and some functions and services are duplicated.	The **central government** only has limited power, which restricts its ability to act on behalf of the confederacy as a whole.

>> Power can be distributed between central (national) and local governments in different ways. **Analyze Charts** Which diagram describes the distribution of power in the United States?

A single central organization, the Parliament, holds all of the government's power. Local governments do exist—but solely to relieve Parliament of burdens it could perform only with much inconvenience. Though unlikely, Parliament could do away with all local government in Britain at any time. This is one of the disadvantages of unitary governments.

Other disadvantages of unitary systems are that the concentration of authority in one central government can lead to an abuse of power. In addition, a far-off central government may not have a good understanding of citizens' needs. The advantages of a unitary system are that its laws are applied uniformly and there is little duplication of effort or conflicts between levels of government.

Note that the central government might not hold all power. In Great Britain, for example, the powers held by the government are limited. British government is unitary and, at the same time, democratic.

Federal Government A **federal government**
is one in which the powers of government are divided between a central government and several local governments. This **division of powers** has a geographic basis, meaning it cannot be changed by either the local or national level acting alone. Both levels of government act directly on the people through their own sets of laws, officials, and agencies.

In the United States, for example, the National Government has certain powers, and the 50 States have others. This division of powers is set out in the Constitution of the United States. The Constitution stands above both levels of government; it cannot be changed unless the people, acting through both the National Government and the States, agree to the change.

Advantages to this model include that both national and State power are limited and preserved under a federal system, that government is closer to the people, and that individualized solutions to issues can be implemented on a State-by-State basis, which also encourages innovation. A clear disadvantage of the federal system of government is that each of the 50 States can have its own policy on the same issue. There can also be frequent conflicts between levels of government.

In the United States, the phrase "the Federal Government" is often used to identify the National Government, the government headquartered in Washington, D.C. Note, however, that each of the 50 State governments in this country is unitary, not federal, in form.

Australia, Canada, Mexico, Switzerland, Germany, India, and some 20 other countries also have federal forms of government today.

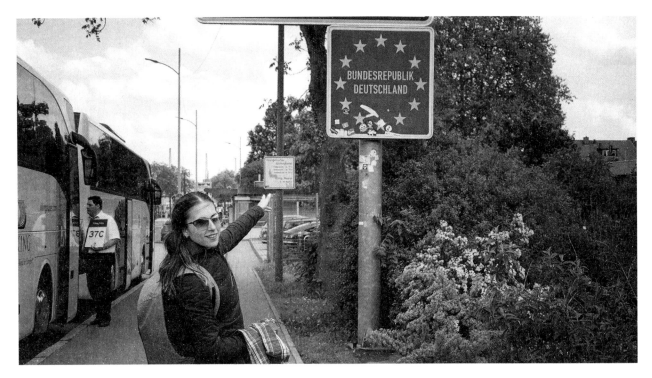

>> A young woman points at the German European Union sign as she crosses the border into Germany. Every EU citizen can travel, work and live in any EU country and citizens can cross internal borders without being subjected to border checks.

Confederation A **confederation** is an alliance of independent states. A central organization has the power to handle only those matters that the member states have assigned to it. Typically, confederate governments have had limited powers and only in such fields as defense and foreign affairs.

Most often, confederate governments have not had the power to make laws that apply directly to individuals, at least not without some further action by the member states. A confederate structure of government makes it possible for the several states to cooperate in matters of common concern and, at the same time, retain their separate identities.

Under this model, government is closer to the people and laws can be written to meet the needs of the individual states. On the other hand, the central government has only limited power, which restricts its ability to act on behalf of the confederacy as a whole.

In our own history, the United States under the Articles of Confederation (1781–1789) and the Confederate States of America (1861–1865) also provide examples of this form of government.

Confederations are rare today. The European Union (EU) is the closest approach to one in modern times. Formed by 12 countries in 1993, it has more than doubled its member nations since that time. The EU has established free trade among its members, launched a common currency, and seeks to coordinate its members' foreign and defense policies.

☑ **IDENTIFY MAIN IDEAS** How is power distributed in a Federal government?

Legislative and Executive Branches

Political scientists also classify governments based on the relationship between their legislative (law-making) and executive (law-executing) agencies. This classification yields two basic forms of government, known as parliamentary and presidential.

Separation of Powers Between Branches of Government A **presidential government** is a system of shared powers in which the executive and legislative branches have separate powers. The two branches are independent of one another and coequal. The chief executive (the President) is chosen by the people, independently of the legislature. He or she holds office for a fixed term and has a number of significant powers that are not subject to the direct control of the legislative branch.

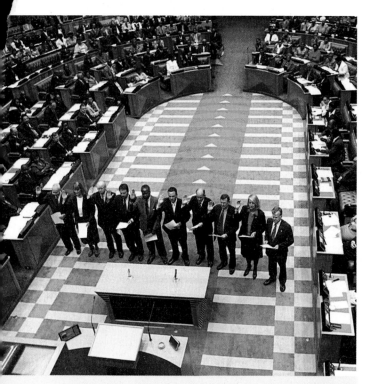

>> Members of the South African parliament are sworn into office. A voter-elected National Assembly and a National Council of Provinces comprise the South African Parliament.

Written Constitution The details of this separation of the powers of these two branches are almost always spelled out in a written constitution—as they are in the United States. This system serves to limit power, as does the fact that each of the branches is regularly given several powers with which it can block actions of the other branch.

The United States is the world's leading example of presidential government. In fact, the United States invented the form. Nearly all of the other presidential systems that exist in the world today are also found in the Western Hemisphere.

Parliamentary Government In a **parliamentary government,** the executive branch is made up of the prime minister or premier, and that official's cabinet. The prime minister and cabinet are themselves members of the legislative branch, the parliament. The prime minister is the leader of the majority party or of a like-minded group of parties (a coalition) and is chosen by that body. With parliament's approval, the prime minister selects the members of the cabinet from among the members of parliament. The executive is thus chosen by the legislature, is a part of it, and is subject to its direct control.

In a parliamentary system, power is limited by the fact that the party in the minority has the duty to challenge the majority party on any actions or positions it opposes. In addition, the prime minister and the cabinet (often called "the government") remain in office only as long as their policies and administration have the support of a majority in parliament. If the parliament defeats the prime minister and cabinet on an important matter, the government may receive a "vote of no confidence," and the prime minister and his cabinet must resign from office. Either parliament chooses a new prime minister or, as often happens, all the seats in parliament go before the voters in a general election.

Advantages and Disadvantages of Presidential and Parliamentary Systems A majority of the governmental systems in the world today are parliamentary, not presidential, in form. Parliamentary government avoids one of the major problems of the presidential form: prolonged conflict and sometimes deadlock between the executive and legislative branches because very often the legislature is controlled by one political party, and the President is a member of a different party. The outcome can be gridlock. However, the protections against arbitrary government found in the checks and balances of presidential government are not a part of the parliamentary system.

☑ **CITE EVIDENCE** Compare and contrast presidential and parliamentary forms of government. Describe advantages and disadvantages of each. Cite evidence from the text to support your answer.

☑ ASSESSMENT

1. **Compare** How does a direct democracy differ from an indirect democracy?

2. **Determine Central Ideas** What do the unitary, federal, and confederate forms of government have in common?

3. **Make Inferences** What is the difference between a democracy and a republican form of government? Which is the United States?

4. **Compare Points of View** Should democracies take action to help prevent dictatorships? Why or why not?

5. **Cite Evidence** How is the executive branch related to the legislative branch in a presidential government?

The U.S. Supreme Court building, completed in 1935, was designed to resemble the classic Greek and Roman temples and to reflect the same values and significance.

Origins of the Modern Democratic State

The roots of democratic government in today's world—including government in the United States—lie deep in human history. They reach back most particularly to ancient Greece and Rome, and also to elements of Judeo-Christian philosophy and later beliefs and practices that emerged elsewhere in Europe.

Building on the Past

Those who built a governmental system for the newly independent United States in the late 1700s were a well-read and well-educated group. They were quite familiar with the political institutions and philosophies of ancient Asia, Africa, and Europe.

Athens: The First Democracy Greek civilization began to develop some 700 to 800 years before the common era B.C.E., and it reached its peak in the fourth century B.C.E. The Greece of that time was a loose collection of many small, independent, and somewhat isolated city-states—a pattern dictated by the geography of the region, where every island, valley, and plain is cut off from its neighbors by the sea or by mountain ranges.

The concept of democracy was born in those city-states, most notably in Athens. By the sixth century B.C., however, the Athenians had overthrown monarchical rule, and they soon replaced it with what they called *demokratia*—literally, "rule by the people."

BOUNCE to Activate Flipped Video

Objectives

Identify the ancient foundations of the state in Athens, in Rome and in the Feudal system.

Analyze the rise of sovereign states.

Explain how governments can achieve legitimacy.

Understand why European nations turned to colonialism.

Understand how Enlightenment ideas helped influence the expansion of popular sovereignty.

Key Terms

patricians
plebeians
feudalism
sovereignty
legitimacy
divine right of kings
colonialism
mercantilism

François-Marie
 Arouet
William Blackstone

Athenian democracy was, at base, direct democracy. Its central feature was an Assembly (the *Ecclesia*) open to all male citizens at least 18 years of age. The Assembly debated public matters and made law. Decisions in the Assembly were made by majority vote. The Assembly's agenda was set by a Council of Five Hundred (the *boule*). That body was composed of 500 citizens who were chosen randomly, served one-year terms, and did the routine day-to-day work of government.

The writings of many ancient Greek political thinkers had a strong influence on the development of American government some two thousand years later. The Greek leader Pericles encapsulated the underlying philosophy behind American democracy when he said "Our constitution ... favors the many instead of the few; this is why it is called a democracy. If we look to the laws, they afford equal justice to all. ..."

Similarly, the American system of representative democracy was developed with a nod to Greek philosophers such as Aristotle and Plato, who viewed direct democracy as rule by the rabble, dangerous and unstable. James Madison and many of the Framers agreed. This is one of the reasons, in addition to the sheer size of the country, that they fashioned a representative, rather than a direct, democracy. Aristotle also described the separation of powers among distinct parts of the government, drew a connection between democracy and liberty, and advocated the rule of law. All these ideas were also later adopted by the United States.

Athens reached the peak of its glory in art, literature, and philosophy in the fifth century B.C., but it had been severely weakened by the long Peloponnesian War (431–404 B.C.) and later conquest by the Macedonians. What remained of Athenian democracy was extinguished by the Romans who overran Greece in 146 B.C.

The Roman Republic At about the time that glimmers of democracy first appeared in Greece, they began to emerge as well in Rome on the Italian peninsula. Rome was founded in 753 B.C. and, like Athens, was originally a city-state ruled by a monarchy. Monarchical rule was overthrown in 509 B.C. and was soon replaced by a crude form of popular government. The Romans referred to their new system as *res publica*, a republic.

The Roman Republic was to last for some 400 years, until it became the Roman Empire at the end of the first century B.C. Over that period, Rome expanded its domain to include most of the lands surrounding the Mediterranean Sea and nearly all of Western Europe.

The Republic was far from democratic in the modern sense. It did introduce the concept of representation, however. Much of the political history of the republican period revolved around an often violent struggle between two social classes: the **patricians**, mostly rich upper-class, landowning aristocrats; and the **plebeians**, the common folk. The Romans did hold elections to choose some public officials, but women, the enslaved, and the foreign-born could not participate.

Government was centered in the Senate, composed of some 300 members, and two consuls chosen by the Senate. Senators were elected by the citizenry. The patricians dominated that body, but, over time, an increasing number of plebeians were elected to the Senate and to a number of lesser assemblies. The consuls were, effectively, the heads of state. They commanded the army and conducted foreign affairs. The consuls also presided over the Senate and enforced its decrees.

The influence of ancient Rome echoed through the centuries, to the founding of the United States. The men who shaped the American government adopted the Roman idea of representative government. They also borrowed a great deal from the writings of Marcus Tullius Cicero, a leading political figure during the Roman Empire, including the notion that the primary goal of public officials should be the welfare of the people.

>> Power in the ancient Athenian government came from the people, not from a single ruler.

STRUCTURE OF THE ROMAN GOVERNMENT DURING THE REPUBLIC

CONSULS

2 CONSULS

ELECTED —BY— LEGISLATIVE ASSEMBLIES

CHIEF **EXECUTIVES** OF **GOVERNMENT**

COMMANDERS OF THE **ARMY IN WARTIME**

SERVED **1**-YEAR TERM

SENATE

300 SENATORS

PROPOSED **LAWS**

CHOSEN BY CONSULS

MOST **POWERFUL GOVERNING BODY**

HAD **VETO** POWER OVER ANY ACTS OF ASSEMBLIES OR CONSULS

ADVISED CONSULS AND **ASSEMBLIES**

MEMBERS — SERVED A — **LIFE TERM**

LEGISLATIVE ASSEMBLIES

— PASSED — **LAWS**

— COUNCIL OF — **PLEBEIANS**

CURIATE ASSEMBLY COMPRISED OF

ASSEMBLY OF TRIBES AND **ASSEMBLY OF CENTURIANS**

ELECTED THE CONSULS FROM **SENATE** ✓

>> During the Roman republic, Plebeians (commoners) were part of the legislative assembly. **Analyze Charts** What kind of power was available to Roman Plebeians?

Feudalism The decline and fall of the Roman Empire in the fifth century A.D. marked the beginning of the Middle Ages—the period from that epochal event on to the 16th century. It also marked the collapse of centralized authority and organized government over vast stretches of the western world. For more than a thousand years, that world would know little or nothing of government in the modern sense of the term.

The feudal system was born in response to that chaos and disorder. It developed in fits and starts and came to hold sway over much of Europe from the ninth through the twelfth centuries. **Feudalism** was a loosely organized system in which powerful lords divided their lands among other, lesser lords. Those with land and power agreed to protect others in exchange for their loyalty, their military service, and a share of the crops they produced. The basic economic units in the feudal system were the lords' manors. Each manor contained all of a lord's land holdings, which often included a town or village, as well.

The Structure of the Feudal System The primary relationship in the feudal chain was that between a lord and his vassals, lesser lords who pledged their loyalty to the ranking lord—who was, in some places, a monarch. The lord ruled and the vassals served him, watching over the lands in their section of the manor. The lord provided protection for his vassals and administered a rough form of justice.

Serfs, the bulk of the population, lived at the bottom of the chain of feudal relationships. They were peasants, bound to the land they farmed. The serfs gave a share of what they grew to their vassals in return for protection in times of war. They led harsh lives. None could leave the land without the lord's permission, and their children inherited their ties and responsibilities to the lord. Most died young, never having journeyed more than a few miles from the lord's manor.

The Roman Catholic Church As the Roman Empire had spread across Western Europe, so had Roman Catholicism. The Church survived the collapse of imperial rule and now, in concert with feudalism, it provided some measure of government-like order to life in the Europe of the Middle Ages.

The Roman Catholic Church, now nearly 2,000 years old, traces its origins to the birth of Christianity and to the death of Jesus in Jerusalem, in the Roman province of Judea, in A.D. 33. Its teachings drew from Biblical texts, including the book of Exodus, in which Moses is described as bringing the Ten Commandments to the people of Israel. Catholicism managed to overcome three centuries of often violent persecution by a succession of hostile emperors. In A.D. 380, the Roman Catholic Church became the official church of the Roman Empire.

As most of Europe was converted to Christianity—that is, as most Europeans became Catholics—the Roman Catholic Church became increasingly powerful. By the late Middle Ages, the pope and his bishops ruled vast land holdings, and they frequently vied with monarchs and lords for political as well as religious influence over people's lives.

☑ **POSE AND ANSWER QUESTIONS** How long did the Roman Republic operate?

Nations and Kings

Feudalism was, at best, a loose, makeshift basis for government. As cracks emerged in the system—between Catholics and Protestants and the feudal manor and the marketplace—the need for a more structured arrangement became apparent. The outlines of the modern, sovereign nation-state began to emerge.

The Commercial Revolution By the end of the Middle Ages, a commercial revolution began to change the ways in which people lived and did business. A horrific plague, the Black Plague of the 1340s, was a major catalyst of that revolution. In all, it killed a third of Western Europe's population. The Plague itself did not destroy the feudal system. Rather its far-reaching effects undercut that system.

After the plague, the manors still depended on the same amount of work, but from the smaller number of serfs who had survived. Serfs and free peasants found strength in the high value of their labor and began to demand higher wages and better conditions.

Because of the vast decrease in population caused by the plague, the prices of food crops fell, and so the lords made less money from their manorial lands. Merchants and artisans became increasingly wealthy and more powerful. The economy became increasingly based on money and trade, rather than land.

The Influence of Towns As you know, feudalism relied on personal relationships and agreements in which people exchanged work and food for security and justice. Over time, lords had to find new ways to gather money. Some lords accepted money from their vassals in place of military service. Others allowed free people to set up towns on their land for a fee under a charter. In this way, towns began to spring up across Europe. Those towns were centers of trade and freedom that tested the limits of feudalism.

The most important of these towns were found in northern Italy, northern Germany, and the Netherlands. Their income came from trade with Central Europe and Asia. The merchants in these towns had uneasy relationships with the lords.

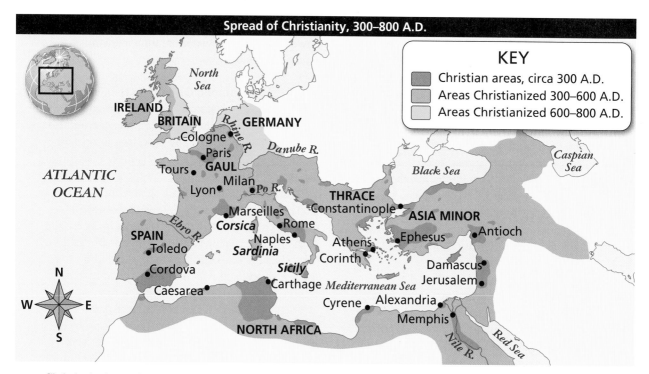

>> Christianity began in the Middle East and diffused across widely settled lands.
Analyze Maps According to the map, how far had Christianity spread by about 800 A.D.?

Monarchical Government During the Middle Ages

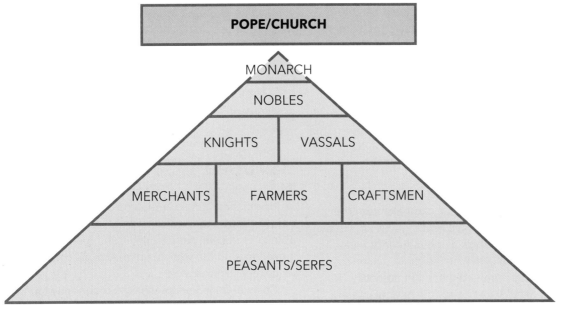

POPE/CHURCH

MONARCH

NOBLES

KNIGHTS

VASSALS

MERCHANTS

FARMERS

CRAFTSMEN

PEASANTS/SERFS

>> During the Middle Ages, kings had absolute power over their subjects. **Analyze Charts** How did the structure of the government support "absolute monarchies?"

Although the merchants were free, they had to pay money to lords for protection, duties on their trade goods, and the right to use roads, rivers, and bridges. Many lords tried to extend their system of justice to the towns. They often failed because they depended on the merchants and bankers of the towns for loans. Trade guilds also developed in the cities and towns, and their members demanded a say in government.

The Rise of Monarchies All of these factors began to undermine the feudal system, weakening the power of the lords. At the same time, the leaders of the towns began to appreciate the benefits of supporting a central authority and they allied themselves with monarchs. The monarchs, in turn, saw the towns as a source of wealth that could free them from dependence on their vassals.

Therefore, by the late 1400s the power of the monarchs was expanding, and feudalism was fast disappearing. In nations such as England, Spain, and France, rulers centralized power, establishing national governments with national legal systems, national identities, and, most important for the monarchs, national taxes. Warfare now was between national armies, not between powerful nobles. Monarchs, whose power was absolute or nearly so, no longer needed the lords to support them and could also ignore popular representative assemblies, if they wished, for long periods of time.

The Power of Absolute Monarchs To help manage the national government, monarchs hired loyal civil servants typically born in the towns and educated at local universities. Their perspectives were national, not regional. The state, in the person of the monarch, now had **sovereignty**, or the utmost authority in decision making and in maintaining order. Everyone, including the nobles, was subordinate to that authority. This form of ultimate power is often referred to as "absolute monarchy."

Because monarchs already existed within the feudal system, they enjoyed the benefits and respect of tradition. A monarch was now recognized as the strongest individual who could best govern a state and protect the people from harm. With sovereignty, the monarch now had the right to make laws for the entire nation and all its people.

☑ **CHECK UNDERSTANDING** Which form of government had become most prevalent in Europe in 1490?

Power, Authority, and Legitimacy

The development of the sovereign state was useful in creating political organization, but claiming sovereignty alone does not establish government. All governments must have legitimacy to rule.

Rulers have strong reasons to seek consent for their rule. This consent is known as **legitimacy**, the belief of the people that a government has the right to make public policy. A legitimate government is one that is accepted by its people and other governments as the sovereign authority of a nation. Leaders may use force to keep power. However, force is difficult to maintain over time.

Forms of Legitimacy Governments may gain legitimacy in several ways. One is by tradition. In this case, people accept a certain form of government because their society has long been governed in that way, and people expect their institutions and traditions to be carried on into the future. One type of traditional legitimacy is known as the **divine right of kings**. For hundreds of years, European monarchs based their right to rule on this belief that God had granted them that authority. To disobey a monarch was to deny the natural order of society and to commit a sin against God. In theory, monarchs who ruled by divine right did not have to answer to parliaments or to the people, only to God. The divine right of kings drew its claim to legitimacy from Europe's deep-rooted Christian values.

Another way for a government, and in particular one leader, to win legitimacy is through the power of personality. A charismatic person with strong leadership skills can often win popular support. The people agree to allow this person to rule them.

The final and most durable form of legitimacy is created when a government binds itself to the rule of law. The law must be seen as fair and effective in order for people to trust their government. Constitutional government in the United States is an excellent example of this form of legitimacy.

☑ **APPLY CONCEPTS** What is a legitimate government?

European Colonialism

Beginning in the late 1400s and early 1500s, several European monarchies embarked on a policy of **colonialism**—the control of one nation over lands abroad. European settlers, laws, and religious beliefs spread around the world as rival nations competed for colonial possessions.

Colonial trade and its wealth brought newfound power to merchants, and monarchs adopted mercantilism to control and profit from that situation. **Mercantilism** is an economic and political theory emphasizing money as the chief source of wealth to increase the absolute power of the monarchy and the nation. The policy stressed the accumulation of precious metals, like gold and silver. It also called for the establishment of colonies and a merchant marine and the development of industry and mining to build a favorable balance of trade with other countries.

ROOTS OF DEMOCRACY

ATHENIAN DEMOCRACY
The Athenians introduced direct democracy. Citizens debated public questions and decided them by majority vote. Courts administered justice.

ROMAN REPUBLIC
The Roman Republic gave decision-making power to an elite Senate and consuls who could check each other and, in theory, represented the people. The laws of Rome were written for all to see.

FEUDALISM
In the Feudal Era, Europe's first parliaments emerged and began to limit the powers of kings. England provided for trial by a jury of one's peers.

SOVEREIGNTY
Sovereignty emerged in the 17th century, with states with fixed borders, a national identity, and a centralized government with broad authority.

DEMOCRACY
Signed on September 17, 1787, the U.S. Constitution established an American government based on Enlightenment philosophies. The Constitution limited the power of the Federal Government and separated it into three branches: executive, legislative, and judicial.

>> Democracy has its roots in governments from ancient Greece to the 1700s. **Analyze Charts** How did prior forms of sovereignty lead to the development of the United States and its Constitution?

Triangular Trade Routes

KEY
- - → First Leg
- - - → Second Leg (Middle Passage)
——→ Third Leg

>> By the 1700s many trade routes were established from Europe across the oceans.
Analyze Maps How does the Triangular Trade illustrate the policy of mercantilism?

Mercantilist policies brought the monarchy and the state deep into the economy. Monarchs taxed imports heavily to protect locally produced goods. Foreigners were required to buy licenses from the state in order to trade with local merchants. Monarchs sought to fill their treasuries and enhance their own and their nations' power.

Colonial Trade Mercantilism expanded when European explorers reached the Western Hemisphere. Their explorations there opened new opportunities for trade and farming, but only monarchs had the wealth and power to establish and control new colonies.

Monarchs soon controlled overseas commerce by setting up companies to monopolize trade with the new regions. The company system allowed monarchs to tap new sources of wealth from distant gold and silver mines and from far-flung trade.

European colonization brought about new developments in modern government. In particular, Britain's colonial efforts eventually led to the American Revolution and the creation of the United States and its constitutional government.

☑ **APPLY CONCEPTS** Why were monarchs able to monopolize overseas commerce?

Power Comes from the People

The period from roughly 1300 to 1600 in Europe is known as the Renaissance, a time of creativity and change in the arts, sciences, economics, and other areas. One product of this era was Niccoló Machiavelli, an Italian philosopher and statesman. Machiavelli's most famous work was *The Prince*. In it, he offered a practical guide to ruling, including the idea that a leader is justified in using any tactics necessary to preserve the state, including a willingness to go beyond the letter of the law. In his other works, Machiavelli discussed the ideas of natural law and the wisdom of allowing the people to choose their own rulers.

These ideas and others of Machiavelli's later found their way into the libraries and minds of the Framers of the United States Constitution. The system of government they designed incorporated some of them and guarded against the sort of tyrant to whom *The Prince* was addressed.

By the beginning of the eighteenth century, scientific discoveries and new thinking had led to an intellectual movement based on reason and known as the Enlightenment. Some of the most important ideas about modern government, economics, and society were developed at the time, as people began

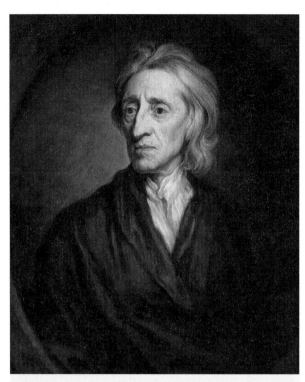

>> John Locke believed "the end of law is not to abolish or restrain, but to preserve and enlarge freedom."

to discuss the rights of individuals to control their own fates and to have a meaningful say in their governance.

Major Enlightenment Figures Early in the movement, English political theorist John Locke (1632–1704) put forth the notion of the natural rights of all men, including the rights to life, liberty, and property—ideas that later formed the basis for the Declaration of Independence. Locke, whose idea of natural rights was limited to white men, built on the view of fellow Englishman Thomas Hobbes (1588–1679): that the people and their rulers are parties to a social contract that defines the rights and powers of each. Economists, including Adam Smith (1723–1790) and David Ricardo (1772–1823), criticized those economic policies that had helped monarchs grow wealthier while most of their subjects became steadily poorer and less free.

In France, the philosopher **François-Marie Arouet** (1694–1778), known as Voltaire, advocated reason, freedom of religion, the importance of scientific observation, and the idea of human progress. The ideas of the Baron de Montesquieu (1689–1755) were crucial to political theory during the Enlightenment. His theories about the separation of powers of government, so that the different branches might check and balance one another, were integral to what was to become the Constitution of the United States. Another major Enlightenment figure who influenced the American Constitution was English jurist **William Blackstone**. Blackstone believed strongly in "common law"—the idea that legal decisions should be made on the basis of similar decisions made in the past.

As reason and secular thinking began to supersede religious belief, monarchs lost some of their divine legitimacy, and their God-given sovereignty came into question. More and more people began to feel that even monarchs governed only because the people granted them the power to do so. If a monarch abused his or her power, he or she broke the social contract with the people and no longer deserved to rule. In this way, popular sovereignty became increasingly important, even in a monarchy. Recall that popular sovereignty is the idea that governments can exist only with the consent of the governed.

Popular sovereignty would eventually form the basis for the many republics and democracies in the world today. Since the eighteenth century, almost every government has had to address issues of popular sovereignty in one way or another.

☑ **APPLY CONCEPTS** What is the purpose of a "social contract"?

☑ ASSESSMENT

1. **Contrast** How is feudalism different from popular sovereignty?

2. **Hypothesize** How might Europe be different if the Black Plague had never occurred?

3. **Identify Cause and Effect** What events were influential in the development of the Enlightenment?

4. **Apply Concepts** How did the Catholic Church support the claims of monarchs?

5. **Support Ideas with Examples** Provide an example of how the rise of monarchs led to colonialism.

Enlightenment Ideas

In 1748, the French aristocrat Baron de Montesquieu (1689–1755) wrote *The Spirit of Laws,* in which he concluded that the separation of the executive, legislative, and judicial powers was in the best interests of the people. Much earlier, English philosopher John Locke (1632–1704) had published *Two Treatises of Government* (1690). Locke believed that all people had the same natural rights of life, liberty, and property. Locke's ideas greatly influenced the American revolutionaries in the 1770s, and both Locke and Montesquieu inspired the Framers of the United States Constitution.

>> Baron de Montesquieu

The Spirit of Laws: Baron de Montesquieu

The principle of democracy is corrupted not only when the spirit of equality is extinct, but likewise when they fall into a spirit of extreme equality, and when each citizen would fain be [be satisfied] upon a level with those whom he has chosen to command him. Then the people, incapable of bearing the very power they have delegated, want to manage everything themselves, to debate for the senate, to execute for the magistrate [judicial officer], and to decide for the judges.

When this is the case, virtue can no longer subsist [survive] in the republic. The people are desirous of exercising the functions of the magistrates, who cease to be revered. . . .

Democracy has, therefore, two excesses to avoid—the spirit of inequality, which leads to aristocracy or monarchy, and the spirit of extreme equality, which leads to despotic [authoritarian; tyrannical] power, as the latter is completed by conquest. . . .

☑ **DETERMINE CENTRAL IDEAS** What two excesses does Montesquieu say a democracy should avoid? What does he say will happen if it does not?

In the state of nature, indeed, all men are born equal, but they cannot continue in this equality. Society makes them lose it, and they recover it only by the protection of the laws.

Such is the difference between a well-regulated democracy and one that is not so, that in the former men are equal only as citizens, but in the latter they are equal also as magistrates, as senators, as judges, as fathers, as husbands, or as masters.

The natural place of virtue is near to liberty; but it is not nearer to excessive liberty than to servitude. . . .

☑ **DETERMINE AUTHOR'S POINT OF VIEW** What are Montesquieu's views on equality as they pertain to a democracy? Do you agree or disagree with him?

Democratic and aristocratic states are not in their own nature free. Political liberty is to be found only in moderate governments; and even in these it is not always found. It is there only when there is no abuse of power. . . .

To prevent this abuse, it is necessary from the very nature of things that power should be a check to power. A government may be so constituted, as no man shall be compelled to do things to which the law does not oblige him, nor forced to abstain from things which the law permits. . . .

Primary Sources

☑ **PARAPHRASE** Using your own words, explain what Montesquieu says is the best way to avoid the abuse of power by governmental officials.

When the legislative and executive powers are united in the same person, or in the same body of magistrates, there can be no liberty; because apprehensions may arise, lest the same monarch or senate should enact tyrannical laws, to execute them in a tyrannical manner. . . .

Again, there is no liberty, if the judiciary power be not separated from the legislative and executive. Were it joined with the legislative, the life and liberty of the subject would be exposed to arbitrary control; for the judge would be then the legislator. Were it joined to the executive power, the judge might behave with violence and oppression.

There would be an end of everything, were the same man or the same body, whether of the nobles or of the people, to exercise those three powers, that of enacting laws, that of executing the public resolutions, and of trying the causes of individuals.

Two Treatises of Government: John Locke

But though men, when they enter into society give up the equality, liberty, and executive power they had in the state of Nature into the hands of society . . . the power of the society or legislative constituted by them can never be supposed to extend farther than the common good. . . . Whoever has the legislative or supreme power of any commonwealth, is bound to govern by established standing laws, promulgated [published or made known] and known to the people, and not by extemporary [without any preparation] decrees, by indifferent and upright judges, who are to decide controversies by those laws; and to employ the force of the community at home only in the execution of such laws, or abroad to prevent or redress foreign injuries and secure the community from inroads [advances at the expense of someone] and invasion. And all this to be directed to no other end but the peace, safety, and public good of the people. . . .

☑ **DETERMINE AUTHOR'S POINT OF VIEW** When does Locke say it is appropriate to use military force? Do you agree with him? Explain your reasoning.

The reason why men enter into society is the preservation of their property; and the end while they choose and authorize a legislative is that there may be laws made, and rules set, as guards and fences to the properties of all the society. . . .

Whensoever, therefore, the legislative [power] shall transgress [go beyond; break] this fundamental rule of society, and either by ambition, fear, folly, or corruption, endeavor to grasp themselves, or put into the hands of any other, an absolute power over the lives, liberties, and estates of the people, by this breach of trust they forfeit the power the people had put into their hands for quite contrary ends, and it devolves [passes] to the people; who have a right to resume their original liberty, and by the establishment of a new legislative (such as they shall think fit), provide for their own safety and security. . .

☑ ASSESSMENT

1. **Summarize** What does Locke say is the duty of government? How does this relate to his main idea?

2. **Assess an Argument** Evaluate Locke's claim that "The reason why men enter into society is the preservation of their property" by comparing it to the theory put forward by Jean-Jacques Rousseau in *The Social Contract:* The individual gives up some of his or her freedom in exchange for the protection and benefits offered by the group.

3. **Determine Author's Purpose** For what reasons does Montesquieu promote the separation of powers?

1.4

Young people wave American flags to show their patriotism while attending the inauguration of U.S. President Barack Obama.

The Basics of Democracy

What do you make of this assessment of democracy by British statesman James Bryce: "No government demands so much from the citizen as Democracy, and none gives so much back"? What does democratic government demand from you? What does it give you in return?

Foundations of Democracy

Democracy is not inevitable. It does not exist in the United States simply because Americans regard it as the best of all possible political systems. Rather, democracy exists in this country because the American people believe in its basic concepts. It will continue to exist only for as long as we, the people, continue to subscribe to and practice those concepts.

Sir **Winston Churchill** (1874–1965) once put the argument for democracy this way: "No one pretends that democracy is perfect or all-wise. Indeed, it has been said that democracy is the worst form of government except all those other forms that have been tried from time to time."

The American concept of democracy—what we believe democracy means—rests on these basic notions:

1. Recognition of the fundamental worth and dignity of every person; 2. Respect for the equality of all persons; 3. Faith in majority rule and an insistence upon minority rights; 4. Acceptance of the necessity of compromise; and 5. Insistence upon the widest possible degree of individual freedom.

Of course, these concepts can be worded in other ways. No matter what the wording, however, they form the very minimum

 BOUNCE to Activate Flipped Video

Objectives

Understand the foundations of democracy.

Analyze the connections between democracy and the free enterprise system.

Key Terms

majority rule
compromise
citizen
free enterprise
  system
James Bryce
Winston Churchill
Oliver Wendell
  Holmes, Jr.
Theodore Roosevelt
George Washington

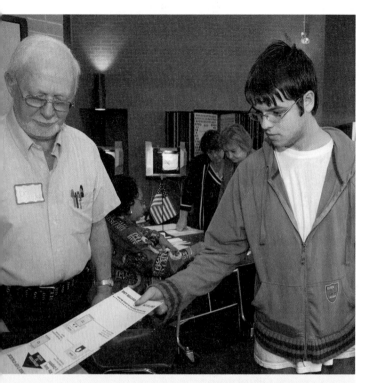

>> A first-time voter casts a ballot in a presidential election. To work, democracy requires an educated and informed population of voters who participate in the election process.

>> Elizabeth Eckford was an African American who enrolled at Central High School, an all-white school in Arkansas, after the Supreme Court ruled that segregation denied African Americans their guaranteed equality.

with which anyone who professes to believe in democracy must agree.

Worth of the Individual Democracy is firmly based upon a belief in the fundamental importance of the individual. Each individual, no matter what his or her station in life, is a separate and distinct being.

This concept of the dignity and worth of the individual is of overriding importance in democratic thought. At various times, of course, the welfare of one or a few individuals is subordinated to the interests of the many in a democracy. People can be forced to do certain things whether they want to or not. Examples range from paying taxes to registering for the draft to stopping at a stop sign.

When a democratic society forces people to pay a tax or obey traffic signals, it is serving the interests of the many. However, it is not simply serving the interests of the many who as a mass of people happen to outnumber the few. Rather, it is serving the many who, as individuals, together make up that society.

The distinction we are trying to make here between *an* individual and *all* individuals may be difficult to grasp. It is, however, critically important to a real understanding of the meaning of democracy.

Equality of All Persons Hand in hand with the belief in the worth of the individual, democracy stresses the equality of all individuals. It holds, with Jefferson, that "all men are created equal."

Certainly, democracy does not imply an equality of condition for all persons. Thus, it does not claim that all are born with the same mental or physical abilities. Nor does it hold that all persons have a right to an equal share of worldly goods.

Rather, the democratic concept of equality means that every person is entitled to (1) equality of opportunity and (2) equality before the law. That is, the democratic concept of equality holds that no person should be held back for any such arbitrary reasons as those based on race, color, religion, or gender.

Note that democratic governments must constantly balance liberty and equality. For example, the government might promote equality by requiring employers to hire a certain percentage of people who claim a particular religious affiliation. Such a requirement, however, would infringe unreasonably on the freedom of business owners to run their companies as they wish.

Majority Rule, Minority Rights In a democracy, the will of the people and not the dictate of the ruling few determines public policy. What is the popular will, and how is it determined? Some device must exist by which these crucial questions can be answered. The only satisfactory device democracy knows is that of **majority rule**. Democracy holds that a majority will be right more often than it will be wrong, and that the majority will also be right more often than any one person or small group will.

Democracy can be described as an experiment or a trial-and-error process designed to find satisfactory ways to order human relations. Democracy does not dictate that the majority will always arrive at the best decisions on public matters. In fact, the democratic process is not meant to come up with "right" or "best" answers. Rather, the democratic process is a search for *satisfactory* solutions to public problems.

Of course, in a democracy the majority's decisions will usually be more, rather than less, satisfactory. Democracy does admit the possibility of mistakes; there is the possibility that "wrong" or less satisfactory answers will sometimes be found. Democracy also recognizes that seldom is any solution to a public problem so satisfactory that it cannot be improved upon, and that circumstances can change over time. So, the process of experimentation, of seeking answers to public questions, is a never-ending one.

Certainly, a democracy cannot work without the principle of majority rule. Unchecked, however, a majority could destroy its opposition and, in the process, destroy democracy itself. Thus, democracy requires majority rule restrained by minority rights. The majority must always recognize the right of any minority to become, if it can by fair and lawful means, the majority. The majority must always be willing to listen to a minority's argument, to hear its objections, to bear its criticisms, and to welcome its suggestions.

Necessity of Compromise In a democracy, public decision making must be largely a matter of give-and-take among the various competing interests. It is a matter of compromise in order to find the position most acceptable to the largest number. **Compromise** is the process of blending and adjusting competing views and interests.

Compromise is an essential part of the democratic concept for two major reasons. First, remember that democracy puts the individual first and, at the same time, insists that each individual is the equal of all others. In a democratic society made up of many individuals and groups with many different opinions and interests, how can the people make public decisions except by compromise?

>> Politics involves an element of compromise. **Analyze Political Cartoons** Who do the chefs represent in this cartoon?

Second, few public questions have only two sides. Most can be answered in several ways. Take the apparently simple question of how a city should pay for the paving of a public street. Should it charge those who own property along the street? Or should the costs be paid from the city's general treasury? Or should the city and the adjacent property owners share the costs? What about those who will use the street but do not live in the city? Should they have to pay a toll?

Remember, compromise is a process, a way of achieving majority agreement. It is never an end in itself. Not all compromises are good, and not all are necessary.

Insistence upon Individual Freedom It should be clear by this point that democracy can thrive only in an atmosphere of individual freedom. However, democracy does not and cannot insist on complete freedom for the individual. Absolute freedom can exist only in a state of anarchy—the total absence of government. Anarchy can only lead, inevitably and quickly, to rule by the strong and ruthless.

Democracy does require that each individual must be as free to do as he or she pleases as far as the freedom of all will allow. Justice **Oliver Wendell Holmes, Jr.,** is often attributed with saying this about the relative nature of each individual's rights: "The right to swing my fist ends where the other man's nose begins."

Drawing a line between the rights of one individual and those of another is not easy. Still, the drawing of that line is a continuous and vitally important function of democratic government.

Striking the proper balance between freedom for the individual and the rights of society as a whole is similarly difficult—and vital. Abraham Lincoln described democracy's problem by asking a question.

> Must a government, of necessity, be too strong for the liberties of its own people, or too weak to maintain its own existence?
>
> —Message to Congress, July 4, 1861

Human beings desire both liberty and authority. Democratic government must work constantly to strike the proper balance between the two. The authority of government must be adequate to the needs of society. At the same time, that authority must never be allowed to become so great that it restricts the individual beyond what is absolutely necessary.

☑ **SUMMARIZE** To what are citizens entitled under the democratic concept of equality?

>> As John F. Kennedy, the 35th President of the United States said, "The rights of every man are diminished when the rights of one man are threatened."

Responsibilities, Duties, and Obligations of Citizenship

Over the centuries, any number of statesmen, philosophers, and others have told us that citizenship carries with it both duties and responsibilities. **Theodore Roosevelt** put that point this way in 1902: "The first requisite of a good citizen in our republic is that he should be able and willing to pull his weight."

Why is political and civic participation important? The answer is simple. As you will recall, the United States is a government by the people. Therefore, the very survival of our democratic government depends on the active involvement of the people.

Being a "Good Citizen" In a democratic society, the *duties* of "a good citizen" all revolve around his or her commitment to obey the law—a point long accepted in this country. In his Farewell Address in 1796, **George Washington** put that obligation this way: "the very idea of the power and right of the People to establish Government presupposes the duty of every individual to obey the established Government."

The several *responsibilities* of "a good citizen" in a free society all come down to this: an abiding respect for each of the core beliefs on which democracy is based in this country. A **citizen** is one who holds both rights and responsibilities in a state. Ask yourself this question: Do I understand and am I committed to honoring the basic concepts of American democracy?

What is the difference between personal and civic responsibilities? Personal responsibilities mean being responsible for your own behavior, taking care of your family, being considerate of others. Civic responsibilities involve your role as a citizen of a larger community. They include obeying the law, paying taxes, being informed and voting, respecting the rights of others, serving as a juror, and serving in the armed forces. All of these civic responsibilities serve to strengthen and support the community.

In a democracy, part of every citizen's responsibility is to serve the public good. This involves caring for the welfare of the community including its environment, safety, and education. Volunteering, participating in public service organizations, and seeking opportunities to serve the community are all ways to meet this important obligation.

Making a Difference For many, the most effective form of participation in a democracy is to seek elected office. The decisions being made, the compromises necessary, are all made by individuals who have been selected by their fellow citizens to guide the hand of authority in the ways that best serve their country. Another effective method is to take part in the working of the government itself. From the smallest towns and villages to the grand scope of an entire nation, there must be those who implement the decisions being made.

Similarly, those who draw up petitions or form action groups to address issues can have a very real effect on public policy. Letters can be written to government leaders including city council members, State legislators, and members of Congress. Joining political parties, working on campaigns, and contributing time and money towards political causes can also be useful ways to participate, because working to make a party stronger or get a certain candidate elected can have a real impact on laws and policies at all levels of government.

The simplest way to participate in politics is to vote, to exercise the right to speak and be heard. Voting at every level, from national to local, helps to ensure that the needs of the people are being heard and addressed. Being informed and participating are rights and responsibilities of every citizen.

Civil Society As you have seen, the American democratic system provides citizens with many ways to fulfill their responsibility to participate in the political process. Other useful vehicles for participation are the many associations and groups that constitute civil society.

Civil society is that private area of American life outside of governmental institutions or interference. It includes any voluntary activity in which people join together for social, cultural, religious, economic, or political purposes, and it functions on the basis of trust and shared values.

Civil society provides opportunities for people to join together to advocate for things they believe in and to make life better. They do this in many ways— by improving living standards and neighborhoods, undertaking charitable work, joining international organizations such as the Red Cross, joining interest groups, working to improve human rights, and so on. The 1963 March on Washington for civil rights is an example of civil society in action, as is the Ten Point Coalition, a national group of Black American ministers targeting at-risk youth in their communities.

A constitutional democracy like the United States recognizes and protects the existence of civil society, because the exchange of ideas and positive actions makes for a better functioning, more effective, more stable nation. Government does so in

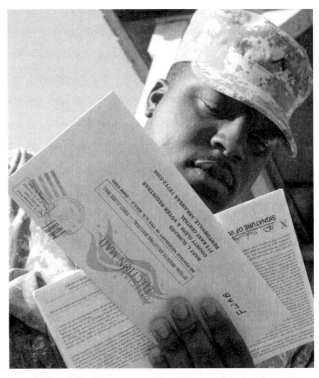

>> This soldier, like many active-duty service members, is casting his vote by absentee ballot.

many ways—through constitutional guarantees such as the freedom of speech and assembly, for example, or by helping to create a safe environment in which citizens can thrive.

At the same time, civil society makes it possible for citizens to influence government in ways other than voting and elections. In non-democratic nations, the associations and activities of civil society are often undermined or even illegal. In these societies, people cannot work to improve their situations or those of others.

☑ **INTERPRET** What is the most basic duty of a U.S. citizen?

Democracy and the Free Enterprise System

The American commitment to freedom for the individual is deep-rooted, and it is as evident in the nation's economic system as it is in the political system. The American economic system is often called the **free enterprise system**. It is an economic system characterized by the private ownership of capital goods; investments made by

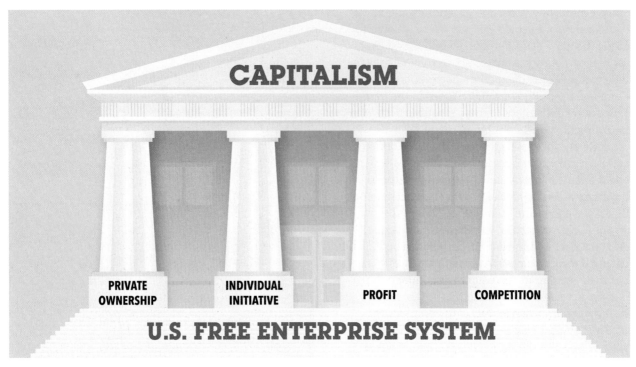

CAPITALISM

PRIVATE OWNERSHIP | INDIVIDUAL INITIATIVE | PROFIT | COMPETITION

U.S. FREE ENTERPRISE SYSTEM

>> The four pillars are the basis for free enterprise, or capitalism, in the United States. **Analyze Charts** What are some examples of each pillar, such as home ownership or starting a business?

private decision, not by government directive; and success or failure determined by competition in the marketplace. The free enterprise system is based on four fundamental factors: private ownership, individual initiative, profit, and competition.

How the System Works The free enterprise system is often called capitalism. It is also known as the private enterprise system and as a market-based system. It does not rely on government to decide what items are to be produced, how much of any particular item should be produced, or how much any item is to sell for. Rather, those decisions are made in the marketplace. Millions of producers and consumers obey the unwritten law of supply and demand: When supplies of goods and services become plentiful, prices will tend to drop; when, on the other hand, supplies become scarce, prices will very likely rise.

Democracy and the free enterprise system are not the same thing. One is a political system, and the other is an economic system. However, both are firmly based on the concept of individual freedom. America's experience with both systems clearly suggests that the two reinforce one another in practice.

Because the United States is a democracy, Americans enjoy a long list of economic rights. These include the right to choose one's work, the right to join or not join labor unions, and the right to

acquire, use, transfer, and dispose of property as one wishes (while abiding by any local zoning laws).

These rights are important to individuals and society because they promote equality and ensure just and favorable conditions for all. They have been secured through constitutional guarantees such as the 5th and 14th Amendments, and through court cases and legislation throughout the nation's history.

That is not to say that the American free enterprise system is without flaws. Many Americans believe that society as a whole benefits through the continuous creation of new businesses, new jobs, and increased wealth when individuals can pursue their own interests and have opportunities to use private property to create jobs and generate income. Yet, this American ideal is not always fulfilled in practice. Historically, racial and gender discrimination have limited opportunities for many Americans to find good jobs or start their own businesses. Growing disparities between the rich and poor, the favoring of some industries over others by government policies, and the takeover of businesses by larger companies or private investors, have led to occasional calls for a change in the American economic system. For the most part, however, criticisms are focused on revising specific aspects of capitalism, rather than attempting to replace that system entirely.

Government and the Free Enterprise System

The basis of the American economic system is the free market. However, government does play a role in the American economy, and it always has. Government's participation in the economy serves a two-fold purpose: to protect the public and to preserve private enterprise.

Government's participation in the economy can be seen at every level in this country: national, State, and local. Here are but a few examples: Economic activities are regulated by government through antitrust laws, pure food and drug laws, antipollution standards, and city and county zoning ordinances and building codes.

The nation's economic life is promoted in a great number of public ways. Congress grants copyrights and patents to artists and inventors to protect their ideas and work, thereby fostering competition and entrepreneurship in the United States. The government also grants money for transportation systems and the growing of particular food crops, builds roads and operates public schools, provides services such as the postal system and weather reports, and much more.

Thus, some activities that might be carried out privately are in fact conducted by government. Public education, local fire departments, and city bus systems are longstanding examples of the point.

How much should government participate, regulate, promote, police, and serve? Many heated debates in American politics center on that question, and we are often reminded of Abraham Lincoln's advice about the object of government.

> The legitimate object of government, is to do for a community of people, whatever they need to have done, but can not do, at all, or can not, so well do, for themselves— in their separate, and individual capacities.
>
> —Abraham Lincoln

☑ **LIST** What are the four factors of the free enterprise system?

>> This cartoon shows a train being sidetracked by a monopoly. **Analyze Political Cartoons** Why might there be tension in the economy between the government and private enterprise?

☑ ASSESSMENT

1. **Draw Conclusions** Why is democracy the political system of the U.S. government?

2. **Apply Concepts** Explain the ideas behind majority rule and minority rights.

3. **Explain** Why are civic and political participation important?

4. **Analyze** Analyze the impact of citizen participation as a means of achieving political and social change.

5. **Apply Concepts** How does supply and demand work?

LESSON SUMMARIES

Use these Lesson Summaries, and the longer versions available online, to review the key ideas for each lesson in this Topic.

Lesson 1: Principles of Government

Governments are institutions that make and enforce laws. Their structure is often outlined in a constitution. Today, the world's dominant political unit is the state. A variety of theories explain how states arose, including the divine right and social contract theories.

Lesson 2: Types of Government

Governments can be classified into different types. One method of classification looks at who participates in government. Another looks at how power is shared geographically. A third considers how the legislative and executive branches are connected.

Lesson 3: Origins of the Modern Democratic State

The roots of modern democracies go back to ancient Athens and the Roman republic. During the Middle Ages in Europe, a feudal system developed. Eventually, absolute monarchs took control and founded colonies around the world. Enlightenment thinkers developed ideas about democracy, helping lead to the American and French revolutions.

Lesson 4: The Basics of Democracy

American democracy rests on the belief by the American people in important principles, such as individual rights. These principles are also important to the country's free enterprise economic system. American citizens have important duties and obligations that help democracy function, including obeying the law, voting, and paying taxes.

VISUAL REVIEW

Use these graphics to review some of the key terms, people, and ideas from this Topic.

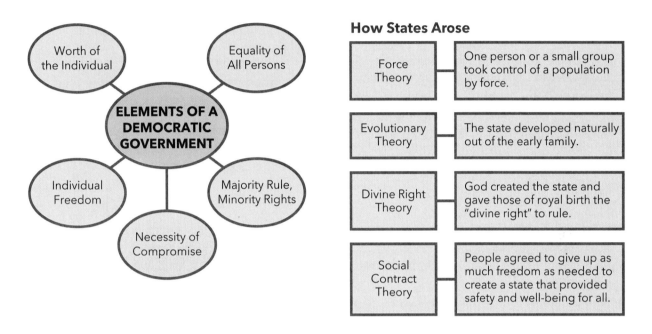

ELEMENTS OF A DEMOCRATIC GOVERNMENT
- Worth of the Individual
- Equality of All Persons
- Individual Freedom
- Majority Rule, Minority Rights
- Necessity of Compromise

How States Arose

Force Theory	One person or a small group took control of a population by force.
Evolutionary Theory	The state developed naturally out of the early family.
Divine Right Theory	God created the state and gave those of royal birth the "divine right" to rule.
Social Contract Theory	People agreed to give up as much freedom as needed to create a state that provided safety and well-being for all.

Timeline of the Modern State

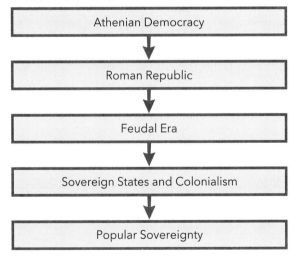

- Athenian Democracy
- Roman Republic
- Feudal Era
- Sovereign States and Colonialism
- Popular Sovereignty

Who Can Participate in Government?

TYPE OF GOVERNMENT	WHO CAN PARTICIPATE?
Democracy	The people, either directly or through representatives
Autocracy	A single person who holds complete power
Oligarchy	A small group that holds complete power
Theocracy	Religious leaders

Topic 1 Assessment

KEY TERMS, PEOPLE, AND IDEAS

1. List the three kinds of power that every **government** has.

2. Compare and contrast a **presidential government** and a **parliamentary government**.

3. What is a **constitution** and why is it important?

4. What are the advantages and disadvantages of **unitary, federal,** and **confederate** governments?

5. **Thomas Hobbes** and **Baron de Montesquieu** are best known for what ideas about government?

6. What are the four characteristics of the **state**?

7. Compare and contrast an **autocracy**, an **oligarchy**, and a **theocracy**.

8. What are the responsibilities of a **citizen**?

CRITICAL THINKING

9. **Evaluate** What effect did the Enlightenment have on the concepts of liberty, rights, and the responsibilities of individuals?

10. **Formulate Questions and Defend Analysis** What do the terms *liberty* and *equality* mean? How do they relate to each other? Define these terms, and then formulate three questions about the relationship between liberty and equality and the importance of maintaining a balance between them. Then answer one of the questions, giving examples to defend your response.

11. **Summarize** How does the Constitution both safeguard and limit individual rights?

12. **Contrast** Write a paragraph comparing the U.S. government to dictatorships. Describe how the structure, powers, and leadership of each government differ.

13. **Explain** Rights are not absolute. Why do they have limits?

14. **Evaluate** Why are political and civic participation important for citizens of a democratic society?

15. **Analyze** How does citizen participation help achieve political and social change and shape public policy?

16. **Synthesize** How does the Declaration of Independence reflect the political principle described in the "Social Contract Theory" art in the next column?

SOCIAL CONTRACT THEORY

A population in a given territory gave up as much power to a government as needed to promote the well-being of all. In doing so, they created a sovereign state.

17. **Synthesize** In what ways can citizens participate in the political process?

18. **Evaluate** Explain how the following duties and responsibilities of citizenship contribute to the good of all: paying taxes, voting, and volunteering. Which do you think is the most important? Why?

19. **Summarize** Explain the constitutional principle of representative government, including consent of the governed, and the rule of law.

20. **Writing Activity** You are the leader of a group of formerly independent states now coming together to form a new country. The new country will be large in area, with a large population. Choose a form of government that you think would best suit this situation and work out the details of your new government based on information in this topic. Write an organizational plan for your government.

DOCUMENT-BASED QUESTIONS

Democracy existed well before the Greeks coined the term around 2,500 years ago. The Greeks, however, wrote extensively on the subject.

DOCUMENT A

In this excerpt, the Greek philosopher Aristotle discusses the ideal—or most stable—type of political community.

> Thus it is manifest that the best political community is formed by citizens of the middle class, and that those states are likely to be well-administered in which the middle class is large, and stronger if possible than both the other classes, or at any rate than either singly; for the addition of the middle class turns the scale, and prevents either of the extremes from being dominant. Great then is the good fortune of a state in which the citizens have a moderate and sufficient property; for where some possess much, and the others nothing, there may arise an extreme democracy, or a pure oligarchy; or a tyranny may grow out of either extreme.
>
> —*Aristotle, Politics, Book Four, Part XI, c. 350 B.C.E*

DOCUMENT B

Aristotle was taught by Plato, who gives his opinion of democracy in this excerpt.

> To How grandly does [democracy] trample all these fine notions of ours under her feet, never giving a thought to the pursuits which make a statesman, and promoting to honor any one who professes to be the people's friend. . . .
>
> And when they [democratic principles] have emptied and swept clean the soul of him who is now in their power and who is being initiated by them in great mysteries, the next thing is to bring back to their house insolence [rudeness] and anarchy [lawlessness] and waste and impudence in bright array having garlands on their heads, and a great company with them, hymning their praises and calling them by sweet names. . . .
>
> —*Plato, Republic, Book VIII, c. 360 B.C.E*

DOCUMENT C

This stone relief shows Democracy crowning the people of Athens with a wreath. It was placed in the marketplace, where citizens could see it every day.

DOCUMENT D

An anonymous Greek who called himself the Old Oligarch wrote this excerpt about democracy.

> . . . [A]s for the fact that the Athenians have chosen the kind of constitution that they have, I do not think well of their doing this inasmuch as in making their choice they have chosen to let the worst people be better off than the good. Therefore, on this account I do not think well of their constitution. . . .
>
> And everywhere on earth the best element is opposed to democracy. For among the best people there is minimal wantonness and injustice but a maximum of scrupulous care for what is good, whereas among the people there is a maximum of ignorance, disorder, and wickedness; for poverty draws them rather to disgraceful actions, and because of a lack of money some men are uneducated and ignorant.
>
> —*Old Oligarch, The Constitution of the Athenians, c. 424 B.C.E*

21. Which of the following does Aristotle believe to be best for democracy?
   A. a well-educated population
   B. a large and stable middle class
   C. a pure oligarchy
   D. a wealthy ruling class

22. Analyze Images Does Document C corroborate or challenge Document B? What does Document C say about whether most Athenians agreed or disagreed with Plato's viewpoint?

23. How do the claims and reasoning in Document B differ from those in Document D?
   A. Document B gives opinions rather than facts.
   B. Document D gives opinions rather than facts.
   C. Document D appeals to readers' emotions.
   D. Document B appeals to reader's emotions.

24. Writing Task Integrate the information from these documents to give an overview of how the ancient Greeks viewed democracy.

The Beginnings of American Government

ESSENTIAL QUESTION How much power should a government have?

Painting of George Washington, the first President of the United States

Connections to Today

Do you play online games? If so, you may sometimes wish that virtual currency has real-life value. In fact, some virtual assets *are* real. Cryptocurrency exists only as a digital "asset" that is not regulated by the Federal Government (but it must be purchased with real money).

In this Topic, you'll learn that under the Articles of Confederation, the Federal Government faced similar issues. Decentralized States printed their own money with no national oversight. What are the pros and cons of a strong central government?

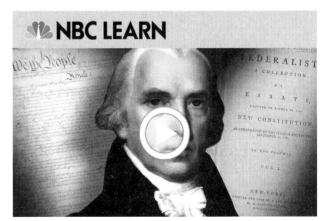

Learn about one of the most important political thinkers in U.S. history, James Madison.

 BOUNCE to Activate My Story Video

Topic 2 Overview

In this Topic, you will learn about the American Revolution, the early years of the American government, and the drafting and ratification of the Constitution of the United States. Look at the lesson outline and explore the timeline. As you study this Topic, you'll complete the Quest Inquiry.

LESSON OUTLINE

2.1 Origins of American Political Ideals

2.2 Independence

2.3 First Steps

2.4 Creating and Ratifying the Constitution

The Road to Independence

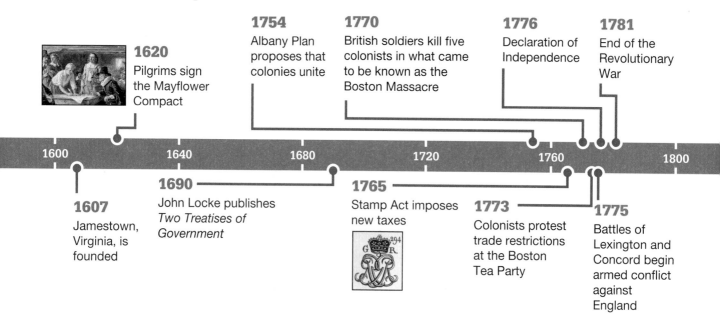

1620 Pilgrims sign the Mayflower Compact

1754 Albany Plan proposes that colonies unite

1770 British soldiers kill five colonists in what came to be known as the Boston Massacre

1776 Declaration of Independence

1781 End of the Revolutionary War

1600   1640   1680   1720   1760   1800

1607 Jamestown, Virginia, is founded

1690 John Locke publishes *Two Treatises of Government*

1765 Stamp Act imposes new taxes

1773 Colonists protest trade restrictions at the Boston Tea Party

1775 Battles of Lexington and Concord begin armed conflict against England

QUEST!

Document-Based Question:
Should the Constitution Be Ratified?

The delegates to the Constitutional Convention have written a new constitution. State ratifying conventions are under pressure from both sides. Should they support the proposed plan? In this Quest, you will weigh the viewpoints of the Federalists and Anti-Federalists as you decide how to cast your vote.

STEP

List your questions and answers related to the debate between the Federalists and Anti-Federalists. What did ratification mean for both groups?

STEP

Examine the documents relating to the debate. Determine the central idea of each and evaluate the authors' differing points of view.

STEP

Write a coherent essay arguing for or against ratification. Point out the strengths and limitations of your position and the opposing position.

STEP

Revise your writing. Did you cite specific evidence from the documents to support your argument? Share your finished work with the class.

2.1

Ships such as the *Mayflower* brought English colonists to North America, where they established governments based on political traditions and ideas from Europe and elsewhere.

BOUNCE to Activate Flipped Video

Objectives

Explain how constitutional government in the United States has been influenced by centuries of political ideas and traditions from England and elsewhere.

Analyze the significance of three landmark historical documents to the American system of government.

Describe the three types of colonies that the English established in North America and explain why they are important to the study of American government.

Key Terms

limited government
representative
    government
Magna Carta
due process
Petition of Right
Glorious Revolution
English Bill of Rights
charter
bicameral
proprietary

unicameral
Jamestown
King John
King Charles I
William and Mary of
    Orange
King George II
George Calvert,
    Lord Baltimore
William Penn

Origins of American Political Ideals

The American system of government did not suddenly spring into being with the signing of the Declaration of Independence in 1776. Nor was it created by the Framers of the Constitution in 1787. Instead, the beginnings of what was to become the United States can be found in the mid-sixteenth century, when explorers, traders, and settlers first made their way to North America.

Origins of American Constitutional Government

The French, Dutch, Spanish, Swedes, and others came to explore and settle what would become this nation—and, in the process, to decimate those Native Americans who were here for centuries before the arrival of the first Europeans. It was the English, however, who came in the largest numbers. And it was the English who soon controlled the 13 colonies that stretched for some 1,300 miles along the Atlantic seaboard.

The earliest English settlers brought with them knowledge of a political system that had been developing in England for centuries. English common law, for example, which is unwritten, judge-made law developed over centuries, was one integral part of that system. English constitutionalism, the notion that government leaders are subject to the limitations of the law, had also been developing for hundreds of years in England. These traditions of common law and constitutionalism, like many other major intellectual, philosophical, political, and religious traditions, would later influence the founding of America.

The origins of many of these fundamental ideas stretch back into ancient times and across many lands. Thus, the concept of the rule of law that influenced English political ideas, for example, has roots in the early civilizations of Africa and Asia.

King Hammurabi of Babylonia, for example, developed a system of laws known as Hammurabi's Code around 1750 B.C. Jewish legal concepts relating to individual worth, fair trial, and the rule of law were detailed in the Hebrew Bible. The English were quite familiar with and devoutly attracted to the biblical concept of the rule of law, the idea that government is always subject to, never above, the law.

Even more directly, the ancient Romans occupied much of England from A.D. 43 to 410. They left behind a legacy of law, religion, and custom. From this rich political history, the English colonists brought to North America three basic notions that were to loom large in the shaping of government in the United States.

Ordered Government The English colonists saw the need for an orderly regulation of their relationships with one another—that is, a need for government. They created local governments, based on those they had known in England. Many of the offices and units of government they established are with us yet today: the offices of sheriff and justice of the peace, the grand jury, counties, and several others.

Limited Government The colonists also brought with them the idea that government is restricted in what it may do. This concept is called **limited government**, and it was deeply rooted in English belief and practice by the time the first English ships set sail for America.

The colonists also believed firmly that every individual has certain rights—unalienable rights—that government cannot take away. These concepts had been planted in England centuries earlier and had been developing there for nearly 400 years before **Jamestown** was settled in 1607.

Representative Government The early English settlers carried another important concept across the Atlantic: **representative government**. This idea that government should serve the will of the people had also been developing in England for several centuries. With it had come a growing insistence that the people should have a voice in deciding what government should and should not do. As with the concept of limited government, the idea of

"government of, by, and for the people" flourished in America.

☑ **IDENTIFY CENTRAL ISSUES** In what way did the local governments established by the English colonists reflect major political ideas and traditions in history?

Influential Documents and Ideas

These basic notions of ordered, limited, and representative government can be traced to ideas that began to emerge hundreds of years before the English reached North America, as well as to several landmark documents in English history.

The Magna Carta A group of determined barons forced **King John** to sign the **Magna Carta**—the Great Charter—at Runnymede in 1215. Weary of John's military campaigns and heavy taxes, the barons who prompted the Magna Carta were seeking protection against heavy-handed and arbitrary acts by the king.

The Magna Carta included guarantees of such fundamental rights as trial by jury and **due process**

Basic Concepts of Government

Ordered	• Government regulates affairs among people. • Government maintains order and predictability.
Limited	• Government is restricted in what it may do. • Every individual has certain rights government cannot take away.
Representative	• Government should serve the will of the people. • People should have a voice in deciding what government can and cannot do.

>> The English settlers brought ideas about government with them to North America. **Analyze Charts** How is representative government practiced in the United States today?

of law (protection against the arbitrary taking of life, liberty, or property). Those protections against the absolute power of the king were originally intended for the privileged classes only. Over time, however, they became the rights of all English people and were incorporated into other documents. The Magna Carta established the critical idea that the monarchy's power was not absolute.

The Petition of Right The Magna Carta was respected by some monarchs and ignored by others for 400 years. Over that period, England's Parliament slowly grew in influence. In 1628, when **Charles I** asked Parliament for more money in taxes, Parliament refused until he agreed to sign the **Petition of Right**.

The Petition of Right limited the king's power in several ways. Most importantly, it demanded that the king no longer imprison or otherwise punish any person but by the lawful judgment of his peers or by the law of the land. The document also insisted that the king may not impose martial law, or military rule, in times of peace, or require homeowners to shelter the king's troops without their consent. The Petition declared that no man should be

compelled to make or yield any gift, loan, benevolence, tax, or such like charge, without common consent by act of parliament.

—Petition of Right

The Petition challenged the idea of the divine right of kings, declaring that even a monarch must obey the law of the land.

The English Bill of Rights In 1689, after years of revolt and turmoil, Parliament offered the crown to **William and Mary of Orange**. The events surrounding their ascent to the throne are known as the **Glorious Revolution**. To prevent abuse of power by William and Mary and all future monarchs, Parliament that same year drew up a list of provisions to which William and Mary had to agree.

This document, the **English Bill of Rights**, prohibited a standing army in peacetime, except with the consent of Parliament, and required that all parliamentary elections be free. In addition, the document declared

that the pretended power of suspending the laws, or the execution of laws, by regal authority, without consent of Parliament is illegal . . . that levying money for or to the use of the Crown . . . without grant of Parliament . . . is illegal . . . that it is the right of the subjects to petition the king . . . and that prosecutions for such petitioning are illegal . . .

—English Bill of Rights

The English Bill of Rights also included such guarantees as the right to a fair trial, as well as freedom from excessive bail and from cruel and unusual punishment.

Our nation has built upon, changed, and added to those ideas and institutions that settlers brought here from England. Still, much in American government and politics today bears the stamp of those early English ideas. Surely, this is not so strange when you recall that the colonial period of American history lasted for some 170 years and that

>> The English Bill of Rights, presented to William and Mary in 1689, is still in force today. A century later, it influenced a similar declaration of rights in the newly formed United States.

Colonial America, 1775

KEY

- Charter Colonies/ Bicameral Legislatures
- Proprietary Colonies/ Bicameral Legislatures
- Proprietary Colonies/ Unicameral Legislatures
- Royal Colonies/ Bicameral Legislatures

Huron Native American group

Albers Conic Equal-Area Projection

>> Despite the varying government systems of the colonies, they were all influenced by their English roots. **Analyze Maps** How were the legislatures of the proprietary colonies structured?

the United States has existed as an independent nation for only a slightly longer period.

☑ **DESCRIBE** Explain the ways in which the English Bill of Rights limited the power of the monarch.

Three Types of Colonies

England's colonies in North America have been described as "schools of government," because they were the settings in which Americans first began to learn the difficult art of government. Later, the lessons learned by the colonists would help inform the development of the government of the new United States.

The English and other Europeans did not introduce the idea of government to the Americas, however. Several Native American societies already had developed complex systems. For example, five Native American groups in what is now New York State—the Seneca, Cayuga, Oneida, Onondaga, and Mohawk—formed a confederation known as the Iroquois League. The League was originally created to end conflicts among the tribes. It proved so successful as a form of government that it lasted for some 200 years.

Thirteen of England's North American colonies would eventually break away from Great Britain and the other colonies. These 13 were established, separately, over a span of some 125 years. During that long period, outlying trading posts and isolated farm settlements developed into organized communities. The first of these colonies, Virginia, was founded with the first permanent English settlement in North America at Jamestown in 1607. Georgia was the last to be formed, with the settlement of Savannah in 1733.

Each of the colonies was born out of a particular set of circumstances. Virginia was originally organized as a commercial venture. Its first colonists were employees of the Virginia Company of London (also called the London Company), a private trading corporation. Massachusetts was first settled by people who came to North America in search of greater personal and religious freedom. **King George II** granted Georgia to 21 trustees, who governed the colony.

But the differences among the colonies are of little importance. Of much greater significance is the fact that all of them were shaped by their English origins. The many similarities among these colonies far outweighed their differences.

>> In 1619, Virginia's colonial legislature became the first representative body to meet in the North American English colonies. Its lower house was called the House of Burgesses.

>> After receiving a charter from Charles II, William Penn (right) came to North America in 1682 and established the Pennsylvania colony as a haven for Quakers and other religious minorities.

Each colony was established on the basis of a **charter**, a written grant of authority from the king. This grant gave colonists or companies a grant of land and some governing rights, while the Crown retained a certain amount of power over a colony. Over time, these instruments of government led to the development of three different types of colonies: royal, proprietary, and charter.

Royal Colonies The royal colonies were subject to the direct control of the Crown. On the eve of the American Revolution in 1775, there were eight: New Hampshire, Massachusetts, New York, New Jersey, Virginia, North Carolina, South Carolina, and Georgia.

The Virginia colony did not enjoy the quick success its sponsors had promised. In addition, the colony's government was evolving into one of popular rule. The king disapproved of the local government's methods, as well as their attempt to grow tobacco. So, in 1624, the king revoked the London Company's charter, and Virginia became the first of the royal colonies. Later, as the charters of other colonies were canceled or withdrawn for a variety of reasons, they became royal colonies.

A pattern of government gradually emerged for each of the royal colonies. The king named a governor to serve as the colony's chief executive. A council, also named by the king, served as an advisory body to the royal governor. Later, the governor's council became both the upper house of the colonial legislature and the colony's highest court. The lower house of a **bicameral** (two-house) legislature was elected by those property owners qualified to vote. It owed much of its influence to the fact that it shared with the governor and his council the power of the purse—the power to tax and spend. The governor, advised by the council, appointed judges for the colony's courts.

The laws passed by the legislatures in the royal colonies had to be approved by the governor and the Crown. Royal governors often ruled with a stern hand, following instructions from London. Much of the resentment that finally flared into revolution was fanned by their actions.

The Proprietary Colonies By 1775, there were three **proprietary** colonies: Maryland, Pennsylvania, and Delaware. These colonies were organized by a proprietor, a person to whom the king had made a grant of land. By charter, that land could be settled and governed much as the proprietor chose. In 1632, the king granted Maryland to **George Calvert, Lord Baltimore**, which was intended as a haven for Catholics. In 1681, Pennsylvania was granted to **William Penn**. In 1682, Penn also acquired Delaware.

The governments of these three colonies were much like those in the royal colonies. The governor, however, was appointed by the proprietor. In Maryland and Delaware, the legislatures were bicameral. In Pennsylvania, the legislature was a **unicameral** body. The Frame of Government, a constitution that William Penn drew up for that colony in 1682, was, for its time, exceedingly democratic. As in the royal colonies, appeals of decisions in the proprietary colonies could be carried to the king in London.

The Charter Colonies The Massachusetts Bay Colony was established as the first charter colony in 1629. Its charter was later revoked, and Massachusetts became a royal colony in 1691.

Connecticut and Rhode Island were charter colonies founded by religious dissidents from Massachusetts. Connecticut was founded in 1633, and granted a charter in 1662. Rhode Island was founded in 1636 and granted a charter in 1663. Both colonies were largely self-governing.

The governors of Connecticut and Rhode Island were elected each year by the white, male property owners in each colony. Although the king's approval was required before the governor could take office, it was not often asked. Laws made by their bicameral legislatures were not subject to the governor's veto, nor was the Crown's approval needed. Judges in the charter colonies were appointed by the legislature, but appeals could be taken from the colonial courts to the king.

The Connecticut and Rhode Island charters were so liberal for their time that, after independence, they were kept with only minor changes as State constitutions until 1818 and 1843, respectively. In fact, many historians say that if Britain had allowed the other colonies the same freedoms and self-government found in the charter colonies, the Revolution might never have occurred.

☑ **CONNECT** In what way did the different types of governments present in the English colonies influence the political ideas and institutions of the United States?

>> Legend has it that colonists hid Connecticut's royal charter in this oak tree to protect it from confiscation by the English governor general. The tree later became known as the Charter Oak.

☑ ASSESSMENT

1. **Apply Concepts** How was the concept of representative government reflected in the royal colonies? What aspects of these governments did NOT reflect the concept of representative government?

2. **Cite Evidence** The Petition of Right challenged the traditional idea of the divine right of kings. Give at least one specific example that supports this statement, and explain how its underlying message weakened the divine right theory.

3. **Connect** How did the barons who forced King John to sign the Magna Carta in 1215 have an impact on the governments established in the English colonies founded centuries later?

4. **Compare and Contrast** In what ways were the charter colonies more democratic than either the royal or proprietary colonies?

5. **Draw Conclusions** In the royal colonies, why might the colonists resent the "stern hand" of a royal governor?

Groundbreaking English Documents

During King John's troubled reign over England (1199–1216), he found himself in conflict with the feudal barons. In 1215, the barons forced John to sign the Magna Carta, or Great Charter. This document consists of a series of promises granted by the king, referring to himself with the royal "we" and "our." Nearly five hundred years later, Parliament forced William and Mary to submit to a bill of rights in exchange for the crown. This document sums up the powers that Parliament had been seeking since the 1628 Petition of Right. When English colonists came to North America, they brought with them the idea of limited government found in these documents.

>> King John signs the Magna Carta in 1215

The Magna Carta (1215)

John, by the grace of God, king of England, . . . to the archbishop, bishops, abbots, earls, barons, justiciaries, foresters, sheriffs, stewards, servants, and to all his bailiffs and liege subjects, greetings. . . .

1. In the first place we have granted to God, . . . that the English Church shall be free, and shall have her rights entire, and her liberties inviolate; . . . We have also . . . granted to all freemen of our kingdom, for us and our heirs forever, all the underwritten liberties, to be had and held by them and their heirs, of us and our heirs forever.

12. No [tax] nor aid shall be imposed on our kingdom, unless by common counsel [consent] of our kingdom, except for ransoming our person, for making our eldest son a knight, and for once marrying our eldest daughter; and for these there shall not be levied more than a reasonable aid. . . .

☑ **SUMMARIZE** What promise is made in Clause 12?

30. No sheriff or bailiff [tax collector] of ours, or other person, shall take the horses or carts of any freeman for transport duty, against the will of the said freeman.

31. Neither we nor our bailiffs shall take, for our castles or for any other work of ours, wood which is not ours, against the will of the owner of that wood. . . .

38. No bailiff for the future shall, upon his own unsupported complaint, put any one to his "law," without credible [believable] witnesses brought for this purpose.

39. No freeman shall be taken or imprisoned . . . or exiled or in any way destroyed, nor will we go upon him nor send upon him, except by the lawful judgment of his peers [people of equal rank] or by the law of the land.

40. To no one will we sell, to no one will we refuse or delay, right or justice. . . .

45. We will appoint as justices, constables, sheriffs, or bailiffs only such as know the law of the realm [kingdom] and mean to observe it well. . . .

63. Wherefore it is our will, and we firmly enjoin [order], that the English Church be free, and that the men in our kingdom have and hold all the

aforesaid liberties, rights, and concessions, well and peaceably, freely and quietly, fully and wholly, for themselves and their heirs, of us and our heirs, in all respects and in all places for ever, as is aforesaid.

☑ **COMPARE AND CONTRAST** How do the principles expressed in Clauses 38–40 apply to the U.S. justice system?

English Bill of Rights (1689)

Whereas, the late King James II . . . did endeavor to subvert and extirpate [eliminate] the Protestant religion and the laws and liberties of this kingdom; . . .

- By assuming and exercising a power of dispensing with and suspending of laws and the execution of laws without consent of Parliament; . . .
- By raising and keeping a standing army within this kingdom in time of peace without consent of Parliament, . . . ;
- And excessive bail hath been required of person committed in criminal cases . . .
- And excessive fines have been imposed;
- And illegal and cruel punishments inflicted; . . .
- All which are utterly and directly contrary to the known laws and statutes and freedom of this realm;

And whereas the said late king James II having abdicated the government, and the throne being vacant. . . . The said Lords [Parliament] . . . being now assembled in a full and free representative [body] of this nation . . . do in the first place . . . declare

- That the pretended [untruthfully claimed] power of suspending the laws or the execution of laws by regal authority without consent of Parliament is illegal;
- That the pretended power of dispensing with laws or the execution of laws by regal authority, as it hath been assumed and exercised of late, is illegal; . . .
- That levying [collecting] money for or to the use of the Crown by pretence of prerogative [a right exclusive to a king or queen], without grant of Parliament, for longer time, or in other manner than the same is or shall be granted, is illegal;
- That it is the right of the subjects to petition [make a request of] the king, and

all commitments and prosecutions for such petitioning are illegal;

- That the raising or keeping a standing army within the kingdom in time of peace, unless it be with consent of Parliament, is against law;
- That the subjects which are Protestants may have arms for their defence suitable to their conditions and as allowed by law;
- That election of members of Parliament ought to be free;
- That the freedom of speech and debates or proceedings in Parliament ought not to be impeached [discredited] or questioned in any court or place out of Parliament;
- That excessive bail ought not to be required, nor excessive fines imposed, nor cruel and unusual punishments inflicted;
- That jurors ought to be duly [done at a proper time] impaneled [registered on a panel of jurors] and returned [released from service], and jurors which pass upon men in trials for high treason ought to be freeholders [property owners with unconditional rights]; . . .
- And that for redress [correction] of all grievances, and for the amending, strengthening and preserving of the laws, Parliaments ought to be held frequently.

☑ **DRAW CONCLUSIONS** Why might Parliament have included the point that its members should be elected freely? What larger concept is supported by this point?

☑ ASSESSMENT

1. **Determine Author's Purpose** Why did the barons write the Magna Carta, and how did it affect the power of the king?

2. **Cite Evidence** How did the English Bill of Rights expand the rights of common Englishmen? Cite specific examples from the text to support your answer.

3. **Determine Central Ideas** How did the English Bill of Rights make Parliament more powerful? Provide specific examples from the text in your response.

2.2

The Second Continental Congress met just weeks after the battles of Lexington and Concord. One of their first tasks was to appoint George Washington as commander in chief of the new army.

 BOUNCE to Activate Flipped Video

Objectives

Explain how Britain's policies contributed to the growth of self-government in the colonies.

Identify the major steps that led to growing feelings of colonial unity.

Consider the ways the colonists organized to protest British policies, and the contributions of significant individuals, including Thomas Jefferson, Samuel Adams, John Adams, Roger Sherman, John Jay, and George Washington.

Examine the debates that impacted the creation of the Declaration of Independence.

Understand the major ideas of the Declaration of Independence, including unalienable rights, the social contract theory, and the right of resistance to illegitimate government.

Key Terms

confederation
Albany Plan of Union
delegate
duty
popular sovereignty
Samuel Adams
Roger Sherman
John Jay
George Washington
John Adams
James Wilson
Thomas Jefferson
John Locke

Independence

"We must all hang together, or assuredly we shall all hang separately." Benjamin Franklin is said to have spoken these words on July 4, 1776, as he and the other members of the Second Continental Congress approved the Declaration of Independence. Those who heard him may have chuckled, but they also may have felt a shiver, for Franklin's humor carried a deadly serious message. In this section, you will follow the events that led to the momentous decision to break with Great Britain. You will also consider the new State governments that were established with the coming of independence.

British Colonial Policies

Much of British political history can be told in terms of the century-long struggle for supremacy between the monarch and Parliament. That conflict was largely settled by England's Glorious Revolution of 1688, but it did continue through the American colonial period and into the nineteenth century.

In the midst of this struggle, Parliament paid little attention to the American colonies until late in the colonial period. Instead, they were separately controlled under the king, largely through the Privy Council and the Board of Trade in London. Although Parliament did become increasingly interested in matters of trade, it often left administrative matters to the Crown.

Over the century and a half that followed the first settlement at Jamestown, the colonies developed within that framework of royal control. In theory, they were governed from London. But London was more than 3,000 miles away, and it took nearly two months to sail that distance. The colonists became used to a large measure of self-government.

Each colonial legislature began to assume broad lawmaking powers. Many found the power of the purse to be an effective way to circumvent the king's appointed officers. They often bent a royal governor to their will by not voting the money for his salary until he came to terms with them. As one member of New Jersey's assembly put it: "Let us keep the dogges poore, and we'll make them do as we please."

By the mid-1700s, the relationship between Britain and the colonies had become, in fact if not in form, federal. This meant that the central government in London was responsible for colonial defense and for foreign affairs. It also provided a uniform system of money and credit and a common market for colonial trade. Beyond that, the colonies were allowed a fairly wide amount of self-rule. Little was taken from them in direct taxes to pay for the central government. The few regulations set by Parliament, mostly about trade, were largely ignored.

Shortly after George III came to the throne in 1760, however, Britain began to deal more firmly with its colonies. New taxes were levied to help pay the heavy costs incurred by the British during the French and Indian War (1754–1763). Since the war had been fought to protect the colonies, Parliament and King George III reasoned that the colonists should have to pay a share of those costs. In addition to the new taxes, restrictive trading acts were expanded and enforced.

Many colonists took strong exception to those policies. They objected to taxes imposed on them from afar. Because the colonies had no representatives in Parliament, they claimed such taxes amounted to "taxation without representation." They saw little need for the costly presence of British troops on North American soil, since the French had been defeated. Yet at the same time, the colonists still considered themselves British subjects loyal to the Crown.

The king's ministers were poorly informed and stubborn. They pushed ahead with their policies, despite the resentments they stirred in America. Within a few years, the colonists faced a fateful choice: submit or revolt.

☑ **DEFINE** What does the term *taxation without representation* mean?

Growing Colonial Unity

A decision to revolt was not one to be taken lightly— or alone. The colonies would need to learn to work together if they wanted to succeed. Indeed, long before the 1770s, several attempts had been made to promote cooperation among the colonies.

Early Attempts In 1643, the Massachusetts Bay, Plymouth, New Haven, and Connecticut settlements formed the New England **Confederation**, a "league of friendship" for defense against Native American tribes. As the danger passed and frictions among the settlements grew, the confederation lost importance and finally dissolved in 1684.

British Colonial Policies, 1761–1774

YEAR	ACT
1761	**Writs of Assistance** allowed British officials to search homes and businesses for smuggled goods.
1763	**Proclamation of 1763** restricted white settlers from land west of Appalachian mountains and required a license for trade with Native Americans.
1764	**Sugar Act** required and heavily enforced taxes on sugar and other goods imported into America.
1765	**Stamp Act** taxed printed paper, including legal documents, newspapers, and playing cards.
1767	**Townshend Acts** taxed glass, lead, paint, paper, and tea.
1773	**Tea Act** manipulated the tax on tea to favor the East India Company, giving them a monopoly and undercutting local merchants.
1774	**"Intolerable Acts,"** so named by the colonists, included closing the port of Boston until colonists paid for the tea dumped during the Boston Tea Party, restricting town meetings in Massachusetts, and allowing for British soldiers to be housed in private homes.

>> During the latter 1700s, the British began to implement new policies in its North American colonies. **Analyze Charts** Who benefited from these British policies?

>> Members of a New England Confederation militia return home after responding to a false alarm of a Native American attack.

JOIN, or DIE.

>> This famous political cartoon was published by Benjamin Franklin in 1754. **Analyze Political Cartoons** What does it suggest about the importance of colonial unity?

In 1696, William Penn offered an elaborate plan for intercolonial cooperation, largely in trade, defense, and criminal matters. It received little attention and was very quickly forgotten.

The Albany Plan In 1754, the British Board of Trade called a meeting of seven of the northern colonies at Albany. The main purpose of the meeting was to discuss the problems of colonial trade and the danger of attacks by the French and their Native American allies. Here, Benjamin Franklin offered what came to be known as the **Albany Plan of Union**.

In his plan, Franklin proposed the creation of an annual congress of **delegates** from each of the 13 colonies. That body would have the power to raise military and naval forces, make war and peace with the Native Americans, regulate trade with them, tax, and collect customs **duties**.

Franklin's plan was ahead of its time. It was agreed to by the representatives attending the Albany meeting, but it was turned down by the colonies and by the Crown.

The Stamp Act Congress Britain's harsh tax and trade policies fanned resentment in the colonies. Parliament had passed a number of new laws, among them the Stamp Act of 1765. That law required the use of tax stamps on all legal documents, on certain business agreements, and on newspapers.

The new taxes were widely denounced, in part because the rates were perceived as severe, but largely because they amounted to "taxation without representation." In October of 1765, nine colonies—all except Georgia, New Hampshire, North Carolina, and Virginia—sent delegates to a meeting in New York, the Stamp Act Congress. There, they prepared a strong protest, called the Declaration of Rights and Grievances, against the new British policies and sent it to the king. The Stamp Act Congress marked the first time a significant number of the colonies had joined to oppose the British government.

Parliament repealed the Stamp Act, but new laws and policies tied the colonies more closely to London. Colonists showed their anger by completely evading the laws. Mob violence erupted at several ports, and many colonists supported a boycott of English goods. On March 5, 1770, British troops in Boston fired on a jeering crowd, killing five, in what came to be known as the Boston Massacre.

Organized resistance was carried on through Committees of Correspondence, which had grown out of a group formed by political leader **Samuel Adams** in Boston in 1772. Those committees soon spread throughout the colonies, providing a network for cooperation and the exchange of information among the patriots.

Protests multiplied. The Boston Tea Party took place on December 16, 1773. A group of men, disguised as Native Americans, boarded three tea ships in Boston Harbor. They broke open the chests and dumped the ship's cargo into the sea to protest British control of the tea trade.

☑ **SEQUENCE** What did the Stamp Act Congress accomplish? In what way did it mark a turning point in colonial-British relations?

The First Continental Congress

In the spring of 1774, Parliament passed yet another set of laws, this time to punish the colonists for the troubles in Boston and elsewhere. These new laws, denounced in America as the Intolerable Acts, prompted widespread calls for a meeting of the colonies.

Delegates from every colony except Georgia met in Philadelphia on September 5, 1774. Many of the ablest men of the day were there: Samuel Adams of Massachusetts; **Roger Sherman** of Connecticut; Stephen Hopkins of Rhode Island; John Dickinson and Joseph Galloway of Pennsylvania; **John Jay** and Philip Livingston of New York; and John Rutledge of South Carolina.

Virginia sent **George Washington**, Richard Henry Lee, and Patrick Henry. At the time, Washington, a former colonel in the French and Indian War, was serving as a Virginia legislator. He had voted against British policies, defied royal orders for the legislature to stop meeting, and helped organize a boycott of British trade in Virginia.

John Adams, a rising lawyer in Boston, was also present. Adams had defended the British officers accused of murder in the Boston Massacre, despite his opposition to British colonial policies. By the time of the First Continental Congress, he had become a staunch supporter of independence as well as a brilliant political analyst.

Lawyer **James Wilson** was one of Pennsylvania's delegates. His essay, *Considerations on the Nature and Extent of the Legislative Authority of the British Parliament*, circulated among the other delegates. In it, Wilson proposed the idea that the British government had no authority to govern the colonies.

>> The 340 chests of tea destroyed during the Boston Tea Party would be worth about $1.7 million today. The colonists took great care, however, not to harm the crew or damage other property.

For nearly two months, these and other members of that First Continental Congress discussed the worsening situation and debated plans for action. Most of the delegates, many of whom would later be considered Founding Fathers of the United States, were opposed to independence. There was still great hope that a compromise could be reached. To this end, the delegates sent a Declaration of Rights, protesting Britain's colonial policies, to King George III. In it, they wrote:

Resolved, . . . That our ancestors, who first settled these colonies, were at the time of their emigration from the mother country, entitled to all the rights, liberties, and immunities of free and natural-born subjects, within the realm of England.

Resolved, . . . That by such emigration they by no means

forfeited, surrendered, or lost any of those rights. . . .

—The Declaration of Rights and Grievances, 1774

The term "natural-born subjects" relates to the ideas of English philosopher Thomas Hobbes (1588–1679). Hobbes wrote that, according to the laws of nature, humans live freely and without authority, leaving weak people vulnerable to the aggression of others. They voluntarily create governments to promote their safety and well-being.

The delegates also urged the colonies to refuse all trade with England until the hated taxes and trade regulations were repealed. Finally, the delegates called for the creation of local committees to enforce that boycott.

The meeting adjourned on October 26, 1774, with a call for a second congress to be convened the following May. Over the next several months, all 13 colonial legislatures gave their support to the actions of the First Continental Congress.

☑ **GENERATE EXPLANATIONS** Why do you think the delegates to the First Continental Congress believed that refusing to buy British goods would help their cause?

The Second Continental Congress

During the fall and winter of 1774–1775, the British government continued to refuse to compromise, let alone reverse, its colonial policies. It reacted to the Declaration of Rights as it had to other expressions of colonial discontent—with even stricter and more repressive measures.

The Second Continental Congress met in Philadelphia on May 10, 1775. By then, the Revolution had begun. The "shot heard 'round the world" had been fired. The battles of Lexington and Concord had been fought three weeks earlier, on April 19. With this bloodshed, many delegates believed that compromise with Great Britain was no longer possible.

The Nation's Founding Fathers Each of the 13 colonies sent representatives to the Congress. Most of those who had attended the First Continental Congress were again present. Notable among the newcomers were Benjamin Franklin of Pennsylvania and John Hancock of Massachusetts.

Hancock was chosen president of the Congress. In just over a month, a continental army was created, and George Washington appointed its commander-in-chief. Thirty-two-year-old **Thomas Jefferson** joined the Virginia delegation in June 1775. New York lawyer John Jay favored a course of moderation,

Key Delegates to Second Continental Congress, 1775

COLONY	DELEGATES	KEY CONTRIBUTIONS
Massachusetts	John Hancock	President of the Continental Congress
	John Adams	Nominated George Washington to command Continental Army; served on committee that drafted the Declaration of Independence
Connecticut	Roger Sherman	Served on the committee that drafted the Declaration of Independence
New York	John Jay	Favored a course of moderation toward Great Britain; helped draft the Olive Branch petition
Virginia	Thomas Jefferson	Primary author of the Declaration of Independence
	Richard Henry Lee	Made motion calling for independence
Pennsylvania	James Wilson	Argued passionately for independence
	Benjamin Franklin	Served on the committee that drafted the Declaration of Independence

>> This chart shows just a few of the key delegates to the Second Continental Congress. **Analyze Charts** What qualifications did these men have to suit them to the task of leading the colonies?

and drafted an early version of an Olive Branch petition as a last attempt to make peace with Great Britain. John Dickinson of Pennsylvania wrote the final draft, which Jay signed. John Hancock also signed it, as did John Adams, Roger Sherman, Benjamin Franklin, and Thomas Jefferson. When King George III rejected the petition, the delegates began discussing other strategies.

First Government The Second Continental Congress became, by force of circumstance, the nation's first national government. However, it rested on no constitutional base. It was condemned by the British as an unlawful assembly and a den of traitors. But it was supported by the force of public opinion and practical necessity.

The Second Continental Congress served as the first government of the United States for five fateful years, from the formal adoption of the Declaration of Independence in July 1776 until the Articles of Confederation went into effect on March 1, 1781. During that time, the Second Continental Congress fought a war, raised armies and a navy, borrowed funds, bought supplies, created a money system, made treaties with foreign powers, and did other things that any government would have had to do in those circumstances.

The unicameral Congress had both legislative and executive powers. In legislative matters, each colony—later, State—had one vote. Executive functions were handled by committees of delegates.

☑ **ANALYZE** Why did the British call the Second Continental Congress "a den of traitors"?

The Declaration of Independence

About a year after the Revolution began, Virginia's Richard Henry Lee proposed to the Congress:

> Resolved, That these United Colonies are, and of right ought to be, free and independent States, that they are absolved from all allegiance to the British Crown, and that all political connection between them and the State of Great Britain is, and ought to be, totally dissolved.

—Resolution of June 7, 1776

>> Congressional delegates thought the move for independence should be unanimous, so they delayed the final vote until 12 colonial delegations favored it. New York abstained.

As debate on Lee's resolution began, Congress named a committee of five—Benjamin Franklin, John Adams, Roger Sherman, Robert Livingston, and Thomas Jefferson—to prepare a proclamation of independence. Their momentous product, the Declaration of Independence, was very largely the work of Jefferson.

Jefferson's Work Thomas Jefferson was a young delegate, well-respected though shy. As a lawyer, he had gained early notoriety through an essay he wrote in 1774 in which he argued for colonial independence. He was also a man of contradictions, embracing the idea of equality at the same time that he enslaved others. As a member of the Second Continental Congress, he spoke rarely but nonetheless impressed his colleagues with his passionate belief in the cause of independence. The document he crafted drew from the political philosophies of Enlightenment thinker **John Locke**, in particular the ideas of natural rights and the social contract theory.

Locke believed that people have natural rights— rights that belong to them simply because they are human, not because kings or governments have granted them these rights. He also put forward his own view of the social contract theory. According to Locke, people form governments to protect their natural rights, but they do not surrender control over their government. If a government fails to act in the best interests of the people, they have the right to revolt and replace that government with a new one.

Jefferson drew upon these ideas to validate the colonists' dissatisfaction with the king's governance. In what became known as the list of "grievances," Jefferson delineated the ways in which the king had violated the colonists' individual and natural rights, due process of law, and popular sovereignty, which effectively nullified their social contract with the king.

Debates and Compromises As Thomas Jefferson worked, the delegates continued to debate Lee's resolution. Many of them had serious doubts about the wisdom of a complete separation from England. Could the colonies survive on their own? Others had grave reservations about remaining British subjects. They believed that the British government clearly did not have the best interests of the colonies at heart. On July 2, the delegates finally reached a decision. They agreed to Lee's resolution and quickly took up consideration of Jefferson's work.

Spirited debate again ensued. Should Jefferson's lines criticizing the English people remain? Many

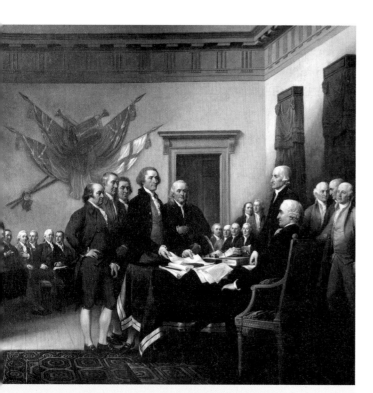

>> The Second Continental Congress adopted the Declaration of Independence on July 4, 1776, but the document wasn't actually signed until the first week of August.

delegates feared that such language would offend those they still considered friends, and it was removed from the first draft. So too were the lines condemning the trade in enslaved people, in deference to southern enslavers and to the general views of many delegates about Black people. The debates continued for more than two days, but on July 4, 1776, in one of the most historic votes of all time, the Congress adopted the revised Declaration of Independence.

At its heart, the Declaration proclaims:

> We hold these truths to be self-evident, that all men are created equal, that they are endowed by their Creator with certain unalienable Rights, that among these are Life, Liberty and the pursuit of Happiness. That to secure these rights, Governments are instituted among Men, deriving their just powers from the consent of the governed; That whenever any Form of Government becomes destructive of these ends it is the Right of the People to alter or to abolish it, and to institute new Government, laying its foundations on such principles and organizing its powers in such form, as to them shall seem most likely to effect their Safety and Happiness.
>
> —The Unanimous Declaration of the Thirteen United States of America

Revolutionary Ideas In these opening lines, the Declaration of Independence reflects the political principles of natural rights and the social contract theory: "all men are . . . endowed by their Creator with certain unalienable Rights." Notice that these rights come from "the Laws of Nature and of Nature's God"—not from a government or a king. In its conclusion, the Declaration affirms that the members of the Second Continental Congress act "by Authority of the good People of these Colonies."

The Declaration goes on to embrace the social contract theory by insisting that "to secure these rights, Governments are instituted among Men, deriving their just powers from the consent of the governed"—that is, a social contract is formed.

FEATURES OF STATE CONSTITUTIONS

1 POPULAR SOVEREIGNTY

2 LIMITED GOVERNMENT

3 CIVIL RIGHTS AND LIBERTIES

4 SEPARATION OF POWERS

5 CHECKS AND BALANCES

1776
DECLARATION OF INDEPENDENCE

123

"...all men are created equal, ... they are endowed by their Creator with certain unalienable Rights, ...among these are Life, Liberty, and the pursuit of Happiness."

1781
ARTICLES OF CONFEDERATION

2

"Each state retains its sovereignty, freedom and independence, and every Power, Jurisdiction and right, which is not by this confederation expressly delegated to the United States..."

1788
— U.S. — CONSTITUTION

12345

"We the People of the United States... do ordain and establish this Constitution...."

>> The initial State constitutions had several features in common with America's founding documents. **Analyze Charts** What features were most common?

Further, "That whenever any Form of Government becomes destructive of these ends it is the Right of the People to alter or to abolish it." Should the government not act in the people's best interest, the people can end the social contract.

The Declaration also reflects the principles of popular sovereignty and individual rights. **Popular sovereignty** means that the people are the *only* source of governmental authority. The Declaration makes it clear that government in the new nation would be by the people: "Governments are instituted among Men, deriving their just powers from the consent of the governed." Further, the "governed"— that is, the people—have individual rights, including the right to "Life, Liberty and the pursuit of Happiness." These principles form the philosophical basis of our government. So, too, do the "self-evident truths" that all are created equal and have certain "unalienable rights" and the idea of due process of law, so clearly expressed in the Declaration's list of grievances.

With the adoption of the Declaration of Independence, the United States was born. The 13 colonies became free and independent States, and the American Revolution became more than a war for independence. No political system had ever been founded on the notion that the people, born free and equal, should rule instead of being ruled.

☑ **SUMMARIZE** What gave the signers of the Declaration the authority to dissolve their status as a British colony and create a new government?

The First State Constitutions

In January 1776, New Hampshire adopted a constitution to replace its royal charter. Less than three months later, South Carolina followed suit. Then, on May 10, nearly two months before the adoption of the Declaration of Independence, the Congress urged each of the colonies to adopt "such governments as shall, in the opinion of the representatives of the people, best conduce to the happiness and safety of their constituents."

Drafting State Constitutions In 1776 and 1777, most of the States adopted written constitutions— bodies of fundamental laws setting out the principles, structures, and processes of their governments. Assemblies or conventions were commonly used to draft and then adopt these new documents.

Massachusetts set a lasting example in the constitution-making process. There, a popularly elected convention submitted its work to the voters

>> In order to vote in the United States following the Revolutionary War, a person had to be a white male who owned property.

rights that government must at all times respect. Seven of the new documents began with a bill of rights, setting out these "unalienable rights" held by the people.

Separation of Powers, Checks and Balances. The powers granted to the new State governments were divided among three distinct branches: executive, legislative, and judicial. Each branch was given powers with which to check, or restrain the actions of, the other branches of the government.

Beyond those basics, the new State constitutions were rather brief documents. They were, for the most part, declarations of principle and statements of limitation on governmental power. Memories of the royal governors were fresh, and State governors were given little real power. Most of the authority that was granted to government was placed in the legislature. Elective terms of office were made purposely short, seldom more than one or two years. The right to vote was limited to those adult white males who could meet rigid qualifications, including property ownership.

☑ **GENERATE EXPLANATIONS** Why were elective terms of office made purposely short?

for ratification. The Massachusetts constitution of 1780, authored by John Adams, is the oldest of the present-day State constitutions. It also is the oldest written constitution in force in the world today. John Jay helped draft New York's State constitution.

Common Features The first State constitutions differed, sometimes widely, in their details. Yet they were on the whole more alike than not. The most common features were the principles of popular sovereignty, limited government, civil rights and liberties, separation of powers, and checks and balances. Most importantly, the basic principles set out in the earliest of those documents were, within a very few years, to have a marked impact on the drafting of the Constitution of the United States.

Popular Sovereignty. Everywhere, the people were recognized as the only source of governmental authority. In the new United States, government could be conducted only with the consent of the governed.

Limited Government. The new State governments could exercise only those powers granted to them by the people through the constitution. The powers that were given were hedged with many restrictions to protect the rights of individual citizens.

Civil Rights and Liberties. In every State, it was made clear that the sovereign people held certain

☑ ASSESSMENT

1. **Analyze Information** How did "taxation without representation" conflict with John Locke's social contract idea of government?

2. **Identify Central Ideas** Who was Thomas Jefferson, and what was his contribution toward the development of the United States government?

3. **Sequence Events** The Declaration of Independence was issued *after* the Revolutionary War had already started. What was the focus of debate about the war at the Second Continental Congress?

4. **Infer** The ideas in the Declaration of Independence created a new national identity that united colonists behind a core set of beliefs and set the new nation apart from other countries throughout the world. Why else was it significant that the ideas in the Declaration of Independence created a new national identity?

5. **Draw Conclusions** How was the Revolutionary War much more than just a war for independence?

Voices of American Patriots

Virginia lawyer Patrick Henry (1736–1799) became known for his remarkable speaking skills while still a young man. He was elected to the Virginia House of Burgesses in 1765 and strongly opposed the Stamp Act. In a speech related to the crisis, he declared, "If this be treason, make the most of it." Bitter criticism from delegates forced him to apologize for the statement and affirm his loyalty to the king. When Henry spoke in favor of liberty in 1775, members of the assembly jumped from their seats and shouted, "To Arm! To Arms!"

In 1776, after the battles at Lexington and Concord, another American who had a way with words inspired his fellow patriots. Thomas Paine published a fiery fifty-page pamphlet that challenged the authority of the British government and appealed to Americans to seek independence from Great Britain.

>> The American Revolution was fought from 1775–1783.

"Give Me Liberty or Give Me Death": Patrick Henry

. . . They tell us, sir, that we are weak; unable to cope with so formidable an adversary [enemy; opponent]. But when shall we be stronger? Will it be the next week, or the next year? Will it be when we are totally disarmed, and when a British guard shall be stationed in every house? Shall we gather strength by irresolution [uncertainty on how to act] and inaction? Shall we acquire the means of effectual resistance by lying supinely [reclining] on our backs and hugging the delusive [unreal; misleading] phantom of hope, until our enemies shall have bound us hand and foot? Sir, we are not weak if we make a proper use of those means which the God of nature hath placed in our power. Three millions of people armed in the holy cause of liberty, and in such a country as that which we possess, are invincible by any force which our enemy can send against us. . . . The battle, sir, is not to the strong alone; it is to the vigilant [on the alert for danger], the active, the brave.

☑ **ANALYZE STYLE AND RHETORIC** How does Patrick Henry make effective use of rhetorical questions in this passage? What effect do you think this style had on his audience?

Besides, sir, we have no election. If we were base enough to desire it, it is now too late to retire from the contest. There is no retreat but in submission and slavery! Our chains are forged! Their clanking may be heard on the plains of Boston! The war is inevitable—and let it come! I repeat, sir, let it come!

It is vain, sir, to extenuate [to excuse; to make light of] the matter. The gentlemen may cry, Peace, peace! But there is no peace. The war has actually begun! The next gale that sweeps from the north will bring to our ears the clash of resounding arms! Our brethren are already in the field! Why stand we here idle? What is it that gentlemen wish? What would they have? Is life so dear or peace so sweet as to be purchased at the price of chains and slavery? Forbid it, almighty God. I know not what course others may take, but as for me, give me liberty or give me death!

☑ **ANALYZE WORD CHOICES** What does Henry mean, exactly, when he says that the colonists "have no election"?

Common Sense: Thomas Paine

. . . To the evil of monarchy we have added that of hereditary succession; and as the first is a degradation and lessening of ourselves, so the second, claimed as a matter of right, is an insult and imposition on posterity. For all men being originally equals, no one by birth could have a right to set up his own family in perpetual preference to all others for ever . . .

. . . As to the government matters, it is not in the power of Britain to do this continent justice: The business of it will soon be too weighty, and intricate, to be managed with any tolerable degree of convenience, by a power, so distant from us, and so very ignorant of us; for if they cannot conquer us, they cannot govern us. To be always running three or four thousand miles with a tale or a petition, waiting four or five months for an answer, which when obtained requires five or six more to explain it in, will in a few years be looked upon as folly and childishness—There was a time when it was proper, and there is a proper time for it to cease. . . .

☑ **CITE EVIDENCE** What two pieces of evidence does Paine provide to support his thesis?

If there is any true cause of fear respecting independence, it is because no plan is yet laid down: men do not see their way out. Wherefore, as an opening into that business, I offer the following hints. . . .

[L]et a Continental Conference be held. . . . The conferring members being met, let their business be to frame a Continental Charter. . . .

[L]et a day be solemnly set apart for proclaiming the charter; . . . let a crown be placed thereon, by

which the world may know, that so far as we approve of monarchy, that in America the law is king. For as in absolute governments the King is law, so in free countries the law ought to be King; and there ought to be no other. But lest any ill use should afterwards arise, let the crown at the conclusion of the ceremony be demolished, and scattered among the people whose right it is.

☑ **ANALYZE STYLE AND RHETORIC** Some people might say Paine was employing hyperbole in this passage. Would you agree? Why or why not?

A government of our own is our natural right: And when a man seriously reflects on the precariousness of human affairs, he will become convinced, that it is infinitely wiser and safer, to form a constitution of our own in a cool deliberate manner, while we have it in our power, than to trust such an interesting event to time and chance.

☑ **ANALYZE WORD CHOICE** In the first sentence of this passage, Paine could have written, "A government of our own is our right." Why do you think he included the word *natural*?

☑ ASSESSMENT

1. **Analyze Word Choices** What militaristic words does Henry use when making his argument? How do they impact the effectiveness of his speech?

2. **Evaluate** Evaluate Patrick Henry's point of view, reasoning, and use of evidence and rhetoric. In your answer consider the following: Henry's stance, premises, links among ideas, word choice, points of emphasis and tone.

3. **Synthesize** How do specific details in the text of *Common Sense* contribute to an understanding of the text as a whole?

George Washington leads troops across the Delaware River on December 25, 1776. As the fight for independence continued, Congress worked on a plan of government for the new nation.

First Steps

The First and Second Continental Congresses rested on no legal base. They were called in haste to meet an emergency, and they were intended to be temporary. Something more regular and permanent was clearly needed. In this reading, you will look at the first attempt to establish a lasting government for the new nation.

The Articles of Confederation

Richard Henry Lee's resolution that led to the Declaration of Independence also called on the Second Continental Congress to propose "a plan of confederation" to the States. Off and on, for 17 months, Congress debated the best organization for the new government.

One widely discussed issue centered around the amount of money each State should pay into a common treasury. The northern States proposed that the sum should be in proportion to a State's total population, which they said should include enslaved people but not untaxed Native Americans. The southern States objected to this proposal because they considered enslaved people to be "property, not persons," and they were attempting to limit their required contribution to the treasury. After much debate, Congress decided to base contributions not on population, but instead on the value of land within each State.

A second area of debate involved the voting power of the States in Congress. The original plan provided that each State would have one vote. Some delegates proposed instead that on financial questions, each State should have votes in proportion to its population. This amendment eventually failed, and the original article was accepted. Finally, on November 15, 1777, after

BOUNCE to Activate Flipped Video

Objectives

Describe the debates that impacted the creation of the Articles of Confederation, the structure of the government set up under the Articles, and how that government was influenced by ideas, people, and historical documents.

Explain why the weaknesses of the Articles led to a critical period for the country in the 1780s.

Describe how a growing need for a stronger national government led to plans for a Constitutional Convention.

Key Terms

Articles of
   Confederation
ratification
full faith and credit
Shays' Rebellion
Daniel Shays
Alexander Hamilton
James Madison

various other issues were resolved, the **Articles of Confederation** were approved at last.

The Articles of Confederation established "a firm league of friendship" among the States. Each State kept "its sovereignty, freedom, and independence, and every Power, jurisdiction, and right . . . not . . . expressly delegated to the United States, in Congress assembled." The States came together "for their common defense, the security of their Liberties, and their mutual and general welfare. . . ." In effect, the Articles created a structure that more closely resembled an alliance of independent states than a government "of the people."

The Articles did not go into effect immediately, however. The **ratification** of each of the 13 States was needed first. Eleven States approved the document within a year. Delaware added its approval in February 1779. Maryland did not ratify until March 1, 1781. The Second Continental Congress declared the Articles effective on that date.

A Simple Structure The government set up by the Articles was quite simple. A Congress was the sole body created. It was unicameral, made up of delegates chosen yearly by the States in whatever way their legislatures might direct. Each State

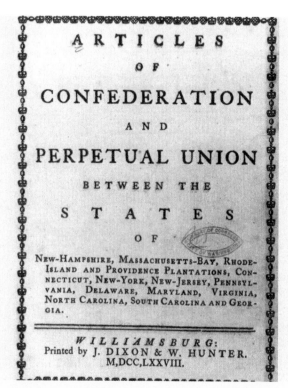

>> The Articles of Confederation sought to unify the former colonies, while balancing States' rights and the powers of the federal government.

had only one vote in the Congress, regardless of its population or wealth.

The Articles established no executive or judicial branch. These functions were to be handled by committees of the Congress. Each year, the Congress would choose one of its members as its president. That person would be its presiding officer, but not the President of the United States. Civil officers such as postmasters were to be appointed by the Congress.

Congressional Powers Several important powers were given to the Congress. It could make war and peace, send and receive ambassadors, make treaties, borrow money, set up a money system, establish post offices, build a navy, raise an army by asking the States for troops, fix uniform standards of weights and measures, and settle disputes among the States.

The States Under the Articles By agreeing to the Articles, the States pledged to obey both the Articles and acts of the Congress. They promised to provide the funds and troops requested by Congress; treat citizens of other States fairly and equally within their own borders; and give **full faith and credit** to the public acts, records, and judicial proceedings of every other State. In addition, the States agreed to surrender fugitives from justice to one another, submit their disputes to Congress for settlement, and allow open travel and trade among the States.

Beyond those few obligations, the States retained those powers not explicitly given to the Congress. They, not the Congress, were primarily responsible for protecting life and property, and for promoting "the safety and happiness of the people."

Major Weaknesses Surface The powers of the Congress appear, at first glance, to have been considerable. Several important powers were missing, however. Their omission, together with other weaknesses, soon proved the Articles inadequate for the needs of the time.

The Congress did not have the power to tax. It could raise money only by borrowing and by asking the States for funds. Borrowing was, at best, a poor source. The Second Continental Congress had borrowed heavily to support the Revolution, and many of those debts had not been paid. And, while the Articles remained in force, not one State came close to meeting the financial requests made by the Congress.

Nor did the Congress have the power to regulate trade among the States. This lack of a central mechanism to regulate the young nation's growing commerce was one of the major factors that soon led to the adoption of the Constitution.

The Congress was further limited by a lack of power to make the States obey the Articles of Confederation or the laws it made. Congress could exercise the powers it did have only with the consent of 9 of the 13 State delegations. Finally, the Articles themselves could be changed only with the consent of all 13 of the State legislatures.

☑ **SUMMARIZE** What two main issues were debated that impacted the creation of the Articles of Confederation?

A Time of Troubles, the 1780s

The long Revolutionary War finally ended on October 19, 1781. America's victory was confirmed by the signing of the Treaty of Paris in 1783. Peace, however, brought the new nation's economic and political weaknesses into sharp focus.

Problems, made even more difficult by the weaknesses of the Articles, soon surfaced. With a central government unable to act, the States bickered among themselves. They grew increasingly jealous and suspicious of one another. They often refused to support the new central government, financially and in almost every other way. Several of them made agreements with foreign governments without the approval of the Congress, even though that was forbidden by the Articles. Most organized their own military forces. George Washington complained, ". . . we are one nation today and 13 tomorrow. Who will treat with us on such terms?"

The States taxed one another's goods and even banned some trade. They printed their own money, often with little backing. Economic chaos spread throughout the colonies as prices soared and sound credit vanished. Debts, public and private, went unpaid. Violence broke out in a number of places.

The most spectacular of these events played out in western Massachusetts in a series of incidents that came to be known as **Shays' Rebellion**. As economic conditions worsened there, property holders, many of them small farmers, began to lose their land and possessions for lack of payment on taxes and other debts.

In the fall of 1786, **Daniel Shays**, who had served as an officer in the War for Independence, led an armed uprising that forced several State judges to close their courts. Early the next year, Shays mounted an unsuccessful attack on the federal

>> Many State legislatures forgave debt and printed more money during the 1780s, but not Massachusetts. Shays' Rebellion was a desperate protest against high taxes and unresponsive government.

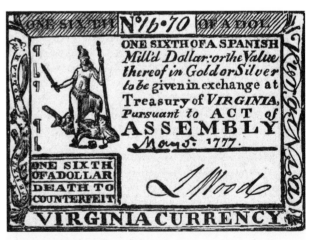

>> States often printed their own money, which was not backed by silver or gold and did not hold its value. Banks and merchants often refused to accept this money, leading to economic chaos.

arsenal at Springfield. State forces finally moved to quiet the rebellion and Shays fled to Vermont. In response to the violence, the Massachusetts legislature eventually passed laws to ease the burden of debtors.

☑ **INTERPRET** What did George Washington mean when he said ". . . we are one nation today and 13 tomorrow"?

A Demand for Stronger Government

The Articles had created a government unable to deal with the nation's troubles. Inevitably, demand grew for a stronger, more effective national government. Those who were most threatened by economic and political instability—large property owners, merchants, traders, and other creditors—soon took the lead in efforts to that end. The movement for change began to take concrete form in 1785.

First Steps Toward Change Maryland and Virginia, plagued by bitter trade disputes, took the first step in the movement for change. Ignoring the Congress, the two States agreed to a conference to resolve conflicts over commerce and navigation on the Potomac River and Chesapeake Bay.

Representatives from the two States met at Alexandria, Virginia, in March 1785. At George Washington's invitation, they moved their sessions to his home at nearby Mount Vernon. Their negotiations proved so successful that on January 21, 1786, the Virginia General Assembly called for "a joint meeting of [all of] the States to consider and recommend a federal plan for regulating commerce."

A Call for Action That joint meeting opened at Annapolis, Maryland, on September 11, 1786. Turnout was poor, with representatives from only 5 of the 13 States attending: New York, New Jersey, Pennsylvania, Delaware, and Virginia. Although New Hampshire, Massachusetts, Rhode Island, and North Carolina had appointed delegates, none attended the Annapolis meeting. Disappointed but still hopeful, **Alexander Hamilton**, a delegate from New York, and Virginia's **James Madison** persuaded the gathering to call for yet another meeting of the States.

By mid-February of 1787, seven of the States had named delegates to the Philadelphia meeting: Delaware, Georgia, New Hampshire, New Jersey, North Carolina, Pennsylvania, and Virginia. On February 21, the Congress, which had been hesitating, also called upon the States to send delegates to Philadelphia

> . . . for the sole and express purpose of revising the Articles of Confederation and reporting to Congress and the several legislatures such alterations and provisions therein as shall when agreed to in Congress and confirmed by the States render the [Articles] adequate to the exigencies of Government and the preservation of the Union.
>
> —The United States in Congress Assembled, February 21, 1787

That Philadelphia meeting became known as the Constitutional Convention. What began as an assembly to revise the existing Articles of Confederation soon evolved into a meeting dedicated to a different purpose—the creation of an entirely new kind of government for the United States of

>> Representatives from Virginia and Maryland moved their discussions to Mount Vernon (shown here) in 1785. This Mount Vernon Conference began a new era of interstate cooperation.

America. This government would derive its power from a constitution.

☑ **DRAW CONCLUSIONS** What weakness in the Articles of Confederation led to conflicts regarding trade and navigation between Virginia and Maryland?

☑ ASSESSMENT

1. **Identify Central Issues** Describe the major debates that impacted the creation of the Articles of Confederation.

2. **Make Generalizations** How did the government structure set up under the Articles of

Confederation reflect the ideas and experiences of the English colonists who had so recently been embroiled in a fight for independence?

3. **Infer** Why did Congress refrain from including the power to tax in the Articles of Confederation?

4. **Identify Cause and Effect** In what ways was Shays' Rebellion a result of weaknesses in the Articles of Confederation?

5. **Support Ideas with Evidence** When the States ratified the Articles, they agreed to obey the Articles and all acts of Congress. Did the States honor that agreement? Give evidence to support your answer.

This painting, *The Signing of the Constitution,* by Howard Chandler Christy, depicts the scene on the day the U.S. Constitution was signed after four long months of debate and compromise.

BOUNCE to Activate Flipped Video

Objectives

Identify the Framers of the Constitution, the individuals, principles, and ideas that influenced them, how they organized the Constitutional Convention, and their contributions to the creation of the United States Constitution.

Compare and contrast the Virginia and New Jersey plans for the new government.

Examine the convention's major debates and compromises.

Identify the opposing sides in the fight for ratification and describe the major arguments for and against the proposed Constitution.

Key Terms

Framers	Federalists
quorum	Anti-Federalists
Virginia Plan	Baron de
veto	Montesquieu
New Jersey Plan	Jean Jacques
Connecticut	Rousseau
Compromise	William Blackstone
Three-Fifths	George Mason
Compromise	
Commerce and	
Slave Trade	
Compromise	

Creating and Ratifying the Constitution

Picture the scene. It is hot—sweltering, in fact. Yet all of the windows of the State House are closed and shuttered to discourage eavesdroppers. Outside, soldiers keep curious onlookers and others at a distance. Inside, the atmosphere is frequently tense, as fifty or so men exchange sometimes heated views. Indeed, some who are there become so upset that they threaten to leave the hall, and a few actually do so.

The Framers Meet

This was often the scene at the Philadelphia meeting, which finally began on May 25, 1787. Over the long summer months, until mid-September, the Framers of what was to become the Constitution worked to build a new government that could meet the needs of the nation.

The Delegates Many of the men attending the meeting had studied the writings of John Locke, **Baron de Montesquieu**, **Jean Jacques Rousseau**, and **William Blackstone**. Like these great thinkers, the Framers of the Constitution believed that government should exist only by the consent of the governed. They also subscribed to such Enlightenment ideas as natural rights, the social contract, separation of powers, and checks and balances. It is no surprise, then, that these principles formed the basis of their new plan of government.

Twelve of the thirteen States, all but Rhode Island, sent delegates to Philadelphia. In total, 74 delegates were chosen by the legislatures in those 12 States. For a number of reasons, however, only 55 of them actually attended the convention.

Of that 55, this much can be said: Never, before or perhaps even since, has so remarkable a group been brought together in this country. Thomas Jefferson, who was not among them, later called the delegates "an assembly of demigods."

A New Generation in American Politics

The delegates who attended the Philadelphia Convention, known as the **Framers** of the Constitution, included many outstanding individuals. These were men of wide knowledge and public experience.

Many of the Framers had fought in the Revolution; 46 had been members of the Continental Congress or the Congress of the Confederation, or both. Eight had served in constitutional conventions in their own States, and seven had been State governors. Eight had signed the Declaration of Independence. Thirty-four of the delegates had attended college in a day when there were but a few colleges in the land. Two were to become Presidents of the United States, and one a Vice President. Nineteen later served in the Senate and thirteen in the House of Representatives.

Is it any wonder that the product of such a gathering was described by the English statesman William E. Gladstone, nearly a century later, as "the most wonderful work ever struck off at a given time by the brain and purpose of man"?

Remarkably, the average age of the delegates was only 42, and most of the leaders were in their thirties—James Madison, arguably the principal architect of the Constitution, was 36, Gouverneur Morris was 35, Edmund Randolph was 34, and Alexander Hamilton was 30. At 81, Benjamin Franklin was the oldest, and although his health was failing, he nonetheless managed to attend many of the meetings. George Washington, at 55, was one of the few older members who played a key role at the convention. Jonathan Dayton of New Jersey was, at 26, the youngest delegate.

James Wilson of Pennsylvania was 45 when the convention began. He was one of the most active delegates at the meeting, arguing for a strong central government and other provisions he thought would best guarantee a government by the people.

By and large, the Framers of the Constitution were of a new generation in American politics. Several of the leaders of the Revolutionary period were not in Philadelphia. Patrick Henry said he "smelt a rat" and refused to attend. Samuel Adams, John Hancock, and Richard Henry Lee were not

Selected Framers of the Constitution

VIRGINIA	CONNECTICUT	NEW YORK	VIRGINIA	VIRGINIA
George Washington	**Roger Sherman**	**Alexander Hamilton**	**James Madison**	**George Mason**
• Planter • Commander of the Continental Army • Continental Congress • Presence lent respectability to the Convention	• Merchant • Continental Congress; Confederation Congress • Member of Declaration of Independence and Articles of Confederation committees	• Soldier in the Revolutionary War; lawyer • Continental Congress; Confederation Congress • Favored a strong national government	• Involved in state and local politics • Continental Congress; Confederation Congress • Leading figure in movement to replace Articles of Confederation	• Planter • Author of Virginia's Declaration of Rights • Concerned with the absence of a declaration of rights in the Constitution

>> The Framers of the Constitution were accomplished men who came from different backgrounds. **Analyze Charts** How might their experiences have helped the Framers to create the Constitution?

selected as delegates by their States. Thomas Paine was in Paris. So was Thomas Jefferson, as American minister to France. John Adams was the envoy to England and Holland at the time.

☑ **ASSESS CREDIBILITY** Suppose you lived in 1787 and wanted to defend the delegates to the Constitutional Convention in terms of their suitability for the job of drafting a new Constitution. What facts might you use to back up your argument?

The Delegates Adopt Rules of Procedure

The Framers met in the Pennsylvania State House (now Independence Hall), probably in the same room in which the Declaration of Independence had been signed 11 years earlier. Not enough States were represented on the date Congress had set, May 14, to begin the meeting. The delegates who were present met until the 25th, when a **quorum** of the States was finally on hand.

On that date, the delegates unanimously elected George Washington president of the convention. Then, and at the second session on Monday, May 28, they adopted several rules of procedure. A majority

of the States would be needed to conduct business. Each State delegation was to have one vote on all matters, and a majority of the votes cast would carry any proposal.

The Framers met on 92 of the 116 days from May 25 through their final meeting on September 17. They did most of their work on the floor of the convention. They handled some matters in committees, but the full body ultimately settled all questions.

Remember, Congress had called the Philadelphia Convention "for the sole and express purpose" of recommending revisions to the Articles of Confederation. However, almost at once the delegates agreed that they were meeting to create an entirely new government for the United States. On May 30 they adopted this proposal:

> Resolved, . . . that a national Government ought to be established consisting of a supreme Legislative, Executive and Judiciary.
>
> —Edmund Randolph, Delegate from Virginia

With this momentous decision, the Framers redefined the purpose of the convention. From that point on, they set about writing a new constitution, intended to replace the Articles of Confederation. (However, much that would go into this new constitution would come directly from the Articles of Confederation.) Their debates were spirited, even bitter. At times the convention seemed near collapse. Once they had passed Randolph's resolution, however, the resolve of most of the delegates never wavered.

☑ **SUMMARIZE** How did the goal of the Philadelphia meeting change from the time the meeting was called to the first week of the convention?

Two Plans of Government

Once the Framers resolved to replace the Articles of Confederation, two major plans were offered for the new government, the Virginia Plan and the New Jersey Plan.

The Virginia Plan No State had more to do with the calling of the convention than Virginia. It was not surprising, then, that its delegates should offer the first plan for a new constitution. On May 29, the **Virginia Plan**, largely the work of James Madison, was presented by Edmund Randolph.

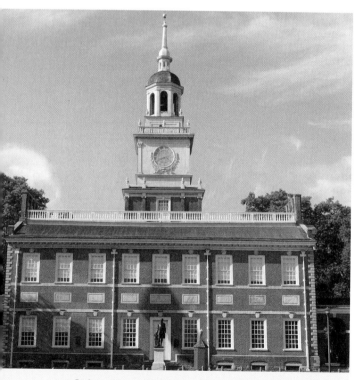

>> Independence Hall, often referred to as the birthplace of the United States, was originally home to all three branches of Pennsylvania's colonial government.

HIGHLIGHTS OF THE VIRGINIA PLAN

CREATED A
NEW GOVERNMENT WITH THREE SEPARATE BRANCHES:
EXECUTIVE, LEGISLATIVE, JUDICIAL

MEMBERS OF THE **LOWER HOUSE** WOULD BE ELECTED BY **POPULAR VOTE** ✓

MEMBERS OF THE SENATE WOULD BE **CHOSEN BY THE HOUSE** FROM A LIST SUGGESTED BY THE **STATE LEGISLATURES**

CONGRESS COULD TAKE CONTROL OF INDIVIDUAL STATES IN EXTREME CASES

REPRESENTATION BASED ON **POPULATION OR THE AMOUNT OF MONEY** EACH STATE GAVE TOWARD **THE CENTRAL GOVERNMENT**

CONGRESS WOULD BE BICAMERAL

A NATIONAL EXECUTIVE AND A NATIONAL JUDICIARY, CHOSEN BY CONGRESS, WOULD HAVE THE **POWER TO VETO** CONGRESSIONAL ACTS

>> Edmund Randolph proposed the Virginia Plan to the convention, but it was written largely by James Madison. **Analyze Charts** How many branches would the government have under the Virginia Plan?

The Virginia Plan called for a new government with three separate branches: legislative, executive, and judicial. The legislature—Congress—would be bicameral. Representation in each house was to be based either on each State's population or on the amount of money it gave for the support of the Federal Government. The members of the lower house, the House of Representatives, were to be popularly elected in each State. Those of the upper house, the Senate, were to be chosen by the House from lists of persons nominated by the State legislatures.

Congress was to be given all of the powers it held under the Articles. In addition, it would have the power "to legislate in all cases to which the separate States are incompetent" to act, to veto any State law in conflict with national law, and to use force if necessary to make a State obey national law.

Under the proposed Virginia Plan, Congress would choose a "National Executive" and a "National Judiciary." Together, these two branches would form a "Council of revision." They could **veto** acts passed by Congress, but a veto could be overridden by the two houses. The executive would have "a general authority to execute the National laws." The judiciary would "consist of one or more supreme tribunals [courts], and of inferior tribunals."

The Virginia Plan also provided that all State officers should take an oath to support the Union, and that each State be guaranteed a republican form of government. Under the plan, Congress would have the exclusive power to admit new States to the Union.

The Virginia Plan, then, would create a new constitution by thoroughly revising the Articles. Its goal was the creation of a truly national government with greatly expanded powers and, importantly, the power to enforce its decisions.

The Virginia Plan set the agenda for much of the convention's work. Its major support came from the three most populous States: Virginia, Pennsylvania, and Massachusetts. But some delegates—especially those from New York (then only the fifth most populous State) and the smaller States of Delaware, Maryland, and New Jersey—found it too radical. Soon they developed their counter proposals. On June 15, William Paterson of New Jersey presented the position of the smaller States.

The New Jersey Plan Paterson and his colleagues offered several amendments to the Articles, but not nearly so thorough a revision as that proposed by the Virginia Plan. The **New Jersey Plan** retained the unicameral Congress of the Confederation, with each of the States equally represented. In addition to those powers Congress already had, the plan would add closely limited powers to tax and to regulate trade between the States.

The New Jersey Plan also called for a "federal executive" of more than one person. This plural executive would be chosen by Congress and could be removed by it at the request of a majority of the States' governors. The "federal judiciary" would be composed of a single "supreme Tribunal," appointed by the executive.

The major point of disagreement between the two plans centered on this question: How should the States be represented in Congress? Would it be on the basis of their populations or financial contributions, as in the Virginia Plan? Or on the basis of State equality, as in the Articles and the New Jersey Plan?

For weeks the delegates returned to this conflict, debating the matter again and again. The lines were sharply drawn. Several delegates on both sides of the issue threatened to withdraw. Finally, the dispute was settled by one of the key compromises the Framers were to make as they built the Constitution.

☑ **COMPARE AND CONTRAST** Explain the major difference between the Virginia Plan and the New Jersey Plan.

Debates and Compromises

The disagreement over representation in Congress was critical. The larger States expected to dominate the new government. The smaller States feared that they would not be able to protect their interests. Tempers flared on both sides. The debate became so intense that Benjamin Franklin was moved to suggest that "henceforth prayers imploring the assistance of Heaven . . . be held in this Assembly every morning before we proceed to business."

The Connecticut Compromise The Connecticut delegates—Roger Sherman, Oliver Ellsworth, and William Samuel Johnson—presented their compromise to the convention as a means to end the deadlock between the supporters of the rival New Jersey and Virginia plans. Roger Sherman had been one of the most active members of the Continental Congress and, during the convention, he actively defended the rights of the smaller States. He was also the main architect of the **Connecticut Compromise**.

The compromise proposed that Congress should be composed of two houses. In the smaller Senate,

HIGHLIGHTS OF THE NEW JERSEY PLAN

SUGGESTED **CHANGES** TO THE
★★★ **ARTICLES OF** ★★★
CONFEDERATION
BUT **NOT AS COMPLETE A REVISION**
AS THE VIRGINIA PLAN

— EACH STATE —
EQUALLY
REPRESENTED
IN CONGRESS

FEDERAL EXECUTIVE OF
MORE THAN
ONE PERSON
CHOSEN BY CONGRESS,
—— AND WHO COULD BE ——
REMOVED
AT THE REQUEST OF A MAJORITY OF THE
STATES' GOVERNORS

CONGRESS WOULD GAIN
—— THE POWERS TO ——
TAX
AND
REGULATE TRADE
BETWEEN THE STATES

RETAINED THE
UNICAMERAL
CONGRESS
SET UP IN THE ARTICLES
OF CONFEDERATION

FEDERAL JUDICIARY
—— WOULD BE ——
APPOINTED BY THE
FEDERAL EXECUTIVE

>> The smaller States proposed that the New Jersey Plan be substituted for the plan proposed by Randolph. **Analyze Charts** How many branches would the government have under this plan?

the States would be represented equally. In the House, the representation of each State would be based upon its population.

By combining basic features of the plans, the convention's most serious dispute was resolved—the States, regardless of size, would be equally represented in Congress. The agreement satisfied the smaller States in particular, allowing them to support the creation of a strong central government. The Connecticut Compromise was so pivotal to the writing of the Constitution that it has often been called the Great Compromise. It could even be said that had the compromise not been reached, the Constitution may not have been written and the American federal system of fifty equal states may never have developed.

The Three-Fifths Compromise Once it had been agreed to base the seats in the House on each State's population, this question arose: Should enslaved people be counted in figuring the populations of the States?

Most delegates from the southern States argued that enslaved people should be counted. Most of the northerners took the opposing view. All could see the contradictions between slavery and the sentiments expressed in the Declaration of Independence, but slavery was legal in every State except Massachusetts and nearly half of the delegates were themselves enslavers. The enslaved population was concentrated in the southern States, however, therefore those States stood to gain or lose the most.

Again, debate on the issue was fierce. Finally, the Framers agreed to the **Three-Fifths Compromise**. It provided that all "free persons" should be counted, and so, too, should "three fifths of all other persons" (Article I, Section 2, Clause 3; by "all other persons," the delegates meant enslaved people). For the three-fifths won by the southerners, the northerners exacted a price. That formula was also to be used in fixing the amount of money to be raised in each State by any direct tax levied by Congress. In short, the southerners could count the enslaved members of their population, but they would have to pay for them. This compromise disappeared from the Constitution with the adoption of the 13th Amendment of 1865, which abolished slavery.

The Commerce and Slave Trade Compromise The Framers generally agreed that Congress must have the power to regulate foreign and interstate trade. But to many southerners, that power carried a real danger. They worried that Congress, likely

>> The Connecticut Compromise established a legislature with a population-based House of Representatives per the Virginia Plan and a Senate with equal representation per the New Jersey Plan.

>> The South relied on labor provided by enslaved people. Therefore, the Three-Fifths Compromise was a critical step towards a Constitution all delegates would sign.

to be controlled by northern commercial interests, would act against the interests of the agricultural South.

They were particularly fearful that Congress would try to pay for the new government out of export duties, and southern tobacco was the major American export of the time. They also feared that Congress would interfere with the trade in enslaved people. In addition, a growing abolitionist movement in Europe led many enslavers to fear that the new government might move to end slavery in the United States.

Before they would agree to the commerce power, the southerners insisted on certain protections. So, according to the **Commerce and Slave Trade Compromise,** Congress was forbidden the power to tax the export of goods from any State. It was also forbidden the power to act on the trade in enslaved people for a period of at least 20 years. To understand this provision, it is necessary to realize that southern enslavers viewed Black people as property. They also feared what would happen if the enslaved were freed by an act of Congress. This compromise, in a very real and direct way, solidified the position of slavery in the new nation.

A "Bundle of Compromises" The convention spent much of its time, said Franklin, "sawing boards to make them fit." The Constitution drafted at Philadelphia has often been called a "bundle of

compromises." These descriptions are apt, if they are properly understood.

There were differences of opinion among the delegates, certainly. After all, the delegates came from 12 different States widely separated in geographic and economic terms, and the delegates often reflected the particular interests of their own States. Bringing those interests together did require compromise. Indeed, final decisions on issues such as the selection of the President, the treaty-making process, the structure of the national court system, and the amendment process were all reached as a result of compromise.

But by no means did all, or even most, of what shaped the document come from compromises. The Framers were agreed on many of the basic issues they faced. Thus, nearly all the delegates were convinced that a new national government, a federal government, had to be created, and that it had to have the powers necessary to deal with the nation's grave social and economic problems. The Framers were also dedicated to the concepts of popular sovereignty and limited government. None questioned for a moment the wisdom of representative government. The principles of separation of powers and of checks and balances were accepted almost as a matter of course.

Many disputes did occur, and the compromises by which they were resolved came only after hours, days, and even weeks of heated debate. The point

Major Compromises of the Constitutional Convention

COMPROMISE	ISSUE TO RESOLVE	COMPROMISE REACHED	PROS/CONS
The Connecticut Compromise	How should the States be represented in Congress?	Congress should have two houses. In the Senate, States would be represented equally. In the House, representation would be based on population.	Enabled the small States to support the creation of a strong central government
The Three-Fifths Compromise	Should the enslaved be counted when figuring the populations of the States?	All free persons in each State would be counted, and "three fifths of all other persons" would also be counted. "Three fifths of all other persons" was generally recognized to be referring to those who were enslaved.	The southern States were able to count a portion of the enslaved, but they also had to count them when figuring any direct tax that was levied by Congress.
The Commerce/ Slave Trade Compromise	Should Congress have the power to regulate foreign and interstate trade?	Congress could not tax the export of goods from any State or interfere with the trade in enslaved people for at least 20 years.	Southerners agreed to the inclusion of the commerce power, but northerners had to wait 20 years to ban the trade in enslaved people.

>> The delegates spent weeks hammering out compromises during the convention.
Analyze Charts Why were these compromises important in the creation of the Constitution?

here, however, is that the differences were not over the most fundamental of questions. They involved, instead, such vital but lesser points as these: the details of the structure of Congress, the method by which the President was to be chosen, and the practical limits that should be put on the several powers to be given to the new central government.

The Constitution in its Final Form For several weeks, through the hot Philadelphia summer, the delegates took up resolution after resolution. On September 8, a committee was named "to revise the stile of and arrange the articles which had been agreed to" by the convention. That committee, the Committee of Stile and Arrangement, put the Constitution into its final form.

Finally, on September 17, the convention approved its work and 39 names were placed on the finished document. Three of the 41 delegates present on the last day refused to sign the proposed Constitution: Edmund Randolph of Virginia, who later supported ratification and served as Attorney General and then Secretary of State under President Washington; Elbridge Gerry of Massachusetts, who later became Vice President under Madison; and **George Mason** of Virginia, who opposed the Constitution because he believed it did not give enough attention to citizens' rights.

George Read of Delaware signed both for himself and for his absent colleague John Dickinson. Because not all of the delegates were willing to sign the Constitution, its final paragraph was very carefully worded to give the impression of unanimity: "Done in Convention by the Unanimous Consent of the States present. . . ."

Perhaps none of the Framers was completely satisfied with their work. Nevertheless, wise old Benjamin Franklin put into words what many of them must have thought on that final day:

Sir, I agree with this Constitution with all its faults, if they are such; because I think a general Government necessary for us . . . I doubt . . . whether any other Convention we can obtain, may be able to make a better Constitution. For when you assemble a number of men to have the advantage of their joint wisdom, you inevitably assemble with those men, all their prejudices,

>> Benjamin Franklin is called the "First American" for many reasons, including his qualities of industriousness, self-reliance, and commitment to the vision of an independent America.

their passions, their errors of opinion, their local interests, and their selfish views. From such an assembly can a perfect production be expected? It therefore astonishes me, Sir, to find this system approaching so near to perfection as it does . . .

—*Notes* of Debates in the Federal Convention of 1787, James Madison

On Franklin's motion, the Constitution was signed. Madison tells us that

. . . Doctor Franklin, looking towards the President's chair, at the back of which a rising sun happened to be painted, observed to a few members near him, that painters had found it difficult to distinguish in their art a rising sun from a setting sun. 'I have,' said he, 'often and often in the course of the Session . . . looked at that behind the President without being able to tell whether it was rising or setting: But now at length I have the happiness to know that it is a rising and not a setting Sun.'

—*Notes* of Debates in the Federal Convention of 1787, James Madison

☑ **MAKE GENERALIZATIONS** Why was it said that the Constitution was a "bundle of compromises"? Was this aspect of the document positive or negative for the nation?

The Fight for Ratification

Today, the Constitution of the United States is the object of unparalleled admiration and respect, both here and abroad. But in 1787 and 1788, it was widely criticized, and in every State there were many who opposed its adoption. The battle over the ratification of the document was not easily decided.

Remember, the Articles of Confederation provided that changes could be made to them only if *all* of the State legislatures agreed. But the Framers had determined that the new Constitution would replace, not amend, the Articles. They had seen how crippling the requirement of unanimity could be. So, the new Constitution provided that

> The ratification of the conventions of nine States shall be sufficient for the establishment of this Constitution between the States so ratifying the same.

—Article VII

The Congress of the Confederation agreed to this irregular procedure. On September 28, 1787, it sent copies of the new document to the States.

Federalists and Anti-Federalists The Constitution circulated widely and was debated vigorously. Two groups quickly emerged in each of the States: the **Federalists**, who favored ratification, and the **Anti-Federalists**, who opposed it.

The Federalists were led by many of those who attended the Philadelphia Convention. Among the most active were James Madison and Alexander Hamilton. The opposition was headed by such well-known Revolutionary War figures as Patrick Henry, Richard Henry Lee, John Hancock, and Samuel Adams.

TWO SIDES OF RATIFICATION

FEDERALIST

The Articles of Confederation are too weak.

Only a stronger national government can overcome the difficulties the Republic faces.

Liberties that could be included in a bill of rights are covered in the State constitutions.

ANTI-FEDERALIST

The States would no longer have the power to print money.

The national government would be given too much power.

There should be a bill of rights.

"The subject speaks its own importance; comprehending in its consequences **nothing less than the existence of the Union,**

the safety and welfare of the parts of which it is composed, the fate of an empire in many respects the most interesting in the world.

–Alexander Hamilton, *The Federalist*, No. 1, 1787

"The fate of this question and America may depend on this: **Have they said, we the States?**

Have they made a proposal of a compact between States? If they had this would be a confederation....

–Patrick Henry, Speech before the Virginia Ratifying Convention, June 5, 1788

>> Both the Federalists and Anti-Federalists felt strongly about the proposed Constitution. **Analyze Charts** What do these comments reveal about the sentiments of the time?

Ratification of the Constitution

STATE	DATE	VOTE	STATE	DATE	VOTE
Delaware	Dec. 7, 1787	30-0	South Carolina	May 23, 1788	149-73
Pennsylvania	Dec. 12, 1787	46-23	New Hampshire	June 21, 1788	57-46
New Jersey	Dec. 18, 1787	38-0	Virginia	June 25, 1788	89-79
Georgia	Jan. 2, 1788	26-0	New York	July 26, 1788	30-27
Connecticut	Jan. 9, 1788	128-40	North Carolina*	Nov. 21, 1789	195-77
Massachusetts	Feb. 6, 1788	187-168	Rhode Island	May 29, 1790	34-32
Maryland	April 28, 1788	63-11	* Second vote; ratification was originally defeated on August 4, 1788, by a vote of 184-84.		

>> The battle between Federalists and Anti-Federalists continued throughout the ratification process. **Analyze Charts** In which States was ratification won by only a narrow margin?

The Federalists stressed the weaknesses of the Articles. They argued that the many difficulties facing the Republic could be overcome only by the creation of a new government based on the Constitution.

The Anti-Federalists attacked nearly every part of the document. Many objected to the ratification process. Several worried that the presidency could become a monarchy and that Congress would become too powerful. In Massachusetts, Amos Singletary, a delegate to the ratifying convention, condemned the Federalists:

> These lawyers, and men of learning, and monied men, that talk so finely and gloss over matters so smoothly, to make us poor illiterate people, swallow down the pill, expect to get into Congress themselves; they expect to . . . get all the power and all the money into their own hands, and then they will swallow up all us little folks . . . just as the whale swallowed up Jonah.

—Amos Singletary

The lack of one major feature of the proposed Constitution drew the heaviest fire: a bill of rights. The new document did contain some protections of individual rights—for example, a provision for the writ of habeas corpus, which is a protection against arbitrary arrest. The Framers had made no provision for such basic liberties as freedom of speech, press, and religion, however—largely because those matters were covered by the existing State constitutions. They also believed that because the powers to be granted to the new government would be fragmented among three branches, no branch of the government could become powerful enough to threaten the rights of the people.

Everywhere, the Anti-Federalists bore down on the absence of a bill of rights. At Virginia's ratifying convention, Patrick Henry said of the proposed Constitution, "I look on that paper as the most fatal plan that could possibly be conceived to enslave a free people." Stung by the criticism, the Federalists promised that the Constitution, once adopted, would be amended to overcome this fault.

The Battle on Paper Over the course of the struggle for ratification, an extraordinary number of essays, speeches, letters, and other commentaries were printed. Of them all, the most remarkable were a series of 85 essays that first appeared in various newspapers in New York in the fall of 1787 on into the spring of 1788.

Those essays, supporting the Constitution, were written by Alexander Hamilton, James Madison, and John Jay, and they were soon published in book form as *The Federalist: A Commentary on the Constitution of the United States.* All of the essays bore the pen

CENTINEL

VOL. IX

REDEUNT SATURNIA REGNA.
On the erection of the Eleventh PILLAR of the great national DOME, we beg leave most sincerely to felicitate "OUR DEAR COUNTRY."

Rise it will.

The foundation good—it may yet be SAVED.

The FEDERAL EDIFICE.

ELEVEN STARS, in quick succession rise—
ELEVEN COLUMNS strike our wond'ring eyes,
Soon o'er the whole, shall swell the beauteous DOME,
COLUMBIA's boast—and FREEDOM's hallow'd home.
Here shall the ARTS in glorious splendour shine !
And AGRICULTURE give her stores divine !
COMMERCE refin'd, dispense us more than gold,
And this new world, teach WISDOM to the old—
RELIGION here shall fix her blest abode,
Array'd in mildness, like its parent GOD !
JUSTICE and LAW shall endless PEACE maintain,
And the "SATURNIAN AGE," return again.

>> Columns representing the States that had ratified the Constitution are placed in a row by the hand of God. **Analyze Political Cartoons** Is this a Federalist or Anti-Federalist cartoon?

>> New Yorkers welcomed ratification with celebrations. This parade float celebrates the key role played by Alexander Hamilton in the ratification process.

name "Publius" (Latin for "Public Man"), and they were reprinted throughout the 13 States. They remain an excellent commentary on the Constitution and rank among the finest of all political writings in the English language. If one wants to know what the Framers were thinking about different aspects of the Constitution, the *Federalist Papers* is the best place to start.

The Anti-Federalists' attacks were also published widely. Among the best of their works were several essays usually attributed to Robert Yates, who had been one of New York's delegates to the Philadelphia Convention; they were signed by "Brutus" and appeared in the New York Journal at the same time that the paper carried several of the Federalist essays. The Anti-Federalists' views were also presented in pamphlets and letters written by Richard Henry Lee of Virginia, who used the pen name "The Federal Farmer."

It is noteworthy that this critically important debate—whether or not to ratify the Constitution— was conducted vehemently but peacefully. Each side offered reasoned, thoughtful arguments, and when it was all said and done, the people of the 13 States were left to decide.

Nine States Ratify Ratification came fairly quickly in a few States and only after a bitter struggle in others. Delaware was the first to approve the Constitution, on December 7. Pennsylvania followed five days later. In Pennsylvania, however, where the legislature had been slow to call a ratifying convention, several Federalists, angered by Anti-Federalist delays, took matters into their own hands. They broke into a Philadelphia boarding house, seized two legislators hiding there, and forcibly marched them to the State house so the assembly could vote to schedule the convention.

The contest for ratification was close in several States, but the Federalists finally prevailed in all of them. On June 21, 1788, New Hampshire brought the number of ratifying States to nine.

Under Article VII, New Hampshire's ratification should have brought the Constitution into effect, but it did not. Neither Virginia nor New York had yet ratified. Without either of those key States the new government could not hope to succeed.

Virginia's Ratification Virginia's vote for ratification followed New Hampshire's by just four days. The brilliant debates in its convention were followed closely throughout the State. The Federalists were led by Madison, John Marshall, and Governor Edmund Randolph (even though he had refused to sign the Constitution at Philadelphia). Patrick Henry, leading the opposition, was joined by James Monroe, Richard Henry Lee, and George Mason (another of the nonsigners).

Although George Washington was not one of the delegates to Virginia's convention, his strong support for ratification proved vital. With Madison, he was able to get a reluctant Thomas Jefferson to support the document. Had Jefferson fought as did other Anti-Federalists, Virginia might never have ratified the Constitution.

New York, The Last Key State In New York, the ratifying convention was bitterly divided. The Anti-Federalists were led by Governor George Clinton and two of the State's three delegates to the Philadelphia convention: Robert Yates and John Lansing, who had quit Philadelphia in late July, claiming that the convention had gone beyond its authority.

New York's approval of the Constitution was absolutely necessary, for that large commercial State effectively separated New England from the rest of the nation. Its ratification of the Constitution, on July 26, brought the number of ratifying States to 11. The victory there was largely won by Alexander Hamilton.

Inauguration of the New Government On September 13, 1788, with 11 of the 13 States "under the federal roof," the Congress of the Confederation paved the way for its successor. It chose New York City as the temporary capital. It set the first Wednesday in January as the date on which the States would choose presidential electors. The first Wednesday in February was set as the date on which those electors would vote, and the first Wednesday in March as the date for the inauguration of the new government.

The new Congress convened on March 4, 1789. It met in Federal Hall, on Wall Street in New York City. But because it lacked a quorum, it could not count the electoral votes until April 6. Finally, on that day,

it found that George Washington had been elected President by a unanimous vote. John Adams was elected Vice President by a large majority.

On April 30, after a historic trip from Mount Vernon to New York, Washington took the oath of office as the first President of the United States.

☑ **IDENTIFY CENTRAL ISSUES** On what main point did the Anti-Federalists focus their arguments against ratification of the Constitution?

☑ ASSESSMENT

1. **Make Generalizations** In what way did the principles of Enlightenment thinkers John Locke, Baron de Montesquieu, Jean Jacques Rousseau, and William Blackstone influence the American founding documents?

2. **Determine Relevance** What was the Connecticut Compromise, and why was it so important to the future of the new government?

3. **Summarize** In what ways did George Mason influence the U.S. Constitution?

4. **Identify Supporting Details** What was a common element in the two key debates at the convention—one regarding representation in Congress and the other regarding slavery? Give details to support your answer.

5. **Support Ideas with Evidence** Read the following quotation: "Six years is a long period for a man to be absent from his home, it would have a tendency to wean him from his constituents." What is this quotation referring to and what does it mean? Do you believe this quotation came from a Federalist or an Anti-Federalist? Support your answer with evidence.

Topic 2 Quick Study Guide

LESSON SUMMARIES
Use these Lesson Summaries, and the longer versions available online, to review the key ideas for each lesson in this Topic.

Lesson 1: Origins of American Political Ideals

The English colonists who came to North America in the 1600s and 1700s brought with them a long tradition of ordered, limited government. English government has long been bound by documents like the Magna Carta. The governments set up in each of the colonies reflected this tradition.

Lesson 2: Independence
In the 1760s, the British government tried to tighten its control over its North American colonies and impose new taxes. Colonists objected to these policies and organized to oppose them. Tensions escalated, and British policy grew harsher. The colonies declared their independence and fought for it, leading to the creation of the United States of America.

Lesson 3: First Steps
During the Revolutionary War, the United States formed its first national government under the Articles of Confederation. It had a simple structure that kept the national government weak and the states largely self-governing. It proved too weak to deal with the serious problems facing the new nation.

Lesson 4: Creating and Ratifying the Constitution

Delegates gathered in Philadelphia in 1787 to address the Articles of Confederation's problems. They produced a new framework for the national government, the Constitution. It was the result of debate and compromise over issues like representation. After a struggle, the new Constitution was eventually ratified by the states.

VISUAL REVIEW

Use these graphics to review some of the key terms, people, and ideas from this Topic.

The Articles of Confederation

STRUCTURE	WEAKNESSES
• The only branch of government was the Congress. • Congress chose its leader and various lower officers. • Congress had limited powers including making treaties, declaring war, and settling disputes between states. • Congress could ask the states for money or troops. • Congress could not raise taxes or regulate trade.	• Congress did not have the power to make states obey the Articles. • States failed to send Congress the money it requested. • States made illegal agreements with foreign countries. • States taxed one another's goods and printed their own money, leading to economic chaos. • Economic problems led to a rebellion in Massachusetts.

Types of Colonial Governments

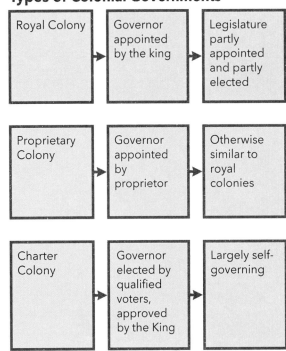

Royal Colony	Governor appointed by the king	Legislature partly appointed and partly elected
Proprietary Colony	Governor appointed by proprietor	Otherwise similar to royal colonies
Charter Colony	Governor elected by qualified voters, approved by the King	Largely self-governing

CONSTITUTION: KEY FACTS

- The New Jersey Plan: A unicameral Congress with each State equally represented

- The Virginia Plan: A bicameral Congress with representation based on population or the amount of money each State contributed to Congress each year

- The Connecticut Compromise: A bicameral Congress with each State equally represented in the Senate and represented by population in the House

- The Three-Fifths Compromise: Three fifths of the slave population was counted for representation in the House and for taxation

- The Constitution was hotly debated by Federalists and Anti-Federalists

The Road to the Constitution

1215: Magna Carta
1628: Petition of Right
1689: English Bill of Rights

1765: Parliament passes the Stamp Act.
1774: The First Continental Congress meets.
1775: The American Revolution begins.
1776: The Declaration of Independence.
1777: Articles of Confederation approved.

1787: The Framers sign the Constitution.
1789: The Constitution takes effect.

Topic 2 Assessment

KEY TERMS, PEOPLE, AND IDEAS

1. What guarantees and protections did the **Magna Carta** provide?

2. What is a **representative government**?

3. How did royal colonies and **proprietary** colonies differ?

4. What is the principle of **popular sovereignty**?

5. Compare and contrast the **Virginia Plan** and the **New Jersey Plan**.

6. What was the **Three-Fifths Compromise**?

7. How did the social contract theory influence **Thomas Jefferson's** writing of the Declaration of Independence?

8. Why did the **Articles of Confederation** fail?

CRITICAL THINKING

9. **Explain** How did the grievances listed in the Declaration of Independence reflect the political principles of popular sovereignty, social contract, natural rights, and individual rights?

10. **Evaluate** the ideals and principles of the founding documents (including the Declaration of Independence, the Articles of Confederation, and the Federalist Papers) that shaped American democracy. In what ways are these documents connected?

11. **Draw Conclusions** Name and explain the three concepts of government that the English brought with them to North America. How did these ideas shape the creation of the 13 colonies?

12. **Summarize** How did the Magna Carta, the Petition of Right, and the English Bill of Rights influence American colonists' ideas about government?

13. **Compare and Contrast** the viewpoints presented by the Federalists and the Anti-Federalists concerning ratification of the Constitution and inclusion of a bill of rights.

14. **Summarize** Describe the structure of the government established by the Articles of Confederation.

15. **Identify Central Issues** Why did the Framers consider it necessary to replace the Articles of Confederation? What obstacles did they face in creating a strong central government?

16. **Draw Conclusions** Why was a bill of rights not included in the original Constitution? Why might the Anti-Federalists have wanted a bill of rights in the document?

17. **Summarize** Why did nine colonies send delegates to the Stamp Act Congress? What made this meeting a significant event in the relationship between the colonies and the British government?

18. **Analyze Data** The chart below shows the votes by which the States ratified the Constitution. List the States in order of voting margin, from narrowest margin (Rhode Island, 2 votes) to greatest (North Carolina, 118 votes).

Ratification of the Constitution

STATE	DATE	VOTE
Delaware	Dec. 7, 1787	30-0
Pennsylvania	Dec. 12, 1787	46-23
New Jersey	Dec. 18, 1787	38-0
Georgia	Jan. 2, 1788	26-0
Connecticut	Jan. 9, 1788	128-40
Massachusetts	Feb. 6, 1788	187-168
Maryland	April 28, 1788	63-11
South Carolina	May 23, 1788	149-73
New Hampshire	June 21, 1788	57-46
Virginia	June 25, 1788	89-79
New York	July 26, 1788	30-27
North Carolina*	Nov. 21, 1789	195-77
Rhode Island	May 29, 1790	34-32

* Second vote; ratification was originally defeated on August 4, 1788, by a vote of 184-84.

19. **Writing Activity** Write a one-page essay in which you describe the events surrounding the ratification of the Constitution. Organize the essay so that each new element builds on that which precedes it to create a unified whole. Include headings and at least one image, graph, or table. Develop the topic thoroughly by selecting the most significant facts. Define key terms and include at least one quotation. Provide a concluding paragraph that follows from and supports the information in your essay.

DOCUMENT-BASED QUESTIONS

The Boston Tea Party was an act of colonial defiance against the British. It took place in 1773.

DOCUMENT A

Bostonian Ebenezer Stevens was 22 years old and a member of the Sons of Liberty at the time of the Boston Tea Party.

> I left that vessel with some of my comrades, and went on board the other vessel which lay at the opposite side of the wharf. . . . We commenced handing the boxes of tea on deck, and first commenced breaking them with axes, but found much difficulty, owing to the boxes of tea being covered with canvass—the mode that this article was then imported in. I think that all the tea was discharged in about two hours. We were careful to prevent any being taken away; none of the party were painted as Indians, nor, that I know of disguised, excepting that some of them stopped at a paint shop on the way and daubed their faces with paint.
> —Ebenezer Stevens

DOCUMENT B

Joshua Wyeth was 16 years old when he participated in the Boston Tea Party.

> To prevent discovery we agreed to wear ragged clothes and disfigure ourselves, dressing to resemble Indians. . . . We boarded the ship moored by the wharf, and ordered the captain and crew to open the hatchways, and hand us the hoisting tackle and rope, assuring them that no harm was intended them. Some of our numbers then jumped into the hold, and passed the chests to the tackle. As they were hauled on deck others knocked them open with axes, and others raised them to the railings and discharged their contents overboard. All who were not needed on this ship went on board the others where the same ceremonies were repeated. We were merry, in an undertone, at the idea of making so large a cup of tea for the fishes but we used not more words than absolutely necessary.
> —Joshua Wyeth

DOCUMENT C

Thomas Hutchinson was the British governor of Massachusetts colony in 1773.

> . . . [T]he people . . . gave a loud huzza and many of them cried out a mob a mob and broke up and in great numbers ran to the wharffe where three of the Vessels having on board 340 Chests of Tea lay and in about two hours the whole of it was hoisted out and thrown into the dock the chestes being first opened. It appears to have been a concerted plan for a sufficient number of men to do the work were prepared and disguised before the people came down from the meeting and guards were placed to prevent any spies and the whole conducted with very little tumult nor was there any suspicion of an intention in the conductors of the affair that the Tea should be destroyed.
> —Thomas Hutchinson, report to the East India Company, 1773

DOCUMENT D

Participant Samuel Cooper later fought in the battles of Lexington and Concord, Bunker Hill, and others.

> Arrived at the wharves they divided into three troops each with a leader gained possession of the ships quietly and proceeded to lighten them of their cargo by hoisting out the boxes and emptying their contents into the dock. No noise was heard except the occasional clink of the hatchet in opening the boxes and the whole business was performed with so much expedition that before 10 o'clock that night the entire cargo of the three vessels were deposited in the docks.
> —Samuel Cooper

20. On which of the following points do all the excerpts agree?
    A. that it took about two hours to throw all the tea into the harbor
    B. that no one was allowed to steal any of the tea
    C. that the chests of tea were opened before being thrown into the harbor
    D. that there were 340 chests of tea thrown overboard

21. Which document(s) offer evidence that corroborates Governor Hutchinson assertion that the events of the Tea Party were "conducted with very little tumult"?
    A. Document A only
    B. Document B only
    C. Documents A and D
    D. Documents B and D

22. **Examine Evidence** Which document(s) corroborate the assertion in Document C that the plot appeared to have been planned out in advance? In what way?

23. **Writing Task** Evaluate these various accounts of the Boston Tea Party. Which account(s) best accord with the description of the Tea Party you read about in this topic? Which do (does) not agree with that account? In what way? Does that fact leave your understanding of any aspect of the event uncertain? Why or why not?

The Constitution

ESSENTIAL QUESTION What Is the Right Balance of Power in Good Government?

The birthplace of the U.S. Constitution: Independence Hall, Philadelphia

Connections to Today

Repressive governments around the world censor information. They operate state-owned media, criticizing or harassing independent media outlets in order to weaken their critics and erode the public's trust in objective reporting.

In this Topic, you'll read about the Constitution, which protects many rights, including freedom of the press. Because of this we, the people, can criticize our leaders without fear. In what other ways is the Constitution still relevant today?

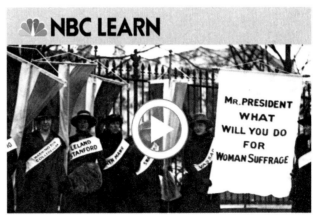

Learn more about the long battle to win the right to vote for American women.

BOUNCE to Activate My Story Video

In this Topic, you will learn about the Constitution of the United States and the structure and principles of the government it establishes. Look at the lesson outline and explore the diagram. As you study this Topic, you can work on your Quest Inquiry.

LESSON OUTLINE

3.1 An Overview of the Constitution

3.2 Amending the Constitution

3.3 Federalism: Powers Divided

3.4 The National Government and the States

Bill of Rights

Amendment 1
Freedom of religion, speech, and the press; rights of assembly and petition

Amendment 3
Housing of troops

Amendment 5
Rights in criminal cases

Amendment 7
Rights in civil cases

Amendment 9 and 10
Rights retained by the people; powers retained by the States and the people

Amendment 2
Right to keep and bear arms

Amendment 4
Search and seizure; warrants; probable cause

Amendment 6
Right to fair trial

Amendment 8
Bails, fines; no cruel, unusual punishments

Inquiry Center

Want to become an active and effective citizen? Make a difference in your community and beyond by using the **Inquiry Center** on the digital course.

Connect with issues you're passionate about by using the **Interest Finder**.

Investigate public policies, get involved in your community, influence public opinion, and develop leadership skills.

Synthesize the work you've done and what you've learned along the way.

Demonstrate what you've learned once you've finished your project by sharing your work.

3.1

The U.S. Constitution is on display in the Rotunda of the National Archives Building in Washington, D.C. At night, it is stored in a highly secure underground vault.

 BOUNCE to Activate Flipped Video

Objectives

Understand the basic outline of the Constitution.

Understand the basic principles of the Constitution: popular sovereignty, limited government, and separation of powers.

Understand the basic principles of the Constitution: checks and balances, judicial review, and federalism.

Key Terms

bicameral	veto
Executive Article	judicial review
inferior courts	unconstitutional
popular sovereignty	federalism
limited government	James Madison
constitutionalism	Alexander Hamilton
rule of law	Andrew Johnson
separation of powers	Donald Trump
checks and balances	

An Overview of the Constitution

The Articles of Confederation had provided the new nation with domestic and international legitimacy, at the price of a weak general government. The new Constitution created a stronger federal government with a chief executive, the power to tax, and a court system.

An Outline of the U.S. Constitution

The Constitution of the United States begins with the Preamble.

> "We the People of the United States, in Order to form a more perfect Union, establish Justice, insure domestic Tranquility, provide for the common defence, promote the general Welfare, and secure the Blessings of Liberty to ourselves and our Posterity, do ordain and establish this Constitution for the United States of America."

—United States Constitution

The Constitution of the United States dates from the latter part of the eighteenth century. Written in 1787, it took effect in 1789. The fact that it is more than 200 years old does not mean, however, that in the twenty-first century, it is only an interesting historical artifact, best left to museums and dusty shelves. On the contrary, it remains a vitally important and vibrant document.

The Constitution is this nation's fundamental law. It is, by its own terms, "the supreme Law of the Land"—the highest form of law in the United States.

Sets the Rules The Constitution sets out the basic principles upon which government in the United States was built and operates today. The document lays out the ways in which the Federal Government is organized, how the leaders of that government are selected, and many of the procedures those leaders must follow as they perform their duties. Of utmost importance, it sets out the limits within which government must conduct itself.

The Constitution also lays out the basic rules of American politics. By doing so, it helps to determine who wins and who loses in the political arena. To really understand government and politics in this country, we must know a good deal about the Constitution and how it has been interpreted and applied throughout our history.

Amendments Even with its 27 amendments, the Constitution is a fairly brief document. Its little more than 7,000 words can be read in half an hour. Remember that this document has successfully guided this nation through more than two centuries of tremendous growth and change. One of the Constitution's greatest strengths is that it deals largely with matters of basic principle. Unlike most other constitutions—those of the 50 States and those of other nations—the Constitution of the United States is not weighted down with detailed and cumbersome provisions.

As you read the Constitution, you will also see that it is organized in a simple and straightforward way. It begins with a short introduction, the Preamble. The balance of the original document is divided into seven numbered sections called articles.

The first three articles deal with the three branches of the National Government: Congress, the presidency, and the federal court system. These articles outline the basic organization and powers of each branch, and the methods by which the members of Congress, the President and Vice President, and federal judges are chosen.

Article IV deals mostly with the place of the States in the American Union and their relationships with the National Government and with one another. Article V indicates how formal amendments may be added to the document. Article VI declares that the Constitution is the nation's supreme law; Article VII provided for the ratification of the Constitution.

Articles of the Constitution

SECTION	SUBJECT
Preamble	States the purpose of the Constitution
Article I	Creates the Legislative branch
Article II	Creates the Executive branch
Article III	Creates the Judicial branch
Article IV	Relations among the States
Article V	Amending the Constitution
Article VI	National debts, supremacy of national law, and oaths of office
Article VII	Ratifying the Constitution

>> The body of the Constitution is made up of seven articles. These articles set out the basic shape of the Federal Government. **Analyze Charts** What is the purpose of the first three articles?

The 7 articles of the original document are followed by 27 amendments, printed in the order in which each provision was adopted.

☑ **CATEGORIZE** Describe the basic organization of the Constitution and why this organization was used by the Framers.

Article I

Immediately, the Constitution establishes a **bicameral** legislature—that is, a legislature made up of two houses. It does so for historical, practical, and theoretical reasons.

Historical The British Parliament had consisted of two houses since the 1300s. The Framers and most other Americans knew the British system of bicameralism quite well. Most of the colonial assemblies and, in 1787, all but two of the new State legislatures were also bicameral. Among the original 13 colonies, only Georgia and Pennsylvania had unicameral colonial and then State legislatures. Georgia's legislature became bicameral in 1789 and Pennsylvania's in 1790. (Only one State, Nebraska, has a unicameral legislature today.)

Practical The Framers had to create a two-chambered body to settle the conflict between the Virginia and the New Jersey Plans at Philadelphia in 1787. Recall, the most populous States wanted to distribute the seats in Congress in proportion to the population of each State, while the smaller States demanded an equal voice in Congress.

Bicameralism is a reflection of federalism. Each of the States is equally represented in the Senate and each is represented in line with its population in the House.

Theoretical The Framers favored a bicameral Congress in order that one house might act as a check on the other.

A leading constitutional historian recounts a conversation between Thomas Jefferson and George Washington at Mount Vernon. Jefferson, who had just returned from France, told Washington that he was opposed to a two-chambered legislature. As he made his point, he poured his tea into his saucer, and Washington asked him why he did so. "To cool it," replied Jefferson. "Even so," said Washington, "we pour legislation into the senatorial saucer to cool it."

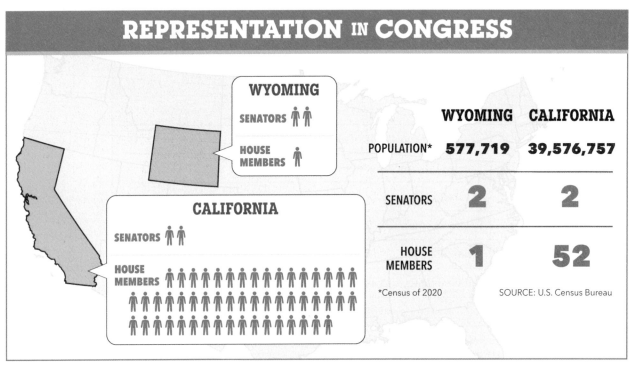

REPRESENTATION IN CONGRESS

WYOMING
SENATORS
HOUSE MEMBERS

CALIFORNIA
SENATORS
HOUSE MEMBERS

	WYOMING	CALIFORNIA
POPULATION*	577,719	39,576,757
SENATORS	2	2
HOUSE MEMBERS	1	52

*Census of 2020

SOURCE: U.S. Census Bureau

>> Each State has two U.S. senators while the number of representatives in the House vary from State to State. **Analyze Charts** How does the number of Senate seats per State illustrate the principle of federalism?

As a whole, the Framers were convinced that the legislature would dominate the new National Government. As **Madison** observed,

> In republican government, the legislative authority necessarily predominates. The remedy for this inconveniency is to divide the legislature into different branches.

—*The Federalist* No. 51

The Framers saw bicameralism as a way to diffuse the power of Congress and so prevent it from overwhelming the other two branches of government.

For more than 200 years now, some people have argued that equal representation of the States in the Senate is undemocratic and should be eliminated. They often point to the two extremes to make their case. The State with the least population, Wyoming, only has around 600,000 residents. The most populous State, California, now has a population of around 40 million. Yet each of these States has two senators.

Those who object to State equality in the Senate ignore a vital fact. The Senate was purposely created as a body in which the States would be represented as coequal members and partners in the Union. Also recall that if the Framers had been unable to agree that the States would be equally represented in the Senate, the Constitution might never have been written.

☑ **SYNTHESIZE** What practical problem did the Framers solve by creating a bicameral legislature?

Article II

Article II of the Constitution is known as the **Executive Article**, which in only a few words established the presidency. It begins this way:

> The executive Power shall be vested in a President of the United States of America.

—Article II, Section 1

With this one sentence, the Framers laid the basis for the vast power and influence that the nation's chief executive possesses today.

The Constitution also sets out other, somewhat more specific grants of presidential power. Thus, the President is given the power to command the armed

>> Patricia Schroeder (D., Colorado) was the first woman from Colorado to be elected to Congress. She served in the House of Representatives from 1973 to 1997.

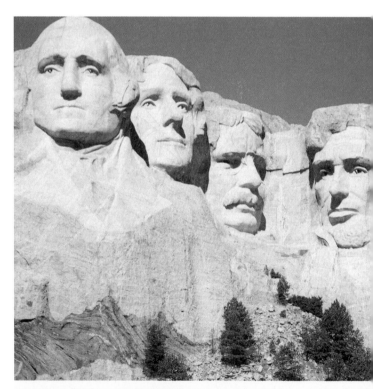

>> Mount Rushmore in South Dakota features four U.S. Presidents—George Washington, Thomas Jefferson, Theodore Roosevelt, and Abraham Lincoln—representing the first 130 years of U.S. history.

forces, to make treaties, to approve or veto acts of Congress and call special sessions of that body, to send and receive diplomatic representatives, and to "take Care that the Laws be faithfully executed."

Still, the Constitution lays out the powers of the presidency in a very sketchy fashion. Article II reads almost like an outline. It has been called "the most loosely drawn chapter" in the nation's fundamental law. It does not define "the executive Power," and the other grants of presidential power are couched in similarly broad terms.

Much of our political history can be told in terms of the struggle over the meaning of the constitutional phrase "executive Power"—that is, over the extent of presidential power. That struggle has pitted those who have argued for a weaker presidency, subordinate to Congress, against those who have pressed for a stronger, independent, coequal chief executive.

That never-ending contest began at the Philadelphia Convention in 1787. There, several of the Framers agreed with Roger Sherman of Connecticut, who, according to James Madison,

. . . considered the Executive Magistracy as nothing more than an institution for carrying the will of the legislature into effect, that the person or persons [occupying the presidency] ought to be appointed by and accountable to the Legislature only, which was the depository of the supreme will of the Society.

—James Madison, *Notes of Debates in the Federal Convention of 1787*

As you know, those delegates who argued for a stronger executive carried the day. The Framers established a single executive, chosen independently of Congress and with its own distinct field of powers.

☑ **COMPARE POINTS OF VIEW** What two points of view of the presidency were debated by the Framers?

Article III

During the years the Articles of Confederation were in force (1781–1789), there was no provision for federal courts or a national judiciary. The laws of the United States were interpreted and applied as each State saw fit, and sometimes not at all. Disputes between States and between persons who lived in different States were decided, if at all, by the courts in one of the States involved. Often, decisions by the courts in one State were ignored by courts in the other States.

Alexander Hamilton spoke to the point in *The Federalist* No. 22. He described "the want of a judiciary power" as a "circumstance which crowns the defects of the Confederation." Arguing the need for a federal court system, he added, "Laws are a dead letter without courts to expound and define their true meaning and operation." The Framers created a national judiciary for the United States in a single sentence in the Constitution:

The judicial Power of the United States shall be vested in one supreme Court, and in such inferior Courts as the Congress may from time to time ordain and establish.

—Article III, Section 1

Congress also is given the expressed power "to constitute Tribunals inferior to the supreme Court"—

>> Until the late 1700s, U.S. laws were interpreted by State courts. In a 1735 trial, Andrew Hamilton's successful defense of John Peter Zenger set a precedent for freedom of the press.

that is, create the rest of the federal court system—in Article I, Section 8, Clause 9.

Keep in mind this important point: There are *two* separate court systems in the United States. On one hand, the national judiciary spans the country with its more than 100 courts. On the other hand, each of the 50 States has its own system of courts. Their numbers run well into the thousands, and most of the cases that are heard in court today are heard in those State, not the federal, courts.

The Constitution establishes the Supreme Court and leaves to Congress the creation of the **inferior courts**—the lower federal courts under the Supreme Court. Over the years, Congress has created two distinct types of federal courts: (1) the constitutional courts, and (2) the special courts.

The constitutional courts are those federal courts that Congress has formed under Article III to exercise "the judicial Power of the United States." Together with the Supreme Court, they now include the courts of appeals (also called circuit courts), the district courts, and the U.S. Court of International Trade. The constitutional courts are also called the regular courts and, sometimes, Article III courts.

The special courts do not exercise the broad "judicial Power of the United States." Rather, they have been created by Congress to hear cases arising out of some of the expressed powers given to Congress in Article I, Section 8. The special courts hear a much narrower range of cases than those that may come before the constitutional courts.

These special courts are also called the legislative courts and, sometimes, Article I courts. Today, they include the U.S. Court of Appeals for the Armed Forces, the U.S. Court of Appeals for Veterans Claims, the U.S. Court of Federal Claims, the U.S. Tax Court, the various territorial courts, and the courts of the District of Columbia.

☑ **EXPRESS PROBLEMS CLEARLY** Why did the Framers see a need for the creation of a national judiciary?

Basic Principles

The Constitution is built around six basic principles. The first three are popular sovereignty, limited government, and separation of powers.

Popular Sovereignty In the United States, all political power resides in the people, a concept known as **popular sovereignty**. The people are the *only* source for any and all governmental power.

>> Outside the federal courthouse in New York City during the hearing of the high profile case of Mexican drug kingpin Joaquin "El Chapo" in 2019

>> The principle of popular sovereignty was set out in the Constitution. **Analyze Political Cartoons** According to the cartoon, what is citizens' role in the government?

>> Another basic principle of the Constitution is that of limited government. **Analyze Political Cartoons** How are limited government and popular sovereignty related?

>> The Constitution also specifies the separation of powers. **Analyze Political Cartoons** How does the separation of powers keep government from becoming too powerful?

Government can govern only with the consent of the governed.

The principle of popular sovereignty is woven throughout the Constitution. In its opening words—the Preamble—that document declares: "We the People of the United States . . . do ordain and establish this Constitution for the United States of America."

Thus, the people have given the United States government whatever powers it has, through the Constitution. That government exercises those powers through popularly elected leaders who are chosen by the people, which is essentially what James Madison referred to as republicanism.

Limited Government The principle of **limited government** holds that no government is all-powerful. That government may do *only* those things that the people have given it the power to do.

In effect, the principle of limited government is the other side of the coin of popular sovereignty. It is that principle stated the other way around: The people are the only source of any and all of government's authority; and government has only that authority the people have given to it.

The concept of limited government can be put another way: Government must obey the law. Stated this way, the principle is often called **constitutionalism**—that is, government must be conducted according to constitutional principles. The concept of limited government is also frequently described as the **rule of law**, which holds that government and its officers, in all that they do, are always subject to—never above—the law.

Under the rule of law, government officials are held accountable for any crimes or civil offenses they may commit. The Supreme Court limited the scope of what constitutes corruption in a 2016 case, *McDonnell* v. *United States*, but elected and appointed officials still face consequences for illegal actions. One State representative, for example, was convicted of receiving kickbacks from State grant monies. Or consider the federal judge who was ordered to undergo counseling related to a domestic violence misdemeanor charge.

The official actions of government officers are also subject to the rule of law in this country. It is fairly rare, but the federal courts sometimes halt a presidential action because the maneuver is considered unconstitutional or contrary to existing statutes or case law. The acts of Congress and of the States are also sometimes nullified by court decisions.

In large part, the entire Constitution is a statement of limited government. Much of it reads as prohibitions of power to government. For example, notice the Constitution's guarantees of freedom of expression. Those great guarantees—of freedom of religion, of speech, of the press, of assembly, and of petition—are vital to democratic government. They are enshrined in the 1st Amendment, which begins with the words: "Congress shall make no law. . . ."

Separation of Powers Recall that in a parliamentary system, the legislative, executive, and judicial powers of government are all gathered in the hands of a single agency. British government is a leading example of the form. In a presidential system, these basic powers are distributed—separated—among three distinct and independent branches of the government.

This concept is known as **separation of powers**. It was first found in each of the State constitutions adopted during the Revolution.

The Constitution of the United States distributes the powers of the National Government among the Congress (the legislative branch), the President (the executive branch), and the courts (the judicial branch). This separation of powers is clearly set forth in the opening words of each of the first three Articles of the Constitution.

Article I, Section 1 declares: "All legislative Powers herein granted shall be vested in a Congress of the United States. . . ." Thus, Congress is the lawmaking branch of the National Government.

Article II, Section 1 declares: "The executive Power shall be vested in a President of the United States of America." Thus, the President is given the law-executing, law enforcing, and law-administering powers of the National Government.

Article III, Section 1 declares: "The judicial Power of the United States shall be vested in one supreme Court, and in such inferior Courts as the Congress may from time to time ordain and establish." Thus, the federal courts, and most importantly the Supreme Court, interpret and apply the laws of the United States in cases brought before them.

Remember, the Framers intended to create a stronger central government for the United States. Yet they also intended to limit the powers of that government. The doctrine of separation of powers was designed to accomplish just that.

In *The Federalist,* No. 47, James Madison wrote of this arrangement: "The accumulation of all powers, legislative, executive, and judiciary, in the same hands, whether of one, a few, or many . . . may justly be pronounced the very definition of tyranny."

The earliest of the State constitutions provided for a separation of powers among the legislative, executive, and judicial branches of

>> The legislative, executive, and judicial branches are connected by a system of checks and balances. **Analyze Political Cartoons** What is one way the President can check the powers of Congress?

the new governments they established. This was a reflection of the mistrust and suspicion toward any government common to the people of the new United States in the late 1700s. Thus, the inclusion of the doctrine of separation of powers was both natural and inevitable in the writing of the Constitution.

☑ **EXPRESS IDEAS CLEARLY** Explain the concept of popular sovereignty in your own words.

More Basic Principles

The remaining three basic principles of the Constitution are checks and balances, judicial review, and federalism.

Checks and Balances The National Government is organized around three separate branches. As you have just seen, the Constitution gives to each branch its own field of governmental authority: legislative, executive, and judicial.

These three branches are not entirely separated nor completely independent of one another. Rather, they are tied together by a complex system of **checks and balances**. This means that each branch is subject to a number of constitutional checks, or restraints, by the other branches. In other words, each branch has certain powers with which it can check the operations of the other two.

Congress has the power to make laws, but the President may **veto** (reject) any act of Congress. In its turn, Congress can override a presidential veto by a two-thirds vote in each house. Congress can refuse to provide funds requested by the President, or the Senate may refuse to approve a treaty or an appointment made by the chief executive. The President is the commander in chief of the armed forces, but Congress provides that military force; and so on.

The system of checks and balances links the judicial branch to the legislative and the executive branches. The President has the power to name all federal judges. Each appointment, however, must be approved by a majority vote in the Senate. At the same time, the courts have the power to determine the constitutionality of acts of Congress and of presidential actions, and to strike down those they find unconstitutional.

Head-on clashes between the branches of government do not often happen. The check-and-balance system operates all the time, however, and in routine fashion. The very fact that it exists affects much of what happens in Washington, D.C.

For example, when the President picks someone to serve in some important office in the executive branch—as, say, secretary of state or director of the Office of National Intelligence—the President is quite aware that the Senate must confirm that appointment. So, the chief executive is apt to pick someone who very likely will be approved by the Senate. In a similar sense, when Congress makes a law, it does so with a careful eye on both the President's veto power and the power of the courts to review its actions.

Spectacular clashes—direct applications of the check-and-balance system—do sometimes occur, of course. The President does veto some acts of Congress. On rare occasions, Congress does override a veto. And, even more rarely, the Senate does reject a presidential appointee. Four times in the nation's history, the House of Representatives has impeached (brought charges against) a President, seeking his removal: **Andrew Johnson** in 1868, Bill Clinton in 1998 and **Donald Trump** in 2019 and 2021. On each occasion, the President was acquitted by the Senate.

But, again, these and other direct confrontations are not common. Congress, the President, and even the courts try to avoid them. The check-and-balance system makes compromise necessary—and, remember, compromise is a vital part of democratic government.

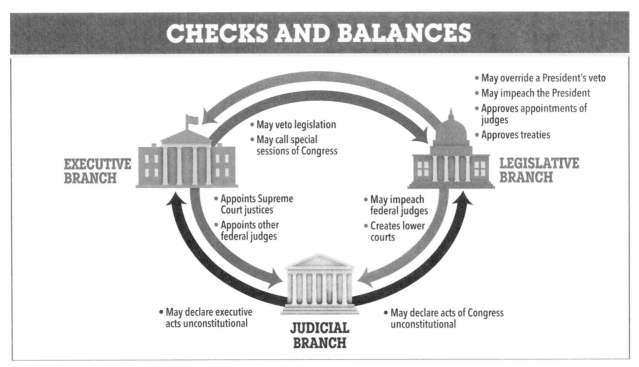

CHECKS AND BALANCES

EXECUTIVE BRANCH

- May veto legislation
- May call special sessions of Congress

- Appoints Supreme Court justices
- Appoints other federal judges

LEGISLATIVE BRANCH

- May override a President's veto
- May impeach the President
- Approves appointments of judges
- Approves treaties

- May impeach federal judges
- Creates lower courts

JUDICIAL BRANCH

- May declare executive acts unconstitutional
- May declare acts of Congress unconstitutional

>> The system of checks and balances allows each branch of government to limit the actions of the others. **Analyze Diagrams** How can the executive branch be checked by the other two branches?

Over time, the checks-and-balances system has generally worked well. It has done what the Framers intended it to do; it has prevented "an unjust combination of a majority." At the same time, the system of checks and balances has not often forestalled a close working relationship between the executive and legislative branches of the Federal Government.

Note, however, that the balance of power among the branches has shifted over time, particularly with regard to the legislative and executive branches. Beginning with President Franklin Roosevelt's New Deal programs of the 1930s, the scope of presidential powers has grown by leaps and bounds. From that new vantage point, both Congress and the President have engaged in a long-term tug-of-war, in which each branch has fought for supremacy. The results of that ongoing struggle have swung first in one direction then the other. In 1973, for example, Congress took the upper hand by significantly limiting presidential war powers by means of the War Powers Resolution.

Various factors influence the balance of power, including the personality and beliefs of the President, specific domestic and foreign events, and party politics. In fact, the working relationship between the executive and legislative branches runs more smoothly when the President and a majority in both houses of Congress are of the same political party. When the other party controls one or both houses, partisan friction and conflict play a larger-than-usual part in that relationship.

Through most of our history, the President and a majority of the members of both houses of Congress have been of the same party. Over the past several decades, however, the American people have become quite familiar with divided government—that is, a political environment in which one party occupies the White House and the other controls one or both houses of Congress.

In this situation, the system of checks and balances sometimes prevents the government from accomplishing anything. Some observers say that the resulting gridlock (stability) is good for the economy. Others say that government spending falls and that any programs that are enacted tend to last. On the other hand, opponents say that the people's business is stalled during divided governments and much-needed economic or other reforms fall victim to partisan fighting.

Judicial Review One aspect of the principle of checks and balances is of such importance in the American constitutional system that it stands by

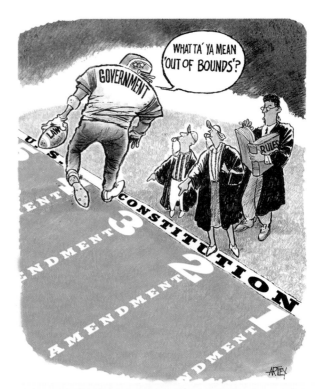

>> Judicial review is one of the six principles of government established by the Constitution. **Analyze Political Cartoons** According to this cartoon, what is the role of the judicial branch?

itself, as one of that system's basic principles. The power of **judicial review** may be defined as the power of a court to determine the constitutionality of a governmental action.

In part, then, judicial review is the power to declare **unconstitutional**—to declare illegal, null and void, of no force and effect—a governmental action found to violate some provision in the Constitution. The power of judicial review is held by all federal courts and by most State courts, as well.

The Constitution does not provide for judicial review in so many words. Yet it seems clear that the Framers intended that the federal courts, and in particular the Supreme Court, should have that power. In *The Federalist* No. 51, James Madison described the judicial power as one of the "auxiliary precautions" against the possible domination of one branch of the government over another.

In *The Federalist* No. 78, Alexander Hamilton wrote:

"The interpretation of the laws is the proper and peculiar province of the courts. A constitution is, in fact, and must be regarded by the judges as a fundamental law. It therefore belongs to them to ascertain its meaning, as well as the meaning of any particular act proceeding from the legislative body. If there should happen to be an irreconcilable variance between the two, that which has the superior obligation and validity ought, of course, to be preferred; or, in other words, the Constitution ought to be preferred to the statute...."

—*The Federalist* No. 78

In practice, the Supreme Court established the power of judicial review in the landmark case of *Marbury* v. *Madison* in 1803. Since *Marbury*, the Supreme Court and other federal and State courts have used the power in thousands of cases. For the most part, those courts have upheld challenged governmental actions. That is, in most cases in which the power of judicial review is exercised, the actions of government are found to be constitutional.

That is not always true, however. The Supreme Court has decided roughly 200 cases in which it has found an act or some part of an act of Congress to be unconstitutional. It has struck down several presidential and other executive branch actions as well. The Court has also voided more than 1,000 State laws and local government ordinances.

Federalism As you know, the American governmental system is federal in form. The powers held by government are distributed on a territorial basis. The National Government holds some of those powers, which it uses to fulfill responsibilities for domestic policy (such as healthcare, education, and business) and foreign policy, which includes international trade and alliances with other countries. Other powers belong to the 50 States.

The principle of **federalism**—the division of power among a central government and several regional governments—came to the Constitution out of both experience and necessity. At Philadelphia, the Framers faced a number of difficult problems, not the least of them: How to build a new, stronger, more effective National Government while preserving the existing States and the concept of local self-government.

The colonists had rebelled against the harsh rule of a powerful and distant central government. They had fought for the right to manage their own local affairs without the meddling and dictation of the king and his ministers in far-off London. Surely, the colonists would not now agree to another such government.

Who has the Power?

FEDERAL POWERS
- To maintain an army and a navy
- To declare war
- To coin money
- To regulate trade between States and with foreign nations
- To make treaties

SHARED POWERS
- To enforce laws
- To establish courts
- To borrow money
- To secure the population
- To build an infrastructure
- To collect taxes
- To make laws

STATE POWERS
- To conduct elections
- To establish schools
- To regulate business within a State
- To establish local governments
- To regulate marriage, divorce
- To assume other powers not given to the Federal Government nor denied to the States, by the Constitution

>> The Constitution divides power among the State and Federal governments.
Analyze Diagrams Which government has the power to provide aid to victims of a California earthquake?

The Framers found their solution in federalism. In short, they constructed the federal arrangement, with its division of powers, as a compromise. It was an alternative to both the system of nearly independent States, loosely tied to one another in the weak Articles of Confederation, and to a much feared, too powerful central government.

Keep in mind that federalism is an important part of the Constitution's web of protections of individual freedom. Remember, the Framers were dedicated to the concept of limited government. They were convinced (1) that governmental power poses a threat to individual liberty, (2) that, therefore, the exercise of governmental power must be restrained, and (3) that to divide governmental power, as federalism does, is to curb it and so prevent its abuse. James Madison addressed this point in this passage from *The Federalist Papers:*

> In the compound republic of America, the power surrendered by the people is first divided between two distinct governments, and then the portion allotted to each is subdivided among distinct and separate departments. Hence a double security arises to the rights of the people. The different governments will control each other, at the same time that each will be controlled by itself.

—*The Federalist* No. 51

☑ **EXPRESS IDEAS CLEARLY** Explain the concept of judicial review and why it is important.

☑ ASSESSMENT

1. **Evaluate Arguments** Why might some argue that the organization of the Senate is undemocratic?

2. **Draw Conclusions** In 2006, the Supreme Court struck down President Bush's plan to use military tribunals to prosecute persons captured in the war against terrorism, deciding that only Congress has the power to provide for the creation of such court-like bodies. On what constitutional principle was this decision based?

3. **Interpret** Suppose two people who live in adjoining states are having a land dispute. Identify the article of the Constitution that addresses this issue, and explain how it addresses the problem.

4. **Infer** Why is it in the President's best interest to nominate federal judges favored by most Senators?

5. **Synthesize** How did the principle of federalism resolve the issue of national versus States' rights?

Students in Seattle march in a rally in support of the 26th Amendment. Congress passed the amendment in March 1971, and the States ratified it in just four months.

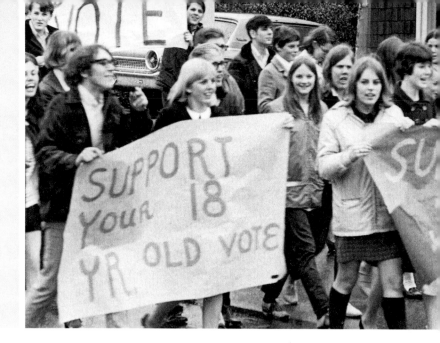

🅑 BOUNCE to Activate Flipped Video

Objectives

Describe the constitutionally prescribed procedures by which the Constitution may be formally changed.

Explain how the amendment process illustrates federalism and popular sovereignty.

Understand the 27 amendments that have been added to the Constitution, and several that have been proposed but not ratified.

Identify how legislation has added to our understanding of the Constitution over time.

Analyze how interpretation of the Constitution has changed through the actions of the executive and judicial branches, and by party practices and customs.

Key Terms

amendment	Cabinet
ratification	senatorial courtesy
formal amendment	Thomas Jefferson
Bill of Rights	Franklin D. Roosevelt
executive agreement	James Madison
treaty	George Washington
electoral college	Lyndon Johnson

Amending the Constitution

The Constitution of the United States has now been in force for more than 200 years—longer than the written constitution of any other nation in the world.

Formal Amendment Process

When the Constitution became effective in 1789, the United States was a small agricultural nation of fewer than four million people. That population was scattered for some 1,300 miles along the eastern edge of the continent. The 13 States, joined together mostly by travel on horseback and sailing ships, struggled to stay alive in a generally hostile world.

An Enduring Document Today, well over 300 million people live in the United States. The now 50 States stretch across the continent and beyond, and the country has many far-flung commitments. The United States is the most powerful nation on Earth, and its modern, highly industrialized and technological society has produced a standard of living that has long been the envy of many other countries.

How has the Constitution, written in 1787, endured and kept pace with that astounding change and growth? The answer lies in this highly important fact: The Constitution of today is, and at the same time is not, the document of 1787. Many of its words are the same, and much of their meaning remains the same. But some of its words have been changed, some have been eliminated, and some have been added. And, very importantly, the meanings of many of its provisions have been modified, as well.

This process of constitutional change, of modification and growth, has come about in two basic ways: (1) by formal amendment and (2) by other, informal means. In this section, you will look at the first of them: the addition of formal amendments to the Constitution.

The Framers knew that even the wisest of constitution makers cannot build for all time. Thus, the Constitution provides for its own **amendment**—that is, for changes in its written words.

Methods of Formal Amendment Article V sets out two methods for the proposal and two methods for the **ratification** of amendments. So, there are four possible methods of **formal amendment**—changes or additions that become part of the written language of the Constitution itself.

First, an amendment may be proposed by a two-thirds vote in each house of Congress and ratified by three fourths of the State legislatures.

Today, at least 38 State legislatures must approve an amendment to make it a part of the Constitution. Of the Constitution's 27 amendments, 26 were adopted in this manner.

Second, an amendment may be proposed by Congress and ratified by conventions, called for that purpose, in three fourths of the States. Only the 21st Amendment (1933) was adopted in this way.

When Congress proposes an amendment, it chooses the method of ratification. State conventions were used to ratify the 21st Amendment, largely because the lawmakers felt that the conventions' popularly elected delegates would be more likely to reflect public opinion on the question of the repeal of nationwide prohibition than would State legislators.

Third, an amendment may be proposed by a national convention, called by Congress at the request of two thirds (34) of the State legislatures. It must then be ratified by three fourths of the State legislatures. To this point, Congress has not called such a convention.

And fourth, an amendment may be proposed by a national convention and then ratified by conventions in three fourths of the States. Remember, the

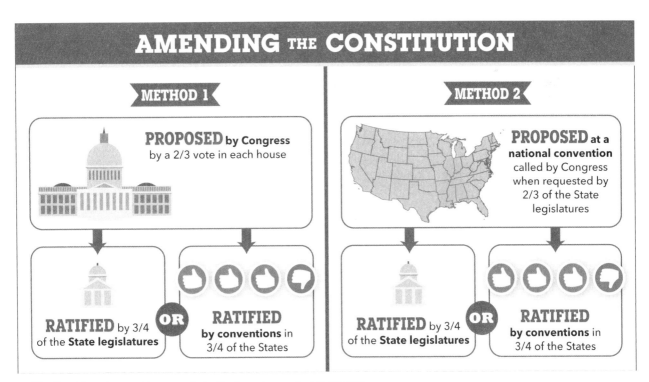

AMENDING THE CONSTITUTION

METHOD 1

PROPOSED by Congress
by a 2/3 vote in each house

RATIFIED by 3/4 of the **State legislatures** OR **RATIFIED** by conventions in 3/4 of the States

METHOD 2

PROPOSED at a **national convention** called by Congress when requested by 2/3 of the State legislatures

RATIFIED by 3/4 of the **State legislatures** OR **RATIFIED** by conventions in 3/4 of the States

>> The President does not have a role in the formal amendment process.
Analyze Charts Why do you think the Constitution outlines amendment methods involving Congress and State legislatures?

>> A senator stands atop a pyramid of the groups that got him elected. **Analyze Political Cartoons** How might each group have contributed to his election?

>> Inez Milholland was a labor lawyer and activist who rode in the Woman Suffrage Parade in 1913 as part of her fight to amend the Constitution to give women the right to vote.

Constitution itself was adopted in much this same way.

☑ **IDENTIFY MAIN IDEAS** How does the formal amendment process reflect the concept of federalism?

Federalism and Popular Sovereignty

Note that the formal amendment process emphasizes the federal character of the governmental system. Proposal takes place at the national level and ratification is a State-by-State matter. Also note that when the Constitution is amended, that action represents the expression of the people's sovereign will.

Some criticize the practice of sending proposed amendments to the State legislatures rather than to ratifying conventions, especially because it permits a constitutional change without a clear-cut expression by the people.

The critics point out that State legislators, who do the ratifying, are elected to office for a mix of reasons, including party membership, name familiarity, and their stances on certain issues. They are almost never chosen because of their stance on a proposed amendment. On the other hand, the delegates to a ratifying convention would be chosen by the people on the basis of only one factor: a yes-or-no stance on the proposed amendment.

The Supreme Court has held that a State cannot require an amendment proposed by Congress to be approved by a vote of the people of the State before it can be ratified by that State's legislature. It made that ruling in *Hawke* v. *Smith*, in 1920. However, a State legislature can call for an advisory vote by the people before it acts, as the Court held in *Kimble* v. *Swackhamer*, in 1978.

☑ **CHECK UNDERSTANDING** Why have some people criticized sending proposed amendments to the State legislatures rather than to ratifying conventions?

Proposing an Amendment

The Constitution places only one restriction on the subjects with which a proposed amendment may deal. Article V declares that "no State, without its Consent, shall be deprived of its equal Suffrage in the Senate."

The Bill of Rights

1	• Freedom of religion, speech and the press • Freedom to peaceably assemble and to petition the government	6	The right to: • a speedy trial by an impartial jury • be informed of the charges, to cross-examine witnesses, and to present favorable witnesses • an attorney
2	• The right to maintain a militia • The right to bear arms	7	The right to trial by jury in any civil case where the amount of money involved is $20 or more
3	Protection from having to quarter (house) soldiers in a time of peace without the consent of the owner, nor in a time of war except as provided by law	8	Protection from: • excessive bail or fines • cruel and unusual punishment
4	Protection against arbitrary searches and seizures without a proper warrant	9	The fact that the Constitution spells out a number of civil rights does not mean that there are not other, unwritten, rights held by the people.
5	Protection from: • prosecution without an indictment • being tried for the same crime twice • having to testify against oneself • the loss of life, liberty, or property without due process of law • loss of property without just compensation	10	The powers not delegated to the Federal Government may be exercised by the States, as long as they are not prohibited by the Constitution.

>> The first ten amendments protect many fundamental rights held by the people.
Generate Explanations Why is it important to spell out these rights?

When both houses of Congress pass a resolution proposing an amendment, Congress does not send it to the President to be signed or vetoed, though the Constitution would seem to require it—because when Congress proposes an amendment, it is not making law (not legislating). Although the chief executive has no formal role in the amendment process, his or her political influence can affect the success or failure of any attempt to amend the Constitution, of course.

If a State rejects a proposed amendment, it is not forever bound by that action. It may later reconsider and ratify the proposal. Most constitutional scholars agree that the reverse is not true, however. Once a State has approved an amendment, that action cannot be undone; and no governor's veto power extends to the ratification of a proposed amendment.

Proposed Amendments Over 10,000 joint resolutions calling for amendments to the Constitution have been proposed in Congress since 1789. Only 33 of them have been sent on to the States. Of those, only 27 have been finally ratified. One of the unratified amendments had been offered by Congress in 1789—along with 10 other proposals that became the Bill of Rights in 1791, and another that became the 27th Amendment in 1992.

The unratified amendment of 1789 dealt with the distribution of seats in the House of Representatives. A second, proposed in 1810, would have voided the citizenship of anyone accepting any foreign title or other honor. Another, in 1861, would have prohibited forever any amendment relating to slavery. A fourth, in 1924, was intended to give Congress the power to regulate child labor. A fifth one, proclaiming the equal rights of women (ERA), was proposed in 1972; it fell three States short of ratification and died in 1982. An amendment to give the District of Columbia seats in Congress was proposed in 1978; it died in 1985.

Reasonable Time Limit When Congress proposed the 18th Amendment in 1917, it set a seven-year deadline for its ratification. The Supreme Court held that Congress can place "a reasonable time limit" on the ratification process in a case from California, *Dillon* v. *Gloss*, in 1921. Congress has set a similar limit on the ratification period for each of the amendments (except the 19th) that it has proposed since then. It also granted a three-year extension of the deadline for the Equal Rights Amendment in 1979.

☑ **DESCRIBE** How can the chief executive impact the formal amendment process?

The 27 Amendments

The Constitution's amendments are quite significant. Yet they are also quite few in number. Over more than two centuries, only 27 formal amendments have been added to the document crafted in 1787.

The Bill of Rights The first ten amendments were added to the Constitution less than three years after it became effective. They were proposed by the First Congress in 1789 and were ratified by the States in late 1791. Each of these amendments arose out of the controversy surrounding the ratification of the Constitution itself. Many people, including Thomas Jefferson, had agreed to support the Constitution only if a listing of the basic rights held by the people were added to it, immediately.

Collectively, the first ten amendments are known as the **Bill of Rights**. They set out the great constitutional guarantees of freedom of belief and expression, of freedom and security of the person, and of fair and equal treatment before the law.

We shall look at the 1st through the 9th amendments at some length in later readings. The 10th Amendment does not deal with civil liberties, as such. Rather, it spells out the concept of reserved powers held by the States in the federal system.

>> The Buffalo Soldiers were members of the first all-Black regiments to serve in the U.S. Army during peacetime. Because of the 13th and 14th Amendments, they were free men and U.S. citizens.

The Bill of Rights limits the powers of the Federal Government by guaranteeing the safety of persons, opinions, and property from arbitrary acts of government. Over the years, the Supreme Court has held that the Bill of Rights also limits the power of the States. It does, says the Court, because of the 14th Amendment, which says "No State shall . . . deprive any person of life, liberty, or property, without due process of law. . . ."

The Later Amendments Each of the other amendments that have been added to the Constitution over the past 200 years also grew out of some particular, and often interesting, set of circumstances. For example, the 11th Amendment declares that no State may be sued in the federal courts by a citizen of another State or by a citizen of any foreign state. It was proposed by Congress in 1794 and ratified in 1795, after the State of Georgia had lost a case in the United States Supreme Court. The case (*Chisholm* v. *Georgia*, decided by the Court in 1793) arose out of a dispute over the ownership of some land in Georgia. It had been brought to the brand new federal court system by a man who lived in South Carolina.

The 12th Amendment was added in 1804 after the electoral college had failed to produce a winner in the presidential election of 1800. **Thomas Jefferson** became the third President of the United States in 1801, but only after a long, bitter fight in the House of Representatives. The 13th Amendment, added in 1865, provides another example. It abolished slavery in the United States and was a direct result of the Civil War.

Enslaved people freed under the 13th Amendment were legally in limbo in regards to their rights. The 14th Amendment, adopted in 1868, defined citizenship as "all persons born or naturalized in the United States," granting citizenship to formerly enslaved people.

Passage of the 14th Amendment was bitterly contested by the southern States, who were forced to ratify it in order to regain representation in Congress. The 15th Amendment later prohibited denying the vote based on a citizen's "race, color, or previous condition of servitude," which granted those previously enslaved the right to vote.

The 18th Amendment, establishing a nationwide prohibition of alcohol, was ratified in 1919. Known as "the noble experiment," it was repealed by the 21st in 1933.

The 22nd Amendment (1951), limiting the number of terms in which a President may serve to two, was proposed in 1947, soon after the Republican Party had gained control of Congress for the first time in 16 years. Over that period, **Franklin D. Roosevelt**, a Democrat, had won the presidency four times.

The 26th Amendment was added in 1971. It lowered the voting age to 18 in all elections in the United States. Many who backed the amendment began to work for its passage during World War II, creating the slogan "Old enough to fight, old enough to vote." Its ratification was spurred by the war in Vietnam.

The most recent amendment, the 27th, was written by **James Madison** and was among the first to be offered by Congress, in 1789. It forbids members of Congress from raising their own pay during that term. It finally became a part of the Constitution in 1992, when the 38th State, Michigan, ratified it.

☑ **SYNTHESIZE** Many of the 27 current amendments were proposed in response to legal disputes, social conflicts, or perceived constitutional problems. What problem was resolved by the 12th Amendment?

Change by Other Means

Surely, the Framers would be surprised to learn that only 17 amendments have been added to their handiwork since the adoption of the Bill of Rights more than two centuries ago. That so few formal changes have been made is, in part, a tribute to the wisdom of the Framers. But it is also due, in no small part, to the fact that many of the Constitution's provisions are cast in almost outline-like form; they are brief and seldom very detailed or specific. In short, their skeletal nature virtually guarantees interpretation.

So, to understand the Constitution, you must grasp this key point: There is much in that document—in fact, a great deal—that cannot be seen with the naked eye.

To put this essential point another way: Over time, many interpretations have been made in the Constitution that have not involved any changes in its written words.

This vital process of constitutional change by means other than formal amendment has taken place—and continues to occur—in five key ways: through (1) the passage of basic legislation by Congress; (2) actions taken by the President; (3) key decisions of the Supreme Court; (4) the activities of political parties; and (5) custom and usage.

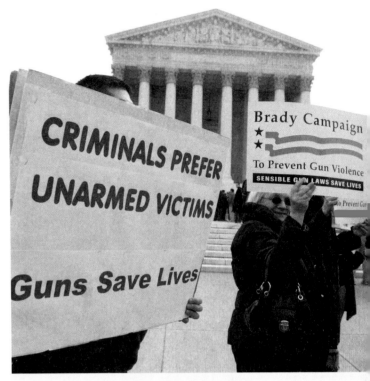

>> Gun control advocates and opponents protest outside the U.S. Supreme Court. The role of the Court is to interpret the Constitution and determine the constitutionality of federal laws.

>> The Judiciary Act of 1789 established the federal court system and gave Congress the power to create the courts.

>> In 1947, President Harry S. Truman signed the Presidential Succession Act, which designated the Speaker of the House to succeed the President and Vice President if neither is able to serve.

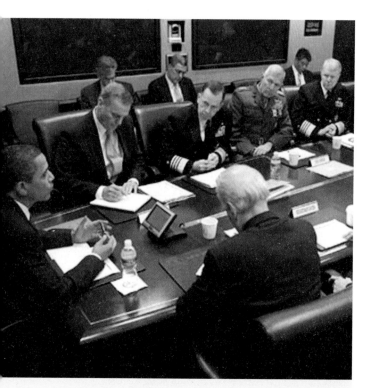

>> President Obama meets in the Situation Room to plan for the war in Afghanistan. As commander in chief, the President can send U.S. troops into combat without an official declaration of war.

Basic Legislation Congress has been a major agent of constitutional change in two important ways. First, it has passed a number of laws to clarify several of the Constitution's brief provisions. That is, Congress has added flesh to the bones of those sections of the Constitution that the Framers left purposely skeletal—provisions they left for Congress to detail as circumstances required.

Take the structure of the federal court system as an example. In Article III, Section 1, the Constitution provides for "one supreme Court, and . . . such inferior Courts as the Congress may from time to time ordain and establish." Beginning with the Judiciary Act of 1789, all of the federal courts, except the Supreme Court, have been created by acts of Congress. Or, similarly, Article II creates only the offices of President and Vice President. The many departments, agencies, and offices in the now huge executive branch have been created by acts of Congress.

As an additional example, the Constitution deals with the matter of presidential succession, but only up to a point. The 25th Amendment says that if the presidency becomes vacant, the Vice President automatically succeeds to the office. But who becomes President if both the presidency and the vice presidency are vacant? Thus, the Constitution leaves the answer to that question to Congress.

Second, Congress has added to the Constitution by the way in which it has used many of its powers. The Constitution gives to Congress the expressed power to regulate foreign and interstate commerce. But what is "foreign commerce" and "interstate commerce"? What, exactly, does Congress have the power to regulate? The Constitution does not say. Congress has done much to define those words, however, by exercising its commerce power with the passage of literally thousands of laws. As it has done so, Congress has, in a very real sense, clarified parts of the Constitution.

Executive Action The manner in which various Presidents, especially the more vigorous ones, have used their powers has also contributed to the growth of the Constitution. For example, the document says that only Congress can declare war. But the Constitution also makes the President the commander in chief of the nation's armed forces. Acting under that authority, several Presidents have made war without a declaration of war by Congress. In fact, Presidents have used the armed forces abroad in combat without such a declaration on several hundred occasions in our history.

Take the use of executive agreements in the conduct of foreign affairs as another example. An **executive agreement** is a pact made by the President directly with the head of a foreign state. A **treaty**, on the other hand, is a formal agreement between two or more sovereign states.

The principal difference between agreements and treaties is that executive agreements need not be approved by the Senate. They are as legally binding as treaties, however. Recent Presidents have often used them in our dealings with other countries, instead of the much more cumbersome treaty-making process outlined in Article II, Section 2 of the Constitution.

Additionally, most Presidents have insisted that the phrase "executive power" in Section 1 of Article II includes much more than the particular presidential powers set out in that article. Thus, Thomas Jefferson engineered the Louisiana Purchase in 1803, doubling the size of the United States—even though the Constitution does not say that the President has the power to acquire territory.

Court Decisions The nation's courts, most tellingly the United States Supreme Court, interpret and apply the Constitution in many of the cases they hear. You have already encountered several of these instances of constitutional interpretation by the Court, most notably in *Marbury* v. *Madison*, 1803.

Recall that the Court established the power of judicial review—which is not specifically mentioned in the Constitution. You will find many more instances of constitutional interpretation—for the Supreme Court is, as Woodrow Wilson once put it, "a constitutional convention in continuous session."

Party Practices The nation's political parties have been a major agent of constitutional change over the course of our political history, despite the fact that the Constitution makes no mention of them. In fact, most of the Framers were opposed to political parties. In his Farewell Address in 1796, **George Washington** warned the people against what he called "the baneful effects of the spirit of party."

He and many others feared the divisive effect of party politics on government. Yet, even as he spoke, parties were developing. They have had a major place in the shaping of government and its processes ever since. Illustrations of that point are almost endless.

Neither the Constitution nor any law provides for the nomination of candidates for the presidency. From the 1830s on, however, the major parties have held national conventions to do just that. The parties

>> After succeeding to the office of President after John F. Kennedy's 1963 assassination, Lyndon Johnson was elected President in his own right in 1964.

have converted the **electoral college**, the body that makes the formal selection of the nation's President, from what the Framers intended into a "rubber stamp" for each State's popular vote in presidential elections. Both houses of Congress are organized and conduct much of their business on the basis of party. The President makes appointments to office with an eye to party politics. In short, government in the United States is in many ways government through party.

Custom and Usage Unwritten customs may be as strong as written law, and many of them have developed in our governmental system. Again, there are many examples. By custom, not because the Constitution says so, the heads of the 15 executive departments make up the **Cabinet**, an advisory body to the President.

On each of the eight occasions when a President died in office, the Vice President succeeded to that office—most recently **Lyndon Johnson**, following John Kennedy's assassination in 1963. Yet, the written words of the Constitution did not provide for this practice until the adoption of the 25th Amendment in 1967. Until then, the Constitution said only that the powers and duties of the presidency—but not the office itself—"shall devolve on" (be transferred to) the Vice President.

It is a long-established custom that the Senate will approve only those presidential appointees, such as a federal judge or a United States marshal, who are acceptable to the senator or senators of the President's party from the State involved. This practice is known as **senatorial courtesy**, and it amounts to an unwritten rule that is closely followed in the Senate. Notice that its practical effect is to shift a portion of the appointing power from the President, where the formal wording of the Constitution puts it, to certain members of the Senate.

Both the strength and the importance of unwritten customs can be seen in the reaction to the rare circumstances in which one of them has not been observed. For nearly 150 years, the "no-third-term tradition" was a closely followed rule in presidential politics. The tradition began in 1796, when George Washington refused to seek a third term as President, and several later Presidents followed that lead. In 1940, and again in 1944, however, Franklin Roosevelt broke the no-third-term custom. He sought and won a third and then, four years later, a fourth term in the White House. As a direct result, the 22nd Amendment was added to the Constitution in 1951, limiting the President to two terms. What had been an unwritten custom, an informal rule, became part of the written Constitution itself.

☑ **IDENTIFY CAUSE AND EFFECT** How has the general way the Framers laid out the provisions of the Constitution eased change throughout the last two centuries?

☑ ASSESSMENT

1. **Make Generalizations** How do the constitutionally prescribed procedures by which the U.S. Constitution can be changed reflect the concepts of federalism and sovereignty?

2. **Draw Conclusions** What is the purpose of the Bill of Rights?

3. **Synthesize** Woodrow Wilson called the Supreme Court "a constitutional convention in continuous session." What did Wilson mean by this?

4. **Generate Explanations** Why do you think only 27 amendments have been added to the Constitution since its ratification, even though thousands have been proposed?

5. **Cite Evidence** The Framers wrote the Constitution knowing that needs and customs would change over time. What techniques did they use to ensure that the Constitution would, in fact, be relevant for hundreds of years?

Virginia Declaration of Rights

The Virginia Declaration of Rights was largely the work of George Mason (1725–1792), one of Virginia's wealthiest planters and a neighbor and friend of George Washington. The Declaration was adopted unanimously by the Virginia Convention of Delegates on June 12, 1776, and was later incorporated within the Virginia State constitution. It influenced a number of later documents, including the Declaration of Independence and the Bill of Rights.

>> Virginia patriot George Mason

A declaration of rights made by the representatives of the good people of Virginia, assembled in full and free convention; which rights do pertain to them and their posterity, as the basis and foundation of government.

I That all men are by nature equally free and independent, and have certain inherent rights . . . ; namely, the enjoyment of life and liberty, with the means of acquiring and possessing property, and pursuing and obtaining happiness and safety.

II That all power is vested in, and consequently derived from, the people; that magistrates [government officials] are their trustees and servants, and at all times amenable to them.

III That government is, or ought to be, instituted for the common benefit, protection, and security of the people, nation or community; of all the various modes and forms of government that is best, which is capable of producing the greatest degree of happiness and safety and is most effectually secured against the danger of maladministration; and that, whenever any government shall be found inadequate or contrary to these purposes, a majority of the community hath an indubitable [unquestionable], unalienable [incapable of being transferred or surrendered], and indefeasible [not able to be lost] right to reform, alter or abolish it, in such manner as shall be judged most conducive to the public weal [well-being]. . . .

V That the legislative and executive powers of the state should be separate and distinct from the judicative; and, [in order] that the members of the two first may be restrained [shielded] from oppression by feeling and participating the burthens [burdens] of the people, they should, at fixed periods, be reduced to a private station, return into that body from which they were originally taken, and the vacancies be supplied by frequent, certain, and regular elections in which all, or any part of the former members, to be again eligible, or ineligible, as the laws shall direct.

☑ **DETERMINE MEANING** What does *judicative* mean as it is used in Article V? Tell how you determined the meaning.

VI That elections of members to serve as representatives of the people in assembly ought to be free; and that all men, having sufficient evidence of permanent common interest with, and attachment to, the community have the right of suffrage [voting] and cannot be taxed or deprived of their property for public uses without their own consent or that of their representatives so elected, nor bound by any law to which they have not, in like manner, assented, for the public good.

VII That all power of suspending laws, or the execution of laws, by any authority without consent of the representatives of the people is injurious to their rights and ought not to be exercised.

VIII That in all capital or criminal prosecutions a man hath a right to demand the cause and nature of his accusation to be confronted with the accusers and witnesses, to call for evidence in his favor, and to a speedy trial by an impartial jury of his vicinage [neighbors], without whose unanimous consent he cannot be found guilty, nor can he be compelled [forced] to give evidence against himself; that no man be deprived of his liberty except by the law of the land or the judgement of his peers.

☑ **DRAW INFERENCES** Based on Article VIII, what do you think are some of the ways that the colonists felt they were being mistreated by the colonial government?

IX That excessive bail ought not to be required, nor excessive fines imposed; nor cruel and unusual punishments inflicted.

X That general warrants, whereby any officer or messenger may be commanded to search suspected places without evidence of a fact committed, or to seize any person or persons not named, or whose offense is not particularly [specifically] described and supported by evidence, are grievous and oppressive and ought not to be granted.

XI That in controversies respecting property and in suits between man and man, the ancient trial by jury is preferable to any other and ought to be held sacred.

☑ **DETERMINE MEANING** What does "suits between man and man" mean in Article XI?

XII That the freedom of the press is one of the greatest bulwarks of liberty and can never be restrained but by despotic governments.

XIII That a well regulated militia, composed of the body of the people, trained to arms, is the proper, natural, and safe defense of a free state; that standing [permanent] armies, in time of peace, should be avoided as dangerous to liberty; and that, in all cases, the military should be under strict subordination to, and be governed by, the civil power.

XIV That the people have a right to uniform government; and therefore, that no government separate from, or independent of, the government of Virginia, ought to be erected or established within the limits thereof.

XV That no free government, or the blessings of liberty, can be preserved to any people but by a firm adherence to justice, moderation, temperance, frugality, and virtue and by frequent recurrence to fundamental principles.

XVI That religion, or the duty which we owe to our Creator and the manner of discharging it, can be directed by reason and conviction, not by force or violence; and therefore, all men are equally entitled to the free exercise of religion, according to the dictates of conscience; and that it is the mutual duty of all to practice Christian forbearance, love, and charity towards each other.

☑ ASSESSMENT

1. **Examine Information** Identify how the Virginia Declaration of Rights helped lead to an expansion of civil rights, both in the State of Virginia and, later, in the entire United States.

2. **Integrate Information from Diverse Sources** How might Mason's words in Article I have influenced Thomas Jefferson when he wrote the preamble to the Declaration of Independence? Cite specific examples from one or both documents in your answer.

3. **Cite Evidence** How might the first part of Article V lead someone to believe that Virginia Declaration of Rights influenced the writing of the U.S. Constitution?

3.3

The President is the commander in chief of the Armed Forces, but governors fulfill that duty for their States' National Guard, unless it is called to active duty by the President.

Federalism: Powers Divided

You know that federal law requires young men to register for military service at age 18, that most employers must pay their workers at the least a minimum wage set by act of Congress, and that no person can be denied a job on the basis of his or her race or ethnicity.

The Founders Choose Federalism

You also know that State law says that you must have a driver's license in order to drive a car, that it is illegal for anyone under 21 to buy alcoholic beverages, and that only those persons who can satisfy certain requirements can buy or own firearms.

Those three examples illustrate a very complex matter: the division of the powers of government in this country between the National Government, on the one hand, and the 50 States on the other. This section will help you to better understand that sometimes complicated, but very important, arrangement.

Balancing National and State Powers When the Framers of the Constitution met at Philadelphia in 1787, they faced a number of difficult questions. Not the least of them: How could they possibly create a new central government that would be strong enough to meet the needs of the day and would, at the same time, preserve the already existing States? Even those Founders who, like Thomas Jefferson, were not part of the constitutional writing

🔲 BOUNCE to Activate Flipped Video

Objectives

Define federalism and explain why the Framers adopted a federal system instead of a unitary system.

Categorize powers delegated to and denied to the National Government, and powers reserved for and denied to the States, and the difference between exclusive and concurrent powers.

Summarize the obligations that the Constitution, as the "the supreme Law of the Land," places on the National Government with regard to the States.

Key Terms

federalism
division of powers
delegated powers
expressed powers
implied powers
inherent powers
reserved powers

exclusive powers
concurrent powers
Supremacy Clause
John Marshall

process, took an active interest in designing the document to meet the needs of a growing nation.

Few of the Framers favored a strong central government based on the British model, and all of them knew that the Revolution had been fought in the name of local self-government. They also knew that the government established under the Articles of Confederation had proved too weak to deal with the new nation's many problems.

While the Framers favored a stronger national government, they also knew firsthand the importance of limiting federal powers. They were convinced that (1) governmental power inevitably poses a threat to individual liberty, (2) that therefore the exercise of governmental power must be restrained, and (3) that to divide governmental power, as federalism does, is to prevent its abuse.

☑ **SUMMARIZE** What set of contradictions made the development of a Constitution so complex?

What Is Federalism?

Federalism Defined **Federalism** is a system of government in which a written constitution divides the powers of government on a territorial basis,

between a central government and several regional governments, usually called states or provinces. Each of those basic levels of government has its own substantial set of powers. Neither level, acting alone, can change the basic division of powers the Constitution has created. Additionally, each level of government operates through its own agencies and acts directly through its own officials and laws.

The American system of government stands as a prime example of federalism. The basic design of that system is set out in the Constitution. The document provides for a **division of powers** between the National Government and the governments of the 50 States. That is, it assigns certain powers to the National Government and reserves others to the States. This division of powers was implied in the original Constitution and then spelled out in the 10th Amendment.

In effect, federalism produces a dual system of government. That is, it provides for two basic levels of government, each with its own field of authority, and each operating over the same people and the same territory at the same time.

In the American federal system, each of the two basic levels of government can make certain decisions and do certain things that the other level cannot. For example, only the Federal Government can regulate interstate commerce—that is, trade conducted between and among the various States. On the other hand, each of the States decides for itself whether those who commit certain crimes in that State can be put to death.

A Closer Look at Federalism Federalism's major strength lies in this central fact: It allows local action in matters of local concern and national action in matters of wider concern. Local traditions, needs, and desires vary from one State to another, and federalism allows for differing circumstances among the States. In addition, geographic differences can have a significant impact on States' policies.

States located in earthquake zones, for example, may need to enact laws regarding earthquake-resistant building codes, while States located along the coasts may need to enact policies related to flooding, fisheries, or maritime commerce.

Illustrations of this point are nearly endless. Self-service gas stations, voter registration, the sales tax, legalized physician-assisted death, and

>> The American Revolution was fought for freedom from British control, fueling the desire of the Framers of the Constitution to create the right balance between local and central government.

The Role of State and Federal Governments in Welfare Reform

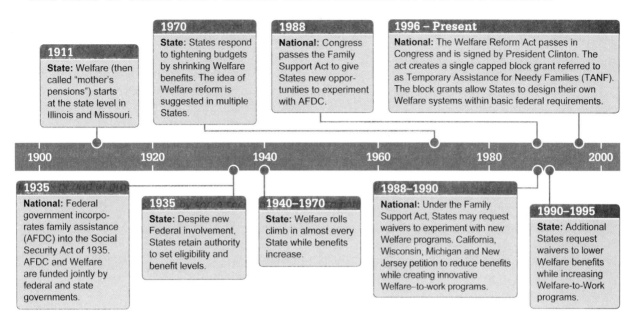

1911
State: Welfare (then called "mother's pensions") starts at the state level in Illinois and Missouri.

1970
State: States respond to tightening budgets by shrinking Welfare benefits. The idea of Welfare reform is suggested in multiple States.

1988
National: Congress passes the Family Support Act to give States new opportunities to experiment with AFDC.

1996 – Present
National: The Welfare Reform Act passes in Congress and is signed by President Clinton. The act creates a single capped block grant referred to as Temporary Assistance for Needy Families (TANF). The block grants allow States to design their own Welfare systems within basic federal requirements.

1900   1920   1940   1960   1980   2000

1935
National: Federal government incorporates family assistance (AFDC) into the Social Security Act of 1935. AFDC and Welfare are funded jointly by federal and state governments.

1935
State: Despite new Federal involvement, States retain authority to set eligibility and benefit levels.

1940–1970
State: Welfare rolls climb in almost every State while benefits increase.

1988–1990
National: Under the Family Support Act, States may request waivers to experiment with new Welfare programs. California, Wisconsin, Michigan and New Jersey petition to reduce benefits while creating innovative Welfare–to-work programs.

1990–1995
State: Additional States request waivers to lower Welfare benefits while increasing Welfare-to-Work programs.

>> Welfare reform has alternated between State and National governments for many years. **Analyze Charts** How are welfare programs now managed at both levels of government?

many other issues are governed by different laws depending on which State you live in. The same was true of States' differing responses to the COVID-19 pandemic that struck the United States in early 2020. Shutdown and mask-wearing orders during that public emergency, for example, varied from State to State.

Federalism also allows for experimentation and innovation in solving public policy problems. Indeed, the several States have long been described as so many "laboratories of government." New approaches to difficult matters may originate in one State and then be adopted in another or even be put in place at the national level.

The Welfare Reform Act passed by Congress in 1996 affords a useful illustration of the point. That landmark statute revolutionized the Federal Government's approach to providing welfare assistance to millions of Americans on the lower rungs of the nation's economic ladder—and its basic features were first suggested by welfare administrators in the States of Wisconsin, California, and Michigan.

While federalism allows individual States to handle State and local matters, it also provides for the strength that comes from union. National defense and foreign affairs offer useful illustrations of this point. So, too, do domestic affairs. Take, for example, a natural disaster. When a flood, drought, hurricane, or other catastrophe hits a particular State, the resources of the National Government and all of the other States can be mobilized to aid the stricken area.

Some disadvantages of federalism, however, are the redundancy and/or lack of coordination that can occur due to overlapping jurisdictions. One prime example of this is the handling of Hurricane Katrina, a tropical storm that decimated parts of Florida, Louisiana, and Mississippi in 2005. Katrina cost the region nearly 2,000 lives and over a billion dollars in damages as local, State, and Federal governments struggled to coordinate their efforts.

Deciding when the Federal Government should become involved in State affairs can be controversial. Air pollution caused by industry in one State can spread to other States. Water usage in one State may impact down river communities in other States. Even more controversial are cases when civil liberties are violated at the State level. A prime example of this was the systematic discrimination against Black Americans in the South for more than 100 years after the Civil War and Reconstruction.

☑ **APPLY CONCEPTS** Why are the States sometimes described as "laboratories of government?"

Three Types of Federal Powers

The National Government is a government of **delegated powers**. That is, that government has only those powers delegated (granted) to it in the Constitution. There are three distinct types of delegated powers: expressed, implied, and inherent.

The Expressed Powers The **expressed powers** are those powers delegated to the National Government in so many words—spelled out, expressly, in the Constitution. Those powers are also sometimes called the "enumerated powers."

You can find most of the expressed powers in Article I, Section 8. There, in 18 separate clauses, the Constitution expressly gives 27 powers to Congress. They include the power to lay and collect taxes, to coin money, to regulate foreign and interstate commerce, to raise and maintain armed forces, to declare war, to fix standards of weights and measures, to grant patents and copyrights, and to do many other things.

Several other expressed powers are set out elsewhere in the Constitution, as well. Article II, Section 2 gives several powers to the President—

including the power to act as commander in chief of the armed forces, to grant reprieves and pardons, to make treaties, and to appoint major federal officials. Article III grants "the judicial Power of the United States" to the Supreme Court and other courts in the federal judiciary. And, finally, several expressed powers also are found in various amendments to the Constitution; thus, the 16th Amendment gives Congress the power to levy an income tax.

The Implied Powers The **implied powers** are not expressly stated in the Constitution, but they are reasonably suggested—implied—by the expressed powers. The constitutional basis for the implied powers is found in one of the expressed powers. Article I, Section 8, Clause 18 gives Congress the "necessary and proper power." The Necessary and Proper Clause says that Congress has the power

> . . . to make all Laws which shall be necessary and proper for carrying into Execution the foregoing Powers and all other Powers vested by this Constitution in the Government of the United States, or in any Department or Officer thereof.
>
> —Article I, Section 8, Clause 18

Through decades of congressional and court interpretation, the words *necessary and proper* have come to mean, in effect, "convenient and useful." Indeed, the Necessary and Proper Clause is sometimes called the Elastic Clause, because, over time, it has been stretched to cover so many different situations.

Here are but a few of the thousands of examples of the exercise of implied powers: Congress has provided for the regulation of labor-management relations, the building of hydroelectric power dams, and the building of the 42,000-mile interstate highway system. It has made federal crimes of such acts as moving stolen goods, gambling devices, and kidnapped persons across State lines. It has prohibited racial discrimination in granting all people access to such places as restaurants, theaters, hotels, and motels. Congress has taken these actions, and many more, because the power to do so is reasonably implied by just one of the expressed powers: the power to regulate interstate commerce.

The Inherent Powers The **inherent powers** are those powers that belong to the National Government because it is the national government of

>> President Woodrow Wilson walking with other world leaders while negotiating the Treaty of Versailles. The Constitution gives the Federal Government the power to negotiate and sign treaties.

Examples of Powers Expressly Denied to the Federal Government

POWER DENIED	EXAMPLE OF ILLEGAL USE OF POWER
Levy taxes on exports	The Federal Government levies a tax on coal exports from Pennsylvania to Canada.
Take private property for public use without payment of compensation	The Federal Government appropriates a farmer's land to build a highway, and offers him no compensation.
Prohibit freedom of religion, speech, press, or assembly	The Federal Government enacts a law stating that no one may make a speech outside of public buildings.
Conduct illegal search or seizure	The Federal Government sends an agent without a warrant to find and confiscate a business's financial records.
Deny a speedy trial to an accused person	The Federal Government holds a suspected criminal in jail without trial for two years.

>> The powers denied to the National Government are varied and extensive.
Analyze Charts How is federalism preserved by the denial of these powers?

a sovereign state in the world community. Although the Constitution does not expressly provide for them, they are powers that, over time, all national governments have come to possess. It stands to reason that the Framers of the Constitution intended the National Government they created would also hold those several constitutional powers.

The inherent powers are few in number. The major ones include the power to regulate immigration, to deport unauthorized immigrants, to acquire territory, to grant diplomatic recognition to other states, and to protect the nation against rebellion or other attempts to overthrow the government by force or violence.

One can argue that most of the inherent powers really are implied by one or more of the expressed powers. For example, the power to regulate immigration is suggested by the expressed power to regulate foreign trade. The power to acquire territory can be drawn from the treaty-making power and the several war powers. But the doctrine of inherent powers holds that it is not necessary to go to these lengths to find these powers in the Constitution. In short, these powers exist because the United States exists.

☑ **DRAW CONCLUSIONS** Why would it be unacceptable for a State to deport unauthorized immigrants?

Powers Denied to the Federal Government

Although the Constitution delegates certain powers to the National Government, it also denies certain powers to that level of government in order to keep federalism intact. It does so in three distinct ways.

First, the Constitution denies some powers to the National Government in so many words—expressly. Among them are the powers to levy duties on exports; to take private property for public use without the payment of just compensation; to prohibit freedom of religion, speech, press, or assembly; to conduct illegal searches or seizures; and to deny to any person accused of a crime a speedy and public trial or a trial by jury.

Second, several powers are denied to the National Government because of the *silence* of the Constitution. Recall that the National Government is a government of delegated powers; it has only those powers the Constitution gives to it.

While some disagree, many others argue that the powers not granted to the National Government include such things as creating a public school system for the nation, enacting uniform marriage and divorce laws, and setting up units of local government. The Constitution says little that would give the National Government the power to do any of those things, expressly, implicitly, or inherently. In short, the lack of any such provision—the silence of the Constitution—denies power to the National Government.

>> One reserved State power is the right to issue licenses to various professionals, such as nurses and physicians. Such a license is required to practice in that particular State.

>> The Texas Ranger Division is the oldest State law enforcement agency in the country and is an example of a State's right to enforce order among its own people.

Third, some powers are denied to the National Government because of the federal system itself. Clearly the Constitution does not intend that the National Government should have the power to take any action that would threaten the existence of that system. For example, in the exercise of its power to tax, Congress cannot tax any of the States or any of their local units in the conduct of their various governmental functions. If it could, it would have the power to destroy—tax out of existence—one or more, or all, of the States.

☑ **APPLY CONCEPTS** Explain why the U.S. Government cannot break into your home to search for stolen goods without a warrant.

Powers of the Fifty States

The 50 States are the other half of the very complicated equation we call federalism. Their many-sided role in the American federal system is no less important than that of the National Government.

Powers Reserved to the States Recall, the 10th Amendment states that the States are governments of **reserved powers**. The reserved powers are those powers that the Constitution does not grant to the National Government and does not, at the same time, deny to the States.

Thus, any State can forbid persons under 18 to marry without parental consent. It can ban the sale of obscene materials, outlaw prostitution, and permit some forms of gambling and prohibit others. A State can require that doctors and plumbers be licensed in order to practice in the State. It can establish public schools, enact land use laws, regulate the services and restrict the profits of such public utilities as natural gas, oil, electric power, and telephone companies, and do much, much more.

In short, the sphere of powers held by each State—the scope of the reserved powers—is huge. The States can do all of those things just mentioned, because the Constitution does not give the National Government the power to do those things, and it does not deny the States the power to do them. In effect, the reserved powers set aside particular issues as matters for the State governments. And as matters for the State governments, they are also necessarily matters for the people who established those governments.

How broad the reserved powers really are can be understood from the fact that most of the rules and regulations we live under are created by the State and local governments, not by the National Government. The reserved powers also include the vitally important police power—the power of a State to protect and promote the public health, the public morals, the public safety, and the general welfare.

The Constitution does not grant expressed powers to the States, with one exception. Section 2 of the 21st Amendment gives the States a virtually unlimited power to regulate the manufacture, sale, and consumption of alcoholic beverages.

Powers Denied to the States Just as the Constitution denies many powers to the National Government, so it denies many powers to the States. Some of those powers are denied to the States in so many words, in Article I. For example, no State can enter into any treaty, alliance, or confederation. Nor can a State print or coin money or keep a standing army or navy.

Some powers are denied to the States inherently—that is, by the existence of the federal system. Thus, no State (and no local government) can tax any of the agencies or functions of the National Government. Remember, too, each State has its own constitution. Those documents also deny many powers to the States. Additionally, recall that, as a result of the Court's interpretation of the 14th Amendment, the States cannot deny individuals the civil liberties outlined in the Constitution.

☑ **CHECK UNDERSTANDING** Describe the breadth of powers provided to the States.

The Exclusive and the Concurrent Powers

Exclusive Powers Most of the powers that the Constitution delegates to the National Government are **exclusive powers**. That is, they can be exercised only by the National Government and not by the States under any circumstances.

Some of these powers are expressly denied to the States—for example, the power to coin money and to make treaties with foreign states. Some of them are not expressly denied to the States but are, nonetheless, among the exclusive powers of the Federal Government because of the nature of the power involved. The power to regulate interstate commerce is a leading example of this point. If the States could exercise that power, trade between and among the States would be at best chaotic and at worst impossible.

Concurrent Powers Some of the powers delegated to the National Government are **concurrent**

>> The 1897 Dingly Tariff Act is an example of the exclusive power to lay duties on imports. **Analyze Political Cartoons** What was the impact of this act according to this cartoon?

>> Some reservoirs, such as Shasta Lake in California, were created on land with existing homes. The land was claimed through eminent domain, a power shared by federal and State governments.

powers. That is, they are powers that both the National Government and the States possess and exercise. Those powers include the power to levy and collect taxes, to make laws, to define crimes and set punishments for them, to condemn (take) private property for public, and build roads.

The concurrent powers are held and exercised separately and simultaneously by the two basic levels of government. That is, the concurrent powers are those powers that the Constitution does not grant exclusively to the National Government and that, at the same time, does not deny to the States. The concurrent powers, in short, are those powers that make it possible for a federal system of government to function.

Although government in the United States is often discussed in terms of three levels—national, State, and local—there are, in fact, only two basic levels in the federal system: the National Government and the State governments. The approximately 90,000 units of local government in the United States today are subunits of the various State governments. Local governments can provide services, regulate activities, collect taxes, and do many other things only because the State has given them the power to do so. In short, when local governments exercise their powers, they are actually exercising State powers.

Another way of putting all of this is to remind you of a point that we first made in Topic 1. Each of the 50 States has a *unitary* form of government—an arrangement in which a central government that creates local units of government for its own convenience.

☑ **EXPRESS IDEAS CLEARLY** How do local governments relate to State governments?

The Constitution Reigns Supreme

As you have just seen, the division of powers in the American federal system produces a dual system of government, one in which two basic levels of government operate over the same territory and the same people at the same time. Such an arrangement is bound to result in conflicts between national and State law.

The Supremacy Clause The Framers anticipated those conflicts—and so they wrote the **Supremacy Clause** into the Constitution. That provision declares that

> This Constitution, and the Laws of the United States which shall be made in Pursuance thereof; and all Treaties made, or which shall be made, under the Authority of the United States, shall be the supreme Law of the Land; and the Judges in every State shall be bound thereby, anything in the Constitution or Laws of any State to the Contrary notwithstanding.
>
> —Article VI, Section 2

The Constitution and the laws and treaties of the United States are "the supreme Law of the Land." This means that the Constitution ranks above all other forms of law in the United States. Acts of Congress and treaties stand immediately beneath the Constitution.

The Supremacy Clause has been called the "linchpin of the Constitution" because it joins the National Government and the States into a single

>> Local governments can collect taxes and provide some local services like fire departments, but their authority comes from the State.

governmental unit, a federal government. The Supremacy Clause is the provision in the Constitution that makes the complex federal system a working reality.

Our political history is studded with challenges to the concept of national supremacy. In the 1950s, for example, several southern states defied a Supreme Court ruling that schools must desegregate. It was not until 1964 and the passage of the Civil Rights Act that desegregation began in any meaningful way.

Those who have rejected the concept of national supremacy have insisted that the Constitution is a compact among sovereign States, rather than one among "We the People of the United States." They believe that the powers that compact gives to the Federal Government should be narrowly defined and applied. Variations of that view can still be found in contemporary American politics.

The Supreme Court and Federalism

The Supreme Court is the umpire in the federal system. One of its chief duties is to apply the Constitution's Supremacy Clause to the conflicts that the dual system of government inevitably produces.

The Court was first called to settle a clash between a national and a State law in 1819. The case, *McCulloch* v. *Maryland*, involved the controversial Second Bank of the United States. The bank had been chartered by Congress in 1816. In 1818, the Maryland legislature, hoping to cripple the bank, placed a tax on all notes issued by its Baltimore branch. James McCulloch, the branch cashier, refused to pay the tax, and the Maryland courts convicted him for that refusal. The Supreme Court unanimously reversed that decision.

Speaking for the Court, Chief Justice **John Marshall** based the decision squarely on the Constitution's Supremacy Clause:

> [If] any one proposition could command the universal assent of mankind, we might expect it would be this—that the government of the Union, though limited in its powers, is supreme within its sphere of action.

> [If] any one proposition could command the universal assent of mankind, we might expect it would be this—that the government of the Union, though limited in its powers, is supreme within its sphere of action.
>
> —*McCulloch* v. *Maryland,* 1819

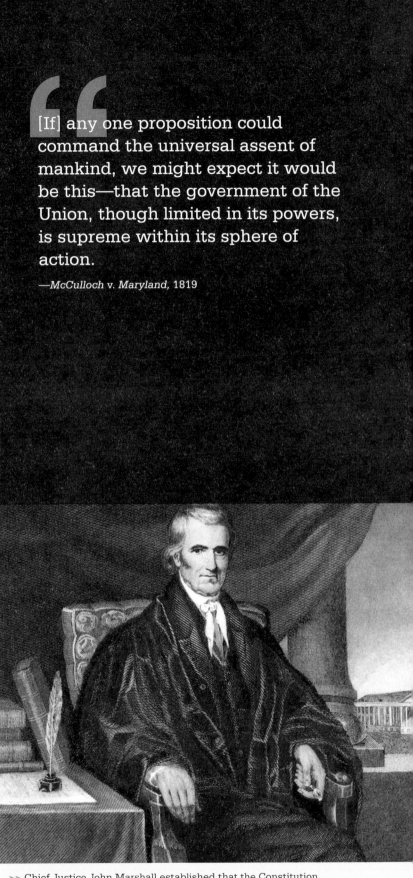

>> Chief Justice John Marshall established that the Constitution grants the Federal Government implied powers for implementing its express powers, and that States cannot impede those powers.

. . . [T]he states have no power . . . to retard, impede, burden, or in any manner control, the operations of the constitutional laws enacted by Congress. . . .

—*McCulloch* v. *Maryland*, 1819

Marshall, a strong Federalist, served on the Supreme Court for more than 30 years, and he believed strongly in the importance of the Supreme Court as a force in determining the law of the land. Since the decision in this landmark case, it has been impossible to overstate the significance of the role of the Court as the umpire of the federal system.

Had the Court not assumed this role, the American federal system and probably the United States itself could not have survived its early years. Justice Oliver Wendell Holmes once made that point in these words:

I do not think the United States would come to an end if we [the Court] lost our power to declare an Act of Congress void. I do think the Union would be imperiled if we could not make that declaration as to the laws of the several States.

—Collected Legal Papers

The Supreme Court first held a State law to be unconstitutional in a case from Georgia, *Fletcher* v. *Peck*, in 1810. The Court found that a Georgia law passed in 1794 that sold some 35 million acres of public land for 1.5 cents an acre amounted to a contract between the State and Peck and other buyers. Despite the obvious corruption involved, it found that the legislature's later (1796) repeal of the law violated the Constitution's Contract Clause (Article I, Section 10, Clause 1). That provision prohibits the States the power to pass any "Law impairing the Obligation of Contracts." Over the centuries since then, the High Court has found thousands of State laws and local ordinances unconstitutional, but it has upheld the constitutionality of thousands of others.

The Supreme Court's role as umpire in the federal system was also called upon in *National Federation of Independent Business* v. *Sebelius* (2012). One of the issues in this landmark case centered on a provision of the Affordable Care Act (ACA) that required States to comply with a requirement to expand Medicaid coverage or else forfeit all federal Medicaid funding.

The States argued that the expansion was coercive and violated the principle of federalism by pressuring State governments "into accepting conditions that Congress could not impose directly." The Court concurred, in part. It agreed that the federal government's demand to comply or lose all funding was unconstitutional. However, the Court held that the Medicaid provision was valid under Congress's Spending Clause as long as the threat of losing all funding was removed. Some states' rights advocates praised the limitation on funding conditions, but the constitutionality of the ACA is still under scrutiny.

☑ **RECALL** Why is the Supremacy Clause often called the "linchpin" of the Constitution?

☑ ASSESSMENT

1. **Connect** How does the Supremacy Clause impact disputes among States or between States and the National Government?

2. **Compare** How do the powers of the National Government compare in breadth to the powers of the States?

3. **Identify** How would President Lyndon Johnson be able to justify the use of federal troops to manage riots during the summer of 1967?

4. **Apply** Anna wanted to apply for a license to become a lawyer in the State of Alabama. Would she apply to the federal or State government for the license? Why?

5. **Check Understanding** What approach did the Framers of the Constitution use to limit the powers of the National Government, and why was that approach successful?

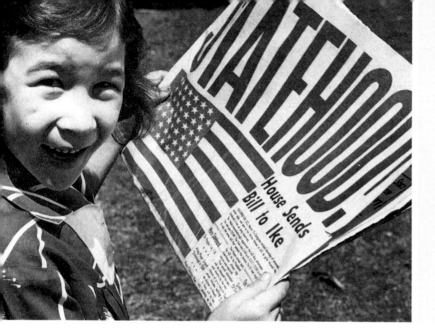

Hawaii became the 50th State in 1959, following a precedent established by the 1787 Northwest Ordinance: the U.S. would grow by forming new States rather than expanding existing States.

The National Government and the States

Have you ever really focused on the words *United States*, and what those two words say? The United States is a union of States, the several States joined together, the States united.

The Nation's Obligations Under the Constitution

The Framers of the Constitution created that union of States, and they intended to preserve it. To that end, the Constitution (1) requires the National Government to guarantee certain things to the States and (2) makes it possible for the National Government to do certain things for the States.

The Constitution places several obligations on the National Government for the benefit of the States. Most of them are found in Article IV.

Republican Form of Government The Constitution requires the National Government to "guarantee to every State in this Union a Republican Form of Government." The Constitution does not define "Republican Form of Government," and the Supreme Court has regularly refused to do so. The term is generally understood to mean a "representative government."

BOUNCE to Activate Flipped Video

Objectives

Explain the process for admitting new States to the Union.

Examine the many and growing areas of cooperative federalism.

Explain why States make interstate compacts.

Understand the purpose of the Full Faith and Credit Clause, the Extradition Clause, and the Privileges and Immunities Clause.

Key Terms

enabling act
act of admission
grants-in-aid
  programs
categorical grants
block grants
project grants
interstate compacts
Full Faith and Credit
  Clause

extradition
Privileges and
  Immunities Clause
William Howard Taft

Take it quietly UNCLE ABE and I will draw it closer than ever!!!

A few more stitches ANDY and the good old UNION will be mended!

THE "RAIL SPLITTER" AT WORK REPAIRING THE UNION.

>> President Lincoln planned to quickly reunite the nation after the Civil War. **Analyze Political Cartoons** How might his assassination have affected reconciliation?

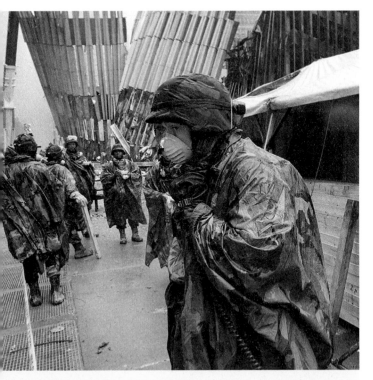

>> The Constitution guarantees the Federal Government will assist States that are attacked. U.S. Army soldiers helped patrol New York City after the 2001 attack on the World Trade Center.

The Supreme Court has held that the question of whether a State has a republican form of government is a "political question." That is, it is one to be decided by the political branches of the government—the President and Congress—and not by the courts.

The only extensive use ever made of the republican-form guarantee came in the years immediately following the Civil War. Congress declared that several southern States did not have governments of a republican form, and refused to admit senators and representatives from those States until they had ratified the 13th, 14th, and 15th amendments and broadened their laws to recognize the voting and other rights of African Americans.

Making War, Keeping Peace The Constitution states that the National Government must also

> protect each of them [the States] against Invasion; and on Application of the Legislature, or of the Executive (when the Legislature cannot be convened) against domestic Violence.
>
> —Article IV, Section 4

Today it is clear that an invasion of any one of the States would be met as an attack on the United States itself. This constitutional guarantee is therefore now of little significance.

That was not the case in the late 1780s. Then it was not at all certain that all 13 States would stand together if a foreign power attacked one of them. So, before the States agreed to give up their war-making powers, each demanded that an attack on any one of the States would be met as an attack on all of them.

The federal system assumes that each of the 50 States will keep the peace within its own borders. Thus, the primary responsibility for curbing insurrection, riot, or other internal disorder rests with the individual States. However, the Constitution does recognize that a State might not be able to control some situations. It therefore guarantees protection against internal disorder, or what the Constitution calls "domestic Violence."

The use of federal force to restore order within a State has been a rare event historically. Several instances did occur in the 1960s, however. When racial unrest exploded into violence in Detroit during the "long, hot summer" of 1967, President Lyndon Johnson ordered units of the United States Army into the city. He acted at the request of the governor of Michigan, George Romney, and only after Detroit's police and firefighters, supported by State police and National Guard units, could not control riots, arson, and looting in the city.

In 1968, again at the request of the governors involved, federal troops were sent into Chicago and Baltimore to help put down the violence that erupted following the assassination of Martin Luther King, Jr. In 1992, President George H.W. Bush ordered members of the National Guard, the Army, and the Marines to Los Angeles to restore order after three days of rioting. The violence was sparked by the acquittal of four white officers charged with beating Rodney King, a Black motorist, after he led them on a highspeed chase.

Normally, a President has sent troops into a State only in answer to a request from its governor or legislature. If national laws are being broken, national functions interfered with, or national property endangered, however, a President does not need to wait for such a plea.

President Grover Cleveland ordered federal troops to end rioting in the Chicago rail yards during the Pullman Strike in 1894 despite the objections of Illinois Governor William Altgeld. The Supreme Court upheld his actions in *In re Debs* (1895). The Court found that rioters had threatened federal property and impeded the flow of the mail and interstate commerce. Thus, more than "domestic Violence" was involved. Since then, several Presidents have acted without a request from the State involved. President Dwight Eisenhower did so at Little Rock, Arkansas, in 1957, and President John Kennedy did so at the University of Mississippi in 1962 and at the University of Alabama in 1963. In each of those instances, the President acted to halt the unlawful obstruction of school integration orders issued by the federal courts.

The ravages of nature—storms, floods, drought, forest fires, and the like—can be far more destructive than human violence. Here, too, acting to protect the States against "domestic Violence," the Federal Government stands ready to aid stricken areas.

Respect for Territorial Integrity The National Government is constitutionally bound to respect the territorial integrity of each of the States. That is, the National Government must recognize the legal existence and the physical boundaries of each State.

The basic scheme of the Constitution imposes this obligation. Several of its provisions do so, as well. For example, Congress must include, in both of its houses, members chosen in each one of the States. Recall, too, that Article V of the Constitution

>> In 1963, President Kennedy sent federal troops to intervene when Governor George Wallace blocked the door of the University of Alabama to prevent African American students from entering.

declares that no State can be deprived of its equal representation in the United States Senate without its own consent.

☑ **INFER** What compromise made it possible for States to agree to give up their power to make war?

Admitting New States

That new States would soon join the original 13 as members of the new United States was generally accepted as fact in the 1780s. To that end, the Congress of the Confederation, meeting as the Framers were drafting what was to become the Constitution, enacted the Northwest Ordinance of 1787—clearly, the most important measure passed by that body in its eight years as the government of the United States.

The ordinance anticipated the creation of new States in what was then known as the Northwest Territory—a roughly defined area lying north of the Ohio River and west of New York, Pennsylvania, and Virginia. The measure provided for the eventual Statehood of any sector in that region that acquired a population of at least 60,000 persons.

Understanding that geographical differences would require unique laws and policies, it made provisions for local self-government, for civil and political rights, and for the support of education. An earlier measure, the Ordinance of 1785, had created the township system for the dividing of land for the support of local schools. Its provisions were folded into the 1787 enactment.

The Northwest Ordinance was re-adopted by the new Congress under the Constitution in 1790, and it served as the basis for later legislation regarding the nation's territorial possessions. It established that those territories were not to be kept in a second-class status but were to be groomed for Statehood on an equal footing with the existing States.

Congress and New States Only Congress has the power to admit new States to the Union, and the Constitution places only one restriction on that power: A new State cannot be created by taking territory from one or more of the existing States without the consent of the legislature(s) of the State(s) involved.

Congress has admitted 37 States since the original 13 formed the Union, as the map shows. Four States (Kentucky, Tennessee, Maine, and West Virginia) were created from parts of already existing States. Texas and Vermont were independent republics before admission. California was admitted shortly after being ceded to the United States by Mexico. Each of the other 30 States entered the Union only after a longer period of time, frequently more than 15 years, as an organized territory.

Admission Procedure The process of admission to the Union is usually simple. The area desiring Statehood first asks Congress for admission. If and when Congress chooses, it passes an **enabling act**, an act directing the people of the territory to frame a proposed State constitution. A territorial convention prepares the constitution, which is then put to a popular vote in the proposed State. If the voters approve the document, it is submitted to Congress for its consideration. If Congress still agrees to Statehood after reviewing the proposed constitution, it passes an **act of admission**, an act creating the new State. If the President signs the act, the new State enters the Union.

The two newest States, Alaska and Hawaii, shortened the usual admission process. Each adopted a proposed constitution without waiting for an enabling act, Hawaii in 1950 and Alaska in 1956. Both became States in 1959.

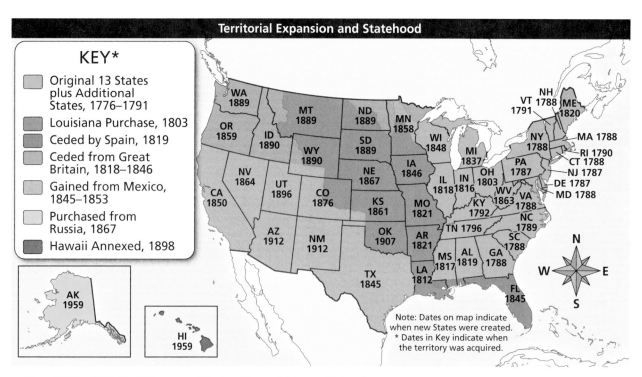

Territorial Expansion and Statehood

KEY*

- Original 13 States plus Additional States, 1776–1791
- Louisiana Purchase, 1803
- Ceded by Spain, 1819
- Ceded from Great Britain, 1818–1846
- Gained from Mexico, 1845–1853
- Purchased from Russia, 1867
- Hawaii Annexed, 1898

WA 1889
MT 1889
ND 1889
MN 1858
NH
VT 1788 1791
ME 1820
OR 1859
ID 1890
SD 1889
WI 1848
NY 1788
MA 1788
RI 1790
CT 1788
WY 1890
IA 1846
MI 1837
PA 1787
NJ 1787
NV 1864
UT 1896
NE 1867
IL 1818
IN 1816
OH 1803
WV 1863
VA 1788
DE 1787
MD 1788
CA 1850
CO 1876
KS 1861
MO 1821
KY 1792
NC 1789
AZ 1912
NM 1912
OK 1907
AR 1821
TN 1796
SC 1788
TX 1845
MS 1817
AL 1819
GA 1788
LA 1812
FL 1845

AK 1959

HI 1959

N
W E
S

Note: Dates on map indicate when new States were created.
* Dates in Key indicate when the territory was acquired.

>> From 1776 to 1898, the U.S. acquired the land from which new States were eventually formed. **Analyze Maps** From which acquisition were the most States formed?

Conditions for Admission Before finally admitting a new State, Congress has often set certain conditions. For example, in 1896, Utah was admitted on condition that its constitution outlaw polygamy, the practice of having more than one spouse at a time. In admitting Alaska to the Union, Congress forever prohibited that State from claiming title to any lands legally held by any Native American.

Each State enters the Union on an equal footing with each of the other States. Thus, although Congress can set certain conditions like those just described, it cannot impose conditions of a political nature. For example, when Oklahoma was admitted to the Union in 1907, Congress said the State could not move its capital from Guthrie to any other place before 1913. In 1910, however, the Oklahoma legislature moved the State's capital to Oklahoma City. When that step was challenged, the Supreme Court held, in *Coyle* v. *Smith* (1911) that Congress can set conditions for a prospective State's admission, but those conditions cannot be enforced if they compromise the independence of a State to manage its own internal affairs.

Consider one more example: President **William Howard Taft** vetoed a resolution to admit Arizona to the Union in 1911. He did so because Arizona's proposed constitution provided that members of the State's judiciary could be recalled (removed from office) by popular vote. This provision meant, said Taft, that in deciding cases a judge would have to keep one eye on the law and the other on public opinion. In response to the President's concern, Arizona removed the recall section from the document. In 1912 Congress passed, and the President signed, another act of admission for Arizona. Almost immediately after admission, however, the new State amended its new constitution to provide for the recall of judges. That provision remains a valid part of Arizona's constitution today.

☑ **IDENTIFY STEPS IN A PROCESS** What are the usual steps required to admit a new State to the United States of America?

States and Federal Government Sharing Resources

Remember, federalism produces a dual system of government, one in which *two* basic levels operate over the same people and the same territory at the

>> Passed in 1971, the Alaska Native Claims Settlement Act gave Alaska Natives title to lands they had used for generations. The United States paid them to give up claims to other lands.

"Sorry, but all my power's been turned back to the states."

>> A superhero, representing the Federal Government, is ineffective due to a shift in power to the States. **Analyze Political Cartoons** How does the Constitution prevent this from happening?

>> In 1984, the Federal Government withheld partial funding for highway maintenance to encourage States to raise the minimum drinking age to 21. States depend on federal funds for road repairs.

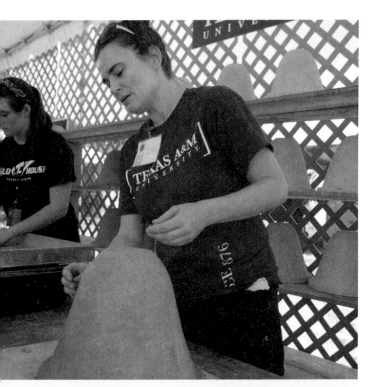

>> The Morrill Act established land-grant colleges, such as Texas A & M, to provide a practical education to students. Classes originally covered agriculture, military science, and engineering.

same time. As a result of this complex arrangement, competition, tensions, and conflict are a regular and ongoing part of American federalism. In short, the American federal system is much like a tug-of-war, a continuing power struggle between the National Government and the States.

The American federal system also involves a broad area of *shared* powers. That is, in addition to the two separate spheres of power held and exercised by the two basic levels of government, there are large and growing areas of cooperation between them.

Federal Grants-in-Aid Perhaps the best known examples of this intergovernmental cooperation are the many federal **grants-in-aid programs**—grants of federal money or other resources to the States and their cities, counties, and other local units. Many of these governments are regularly strapped for funds; these grants often help them perform a large share of their everyday functions.

The history of grants-in-aid goes back more than 200 years, to the period before the Constitution. In the Northwest Ordinance, the Congress under the Articles of Confederation provided for the government of the territory beyond the Ohio River and set aside sections of land for the support of public education in those future States.

On through the nineteenth century, most States received grants of federal lands for a number of purposes: schools and colleges, roads and canals, flood control work, and several others. A large number of the major State universities, for example, were founded as land-grant colleges. These schools were built with the money that came from the sale of public lands given to the States by the Morrill Act of 1862.

Congress began to make grants of federal money quite early, too. In 1808, it gave the States $200,000 to support the militia, the forerunner of the present-day National Guard. Cash grants did not play a large role, however, until the Depression years of the 1930s. Many of the New Deal programs aimed at bringing the nation out of its economic crisis were built around grants of money.

Since then, Congress has set up hundreds of grants-in-aid programs. In fact, more than 1,000 are now in operation. Dozens of programs function in a variety of areas: education, mass transit, highway construction, healthcare, and many others.

Grants-in-aid are based on the National Government's taxing power. The Constitution gives Congress that power in order

TYPES OF FEDERAL GRANTS TO STATES

BLOCK

Funds used for **BROAD PURPOSES** where States have freedom to decide how to spend the money.

EXAMPLES
- Social Services
- Transportation
- Education

CATEGORICAL

Funds used for **CLOSELY DEFINED PURPOSES** with conditions set by Federal Government.

EXAMPLES
- Construction of airports
- Distribution of school lunches
- Construction of wastewater plants
- Support for senior centers

PROJECT

Funds used for **INDIVIDUAL PROJECTS** that States, localities, and private agencies compete for.

EXAMPLES
- Research into diabetes treatments
- Implementation of an innovative educational program
- Digitization of a local library

>> Congress has the implied power to make grants-in-aid to States and their local governments. **Analyze Charts** What kinds of organizations might receive a block grant?

to pay the Debts and provide for the common Defense and general Welfare of the United States. . . .

—Article I, Section 8, Clause 1

Today, these grants total in the hundreds of billions and account for about a third of all State and local government spending each year.

In effect, grants-in-aid blur the division-of-powers line in the federal system. They make it possible for the Federal Government to operate in many policy areas in which it would otherwise have no constitutional authority—for example, in such fields as education, low-income housing, local law enforcement, and mental health.

Critics of grants-in-aid have long made this point. They also argue that the grants, which usually come with strings attached, often give Washington a major—and, they say, an unwarranted—voice in the making of public policy at the State and local levels. Conversely, proponents of grants-in-aid maintain that the many programs and projects made possible by grants-in-aid offset any negatives associated with the funds.

Types of Federal Grants Today, Congress appropriates money for three types of grants-in-aid: categorical grants, block grants, and project grants.

Over time, most grants have been categorical. **Categorical grants** are made for some specific, closely defined purpose—for school lunches or for the construction of airports or wastewater treatment plants, for example. Categorical grants are usually made with conditions attached. These "strings" require the State to (1) use the federal monies only for the specific purpose involved; (2) make its own monetary contribution, often a matching amount but sometimes much less; (3) provide an agency to administer the grant; and (4) obey a set of guidelines tailored to the particular purpose for which the monies are given.

Block grants have come into wide use over the last several years. They are made for much more broadly defined purposes than are categorical grants—for healthcare, social services, or welfare, for example. They are also made with fewer strings attached, so State and local governments have greater freedom in deciding just how and on what to spend block grant dollars. From the 1980s on, many programs once supported by separate and fragmented categorical grants have been merged into broader block grants.

Congress also provides money for **project grants**. These are grants made to States, localities, and sometimes private agencies that apply for the grants. The Department of Health and Human

Services makes many project grants—through its National Institutes of Health, for example, to support scientists engaged in research on cancer, diabetes, neurological disease, and other medical issues. Many State and local governments also apply for these grants to fund their job training and employment programs.

Other Forms of Federal Aid The National Government aids the States in several other important ways. For example, the FBI gives extensive help to State and local police. The army and the air force equip and train each State's National Guard units. The Census Bureau's data are essential to State and local school, housing, and transportation officials as they plan for the future.

Many other forms of aid are not nearly so visible. "Lulu payments," for example, are federal monies that go to local governments in those areas in which there are large federal landholdings. These direct payments are made in lieu of (to take the place of) the property taxes that those local governments cannot collect from the National Government. These payments are also known as PILTs (payment in lieu of taxes).

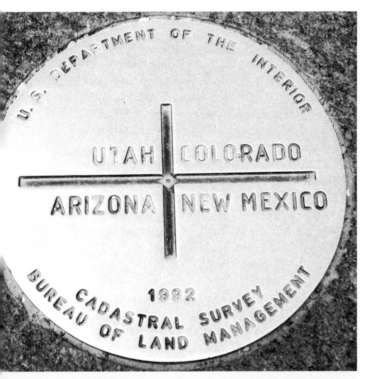

>> The Four Corners monument marks the legally accepted intersection of Arizona, New Mexico, Utah and Colorado. The location was surveyed in 1868 and was upheld by the Supreme Court in 1925.

State Aid to the National Government
Intergovernmental cooperation is a two-way street. That is, the States and their local governments also aid the National Government in many ways. Thus, State and local election officials conduct national elections. These elections are financed with State and local funds, and they are regulated largely by State laws.

The legal process by which foreign-born residents can become citizens, called naturalization, takes place most often in State courts. The examples go on and on.

☑ **INTERPRET** In what way is the American government like a "tug of war?"

Agreements Among States

The Constitution Reduces Interstate Frictions
Rivalries, conflicts, and jealousies among the newly independent States were a principal reason for the adoption of the Constitution. The fact that the new document strengthened the hand of the National Government, especially with regard to interstate trade, reduced many of those frictions. So, too, did several of the new Constitution's provisions dealing with the States' relationships with one another.

Interstate Compacts No State can enter into any treaty, alliance, or confederation, says the Constitution. However, the States can, with the consent of Congress, enter into **interstate compacts**—agreements among themselves and with foreign states.

The States made few of these agreements for several decades—only 36 of them by 1920. The number has grown steadily since then, however. New York and New Jersey led the way in 1921 with a pact creating what is now the Port Authority of New York and New Jersey to manage the harbor facilities bordering both States. Hundreds of compacts are now in force; and many involve several States and more and more are related to environmental issues.

There are several interstate compacts that all 50 States have signed onto, such as the Compact for the Supervision of Parolees and Probationers and the Compact on Juveniles. These two compacts enable States to share important law-enforcement data.

Other agreements cover a widening range of subjects. They include pacts that coordinate the development and conservation of such resources as water, oil, wildlife, and fish; counter the effects of global climate change; and encourage the cooperative use of public universities.

☑ **ANALYZE INFORMATION** For what purpose have all fifty States joined together in interstate compacts?

How the Law Crosses State Lines

In Article IV, Section 1, the Constitution commands that: "Full Faith and Credit shall be given in each State to the public Acts, Records, and judicial Proceedings of every other State."

The term *public acts* refers to the laws of a State. *Records* refers to such documents as birth certificates, marriage licenses, deeds to property, car registrations, and the like. The words *judicial proceedings* relate to the outcome of court actions: damage awards, the probating of wills, divorce decrees, and so forth.

The **Full Faith and Credit Clause** most often comes into play in court matters. Take this example: José sues Daniel in California, and the California court awards José $50,000 in damages.

Daniel cannot escape payment of the damages by moving to Nevada, because José could simply ask the Nevada courts to enforce the damage award. Nor would the case have to be retried in Nevada. Instead, the Nevada courts would have to give full faith and credit to—recognize and respect the validity of—the judgment made by the California court.

In a similar vein, a person can prove age, place of birth, marital status, title to property, and similar facts by securing the necessary documents from the State where the record was made. The validity of these documents will be recognized in each of the 50 States.

Exceptions The Full Faith and Credit Clause is regularly observed, and it usually operates routinely between the States. There are two notable exceptions to the rule, however. First, it applies only to *civil*, not *criminal*, matters. One State cannot enforce another State's criminal law. Second, full faith and credit need not be given to certain divorces granted by one State to residents of another State.

On the second exception, the key question is always this: Was the person who obtained the divorce in fact a resident of the State that granted it? If so, the divorce will be accorded full faith and credit in other States. If not, the State granting the divorce

>> When Richard and Mildred Loving were married in 1958, interracial marriage was illegal in some States. In 1967, the Supreme Court ruled that all States must recognize interracial marriage.

did not have the authority to do so, and another State can refuse to recognize it.

Marriage and Divorce The matter of interstate "quickie" divorces has been troublesome for decades, and especially since the Supreme Court's decision in a 1945 case, *Williams* v. *North Carolina*. In that case, a man and a woman traveled to Nevada, where each wanted to obtain a divorce so they could marry one another. They lived in Las Vegas for six weeks, the minimum period of State residence required by Nevada's divorce law. The couple were granted their divorces, were married, and returned to North Carolina the next day.

Problems arose when that State's authorities refused to recognize their Nevada divorces. North Carolina brought the couple to trial and a jury convicted each of them of the crime of bigamous cohabitation (marrying and living together while a previous marriage is still legally in effect).

On appeal, the Supreme Court upheld North Carolina's denial of full faith and credit to the Nevada divorces. It ruled that the couple had not in fact established *bona fide*—good faith, valid—residence in Nevada. Rather, the Court held that the couple had remained legal residents of North Carolina. In short, it found that Nevada lacked the authority to grant their divorces.

A divorce granted by a State court to a *bona fide* resident of that State must be given full faith and credit in all other States. To become a legal resident of a State, a person must intend to reside there permanently, or at least indefinitely. Clearly, the Williamses had not intended to do so.

The *Williams* case, and later ones like it, have cast dark clouds of doubt over the validity of thousands of other interstate divorces. The later marriages of people involved in these divorces, and the frequently tangled estate problems produced by their deaths, suggest the serious nature of the matter.

Same-Sex Marriage For years, the legality of same-sex marriages also posed an exception to the Full Faith and Credit Clause, though some argued that it should not. The controversy began in 2003, when the Supreme Judicial Court of Massachusetts held that same-sex couples had exactly the same marriage rights as those enjoyed by male-female couples in Massachusetts. Soon after, the States of Connecticut (2005) and then New Jersey and New Hampshire (2007) came to the same position. The

movement gradually gained momentum over the following years, with the legalization of same-sex marriages by 17 States in 2014 alone. A year later, by court decision, legislation, or ballot initiative, 37 States and the District of Columbia had legalized same-sex marriages within their borders. The last State to do so was Florida, where a district judge ruled the State's ban on same-sex unions to be unconstitutional in early 2015.

Throughout the early 2000s, one question related to same-sex marriage arose again and again: If a same-sex couple, legally married to one another in one State, moves to a State where those unions are outlawed, does the Full Faith and Credit Clause require the second State to recognize the validity of that couple's marriage?

That thorny question finally reached the Supreme Court in 2013, in the case of *United States* v. *Windsor*. In a 5–4 decision, the justices ruled that same-sex couples who were legally married in any State would be treated as married by the Federal Government—even if they lived in a State which did not recognize same-sex marriage. In other words, anyone who was legally married in any State could receive federal tax, health, and pension benefits.

That decision overturned part of the existing Defense of Marriage Act (DOMA), which had been enacted in 1996. DOMA declared that only those marriages that unite a man and a woman are legal in the United States. It also provided that no State can be required to give full faith and credit to any same-sex marriage performed in any other State.

While *U.S.* v. *Windsor* struck down part of DOMA, it did not comment on the constitutionality of same-sex marriage. The Supreme Court took that historic step in 2015, in the landmark case *Obergefell* v. *Hodges*, in which it legalized same-sex marriage throughout the nation. The ruling effectively invalidated DOMA and any remaining State laws banning same-sex marriage. It also meant that every State must now recognize lawful same-sex marriages performed in other States.

☑ **APPLY CONCEPTS** Barnaby stole a car in one State and fled to another. The State in which he stole the car demanded that the State in which he now resides must enforce its law against auto theft. Does the Full Faith and Credit Clause apply in this situation?

>> James Obergefell, the plaintiff in *Obergefell* v. *Hodges*, speaks to reporters following the Supreme Court's decision to legalize same-sex marriage.

Extradition

Definition of Extradition The Constitution makes provisions for those who flee to another State to avoid punishment for a crime:

> A Person charged in any State with Treason, Felony, or other Crime, who shall flee from Justice, and be found in another State, shall on Demand of the executive Authority of the State from which he fled, be delivered up, to be removed to the State having Jurisdiction of the Crime.
>
> —Article IV, Section 2, Clause 2

This clause refers to **extradition**, the legal process by which a fugitive from justice in one State can be returned to that State. Extradition is designed to prevent a person from escaping justice by fleeing a State.

>> James Earl Ray assassinated Martin Luther King, Jr., in June of 1968. Less than two months later, he was caught in England with a fake Canadian passport and extradited to the United States.

Changes in Extradition Law The return of a fugitive from justice is usually a routine matter; governors regularly approve the extradition requests they receive from other States' chief executives. Some of those requests, however, are contested. This is especially true in cases with strong racial or political overtones, and in cases of parental kidnapping of children involved in custody disputes.

Until the 1980s, governors could, and on occasion did, refuse to return fugitives. In *Kentucky* v. *Dennison* (1861) the Supreme Court had held that the Constitution did not give the Federal Government any power with which to compel a governor to act in an extradition case. So, for more than a century, the Constitution's word *shall* in the Extradition Clause had to be read as "may."

The Court overturned that ruling in 1987, however. In *Puerto Rico* v. *Branstad*, a unanimous Court held that the federal courts can indeed order an unwilling governor to extradite a fugitive.

☑ **SUPPORT IDEAS WITH EXAMPLES** Provide an example of a situation in which the return of a fugitive from justice might be contested.

>> Convicted murderer Chadrick Fulks being escorted from Indiana to West Virginia by U.S. Marshals in 2013, in order to assist the FBI in their search for the body of one of his victims.

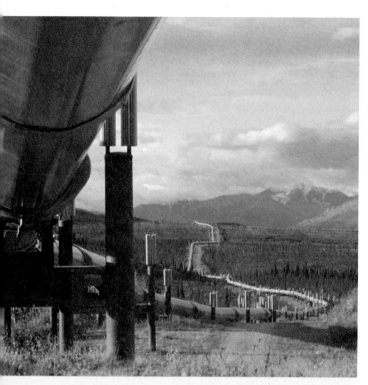

>>In the three years it took to complete the Trans-Alaska pipeline, workers on the project from Alaska and other States earned high salaries and endured brutal conditions.

Privileges and Immunities

The Constitution also protects citizens who move between the States.

> The Citizens of each State shall be entitled to all Privileges and Immunities of Citizens in the several States.

—Article IV, Section 2, Clause 1

This clause, known as the **Privileges and Immunities Clause**, means that no State can draw unreasonable distinctions between its own residents and those who happen to live in another State.

States must recognize the right of Americans to travel in or become a resident of that State. It must also allow any citizen, no matter where he or she lives, to use its courts and make contracts; buy, own, rent, or sell property; or marry within its borders.

Unreasonable Distinctions However, a State cannot do such things as try to relieve its unemployment problems by requiring employers to hire in-State residents first. Thus, the Supreme Court struck down an Alaskan law requiring employers

to prefer Alaskan workers to construct that State's oil and gas pipelines (*Hicklin* v. *Orbeck*, 1978). The Court overturned a California law that set the welfare benefits for new residents from States with lower welfare benefit levels at a lower level than those paid to long-term residents (*Saenz* v. *Roe*, 1999).

Reasonable Distinctions The Privileges and Immunities Clause does allow States to draw *reasonable* distinctions between its own residents and those of other States. Thus, any State can require that a person live within the State for some time before he or she can vote or hold public office. It also can require some period of residence before one can be licensed to practice law, medicine, dentistry, and so on.

In another example, wild fish and game in a State are considered common property of the people of that State. So, a State can require nonresidents to pay higher fees for fishing or hunting licenses than those paid by residents—who pay taxes to provide fish hatcheries, enforce game laws, and so on. Similarly, State colleges and universities can set higher tuition rates for out-of-State students.

☑ **APPLY CONCEPTS** Describe an example of reasonable distinction under the Privileges and Immunities Clause.

☑ ASSESSMENT

1. **Generate Explanations** The Constitution requires the National Government to "guarantee to every State in this Union a Republican Form of Government," but the Supreme Court has refused to define the term "Republican Form of Government." Why is this the case?

2. **Infer** Would it be legal for Congress to allow a territory of the United States to become a full State on the condition that it choose a new governor? Why or why not?

3. **Identify Cause and Effect** Federal grants of land were common during the 19th century, but cash grants-in-aid were not made until the next century. What was the reason for this change?

4. **Infer** What might keep a State from accepting a categorical grant-in-aid?

5. **Apply Concepts** When Wilma moved from Tennessee to Michigan, she expected no legal obstacles to buying or renting a home in Michigan. Was Wilma correct? Why?

GO ONLINE to www.SavvasRealize.com and access your digital course

Use the following online resources to practice citizenship skills and prepare for the Topic Test.

Case Studies

Current Connections

Quest Inquiries

Quizzes

Interactivities

Texts

Flipped Videos

While online you can also check the progress you've made learning the topic and course content by viewing your grades, test scores, and assignment status.

LESSON SUMMARIES
Use these Lesson Summaries, and the longer versions available online, to review the key ideas for each lesson in this Topic.

Lesson 1: An Overview of the Constitution

The Constitution creates a strong national government. It is built around the principles of popular sovereignty, limited government, and separation of powers. Its first three articles establish the three branches of the Federal Government. Other articles outline how to amend the Constitution and define the role of State governments.

Lesson 2: Amending the Constitution
The Constitution provides a process for making formal amendments, or changes. Since 1789, 27 amendments have been ratified by the States, including the ten that make up the Bill of Rights. Constitutional change can also happen without amendment, through legislation, executive action, court decisions, custom, and other means.

Lesson 3: Federalism: Powers Divided
Federalism is a system of government that divides power between a central government and state or provincial governments, as the Constitution specifies. Federal powers include managing foreign affairs, providing for defense, coining money, and regulating commerce. State powers include nearly all other functions of government.

Lesson 4: The National Government and the States

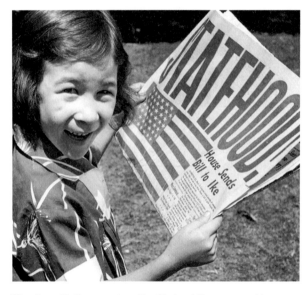

The Constitution requires the Federal Government to defend the States and guarantee that they have republican forms of government. States, likewise, are required to honor one another's public acts and records and must extradite fugitives to other States. States are also forbidden to discriminate against residents of other States.

VISUAL REVIEW

Use these graphics to review some of the key terms, people, and ideas from this Topic.

THE FORMAL AMENDMENT PROCESS

By Congress	By a National Convention
• **Proposal** by a 2/3 vote in each house of Congress • **Ratification** by 3/4 of State legislatures or by conventions in 3/4 of the States	• **Proposal** by a national convention called by Congress • **Ratification** by 3/4 of State legislatures or by conventions in 3/4 of the States

The Bill of Rights

1	Freedom of religion, speech and press; rights of assembly and petition
2	The right to maintain a militia, bear arms
3	Housing of troops
4	Search and seizure; warrants; probable cause
5	Rights of those accused of crimes; just compensation
6	Right to a speedy and fair trial
7	The right to trial by jury in civil cases
8	No excessive bail or fines; no cruel or unusual punishment
9	Rights held by the people not listed here
10	Powers retained by the States and the people

Basic Principles of the Constitution

Popular Sovereignty	The people give the government its power.
Limited Government	Government has only those powers that the people give it.
Separation of Powers	The powers of government are split among the judicial, legislative, and executive branches.
Checks and Balances	Each branch has the power to check the other two branches.
Judicial Review	The courts have the power to determine if government actions violate the Constitution.
Federalism	The powers of government are divided between the Federal Government and the States.

Division of Power

FEDERAL POWERS	CONCURRENT POWERS	STATE POWERS
• Coin money • Declare war • Make laws that are "necessary and proper" • Regulate interstate commerce • Control immigration • Acquire territory • Conduct diplomatic relations with other countries	• Levy and collect taxes • Borrow money • Establish courts • Define crimes and set punishments • Claim private property for public use • Establish a police force • Set environmental and health standards	• Maintain public schools • License drivers • Ratify amendments to the Constitution • Regulate elections • Set speed limits • Exercise those powers not given to the Federal Government and not restricted by the Constitution

Topic 3 Assessment

KEY TERMS, PEOPLE, AND IDEAS

1. Define **federalism**.

2. What is **judicial review**, and why is it an important principle?

3. What are **expressed powers** and **implied powers**? Give an example of each.

4. How do **reserved powers** and **concurrent powers** differ?

5. What does the concept of **popular sovereignty**, also known as the consent of the governed, mean?

6. How are the concepts of **limited government** and **rule of law** related?

7. How does the **Bill of Rights** protect individual rights?

8. What does **separation of powers** refer to?

CRITICAL THINKING

9. **Evaluate** How do the Constitution and its amendments reflect the political principles of rule of law, checks and balances, separation of powers, republicanism, democracy, and federalism?

10. **Compare** the roles of the expressed, implied, concurrent, and reserved powers in the American federalist system of government.

11. **Analyze Primary Sources** How did civil rights and civil liberties expand over time? Use examples from the Constitution, which you can find in the reference section of this textbook, to support your answer.

12. **Contrast** How does the Constitution safeguard and limit individual rights?

13. **Discuss** Prepare notes for a class discussion on the structure and function of the legislative branch as described in Article I of the Constitution.

14. **Analyze** the structure and function of the executive branch as described in Article II of the Constitution.

15. **Analyze** the structure and function of the judicial branch as described in Article III of the Constitution.

16. **Draw Conclusions** This table lists the first ten amendments to the Constitution, known as the Bill of Rights. Why are these ten amendments so important to the American system of government? Which Constitutional principles do they uphold?

The Bill of Rights

1	Freedom of religion, speech and press; rights of assembly and petition
2	The right to maintain a militia, bear arms
3	Housing of troops
4	Search and seizure; warrants; probable cause
5	Rights of those accused of crimes; just compensation
6	Right to a speedy and fair trial
7	The right to trial by jury in civil cases
8	No excessive bail or fines; no cruel or unusual punishment
9	Rights held by the people not listed here
10	Powers retained by the States and the people

17. **Evaluate** Summarize the rights protected by the Constitution and the Bill of Rights. Which right or rights do you think are the most important to protect? Give details to defend your answer.

18. **Interpret** Why are *McCulloch* v. *Maryland* (1819) and *Fletcher* v. *Peck* (1810) considered to be landmark Supreme Court cases?

19. **Summarize** How are power and responsibility distributed, shared, and limited by the Constitution?

20. **Writing Activity** Describe the founding ideals and principles in American constitutional government. In your opinion, which principle or principles have been the most significant in shaping our system of government? Use details and reasoning to defend your position.

DOCUMENT-BASED QUESTIONS

Discussion over the extent of the powers of the National Government began during the debate over ratification of the Constitution. Today, that debate continues, as some of the documents here illustrate.

DOCUMENT A

On June 4, 1788, George Mason spoke before the Virginia ratifying convention about the proposed constitution.

> The very idea of converting what was formerly confederation, to a consolidated Government, is totally subversive of every principle which has hitherto governed us. This power is calculated to annihilate totally the State Governments. Will the people of this great community submit to be individually taxed by two different and distinct powers? Will they suffer themselves to be doubly harassed? These two concurrent powers cannot exist long together; the one will destroy the other: The General Government being paramount to, and in every respect more powerful than, the State governments, the latter must give way to the former.
>
> —*George Mason, Speech to the Virginia ratifying convention, 1788*

DOCUMENT B

This cartoon comments on the relative power of the States versus the Federal Government.

DOCUMENT C

Chief Justice John Marshall addresses the extent of the powers of the National Government in this excerpt.

> America has chosen to be, in many respects and to many purposes, a nation, and for all these purposes her government is complete; to all these objects, it is competent. The people have declared that in the exercise of all powers given for these objects, it is supreme. . . . The Constitution and laws of a State, so far as they are repugnant to [in conflict with] the Constitution and laws of the United States, are absolutely void. These States are constituent parts of the United States. They are members of one great empire—for some purposes sovereign, for some purposes subordinate.
>
> —*Opinion of the Court, Cohens v. Virginia, 1821*

DOCUMENT D

Environmental issues have frequently caused clashes between States and the Federal Government.

> . . . I promote states' rights; I do not want an all-powerful central government. But, in certain cases, a national law is necessary. Environmental policy is one of these cases.
>
> . . . [M]any environmental issues travel across state borders. For example, mercury emissions pass over many states. Pollution from a factory in Philadelphia travels easily, infecting nearby states. Additionally, waterways do not end at state lines. Rivers, lakes, and streams flow from state to state, allowing industry-polluted water from the Rio Grande to infect not only Colorado, but also New Mexico and Texas. If one state falters on strong laws, all other states will suffer.
>
> —*Meredith Medoway, "Why the Federal Government, Not States, Should Regulate the Environment," Policy.Mic, 2012*

21. What main point is made by Document D?
    - **A.** The Federal Government should not be all-powerful.
    - **B.** It is unconstitutional for citizens to be taxed at both the State and federal levels.
    - **C.** Environmental issues cross State borders.
    - **D.** The American people have chosen a federal form of government.

22. **Analyze Political Cartoons** What point is the cartoonist making about the power of the States versus that of the Federal Government?

23. **Writing Task** Would the cartoonist (Document B) likely agree or disagree with the opinion expressed by Document A? Explain your answer in a paragraph.

The Legislative Branch

ESSENTIAL QUESTION How should government meet the needs of its people?

United States Capitol,
Washington, D.C.

Connections to Today

Ever follow the tweets of celebrities? These posts are meant to create favorable impressions and to gain our trust. In turn, we'll be more likely to support their efforts—whether it is performing or selling a brand.

Generally, public approval of and trust in Congress has been low. Congress is perceived as not doing enough or doing everything wrong. In this Topic, you'll learn about how Congress does its work. How difficult is it to transform the public will into public policy?

NBC LEARN

Explore the unusual success story of lawmaker Loretta Sanchez.

BOUNCE to Activate My Story Video

Topic 4 Overview

As Representative Thaddeus Stevens said in 1867: "this is . . . a government of the people, and . . . Congress is the people." In this Topic, you will learn about Congress—the law-making branch of the Federal Government. Look at the lesson outline and explore the drawing. As you study this Topic, you'll complete the Quest Inquiry.

LESSON OUTLINE

4.1 National Legislature Overview

4.2 The Two Houses

4.3 The Expressed Powers

4.4 The Implied and Nonlegislative Powers

4.5 Congress at Work—Organization and Committees

4.6 Congress at Work—Making Laws

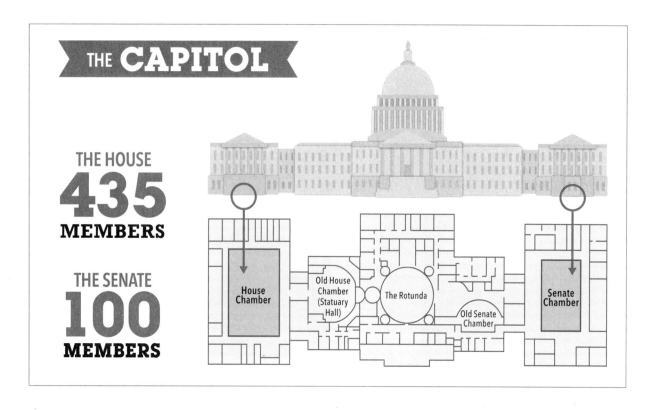

THE **CAPITOL**

THE HOUSE
435
MEMBERS

THE SENATE
100
MEMBERS

House Chamber

Old House Chamber (Statuary Hall)

The Rotunda

Old Senate Chamber

Senate Chamber

QUEST! INQUIRY

Civic Discussion: The Filibuster

These senators are resting during a marathon filibuster of civil rights legislation in 1960. A filibuster prevents a vote on a bill until at least 60 Senators agree to move forward. Is this good or bad for democracy? In this Quest, you will consider various viewpoints on that question and hold a discussion with your classmates about whether the filibuster should be abolished.

STEP 1

Read the Discussion Launch and work with your group to identify the major points in the reading.

STEP 2

Read and analyze the source documents relating to the debate. Determine the central idea of each and evaluate the authors' differing points of view.

STEP 3

Find evidence that supports your assigned position. Prepare for the discussion by formulating arguments, considering both sides of the question, and posing and responding to questions.

STEP 4

Participate in a thoughtful, well-reasoned exchange of ideas with group members. Present your arguments and evidence and consider and challenge those presented by others.

4.1

The freshman class of a new Congress poses for an official portrait on the steps of the Capitol.

 BOUNCE to Activate Flipped Video

Objectives

Explain the role of Congress.

Describe the duties performed by those who serve in Congress.

Identify the personal and political backgrounds of members of Congress.

Explain the difference between a term and a session of Congress.

Describe a situation in which the President may convene or end a session of Congress.

Describe the compensation and privileges of members of Congress.

Key Terms

delegates
trustees
partisans
politicos
bills
floor consideration
oversight function
term
session
convene
adjourn
recess
prorogue
special session
franking privilege
Luther Patrick
Nancy Pelosi
Harry Truman

National Legislature Overview

The Framers of the Constitution were well versed in the history of government. They knew that throughout world history, heads of state—usually kings—often abused their power. Indeed, the "list of grievances" in the Declaration of Independence was aimed squarely at King George III. "The history of the present King of Britain," wrote Thomas Jefferson, "is a history of repeated injuries and usurpations. . . ."

The Role of Congress in a Democracy

Because of this distrust of a powerful executive, coupled with an emerging view that just governments derive their powers from the will of the people, the colonists put great stock in representative assemblies. As alarms about oppression by the British government grew, sentiments like "no taxation without representation" reflected this belief. The nation's first such assembly was the Second Continental Congress, which governed the nation from the Declaration of Independence until the Confederation Congress convened in 1781, and was composed of delegates from every colony.

National Government The individual colonies (and later, States) put their faith in this representative body to guide them through both war with Great Britain and the United States' early days as a sovereign nation. Even so, the Framers worried about vesting too much power in a body chosen directly by the people. The average citizen can be overly passionate and driven by self-interest, they argued. So, they designed a National Government that couched the legislature's powers within both a broader system of checks and balances and a federal system where a good deal would be left to the States. It would be the job of each representative to "enlarge and refine the public views," as suggested by James Madison in *The Federalist* No. 10. It is the job of a legislator to help citizens look beyond their immediate concerns to the national interest.

☑ MAKE GENERALIZATIONS

The Framers distrusted a powerful executive, putting great trust in representative assemblies, but they were also concerned about vesting too much power in a body chosen directly by the people. Does this idea still hold true today?

Congress: The Job

One leading commentary on American politics describes Congress and the job of a member of Congress this way:

> Congress has a split personality. On the one hand, it is a lawmaking institution and makes policy for the entire nation. In this capacity, all the members are expected to set aside their personal ambitions and perhaps even the concerns of their constituencies. Yet Congress is also a representative assembly, made up of 535 elected officials who serve as links between their constituents and the National Government. The dual roles of making laws and responding to constituents' demands forces members to balance national concerns against the specific interests of their States or districts.
>
> —James M. Burns, et al., *Government by the People*

Members of both houses of Congress fulfill five major roles. They are most importantly (1) legislators and (2) representatives of their constituents.

> ❝❝
> **Congress** has a split personality. On the one hand, it is a lawmaking institution and makes policy for the entire nation. In this capacity, all the members are expected to set aside their personal ambitions and perhaps even the concerns of their constituencies. Yet Congress is also a representative assembly, made up of 535 elected officials who serve as links between their constituents and the National Government. The dual roles of making laws and responding to constituents' demands forces members to balance national concerns against the specific interests of their States or districts.
>
> —James M. Burns, et al., *Government by the People*

>> Nancy Pelosi, the first woman Speaker of the House in United States history, and President George W. Bush shake hands on the floor of the House. The Framers envisioned Congress as a body "whose wisdom may best discern the true interest of their country."

Beyond those roles, they are also (3) committee members, (4) servants of their constituents, and (5) politicians. Here, we consider their representative, committee member, and servant functions.

Representatives of the People Senators and representatives are elected to represent the people. What does that really mean? The members of both houses cast hundreds of votes during each session of Congress. Many of those votes involve quite routine, relatively unimportant matters; for example, a bill to designate a week in May as National Wildflower Week. But many of those votes, including some on matters of organization and procedure, do involve questions of far reaching importance.

Therefore, no questions about the lawmaking branch can be more vital than these: How do the people's representatives represent the people? On what basis do they cast their votes?

In broadest terms, each lawmaker has four voting options. He or she can vote as a delegate, a trustee, a partisan, or a politico.

Delegates see themselves as the agents of the people who elected them. They believe that they should discover what "the folks back home" think about an issue and vote that way. They are often willing to suppress their own views, ignore those of their party's leadership, and turn a deaf ear to the arguments of their colleagues and of special interests from outside their constituencies.

Trustees believe that each question they face must be decided on its merits. Conscience and judgment are their guides. They reject the notion that they must act as robots or rubber stamps. Instead, they call issues as they see them, regardless of the views held by a majority of their constituents or by any of the other groups that seek to influence their decisions.

Partisans believe that they owe their first allegiance to their political party. They feel duty-bound to cast their votes in line with the party platform and the views of their party's leaders. Most studies of legislators' voting behavior indicate that partisanship is the leading factor influencing lawmakers' votes on most important questions.

Politicos attempt to combine the basic elements of the delegate, trustee, and partisan roles. They try to balance these often conflicting factors: their own view of what is best for their constituents and/or the nation as a whole, the political facts of life, and the peculiar pressures of the moment.

Current Trends Which model is the most popular today? Scholars generally agree that a growing number of legislators adhere to the delegate model. This fact is largely due to the marvels of modern-day polling, which gives legislators, the media, and voters a much clearer picture of "the will of the people" than was possible in the past. In addition, the Internet has given constituents the ability to check the voting records of their legislators with a few quick clicks, making lawmakers much more accountable to the public than in earlier times. Finally, today's senators and representatives

Roles of Members of Congress

ROLES	DUTIES
Legislator	• Study proposals and draft legislation • Frame public policies
Agent of Constituents	• Be the people's representative on important matters
Committee Member	• Serve on committees that screen proposals for floor consideration
Servant of Constituents	• Assist constituents with bureaucratic and ceremonial tasks
Politician	• Balance interests of constituents and political party

>> Members of both houses of Congress have many roles to play. **Analyze Charts** Why are the legislative and agent of constituent roles the most important?

often enter Congress with the goal of remaining in Washington for years to come. Throughout the nation's early history, a stint in the House or Senate was viewed as a public service, and legislators returned to private life after a few terms. Today, however, lawmakers often view membership in Congress as a long-term career, giving rise to a new era that has been dubbed the "rise of career legislators." And of course, the surest way to stay in office is to rarely, if ever, buck public opinion.

Another recent trend is the growing tide of partisan voting. The degree to which members of the same party vote together is called the *party unity score*. That figure has reached historic levels in recent years, suggesting that the partisan model has also become prominent.

Committee Members In every session of Congress, proposed laws, known as **bills**, are referred to committees in each chamber. As committee members, senators and representatives must screen those proposals. They decide, in committee, which measures will go on to **floor consideration**— that is, be considered and acted upon by the full membership of the House or Senate.

Although Congress enacts laws and appropriates the money to implement them, the Constitution assigns the task of executing those laws to the executive branch. Congress must see that executive agencies carry out those laws faithfully and spend that money properly. It does so through the exercise of its critically important **oversight function,** the process by which Congress, through its committees, checks to see that the executive branch agencies are carrying out the policies that Congress has enacted.

Servants of the People Members of both the House and the Senate act as servants of their constituents. Most often, they do this as they (and their staff aides) try to help people in various dealings with the federal bureaucracy. Those interactions may involve a Social Security benefit, a passport application, a small business loan, or any one of a thousand other matters.

Some of "the folks back home" seem to think that members of Congress are sent to Washington mostly to do favors for them. Most members are swamped with constituent requests from the moment they take office. The range of these requests is almost without limit—everything from help in securing a government contract or an appointment to a military academy, to asking for a free sightseeing tour of Washington or even a personal loan. Consider this job description offered only half-jokingly by a former representative. He notes that every member of Congress

>> Romualdo Pacheco (R., California) served in the House from 1877 to 1883, where he passionately supported landowners' rights and laws limiting immigration.

. . . has become an expanded messenger boy, an employment agency, getter-outer of the Navy, Army, Marines, ward heeler, wound healer, trouble shooter, law explainer, bill finder, issue translator, resolution interpreter, controversy oil pourer, gladhand extender, business promoter, convention goer, civil ills skirmisher, veterans' affairs adjuster, ex-serviceman's champion, watchdog for the underdog, sympathizer with the upper dog, namer and kisser of babies, recoverer of lost luggage, soberer of delegates, adjuster for traffic violators, voter straying into Washington and into toils of the law, binder up of broken hearts, financial wet nurse, Good Samaritan, contributor to good causes—there are

>> Jeannette Rankin of Montana, the first woman elected to Congress (1916), is presented with the flag that flew at the House of Representatives during the passage of the woman's suffrage amendment in 1920.

so many good causes—cornerstone layer, public building and bridge dedicator, ship christener—to be sure he does get in a little flag waving—and a little constitutional hoisting and spread-eagle work, but it is getting harder every day to find time to properly study legislation—the very business we are primarily here to discharge, and that must be done above all things.

—Rep. Luther Patrick (D., Alabama)

Most members of Congress know that to deny or fail to respond to most of these requests would mean to lose votes in the next election. This is a key fact, for all of the roles a member of Congress plays—legislator, representative, committee member, constituent servant, and politician—are related, at least in part, to their efforts to win reelection.

A Profile of Congress Whatever else they may be, the 535 members of Congress are *not* a representative cross section of the American people. Rather, the average member is a white male in his late 50s with considerable political experience. The average senator is serving a second term, and the typical representative has served four terms. Many senators once sat in the House. And in any given Congress, several members are former governors, State legislators, or mayors. Often, a few have held Cabinet seats or other high posts in the executive branch of the Federal Government.

Women and minorities have not been well represented in Congress. No women served in the legislature until Jeannette Rankin of Montana was elected to the House of Representatives in 1916. After that, it was not until the early 1960s that women held 20 of the 535 seats in Congress. In the late 1980s, those numbers finally began to rise, but women still hold only about a quarter of the seats in Congress.

Black Americans have been even more underrepresented. The first Black Americans, Hiram Revels of Mississippi and Joseph Rainey of South Carolina, served in the Senate beginning in 1870, during the years when the Federal Government regulated elections in southern States as part of Reconstruction. After that, numbers remained in the single digits until the late 1960s. Moreover, there were long stretches during which no Black Americans sat in Congress, including one in the

>> The United States had not had a single Black senator since 1881 when Edward Brooke, shown here campaigning, was chosen to represent Massachusetts in the upper house in 1966.

Terms and Sessions of Congress

SENATE

Senate Class I

Senate Class III

Senate Class II

| JAN 1935 | JAN 1937 | JAN 1939 | JAN 1941 | JAN 1943 | JAN 1945 |

HOUSE

74th Congress — 75th Congress — 76th Congress — 77th Congress — 78th Congress

>> The Senate is divided into three equal classes so that only a third of the Senate seats may change hands in an election. **Analyze Charts** Why do you think this chart focuses on the year 1935 as its beginning point?

Senate that lasted some 90 years. Other minorities have also been underrepresented in Congress.

Nearly all members of Congress are married and most are Protestants. A large percentage are lawyers, but every Congress usually also includes a substantial number of business professionals, educators, and veterans. Nearly all have a college degree and most have advanced degrees.

Many other personal and political generalizations can be made about members of Congress. At the same time, some unconventional members also always serve, such as sheriffs, physicians, and people born outside the United States.

☑ **DISTINGUISH** A representative is preparing to vote on a bill that includes benefits for her State, but also results in greater deficit spending. Most of her constituents support the bill. Under what circumstances do you think she would choose to vote as a partisan or a trustee, rather than a delegate, on this bill?

Terms and Sessions of Congress

It is said that a woman, incensed at something her senator had done, said to him, "You know, the 535 of you people in Congress meet every two years. Well, Senator, there are some of us who think that it would be much better if just two of you met every 535 years."

Whether that story is true or not, that woman's advice has never been followed. Ever since 1789, Congress has met for two-year terms.

Terms of Congress Each **term** of Congress lasts for two years, and each of those two-year terms is

numbered consecutively (Article I, Section 2, Clause 1). Congress began its first term on March 4, 1789. That term ended two years later, on March 3, 1791.

The date for the start of each new term was changed by the 20th Amendment in 1933. In an earlier era, the several months from election to March 4 allowed for delays in communicating election results, and it gave newly chosen lawmakers time to arrange their affairs and travel to Washington. The March date gave Congress less time to accomplish its work each year, however, and by the 1930s travel and communications were no longer an issue.

Sessions of Congress A **session** of Congress is that period of time during which, each year, Congress assembles and conducts business. There are two sessions to each term of Congress—one session each year. The Constitution provides that:

> The Congress shall assemble at least once in every year, and such meeting shall begin at noon on the 3d day of January, unless they shall by law appoint a different day.
>
> —20th Amendment, Section 2

In fact, Congress often does "appoint a different day." The second session of each two-year term frequently **convenes** a few days or even a few weeks after the third of January.

Congress **adjourns,** or suspends until its next session, each regular session as it sees fit. Until World War II, the nation's lawmakers typically met for four or five months each year. Today, the many pressing issues facing Congress force it to remain

>> When Congress is not in session, the House of Representatives is empty and legislators may be working in their home States. The 2014 schedule called for Congress to be in session 113 days.

>> During a special joint session of Congress the day after the Japanese attack on Pearl Harbor, President Franklin D. Roosevelt asked Congress to declare war on Japan.

in session through most of each year. Both houses do **recess** for several short periods during a session. That is, they temporarily suspend business.

Neither house may adjourn *sine die* (finally, ending a session) without the other's consent. The Constitution provides that

> Neither House . . . shall, without the Consent of the other, adjourn for more than three days, nor to any other Place than that in which the two Houses shall be sitting.
>
> —Article I, Section 5, Clause 4

Article II, Section 3 of the Constitution does give the President the power to **prorogue** a session, but only when the two houses cannot agree on a date for adjournment. No President has ever had to use that power.

Special Sessions Only the President may call Congress into **special session** (Article II, Section 3). Only 27 of these special joint sessions of Congress have ever been held. President **Harry Truman** called the most recent one in 1948, to consider anti-inflation and welfare measures in the aftermath of World War II.

Note that the President can call Congress or either of its houses into a special session. The Senate has been called alone on nearly 50 occasions, to consider treaties or presidential appointments. The House has never been called alone.

Of course, the fact that Congress now meets nearly year-round reduces the likelihood of special sessions. That fact also lessens the importance of the President's power to call one. Still, as Congress nears the end of a session, the President sometimes finds it useful to threaten a special session if the two chambers do not act on some measure high on the administration's legislative agenda.

☑ **DRAW CONCLUSIONS** What option does the Constitution give the President if Congress adjourns without an approved budget?

Congressional Compensation

The Constitution says that members of Congress "shall receive a Compensation for their Services, to be ascertained by Law. . . (Article I Section 6, Clause 1)." That is, the Constitution says that

Congress votes for another pay raise — News item

all in favor of our congressional pay raise say Shhhhh

ED FISCHER

>> The 27th Amendment prevents any salary change for Congress taking effect during that same term. Since most members of Congress get reelected, however, they are still essentially voting themselves a pay raise. **Analyze Political Cartoons** Why would members of Congress want to avoid drawing attention to a raise in their pay?

Congress fixes its own pay. The late Senator Russell Long (D., Louisiana) once characterized this provision as one that gives to members of Congress "a power that no good man would want and no bad man should have." The 27th Amendment modified this pay-setting authority. It declares that no increase in members' pay can take effect until after the next congressional election—that is, not until after voters have had an opportunity to react to the pay raise.

Salary The salary for senators and representatives has been set at $174,000 per year since 2009. The Speaker of the House, the Vice President, and the Senate's president pro tem are paid somewhat more. Information about salaries is public and is available on the Senate and House websites.

Nonsalary Compensation Members receive a number of "fringe benefits," and some are quite substantial. For example, each member has a special tax deduction. That deduction recognizes the fact that most members of Congress must maintain two residences, one in his or her home State and one in Washington.

Generous travel allowances offset the cost of several round trips each year between home and Washington. Members pay relatively small amounts for life and health insurance and for outpatient

care by a medical staff on Capitol Hill; they can get full medical care, at very low rates, at any military hospital. They also have a generous retirement plan, to which they contribute. The plan pays a pension based on years of service in Congress, and longtime members can retire with an income of more than $100,000 per year. The lawmakers are also covered by Social Security's retirement and Medicare programs.

Members are also provided with offices in one of the several Senate and House office buildings near the Capitol and allowances for offices in their home State or district. Each member is given funds for hiring staff and for the operating costs related to running those offices. The **franking privilege** is a well-known benefit that allows them to mail letters and other materials postage-free by substituting their facsimile signature (frank) for the postage.

Congress has also provided its members with the free printing—and through franking, the free distribution—of speeches, newsletters, and the like. Radio and television tapes can be produced at very low cost. Each member can choose among several fine restaurants and two first-rate gymnasiums. Members receive still more privileges, including such things as the help of the excellent services of the Library of Congress and free parking in spaces reserved for them at the Capitol and also at Washington's major airports.

>> Those who want a seat in Congress must spend a good part of each year fundraising, in order to pay for campaign costs at election time.

Why Serve? Despite these many fringe benefits, few citizens choose to run for Congress. In addition to the costs such a venture entails, the reluctance to serve can be traced to the enormous challenges of the job, weighed against the relatively modest compensation enjoyed by the nation's lawmakers. While it is true that millions of Americans would view what members of Congress are paid as a hefty salary, the fact is that many of the men and women who serve in Congress are at the top of their professions and actually take a pay cut to serve. Several are also already millionaires. The work entails long hours and intense public scrutiny. Additionally, running for office can be expensive and exhausting and can sometimes draw a candidate's family into the fray. So why *does* anyone serve in Congress?

Many members of Congress are anxious to make a difference—to bring about changes they care about and to help their communities. In addition, the prestige of office is also an appealing part of the job. Congress, as an institution, is sometimes held in low regard, but individual members are well respected. Not everyone in office cares about being a "big shot," but many do. In fact, some speculate that Congress is filled with a disproportionately large number of folks who care about prestige. But that might not be a bad thing. Even the Framers knew that the desire to be held in high regard by constituents can serve to keep legislators, as they say, "on task."

The Politics of Pay There are only two real limits on the level of congressional pay. One is the President's veto power. The other and more potent limit is the fear of voter backlash, an angry reaction by constituents at the ballot box. That fear of election-day fallout has always made most members reluctant to vote to raise their own salaries.

Congress has often tried to skirt the politically sensitive pay question. It has done so by providing for such fringe benefits as a special tax break for those who must maintain two residences, a liberal pension plan, more office and travel funds, and other perquisites, or "perks"—items of value that are much less apparent to "the folks back home."

☑ **IDENTIFY CENTRAL ISSUES** The Constitution specifies that Congress has the power to fix its own pay. Why was it important to modify this authority with the 27th Amendment?

☑ ASSESSMENT

1. **Identify Central Issues** A poll showed voters prefer that members of Congress act as delegates. How might we expect the effect of this to differ between senators and representatives?

2. **Make Generalizations** What is the *most likely* reason that the Constitution placed limits on the President's power to convene and dismiss Congress?

3. **Interpret** In what way does Congress's oversight function provide a process of checks and balances?

4. **Support Ideas with Examples** What aspects of the National Government exemplify the Framers' plan to have representatives focused on national, rather than personal, interests?

5. **Identify Cause and Effect** Lawmakers often view membership in Congress today differently than during the nation's early history. How and why might this be reflected in the way today's members of Congress vote?

Former senators Ted Kennedy (D., Massachusetts, seated), John McCain (R., Arizona, right) and Joseph Lieberman (Indep. D., Connecticut, left) converse during a session.

The Two Houses

Article I of the Constitution directs that, "All legislative Powers herein granted shall be vested in a Congress of the United States, which shall consist of a Senate and House of Representatives." Thus, Congress is bicameral, meaning it has two houses. In election years, candidates for both houses try to win votes on social media, on Web sites, and with yard signs, billboards, flyers, buttons, and radio and television spots.

The House

The exact size of the House of Representatives—today, 435 members—is not fixed by the Constitution. Rather, it is set by Congress. The Constitution provides that the total number of seats in the House of Representatives shall be **apportioned** among the States on the basis of their respective populations (Article I, Clause 3). Each State is guaranteed at least one seat no matter what its population.

Voters in the District of Columbia, Guam, the Virgin Islands, and American Samoa each elect a delegate to represent them in the House, and Puerto Rico chooses a resident commissioner. Those officials are not full-fledged members of the House of Representatives and do not vote on bills. Despite this fact, they have played important roles throughout the years.

Terms for Representatives Article I, Section 2, Clause 1 of the Constitution provides that "Representatives shall be . . . chosen every second Year"—that is, they are elected for two-year terms. This rather short term means that, for House members, the next election is always just around the corner. That fact tends to make them pay close attention to "the folks back home."

[BOUNCE to Activate Flipped Video]

Objectives

Explain how House seats are distributed and describe the length of a term in the House.

Explain how House seats are reapportioned among the States after each census.

Describe a typical congressional election and congressional district.

Analyze the formal and informal qualifications for election to the House and the Senate.

Compare the size of the Senate to the size of the House of Representatives.

Explain how and why a senator's term differs from a representative's term.

Key Terms

apportioned
reapportion
single-member
   district
at-large
gerrymandering
off-year elections
incumbent
continuous body
constituencies
James Madison
Woodrow Wilson
Robert C. Byrd

There is no constitutional limit on the number of terms any member of Congress may serve. A considerable effort was made in the 1990s to persuade Congress to offer a constitutional amendment to limit congressional terms. Most versions of such an amendment would have put a three- or four-term limit on service in the House and a two-term limit for the Senate. The federal courts ruled these moves unconstitutional, however, because Article I says nothing about limiting congressional terms.

☑ **IDENTIFY CENTRAL ISSUES** Why did the Constitution provide that the total number of seats in the House of Representatives should be apportioned among the States based on population, rather than being set at a fixed number?

Reapportionment of Congress

Article I of the Constitution directs Congress to **reapportion** the seats in the House every ten years, after each census (Article I, Section 2, Clause 3). Until a first census could be taken, the Constitution set the size of the House at 65 seats. That many members served in the First and Second Congresses (1789–1793). The census of 1790 showed a national population of 3,929,214 persons; so in 1792, Congress increased the number of House seats by 41, to 106.

A Growing Nation As the nation's population grew over the decades, and as the number of States also increased, so did the size of the House. It went to 142 seats after the census of 1800, to 182 seats 10 years later, and so on. By 1912, following the census of 1910 and the admission of Arizona and then New Mexico to the Union, the House had grown to 435 seats.

With the census of 1920, Congress found itself in a difficult political position. The House had long since grown too large for effective floor action. To reapportion without adding seats, however, would mean that some States would have to lose seats.

Congress met the problem by doing nothing. So, despite the Constitution's command, there was no reapportionment on the basis of the 1920 census.

Reapportionment Act of 1929 Faced with the 1930 census, Congress avoided repeating its earlier lapse by passing the Reapportionment Act of 1929. That law, still on the books, sets up what is often called an "automatic reapportionment." It provides:

1. The "permanent" size of the House is 435 members. Of course, that figure is permanent only so long as Congress does not decide to change it. Congress did enlarge the House temporarily in 1959 when Alaska and then Hawaii became States.

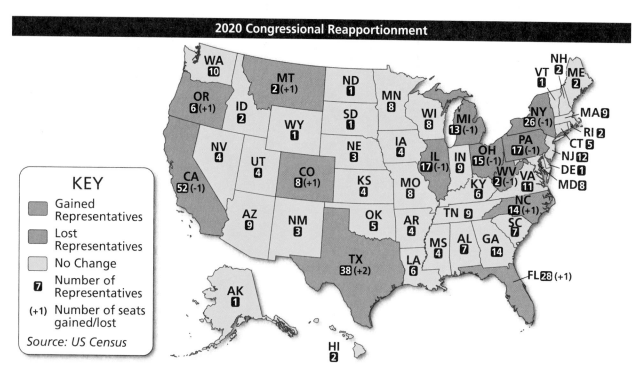

2020 Congressional Reapportionment

KEY
- Gained Representatives
- Lost Representatives
- No Change
- **7** Number of Representatives
- (+1) Number of seats gained/lost

Source: US Census

WA **10**
MT **2** (+1)
ND **1**
MN **8**
NH **2**
VT **1**
ME **2**
OR **6** (+1)
ID **2**
WY **1**
SD **1**
WI **8**
MI **13** (-1)
NY **26** (-1)
MA **9**
NV **4**
UT **4**
NE **3**
IA **4**
IL **17** (-1)
IN **9**
OH **15** (-1)
PA **17** (-1)
RI **2**
CT **5**
NJ **12**
DE **1**
CA **52** (-1)
CO **8** (+1)
KS **4**
MO **8**
KY **6**
WV **2** (-1)
VA **11**
MD **8**
AZ **9**
NM **3**
OK **5**
AR **4**
TN **9**
NC **14** (+1)
SC **7**
MS **4**
AL **7**
GA **14**
TX **38** (+2)
LA **6**
FL **28** (+1)
AK **1**
HI **2**

>> The 2020 census determined how the 435 seats in the House were reapportioned among the States. **Analyze Maps** What regions gained or lost representation? What does that tell you about those regions?

2. After each census, the Census Bureau is to determine the number of seats each State will have.

3. When the Bureau's plan is ready, the President must send it to Congress.

4. If neither house rejects the Census Bureau's plan within 60 days, it becomes effective.

The plan set out in the 1929 law has worked quite well through eight reapportionments. The law leaves to Congress its constitutional responsibility to reapportion the House, but it gives to the Census Bureau the mechanical chores and the political "heat" that go with that task.

Congressional Districts The 435 members of the House are chosen by the voters in 435 separate congressional districts across the country. Six States each have only one seat in the House. There are, then, 429 congressional districts within the other 44 States.

The Constitution makes no mention of congressional districts. For more than half a century, Congress allowed each State to decide whether to elect its members by a general ticket system or on a **single-member district** basis. Under the single-member district arrangement, the voters in each district elect one of the State's representatives from among a field of candidates running for a seat in the House from that district.

Most States quickly set up single-member districts. However, several States used the general ticket system. Under that arrangement, all of the State's seats were filled **at-large**—that is, elected from the State as a whole, rather than from particular districts. Every voter could vote for a candidate for each one of the State's seats in the House.

At-large elections proved grossly unfair. A party with even a very small plurality of voters statewide could win all of a State's seats in the House. Congress finally did away with the general ticket system in 1842. Thereafter, all of the seats in the House were to be filled from single-member districts. Since the six States with the fewest residents each have only one representative in the House, these representatives are said to be elected "at-large." Although each of them does represent a single-member district, that district covers the entire State.

Redistricting While reapportionment defines the number of congressional districts that each State will have, precisely what those districts will look like—their size and shape—is a different matter. The process of creating congressional districts in each State after the census is called redistricting.

The 1842 law that ended the general ticket system also gave each State legislature the

>> In 1812, Massachusetts governor Elbridge Gerry persuaded the State legislature to redraw districts to favor his party. Allegedly, an artist spied the new district map hanging over the desk of a newspaper editor and added a head, wings, and claws to it. "That will do for a salamander," he noted. "Better say Gerrymander," growled the editor. **Analyzing Political Cartoons** What point does the drawing make?

responsibility of drawing congressional district lines. It also required each district to be "contiguous," meaning that it must be one piece, not several disconnected pieces. In 1872, Congress added the requirement that every district boast roughly the same number of inhabitants when practical. But does "inhabitants" mean voters or residents? Many who live in a community might not be voters. In *Evenwel* v. *Abbott*, 2016, the Supreme Court ruled that the Equal Protection Clause of the 14th Amendment allows States to use total population when calculating inhabitants.

In 1901, Congress further directed that districts be made up of "compact territory." In other words, they must be comparatively small.

These requirements of contiguity, population equality, and compactness have often been disregarded by State legislatures, probably because Congress has made little effort to enforce them.

Gerrymandering Congressional district maps have often been peculiarly shaped. Some look like the letters *S* or *Y*, some resemble a squiggly piece of spaghetti, and some defy description. This is often the result of **gerrymandering**, the drawing of legislative districts for partisan advantage. That is, the odd shapes spring from an effort by the political party that controls the State legislature to gain an advantage in subsequent elections. Gerrymandering is widespread today. It is used in most places where lines are drawn for the election of public officials— not just at the congressional district level, but also in cities, counties, school districts, and elsewhere.

Most often, gerrymandering takes one of two forms. "Packing" concentrates the opposition's voters in one or a few districts, thus leaving the other districts comfortably safe for the dominant party. "Cracking" is designed to spread the opposition as thinly as possible among several districts, limiting their ability to win anywhere in the region. The goal is to create as many "safe" districts as possible— districts almost certain to be won by the party in control of the line-drawing process. The computer-driven mapmaking techniques of today make the practice more effective than ever. This is why, presently, only about 50 districts (out of 435) are competitive in any given election.

For decades, gerrymandering also led to districts that differed widely in terms of population. Most States were carved up on a rural versus urban basis, as well as a partisan one. The typical State legislature was dominated by the State's less-populated (and over-represented) rural areas.

Redistricting and the Courts The creation of districts of widely varying population sizes came to an abrupt end in the 1960s. In an historic case from Georgia, *Wesberry* v. *Sanders*, 1964, the Court held that the Constitution demands congressional districts with populations that are roughly equal in size.

This "one person, one vote" ruling had an immediate and extraordinary impact on the makeup of the House, on the content of public policy, and on the shape of electoral politics in general. The nation's cities and suburbs now speak with a much louder voice in Congress. But notice, it remains quite possible for States to draw their congressional (or any other) district lines in accord with the "one person, one vote" rule and, at the same time, to gerrymander those districts.

Political parties also use gerrymandering to minimize the voting power of racial or ethnic groups because those groups tend to vote for candidates of a particular party. Areas with a high density of Black voters, for example, have been "cracked" into several districts or "packed" into a small number.

Gerrymandering based solely on race has been found to be a violation of the 15th Amendment. But what if a State is interested in enhancing the voting strength of minority groups—perhaps to overcome historic discrimination? So-called "majority-minority districts" were drawn in some States following the 1990 census. Those districts were crafted to include a majority of Black Americans and/or Latinos and, as a result, were likely to send Black Americans and Latinos to Congress. In *Shaw* v. *Reno*, 1993, the Supreme Court struck down those race-based districts. While race can be one of many factors in drawing district lines, said the Court, it cannot be the predominate factor.

Another important redistricting case was handed down by the Supreme Court in 2017. Seeking a partisan advantage, the North Carolina legislature had packed Black Americans—who tend to vote Democratic—into two very oddly shaped districts. In *Cooper* v. *Harris*, the Court said that this use of race violates the Equal Protection Clause and provisions of the Voting Rights Act. As such, the scheme was unconstitutional.

In 2019, however, the Supreme Court ruled that claims of partisan gerrymandering lie "beyond the reach of the federal courts." In that decision, the Court noted that the courts may not second-guess decisions made by State legislators (*Rucho* v. *Common Cause* and *Lamone* v. *Benisek*). The Court also pointed out that the Framers of the Constitution gave Congress the means to curb partisan

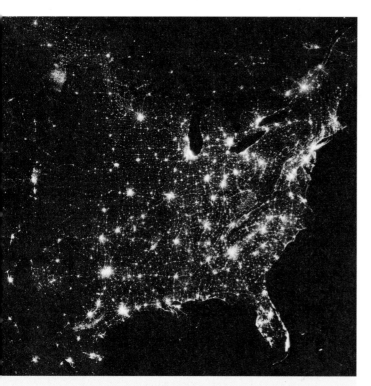

>> A view of the United States at night shows the differences in regional populations. Urban and rural populations have different needs and interests, which Congress struggles to balance.

gerrymandering in Article I Section 4, which lays out the power to "make or alter" State regulations regarding congressional elections.

Nonpartisan Redistricting Commissions

Because of the historic problems of partisan-based redistricting, many States in recent years have introduced nonpartisan commissions. In Iowa, for example, a complex computer program administered by a nonpartisan commission is used to draw geographically compact and equal districts. The State legislature then votes these districts up or down, but it cannot amend them. This process has spared Iowa from court challenges and has generally produced competitive congressional races.

In 2008, California voters passed a ballot measure allowing the creation of a nonpartisan Citizens Redistricting Commission. A significant number of other States have made similar moves. In some States, "backup commissions" have been established in the event that the State legislature is unable to agree on a redistricting plan. New research suggests that districts drawn by commissions are typically much more competitive than legislatively drawn districts. It appears that any check on State legislatures likely will have to come from this type of commission, the State courts, or Congress.

☑ **DRAW CONCLUSIONS** What impact do you think it would have on the way Congress operates if all States adopted nonpartisan redistricting commissions?

House Elections

According to the Constitution, any person whom a State allows to vote for members of "the most numerous Branch" of its own legislature is qualified to vote in congressional elections (Article I, Section 2, Clause 1). The Constitution also provides that

> The Times, Places and Manner of holding [Congressional] Elections . . . shall be prescribed in each State by the Legislature thereof; but the Congress may at any time by Law make or alter such Regulations. . . .
>
> —Article I, Section 4, Clause 1

Setting the Date Elections for Congress are held on the same day in every State. Since 1872 Congress has required that those elections be held on the Tuesday following the first Monday in November of

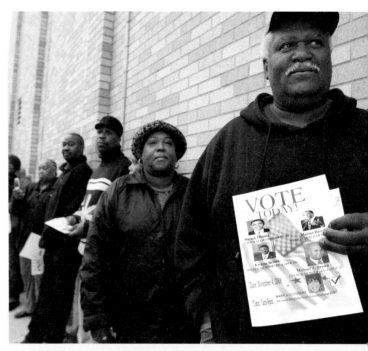

>> People wait patiently to vote in a presidential election. Gerrymandering affects the political influence of a group of people by putting them in a single district, or by splitting them among several districts.

each even-numbered year. Congress has made an exception for Alaska, which may hold its election in October. To date, however, Alaskans have chosen to use the November date.

Off-Year Elections Those congressional elections that occur in nonpresidential years—that is, between presidential elections—are called **off-year elections.**

Far more often than not, the party that holds the presidency loses seats in the off-year elections. The most dramatic example of this fact happened in the election of 1894. That year, the country was in the midst of a deep recession and railroad workers were striking. President Grover Cleveland's Democratic Party lost more than 100 seats in the House and he spent the remainder of his presidency with a Republican majority in Congress.

Generally, mid-term elections are a way for voters to express dissatisfaction with the President. But if the President's supporters are generally satisfied, they may tend to not vote in off-year elections. This results in better turnout among opponents, and thus a loss of seats in Congress for the President's party.

☑ **INFER** The author has stated that "far more often than not, the party that holds the presidency loses seats in the off-year elections." What can you infer causes this loss?

Qualifications for Office in the House

You know that there are 435 members of the House of Representatives, and that each one of them had to win an election to get there. Each one of them also had to meet two quite different sets of qualifications to win office: the formal qualifications for membership in the House set out in the Constitution and a number of informal qualifications imposed by the realities of politics.

Formal Qualifications The Constitution says that a member of the House must (1) be at least 25 years of age, (2) have been a citizen of the United States for at least 7 years, and (3) be an inhabitant of the State from which he or she is elected (Article I, Section 2, Clause 2; see also Article I, Section 6, Clause 2).

Custom, not the Constitution, also requires that a representative must live in the district he or she represents. The custom is based on the belief that the legislator should be familiar with the locale he or she represents, its people, and its problems. Rarely, then, does a district choose an outsider to represent it.

The Constitution makes the House "the Judge of the Elections, Returns and Qualifications of its own Members" (Article I, Section 5, Clause 1) Thus, when the right of a member-elect to be seated is challenged, the House has the power to decide the matter. Challenges are rarely successful.

The House may refuse to seat a member-elect by majority vote. It may also "punish its Members for disorderly Behavior" by majority vote, and "with the Concurrence of two thirds, expel a Member"(Article 1, Section 5, Clause 2).

Imposing Additional Standards For decades, the House viewed its power to judge the qualifications of members-elect as the power to impose additional standards. It did so several times. In 1900, it refused to seat Brigham H. Roberts of Utah because he was a polygamist—that is, he had more than one wife. In 1919 and again in 1920, the House excluded Victor L. Berger of Wisconsin, the first Socialist Party candidate to win a House seat. During World War I, Mr. Berger wrote several newspaper articles denouncing America's participation in that conflict. In 1919, he was convicted of sedition for obstructing the war effort and sentenced to 20 years in prison. The Supreme Court reversed that conviction in 1921. Mr. Berger was reelected to the House three more times and seated each time without challenge. In *Powell* v. *McCormack*, 1969, however, the Supreme Court held that the House could not exclude a member-elect who meets the Constitution's standards of age, citizenship, and residence. The House has not excluded anyone since that decision.

Over the years, the House has expelled very few members. Three were ousted in 1861 for their "support of rebellion." Michael Myers (D., Penn.) was expelled for corruption in 1980. James Traficant (D., Ohio) was ejected after his conviction for bribery, fraud, and tax evasion in 2002. Over time, a few members have resigned to avoid almost certain expulsion. For example, Randy "Duke" Cunningham (R., Calif.) resigned after pleading guilty to bribery charges in 2005.

The House has not often punished a member for "disorderly Behaviour," but such actions are not nearly so rare as expulsions. For example, the House voted to reprimand Addison Graves Wilson (R., South Carolina) in 2009 for interrupting President Obama's remarks before a joint session of Congress, calling it a "breach of decorum" that "degraded the proceedings" of Congress.

Informal Qualifications The realities of politics produce a number of informal qualifications for membership in the House, beyond those

>> Victor Berger won two separate elections to the House in 1919, but was denied his seat because he opposed U.S. participation in World War I. He later served three terms in Congress.

Growth of Seats in Congress, Selected Years

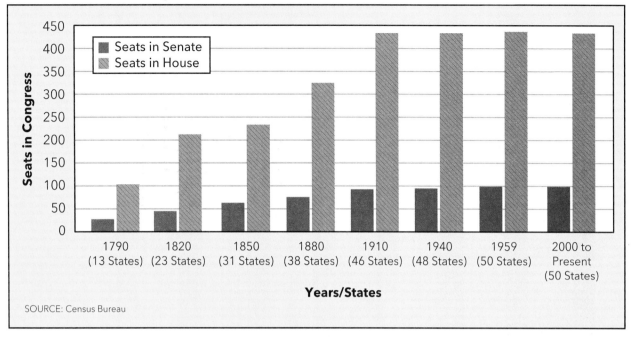

Seats in Congress

■ Seats in Senate
▨ Seats in House

Years/States

1790 (13 States), 1820 (23 States), 1850 (31 States), 1880 (38 States), 1910 (46 States), 1940 (48 States), 1959 (50 States), 2000 to Present (50 States)

SOURCE: Census Bureau

>> The number of seats in the House grew rapidly until 1929. The number of seats in the Senate grew more slowly and then leveled off. **Analyze Graphs** What are the reasons for these trends?

requirements set out in the Constitution. Those informal yardsticks vary from time to time, sometimes from State to State, and even from one congressional district to another within the same State. Clearly, some of those factors that attract or repel voters in a heavily urbanized district differ from some of those that influence how voters see candidates in a largely rural setting.

These informal qualifications have to do with a candidate's vote-getting abilities. They include such considerations as party identification, name familiarity, gender, ethnic characteristics, and political experience. Being the **incumbent,** the person who currently holds the office, almost always helps. Regularly, well over 90 percent of those members of the House who seek reelection do so successfully.

Much more so today than in the past, a candidate's fundraising abilities also figure into the mix of informal qualifications. Like all other races, congressional campaigns have become very expensive. The average amount spent on a winning bid for the House is over two million dollars. Several winners, and some losers, spend even more than that.

The "right" combination of these informal measurements will help a candidate win nomination and then election to the House of Representatives. The "wrong" mix will almost certainly spell defeat.

☑ **MAKE GENERALIZATIONS** What is the significance of the 1969 Supreme Court's decision in *Powell* v. *McCormack* to uphold the Constitution's formal qualifications of age, citizenship, and residency for a member of the House?

The Senate: Size, Election, and Terms

You should not be very surprised by these facts: A large number of the present members of the Senate once served in the House of Representatives; none of the current members of the House has ever served in the Senate. Indeed, many of the men and women who now serve in the House look forward to the day when, they hope, they will sit in the Senate. As you read, you will come to see why the Senate is often called the "upper house."

Why are there 100 members of the United States Senate? Have the members of the Senate always been elected by the voters of their States? Why do senators serve six-year terms? What qualifications must candidates for the Senate meet? Read on to find the answers to these and other questions.

Senate Size The Constitution says that the Senate "shall be composed of two senators from each State," and so the Senate is a much smaller body than the House of Representatives (Article I, Section 3, Clause 1 and the 17th Amendment). Today, however, the Senate is a much larger body than the Framers imagined. The Senate had only 22 members when it held its first session in March of 1789, and 26 members by the end of the 1st Congress in 1791. Like the House, the size of the upper chamber has grown with the country. Today, 100 senators represent the 50 States. The Framers hoped that the smaller Senate would be a more enlightened and responsible body than the House. Many of them thought that the House would be too often swayed by the immediate impact of events and by the passions of the moment, mostly because of the short term of office for members of the lower chamber. They reinforced that hope by giving senators a longer term of office and by setting the qualifications for membership in the Senate a cut above those they set for the House.

James Madison saw those provisions as "a necessary fence" against the "fickleness and passion" of the House of Representatives. Nearly a century later, **Woodrow Wilson** agreed with Madison:

> It is indispensable that besides the House of Representatives which runs on all fours with popular sentiment, we should have a body like the Senate which may refuse to run with it at all when it seems to be wrong—a body which has time and security enough to keep its head, if only now and then and but for a little while, till other people have had time to think.
>
> —Woodrow Wilson, *Congressional Government*

Each one of the 100 members of the upper house represents an entire State. That same thing can be said of only a few members of the lower house—the seven representatives from those States with only one seat in the House.

Consequently, nearly all of the members of the Senate represent a much larger and more diverse population and a much broader range of interests than do the several representatives from their State. If you look at your own State—at the size, diversity, and major characteristics of its population and at its history, geography, and economy—you will see the point.

Election to the Senate Originally, the Constitution provided that the members of the Senate were to be chosen by the State legislatures. Since the ratification of the 17th Amendment in 1913, however, senators have been picked by the voters in each State at the regular November elections. Only one senator is elected from a State in any given election, except when the other seat has been vacated by death, resignation, or expulsion.

Before the coming of popular election, the State legislatures often picked well-liked and qualified men to be senators. On other occasions, however, their choice was the result of maneuvering and infighting among the leaders of various factions in the State. These personalities all spent a great deal of energy trying to gain (and sometimes buy) enough legislators' votes to win a seat in the United States Senate. In fact, by the late 1800s, the Senate was often called the "Millionaires' Club," because so many wealthy party and business leaders sat in that chamber.

The Senate twice defeated House-passed amendments to provide for popular election. In 1912, it finally bowed to public opinion and agreed to what became the 17th Amendment the next year. The Senate was also persuaded by the fact that several

>> President Woodrow Wilson once argued, "Just what is it that America stands for? If she stands for one thing more than another, it is for the sovereignty of self-governing people."

States had already devised ways to ensure that their legislatures would choose senators who were supported by the people of the State.

Each senator is elected from the State at-large. The 17th Amendment declares that all persons whom the State allows to vote for members of "the most numerous Branch" (the larger house) of its legislature are automatically qualified to vote for candidates for the U.S. Senate.

Term of Office Senators serve for six-year terms, three times the length of those for which members of the House are chosen (Article I, Section 3, Clause 1). The Constitution puts no limit on the number of terms any senator may serve. The late **Robert C. Byrd** was first elected to the upper house in 1958 and holds the all-time record for length of service there—more than 51 years.

Senators' terms are staggered. Only a third of them—33 or 34 terms—expire every two years. The Senate is, then, a **continuous body.** That is, all of its seats are never up for election at the same time.

The six-year term gives senators somewhat greater job security than that enjoyed by members of the lower house. Those six years give senators some insulation from the rough-and-tumble of day-to-day politics. The six-year term also tends to make senators less subject to the pressures of public opinion and less susceptible to the pleas of special interests than their colleagues in the House.

The larger size and the geographic scope of their **constituencies**—the people and interests the senators represent—are designed to have much the same effect. That is to say, senators are supposed to be less concerned with the interests of some particular small locality and more focused on the "big picture" of national concerns. Indeed, senators are much more likely to be regarded as national political leaders than are most House members.

The large size of the House generally prevents representatives from gaining as much notice and public exposure as most members of the Senate attract. Senators, and especially those who have presidential ambitions, are better able to capture national media attention. Over the past several elections, the Senate has emerged as a prime source of contenders for the presidential nomination in both parties. Senators also find it easier to establish themselves as the champions of public policies that appeal to large segments of the American people— for example, social security or national health care.

Senators are also more likely to be covered by the media in their States. And they tend to have more

COMMITTEE TO RE-RE-RE-RE-RE-RE-ELECT Senator Smoot

WILOT

"We all know the Senator's position regarding term limits."

>> Many members of Congress are elected to successive terms; for them, legislating becomes a lifelong career. **Analyze Political Cartoons** What is the cartoonist's opinion about the need to limit the number of terms a member of Congress is allowed to serve?

clout in their State's politics than that enjoyed by members of the House of Representatives.

☑ **IDENTIFY CAUSE AND EFFECT** Representative Jones, acting as a delegate, votes for a spending bill favored by his constituents, even though he is not in favor of the bill. Senator Miller votes against it as a partisan, even though his constituents favor the bill. What effect does each Congressman's term length have on their voting decision?

Qualifications for Office in the Senate

A senator must meet a higher level of qualifications for office than those the Constitution sets for a member of the House. A senator must (1) be at least 30 years of age, (2) have been a citizen of the United States for at least nine years, and (3) be an inhabitant of the State from which he or she is elected (Article I, Section 3, Clause 3. Note that a senator need not have lived in the State for any particular period of time).

Senators must satisfy a number of informal qualifications for office—various extralegal

>> Congresswomen and staff members who accused Senator Bob Packwood of making inappropriate advances hold a press conference urging women to speak out about sexual harassment.

yardsticks based on such factors as party, name familiarity, gender, ethnic characteristics, and political experience. Both incumbency and a talent for fundraising are also major assets in Senate races.

The Senate can also judge the qualifications of its members when and if they are challenged, and it may exclude a member-elect by a majority vote (Article I, Section 5, Clause 1). The upper house has refused to seat someone on three occasions. It has not exercised that power since 1867, however. The chamber may also "punish its Members for disorderly Behaviour" by majority vote and "with the Concurrence of two thirds, expel a Member" (Article 1, Section 5, Clause 2).

Fifteen members of the Senate have been expelled by that body, one in 1797 and 14 during the Civil War. Senator William Blount of Tennessee was expelled in 1797 for conspiring to lead two Native American tribes, supported by British warships, in attacks on Spanish Florida and Louisiana. The 14 senators ousted in 1861 and 1862 were all from States of the Confederacy and had supported secession.

Over time, a few senators have resigned in the face of almost certain expulsion. Senator Bob Packwood (R., Oregon), for example, resigned in

1995 amid allegations of sexual harassment. In 2011, Senator John Ensign (R., Nevada) resigned from the Senate during an ongoing Senate Ethics Committee investigation into allegations that he had broken Senate rules and possibly federal law while attempting to cover up an extramarital affair with an aide. After his resignation, the committee took the rare step of referring the case to federal investigators. In the end, however, the Justice Department did not prosecute Mr. Ensign.

The punishing of a senator for "disorderly Behaviour" has also been rare. In one case in 1990, for example, the Senate formally "denounced" Senator David Durenberger (R., Minnesota). The Ethics Committee had found him guilty on several counts of financial misconduct. The Senate called Senator Durenberger's conduct "reprehensible" and declared that he had "brought the Senate into dishonor and disrepute." Senator Durenberger chose not to seek reelection to a third term in 1994.

☑ **INTERPRET** What did the Constitution intend when it provided procedures for the Senate to judge the conduct of its members?

☑ ASSESSMENT

1. **Predict Consequences** How did the 17th Amendment change the selection of senators?

2. **Support Ideas with Examples** In what way might gerrymandering thwart the purpose of members being elected on a single-member district basis?

3. **Make Predictions** What effect would you expect the 1964 Supreme Court case, *Wesberry* v. *Sanders*, to have on the likelihood of a group of small rural farmers being heard in Congress and why?

4. **Support a Point of View with Evidence** James Madison saw the organization of Congress as "a necessary fence" against the "fickleness and passion" of the House of Representatives. How does this view compare with that of the Framers?

5. **Test Conclusions** The 2020 census showed that population growth has increased in the South and West, and decreased in the Northeast and Midwest regions of the country. How do provisions in the Constitution address the shifting population?

Wesberry v. Sanders, 1964

In *Wesberry v. Sanders,* James Wesberry sued the State of Georgia for not reapportioning, or adjusting, voting districts to ensure they had populations of a similar size. Every ten years, a national census is taken to ascertain state population, which in turn is used to determine how many districts (delegates) each state will have in Congress. Even though the population in Mr. Wesberry's district grew greatly, district lines had not been adjusted in thirty years. Mr. Wesberry alleged that compared to those in less populous districts in Georgia, his vote had less impact because each district, regardless of population, elects a single representative.

As you read, look for how the Constitution is used as the basis for both the majority and dissenting opinions.

>> "One Man, One Vote" was the overall effect of the *Wesberry* v. *Sanders* decision. Here, civil rights activists advocate in 1965 for the ruling to be applied fairly in all congressional districts across the country.

Majority Opinion, Justice Hugo Black

Appellants [those appealing the decision of the lower court] are citizens and qualified voters of Fulton County, Georgia, and as such are entitled to vote in congressional elections in Georgia's Fifth Congressional District. That district, one of ten created by a 1931 Georgia statute, . . . has a population according to the 1960 census of 823,680. The average population of the ten districts is 394,312, less than half that of the Fifth. One district, the Ninth, has only 272,154 people, less than one-third as many as the Fifth. Since there is only one Congressman [In 1964, there were 14 women in Congress, but many people still referred to all members of Congress as "Congressmen."] for each district, this inequality of population means that the Fifth District's Congressman has to represent from two to three times as many people as do Congressmen from some of the other Georgia districts. . . .

. . . The complaint alleged that appellants were deprived of the full benefit of their right to vote, in violation of (1) Art. I, Section 2, of the Constitution of the United States, which provides that "The House of Representatives shall be composed of Members chosen every second Year by People of the several States . . ."; (2) the Due Process, Equal Protection, and Privileges and Immunities Clauses of the Fourteenth Amendment; and (3) that part of Section 2 of the Fourteenth Amendment which provides that "Representatives shall be apportioned [distributed] among the several States according to their respective numbers. . . .".

☑ **IDENTIFY MAIN IDEA** Why are the appellants suing the State of Georgia?

We hold that, . . . the command of Art. I, Section 2, that Representatives be chosen "by the People of the several States" means that as nearly as is practicable one man's vote in a congressional election is to be worth as much as another's. . . .

While it may not be possible to draw congressional districts with mathematical precision, that is no excuse for ignoring our Constitution's plain objective of making equal representation for equal numbers of people the fundamental goal for the House of Representatives. That is the high standard of justice and common sense which the Founders set for us.

Dissenting Opinion, Justice John Marshall Harlan

I had not expected to witness the day when the Supreme Court of the United States would render a decision which casts grave doubt on the constitutionality of the composition of the House of Representatives. . . . The Court's holding that the Constitution requires States to select Representatives either by elections at large or by elections in districts composed "as nearly as is practicable" of equal population places in jeopardy the seats of almost all the members of the present House of Representatives.

In the last congressional election, in 1962, Representatives from 42 States were elected from congressional districts. In all but five of those States, the difference between the populations of the largest and smallest districts exceeded 100,000 persons. A difference of this magnitude. . . is presumably not equality among districts "as nearly as is practicable," although the Court does not reveal its definition of that phrase. Thus, today's decision impugns [challenges] the validity of the election of 398 Representatives from 37 States, leaving a "constitutional" House of 37 members now sitting. . . .

☑ **CAUSE AND EFFECT** According to Justice Harlan's dissent, what might logically happen based on the Court's ruling that districts must have approximately equal populations?

In short, in the absence of legislation providing for equal districts by the Georgia Legislature or by Congress, these appellants have no right to the judicial relief which they seek. It goes without saying that it is beyond the province of this Court to decide whether equally populated districts is the preferable method for electing Representatives, whether state legislatures would have acted more fairly or wisely had they adopted such a method, or whether Congress has been derelict [irresponsible] in not requiring state legislatures to follow that course. Once it is clear that there is no *constitutional* right at stake, that ends the case.

☑ **IDENTIFY AUTHOR'S POINT OF VIEW** Why does Justice Harlan reject the suit by the appellants?

What is done today saps the political process. The promise of judicial intervention in matters of this sort cannot but encourage popular inertia [lack of motivation] in efforts for political reform through the political process, with the inevitable result that the process is itself weakened. . . .

☑ **ASSESSMENT**

1. **Summarize** Which statement summarizes the decision of the Supreme Court in *Wesberry* v. *Sanders*?

   A. Districts must be of similar geographic size.
   B. Districts must be of similar population size.
   C. Districts must have similar representations by Democrats and Republicans.
   D. Districts must have similar representations for different ethnic/racial groups.

2. **Analyze Information** According to Justice Harlan, how does this decision "sap the political process"?

3. **Compare and Contrast** Based on these opinions, what is the role of the Supreme Court in redistricting?

In 1968, Representative Shirley Chisholm (D., New York) became the first Black woman elected to Congress. She served in the House until 1983.

The Expressed Powers

A typical day in either chamber of Congress might suggest that there is no limit to what Congress can do. On any given day, the House might consider bills dealing with such varying matters as the interstate highway system, an increase in the minimum wage, and grazing on public lands. Meanwhile, the Senate might be considering aid to a famine-stricken country in Africa, the President's nomination of someone to fill a vacancy on the Supreme Court, or any number of other matters.

Types of Congressional Powers

Still, there are very real limits on what Congress can do. It is important to note that (1) the government in the United States is a limited government, and (2) the American system of government is federal in form. These two fundamental facts work to shape and also to limit the powers of Congress.

The Delegated Powers Congress has only those powers delegated (granted, given) to it by the Constitution. Large areas of power are denied to Congress (1) in so many words in the Constitution, (2) by the Constitution's silence on many matters, and (3) because the Constitution creates a federal system.

There is much that Congress cannot do. It cannot create a national public school system, require people to vote or attend church, or set a minimum age for marriage or drivers' licenses. It cannot abolish jury trials, confiscate all handguns, or authorize the censorship of newspapers or radio or television broadcasts. Congress cannot do these and a great many other things because the Constitution does not delegate to it any power to do so.

BOUNCE to Activate Flipped Video

Objectives

Describe the three types of powers delegated to Congress.

Understand the expressed powers of Congress.

Identify the key sources of the foreign relations powers of Congress.

Describe the power-sharing arrangement between Congress and the President on the issues of war and national defense.

List other key domestic powers exercised by Congress.

Key Terms

expressed powers
implied powers
inherent powers
commerce power
tax
public debt
deficit financing
bankruptcy
legal tender
copyright
patent
territory

eminent domain
naturalization
Hudson River
John Marshall
District of Columbia
Bill Clinton
Boston
Philadelphia
Benjamin Franklin
Lyndon Johnson
Richard Nixon

Still, Congress does have the power to do many things. The Constitution grants it a number of specific powers—and, it delegates those powers in three different ways: (1) explicitly, in its specific wording—the **expressed powers;** (2) by reasonable deduction from the expressed powers—the **implied powers;** and (3) by creating a national government for the United States—the **inherent powers.**

The Framers very purposefully created a limited government. Given that fact, it is understandable that the existence and the scope of both the implied and the inherent powers have been the subject of dispute ever since the adoption of the Constitution.

The Expressed Powers Most, but not all, of the expressed powers of Congress are found in Article I, Section 8 of the Constitution. There, in 18 separate clauses, 27 different powers are explicitly given to Congress.

These grants of power are brief. What they do and do not allow Congress to do often cannot be discovered by merely reading the few words involved. Rather, their meaning is found in the ways in which Congress has exercised its powers since 1789, and in scores of Supreme Court cases arising out of the measures Congress has passed.

As a case in point, take the Commerce Clause, in Article I, Section 8, Clause 3. It gives Congress the power "to regulate Commerce with foreign Nations, and among the several States, and with the Indian Tribes." What do these words mean? Over the past two centuries, Congress and the Court have had to answer hundreds of questions about the scope of the Commerce Clause. Here are but a few examples: Does "commerce" include people crossing State lines or entering or leaving the country? What about business practices? Working conditions? Radio and television broadcasts? The Internet? Does Congress have the power to ban the shipment of certain goods from one State to another? To prohibit discrimination? What trade is "foreign" and what is "interstate"? And what trade is neither?

In answering these and dozens of other questions arising out of this one provision, Congress and the Court have defined—and are still defining—the meaning of the Commerce Clause. So it is with most of the other constitutional grants of power to Congress.

The commerce power and, with it, the expressed power to tax have provided much of the basis upon which Congress and the courts have built nearly all of the implied powers. Most of what the Federal Government does, day to day and year to year, it does as the result of legislation enacted by Congress in the exercise of those two powers.

☑ **DESCRIBE** Explain why the Constitution limits the powers of Congress.

The Commerce Power

Commerce, generally, is the buying and selling of goods and services. The **commerce power**—the power of Congress to regulate interstate and foreign trade—is vital to the welfare of the nation. Its few words have prompted the growth of the greatest open market in the world. The Commerce Clause proved to be more useful for the building of a strong and United States out of a weak confederation than any other provision in the Constitution.

The Delegated Powers

INHERENT	EXPRESSED	IMPLIED
Inherent powers are those that belong to all sovereign nations—for example, the power to control a nation's borders.	Expressed powers are those stated in the Constitution—for example, the power to regulate both foreign and interstate commerce.	Implied powers are not stated in the Constitution, but drawn from the expressed powers. Based on the expressed power to regulate commerce, Congress has set a minimum wage for hourly workers.

>> This chart gives an example of each type of congressional power.
Analyze Charts How do these powers help to create a limited government?

>> New technologies, such as the steamboat, brought with them new legal issues and implications for the growing nation in the 1800s.

Gibbons v. Ogden, 1824 The first case involving the Commerce Clause to reach the Supreme Court, *Gibbons* v. *Ogden*, was decided in 1824. The case arose out of a clash over the regulation of steamboats by the State of New York, on the one hand, and the Federal Government, on the other. In 1807, Robert Fulton's steamboat, the *Clermont*, had made its first successful run up the **Hudson River**, from New York City to Albany. The State legislature then gave Fulton an exclusive, long-term grant to navigate the waters of the State by steamboat. Fulton's monopoly then gave Aaron Ogden a permit for steamboat navigation between New York City and New Jersey.

Thomas Gibbons, operating with a coasting license from the Federal Government, began to carry passengers on a competing line. Ogden sued, and the New York courts ruled in his favor, holding that Gibbons could not sail by steam in New York waters.

Gibbons appealed that ruling to the Supreme Court. He claimed that the New York grant conflicted with the congressional power to regulate interstate commerce. The Court agreed. It rejected Ogden's argument that "commerce" should be defined narrowly, as simply "traffic" or the mere buying and selling of goods. Instead, the Court read the Commerce Clause in very broad terms. Chief Justice **John Marshall,** speaking for the majority, wrote:

Commerce, undoubtedly, is traffic, but it is something more; it is intercourse. It describes the commercial intercourse between nations, and parts of nations, in all its branches, and is regulated by prescribing rules for carrying on that intercourse.

—*Gibbons* v. *Ogden*, 1824

The Court's ruling was widely popular at the time because it dealt a death blow to steamboat monopolies. Freed from restrictive State regulation, many new steamboat companies came into existence. As a result, steam navigation developed rapidly. Within a few years, the railroads were similarly freed, which revolutionized transportation within the United States.

Over the decades, the Court's sweeping definition of commerce has brought an extension of federal authority into many areas of American life—a reach of federal power beyond anything the Framers could have imagined.

As another of the many examples of the point, note this: It is on the basis of the commerce power that the Civil Rights Act of 1964 prohibits discrimination in access to or service in hotels, motels, theaters, restaurants, and in other public accommodations on grounds of race, color, religion, or national origin.

The Supreme Court upheld this use of the commerce power in *Heart of Atlanta Motel* v. *United States* in 1964. The unanimous Court noted that there was "overwhelming evidence of the disruptive effect that racial discrimination has had on commercial intercourse."

Limits on the Commerce Power The congressional power to regulate commerce is not unlimited. It, too, must be exercised in accord with all other provisions in the Constitution. As but one example: the Supreme Court struck down the Gun-Free School Zone Act of 1990 in *United States* v. *Lopez,* 1995. That act had made it a federal crime for anyone other than a police officer to possess a firearm in or around a school. The Court could find no useful connection between interstate commerce and guns at school. It held that Congress had in this case invaded the reserved powers of the States.

In more specific terms, the Constitution places four explicit limits on the use of the commerce power. The Constitution declares that Congress

1. cannot tax exports (Article I, Section 9, Clause 5);

2. cannot favor the ports of one State over those of any other in the regulation of trade (Article I, Section 9, Clause 6);

3. cannot require that "Vessels bound to, or from, one State be obliged to enter, clear, or pay Duties in another" (Article I, Section 9, Clause 6); and finally,

4. could not interfere with the trade in enslaved people until at least the year 1808 (Article I, Section 9, Clause 1). This last limitation, part of the curious Slave-Trade Compromise the Framers struck at Philadelphia, has been a dead letter for more than two centuries.

☑ **ANALYZE INFORMATION** What was the long-term impact of *Gibbons* v. *Ogden* on the commerce power of Congress?

The Money Powers

Congress has several expressed powers related to money, including the power to tax, the power to borrow, the power to establish laws on bankruptcy, and the power to coin money. These congressional powers have played an important role in the forming of our nation.

The Power to Tax The Constitution gives Congress the power

> To lay and collect Taxes, Duties, Imposts and Excises, to pay the Debts and provide for the common Defense and general Welfare of the United States. . . .

—Article I, Section 8, Clause 1

The Articles of Confederation had not given Congress the power to tax. Congress did have the power to requisition funds from the States; that is, Congress could ask (in reality, beg) each of the 13 States for money.

But, through the 1780s, not a single State came even remotely close to meeting the few requests that Congress made, and a number of them paid nothing at all. The government was impotent, and the lack of a power to tax was a leading cause for the creation of the Constitution.

The Purpose of Taxes Here are a number of important points regarding the taxing power: The Federal Government takes in trillions of dollars each year. The vast majority of that money comes from the various taxes levied by Congress.

A **tax** is a charge levied by government on persons or property to raise money to meet public needs. But notice, Congress does sometimes impose taxes for other purposes as well. The protective tariff is perhaps the oldest example of this point. Although

>> Because of the Court's broad interpretation of the Commerce Clause, Congress can regulate practices that disrupt commerce, such as lack of accessibility.

HISTORICAL SNAPSHOT OF FEDERAL TAXES

1800 100%=$10.8 million

		1% VETERANS' BENEFITS	
55.7% MILITARY	31.3% INTEREST ON PUBLIC DEBT		12.4% ALL OTHER

1900 100%=$521 million

36.6% MILITARY	8% INTEREST	27.1% VETERANS' BENEFITS	28.6% ALL OTHER	

2000 100%=$1.8 trillion

			3% VETERANS' BENEFITS	
16.5% MILITARY	12.5% INTEREST	59.7% HEALTH, SOCIAL SECURITY, & PUBLIC WELFARE		8.3% ALL OTHER

SOURCE: Treasury Department

>> The way the Federal Government spends tax revenues has changed over time.
Analyze Charts What 2000 category(ies) of spending did not exist in 1800 or 1900?

it does bring in some revenue every year, its real goal is to "protect" domestic industry against foreign competition by increasing the cost of imported goods.

Taxes are also sometimes levied to protect the public health and safety. The Federal Government's regulation of narcotics is a case in point. Only those who have a proper federal license can legally manufacture, sell, or deal in those drugs—and licensing is a form of taxation.

Limits on the Taxing Power Congress does not have an unlimited power to tax. As with all other powers, the taxing power must be used in accord with all other provisions of the Constitution. Thus, Congress cannot lay a tax on church services, for example—because such a tax would violate the 1st Amendment. Nor could it lay a poll tax as a condition for voting in federal elections, for that would violate the 24th Amendment.

More specifically, the Constitution places four explicit limitations on the congressional power to tax:

1. Congress may tax only for public purposes, not for private benefit. Article I, Section 8, Clause 1 says that taxes may be levied only "to pay the Debts and provide for the common Defence and general Welfare of the United States. . . ."

2. Congress may not tax exports. Article I, Section 9, Clause 5 declares "[n]o Tax or Duty shall be laid

on Articles exported from any State." Thus, customs duties (tariffs), which are taxes, can be levied only on goods brought into the country (imports), not on those sent abroad (exports).

3. Direct taxes must be apportioned among the States, according to their populations:

> No Capitation, or other direct, Tax shall be laid, unless in Proportion to the Census of enumeration herein before directed to be taken.

—Article I, Section 9, Clause 4

A direct tax is one that must be paid directly to the government by the person on whom it is imposed—for example, a tax on the ownership of land or buildings, or a capitation (head or poll) tax.

An income tax is a direct tax, but it may be laid without regard to population:

> The Congress shall have power to lay and collect taxes on incomes, from whatever source derived, without apportionment among the several States, and without regard to any census or enumeration.

—16th Amendment

"I assure you, Madam, that every penny you pay in taxes goes straight into the government's pocket."

>> An IRS agent assures a taxpayer that every cent she pays "goes straight into the government's pockets." **Analyze Political Cartoons** What is ironic about his statement?

>> The war in Iraq cost trillions of dollars, much of which was borrowed and must now be repaid with interest.

Wealth (which translates to the ability to pay taxes) is not evenly distributed among the States. So, a direct tax levied in proportion to population would fall more heavily on the residents of some States than it would on others—and would, therefore, be grossly unfair. Consequently, Congress has not levied any direct tax—except for the income tax—outside the **District of Columbia** since 1861.

Article I, Section 8, Clause 1 provides that "all Duties, Imposts and Excises shall be uniform throughout the United States." That is, all indirect taxes levied by the Federal Government must be levied at the same rate in every part of the country. Those indirect taxes include the federal levies on gasoline, alcoholic beverages, and tobacco products.

As a general rule, an indirect tax is one first paid by one person but then passed on to another. It is indirectly paid by that second person. Take, for example, the federal tax on cigarettes. It is paid to the Treasury by the tobacco company but is then passed on through the wholesaler and retailer to the person who finally buys the cigarettes.

The Borrowing Power Article I, Section 8, Clause 2 gives Congress the power "[t]o borrow Money on the credit of the United States." There are no constitutional limits on the amount of money Congress may borrow and no restrictions on the purposes for borrowing.

The Treasury does the actual borrowing. Usually, it issues Treasury Notes (T-bills) for short-term borrowing and bonds for long-term purposes. Those securities are, in effect, promissory notes—IOUs—for which the government agrees to pay investors a certain sum plus interest on a certain date.

Congress has put a statutory ceiling on the public debt, however. The **public debt** is all of the money borrowed by the Federal Government over the years and not yet repaid, plus the accumulated interest on that money. That legal ceiling has never amounted to much more than a political gesture, however. Congress regularly raises the limit whenever the debt threatens to overtake it.

For decades, the Federal Government has practiced **deficit financing**. That is, it regularly spends more than it takes in each year and then borrows to make up the difference. Thus, the government has relied on deficit financing—on borrowing—to deal with the economic Depression of the 1930s, to meet the extraordinary costs of World War II, and to pay for wars and social programs over the decades since then.

In fact, the government's books showed a deficit in all but seven years from 1930 to 1969. And they were in the red every year from 1969 to 1998. A concerted effort by a Republican-controlled Congress and President **Bill Clinton** curbed the soaring debt and produced four straight years of budget surpluses from 1998 to 2002. In subsequent years, however, deficits once again became the norm.

Congress has been entrusted with determining how much debt the country should carry, always bearing in mind the cautionary words of President George Washington in his Farewell Address: "As a very important source of strength and security, cherish public credit. One method of preserving it is to use it as sparingly as possible."

The Bankruptcy Power Article I, Section 8, Clause 4 gives Congress the power "[t]o establish . . . uniform Laws on the subject of Bankruptcies throughout the United States." A bankrupt individual or company or other organization is one a court has found to be insolvent—that is, unable to pay debts in full. **Bankruptcy** is the legal proceeding in which the bankrupt's assets—however much or little they may be—are distributed among those to whom a debt is owed. That proceeding frees the bankrupt from legal responsibility for debts acquired before bankruptcy.

The States and the National Government have concurrent power to regulate bankruptcy. Today, however, federal bankruptcy law is so broad that it all but excludes the States. Nearly all bankruptcy cases are now heard in federal district courts.

The Currency Power Article I, Section 8, Clause 5 gives Congress the power "[t]o coin Money [and] regulate the Value thereof." The States are expressly denied that power. (Article I, Section 10, Clause 1)

Until the Revolution, the English money system, built on the shilling and the pound, was in general use in the colonies. With independence, that stable currency system collapsed. The Second Continental Congress and then the Congress under the Articles issued paper money. Without sound backing, and with no taxing power behind it, however, the money was practically worthless. Each of the 13 States also issued its own currency. Adding to the confusion, people still used English coins, and Spanish money circulated freely in the southern States.

Nearly all the Framers agreed on the need for a single, national system of "hard" money. So the Constitution gave the currency power to Congress, and it all but excluded the States from that field. Currency is money in any form when it is in use as a medium of exchange. From 1789 on, among the most important of all of the many tasks performed by the Federal Government has been that of providing the nation with a uniform, stable monetary system.

>> Cooperation between the Clinton-Gore administration and Republican senators like Bob Dole (left) and Newt Gingrich (right) helped keep the national debt in check for four years.

From the beginning, the U.S. has issued coins in gold, silver, and other metals. Congress chartered the first Bank of the United States in 1791 and gave it the power to issue bank notes—that is, paper money. Those notes were not legal tender, however. **Legal tender** is any kind of money that a creditor must by law accept in payment for debts.

Congress did not create a national paper currency, and make it legal tender, until 1862. Its new national notes, known as Greenbacks, had to compete with other paper currencies already in the marketplace. Although the States could not issue paper money themselves, State governments could and did charter (license) private banks, whose notes did circulate as money. When those private bank notes interfered with the new national currency, Congress (in 1865) laid a ten percent tax on their production. The private bank notes soon disappeared. The Supreme Court upheld the 1865 law as a proper exercise of the taxing power in *Veazie Bank* v. *Fenno,* 1869.

At first, the Greenbacks could not be redeemed for gold or silver. Their worth fell to less than half their face value on the open market. Then, in 1870, the Supreme Court held their issuance to be unconstitutional. In *Hepburn* v. *Griswold* it said "to coin" meant to stamp metal and so the Constitution

> "To promote the Progress of Science and useful Arts, by securing for limited Times to Authors and Inventors the exclusive Right to their respective Writings and Discoveries."

—Article I, Section 8, Clause 8

T. A. EDISON.
Electric-Lamp.

No. 223,898.   Patented Jan. 27, 1880.

>> A patent drawing by Thomas Edison for an improvement to electric lamps. By assigning rights to intellectual property, patents and copyrights encourage creativity and progress.

did not authorize the National Government to issue paper money.

The Court soon changed its mind, however, in the *Legal Tender Cases* in 1871 and again in *Juliard* v. *Greenman* in 1884. In both cases, it held the issuing of paper money as legal tender to be a proper use of the currency power. The Court also declared this a power properly implied from both the borrowing and the war powers.

☑ **IDENTIFY STEPS IN A PROCESS**
What steps would you expect that President Clinton and a Republican-controlled Congress took in order to produce four years of budget surpluses from 1998 to 2002?

Other Domestic Powers

The other expressed powers relate to domestic matters. Each of them has a direct and a considerable effect on the daily lives of the American people.

Copyrights and Patents The Constitution gives Congress the power

> To promote the Progress of Science and useful Arts, by securing for limited Times to Authors and Inventors the exclusive Right to their respective Writings and Discoveries.

—Article I, Section 8, Clause 8

A **copyright** is the exclusive right of an author to reproduce, publish, and sell his or her creative work. That right may be assigned—transferred by contract—to another, as to a publishing firm by mutual agreement between the author and the other party.

Copyrights are registered by the Copyright Office in the Library of Congress. Under present law, they are good for the life of the author plus 70 years. They cover a wide range of creative efforts: books, magazines, newspapers, musical compositions and lyrics, dramatic works, paintings, sculptures, cartoons, maps, photographs, motion pictures, sound recordings, and much more. The Office registers hundreds of thousands of copyrights each year.

The Copyright Office does not enforce the protections of a copyright. If the holder thinks a copyright has been violated, he or she may bring a suit for damages in the federal courts.

A **patent** grants a person the sole right to manufacture, use, or sell "any new and useful process, machine, manufacture, or composition of matter, or any new and useful improvement thereof." A patent is good for up to twenty years. The term of a patent may be extended only by a special act of Congress. The Patent and Trademark Office in the Department of Commerce administers patent laws.

Patent protection has played an important role in fostering competition and entrepreneurship. Having a patent often increases the value of an invention, scientific discovery, or technological advancement. Many industries, particularly pharmaceuticals, have grown and experienced economic success due to the patents that they hold. A patent can also increase the value of a company and gives that company a competitive advantage for a period of time. In short, the patent system produces monetary incentives to pursue inventions and to make important scientific discoveries.

The Postal Powers Article I, Section 8, Clause 7 gives Congress the power "[t]o establish Post Offices and Post roads"—in effect, the power to provide for the carrying of the mail. "Post roads" are all postal routes, including rail lines, airways, and waters within the United States, during the time mail is being carried on them.

Carrying the mail is among the oldest of all governmental functions. Its origins date back at least to Egyptian practice before 4000 B.C. The first post office in America was established in **Boston** in 1639, by the General Court of the Massachusetts Bay Colony. The first successful postal system in the colonies, the Penn Post, was begun by William Penn in 1683. He established a post office in **Philadelphia** and provided a regular weekly service along a 30-mile route from there to New Castle, Delaware.

The United States Postal Service traces its history back to the early colonial period. The remarkable **Benjamin Franklin** is generally recognized as the father of the present-day postal system. He served as Co-Deputy Postmaster of the British Colonies in North America from 1753 to 1774, when the British removed him from office because of his political activities. In 1775, he became, by unanimous

>> These workers are preparing a bag of mail for rail delivery. The U.S. Post Office played a crucial role in the country's westward expansion by helping businesses establish cross-country relationships.

choice of the Second Continental Congress, the first Postmaster General of the United States.

Today, the Postal Service functions as an independent agency in the executive branch. It serves the nation through tens of thousands of post offices. Hundreds of thousands of Postal Service employees handle billions of pieces of mail every year.

Congress has established a number of crimes based on the postal power. It is, for example, a federal crime for anyone to obstruct the mails or to use the mails to commit any criminal act. It has also prohibited the mailing of many items, among them poisons, explosives, intoxicating liquors, some live animals, libelous or obscene matter, lottery tickets, and any dangerous articles. Any article prohibited by a State's laws—for example, switchblade knives or firecrackers—cannot be sent into that State by mail.

The States and their local governments cannot interfere with the mails in any unreasonable way. Nor can they require licenses for Postal Service vehicles, tax the gas they use, or tax post offices or any other property of the United States Postal Service.

Territories and Other Areas In two places—in Article I, Section 8, Clause 17 and in Article IV, Section 3, Clause 2—the Constitution delegates to Congress the power to acquire, manage, and dispose of various federal areas. That power relates to the District of Columbia and to the several federal **territories,** parts of the United States that are not admitted as States and that have their own systems of government, including Puerto Rico, Guam, and the Virgin Islands. It also covers hundreds of military and naval installations, arsenals, dockyards, post offices, prisons, parks and forest preserves, and many other federal holdings.

The Federal Government may acquire property by purchase or gift. It may also do so through the exercise of the power of **eminent domain,** the inherent power to take private property for public use. Notice that the Taking Clause in the 5th Amendment restricts the Federal Government's use of the power with these words: "nor shall private property be taken for public use, without just compensation." Private property may be taken by eminent domain only (1) for a public use, (2) with proper notice to the owner, and (3) for a fair price. What in fact constitutes a public use, proper notice, or a fair price often becomes a matter for courts to decide.

Territory may also be acquired from a foreign state as the result of the exercise of the power of Congress to admit new States (in Article IV), the war powers, or the President's treaty-making power (in Article II). Under international law, any sovereign state may acquire unclaimed territory by discovery.

Weights and Measures Article I, Section 8, Clause 5 gives Congress the power to "fix the Standard of Weights and Measures" throughout the United States. The power reflects the absolute need for accurate, uniform gauges of time, distance, area, weight, volume, and the like.

In 1838, Congress set the English system of pound, ounce, mile, foot, gallon, quart, and so on, as the legal standards of weights and measures in this country. In 1866, Congress also legalized the use of the metric system of gram, meter, kilometer, liter, and so on.

In 1901, Congress created the National Bureau of Standards in the Commerce Department. Now known as the National Institute of Standards and Technology, the agency keeps the original standards for the United States. It is these standards by which all other measures in the United States are tested and corrected.

Naturalization Citizens of one country become citizens of another through a process called **naturalization**. Article I, Section 8, Clause 4 gives Congress the exclusive power "[t]o establish an uniform Rule of Naturalization," and the nation's population includes tens of millions of naturalized citizens.

Judicial Powers As a part of the system of checks and balances, the Constitution gives Congress several judicial powers. Thus, it has the power to create all of the federal courts below the Supreme Court and otherwise provide for the organization and composition of the federal judiciary.

Congress also has the power to define federal crimes and set the punishments that may be imposed on those who violate federal law. The Constitution mentions only four offenses. Three are found in Article I, Section 8: counterfeiting, piracies and felonies committed on the high seas, and offenses against international law. Treason is listed in Article III, Section 3. In addition to these, Congress has used its implied powers to establish more than 100 other federal crimes.

>> Used in the atomic clock, this device was developed by Charles Townes, James Gordon, and H.J. Zeiger (not shown). The Weights and Measures Clause lets Congress set standards for measuring time.

☑ **APPLY CONCEPTS** How do copyrights and patents "promote the Progress of Science and useful Arts?" Why do you think the Framers granted this power to Congress?

Congress and Foreign Policy

The Federal Government has greater powers in the field of foreign affairs than it does in any other area of public policy. The 50 States that comprise the Union are not sovereign, so they have no standing in international law. In short, the Constitution does not allow them to take part in foreign relations. (See Article I, Section 10, Clauses 1 and 3.)

The Constitution gives the President primary responsibility for the conduct of American foreign policy. As the Supreme Court put that point in a leading case, *United States* v. *Curtiss-Wright Export Corp.* in 1936, the chief executive is "the sole organ of the Federal Government in the field of international relations."

Still, the Constitution does give Congress a significant place in the field of foreign affairs. Its authority in that area arises from two sources: (1) from a number of the expressed powers, most especially the spending, the commerce, and the war powers; and (2) from the fact that the United States is a sovereign state in the world community. As the lawmaking body of the sovereign United States, Congress has the inherent power to act on matters affecting the security of the nation—for example, the regulation of immigration and the enactment of measures to combat terrorism here and abroad.

☑ **SUPPORT IDEAS WITH EVIDENCE** How do the foreign policy powers of the legislative and executive branches establish a system of checks and balances between these two branches of government?

>> In *United States* v. *Curtiss-Wright Export Corp.,* an American plane builder was charged with illegally selling arms to Bolivia after President Franklin D. Roosevelt had declared an embargo.

The War Powers

Six of the 27 expressed powers set out in Article I, Section 8 deal explicitly with the subject of war and national defense. Remember that here, too, Congress shares power with the chief executive. The Constitution makes the President commander in chief of the nation's armed forces, (Article II, Section 2, Clause 1) and, as such, the President dominates the field.

The congressional war powers are, however, both extensive and substantial. Only Congress can declare war. It alone has the power to raise and support armies, to provide and maintain a navy, and to make rules for the governing of the nation's military forces. Congress also has the power to provide for "calling forth the Militia" (today, the National Guard), and for the organizing, arming, and disciplining of that force. And Congress is also given

>> The U.S. Coast Guard inspects a boat suspected of smuggling illegal drugs. Administration of the Coast Guard falls under the war powers granted to Congress by Article I, Section 8.

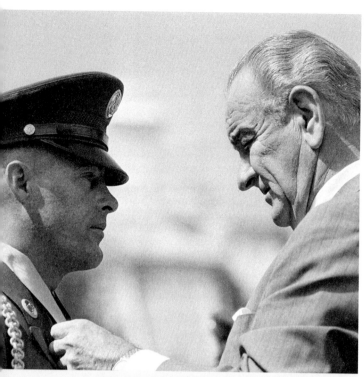

>> President Lyndon Johnson gives the Medal of Honor to Army Staff Sergeant Jennings in 1968. Congress gave Johnson power to use military force in Vietnam, later reversed in 1973.

the power to grant letters of marque and reprisal, and to make rules concerning captures on land and water.

As you think about congressional war powers, consider this question: Does the Constitution give the President the power to make war in the absence of a declaration of war by Congress? Many argue that it does not, but more than 200 years of American history argue otherwise. Indeed, most Presidents have used the armed forces of the United States abroad, in combat, without a congressional declaration of war.

In today's world, no one can doubt that the President must have the power to respond, rapidly and effectively, to any threat to the nation's security. Still, many people have long warned of the dangers inherent in a presidential power to involve the country in undeclared wars.

The War Powers Resolution In the context of the war powers of Congress, we must examine the War Powers Resolution, a statute enacted by Congress in 1973.

The war-making power as it was exercised by Presidents **Johnson** and **Nixon** during the

undeclared war in Vietnam (1964–1973) moved Congress to enact the War Powers Resolution. That law provides that the chief executive can commit American military forces to combat abroad only (1) if Congress has declared war, or (2) when Congress has specifically authorized a military action, or (3) when an attack on the United States or any of its armed forces has occurred.

If troops are ordered into combat in the third circumstance, the President is directed to report that fact to Congress within 48 hours. Any such commitment of military forces must end within 60 days, unless Congress agrees to a longer involvement. And Congress can end a commitment at any time.

The constitutionality of the War Powers Resolution remains in dispute. A determination of the question must await a situation in which Congress demands that its provisions be obeyed but the President refuses to do so.

☑ **ANALYZE INFORMATION** How is the balance of power between Congress and the President reinforced through the limits placed on the President's war powers?

☑ ASSESSMENT

1. **Describe** Describe how the meanings of the constitutional clauses that grant powers to Congress have been defined.

2. **Compare and Contrast** Compare *Gibbons v. Ogden*, 1824 and *United States v. Lopez*, 1995, and how the Commerce Clause has been interpreted by the Supreme Court in these two cases.

3. **Analyze Information** Why did the Framers explicitly grant the powers of currency, borrowing, and bankruptcy to Congress? What might be the outcome if these powers had not been granted to Congress?

4. **Apply Concepts** Describe the manner in which Congress and the President share power in the fields of foreign affairs, war, and national defense. Is the division of power reasonable?

5. **Interpret** Why did the Framers grant Congress sole power to declare war? What tensions may arise from the division of the war powers?

4.4

Senator Joseph McCarthy and his aide listen to proceedings at a 1954 Senate investigation into alleged attempts to obtain an Army reserve officer commission for McCarthy's political ally.

The Implied and Nonlegislative Powers

What does the Constitution have to say about education? Nothing, not a word. Still, Congress provides hundreds of billions of dollars every year for the Department of Education to spend in a variety of ways throughout the country. Look around you. What indications of these federal dollars can you find in your local school? If you attend a public school anywhere in the United States, that evidence should not be hard to spot.

The Necessary and Proper Clause

How can this be? Congress has only those powers delegated to it by the Constitution, and that document says nothing about education. The answer to that question lies in the implied powers of Congress.

Implied powers are those powers that are not set out in so many words in the Constitution but are, rather, implied by (drawn from) those that are. The constitutional basis for the existence of the implied powers is found in one of the expressed powers. The **Necessary and Proper Clause,** the final clause in the lengthy Section 8 of Article I in the Constitution, gives to Congress the expressed power

> To make all Laws which shall be necessary and proper for carrying into Execution the

 BOUNCE to Activate Flipped Video

Objectives

Explain how the Necessary and Proper Clause gives Congress flexibility in lawmaking.

Compare the strict construction and liberal construction positions on the scope of congressional power.

Describe the ways in which the implied powers have been applied.

Describe the investigatory and executive powers of Congress.

Describe the power of Congress to impeach.

Describe the role of Congress in amending the Constitution and its electoral duties.

Key Terms

Necessary and Proper Clause	subpoena
	successor
strict constructionist	Thomas Jefferson
liberal constructionist	Alexander Hamilton
consensus	George W. Bush
appropriate	Samuel Alito
impeach	Andrew Johnson
acquit	Abraham Lincoln
perjury	Richard Nixon
censure	John Quincy Adams

foregoing Powers, and all other Powers vested by this Constitution in the Government of the United States, or in any Department or Officer thereof.

—Article I, Section 8, Clause 18

Much of the vitality and adaptability of the Constitution can be traced directly to this provision, and even more so to the ways in which both Congress and the Supreme Court have interpreted and applied it over the years. In effect, the Necessary and Proper Clause allows Congress to choose the means "for carrying into Execution" the many powers given to it by the Constitution.

The manner in which Congress has viewed the concept, together with the supporting decisions of the Supreme Court, have made the final clause in Article I, Section 8, truly the "Elastic Clause." It has earned that name, for it has been stretched so far and made to cover so much over the years.

Strict vs. Liberal Construction The Constitution had barely come into force when the meaning of the Elastic Clause became the subject of one of the most important disputes in American political history. The Framers of the Constitution intended to create a new and stronger National Government. The ratification of their plan was opposed by many, and that opposition was not stilled by the adoption of the Constitution. Rather, the conflict between the Federalists and the Anti-Federalists continued into the early years of the Republic. Much of that conflict centered on the powers of Congress and the meaning of the Elastic Clause. Just how broad, in fact, were those powers?

The **strict constructionists,** led by **Thomas Jefferson,** continued to argue the Anti-Federalist position after the ratification period. They insisted that Congress should be able to exercise (1) its expressed powers and (2) only those implied powers absolutely necessary to carry out those expressed powers. They maintained that the States should keep as much power as possible. They agreed with a quotation often attributed to Jefferson that "that government is best which governs least."

Most of these Jeffersonians did acknowledge a need to protect interstate trade, and they recognized the need for a strong national defense. At the same time, they feared the consequences of a strong National Government. They believed, for instance, that the interests of the people of Connecticut were not the same as those of South Carolinians

THE IMPLIED POWERS OF CONGRESS

THE EXPRESSED POWER TO	IMPLIES THE POWER TO
💲 LAY AND COLLECT TAXES	• Punish tax evaders • Regulate some commodities and outlaw the use of others • Set conditions to qualify for federal funding
BORROW MONEY	• Establish the Federal Reserve System of banks
CREATE NATURALIZATION LAW	• Regulate and limit immigration
RAISE ARMIES AND A NAVY	• Draft Americans into the military
REGULATE COMMERCE	• Establish a minimum wage • Ban discrimination in workplaces and public facilities • Pass laws protecting the disabled • Regulate banking
ESTABLISH POST OFFICES	• Prohibit mail fraud and obstruction of the mails • Bar the shipping of certain items through the mail

>> Modern lawmakers must try to interpret the Framers' intent in light of modern circumstances. **Analyze Charts** Without its implied powers, how effectively could Congress address new situations?

Strict vs. Liberal Constructionists

STRICT CONSTRUCTIONISTS	LIBERAL CONSTRUCTIONISTS
Thomas Jefferson	**Alexander Hamilton**
• Favored a very limited role for the new government created by the Constitution • Majority of power would remain with the States and the people • Based on a strict reading of the Necessary and Proper Clause in the Constitution to prevent the government from gaining too much power	• Favored a powerful government that could exercise implied powers • Favored vigorous executive leadership • Based on a liberal interpretation of the Constitution because the Constitution did not specifically grant the government these powers

>> Strict constructionists battled with liberal constructionists over congressional powers. **Analyze Charts** How would each want Congress to address new situations not originally anticipated?

or Marylanders or Pennsylvanians. They argued that only the States—not the far-off National Government—could protect and preserve those differing interests.

The **liberal constructionists,** led by **Alexander Hamilton,** had led the fight to adopt the Constitution. Now they favored a liberal interpretation of that document, a broad construction of the powers it gives to Congress. They believed that the country needed, as Hamilton put it in *The Federalist* No. 70, "an energetic government."

The strict constructionists were sorely troubled by that broad view of the powers of Congress. They were sure that it would all but destroy the reserved powers of the States.

Liberal Construction Prevails The Supreme Court upheld the concept of implied powers in *McCulloch* v. *Maryland* in 1819. At the time, a Maryland law required all banks not chartered by the State to print their currency on special paper stamped by the State, which amounted to a tax. James McCulloch, the cashier of the Baltimore branch of the Second Bank of the United States, refused to use the paper, claiming that States could not tax the Federal Government. The Court declared the Maryland law unconstitutional.

That victory for the liberal constructionists set a pattern that, in general, has been followed ever since. Over the years, the powers wielded by the National Government have grown to a point that even the most ardent supporters of liberal construction could not have imagined. It is impossible to see how the United States could have developed as it has over the past two centuries had the Court not ruled as it did in *McCulloch*.

Several factors, working together with the liberal construction of the Constitution, have been responsible for that marked growth in national power. They have included wars, economic crises, and other national emergencies. Spectacular advances, especially in transportation and communication, have also had a real impact on the size and the scope of government. Equally important have been the demands of the people for more and still more services from government.

Congress has been led by these and other factors to view its powers in broader and broader terms. Most Presidents have regarded their powers in like fashion. The Supreme Court has generally taken a similar position in its decisions in cases involving the powers of the National Government.

Moreover, the American people have generally agreed with a broader rather than a narrow reading of the Constitution. This **consensus,** or

>> The 2009 government bailout and subsequent takeover of failing automotive companies Chrysler, Ford, and General Motors was an example of the exercise of the doctrine of implied powers.

Get out!
New York gave me the <u>exclusive</u> right to operate steamships in New York waters.

Wrong.
New York gave the United States the <u>exclusive</u> right to regulate interstate commerce.

stus.com

>> An illustration of the conflict over interstate commerce in the case of *Gibbons* v. *Ogden.* **Analyze Political Cartoons** Did that Supreme Court ruling reflect strict or liberal constructionist views?

general agreement, has prevailed even though our political history has been marked, and still is, by controversies over the proper limits of national power.

☑ **APPLY CONCEPTS** How has the doctrine of implied powers increased the powers of Congress?

The Doctrine in Practice

The ways in which the Necessary and Proper Clause has been construed (interpreted) and applied over the last 200 years has enabled the National Government to meet the changing needs of the times. As a result, it has virtually eliminated the need for frequent amendment of the Constitution.

Instances of the exercise of the doctrine of implied powers are almost too numerous to count. The concept of implied powers has made it possible for the Government of the United States to meet any number of problems that could not possibly have been foreseen by the Framers. It does not stretch matters too much to say that, today, the Constitution's words "necessary and proper" really mean "convenient and useful."

Every exercise of implied powers must be based on at least one of the expressed powers. Thus, in *McCulloch* v. *Maryland* the Supreme Court found that the creation of the Bank of the United States was "necessary and proper" to the execution of four expressed powers held by Congress: the taxing, borrowing, currency, and commerce powers.

Over the years, Congress has most often found a basis for the exercise of implied powers in (1) the commerce power, (2) its power to tax and spend, and (3) the war powers.

The Commerce Clause The Commerce Clause gives Congress the power to regulate both foreign and interstate trade. The Supreme Court's hugely expansive reading of that provision began in 1824 with *Gibbons* v. *Ogden* when the Court found in favor of Gibbons, ruling that the State of New York could not prevent him from carrying passengers on his steamboat between New York and New Jersey. The word "commerce" has been held to include the production and the buying and selling of goods as well as the transportation of people and commodities.

Commerce has been defined so broadly that it encompasses virtually every form of economic activity today. Congress has the authority to regulate manufacturing, wages and hours, labor-management

Constitutional Limits on the Commerce Power

Congress cannot tax exports. (Article I, Section 9, Clause 5)
Congress cannot favor the ports of one State over those of any other in the regulation of trade. (Article I, Section 9, Clause 6)
Congress cannot require that "Vessels bound to, or from, one State, be obliged to enter, clear, or pay Duties in another." (Article I, Section 9, Clause 6)
Congress could not interfere with the trade in enslaved people, at least not until the year 1808 (Article I, Section 9, Clause 1). This last limitation, part of the curious Slave-Trade Compromise the Framers struck at Philadelphia, has been a dead letter for more than two centuries.

>> Congress' expressed and implied use of the commerce power is not unlimited.
Analyze Charts Why are limits on the commerce power important?

relations, foods and drugs, air travel, and much more. It can provide for the building of interstate highways, consumer protection, the protection of the environment—the list goes on and on.

In 1938, for example, Congress used its commerce power to abolish child labor when it passed the Fair Labor Standards Act, which stated, in part, that:

> "No producer, manufacturer, or dealer shall ship or deliver for shipment . . . any goods produced in an establishment . . . in or about which . . . any oppressive child labor has been employed."

In 1941 the Supreme Court upheld the law, ruling that it properly fell under the Commerce Clause because child labor and other unfair labor practices have a significant impact on interstate commerce (*United States* v. *Darby*).

Limits on the Commerce Power Still, Congress is not free to use the Commerce Clause to do whatever it chooses. The Constitution places four explicit limitations on the exercise of the commerce power. And the Supreme Court does, at least on occasion, find that the lawmaking branch has overstepped its authority under that provision. Congress cannot pass a law based solely on the grounds that a measure will somehow promote "the general Welfare of the United States." But it can and does levy taxes and provide for the spending of money for that purpose. Thus, for example, as discussed earlier, Congress **appropriates**—assigns to a particular use— hundreds of billions of dollars per year to support education. And, similarly, it does so to provide for such things as farm subsidies, unemployment

compensation, Social Security, Medicare, and a host of other programs.

The War Powers The several war powers reflect the fact that the National Government is responsible for the protection of this country against aggression and, when necessary, for the waging of war. As with its other expressed powers, Congress has the authority to do whatever is necessary and proper for the execution of its war power—with the exception that, in doing so, it cannot violate any other provision of the Constitution. Among many other examples of the point, Congress has the power to provide for compulsory military service—a draft—because Article I, Section 8 gives it the expressed power "[t]o raise and support Armies" (in Clause 12) and "[t]o provide and maintain a Navy" (in Clause 13). The Supreme Court originally upheld the constitutionality of a draft in a series of cases challenging the Selective Service Act of 1917 (*Selective Draft Law Cases*, 1918).

☑ **SUMMARIZE** Explain how Congress has used each of the following expressed powers as a basis for the exercise of implied powers: the commerce powers, the tax powers, the war powers.

The Power to Investigate

Congress has the power to investigate—to inquire into, or inform itself on—any matter that falls within the scope of its lawmaking authority. The authority to do so is implied by the Constitution's grant of the legislative power to Congress, in Article I, Section 1. Both the House and Senate exercise that power through the standing committees and their subcommittees and often through special committees, as well.

Both houses may choose to conduct investigations for any one or a number of reasons. Most often, those inquiries are held to (1) gather information necessary to the framing of legislation, (2) oversee the operations of various agencies in the executive branch, (3) focus public attention on some particular matter, (4) expose the questionable activities of some public official or private person or group, and/or (5) promote the particular interests of some members of Congress.

Notice that the second of these motives, oversight, is a little-noted but quite important aspect of the constitutional system of checks and balances. Note, too, that Congress is more inclined to exercise its oversight function when one or both of its chambers is controlled by the party that does not hold the presidency.

Exercising Oversight Over the years, Congress has improved its ability both to inform itself and to perform its oversight responsibilities by increasing the staff resources available to the standing committees of both houses. The three little-known agencies in the legislative branch which also add to that capability are:

1. the Congressional Budget Office, which committees of both houses rely on quite heavily in taxing, spending, and other budget-related matters;
2. the Congressional Research Service, in the Library of Congress, whose several hundred staff specialists provide members with factual information on virtually any subject; and
3. the Government Accountability Office, also called Congress' watchdog because it has broad authority to monitor the work of the Federal Government and report its findings to Congress.

One notable investigation was a year-long Senate probe into the activities of intelligence agencies beginning in 1975. The investigation revealed that the CIA, FBI, and NSA had abused their powers by wiretapping, monitoring mail, and otherwise monitoring U.S. citizens. The investigation led to the creation of a special court to ensure oversight of surveillance activities. Another example is a lengthy House probe related to the 2012 attack on an American diplomatic building in Benghazi, Libya, and the Obama administration's handling of the events before and after the attack. In its final report, the House Select Committee on Benghazi issued a rebuke to officials in the State Department, the Defense Department, and the Central Intelligence Agency.

Examples of Senate Rejections of Cabinet Nominees

PRESIDENT	NOMINEE, YEAR	POSITION	REASON FOR REJECTION
Andrew Jackson	Roger B. Taney, 1834	Secretary of the Treasury	The pro-bank majority in the Senate rejected Taney, who planned to dismantle the Second Bank of the United States.
John Tyler	Caleb Cushing, 1843	Secretary of the Treasury	The Senate Whig majority opposed President Tyler and rejected his nominations in contentious and partisan voting.
	David Henshaw, 1844	Secretary of the Navy	
	James M. Porter, 1844	Secretary of War	
	James S. Green, 1844	Secretary of the Treasury	
Dwight Eisenhower	Lewis L. Strauss, 1959	Secretary of Commerce	Rejected due to Strauss's antagonistic treatment of the Senate Commerce Committee members during his confirmation hearings.
George H. W. Bush	John G. Tower, 1989	Secretary of Defense	Allegations of misconduct led to Tower's rejection.

SOURCE: Senate.gov

>> Even though it has not occurred often, Congress has rejected several presidential cabinet nominees. **Analyze Charts** How does the political climate play a role in the reason for rejection?

Congressional Influence

CONGRESSIONAL CHECKS ON THE PRESIDENTIAL TREATY-MAKING POWER			
The Senate approves high-level appointments by the President, including the secretary of state, as well as ambassadors to foreign nations, who often play a role in the treaty-making process.	The President often consults with members of Congress as he makes treaties with other nations.	Presidents may need to make changes in a treaty at the behest of Congress. This ensures that there is broad consensus for any such agreement among the American people.	Even after a treaty has been approved, Congress can abrogate (repeal) it by passing a law that is inconsistent with its terms, or by directing the President to abrogate.

>> Congressional powers related to treaties are part of the checks and balances built into our political system. **Analyze Charts** Why is it important for Congress to have these powers?

☑ **APPLY CONCEPTS** From what source does Congress get its investigative powers? List the five main reasons that committees in Congress conduct investigations.

Executive Powers

The Constitution gives two executive powers to the Senate. One of those powers has to do with appointments to office, and the other with treaties (Article II, Section 2, Clause 2).

Appointments All major appointments made by the President must be confirmed by the Senate by majority vote. Each of the President's nominations is referred to the appropriate standing committee of the Senate. That committee may then hold hearings to decide whether or not to make a favorable recommendation to the full Senate for that appointment. When the committee's recommendation is brought to the floor of the Senate, it may be, but seldom is, considered in executive (secret) session.

The appointment of a Cabinet officer or of some other top member of the President's "official family" is rarely rejected by the Senate. It is worth noting, however, that during times of divided government, the confirmation process can be characterized by a great deal of partisanship and contention. But throughout history, the Senate has rejected only a few Cabinet appointments. One such rejection came in 1989, when the Senate refused President George H.W. Bush's nomination of John Tower as secretary of defense. More commonly, the President will withdraw a nomination if the Senate sends signals that it will reject the nominee. In 2005, for example, President **George W. Bush** withdrew the nomination of Harriet Miers, his White House Counsel, to the Supreme Court. He later nominated **Samuel Alito,** who was confirmed by the Senate.

During the President's appointment of federal officers who serve in the various States (for example, U.S. attorneys and federal marshals), the unwritten rule of "senatorial courtesy" comes into play. The Senate will turn down such a presidential appointment if it is opposed by a senator of the President's party from the State involved. The Senate's observance of this unwritten rule has a significant impact on the President's exercise of the power of appointment; in effect, this rule means that some senators virtually dictate certain presidential appointments.

Treaties The President makes treaties "by and with the Advice and Consent of the Senate, . . . provided two thirds of the Senators present concur" (Article II, Section 2, Clause 2). For a time after the adoption of the Constitution, the President asked the advice of the Senate when a treaty was being negotiated and prepared. Now the President most often consults the members of the Senate Foreign Relations Committee and other influential senators of both parties.

The Senate may accept or reject a treaty as it stands, or it may decide to offer amendments, reservations, or understandings to it. Treaties are sometimes considered in executive session. Because the House has a hold on the public purse strings, influential members of that body are often consulted in the treaty-making process, too.

☑ **SUMMARIZE** What is the unwritten rule of senatorial courtesy and how does it affect the President's power of appointments?

Impeachment

The Constitution provides that the President, Vice President, and all civil officers of the United States may "be removed from Office on Impeachment for, and Conviction of, Treason, Bribery, or other high Crimes and Misdemeanors." (Article II, Section 4) A close reading of those words suggests that the Framers expected that only serious criminal offenses, not political disagreements, would lead to impeachment.

The House has the sole power to **impeach**—to accuse, bring charges. The Senate has the sole power to try—to judge, to sit as a court—in impeachment cases. (Article I, Section 2, Clause 5; Section 3, Clause 6)

Impeachment requires only a majority vote in the House; conviction requires a two-thirds vote in the Senate. The Chief Justice presides over the Senate when a President is to be tried. The penalty for conviction is removal from office. The Senate may also prohibit a convicted person from ever holding federal office again; and he or she can be tried in the regular courts for any crime involved in the events that led to the impeachment. To date, there have been some twenty impeachments and only a few convictions; all of the people removed by the Senate were federal judges.

Three Presidents have been impeached by the House: **Andrew Johnson** in 1868, Bill Clinton in 1998, and Donald Trump in 2019 and 2021. The Senate voted to **acquit** in all four instances—that is, it returned a verdict of not guilty.

Andrew Johnson The unsuccessful attempt to remove Andrew Johnson grew out of the turmoil that followed the Civil War. Mr. Johnson had become the nation's 17th President when **Abraham Lincoln** was assassinated in April of 1865, and he soon became enmeshed in a series of disputes with the Radical Republicans who controlled both houses of Congress. Many of those disagreements centered around the treatment of the defeated Southern States in the immediate post-war period.

President Johnson tried to carry out the conciliatory Reconstruction policies favored by Abraham Lincoln—policies that Mr. Lincoln has summarized in these memorable words in his Second Inaugural Address on March 4, 1865: "With malice toward none, with charity for all... " The Radical Republicans supported a much harsher approach to Reconstruction.

Matters came to a head when Congress passed the Tenure of Office Act, over the President's veto, in 1867. President Johnson's violation of that law triggered his impeachment by a House bent on political revenge. The Senate fell just one vote short of removing him from office.

Richard Nixon A few officeholders have resigned in the face of almost certain impeachment—most notably, **Richard Nixon**, who resigned the presidency in mid-1974. President Nixon's second term in office was cut short by the Watergate scandal.

The term *Watergate* comes from a June 1972 attempt by Republican operatives to break into the Democratic Party's national headquarters in the Watergate office complex in Washington, D.C. The investigation of that incident, by the *Washington Post* and then by other media, led to official investigations by the Department of Justice and by the Senate's Select Committee on Presidential Campaign Activities, popularly known as the Senate Watergate Committee.

The probes unearthed a long list of illegal acts, including bribery, perjury, income tax fraud, and illegal campaign contributions. They also revealed the use of the Federal Bureau of Investigation, the Internal Revenue Service, and other government agencies for personal and partisan purposes.

The House Judiciary Committee voted three articles of impeachment against President Nixon in

>> Richard Nixon makes a "V" for victory sign following his 1974 resignation. He first used the trademark gesture after his nomination as the 1968 Republican presidential candidate.

late July 1974. He was charged with obstruction of justice, abuse of power, and failure to respond to the Judiciary Committee's **subpoenas.** A committee's subpoena is a legal order directing one to appear before that body and/or to produce certain evidence. Mr. Nixon had ignored the committee's subpoena of several tape recordings of Watergate-related conversations in the Oval Office.

It was quite apparent that the full House would impeach the President and that the Senate would convict him. Those facts prompted Mr. Nixon to resign the presidency on August 9, 1974.

Beyond doubt, the Watergate scandal involved the most extensive and the most serious violations of public trust in the nation's history. Among its other consequences, several Cabinet officers, presidential assistants, and others were convicted of various felonies and misdemeanors—and many of them served jail time.

Bill Clinton Bill Clinton was impeached by the House in 1998. In proceedings steeped in partisanship, the House voted two articles of impeachment against him on December 19. Both articles arose out of the President's admitted "inappropriate relationship" with a White House intern. The first article charged the President with **perjury**—that is, lying under oath. The second article accused him of obstruction of justice because he had withheld information about his affair with the intern.

Members of the House who supported the articles of impeachment contended that the acts of lying under oath and of withholding evidence were within the meaning of the Constitution's phrase "other high Crimes and Misdemeanors." Therefore, they argued, the President's immediate removal from office was justified.

Their opponents argued that the facts involved in the case did not justify either charge. They insisted that, while the President's conduct was deplorable and should be condemned, that conduct did not rise to the level of an impeachable offense. Many of them pressed, instead, for a resolution to **censure** the President—that is, for a formal condemnation of his behavior.

The Senate received the articles of impeachment when the new Congress convened in 1999, and it began to sit in judgment of the President on January 7. The President was acquitted on both articles on February 12, 1999, with ten Republicans joining the Democrats in voting against the first article, and five in voting against the second.

Donald Trump In September 2019, the House of Representatives began impeachment proceedings against President Donald Trump, charging him with abuse of power and obstruction of Congress. The charges stemmed from a telephone conversation the President had had with the president of Ukraine, Volodymyr Zelensky, in July 2019. According to a CIA whistleblower, the President had pressured Zelensky to dig up damaging information on his main political rival, Joseph Biden, by threatening to withhold American military aid to Ukraine, despite the fact that Congress had already appropriated these funds. The charges also alleged that the President later obstructed the congressional investigation into his misconduct by blocking subpoenas and refusing to allow key senior officials to testify before Congress.

Throughout the impeachment proceedings, the President and his supporters in Congress claimed that no wrongdoing had taken place. The President insisted that the impeachment was politically motivated by Democrats in Congress.

After three months of hearings and testimony, the Democratically-controlled House adopted both articles of impeachment against the President in December, overwhelmingly along party lines. The proceedings then moved to the Republican-controlled Senate, where it was generally acknowledged that Republicans would support the President and vote against conviction. This proved to be the case when, in February 2020, the Senate acquitted the President on both articles of impeachment.

The nation was still reeling from those events when, on January 13, 2021, just one week before President-elect Joseph Biden was scheduled to be sworn in as President, Donald Trump became the only chief executive in the nation's history to be impeached a second time. The impeachment charges stemmed from the President's claims of election fraud and a speech he delivered to supporters outside the White House on January 6. After the speech, the mob broke into the Capitol, ransacked offices, and left widespread destruction in their wake. Their actions forced lawmakers to suspend certification of the presidential election results until later that evening, after the Capitol had been cleared of the danger.

Days later, the House of Representatives opened impeachment hearings against the President. The charges alleged that he had incited insurrection with his January 6 speech, in which he pressured lawmakers to overturn the legal results of the 2020 presidential election and urged supporters to march on the Capitol. Lawmakers voted 232–197 in favor of impeachment. The vote included ten Republicans, making it the most bipartisan impeachment vote in United State history.

When the case moved to the Senate, all 50 Democrats and seven Republicans voted to convict. The vote did not meet the two thirds necessary for a guilty verdict, but was the most bipartisan among the four presidential trials in American history.

☑ **IDENTIFY STEPS IN A PROCESS** Describe the steps in the impeachment process.

Other Powers

Congress is a legislative body; its primary function is to make law. But the Constitution does give it some other chores to perform as well.

Constitutional Amendments Article V says that Congress may propose amendments to the Constitution by a two-thirds vote in each house. All 27 of the amendments thus far added to the document have been proposed by Congress. Article V also provides that Congress may call a national convention of delegates from each of the States to propose an amendment—but only if requested to do so by at least two thirds (34) of the State legislatures. No such convention has ever been called.

In recent years, several State legislatures have petitioned Congress for amendments—among them measures that would require Congress to balance the federal budget each year, prohibit flag burning, permit prayer in public schools, outlaw abortions, impose term limits on members of Congress, and regulate campaign spending.

Electoral Duties The Constitution gives certain electoral duties to Congress. But they are to be exercised only in very unusual circumstances.

The House may be called on to elect a President. The 12th Amendment says that if no one receives a majority of the electoral votes for President, the House, voting by States, is to decide the issue. It must choose from among the three highest contenders in the electoral college balloting. Each State has but one vote to cast, and a majority of the States is necessary for election.

The Senate must choose a Vice President if no candidate wins a majority of the electoral votes for that office. In that situation, the vote is by individual senators, with a majority of the full Senate necessary for election.

The House has had to choose a President twice: Thomas Jefferson in 1801 and **John Quincy Adams** in 1825. The Senate has had to pick a Vice President only once: Richard M. Johnson in 1837.

The 25th Amendment provides for the filling of a vacancy in the vice presidency. When one

ELECTORAL DUTIES OF CONGRESS ▶ WHO WINS? ◀

STEP 1
No candidate receives a majority of the **electoral college votes.**

267 VOTES | 246 VOTES
└ **25** VOTES
CANDIDATES

STEP 2
Each State's **House** delegation must decide which of the top three candidates to support. Each State has **one vote** in the contest. Failure to agree means the loss of that State's vote.

CANDIDATES

ONE VOTE

STEP 3
A candidate who wins a **majority** (26) of the votes of the States' delegations **wins the presidency.** If no candidate wins a majority of the States' votes, another vote must be taken.

WINNER

>> One presidential candidate must receive the majority of the electoral college votes. **Analyze Charts** What is an example of a situation that might prevent any candidate from winning a majority?

VICE-PRESIDENTIAL VACANCY

The 25th Amendment provides, in part: "Whenever there is a vacancy in the office of the Vice President, the President shall nominate a Vice President who shall take office upon confirmation by a majority vote of both Houses of Congress."

—25th Amendent, Section 2

 1 - - - - - - - - - - - - -> **2** - - - - - - - - - - - - -> **3**

A vacancy occurs. | The President selects a successor. | Both Houses of Congress vote to confirm or reject the nominee. A majority vote is required.

VICE PRESIDENT SPIRO AGNEW RESIGNS
AFTER A CONVICTION FOR INCOME TAX EVASION.

PRESIDENT NIXON NOMINATES
HOUSE MINORITY LEADER GERALD FORD (R., MI) TO SUCCEED SPIRO AGNEW AS VICE PRESIDENT.

CONGRESS CONFIRMS GERALD FORD TO SUCCEED SPIRO AGNEW AS **VICE PRESIDENT.**

>> Congress' electoral duties include selecting a successor if the vice presidency becomes vacant. **Analyze Charts** Why is it important that Congress is involved in filling such a vacancy?

occurs, the President nominates a **successor**—a replacement, someone to fill the vacancy, subject to a majority vote in both houses of Congress. That process has also been used twice: Gerald Ford was confirmed as Vice President in 1973 and Nelson Rockefeller in 1974.

☑ **SUMMARIZE** Summarize the processes Congress may take to amend the Constitution and discuss how each has been used.

☑ ASSESSMENT

1. **Compare and Contrast** How do strict constructionists and liberal constructionists differ in their attitude toward congressional power?

2. **Interpret** What is the significance of the court's decision in *McCulloch* v. *Maryland*, 1819?

3. **Analyze Information** How do each of the nonlegislative powers of Congress illustrate the principle of checks and balances?

4. **Apply Concepts** What is the Necessary and Proper Clause? Why has it been called the Elastic Clause?

5. **Draw Conclusions** Why is the Commerce Clause, written in 1787, still adequate to meet the needs of the nation in the 21st century?

4.5

Senate Watergate Committee chair Sam Ervin confers with colleagues during the 1974 hearings. Ervin also chaired the committee that investigated Senator Joe McCarthy in 1954.

 BOUNCE to Activate Flipped Video

Objectives

Describe how and when Congress convenes.

Compare the roles of the presiding officers in the Senate and the House.

Identify the duties of the party officers in each house.

Describe how committee chairs are chosen and explain their role in the legislative process.

Explain how standing committees function.

Describe the role of select committees.

Compare the functions of joint and conference committees.

Key Terms

Speaker of the
  House
president of the
  Senate
president pro
  tempore
party caucus
floor leader
majority leader
minority leader
whip
committee chair
seniority rule
standing committee

subcommittee
select committee
joint committee
conference
  committee
Joseph Biden

Congress at Work— Organization and Committees

What comes to mind when you hear the word *Congress*? The Capitol? Your members of Congress? Some particular bill? Those senators and representatives you often see on the evening news? Of course, you know that the nation's lawmaking body is much more than that. It is, in fact, a very complex enterprise, and much larger than most people realize. Tens of thousands of men and women work for the legislative branch today, and Congress appropriates billions every year to finance its own many-sided operations.

Congress Convenes

Congress convenes—begins a new term—every two years, on January 3 of every odd-numbered year. Each new term follows the general elections in November.

Opening Day in the House Every other January, the 435 men and women who have been elected to the House come together at the Capitol to begin a new term. Because all 435 of its seats are up for election every two years, the House technically has no sworn members, no rules, and no organization until its opening-day ceremonies are held.

Senator Sherrod Brown (D., Ohio) sat in the House for seven terms before he won election to the Senate in 2006. He remembers his first opening day, in 1993, this way:

> Walking around the chamber the first day, I was awed and nervous. . . . [Q]uestions gnawed

at me when I walked into that august [grand] room, when I met several members about whom I had read and whom I had seen on television. And then I thought about the President of the United States coming to address us— 'Do I deserve to be here with all these people? How did I get here? Will I measure up?'

—Sherrod Brown, *Congress From the Inside*

The clerk of the House in the preceding term calls the chamber to order and checks the roll of representatives elect. Those members-to-be then choose a Speaker, who will be their permanent presiding officer. By custom, the Speaker is a long-standing member of the majority party, and election on the floor is only a formality. The majority party's members in the House have settled the matter beforehand.

The Speaker then takes the oath of office. By tradition, the oath is administered by the Dean of the House, the member-elect with the longest record of service in the House. With that accomplished, the Speaker swears in the rest of the members, as a body. The Democrats take their seats to the right of the center aisle; the Republicans, to the left.

Next, the House elects its clerk, parliamentarian, sergeant at arms, chief administrative officer, and chaplain. None of these people are members of the House, and their elections are also a formality. The majority party has already decided the matter.

Then, the House adopts the rules that will govern its proceedings through the term. The rules of the House have been developing for over 200 years, and they take up hundreds of pages of the *House Rules and Manual*. They are readopted, most often with little or no change, at the beginning of each term, though they are occasionally and sometimes extensively amended during a term. Thus, before one session of Congress, the rules were amended to require the Congressional Budget Office and the Joint Committee on Taxation to calculate the impact of potential economic growth that might result from legislation. Republicans saw the change as a way to help get tax reform legislation passed, while Democrats called it a "smoke-and-mirrors budget gimmick."

Finally, members of the House permanent committees are appointed by a floor vote. With that, the House is organized.

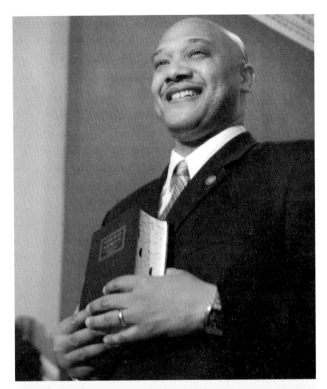

>> Newly elected Indiana Representative Andre Carson used the *House Rules and Manual* for his ceremonial swearing-in, which followed his official swearing-in held earlier in the day.

>> A long-standing tradition in the House of Representatives, the chaplain is one of its officers. In addition to leading opening prayers, the chaplain performs ceremonial and pastoral duties.

> "He shall from time to time give to the Congress Information of the State of the Union, and recommend to their Consideration such Measures as he shall judge necessary and expedient . . .
>
> —Article II, Section 3

>> President Woodrow Wilson gives his State of the Union address to a joint session of Congress in 1918. Before Wilson's first 1913 address, these addresses were always delivered in writing.

Opening Day in the Senate The Senate is a continuous body. It has been organized without interruption since its first session in 1789. Recall that only one third of the seats are up for election every two years. Two thirds of the Senate's membership is carried over from one term to the next. As a result, the Senate does not face large organizational problems at the beginning of a term. Its first-day session is nearly always fairly short and routine, even when the elections have brought a change in the majority party. Newly elected and reelected members must be sworn in, vacancies in Senate organization and on committees must be filled, and a few other details attended to.

State of the Union Message When the Senate is notified that the House of Representatives is organized, a joint committee of the two chambers is appointed and instructed "to wait upon the President of the United States and inform him that a quorum of each House is assembled and that the Congress is ready to receive any communication he may be pleased to make."

Within a few weeks—in late January or early February—the President delivers the annual State of the Union message to a joint session of Congress. The speech is a major political event and is based on this constitutional command:

> He shall from time to time give to the Congress Information of the State of the Union, and recommend to their Consideration such Measures as he shall judge necessary and expedient . . .
>
> —Article II, Section 3

From Woodrow Wilson's first message in 1913, the President has almost always presented his annual assessment in person. Members of Congress, together with the members of the Cabinet, the justices of the Supreme Court, the foreign diplomatic corps, and other dignitaries, assemble in the House chamber to hear him.

In the address, the President reports on the state of the nation as he or she sees it, in both domestic and foreign policy terms. The message is widely covered by the news media, and it is very closely followed both here and abroad. In fact, the chief executive's speech is as much a message to the American people, and to the world, as it is an address to Congress. In it, the President lays out the broad shape of the policies the administration expects to follow and the course the chief executive has charted for the nation. The message regularly includes a number of specific legislative recommendations, along with a plea that Congress will enact them. Its presentation is soon followed by scores of bills drawn up in the executive branch and introduced in the House and Senate by various members of the President's party.

With the conclusion of the speech, the joint session is adjourned. Each house then separately turns to the legislative business that will come before it.

☑ **INFER** What is the purpose of the organization of the House, where all 435 seats are up for election every two years, and the Senate, which is a continuous body?

>> Sam Rayburn (D., Texas; left) served as Speaker of the House for nearly 17 years, making him the longest serving Speaker in history. His time as Speaker spanned the years 1940 to 1961, with the exception of only two Congresses.

The Presiding Officers

The Constitution provides for the presiding officers of each house of Congress—the Speaker of the House and the president of the Senate. Article I, Section 2, Clause 5 directs that "The House of Representatives shall choose their Speaker and other Officers. . . ." And Article I, Section 3, Clause 4 declares: "The Vice President of the United States shall be President of the Senate. . . ."

The Speaker of the House Of the two positions, the **Speaker of the House** is by far the more important and more powerful within the halls of Congress. This is particularly so because the Speaker is both the elected presiding officer of the House and the acknowledged leader of its majority party. Although neither the Constitution nor its own rules require it, the House has always chosen the Speaker from among its own members. The first woman Speaker of the House was elected in 2007, Nancy Pelosi (D., California).

The Speaker is expected to preside in a fair and judicious manner and regularly does. The Speaker is also expected to aid the fortunes of the majority party and its legislative goals, and regularly does that, too.

Nearly all of the Speaker's powers revolve around two duties: to preside and to keep order. The Speaker chairs most sessions of the House but often appoints another member as temporary presiding officer. No member may speak until he or she is recognized by the Speaker. The presiding officer also interprets and applies the rules, refers bills to committee, rules on points of order (questions of procedure raised by members), puts motions to a vote, and decides the outcome of most votes taken on the floor of the House. (The Speaker can be overridden by a vote of the House, but that almost never happens.) The Speaker also names the members of all select and conference committees and must sign all bills and resolutions passed by the House.

As an elected member of the House, the Speaker may debate and vote on any matter before that body. That seldom happens, but when it does, the Speaker appoints another member as the temporary presiding officer and he or she then occupies the Speaker's chair. The Speaker does not often vote,

>> Whatever influence the president of the Senate has comes from a personal relationship with other senators. Vice President Dan Quayle once represented Indiana in the Senate.

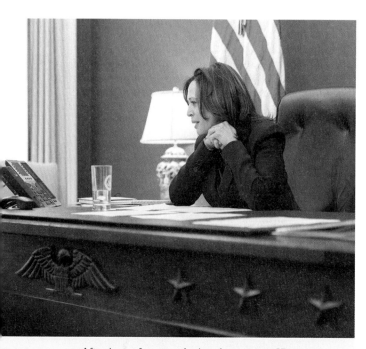

>> After just a few months into her term as Vice President, Kamala Harris had already been called upon to break four tied votes in the Senate. **Analyze Information** What does this tell you about the party breakdown in the Senate at that time?

and the House rules say only that the Speaker *must* vote to break a tie. Notice then, that because a tie vote defeats a question, the Speaker occasionally votes to cause a tie and so defeat a proposal.

The Speaker of the House follows the Vice President in the line of succession to the presidency. That fact is a considerable testimony to the power and importance of both the office and the person who holds it.

The President of the Senate The Constitution makes the Vice President the **president of the Senate,** the Senate's presiding officer. This means that (1) unlike the House, the Senate does not choose its own presiding officer and (2) unlike the Speaker of the House, the Senate's presiding officer is not in fact a member of that body. Indeed, the Vice President might not even be a member of the party that controls the Senate.

All of this adds up to the major reason why the Vice President plays a much less powerful role in the Senate than that played by the Speaker in the House. Also note this important point: the Vice President's career path, the route traveled to the post, is a much different path than the one the Speaker has followed. The Vice President has not become the Senate's presiding officer out of long service in that body. He has, instead, come to the post out of a much different process.

The president of the Senate does have the usual powers of a presiding officer: to recognize members, put questions to a vote, and so on. However, the Vice President cannot take the floor to speak or debate and may vote *only* to break a tie.

Any influence a Vice President may have in the Senate is largely the result of personal abilities and relationships. Several Vice Presidents came to that office from the Senate. Examples include Harry Truman, Alben Barkley, Richard Nixon, Lyndon Johnson, Hubert Humphrey, Walter Mondale, Dan Quayle, Al Gore, **Joseph Biden**, and Kamala Harris. Each was able to build at least some power into the position out of that earlier experience.

The Senate does have another presiding officer, one who serves in the Vice President's absence. The **president pro tempore**, or president pro tem for short, is elected by the Senate itself and is always a leading member of the majority party—usually its longest-serving member. Unlike the Vice President, the president pro tempore (meaning "for a time") may speak and vote on any issue that comes before the Senate.

The president pro tem follows the Speaker of the House in the line of presidential succession. Other

>> Congressional leaders are chosen at the start of each session of Congress. Here (from left), Republican Minority Whip Leslie Arends, Majority Whip Hale Boggs, House Speaker John McCormack, Majority Leader Carl Albert, and Minority Leader Gerald Ford celebrate the start of the second session of the 90th Congress in 1968.

senators do frequently preside over the Senate, on a temporary basis; newly elected members regularly do so early in their terms.

☑ **INFER** The Constitution specifies that the Senate's presiding officer is not a member of that body. In what ways does this affect his or her influence in the Senate?

Party Officers

Congress is a *political body*. This is so for two leading reasons: (1) Congress is the nation's central *policy*-making body, and (2) Congress is *partisan*. Reflecting its political character, both houses of Congress are organized along party lines.

The Party Caucus The **party caucus** is a closed meeting of the members of each party in each house. These meetings are regularly held just before Congress convenes in January and occasionally during a session. In recent years the Republicans have called their caucus in each house the *party conference*, and the Democrats now use this term in the Senate, too.

A caucus deals mostly with matters related to party organization, such as the selection of the

party's floor leaders and questions of committee membership. It sometimes takes stands on particular bills, but neither party tries to force its members to follow its caucus decisions, nor can it.

The policy committee is composed of the party's top leadership. It acts as an executive committee for the party caucus. That body is known as the *policy committee* in each party's structure in the Senate and in the Republicans' organization in the House. However, it is called the *steering and policy committee* by the Democrats in the lower chamber.

The Floor Leaders Next to the Speaker, the **floor leaders** in the House and Senate are the most important officers in Congress. They do not hold official positions in either chamber. Rather, they are party officers, picked for their posts by their party colleagues.

The floor leaders are legislative strategists. Assisted by paid staff, they try to carry out the decisions of their parties' caucuses and steer floor action to their parties' benefit. Each of them is also the chief spokesman for his party in his chamber. All of that calls for political skills of a high order. Senator Howard Baker (R., Tennessee), one of the Senate's most effective floor leaders, often likened his job to that of "herding cats."

The floor leader of the party that holds the majority of seats in each house of Congress is known as the **majority leader.** The floor leader of the party that holds the minority of seats in each house is the **minority leader.** The majority leader is the more powerful in each house—for the obvious reason that the majority party has more seats (more votes) than the other party has. And, the majority leader very largely controls the order of business on the floor in his or her chamber.

The two floor leaders in each house are assisted by party **whips.** The majority whip and the minority whip are, in effect, assistant floor leaders. Each of them is chosen at the party caucus, almost always at the floor leader's recommendation. A number of assistant whips serve in the House.

Whips serve as a liaison—a two-way link—between the party's leadership and its rank-and-file members. The term *whip* was borrowed from British politics. There, it came from the "whipper-in" in a fox hunt, the rider who is supposed to keep the hounds bunched in a pack. The whips check with party members and tell the floor leader which members, and how many votes, can be counted on in any particular matter. The whips also see that all members of the party are present for important votes and that they vote with the party leadership. If a member must be absent for some reason, a whip sees that that member is paired with a member of the other party who will also be absent that day or who agrees not to vote on certain measures at that day's session—so one non-vote cancels out another.

☑ **DRAW CONCLUSIONS** Why can't a party force its members to take a particular stand on a bill during the party's caucus?

Committee Chairs

The bulk of the work of Congress, especially in the House, is really done in committee. Thus, **committee chairs**—those members who head the standing committees in each chamber—hold very strategic posts. The chair of each of these permanent committees is chosen from the majority party by the majority party caucus. These men and women are always ranking members of the majority party.

Although committee chairs are less powerful now than in years past, they still have a major say in such matters as which bills a committee will consider and

>> Committee and subcommittee chairs, including Representatives John Lewis (D., Georgia; second from left) and Kevin Brady (R., Texas; right) listen while another representative speaks during a congressional hearing.

in what order and at what length, whether public hearings are to be held, and what witnesses the committee will call. When a committee's bill has been reported—approved for consideration—to the floor, the chair usually manages the debate and tries to steer it to final passage.

We shall take a closer look at committees and their chairs in a moment. But, first, consider the seniority rule.

The Seniority Rule The **seniority rule** is, in fact, an unwritten custom. It dates from the late 1800s, and is still more or less followed in both houses today. The seniority rule provides that the most important posts in Congress, in both the formal and the party organizations, usually will be held by those party members with the longest records of service. (Notice that seniority rule does not apply to the presiding officers or to the floor leaders in either chamber. As you've seen, their selection is otherwise provided for.)

The rule is applied most strictly to the choice of committee chairs. The head of each committee is almost always the longest-serving majority party member of that committee. The rule is also followed quite closely in the selection of those members who chair the several subcommittees into which nearly all the standing committees are divided.

Criticism of the Seniority Rule Critics of the seniority rule are many, and they do make a strong case. They insist that the seniority system ignores ability, rewards mere length of service, and works to discourage younger members. Its opponents also note that the rule means that a committee head often comes from a "safe" constituency—a State or district in which one party regularly wins the seat. With no play of fresh and conflicting forces in those places, critics claim, the chair of a committee is often out of touch with current public opinion.

Defenders of the seniority rule argue that it ensures that a powerful and experienced member will head each committee. They also say that the rule encourages members to stay on a particular committee and so, over time, gain a wide-ranging knowledge of matters that fall within that committee's jurisdiction. In addition, they note that the rule is fairly easy to apply and that it very nearly eliminates the possibility of fights within the party.

The rule's opponents have gained some ground in recent years. Thus, the House Republican Conference (caucus) now picks several GOP members of House committees by secret ballot.

>> In a 2016 interview, Senator Nancy Kassebaum (R., Kansas) noted that "Seniority really does matter. You can stay sometimes too long, but you also have to be cognizant of where you have some voice."

House Democrats use secret ballots to choose a committee chair whenever 20 percent of their caucus requests that procedure.

Whatever the arguments against the seniority rule, it is unlikely to be eliminated. Those members with the real power to abolish the rule are also the ones who reap the largest benefits from it.

☑ **IDENTIFY CAUSE AND EFFECT** In what ways do seniority practices within congressional committees minimize the impact of changes in voters' choices?

Standing Committees

Do you know the phrase "a division of labor"? It means dividing the work to be done, assigning the several parts of the overall task to various members of the group. The House and the Senate are both so large, and their agendas are so crowded with so many different matters, that both chambers must rely on a division of labor. That is to say, much of the work that Congress does is in fact done by committees. Indeed, Representative Clem Miller (D., California) once described Congress as "a collection of committees that come together in a chamber periodically to approve of one another's actions."

In 1789, the House and Senate each adopted the practice of naming a special committee to consider each bill as it was introduced. By 1794, there were more than 300 committees in each chamber. Each house then began to set up permanent panels, **standing committees,** to which all similar bills can be sent. The number of these committees has varied over the years, but it generally hovers around 15 to 20. Each House committee has anywhere from a handful of members to more than fifty. Senate committees usually have between 15 and 30 members. Representatives are normally assigned to one or two standing committees and senators to three or four.

The pivotal role these committees play in the lawmaking process cannot be overstated. Most bills receive their most thorough consideration in these bodies. Members of both houses regularly respect the decisions and follow the recommendations they make. Thus, the fate of most bills is usually decided in the various standing committees, not on the floor of either house. More than a century ago, Woodrow Wilson described "Congress in its committee rooms" as "Congress at work," and that remains true today.

Some panels are more prominent and more influential than others. As you would expect, most members try to win assignments to one of these major panels. Some leading committees in the House are the Rules, Ways and Means, Appropriations, Armed Services, Judiciary, Foreign Affairs, and Agriculture committees. In the Senate, senators usually compete for places on the Foreign Relations; Appropriations; Finance; Judiciary; Armed Services; and Banking, Housing, and Urban Affairs committees.

Of course, some of the other committees are particularly attractive to some members. Thus, a representative whose district lies wholly within a major city might want to sit on the House Committee on Education and the Workforce. A senator from one of the western States might angle for assignment to the Senate's Committee on Energy and Natural Resources.

Most of the standing committees review bills dealing with particular policy matters—say, public lands, taxes, or veterans' affairs. However, there are three standing committees that are not organized as subject-matter bodies: in the House, the Rules Committee and the Committee on House Administration, and in the Senate, the Committee on Rules and Administration.

When a bill is introduced in either house, the Speaker or the president of the Senate refers the measure to the appropriate standing committee.

A BILL IN THE HOUSE

①

Introduced in the House

② **Speaker Referred Bill**
• The Speaker of the House sends the bill to two committees.

③ **Subcommittees**

Committee on Agriculture
• Conservation, Energy, and Forestry
• Department Operations, Oversight, and Nutrition
• General Farm Commodities and Risk Management
• Horticulture, Research, Biotechnology, and Foreign Agriculture
• Livestock, Rural Development, and Credit

Committee on Foreign Affairs
• Quickly discharged; not referred to subcommittee

④ **Bill Was Reported**
• The bill was discharged from the Committee on Foreign Affairs and reported by the Committee on Agriculture. Then it went to the Rules Committee.
• The Rules Committee set aside one hour for general debate, plus time to consider amendments. It also instructed the House to consider the bill in the Committee of the Whole (Section 3).

⑤ **Bill Was Sent to Full House**
• The bill was considered in the Committee of the Whole—that is, the full House sitting as a committee of itself.

>> This chart shows the path of one bill, the 2007 Food and Energy Security Act, through the House.
Analyze Charts How many committees and subcommittees studied the bill?

Congressional Committees*

HOUSE COMMITTEES		SENATE COMMITTEES	
Agriculture	Judiciary	Agriculture, Nutrition, and Forestry	Finance
Appropriations	Natural Resources	Appropriations	Foreign Relations
Armed Services	Oversight and Reform	Armed Services	Health, Education, Labor, and Pensions
Budget	Rules	Banking, Housing, and Urban Affairs	Homeland Security and Governmental Affairs
Education and Labor	Science, Space, and Technology	Budget	Indian Affairs
Energy and Commerce	Small Business	Commerce, Science, and Transportation	Judiciary
Ethics	Transportation and Infrastructure	Energy and Natural Resources	Rules and Administration
Financial Services	Veterans' Affairs	Environment and Public Works	Small Business and Entrepreneurship
Foreign Affairs	Ways and Means		Veterans' Affairs
Homeland Security			
House Administration			

*Names and number of committees can vary slightly from Congress to Congress
SOURCES: house.gov; senate.gov

>> Each congressional committee has its own budget and staff. **Analyze Charts** A representative introduces a bill seeking to build a high-speed rail between two major cities. To which House committee might this bill be sent? To which Senate committee?

Thus, the Speaker sends all tax measures to the House Ways and Means Committee; in the Senate, tax measures go to the Finance Committee. A bill dealing with the creation of additional federal district judgeships will be sent to the Judiciary Committee in both chambers, and so on.

Recall that the chair of each of the standing committees is chosen according to the seniority rule. As a consequence, most committee chairs have served in Congress for at least 12 years and some much longer. The seniority rule is also closely applied in each house when it elects the other members of each of its committees.

The members of each standing committee are formally elected by a floor vote at the beginning of each term of Congress. In fact, each party has already drawn up its own committee roster before that vote, and the floor vote merely ratifies those party choices. The majority party always holds a majority of the seats on each standing committee. The other party is well represented, however.

Subcommittees Most standing committees are divided into **subcommittees**—divisions of standing committees that do most of the committees' work. Each subcommittee is responsible for a portion of the committee's workload. There are generally some 150 subcommittees between the two houses.

Take a look at the Senate's Judiciary Committee, for example. It does most of its work in its subcommittees, and each member serves on at least two of them. Although their names change from time to time, they usually describe the subcommittee's focus. Consider the following examples: Antitrust, Competition Policy and Consumer Rights; The Constitution; Crime and Terrorism; Border Security and Immigration; Oversight, Agency Action, Federal Rights, and Federal Courts; and Privacy, Technology, and the Law.

The House Rules Committee The House Committee on Rules is the Speaker's "right arm." It controls the flow of bills to the floor and sets the conditions for their consideration there. The panel is often described as the "traffic cop" in the lower house. So many measures are introduced in the House each term that some sort of screening device is absolutely necessary.

Most bills die in the committees to which they are referred. Still, several hundred are reported out every year. So, before most of these bills can reach the floor of the House, they must also clear the Rules Committee. Normally, a bill gets to the floor only if it has been granted a rule—been scheduled for floor consideration—by the Rules Committee. The committee decides whether and under what conditions the full House will consider a measure.

As you will see, this means that the powerful Rules Committee can speed, delay, or even prevent House action on a measure. In the smaller Senate, where the process is not so closely regulated, the majority leader controls the appearance of bills on the floor.

☑ **INFER** How can party control of the legislature impact the passage of a bill through committee to floor consideration?

Select Committees

At times, each house finds a need for a **select committee,** sometimes called special committees. They are panels set up for some specific purpose and, most often, for a limited time. The Speaker of the House or the president of the Senate appoints the members of these special committees, with the advice of the majority and minority leaders.

The congressional power to investigate is an essential part of the lawmaking function. Congress must decide on the need for new laws and gauge the adequacy of those already on the books. It also must exercise its vital oversight function, to ensure that federal agencies are following the laws it has

already passed. At times, too, a committee may conduct an investigation of an issue—for example, the threat of domestic terrorism—in order to focus public attention on that matter. Most investigations are conducted by standing committees, or by their subcommittees.

However, select committees are sometimes formed to investigate a current issue, such as one investigation by the Senate's Select Committee on Indian Affairs. That panel spent nearly three years investigating the behavior of a number of well-connected lobbyists who represented several Native American tribes as they sought to establish gambling casinos. The committee's extensive probe uncovered massive instances of fraud, bribery, tax evasion, and other illegal activities for which several offenders began to serve long prison sentences in 2006 and 2007. The most prominent of those miscreants were Washington-based lobbyist Jack Abramoff and a member of Congress, Representative Robert Ney (R., Ohio), who had been chairman of the House Committee on Administration.

At times, select committees have been spectacularly important. This happened, for example, with the Senate's Select Committee on Presidential Campaign Activities, popularly known as the Senate Watergate Committee. As the Watergate scandal began to unfold in 1973, the Senate created that committee. Chaired by Senator Sam Ervin (D., North Carolina), its job was to investigate "the extent, if any, to which illegal, improper, or unethical activities were engaged in by any persons . . . in the presidential election of 1972." Its sensational hearings riveted the nation for months. Eventually, they formed a key link in the chain of events that led to President Richard Nixon's resignation from office in mid-1974.

Another notable instance came in 1987, with the work of two panels: the Senate's Select Committee on Secret Military Assistance to Iran and the Nicaraguan Opposition, and the House Select Committee to Investigate Covert Arms Transactions with Iran. These twin committees, often referred to jointly as the Iran-Contra Committee, probed the Reagan administration's conduct of two highly secret projects abroad: the sale of arms to Iran and efforts to give military aid to the Contra rebels in Nicaragua.

The operation in Iran was intended, at least in part, as an arms-for-hostages deal, and it failed. The aid to the Contras was funded in part with money from the Iranian arms sales, despite an act of Congress that expressly prohibited such aid by the United States.

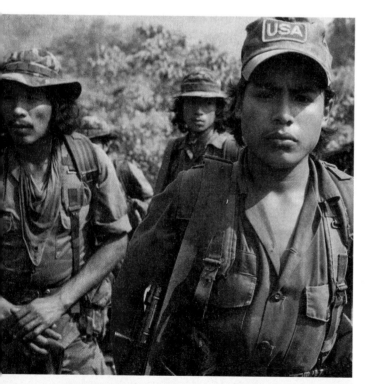

>> A group of Contras on patrol in northern Nicaragua. Congress later formed a committee to investigate weapon sales to the Contras.

Another notable select committee investigation happened in 2014, when the House studied the events surrounding the 2012 terrorist attacks on the U.S. diplomatic compound and a nearby CIA compound in Benghazi, Libya. U.S. ambassador Christopher Stevens and three other Americans were killed in the attacks. Some Republicans in Congress charged the White House and the State Department with attempting to cover up what actually happened in Benghazi, while some Democrats said that the committee was motivated by partisan politics. In its final report, the House Select Committee on Benghazi issued a rebuke to officials in the State Department, the Defense Department, and the Central Intelligence Agency.

Most congressional investigations are not nearly so visible, nor so historic. Their more usual shape can be seen when, for example, the House Committee on Agriculture probes the spruce budworm problem (an infestation affecting trees in the Pacific Northwest) or the Senate's Armed Services Committee looks at the Army's recruiting programs.

☑ **INFER** Why would a select committee need to focus public attention on a particular issue?

Joint and Conference Committees

A **joint committee** is one composed of members of both houses. Some of these are select committees set up to serve some temporary purpose. Most are permanent groups that serve on a regular basis. Because the standing committees of the two houses often duplicate one another's work, many have long urged that Congress make much greater use of the joint committee device.

Some joint committees are investigative in nature and issue periodic reports to the House and Senate—for example, the Joint Committee on Taxation. It conducts in depth studies of the federal tax system and presents its findings to the House Ways and Means Committee and the Senate's Finance Committee. Most often, those committees perform more routine duties—for example, the Joint Committee on the Library oversees the administration of that remarkable institution, the Library of Congress.

Before a bill may be sent to the President, each house must pass it in identical form. Sometimes, the two houses pass differing versions, and the first house will not agree to the changes the other has made. When this happens, a **conference committee**—a temporary, joint body—is created to iron out the differences in the bill. Its job is to produce a compromise bill that both houses will accept—as you will see shortly.

☑ **GENERATE EXPLANATIONS** What is the purpose of having both the House of Representatives and the Senate debate the same bill?

☑ ASSESSMENT

1. **Describe** Describe how and when Congress convenes.

2. **Compare and Contrast** Compare the roles of the Speaker of the House and the president of the Senate.

3. **Identify** Identify the party officers in each house and what their roles are.

4. **Compare** Compare the functions of a standing committee, the House Rules Committee, a select committee, a joint committee, and a conference committee.

5. **Describe** Describe how committee chairs are chosen and their role in the legislative process.

4.6

In the 1930s, Speaker of the House John Nance Garner appealed to the House Ways and Means Committee to pass his bill providing relief for the unemployed.

 BOUNCE to Activate Flipped Video

Objectives

Identify the first steps in the introduction of a bill to the House.

Describe what happens to a bill once it is referred to a committee.

Explain what happens to a bill on the House floor.

Describe how a bill is introduced in the Senate.

Compare the Senate's rules for debate with those in the House.

Describe the role of conference committees in the legislative process.

Evaluate the actions the President can take after both houses have passed a bill.

Key Terms

bill
joint resolution
concurrent resolution
resolution
rider
pigeonholed
discharge petition
quorum
engrossed
filibuster
cloture
veto
pocket veto
omnibus measure
Huey Long
Strom Thurmond

Congress at Work— Making Laws

These numbers may surprise you: From 6,000 to 9,000 bills and resolutions are introduced in the House and Senate during each session of Congress. Only about ten percent become law. Where do all those measures come from? Why are so few of them passed? How, by process, does Congress make law?

The First Steps

A **bill** is a proposed law presented to the House or Senate for consideration. Most of the bills introduced in either house do not originate with members themselves. Instead, many of the most important bills are born in the executive branch. Business, labor, agriculture, and other interest groups often draft measures, as well. And the ideas for some come from private citizens who think "there ought to be a law. . . ." Many others are born in the standing committees of Congress.

According to Article I, Section 7, Clause 1 of the Constitution, "bills for raising Revenue shall originate in the House." In other words, tax bills must first be acted upon by the House. Measures dealing with any other matter may be introduced in either chamber. Only members can introduce bills in the House, and they do so by dropping them into the hopper, a box hanging on the edge of the clerk's desk.

Often, before a member introduces a bill, he or she will circulate a letter informing other members about the measure and why its sponsor thinks it should become law. That is, he or she hopes to persuade several other members to become cosponsors, thereby increasing the chances that the bill will be passed. By the time many measures are introduced, in either house, a number of members are listed on them as cosponsors.

Public and Private Bills The thousands of measures—bills and resolutions—Congress considers take several forms. To begin with, there are two types of bills: public bills and private bills.

Public bills are measures applying to the nation as a whole—for example, a tax measure. Private bills are measures that apply to certain persons or places rather than to the entire nation. As an example, Congress once passed an act to give a sheep rancher $85,000 for his losses resulting from attacks by grizzly bears. The bears had been moved from Yellowstone National Park to other public lands on which the rancher grazed his flock.

Joint resolutions are similar to bills, and, when passed, have the force of law. They most often deal with unusual or temporary matters—for example, to appropriate money for the presidential inauguration ceremonies. Joint resolutions are used as well to propose constitutional amendments, and they have also been used to annex territories.

Concurrent resolutions deal with matters in which the House and Senate must act jointly. However, they do not have the force of law and do not require the President's signature. Concurrent resolutions are used most often by Congress to state a position on some matter—for example, in foreign affairs.

Resolutions, often called "simple resolutions," deal with matters concerning either house alone and are taken up only by that body. They are regularly used for such matters as the adoption of a new rule of procedure or the amendment of some existing rule. Like concurrent resolutions, a resolution does not have the force of law and is not sent to the President for approval.

A bill or resolution usually deals with a single subject, but sometimes a rider dealing with an unrelated matter is included. A **rider** is a provision not likely to pass on its own merit that is attached to an important measure certain to pass. Its sponsors hope that it will "ride" through the legislative process on the strength of the main measure.

Most riders are tacked onto appropriations measures, and are often called "earmarks." In fact, some money bills have so many riders attached that they are called "Christmas trees." The opponents of those "decorations" and the President are almost

>> House Doorkeeper Ralph Roberts shows freshman Congressman Richard Nixon the hopper where new House bills are placed. The role of Doorkeeper was abolished in 1995; the hopper was not.

>> In politics, "pork" refers to benefits a politician arranges for his or her home district. **Analyze Political Cartoons** What does this cartoon imply about the military spending bill?

always forced to accept them if they want the bill's major provisions to become law.

Introduction and First Reading The clerk of the House numbers each bill as it is introduced. Thus, H.R. 3410 would be the 3,410th measure introduced in the House during the congressional term. Bills originating in the Senate receive the prefix S.—such as S. 210. Resolutions are similarly identified in each house in the order of their introduction.

The clerk also gives each bill a short title—a brief summary of its principal contents. Having received its number and title, the bill is then entered in the House *Journal* and in the *Congressional Record* for the day.

The *Journal* contains the minutes, the official record, of the daily proceedings in the House or Senate. The *Congressional Record* is a voluminous account of the daily proceedings (speeches, debates, other comments, votes, motions, etc.) in each house. The Record is not quite a word-for-word account, however. Members have five days in which to make changes in each temporary edition. They often insert speeches that were in fact never made, reconstruct "debates," and revise thoughtless or inaccurate remarks.

With these actions the bill has received its first reading. All bills are printed immediately after introduction and distributed to all members of the House.

Each bill that is finally passed in either house is given three readings along the legislative route. In the House, second reading comes during floor consideration, if the measure gets that far. Third reading takes place just before the final vote on the measure. Each reading is usually by number and title only: "H.R. 3410, A bill to provide. . . ." However, the more important or controversial bills are read in full and taken up line by line, section by section, at second reading.

The three readings, an ancient parliamentary practice, are intended to ensure careful consideration of bills. Today, the readings are little more than way stations along the legislative route. They were quite important in the early history of Congress, however, when some members could not read.

After the first reading, the Speaker refers the bill to one or more of the standing committees. A bill's content largely determines where it will go. The Speaker does have some discretion, however, particularly over complex measures with provisions covering a number of subjects. Which committee gets a bill can matter. For example, a controversial provision in the bill might receive a more favorable welcome in one committee than it might in another.

☑ **CHECK UNDERSTANDING** Would a rider be likely to be attached to a bill proposing abolishing the federal income tax and the Internal Revenue Service? Why or why not?

The Bill in Committee

The Constitution makes no mention of standing committees. These bodies do play an absolutely essential role in the lawmaking process, however— and in both houses of Congress. Indeed, their place is so pivotal that they are sometimes called "little legislatures."

The standing committees act as sieves. They sift through all of the many bills referred to them— rejecting most, considering and reporting only those they find to be worthy of floor consideration. In short, the fate of most bills is decided in these committees rather than on the floor of either house.

Most of the thousands of bills introduced in each session of Congress are **pigeonholed.** That is, they are buried; they die in committee. They are simply put away, never to be acted upon. The

>> The term *pigeonholed* originally referred to the practice of shelving items in the pigeonholes of a desk.

term comes from the old-fashioned rolltop desks with pigeonholes—slots into which papers were put and often soon forgotten. Most "by request" bills are routinely pigeonholed; they are the measures that members introduce but only because some constituent or some interest group has asked them to do so.

Most pigeonholed bills do deserve their fate. On occasion, however, a committee buries a measure that a majority of the members of the House want to consider. When that happens, the bill can be blasted out of the committee with a discharge petition.

A **discharge petition** enables members to force a bill that has remained in committee 30 days (7 in the Rules Committee) onto the floor for consideration. Any member may file a discharge motion. If that motion is signed by a majority (218) of House members, the committee has seven days to report the bill. If it does not, any member who signed the motion may, on the second and fourth Mondays of each month, move that the bill be discharged from the committee—that is, sent to the floor. If the motion carries, the rules require the House to consider the bill at once. This maneuver is not often tried, and it seldom succeeds.

When the tactic does succeed, however, it is often in relation to an historic piece of legislation. In 2002, for example, what went on to become the Bipartisan Campaign Reform Act of 2002 was blasted out of the Committee on House Administration—where the House leadership had managed to bury it for several years. That measure marked the first major change in federal campaign finance law in 23 years.

A Subcommittee's Work Once a bill reaches a committee, the chair almost always refers it to one of several subcommittees. For an important or controversial measure, a committee, or most often one of its subcommittees, holds public hearings. Interested parties, including the representatives of interest groups, public officials, and others, are invited to testify at these information-gathering sessions. If necessary, a committee can issue a subpoena, forcing a witness to testify. A subpoena is an order compelling one to testify and/or produce evidence. Failure to obey a subpoena may lead the House or Senate to cite the offender for contempt of Congress—a federal crime punishable by fine and/or imprisonment.

Occasionally, a subcommittee will make a trip to locations affected by a measure. Thus, several members of the House Foreign Affairs Committee's Subcommittee on the Western Hemisphere

>> U.S. Senators Jeanne Shaheen (D., NH, left), Rob Portman (R., OH, center) and Chris Murphy (D., CT, right) hold a press conference following a meeting with the Ukrainian President in Kiev. The senators visited Ukraine to reaffirm bipartisan support for Ukraine's reform agenda.

may visit Rio de Janero for a firsthand look at Brazil's successful efforts to reduce that country's dependence on foreign oil.

These trips are made at public expense, and members of Congress are sometimes criticized for taking them. Some of these junkets deserve criticism. But an on-the-spot investigation often proves to be among the best ways a committee can inform itself.

Committee Actions When a subcommittee has completed its work on a bill, the measure goes to the full committee. At the chair's direction, that body may do one of several things. It may:

1. Report the bill favorably, with a "do pass" recommendation. It is then the chair's job to steer the bill through debate on the floor.

2. Refuse to report the bill—that is, pigeonhole it. Again, this is the fate suffered by most measures in both houses.

3. Report the bill in amended form. Many bills are changed in committee, and several bills on the same subject may be combined into a single measure.

4. Report the bill with an unfavorable recommendation. This does not often happen. Occasionally, however, a committee feels that the

full House should have a chance to consider a bill or does not want to take the responsibility for killing it.

5. Report a committee bill. The panel produces a substantially rewritten measure as a substitute for one or several of the bills referred to it.

☑ **DRAW CONCLUSIONS** The U.S. Constitution does not state that Congress needs to form committees to handle business. Why did the House add them?

Scheduling Floor Debate

Before it goes to the floor for consideration, a bill reported by a standing committee is placed on one of several calendars in the House. A calendar is a schedule of the order in which bills will be taken up on the floor.

The Purpose of Five Calendars There are five calendars in the lower house. The *Calendar of the Committee of the Whole House on the State of the Union,* commonly known as the *Union Calendar,* is for all bills having to do with revenues, appropriations, or government property. The *House Calendar* is for all other public bills. The *Private Calendar* is for all private bills. The *Corrections Calendar* is for all bills from the Union or House Calendar taken out of order by unanimous consent of the House of Representatives. These are most often minor bills to which there is no opposition. The *Discharge Calendar* is for petitions to discharge bills from committee.

Under the rules of the House, bills are taken from each of these calendars for consideration on a regularly scheduled basis. For example, bills from the Corrections Calendar are supposed to be considered on the second and fourth Tuesdays of each month. Measures relating to the District of Columbia can be taken up on the second and fourth Mondays, and private bills on the first and third Tuesdays. On "Calendar Wednesdays," the various committee chairmen may each call up one bill from the House or Union calendars that has cleared their committees.

The Powerful Rules Committee None of these arrangements is followed too closely, however. What most often happens is even more complicated. Remember that the Rules Committee plays a critical role in the legislative process in the House.

It must grant a rule before most bills can in fact reach the floor. That is, before most measures can be taken from a calendar, the Rules Committee must approve that step and set a time for its appearance on the floor.

By not granting a rule for a bill, the Rules Committee can effectively kill it. Or, when the Rules Committee does grant a rule, it may be a special rule—one setting conditions under which the members of the House will consider the measure. A special rule often sets a time limit on floor debate. It may even prohibit amendments to certain, or even to any, of the bill's provisions.

Then, too, certain bills are privileged. That is, they may be called up at almost any time, ahead of any other business before the House. The most privileged measures include major appropriations (spending) and general revenue (tax) bills, conference committee reports, and special rules granted by the Rules Committee.

On certain days, the House may suspend its rules. A motion to that effect must be approved by a two-thirds vote of the members present. When that happens, as it sometimes does, the House moves so far away from its established operating procedures that a measure can go through all the many steps necessary to enactment in a single day.

All of these—the calendars, the role of the Rules Committee, and the other complex procedures—

>> This cartoon shows one interpretation of the lawmaking process in Congress. **Analyze Political Cartoons** What is the purpose of the tangled and hopelessly complex maze in the bottom half of the cartoon?

have developed over time to help members of the House manage their heavy workload. Because of the large size of the House and the sheer number and variety of bills its members introduce, no one member could possibly know the contents, let alone the merits, of every bill on which he or she has to vote.

☑ **INTERPRET** Does the Rules Committee or a standing committee have more influence on whether a bill is debated on the floor of the House?

The Bill on the House Floor

If a bill finally reaches the floor, it receives its second reading in the House. Many bills the House passes are minor ones, with little or no opposition. Most of these less important measures are called from the Corrections Calendar, get their second reading by title only, and are quickly disposed of.

Nearly all of the more important measures are dealt with in a much different manner. They are considered in the Committee of the Whole, an old parliamentary device for speeding business on the floor.

The Committee of the Whole includes all the members of the House, sitting as one large committee of the House, not as the House itself. The rules of the Committee of the Whole are much less strict than the rules of the House, and floor action moves along at a faster pace. For example, a **quorum,** which is a majority of the full membership (218), must be present in order for the House to do business. Only 100 members need be present in the Committee of the Whole.

When the House resolves itself into the Committee of the Whole, the Speaker steps down because the full House of Representatives is no longer in session. Another member presides. General debate begins, and the bill receives its second reading, section by section. As each section is read, amendments may be offered. Under the five-minute rule, supporters and opponents of each amendment have just that many minutes to make their cases. Votes are taken on each section and its amendment as the reading proceeds.

When the bill has been gone through—and many run to dozens and sometimes hundreds of pages—the Committee of the Whole has completed its work. It then rises, that is, dissolves itself. Presto! The House is now back in session. The Speaker resumes the chair, and the House formally adopts the committee's work.

>> Although the Committee of the Whole, a concept taken from Great Britain's Parliament (shown here), is still used in the House, it is no longer used in the Senate.

Debate Its large size has long since forced the House to impose severe limits on floor debate. A rule first adopted in 1842 forbids any member from holding the floor for more than one hour without unanimous consent to speak for a longer time. Since 1880, the Speaker has had the power to force any member who strays from the subject at hand to give up the floor.

The majority and minority floor leaders generally decide in advance how they will split the time to be spent on a bill. But at any time, any member may "move the previous question." That is, any member can demand a vote on the issue before the House. If that motion is adopted, debate ends. An up-or-down vote must be taken. This device is the only motion that can be used in the House to close (end) debate, but it can be a very effective one.

Voting A bill may be the subject of several votes on the floor. If amendments are offered, as they frequently are, members must vote on each of them. Then, too, a number of procedural motions may be offered, for example, one to table the bill (lay it aside), another for the previous question, and so on. The members must vote on each of these motions. These several other votes are very often a better guide to a bill's friends and foes than is the final vote itself.

>> In the House, members vote by inserting their voting cards into a slot and pressing the appropriate button. The machines record the votes and tally the results.

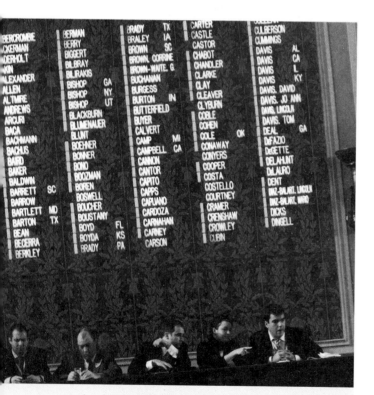

>> An electronic tally board shows votes made in the House of Representatives. The first electronic roll-call vote, in January 1973, took fifteen minutes, compared to 30 to 45 minutes previously.

Sometimes, a member votes for a bill that is now certain to pass, even though he or she had supported amendments to it that, had they been adopted, would have in fact defeated the measure.

The House uses four different methods for taking floor votes: In a voice vote, the Speaker calls for the "ayes" and then the "noes," the members answer in chorus, and the Speaker announces the result. If any member thinks the Speaker has erred in judging a voice vote, he or she may demand a standing vote, also known as a division of the House. All in favor, and then all opposed, stand and are counted by the clerk.

One fifth of a quorum (44 members in the House or 20 in the Committee of the Whole) can demand a teller vote. When this happens, the Speaker names one teller from each party. The members pass between the tellers and are counted, for and against. Teller votes are rare today. The practice has been replaced by electronic voting.

A roll-call vote, also known as a record vote, may be demanded by one fifth of the members present.

In 1973, the House installed a computerized voting system for all quorum calls and record votes to replace the roll call by the clerk. In 1977, the system was modified to work with C-SPAN television cameras so that votes could be recorded in real time. In 2018, Braille and LCD screens displaying each member's name were added.

Members now vote at any of the 48 stations on the floor by inserting a personalized digital card in a box and then pushing one of three buttons: "Yea," "Nay," or "Present." The "Present" button is most often used for a quorum call—a check to make sure that a quorum of the members is in fact present. Otherwise, it is used when a member does not wish to vote but still wants to be recorded as present. A "present" vote is not allowed on some questions, however—for example, a vote to override a veto.

A large master board above the Speaker's chair shows instantly how each member has voted. The House rules allow the members 15 minutes to answer quorum calls or cast record votes. Voting ends when the Speaker pushes a button to lock the electronic system, producing a permanent record of the vote at the same time. Under the former roll-call process, it took the clerk up to 45 minutes to call each member's name and record his or her vote. Before 1973, roll calls took up about three months of House floor time each session.

Voting procedures are much the same in the Senate. The upper house uses voice, standing, and roll-call votes, but does not take teller votes or use an electronic voting process. Only six or seven minutes are needed for a roll-call vote in the smaller upper chamber.

Final Steps Once a bill has been approved at second reading, it is **engrossed,** or printed in its final form Then it is read a third time, by title, and a final vote is taken. Invariably, a bill is approved at third reading, and then the Speaker signs it. A page—a legislative aide—then carries it to the Senate side of the Capitol and places it on the Senate president's desk.

☑ **INTERPRET** Once a bill reaches the House for debate, what can a representative do to try to prevent that bill from passing? Should the rules be changed to prevent this kind of last-minute maneuvering?

>> Then Speaker of the House Nancy Pelosi hands the College Cost Reduction Act of 2007 to House Clerk Lorraine Miller after signing it, for delivery to the Senate for consideration.

The Bill on the Senate Floor

The House and the Senate really are two quite different places. Overall, however, the basic steps in the lawmaking process are much the same in the two chambers. Still, there are a few critical differences in their processes.

The chief differences between House and Senate procedures involve the consideration of measures on the floor. With introduction by a senator formally recognized for the purpose, a measure is given a number, read twice, and then referred to a standing committee, where it is dealt with much as are bills in the House. The Senate's proceedings are less formal and its rules less strict than those in the much larger lower house. For example, the Senate has only one calendar for all bills reported out of its committees. (Recall, there are five of these schedules in the House.) Bills are called to the Senate floor by the majority leader, usually, but not always, in consultation with the minority leader.

Where debate in the House is strictly limited, it is almost unrestrained in the Senate. Indeed, most members of the Senate are intensely proud of belonging to what has often been called "the greatest deliberative body in the world."

As a general matter, a senator may speak on the floor for as long as he or she pleases. Unlike the House, the Senate has no rule that requires a member to speak only to the measure before the chamber. In short, a senator can talk about anything he or she wants to. And the Senate's rules do not allow any member to move the previous question.

Many bills, and particularly the most important pieces of legislation, come to the Senate floor under a unanimous consent agreement. The majority leader regularly negotiates these agreements with the minority leader, and they become effective only if no senator objects. Unanimous consent agreements usually limit the amount of floor time to be devoted to a particular measure and the number and content of amendments that may be offered to it.

The Senate does have a "two-speech rule." No senator may speak more than twice on a given question on the same legislative day. By recessing rather than adjourning a day's session, the Senate can prolong a "legislative day" indefinitely. Thus, the two-speech rule can successfully limit the amount of time the Senate spends on some matters.

The Senate's dedication to freedom of debate is almost unique among modern legislative bodies. That freedom is intended to encourage the fullest possible discussion of matters on the floor. But, notice, the great latitude it allows also gives rise to the filibuster.

The Filibuster Essentially, a **filibuster** is an attempt to "talk a bill to death." It is a stalling tactic by which a minority of senators seeks to delay or prevent Senate action on a measure. The filibusterers try to monopolize the Senate floor and its time so that the Senate must either drop the bill or change it in some manner acceptable to the minority.

Talk—and more talk—is the filibusterers' major weapon. In addition, senators may use time-killing motions, quorum calls, and other parliamentary maneuvers. Indeed, anything to delay or obstruct is grist for the minority's mill as it works to block a bill that would very likely pass if brought to a vote.

Among the many better-known filibusterers, Senator **Huey Long** (D., Louisiana) spoke for more than 15 hours in 1935. He stalled by reading from the Washington telephone directory and giving his colleagues his recipes for "pot-likker," corn bread, and turnip greens. Senator **Strom Thurmond** (R., South Carolina) set the current filibuster record for an individual. He held the floor for 24 hours and 18 minutes in an unsuccessful, one-person effort against what, despite his arguments, became the Civil Rights Act of 1957.

A few later efforts have come close to Senator Thurmond's record. In 1986, for example, Senator Alfonse D'Amato (R., New York) staged a successful 23-1/2-hour filibuster against a military spending bill that would have cut funding for a warplane built by a company in his district. Hundreds of other measures have been killed by the filibuster. In fact, just the *threat* of a filibuster has resulted in the Senate's failure to consider a number of bills and the amending of many others.

The Senate often tries to beat off a filibuster with lengthy, even day-and-night, sessions to wear down the participants. At times, some little-observed rules are strictly enforced. Among them are the requirements that senators stand—not sit, lean on their desks, or walk about—as they speak and that they not use "unparliamentary language" on the floor. These countermeasures seldom work.

The Cloture Rule The Senate's real check on the filibuster is its Cloture Rule, Rule XXII in the Standing Rules of the Senate. It was first adopted in 1917, after one of the most notable of all filibusters in Senate history. That filibuster, which lasted for three weeks, took place less than two months before the United States entered World War I.

German submarines had renewed their attacks on shipping in the North Atlantic, so President Wilson asked Congress to permit the arming of American merchant vessels. The bill, widely supported in the country, quickly passed the House, by a vote of 403–13. The measure died in the Senate, however, because twelve senators filibustered it until the end of the congressional term on March 4th.

The public was outraged. President Wilson declared: "A little group of willful men, representing no opinion but their own, has rendered the great Government of the United States helpless and contemptible." The Senate passed the Cloture Rule at its next session.

Rule XXII provides for **cloture**—limiting debate. The rule is not in regular, continuing force; it can be brought into play only by a special procedure. A vote to invoke the rule must be taken two days after a petition calling for that action has been submitted

The Longest Filibusters

NAME OF SENATOR	YEAR	TOPIC	LENGTH OF FILIBUSTER
Strom Thurmond	1957	opposed Civil Rights Act of 1957	24 h, 18 m
Alfonse D'Amato	1986	opposed military spending bill	23 h, 30 m
Wayne Morse	1953	opposed Tidelands oil bill	22 h, 26 m
Robert LaFollette	1908	opposed a currency bill	18 h, 23 m
William Proxmire	1981	opposed a debt ceiling increase	16 h, 12 m

SOURCE: Washingtonpost.com
*Ted Cruz (R., TX) spoke for 21 h, 19 m in 2013 against a healthcare bill, but there is debate about whether his speech qualified as a filibuster due to Senate rules.

>> In a filibuster, a senator speaks until a cloture vote passes or until the senator runs out of energy. **Analyze Charts** How does the filibuster protect the rights of the minority?

More Filibusters, More Cloture: Selected Congresses

CONGRESS	YEAR	CLOTURE MOTIONS FILED	CLOTURE INVOKED
65	1917–1918	2	0
73	1933–1934	0	0
78	1943–1944	1	0
89	1965–1966	7	1
100	1987–1988	54	12
105	1997–1998	69	18
116	2019–2020	328	270

SOURCE: Senate.gov

>> Since the Senate adopted the cloture rule in 1917, its use has grown as filibusters have become more common. **Analyze Charts** Why do you think cloture motions are filed more often than cloture is actually invoked?

by at least 16 members of the Senate. If at least 60 senators—three fifths of the full Senate—vote for the motion, the rule becomes effective. From that point, no more than another 30 hours of floor time may be spent on the measure. Then it *must* be brought to a final vote.

Quite often, attempts to invoke cloture meet with failure. Many senators hesitate to vote for cloture because (1) they honor the tradition of free debate and/or (2) they worry that frequent use of cloture will undercut the value of the filibuster that they may someday want to use.

Modern Uses of the Filibuster Filibusters have become much more common in modern times because party control of the upper house has often been a very narrow thing. In this type of situation, the minority party, at times the Republicans, and other times the Democrats, make frequent use of the filibuster to block legislation backed by the majority party. And these filibusters are often successful. This is because, given the Cloture Rule, the minimum number of votes necessary to pass an important bill in the Senate today is not 51 or a simple majority of the members present and voting. It is, instead, 60, the minimum number of votes necessary to invoke cloture (end debate).

In 2013, frustrated with Republican filibusters of President Obama's appointees, Democrats changed longstanding rules. Under the new procedures,

nominees for all executive branch and lower court vacancies can be approved by a simple majority of 51 votes. The Republicans took this a step further in 2017, allowing even Supreme Court nominees to be approved with a simple majority.

These changes effectively eliminate senators' ability to filibuster nearly all presidential nominations. Most legislation, however, still must pass the 60-vote threshold.

Some members of Congress and political observers believe that the filibuster should be eliminated because it can derail the making of laws to the point that nothing can be accomplished. Others believe it is still an important fence against too hasty legislating and that it fosters compromise. Only a majority vote in the Senate is required to change the rules, but doing so would be a massive shift. Here again, partisan considerations are a key part of each side's calculations.

☑ **COMPARE AND CONTRAST** Name two major differences between House and Senate debate.

House-Senate Conference Committees

As you have seen, a bill must survive any number of challenges in order to become a law. Most don't. A measure can be killed, or simply buried, in a subcommittee, in the full committee, in the

House Rules Committee, or in any of the parallel committees in the Senate. The remainder must make it through votes on the floor in both houses.

Any measure that does survive the legislative process *must* have been passed by both houses in identical form. Most often, a bill approved by one house and then passed by the other is left unchanged by the second. When the House and Senate do pass different versions of the same bill, the first house usually concurs in the other's amendments, and congressional action is completed.

When one house will not accept the other's version of a bill, the measure is sent to a conference committee—a temporary joint committee of the two chambers. It seeks to produce a compromise bill acceptable to both houses. Conferees—managers— are named by the respective presiding officers. Mostly, they are leading members of the standing committee that first handled the measure.

Both chambers' rules say that a conference committee can consider only those parts of a bill on which the two houses have disagreed. In practice, however, conferees often add provisions never considered in either the House or Senate.

Once the conferees agree, their report, the compromise bill, is submitted to both houses. It must be accepted or rejected without amendment. Only rarely does either house turn down a conference committee's work. This is not surprising, for two major reasons: (1) the powerful membership of the typical conference committee, and (2) the fact that its report usually comes in the midst of the rush to adjournment at the end of a congressional session.

The conference committee stage is a most strategic step. A number of major legislative decisions and compromises are often made at that point. Indeed, the late Senator George Norris (R., Nebraska) once quite aptly described conference committees as "the third house of Congress."

☑ **GENERATE EXPLANATIONS** Why do members of a House and Senate conference committee sometimes add provisions to a bill as they work on it?

The President Acts on a Bill

The Constitution requires that bills and resolutions be sent to the President after they have passed both houses of Congress. The President has four options at this point:

The President may sign the bill, and it then becomes law.

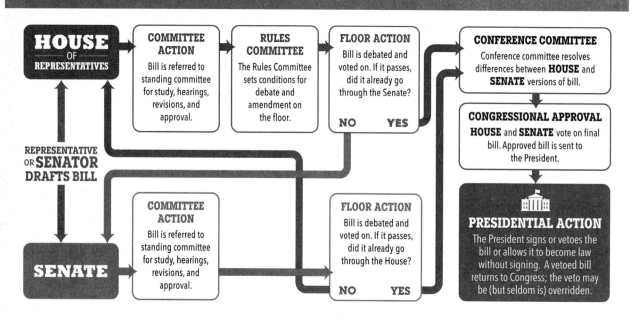

HOW A BILL BECOMES A LAW

HOUSE OF **REPRESENTATIVES**

REPRESENTATIVE OR **SENATOR** DRAFTS BILL

SENATE

COMMITTEE ACTION
Bill is referred to standing committee for study, hearings, revisions, and approval.

RULES COMMITTEE
The Rules Committee sets conditions for debate and amendment on the floor.

FLOOR ACTION
Bill is debated and voted on. If it passes, did it already go through the Senate?
NO   YES

COMMITTEE ACTION
Bill is referred to standing committee for study, hearings, revisions, and approval.

FLOOR ACTION
Bill is debated and voted on. If it passes, did it already go through the House?
NO   YES

CONFERENCE COMMITTEE
Conference committee resolves differences between **HOUSE** and **SENATE** versions of bill.

CONGRESSIONAL APPROVAL
HOUSE and **SENATE** vote on final bill. Approved bill is sent to the President.

PRESIDENTIAL ACTION
The President signs or vetoes the bill or allows it to become law without signing. A vetoed bill returns to Congress; the veto may be (but seldom is) overridden.

>> A bill may be introduced first in either the House or the Senate. **Analyze Sequence** In what ways does the lawmaking process in the House differ from that in the Senate?

The President may **veto**—refuse to sign—the bill. The measure must then be returned to the house in which it originated, together with the President's objections (a veto message). Although it seldom does, Congress may then pass the bill over the President's veto, by a two-thirds vote of the full membership of each house.

The President may allow the bill to become law without signing it—by not acting on it within 10 days, not counting Sundays, of receiving it.

The fourth option is a variation of the third, called the **pocket veto.** If Congress adjourns its session within 10 days of submitting a bill to the President, and the President does not act, the measure dies. (Sundays are not counted.) Congress added another element to the President's veto power with the passage of the Line Item Veto Act of 1996. That law gave the chief executive the power to reject individual items in appropriations bills. The Supreme Court held the law unconstitutional, however, in *Clinton* v. *City of New York,* 1998.

Because Congress can seldom muster enough votes to override a veto, the power can play an extremely effective part in the President's dealings with Congress. The weight of that power in the executive-legislative relationship is underscored by this fact: The mere threat of a veto is often enough to defeat a bill or to prompt changes in its provisions as it moves through the legislative process.

☑ **INFER** Why might a President use a pocket veto instead of a regular veto for bill?

Unorthodox Lawmaking and Emergency Legislation

The steps outlined by the Constitution explain the process used throughout most of our nation's history for a bill to become law. However, a number of adjustments in recent decades have continued to transform the lawmaking process. For example, it is increasingly common for each chamber to pass generic bills, knowing that the true details of the legislation will be ironed-out in conference committee. Another approach to reconciling differences, often called "ping-ponging," is for each chamber to take turns adding amendments until disagreements are resolved. On occasion, particularly at the end of the legislative session, when there is a push to tie up loose ends, bills can "ping-pong" back and forth between the House and

>> This illustration, which appeared in *The Washington Post* in 1906, depicts the Hepburn Bill, which was amended so much in the Senate that it was practically unrecognizable to its original House author. **Analyze Political Cartoons** How does the artist portray the amended bill?

>> President George W. Bush signs the Patriot Act Anti-Terrorism bill on October 26, 2001. The bill was introduced on October 23, passed the House on October 24, and the Senate on October 25.

Senate on an hourly basis. **Omnibus measures**, where one bill contains numerous issues and topics, have also become much more common.

Why have these changes to the traditional lawmaking process occurred? Simply stated, the two major parties have found less and less common ground in recent years. In addition, majority party leaders have been granted greater leeway from their members to insert themselves more directly into key stages of the process, with an eye toward producing results. There is no question that both parties are using unorthodox approaches to advance their initiatives in the modern Congress.

Also, emergencies occasionally arise during which the legislature is called upon to act quickly. With such events, Congress does not have the luxury to follow every step strictly by the book.

Such was the case with the Emergency Economic Stabilization Act of 2008, the so-called "Wall Street Bailout Bill," passed in response to the devastating economic crisis in September of that year. President George W. Bush's advisors proposed a plan by which the U.S. Treasury would acquire up to $700 billion worth of mortgage-backed securities. By doing so, they argued, banks would again start lending money.

Congress acted quickly, but not as fast as the Bush administration had hoped. On the one hand, many legislators understood that a massive governmental intervention was the only hope to stave off a financial collapse. On the other hand, many also knew that average citizens saw the proposed measure as helping the business elite. As a result, the plan was very unpopular back in many lawmakers' home districts, leading to some minor delays in its passage.

In short, when emergencies arise, Congress can move quickly, but not nearly as rapidly as the executive branch. This is exactly what the Framers envisioned—immediate action from the executive branch, but slower deliberations in the legislature. Also, unlike Presidents, members of Congress face direct constituencies, and what is good for the nation might be unpopular back home.

Case Study: Environmental Legislation
A look at the passage of one law in particular, the Clean Air Act Amendments of 1990, will help demonstrate why getting a law passed is often difficult.

In the 1970s, pollution levels in Los Angeles, California, hit unhealthy levels 200 days out of the year. While Los Angeles had the worst air quality among American cities, smog was nonetheless a growing problem across the nation by the mid 1900s.

Increasing awareness of the ill effects of pollution had led Congress to pass a landmark piece of legislation, the Clean Air Act, in 1970. While the act made significant progress toward cleaning up the air, work remained to be done. Forests and lakes were threatened by acid rain and many cities still battled unhealthy smog.

Despite their best efforts to pass legislation that would curb acid rain and vehicle emissions in the 1980s, lawmakers were unable to get a new bill passed. According to Representative Henry Waxman (D., California), "Throughout the 1980s, thousands of hours were spent developing, debating and blocking legislative proposals; hundreds of witnesses testified at hearings; and millions of dollars were spent on lobbying by interest groups."

It was not until George H.W. Bush became President in 1989 that things began to change. Spurred on by a looming Clean Air Act compliance deadline and the President's campaign promise to be the "environmental president," congressional leaders found new momentum for a bill.

To craft legislation that could make it through hurdles in both houses, as well as win support across the States, compromises were made and deals were struck. After months of negotiations, bills cleared the House and Senate, despite strong lobbying against them by industry. "The oil companies said doing the reformulated gasoline would drive them out of business; the chemical companies said the ozone depletion rules were going to cause widespread havoc and shut down hospitals and office buildings," recalls a member of Representative Waxman's staff.

During the conference committee process, further refinements were made to the bill. The final version, according to Senator Mitch McConnell (R., Kentucky), "was dramatically improved from the time it emerged from the Environment Committee to final passage." Despite those improvements, some members from coal-mining States such as West Virginia and Illinois voted against the bill. They believed it would harm the economy in their States.

In the end, the bill passed by a wide margin in both houses. President George H.W. Bush signed the Clean Air Act Amendments of 1990 into law on November 15, 1990, noting that "the 13-year legislative logjam has now been broken."

☑ **ANALYZE INFORMATION** Why did the Framers of the Constitution envision immediate action from the executive branch but slower deliberation in Congress? What is one advantage and one disadvantage of each type of decision making?

1. **Synthesize** Does the Rules Committee influence the outcome of a bill more than its sponsor?

2. **Explain** Why would government observers complain that the filibuster allows a minority to control the Senate?

3. **Check Understanding** The House of Representatives uses five calendars to schedule bills, yet the schedule is often ignored. What is the purpose of special procedures to bring bills to the floor?

4. **Compare and Contrast** Explain the similarities and differences between pigeonholing a bill and exercising a pocket veto.

5. **Synthesize** Who is most important in the passage of a law—the bill's sponsor, the committee that considers the bill, or the President? Explain your answer.

Passing the USA PATRIOT Act

Mere days after the 9/11 attacks, Congress was asked to create legislation that would deter terrorists from ever attacking the United States again. The Senate put forward a bill called the Uniting and Strengthening America (USA) Act. The House incorporated much of that bill into its version under the same title. However, both chambers could not agree on either version. On October 23, 2001, the House submitted a compromise bill entitled the Uniting and Strengthening America by Providing Appropriate Tools Required to Intercept and Obstruct Terrorism (USA PATRIOT) Act. On October 24, by a vote of 347-66, it passed in the House. With only one "no" vote (Senator Russ Feingold), it passed in the Senate on October 25.

As you read, pay attention to the constitutional issues each senator raises as he tries to persuade other senators to support or oppose the bill.

>> The terrorist attacks on September 11, 2001, shook the nation to the core. To many, it felt like the threat of terrorism was now on every Americans' doorstep.

Primary Source 1

Senator Russ Feingold (D., WI), Senate Floor Debate, October 25, 2001

One provision would greatly expand the circumstances in which law enforcement agencies can search homes and offices without notifying the owner prior to the search. The longstanding practice under the fourth amendment of serving a warrant prior to executing a search could be easily avoided in virtually every case, because the government would simply have to show that it had "reasonable cause to believe" that providing notice "may" "seriously jeopardize an investigation." This is a significant infringement on personal liberty.

. . . If you're not home, and the police have received permission to do a "sneak and peek" search,
they can come in your house, look around, and leave, and may never have to tell you that ever happened.

That bothers me. I bet it bothers most Americans. . . .

☑ **DEVELOP EMPATHY** How do you feel about the ability of the police to conduct a "sneak and peek" in your home?

Another provision that troubles me a lot is one that permits the Government . . . to compel the production of records from any business regarding any person if that information is sought in connection with an investigation of terrorism or espionage. . . .

Under this provision, the Government can apparently go on a fishing expedition and collect information on virtually anyone. All it has to allege [assert without proof], in order to get an order for these records from the court, is that the information is sought for an investigation of international terrorism or clandestine [secret] intelligence gathering. . . .

Protecting the safety of the American people is a solemn duty of the Congress. . . . But the Congress will fulfill its duty only when it protects both the American people and the freedoms at the foundation of American society.

☑ **DETERMINE CENTRAL IDEAS** What is the greatest concern expressed in Source 1?

Primary Source 2

Senator Orrin Hatch (R., UT), Senate Floor Debate, October 25, 2001

[W]hat he called a "sneak and peek" search warrant, these warrants are already used throughout the United States, throughout our whole country. The bill simply codifies and clarifies the practice. . . .

As the past few weeks have made clear, these terrorists still have a gun pointed at the heads of all the American people. Under such circumstances, it is our sworn duty to do everything in our power, within the bounds of the Constitution, to protect and defend our people. That is what this bill does.

The Senator from Wisconsin worries about the "possible" loss of civil liberties. That is laudable [worthy of praise]. But I am more concerned about the actual loss of the thousands of lives that have been lost and the potential of other lives that may be lost because we don't give law enforcement the tools they need. . . .

I think most people in this country would be outraged to know that various agencies of Government, the intelligence community, and law enforcement community, under current law—until this bill is passed—cannot exchange information that might help interdict [prohibit] and stop terrorism. . . .

☑ **ANALYZE WORD CHOICES** What words or phrases does Senator Hatch use to convey a sense of urgency and necessity in passing the Act?

I think they would be outraged to know that . . . you cannot electronically surveil a terrorist unless there is some underlying criminal predicate [basis or foundation]. In many cases, there is no underlying criminal predicate, so you can't do to terrorists what we can do for health care fraud, or for sexual exploitation of children, or for the Mafia, or for drug dealers. . . .

We have to be able to track terrorists. Under current law, we cannot do that with the efficiency that needs to be used here. I don't see any civil liberties violated there, but I see some of them protected. I think of the civil liberties of those approximately 6,000 people who lost their lives, and potentially many others if we don't give law enforcement the tools they need to do the job. That is what this bill does.

☑ **ANALYZE STYLE AND RHETORIC** Why do you think Senator Hatch repeats "that is what this bill does"?

☑ **ASSESSMENT**

1. **Compare and Contrast** How was the passage of this bill similar to and different from the usual lawmaking process?

2. **Analyze Arguments** Do the arguments in Source 2 support the need to put safety first over individual rights? Why or why not?

3. **Contrast** How would you describe the tone in both sources? Which do you think would gain the most support at the time?

4. **Draw Conclusions** The Patriot Act was written and passed within six weeks of the 9/11 attacks. Do you think this speed had any effect on the quality of the law?

LESSON SUMMARIES

Use these Lesson Summaries, and the longer versions available online, to review the key ideas for each lesson in this Topic.

Lesson 1: National Legislature Overview

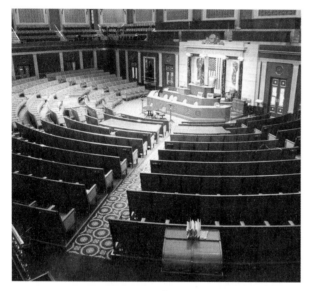

The Framers designed a national government with a powerful legislative branch, the Congress, meant to represent the people. Congress members must decide how best to do this. Senators and representatives are paid a salary plus substantial fringe benefits.

Lesson 2: The Two Houses

The House of Representatives, the lower house of Congress, has 435 members today. States are assigned a set number of representatives based on their population according to the latest census. They draw their own congressional districts, which can be unfair. Each state elects two senators, regardless of population.

Lesson 3: The Expressed Powers

Congressional powers come from the Constitution. Some are those inherent in sovereign nations. Others, the expressed powers, are stated specifically. They include the power to regulate interstate and foreign trade, coin money, declare war, fund the military, and grant copyrights.

Lesson 4: The Implied and Nonlegislative Powers

In addition to the expressed powers, Congress also has authority to take actions implied by these powers. These implied powers include the ability to regulate most economic activity. The Constitution also gives Congress nonlegislative powers to approve or reject the President's major appointees and to remove high officials from office when necessary.

Lesson 5: Congress at Work— Organization and Committees

Presiding and party officers lead the two houses of Congress. The Speaker of the House presides over debate and assigns committee memberships. Majority and minority leaders and whips also play an important role in both houses. Congress does much of its work in different types of committees. The leadership assigns bills to these committees for review before the full House or Senate votes them on.

Lesson 6: Congress at Work—Making Laws

Bills in Congress must clear many obstacles before becoming laws. Fewer than 10 percent succeed. Bills are introduced and referred to committees, where many are rejected or ignored. If approved in committee, bills are debated on the House or Senate floor. Eventually, once both houses have approved an identical version of the bill, the President may sign it into law or veto it.

VISUAL REVIEW

Use these graphics to review some of the key terms, people, and ideas from this Topic.

Types of Bills and Resolutions

Bill	A proposed law: a public bill applies to the entire nation; a private bill applies only to certain people or places
Joint Resolution	A proposal for some action that has the force of law when passed; usually deals with special circumstances or temporary matters
Concurrent Resolution	A statement of position on an issue, adopted by the House and Senate in identical form
Resolution	A measure dealing with some matter in one house; does not have the force of law and does not require the President's signature

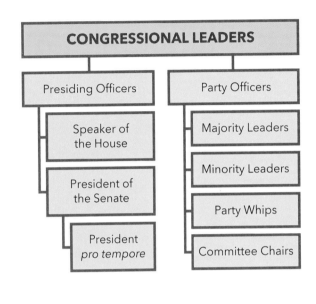

Congressional Powers

Expressed Powers	• Regulating commerce • Collecting taxes and coin money • Defining Federal crimes • Raising armies and a navy and declaring war
Implied Powers	• Spending tax money to "promote the general welfare" • Regulating activities that affect interstate commerce such as, manufacturing, wages, and air travel
Nonlegislative Powers	• Conducting investigations • Approving appointments • Impeaching officials

Comparing the House and the Senate

HOUSE OF REPRESENTATIVES	SENATE
• Smaller personal staffs • Fewer committee assignments • More formal, less flexible rules • Committee work usually more important than floor debate in shaping outcome of legislation • Floor debate strictly limited	• Larger personal staffs • More committee assignments • Fewer, more flexible rules • Floor debate often more important than committee work in shaping outcome of legislation • Floor debate largely unlimited, but subject to cloture vote by 60 senators to end debate

KEY TERMS, PEOPLE, AND IDEAS

1. Why is the role of **committee chair** so powerful?

2. Describe the **commerce power**.

3. Does the concept of **implied powers** undercut federalism? Why or why not?

4. Describe the process outlined in the Constitution to **impeach** the President.

5. How often does a new **term** of Congress begin?

6. How do **strict constructionists** and **liberal constructionists** differ?

7. What is a **filibuster**?

8. How are **reapportionment** and **gerrymandering** related?

CRITICAL THINKING

9. **Hypothesize** Under what circumstances might a senator's role as a national leader conflict with his or her role as a representative of a State?

10. **Integrate Information** Conduct research on a bill that is currently under consideration in Congress. Evaluate the resources you find in terms of their reliability. Choose the most trustworthy sources and use them to consider the predicted outcomes and consequences of the proposed legislation. Write a letter or email to your representative in Congress in which you state your position on the proposed legislation and give reasons to support your viewpoint.

11. **Summarize** Why did the Framers grant Congress the power to tax? What is the purpose of taxes?

12. **Express Ideas Clearly** List five of the expressed powers of Congress as set out in the Constitution.

13. **Classify** Identify the three different types of congressional powers, and explain how the Constitution limits the powers of Congress.

14. **Summarize** Describe the conflict over the meaning of the Necessary and Proper Clause.

15. **Compare and contrast** the makeup of the House of Representatives and the Senate in terms of number of seats, qualifications for office, and length of terms.

16. **Hypothesize** The map in the next column shows reapportionment in the House of Representatives based on the 2020 census. Why is reapportionment an important process? If the Framers had not provided for reapportionment, what might have happened to the representation of different States over time?

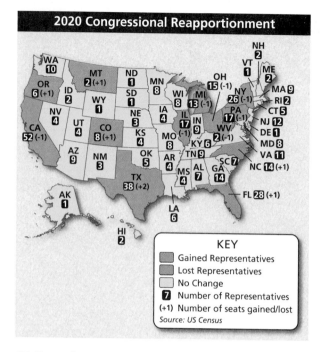

2020 Congressional Reapportionment

KEY
- Gained Representatives
- Lost Representatives
- No Change
- **7** Number of Representatives
- (+1) Number of seats gained/lost

Source: US Census

17. **Draw Conclusions** What problems can gerrymandering cause?

18. **Summarize** How can committee chairs influence legislation?

19. **Identify Cause and Effect** Research the War Powers Act of 1973, including the reason(s) it was originally proposed and any real-life effects it has had on the President's ability to order troops into combat in the years since its passage. Write a brief summary of your findings.

20. **Express Ideas Clearly** In the decisions *Gibbons* v. *Ogden* (1824) and *Heart of Atlanta Motel* v. *United States* (1964), the Supreme Court based its rulings on the same provision in the Constitution. What power of Congress did the Court base its decisions on, and what made these cases landmark decisions?

21. **Writing Activity** Identify your current representative and senators in the United States Congress. Consulting numerous sources, create a chart that lists the following information for each: Name, hometown, length of time in Congress, and congressional committees on which he or she serves. Next, choose one of these legislators and write a one-page essay in which you explore his or her major accomplishments in Congress. Incorporate at least one quotation from the representative or senator and at least one newspaper article in which he or she is mentioned.

DOCUMENT-BASED QUESTIONS

A major part of the Federal Government's response to the Great Recession of the early 2000s was Secretary of the Treasury Henry Paulson's proposed bailout plan, the Troubled Asset Relief Program, or TARP. TARP provoked strong reactions from the public.

DOCUMENT A

The U.S. Treasury established several programs under TARP to help stabilize the U.S. financial system.

- Approximately $250 billion was committed in programs to stabilize banking institutions…
- Approximately $27 billion was committed through programs to restart credit markets.
- Approximately $82 billion was committed to stabilize the U.S. auto industry…
- Approximately $70 billion was committed to stabilize American International Group (AIG)…
- Approximately $46 billion was committed for programs to help struggling families avoid foreclosure…

—*www.treasury.gov*

DOCUMENT B

This excerpt is from an article opposing the bill that established TARP.

Congress votes this week on the biggest giveaway of our tax dollars to the financial sector in our nation's history. Despite attempts by legislators to portray this as a compromise bill that helps both Wall Street and Main Street, in reality it represents an appalling transfer of wealth upward.

—*Medea Benjamin and Arun Gupta, "Time for a Taxpayer Revolt," The Nation, September 29, 2008*

DOCUMENT C

This excerpt is from an article written two years after TARP was established.

TARP was an essential piece of a necessary evil….

People who are opposed to bailouts of any kind like to argue that TARP was not really necessary. Banks could have been allowed to fail and the economic fallout around the world would not have been so dramatic.

This was, of course, the view taken by policy makers in 1929-31, after the Great Crash….

The result was the Great Depression. No responsible policy maker would want to run that risk again.

—*Simon Johnson, "TARP, the Long Goodbye," The New York Times, September 30, 2010*

DOCUMENT D

This is an excerpt from an article written when TARP officially expired.

[T]he TARP bailout was a terrible idea that will cost taxpayers both directly and indirectly through its perverse incentives….

The TARP was crooked from the very start, using taxpayer funds to bail out some of the world's richest people from their own foolish investments….Even worse, TARP taught investment bankers an important lesson: During a boom, make as much money as you can, no matter how short-term the profits will be. When the bubble pops, the Treasury and Fed will be there with a taxpayer-funded pillow.

—*Robert P. Murphy, "Was TARP Good for the Taxpayers?" Ludwig Von Mises Institute, October 7, 2010*

22. Which view of TARP would Simon Johnson most likely agree with?
    A. It was essential to avoid severe economic problems.
    B. It was a reward to the wealthy.
    C. It was inadequate in scope.
    D. It was an excessive burden on the taxpayers.

23. Which view of TARP is shared by the writers Benjamin, Gupta, and Murphy?
    A. It represented a dangerous move toward central planning.
    B. It was an economic necessity.
    C. Its main effect was to bail out the wealthy.
    D. It was a plan to redistribute wealth from the rich to the poor.

24. **Writing Task** Use the data given in Document A to create a pie chart showing how the $475 billion in TARP funding was allocated to various programs. Be careful when specifying units of measure and calculate your chart accurately. Then write a paragraph in which you use the information in your chart and Documents B-D to take a position on the following question: Which writer or writers do you think make the most effective points regarding TARP? Why?

The Executive Branch: The Presidency and Vice Presidency

ESSENTIAL QUESTION What makes a good leader?

Barack Obama, the nation's first Black President, in the Oval Office

Connections to Today

When did you last see the President of the United States performing official duties on television or online? Chances are that whatever the occasion, it was of great importance to the country. This isn't only true within the United States, either. Every word the President utters in public is broadcast around the world and analyzed and can set in motion policies that affect millions of people. Has this always been the case? Is the amount of power that the President has today good or bad for the people of the United States?

NBC LEARN

Examine the qualities that make a good President by exploring the presidencies of Theodore Roosevelt and Ronald Reagan.

 BOUNCE to Activate My Story Video

Topic 5 Overview

In this Topic, you will learn about the President of the United States, including the many powers that come with the office. You will also learn about the roles played by the Vice President and the First Lady. Look at the lesson outline and explore the timeline. As you study this Topic, you can work on your Quest Inquiry.

LESSON OUTLINE

5.1 The Presidency—An Overview

5.2 The Vice President and the First Lady

5.3 The President's Domestic Powers

5.4 The President's Foreign Affairs Powers

The Growth of Presidential Power

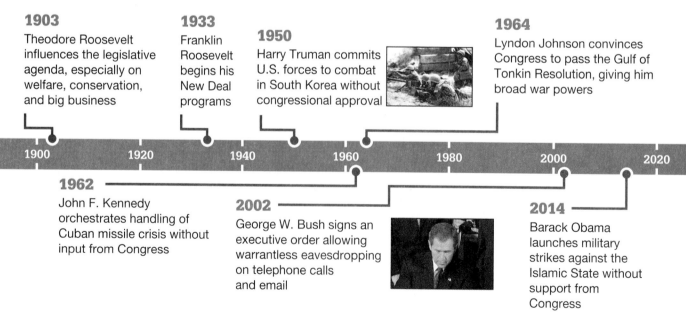

1903
Theodore Roosevelt influences the legislative agenda, especially on welfare, conservation, and big business

1933
Franklin Roosevelt begins his New Deal programs

1950
Harry Truman commits U.S. forces to combat in South Korea without congressional approval

1964
Lyndon Johnson convinces Congress to pass the Gulf of Tonkin Resolution, giving him broad war powers

1900   1920   1940   1960   1980   2000   2020

1962
John F. Kennedy orchestrates handling of Cuban missile crisis without input from Congress

2002
George W. Bush signs an executive order allowing warrantless eavesdropping on telephone calls and email

2014
Barack Obama launches military strikes against the Islamic State without support from Congress

Inquiry Center

Want to become an active and effective citizen? Make a difference in your community and beyond by using the **Inquiry Center** on the digital course.

Connect with issues you're passionate about by using the **Interest Finder**.

Investigate public policies, get involved in your community, influence public opinion, and develop leadership skills.

Synthesize the work you've done and what you've learned along the way.

Demonstrate what you've learned once you've finished your project by sharing your work.

5.1

President Lyndon Johnson meets with civil rights leaders at the White House.

 BOUNCE to Activate Flipped Video

Objectives

Describe the President's many roles.

Understand the formal qualifications necessary to become President.

Explain how the number of terms for which a President may serve has changed over time.

Key Terms

chief of state
chief executive
domestic affairs
foreign affairs
chief administrator
chief diplomat
chief legislator
commander in chief
chief economist
chief of party
chief citizen
presidential
  succession
impeachment
Presidential
  Succession Act of
  1947
president pro
  tempore
William Howard Taft
Harry Truman
Franklin D. Roosevelt
Lyndon B. Johnson
Richard Nixon
Herbert Hoover
Dwight Eisenhower
Alexander Hamilton
George Washington
George H.W. Bush
William Henry
  Harrison
Woodrow Wilson
George W. Bush

The Presidency—An Overview

Do you know what the President does? Who takes over if a President dies while in office? Whether a person born abroad can become President? You will find the answers to these questions, and much more, in this section, which provides a basic overview of the presidential office.

The President's Many Roles

At any given time, of course, only one person is the President of the United States. The office, with all of its awesome powers and duties, belongs to that one individual. Whoever that person may be, he—and most likely someday she—must fill several different roles, and all of them at the same time. The President is simultaneously (1) chief of state, (2) chief executive, (3) chief administrator, (4) chief diplomat, (5) chief legislator, (6) commander in chief, (7) chief economist, (8) chief of party, and (9) chief citizen.

Chief of State To begin with, the President is **chief of state**, the ceremonial head of the government of the United States. He or she is, then, the symbol of all of the people of the nation—in President **William Howard Taft's** words, "the personal embodiment and representative of their dignity and majesty."

In many countries, the chief of state reigns but does not rule. That is certainly true of the queens of England, Denmark, and the Netherlands; the kings of Norway, Sweden, and Belgium; the emperor of Japan; and the presidents of Italy and Germany. It is just as certainly *not* true of the President of the United States. The President both reigns and rules.

Chief Executive The President is the nation's **chief executive**, vested by the Constitution with "the executive Power" of the United States. That power is immensely broad in **domestic affairs** as well as **foreign affairs**. Indeed, the American presidency is often described as "the most powerful office in the world."

But remember, the President is not all-powerful. He or she must abide by constitutional checks and balances that place many practical limits on what he or she can and cannot do.

Chief Administrator The President is also the **chief administrator**, the director of the huge executive branch of the Federal Government. He or she heads one of the largest governmental machines the world has ever known. Today, the President directs an administration that employs millions of civilians and spends trillions of dollars each year.

Managing the sprawling executive branch is only one of the President's several jobs. **Harry Truman** complained that he had to spend too much of his time "flattering, kissing, and kicking people to get them to do what they were supposed to do anyway."

Chief Diplomat Every President is also the nation's **chief diplomat**, the main architect of American foreign policy and the nation's chief spokesman to the rest of the world. "I make foreign policy," President Truman once said—and he did. Everything the President says and does is closely followed, both here and abroad.

Chief Legislator The President is also the nation's **chief legislator**, the principal author of its public policies. Most often, it is the President who sets the overall shape of the congressional agenda—initiating, suggesting, requesting, insisting, and demanding that Congress enact most of the major pieces of legislation that it does.

The President and Congress do sometimes clash, and the President does not always get his or her way on Capitol Hill. Still, working with Congress occupies a major part of the President's time.

These six presidential roles all come directly from the Constitution. Yet they do not complete the list. The President has still other vital roles to play.

Commander in Chief In close concert with his or her role in foreign affairs, the Constitution also

>> President George W. Bush wears a traditional jacket at a meeting with Chinese President Jiang Zemin. As chief diplomat, the U.S. President meets with world leaders and shapes foreign policy.

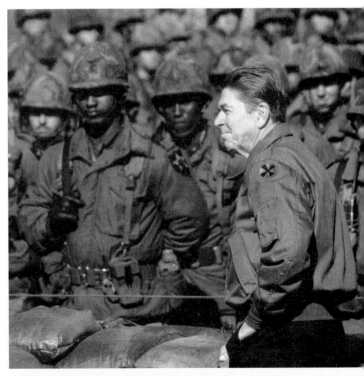

>> In his role as commander in chief of U.S. forces, President Ronald Reagan speaks to U.S. Army troops stationed in South Korea in 1983.

makes the President the **commander in chief** of the nation's armed forces. More than one million men and women in uniform and all of the nation's military might are subject to the President's direct and immediate control. The Constitution does give Congress some significant powers in foreign affairs and over the military, but the President has long since become dominant in both fields.

Chief Economist Some observers have suggested that modern Presidents must also be the nation's **chief economist**. That is, the President is expected to keep a close eye on the nation's economy and to take immediate and effective action when conditions dictate. Since the collapse of communism in the Soviet Union and Eastern Europe in 1989, and paralleling the rapid expansion of Asian economies (especially those of China and India), the management of America's trade relationships has been an expanding aspect of presidential responsibilities. This change has created unique challenges for the President. Opening foreign markets for American goods requires lowering or removing trade restrictions and tariffs on goods imported into the United States.

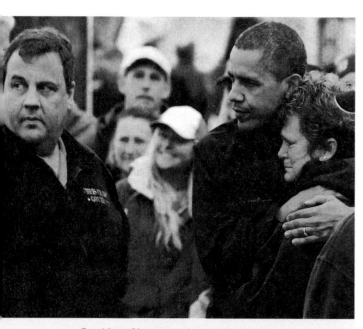

>> President Obama comforts a New Jersey resident as he and Governor Chris Christie survey hurricane damage in 2012. As chief citizen, the President fights for the people's best interests.

As chief economist, the President must constantly balance many conflicting demands, including those of consumers, labor unions, and manufacturers. At the same time, the President must remain ever sensitive to the effect that American economic policies can have on our relationships with countries around the world.

Chief of Party The President is, automatically, the **chief of party**, the acknowledged leader of the political party that controls the executive branch— and is virtually unchallengeable in that role. As you know, parties are not mentioned in the Constitution, but they do have a vital place in the workings of the American governmental system. Much of the real power and influence of the President depends on his or her ability to play this critical role.

Chief Citizen The office also automatically makes its occupant the nation's **chief citizen**. The President is expected to be "the representative of all the people." He or she is expected to take the high road and champion the public interest against the many different and competing private interests. "The presidency," said **Franklin Roosevelt**, "is not merely an administrative office. That is the least of it. It is, preeminently, a place of moral leadership."

Listing the President's roles is a useful way to describe the President's job. But, remember, the President must juggle all of these roles simultaneously, and they are all interconnected. In addition, as presidential power has grown over time, so has the number and scope of the roles he or she must fulfill. Note, too, that none of them can be performed in isolation. The manner in which a President plays any one role can affect his or her ability to execute the others.

As but two illustrations of the point, take the experiences of Presidents **Lyndon Johnson** and **Richard Nixon**. Each was a strong and relatively effective President during his first years in office. But Mr. Johnson's actions as commander in chief during the agonizing and increasingly unpopular war in Vietnam seriously damaged his stature and effectiveness in the White House. In fact, the damage was so great that it helped persuade LBJ not to run for reelection in 1968.

The many-sided and sordid Watergate scandal brought President Nixon's downfall. The manner in which he filled the roles of party leader and chief

Presidential Rankings

LEADERSHIP CHARACTERISTICS		PRESIDENTS AND RANKINGS			
• Public Persuasion	• Administrative Skills	Abraham Lincoln	1*	Harry S. Truman	6
• Crisis Leadership	• Relations with Congress	George Washington	2	Thomas Jefferson	7
• Economic Management	• Vision/Setting an Agenda	Franklin D. Roosevelt	3	John F. Kennedy	8
• Moral Authority	• Pursued Equal Justice for All	Theodore Roosevelt	4	Ronald Reagan	9
• International Relations	• Performance within Context of Times	Dwight D. Eisenhower	5	Barack Obama	10

SOURCE: C-SPAN 2021 Presidential Historians Survey *1 = Highest score

>> A panel of more than 100 historians ranked the Presidents based on the characteristics on the left. **Analyze Charts** Can you match each of these characteristics with a presidential role?

citizen so destroyed Mr. Nixon's presidency that he was forced to leave office in disgrace in 1974.

☑ **IDENTIFY MAIN IDEAS** The President fills several different roles simultaneously. Analyze how the roles of chief of state, chief diplomat, and commander in chief are related.

Qualifications for the Presidency

Whatever else a President must be, the Constitution says that he—and likely one day, she—must meet three formal qualifications for office (Article II, Section 1, Clause 5). These qualifications are related to a candidate's citizenship, age, and residency.

Citizenship Any man or woman who seeks the presidency must first be "a natural born Citizen . . . of the United States." But what exactly do the words "natural born" mean? Do they refer to being "native born"—that is, born in the United States? By law, a person born abroad to an American-citizen parent becomes an American citizen at birth. That law leads many to argue that it is therefore possible for a person born outside the United States to become President. Some dispute that view, however. The question of what the Constitution means here cannot

be answered until someone born a citizen, but born abroad, does in fact seek the presidency. Naturalized citizens cannot run for the presidency, no matter how distinguished their qualifications may be.

Age The Constitution also states that in order to serve as President, a person must "have attained . . . the Age of 35 years." During the writing of the Constitution in 1787, there was no public discussion about this age requirement for the President. In modern times, some have called for an age *limit* rather than a minimum age for the presidency. However, given that most people live longer and are healthier than in times past, this proposal has not won any serious support in Congress. Most chief executives have been in their 50s when they reached the White House, but several, such as Ronald Reagan and Joseph Biden, have been considerably older.

Residency Finally, to hold the office of President of the United States, a person must "[H]ave . . . been fourteen years a Resident within the United States." Given the elections of **Herbert Hoover** (in 1928) and **Dwight Eisenhower** (in 1952), we know that here the Constitution means any 14 years in a person's life. Both men spent several years outside the country before winning the White House.

While these formal qualifications do have some importance, they are really not very difficult to meet.

Indeed, millions of Americans do so today. Several other *informal* and important qualifications for the presidency exist as well, however. These include such requirements as political experience and speaking ability.

☑ **DRAW CONCLUSIONS** Why do you think the Framers chose to provide formal qualifications for the office of the President?

The Presidential Term of Office

The Framers considered a number of different limits on the length of the presidential term. Most of their debate centered on a four-year term, with the President eligible for reelection, versus a single six-year or seven-year term without being eligible for reelection. They finally settled on a four-year term (Article II, Section 1, Clause 1). They agreed, as **Alexander Hamilton** wrote in The *Federalist* No. 71, that four years was a long enough period for a President to have gained experience, demonstrated his abilities, and established stable policies.

>> After Franklin Roosevelt was elected President four times, Congress passed the 22nd Amendment to limit the number of presidential terms. **Infer** What are the pros and cons of term limits?

Until 1951, the Constitution placed no limit on the number of terms a President might serve. Several Presidents, beginning with **George Washington,** refused to seek more than two terms, however. Soon, the "no-third term tradition" became an unwritten rule.

Franklin D. Roosevelt broke the tradition by seeking and winning a third term in 1940, and then a fourth in 1944. To prevent this from recurring, the 22nd Amendment made the unwritten custom limiting presidential terms a part of the written Constitution.

Each President may now serve a maximum of two full terms—eight years—in office. A President who succeeds to the office after the midpoint in a term could possibly serve for more than eight years. In that case, the President may finish out the predecessor's term and then seek two full terms of his or her own. However, no President may serve more than ten years in the office.

Many people, including Presidents Truman, Eisenhower, and Reagan, have called for the repeal of the 22nd Amendment. They insist that the two-term rule is undemocratic because it places an arbitrary limit on the people's right to decide who should be President. Critics also say that it undercuts the authority of a two-term President, especially in the latter part of a second term. Supporters of the amendment defend it as a reasonable safeguard against "executive tyranny."

Several Presidents have urged a single six-year term. They and others have argued that a single, nonrenewable term would free a President from the pressures of a campaign for a second term—and so would allow the chief executive to focus on the pressing demands of the office.

☑ **IDENTIFY CAUSE AND EFFECT** Who was Franklin D. Roosevelt, and what effect did he have on the development of the 22nd Amendment?

Presidential Succession and Disability

The vice presidency can be a stepping stone to winning a presidential election, as it was, for example, for **George H.W. Bush** in 1989. Or, it may instead be the means by which a Vice President is catapulted into the White House should the presidency become vacant for some reason.

Methods of Filling Vacancies Presidential succession is the scheme by which a presidential vacancy is filled. If a President dies, resigns, or is

The Line of Succession

1	Vice President	10	Secretary of Commerce
2	Speaker of the House	11	Secretary of Labor
3	President pro tempore of the Senate	12	Secretary of Health and Human Services
4	Secretary of State	13	Secretary of Housing and Urban Development
5	Secretary of the Treasury	14	Secretary of Transportation
6	Secretary of Defense	15	Secretary of Energy
7	Attorney General	16	Secretary of Education
8	Secretary of the Interior	17	Secretary of Veterans Affairs
9	Secretary of Agriculture	18	Secretary of Homeland Security

>> By tradition, one of the people in the line of succession does not attend the President's State of the Union address with the others. **Analyze Charts** Why do you think this is done?

removed from office by **impeachment**, the Vice President succeeds to the office. Originally, the Constitution did not provide for the succession of a Vice President. Rather, it declared that "the powers and duties" of the office—not the office itself—were to "devolve on [transfer to] the Vice President" (read carefully Article II, Section 1, Clause 6).

In practice, however, the Vice President did succeed to the office when it became vacant. Vice President John Tyler was the first to do so. He set the precedent in 1841 when he succeeded President **William Henry Harrison**, who died of pneumonia just one month after taking office. After Vice President Tyler, seven more Vice Presidents succeeded to the office due to a President's death. At age 42, Theodore Roosevelt became the youngest President to hold the office as a result of the assassination of President William McKinley in 1901.

What had been practice became a part of the written Constitution with the 25th Amendment in 1967, which states, "In case of the removal of the President from office or of his death or resignation, the Vice President shall become President."

Order of Succession According to Article II, Section 1, Clause 6 of the Constitution, Congress fixes the order of succession following the Vice President. The present law on the matter is the **Presidential Succession Act of 1947**. By its terms, the Speaker of the House and then the **president pro tempore** of the Senate are next in line. They are followed, in turn, by the secretary of

state and then by each of the other 14 heads of the Cabinet departments, in order of each position's precedence—that is, the order in which their offices were created by Congress.

Disability of the President Until the 25th Amendment was adopted in 1967, the arrangement for presidential succession had serious gaps. Neither the Constitution nor Congress had made any provision for deciding when a President was so disabled that he could not perform the duties of the office. Nor was there anything in the Constitution or federal law to indicate by whom such a decision was to be made.

For nearly 180 years, then, the nation played with fate. President Eisenhower suffered three serious but temporary illnesses while in office: a heart attack in 1955, ileitis in 1956, and a mild stroke in 1957. Two other Presidents were disabled for much longer periods. James Garfield lingered for 80 days before he died from an assassin's bullet in 1881. **Woodrow Wilson** suffered a paralytic stroke in September of 1919 and was an invalid for the rest of his second term. In fact, he was so ill that he could not meet with his Cabinet for seven months after his stroke. And, in 1981, Ronald Reagan was gravely wounded in an assassination attempt.

Filling the Disability Gap Sections 3 and 4 of the 25th Amendment fill the disability gap, and in detail. The Vice President is to become Acting President if (1) the President informs Congress, in writing, "that he is unable to discharge the powers and duties of his office," or (2) the Vice President and a majority of the members of the Cabinet inform Congress, in writing, that the President is so incapacitated.

The President may resume the powers and duties of the office by informing Congress by "written declaration" that no inability exists. However, the Vice President and a majority of the Cabinet may challenge the President on this score. If they do, Congress has 21 days in which to decide the matter.

Transferring Power Thus far, the disability provisions of the 25th Amendment have come into play on three occasions: In 1985, Ronald Reagan transferred the powers of the presidency to Vice President George H.W. Bush for nearly eight hours, while surgeons removed a tumor from Mr. Reagan's large intestine. In 2002, and again in 2007, President **George W. Bush** conveyed his powers to Vice President Dick Cheney for some two hours, while Mr. Bush was anesthetized during a routine medical procedure.

☑ **INFER** Why do you think the nation felt it was necessary to add the 25th Amendment to the Constitution when the practice of succession had already been established by Vice President Tyler?

☑ ASSESSMENT

1. **Apply Concepts** In what way is the President's effectiveness as chief economist dependent on his or her expertise as chief diplomat?

2. **Draw Conclusions** Who were Ronald Reagan and Franklin D. Roosevelt, and what viewpoint did they share about the presidential term of office?

3. **Identify Cause and Effect** Who was Theodore Roosevelt, and how was he affected by succession?

4. **Make Generalizations** Why was the 25th Amendment necessary?

5. **Interpret** At the national level, public offices can be filled by election or appointment. Why do you think the Constitution does not provide for the presidency to be filled by appointment if the office becomes vacant?

Laura Bush encouraged First Ladies "to speak out and speak up… you can be so constructive for your country if you speak up about issues that you think are important."

The Vice President and the First Lady

"I am Vice President. In this I am nothing, but I may be everything." So said John Adams, the nation's first Vice President. Those words could have been repeated, very appropriately, by each of the men who held that office through the first 150 years of the nation's history. After World War II, however, the status of the vice presidency began to change.

The Structure and Function of the Vice Presidency

Early Vice Presidents The Constitution pays little attention to the office of the Vice President. It assigns the position only two formal duties. Article I, Section 3, Clause 4 says that the Vice President will preside over the Senate, and the 25th Amendment directs him or her to help decide the question of presidential disability. Beyond those duties, the Constitution makes the Vice President, in effect, a "President-in-waiting," ready to step into that office should the President become unable to fulfill his duties.

Despite the fact that the Vice President is literally "only a heartbeat away from the presidency," the office has been treated as one of little real consequence throughout much of the nation's history. Benjamin Franklin once quipped that the Vice President should be addressed as "your Superfluous Excellency." Thomas Marshall, Vice President under Woodrow Wilson, once told a story of two brothers: "One ran away to sea; the other was elected Vice President. And nothing was heard of either of them again."

BOUNCE to Activate Flipped Video

Objectives

Analyze the functions of the executive branch of government in terms of the formal duties the Constitution assigns to the Vice President.

Describe how the role of the Vice President has changed over time.

Explain the part played by First Ladies throughout the nation's history.

Key Terms

balance the ticket
First Lady

Much of the blame for the low status of the vice presidency can be laid on the two major parties and the way they have chosen their candidates for the office. Traditionally, each national convention names the handpicked choice of its just-nominated presidential candidate. Usually, the newly minted presidential candidate picks someone who will **"balance the ticket."** That is, the nominee chooses a running mate who can strengthen his or her chance of being elected by virtue of certain ideological, geographic, racial, ethnic, gender, or other characteristics. In short, fate—presidential succession—does not very often have a high priority in the vice presidential candidate selection process.

The Transformation of the Vice Presidency

With the advent of the cold war in the late 1940s and the proliferation of nuclear weapons, concerns grew about the Vice President's readiness to take the helm at a moment's notice, fully abreast of world and military developments. Harry Truman, who became President following Franklin Roosevelt's sudden death in April 1945, had been kept in the dark about the American project to build an atomic bomb. He was also not fully apprised of the rapidly mounting tension between the United States and

its ally, the Soviet Union, as World War II drew to a close. On President Roosevelt's death, Harry Truman was forced to step into the presidency with little preparation for handling the grave issues confronting the nation at that time.

By the 1950s, in a new age of nuclear missiles, many Americans believed that such a situation should never be allowed again. Dwight Eisenhower remarked, "Even if [Vice President] Nixon and I were not good friends, I would still have him in every important conference of government, so that if the Grim Reaper [death] would find it time to remove me from the scene, he is ready to slip in without any interruption." Thus began a move toward bringing Vice Presidents into the inner circle of the administration. As a result of this shift, the job of the Vice President changed.

By the 1990s, Al Gore, Vice President under Bill Clinton, was given several important responsibilities, including studying the Federal Government to pinpoint waste. Vice President Gore also had full access to the President, including weekly one-on-one lunch meetings. Dick Cheney, who served with George W. Bush from 2001 to 2009, also played a central role in the White House; in fact, some have suggested that he was the most influential Vice President in American history. Since that time, Presidents have continued to delegate important jobs to their Vice Presidents, ranging from heading up task forces to serving as liaisons with Congress and constituents to developing policy.

Filling a Vice-Presidential Vacancy The vice presidency has been vacant 18 times thus far: nine times by succession to the presidency, seven times by death, and twice by resignation. John C. Calhoun resigned to become a senator from South Carolina in 1832, and Spiro T. Agnew resigned in 1973, after a conviction for income tax evasion.

Yet not until 1967 and the 25th Amendment did the Constitution deal with the matter of vice presidential vacancies. The amendment provides, in part:

> Whenever there is a vacancy in the office of the Vice President, the President shall nominate a Vice President who shall take office upon confirmation by a majority vote of both Houses of Congress.
>
> —25th Amendment, Section 2

>> The vice presidency changed significantly during the cold war as the nuclear arms race made Americans aware of the importance of an involved and informed Vice President.

This provision was first implemented in 1973. In that year, President Richard Nixon selected and Congress confirmed Gerald R. Ford to succeed Spiro Agnew as Vice President. It came into play again in 1974 when, following Mr. Nixon's resignation, President Ford named and Congress approved Nelson Rockefeller for the post.

☑ **SUMMARIZE** Summarize how the overall nature of the vice presidency has changed over time.

The First Lady

First Lady is the official title for the President's wife or the White House hostess. Not all First Ladies were wives of a President; one such example is Harriet Lane, First Lady for her uncle, President James Buchanan.

First Ladies are not elected by the American people, which means they do not have a direct role in the President's administration. From Martha Washington onward, these women have made their mark on American history, however, by providing informal advice, advocating for particular policies, and undertaking a host of symbolic (yet important) functions. They have lobbied lawmakers, met with foreign dignitaries, coaxed members of their husband's Cabinet, spoken at national conventions, and cultivated public sympathies. Today, First Ladies even have their own staff within the White House Office, called The Office of the First Lady.

Champions for Many Causes During the early part of our nation's history, First Ladies limited their work to informal, behind-the-scenes advice and social functions. Abigail Adams was a prime example, serving as a trusted friend and confidant to her husband John throughout his long, distinguished political career, including his term as President.

As time went on, First Ladies began to take on a more public role. Edith Wilson, for example, spoke on her husband Woodrow's behalf and filtered all communications after he was left partially paralyzed by a stroke in 1919. Jacqueline Kennedy undertook an historic restoration of the White House and used her position to support the arts in general, hosting opera, ballet, Shakespeare, and other White House performances. President Nixon's First Lady, Pat Nixon, spent up to five hours a day responding to letters from voters, promoted a national volunteer program, and championed the cause of those with special needs. First Lady Laura Bush helped buttress support for military personnel and their families

>> In recent years, Vice Presidents have often taken on a larger role and become close presidential advisors. Here, President Bush and Vice President Dick Cheney confer over lunch.

>> The First Lady is a very visible national figure. This photograph shows, left to right, former First Ladies Michelle Obama, Laura Bush, Hillary Clinton, Barbara Bush, and Rosalynn Carter.

>> Former First Lady Hillary Clinton testifies before a Senate committee in 1993 as part of her efforts to lead the reform of the nation's healthcare system.

during wars in Iraq and Afghanistan, and she also promoted education reform.

Beginning with Eleanor Roosevelt, more First Ladies have become openly involved in political issues. Mrs. Roosevelt, the wife of Franklin D. Roosevelt, traveled extensively and spoke on behalf of her husband's policies, as well as her own concerns. She wrote a weekly newspaper column and worked tirelessly for Democratic candidates.

The Evolving Role of First Ladies Many First Ladies since Mrs. Roosevelt have played important roles in American society. Betty Ford, for example, was known for her support of equal rights for women, while Barbara Bush launched a national effort to end illiteracy. Other examples include First Lady Claudia "Lady Bird" Johnson's national beautification program, Rosalynn Carter's mental health advocacy, Nancy Reagan's "Just Say No" to drugs campaign, Hillary Clinton's leadership of administration efforts to overhaul the nation's healthcare system, and Michelle Obama's advocacy of healthy eating and lifestyles.

Clearly, the role of presidential spouses will continue to evolve in the coming years. As more and more women move into positions of authority and lead high-profile professional lives, the role of behind-the-scenes advisor and ceremonial figure will almost certainly become a thing of the past. In fact, the real question in today's society is this: What role will the nation's "first gentlemen" perform in the future?

☑ **SUMMARIZE** Summarize how the role of First Ladies has changed over time.

☑ ASSESSMENT

1. **Identify** Do you think it is a positive or negative development that the responsibilities of the Vice President have increased from the original responsibilities listed in the Constitution?

2. **Evaluate Arguments** Do you think an attempt to "balance the ticket" is an acceptable method of selecting a Vice President? Why or why not?

3. **Identify Steps in a Process** Suppose that it is 2007 and Dick Cheney is Vice President. He resigns to become a senator from Wyoming. Describe the steps that would be taken to fill this vacancy.

4. **Identify Cause and Effect** Explain the impact of the nuclear arms race on the role of the Vice President.

5. **Compare and Contrast** Compare and contrast the way Abigail Adams handled the role of First Lady to the way Eleanor Roosevelt approached it.

President Johnson signs a bill to create the Department of Housing and Urban Development in 1965. Multiple pens are used to sign important bills because they often become historical artifacts.

The President's Domestic Powers

The presidency is regularly called "the most powerful office in the world," and it is. However, is this what the Framers had in mind when they created the post in 1787? In Philadelphia, they purposely created a single executive with very broadly stated powers. Still, they agreed with the sentiment expressed by Thomas Jefferson in the Declaration of Independence that a tyrant "is unfit to be the ruler of a free people."

The Growth of Presidential Power

The Framers Debate Indeed, few issues took up more time at the Constitutional Convention than the presidency. The first debate centered around whether there should even be a President. If so, should the office consist of one person or a small group of leaders? Should the President be subordinate to the legislature or have the power to check congressional actions? How much influence should the President have in military matters?

In the end, the Framers created a one-person executive. Presidential powers would be broad in some respects, particularly foreign affairs, but limited in other areas. Even so, the very idea of a "chief executive" sent shivers down the spines of many citizens during the ratification period. Had it not been generally understood that George Washington, who had voluntarily resigned from his post as commander of the Continental Army, would be the first President, it is quite possible that this issue might have seriously derailed the ratification of the new Constitution.

BOUNCE to Activate Flipped Video

Objectives

List the reasons for the growth of presidential power and explain how the systems of checks and balances limits that growth.

Understand the constitutional powers of the President, including the President's power to execute the law and issue executive orders.

Explain how certain provisions of the Constitution provide for checks and balances among the three branches of government.

Examine the powers of executive privilege and clemency.

Explain the legislative powers and why they are an important part of the system of checks and balances.

Key Terms

executive order
ordinance power
executive privilege
reprieve
pardon
clemency
commutation
amnesty
veto
pocket veto

line-item veto
Andrew Jackson
Abraham Lincoln
Andrew Johnson
Gerald Ford
James Madison
James Monroe
Ulysses S. Grant

BORN TO COMMAND.

OF VETO MEMORY.

HAD I BEEN CONSULTED.

KING ANDREW THE FIRST.

>> This cartoon depicts President Jackson as a power-hungry tyrant. **Analyze Political Cartoons** What symbols does the cartoonist use to convey this point?

The Constitution's formal grants of power to the President have not been changed since those early years. Yet presidential power has grown remarkably over the past two centuries. Today, that change represents one of the most significant developments in the American political system.

The Whig Theory Throughout the nineteenth century, most Presidents took a restrained approach to leadership. This was called the Whig theory, which assumed that Congress would lead the policy process, while Presidents were limited to the powers expressly granted to them in the Constitution.

While this was the general approach to the office, a few exceptions can be noted. **Andrew Jackson**, first elected in 1828, regularly became involved in important policy questions, and he used the veto much more often than prior Presidents. During the Civil War, **Abraham Lincoln** took bold, far-reaching steps that stretched the limits of presidential power. His 1863 Emancipation Proclamation is a prime example. It freed those still enslaved by the Confederacy but scholars still debate whether it rested on any firm constitutional foundation.

The Stewardship Theory The restrained approach to presidential power also was challenged by President Theodore Roosevelt, who served from

1901 to 1908. According to Roosevelt's "stewardship theory," Presidents should not merely carry out the will of Congress but instead should build public support for particular policy agendas:

"My view was that every executive officer . . . was a steward of the people bound actively and affirmatively to do all that he could for the people. . . . My belief was that it was not only [a President's] right but his duty to do anything that the needs of the Nation demanded unless such action was forbidden by the Constitution or by the laws. . . . I did not usurp power, but I did greatly broaden the use of executive power."

—Theodore Roosevelt, *Theodore Roosevelt: An Autobiography*, 1913

Not everyone agreed with Roosevelt's approach. Ironically, the most strongly worded presidential statement of the opposing view came from Roosevelt's handpicked successor in the office, William Howard Taft. Looking back on his years in the White House, Mr. Taft had this to say:

"The true view of the Executive function is, as I conceive it, that the President can exercise no power which cannot be fairly and reasonably traced to some specific grant of power. . . . Such specific grant must be either in the Federal Constitution or in an act of Congress. . . . There is no undefined residuum of power which he can exercise because it seems to him to be in the public interest. . . ."

—William Howard Taft, *Our Chief Magistrate and His Powers*, 1916

It was not until Teddy Roosevelt's cousin, Franklin D. Roosevelt, was elected in 1932 that the limited approach to the presidency was shattered for good. FDR came into office during the Great Depression and immediately set in motion aggressive government programs in an attempt to lift the nation from its economic woes. By doing so, he forever changed the nature of the presidency.

Case Studies: Great Society Programs and the Persian Gulf War President Lyndon Johnson took an expansive view of the scope of presidential power and decision-making when he pushed Congress to pass his Great Society programs. During the 1960s, the President signed an avalanche of bills related to education, housing, poverty, civil rights, and the environment—his attempt to build a society in which "freedom from the wants of the body can help fulfill the needs of the spirit."

To that end, many new government agencies and programs were established, including the Department of Housing and Urban Development, Medicaid, Head Start, the Volunteers in Service to America (VISTA) program, a National Teachers Corps, and the Office of Economic Opportunity.

Some 25 years later, President George H.W. Bush was considerably more restrained in his use of presidential power. When Iraq invaded the neighboring country of Kuwait in 1990, for example, President Bush did not respond unilaterally. He waited for both Congress and the United Nations to pass resolutions authorizing the use of force against Iraq before proceeding with Operation Desert Storm—the U.S.-led campaign to wrest Kuwait from Saddam Hussein, the leader of Iraq.

The coalition achieved its objective in less than two months. Some called for the President to expand the original, narrow objective of the war and remove Hussein from power. In an example of the restrained use of presidential power, however, President Bush refused to do so. While some criticized the President for this decision, others applauded his refusal to embroil the United States in what would likely have been a longer military campaign with a greater loss of American life.

Reasons for the Expansion There are several reasons for the dramatic expansion of presidential powers. First, these changes were due, in no small part, to Presidents themselves, and especially the stronger ones—Abraham Lincoln and the two Roosevelts, for example. The Constitution is vague on some aspects of presidential powers, so certain Presidents simply filled the void as they saw fit.

Also, as each chief executive inserted himself into policy disputes, subsequent Presidents were expected to do the same. Conversely, those Presidents who remained on the sidelines were deemed poor leaders.

Second, the ability for Presidents to exert their power has grown due to the expansion of the executive branch. Beginning with FDR and the

>> This cartoon depicts Theodore Roosevelt and William Howard Taft as bickering schoolchildren. **Analyze Political Cartoons** How did Taft's view of the presidency differ from Roosevelt's?

>> The Works Progress Administration (WPA) was one of President Roosevelt's New Deal programs. At its peak, the WPA put some three million Americans back to work during the Great Depression.

>> President Bill Clinton, with Hillary and Chelsea Clinton, pose with White House staff members. Unlike earlier Presidents, today's chief executive has a huge staff at his or her disposal.

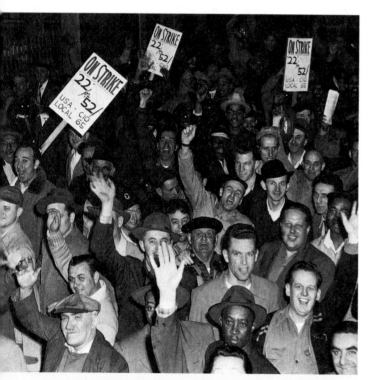

>> Presidential power is not unlimited. An attempt by President Truman to prevent a strike during the Korean War by seizing control of steel mills was ruled unconstitutional by the Supreme Court.

creation of the Executive Office of the President, the number and size of support agencies and office personnel has mushroomed. Because Presidents have so many agencies, offices, and staff working on their behalf, they have been able to exert more control over nearly all aspects of domestic and foreign policy.

Third, the nation's increasingly complex economy and society have also had a telling effect on presidential power. As the United States has become more industrialized and technologically advanced, many citizens wanted the Federal Government to take a larger and larger role in transportation, communications, health, welfare, employment, education, civil rights, and a host of other fields. And they have looked especially to the President for leadership in those matters.

Fourth, the need for immediate and decisive action in times of crisis, and most notably in times of war, has also had a major impact here. The ability of the President—the single, commanding chief executive—to act in those situations has done much to strengthen "the executive Power."

Finally, Congress has also been involved, as it has passed the thousands of laws that have been a key part of the historic growth of the Federal Government, especially since the 1930s. Congress has neither the time nor the specialized knowledge to provide much more than basic outlines of public policy. Out of necessity, it has delegated substantial authority to the executive branch to carry out the laws it has enacted.

Limits to Power Despite the expanded scope of the presidency, no President can become all-powerful. The Constitution, which grants much power to the President, also provides for a number of restraints on the exercise of that power. Here are just two illustrations of that crucial point.

In 1952, at the height of the Korean War, a labor dispute threatened to shut down the nation's steel industry and imperil the war effort. To avert a strike, President Harry Truman, acting as commander in chief, ordered the Secretary of Commerce to seize and operate several steel mills.

The Supreme Court found that the President had overstepped his constitutional authority. It held that only Congress, acting under its commerce power, could authorize the seizure of private property in time of war, and it had not done so.

In another example, President Barack Obama tried to get around the increasingly contentious Senate confirmation process for three appointees to the National Labor Relations Board in 2013. He chose to use what is referred to as "recess appointments," a mechanism occasionally used by Presidents to fill posts when senators are away from Washington. The federal courts, however, ruled that Obama's move was unconstitutional.

Congressional Oversight In addition, congressional oversight can be a powerful check on executive power. Congressional oversight occurs as Congress keeps a close watch over the executive branch to ensure that it acts in compliance with previously passed laws and appropriations. The ability of Congress to limit presidential actions through oversight can be real and significant—and quite frustrating to Presidents at times.

Noteworthy investigations of executive branch actions stretch back through the centuries. In the early 1920s, for example, a Senate committee investigated a Cabinet secretary's secret leasing of federal oil reserves to private companies. In the 1960s, both the House and the Senate investigated various aspects of the conduct of the Vietnam War. After President Nixon resigned in 1974 as the result of a congressional investigation, another investigation looked into President Ford's pardon of Nixon.

In the years since, congressional investigations have focused on a wide range of issues; for example, a Marine barracks bombing in Beirut (1983), arms sales to anti-communists in Nicaragua (1987), arms shipments to Bosnia (1996), the conduct of the Iraq War (2003), the handling of the government's response to Hurricane Katrina (2005), the 2008 financial crisis, the Gulf oil spill (2010), a failed operation to stop the flow of firearms from the United States to Mexico (2011), the issuing of security clearances (2019), and immigration policies (2019).

Critics and Supporters In recent times, critics of what they see as a too-powerful chief executive have condemned what has been called "the imperial presidency." The term paints a picture of the President as a strong-willed emperor, taking various actions without consulting Congress or seeking its approval—sometimes acting in secrecy to evade or even deceive Congress. Critics of the imperial presidency worry that Presidents have shifted the balance of power between the executive and legislative branches.

On the other side of the debate are those who believe that in today's complex and globally interconnected world, the President must be able to react quickly to events at home and abroad, in consultation with advisors and members of Congress. Supporters of a strong presidency say the

>> President Ronald Reagan exercised his power to enforce federal laws in 1981 by firing striking air traffic controllers. The strike was illegal according to a 1955 law passed by Congress.

chief executive must have the power to shepherd the country through the challenges and opportunities of the 21st century.

☑ **DESCRIBE** In 2006, President George W. Bush ordered the formation of military tribunals to prosecute suspected terrorists held at Guantanamo Bay. This action might be seen as an example of which approach to the presidency?

The Power to Execute the Law

Thomas Jefferson wrote this to a friend in 1789: "The execution of the laws is more important than the making of them." Whether Jefferson was right about that or not, in this section you will see that the President's power to execute the law endows the chief executive with extraordinary authority.

As chief executive, the President executes (enforces, administers, carries out) the provisions of federal law. The power to do so rests on two brief constitutional provisions. The first of them is the oath of office sworn by the President on the day he or she takes office:

> I do solemnly swear (or affirm) that I will faithfully execute the Office of President of the United States, and will to the best of my Ability, preserve, protect and defend the Constitution of the United States.

—Article II, Section 1, Clause 8

The other provision is the Constitution's command in Article II, Section 3 that "he shall take Care that the Laws be faithfully executed." This provision is sometimes called the "take care power."

The President's power to execute the law covers all federal laws. In fact, the Constitution requires the President to execute *all* federal laws, no matter what the chief executive's own views of any of them may be. Their number, and the many subjects they cover, nearly boggle the mind. Social Security, gun control, affirmative action, immigration, minimum wages, terrorism, environmental protection, taxes—these only begin the list. There are scores of others.

The President—and, importantly, the President's subordinates—have much to say about the meaning of laws, as do Congress and the courts. In executing and enforcing law, the executive branch also interprets it.

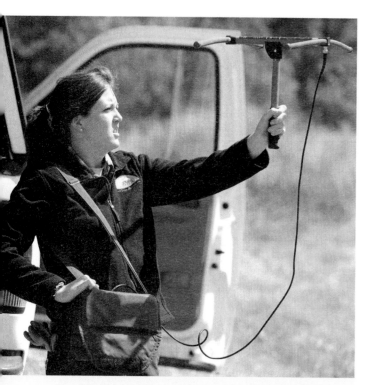

>> Executive orders can be used for such purposes as increasing federal job opportunities for college graduates. This graduate is scanning for a black bear as part of a federal study.

To look at the point more closely: Many laws that Congress enacts are written in fairly broad terms. Congress sets out the basic policies and standards to be followed. The specific details—much of the fine print necessary to the actual, day-to-day administration of the law—are usually left to be worked out by the executive branch.

For example, immigration laws require that all immigrants seeking permanent admission to this country must be able to "read and understand some dialect or language." But what does this broadly worded requirement mean in day-to-day practice? How well must an alien be able to "read and understand"? The law does not say. Rather, the details come from within the executive branch—from the U.S. Citizenship and Immigration Services in the Department of Homeland Security.

☑ **IDENTIFY CENTRAL IDEAS** In what way does the executive branch influence the laws passed by Congress?

Executive Orders and Executive Privilege

The job of administering and applying most federal law is the day-to-day work of all of the many departments, commissions, and other agencies of the Federal Government. All of the millions of civilian men and women who staff those agencies are subject to the President's control and direction.

The chief executive has the power to issue **executive orders**, which are directives, rules, or regulations that have the effect of law. The power to issue these orders, the **ordinance power**, arises from two sources: the Constitution and acts of Congress.

The Constitution does not mention the ordinance power in so many words, but that power is clearly intended. In granting certain powers to the President, the Constitution obviously anticipates their use. In order to exercise those powers, the chief executive must have the power to issue the necessary orders, and, as well, the power to implement them.

The number, the scope, and the complexity of the problems that face the government of the United States have grown over time. As a result, Congress has found it necessary to delegate more and yet more discretion to the President and to top-level subordinates in the executive branch to spell out the policies and programs it has approved. As a result, presidential executive orders deal with a dizzying array of subjects, from establishing a White

United States v. Nixon, 1974

ARGUMENTS FOR NIXON	ARGUMENTS FOR THE UNITED STATES
1. According to the doctrine of separation of powers, no court has the authority to question a President's executive privilege.	1. Article III vests judicial power in the federal courts; their ability to exercise that power would be harmed without the authority to review acts of the executive branch.
2. Without a guarantee of confidentiality, presidential aides might not speak freely, and the President's decision-making ability would be harmed.	2. The 6th Amendment guarantees a fair trial to all criminal defendants. If important evidence is withheld from a court, it would be impossible to conduct trials.
3. The disclosure of communications between the President and his advisors could threaten the nation's security.	3. The protection of the secrecy of presidential communications should be limited to military and diplomatic matters.

>> *United States* v. *Nixon* was a landmark case related to the power of executive privilege.
Analyze Charts What basic principles of government were involved in the case?

House Council on Women and Girls, to setting out medical countermeasures to be taken in the event of a biological weapons attack. Another example: President Truman's 1948 Executive Order 9981, which expanded the civil rights of people of color by desegregating the nation's armed forces.

The Power of Executive Privilege Since 1796, the nation's chief executives have at times insisted that the Constitution gives the President the inherent power to refuse to disclose certain information to Congress or to the federal courts. That is, they have claimed the power of **executive privilege**. Most often, this claim has been made with regard to conversations and other communications between Presidents and their closest advisors.

The chief executive must, of necessity, rely on the information and advice received from key staff and their ability to speak with utmost candor, which depends on the confidential nature of their relationship with the President. These officials must be sure that what they say will become known publicly only if and when the President chooses to disclose that information.

Congress has never recognized executive privilege. It has often tried to compel executive officials to testify at congressional committee hearings, and Presidents have frequently resisted those efforts, citing executive privilege.

The federal courts have been reluctant to become involved in this dispute between the executive and legislative branches. However, the Supreme Court has recognized both the existence of and the need for executive privilege in a historic case, *United*

States v. *Nixon*, in 1974. There, a unanimous Court said that although the President might legitimately claim executive privilege in matters involving national security, that privilege cannot be used to prevent evidence from being heard in a criminal proceeding. This decision was a key factor in Mr. Nixon's resignation.

☑ **MAKE GENERALIZATIONS** How has the growth of the nation affected the President's ordinance power?

The Powers of Appointment and Removal

A President cannot hope to succeed without loyal subordinates who support the policies of the President's administration. To that end, the Constitution says that the President

> by and with the Advice and Consent of the Senate . . . shall appoint Ambassadors, other public Ministers and Consuls, Judges of the supreme Court, and all other Officers of the United States, whose Appointments are not herein otherwise provided for . . .
>
> —Article II, Section 2, Clause 2

Those "Officers of the United States whose Appointments are . . . otherwise provided for" are the Vice President, members of Congress, and presidential electors.

Acting alone, the President names fewer than 1,000 of the millions of civilians who work for the Federal Government. The vast majority of the rest of the federal workforce is hired under the civil service laws.

Appointees The President names most of the top-ranking officers of the Federal Government. Among them are (1) ambassadors and other diplomats; (2) Cabinet members and their top aides; (3) the heads of independent agencies; (4) all federal judges, U.S. marshals, and attorneys; and (5) all officers in the armed forces. When the President makes one of these appointments, the nomination is sent to the Senate. There, the support of a majority of the senators is needed for confirmation.

The unwritten rule of senatorial courtesy plays an important part in this process. That rule applies to the choice of those federal officers who serve within a State—a federal district judge or a U.S. marshal, for example. The rule holds that the Senate will approve only those federal appointees acceptable to the senator or senators of the President's party from the State involved. The practical effect of this custom, which is closely followed in the Senate, is to place a meaningful part of the President's appointing power in the hands of particular senators.

Recess Appointments The Constitution does allow the President to make "recess appointments," that is, appointments "to fill up all Vacancies that may happen during the Recess of the Senate" (Article II, Section 2, Clause 3). Any such appointment automatically expires at the end of the congressional term in which it is made.

Recess appointments have often been a matter of contention—because they make it possible for the President to bypass the Senate confirmation process. Over time, Presidents have made very few recess appointments. The number tends to increase when the President's party does not control the Senate.

In 2014, the Supreme Court weighed in on recess appointments. In *National Labor Relations Board* v. *Noel Canning*, the Court held that Congress must have recessed for a substantial length of time—at least ten days—for the President to use the recess appointment clause. Short breaks of less than ten days during a congressional session do not count as recesses.

The Removal Power The power to remove is the other side of the appointment coin, and is as important to presidential success as is the power to appoint. Yet, except for mention of the little-used impeachment process, the Constitution says nothing about how, by whom, or why an appointed officer may be dismissed.

Recess Appointments, Selected Presidents

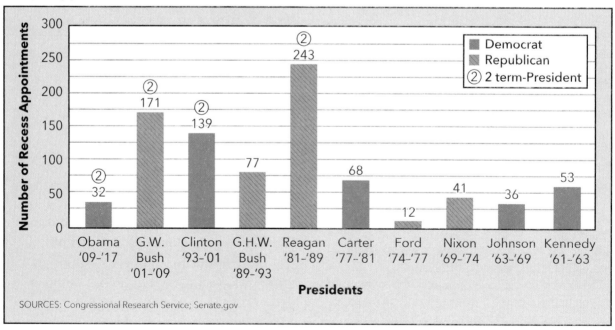

SOURCES: Congressional Research Service; Senate.gov

>> Some critics argue that recess appointments shift the balance of power in the government. Others say they break the logjam of nominees awaiting Senate approval. **Analyze Graphs** How does the length of a President's term affect the number of recess appointments he made?

The matter was hotly debated in the first session of Congress, in 1789. Several members argued that, if an appointment required Senate approval, Senate consent should also be required for removal. They insisted that this restriction on presidential authority was essential to congressional supervision (oversight) of the executive branch. But others argued that the President could not "take Care that the Laws be faithfully executed" without a free hand to dismiss those who were incompetent or otherwise unsuited to office.

The latter view prevailed. The First Congress gave the President the power to remove any officer he appointed, except federal judges. Over the years since then, Congress has sometimes tried, with little success, to restrict the President's freedom to dismiss.

One notable instance occurred in 1867. Locked with Democratic President **Andrew Johnson** in the fight over Reconstruction, Congress passed the Tenure of Office Act. That law's plain purpose was to prevent President Johnson from removing several top officers in his administration, in particular the Republican secretary of war, Edwin M. Stanton. The law provided that any person holding an office by presidential appointment with Senate consent should remain in that office until a successor had been confirmed by the Senate.

The President vetoed the bill, charging that it was an unconstitutional invasion of executive authority. The veto was overridden, but Mr. Johnson ignored Congress and fired Stanton anyway. The veto and Stanton's removal sparked the move for Johnson's impeachment. Ultimately, the Senate acquitted the President by one vote, and the law was ignored in practice. It was finally repealed in 1887.

Removal and the Court The question of the President's removal power did not reach the Supreme Court until *Myers* v. *United States*, 1926. That case began when Congress passed a law in 1876 requiring Senate consent before the President could dismiss any first-class, second-class, or third-class postmaster.

In 1920, without consulting the Senate, President Woodrow Wilson removed Frank Myers as the postmaster at Portland, Oregon. The deposed postmaster then sued for the salary for the rest of his four-year term. He based his claim on the point that he had been removed in violation of the 1876 law.

The Court, led by a former President, Chief Justice Taft, found the law unconstitutional. It held that the removal power was an essential part of executive power, clearly necessary to the faithful execution of the laws.

"Do you have any 'Congratulations on Your Presidential Pardon' cards?"

>> Presidents receive thousands of requests for clemency during their time in office. **Analyze Political Cartoons** What does this cartoon imply about the number of pardons given by Presidents?

The Supreme Court did place some limits on the President's removal power in 1935, in *Humphrey's Executor* v. *United States*. President Herbert Hoover had appointed William Humphrey to a seven-year term on the Federal Trade Commission (FTC) in 1931. When Franklin D. Roosevelt took office in 1933, he found Commissioner Humphrey to be in sharp disagreement with many of his policies. He asked the commissioner to resign, saying that his administration would be better served with someone else on the FTC. When Mr. Humphrey refused, President Roosevelt removed him. Humphrey soon died, but his heirs filed a suit for back salary.

The Supreme Court upheld the heirs' claim. It based its decision on the act creating the FTC. That law provides that a member of the commission may be removed only for "inefficiency, neglect of duty, or malfeasance in office."

The Court further held that Congress does have the power to set the conditions under which a member of the FTC and other such agencies might be removed by the President. It did so because those agencies, the independent regulatory commissions, are not purely executive agencies.

As a general rule, the President may remove those whom the President appoints. Occasionally, a presidential appointee does have to be fired. Most often, however, what was in fact a dismissal is called a "resignation."

☑ **INTEGRATE INFORMATION** What is the significance of the Supreme Court decision *Humphrey's Executor* v. *United States*?

The Powers of Clemency

The President has been given certain judicial powers. Specifically, the Constitution gives the President the power to

> . . . Grant Reprieves and Pardons for Offenses against the United States, except in Cases of Impeachment.

—Article II, Section 2, Clause 1

A **reprieve** is the postponement of the execution of a sentence. A **pardon** is legal forgiveness of a crime.

The President's power to grant reprieves and pardons is absolute, except in cases of impeachment, where they may never be granted. These powers of **clemency** (mercy or leniency) may be used only in cases involving *federal* offenses.

Presidential pardons are usually granted after a person has been convicted in court. Yet the President may pardon a federal offender before that person is tried, or even before that person has been formally charged.

Notable Pardons Pardons in advance of a trial or charge are rare. The most noteworthy pardon, by far, was granted in 1974. In that year, President

Gerald Ford gave "a full, free and absolute pardon unto Richard Nixon for all offenses against the United States which he . . . has committed or may have committed or taken part in during the period from January 20, 1969, through August 9, 1974." Of course, that pardon referred to the Watergate scandal.

To be effective, a pardon must be accepted by the person to whom it is granted. When a pardon is granted prior to a charge or conviction, as in the Nixon case, its acceptance is regularly seen as an admission of guilt by the person to whom it is given.

Nearly all pardons are accepted, of course, and usually gratefully. A few have been rejected, however. One of the most dramatic refusals led to a Supreme Court case, *Burdick* v. *United States*, 1915. George Burdick, a New York newspaper editor, had refused to testify before a federal grand jury regarding the sources for certain news stories his paper had printed.

Those stories reported fraud in the collection of customs duties. He invoked the 5th Amendment, claiming that his testimony could incriminate him. President Woodrow Wilson then granted Burdick "a full and unconditional pardon for all offenses against the United States" that he might have committed in obtaining material for the news stories.

Interestingly, Burdick refused to accept the pardon, and he continued to refuse to testify. With that, the federal judge in that district fined and jailed him for contempt. The judge ruled that (1) the President's pardon was fully effective, with or without Burdick's acceptance and (2) there was, therefore, no basis for Burdick's continued claim of protection against self-incrimination.

The Supreme Court overturned the lower court's action. It unanimously upheld the rule that a pardon must be accepted in order to be effective, and it ordered Burdick's release from jail.

Commutation and Amnesty The pardoning power includes the power to grant conditional pardons, provided the conditions are reasonable. It also includes the power of **commutation**, or the power to reduce a fine or the length of a sentence imposed by a court.

The pardoning power also includes the power of **amnesty**, which is in effect a blanket pardon offered to a group of law violators. Thus, in 1893, President Benjamin Harrison issued a proclamation of amnesty forgiving all Mormons who had violated the antipolygamy (multiple marriage) laws in the federal territories. And in 1977, President Jimmy Carter granted amnesty to those who evaded the draft during the war in Vietnam.

>> Do journalists have to reveal their sources to the courts? Journalist George Burdick said "no" and emphasized his point by rejecting President Wilson's pardon.

The Power to Recommend Legislation

In *The Federalist* No. 51, **James Madison** analyzes the Constitution's elaborate system of checks and balances. Its "constant aim," he says, "is to divide and arrange the several [branches] in such a manner as that each may be a check on the other." And, he adds, "the great security against a gradual concentration of the several powers in the same department consists in giving to those who administer each department the necessary constitutional means and personal motives to resist encroachments of the others. . . . "

The Constitution gives the President certain legislative powers. They are, in Madison's phrase, "the constitutional means" that make it possible for the President to check the actions of Congress.

The President's legislative powers, exercised in combination with a skillful playing of the roles of chief of party and chief citizen, have made the President, in effect, the nation's chief legislator. It is the President who initiates, suggests, and demands that Congress enact much of the major legislation that it produces. However, a President whose party controls both houses on Capitol Hill may have an easier time of it than one who faces a hostile Congress.

The Message Power Article II of the Constitution gives the President what is often called the message power. This provision says that the President

> shall from time to time give to the Congress Information of the State of the Union, and recommend to their Consideration such Measures as he shall judge necessary and expedient.
>
> . . .
>
> —Article II, Section 3

The chief executive regularly sends three major messages to Capitol Hill each year. The first is the State of the Union message, a speech almost always delivered in person to a joint session of Congress. The President's budget message and then the annual Economic Report soon follow. The President often

>> President James Madison praised the Constitution's system of checks and balances as a way of preventing any one branch of government from wielding too much power.

sends the lawmakers a number of other messages on a wide range of topics.

Other Legislative Powers According to Article II, Section 3 of the Constitution, only the President can call Congress into special session. The fact that Congress is now in session through most of each year practically eliminates the likelihood of special sessions and also lessens the importance of the President's power to call one. Still, as Congress nears the end of a regular session, Presidents have sometimes found it useful to threaten a special session if lawmakers do not act on some particular measure. President Harry Truman called the most recent special session in 1948, in an effort to force Congress to consider anti-inflation and welfare measures in the post-World War II period.

The same constitutional provision also gives the chief executive the power to prorogue (adjourn) Congress in the event the two houses cannot agree on a date for their adjournment. That has never happened.

☑ **CHECK UNDERSTANDING** Why might a President whose party controls Congress have an easier time as "chief legislator" than a President who does not have support in Congress?

The Power of the Veto

The Constitution says that "Every Bill" and "Every Order, Resolution, or Vote to which the Concurrence of the Senate and House of Representatives may be necessary (except on a question of Adjournment) shall be presented to the President" (Article I, Section 7, Clauses 2 and 3). Remember, the Constitution presents the President with four options once a measure has been approved by Congress.

First, he or she may sign the bill, making it law, which is what usually happens. Or the President can **veto** the bill, and the measure must then be returned to Congress. The word *veto* comes from the Latin meaning "I forbid." Congress can then override that veto, by a two-thirds vote in each of its two chambers, but it seldom does.

As a third option, the President may allow a bill to become law by not acting on it, neither signing nor vetoing it, within ten days (excluding Sundays). This rarely happens.

The fourth option, the **pocket veto**, can be used only at the end of a congressional session. If Congress adjourns within ten days (not counting Sundays) of sending a bill to the White House and the President does not act on it, the measure dies.

The veto power is an exceedingly valuable tool in the President's dealings with the legislative branch.

Even the mere *threat* of a veto can defeat a bill or, at the least, prompt changes in its provisions as it moves through the legislative mill. When the chief executive makes such a threat, congressional leaders must do the math: Can they find enough votes in both houses to overcome a presidential veto?

George Washington rejected only two measures in his eight years in the presidency, and for nearly seven decades his successors also used their veto pens infrequently. But from Andrew Johnson in the 1860s onward, most chief executives have been much more willing to reject measures.

Signing Statements From **James Monroe** in the 1820s to today, various Presidents have issued "signing statements" as they approved some measures. On occasion, those statements were used to point out constitutional or other problems the President saw in a newly enacted law. More often, the statements have been used to do such things as to direct the manner in which a new law is to be enforced.

President George W. Bush stirred controversy during his time in office by using signing statements differently than his predecessors. In doing so, he claimed a power, on one hand, to refuse to enforce those provisions or, on the other, to interpret them "in a manner

THE POWER OF THE VETO

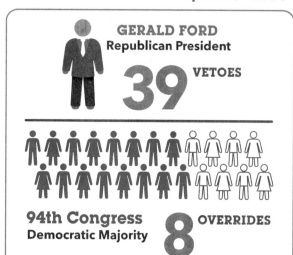

DIVIDED GOVERNMENT, 1975–1977

GERALD FORD
Republican President

39 VETOES

94th Congress
Democratic Majority

8 OVERRIDES

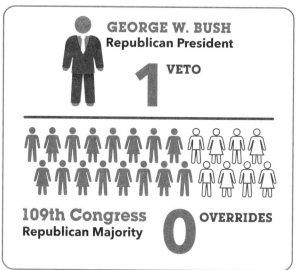

UNITED GOVERNMENT, 2005–2007

GEORGE W. BUSH
Republican President

1 VETO

109th Congress
Republican Majority

0 OVERRIDES

>> When the President and the majority of Congress are of the same party, vetoes tend to be rare. **Analyze Charts** How can Congress check the President's veto power?

consistent with" his view of "the constitutional authority of the President."

His critics claimed that Mr. Bush, in effect, used these statements as a substitute for the veto power, deciding which new laws he would execute and how those laws would be interpreted and applied. Defenders argued that signing statements have been used by Presidents throughout the nation's history, that they are an important means for the President to express his reservations about a piece of legislation, and that the national security issues that arose during the Bush administration warranted any increased use.

A 2012 report by the Congressional Research Service concluded that signing statements are constitutional and further, that they do not necessarily affect how laws enacted by Congress are actually carried out. Instead, concern regarding signing statements should be focused on the fact that Presidents "have employed these instruments in an attempt to leverage power and control away from Congress by establishing these broad assertions of authority as a constitutional norm."

The Line-Item Veto If the President decides to veto a bill, he or she must reject the *entire* measure and not just a portion of it.

Since **Ulysses S. Grant's** day, most Presidents have favored expanding the veto power to include a **line-item veto**. That is, they have sought the power to cancel out some provisions in a measure while approving others. Most often, those who have proposed this device would restrict its application to specific dollar amounts (line items) in spending bills enacted by Congress. Many supporters argue that the line-item veto would be a potent weapon against wasteful and unnecessary federal spending.

Opponents of the line-item veto have long argued that the move would bring a massive and dangerous shift of power from the legislative branch to the executive branch. To this point, efforts to persuade Congress to propose a line-item veto amendment to the Constitution have failed.

In 1996, Congress did pass a Line-Item Veto Act. The Supreme Court struck it down, however, holding that Congress lacked the power to give the President a line-item veto, in *Clinton* v. *New York City*, 1998. If the chief executive is to have that authority, said the Court, it can come only as the result of an amendment to the Constitution.

☑ **INTERPRET** What are the pros and cons of signing statements?

>> Ulysses Grant was the first President to ask for the line-item veto power, but it took until 1996 for Congress to grant that power. Just two years later, the Court ruled it unconstitutional.

☑ ASSESSMENT

1. **Compare Points of View** How are Theodore Roosevelt and the idea of the "imperial presidency" related?

2. **Infer** The number and scope of the executive orders issued by the President have increased dramatically. What does this suggest about the presidency?

3. **Apply Concepts** In what way are presidential appointments an example of the system of checks and balances?

4. **Interpret** In *United States* v. *Nixon*, the Supreme Court based its decision in the case on Article III and the 6th Amendment to the Constitution. Use language from these parts of the Constitution to justify that decision.

5. **Make Generalizations** Which branch of the government has often been charged with interpreting the proper extent of presidential powers? Give one example.

Youngstown Sheet & Tube Company v. Sawyer, 1952

During the Korean War, President Truman feared an impending steelworker strike would disrupt production of the steel needed for guns and ammunition. To prevent this, he issued Executive Order 10340 commanding the Federal Government to seize control of several steel mills. The workers filed suit to prevent this on the grounds that the President did not have such authority. In *Youngstown Sheet & Tube Company* v. *Sawyer*, the Court agreed with the workers. In doing so, it set a limit on presidential powers and reaffirmed the separation of powers between the executive and legislative branches.

As you read, look for the constitutional arguments offered by each side.

>> During the height of the Korean War, steelworkers such as those pictured here went on strike to win higher wages.

Majority Opinion, Justice Hugo Black

The President's power . . . to issue the order must stem either from an act of Congress or from the Constitution itself. There is no statute that expressly authorizes the President to take possession of property as he did here. Nor is there any act of Congress to which our attention has been directed from which such a power can fairly be implied. . . .

Moreover, . . . prior to this controversy, Congress had refused to adopt that method of settling labor disputes. When the Taft-Hartley Act was under consideration in 1947, Congress rejected an amendment which would have authorized such governmental seizures in cases of emergency. . . .

☑ **IDENTIFY CENTRAL IDEAS** Why does Justice Black find the President's actions to be especially disturbing?

The order cannot properly be sustained as an exercise of the President's military power as Commander in Chief of the Armed Forces. . . . we cannot with faithfulness to our constitutional system hold that the Commander in Chief of the Armed Forces has the ultimate power as such to take possession of private property in order to keep labor disputes from stopping production. This is a job for the Nation's lawmakers, not for its military authorities.

. . . In the framework of our Constitution, the President's power to see that the laws are faithfully executed refutes [contradicts] the idea that he is to be a lawmaker. The Constitution limits his functions in the lawmaking process to the recommending of laws he thinks wise and the vetoing of laws he thinks bad. . . .

The Founders of this Nation entrusted the lawmaking power to the Congress alone in both good and bad times. . . . [T]his seizure order cannot stand.

Dissenting Opinion, Chief Justice Fred Vinson

Those who suggest that this is a case involving extraordinary powers should be mindful that these are extraordinary times. . . .

. . . For almost two full years, our armed forces have been fighting in Korea, suffering casualties of over 108,000 men. Further efforts to protect the free world from aggression are found in the congressional enactments of the Truman Plan for assistance to Greece and Turkey and the Marshall Plan for economic aid needed to build up the strength of our friends in Western Europe. In 1949, the Senate approved the North Atlantic Treaty under which each member nation agrees that an armed attack against one is an armed attack against all. . . .

Even this brief review of our responsibilities in the world community discloses the enormity of our undertaking. . . . Alert to our responsibilities, . . . Congress has enacted a large body of implementing legislation. . . .

Over $5-1/2 billion were appropriated for military assistance for fiscal year 1952, the bulk of that amount to be devoted to purchase of military equipment. . . .

Appropriations for the Department of Defense, which had averaged less than $13 billion per year for the three years before attack in Korea, were increased by Congress to $48 billion for fiscal year 1951 and to $60 billion for fiscal year 1952. . . . The bulk of the increase is for military equipment and supplies—guns, tanks, ships, planes and ammunition—all of which require steel. . . .

The President has the duty to execute the foregoing legislative programs. Their successful execution depends upon continued production of steel and stabilized prices for steel. . . .

☑ **DRAW CONCLUSIONS** What was the increase in military spending between 1947 and 1952 in dollars? In percentage? What does this indicate?

One is not here called upon even to consider the possibility of executive seizure of a farm, a corner grocery store or even a single industrial plant. . . . the Nation's entire basic steel production would have shut down completely if there had been no Government seizure. . . .

Accordingly, if the President has any power under the Constitution to meet a critical situation in the absence of express **statutory** [legal] authorization, there is no basis whatever for criticizing the exercise of such power in this case.

. . . A sturdy judiciary should not be swayed by the unpleasantness or unpopularity of necessary executive action, but must independently determine for itself whether the President was acting, as required by the Constitution, to "take Care that the Laws be faithfully executed."

☑ **DETERMINE AUTHOR'S POINT OF VIEW** What does Chief Justice Vinson say is the role of the Court?

☑ ASSESSMENT

1. **Identify Supporting Details** In his dissent, what reason does Justice Vinson give for allowing the President to seize the mills?

2. **Identify** Cite the passage in Justice Black's opinion that explains why separation of powers prohibits the President's actions.

3. **Identify Supporting Details** Under what provisions does the Court say the President would have the power to seize the steel mills?

This photograph of President John F. Kennedy in the Oval Office symbolizes the enormous burden shouldered by every President of the United States, especially with regard to foreign affairs.

 BOUNCE to Activate Flipped Video

Objectives

Explain how treaties are negotiated by the President, approved by the Senate, and ratified by the President under the system of checks and balances.

Explain why and how executive agreements are made.

Summarize how the power of recognition is used by the President.

Describe the President's constitutional powers as commander in chief.

Key Terms

treaty
executive agreement
recognition
persona non grata
John Tyler
William McKinley

The President's Foreign Affairs Powers

In a 1961 radio broadcast, John F. Kennedy described the pressures of the presidency this way: "When I ran for the presidency . . . I knew the country faced serious challenges, but I could not realize—nor could any man who does not bear the burdens of this office—how heavy and constant would be those burdens."

The President's Diplomatic Powers

When President Kennedy made that comment, he had in mind the subject of this section: the President's awesome responsibilities as chief diplomat and commander in chief.

The Constitution does not say, in so many words, that the President is the nation's chief diplomat. Rather, Presidents have come to dominate the field of foreign affairs through the use of the powers of the office. In major part, they were able to do so because the Constitution makes the President the commander in chief of the nation's armed forces—and several centuries of relationships between sovereign states tells us that military force is the ultimate language of diplomacy.

The Power to Make Treaties A **treaty** is a formal agreement between two or more sovereign states. The President, usually acting through the secretary of state, negotiates these international agreements. The Senate must give its approval by a two-thirds vote of the members present before a treaty made by the President can become effective. Recall, the Constitution, in Article VI, makes treaties a part of "the supreme Law of the Land."

Contrary to popular belief, the Senate does not ratify treaties. The Constitution requires the Senate's "Advice and Consent" to a treaty made by the President. Once the Senate has given its consent, the President ratifies a treaty by the exchange of formal notifications with the other party or parties to the agreement.

Treaties have the same legal standing as acts of Congress, and their provisions are enforceable in the courts. Congress may abrogate (repeal) a treaty by passing a law contrary to its provisions, and an existing law may be repealed by the terms of a treaty. When the provisions of a treaty and an act of Congress conflict, the courts consider the latest enacted to be the law (*The Head Money Cases*, 1884). The terms of a treaty cannot conflict with any provision in the Constitution (*Missouri* v. *Holland*, 1920); but the Supreme Court has never found a treaty provision to be unconstitutional.

Checks and Balances: Treaties and the Senate

The Framers considered the Senate—with, originally, only 26 members—a suitable council to advise the President in foreign affairs. Secrecy was thought to be necessary and was seen as an impossibility in a body as large as the House.

The two-thirds rule for treaty approval creates the possibility that a relatively small Senate minority can kill an international agreement. For example, in 1920, the Senate rejected the Treaty of Versailles, the general peace agreement negotiated by Woodrow Wilson to end World War I. The treaty included provisions for the League of Nations. Forty-nine senators voted for the pact and 35 against, but the vote was 7 short of the necessary two thirds. More than once, a President has been forced to bow to the views of a few senators in order to get a treaty approved, even when this has meant making concessions opposed by the majority.

At times, a President has had to turn to roundabout methods in order to achieve his goals. When a Senate minority defeated a treaty to annex Texas, President **John Tyler** was able to bring about annexation in 1845 by encouraging passage of a joint resolution—a move that required only a majority vote in each house. In 1898, President **William McKinley** used the same tactic to annex

>> The President's words and actions related to the leaders of other nations carry great weight, both in the U.S. and around the world. Here, President Trump meets with the emir of Qatar, a small country located in the Middle East.

>> During his presidency, Ronald Reagan (right) negotiated and signed—with the approval of the Senate—an arms control treaty with Soviet leader Mikhail Gorbachev.

>> In 1940, President Franklin Roosevelt negotiated the destroyers-for-bases deal with Great Britain, which he accomplished through the use of an executive agreement.

>> President Theodore Roosevelt used the power of recognition to legitimize and support Panama's independence from Colombia in 1903, thus paving the way for U.S. control of the Panama Canal.

Hawaii, again after a treaty his administration had negotiated failed in the Senate.

Executive Agreements Recent Presidents have relied more heavily on executive agreements than on formal treaties in their dealings with foreign governments, especially in routine matters. An **executive agreement** is a pact between the President and the head of a foreign state, or their subordinates. Unlike treaties, these agreements do not have to be approved by the Senate.

These pacts have the same standing as treaties in the relationships between sovereign states, but they do not supersede federal law or the laws of any State. However, they are otherwise binding on the United States.

Most executive agreements flow out of legislation already passed by Congress or out of treaties to which the Senate has agreed. However, the President can make these agreements without any congressional action. Treaties, once made, become a permanent part of American law. Executive agreements do not. When a change of administrations occurs, only those the new President agrees to remain in force.

A few executive agreements have been extraordinary, most notably the destroyers-for-bases deal of 1940. Under its terms, the United States gave Great Britain 50 "over-age" U.S. destroyers, naval vessels that the British needed to combat German submarine attacks in the North Atlantic. In return, the United States received 99-year leases to a string of air and naval bases extending from Newfoundland to the Caribbean. At a time when the official American policy in World War II was one of neutrality, this bold move by President Franklin Roosevelt put the United States squarely on the side of Great Britain.

The Power of Recognition When the President receives the diplomatic representatives of another sovereign state, the President exercises the power of **recognition**. That is, the chief executive, acting for the United States, acknowledges the legal existence of that country and its government. The President's action indicates that the United States accepts that country as an equal member of the family of nations. Sovereign states generally recognize one another through the exchange of diplomatic representatives. Recognition also may be accomplished by proposing to negotiate a treaty, since in international law only sovereign states can make such agreements.

Recognition does not mean that one government approves the character or the conduct of another. The United States recognizes several governments about which it has serious misgivings. Among the most notable examples is the People's Republic of China. The facts of life in world politics make relations with these governments necessary.

Recognition can be used to gain some advantage in world affairs. President Theodore Roosevelt's quick recognition of Panama in 1903 is a classic example of that point. He recognized the new state less than three days after the Panamanians had begun a revolt against Colombia, of which Panama had been a part. Roosevelt's action guaranteed their success. Similarly, President Harry Truman's dramatic recognition of Israel, within minutes of its creation in 1948, helped that new state to survive among its hostile Arab neighbors.

The President may show American displeasure with the conduct of another country by asking for the recall of that nation's ambassador or other diplomatic representatives in this country. The official recalled is declared to be **persona non grata**, an unwelcome person. The same point can be made by the recalling of an American diplomat from a post in another country. The withdrawal of recognition is the sharpest diplomatic rebuke one government may give to another and can be a step on the way to war.

☑ **POSE AND ANSWER QUESTIONS** The system of checks and balances is part of the treaty-making process. In order to avoid clashes with the legislative or judicial branches, what questions might a President ask advisors prior to negotiating a treaty? What answers might convince the President to proceed with the negotiations?

Commander in Chief

The Constitution makes the chief executive the commander in chief of the nation's armed forces (Article II, Section 2, Clause 1), although Congress does have extensive war powers. However, the President dominates the field of military policy. In fact, the President's powers as commander in chief have often been the source of conflict between the legislative and executive branches.

Consider this illustration of the point: In 1907, Theodore Roosevelt sent the Great White Fleet around the world. He did so partly as a training exercise for the Navy but mostly to impress other nations with America's naval might. Several members of Congress objected to the cost and threatened to block funds for the President's project. To this, Roosevelt is said to have replied, "Very well, the existing appropriation will carry the Navy halfway around the world and if Congress chooses

>> As commander in chief, President Lincoln often visited soldiers in the field and was known for taking a personal interest in the men. Here, he meets with officers at Antietam in 1862.

to leave it on the other side, all right." Congress was forced to give in.

Presidents delegate much of their command authority to military subordinates. They are not required to do so, however. George Washington actually took command of federal troops and led them into Pennsylvania during the Whiskey Rebellion of 1794. Abraham Lincoln often visited the Army of the Potomac and his generals in the field during the Civil War.

Most Presidents have not become so directly involved in military operations. Still, the President has the final authority over and responsibility for all military matters, and the most critical decisions are invariably made by the commander in chief.

Making Undeclared War Does the Constitution give the President the power to make war without a declaration of war by Congress? Although many argue that it does not, American history argues otherwise. Presidents have often used the armed forces abroad, in combat, without a declaration of war. In fact, most Presidents have done so, and on several hundred occasions.

John Adams was the first to do so, in 1798. At his command, the Navy fought and won a number of battles with French warships harassing American merchantmen in the Atlantic and the Caribbean. There have been a great many other foreign adventures since then. The long military conflicts in Korea, Vietnam, and Afghanistan stand as the most extensive of these "undeclared wars."

Congressional Resolutions to Balance Executive Power

Congress has not declared war since World War II. On several occasions since then, however, it has enacted joint resolutions to authorize the President to meet certain international crises with military force.

President Dwight Eisenhower sought the first of these measures in 1955, to block the designs the People's Republic of China had (and still has) on Taiwan. That show of American resolve, and the presence of American warships, defused the situation.

Another authorization of force occurred in 2002, when Congress agreed that President George W. Bush should take those measures "necessary and appropriate" to eliminate the threat posed by Saddam Hussein and his Iraqi dictatorship. Operation Iraqi Freedom lasted nearly nine years and sacrificed the lives of nearly 4,500 American troops. Costing hundreds of billions of dollars, the mission ousted Hussein from power and oversaw the installation of a fledgling democracy in Iraq.

Continued violence and unrest plague the nation, however.

Other Uses of Military Power

Since the end of World War II, there have been many other dire situations in which Presidents have deployed the nation's armed forces without a congressional resolution. Certainly, the Korean War stands as the foremost illustration of that fact. Among other notable instances: the dispatch of U.S. forces to the Balkans in 1995 and 1999 by Bill Clinton as part of NATO's response to a vicious civil war and Serbian President Slobodan Milosevic's horrific "ethnic cleansing" campaign and President Obama's 2011 use of the American military, in conjunction with other NATO forces, to support democratic uprisings in the North African nation of Libya.

Limiting Presidential War Powers

The war-making power as it was exercised by Presidents Johnson and Nixon during the undeclared war in Vietnam moved Congress to enact (over President Nixon's veto) the War Powers Resolution of 1973. That statute provides that the President can commit American military forces to combat only (1) if Congress has declared war, (2) if Congress has authorized that action, or (3) when an attack on the nation or its armed forces has occurred.

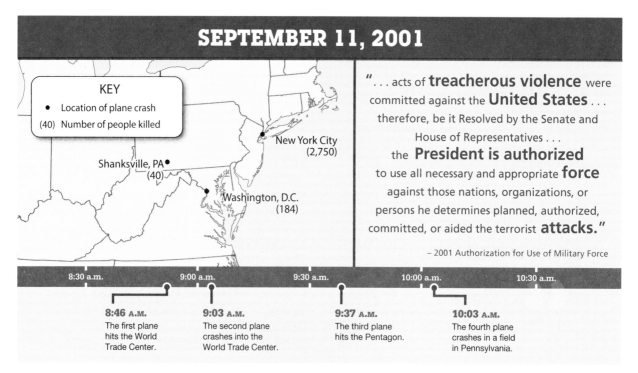

SEPTEMBER 11, 2001

KEY
- Location of plane crash
- (40) Number of people killed

New York City (2,750)

Shanksville, PA (40)

Washington, D.C. (184)

"... acts of **treacherous violence** were committed against the **United States** ... therefore, be it Resolved by the Senate and House of Representatives ... the **President is authorized** to use all necessary and appropriate **force** against those nations, organizations, or persons he determines planned, authorized, committed, or aided the terrorist **attacks.**"

– 2001 Authorization for Use of Military Force

| 8:30 a.m. | 9:00 a.m. | 9:30 a.m. | 10:00 a.m. | 10:30 a.m. |

8:46 A.M. The first plane hits the World Trade Center.

9:03 A.M. The second plane crashes into the World Trade Center.

9:37 A.M. The third plane hits the Pentagon.

10:03 A.M. The fourth plane crashes in a field in Pennsylvania.

>> When the World Trade Center was attacked on 9/11, its 110-stories collapsed within two hours. Sources vary as to the number of people who died in New York City and at the Pentagon.

If troops are ordered into combat in the third circumstance, the President must report it to Congress within 48 hours. Any such commitment of American forces must end within 60 days, unless Congress agrees to a longer involvement. At any time, Congress can end a commitment by the passage of a concurrent resolution (which is not subject to veto). The constitutionality of the War Powers Resolution remains in dispute.

☑ **SYNTHESIZE** What power allows the President to enter into a military conflict without congressional approval? Give an example of how a President has used this power.

☑ ASSESSMENT

1. **Explain** A President has signed an arms control treaty approved by the Senate, but 20 years later, a different President thinks the terms are not stringent enough. What, if anything, can the new President do to change the situation?

2. **Sequence** When Panama was created in 1903, why did President Theodore Roosevelt use his power to recognize the new nation so quickly?

3. **Interpret** How does President Theodore Roosevelt's comment, "speak softly and carry a big stick" relate to the President's powers as a diplomat and as commander in chief? Do you agree with this approach? Why or why not?

4. **Determine Author's Purpose** When President Nixon vetoed the War Powers Resolution in 1973, he noted: "If the [War Powers] resolution had been in operation, America's effective response to a variety of challenges in recent years would have been vastly complicated or even made impossible. We may well have been unable to respond in the way we did during the Berlin crisis of 1961, the Cuban missile crisis of 1962, the Congo rescue operation in 1964, and the Jordanian crisis of 1970—to mention just a few examples." How do the examples given by President Nixon support his decision to veto the War Powers Act?

5. **Analyze** Reflect on the power of the President as the commander in chief. Why do you think the Framers gave this power to the President, rather than Congress?

Desegregation of the Armed Forces

During World War II, civil rights leaders had drawn attention to the unequal treatment of Black servicemen and -women compared to their white counterparts. After the war, President Truman created a committee to recommend what should be done to safeguard civil rights. The committee's report recounted the obstacles that prevented people of color from enjoying equal participation in American life. In response, President Truman issued Executive Order 9981. Despite resistance from the military, the order had far-reaching consequences, leading to the desegregation of the armed forces and helping to set in motion a drive for civil rights protections for Black Americans, Native Americans, Hispanic Americans, women, and immigrants.

As you read, look for how these excerpts take different approaches to achieving a strong America.

>> During World War II, an officer inspects a group of "Buffalo Soldiers," a traditionally Black division in the segregated U.S. Army.

Primary Source 1

Executive Order 9981, July 26, 1948

. . . 1. It is hereby declared to be the policy of the President that there shall be equality of treatment and opportunity for all persons in the armed services without regard to race, color, religion or national origin. This policy shall be put into effect as rapidly as possible, having due regard to the time required to effectuate [put into effect] any necessary changes without impairing efficiency or morale.

2. There shall be created in the national Military Establishment an advisory committee to be known as the President's Committee on Equality of Treatment and Opportunity in the Armed Services. . . .

3. The Committee is authorized on behalf of the President to examine into the rules, procedures and practices of the armed services in order to determine in what respect such rules, procedures and practices may be altered or improved with a view to carrying out the policy of this order. The Committee shall confer and advise with the Secretary of Defense, the Secretary of the Army, the Secretary of the Navy, and the Secretary of the Air Force, and shall make such recommendations to the President and to said Secretaries as in the judgment of the Committee will effectuate the policy hereof. . . .

☑ **IDENTIFY THE MAIN IDEA** What was the goal of Executive Order 9981?

Primary Source 2

Note: *Negro* is a term meaning Black American that is no longer favored today but was considered appropriate in the 1940s.

Statement by General Omar Bradley, March 28, 1949

. . . I would like to say that I personally have no prejudice in this matter and my only concern is that nothing be done which might adversely [negatively] affect our ability to carry out our mission. . . .

Any system of handling manpower and any principles of organization must be based upon what will obtain best results in carrying out our mission, i.e., winning battles in case of war. We must not do anything that will jeopardize National Security. . . .

Complete integration of units would greatly simplify our administrative problems and I believe that steps towards such integration should be taken as fast as our social customs will permit. I think that we have made great strides towards further integration in the last few years. However, we still have great divergence in customs in different parts of the country. . . .

Neither is integration in a military unit as simple as integration in public gatherings or places of work during the day. The big problems arise after work or training, in living quarters and social gatherings. At the same time we must have equality of opportunity, of facilities and of treatment. This is being provided under present policies.

I believe that the Negro soldier, in general, considers his lot, from his viewpoint, a good one. Our high rate of re-enlistment indicates this. . . .

I would say that some of the principal advantages of complete integration are that it might remove any false charges that equal opportunities are not provided. It would simplify administration and the use of manpower, and it would distribute our losses in battle more nearly in proportion to the percentage of the two races.

Among the principal disadvantages I might mention that complete integration might very seriously affect voluntary enlistments, both Negro and White. . . .

In addition . . . complete integration might seriously affect morale and thus affect battle efficiency. I consider that a unit has high morale when the men have confidence in themselves, confidence in their fellow-members of their unit, and confidence in their leaders. If we try to force integration on the Army before the country is ready to accept these customs, we may have difficulty attaining high morale along the lines I have mentioned.

. . . The ultimate winning or losing of battles . . . is our military problem. I am sure you realize that any radical changes in this Army which might seriously affect its ability to accomplish this mission would be a very serious one.

☑ **DETERMINE MEANING** According to General Bradley, why is Army integration not simple?

☑ ASSESSMENT

1. **Predict** In what way might the Executive Order have affected Black Americans, immigrants, Native Americans, women, and other groups despite the fact that they were not in the armed forces?

2. **Cite Evidence** How did the Executive Order plan to enforce the new regulations?

3. **Compare Points of View** The 1946 report of the President's Committee on Civil Rights noted that "Almost 80 percent of the Negro sailors are serving as cooks, stewards, and steward's mates; less than two percent of the whites are assigned to duty in the same capacity. Almost 15 percent of all white enlisted marines are in the three highest grades; less than 2 1/2 percent of the Negro marines fall in the same category. The disparities in the Coast Guard are similarly great." How does this compare to General Bradley's view of the treatment of Black Americans in the military?

Topic 5 Quick Study Guide

LESSON SUMMARIES

Use these Lesson Summaries, and the longer versions available online, to review the key ideas for each lesson in this Topic.

Lesson 1: The Presidency—An Overview

The President serves many roles. He or she is ceremonial head of state and the day-to-day chief executive. The President runs the administration, serves as commander in chief of the military, guides legislation and the economy, and leads his or her political party.

Lesson 2: The Vice President and the First Lady

The roles of the Vice President and First Lady have changed over time. In the past, Vice Presidents were limited to their constitutional roles as leader of the senate and "President-in-waiting." More recently, they have served as key advisors to the President. Likewise, First Ladies have moved from playing a social role to championing important causes.

Lesson 3: The President's Domestic Powers

In domestic affairs, the President is charged with executing federal laws, working out exactly how laws should operate, issuing orders to executive branch employees, and appointing and removing officials. He or she also has the power to grant clemency, recommend legislation, and veto laws.

Lesson 4: The President's Foreign Affairs Powers

The President holds enormous power over the nation's foreign affairs. He or she directs diplomacy, makes treaties and executive agreements, and recognizes foreign governments. The President is also the commander in chief of the armed forces. Still, Congress has some authority to check the President's actions in these areas.

VISUAL REVIEW

Use these graphics to review some of the key terms, people, and ideas from this Topic.

Changing Roles

The Vice President

Early Vice Presidents had little political role. → More recent Vice Presidents have taken on important responsibilities. → Today, the Vice President may be one of the President's most trusted advisors.

The First Lady

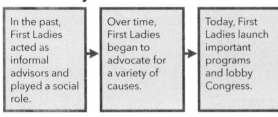

In the past, First Ladies acted as informal advisors and played a social role. → Over time, First Ladies began to advocate for a variety of causes. → Today, First Ladies launch important programs and lobby Congress.

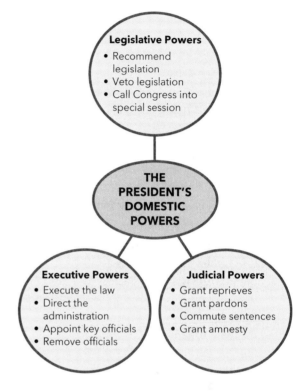

Legislative Powers
- Recommend legislation
- Veto legislation
- Call Congress into special session

THE PRESIDENT'S DOMESTIC POWERS

Executive Powers
- Execute the law
- Direct the administration
- Appoint key officials
- Remove officials

Judicial Powers
- Grant reprieves
- Grant pardons
- Commute sentences
- Grant amnesty

Commander in Chief

Makes treaties

Deploys armed forces

President

FOREIGN POLICY POWERS

Congress

War Powers Act

Funds military

Approves treaties (Senate only)

The Presidency

22nd Amendment: Presidency limited to two four-year terms

25th Amendment: Vice President succeeds to the office if presidency becomes vacant

PRESIDENT

Fulfills many roles: chief of state, chief executive, chief administrator, chief diplomat, chief legislator, commander in chief, chief economist, chief of party, chief citizen

Must be a natural-born citizen, at least 35 years old, and U.S. Resident for 14 years

Topic 5 Assessment

KEY TERMS, PEOPLE, AND IDEAS

1. What is the difference between a **veto** and a **line-item veto**?

2. What is an **executive order**, and how is it related to the **ordinance power**?

3. What is the power of **recognition**? Does recognition necessarily mean that one government approves of the conduct of another?

4. The President is the nation's **chief of state** as well as its **chief executive**. How do those roles differ?

5. What does it mean for a vice presidential candidate to **balance the ticket**?

6. What is the difference between a **treaty** and an **executive agreement**?

7. How do **amnesty** and a **pardon** differ?

8. What is a **pocket veto**?

CRITICAL THINKING

9. **Summarize** How does the President direct foreign policy? How can Congress check presidential power in this area?

10. **Evaluate Arguments** Some critics of the 22nd Amendment claim it is undemocratic. What does the 22nd Amendment do? Does it put an unreasonable burden on the ability of the voters to pick the most qualified person for President?

11. **Interpret** From what two sources in the Constitution does the President get the power to execute the law? How can a President affect the meaning of a law? Do you think Congress gives the executive branch too much authority to interpret laws?

12. **Draw Conclusions** What are the President's legislative powers? What are the President's judicial powers? How do these powers illustrate the principle of checks and balances?

13. **Compare and contrast** the roles of early and modern First Ladies. Use specific examples in your response.

14. **Infer** What competing views of the presidency were held by the Framers, and which view did they finally adopt? Do you think the Framers' decision helped to shape the nature of presidential power? Why or why not?

15. **Evaluate** What presidential power did the Supreme Court recognize in the case *United States* v. *Nixon* (1974)? Why was this a significant case, and how did the decision reflect separation of powers?

16. **Analyze** The map below shows some of the conflicts since World War II that have taken place without a congressional declaration of war. Does the Constitution give the President the power to make war without a declaration of war by Congress? Analyze the history of the presidential use of military force, including the War Powers Resolution of 1973. Why did Congress enact this resolution?

17. **Describe** What are the duties of the Vice President? How has the overall nature of the vice presidency changed over time?

18. **Summarize** Summarize Article II of the Constitution, including its requirements regarding eligibility for office, length of term, election to and removal from office, the oath of office, and executive powers.

19. **Summarize** What powers does the President have to appoint and remove officials? How is Congress involved in this process?

20. **Writing Activity** Consider the various uses of executive powers that you've read about in this Topic. Then write a paragraph in which you explain how the civil rights of people of color were expanded through President Lincoln's Emancipation Proclamation and President Truman's Executive Order 9981. Do you think either of these executive actions affected the civil rights of women? Explain your answer as part of your paragraph.

DOCUMENT-BASED QUESTIONS

President Truman's decision to use the atomic bomb against Japan in World War II continues to stir controversy. Read the documents below, then answer the questions.

DOCUMENT A

This excerpt is from a petition signed by 154 of the scientists who developed the atomic bomb.

> The war has to be brought speedily to a successful conclusion and attacks by atomic bombs may very well be an effective method of warfare. We feel, however, that such attacks on Japan could not be justified, at least not until the terms which will be imposed after the war on Japan were made public in detail and Japan were given an opportunity to surrender. . . .
>
> The development of atomic power will provide the nation with new means of destruction. The atomic bombs at our disposal represent only the first step in this direction, and there is almost no limit to the destructive power which will become available in the course of their future development.
>
> —*Leó Szilárd, Petition to the President of the United States, July 17, 1945*

DOCUMENT B

This photograph shows Hiroshima after the bombing on August 6, 1945. The single bomb destroyed 4.7 square miles of Hiroshima and some 68% of its buildings. Between 70,000 and 80,000 people were killed by the explosion or its aftereffects.

DOCUMENT C

This excerpt is from a letter written by President Truman after the war, explaining why he decided to use the atomic bomb.

> When the message came to Potsdam that a successful atomic explosion had taken place in New Mexico, there was much excitement and conversation about the effect on the war then in progress with Japan. . . . I asked Gen. Marshall what it would cost in lives to land on the Tokyo plain and other places in Japan. It was his opinion that ¼ million casualties would be the minimum cost as well as an equal number of the enemy.
>
> We sent an ultimatum to Japan. It was ignored. . . . Dropping the bombs ended the war, saved lives, and gave the free nations a chance to face the facts.
>
> —*Harry Truman, January 12, 1953*

DOCUMENT D

This excerpt is from a book written by a onetime historian for the Nuclear Regulatory Commission.

> The use of atomic bombs was decisive in ending the war. After Hiroshima, the emperor for the first time came out unequivocally for surrender, and he soon intervened directly to persuade the cabinet to accept the Potsdam Declaration. . . .
>
> Even without the use of the atomic bombs, the war would probably have ended before an American invasion of Kyushu [one of Japan's main islands] became necessary. Conditions in Japan were steadily deteriorating before the atomic attacks and would have continued to worsen as the war dragged on. The destruction of cities from B-29 raids, diminishing food supplies, and decreasing public morale fostered enough discontent to worry the emperor and his advisers. . . .
>
> —*J. Samuel Walker, Prompt and Utter Destruction, 1997*

21. The scientists who signed the petition believed that atomic weapons
    A. would not help bring the war to a quick end.
    B. should be used immediately to end the war.
    C. might be used if there was no other option.
    D. were too dangerous to use for any reason.

22. **Analyze Photographs** Based on Document B, what effect do you think the bombing might have had on those who witnessed it?

23. According to Truman, his main goal in deciding to use the atomic bomb was to
    A. save American and Japanese lives.
    B. punish Japan for carrying on the war.
    C. demonstrate the power of nuclear weapons.
    D. destroy the nation of Japan.

24. **Writing Task** Write a paragraph evaluating the various explanations in these documents. Which facts in the documents best agree with one another? What discrepancies, if any, do you find among the documents?

The Executive Branch at Work

ESSENTIAL QUESTION What Should Governments Do?

A White House ceremony welcomes home the recently freed hostages from Iran in 1981.

Connections to Today

Superhero movies are some of the most popular of all time, with their battles between good and evil and their superhuman characters. Does this have any relation to the term *superpower* that is sometimes used to describe the United States? That label means a lot of things, but superhuman abilities is not one of them! But one thing it does mean is that the United States is a global powerhouse with hundreds of military bases around the world. Some of these bases have their roots back in the late 1800s, when the country first began to grow into a world power.

NBC LEARN

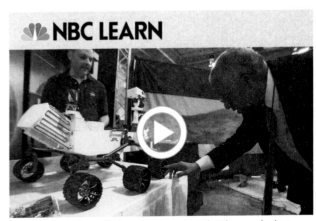

Learn more about independent agencies by exploring NASA's role in advancements in technology.

 BOUNCE to Activate My Story Video

Topic 6 Overview

In this Topic, you will take a look at the huge executive branch of the Federal Government, which handles matters ranging from space exploration to food safety to international treaties. Look at the lesson outline and explore the chart. As you study this Topic, you can work on your Quest Inquiry.

LESSON OUTLINE

6.1 The Federal Bureaucracy

6.2 The EOP and the Executive Departments

6.3 The Independent Agencies

6.4 Foreign Policy Overview

6.5 Diplomacy

6.6 National Security

The Executive Branch

EXECUTIVE OFFICE OF THE PRESIDENT	EXECUTIVE DEPARTMENTS		SELECTED INDEPENDENT AGENCIES
• White House Office	• State	• Housing and Urban Development	• Amtrak
• Office of the Vice President	• Treasury		• Central Intelligence Agency
• Council of Economic Advisors	• Defense	• Transportation	• Environmental Protection Agency
• Council on Environmental Quality	• Justice	• Energy	• Federal Reserve System
• National Security Council	• The Interior	• Education	• National Aeronautics and Space Administration
• Office of Administration	• Agriculture	• Veterans Affairs	• National Endowment for the Arts
• Office of Management and Budget	• Commerce	• Homeland Security	• National Science Foundation
• Office of National Drug Control Policy	• Labor		• Peace Corps
• Office of Science and Technology Policy	• Health and Human Services		• Social Security Administration
• Office of the United States Trade Representative			• United States Agency for International Development
			• United States Postal Service

Inquiry Center

Want to become an active and effective citizen? Make a difference in your community and beyond by using the **Inquiry Center** on the digital course.

Connect with issues you're passionate about by using the **Interest Finder**.

Investigate public policies, get involved in your community, influence public opinion, and develop leadership skills.

Synthesize the work you've done and what you've learned along the way.

Demonstrate what you've learned once you've finished your project by sharing your work.

The Internal Revenue Service is part of the huge executive branch bureaucracy, responsible for processing all federal tax returns. The agency handles millions of pages of paperwork each year.

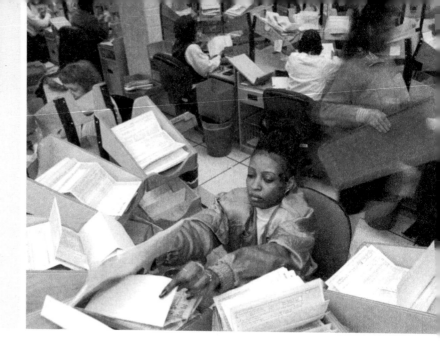

BOUNCE to Activate Flipped Video

Objectives

Define a bureaucracy.

Identify the major elements of the federal bureaucracy.

Explain how groups within the federal bureaucracy are named.

Describe the difference between a staff agency and a line agency.

Key Terms

bureaucracy
bureaucrat
administration
staff agency
line agency
James Madison

The Federal Bureaucracy

The Federal Government is an immense organization. Its employees deliver the mail, regulate business practices, collect taxes, defend the nation, administer Social Security programs, manage the national forests, explore outer space, and do dozens of other things every day. Indeed, you cannot live through a single day without somehow encountering the federal bureaucracy.

What Is a Bureaucracy?

A **bureaucracy** is a large, complex administrative structure that handles the everyday business of an organization. To many Americans, the word *bureaucracy* suggests such things as waste, red tape, and delay. While that image is not altogether unfounded, it is quite lopsided. At its best, bureaucracy can be an efficient and effective way to organize people (bureaucrats) to do work.

Bureaucracies are found wherever there are large organizations, in both the public and the private sectors of this country. Thus, the United States Air Force, McDonald's, the Social Security Administration, MTV, your city government, Yahoo!, the Boy Scouts of America, Twitter, and the Roman Catholic Church are all bureaucracies. Even your school is a bureaucracy.

Defining Bureaucracy By definition, a bureaucracy is a system of organization built on three principles: hierarchical authority, job specialization, and formalized rules.

Hierarchical authority. The word *hierarchical* describes any organization structured as a pyramid, with a chain of command running from the top of the pyramid on down to its base. The few officials and units at the top of the structure have authority over those officials and units at the larger middle level, who in turn direct the activities of the many at the bottom level.

Job specialization. Each **bureaucrat,** each person who works for the organization, has certain defined duties and responsibilities. There is, then, a precise division of labor within the organization.

Formalized rules. The bureaucracy does its work according to a number of established regulations and procedures. Those rules are set out in written form and so can be known by all who are involved in that work.

The Benefits and Drawbacks of Bureaucracy

Those three principles—hierarchical authority, job specialization, and formalized rules—can make bureaucracy the most effective way for people to work together on large and complex tasks, whether public or private.

The hierarchy can speed action by reducing conflicts over who has the power and the appropriate authority to make decisions. The higher a person's rank in the organization, the greater the decision-making power he or she has.

Job specialization promotes efficiency because each person in the organization is required to focus on one particular job. Each worker thus gains a set of specialized skills and knowledge.

Formalized rules mean that workers can act with some speed and precision because decisions are based on a set of known standards, not on someone's likes, dislikes, or inclinations. Those rules also enable work to continue with little interruption even as some workers leave an organization and new workers are hired to replace them.

At the same time, however, bureaucracies can suffer from several important flaws. Among them are the inefficiency and waste that can result from too many levels in the hierarchy or unnecessarily complex procedures that result from formalized rules. In addition, it is important to recognize this very important point about public bureaucracies: their bureaucrats hold appointive offices. Bureaucrats are *unelected* makers and implementers of public policy. This is not to say that bureaucracies are undemocratic. However, in a democracy, much depends on how effectively the bureaucracy is controlled by those whom the people do elect—the President and Congress. Listen to **James Madison** on the point:

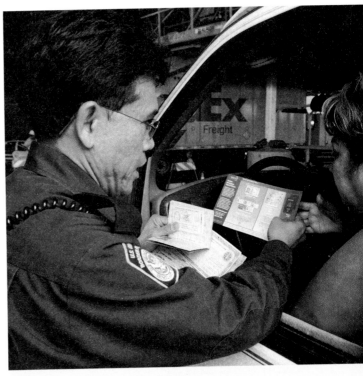

>> A U.S. border patrol officer checks a driver's documents. He is one of millions of people who work for the agencies and organizations that make up the federal bureaucracy.

THE GOVERNMENT WANTS TO ANNOUNCE A TARGET DATE FOR ANNOUNCING A TARGET NUMBER OF TARGETS THEY WANT TO GET RID OF!

>> Bureaucracy and its sometimes convoluted procedures are often criticized as an inefficient way to run the government. **Analyze Political Cartoons** How does the cartoon illustrate this point?

> In framing a government which is to be administered by men over men, the great difficulty lies in this: you must first enable the government to control the governed; and in the next place oblige it to control itself.

—The *Federalist Papers*, No. 51

☑ **GENERATE EXPLANATIONS** If a furniture manufacturer with a bureaucratic organization undergoes a large turnover of employees from one year to the next, what feature of the bureaucratic structure enables that organization to continue to produce furniture, despite the changes to its staff? Explain your answer.

Executive Branch Bureaucracy

The federal bureaucracy is all of the agencies, people, and procedures through which the Federal Government operates. It is the means by which the government makes and administers public policy—the sum of all of its decisions and actions. Nearly all of that huge bureaucracy is located in the executive branch. Not all of it, however, because both Congress and the federal court system are bureaucracies, as well.

The Constitution makes the President the chief administrator of the Federal Government. Article II, Section 3 declares that "he shall take Care that the Laws be faithfully executed." But the Constitution makes only the barest mention of the administrative machinery (the bureaucracy) through which the President is to exercise that power.

Article II does suggest executive departments by giving to the President the power to "require the Opinion, in writing, of the principal Officer in each of the executive Departments" (Article II, Section 2, Clause 1). A reference to "Heads of Departments" is in Clause 2, and to "any Department or Officer" of the government is in Article I, Section 8, Clause 18.

Article II anticipates two departments in particular, one for military and one for foreign affairs. It does so by making the President the "Commander in Chief of the Army and Navy," and by giving the chief executive both the power to make treaties and to appoint "Ambassadors, other public Ministers, and Consuls" (Article II, Section 2, Clauses 1 and 2).

Beyond those references, the Constitution is silent on the organization of the executive branch. The Framers certainly intended that administrative agencies be created, however. They understood that no matter how wise the President and Congress, their decisions still had to be carried out in order to be effective. Without an **administration**—the government's many administrators and agencies—even the best policies would amount to just so many words and phrases. The President and Congress need millions of men and women to put policies into action in Washington, D.C., and in offices all around the country and the world.

The chief organizational feature of the federal bureaucracy is its division into areas of specialization. The executive branch is composed of three broad groups of agencies: (1) the Executive Office of the President, (2) the 15 Cabinet departments, and (3) a large number of independent agencies.

☑ **ANALYZE INFORMATION** On what basis has the federal bureaucracy been established?

>> President Reagan is saluted by members of the U.S. Navy. The Constitution suggests the creation of a federal military by making the President the commander in chief of the army and navy.

The Executive Branch

EXECUTIVE OFFICE OF THE PRESIDENT	EXECUTIVE DEPARTMENTS		SELECTED INDEPENDENT AGENCIES
• White House Office • Office of the Vice President • Council of Economic Advisors • Council on Environmental Quality • National Security Council • Office of Administration • Office of Management and Budget • Office of National Drug Control Policy • Office of Science and Technology Policy • Office of the United States Trade Representative	• State • Treasury • Defense • Justice • The Interior • Agriculture • Commerce • Labor • Health and Human Services	• Housing and Urban Development • Transportation • Energy • Education • Veterans Affairs • Homeland Security	• Amtrak • Central Intelligence Agency • Environmental Protection Agency • Federal Reserve System • National Aeronautics and Space Administration • National Endowment for the Arts • National Science Foundation • Peace Corps • Social Security Administration • United States Agency for International Development • United States Postal Service

>> Each executive branch agency is created by act of Congress to execute the nation's laws. **Analyze Charts** Why do you think the executive branch is the largest part of the federal bureaucracy?

How Units Are Named

The titles given to the many units that make up the executive branch vary a great deal. The name *department* is reserved for agencies of Cabinet rank. Beyond the title of *department*, however, there is little standardized use of titles among the agencies.

Common Names The most commonly used titles for units in the executive branch include *agency, administration, commission, corporation, authority, bureau, service, office, branch*, and *division*. The term *agency* is often used to refer to any governmental body. It is sometimes used to identify a major unit headed by a single administrator of near-cabinet status, such as the Environmental Protection Agency. But so, too, is the title *administration*; for example, the National Aeronautics and Space Administration and the General Services Administration.

The name *commission* is usually given to agencies charged with the regulation of business activities, such as the Federal Communications Commission and the Securities and Exchange Commission. Top-ranking officers called commissioners head these units. The same title, however, is given to some investigative, advisory, and reporting bodies, including the U.S. Commission on Civil Rights and the Federal Election Commission.

Either *corporation* or *authority* is the title most often given to those agencies that conduct businesslike activities. Corporations and authorities are regularly headed by a board and a manager—as is the case with the Federal Deposit Insurance Corporation, the Commodity Credit Corporation, and the Tennessee Valley Authority.

Irregular Names Within each major agency, the same confusing lack of uniformity in the use of names is common. *Bureau* is the name often given to the major elements in a department, but *service, administration, office, branch*, and *division* are often used for the same purpose. For example, the major units within the Department of Justice include the Federal Bureau of Investigation, the United States Marshals Service, the Drug Enforcement Administration, the Office of the Pardon Attorney, the Criminal Division, and the National Drug Intelligence Center.

Acronyms as Names Many federal agencies are often referred to by their initials. The EPA, IRS, FBI, CIA, FCC, NASA, and TVA are but a few of the dozens of familiar examples we hear and read about every day. A few are also known by nicknames.

For example, the Government National Mortgage Association is often called "Ginnie Mae," and the National Railroad Passenger Corporation is better known to us as Amtrak.

The use of acronyms can sometimes cause problems. When the old Bureau of the Budget was reorganized in 1970, it was also renamed. It is now the Office of Management and Budget (OMB). However, it was for a time slated to be known as the Bureau of Management and Budget (BOMB).

☑ **CONNECT** Unlike the numerous other titles given to various units in the executive branch, the name *department* is reserved for a special use. What is that use?

Staff and Line Agencies

The units that make up any administrative organization can be classified as either staff or line agencies. The Federal Government units are also described as such.

Staff agencies serve in a support capacity. They aid the chief executive and other administrators by offering advice and assistance in the management of the organization. **Line agencies,** on the other hand, actually perform the tasks for which the organization exists.

Congress and the President give the line agencies goals to meet, and the staff agencies help the line agencies meet these goals as effectively as possible through advising, budgeting, purchasing, planning, and management. The general public is much more aware of the work of line agencies than it is of that of most of the staff units. It is for a rather obvious reason: it is the line agencies that carry out public policies and, in doing so, deal directly with the public.

Two illustrations of the distinction here can be found in the several agencies that make up the Executive Office of the President and, in contrast, the Environmental Protection Agency. The agencies that make up the Executive Office of the President (The White House, the National Security Council, the Office of Management and Budget, the Office of Policy Development, and others) each exist as staff support to the President. Their primary mission is to assist the President in the exercise of the executive power and in the overall management of the executive branch. They are not operating agencies. That is, they do not actually administer public programs.

The Environmental Protection Agency (EPA), on the other hand, has an altogether different mission. It is responsible for the day-to-day enforcement of the many antipollution laws Congress has enacted over

Staff and Line Agencies

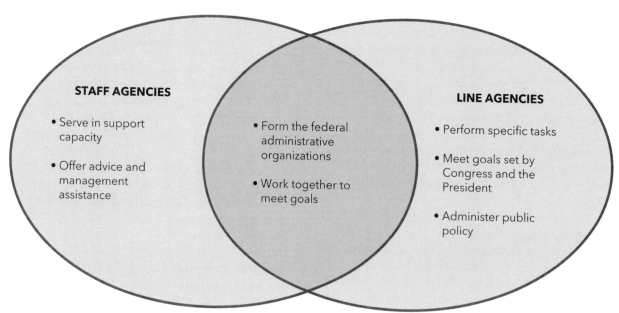

STAFF AGENCIES
- Serve in support capacity
- Offer advice and management assistance

- Form the federal administrative organizations
- Work together to meet goals

LINE AGENCIES
- Perform specific tasks
- Meet goals set by Congress and the President
- Administer public policy

>> The federal bureaucracy is made up of both staff and line agencies. **Analyze Charts** What are some examples of each type of agency?

the years. The EPA operates "on the line," where the action is.

This difference between staff agencies and line agencies can help you find your way through the complex federal bureaucracy. The distinction between the two can be oversimplified, however. For example, most line agencies do have staff units to aid them in their line operations. Thus, the Environmental Protection Agency's Office of Civil Rights is a staff unit. Its job is to ensure that the agency's hiring and other personnel practices do not violate the Federal Government's anti-discrimination policies.

☑ CONTRAST When the Department of Education conducts research on learning styles, is it functioning as a staff or a line agency? Explain your answer.

☑ ASSESSMENT

1. **Analyze Information** Explain how the defining features of a bureaucracy both help and hurt the effectiveness and efficiency of the Federal Government.

2. **Synthesize** Why does the bottom level of the bureaucratic hierarchy have the most employees?

3. **Infer** Why does the Federal Government need an administration, despite the fact that the Constitution says little about it?

4. **Generate Explanations** Why do some people argue that the federal bureaucracy is undemocratic? What is the opposing argument?

5. **Apply Concepts** The Council of Economic Advisors is a staff agency in the Executive Office of the President. Based on its title and the definition of a staff agency, what do you think this group does?

The White House Situation Room is a highly secure complex of rooms in which the President can meet with advisors to handle domestic and international emergencies.

BOUNCE to Activate Flipped Video

Objectives

Analyze the structure and functions of the executive branch of government.

Describe the Executive Office of the President.

Explain the duties of the White House, the National Security Council, and the Office of Management and Budget.

Identify other agencies that make up the Executive Office of the President.

Describe the role of the Cabinet and executive departments in the executive branch.

Key Terms

Executive Office of
  the President
federal budget
fiscal year
domestic affairs
executive
  department
civilian
secretary
attorney general
George Washington
Abraham Lincoln

The EOP and the Executive Departments

Thomas Jefferson performed his presidential duties with the help of two aides, one a messenger and the other his secretary. Like other early Presidents, he paid their salaries out of his own pocket. Indeed, Congress did not provide any money for presidential staff until 1857, when it gave President James Buchanan $2,500 for one clerk.

Structure of the Executive Office of the President

President Jefferson presided over an executive branch that employed, altogether, only some 2,100 people. The situation is remarkably different today. About 2 million men and women work in a modern presidential administration. Two institutions—the Executive Office of the President and the President's Cabinet—are at the center of today's huge executive branch.

Every officer, every employee, and every agency in the executive branch of the Federal Government is legally subordinate to the President. They all exist to help the President—the chief executive—in the exercise of the executive power.

The President's right arm, however, is the **Executive Office of the President** (the EOP). The Executive Office of the President is, in fact, an umbrella agency, a complex organization of several separate agencies staffed by some 2,000 of the President's key advisers and assistants. President Franklin Roosevelt persuaded Congress to establish the EOP in 1939. It has been reorganized in every administration since it was established.

The Role of the White House

The EOP's nerve center—in fact, the nerve center of the entire executive branch—is an agency now called the White House. Most of the President's key personal and political aides work there.

The two wings on either side of the White House hold the offices of most of the President's staff. These presidential assistants occupy much of the crowded West Wing, which the public seldom sees and where the legendary Oval Office and the Cabinet Room are located.

The White House chief of staff to the President directs all of the operations of the EOP and is among the most influential presidential aides. The counselor to the President and a number of senior advisers are also key members of the President's inner circle.

Several top officials work in the White House Office. A number of assistants and deputy assistants to the President aid the chief executive in such vital areas as foreign policy, defense, homeland security, the economy, political affairs, congressional relations, speech writing, and contacts with the news media and the public.

The staff of the White House Office also includes such major presidential aides as the press secretary, the appointments and scheduling assistant, and the President's physician. The First Lady's very visible place in public life today is reflected by the fact that one of the assistants to the President serves as her chief of staff and one of the several deputy assistants is her press secretary.

The staff of the White House Office includes some 450 men and women. The titles of some of the subunits they work for indicate the scope of their responsibilities: The Office of Digital Strategy, Oval Office Operations, the Office of the First Lady, the Office of Cabinet Affairs, the Office of Urban Affairs, and the Office of the Press Secretary.

The National Security Council

Most of the President's major steps in foreign affairs are taken in close consultation with the National Security Council (NSC). It meets at the President's call, often on short notice, to advise him in all domestic, foreign, and military matters that relate to the nation's security.

The President chairs the Council. Its other members include the Vice President and the secretaries of state, treasury, and defense. The Director of National Intelligence and the chairman of the Joint Chiefs of Staff regularly attend its meetings.

>> James Baker (right) served as the chief of staff for two Presidents, Ronald Reagan (left) and George H.W. Bush.

>> A U.S. delegation in Jordan in 2003. From left: Secretary of State Colin Powell, National Security adviser Condoleezza Rice, Jordanian Queen Rania Al Abdullah, and chief of staff Andy Card.

The NSC has a small staff of foreign and military policy experts. They work under the direction of the President's national security adviser. The government's several intelligence agencies do much of their often super-secret work at the direction of the National Security Council.

The National Security Council is a staff agency. That is, its job is to advise the President in all matters affecting the nation's security. However, during the Reagan administration in the 1980s, the NSC's staff actually conducted a number of secret operations, including the sale of arms to Iran. The disclosure of the NSC's role in this sale led to the Iran-Contra scandal of the mid-1980s.

The Office of Management and Budget The Office of Management and Budget (OMB) is the largest and, after the White House, the most influential unit in the Executive Office. The OMB is headed by a director who is appointed by the President and confirmed by the Senate. The OMB's major task is the preparation of the federal budget, which the President must submit to Congress every year.

The **federal budget** is a very detailed estimate of receipts and expenditures, an anticipation of federal income and outgo, during the next fiscal year. A **fiscal year** is the 12-month period used by government and business for record keeping, budgeting, and other financial management purposes. The Federal Government's fiscal year runs from October 1 through September 30.

The budget is more than just a financial document. It is a plan—a carefully drawn, closely detailed work plan for the conduct of government. It is an annual statement of the public policies of the United States, expressed in dollar terms.

The creation of each fiscal year's budget is a lengthy process that begins more than a year before the start of the fiscal year for which it is intended. Each federal agency prepares detailed estimates of its spending needs for that 12-month period. The OMB reviews those proposals and gives agency officials the opportunity to defend their dollar requests. Following that agency-by-agency review, the revised (and usually lowered) spending estimates are fitted into the President's overall program before it is sent to Congress. The OMB then monitors the spending of the funds Congress appropriates.

Beyond its budget chores, the OMB is a sort of presidential "handyman" agency. It makes continuing studies of the organization and management of the executive branch and keeps the President up to date on the work of all its agencies. The OMB checks and clears agency stands on all legislative matters to make certain they agree with the President's policy positions. It also helps prepare the hundreds of executive orders the President must issue each year and the veto messages the chief executive occasionally sends to Congress.

The Office of National Drug Control Policy
The EOP's umbrella covers several other—and

The OMB and the Budget

FACTORS THE OMB CONSIDERS WHEN CREATING THE PRESIDENT'S BUDGET PROPOSAL	
What can the government spend?	The OMB must estimate how much income, principally from taxes, the government will receive in an upcoming fiscal year. Much of that sum must be spent for purposes and at levels previously set by Congress (mandatory spending).
What do the people want?	The people expect the Federal Government to maintain most existing programs. Only about 20 percent of all federal spending can be directed to expanding these programs and/or the creation of new ones (discretionary spending).
What does the President want?	Some spending has a higher priority in the give-and-take of the budget-making process than others—in particular, spending for those programs that are, for whatever reason, important to the President.

>> The Office of Management and Budget considers many factors when creating the President's final budget proposal. **Analyze Charts** Which of these factors might be the most difficult to quantify?

COST OF DRUG ABUSE

$120 billion lost productivity

$11 billion healthcare costs

$61 billion criminal justice costs

— Office of National Drug Control Policy EOP

" ONDCP seeks to foster healthy individuals and safe communities by effectively leading the Nation's effort to reduce drug use and its consequences. "

— Executive Office of the President
Office of National Drug Control Policy

>> The Office of National Drug Control Policy provides resources such as community-based prevention programs and interventions to help recovering drug offenders and to promote public safety.

quite important— agencies. Each of those agencies provides essential staff help to the chief executive.

The Office of National Drug Control Policy was established in 1988. It is headed by a director who is appointed by the President, with Senate approval. The Office prepares an annual national drug control strategy, which the President sends on to Congress. The director also coordinates the ongoing efforts of the more than 50 federal agencies that participate in the continuing war on drugs.

The Council of Economic Advisers Three of the country's leading economists, chosen by the President with Senate consent, make up the Council of Economic Advisers. This Council is the chief executive's major source of information and advice on the state of the nation's economy. It also helps the President prepare the annual Economic Report to Congress, which goes to Capitol Hill in late January or early February each year.

The Roles of Other EOP Units A number of other agencies in the Executive Office house key presidential aides. These men and women make it possible for the President to meet the many-sided responsibilities of the presidency.

The Domestic Policy Council advises the chief executive on all matters relating to the nation's

domestic affairs—that is, all matters not directly connected to the realm of foreign affairs.

The Council on Environmental Quality aids the President in environmental policy and in writing the annual "state of the environment" report to Congress. It sees that federal agencies comply with presidential policy and the nation's environmental laws. The President, with Senate consent, appoints the three members of the council.

The Office of the Vice President houses the now more than fifty men and women who help the Vice President perform the duties of that office. The marked growth in the size of that staff in recent years illustrates the increase in the importance and political clout of the vice presidency.

The Office of United States Trade Representative advises the chief executive in all matters of foreign trade. The trade representative, appointed by the President and confirmed by the Senate, carries the rank of ambassador and represents the President in foreign trade negotiations.

The Office of Science and Technology Policy is the President's major adviser in all scientific, engineering, and other technological matters. Its director is drawn from the nation's scientific community.

The Office of Administration is the general housekeeping agency for all the other units in the

Executive Office. It provides them with the many support services they must have in order to do their jobs.

☑ **ANALYZE INFORMATION** Analyze the reasons for creating different offices within the EOP.

The Executive Departments

In *The Federalist* No. 76, Alexander Hamilton declared that "the true test of a good government is its aptitude and tendency to produce a good administration." Given that comment, it seems strange that Hamilton and the other Framers of the Constitution spent so little time on the organization of the executive branch of the government they were creating. Instead, the machinery of federal administration has been built over time to meet the changing needs of the country.

Much of the work of the Federal Government is done by the 15 **executive departments.** Often called the Cabinet departments, they employ nearly two thirds of the Federal Government's **civilian** workforce. They are the traditional units of federal administration, and each of them is built around some broad field of activity.

The First Congress created three of these departments in 1789: the Departments of State, Treasury, and War. As the size and the workload of the Federal Government grew, Congress added new departments. Some of the newer ones took over various duties originally assigned to older departments, and gradually assumed new functions, as well. Over time, Congress has also created and later combined or abolished some departments.

The work done by the executive departments is diverse, covering a vast array of responsibilities. Above all, however, note this: These departments are the major mechanism through which the domestic and foreign policies crafted by Congress and the President are carried out. Domestic policies are those concerned with matters at home, while foreign policies are concerned with matters abroad.

Executive Officers and Their Staffs Each department is headed by a **secretary,** except for the Department of Justice, whose work is directed by the **attorney general.** As you will see, those department heads serve in the President's Cabinet. Their duties as the chief officers of their specific department take up most of their time, however.

Each department head is the primary link between presidential policy and his or her own department. Just as importantly, each of them also strives to promote and protect his or her department with the White House, with Congress and its committees, with the rest of the federal bureaucracy, and with the media and the public.

An under secretary or deputy secretary and several assistant secretaries aid the secretary in his or her multidimensional role. These officials are also named by the President and confirmed by the Senate. Staff support for the secretary comes from assistants and aides with a wide range of titles in such areas as personnel, planning, legal advice, budgeting, and public relations.

Subunits in the Executive Departments Each department is made up of a number of subunits, both staff and line. Each of these subunits, or agencies, is usually further divided into smaller working units. Thus, the Occupational Safety and Health Administration (OSHA) in the Department of Labor is composed of a number of sections, including, for example, the Standards and Guidance Section and the Whistleblower Protection Programs. OSHA is the main federal agency charged with the enforcement of the safety and health legislation passed by

>> Janet Reno was the first woman to serve as U.S. Attorney General after her nomination by President Bill Clinton was approved by the Senate in 1993.

The Executive Departments Over Time

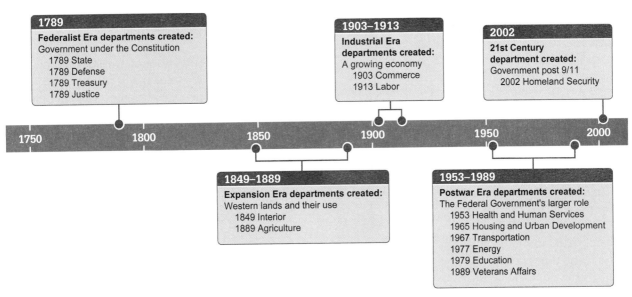

1789

Federalist Era departments created:
Government under the Constitution
1789 State
1789 Defense
1789 Treasury
1789 Justice

1903–1913

Industrial Era departments created:
A growing economy
1903 Commerce
1913 Labor

2002

21st Century department created:
Government post 9/11
2002 Homeland Security

1849–1889

Expansion Era departments created:
Western lands and their use
1849 Interior
1889 Agriculture

1953–1989

Postwar Era departments created:
The Federal Government's larger role
1953 Health and Human Services
1965 Housing and Urban Development
1967 Transportation
1977 Energy
1979 Education
1989 Veterans Affairs

>> The number of executive departments has more than tripled since 1789.
Analyze Charts What can you conclude about the reasons for creating executive departments?

Congress. Approximately 80 percent of the men and women who head OSHA, as well as all the other bureaus, divisions, and major units within each of the executive departments, are career people, not political appointees.

Many of the agencies in the executive departments are structured geographically. Their regional and district offices direct the activities of their employees in the field. In fact, some 90 percent of all civilian employees of the Federal Government are stationed outside the nation's capital.

Like any other government entity, the work of the executive departments and their various subunits can sometimes be controversial. Some people, for example, strongly believe that OSHA is necessary to protect the health and safety of American workers. Others, however, believe just as strongly that the agency's rules are confusing, its policies too rigid, and its penalties unreasonable. Still others think that the agency does not do enough to protect workers' rights.

The Executive Departments Today Today, the executive departments vary a great deal in terms of visibility, size, and importance. The Department of State is the oldest and the most prestigious department; but it is also among the smallest. The Department of Defense is by far the largest, with its civilian workforce approaching one million plus the over one million men and women on active duty.

The Department of Health and Human Services (HHS) has the largest budget; it accounts for just about a fourth of all federal spending each year. HHS is the major government agency charged with establishing public health policies and regulations to promote health and prevent disease. Among other priorities, HHS works to detect potential disease outbreaks or public health emergencies, requires nutritional labeling on foods, and regulates food safety and tobacco products. The Centers for Disease Control and Prevention and the Food and Drug Administration are agencies within HHS.

The Department of Homeland Security became the newest of the executive departments when Congress created it in 2002. The department was formed by combining all or part of 22 existing federal agencies into one unit.

☑ **IDENTIFY MAIN IDEAS** Analyze the reasons why the executive departments have changed over time.

The Cabinet and Its Functions

The Cabinet is an informal advisory body brought together by the President to serve his needs. The Constitution makes no mention of this group of advisors, nor did Congress create it.

The closest approach to it is in Article II, Section 2, Clause 1, where the President is given the power to "require the Opinion, in writing, of the principal Officer in each of the executive Departments, upon any Subject relating to the duties of their respective Offices." The Cabinet was first mentioned in an act of Congress in 1907, well over a century after its birth.

At its first session in 1789, Congress established four top-level executive posts: secretary of state, secretary of the treasury, secretary of war, and attorney general. By his second term, President **George Washington** was regularly seeking the advice of the four outstanding people he had named to those offices: Thomas Jefferson (State), Alexander Hamilton (Treasury), Henry Knox (War), and Edmund Randolph (attorney general). So the Cabinet was born, and it has grown over time.

By tradition, the heads of the now 15 executive departments form the Cabinet. Each of the last several Presidents has regularly added a number of other top officials to the group, including the director of the Office of Management and Budget and the President's chief domestic policy advisor. The Vice President is a regular participant, and several other major figures usually attend Cabinet meetings— today, in particular, the counselor to the President,

>> George Washington's 1789 Cabinet consisted of just the secretaries of state, treasury, and war, and the attorney general. The modern-day presidential Cabinet is nearly four times that size.

the White House chief of staff, the United States trade representative, the director of the Office of National Drug Control Policy, and the administrator of the Environmental Protection Agency.

How the President Chooses Cabinet Members

The President appoints the head of each of the 15 executive departments. Each of these appointments is subject to confirmation by the Senate, but rejections have been exceedingly rare. Of the more than 600 appointments made since 1789, less than a dozen have been rejected. One such rejection occurred in 1989, when the Senate refused to confirm President George H.W. Bush's selection of John Tower as secretary of defense.

Many factors influence the President's Cabinet choices. Party is almost always important. Republican Presidents do not often pick Democrats, and vice versa. One or more of a new President's appointees invariably come from among those who played a major role in the recent presidential campaign.

Of course, professional qualifications and practical experience are also taken into account in the selection of Cabinet secretaries. Geography plays a part as well. Each President tries to give some regional balance to the Cabinet. Thus, the secretary of the interior regularly comes from the West, where most of that department's wide-ranging work is carried out. The secretary of agriculture usually comes from one of the farm States in the Midwest and the secretary of housing and urban development often comes from one of the nation's major metropolitan centers.

Interest groups care about Cabinet appointments, and they influence some choices. The secretary of the treasury regularly comes out of the financial world, the secretary of commerce from the ranks of business, the secretary of education from among professional educators, the attorney general from the legal community, and so on.

Other considerations also guide the President's choices, such as management abilities and experience, personal characteristics, and a host of other factors.

Cabinets Today Today, Presidents may also make Cabinet choices with an eye toward ensuring that the nation's diverse population has a voice at the top levels of government. This has not always been the case, however. Thirty-one Presidents had named more than 300 Cabinet officers before Franklin Roosevelt appointed the first woman to that body: Frances T. ("Ma") Perkins, who served as secretary of labor from 1933 to 1945. In 1966, the first African American, Robert C. Weaver, was selected by Lyndon Johnson to head the Department of Housing and Urban Development. Ronald Reagan named the first Hispanic Cabinet officer, Lauro F. Cavazos, as secretary of education in 1988. Bill Clinton's nomination of Norman Mineta as secretary of commerce in 2000 marked the first time an Asian American had served in a Cabinet post.

Also notable is the fact that both President Donald Trump and President Joe Biden chose secretaries of defense who had to be granted waivers by Congress in order to serve. Because civilian control of the military is a pillar of American democracy, service members must ordinarily wait seven years before they are eligible to serve as secretary of defense. President Trump's selection, General James Mattis, had only been retired for three years at the time of his nomination. President Biden's choice, General Lloyd Austin, had been retired for four years. The only other instance was for General George Marshall following World War II.

One of the first things a President-elect does after winning the election in November is to start naming Cabinet secretaries, so that the administration can hit the ground running on the day after the President is inaugurated. Of course, those selections must be confirmed by the Senate. Usually, that confirmation happens, unless a candidate has a major controversy marring his or her reputation.

The Role of the Cabinet Cabinet members have two major responsibilities. Individually, each is the head of one of the executive departments. Collectively, they are advisors to the President.

Once a central cog in the executive branch, the Cabinet has declined in importance over time. Through much of our history, the Cabinet was a principal source of presidential advice. It met frequently, sometimes as often as twice a week, to offer counsel to the chief executive, and its influence could be seen in virtually all areas of public policy.

The growth of other presidential resources—particularly the vast amount of staff assistance centered in the Executive Office of the President—began to eclipse the Cabinet's role, however. Indeed, during his presidency, John Kennedy said that he could see no need to discuss, say, Defense Department matters with his secretaries of labor and agriculture, and he found Cabinet meetings to be "a waste of time."

This trend continued under President Johnson and was fully embraced by President Nixon, who

>> President John Kennedy meets with his Cabinet during the Cuban missile crisis of 1962. The Cabinet is often called together in times of crisis to advise the President.

centralized control in the White House and regularly declined to involve his Cabinet in key decisions. Since Nixon's time, every President has relied more fully on White House staff and advisors than they have on their Cabinets.

Given the limited number of hours in the day and the seemingly limitless number of issues that need to be addressed, should policy experts trump political strategists, or the other way around? It is often a mix, but there is evidence to suggest that the political strategists are winning out. Many reasons can be cited for this state of affairs, but chief among them is the belief that policy experts—i.e., Cabinet secretaries—often do a poor job of promoting or sticking to the President's political agenda. Additionally, the President has more control over the White House staff than the Cabinet, and that staff can respond much more quickly to issues than the executive departments can. Finally, Cabinet secretaries can be seen as causing headaches for the President—when they propose a controversial new rule, for example, or make a proposal that contradicts administration goals or raises a firestorm of unwanted media attention.

>> President George H.W. Bush speaks to reporters in Kennebunkport, Maine, in 1990, with members of his Cabinet, including Vice President Dan Quayle (left) and Defense Secretary Dick Cheney (far right).

After leaving his post as secretary of labor in the Clinton administration, Robert Reich wrote a 1997 book that spoke to this point, aptly titled *Locked in the Cabinet*. Even though Reich had been friends with both Bill and Hillary Clinton, as a member of the Cabinet he found it difficult to get even a few minutes of the President's time.

Still, Presidents do continue to call Cabinet meetings, though certainly not nearly as frequently as was once the case. More often than not, those sessions are held to do such things as show the administration's unified support for some particular presidential policy, rather than to thrash out the details of that matter. Cabinet members still do offer their advice—which need not be taken, of course—to the chief executive. President **Abraham Lincoln** once laid a proposition he favored before his seven-member Cabinet.

Each member opposed it, whereupon Lincoln, who was for it, declared: "Seven nays, one aye: the ayes have it."

William Howard Taft put the role of the President's Cabinet in its proper light nearly a century ago:

The Constitution . . . contains no suggestion of a meeting of all the department heads, in consultation over general governmental matters. The Cabinet is a mere creation of the President's will. . . . It exists only by custom. If the President desired to dispense with it, he could do so.

—William Howard Taft, *Our Chief Magistrate and His Powers*

No President has ever suggested eliminating the Cabinet. However, several Presidents have leaned on other, unofficial advisory groups and sometimes depended upon them more heavily than on the Cabinet. Andrew Jackson began the practice when he became President in 1829. Several of his close friends often met with him in the kitchen at the White House and, inevitably, came to be known as the Kitchen Cabinet.

Franklin Roosevelt's Brain Trust of the 1930s and Harry Truman's Cronies in the late 1940s were in the same mold.

☑ **GENERATE EXPLANATIONS** Is it appropriate for the President to pick Cabinet members with an eye toward racial, ethnic, and gender diversity? Why or why not?

☑ ASSESSMENT

1. **Cite Evidence** At different times in history, the National Security Council has acted as both a line and a staff agency. Give evidence to support this statement.

2. **Explain** The President wishes to consult with a member of his staff regarding the possibility of expanding trade with Indonesia. Which agency in the EOP would the President consult and why?

3. **Support Ideas with Examples** Given the past history of Presidents and their Cabinets, what do you predict might be the role of the Cabinet under the next President? Is the past an accurate predictor of the future relationship between the President and the Cabinet? Explain your answer, citing details from the text.

4. **Generate Explanations** Why is it important for the President to select the heads of the executive departments?

5. **Compare** How is the Cabinet of today similar to the Cabinet during the presidency of George Washington?

6.3

An FDA agent inspects food products at a processing plant. What might be the result if the FDA did not regulate food safety?

The Independent Agencies

Until the 1880s, nearly all the Federal Government did was done through its Cabinet departments. Since then, however, Congress has created a large number of additional agencies—the independent agencies—located outside the departments. In addition to the executive departments, these agencies are the major mechanism through which the Federal Government carries out the nation's domestic policies.

The Purpose of Independent Agencies

Several **independent agencies** administer programs similar to those of the Cabinet departments. The work of the National Aeronautics and Space Administration (NASA), for example, is not unlike that of a number of agencies in the Department of Defense. NASA's responsibilities are also not very far removed from those of the Department of Transportation.

Neither the size of an independent agency's budget nor the number of its employees provides a good way to distinguish these agencies from the executive departments. For example, the Social Security Administration (SSA) is the largest of the independent agencies today. Only one Cabinet department, Health and Human Services, has a larger budget. The SSA employs over 50,000 people—more than work for several Cabinet departments.

The Reasons Congress Created Independent Agencies The reasons these agencies exist outside of the Cabinet departments are nearly as many as the agencies themselves. A few major reasons stand out, however. Some have been set up outside the regular

 BOUNCE to Activate Flipped Video

Objectives

Explain why Congress created the independent agencies.

Identify the characteristics of independent executive agencies.

Describe the history, purpose, and effect on private enterprise of selected independent executive agencies and regulatory commissions, including NASA and the EPA.

Explain the structure and function of government corporations.

Key Terms

independent agencies
independent executive agencies
civil service
patronage
spoils system
draft
independent regulatory commissions

government corporations
Andrew Jackson
James Garfield
Chester Arthur
Theodore Roosevelt
Jimmy Carter

departmental structure simply because they do not fit well within any of the departments.

The General Services Administration (GSA) is a leading example of the point. The GSA is the Federal Government's major housekeeping agency. Its main chores include the construction and operation of public buildings, purchase and distribution of supplies and equipment, management of real property, and a host of similar services to most other federal agencies.

Congress has given some agencies, such as the Social Security Administration, the Federal Election Commission, and the U.S. Commission on Civil Rights, an independent status to protect them from the influence of both partisan and pressure politics. But, notice, this point can be turned on its head: Congress has located some of these agencies outside any of the Cabinet departments because that is exactly where certain special interest groups want them.

Some agencies were born as independents largely by accident. In short, no thought was given to the problems of administrative confusion when they were created. Finally, some agencies are independent because of the peculiar and sensitive nature of their functions. This is especially true of the independent regulatory commissions.

The Independent Agency Umbrella The label *independent agency* is really a catchall. Most of these agencies are independent only in that they are not located within any of the 15 Cabinet departments. They are not independent of the President and the executive branch. A handful of them are independent in a much more concrete way, however. For most purposes, they do lie outside the executive branch and are largely free of presidential control.

Perhaps the best way to understand all of these many independent agencies is to divide them into three main groups: (1) the independent executive agencies, (2) the independent regulatory commissions, and (3) the government corporations.

☑ **INFER** Why would certain special interest groups want particular independent agencies located outside of the Cabinet departments? Why might Congress concede to their wishes?

Independent Executive Agencies

The **independent executive agencies** include most of the non-Cabinet agencies. Some are huge, with thousands of employees, multimillion-dollar

Types of Independent Agencies

	INDEPENDENT EXECUTIVE AGENCIES	INDEPENDENT REGULATORY COMMISSIONS	GOVERNMENT CORPORATIONS
DESCRIPTION	Non-Cabinet agencies with specialized functions	Agencies that regulate various aspects of the economy; outside presidential control	Agencies that operate like businesses but are financed with public funds and subject to congressional and presidential oversight
EXAMPLES	• National Aeronautics and Space Administration (NASA) • Environmental Protection Agency (EPA) • Food and Drug Administration (FDA) • Peace Corps • Office of Personnel Management (OPM)	• Federal Communications Commission (FCC) • Securities and Exchange Commission (SEC) • Consumer Financial Protection Bureau (CFPB) • Federal Reserve System • Consumer Product Safety Commission	• Federal Deposit Insurance Corporation (FDIC) • Export-Import Bank of the United States • U.S. Postal Service (USPS) • National Railroad Passenger Corporation (AMTRAK) • Tennessee Valley Authority (TVA)

>> The three types of independent agencies are distinctly different, but they do share some common features. **Analyze Charts** What features do these three types of agencies share?

or even multibillion-dollar budgets, and extremely important public tasks to perform.

The GSA, NASA, and the Environmental Protection Agency (EPA) are, for example, three of the largest of the independent executive agencies. They are organized much like the Cabinet departments: they are headed by a single administrator with subunits operating on a regional basis, and so on. The most important difference between these independent executive agencies and the 15 executive departments is simply in the fact that they do not have Cabinet status.

These larger agencies, such as the EPA and the Food and Drug Administration (FDA), play a large role in American life today. The EPA establishes and enforces pollution and other standards in order to protect the environment and also sets and enforces regulations to protect public health. Similarly, the FDA protects citizens by regulating safety standards for food, drugs, medical devices, vaccines, veterinary supplies, tobacco, and cosmetics. While many Americans see the work done by these agencies as valuable and necessary, they are not without their critics. Some people argue that the standards and regulations imposed by the EPA and the FDA place too heavy a burden on private businesses, thereby restricting economic growth.

Most independent executive agencies operate far from the limelight. They have few employees, have comparatively small budgets, and rarely attract any attention. The American Battle Monuments Commission, the Citizens' Stamp Advisory Committee, and the National Indian Gaming Commission are typical of the dozens of these seldom seen or heard public bodies.

Neither the scope nor the effects of the many tasks performed by a number of these independent bureaucracies can be overstated. To make the point, take a quick look at a few specific examples.

The National Science Foundation: Scientific Discoveries and Technological Innovations

The National Science Foundation (NSF) is an independent federal agency created by Congress in 1950. Some of the scientific discoveries and technological innovations the NSF has helped to fund include the bar codes used at checkout counters, magnetic resonance imaging (MRI) technology, air bags in vehicles, touch-screen technology, and biometric identification.

The potential impact has yet to be realized for some recent scientific discoveries. For example, scientists are studying the purple sea fan, a type of coral, to discover how it fights pathogens and

>> Members of the Citizens' Stamp Advisory Committee unveil art for a new stamp honoring baseball great Willie Stargell. The CSAC is one of many independent agencies in the executive branch.

how it repairs injured tissue. What these scientists discover could hold clues for all of us about fighting and recovering from disease. Scientists have also discovered a bacterium in the hot springs at Yellowstone National Park that allows them to more quickly and easily study DNA. Among other uses, improved DNA technology helps law enforcement officials identify a suspect's involvement in a crime or demonstrate his or her innocence.

Many technological innovations also have a potentially great future impact for society. For example, 3-D printing is being used to make a variety of custom-made objects from metal, ceramics, and other materials. Some researchers are starting to use the technology to create custom medical implants to fix complicated injuries that can't be helped by conventional implants.

Another example of a recent innovation with a potentially large impact is nanogrids. These are large metal grids that, when activated by sunlight, break down oil from a spill, leaving behind only biodegradable compounds. This technology has the potential to avoid the devastating consequences on wildlife and local economies that have resulted from recent oil spills.

NASA—An Independent Executive Agency The National Aeronautics and Space Administration (NASA) was created by Congress in 1958 to handle this nation's space programs. Today, the scope of those programs is truly astounding. NASA's work ranges from basic scientific research focusing on the origin, evolution, and structure of the universe, to ongoing explorations of outer space.

The military importance of NASA's work can hardly be exaggerated. Still, Congress has directed the space agency to bend its efforts "to peaceful purposes for the benefit of all humankind," as well. Its wide-ranging research and development efforts have opened new frontiers in a great many areas: in astronomy, physics, and the environmental sciences; in communication, medicine, and weather forecasting; and many more. Many scientific advances, pioneered by NASA, have been put to productive use in the civilian realm.

For example, lifesaving heart and other computer monitoring systems were originally created to observe the effects of space travel on astronauts. Similarly, weather forecasters use NASA-based technology to monitor the weather using 3-D maps in real time, and firefighters regularly use two-way radios that incorporate NASA's technology to communicate with each other during fire emergencies.

NASA's Space Shuttle Program In the 1980s, NASA developed the space shuttle program. This program was so successful that NASA spaceflights and other extraterrestrial projects became fairly routine and attracted little public notice. That changed in 1986, however, following the shocking and tragic explosion of the shuttle *Challenger*. NASA's space activities were put on hold for several years, extended when another tragedy, involving the shuttle *Columbia*, shook the nation in 2003.

For decades, shuttles have delivered personnel and supplies to the international space station. Rotating two- to eight-member international crews have lived aboard the outpost since late 2000.

In the near future, NASA plans to capture an asteroid from deep space, redirect it to orbit the moon, and send humans to explore it. Information gained from these missions will be used to send humans to Mars. The potential future impact of these efforts will likely be seen in advances in medicine, disaster relief, and many other areas.

The Office of Personnel Management (OPM) The Federal Government is the nation's largest

NASA TECHNOLOGIES

GOVERNMENT RESEARCH BENEFITS THE PRIVATE SECTOR

ULTRASOUND MACHINES — WERE — FIRST USED TO **DIAGNOSE MEDICAL CONDITIONS IN SPACE**

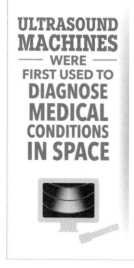

NASA SATELLITES ARE USED TO MEASURE THE **DEPLETION** — OF THE — **OZONE LAYER**

EMERGENCY FOOD PACKS EMERGED FROM THE TYPE OF FOOD THAT ASTRONAUTS EAT ABOARD — THE — **SPACE SHUTTLE**

CORDLESS DRILLS WERE DEVELOPED FOR COLLECTING **SOIL SAMPLES** — ON THE — **MOON**

MEMORY FOAM WAS FIRST USED IN **NASA** AIRCRAFT SEATS TO CUSHION LANDINGS

>> NASA's technological advances have ensured successful space travel and benefited the general public. **Analyze Information** How have each of these NASA innovations benefited civilians?

employer. Around 3 million civilians now work for Uncle Sam, including all branches of the government (and, recall, another million or so men and women serve in the military). Their ranks include computer programmers, forest rangers, electricians, chemists, physicists, FBI agents, security guards, engineers, librarians, truck drivers, botanists, and men and women in literally hundreds of other occupations.

Most of the civilians who work for the Federal Government are members of the **civil service.** That is, they are career employees who were hired, and who are paid and promoted, in accord with acts of Congress administered by an independent agency, the Office of Personnel Management.

The Spoils System For most of the first century following the adoption of the Constitution, federal employees were hired according to the **patronage** system. That practice, often called the **spoils system**, was expanded by President **Andrew Jackson.** In fact, the phrase comes from a comment made by Senator William Learned Marcy of New York in 1832, as he defended President Jackson's appointment of an ambassador. Speaking from the floor of the Senate, Marcy declared: "To the victor belongs the spoils of the enemy."

Every change of administration brought a new round of patronage-based rewards and punishments. Inefficiency, even corruption, became the order of the day. Able people, in and out of government, pressed for reform, but little came of their efforts.

The Pendleton Act Unfortunately, it was a tragedy that at last brought about fundamental changes. In 1881, President **James Garfield** was fatally shot by a disappointed office seeker, Charles J. Guiteau. Garfield had rejected the mentally unstable Guiteau's request that he be appointed to a high diplomatic post. Congress, pushed hard by Garfield's successor, **Chester Arthur**, passed the Pendleton Act—the Civil Service Act of 1883.

The Pendleton Act laid the foundation for the present federal civil service system. The law set up two categories of employment in the executive branch: the classified and the unclassified services. All hiring for positions in the classified service was to be based on merit. That quality was to be measured by "practical" examinations given by an independent agency, the Civil Service Commission (since 1978, the OPM).

The Pendleton Act placed only about 10 percent of the Federal Government's then 130,000 employees in the classified service; it did give the President the

>> This cartoon shows former President Hayes leaving a baby on President Garfield's doorstep. **Analyze Political Cartoons** What symbol does the cartoonist use to represent civil service reform? Why?

power to extend that coverage, however. **Theodore Roosevelt** championed the merit system, and by the end of his term in 1909, the classified umbrella covered two thirds of the federal workforce. Today, not counting the United States Postal Service and a few other federal agencies, nearly 90 percent of all the men and women who work for the executive branch agencies are covered by the merit system.

Today's Civil Service The first goal of civil service reform—the elimination of the spoils system—was largely achieved in the early years of the last century. Gradually, a new purpose emerged: recruiting and keeping the best available people in the federal workforce. On the whole, efforts to reach that newer goal have succeeded. Today, most federal employees are hired through a competitive process. They are paid and promoted on the basis of written evaluations by their superiors. They are generally protected from disciplinary actions or dismissal for partisan reasons.

Still, the federal civil service is not perfect. Critics often claim that not enough attention is paid to merit in the merit system. Another independent agency, the Merit Systems Protection Board, actually enforces the merit principle in the federal bureaucracy. The Board is bipartisan—that is, its five members, appointed by the President and Senate, must include members of both major political parties. It hears appeals from those federal workers who have complaints about personnel actions—for example, denials of pay increases, demotions, or firings.

The Selective Service System Enlisting in the military—that is, signing up voluntarily—is one option for a citizen who wishes to serve his or her country. "Alternative service" is sometimes chosen by those who object to military service on moral or religious grounds. It may involve noncombatant duties in the military or public service related to the environment, the elderly, health care, and the like. Those who serve in combat roles in the military have pledged to defend the nation by sacrificing their lives if necessary.

Through most of our history, the armed forces have depended on voluntary enlistments to fill their ranks. From 1940 to 1973, however, the **draft**—also called conscription, or compulsory military service—was a major source of manpower.

Conscription has a long history in this country. Several colonies and later nine States required all able-bodied males to serve in their militias. However, in the 1790s, Congress rejected proposals for national compulsory military service.

Both the North and the South did use limited conscription programs during the Civil War. It was not until 1917, however, that a national draft was first used in this country, even in wartime. More than 2.8 million of the 4.7 million men who served in World War I were drafted under the terms of the Selective Service Act of 1917.

The nation's first peacetime draft came with the Selective Training and Service Act of 1940, as World War II raged in Europe but before the United States entered the war. Eventually, more than 10 million of the 16.3 million Americans in uniform during World War II entered the service under that law.

The World War II draft ended in 1947. The crises of the postwar period, however, quickly moved Congress to revive the draft, which was reestablished by the Selective Service Act of 1948. From 1948 through 1973, nearly 5 million young men were drafted.

The Draft Today Mounting criticisms of compulsory military service, fed by opposition to our Vietnam policy, led many Americans to call for an end to the draft in the late 1960s. By 1972, fewer than 30,000 men were being drafted per year, and selective service was suspended in 1973. Nevertheless, the draft law is still on the books, and is administered by an independent agency, the Selective Service System.

In 1980, President **Jimmy Carter** reactivated the registration requirement, and his executive order is still in force. All young males are required to sign up soon after they reach their 18th birthday. The President's power to order the actual induction of men into the armed forces expired on June 30, 1973, however. If the draft is ever to be reactivated, Congress must first renew that presidential authority.

☑ **CONNECT** Why do you think the draft was suspended instead of cancelled? Describe the steps that would be taken to reactivate the draft.

Independent Regulatory Commissions

The **independent regulatory commissions** stand out among the independent agencies because they are largely beyond the reach of presidential control. These agencies were created to regulate important aspects of the nation's economy. A notable example is the Federal Communications Commission

>> When young men turn 18, they are required to register for the draft. Although females can serve in the U.S. military, they are not required to register with the Selective Service.

(FCC). It regulates interstate and international communications by radio, television, wire, satellite, and cable while ensuring reasonable rates. A second example is the National Labor Relations Board (NLRB) that works to protect employee and employer rights as well as addresses unfair labor practices.

Structured for Independence The independent regulatory commissions' large measure of independence from the White House comes mainly from the way in which Congress has structured them. Each is headed by a board or commission made up of five to seven members appointed by the President with Senate consent; those officials have terms of such length that it is unlikely a President will gain control over any of these agencies through the appointment process.

Several other features of these boards and commissions put them beyond the reach of presidential control. No more than a bare majority of the members of each board or commission may belong to the same political party. Thus, several of those officers must belong to the party out of power.

Moreover, the appointed terms of the members are staggered so that the term of only one member on each board or commission expires in any one year. In addition, the officers of five of these agencies can be removed by the President only for those causes Congress has specified.

Executive, Legislative, and Judicial Powers
As with the other independent agencies, the regulatory commissions are executive bodies. That is, Congress has given them the power to administer the programs for which they were created. However, unlike other independent agencies, the regulatory commissions are also quasi-legislative and quasi-judicial bodies. That is, Congress has also given these agencies certain legislative-like and judicial-like powers.

These agencies exercise their quasi-legislative powers when they make rules and regulations, which have the force of law. They implement and spell out the details of the laws that Congress has directed these regulatory bodies to enforce.

Securities and Exchange Commission To illustrate the point: Congress has said that those who want to borrow money by issuing stocks, bonds, or other securities must provide a "full and fair disclosure" of all pertinent information to prospective investors. The Securities and Exchange Commission (SEC) makes that requirement effective and indicates how those who offer securities are to meet it by issuing rules and regulations.

>> A radio station host talks to listeners on the air. The radio waves, as well as any content transmitted over them, are regulated by the Federal Communications Commission (FCC).

>> Traders at work on the floor of the New York Stock Exchange. The Securities and Exchange Commission sets and enforces regulations for individuals and companies involved in stock trading.

The regulatory commissions exercise their quasi-judicial powers when they decide disputes in those fields in which Congress has given them policing authority. For example, if an investor in Iowa thinks a local stockbroker has cheated him, he may file a complaint with the SEC's regional office in Chicago. SEC agents will investigate and report their findings, and the agency will judge the merits of the complaint much as a court would do. Decisions made by the SEC, and by the other independent regulatory bodies, can be appealed to the United States courts of appeals.

Filling In for Congress In a sense, Congress has created these agencies to act in its place. Congress could hold hearings and set interest rates, license radio and TV stations and nuclear reactors, check on business practices, and do the many other things it has directed the regulatory commissions to do. These activities are complex and time-consuming, however, and they demand constant and expert attention. If Congress were to do all of this work, it would have no time for its other important legislative work.

Note that because these regulatory bodies possess all three of the basic governmental powers—executive, legislative, and judicial—they are exceptions to the principle of separation of powers. Technically, they should not be grouped with the other independent agencies. Instead, they should be located somewhere between the executive and legislative branches, and between the executive and judicial branches, as well.

Impact of Independent Regulatory Agencies

What impact do these agencies have on the American economy and government? Many believe that governmental goals such as ensuring competition and fairness in the marketplace, protecting consumers and the environment, maintaining fair prices, and ensuring the safety of workers can only be accomplished through government regulation.

Some experts and even recent Presidents, however, believe that government regulations have become unnecessarily complex and burdensome—that they are, in fact, stumbling blocks to economic growth and the startup of new businesses. They point out that these effects are felt not only at the national level, but at the State and local levels as well.

Many pressing questions about the impact of regulations demand answers. For example, have some regulatory commissions been unduly influenced by those they are expected to regulate? Do some regulations stifle competition in the free enterprise system? Do some of them add unreasonably to the cost of doing business and therefore to the prices that consumers must pay?

Congress sets the basic policies of regulatory agencies, and so it has a major responsibility to answer these questions. Beginning in the late 1970s, it did so by focusing on one area: the deregulation of the transportation industry. As a result, airlines, bus companies, truckers, and railroads have greater freedom to operate today than they once did.

In the 1990s, Congress acted again, this time to deregulate some aspects of the communications industry, notably with regard to cable television. More recently, Congress has moved toward deregulating the natural gas and electricity industries as well, at both the national and State levels.

While regulations have been loosened on some industries, problems in others have led to more government regulation. The severe recession that struck the nation's economy in 2007–2008 prompted the passage of the Dodd-Frank Wall Street Reform and Consumer Protection Act in 2010.

In addition to implementing the most sweeping financial reforms since the Great Depression, the law established a new independent regulatory

>> The Dodd-Frank Act was passed to try to help avoid another financial crisis like the one that occurred in 2008. **Analyzing Political Cartoons** What point does the cartoon make about the act?

Government vs. Private Corporations

GOVERNMENT CORPORATIONS	PRIVATE CORPORATIONS
Produces income that goes back into the agency's programs	Makes a profit beyond what is invested back into the business
Congress decides agency's purpose and functions	Investors decide purpose and function of the corporation
Officers and workers are public employees	Executives and other employees are private individuals, not government workers
President selects top officers with Senate approval	Investors or directors choose top officers
Financed by public funds	Financed by private investors
Federal Government owns stock	Shareholders own stock

>> Government corporations blur the line between public and private businesses.
Analyze Charts What are some ways that government and private corporations are similar?

commission, the Consumer Financial Protection Bureau (CFPB). As a "watchdog for the American consumer," the CFPB has the authority to make rules and regulations for all institutions that offer consumers financial services or products. It also has the task of educating the public on financial matters. The commission is funded by the Federal Reserve, rather than by Congress, in an effort to keep it free from the influence of special interests.

Like most major laws passed by Congress, Dodd-Frank has both supporters and detractors. Many applaud greater control over the financial industry, including discouraging risky behaviors, reforming the mortgage industry, requiring transparency from lenders, and slashing the fees that banks charge merchants for debit card use.

Others, however, have complained that Dodd-Frank does not do enough to prevent the financial industry from taking advantage of consumers. Still others maintain that it has cost millions, mired financial institutions in red tape, hurt small banks, and made access to credit—a key part of starting a new business or obtaining a mortgage—unnecessarily difficult.

☑ **HYPOTHESIZE** In what ways might the Federal Communications Commission (FCC) use its legislative and judicial powers?

Government Corporations

A number of independent agencies are **government corporations.** They, too, are located within the vast executive branch and are subject to presidential direction and control. Unlike the other independent agencies, however, they were set up by Congress to carry out certain businesslike activities.

Congress established the first government corporation when it chartered the Bank of the United States in 1791. However, government corporations were little used until World War I and then during the Great Depression. In both periods, Congress set up dozens of corporations to carry out emergency programs. Several still exist—among them, the Federal Deposit Insurance Corporation (FDIC), which insures bank deposits, and the Export-Import Bank of the United States (Eximbank), which makes loans to help the export and sale of American goods abroad.

The various government corporations do such things as provide intercity rail passenger service (Amtrak); protect pension benefits (the Pension Benefit Guaranty Corporation); and generate, sell, and distribute electric power (the Tennessee Valley Authority).

Differences Between Government and Private Corporations The typical government corporation is set up much like a corporation in the private sector.

>> Operated by the Army Corps of Engineers, the Center Hill Hydroelectric Dam in Tennessee features the ACOE's second largest flood control reservoir. The TVA operates 47 similar dams in the area.

It is run by a board of directors, with a general manager who directs the corporation's operations according to the policies laid down by the board. Most government corporations produce income that is plowed back into the agency's programs.

There are several differences between government and private corporations, however. Congress decides the purpose for which the public agencies exist and the functions they perform. Their officers are public officers; in fact, all who work for these corporations are public employees. The President selects most of the top officers of government corporations with Senate approval.

In addition, these public agencies are financed by public funds appropriated by Congress, not by private investors. The Federal Government, representing the American people, owns the stock.

The advantage most often claimed for these agencies is their flexibility. It is said that the government corporation, freed from the controls of regular departmental organization, can carry on its activities with the incentive, efficiency, and ability to experiment that make many private concerns successful. Whether that claim is valid or not is open to question. At the very least, it raises this complex

issue: Is a public corporation's need for flexibility compatible with the basic democratic requirement that all public agencies be held responsible and accountable to the people?

Varying Levels of Independence The degree of independence and flexibility government corporations have varies considerably. In fact, some corporations are not independent at all. They are attached to an executive department.

The Commodity Credit Corporation (CCC), for example, is the government's major crop-loan and farm-subsidy agency. It is located within the Department of Agriculture, and the secretary of agriculture chairs its seven-member board. The CCC carries out most of its functions through a line agency in the Department of Agriculture—the Farm Service Agency—which is also subject to the direct control of the secretary.

Some corporations do have considerable independence, however. The Tennessee Valley Authority (TVA) is a case in point. It operates under a statute that gives it considerable discretion over its own programs. Although its budget is subject to review by the OMB, the President, and Congress, the TVA has a large say in the uses of the income its several operations produce.

☑ **COMPARE** Explain how independent regulatory commissions and government corporations are similar.

☑ ASSESSMENT

1. **Connect** What is the relationship between independent agencies and partisan politics?

2. **Make Generalizations** Make one generalization that is true of *all* independent executive agencies.

3. **Synthesize** How does the Office of Personnel Management help the federal bureaucracy serve the American people?

4. **Apply Concepts** Identify the ways in which the independent regulatory commissions are an exception to both the principle of checks and balances and the principle of separation of powers.

5. **Integrate Information** Describe the several ways that Congress is involved with government corporations.

6.4

U.S. soldiers in Afghanistan board a helicopter that will transport them to their next mission.

Foreign Policy Overview

In *The Federalist* No. 72, Alexander Hamilton noted that the "actual conduct" of America's foreign affairs would be in the hands of "the assistants or deputies of the chief magistrate," the President. Today, most of the President's "assistants or deputies" in the field of foreign affairs are located within the Department of State.

What Is Foreign Policy?

Foreign affairs have been of prime importance from the nation's very beginnings, more than a dozen years before Hamilton penned his comment in *The Federalist*. Indeed, it is important to remember that the United States would have been hard pressed to win its independence without the aid of a foreign ally, France.

Every nation's **foreign policy** is actually many different policies on many different topics. It is made up of all of the stands and actions that a nation takes in every aspect of its relationships with other countries—diplomatic, military, commercial, and all others. To put the point another way, a nation's foreign policy includes everything that that nation's government says and everything that it does in world affairs.

Thus, American foreign policy consists of all of the Federal Government's official statements and all of its actions as it conducts this nation's foreign relations. It involves treaties and alliances, international trade, the defense budget, foreign economic and military aid, the United Nations and other international organizations, nuclear weapons testing, and disarmament negotiations.

🔲 BOUNCE to Activate Flipped Video

Objectives

Explain the major responsibilities of the Federal Government for foreign policy.

Summarize U.S. foreign policy during the first 150 years of its history, including its adherence to isolationism.

Show how World War II finally ended America's traditional policy of isolationism, giving way to internationalism and the principles of collective security and deterrence.

Analyze how today's U.S. foreign policy affects selected places and regions, as well as the significance to the United States of the location and key natural resources of selected global places or regions.

Key Terms

foreign policy	Isthmus of Panama
domestic affairs	Pearl Harbor
foreign affairs	Harry Truman
isolationism	Dwight Eisenhower
collective security	John F. Kennedy
deterrence	Lyndon Johnson
cold war	Richard Nixon
containment	Ronald Reagan
détente	

It also includes the American position on oil imports and grain exports. Human rights, immigration, climate change, space exploration, fishing rights, economic sanctions, computer technology exports, and a great many other matters are also subjects that fall under the heading "foreign policy."

Some aspects of foreign policy remain largely unchanged over time. For example, an insistence on freedom of the seas has been a basic part of American policy from the nation's beginnings. Other policies are more flexible. During most of the late twentieth century, resisting the ambitions of the Soviet Union was a basic part of American foreign policy. Since the turn of the 21st century, however, that focus shifted to counterterrorism and the non-proliferation of nuclear weapons.

Location and natural resources also have a bearing on American foreign policy. Neighboring countries, such as Canada and Mexico, have been a major focus of U.S. policy goals because their proximity makes it essential that the relationship with these countries is on good terms. By the same token, those countries that possess natural resources important to the United States, such as the Middle East, are also critical to U.S. foreign policy.

The United States is now the world's only "superpower." Because of this, other nations look to this country for leadership in world affairs. In addition, American foreign policy has a strong influence on other nations. Thus, when that policy includes, for example, sanctions against a particular country due to human rights abuses, those sanctions are likely to have a crippling effect on the target country's economy. Or, when stability in a particular area of the world is deemed of utmost importance to American interests, U.S. dollars and military aid are used to keep existing governments in power—even, at times, when those governments are oppressive or dictatorial.

Conversely, other nations influence American policies and society. A foreign war, for example, can lead to an influx of refugees to American shores. A financial crisis halfway across the world can cause a loss of jobs at home. The threat of attack from hostile nations can lead to increased spending on defense—which means less money spent on areas such as education or the environment.

☑ **CONNECT** Why is studying a nation's foreign policy important? Give one example to support your answer.

Beginnings Through World War I

The basic purpose of American foreign policy has always been to protect the security and well-being of the United States—and so it is today. It would be impossible to present a full-blown, detailed history of America's foreign relations in this course. But we can review its major themes and highlights here.

With the coming of independence, and then for more than 150 years, the American people were chiefly concerned with **domestic affairs**—with events at home. **Foreign affairs,** this nation's relationships with other nations, were of little or no concern to them. Through that period, America's foreign relations were very largely shaped by a policy of **isolationism**—a purposeful refusal to become generally involved in the affairs of the rest of the world.

Isolationism arose in the earliest years of this nation's history. In his Farewell Address in 1796, George Washington declared that "our true policy" was "to steer clear of permanent alliances with any portion of the foreign world." Our "detached and distant situation," Washington said, made it desirable for us to have "as little political connection as possible" with other nations.

>> Soviet Chairman Nikita Khrushchev shakes President John F. Kennedy's hand during a five-day summit between the two superpowers in 1961.

At the time, and for decades to come, isolationism seemed a wise policy to most Americans. The United States was a new and relatively weak nation with a great many problems, a huge continent to explore and settle, and two oceans to separate it from the rest of the world.

The policy of isolationism did not demand a *complete* separation from the rest of the world, however. From the first, the United States developed ties abroad by exchanging diplomatic representatives with other nations, making treaties with many of them, and building an extensive foreign commerce. In fact, isolationism was, over time, more a statement of our desire for non-involvement outside the Western Hemisphere than a description of United States policy within our own hemisphere.

The Monroe Doctrine James Monroe gave the policy of isolationism a clearer shape in 1823. In a historic message to Congress, he proclaimed what has been known ever since as the Monroe Doctrine.

A wave of revolutions had swept Latin America, destroying the old Spanish and Portuguese empires there. The United States viewed the prospect that other European powers would now help Spain and Portugal to take back their lost possessions as a threat to this country's security and a challenge to its economic interests.

In his message, President Monroe restated America's intentions to stay out of European affairs. He also warned the nations of Europe to stay out of the affairs of both North and South America. He declared that the United States would look on

> any attempt on their part to extend their system to any portion of this hemisphere as dangerous to our peace and safety.
> —Speech by President James Monroe to Congress, December 2, 1823

At first, most Latin Americans took little notice of this doctrine. They knew that it was really the Royal Navy and British interest in Latin American trade that protected them from European domination. But in 1867, the Monroe Doctrine got its first real test. While Americans were immersed in the Civil War, France invaded Mexico. The French leader, Napoleon III, installed Archduke Maximilian of Austria as Mexico's puppet emperor. In 1867, the United States backed the Mexicans in forcing the French to withdraw, and the Maximilian regime fell.

>> President Monroe (standing) is shown with key members of his Cabinet, including John Quincy Adams, who helped draft the Monroe Doctrine. **Describe** What was the intent of the Monroe Doctrine?

Later, as the United States became more powerful, many Latin Americans came to view the Monroe Doctrine differently. They saw it as a selfish policy designed to protect the political and economic interests of the United States, not the independence of other nations in the Western Hemisphere.

Expanding Influence Following its victory in the Revolutionary War, the United States began to expand across the continent almost at once. The Louisiana Purchase in 1803 doubled the nation's size in a single stroke and the Florida Purchase Treaty in 1819 completed its expansion to the south.

Through the second quarter of the nineteenth century, the United States pursued what most Americans believed was this nation's "Manifest Destiny": the mission to expand its boundaries across the continent to the Pacific Ocean. By 1900, the nation had not only accomplished that task, it had spread its influence beyond the continental boundaries to become both a colonial and a world power. The nation's interests now extended to Alaska, to the tip of Latin America, and across the Pacific to the Philippines.

Selected 19th and 20th Century Revolutions

	MEXICO (1910–1917)	CENTRAL AND SOUTH AMERICA (1808–1826)
Ideologies	Overthrow of the Porfirio Díaz dictatorship and creation of a democratic government	Independence from Spain; desire to end the inequalities of Spanish rule
Causes	Poverty, social inequality	Napoleon's invasion of Spain in 1808 and the imprisonment of the Spanish king
Stages	• Revolutionary Francisco Madero successfully ousts Díaz from power • Commander of government forces Victoriano Huerta joins rebels and seizes power • Venustiano Carranza takes control of Mexico and creates Constitution of 1917	• Creole Simón Bolívar leads an uprising in Venezuela • Bolívar moves south into Ecuador, Peru, and Bolivia • Creole revolutionary José de San Martín leads the southern fight for freedom for Argentina and Chile • Bolívar joins forces with José de San Martín
Outcomes	Díaz ousted; democratic constitution adopted; much land redistributed from the wealthy to peasants	Colonial rule ends in much of Latin America; 18 separate republics established

>> During the 1800 and 1900s, Mexico and many countries in Central America sought independence. **Analyze Charts** What connections can you draw between the ideologies behind the revolutions and their ultimate outcomes?

Latin America in the 1900s The threat of European intervention in the Western Hemisphere that troubled President Monroe declined in the second half of the nineteenth century. That threat was replaced by problems within the hemisphere. Political instability, revolutions, unpaid foreign debts, and injuries to citizens and property of other countries plagued Central and South America.

Under what came to be known as the Roosevelt Corollary to the Monroe Doctrine, the United States began to police Latin America in the early 1900s. Several times, the marines were used to quell revolutions and other unrest in Nicaragua, Haiti, Cuba, and elsewhere in Latin America.

In 1903, Panama revolted and became independent of Colombia, with America's blessing. In the same year, the United States gained the right to build a canal across the **Isthmus of Panama**. The canal was significant, because it dramatically shortened the time required to sail between the East and West coasts of the United States, thus making global shipping much cheaper.

In 1917, the United States purchased the Virgin Islands from Denmark to help guard the canal. Many in Latin America resented these and other steps. They complained of "the Colossus of the North," of "Yankee imperialism," and of "dollar diplomacy."

This country's Latin American policies took a dramatic turn in the 1930s. Theodore Roosevelt's Corollary was replaced by Franklin Roosevelt's Good Neighbor Policy, a conscious attempt to win friends to the south by reducing this nation's political and military interventions in the region.

Today, the central provision of the Monroe Doctrine—the warning against foreign encroachments in the Western Hemisphere—is set out in the Inter-American Treaty of Reciprocal Assistance (the Rio Pact) of 1947. Still, the United States is, without question, the dominant power in the Western Hemisphere, and the Monroe Doctrine remains a vital part of American foreign policy.

The United States and China Historically, American foreign-policy interests have centered on Europe and Latin America. But America has also been involved in Asia since the mid-1800s. Forty-five years before the United States acquired territory in the Pacific, the U.S. Navy's Commodore Matthew Perry had opened Japan to American trade.

By the late nineteenth century, however, America's thriving trade in Asia was being seriously threatened. The British, French, Germans, and Japanese were each ready to take slices of the Chinese coast as their own exclusive trading preserves. In 1899, Secretary of State John Hay announced this country's insistence on an Open Door policy in China. That doctrine promoted equal trade access for all nations, and demanded that China's independence and sovereignty over its own territory be preserved.

The other major powers came to accept the American position, however reluctantly. Relations between the United States and Japan worsened from that point on, up to the climax at Pearl Harbor in 1941. Over the same period, the United States built increasingly strong ties with China; but those ties were cut when communists won control of the Chinese mainland in 1949. For nearly 30 years, the United States and the People's Republic of China refused diplomatic recognition of one another.

World War I Germany's submarine campaign against American shipping in the North Atlantic forced the United States out of its isolationist cocoon in 1917. America entered World War I to make the world "safe for democracy."

With the defeat of Germany and the Central Powers, however, America pulled back from the involvements brought on by the war. The United States refused to join the League of Nations, and many Americans were determined to avoid future entanglement in other countries' problems.

☑ **APPLY CONCEPTS** Why did the direction of American foreign policy change in Latin America?

World War II to the End of the Cold War

Some of the seeds of World War II were planted with the growth of a political ideology known as fascism. Fascism arose in southern and central Europe between 1919 and 1945. Leaders such as Benito Mussolini of Italy and Adolf Hitler of Germany advocated this philosophy, which elevated the nation over the individual, an approach also known as hyper-nationalism or extreme nationalism. Fascists sought strength through military might, opposed democratic ideals, believed in traditional gender roles, and advocated rule by a dictator or small group of elites.

Opponents of fascism during this time were suppressed with violence. Tyranny—oppressive, absolute power—prevailed. Human rights—such as physical safety, freedom of speech and the press, and due process of law, to name a few—were not protected and were often violated by these governments. Cultures and ethnic groups outside the national majority were persecuted. In Hitler's Nazi Germany, that persecution led to the systematic attempt to exterminate Jews and other groups Nazi leaders deemed "undesirables."

Fascist Italy and Germany developed centrally planned economies, in which the government controlled all economic activities, the money system, prices, and wages, while still allowing private ownership of property. Fascist governments favored the wealthy and spent heavily on the construction of roads, buildings, and arms production.

Government spending also supported huge social welfare programs, such as help for the unemployed, free higher education, public health programs, pensions, and child support. These programs were aimed at keeping the masses content, so as to minimize any challenges to the ruling elite.

After the war, fascist movements sprang up in various parts of the world. None, however, has rivaled the influence and power of those of the 1920s, 1930s, and 1940s.

World War II In 1939, Nazi Germany attacked Poland, thus beginning World War II. Mussolini's Italy joined forces with Germany in 1940. The United States became directly involved in the war when

>> The attack on Pearl Harbor, which President Roosevelt called "unprovoked and dastardly," left 2,403 Americans dead and the U.S. fleet decimated. It also led to a U.S. declaration of war.

the Japanese attacked the American naval base at **Pearl Harbor** in Hawaii on December 7, 1941. From that point on—along with the British, the Russians, the Chinese, and our other Allies—the United States waged an all-out effort to defeat the Axis Powers (Germany, Italy, and Japan).

Under the direction and leadership of President Franklin Roosevelt, the United States became the "arsenal of democracy." American resources and industrial capacity supplied most of the armaments and other materials needed to win World War II. Within a very short time, the United States was transformed into the mightiest military power in the world—and it has remained so ever since.

Collective Security The coming of World War II brought a historic shift from a position of isolationism to one of internationalism. This nation's foreign policy has been cast in that newer direction ever since. Even so, the overall objective of that policy remains what it has always been: the protection of the security and well-being of the United States.

Following World War II, the United States and most of the rest of a war-weary world looked to the principle of **collective security** to keep international peace and order. America hoped to forge a world community in which at least most nations would agree to act together against any nation that threatened the peace.

To that end, this country took the lead in creating the United Nations in 1945. The organization's charter declares that the UN was formed to promote international cooperation and so "to save succeeding generations from the scourge of war . . . and to maintain international peace and security."

It soon became clear, however, that the UN would not shape the future of the world. Rather, international security would depend largely on the nature of the relations between the two superpowers, the United States and the Soviet Union. Those relations, never very close, quickly deteriorated—and for the next 40 years, American foreign policy was built around that fact.

With the breakup of the Soviet Union, the United States became the only superpower in today's world. Still, collective security remains a cornerstone of American policy. The United States has supported the United Nations and other efforts to further international cooperation. This country has also taken another path to collective security: the building of a network of regional security alliances.

Deterrence The principle of deterrence has also been a part of American foreign policy since World War II. Basically, **deterrence** is the strategy of maintaining military might at so great a level that that very strength will deter—discourage, prevent—an attack on this country by any hostile power.

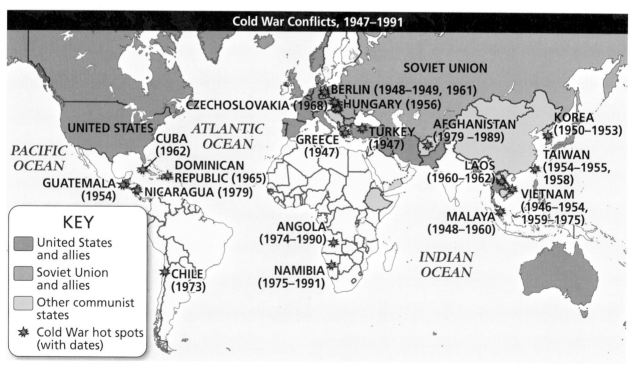

>> Competition between the two superpowers became a source of political tension; nations allied themselves with one or the other. **Analyze Maps** What do most of these locations have in common?

President **Harry Truman** initiated deterrence as U.S.–Soviet relations worsened after World War II. Every President since President Truman's day has reaffirmed the strategy, and deterrence was a key factor in the collapse of the Soviet Union.

The Cold War The **cold war** was a period of more than 40 years during which relations between the two superpowers were at least tense and, more often than not, distinctly hostile. It was, for the most part, not a "hot war" of military action, but rather a time of threats, posturing, and military buildup.

At the Yalta Conference in early 1945, Soviet Premier Josef Stalin had agreed with President Franklin Roosevelt and British Prime Minister Winston Churchill to promote the establishment of "democratic governments" by "free elections" in the liberated countries of Eastern Europe. Instead, the Soviets imposed dictatorial regimes on those countries. The Soviets also looked to exploit postwar chaos in other nations, as well. In 1946, Churchill declared that "an iron curtain" had descended across the continent.

The Truman Doctrine The United States began to counter the aggressive actions of the Soviet Union early in 1947. Both Greece and Turkey were in danger of falling under Soviet control. At President Truman's urgent request, Congress approved a massive program of economic and military aid, and both countries remained free. In a message to Congress, the President declared that it was now

the policy of the United States to support free peoples who are resisting attempted subjugation by armed minorities or by outside pressures.

—Speech by President Harry S Truman to Congress, March 12, 1947

The Truman Doctrine soon became part of a broader American plan for dealing with the Soviet Union. From 1947 through the 1980s, the United States followed the policy of **containment.** That policy was rooted in the belief that if communism could be kept within its existing boundaries, it would collapse under the weight of its own weaknesses.

The United States and the Soviet Union confronted one another often during the cold war years. Two of those confrontations were of major, near-war proportions. The first, the Berlin blockade, occurred in 1948–1949, when the Soviets tried to force the United States and its allies to abandon

the German city of Berlin to Soviet domination. The other major incident, the Cuban missile crisis, arose in 1962. The United States threatened war over the placement of Soviet nuclear missiles on the island of Cuba. In both cases, the Soviets backed down in the face of determined American resistance.

Not all cold war conflicts ended peacefully, however. During the postwar period, the United States fought two hot wars against communist forces in Asia.

Conflict in Korea The Korean War began on June 25, 1950, when communist North Korea attacked South Korea. Immediately, the UN Security Council called on all UN members to help South Korea repel the invasion.

The war lasted for more than three years. It pitted the United Nations Command, largely made up of American and South Korean forces, against Soviet-trained and Soviet-equipped North Korean and communist Chinese troops. Fighting continued until an armistice was signed on July 27, 1953.

The long and bitter Korean conflict did not end in a clear-cut UN victory. Still, the invasion was turned back, and the Republic of Korea remained standing. For the first time in history, armed forces of several nations fought under an international flag against aggression. There is no telling how far the tide of that aggression might have been carried had the United States not come to the aid of South Korea.

>> After World War II, Soviet forces occupied North Korea and U.S. forces occupied South Korea (shown here). Political tension between them led to UN intervention in 1950.

U.S. TROOPS IN VIETNAM

Sources: U.S. Army War College, Department of Defense Manpower Data, Congressional Research Service

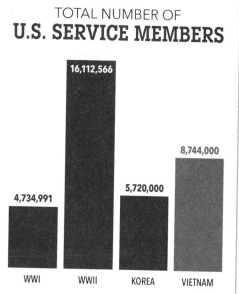

TOTAL NUMBER OF U.S. SERVICE MEMBERS

4,734,991	16,112,566	5,720,000	8,744,000
WWI	WWII	KOREA	VIETNAM

>> The U.S. committed to full-scale war in Vietnam in 1965 and began to end that involvement in 1969. **Analyze Graphs** According to the bar graph, how many total troops served in the wars shown?

The Vietnam War In the years following World War II, a nationalist movement arose in French Indochina—today, Vietnam. Vietnamese nationalists were seeking independence from their French colonial rulers. Made up mostly of communist forces led by Ho Chi Minh, the nationalists fought and defeated the French in a lengthy conflict. Under truce agreements signed in 1954, the country was divided into two zones. The communist-dominated North Vietnam, with its capital in Hanoi, and an anti-communist South Vietnam, with its capital in Saigon.

Almost at once, communist guerrillas (the Viet Cong), supported by the North Vietnamese, began a civil war in South Vietnam. Because President **Dwight Eisenhower** and other foreign policy experts believed that South Vietnam was critical to the security of all of Southeast Asia, the Eisenhower administration responded with economic and then military aid to Saigon. President **John F. Kennedy** increased that aid, and President **Lyndon Johnson** committed the United States to full-scale war in early 1965.

In 1969, President **Richard Nixon** began what he called the "Vietnamization" of the war. Over the next four years, the United States gradually pulled troops out of combat. Finally, the two sides reached a cease-fire agreement in early 1973, and the

United States withdrew its last units. In 1975, South Vietnam fell to the communist North.

The ill-fated war in Vietnam cost more than 58,000 American lives. Over time, millions of Americans came to oppose American involvement in Southeast Asia. Traces of the divisiveness of that period can still be seen in politics today.

Nicaragua The Central American country of Nicaragua illustrates the sometimes murky waters of the cold war struggle between the United States and the Soviet Union. From 1936 to 1979, the Somoza family ruled—and looted—Nicaragua. Due to their strong anti-communist stand, the Somozas enjoyed the support of the United States.

In the 1970s, various groups opposed to Nicaraguan leader Anastasio Somoza joined forces. They called themselves Sandinistas, after Augusto Sandino, a Nicaraguan revolutionary of the 1930s. Like Sandino, they were reform-minded nationalists, thought by some to hold communist beliefs. In 1979, the revolutionaries ousted Somoza. The country soon found itself embroiled in a civil war, however, when the Sandinistas were challenged by guerrilla fighters called Contras.

Many in the United States worried about another Vietnam-like entanglement, and the Democrats who controlled Congress refused to authorize federal funds to help the Contras. Fearing that Nicaragua would fall to the communists, President **Ronald Reagan** secretly backed them. This conflict between Reagan and the Democrats in Congress became known as the Iran-Contra Affair.

Détente: Successes and Failures As the United States withdrew from Vietnam, the Nixon administration embarked on a policy of **détente**. In this case, the policy of détente included a purposeful attempt to improve relations with the Soviet Union and, separately, with China.

President Richard Nixon flew to Beijing in 1972 to begin a new era in American-Chinese relations. His visit paved the way for further contacts and, finally, for formal diplomatic ties between the United States and the People's Republic of China. Less than three months later, Nixon journeyed to Moscow. There, he and Soviet Premier Leonid Brezhnev signed the first Strategic Arms Limitation Talks agreement, SALT I—a five-year pact in which both sides agreed to a measure of control over their nuclear weapons.

Relations with mainland China have improved in fits and starts since the 1970s. Efforts at détente with the Soviets, however, proved less successful. Moscow continued to apply its expansionist pressures and provided economic and military aid to revolutionary movements around the world.

In 1979, an effort by the Soviet Union to impose a communist regime in Afghanistan was met by unexpectedly stiff resistance of armed groups of Afghans and their supporters around the region. The United States, acting largely in secret through the CIA, provided support to some of the groups resisting communist expansion. As was the case in Nicaragua, this type of war by proxy between the United States and the Soviet Union became common during the cold war. After the aggression against Afghanistan, the Carter and then the Reagan administrations placed a renewed emphasis on the containment of Soviet power.

The Cold War Ends Relations between the United States and the USSR improved remarkably after Mikhail Gorbachev came to power in Moscow in 1985. He and President Ronald Reagan met in a series of arms limitation summits that helped pave the way to the end of the cold war.

Certainly, Mikhail Gorbachev deserves much credit for the fundamental change in the Soviets' approach to world affairs. But, just as certainly, that historic change was prompted by deepening political and economic chaos in Eastern Europe and within the Soviet Union itself—by conditions that ultimately brought the collapse of the Soviet Union in late 1991.

The Nicaraguan Revolution, 1978–1979

Ideologies	Overthrow of the Somoza family dictatorship
Causes	Corruption and mass poverty
Stages	• The Sandinista rebel group seizes the national palace • The uprising spreads and the Sandinistas seize and hold several major cities • Civilians join the fight and more cities fall to the Sandinistas • Somoza flees the country
Outcomes	Somoza's rule is ended but the country dissolves into civil war

>> The revolution did not bring peace to Nicaragua. **Analyze Charts** According to the chart, did any of the Nicaraguan people support the Sandinistas? How can you tell?

The fact that the cold war is now a matter of history should also be seen in this light: The American policies of deterrence and containment, first put in place in 1947, finally realized their goals.

☑ **DRAW CONCLUSIONS** How were the U.S. policies of deterrence and containment used during the cold war?

Post-Cold War Foreign Policy Challenges

The coming of World War II finally convinced the American people that neither they nor anyone else can live in isolation—that, in many ways, the world of today is indeed "one world." The well-being of everyone in this country—in fact, the very survival of the United States—is affected by much that happens elsewhere on the globe.

Economic conditions elsewhere in the world, for example, have a direct effect on this country. The American economy has become an intertwined part of a truly global economy, linked by international banking, multinational corporations, and worldwide investments that transcend national boundaries.

Economic issues are not the only ones that cross national borders today. Others, such as the environment and terrorism, do as well. Addressing these threats requires a new international community in which nations work together. They do so through the joint efforts of national governments and through non-governmental organizations (NGOs), multinational alliances, and even the efforts of individual citizens.

Wars and other upheavals abroad have long had an impact on the United States, but in today's "global village," that impact is even more profound. Five times over the past century, the United States fought major wars abroad; and in several other instances, it has committed armed forces to significant conflicts. Political unrest in Afghanistan, terrorists' plots that can strike any country at any time, continuing Arab-Israeli disputes in the Middle East—these and other circumstances around the globe threaten the security of the United States.

Seemingly endless upheavals elsewhere in today's world also pose challenges to foreign policy makers—not the least of them the fact that autocratic North Korea is now a nuclear power, the civil war in Syria, China's strained relationship with other Southeast Asian countries, and the threat from the militant Islamic State of Iraq and Syria (ISIS). In our own neighborhood, the instability of Venezuela and other Central and South American countries are also cause for concern.

Cyber threats also pose an increasing danger in our interconnected world, in which other nations, organizations, or individuals can "attack" the United States by targeting computer networks, information systems, personal computers, and a broad array of Internet-based systems. Hacking into the computer system of a power grid and shutting it down for even a brief period of time, for example, could cost millions of dollars and even lead to the loss of lives.

Foreign governments can wreak havoc on American systems of democracy, as evidenced by the fact that the Russian government, or someone in that government, hacked into the email servers of prominent Democrats during the 2016 presidential campaign. In response to these threats, the Federal Government and many private organizations are scrambling to create better "electronic firewalls" to stop potentially devastating attacks.

The Middle East The Middle East is both oil rich and conflict ridden. America's foreign policy interests in the Middle East have, for decades, been torn in two quite opposite directions: by its long-standing support of Israel and by the critical importance of Arab oil.

The United Nations created Israel as an independent state on May 14, 1948, and the United States recognized the new Jewish state within a matter of minutes. Since that time, this country has been Israel's close ally while also attempting to strengthen its ties with most of the Arab states in the volatile Middle East.

With the active involvement of President Jimmy Carter, Israel and Egypt negotiated the historic Camp David Accords in 1979. That agreement led to the end of more than 30 years of hostilities between those two countries. Israel and Jordan signed a similar pact in 1994.

In 1993, Israel and the Palestinian Liberation Organization (PLO) signed the Oslo Accords. In them, the two nations officially recognized one another and Israel agreed to limited Palestinian self-rule. Beyond those first steps, however, the promise of the Oslo Accords has yet to be realized, despite both UN and United States efforts to bring the two sides together.

The "Arab Spring" revolutions that swept through the Middle East and North Africa in 2010 and 2011 further complicated matters, causing widespread instability in the region and rising hostility to Israel. The uprisings preceded the toppling of authoritarian governments in a dizzying number of countries, including Egypt, Libya, Yemen, Tunisia, and others. In a number of these states, authoritarian forces rebounded in subsequent years.

The worst incarnation of the perilous political environment happened in Syria, where civil war broke out in 2012. The fighting sent massive waves of refugees pouring into neighboring countries and threatened to ignite a larger, regional conflict. The situation deteriorated further when the Islamic

>> In 1948, David Ben-Gurion became the first prime minister of the newly established state of Israel.

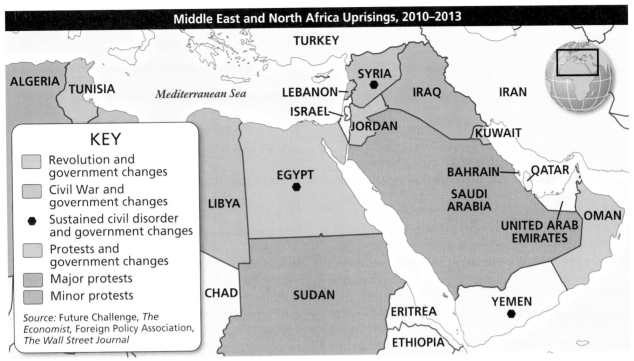

Middle East and North Africa Uprisings, 2010–2013

KEY

- Revolution and government changes
- Civil War and government changes
- Sustained civil disorder and government changes
- Protests and government changes
- Major protests
- Minor protests

Source: Future Challenge, *The Economist,* Foreign Policy Association, *The Wall Street Journal*

>> This map shows the Arab Spring uprisings of 2010–2013. **Analyze Maps** What can you conclude about the threat to nations such as Israel and Turkey?

militant group ISIS (Islamic State of Iraq and Syria) expanded its violence and atrocities into Syria, prompting France, the United Kingdom, the United States, and Arab allies to conduct airstrikes against ISIS targets beginning in 2015. Despite signs that ISIS was losing its grip on the region, many believe an end to the conflict with ISIS and other militant groups is a long way off.

Afghanistan and Iraq The Soviet Union's invasion of Afghanistan in 1979 introduced an era of war and devastation to that Central Asian country. Although the Soviets left Afghanistan in defeat in 1989, the occupation led to civil war. By the late 1990s, an ultraconservative political and religious faction, the Taliban, had gained control over most of Afghanistan. Under the Taliban, Afghanistan became a haven for Islamist militants, including Osama bin Laden, the leader of the Al Qaeda militant organization.

On September 11, 2001, the Al Qaeda Islamist terrorist group hijacked four commercial passenger airplanes and crashed two of them into the World Trade Center in New York City and one into the Pentagon in northern Virginia. A fourth plane, aimed at the White House, crashed into a Pennsylvania field after passengers rushed the hijackers in the cockpit. Nearly 3,000 people died in the attacks. In response, the United States and its NATO allies toppled the

Taliban regime, which had sheltered leader Osama bin Laden and Al Qaeda.

The Taliban reemerged in subsequent years, however. Other militant groups also arose, threatening the hard-won gains the country had made and leading to a protracted U.S. military campaign in Afghanistan.

During the early 2000s, the U.S. waged a second war in Iraq. After the first Gulf War (1991), Iraq's president Saddam Hussein agreed to destroy his country's stock of chemical and biological weapons. By 2003, however, he had failed to convince the international community that he had honored that promise. Consequently, a coalition led by the United States and Great Britain launched the second Gulf War. Iraq was conquered and Saddam Hussein's regime toppled in less than six weeks. Hussein himself was captured, tried, and executed in 2006.

Subsequent efforts to establish a democracy in Iraq and Afghanistan proved difficult, however. As a result, United States troops remained in Iraq until the end of 2011 and in Afghanistan until 2021. The war cost the United States in the trillions of dollars and more than 7,000 American lives.

Russia The relationship between the United States and Russia has generally been positive since the end of the cold war, and the nations have worked together in many areas. In 2011, for example, President Obama and Russian leader Dmitry Medvedev reached an historic agreement to limit both country's nuclear warheads and number of nuclear launch sites. On the economic side, a massive amount of goods are shipped between the United States and Russia.

The relationship has been somewhat strained, however. In 2014, Russia invaded a southeastern region of Ukraine called Crimea. Even though many of the residents of the region consider themselves Russian and actually wanted to join Russia, the move was seen by the United States and other countries as a clear violation of international law. Within a year, Russia had annexed the region. This and other similar moves by Russia in Eastern Europe seemed reminiscent of the tactics used by the Soviet Union during the cold war. In response, the United States and the European Union imposed sanctions on Russian state-owned banks, corporations, and some individuals.

The United States and Russia have also been at odds over what to do to end the civil war in Syria. Since 2014, the United States and several allies have bombed targets inside Syria believed to be held by ISIS, and have also supported Kurdish groups seeking self-rule. Russia, on the other hand, deployed forces to aid the Syrian government—and by so doing helped keep Syrian president Bashar al-Assad in power. The United States has said Assad is a brutal dictator and must go. Russia also bombed several Kurdish areas, claiming that they were centers of terrorist control.

On top of this, U.S. intelligence agencies found that the Russian government tried to influence the outcome of the 2016 presidential election—in part, by hacking into the computers of Democratic Party and other officials. Whether the Trump campaign knew of these actions or even worked with the Russians became a broad investigation during 2017. In 2019, the investigation concluded that Russia had "directed extensive activity" against the election. It also found links between the Russian government and the Trump campaign but did not bring any charges against the President.

The historic friction between the two nations coupled with the fact that each side possesses a huge military and a massive nuclear arsenal, makes this relationship a unique foreign policy challenge. Merge that with growing economic connections and you have the makings of a foreign policy dilemma.

International Terrorism Since the attacks on September 11, 2001, nations across the globe have been fighting terrorism. In this fight, governments must balance aggressive anti-terrorism efforts with the protection of civil liberties. International humanitarian law must also be observed. Because terrorist groups are difficult to identify, surveillance and intelligence are critically important tools in stopping attacks. But does this mean governments should monitor the calls, emails, and social media of their citizens? What sort of security measures should be taken at places where civilians gather? Should a country ban the entry of citizens from countries where terrorists are more common? Nations across the globe are grappling with these sorts of issues. Which anti-terrorism tools can they properly use? These tools often depend on the level of threat, the nation's political culture, and existing civil liberty protections.

There are also a vast number of international organizations aimed at stopping terrorism. The UN Counter-Terrorism Centre, for example, carries out projects around the world to prevent terrorist acts. Dozens of other international initiatives and institutions also work to this same end, by drafting counterterrorism laws and standards and by joining together to gather and share intelligence. Organizations have also been formed to cripple the finances of terrorist groups, including units of the International Monetary Fund and the World Bank.

☑ **CHECK UNDERSTANDING** What foreign policy challenges do the Arab Spring uprisings pose?

☑ ASSESSMENT

1. **Analyze Information** The United States pursued an isolationist foreign policy for its first 150 years as a nation. For what reasons was this approach a reasonable one at the time?

2. **Apply Concepts** Given the interconnected nature of today's world, why might economic chaos and instability in another nation prompt a new direction in American foreign policy?

3. **Express Ideas Clearly** Is the idea of "containment" relevant to American foreign policy today? Why or why not?

4. **Interpret** "The cold war was not just a struggle between the United States and the Soviet Union—it involved the entire world." Do you agree with this statement? Why or why not?

5. **Support a Point of View with Evidence** Has American foreign policy become more or less difficult since the fall of the Soviet Union? Support your position with facts.

Presidents on American Foreign Policy

The transformation of American foreign policy from isolationism to internationalism was a long process. The excerpts here—one from the nation's first President and the other from its 40th—illustrate both ends of the spectrum. As he prepared to leave office in 1796, President George Washington made a speech describing his vision of the nation's future. His Farewell Address deals with a wide range of topics, but one of its most enduring relates to foreign affairs. Nearly two hundred years later, President Ronald Reagan spoke in West Berlin, near the Berlin Wall. His speech acknowledged the new Soviet leader Mikhail Gorbachev's efforts at reform, but challenged the Soviet leader to do more.

>> George Washington

Farewell Address: George Washington

. . . [A] passionate attachment of one nation for another produces a variety of evils. Sympathy for the favorite nation, facilitating the illusion of an imaginary common interest in cases where no real common interest exists, and infusing into one the enmities [hostility] of the other, betrays the former into a participation in the quarrels and wars of the latter without adequate inducement or justification. It leads also to concessions to the favorite nation of privileges denied to others which is apt doubly to injure the nation making the concessions. . . .

Against the insidious wiles of foreign influence (I conjure you to believe me, fellow-citizens) the jealousy of a free people ought to be constantly awake, since history and experience prove that foreign influence is one of the most baneful foes of republican government. But that jealousy to be useful must be impartial, else it becomes the instrument of the very influence to be avoided, instead of a defense against it. Excessive partiality for one foreign nation and excessive dislike of

another cause those whom they actuate [motivate] to see danger only on one side, and serve to veil and even second the arts of influence on the other. Real patriots who may resist the intrigues of the favorite are liable to become suspected and odious [repulsive], while its tools and dupes usurp [take by force] the applause and confidence of the people, to surrender their interests.

☑ **SUMMARIZE** What does Washington say can happen when people have "a passionate attachment" to one nation?

The great rule of conduct for us in regard to foreign nations is, in extending our commercial relations, to have with them as little political connection as possible. So far as we have already formed engagements, let them be fulfilled with perfect good faith. Here let us stop. Europe has a set of primary interests which to us have none; or a very remote relation. Hence she must be engaged in frequent controversies, the causes of which are essentially foreign to our concerns.

Our detached and distant situation invites and enables us to pursue a different course. If we remain one people under an efficient government. the period is not far off when we may defy material injury from external annoyance; when we may take such an attitude as will cause the neutrality we may at any time resolve upon to be scrupulously respected; when belligerent nations, under the impossibility of making acquisitions upon us, will not lightly hazard the giving us provocation; when we may choose peace or war, as our interest, guided by justice, shall counsel.

Why forego the advantages of so peculiar a situation? Why quit our own to stand upon foreign ground? Why, by interweaving our destiny with that of any part of Europe, entangle our peace and prosperity in the toils of European ambition, rivalship, interest, humor or caprice [sudden change in behavior]?

It is our true policy to steer clear of permanent alliances with any portion of the foreign world; so far, I mean, as we are now at liberty to do it; for let me not be understood as capable of patronizing [supporting] infidelity [unfaithfulness] to existing engagements. I hold the maxim [wise saying] no less applicable to public than to private affairs, that honesty is always the best policy. I repeat, therefore, let those engagements be observed in their genuine sense. But, in my opinion, it is unnecessary and would be unwise to extend them.

"Tear Down This Wall": Ronald Reagan

In the 1950s, Khrushchev predicted: "We will bury you." But in the West today, we see a free world that has achieved a level of prosperity and well-being unprecedented in all human history. In the Communist world, we see failure, technological backwardness, declining standards of health, even want of the most basic kind—too little food. Even today, the Soviet Union still cannot feed itself. After these four decades, then, there stands before the entire world one great and inescapable conclusion: Freedom leads to prosperity. Freedom replaces the ancient hatreds among the nations with comity [courtesy] and peace. Freedom is the victor.

And now the Soviets themselves may, in a limited way, be coming to understand the importance of freedom. We hear much from Moscow about a new policy of reform and openness. Some political prisoners have been released. Certain foreign news broadcasts are no longer being jammed. Some economic enterprises have been permitted to operate with greater freedom from state control.

Are these the beginnings of profound changes in the Soviet state? Or are they token gestures, intended to raise false hopes in the West, or to strengthen the Soviet system without changing it? We welcome change and openness; for we believe that freedom and security go together, that the advance of human liberty can only strengthen the cause of world peace. There is one sign the Soviets can make that would be unmistakable, that would advance dramatically the cause of freedom and peace.

General Secretary Gorbachev, if you seek peace, if you seek prosperity for the Soviet Union and Eastern Europe, if you seek liberalization: Come here to this gate! Mr. Gorbachev, open this gate! Mr. Gorbachev, tear down this wall!

☑ **EVALUATE** Use your knowledge of history to evaluate how President Reagan's speech might have influenced later events in Germany.

☑ ASSESSMENT

1. **Evaluate Evidence** In his Farewell Address, George Washington warns about becoming involved in foreign wars and gives reasons for his position. What response might President Reagan make to President Washington's reasons?

2. **Determine Central Ideas** What is the central message of President Washington's address with regard to foreign affairs?

3. **Assess Points of Emphasis** Why do you think President Reagan focused on the Berlin Wall in his speech?

The secretary of state often travels around the world as he or she helps carry out the President's foreign policy. Here, Secretary of State Madeleine Albright participates in a ceremony in Kenya.

Diplomacy

The State Department, headed by the secretary of state, is the President's right arm in foreign affairs. The President names the secretary of state, subject to confirmation by the Senate. It is to the secretary of state and to the Department of State that the President looks for advice and assistance in both the formulation and the conduct of the nation's foreign policy.

America's Representatives to the World

The Secretary of State The secretary of state ranks first among the members of the President's Cabinet. That ranking speaks to the importance of the office, and also to the fact that the State Department was the first executive department that Congress created.

A Department of Foreign Affairs had first been created in 1781 under the Articles of Confederation. Congress re-created it in 1789 as the first major unit in the executive branch under the Constitution. Later that year, its name was changed to the Department of State.

President George Washington appointed **Thomas Jefferson** as the nation's first secretary of state, in 1789. More than two hundred years later, President Bill Clinton appointed the first woman to hold the post, **Madeleine Albright**, in 1997. **Colin Powell**, who served as secretary of state in George W. Bush's first term (2001 to 2005), became the first Black American to occupy the office. His successor, **Condoleezza Rice** (2005–2009), made history as the first Black woman to serve in the post.

🅑 BOUNCE to Activate Flipped Video

Objectives

Describe the functions, components, and organization of the State Department.

Examine how the U.S. government uses economic resources in foreign policy, including foreign aid.

Examine the history, structure, and work of the United Nations and its relationship with the United States.

Key Terms

right of legation
ambassador
diplomatic immunity
passport
visa
foreign aid
regional security alliances
NATO
United Nations
Security Council
Thomas Jefferson
Madeleine Albright

Colin Powell
Condoleezza Rice
Ayatollah Khomeini
George C. Marshall
Balkans
Slobodan Milosevic
Franklin D. Roosevelt
Winston Churchill

Today, the duties of the secretary relate almost entirely to foreign affairs. They center on the making and conduct of policy and on the management of the department, its many overseas posts, and its workforce of tens of thousands.

Some Presidents—most famously, Woodrow Wilson and Franklin Roosevelt—have tended to ignore their secretaries of state and have handled many foreign policy matters personally and quite often directly. Others, notably Richard Nixon, Gerald Ford, and both Bushes, have chosen instead to rely on their national security advisors. Some chief executives—in particular, the earlier ones—have chosen to delegate a large share of the responsibility for matters of foreign policy to the secretary. President Obama, for example, made it clear that he considered Secretary Clinton to be a major player in both the formation and the conduct of American foreign policy.

State Department Organization The State Department is organized along both geographic and functional lines. Some of its agencies, such as the Bureau of African Affairs and the Bureau of Near Eastern Affairs, deal with matters involving particular regions of the world.

Other agencies have broader missions—for example, the Bureau of International Narcotics and Law Enforcement Affairs, sometimes called "Drugs 'n' Thugs." Most bureaus are headed by an assistant secretary and include several offices. Thus, both the Office of Passport Services and the Office of Visa Services are found in the Bureau of Consular Affairs.

The Right of Legation Thousands of men and women represent the United States as members of the Foreign Service, many of them serving abroad. Under international law, every nation has the **right of legation**—the right to send and receive diplomatic representatives. International law consists of those rules and principles that guide sovereign states in their dealings with one another and in their treatment of foreign nationals (private persons and groups). Its sources include treaties, decisions of international courts, and custom. Treaties are the most important source today. The right of legation is an ancient practice. Its history can be traced back to the Egyptian civilization of 6,000 years ago.

The Second Continental Congress named this nation's first foreign service officer in 1778. That year, it chose Benjamin Franklin to be America's minister to France. He served in that capacity for nearly eight years.

American Ambassadors An **ambassador** is the official representative of a sovereign state in the conduct of its foreign affairs. For some five centuries now, most of the formal contacts between sovereign nations—that is, most of their diplomatic relationships—have been conducted through their duly appointed ambassadors.

In this country, ambassadors are appointed by the President, with Senate consent, and they serve at his pleasure. Today, the United States is represented by an ambassador stationed at the capital of each sovereign state this nation recognizes. Thus, American embassies are now located in more than 180 countries around the world.

The United States maintains hundreds of diplomatic and consular offices abroad as well. There, Foreign Service officers promote American interests in a multitude of ways—for example, encouraging trade, gathering intelligence data, advising persons who seek to enter this country, and aiding American citizens who are abroad and in need of legal advice or other help.

>> Secretary of State Henry Kissinger (left) met with communist leader Leonid Brezhnev in 1973, the same year Kissinger received the Nobel Peace Prize for his efforts to end the Vietnam War.

THE IRAN HOSTAGE CRISIS

U.S. EMBASSIES

- Embassies serve diplomatic functions, and are also symbols of the U.S. abroad.

- Tensions between nations have led to attacks on U.S. embassies at times.

AMERICAN HOSTAGES

- In 1979, Iranian students attacked the American embassy in Tehran.

- They held U.S. embassy staff hostage for 444 days.

- The Iran hostage crisis was an unusual assault against both the U.S. and international law.

An American hostage is paraded in front of the media by Iranian militants in 1979.

YELLOW RIBBONS

- During the crisis, yellow ribbons were tied to trees to symbolize public support for the hostages.

>> International law requires the "receiving state" to protect the safety of diplomats and treat them with respect. **Analyze Charts** How did the Iran hostage crisis breach international law?

Some ambassadorships are much desired political plums, and whenever a new President moves into the White House, he typically makes many new appointments. Too often, Presidents have appointed people to ambassadorships and other major diplomatic posts as a reward for those individuals' support—financial and otherwise—of the President's election to office. However, in many cases these ranks are filled with career diplomats in the Foreign Service.

President Harry Truman named the first African American, Edward R. Dudley, as an ambassador to Liberia, in 1949. Later that same year President Truman also appointed the first woman, Eugenie Anderson, as our ambassador to Denmark.

Special Diplomats Those persons whom the President names to certain other top diplomatic posts also carry the rank of ambassador. Examples include the United States representative to the UN and the American member of the North Atlantic Treaty Council. The President also often assigns the personal rank of ambassador to those diplomats who take on special assignments abroad—for example, representing the United States in the ongoing efforts to resolve Arab-Israeli differences.

Diplomatic Privileges In international law, every sovereign state is supreme within its own boundaries. All persons or things found within that state's territory are subject to its jurisdiction.

As a major exception to that rule, ambassadors are regularly granted **diplomatic immunity**—they are not subject to the laws of the state to which they are accredited. They cannot be arrested, sued, or taxed. Their official residences (embassies) cannot be entered or searched without their consent, and all official communications and other properties are protected. All other embassy personnel and their families receive this same immunity.

Diplomatic immunity is essential to the ability of every nation to conduct its foreign relations. The practice assumes that diplomats will not abuse their privileged status. If a host government finds a diplomat's conduct unacceptable, that official may be declared *persona non grata* and expelled from the country. The mistreatment of diplomats is considered a major breach of international law.

Diplomatic immunity is a generally accepted practice. There are exceptions, however. The most serious breach in modern times occurred in Iran in late 1979. Militant followers of the **Ayatollah Khomeini** seized the American embassy in Tehran on November 4 of that year; 66 Americans were taken hostage and 52 were held for 444 days. The Iranians finally released the hostages moments after Ronald Reagan became President on January 20, 1981.

Passports and Visas A **passport** is a legal document issued by a state that identifies a person as a citizen of that state. It grants that person a right of protection while traveling abroad and the right to return to the homeland. Passports entitle their holders to the privileges accorded to them by international custom and treaties. Few countries will admit persons who do not hold valid passports.

The State Department's Office of Passport Services now issues more than ten million passports to Americans each year. Do not confuse passports with visas. A **visa** is a permit to enter another state and must be obtained from the country one wishes to enter. Trips to most foreign countries require visas today. Most visas to enter this country are issued at American consulates abroad.

☑ **APPLY CONCEPTS** To what degree do the Constitution or acts of Congress require that the secretary of state take charge of important international diplomacy?

American Foreign Aid

Do you know this ancient saying: "Those who help others help themselves"? You will see that that maxim underlies two basic elements of present-day American foreign policy: foreign aid and regional security alliances.

What Is Foreign Aid? **Foreign aid**—the economic and military aid given to other countries—has been a basic feature of American foreign policy for decades. It began with the Lend-Lease program of the early 1940s, through which the United States gave nearly $50 billion in food, munitions, and other supplies to its allies in World War II. Since then, this country has sent trillions of dollars in aid to countries around the world.

Foreign aid became an important part of the containment policy beginning with American aid to Greece and Turkey in 1947. The United States also helped its European allies rebuild after the devastation of World War II. Under the Marshall Plan, named for its author, Secretary of State **George C. Marshall**, the United States poured some $13 billion into 16 nations in Western Europe between 1948 and 1952.

Purposes of Foreign Aid Over the years, foreign aid has taken several different directions. Immediately after World War II, American aid was primarily economic. Since that time, however, military assistance has assumed a larger role in aid policy. Until the mid-1950s, Europe received the lion's share of American help. After that time, the largest amounts have gone to nations in the Middle East and Africa.

Most aid, which makes up some one percent of the federal budget, has been sent to those nations regarded as critical to the realization of American foreign policy objectives. Thus, Afghanistan, Israel, Egypt, Jordan, West Bank/Gaza, Kenya, Saudi Arabia, Pakistan, and Indonesia have been major recipients of American help, both economically and militarily. These countries are all of strategic

Travel Documents

PASSPORTS	VISAS
• Issued by a government and identifies the bearer as a citizen or national of the issuing country • Entitles the bearer to consular protection abroad and to return to his or her country of citizenship • Valid for 10 years • Three types: diplomatic, official, tourist	• Issued by the country the individual requests permission to enter • Permits the traveler to remain in a country for a specified period of time, but does not guarantee entry • Valid only for the time period stated • Of many types, including: transit, tourist, business, and student

>> In the past, a valid passport was all one needed to travel abroad and enter most countries. Today, a visa is often required as well. **Analyze Charts** Why do you think this is now the case?

>> NATO summits like this one are only held when there is important business to discuss. Summits have increased in frequency since 1990, largely due to the considerable security challenges of the 21st century.

importance to the United States, in some cases due to their location or natural resources, and in others, due to military or economic ties.

Most foreign aid money must be used to buy American goods and services. So, most of the billions spent for that aid amounts to a substantial subsidy to both business and labor in this country. The independent United States Agency for International Development (USAID) administers most of the economic aid programs, in close cooperation with the Departments of State and Agriculture. Most military aid is channeled through the Defense Department.

☑ **APPLY CONCEPTS** Do you think foreign aid is necessary today?

NATO

Since World War II, the United States has constructed a large network of **regional security alliances** built on mutual defense treaties. In each of those agreements, the United States and the other countries involved have agreed to act to meet any aggression in a particular part of the world. Among these many alliances, the North Atlantic Treaty Organization (NATO) ranks as one of the most significant.

History of NATO The North Atlantic Treaty, signed in 1949, established **NATO,** the North Atlantic Treaty Organization. The alliance was formed initially to promote the collective defense of Western Europe, particularly against the threat of Soviet aggression. NATO was originally composed of the United States and 11 other countries.

With the collapse of the Soviet Union, NATO's mutual security blanket was extended to cover much of Eastern Europe. Though it has grown in size, the alliance remains dedicated to the basic goal of protecting the freedom and security of its members through political and military action. Each member country has agreed that "an armed attack against one or more of them in Europe or in North America shall be considered an attack against them all."

What has changed with NATO since its founding? NATO was formed for defensive purposes and—if defense includes military intervention in conflicts that may destabilize Europe, and with it, the prevention of humanitarian disasters—defense remains its basic charge.

Increasingly, however, NATO is focused on what it calls "crisis management and peacekeeping." Its involvement in the **Balkans** provides a leading illustration of this role. First in Bosnia in 1995 and then in Kosovo in 1999, NATO forces, drawn mostly from the United States, Great Britain, and Canada, ended years of vicious civil war in what was once Yugoslavia. Those military interventions also put an end to the horrific campaigns of "ethnic cleansing," directed by Serbia's President **Slobodan Milosevic**. NATO troops continue to maintain a fragile peace in the Balkans today.

NATO Today In 2003, NATO took command of the International Security Assistance Force (ISAF) in Afghanistan. ISAF troops were drawn from 48 nations, with Americans supplying almost 70 percent of that force. The NATO coalition assumed the leading role in rebuilding Afghanistan and weakening the Taliban. By the end of 2011, NATO forces had begun a gradual transfer of authority to the Afghans. In 2015, ISAF was replaced by the Resolute Support Mission (RSM). Its role is to train, advise, and assist Afghan security forces.

In 2011, NATO forces undertook a seven-month mission to support the pro-democracy movement in the African nation of Libya, during which rebels revolted against the regime of Colonel Muammar al-Qaddafi. In an operation initially led by the United States, NATO used air strikes and sea power to enforce a United Nations-imposed arms embargo and no-fly zone against Libya. The mission ended with the death of Qaddafi and the installation of a transitional government.

In addition to its roles in Kosovo and Afghanistan, NATO patrols the Mediterranean Sea in an effort to deter potential terrorist threats. The organization also has a presence in Eastern Africa, where it combats modern-day piracy off the coast and assists in humanitarian and peacekeeping efforts in the region.

NATO also plays a role in other areas as well, including gender equality and the environment. The multinational organization is engaged in ongoing efforts to react to natural disasters and address the effects of climate change.

However, the security of its member nations is still a key component of NATO's efforts. With the increase of cyber attacks in recent years, NATO now includes cyber defense as part of its "core task of collective defense."

☑ **COMPARE AND CONTRAST** How does NATO's current mission compare with its original mission?

The United Nations

You know that a fundamental change occurred in American foreign policy during and immediately after World War II. That dramatic shift from isolationism to internationalism, is strikingly illustrated by this country's participation in the United Nations. Remember, the United States refused to join the League of Nations after World

RSM Top Troop-Contributing Nations

COUNTRY	TROOPS	COUNTRY	TROOPS
United States	6,800	Romania	650
Georgia	856	Turkey	509
Germany	850	United Kingdom	395
Italy	760	Spain	326
Total troops from all 14 contributing nations			12,905

SOURCE: Resolute Support Mission, NATO.int; December 2015 data

>> As it did for the ISAF, the United States has provided the bulk of NATO troops for the Resolute Support Mission. **Analyze Charts** How do other countries' troop contributions compare to the United States'?

KEY
Founding and Permanent Members
Founding Member, 1945

>> Fifty nations founded the UN in June 1945. Poland is also considered a founding member even though it did not sign the charter until October. **Analyze Maps** Which continent has the fewest founding members? Why do you think that is the case?

War I. With the end of World War II, however, the American people realized that America was a world power with worldwide interests and responsibilities.

The **United Nations** (UN) came into being at the United Nations Conference on International Organization, which met in San Francisco from April 25 to June 26, 1945. There, the representatives of 50 nations—the victorious allies of World War II—drafted the United Nations Charter. The charter is a treaty among all of the UN's member states, and it serves as the body's constitution.

The United States became the first nation to ratify the UN Charter. The Senate approved it by an overwhelming vote, 89–2, on July 24, 1945. The other states that had taken part in the San Francisco Conference then ratified the charter in quick order, and it went into force on October 24, 1945. The UN held the first session of its General Assembly in London on January 10, 1946.

The United Nations Charter The UN's charter is a lengthy document. It opens with an eloquent preamble, which reads in part:

We, the peoples of the United Nations

Determined to save succeeding generations from the scourge of war, which twice in our lifetime has brought untold sorrow to mankind, and . . .

To practice tolerance and live together in peace with one another as good neighbors, and

To unite our strength to maintain international peace and security . . .

Have resolved to combine our efforts to accomplish these aims.

—Charter of the United Nations

The body of the document begins in Article I, with a statement of the organization's purposes: the maintenance of international peace and security, the development of friendly relations between and among all nations, and the promotion of justice and cooperation in the solution of international problems.

The UN has nearly 200 members. Membership is open to those "peace-loving states" that accept the obligations of the charter and are, in the UN's judgment, able and willing to carry out those obligations. New members may be admitted by a two-thirds vote of the General Assembly, upon recommendation by the Security Council.

The charter sets forth the complicated structure of the UN. It is built around six principal bodies: the General Assembly, the Security Council, the Economic and Social Council, the Trusteeship Council (which exists in name only today), the International Court of Justice, and the Secretariat.

The General Assembly The UN's General Assembly has been called "the town meeting of the world." Each of the UN's members has a seat and a vote in the Assembly. It meets once a year, and sessions take place at the UN's permanent headquarters in New York City. The secretary-general may call special sessions, at the request of either the Security Council or a majority of the UN's members.

The Assembly may take up and debate any matter within the scope of the charter, and it may make whatever recommendation it chooses to the Security Council, the other UN organs, and any member-state. The recommendations it makes to UN members are not legally binding on them, but these recommendations do carry some considerable weight, for they have been approved by a significant number of the governments of the world.

>> The UN Security Council must come to a consensus to act on all substantive measures. If one permanent member casts a negative vote, the General Assembly can take up the issue.

The Security Council The UN's **Security Council** is made up of 15 members. Five—the United States, Britain, France, Russia (originally the Soviet Union's seat), and China—are permanent members. The General Assembly chooses the 10 non-permanent members for two-year terms; they cannot be immediately reelected. The council meets in continuous session.

The Security Council bears the UN's major responsibility for maintaining international peace. It may take up any matter involving a threat to or a breach of that peace, and it can adopt measures ranging from calling on the parties to settle their differences peacefully to placing economic and/or military sanctions on an offending nation. The only time the Security Council has undertaken a military operation against an aggressor came in Korea in 1950. It has, however, provided peacekeeping forces in several world trouble spots, with varying degrees of success.

On procedural questions—routine matters—decisions of the Security Council can be made by the affirmative vote of any nine members. On the more important matters, a negative vote by any one of the permanent members is enough to kill a resolution. Because of that veto power, the Security Council is effective only when and if the permanent members are willing to cooperate with one another.

The veto does not come into play in a situation in which one or more of the permanent members abstains. When, on June 25, 1950, the Security Council called on all UN members to aid South Korea in repelling the North Korean invasion, the Soviet delegate was boycotting sessions of the Security Council and so was not present to veto that action.

Economic and Social Council The Economic and Social Council (ECOSOC) is made up of 54 members elected by the General Assembly to three-year terms. It is responsible to the Assembly for carrying out the UN's many economic, cultural, educational, health, and related activities. It coordinates the work of the UN's specialized agencies—a number of independent international bodies that have a working relationship with the world organization. There are now 15 of these independent bodies—among the most notable: the World Health Organization (WHO), the International Monetary Fund (IMF), the World Bank Group, and the Food and Agriculture Organization (FAO).

International Court of Justice The International Court of Justice (ICJ), also known as the World Court, is the UN's judicial arm. A UN member may agree to

>> Many nations provide personnel for UN peacekeeping missions. This photograph shows a UN battalion in Mongolia, which provides nearly one thousand peacekeeping troops to missions in Darfur, the Western Sahara, South Sudan, and elsewhere.

accept the court's jurisdiction over cases in which it may be involved either unconditionally or with certain reservations (exceptions that may not conflict with the ICJ Statute).

The ICJ is made up of 15 judges selected for nine-year terms by the General Assembly and the Security Council. It sits in permanent session at the Peace Palace in The Hague, the Netherlands, and handles cases brought to it voluntarily by both members and nonmembers of the UN.

The Secretariat The civil service branch of the UN is the Secretariat. It is headed by the secretary-general, who is elected to a five-year term by the General Assembly on the recommendation of the Security Council.

The secretary-general heads a staff of tens of thousands who conduct the day-to-day work of the UN in New York and around the globe. Beyond administrative chores, the Charter gives the secretary-general the power to bring before the Security Council any matter that he or she believes poses a serious threat to international peace and security.

The secretary-general prepares the UN's two-year budget, which must be approved by the General Assembly. The budget is in the tens of billions, with nearly twice as much allocated for peacekeeping as for the regular budget. The Assembly apportions the UN's expenses for each two-year period among its member states.

Early on, the secretary-general was seen as little more than the UN's chief clerk. The post amounts to much more than that, however, because the men who have thus far held it transformed the office into a major channel for the negotiated settlement of international disputes.

☑ **CHECK UNDERSTANDING** What world events persuaded the United States to join the United Nations? How did this differ from its previous stance regarding American involvement in an international organization for peace?

The UN's Work

The purpose of the United Nations can be summed up this way: to make the world a better place. To that end, the UN is involved in a wide variety of activities.

Peacekeeping is a primary function of the United Nations. Over 100,000 military and civilian personnel provided by more than 100 member countries are currently engaged in the UN's global peacekeeping operations.

The UN's specialized agencies spend several billion dollars a year for economic and social programs to help the world's poorest nations. Those monies are beyond that loaned by the World Bank, the International Monetary Fund, and the other UN agencies that further development in poorer countries.

Health is the major concern of several UN agencies. A joint program of UNICEF and WHO has immunized 80 percent of the world's children against six killer diseases, and it is estimated that this program saves the lives of more than two million children a year. Smallpox, which plagued the world for centuries, has now been all but eliminated by a WHO-led campaign. Today, that organization coordinates a massive global effort to control the spread of AIDS and helps contend with other international health crises. For example, as the COVID-19 pandemic spread quickly across the globe in 2020, the UN set into motion a comprehensive plan to deal with the crisis.

The health of the environment is also a significant concern of the world organization. United Nations environmental conventions have helped reduce acid rain, lessened marine pollution, and phased out the production of gases that destroy the ozone layer. The UN also helped establish the Intergovernmental Panel on Climate Change. That body was created to examine the large volume of information about climate change generated by the scientific community and to help provide government decision-makers with accurate, balanced analysis of this data.

Human rights have long been a leading priority for the United Nations. In 1948, the UN drafted the Universal Declaration of Human Rights, and it has sponsored more than 80 treaties that help protect specific rights. Various United Nations agencies work to aid and protect refugees and displaced persons, and the international organization raises more than $1 billion a year for assistance to victims of war and natural disasters.

The UN and Nongovernmental Organizations

The UN also works closely with nongovernmental organizations, NGOs, around the world. As the name suggests, NGOs are independent of governments, and the list of issues and topics that they exist to address is nearly endless. On issues ranging from public health to the environment to the status of women, these groups perform valuable work around the world.

The United Nations actively seeks to partner with these organizations as a means of achieving its goals. A prime example is the International Committee of the Red Cross, a humanitarian NGO with which the UN works to assist victims of disasters ranging from military conflicts to those inflicted by Mother Nature. Another is 350.org, a multinational NGO whose efforts focus on ending fossil-fuel dependency and pressuring governments into passing laws that will help stop climate change.

UN Millennium Development Goals

1	Eradicate extreme poverty and hunger
2	Achieve universal primary education
3	Promote gender equality and empower women
4	Reduce child mortality
5	Improve maternal health
6	Combat HIV/AIDS, malaria and other diseases
7	Ensure environmental sustainability
8	Develop a global partnership for economic development

SOURCE: United Nations, un.org

>> The UN's Millennium Development Goals are a blueprint to which all member countries have committed. **Analyze Charts** Which of these goals reflect the UN's human rights objective?

The UN–U.S. Relationship The United States has a long and close relationship with the UN. It was President **Franklin D. Roosevelt** who, with Britain's **Winston Churchill**, first proposed the formation of the UN. The United States occupies a permanent place on the Security Council. Although the United States is one of the nearly 200 members of the UN, it funds almost a quarter of the UN budget. (Each member's contribution is roughly equal in proportion to its share of the world's gross domestic product.)

The relationship with the UN is complex, however. The United States has at times been critical of the UN. In fact, the United States has even withheld payment of funds to the institution. Also, the United States has not always agreed with some formal policy positions taken by the UN. In 2003, for example, the Bush administration was frustrated in its efforts to win UN support for military action against Iraq.

Yet, the United States often works closely with the UN on a variety of issues to further policies that are important to both, including environmental and humanitarian causes. For example, in 2014 the UN was closely involved with American efforts to destroy Syria's chemical weapons stockpiles and bring about a peaceful resolution to the conflict there.

☑ **APPLY CONCEPTS** In some circumstances, the United Nations lacks the resources to provide sufficient aid after a major disaster. How might the UN cope with such a situation?

The Organization of American States

The Organization of American States (OAS) includes the United States and over 30 other countries in North and South America. The OAS, formed in 1948, is a multinational alliance created to promote stability and cooperation in the Americas.

The OAS is concerned with a wide range of issues, among them strengthening democracy, ending poverty, building cybersecurity capabilities, and addressing environmental concerns. The group's environmental initiatives, for example, include efforts to "protect biodiversity, strengthen environmental law, manage water resources, raise awareness on climate change, and promote sustainability."

☑ **CONNECT** Why is ending poverty a key issue for the OAS?

>> Afghan girls take classes at a school funded by American actress Angelina Jolie, a goodwill ambassador for the UN High Commissioner for Refugees.

☑ ASSESSMENT

1. **Compare and Contrast** Compare and contrast the significance of foreign affairs to the United States at the time of its founding with its significance today.

2. **Describe** How and to what degree does the international community ensure the safety and welfare of representatives abroad?

3. **Infer** How does United States foreign aid affect the American economy?

4. **Analyze Information** How has the fall of the Soviet Union affected NATO's work?

5. **Apply Concepts** The UN General Assembly voted in favor of a measure that required action by several member nations. What action, if any, are those nations now likely to take?

6.6

The Salute to Our Troops parade in Hawaii features representatives of the five active duty services— the Army, Marines, Navy, Air Force, and Coast Guard.

 BOUNCE to Activate Flipped Video

Objectives

Summarize the functions, components, and organization of the Defense Department and its military departments.

Explain how the Director of National Intelligence and the Department of Homeland Security contribute to national security.

Key Terms

espionage
terrorism

National Security

How many federal agencies, in addition to the Department of State, are involved with the nation's foreign affairs? Dozens of them. Thus, the FBI combats terrorism and espionage. The Public Health Service works with the UN and foreign governments to conquer diseases in many parts of the world. USAID provides economic help to foreign countries. The Office of the United States Trade Representative promotes this country's interests in international trade.

The Department of Defense

A recitation of this sort could go on and on. But, as you will see, this section deals with those agencies most directly involved in the areas of foreign and defense policy.

Congress established what is today called the Department of Defense (DoD) in the National Security Act of 1947. It is the present-day successor to two historic Cabinet-level agencies: the War Department, created by Congress in 1789, and the Navy Department, created in 1798.

Congress created the Defense Department in order to unify the nation's armed forces. It wished to bring the then-separate Army (including the Air Force) and the Navy under the control of a single Cabinet department. Today, there are over 1 million men and women on active duty in the military, over 1 million in the National Guard and Reserves, and more than 700,000 civilians employed by the Defense Department. Their combined efforts in defending the nation ensure the protection of the rights of every American citizen.

The Framers and the Military The authors of the Constitution understood the importance of the nation's defense. They emphasized that fact clearly in the Preamble, and they underscored it in the body of the Constitution by mentioning defense more frequently than any other governmental function.

The Framers also recognized the dangers inherent in military power and the potential of its abuse. They knew that its very existence can pose a threat to free government. Therefore, the Constitution is studded with provisions to make sure that the military is always subject to the control of the nation's civilian authorities. Thus, the Constitution makes the elected President the commander in chief of the armed forces. To the same end, it gives broad military powers to Congress— that is, to the elected representatives of the people.

The principle of civilian control has always been a major factor in the making of defense policy and in the creation and staffing of the various agencies responsible for the execution of that policy. The importance of civilian control is clearly illustrated by this fact: The National Security Act of 1947 provides that the secretary of defense cannot have served on active duty in any of the armed forces for at least ten years before being named to that post, although that was reduced to seven years in 2008.

The Secretary of Defense The Department of Defense is headed by the secretary of defense, whose appointment by the President is subject to confirmation by the Senate. The secretary, who serves at the President's pleasure, is charged with two major responsibilities. He or she is simultaneously (1) the President's chief aide and advisor in making and carrying out defense policy, and (2) the operating head of the Defense Department.

The secretary's huge domain is often called the Pentagon—because of its massive five-sided headquarters building in Virginia, across the Potomac River from the Capitol. Its operations regularly take a large slice of the federal budget every year. For a time, the global war on terrorism forced vast increases in expenditures for the military. Spending rose from nearly $300 billion in fiscal year 2001, the year of the September 11 attacks, to an all-time high of nearly $680 billion in 2011. That figure dropped somewhat when the nation ended its large-scale operations in Iraq and Afghanistan but in later years it rose again.

The Joint Chiefs of Staff The six members of the Joint Chiefs of Staff serve as the principal military advisers to the secretary of defense, the President, and the National Security Council. This collective body is made up of the chairman of the Joint Chiefs, the vice chairman, the Army chief of staff, the chief of naval operations, the commandant of the Marine Corps, and the Air Force chief of staff. The highest-ranking uniformed officers in the armed

CIVILIAN CONTROL OF THE MILITARY

CIVILIAN

PRESIDENT
Directs the activities of the armed forces as constitutional commander in chief and is the nation's senior military authority

CONGRESS
Provides structure and funding for each of the armed forces

SECRETARY OF DEFENSE
Implements the President's national security policy by managing and directing the activities of the Defense Department

MILITARY

JOINT CHIEFS OF STAFF
Provide advice to the President, the National Security Council, and the Secretary of Defense on all military matters

UNIFIED COMMANDERS
Command the U.S. armed forces around the globe; are the direct link between the military forces and the President, and conduct military operations per their instruction

MILITARY DEPARTMENTS
Provide the Unified Commanders with the army, navy, and air force units for combat, peacekeeping, and humanitarian missions

➡ Chain of Communication ⇨ Chain of Command

>> Concerned about any potential threats to democracy, the Framers placed the military under civilian control. **Analyze Diagrams** In what way is the military able to influence civilian leadership?

>> The U.S. Army conducts maneuvers and special training exercises on a regular basis to improve their skills and maintain readiness.

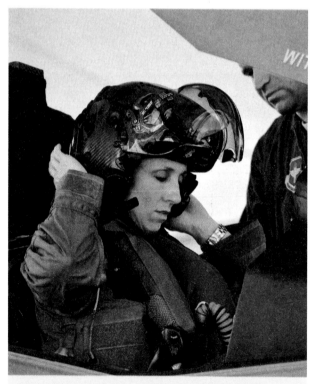

>> Although women have been in the Air Force in different capacities since World War II, it was not until the early 1990s that woman were permitted to become fighter pilots.

services, the members of the Joint Chiefs are named by the President, subject to Senate approval.

☑ **INFER** What might have happened had the Framers not placed control of the military in the hands of civilians?

Branches of the Military

Enlisting in the military is one way people can serve their country. Soldiers endure many hardships, but they also gain highly specialized job and leadership skills.

The three military departments—the Departments of the Army, the Navy, and the Air Force—are major units and sub-Cabinet departments within the Department of Defense. A civilian secretary, named by the President and directly responsible to the secretary of defense, leads each military department. The nation's armed forces—the Army, the Navy, and the Air Force—operate within that unified structure.

The Army The Army is the largest of the armed services, and the oldest. The American Continental Army, now the United States Army, was established by the Second Continental Congress on June 14, 1775.

The Army is essentially a ground-based force, and it is responsible for military operations on land. It must be ready (1) to defeat any attack on the United States itself, and (2) to take swift and forceful action to protect American interests in any other part of the world. To these ends, it must organize, train, and equip its active duty forces—the Regular Army, the Army National Guard, and the Army Reserve.

Over 575,000 Army National Guard soldiers and reservists were called to service between September 11, 2001, and May 2007, most of them for the wars in Afghanistan and Iraq. All of the Army's active duty personnel are under the command of the Army's highest-ranking officer, the Army chief of staff.

The Regular Army is the nation's standing Army, the heart of its land forces. There are now about 500,000 soldiers on active duty—officers and enlisted personnel, professional soldiers, and volunteers. The Army has been downsized in the post–cold war era, however. At the time of the collapse of the Soviet Union in 1991, there were more than 700,000 men and women on active duty.

Women make up less than 20 percent of the Army and now serve in all Army units, including the Special Forces. During the wars in Iraq and Afghanistan, the line between combat and noncombat roles became blurred. As a result, the

>> This painting depicts the 1779 Battle of Flamborough Head, in which the young United States Navy—in one of its first battles ever—overwhelmed two British ships off the northeast coast of Britain during the Revolutionary War.

Pentagon announced in 2015 that it would open all combat jobs to women.

The Army trains and equips its combat units to fight enemy forces. The infantry takes, holds, and defends land areas. The artillery supports the infantry, seeks to destroy enemy concentrations with its heavier guns, and gives anti-aircraft cover. The armored cavalry also supports the infantry, using armored vehicles and helicopters to spearhead assaults and oppose enemy counteroffensives.

Other units of the Army provide the many services and supplies in support of combat troops. Those soldiers could not fight without the help of members of the engineer, quartermaster, signal, ordnance, transportation, military police, and medical corps.

The Navy The United States Navy was first formed as the Continental Navy—a fledgling naval force created by the Second Continental Congress on October 13, 1775. Ever since, its major responsibility has been sea warfare.

The chief of naval operations is the Navy's highest-ranking officer and is responsible for its preparations and readiness for war and for its use in combat. Similar to the Army, the Navy's ranks also have been thinned in the post–cold war period. In 1955, for example, in the midst of the Cold War, there were double the number of officers and enlisted personnel in the Navy than there are today.

The Second Continental Congress established the United States Marine Corps (USMC) in 1775. Today, it operates as a separate armed service within the Navy Department, but it is not under the control of the chief of naval operations. Its commandant answers directly to the secretary of the Navy.

The Marines are a combat-ready land force for the Navy. They have two major combat missions: (1) to seize or defend land bases from which the ships and air power of the Navy and Marines can operate, and (2) to carry out other land operations essential to a naval campaign. The Marines have participated in every United States war. In fact, they have often been the first troops to see combat in those conflicts.

The Air Force The Air Force is the youngest of the military services. Congress established the United States Air Force (USAF) and made it a separate branch of the armed forces in the National Security Act of 1947. However, its history dates back to 1907, when the Army assigned an officer and two enlisted men to a new unit called the Aeronautical Division of the Army Signal Corps.

Although less than cold war levels, the Air Force has over 300,000 active duty members. The USAF is the nation's first line of defense. It has primary responsibility for military air and aerospace operations. In time of war, its major duties are to defend the United States; attack and defeat enemy air, ground, and sea forces; strike military and other war-related targets in enemy territory; and provide transport and combat support for land and naval operations.

The current era of nuclear weapons, delivered by long-range bombers and military drones, means that the Air Force will play a decisive role in any future conflict. The USAF is under the command of the chief of staff of the Air Force.

>> The operations center of the National Counterterrorism Center investigates threat reports and coordinates and shares real-time intelligence on terrorism.

>> This photo shows SIGSALY, a voice encryption system first used during World War II to protect communications between London and Washington, D.C.

The need to maintain dominion over space for national security reasons led to the creation of the U.S. Space Force in 2019, the first new military branch in over 70 years. The Chief of Space Operations commands the over 5,000 members of the USSF.

☑ **DRAW CONCLUSIONS** Over the years, three of the military branches have been downsized. Will they ever need to return to their cold war levels?

The Director of National Intelligence

The Director of National Intelligence (DNI) heads the Office of the Director of National Intelligence, established in 2005. The Office was born out of the pre-9/11 failure of the government's several intelligence agencies to collect and share information that might have warned of al Qaeda's coming attacks.

The Work of the DNI The President, with Senate approval, appoints the DNI, who is now the President's chief advisor in all matters relating to intelligence. The DNI supervises the operations of the agencies that make up the federal intelligence community and directs the work of the National Counterterrorism Center (NCTC). The NCTC's hundreds of specialists receive and evaluate all information gathered by the intelligence community and relay it to all those who have "the need to know." As the first DNI, John Negroponte, put it: "Our job is to integrate foreign, military, and domestic intelligence in defense of the homeland and of United States interests abroad."

Agencies Controlled by the DNI Some of the agencies controlled by the DNI are fairly well known, among them the FBI, the DEA, and the CIA. Indeed, for more than half a century, one of them, the Central Intelligence Agency, was—as its title suggests—the government's principal, its central, intelligence gathering organization. The CIA remains a major "cloak and dagger" agency, but the DNI now holds its once leading role in the intelligence community.

Some of the agencies in this community are little known, however, including the National Geospatial-Intelligence Agency, the Defense Intelligence Agency, and the world's largest spy organization, the National Security Agency. Much of their work involves **espionage**—spying—and is shrouded in deepest secrecy. Even Congress has generally shied away from more than a passing check on their activities, and their operating funds are disguised at several places in the federal budget each year.

Prevent Terrorism or Protect Civil Liberties?

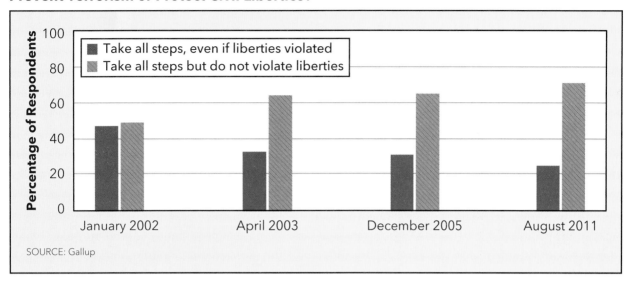

>> After the attacks by the Al Qaeda Islamist terrorist group, polling data showed that Americans were split on preventing terrorism and protecting civil liberties.
Analyze Charts How did these preferences change over the next ten years?

Balancing Security and Liberty Most Americans agree that the work of the several agencies that comprise the intelligence community is absolutely essential to the security of the United States. At the same time, however, both government leaders and the American people recognize the potential dangers of a group of government agencies whose operations are conducted in utmost secrecy.

The American people expect the government, through agencies such as the National Security Agency (NSA), to collect and analyze a vast array of information and to keep the country safe from terrorist attacks. At the same time, however, Americans expect a right to privacy. In fact, the Constitution speaks to this issue in several places, including the 3rd Amendment, which prohibits the quartering of soldiers in times of peace, and the 4th Amendment, which bars unreasonable searches of persons or property. Numerous Supreme Court decisions have also found privacy to be a fundamental right.

The issue of the tricky balance between national security and individual rights came to the fore in 2013, when Edward Snowden, a computer specialist and a former CIA and NSA employee, disclosed classified, top-secret information regarding government surveillance to the press. According to Snowden, he leaked the information because it showed that government intelligence agencies were illegally invading the privacy of innocent Americans. Specifically, his information revealed a secret court order allowing the Federal Government to access the phone records of millions of Americans.

President Obama and others in the administration defended the court order. They argued that the information was not only consistent with laws passed by Congress, but also necessary for national security.

The Snowden controversy underscored the sensitive nature of the work of the DNI and its agencies. It also stressed the need for vigilance on the part of the American people. Democracy requires that citizens are informed about what government is doing, that they participate in discussions about government policies and actions, and that they take the right to vote seriously, so that only the most trustworthy and qualified individuals serve in government. Only in this way can the delicate balance between security and liberty be maintained.

☑ **COMPARE POINTS OF VIEW** What are some of the arguments for and against secret intelligence agencies?

The Department of Homeland Security

The Department of Homeland Security (DHS) is charged with the awesome and complex task of protecting the United States against terrorism. **Terrorism** is the use of violence to intimidate a government or a society, usually for political or ideological reasons.

Congress created the department in 2002, and it became operational in 2003. It is responsible for the

>> Many federal agencies, including customs, immigration, and border patrol, as well as State troopers and private security organizations, work to protect the Trans-Alaska pipeline from terrorist attack.

coordination and the direction of all anti-terrorist activities of all of the public agencies that operate in the field of domestic security—including thousands of police departments, fire departments, emergency medical and search and rescue units, and other disaster response agencies across the country.

The Work of the Department of Homeland Security The Homeland Security Act of 2002 gives the department major operating responsibilities in five specific areas:

- border and transportation security
- infrastructure protection
- emergency preparedness and response
- chemical, biological, radiological, and nuclear defense
- information analysis (intelligence)

The department was built mostly of agencies transferred to it from other Cabinet departments. Those agencies include the Secret Service and the newly entitled U.S. Immigration and Customs Enforcement (ICE), from the Treasury Department; the Coast Guard and the Transportation Security Administration, from the Transportation Department; the renamed U.S. Citizenship and Immigration Services, from the Justice Department; and the independent Federal Emergency Management Agency (FEMA).

A Daunting Task The threat of bioterrorism—the use of such biological agents as smallpox or anthrax as weapons—dramatizes the immensity of the problems facing the Department of Homeland Security. So, too, do these facts: There are more than 600,000 bridges, about 155,000 water systems, and more than 6,000 power plants (with 104 nuclear reactors) in the United States. There are also some 140,000 miles of rail lines, 2.1 million miles of natural gas pipelines, and 25,000 miles of inland waterways. Additionally, there are hundreds of skyscrapers, more than 13,000 airports (including some 300 major facilities), thousands of stadiums and other large gathering places, and more than 7,000 miles of international border with Canada and Mexico.

Add to those fundamental facts such critical matters as the nation's food and water supply, its healthcare system, and its communications networks, and this point becomes clear: The task of protecting the United States against terrorist acts is a daunting one. Despite the enormity of that task, the DHS is charged with (1) preventing most—if not all—terrorist attacks, and (2) bringing those responsible for any attempted attacks to justice.

☑ **INFER** Why is the threat of bioterrorism such an immense issue for the Department of Homeland Security?

☑ ASSESSMENT

1. **Interpret** How did the Framers of the Constitution address the importance of the military?

2. **Analyze Information** A vast increase in defense spending in recent years may be attributed to what events or changes?

3. **Apply Concepts** What is a potential benefit and a potential negative impact of the work of the DNI?

4. **Connect** Why does the author consider the work of the Department of Homeland Security to be such a daunting task?

5. **Compare** Compare the United States Army and Air Force in terms of responsibilities and size.

GO ONLINE to www.SavvasRealize.com and access your digital course

Use the following online resources to practice citizenship skills and prepare for the Topic Test.

Case Studies

Current Connections

Quest Inquiries

Quizzes

Interactivities

Texts

Flipped Videos

While online you can also check the progress you've made learning the topic and course content by viewing your grades, test scores, and assignment status.

Topic 6 Quick Study Guide

LESSON SUMMARIES
Use these Lesson Summaries, and the longer versions available online, to review the key ideas for each lesson in this Topic.

Lesson 1: The Federal Bureaucracy
A bureaucracy is a large, complex structure that handles the everyday business of an organization. The President leads the federal bureaucracy, directing a large number of agencies. These include Cabinet-level departments such as the Departments of State and Defense, and many others.

Lesson 2: The EOP and the Executive Departments

Part of the work of the executive branch is carried out by the Executive Office of the President (EOP) and the executive departments. The EOP includes the President's chief of staff and closest advisors. It manages a variety of offices and agencies. The executive departments are headed by members of the Cabinet.

Lesson 3: The Independent Agencies
Independent agencies are agencies created by Congress outside of the executive departments. Most of these are independent executive agencies, such as the Environmental Protection Agency. Others are independent regulatory commissions, which are largely outside the President's control. Government corporations, such as Amtrak, perform businesslike activities for the government.

Lesson 4: Foreign Policy Overview
Foreign policy includes every aspect of a nation's relationship with other countries. Over time, the United States has moved from a policy of isolationism to one of increasing involvement around the world. Today, the United States faces many foreign policy challenges in the Middle East and elsewhere.

Lesson 5: Diplomacy
The State Department, headed by the Secretary of State, advises the President on foreign affairs and dispatches ambassadors to foreign countries. The United States also engages with the world by providing foreign aid, and through involvement in international organizations such as NATO and the United Nations.

Lesson 6: National Security
Many agencies are responsible for national security. The Department of Defense includes the Army, the Navy, and the Air Force. It is led by the Secretary of Defense, who is appointed by the President. The Department of Homeland Security and the agencies run by the Director of National Intelligence also work to keep the nation secure.

VISUAL REVIEW

Use these graphics to review some of the key terms, people, and ideas from this Topic.

Structure of the Executive Branch

EXECUTIVE OFFICE OF THE PRESIDENT	EXECUTIVE DEPARTMENTS	INDEPENDENT AGENCIES
• The White House comprises the President's key personal and political staff • National Security Council advises on matters relating to national security • OMB prepares federal budget and assists in executive branch management • Other units provide advice on issues ranging from the economy to foreign affairs • Includes: White House Office, National Security Council, Office of Management and Budget	• Traditional units of the federal administration • Built around broad fields of authority • Headed by a department secretary, serving as link between presidential policy and department • Structured geographically, with much work done through regional offices • Includes: State, Treasury, Defense, Commerce	• Located outside the executive departments • Created by Congress to perform specific functions • Nature and purpose vary from agency to agency • These include: Amtrak, CIA, Environmental Protection Agency, United States Post Office

Key American Foreign Policies

MONROE DOCTRINE	Isolates the U.S. from international affairs unless North or South America is threatened.
ROOSEVELT COROLLARY	Extends the Monroe Doctrine by giving the U.S. the authority to intervene in the affairs of Latin America.
GOOD NEIGHBOR POLICY	Reduces American political and military interference in Latin America.
DETERRENCE	Maintains that superior military strength will deter hostile powers from attacking the nation.
TRUMAN DOCTRINE	Affirms that the U.S. will oppose any aggressor's attempt to control another nation and its people.
CONTAINMENT	Prevents the spread of Communism by assisting threatened nations.
DÉTENTE	Reduces tensions between the United States and both the Soviet Union and China.
COLLECTIVE SECURITY	Brings nations together to resist any nation that threatens the peace.

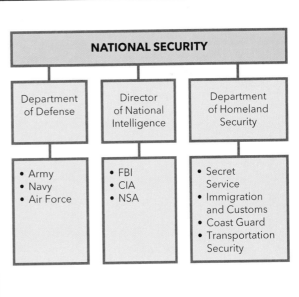

NATIONAL SECURITY

Department of Defense
- Army
- Navy
- Air Force

Director of National Intelligence
- FBI
- CIA
- NSA

Department of Homeland Security
- Secret Service
- Immigration and Customs
- Coast Guard
- Transportation Security

Topic 6 Assessment

KEY TERMS, PEOPLE, AND IDEAS

1. What is the **draft**, and how does it relate to one of the responsibilities of male citizens at the federal level?

2. What is a **bureaucracy**?

3. What is **patronage**?

4. What was the policy of **containment**?

5. Define the policy of **deterrence**.

6. What are **passports** and **visas**?

7. What is the **civil service**?

8. Define **terrorism**.

CRITICAL THINKING

9. **Make Generalizations** Do you think the bureaucratic organization of the Federal Government makes it more or less effective?

10. **Express Ideas Clearly** Identify the impact of independent executive agencies and independent regulatory commissions in the federal bureaucracy, including the Federal Reserve, the Food and Drug Administration (FDA), and the Federal Communications Commission (FCC).

11. **Evaluate** How do public health policies and government regulations influence health promotion and disease prevention? Refer to Health and Human Services (HHS), Centers for Disease Control and Prevention (CDC), the Food and Drug Administration (FDA), and the Occupational Safety and Health Administration (OSHA) in your answer.

12. **Explain** How can nongovernmental organizations improve civil society?

13. **Summarize** How has the United Nations worked to protect human rights around the world?

14. **Support Ideas with Examples** How does government affect the daily life of citizens at the local, State, and national levels? Give examples.

15. **Interpret** How does the government seek to balance national security and individual rights? How does the Constitution speak to this issue?

16. **Evaluate Data** The chart at the top of the next column shows the percentages of federal civilian employment by branch of the federal government. Which branch is the largest? Why is this the case? What does the Constitution say about the organization of this branch?

Federal Civilian Employment by Branch

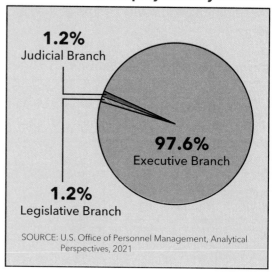

1.2% Judicial Branch

97.6% Executive Branch

1.2% Legislative Branch

SOURCE: U.S. Office of Personnel Management, Analytical Perspectives, 2021

17. **Make Generalizations** How has the United States joined with other countries to combat terrorism around the world? What challenges do these efforts pose in terms of international humanitarian law?

18. **Express Ideas Clearly** What is the difference between isolationism and internationalism? When and why did the United States stop pursuing a largely isolationist foreign policy? What are the advantages and disadvantages of an internationalist foreign policy?

19. **Describe** How do multinational alliances such as the United Nations and NATO work together to combat climate change? What further steps can be taken?

20. **Compare** Compare the United Nation's 1948 Universal Declaration of Human Rights with the Bill of Rights in the American Constitution. Both documents are available in the online resources for this course. What similarities can you find in the two documents? What differences?

21. **Writing Activity** Choose two of the following countries, then research and write a case study in which you describe the conditions that gave rise to tyrannies in these countries during the time periods noted: Italy (1919–1939), Japan (1929–1939), Haiti (1957–1971), Nigeria (1979–1999), Cambodia (1975–1979).

DOCUMENT-BASED QUESTIONS

Spending on American foreign aid has often raised criticism.

DOCUMENT A

When lawmakers proposed reducing foreign aid, Senator Patrick Leahy weighed in.

> Foreign aid today is . . . widely misunderstood. It is viewed by many as a form of charity, or a luxury . . . , or as a sizable part of the federal budget. It is none of those things.
>
> What we call "foreign aid" . . . promotes U.S. exports, supports democratic elections, combats poverty, and helps build alliances with countries to counter terrorism, thwart drug trafficking, protect the environment, and stop cross-border crime. . . .
>
> The world is changing, and we cannot afford to retreat or to succumb to isolationism. Funding that enables us to engage with allies, competitors, and adversaries helps us meet growing threats to our struggling economy and our security.
>
> —Senator Patrick Leahy (D., Vermont), "Cuts to Foreign Aid Cost the U.S. Globally," US News, 2011

DOCUMENT B

Congressman John Mica gives his viewpoint on foreign aid spending on his web site.

> The time to eliminate many of our foreign aid programs is overdue. It is hard for me to understand why we lavish money on foreign countries when the United States continues to work to improve our economy, face recent extraordinary deficit spending and our ever growing large national debt.
>
> I strongly believe that it is time for us to reexamine our entire approach to foreign aid. In my view, we have very limited resources and we should be spending our funds on promoting business, commerce and trade programs that directly benefit job growth here in the United States. . . . Foreign aid can be useful, but we cannot keep playing the rich uncle for every country seeking a handout.
>
> —Representative John Mica (R., Florida), mica.house.gov

DOCUMENT C

This cartoon comments on the amount of foreign aid that intended recipients actually receive.

DOCUMENT D

The information below describes how U.S. foreign aid fits into the overall budget.

> The United States spent $20,975 million on foreign aid in 2015. This was out of total U.S. spending of $3,687,622 million. In comparison, $90,031 million was spent on education and $562,506 million on defense. Over recent years, spending on foreign aid has been as follows, for the years 2007, 2009, 2011, 2013, and 2015: $12,752 million; $14,797 million; $20,583 million; $19,672 million; and $20,950 million.
>
> —Based on Budget of the United States Government, Fiscal Year 2015

22. Does the information in Document D support or refute the statement in Document A that foreign aid is not a sizeable part of the federal budget?
    A. refutes
    B. supports
    C. neither refutes nor supports
    D. refutes in part and supports in part

23. **Analyze Political Cartoons** What point is the cartoonist making about U.S. foreign aid?

24. **Writing Task** Use the information in Document D to draw and label two graphs: 1) a pie graph showing the percentage of foreign aid versus other types of spending; and 2) a line graph showing foreign aid spending from 2007–2015. Then write a paragraph in which you use the information in your graphs and Documents A, B, and C to take a position on foreign aid spending, defend your position, and then critique the opposing position.

The Judicial Branch

ESSENTIAL QUESTION How Should We Handle Conflict?

Contemplation of Justice sits on the west side of the U.S. Supreme Court building

Connections to Today

The Supreme Court and the air you breathe—are they related? After Congress approved the creation of the Environmental Protection Agency in 1970, an argument arose about whether the agency had the authority to regulate greenhouse gases. Massachusetts and other States sued the EPA in 2006 and the case went all the way to the Supreme Court. That one case led to air quality regulations that have had a major impact on the air we breathe. The courts often play a central role in Americans' lives—in ways you may not have expected.

NBC LEARN

Explore the Supreme Court's role in the fight for civil rights and equality.

 BOUNCE to Activate My Story Video

In this Topic, you will learn about the judicial branch of the Federal Government, which consists of the district courts, the courts of appeals, the special courts, and the United States Supreme Court. It is the responsibility of these courts to interpret the laws passed by Congress. Look at the lesson outline and explore the timeline. As you study this Topic, you can work on your Quest Inquiry.

LESSON OUTLINE

7.1 The National Judiciary

7.2 The Supreme Court

7.3 The Inferior Courts and the Special Courts

The Evolution of the National Judiciary

1789

The Judiciary Act of 1789 sets up a federal court system with broad jurisdiction while respecting the role of State courts. Three federal courts are established: Supreme Court, district courts, circuit courts.

1925

Congress mandates that only a few types of cases can be reviewed in the Supreme Court.

1968

Congress establishes the position of magistrate judge, whose job is to oversee pretrial proceedings.

1750   1800   1850   1900   1950   2000

1891

The Evarts Act establishes separate courts of appeals in the nine circuits, in order to relieve the load on Supreme Court justices.

1939

The Administrative Office of the U.S. Courts is established to provide administrative support to the judicial branch.

1988

Congress eliminates nearly all required appellate jurisdiction from the Supreme Court.

Inquiry Center

Want to become an active and effective citizen? Make a difference in your community and beyond by using the **Inquiry Center** on the digital course.

Connect with issues you're passionate about by using the **Interest Finder**.

Investigate public policies, get involved in your community, influence public opinion, and develop leadership skills.

Synthesize the work you've done and what you've learned along the way.

Demonstrate what you've learned once you've finished your project by sharing your work.

7.1

Sandra Day O'Connor, nominated to the Supreme Court by President Ronald Reagan, was rejected by 40 law firms following her graduation from law school because she was a woman.

 BOUNCE to Activate Flipped Video

Objectives

Explain why the Constitution created a national judiciary, and analyze its structure and functions.

Identify the criteria that determine whether a case is within the jurisdiction of a federal court, and compare the types of jurisdiction.

Outline the process for appointing federal judges, and list their terms of office.

Understand the impact of judicial philosophy, and analyze issues raised by judicial activism and judicial restraint.

Examine the roles of court officers.

Key Terms

inferior courts
jurisdiction
concurrent
  jurisdiction
plaintiff
defendant
original jurisdiction
appellate jurisdiction
judicial restraint
precedent

judicial activism
Sandra Day
  O'Connor
Thurgood Marshall
District of Columbia

The National Judiciary

As the ideas of self-government and fundamental civil liberties began to emerge in colonial America, colonists cast a critical eye on the courts. Corrupt, tyrannical leaders throughout history had used many tactics to maintain control, including exerting undue influence on the legal process. Those who acted against these rulers would be arrested and jailed without a trial, for example, quite often without ever being charged with a crime. Even for those lucky enough to stand before the court, a guilty verdict was inevitable. By controlling the court system, corrupt leaders could control the people.

The Courts and Democracy

It is telling that one of the earliest struggles between the colonists and the British involved the court system. In 1733, the British governor of New York, William Cosby, replaced a popular judge with a friend, a person alleged to be both corrupt and incompetent. This caused great indignation among the colonists in New York, and soon a newspaper, the *New York Weekly Journal*, began running a series of articles critical of the governor. Cosby responded by putting the editor of the paper, Peter Zenger, in jail. Even though he was clearly guilty, based on libel laws at the time, the colonial jury found Zenger not guilty because the stories he had printed were based on fact. The trial of Peter Zenger was widely followed and is still important today, not only because it dealt with freedom of the press, but also because it highlights the importance the colonists placed on an impartial court system.

    It is also notable that much of the Bill of Rights addresses the rights of the accused. The 4th Amendment, for example, forbids illegal searches and establishes the need for probable cause; the 6th Amendment speaks to jury trials. These safeguards were put in place to ensure that leaders in the United States could not maintain power by manipulating the courts.

Finally, the Framers of the Constitution thought it essential that federal judges be separated from public pressures, as well as from coercion from the other branches of government. This is why it is stipulated that federal judges be appointed, rather than elected, that they serve for life, and that their pay cannot be reduced while they serve. Judges are to make decisions based on the law, without facing the prospect of removal for issuing an unpopular decision. Put in another way, the Framers of our system believed that in a functioning democracy, the law would rule—not tyrants or popular opinion.

☑ **INTERPRET** How did Zenger's trial demonstrate the need for an impartial court system?

Creation of a National Judiciary

During the years the Articles of Confederation were in force (1781–1789), there were no national courts and no national judiciary. The laws of the United States were interpreted and applied as each State saw fit, and sometimes not at all. Disputes between States and between persons who lived in different States were decided, if at all, by the courts in one of the States involved. Often, decisions by the courts in one State were ignored by courts in the other States.

Alexander Hamilton spoke to the point in *The Federalist* No. 22. He described "the want of a judiciary power" as a "circumstance which crowns the defects of the Confederation." Arguing the need for a federal court system, he added, "Laws are a dead letter without courts to expound and define their true meaning and operation."

The Framers created a national judiciary in the following single sentence in the Constitution.

> The judicial Power of the United States shall be vested in one supreme Court, and in such inferior Courts as the Congress may from time to time ordain and establish.

—Article III, Section 1

Congress also is given the expressed power "to constitute Tribunals inferior to the supreme Court"— that is, create the rest of the federal court system—in Article I, Section 8, Clause 9.

A Dual Court System: Federal Courts and State Courts Keep in mind this important point about the structure of the court systems in the United States: There are *two* separate court systems. On the one hand, the federal court system spans the country with its more than 100 courts. On the other hand, each of the 50 States has its own system of courts. Their numbers run well into the thousands, and most of the cases that are heard in court today are heard in those State, not the federal, courts.

The First Type of Federal Court: Constitutional Courts The Constitution establishes the Supreme Court and leaves to Congress the creation of the **inferior courts**—the lower federal courts, those beneath the Supreme Court. Over the years, Congress has created two distinct types of federal courts: (1) the constitutional courts, and (2) the special courts.

The constitutional courts are those federal courts that Congress has formed under Article III to exercise "the judicial Power of the United States." Together with the Supreme Court, they now include the courts of appeals (also called the circuit courts), the district courts, and the U.S. Court of International Trade. The constitutional courts are also called the regular courts and, sometimes, Article III courts.

>> Alexander Hamilton favored a federal judiciary with the power to settle State disputes and override State laws. He advocated a strong federal court system in several of his *Federalist* essays.

The Second Type of Federal Court: Special Court The special courts do not exercise the broad "judicial Power of the United States." Rather, they have been created by Congress to hear cases arising out of some of the expressed powers given to Congress in Article I, Section 8. The special courts hear a much narrower range of cases than those that may come before the constitutional courts.

These special courts are also called the legislative courts and, sometimes, Article I courts. Today, they include the U.S. Court of Appeals for the Armed Forces, the U.S. Court of Appeals for Veterans Claims, the U.S. Court of Federal Claims, the U.S. Tax Court, the various territorial courts, and the courts of the District of Columbia.

☑ **HYPOTHESIZE** Why did the Framers see a need for a federal court system?

Jurisdiction in the Federal Court System

The constitutional courts hear most of the cases tried in the federal courts. That is to say, those courts have jurisdiction over most federal cases.

>> A ship capsizes, sending its cargo into the sea. Problems caused by accidents, such as oil spills and the recovery of goods and wreckage, fall under the federal umbrella of admiralty law.

Jurisdiction is defined as the authority of a court to hear (to *try* and to *decide*) a case. The term means, literally, the power "to say the law."

The Constitution gives federal courts jurisdiction over only certain cases. Recall, most cases heard in court in the United States are heard in State, not federal, courts. Article III, Section 2 provides that the federal courts may hear cases either because of (1) the *subject matter* or (2) the *parties* involved in those cases.

Subject Matter In terms of subject matter, the federal courts may hear a case if it involves a "federal question"—that is, the interpretation and application of a provision in the Constitution or in any federal statute or treaty—or a question of admiralty or maritime law.

Admiralty law related to matters that arise on the high seas of the navigable waters of the United States, such as a collision at sea or a crime committed aboard a ship. Maritime law relates to matters that arise on land but are directly related to the water, such as a contract to deliver ship supplies and dockside.

The Framers purposefully gave the federal courts exclusive jurisdiction in all admiralty and maritime cases in order to ensure national supremacy in the regulation of all waterborne commerce.

Parties A case falls within the jurisdiction of the federal courts if one of the parties involved in the case is (1) the United States or one of its officers or agencies; (2) an ambassador, consul, or other official representative of a foreign government; (3) one of the 50 States suing another State, a resident of another State, or a foreign government or one of its subjects; (4) a citizen of one State suing a citizen of another State; (5) an American citizen suing a foreign government or one of its subjects; or (6) a citizen of a State suing another citizen of that same State where both claim title to land under grants from different States.

These criteria for determining which cases can be heard in the federal courts may seem quite complicated, and they are. But the matter is also a reflection of Federalism and, so, of the dual system of courts in this country. To put the whole point of the jurisdiction of the federal courts the other way around: those cases that are not heard by the federal courts fall within the jurisdiction of the State courts.

☑ **APPLY CONCEPTS** How is the matter of federal court jurisdiction a reflection of federalism in the United States?

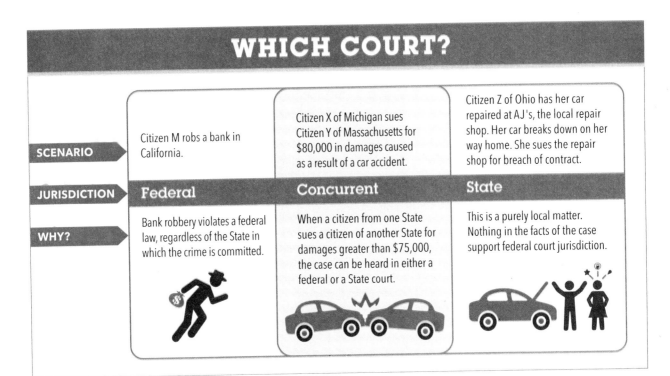

WHICH COURT?

SCENARIO	Citizen M robs a bank in California.	Citizen X of Michigan sues Citizen Y of Massachusetts for $80,000 in damages caused as a result of a car accident.	Citizen Z of Ohio has her car repaired at AJ's, the local repair shop. Her car breaks down on her way home. She sues the repair shop for breach of contract.
JURISDICTION	Federal	Concurrent	State
WHY?	Bank robbery violates a federal law, regardless of the State in which the crime is committed.	When a citizen from one State sues a citizen of another State for damages greater than $75,000, the case can be heard in either a federal or a State court.	This is a purely local matter. Nothing in the facts of the case support federal court jurisdiction.

>> Two separate court systems, federal and State, hear cases in the United States. **Analyze Information** What does this infographic tell you about the jurisdictions of these two court systems?

Types of Jurisdiction

Still more must be said on this quite complex matter of federal court jurisdiction. The federal courts exercise both *exclusive* and *concurrent* jurisdiction and, also, original and appellate jurisdiction.

Exclusive Jurisdiction Most of the cases that can be heard in the federal courts fall within their exclusive jurisdiction. That is, they can be tried *only* in the federal courts. Thus, a case involving an ambassador or some other official of a foreign government cannot be heard in a State court; it *must* be tried in a federal court. The trial of a person charged with a federal crime, or a suit involving the infringement of a patent or a copyright, or one involving any other matter arising out of an act of Congress is also within the exclusive (sole) jurisdiction of the federal courts.

Concurrent Jurisdiction Some cases may be tried in either a federal *or* a State court. Then, the federal and State courts have **concurrent jurisdiction,** meaning they share the power to hear these cases. Disputes involving citizens of different States are fairly common examples of this type of case. Such cases are known in the law as cases in diverse citizenship.

Congress has provided that a federal district court may hear a case of diverse citizenship only when the amount of money involved in that case is at least $75,000. In such a case, the **plaintiff**—the person who files the suit—may bring the case in the proper State or federal court, as he or she chooses. If the plaintiff brings the case in a State court, the **defendant**—the person against whom the complaint is made—can have the trial moved, under certain circumstances, to the federal district court.

Original and Appellate Jurisdiction A court in which a case is first heard is said to have **original jurisdiction** over that case. That court, the trial court, is often described as "the court of first instance." A court that hears a case on appeal from a lower court exercises **appellate jurisdiction** over that case. Appellate comes from the word *appellare*, "meaning to speak to, to call upon, to appeal to."

Appellate courts do not retry cases. Rather, they determine whether a trial court has acted in accord with applicable law. The higher court—the appellate court—may uphold, overrule, or in some way modify the decision appealed from the lower court.

In the federal judiciary, the district courts have only original jurisdiction, and the courts of appeals have only appellate jurisdiction. The Supreme Court exercises both original and (most often) appellate jurisdiction.

☑ **APPLY CONCEPTS** Why would a lawsuit involving the infringement of a patent or a copyright be considered the exclusive jurisdiction of the federal courts?

Federal Judges and Court Officers

Each federal court is headed by a judge. In virtually every type of court, judges have the same general duties.

The Role of Judges The first role of a judge is to preside over the courtroom. This means that he or she ensures that lawyers, plaintiffs, defendants, and witnesses follow proper courtroom procedures. The judge must also interpret the law as it applies to a particular case, including deciding whether the evidence is admissible. In trials that do not use a jury, the judge must rule on the facts and decide the case. Finally, a judge sentences those convicted of crimes or awards damages in a civil trial.

Unlike the members of Congress, who make laws based on the will of the majority, or the President, who carries out the laws passed by Congress, judges are *interpreters* of the law. The Framers purposely separated these powers so that the courts could impartially evaluate the constitutionality of laws and act as a check on the legislative and executive branches. Other elected officials make decisions based on the will of the majority, while judges make decisions based on the law.

Selection The manner in which federal judges are chosen, the terms for which they serve, and even the salaries they are paid are vital parts of the Constitution's design of an independent judicial branch. In Article II, Section 2, Clause 2, the Constitution declares that the President "shall nominate, and by and with the Advice and Consent of the Senate, shall appoint . . . Judges of the supreme Court . . .".

First, in the Judiciary Act of 1789, and ever since, Congress has provided the same procedure for the selection of all federal judges.

The Senate has a major part in the selection of every federal judge. In effect, the Constitution says that the President can name to the federal bench anyone whom the Senate will confirm. The practice of senatorial courtesy gives great weight to the wishes of the senators from a State in which a federal judge is to serve. That unwritten rule means that the President almost always selects someone the senators from that State recommend.

Unlike the qualifications it sets for members of Congress and the President, the Constitution sets no age, residence, or citizenship requirements for

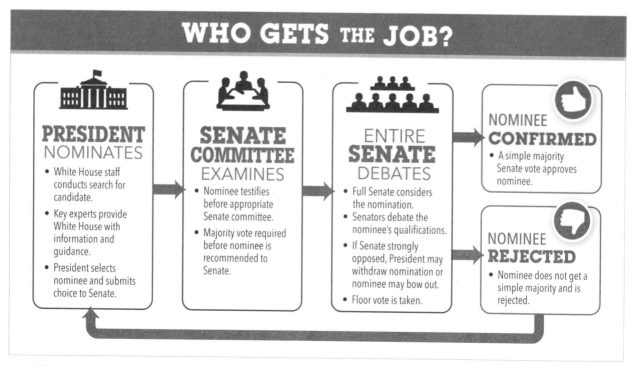

WHO GETS THE JOB?

PRESIDENT NOMINATES
- White House staff conducts search for candidate.
- Key experts provide White House with information and guidance.
- President selects nominee and submits choice to Senate.

SENATE COMMITTEE EXAMINES
- Nominee testifies before appropriate Senate committee.
- Majority vote required before nominee is recommended to Senate.

ENTIRE SENATE DEBATES
- Full Senate considers the nomination.
- Senators debate the nominee's qualifications.
- If Senate strongly opposed, President may withdraw nomination or nominee may bow out.
- Floor vote is taken.

NOMINEE CONFIRMED
- A simple majority Senate vote approves nominee.

NOMINEE REJECTED
- Nominee does not get a simple majority and is rejected.

>> This infographic shows the process by which Supreme Court justices and other presidential appointees are selected and confirmed. **Analyze Charts** Why is this multi-step process necessary?

federal judges. Nor does it require that a judge have a professional background in the law.

Influences on the Selection of Judges The President's closest legal and political aides, especially the Attorney General, take the lead in selecting federal judges. Influential senators—especially those from the nominee's home State and members of the Judiciary Committee, the President's allies and supporters in the legal profession, and various members of the President's political party also play a major role in selecting judges. Several interest groups are also quite influential in the process.

Today, an increasing number of those persons who are appointed to the federal bench have had prior judicial experience. Most federal judges are drawn from the ranks of leading attorneys, legal scholars and law school professors, former members of Congress, and State court judges. Elective office (in particular, a seat in the U.S. Senate) was once a well-traveled path to the Supreme Court; now, most justices reach the High Court from the courts of appeals.

History Concerning Judgeships Since **Sandra Day O'Connor** became the first woman appointed to the Supreme Court in 1981, several other women have also joined the Court: Ruth Bader Ginsburg (1993), Sonia Sotomayor (2009), Elena Kagan (2010), and Amy Coney Barrett (2020). Justice Sotomayor is also the Court's first Hispanic member. Only two Black Americans have thus far become justices: **Thurgood Marshall** (appointed in 1967) and Clarence Thomas (1991).

From George Washington's day, Presidents have looked to their own political party to fill judgeships. Republican Presidents usually choose Republicans; Democrats generally pick Democrats. Every President knows that judges may serve for decades. So chief executives regularly look for ethical, well-versed jurists who tend to agree with their own general views.

The selection and confirmation of Supreme Court justices and federal judges can sometimes cause controversy, particularly in the last few decades. Partisan politics has played a larger-than-usual part in the process, to the point where a longstanding rule requiring 60 votes to confirm an appointee (the number of votes needed to break a Senate filibuster) were changed. Supreme Court appointments now require only a simple majority to be confirmed.

Judicial Philosophies Another major impact on the judicial selection process is judicial philosophy—in particular, the concepts of judicial restraint and judicial activism. All federal judges make decisions in which they must interpret and apply provisions in the Constitution and acts of Congress. That is, they often decide questions of public policy—and, in doing so, they inevitably *shape* public policy.

Although the line between the two judicial philosophies can become blurred, the proponents of **judicial restraint** believe that judges should decide cases on the basis of (1) the original intent of the Framers or those who enacted the statute(s) involved in a case, and (2) **precedent**—a judicial decision that serves as a guide for settling later cases of a similar nature. They say that the courts should defer to policy judgments made in the legislative and executive branches of the government and, in so doing, honor the basic premise of self-government: the right of the majority to determine public policy. In short, they argue that elected legislators, not appointed judges, should make law.

Those who support **judicial activism** take a much broader view of judicial power. They argue that provisions in the Constitution and in statute law should be interpreted and applied in the light of ongoing changes in conditions and values—especially in cases involving civil rights and social welfare issues.

They, too, insist on the fundamental importance of majority rule and the value of precedents, but they believe that judges should be willing to strike down precedents when necessary and to judge the constitutionality of a law or government action in broader terms. In other words, legislators are brought to power through "majority rule" (elections) and this process can sometimes thwart individual civil liberties. For example, most legislators (and their constituents) likely opposed racial desegregation in the 1950s, but cases brought before the Court for review would allow the justices to ensure that civil liberties were not violated.

The Effect of Judicial Philosophies Over time, both judicial philosophies have had far-reaching effects on American society. When the Supreme Court has taken a restrained approach, it has left matters in the hands of the executive and legislative branches.

In *Ling* v. *Northwest Indian Cemetery Protective Association*, 1988, for example, the Court refused to block the U.S. Forest Service from building a road through lands that were of religious importance to Native Americans, ruling that the road did not actually prohibit the free exercise of religion. In the wake of that decision, Congress designated the site a wilderness area, thereby stopping the road construction. In other cases, however, such as *Plessy v. Ferguson*, 1896, which upheld the segregation of African Americans in railroad coaches, Congress refused to act. As a result, segregation remained the law of the land for more than fifty years.

Some Chief Justices have led Courts that tended, throughout their tenure, toward either judicial restraint or judicial activism. The Warren Court (1953–1969) is generally considered to have been an activist court, making decisions that had a profound effect on American society and culture. Its rulings brought about striking change in the areas of minority rights, criminal proceedings, congressional reapportionment, and the separation of church and state, to name a few.

Conversely, the Rehnquist Court (1986–2005), is seen by many as having been more likely to practice judicial restraint, and its decisions were generally more conservative than those of the Warren Court. During the Rehnquist years, the Court sided in favor of States' rights, rather than with federal power. In fact, the Rehnquist Court struck down more federal laws than either the Warren or Burger (1969–1986) courts.

Terms of Judges Article III, Section 1 of the Constitution reads, in part: "The Judges, both of the supreme and inferior Courts, shall hold their Offices during good Behaviour. . . . " This means that the judges of the constitutional courts are appointed for life; they serve until they resign, retire, or die in office. The Framers provided for what amounts to life tenure for these judges quite purposefully, to ensure the independence of the federal judiciary.

The very next words of the Constitution are directed to that same purpose. Article III, Section 1 of the Constitution deals with compensation for federal judges: "and [they] shall, at stated Times, receive for their Services, a Compensation, which shall not be diminished during their Continuance in Office."

Federal judges may be removed from office only through the impeachment process. In 180 years, fewer than 20 have ever been impeached. Of that number, only a handful were convicted and removed by the Senate.

Those judges who sit on the special courts are not appointed for life. They are named, instead, to terms of 8–15 years—and may be, but seldom are, reappointed. In the **District of Columbia**, Superior Court judges are chosen for four-year terms; those who sit on the district's Court of Appeals are chosen for a period of eight years.

Salaries and Duties of Federal Judges Congress sets the salaries of federal judges and has provided a

Types of Inferior Federal Courts

Courts	CONSTITUTIONAL COURTS				SPECIAL COURTS					
	District Courts	U.S. Courts of Appeals	U.S. Court of Appeals for the Federal Circuit	U.S. Court of International Trade	U.S. Court of Federal Claims	U.S. Tax Court	Territorial Courts	U.S. Court of Appeals for the Armed Forces	Courts of the District of Columbia	U.S. Court of Appeals for Veterans Claims
Year Created	1789	1891	1982	1890	1855	1969	n/a	1951	1970s	1988
Number of Courts	94	13	1	1	1	1	3	1	4	1
Number of Judges	678	179	18	9	17	34	n/a	5	n/a	9
Terms of Judges	Life	Life	Life	Life	8-15 years	8-15 years	8-15 years	8-15 years	8-15 years	8-15 years

SOURCES: United States Courts online, United States Tax Court online, United States Court of Appeals for the Armed Forces online, Encyclopedia Britannica Online

>> The inferior courts include the constitutional and the special courts. **Analyze Charts** What events in U.S. history might have contributed to the need for the Court of International Trade?

generous retirement for them. They may retire at age 70, and if they have served for at least 10 years, receive full salary for the rest of their lives. Or, they may retire at full salary at age 65, after at least 15 years of service. The Chief Justice may call any retired judge back to temporary duty in a lower federal court at any time.

Today, federal judges have little involvement in the day-to-day administrative operations of the courts over which they preside. Their primary mission is to hear and decide cases. A clerk, several deputy clerks, bailiffs, court reporters and stenographers, probation officers, and others provide support services.

The judges of each of the 94 district courts appoint one or more United States magistrates, of which there are now more than 400. They are appointed to eight-year terms and handle a number of legal matters once dealt with by the judges themselves. They issue warrants of arrest, and often hear evidence to decide whether or not a person who has been arrested on a federal charge should be held for action by a grand jury. They also set bail in federal criminal cases, and even have the power to try those who are charged with certain minor offenses.

Other Federal Judges and Appointments

Each federal judicial district also has at least one bankruptcy judge. These judges handle bankruptcy cases under the direction of the district court to which they are assigned. There are now some 300 bankruptcy judges, all of them appointed to 14-year terms by the judges of each federal court of appeals.

The President and the Senate appoint a United States Attorney for each federal judicial district. The U.S. Attorneys and their many deputies are the government's prosecutors. They work closely with the FBI and other law enforcement agencies, and they bring to trial those persons charged with federal crimes. They also represent the United States in all civil actions brought by or against the Federal Government in their districts.

The President and Senate also select a United States marshal to serve each of the district courts. These marshals, and their several deputy U.S. marshals, perform duties much like those of a county sheriff.

The marshals make arrests in federal criminal cases, hold accused persons in custody, secure jurors, serve legal papers, keep order in courtrooms, and execute court orders and decisions. They also respond to such emergency situations as riots, mob violence, and other civil disturbances, as well as terrorist incidents. All United States Attorneys and marshals are appointed to four-year terms.

☑ **DRAW CONCLUSIONS** Why did the Framers create a system of judicial selection that requires the cooperation of the President and the Senate?

☑ ASSESSMENT

1. **Support Ideas with Examples** Why did the Framers of the Constitution stipulate that federal judges be appointed, rather than elected, and serve for life?

2. **Infer** Why did the Framers believe that an independent judiciary was so important?

3. **Infer** What are the two general principles that determine whether the federal courts have jurisdiction over a case? Do you think these principles are broad enough? Why or why not?

4. **Analyze Information** What could happen if it is a concurrent jurisdiction situation and the plaintiff files in the State court, rather than in a federal court?

5. **Compare and Contrast** Analyze judicial restraint and judicial activism and their effects over the years.

The Court Chamber of the Supreme Court of the United States is indeed a dignified space. During sessions, the nine Justices of the Supreme Court sit behind the raised bench.

 BOUNCE to Activate Flipped Video

Objectives

Define the concept of judicial review, and identify the roles played by Thomas Jefferson, James Madison, and John Marshall in the case in which the Court first asserted its power of judicial review.

Outline the types of jurisdiction that apply to the Supreme Court.

Explain how cases reach the Supreme Court.

Summarize the way the Supreme Court operates.

Key Terms

judicial review
writ of certiorari
certificate
brief
majority opinion
concurring opinion
dissenting opinion
Thomas Jefferson

William Marbury
James Madison
John Marshall

The Supreme Court

The eagle, the flag, Uncle Sam—you almost certainly recognize these symbols. They are used widely to represent the United States. You probably also know the symbol for justice: the blindfolded woman holding a balanced scale. She represents what is perhaps this nation's loftiest goal: equal justice under the law. Indeed, those words are chiseled in marble above the entrance to the Supreme Court building in Washington, D.C.

What Is Judicial Review?

Composition of the Court The Supreme Court of the United States is the only court specifically created by the Constitution, in Article III, Section 1. The Court is made up of the Chief Justice of the United States, whose office is also established by the Constitution (Article I, Section 3, Clause 6), and eight associate justices.

Congress sets the number of associate justices and thus the size of the Supreme Court. The Judiciary Act of 1789 created a Court of six justices, including the Chief Justice. The Court was reduced to five members in 1801 but increased to seven in 1807, to nine in 1837, and to 10 in 1863. It was reduced to seven in 1866 and increased to the present size of nine in 1869.

The Third Branch of Government The Framers quite purposely placed the Court on an equal plane with the President and Congress. As the highest court in the land, it stands as the court of last resort in all questions of federal law. That is, the Supreme Court of the United States is the final authority in any case involving any question arising under the Constitution, an act of Congress, or a treaty of the United States.

Remember, most courts in this country, both federal and State, may exercise the critically important power of **judicial review**. They have the extraordinary power to decide the constitutionality of an act of government, whether executive, legislative, or judicial.

The ultimate exercise of that power rests with the Supreme Court of the United States. That single fact makes the Supreme Court the final authority on the meaning of the Constitution.

The Constitution does not, in so many words, provide for the power of judicial review. Nevertheless, there is little doubt that the Framers intended that the federal courts—and, in particular, the Supreme Court—should have this power. If, as the Supremacy Clause states, the Constitution is the "supreme law of the land," then judges must have the power to review and strike down any act of government that goes against the Constitution.

Marbury v. Madison The Court first asserted its power of judicial review in *Marbury* v. *Madison* in 1803. Recall that the case arose in the aftermath of the stormy elections of 1800. **Thomas Jefferson** had won the presidency and control of both houses of Congress. The outgoing Federalists, stung by their defeat, then tried to pack the judiciary with loyal party members. Congress created several new federal judgeships in the early weeks of 1801, and President John Adams quickly filled those posts with Federalists.

William Marbury had been appointed a justice of the peace for the District of Columbia. The Senate had promptly confirmed his appointment, and late on the night of March 3, 1801, President Adams signed the commissions of office for Marbury and a number of other new judges. The next day, Jefferson became President and discovered that Marbury's commission and several others had not been delivered.

Angered by the Federalists' attempted court-packing scheme, President Jefferson instructed **James Madison**, the new secretary of state, not to deliver those commissions. William Marbury then went to the Supreme Court to compel an officer of government to issue the commission.

Overturning an Act of Congress Marbury based his suit on the Judiciary Act of 1789, in which Congress had created the federal court system. That law also gave the Supreme Court the right to hear such suits in its original jurisdiction (not on appeal from a lower court).

In a unanimous opinion written by Chief Justice **John Marshall**, the Court refused Marbury's

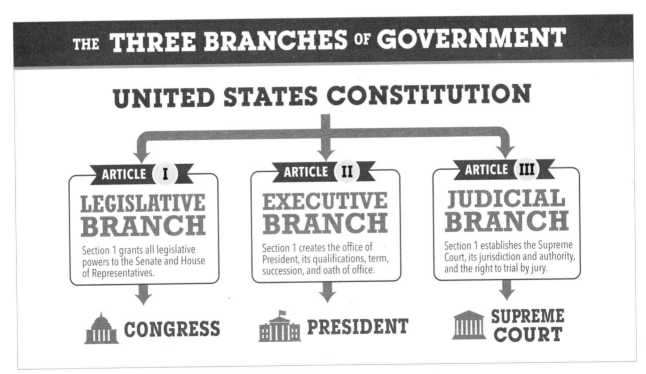

THE **THREE BRANCHES** OF **GOVERNMENT**

UNITED STATES CONSTITUTION

ARTICLE I

LEGISLATIVE BRANCH

Section 1 grants all legislative powers to the Senate and House of Representatives.

CONGRESS

ARTICLE II

EXECUTIVE BRANCH

Section 1 creates the office of President, its qualifications, term, succession, and oath of office.

PRESIDENT

ARTICLE III

JUDICIAL BRANCH

Section 1 establishes the Supreme Court, its jurisdiction and authority, and the right to trial by jury.

SUPREME COURT

>> The U.S. Constitution created three branches of government: legislative, executive, and judicial. **Analyze Information** Why do you think the Framers created the three branches to be equal?

>> Chief Justice John Marshall wrote the Court's opinion in *Marbury* v. *Madison*, saying, "A law repugnant to the Constitution is void."

>> William Marbury, a business executive, was the Marbury of the well-known Supreme Court case *Marbury* v. *Madison*, which established the principle of judicial review.

request. It did so because it found the section of the Judiciary Act that allowed Marbury to take his case directly to the Supreme Court to be in conflict with Article III of the Constitution. In one master stroke, the Court not only avoided ruling on the case, which was a no-win situation, it also established the principle of judicial review by nullifying parts of the Judiciary Act.

How the *Marbury* Decision Affects the Supreme Court Today With the Court's decision, Chief Justice Marshall claimed for the Supreme Court the right to declare acts of Congress unconstitutional, and so laid the foundation for the judicial branch's key role in the development of the American system of government.

The dramatic and often far-reaching effects of the Supreme Court's exercise of the power of judicial review tend to overshadow much of its other work. Each year, the Supreme Court hears dozens of cases in which questions of constitutionality are not raised, but in which federal law is interpreted and applied. Thus, many of the more important statutes that Congress has passed have been brought to the Supreme Court time and again for decisions. So, too, have many of the lesser ones. In interpreting those laws and applying them to specific situations, the Court has had a real impact on both their meaning and their effect.

☑ **COMPARE** How does the Supreme Court's power of judicial review differ from the power of a district court to determine guilt or innocence in a criminal case?

Jurisdiction of the Supreme Court

The Supreme Court has both original and appellate jurisdiction. Most of its cases, however, come on appeal—from the lower federal courts and from the highest State courts. Article III, Section 2 of the Constitution spells out two classes of cases that may be heard by the High Court in its original jurisdiction.

Two Types of Original Jurisdiction Congress cannot enlarge on this constitutional grant of original jurisdiction. Recall, that is precisely what the Supreme Court held in *Marbury*. If Congress could do so, it would in effect be amending the Constitution.

Congress can implement the constitutional provision, however, and it has done so. It has provided that the Supreme Court shall have original and exclusive jurisdiction over (1) all controversies involving two or more States, and (2) all cases brought against ambassadors or other public ministers, but not consuls.

Choosing to Take Original Jurisdiction The Court may choose to take original jurisdiction over any other case covered by the broad wording in Article III, Section 2 of the Constitution. Almost without exception, however, those cases are tried in the lower courts. The Supreme Court hears only a very small number of cases in its original jurisdiction—in fact, no more than a case or two each term.

☑ **INTEGRATE INFORMATION** In 2013, the Supreme Court agreed to hear a case challenging Environmental Protection Agency (a federal agency) regulations related to greenhouse gases. The case had previously been heard in federal court—most recently, by the United States Court of Appeals for the District of Columbia Circuit in 2012. What type of jurisdiction did the Supreme Court have in this case, and why?

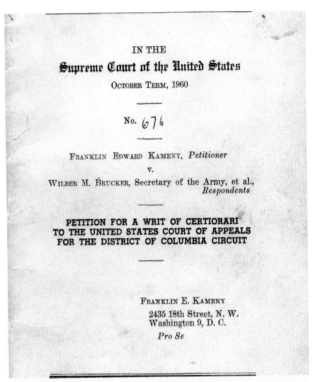

>> A petition for a writ of certiorari can be issued by either party to a case to the Supreme Court. If the Court issues a writ, it means that the Court has agreed to accept the case.

Appealing to the Supreme Court

Thousands of cases are appealed to the Supreme Court each term. Of these, the Court accepts only about a hundred for decision. In most cases, petitions for review are denied, usually because most of the justices agree with the decision of the lower court or believe that the case involves no significant point of law.

In short, the High Court is in the somewhat enviable position of being able to set its own agenda. It decides what it wants to decide. The Court selects those cases that it does hear according to "the rule of four": At least four of its nine justices must agree that a case should be put on the Court's docket.

More than half the cases decided by the Court are disposed of in brief orders. For example, an order may remand (return) a case to a lower court for reconsideration in light of some other recent and related case decided by the High Court. All told, the Court now decides, after hearing arguments and with full opinions, generally fewer than 80 cases per term.

Writs of Certiorari Most cases reach the Supreme Court by **writ of certiorari** (from the Latin, meaning "to be made more certain"). This writ is an

order by the Court directing a lower court to send up the record in a given case for its review. Either party to a case can petition the Court to issue a writ. But, again, "cert" is granted in only a very limited number of instances—typically, only when a petition raises some important constitutional question or a serious problem in the interpretation of a statute.

When certiorari is denied, the decision of the lower court stands in that particular case. Note, however, that the denial of cert is not a decision on the merits of a case. All a denial means is that, for whatever reason, four or more justices could not agree that the Supreme Court should accept that particular case for review.

Certifying Answers to Specific Questions A few cases do reach the Court in yet another way: by **certificate**. This process is used when a lower court is not clear about the procedure or the rule of law that should apply in a case. The lower court asks the Supreme Court to certify the answer to a specific question in the matter.

Most cases that reach the Court do so from the highest State courts and the federal courts of appeals. A very few do come from the federal district courts and an even smaller number from the Court of Appeals for the Armed Forces.

☑ **CONTRAST** How does the procedure for obtaining a writ of certiorari differ from the procedure for obtaining a certificate?

Hearing a Supreme Court Case

A Supreme Court term lasts from the first Monday in October to the first Monday in October of the following year. During that time, the Court actually sits—hears cases and delivers opinions—only until June or July. The remainder of the term is spent analyzing new petitions and preparing for the following term.

Hearing Oral Arguments Once the Supreme Court accepts a case, it sets a date on which that matter will be heard. As a rule, the justices consider cases in two-week cycles from October to early May. They hear oral arguments in several cases for two weeks; then recess for two weeks to consider those cases and handle other Court business.

>> While part of the majority opinion in *National Federation of Independent Business* v. *Sebelius*, 2012, Justice Sonia Sotomayor dissented on the reasoning behind the decision.

On those days on which the Court hears arguments, it convenes at 10:00 a.m. on Mondays, Tuesdays, Wednesdays, and sometimes Thursdays. At those public sessions, the lawyers, representing the parties of those cases the Court has accepted, make their oral arguments. Their presentations are almost always limited to 30 minutes.

The justices usually listen to an attorney's arguments and sometimes interrupt them with pointed questions. After 25 minutes, a white light flashes at the lectern from which an attorney addresses the Court. Five minutes later, a red light signals the end of the presentation and it must stop, even if the lawyer is in mid-sentence.

Filing Briefs Each party files detailed written statements—**briefs**—with the Court before they present their oral arguments. These detailed statements spell out the party's legal position and are built largely on relevant facts and the citation of precedents. Briefs often run to hundreds of pages.

The Court may also receive *amicus curiae* (friend of the court) briefs. These are briefs filed by persons or groups who are not actual parties to a case but who nonetheless have a substantial interest in its outcome.

Thus, for example, cases involving such highly charged matters as abortion or gun rights regularly attract a large number of *amicus* briefs. Notice, however, that these briefs can be filed only with the Court's permission or at its request.

The Solicitor General The solicitor general, a principal officer in the Department of Justice, is often called the Federal Government's chief trial lawyer. He or she represents the United States in all cases to which it is a party in the Supreme Court and may appear and argue for the government in any federal or State court.

The solicitor general also has another extraordinary responsibility. He decides which cases the government should ask the Supreme Court to review and what position the United States should take in those cases it brings before the High Court.

Meeting in Conference On most Fridays through a term, the justices meet in conference. There, in closest secrecy, they consider the cases in which they have heard oral arguments; and there, too, they decide which new cases they will accept for decision.

Only the Chief Justice, who presides, and the eight other members of the Court are present at the conference. The Chief Justice leads the discussion

The Power of Precedent

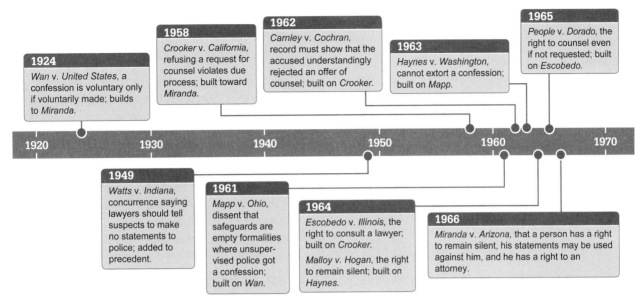

1924 *Wan* v. *United States*, a confession is voluntary only if voluntarily made; builds to *Miranda*.

1958 *Crooker* v. *California*, refusing a request for counsel violates due process; built toward *Miranda*.

1962 *Carnley* v. *Cochran*, record must show that the accused understandingly rejected an offer of counsel; built on *Crooker*.

1963 *Haynes* v. *Washington*, cannot extort a confession; built on *Mapp*.

1965 *People* v. *Dorado*, the right to counsel even if not requested; built on *Escobedo*.

1949 *Watts* v. *Indiana*, concurrence saying lawyers should tell suspects to make no statements to police; added to precedent.

1961 *Mapp* v. *Ohio*, dissent that safeguards are empty formalities where unsupervised police got a confession; built on *Wan*.

1964 *Escobedo* v. *Illinois*, the right to consult a lawyer; built on *Crooker*.
Malloy v. *Hogan*, the right to remain silent; built on *Haynes*.

1966 *Miranda* v. *Arizona*, that a person has a right to remain silent, his statements may be used against him, and he has a right to an attorney.

>> Majority opinions of the Supreme Court stand as precedents. Later Court decisions are often based on these precedents. **Analyze Data** What two main principles guided the Court in *Miranda*?

of each case to be considered—stating the facts, summarizing the questions of law involved, and usually indicating how he or she thinks the Court should dispose of that case. Then each of the associate justices, in order of seniority, present their views and conclusions. A majority must decide which party wins or loses a case and whether a lower court's decision in that matter is to be affirmed or reversed.

About a third of the Court's decisions are unanimous, but most find the Court divided. The High Court is sometimes criticized for its split decisions. However, most of the cases it hears pose difficult and complicated questions, and many present questions on which lower courts have disagreed. In short, most of the Court's cases excite controversy; the easy cases seldom get that far.

Announcing a Decision Once a case has been considered and decided in conference, the Court announces its decision in the matter and, with it, issues one or more written opinions. The decision indicates which party has won the dispute and by what margin among the justices. Where the decision is unanimous, the Chief Justice most often writes the Court's opinion. If there has been a split decision, the Chief Justice may write the majority opinion, or he or she may assign that task to another justice in the majority. When the Chief Justice is in the minority, the senior justice in the majority makes that assignment.

The Majority Opinion The **majority opinion,** officially called "the Opinion of the Court," sets out the facts in a case, identifies the issues it presents, and details the reasons that underpin the majority's decision.

Most majority opinions, and many concurring and dissenting opinions, run to dozens of pages. Some Supreme Court decisions are issued with very brief, unsigned opinions. These *per curiam* (for the court) opinions seldom run more than a paragraph or two and usually dispose of relatively uncomplicated cases. All of the High Court's opinions in every case are published online and in the United States Reports, the official printed record of the decisions.

The Power of Precedent The Court's opinions are exceedingly valuable. Its majority opinions stand as precedents. The lower courts, both federal and State, are expected to follow precedent—that is, decide cases of like nature in a manner consistent with previous rulings.

The doctrine of precedent is often identified as *stare decisis*—Latin for "let the decision stand," or adhere to decided cases. Precedents are powerful guidelines, but on rare occasions they can be overturned. Needless to say, these decisions are especially controversial.

Concurring Opinions One or more of the justices on the majority side may write a **concurring opinion**, usually to make some point not made or not emphasized in the majority opinion. In effect, a justice who writes a concurring opinion agrees with (concurs in) the majority decision as to the winner of a case but offers different reasons for reaching that conclusion.

Dissenting Opinions One or more **dissenting opinions** may be written by those justices who do not agree with the Court's majority decision. Those dissents do not become precedent. They are, instead, expressions of opposition to the majority's views in a case. Chief Justice Charles Evans Hughes once described dissenting opinions as "an appeal to the brooding spirit of the law, to the intelligence of a future day." Rarely, the High Court does reverse itself—and so minority opinion of today could become the Court's majority position on some distant tomorrow.

☑ **MAKE GENERALIZATIONS** Why would a justice refer to precedent while writing an opinion on a case?

☑ **ASSESSMENT**

1. **Draw Conclusions** How does the power of the Supreme Court act as a check on the other branches of government?

2. **Sequence Events** What sequence of events led to the Court hearing the case *Marbury* v. *Madison*?

3. **Compare** Compare the Supreme Court's original jurisdiction with its appellate jurisdiction.

4. **Integrate Information** Use what you have learned in Lessons 1 and 2 of this topic to answer the following question: Is an unelected Supreme Court truly democratic? Why or why not?

5. **Identify Steps in a Process** How does the Supreme Court reach decisions in its cases?

Out of Order: Stories of the History of the Supreme Court

Justice Sandra Day O'Connor, the first female justice of the Supreme Court, served from 1981 to 2006. Her book *Out of Order: Stories of the History of the Supreme Court*, written after her retirement, explores different aspects of the Supreme Court's history and practices. Her aim was to convey how the Court "embodies the bold vision of the Framers" and was "the culmination of the hard work, risks, and sacrifices of many people." In this excerpt, taken from the Introduction of her book, she discusses the unique and ever-evolving role of the Supreme Court and the people who work therein.

>> President Barack Obama presents Justice Sandra O'Connor with the 2009 Medal of Freedom in recognition of her lifetime accomplishments.

The Supreme Court Building is an awe-inspiring sight. Many a visitor each year is stopped in his or her tracks by the grandeur and solemnity of the white marble staircase and the soaring inscription on the Court's façade [front of the building], EQUAL JUSTICE UNDER LAW. An inspiring and profound image of permanence and continuity, the Court stands as a symbol of our commitment as a society to the rule of law. It stands for our Founding Fathers' uniquely American vision of an independent judiciary, in which judges and the Court would stand alone, independent and not beholden to the will of political majorities in their interpretation of the laws and the Constitution. . . .

✔ **MAKE INFERENCES** O'Connor uses the word stand three times in this paragraph. What is the definition of each use and how do they relate to the Supreme Court building?

But why did the Framers envision for the new government a judicial branch whose members, unlike those of the legislative and executive branches, would be unelected? And why was a *federal* judiciary necessary, given the extensive system of state courts in existence at the time of the Founding? . . .

The Framers wished to create an independent federal judiciary because they knew that the new national political branches could not be left unchecked. Our congressmen and President serve as elected representatives. In that role, they are supposed to speak for and answer to the people. For that reason, the Framers did not rely on the political branches to protect minority groups with less popular, more marginal interests. And so they assigned federal courts primary responsibility in guarding against the overreaching and excesses of the political branches, recognizing the benefits of a judiciary that functions as an "outsider" to the system of majority will.

The majestic building on One First Street in our nation's capital stands as a monument to our Founding Fathers' vision. Erected across the street from the Capitol, and across town from the White House, the building stands as a physical testament to the Court's status as an independent, coequal branch of government. The Supreme Court today regularly reviews the legality of laws passed by Congress and enforced by the executive branch. And from time to time, the Justices find themselves compelled by the law to strike down invalid government action by the political branches. The Court's decisions today, though often the subject of public criticism, are followed and adhered to even by those who disagree. . . .

☑ **MAKE CONNECTIONS** To what concept is O'Connor referring with the statement that the Court's decisions are to be "followed and adhered to even by those who disagree?"

. . . The Court was a daring, bold, but risky political experiment, and its beginnings were modest and uncertain. In reflecting on the Court's humble early days, it is striking to note how dramatically the Court and its practices have evolved and how so much of that evolution was born of struggle and serendipity. . . . The many Justices who have come and gone have made contributions . . . to not only the law, but the institution and its internal operations. . . .

From the array of characters who have served as Justices, to the law clerks who have aided them, the advocates who have argued before them, and the staff who have worked behind the scenes, the makeup of the community of the Court has changed dramatically. Just consider the criteria that Presidents have laid out for Supreme Court nominees. President George Washington was looking for men who were strong supporters of the Federalist cause and the Constitution, who had served in the Revolution, who were active in the political life of their states, and who had the blessing of well-known Federalists. . . . President Obama has stated that he looks for men and women with "a sharp and independent mind," who understand "that justice isn't about some abstract legal theory," and who "identif[y] with people's hopes and struggles as an essential ingredient for arriving at just decisions and outcomes." . . .

☑ **CONTRAST** How do the qualities of a Supreme Court justice differ between President Washington and President Obama?

The everyday operations and customs of the Court have evolved as well. The early Court had few cases on its docket. In the days of Chief Justice John Marshall, the Court often sat for cases for only six weeks. Today, the Supreme Court Term runs for nine months. . . . In the late nineteenth century, the Court's docket was inundated with mandatory appeals—cases that the Justices were at least technically obliged to decide on the merits, regardless of their importance or the urgency for review. Today, the Court uses its discretion to select a small subset of cases from approximately eight thousand appeals. . . filed each year.

☑ **IDENTIFY CAUSE AND EFFECT** What do you think was the reason why the Court was eventually able to choose the cases it heard?

Those who practice before the Supreme Court also face a very different scene. Early oral advocates were unconstrained by any time limitations, or indeed, any real rules of practice. When they presented their arguments, they were "heard in silence for hours, without being stopped or interrupted" by the Justices. High-style oratory . . . was in fashion and oral arguments could last for ten days. Today, oral advocates are strictly limited to thirty minutes of argument time per side. Classical oral exposition is discouraged, and advocates are lucky if they get more than two unbroken sentences out of their mouths before the Justices interject with difficult questions.

The Court's dramatic evolution over time is humbling to review. . . . I am reminded of this each time I walk through the Court and admire the succession of portraits . . . gracing its hallways. The Court as it exists today reflects the contributions of those who devoted their lives to it.

☑ ASSESSMENT

1. **Draw Conclusions** Do you think the reduction of time allowed for today's oral arguments before the Court is fair? Why or why not?

2. **Cite Evidence** How is the case *Marbury* v. *Madison* an example of how today's Supreme Court "reflects the contributions of those who devoted their lives to it"?

3. **Predict** O'Connor states that the Court's practices have evolved over time. What changes, if any, do you think will occur in the future?

Army Private Bradley Manning (now known as Chelsea Manning) was court-martialed and convicted in July 2013 of violations of the Espionage Act for giving classified military documents to the website WikiLeaks.

The Inferior Courts and the Special Courts

You know that the particular meaning of a word often depends on the context—the setting—in which it is used. Thus, *pitch* can be either a baseball term or a musical term; it can also refer to setting up a tent or to a high-pressure sales talk. The word *inferior* also has various meanings. Here, it describes the lower federal courts, those courts created by an act of Congress to function beneath the Supreme Court. The inferior courts handle nearly all of the cases tried in the federal courts.

The Structure and Role of the Federal District Courts

The United States district courts are the federal trial courts. Their judges handle more than 350,000 cases per year, about 80 percent of the federal caseload. The district courts were first created by Congress in the Judiciary Act of 1789. There are now 94 of them.

Federal Judicial Districts and Judges The 50 States are divided into 89 federal judicial districts. There are also federal district courts for Washington, D.C., Puerto Rico, the Virgin Islands, Guam, and the Northern Mariana Islands. Each State forms at least one judicial district. Some are divided into two or more districts, however—usually because of the larger amount of judicial business there. At least two judges are assigned to each district, but many districts have several. Thus, New York is divided into four judicial districts; one of them, the United States Judicial District for Southern New York, has over 40 judges.

 BOUNCE to Activate Flipped Video

Objectives

Describe the structure and jurisdiction of the federal district courts, the federal courts of appeals, and other constitutional courts.

Contrast the jurisdiction of the Court of Appeals for the Armed Forces and the Court of Appeals for Veterans Claims.

Explain how a citizen may sue the United States government in the Court of Federal Claims.

Examine the roles of the territorial courts and those of the District of Columbia courts.

Explain what types of cases are brought to the Tax Court.

Key Terms

criminal case
civil case
docket
record
courts-martial
civilian tribunal
redress
Guantanamo Bay,
   Cuba

Cases tried in the district courts are most often heard by a single judge. However, certain cases may be heard by a three-judge panel. Chiefly, these are cases that involve congressional districting or State legislative apportionment questions; those arising under the Civil Rights Act of 1964 or the Voting Rights Acts of 1965, 1970, 1975, and 1982; and certain antitrust actions.

Courts Focused on Terrorism Two little-known multi-judge panels—made up entirely of judges drawn from the district courts—play a key role in ongoing efforts to combat terrorism in this country and abroad. Both are shrouded in secrecy. One is the Foreign Intelligence Surveillance Court, created by Congress in 1978. It is often called the "FISA court" and is composed of 11 federal district court judges, who are appointed to seven-year terms by the Chief Justice of the United States. The court, which meets in secret, has the power to issue search warrants—court orders that allow the FBI and other federal law enforcement agencies to conduct covert surveillance of persons suspected of being spies or members of terrorist organizations.

The other is the Alien Terrorist Removal Court, created by Congress in 1996. It is made up of five district court judges, appointed by the Chief Justice to five-year terms. This court has the power to decide whether those persons identified as "alien terrorists" by the Attorney General of the United States should be expelled from this country.

District Court Jurisdiction The district courts have original jurisdiction over more than 80 percent of the cases that are heard in the federal court system. The only federal cases that do not begin in the district courts are those few that fall within the original jurisdiction of the Supreme Court, as well as those cases heard by the Court of International Trade or by one of the special courts. Thus, the district courts are the principal trial courts, the "courts of first instance," in the federal judiciary.

District Court Cases District court judges hear a wide range of both criminal and civil cases. In the federal courts, a **criminal case** is one in which a defendant is tried for committing some action that Congress has declared by law to be a federal crime. The punishment can be a fine, incarceration, or both. A federal **civil case** involves some noncriminal matter—say, a dispute over the terms of a contract or a suit in which the plaintiff seeks damages (money) for some harm done by the defendant.

The United States is always a party to a federal criminal case, as the prosecutor. Most civil cases are disputes between private parties, but here, too, the United States may be a litigant, as either the plaintiff or the defendant.

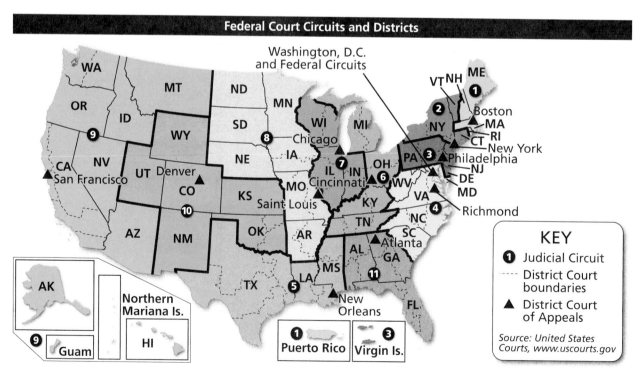

Federal Court Circuits and Districts

KEY
❶ Judicial Circuit
----- District Court boundaries
▲ District Court of Appeals

Source: United States Courts, www.uscourts.gov

>> There are 94 federal district courts. A biannual survey examines whether new district judgeships are needed. **Analyze Maps** What do the States with multiple districts have in common?

THE APPELLATE PATH IN THE FEDERAL COURTS

APPEALS FROM HIGHEST STATE COURTS →→

U.S. COURT OF APPEALS FOR THE ARMED FORCES →→

Military Courts

SUPREME COURT

⇑

U.S. COURT OF APPEALS FOR THE FEDERAL CIRCUIT

U.S. Court of International Trade
U.S. Court of Federal Claims
U.S. Court of Appeals for Veterans Claims

U.S. COURT OF APPEALS ⇐

Appeals from Federal Regulatory Agencies

District Courts

Courts of the District of Columbia
U.S. Tax Court
Territorial Courts

>> Cases originating in various courts can be appealed to the U.S. Supreme Court.
Analyze Charts In which courts do you suppose the largest number of cases originate?

The district courts try criminal cases ranging from bank robbery, kidnapping, and mail fraud to counterfeiting, terrorism, and tax evasion. They hear civil cases arising under bankruptcy, postal, tax, public lands, civil rights, and other laws of the United States. These trial courts are the only federal courts that use grand juries to indict defendants, and petit juries to determine their guilt or innocence.

Final Decisions Most of the decisions made in the 94 federal district courts are final. That is, most federal cases not only begin in those courts, they end there as well. Losing parties do not often appeal a decision to a higher court. Still, a few cases are taken to the court of appeals in that judicial circuit or, in a few instances, directly to the Supreme Court.

☑ **COMPARE AND CONTRAST** How are the two constitutional courts devoted to combating terrorism different from other federal district courts? Do they compare in any way to the federal special courts? Explain.

The Structure and Role of the Federal Courts of Appeals

The courts of appeals were created by Congress in 1891. They were established as "gatekeepers" to relieve the Supreme Court of much of the burden of hearing appeals from the decisions of the district courts. Those appeals had become so numerous that the High Court was more than three years behind on its **docket**—its list of cases to be heard.

There are now 13 courts of appeals in the federal judiciary. These tribunals were originally called the circuit courts of appeals. Before 1891, each Supreme Court justice "rode circuit," hearing appeals from the district courts within that geographic area. Congress renamed these courts in 1948, but they still are often called the "circuit courts."

The country is divided into 12 judicial circuits, including the District of Columbia. There is one court of appeals for each of those circuits, and they hear cases on appeal from the various district courts within their circuit. The Court of Appeals for the Federal Circuit is the thirteenth of these appellate tribunals. It sits in the District of Columbia, but its jurisdiction is nationwide and it is mostly concerned with appeals of decisions in patent, copyright, and international trade cases.

Appellate Court Judges Each of these courts is composed of 6 to 28 judges (roughly 180 in all). In addition, a justice of the Supreme Court is assigned to each. For example, the United States Court of Appeals for the Eleventh Circuit covers Alabama, Florida, and Georgia. The court is composed of 12 circuit judges and Associate Justice Clarence Thomas of the Supreme Court. The judges hold their sessions in a number of major cities within the circuit.

Each court of appeals usually sits in three-judge panels. Occasionally, however, and especially for an important case, a court will sit *en banc*—that is, with all of the judges on that court participating.

Circuit-Based Appellate Court Jurisdiction The 13 courts of appeals have only appellate jurisdiction. For the 12 circuit-based courts, most cases come to them from the district courts within their circuit, but some are appealed from the Tax Court and some from the territorial courts. Recall, they are also empowered to hear appeals from the decisions of several federal regulatory agencies—for example, the Federal Trade Commission and the National Labor Relations Board.

Court of Appeals for the Federal Circuit Jurisdiction Unlike the 12 circuit-based courts, the jurisdiction of the thirteenth, the Court of Appeals for the Federal Circuit, is nationwide in scope. Congress created this court in 1982, with the special purpose of centralizing and speeding up the handling of appeals in certain types of federal civil cases.

The Court of Appeals for the Federal Circuit hears appeals from the decisions rendered in several different courts. Many of its cases come from the other constitutional court, the Court of International Trade, and still others come from two of the special courts: the Court of Federal Claims and the Court of Appeals for Veterans Claims. It also hears the appeals taken in any patent, copyright, or trademark case decided in any of the 94 federal district courts.

An Important Role Again, these 13 tribunals are appellate courts. They do not conduct trials or accept new evidence in the cases they hear. Instead, they review the **record,** the transcript of proceedings made in the trial court, and they ponder the oral and written arguments (the briefs) submitted by attorneys representing parties to a case. The fact that less than one percent of their decisions are appealed to the Supreme Court underscores the importance of the place these tribunals occupy.

☑ **DRAW CONCLUSIONS** Why are two courts of appeals located in Washington, D.C.?

The Court of Appeals for the Federal Circuit

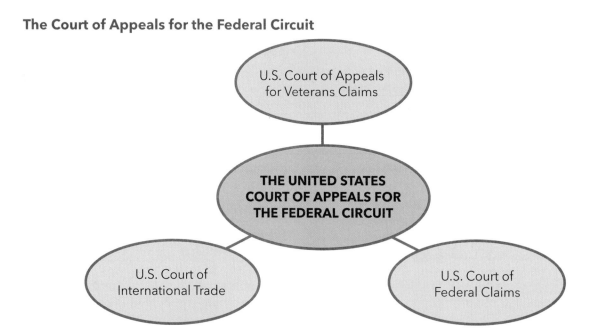

>> The court of appeals is authorized to hear a wide variety of cases outside of Washington, and has convened in many different cities. **Analyze Charts** When might this be necessary?

The Court of International Trade

Congress has established one other Article III court, the Court of International Trade. Often called the Trade Court, this body was originally created in 1890, and was restructured as a constitutional court in 1980.

The Trade Court now has nine judges, including its chief judge, appointed by the President and the Senate. Like the 94 district courts, it is a federal trial court, a court of first instance. It tries all civil (but not criminal) cases that arise out of the nation's customs and other trade-related laws. Its judges sit in panels of three and often hold jury trials in such major ports as New Orleans, San Francisco, Boston, and New York.

☑ **APPLY CONCEPTS** Why wouldn't a case involving the piracy of a merchant vessel be tried in the Court of International Trade?

Military Justice—Special Courts and Commissions

Recall, the national court system is made up of two quite distinct types of federal courts. They are (1) the constitutional courts, sometimes called the regular or Article III courts, already discussed, and (2) the special courts, also known as the legislative or Article I courts.

Each of the special courts was established by Congress acting under the authority delegated to it in Article I, Section 8 of the Constitution—not under the power given to it in Article III to create courts to exercise the broad "judicial Power of the United States." That is to say, each of these courts has a very narrow jurisdiction; each hears only those cases that fall into a very limited class. The special courts differ from the constitutional courts in one other important regard. Although their judges are all appointed by the President and Senate, they serve for a fixed term—not for life "during good Behaviour."

The Purpose of Military Courts Beginning in 1789, Congress has created a system of military courts for each branch of the nation's armed forces, as an exercise of its expressed power to "make Rules for the Government and Regulation of the land and naval Forces." (Article I, Section 8, Clause 14.) These military courts—**courts-martial**—serve the special disciplinary needs of the armed forces and are *not*

>> U.S. military courts, or courts-martial, employ lawyers and judges to try military personnel for crimes such as theft and assault, as well as for military offenses like desertion.

a part of the federal court system. Their judges, prosecutors, defense attorneys, court reporters, and other personnel are all members of the military; most of them are officers. They conduct trials of those members of the military who are accused of violating military law. Today, the proceedings in a court-martial are fairly similar to the trials held in civilian courts across the country. There are some important differences, however. For example, at a court-martial, only two thirds of the panel (the jury in the case) must agree on a guilty verdict, in contrast to the unanimous verdict usually required in cases tried in the civilian courts.

The Court of Appeals for the Armed Forces

In 1950, Congress created the Court of Military Appeals, now titled the Court of Appeals for the Armed Forces, to review the more serious court-martial convictions of military personnel. This appellate court is a **civilian tribunal**, a part of the judicial branch, entirely separate from the military establishment. Appeals from the court's decisions can be taken to the Supreme Court. It is, then, the court of last resort in most cases that involve offenses against military law.

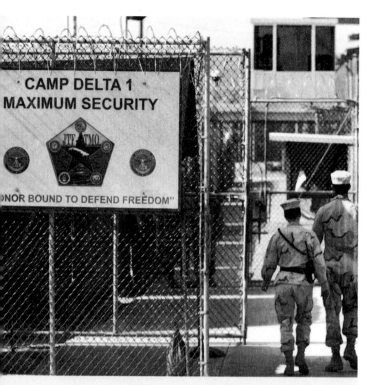

>> Since 2002, the U.S. Naval Station at Guantanamo Bay, Cuba, has housed Camp Delta, a military prison where suspected terrorists can be held indefinitely without a trial.

>> In 2013, the Supreme Court ruled in favor of Maryland's DNA Collection Act. **Analyze Political Cartoons** What is the relationship between the long arm of the law and Lady Liberty?

The Court of Appeals for Veterans Claims

Acting under its power (Article I, Section 8, Clause 9) to "constitute Tribunals inferior to the supreme Court," Congress created the Court of Veterans Appeals in 1988 and changed its name in 1999 to the Court of Appeals for Veterans Claims.

This court has the power to hear appeals from the decisions of an administrative agency, the Board of Veterans' Appeals in the Department of Veterans Affairs (VA). Thus, this court hears cases in which individuals claim that the VA has denied or otherwise mishandled valid claims for veterans' benefits. Appeals from the decisions of the Court of Appeals for Veterans Claims can be taken to the Court of Appeals for the Federal Circuit.

Military Commissions In 2001, President Bush issued a controversial executive order creating several military commissions. These court-like bodies were set up, outside the regular courts-martial system, to try "unlawful enemy combatants"—suspected terrorists captured by American forces in Iraq and Afghanistan. Some 770 of those captives were held over a seven-year period in a military prison at the American naval base at **Guantanamo Bay, Cuba.**

In 2006, the Supreme Court found that those military commissions had been improperly established, in *Hamdan* v. *Rumsfeld*. The Court held that a chief executive could create such tribunals but only if authorized to do so by an act of Congress. Congress responded with the Military Commissions Act of 2006, but the commissions accomplished very little over the next three years.

To some Americans, the holding of prisoners at Guantanamo Bay is itself unconstitutional. They argue that the basic civil rights of those held there are being violated. Others, however, feel their imprisonment is necessary to safeguard the nation's security.

Upon taking office, President Obama suspended the tribunals and ordered the closure of the Guantanamo Bay facility. Congressional resistance soon derailed those plans, however, and the daunting problem of the fate of the detainees still held there remains.

☑ **HYPOTHESIZE** If a case settled in courts-martial is appealed, it is removed from the military system and placed into the federal judicial system. What is the rationale behind this approach?

Other Special Courts

The other special courts also have very narrow jurisdictions. They include the Court of Federal Claims, the territorial courts, the District of Columbia courts, and the U.S. Tax Court.

The Court of Federal Claims The United States government cannot be sued by anyone, in any court, for any reason, without its consent. The government is shielded from suit by the doctrine of sovereign immunity. The doctrine comes from an ancient principle of English public law: "The King can do no wrong." The rule is not intended to protect public officials from charges of wrongdoing; rather it is intended to prevent government from being hamstrung in its own courts. Congress has long since agreed to a long list of legitimate court actions against the government.

The government may be taken to court only in cases in which Congress has declared the United States to be open to suit. Originally, any person with a money claim against the United States could secure **redress**—satisfaction of a claim, payment—only by an act of Congress. In 1855, however, acting under its expressed power to pay the debts of the United States (Article I, Section 8, Clause 1), Congress set up the Court of Claims to hear such pleas. That body was renamed the United States Court of Federal Claims in 1992.

Methods of Compensation The Court of Federal Claims holds trials throughout the country, hearing claims for damages against the Federal Government. Those claims it upholds cannot in fact be paid until Congress appropriates the money, which it does almost as a matter of standard procedure. Appeals from the court's decisions may be carried to the Court of Appeals for the Federal Circuit.

Occasionally, those who lose in the Claims Court still manage to win some compensation. Some years ago, a mink rancher lost a case in which he claimed that low-flying Navy planes had frightened his animals and caused several of the females to become sterile. He asked $100 per mink. He lost, but then his congressman introduced a private bill that eventually paid him $10 for each animal.

The Territorial Courts Acting under its power (Article IV, Section 3, Clause 2) to "make all needful Rules and Regulations respecting the Territory . . . belonging to the United States," Congress has created courts for the nation's territories. These courts sit in the Virgin Islands, Guam, and the Northern Mariana Islands. They function much like the local courts in the 50 States.

The District of Columbia Courts Acting under its power to "exercise exclusive Legislation in all Cases whatsoever, over such District . . . as may . . . become the Seat of the Government of the United States" (Article I, Section 8, Clause 17), Congress has set up a judicial system for the nation's capital. Both the federal district court and the federal Court of Appeals for the District of Columbia hear cases as constitutional courts. Congress has also established two local courts, much like the courts in the States: a superior court, which is the general trial court, and a court of appeals.

The United States Tax Court Acting under its power to tax (Article I, Section 8, Clause 1), Congress created the United States Tax Court in 1969 as "an independent judicial body" in the legislative branch. It is not, in fact, a part of the federal court system. The Tax Court hears civil but not criminal cases involving disputes over the application of the tax laws. Most of its cases, then, are generated by the Internal Revenue Service and other Treasury Department agencies. Its decisions may be appealed to the federal courts of appeals.

☑ **SUMMARIZE** Describe the factors that must fall into place for a U.S. citizen to successfully sue the federal government.

☑ ASSESSMENT

1. **Integrate Information** Identify and describe the different roles of the legislative branch of the federal government with regard to the inferior constitutional courts and special courts of the judicial branch.

2. **Draw Conclusions** How does the large number of appellate courts support a democratic form of government?

3. **Interpret** Congress establishes special courts for particular reasons. These reasons often reflect what is happening in the country. Give an example of how understanding congressional decisions about special courts also reveals your knowledge of current events.

4. **Explain** Why is it necessary to have District of Columbia special courts?

5. **Compare and Contrast** How are the cases heard in the Court of Appeals for Veterans Claims and the Court of Federal Claims alike and different?

LESSON SUMMARIES

Use these Lesson Summaries, and the longer versions available online, to review the key ideas for each lesson in this Topic.

Lesson 1: The National Judiciary

The Constitution created a Supreme Court but left the creation of inferior courts to Congress. Federal courts have limited jurisdiction. They deal with cases that involve interpreting federal laws or the Constitution, or cases between certain kinds of parties. Federal judges are appointed for life by the President and confirmed by the Senate.

Lesson 2: The Supreme Court

The Constitution places the Supreme Court on an equal level with the President and Congress. It is the highest appeals court for all federal cases, and has the power of judicial review. This means that it can decide if an act of government is constitutional. The Court's opinions stand as precedents to be followed by lower courts.

Lesson 3: The Inferior Courts and the Special Courts

Inferior courts try most federal cases. They are organized into geographic districts. They hear a wide variety of criminal and civil cases that come under federal jurisdiction. Some of their cases are appealed to the courts of appeals or the Supreme Court. In addition to these courts, Congress has created a Court of International Trade, a system of military courts, and other special courts.

VISUAL REVIEW

Use these graphics to review some of the key terms, people, and ideas from this Topic.

Which Cases do Federal Courts Hear?

SUBJECT MATTER	PARTIES
• Federal law or the Constitution • Maritime or admiralty law	• Federal government • Foreign ambassador or consul • State suing another State, its resident, or a foreign government • Resident of one State suing another State's government • Citizen suing a foreign government • Residents of the same State if land grants from different States are involved

Structure of the Federal Courts

How Cases Reach the Court

A Supreme Court Case

Topic 7 Assessment

KEY TERMS, PEOPLE, AND IDEAS

1. What is a **concurring opinion**? What is a **dissenting opinion**?

2. What are the **inferior courts?**

3. Define **concurrent jurisdiction**.

4. How do federal **criminal cases** and **civil cases** differ?

5. What are the roles of the **plaintiff** and the **defendant** in a case?

6. What is **original jurisdiction**, and how is it different than **appellate jurisdiction**?

7. What was significant about the appointments of **Thurgood Marshall** and **Sandra Day O'Connor** to the Supreme Court?

8. Define **precedent**.

CRITICAL THINKING

9. **Describe** the role of judicial review in American constitutional government. Is the principle of judicial review consistent with the basic principles of democracy? Why or why not?

10. **Compare and Contrast** Compare the role of judges on the federal level to that of other federal officials.

11. **Discuss** Hold a class discussion on the following topic, making sure to support your ideas with examples: Are Supreme Court or federal judicial appointments and confirmations ever controversial? Why or why not?

12. **Analyze** How do the responsibilities of the different levels of courts in the federal judicial system vary?

13. **Evaluate** What was the outcome of the Supreme Court case *Marbury* v. *Madison* (1803)? Why was this case significant?

14. **Support a Point of View with Evidence** What are the two general principles that determine whether the federal courts have jurisdiction over a case? Do you think these principles are broad enough? Why or why not?

15. **Compare and Contrast** How do supporters of **judicial restraint** differ from supporters of **judicial activism**?

16. **Summarize** The infographic below shows the changes in the federal district courts between 1789 and 2013. How have changes in the United States affected the federal court system?

Federal District Courts

1789	2013
13 Federal districts	94 Federal districts
13 judges	nearly 700 judges
4 sessions per year	over 350,000 cases heard each year
Majority of cases about maritime law	Wide variety of civil and criminal cases

17. **Identify Steps in a Process** Describe the process by which Supreme Court cases are accepted, argued, and decided.

18. **Summarize** What are the roles and responsibilities of the special courts of the U.S. federal court system?

19. **Discuss** Hold a class discussion on the following topic: Why is it important that the judiciary be independent from the other branches of government, as well as from public pressure? Be sure to express your ideas clearly and to listen carefully to the views of others.

20. **Identify Steps in a Process** Outline the process by which Supreme Court justices are nominated and approved. Why did the Framers create a system of judicial selection that requires the cooperation of the President and Senate?

21. **Writing Activity** In Topics 4, 5, 6, and 7, you learned about the three branches of the Federal Government. Given what you now know about the powers of each branch, write an opinion piece that describes your viewpoint on this question: Which branch of government is the most powerful?

DOCUMENT-BASED QUESTIONS

The President nominates and the Senate confirms nominees for the Supreme Court. On what basis are candidates for the bench chosen?

DOCUMENT A

Senator Strom Thurmond was the chairman of the Senate Judiciary committee when President Reagan nominated Sandra Day O'Connor to the Supreme Court.

> We seek, first, a person of unquestioned integrity—honest, incorruptible, and fair. We seek a person of courage—one who has the fortitude to stand firm and render decisions based not on personal beliefs but, instead, in accordance with the Constitution and the will of the people as expressed in the laws of Congress. We seek a person learned in the law. . . . We seek a person of compassion—compassion which tempers with mercy the judgment of the criminal, yet recognizes the sorrow and suffering of the victim; compassion for the individual but also compassion for society in its quest for the overriding goal of equal justice under law.
>
> —Strom Thurmond, (R., So. Carolina), Judiciary Committee hearings, 1981

DOCUMENT B

In 2009, Sonia Sotomayor was nominated by President Obama for a seat on the Supreme Court.

DOCUMENT C

Interest groups such as the National Rifle Association (NRA) voiced their opinions about the nomination of Elena Kagan to the Court in 2010.

> We have carefully examined the career, written documents and public statements of nominee Elena Kagan and have found nothing to indicate any support for the 2nd Amendment. On the contrary, the facts reveal a nominee who opposes 2nd Amendment rights and is clearly out of step with mainstream Americans.

Therefore, the NRA is strongly opposed to Kagan's confirmation to the Court. In testimony before the Senate Judiciary Committee, she refused to declare support for the Second Amendment, saying only that the matter was "settled law." . . .

> —Joint Statement, Wayne LaPierre, NRA Exec. Vice President and Chris Cox, Exec. Dir. NRA Inst. for Legislative Action, June 30, 2010

DOCUMENT D

This chart shows how the Senate voted for three different Supreme Court nominees.

Senate Votes on Supreme Court Nominees

	NOMINATED BY/YEAR	PARTY IN POWER	SENATE VOTE	
CLARENCE THOMAS	Pres. George H.W. Bush (Republican), 1991	Democratic	52 YES	48 NO
			41 R's 11 D's	46 D's 2 R's
SAMUEL ALITO	Pres. George W. Bush (Republican), 2006	Republican	58 YES	42 NO
			54 R's 4 D's	41 D's 1 R's
ELENA KAGAN	Pres. Barack Obama (Democrat), 2010	Democratic	63 YES	37 NO
			58 D's 5 R's	36 R's 1 D

SOURCE: senate.gov

22. What is the main point that can be determined from Document D?

    A. Most Presidents nominate someone from their own political party.

    B. Senators vote almost exclusively along party lines when confirming or rejecting a Supreme Court nominee.

    C. The Senate is not likely to confirm a nominee who is from the opposing party.

    D. Democrats are more likely than Republicans to approve a presidential nomination to the Court.

23. Analyze Political Cartoons Who is the person speaking in Document B? What is the cartoonist's point about presidential nominations to the Supreme Court?

24. Writing Task When President Obama nominated Sonia Sotomayor in 2009, he noted that she would be the only sitting justice with experience as a trial judge. Using this information, as well as the information in all four documents, write several paragraphs about the factors that go into choosing a Supreme Court justice.

Protecting Civil Liberties

ESSENTIAL QUESTION How much power should the government have?

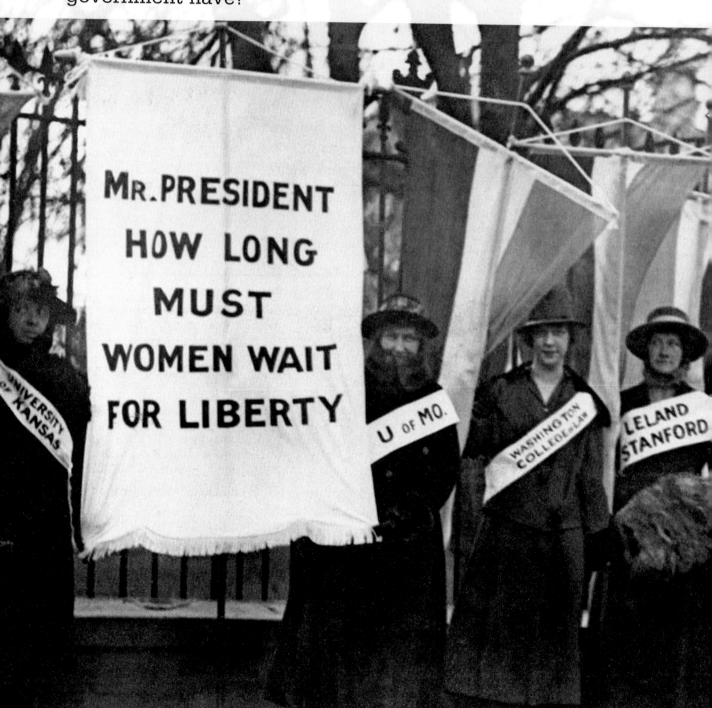

MR. PRESIDENT HOW LONG MUST WOMEN WAIT FOR LIBERTY

National Woman's Party members demonstrate at the White House in 1918.

Connections to Today

Imagine that child labor laws did not exist. Where would you be right now? In some countries, it's possible you might not only have to work, you might actually be enslaved—forced to work for free. Slavery, today often referred to as "human trafficking," takes many forms and affects people worldwide. A large percentage of victims are women and children.

In this Topic, you'll learn how the 13th Amendment ended legal slavery in the United States and how other court cases have sought to guarantee individual freedoms.

Learn how methods of surveillance can affect a person's privacy and security in the United States.

 BOUNCE to Activate My Story Video

Topic 8 Overview

In this Topic, you will take a close look at the fundamental freedoms guaranteed to all Americans in the Bill of Rights. Look at the lesson outline and explore the timeline. As you study this Topic, you can work on your Quest Inquiry.

LESSON OUTLINE

8.1 The Unalienable Rights

8.2 Freedom of Religion

8.3 Freedom of Speech and Press

8.4 Freedom of Assembly and Petition

8.5 Due Process of Law

8.6 Freedom and Security of the Person

8.7 Rights of the Accused

Landmark Supreme Court Cases: Civil Liberties

1963
Gideon v. *Wainwright,* guarantee of counsel for all poor persons facing felony charges

1966
Miranda v. *Arizona,* the accused must be advised of his or her rights

1989
Texas v. *Johnson,* the act of burning the American flag cannot be prosecuted

1960

1970

1980

1990

1962
Engel v. *Vitale,* students cannot be required to recite a prayer

1971
New York Times v. *U.S., the* government may not place prior restraint on the press

1984
Lynch v. *Donnelly,* a city holiday display that includes both religious and secular items is constitutional

Inquiry Center

Want to become an active and effective citizen? Make a difference in your community and beyond by using the **Inquiry Center** on the digital course.

Connect with issues you're passionate about by using the **Interest Finder**.

Investigate public policies, get involved in your community, influence public opinion, and develop leadership skills.

Synthesize the work you've done and what you've learned along the way.

Demonstrate what you've learned once you've finished your project by sharing your work.

Freedom Ride organizer James Farmer helped expand the civil rights of African Americans by contributing to the desegregation of interstate transportation in the United States.

 BOUNCE to Activate Flipped Video

Objectives

Explain how Americans' commitment to freedom led to the creation of the Bill of Rights.

Understand that the obligation of citizenship requires that personal desires and interests be subordinated to the public good.

Describe efforts to extend some of the protections of the Bill of Rights to the States and analyze the impact of that process on the scope of fundamental rights and federalism.

Describe how the 9th Amendment helps protect individual rights.

Key Terms

Bill of Rights
civil liberties
civil rights
alien
Due Process Clause
process of
  incorporation

Robert H. Jackson
Oliver Wendell
  Holmes, Jr.
Pearl Harbor
James G. Blaine

The Unalienable Rights

Have you ever heard of Walter Barnette? How about Toyosaburo Korematsu? Dollree Mapp? Clarence Earl Gideon? Walter Barnette was a Jehovah's Witness in West Virginia who told his children not to salute the American flag or to recite the Pledge of Allegiance in school. Toyosaburo Korematsu was an American citizen interned by the Federal Government during World War II. Dollree Mapp was jailed for keeping "lewd and lascivious books" in her boarding house in Ohio. Clarence Earl Gideon went to prison for breaking into a poolroom in Florida.

A Commitment to Individual Rights

You will encounter these names again as you read about civil rights and liberties in the United States. Each of these people played an important part in building and protecting the rights of all Americans.

Constitutional Guarantees A commitment to personal freedom is deeply rooted in America's colonial past. For centuries, the people of England waged a continuing struggle for individual rights, and the early colonists brought a dedication to that cause with them to America.

Their commitment to freedom took root in the United States, and it flourished. The Revolutionary War was fought to preserve and expand those very rights: the rights of the individual against government. In proclaiming the independence of the new United States, the founders of this country declared:

> We hold these truths to be self-evident, that all men are created equal, that they are endowed by their Creator with certain unalienable Rights, that among these are Life, Liberty and the Pursuit of Happiness. That to secure these rights, Governments are instituted among Men. . . .
>
> —Declaration of Independence

The Framers of the Constitution repeated the justification for the existence of government in the Preamble to the Constitution. That document, they said, was written to "secure the Blessings of Liberty to ourselves and our Posterity."

The Constitution, as it was written in Philadelphia, contained a number of important guarantees. The most notable can be found in Article I, Sections 9 and 10, and Article III. Unlike many of the first State constitutions, however, the new national Constitution did not include a general listing of the rights of the people.

That omission raised an outcry. The objections were so strong that several States ratified the Constitution only with the understanding that a listing of rights would soon be added. The first session of the new Congress proposed a series of amendments. Ten of them, known as the **Bill of Rights,** were ratified by the States and became a part of the Constitution on December 15, 1791. Later amendments, especially the 13th and the 14th, have added to those guarantees of personal freedom.

Civil Rights and Civil Liberties The Constitution guarantees both rights and liberties to the American people. The distinction between civil rights and civil liberties is murky at best. In general, **civil liberties** are protections *against government*. They guarantee the safety of persons, opinions, and property from arbitrary acts of government. Freedom of religion, freedom of speech, and the guarantees of fair trial are prime examples of civil liberties.

In contrast, **civil rights** are often associated with *positive acts of government* that seek to make constitutional guarantees a reality for all people. Viewed from this perspective, laws against discrimination on the basis of race, sex, religious belief, or national origin set out in the Civil Rights Act of 1964 are leading examples of civil rights.

Human Rights Policies At the heart of this country's commitment to civil rights and liberties lies a commitment to basic human rights. These rights include all of the freedoms and protections previously mentioned, as well as such things as internet freedom and human trafficking laws. U.S. human rights policies are enshrined in national documents, including the Declaration of Independence and the Constitution, and in the United Nation's 1948 Universal Declaration of Human Rights.

At the same time that the nation was setting up these guarantees of personal freedoms, however, many people's rights were not protected. Although the Framers of the Constitution referred to "We the People," in reality, at this point in history this did not include all individuals. In fact, over a century after the establishment of the Bill of Rights, racial segregation was legal across the nation, as was discrimination against women. People were still persecuted for their political and religious views.

But over time, the nation's people have waged a protracted struggle to secure human rights in more and more areas. From the abolition of slavery to expanded voting rights, from the end of legal racial segregation to the protection of workers' rights, and through rules against discrimination on the basis of disability—the people, through their representatives, have gradually won equal rights for more and more groups of people.

In 1941, for example, President Franklin Roosevelt gave his Four Freedoms speech, in which he identified freedom of speech and religion and freedom from want and fear as the right of every man and woman. The United States signed the Geneva Convention in 1949, which governs the fair treatment of prisoners of war.

In 1977, the State Department created the Bureau of Human Rights and Humanitarian Affairs, which began issuing reports on human rights around the world. That same year, President Jimmy Carter declared in his inaugural address that "Our commitment to human rights must be absolute, our laws fair, our national beauty preserved; the powerful must not persecute the weak, and human dignity must be enhanced." And at a town hall meeting in China in 2015, President Obama stressed the importance of protecting children from exploitation and called access to information a "universal right": "the more freely information flows, the stronger the society becomes, because then citizens of countries around the world can hold their own governments accountable."

☑ **COMPARE AND CONTRAST** What is the difference between civil liberties and civil rights? Provide an example of each.

Limited Government

Remember, government in the United States is limited. The Constitution is filled with examples of this fact. Chief among them are its many guarantees of personal freedom. Each of those guarantees is either an outright prohibition or a restriction on the power of government to do something.

All governments have and use authority over individuals. The all-important difference between a democratic government and a dictatorial one lies in the extent of that authority.

In a dictatorial regime, the government's powers are practically unlimited. The government regularly suppresses dissent, often harshly. In the United States, however, governmental authority is strictly limited. As Justice **Robert H. Jackson** once put the point:

> If there is any fixed star in our constitutional constellation, it is that no official, high or petty, can prescribe what shall be orthodox in politics, nationalism, religion, or any other matters of opinion or force citizens to confess by word or act their faith therein.
>
> —*West Virginia Board of Education v. Barnette,* 1943

>> Justice Oliver Wendell Holmes, Jr.'s, opinion in *Schenck* v. *United States* set limits on free speech when it established the doctrine of "clear and present danger . . . which Congress has a right to prevent."

Personal Interests and the Public Good The Constitution guarantees many rights to everyone in the United States. Still, no one has the right to do anything he or she pleases. Rather, all persons have the right to do as they please as long as they do not infringe on the rights of others. That is, each person's rights are *relative* to the rights of every other person. In other words, sometimes the public good takes precedence over the personal interests and desires of citizens.

To illustrate the point: Everyone in the United States has a right of free speech, but no one enjoys absolute freedom of speech. A person can be punished for using obscene language, or for using words in a way that causes someone to commit a crime—to riot or to desert from the military, for example. One Supreme Court case dealing with this point is *Federal Communications Commission* v. *Fox Television Stations,* 2009. In its 5–4 decision, the Court upheld the FCC's controversial policy of punishing broadcasters for even the one-time use of gross vulgarities on the air.

Another example can be found in government rationing during World War II. The war disrupted trade, making goods like rubber scarce. Other goods, such as gasoline and sugar, had been diverted to the war effort. Rationing limited people's rights in order to send goods where they were needed, ensure fair distribution of scarce supplies, and win the war.

In this oft-quoted line, Justice **Oliver Wendell Holmes, Jr.,** put the relative nature of each person's rights in this way:

> The most stringent protection of free speech would not protect a man in falsely shouting fire in a theatre and causing a panic.
>
> —*Schenck v. United States,* 1919

To Whom Are Rights Guaranteed? Most constitutional rights are extended to all persons. The Supreme Court has often held that "persons" includes **aliens**, a term formerly used for people who are not citizens of the country in which they live. Not *all* rights are given to noncitizens, however. The right to travel freely throughout the country is guaranteed to all citizens, for example, but travel by noncitizens can be restricted. (See the two Privileges and Immunities clauses, in Article IV, Section 2, and the 14th Amendment.)

After the bombing of **Pearl Harbor** by Japan in 1941, all persons of Japanese descent living on the Pacific Coast were evacuated—forcibly moved— inland. Many suffered economic and other hardships. In 1944, the Supreme Court reluctantly upheld the forced evacuation as a reasonable wartime emergency measure (*Korematsu* v. *United States*, 1944). Still, the relocation was strongly criticized over the years. In 1988, the Federal Government admitted that the wartime relocation had been both unnecessary and unjust. Congress voted to pay $20,000 to each living internee. It also declared, "the Congress apologizes on behalf of the nation."

☑ **PARAPHRASE** Explain the importance of having a limited government like the one found in the United States.

The 14th Amendment, Fundamental Rights, and Federalism

The Framers crafted our Constitution on the principle of federalism—the division of power among a central government and several regional governments. Federalism is a complicated arrangement. It produces any number of problems— including a very complex pattern of guarantees of individual rights in the United States.

The Bill of Rights and the States Remember, the first ten amendments to the Constitution were originally intended as restrictions on the new National Government, not on the already existing States. The Supreme Court first held that the provisions of the Bill of Rights restrict only the National Government in *Barron* v. *Baltimore*, 1833. This was the first case in which the point was raised. The Supreme Court has followed that precedent ever since.

To illustrate this important point: The 5th Amendment says that no person can be charged with "a capital, or otherwise infamous crime" except by a grand jury. As a part of the Bill of Rights, this provision applies only to the National Government. The States may use the grand jury to bring accusations of serious crime—or, if they prefer, they can use some other process to do so. (The grand jury is a part of the criminal justice system in all but two States and the District of Columbia.)

>> More than 100,000 persons of Japanese ancestry were sent to incarceration camps during World War II. **Draw Conclusions** Why did the government take that action?

>> When John Barron sued the city of Baltimore (shown here) because it had deposited sand in the waters near his wharf, the Court ruled that the 5th Amendment did not apply to the States.

Extending the Bill of Rights to the States Again, the provisions of the Bill of Rights apply against the National Government, not against the States. This does *not* mean, however, that the States can deny basic rights to the people.

In part, the States cannot do so because each of their own constitutions contains a bill of rights. In addition, they cannot deny these basic rights because of the 14th Amendment's **Due Process Clause**, which was ratified after the Civil War. It says, in part:

> No State shall . . . deprive any person of life, liberty, or property, without due process of law. . . .
>
> —14th Amendment, Section 1

The Supreme Court has often said that the 14th Amendment's Due Process Clause means that no State can deny to any person any right that is "basic or essential to the American concept of ordered liberty."

But what specific rights are "basic or essential"? The Supreme Court has answered that question in a long series of cases in which it has held that most (but not all) of the protections in the Bill of Rights are also covered by the 14th Amendment's Due Process Clause, and so apply against the States. In deciding those cases, the Court has engaged in what has come to be called the **process of incorporation**. It has incorporated—merged or combined—most of the guarantees in the Bill of Rights into the 14th Amendment's Due Process Clause.

Gitlow v. New York The Court began that historic incorporation in *Gitlow* v. *New York,* 1925. That landmark case involved Benjamin Gitlow, a founding member of the Communist Party USA, who had been convicted of criminal anarchy in the State courts. He had made several speeches and published a pamphlet calling for the violent overthrow of government in this country.

On appeal, the Court upheld Gitlow's conviction and the State law under which he had been tried. In deciding the case, however, the Court made this crucial point: Freedom of speech and press, which the 1st Amendment says cannot be denied by the National Government, are also "among the fundamental personal rights and liberties protected by the Due Process Clause of the 14th Amendment from impairment by the States."

Soon after *Gitlow,* the Court held each of the 1st Amendment's other guarantees to be covered by the 14th Amendment. It struck down State laws involving speech (*Fiske* v. *Kansas*, 1927; *Stromberg* v. *California*, 1931), the press (*Near* v. *Minnesota,* 1931), assembly and petition (*DeJonge* v. *Oregon,* 1937), and religion (*Cantwell* v. *Connecticut,* 1940).

Provisions of the 14th Amendment's Due Process Clause

AMENDMENT	RIGHTS INCORPORATED	RIGHTS NOT INCORPORATED
1st Amendment	Freedoms of speech, press, assembly, petition; Free Exercise Clause; Establishment Clause	
2nd Amendment	Right to bear arms	
3rd Amendment		No quartering of troops
4th Amendment	No unreasonable searches or seizures	
5th Amendment	No self-incrimination; No double jeopardy	Grand jury
6th Amendment	Right to counsel; Right to confront and obtain witnesses; Speedy trial, Trial by jury in criminal cases	
7th Amendment		Trial by jury in civil cases
8th Amendment	No cruel and unusual punishment	

>> The Supreme Court has "nationalized" some rights into the 14th Amendment's Due Process Clause. **Analyze Charts** Why do you think only some of the rights have been incorporated?

A building with features of the Vatican is labeled Tammany Hall, a social organization with political influence in New York City.

Children trapped on the shore near a crumbling U.S. public school. A Bible represents a perceived Protestant influence in public schools.

Alligators representing Catholic bishops climb out of the Ganges, a river with spiritual significance.

THE AMERICAN RIVER GANGES.
THE PRIESTS AND THE CHILDREN.—(See Page 382.)

>> This cartoon reflects the controversy in the 1800s over using public funds for parochial schools. **Analyze Political Cartoons** What do the elements represent? What is the cartoonist's viewpoint?

In each of those cases, the Court declared a State law unconstitutional as a violation of the 14th Amendment's Due Process Clause.

In the 1960s, the Court extended the scope of the 14th Amendment's Due Process Clause even further. In 2010, it added the 2nd Amendment to that coverage when it decided the case of *District of Columbia* v. *Heller*.

Blaine Amendment The Establishment Clause of the 1st Amendment says that the Federal Government cannot pass laws or spend money in ways that promote a religion. This might seem a simple matter, but in reality, it has posed many complex questions. One particularly vexing issue involves government aid to parochial (religious-based) schools.

In the latter half of the nineteenth century, waves of immigrants arrived on American shores. Many were Catholic, and in response to what was perceived as a strong Protestant influence in the public schools, many Catholic schools were created. In some instances, public monies were used to support those schools.

In 1875, the Speaker of the House of Representatives, **James G. Blaine** of Maine, proposed a constitutional amendment that would explicitly prohibit the use of State money for "sectarian" schools. Recall, the Establishment Clause

had not yet been incorporated. The bill passed overwhelmingly in the House but was narrowly defeated in the Senate. In response, many States passed their own "Blaine amendments," making it clear that State funds could not be used for religious schools. Today, some 37 States have these restrictions.

Rather than fade into the history books, however, Blaine amendments have again become relevant as a growing number of States have started school voucher programs. These initiatives allow parents to use their public school allotment (voucher) to send their children to any public or private school to increase parents' choices and encourage competition among schools. Nevertheless, federal court rulings have said that States with explicit prohibitions—Blaine amendments—cannot allow vouchers to be used for parochial schools.

Impact on Fundamental Rights and Federalism
Over the years, the process of incorporation has increased the scope of fundamental rights by extending most of the rights guaranteed by the Bill of Rights to the States. In some respects, the application of the Bill of Rights to the States is noncontroversial. Most agree, for instance, that States should not be allowed to abridge an individual's freedom of speech or right to assemble.

In fact, as you know, most State constitutions detail many of the same protections found in the United States Constitution.

In other ways, however, the incorporation process has had an impact on federalism. Take, for instance, the rights of those accused of committing a crime. Through a series of cases in the 1960s and 1970s, the Supreme Court applied federal-level protections to criminal defendants, thus altering the policies of many State and local law enforcement agencies.

The guarantee of the separation of church and state found in the 1st Amendment's Establishment Clause is another area in which the process of incorporation has had an impact on federalism. Prayer, or even a moment of silence, in public schools has been deemed a violation of the 1st Amendment. Thus, the Federal Government has outlawed a practice despite the fact that wide support for that practice can be found in many communities. Again, in some respects, the incorporation process has been a simple matter, but in other ways, it has broadened federal control in areas traditionally left to the States.

The 9th Amendment The Constitution does *not* contain a complete catalog of all the rights held by Americans. The little-noted 9th Amendment says that there are, in fact, some guarantees beyond those set out in the Constitution:

> The enumeration in the Constitution, of certain rights, shall not be construed to deny or disparage others retained by the people.

—9th Amendment

Over the years, the Supreme Court has found a number of other rights "retained by the people." They include, most notably, the guarantee that an accused person will not be tried on the basis of evidence unlawfully gained, and the right of a woman to choose to have an abortion without undue interference by government.

☑ **SUMMARIZE** What is the process of incorporation? Discuss its impact on federalism.

☑ ASSESSMENT

1. **Identify Central Issues** How does the Constitution protect the rights of individuals against government?

2. **Generate Explanations** How are the Constitution's guarantees of personal freedom and the principle of limited government connected?

3. **Support Ideas with Examples** Why are individual rights not absolute? Cite two examples that support your thinking and explain how that right is not absolute.

4. **Compare and Contrast** Discuss the 14th Amendment and the 9th Amendment. How are they similar? How are they different?

5. **Identify Central Issues** How does federalism complicate guarantees of personal rights? How do the 14th Amendment and various Supreme Court rulings address this complication?

8.2

These demonstrators supported the construction of an Islamic cultural center and mosque near Ground Zero in New York, while others opposed building the center there.

Freedom of Religion

In the early 1830s, Frenchman Alexis de Tocqueville came to America to observe life in the young country. In his classic *Democracy in America,* he later noted that "the spirit of religion and the spirit of freedom" were "intimately united" in America. Wrote de Tocqueville: "I learned with surprise that [the clergy] filled no public appointments; not one of them is to be met with in the administration, and they are not even represented in the legislative assemblies. In several States the law excludes them from political life. . . ." de Tocqueville had discovered the American principle of the separation of church and state.

Religious Liberty

Many of the original 13 colonies were settled by people escaping religious persecution. Pilgrims, Puritans, Separatists, Quakers, Lutherans, Presbyterians, Roman Catholics, and many others made their homes in America. Eventually, however, some colonies, such as Massachusetts, required their residents to practice an official religion. In the years following the American Revolution, state-sponsored churches and discrimination against people of certain religions, such as Catholics and Jews, were fairly common.

It was not until 1784, when James Madison argued in favor of religious freedom in an influential essay, that any State took positive steps toward that goal. Soon after, Thomas Jefferson's bill proposing legal equality for people of all religions—the Virginia Statute for Religious Freedom—was passed by the Virginia legislature.

Madison and Jefferson's ideas made their way into the United States Constitution. Article VI, Section 3 states that public officials, at either the federal or State level, "shall be bound by Oath or Affirmation, to support this Constitution, but no religious Test shall ever be required as a Qualification to any Office or public Trust under the United States."

▶ BOUNCE to Activate Flipped Video

Objectives

Examine the reasons the Founding Fathers protected religious freedom and guaranteed its free exercise.

Understand the meaning of the phrase "separation of church and state."

Analyze Supreme Court interpretations of religious rights guaranteed by the Constitution in selected cases relating to education.

Summarize Establishment Clause rulings in other areas, such as seasonal religious displays and public displays of the Ten Commandments.

Evaluate Supreme Court decisions that have affected a particular religious group, in particular those related to the Free Exercise Clause.

Key Terms

Establishment Clause
Free Exercise Clause
parochial
Alexis de Tocqueville

Later, when the Bill of Rights was passed in 1791, the very first amendment guaranteed that

Congress shall make no law respecting an establishment of religion, or prohibiting the free exercise thereof. . . .

—1st Amendment

Notice that the 1st Amendment sets out *two* guarantees of religious freedom. It prohibits (1) "an establishment of religion" (in the **Establishment Clause**), and (2) any arbitrary interference by government with "the free exercise thereof" (in the **Free Exercise Clause**). Recall, the Supreme Court has incorporated both protections into the 14th Amendment's Due Process Clause, meaning that they apply against the States.

These guarantees were born out of centuries of opposition to government-established churches that had been brought to America by the colonists. They assured the people of the United States, who practiced a multitude of different religions, that they could practice their religions as they saw fit, or practice no religion. These guarantees also meant that religion could not serve as the basis for discrimination of any kind by the government.

Separation of Church and State The Establishment Clause sets up, in Thomas Jefferson's words, "a wall of separation between church and state." That wall is not infinitely high, however, and it is not impenetrable. Church and government are constitutionally separated in this country, but they are neither enemies nor strangers to one another.

Government has done much to encourage churches and religion in the United States. Nearly all property of and contributions to religious sects are free from federal, State, and local taxation. Chaplains serve with each branch of the armed forces. Most public officials take an oath of office in the name of God. Sessions of Congress, most State legislatures, and many city councils open with prayer. The nation's anthem and its coins and currency make reference to God.

The limits imposed by the Establishment Clause remain a matter of continuing controversy. The Supreme Court did not hear its first Establishment Clause case until 1947. A few earlier cases did involve government and religion, but none of them involved a direct consideration of the "wall of separation."

The most important of those earlier cases that dealt with religion, but not the Establishment Clause, was *Pierce* v. *Society of Sisters,* 1925. There, the Court held an Oregon compulsory school attendance law to be unconstitutional. That law required parents to send their children to *public* schools. It was purposely intended to eliminate private and especially **parochial** (church-related) schools. The Court found the law to be an unreasonable interference with "the liberty of parents and guardians to direct the upbringing and education of children" and thus to be in conflict with the Due Process Clause of the 14th Amendment.

☑ **IDENTIFY CENTRAL ISSUES** Why did the Founding Fathers protect religious freedom?

Religion and Education

The foremost area of collision between religion and government has been issues pertaining to education. Can State and local governments give

>> The Establishment Clause does not prohibit members of Congress, such as Keith Ellison (D., Minnesota), from taking an oath of office. Ellison rested his hand on a Quran as he was sworn in.

financial aid to parochial schools, for example? What about providing textbooks or assistance in busing students to these schools? Can public schools open their day or a high school commencement with a prayer, or even a moment of silence? Is it proper for religious student groups to hold meetings at public schools in the evenings?

A 1947 case often called the *New Jersey School Bus Case* (*Everson* v. *Board of Education*) was the Court's first direct ruling on the Establishment Clause. There, the Court upheld a State law that provided for the public, tax-supported busing of students attending any school in the State, including parochial schools.

Aid to Parochial Schools Many Establishment Clause cases have centered on State aid to parochial schools. Those who support this kind of aid argue that parochial schools enroll large numbers of students who would otherwise have to be educated at public expense. Also, they maintain, the State should give some aid to parochial schools in order to relieve parents of some of the double burden they carry because they must pay taxes to support the public schools their children do not attend. Many advocates further insist that schools run by religious organizations pose no real church-state problems because they devote most of their time to secular (nonreligious) subjects.

Opponents of aid to parochial schools argue that parents who choose to send their children to religious-based schools should accept the financial consequences of that choice. Many of these critics also insist that it is impossible to draw clear lines between secular and sectarian courses in parochial schools. They say that religious beliefs are bound to have an effect on the teaching of nonreligious subjects.

The *Lemon* Test In a 1971 case, *Lemon* v. *Kurtzman*, the Supreme Court held that the Establishment Clause is designed to prevent three main evils: "sponsorship, financial support, and active involvement" of the government in religious activity. It struck down a Pennsylvania law that provided for reimbursements (money payments) to private schools to cover their costs for teachers' salaries, textbooks, and other teaching materials in nonreligious courses.

The Court introduced a three-pronged standard, now known as the *Lemon* test, to decide whether a State law amounts to an "establishment" of religion. That standard states: (1) a law must have a secular, not religious, purpose; (2) it must neither

>> Private speech endorsing religion is protected by the Free Exercise Clause. However, a teacher endorsing religion in a public school would violate the Establishment Clause.

advance nor inhibit religion; and (3) it must not foster an "excessive entanglement" of government and religion.

More often than not, the Court has found laws that provide some form of public aid to church-related schools unconstitutional. Thus, it ruled in an Ohio case that public funds cannot be used to pay for such things as field trips for parochial school students. Nor, as it ruled in a Michigan case, can tax monies be used to pay any part of the salaries of parochial school teachers, even those who teach only secular courses. The Court noted in that case that while the contents of, say, a textbook used in a course may be checked easily, the way a teacher handles that course cannot. The Court also invalidated a New York law that purposely created a small school district to benefit handicapped school children in a tight-knit community of Hasidic Jews.

Some State laws have passed the *Lemon* test, however. For example, the Court has held that New York can pay church-related schools what it costs them to administer standardized tests, and that the use of public money in Arizona to provide an interpreter for a deaf student in a Catholic high school does not violate the Establishment Clause.

The Constitution, said the Court, does not lay down an absolute barrier to the placing of a public employee in a religious school.

The High Court went much further in *Zelman* v. *Simmons-Harris* in 2002. There, it upheld Ohio's experimental "school choice" plan. Under that plan, parents in Cleveland can receive vouchers (grants for tuition payments) from the State and use them to send their children to private schools. Nearly all families who take the vouchers send their children to parochial schools. The Court found, 5–4, that the Ohio program is not intended to promote religion but rather to help children from low-income families.

Released Time and Student Groups Many other issues have arisen regarding religion and education. For example, should public schools be allowed to release students during school hours to attend religious classes? The Court said such "released time" programs are unconstitutional if held in public facilities, but not if the religious classes are held in private places off school grounds.

The Equal Access Act of 1984 declares that any public high school that receives federal funds (and nearly all do) must allow student religious groups to meet in the school on the same terms that it sets for other student organizations. The Supreme Court has ruled that the law does not violate the Establishment Clause. The Court has since gone much further than that ruling. In 2001, a school board had refused to allow the "Good News Club," a group of grade-school students, to meet after school to sing, pray, memorize scriptures, and hear Bible lessons. The school board based its action on the Establishment Clause. The Court, however, held that the board had violated Good News Club members' 1st and 14th amendment rights to free speech.

Prayers and the Bible The Court has now decided several major cases involving the recitation of prayers and the reading of the Bible in public schools. In *Engel* v. *Vitale*, 1962, the Court outlawed the use, even on a voluntary basis, of a prayer written by the New York State Board of Regents. The prayer read: "Almighty God, we acknowledge our dependence upon Thee, and we beg Thy blessings upon us, our parents, our teachers, and our country."

In striking down the prayer, the Supreme Court held that

> [T]he constitutional prohibition against laws respecting an establishment of religion must at least mean that, in this country, it is no part of the business of government to compose official prayers for any group of the American people to recite as part of a religious program carried on by government.
>
> —Justice Hugo L. Black

The High Court extended that holding in two 1963 cases. In *Abington School District* v. *Schempp*, it struck down a Pennsylvania law requiring that each school day begin with readings from the Bible and a recitation of the Lord's Prayer. In *Murray* v. *Curlett*, the Court erased a similar rule in Baltimore.

Since then, the Supreme Court has found unconstitutional:

- a Kentucky law that ordered the posting of the Ten Commandments in all public school classrooms, *Stone* v. *Graham*, 1980;
- Alabama's "moment of silence" law, *Wallace* v. *Jaffree*, 1985, which provided for a one-minute period of silence for "meditation or voluntary prayer" at the beginning of each school day;

"When the teacher says 'heaven help me', is that praying in school?"

>> The Supreme Court has consistently ruled against prayer in public schools, but the issue continues to be debated. **Analyze Political Cartoons** Why might school prayer be so controversial?

- the offering of prayer as part of a public school graduation ceremony, in a Rhode Island case, *Lee* v. *Weisman,* 1992;
- a Texas school district's policy that permitted student-led prayer at high school football games, *Santa Fe Independent School District* v. *Doe,* 2000.

To sum up these rulings, the Court has held that public schools cannot sponsor religious exercises. It has *not* held that individuals cannot pray when and as they choose in schools or in any other place. Nor has it held that students cannot study the Bible in a literary or historical context in the schools.

These rulings have stirred a great deal of controversy. Many individuals and groups have long proposed that the Constitution be amended to allow voluntary prayer in the public schools. And, despite these decisions, both organized prayer and Bible readings are found in a great many public school classrooms today. On the other hand, supporters of these rulings maintain that they are necessary to uphold the separation of church and state guaranteed by the Establishment Clause.

Evolution One interesting set of religious liberty cases dealt with the teaching of evolution in public school biology classes. In 1968, the Court struck down a State law forbidding the teaching of the scientific theory of evolution. The Court held that the Constitution

> forbids alike the preference of a religious doctrine or the prohibition of theory which is deemed antagonistic to a particular dogma. . . . 'The State has no legitimate interest in protecting any or all religions from views distasteful to them.'

—Justice Abe Fortas

The Court found a similar law to be unconstitutional in 1987. In *Edwards* v. *Aguilard,* it voided a 1981 Louisiana law that mandated that whenever the theory of evolution was taught, instruction in what the law termed "creation science" had to be offered as well.

☑ **SUMMARIZE** Describe what the Supreme Court has ruled permissible in public schools and what is not permitted.

>> Lawyers Clarence Darrow (left) and William Jennings Bryan faced off in the 1925 trial of John Scopes, a Tennessee teacher accused of violating a State law against the teaching of evolution.

Other Establishment Clause Cases

Most church-state controversies have involved public education, but some have arisen in other policy areas. In 2014, the Court held that town councils may start meetings with a prayer (*Town of Greece* v. *Galloway*), noting that legislative prayers are part of a long-established tradition in the United States.

Seasonal Displays Many public organizations sponsor celebrations of the holiday season with street decorations, programs in public schools, and the like. Can these publicly sponsored observances properly include expressions of religious belief?

In 1984, the Court held that the city of Pawtucket, Rhode Island, could include the Christian nativity scene in its holiday display, which also featured nonreligious objects such as candy canes and Santa's sleigh and reindeer. That ruling, however, left open this question: What about a public display made up *only* of a religious symbol?

The Court faced that question in 1989, when it ruled that if a seasonal display "endorsed Christian doctrine," it violated the 1st and 14th amendments.

A county government had placed a large display celebrating the birth of Jesus on the grand stairway in the county courthouse, with a banner proclaiming "Glory to God in the Highest."

At the same time, however, the Court upheld another holiday display in *Pittsburgh* v. *ACLU.* The city's display consisted of a large Christmas tree, an 18-foot menorah, and a sign declaring the city's dedication to freedom.

The Ten Commandments Public displays of the Ten Commandments have ignited controversy in several places over the years. In one 2005 case, the Court held that the Ten Commandments monument located on the grounds of the Texas State Capitol in Austin does not violate the 1st and 14th amendments.

The Court's 5–4 majority found that the monument (1) was erected in 1961 as part of a private group's campaign against juvenile delinquency, (2) is set among 37 other historical and cultural markers, and (3) had gone unchallenged for some 40 years. In short, the Court found the monument's overall message to be secular rather than religious and therefore acceptable.

In another case, a divided 5–4 majority ruled that the display of the Ten Commandments in Kentucky

>> A court ruling required the city of Duluth, Minnesota, to remove this monument of the Ten Commandments from outside city hall. **Hypothesize** Why do you think this ruling was different from the Texas case?

county courthouses was unacceptable. They were, said the Court, an impermissible endorsement of religion by government. Framed copies of the Commandments were first posted in county courthouses in 1991. Copies of other nonreligious documents, including the Bill of Rights, were added to the display some years later, but only after the original displays' content had been challenged. The Supreme Court found that the original displays had a clear religious purpose. The later additions were merely "a sham," an attempt to mask that unconstitutional religious purpose.

☑ **ANALYZE INFORMATION** Analyze the rulings made by the Supreme Court regarding seasonal religious displays in public places and the public display of the Ten Commandments. What distinctions were made in terms of what was permissible under the Establishment Clause? What was not permitted?

The Free Exercise Clause

The second part of the constitutional guarantee of religious freedom is set out in the Constitution's Free Exercise Clause, which guarantees to each person the right to believe whatever he or she chooses to believe in matters of religion. No law and no other action by any government can violate that absolute constitutional right. It is protected by both the 1st and the 14th amendments.

No person has an absolute right to act as he or she chooses, however. The Free Exercise Clause does *not* give anyone the right to violate criminal laws, offend public morals, or threaten community safety simply because it might be done in the name of religion. The Supreme Court laid down the basic shape of the Free Exercise Clause in the first case it heard on the issue, *Reynolds* v. *United States,* 1879. Reynolds, a Mormon, had two wives. That practice, known as polygamy, was allowed by his church, but was prohibited by federal law in any U.S. territory.

Reynolds was convicted under the law. The Supreme Court held that the 1st Amendment does not forbid Congress the power to punish those actions that are "violations of social duties or subversive of good order."

Limits on Free Exercise Over the years, the Court has approved many regulations of human conduct in the face of free exercise challenges, for the protection of the public good. For example, it has upheld laws that require the vaccination of schoolchildren, laws that forbid the use of poisonous snakes in religious rites, laws that require businesses to be closed on Sundays ("blue laws"), and a law requiring religious groups to have a permit to hold a parade on public streets. Further, the Court has ruled that the Federal Government can draft those who have religious objections to military service, *Welsh* v. *United States*, 1970.

Free Exercise Upheld Nevertheless, over time the Court has found many actions by governments to be incompatible with the free exercise guarantee. The Court did so for the first time in *Cantwell* v. *Connecticut*, 1940. There, the Court struck down a law requiring a person to obtain a license before soliciting money for a religious cause. The Court reaffirmed that holding in 2002.

The Supreme Court has decided a number of other cases in a similar way. Thus, Amish children cannot be forced to attend school beyond the 8th grade, because that sect's centuries-old "self-sufficient agrarian lifestyle is essential to their religious faith and is threatened by the exposure of their children to modern educational influences" (*Wisconsin* v. *Yoder*, 1972). On the other hand, the Amish, who provide support for their own elderly or disabled people, must pay Social Security taxes, as all other employers do.

The Court has also unanimously upheld the free exercise rights of Muslims. In *Holt* v. *Hobbs*, 2015, the justices ruled that a Muslim prison inmate must be allowed to grow the beard his religion requires.

The Jehovah's Witnesses have carried several important religious freedom cases to the High Court. Perhaps the stormiest controversy resulting from these cases arose out of the Witnesses' refusal to salute the flag because they see such conduct as a violation of the Bible's commandment against idolatry. In 1943, and after a series of back-and-forth decisions, the Supreme Court eventually held a compulsory flag-salute law unconstitutional. Justice Robert H. Jackson's words below are from the Court's powerful opinion in that case:

> To believe that patriotism will not flourish if patriotic ceremonies are voluntary and spontaneous, instead of a compulsory routine, is to make an unflattering estimate of the appeal of our institutions to free minds.
>
> —Justice Robert H. Jackson *West Virginia State Board of Education* v. *Barnette*, 1943

☑ **DRAW CONCLUSIONS** Why have the courts upheld the law prohibiting poisonous snakes in religious rites?

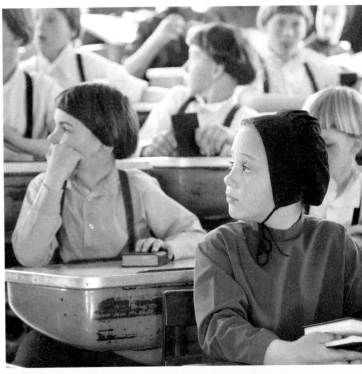

>> In 1972, the Court ruled that the "requirement of compulsory formal education after the eighth grade would gravely endanger, if not destroy, the free exercise of [Amish] religious beliefs."

☑ **ASSESSMENT**

1. **Define** What is the meaning of the phrase "separation of church and state"? What part of the Constitution guarantees this separation?

2. **Check Understanding** The constitutional guarantee of religious freedom has two parts: the Establishment Clause and the Free Exercise Clause. What does each clause create or guarantee? What does each clause prohibit or NOT protect?

3. **Identify Central Issues** What does the *Lemon* test evaluate? How did the test originate?

4. **Compare and Contrast** Describe arguments for and against allowing State aid to parochial schools.

5. **Evaluate Arguments** Describe the Supreme Court decision related to the Jehovah's Witnesses' objection to saluting the flag.

Like other protestors throughout history, a woman exercises her freedom of speech at an Occupy Seattle march, part of a worldwide Occupy movement for economic and social equality.

 BOUNCE to Activate Flipped Video

Objectives

Analyze the purpose and importance of the rights of free speech and press.

Analyze Supreme Court interpretations of rights guaranteed by the Constitution in *Schenck* v. *U.S.*, and other rulings related to seditious and obscene speech.

Define symbolic and commercial speech and describe the limits on their exercise, including Supreme Court interpretations of rights guaranteed by the Constitution in *Texas* v. *Johnson*.

Examine the issues of prior restraint and press confidentiality, and describe the limits the Court has placed on the media.

Key Terms

libel	prior restraint
slander	injunction
sedition	shield laws
seditious speech	John Roberts
symbolic speech	Oliver Wendell
picketing	Holmes, Jr.

Freedom of Speech and Press

Think about this children's verse: "Sticks and stones may break my bones, but names will never hurt me." This rhyme says, in effect, that acts and words are separate things, and that acts can harm but words cannot.

The Right of Free Expression

Is that really true? Certainly not. You know that words can and do have consequences—sometimes powerful consequences. Words, spoken or written, can make you happy, sad, bored, informed, or entertained. They can also expose you to danger, deny you a job, or lead to other serious events.

The guarantees of free speech and press in the 1st and 14th amendments serve two fundamentally important purposes: (1) to guarantee to *each* person a right of free expression, in the spoken and the written word, and by all other means of communication; and (2) to guarantee to *all* persons a wide-ranging discussion of public affairs. That is, the 1st and 14th amendments give people the right to have their say *and* the right to hear what others have to say.

The American system of government depends on the ability of the people to make sound, reasoned judgments on matters of public concern. The people can best make such judgments when they know all the facts and can hear all the available interpretations of those facts.

Unpopular Views, Libel, and Slander Keep two other points in mind. First, the guarantees of free speech and press are intended to protect the expression of unpopular views. The opinions of the majority need little or no constitutional protection. These guarantees ensure, as Justice Holmes put it, "freedom for the thought that we hate," (dissenting opinion, *Schwimmer* v. *United States,* 1929).

In 2011, for example, the Supreme Court issued a controversial 1st Amendment ruling relating to free speech. During the funeral of Matthew Snyder, a Marine killed in Iraq, members of a Baptist church picketed on public property near the church where the funeral was conducted. Finding the picketers' signs and statements insulting and offensive, Snyder's father sued.

In its 8–1 decision, the Court ruled in favor of the protestors, pointing out that they had properly notified authorities before their protest, that the protest took place on public property some distance away from the church, and that the views expressed related to matters of public concern. In the Court's opinion in *Snyder* v. *Phelps*, Chief Justice **John Roberts** wrote:

> "Speech is powerful. It can stir people to action, move them to tears of both joy and sorrow, and . . . inflict great pain. On the facts before us, we cannot react to that pain by punishing the speaker. As a nation, we have chosen a different course— to protect even hurtful speech on public issues to ensure that we do not stifle public debate."
>
> —Chief Justice John Roberts

Second, some forms of expression are not protected by the Constitution. No person has an unbridled right of free speech or free press. Reasonable restrictions can be placed on those rights. The key issue is whether the words trigger an unlawful or dangerous action. Think about Justice Holmes's comment about restricting the right to falsely shout "Fire!" in a crowded theater. Or consider this restriction: No person has the right to libel or slander another. **Libel** is the false and malicious use of printed words; **slander** is the false and malicious use of spoken words. Malicious means that the words are used to injure a person's character or reputation, or to expose that person to public contempt, ridicule, or hatred.

Public Figures and Slander Truth is generally an adequate defense against a claim of libel or slander. The law does not shield public officials nearly as completely as it protects private persons, however. In *New York Times* v. *Sullivan,* 1964, the Supreme Court held that public officials cannot recover damages for a published criticism, even if it is exaggerated or false, "unless that statement was made with actual malice—that is, knowledge that it was false or with a reckless disregard of whether it was false or not."

Several later decisions have extended that ruling to cover "public figures" and even private persons who simply happen to become involved in some newsworthy event.

Similarly, federal law prohibits the use of obscene words, the printing and distributing of obscene materials, and false advertising. It also condemns the use of words to prompt others to commit a crime— for example, to riot or to attempt to overthrow the government by force.

☑ **IDENTIFY CENTRAL ISSUES** Why are "reasonable restrictions" allowed on freedom of expression?

>> Answer Coalition members protest the war in Iraq. Other anti-war groups criticized Answer for its affiliations and tactics, but its members' right to be heard was guaranteed by the Constitution.

Seditious Speech

Sedition is the crime of attempting to overthrow the government by force or to disrupt its lawful activities by violent acts. **Seditious speech** is the advocating, or urging, of such conduct. It is not protected by the 1st Amendment.

The Alien and Sedition Acts Congress first acted to curb opposition to government in the Alien and Sedition Acts of 1798. Those acts gave the President the power to deport undesirable aliens and made "any false, scandalous, and malicious" criticism of the government a crime. The laws were meant to stifle the opponents of President John Adams.

The Alien and Sedition Acts were undoubtedly unconstitutional, but that point was never tested in the courts. Some 25 persons were arrested for violating them; of those, 10 were convicted. The Alien and Sedition Acts expired before Thomas Jefferson became President in 1801, and he soon pardoned those who had run afoul of them.

Sedition Law of 1917 Congress passed another sedition law during World War I, as part of the Espionage Act of 1917. That law made it a crime to encourage disloyalty, interfere with the draft, obstruct recruiting, incite insubordination in the armed forces, or hinder the sale of government bonds. The act also made it a crime to "willfully utter, print, write, or publish any disloyal, profane, scurrilous, or abusive language about the form of government of the United States."

More than 1,000 persons were convicted for violating the Espionage Act. The constitutionality of the law was upheld several times, most importantly in *Schenck* v. *United States,* 1919. Charles Schenck, an officer of the Socialist Party, had been found guilty of obstructing the war effort. He had sent fiery leaflets to some 15,000 draftees, urging them to resist the call to military service.

The Supreme Court upheld Schenck's conviction. The case is particularly noteworthy because in it **Justice Oliver Wendell Holmes, Jr.,** established the "clear and present danger" rule:

> Words can be weapons. . . . The question in every case is whether the words used are used in such circumstances and are of such nature as to create a clear and present danger that they will bring about the substantive evils that Congress has a right to prevent.
>
> —Justice Oliver Wendell Holmes

>> President John Adams used the Sedition Act to silence his opponents, even imprisoning a Vermont Congressman when he accused Adams of having "an unbounded thirst for ridiculous pomp."

>> Women and children protest the imprisonment of relatives who had violated the Espionage Act of 1917.

In short, the rule says that words can be outlawed. Those who utter them can be punished if there is an immediate danger that criminal acts will follow.

The Smith Act of 1940 Congress passed the Smith Act in 1940, just over a year before the United States entered World War II. That law is still on the books. It makes it a crime for anyone to advocate the violent overthrow of the government of the United States, to distribute any material that teaches or advises violent overthrow, or to knowingly belong to any group with such an aim.

The Court upheld the Smith Act in *Dennis* v. *United States*, 1951. There, 11 Communist Party leaders had been convicted of advocating the overthrow of the Federal Government. On appeal, the communist leaders argued that the Smith Act violated the 1st Amendment. They also claimed that no actions of theirs constituted a clear and present danger to this country. The Court disagreed.

Later, however, the Supreme Court modified the *Dennis* ruling in several cases. In *Yates* v. *United States*, 1957, for example, the Court overturned the Smith Act convictions of several Communist Party leaders. It held that merely to urge someone to *believe* something, in contrast to urging that person to *do* something, cannot be made illegal. In *Yates* and other Smith Act cases, the Court upheld the constitutionality of the law, but interpreted its provisions so that enforcing the Smith Act became practically impossible.

☑ **ANALYZE INFORMATION** The Supreme Court case *Schenck* v. *United States* established the "clear and present danger" rule. What is the impact of this ruling on 1st Amendment rights?

The 1st Amendment and Symbolic Speech

People also communicate ideas by their conduct, by the way they do a particular thing. Thus, a person can "say" something with a facial expression or a shrug of the shoulders, or by carrying a sign or wearing an armband. This expression by conduct is known as **symbolic speech**.

Clearly, not all conduct amounts to symbolic speech. If it did, murder or robbery or any other crime could be excused on grounds that the person who committed the act meant to say something by doing so.

>> The U.S. Cavalry escorts a train through picketers during the 1894 Pullman Strike. Picketing became more common after 1932 when laws were passed to limit employers' right to stop strikes.

Picketing Just as clearly, however, some conduct does express opinion. Take picketing in a labor dispute as an example. **Picketing** involves the patrolling of a business site by workers who are on strike. By their conduct, picketers attempt to inform the public of the controversy and to persuade others not to deal with the firm involved. Picketing is, then, a form of expression. If peaceful, it is protected by the 1st and 14th amendments.

The leading case on the point is *Thornhill* v. *Alabama*, 1940. There, the Court struck down a State law that made it a crime to loiter about or to picket a place of business in order to influence others not to trade or work there. Picketing that is "set in a background of violence," however, can be prevented. Even peaceful picketing can be restricted if it is conducted for an illegal purpose—for example, forcing someone to do something that is itself illegal.

Other Symbolic Speech Cases The Court has been sympathetic to the symbolic speech argument, but it has not given blanket 1st Amendment protection to that means of expression. Several key cases illustrate this point.

United States v. *O'Brien*, 1968, involved four young men who had burned their draft cards to protest the war in Vietnam. A court convicted them of violating a federal law that makes that act a crime. O'Brien appealed, arguing that the 1st Amendment protects "all modes of communication of ideas by conduct." The Court disagreed, saying: "We cannot accept the view that an apparently limitless variety of conduct can be labeled 'speech' whenever the person engaging in the conduct intends thereby to express an idea."

Acts of Dissent The Court also held that acts of dissent by conduct can be punished under certain circumstances, and it has sometimes denied claims of symbolic speech. Thus, in *Virginia* v. *Black,* 2003, it upheld a State law that prohibits the burning of a cross as an act of intimidation, a threat that can make a person fear for his safety. The Court also made this point: Those who burn crosses at rallies or parades as acts of political expression (acts not aimed at a particular person) cannot be prosecuted under the law.

Tinker v. *Des Moines School District,* 1969, on the other hand, is one of several cases in which the Court has come down on the side of symbolic speech. In *Tinker*, several students who had worn black armbands to school to dramatize their opposition to the war in Vietnam had been suspended by the district.

>> Mary Beth and John Tinker display the black armbands they wore to symbolize opposition to the Vietnam War. **Apply Concepts** Why did the Court rule in favor of the Tinkers?

The Court found that school officials had overstepped their authority and violated the students' right to free expression. Arguing that the students' conduct did not cause a substantial disruption of normal school activities, the Court stated, "It can hardly be argued that either students or teachers shed their constitutional rights to freedom of speech or expression at the schoolhouse gate."

Campaign Contributions The Court first recognized campaign contributions as protected speech in *Buckley* v. *Valeo* in 1976. In this case, the Court found certain parts of the Federal Election Campaign Act of 1971 were unconstitutional, including limits on candidates' expenditures from their personal funds.

The Court upheld this ruling in *Citizens United* v. *FEC* in 2010. There, the Court ruled that the government ban on political spending by corporations or labor unions violated the 1st Amendment right to free speech. In 2014, the Court went further down this path, striking down limits on how much an individual can contribute to all candidates, political parties, and political action committees combined in any two-year election cycle, on the same 1st Amendment grounds (*McCutcheon* v. *FEC*).

Flag Burning A sharply divided Court has twice held that burning the American flag as an act of political protest is expressive conduct protected by the 1st and 14th amendments. In *Texas* v. *Johnson,* 1989, a 5–4 majority ruled that State authorities had violated a protester's rights by prosecuting him under a law that forbids the "desecration of a venerated object."

Johnson had set fire to an American flag during an anti-Reagan demonstration at the Republican National Convention in Dallas in 1984. Said the Court:

If there is a bedrock principle underlying the 1st Amendment, it is that the government may not prohibit the expression of an idea simply because society finds the idea itself offensive. . . . We do not consecrate the flag by punishing its desecration, for in doing so we dilute the freedom that this cherished emblem represents.

—Justice William J. Brennan, Jr.

The Supreme Court's decision in *Johnson* set off a firestorm of criticism around the country and prompted Congress to pass the Flag Protection Act of 1989. It, too, was struck down by the Court, 5–4, in *United States* v. *Eichman,* 1990. The Court based its decision on the same grounds as those set out a year earlier in *Johnson*. Since *Johnson* and *Eichman*, Congress has rejected several attempts to propose a constitutional amendment to outlaw flag burning.

☑ **COMPARE AND CONTRAST** Compare and contrast the Court's interpretation of symbolic speech in *Virginia* v. *Black*, involving the burning of a cross, with its interpretation in *Texas* v. *Johnson*, involving flag burning.

Prior Restraint on Expression

The Constitution allows government to punish some utterances after they are made—for example, in cases involving libel or slander, or obscenity. With almost no exceptions, however, government cannot curb ideas *before* they are expressed. That is, except in the most extreme situations, government cannot place any **prior restraint** on written or spoken expression.

Prior Restraint and Publications The concept of prior restraint is basic to the meaning of the 1st and 14th amendment protections of freedom of expression. *Near* v. *Minnesota,* 1931, is a leading case in point. There, the Supreme Court struck down a State law that allowed local public officials to prevent the publication of any "malicious, scandalous, and defamatory" periodical. Acting under that law, a local court had issued an order forbidding the publication of *The Saturday Press*. That Minneapolis newspaper had published a series of articles charging public corruption and attacking local officials as "grafters" and "Jewish gangsters."

The Court held that the guarantee of a free press does not allow a prior restraint on publication— *except* in such extreme situations as wartime, or when a publication is obscene or incites its readers to acts of violence. Even "miscreant purveyors of scandal" and anti-Semitism are entitled to the protection of the 1st Amendment, said the Court.

The Constitution does not forbid any and all forms of prior censorship, but "any prior restraint on expression comes to this Court with a 'heavy presumption' against its constitutional validity." The Court made this pronouncement in *Nebraska Press*

>> Daniel Ellsberg (right) and Anthony Russo speak to reporters outside the Federal Building in Los Angeles during their trial for the theft and release of the so-called "Pentagon Papers."

Association v. *Stuart,* 1976, in which a State judge had ordered the media not to report certain details of a murder trial. The Court found the judge's gag order to be unconstitutional.

The Pentagon Papers Since that time, the Court has used this general rule on numerous occasions— for example, in the famous Pentagon Papers Case, *New York Times* v. *United States,* 1971. In that case, several newspapers had obtained copies of a set of classified documents, widely known as the Pentagon Papers. Officially titled *History of U.S. Decision Making Process on Viet Nam Policy*, those documents had been stolen from the Defense Department and then leaked to the press.

The Nixon administration sought an **injunction** to bar their publication, arguing that national security was at stake and the documents (government property) had been stolen. The newspaper argued the "public right to know," and it insisted that the 1st Amendment protected its right to publish the papers.

The Court found that the government had not shown that printing the documents would endanger the nation's security. The government, in effect, had not overcome the "heavy presumption" against prior censorship.

Court-Approved Prior Restraint The few prior restraints the Supreme Court has approved include:

- regulations prohibiting the distribution of political literature on military bases without the approval of military authorities, *Greer* v. *Spock*, 1976;

- a Central Intelligence Agency (CIA) rule that agents must never publish anything about the agency without the CIA's express permission, *Snepp* v. *United States*, 1980;

- a federal prison rule that blocks prisoners who are being punished for misbehavior from access to newspapers and magazines, *Beard* v. *Banks*, 2006.

The Court has also said that public school officials have a broad power to censor school newspapers, plays, and other "school-sponsored expressive activities." It did so in a case from Missouri, *Hazelwood School District* v. *Kuhlmeier*, 1988. There, the principal of a St. Louis high school had prohibited the publication of a series of articles written by student reporters for their school's paper. Those articles explored the impact that various events, among them pregnancy and parents' divorces, can have on teenagers.

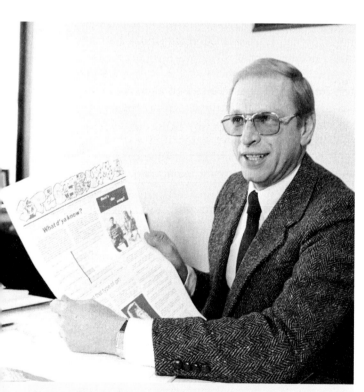

>> Principal Robert Reynolds holds a copy of his high school's newspaper. In *Hazelwood School District* v. *Kuhlmeier*, the Supreme Court ruled that his censorship of the paper was legal.

Three students sued, but they finally lost their case when the High Court held that school administrators can exercise "editorial control over the style and content of student speech in school-sponsored expressive activities so long as their actions are reasonably related to legitimate pedagogical [educational] concerns."

☑ **INFER** What can you infer from the Court's differing decisions in the case of the Pentagon Papers versus *Snepp* v. *United States*?

The Media in a Free Society

The 1st Amendment stands as a monument to the central importance of the media in a free society. That raises this question: To what extent can the media—whether print, radio, television, or the Internet—be regulated by government?

Confidentiality Can news reporters be forced to testify before a grand jury in court or before a legislative committee? Can those government bodies require journalists to name their sources and reveal other confidential information? Many reporters and news organizations insist that they must have the right to refuse to testify in order to protect their sources. They argue that without this right they cannot assure confidentiality, and therefore many sources will not reveal important, sensitive information.

Both State and federal courts have generally rejected the news media argument. Several reporters have refused to obey court orders directing them to give information, and they have gone to jail, thus testifying to the importance of these issues.

In the leading case, *Branzburg* v. *Hayes*, 1972, the Supreme Court held that reporters, "like other citizens, [must] respond to relevant questions put to them in the course of a valid grand jury investigation or criminal trial." If the media are to receive any special exemptions, said the Court, they must come from Congress and the State legislatures.

To date, Congress has not acted on the Court's suggestion, but every State except Wyoming has passed so-called **shield laws.** These laws give reporters some protection against having to disclose their sources or reveal other confidential information in legal proceedings in those States.

Motion Pictures The Supreme Court took its first look at motion pictures early in the history of the movie industry. In 1915, in *Mutual Film Corporation* v. *Ohio,* the Court upheld a State law that barred the showing of any film that was not of a "moral, educational, or amusing and harmless character." The Court declared that "the exhibition of moving pictures is a business, pure and simple," and "not . . . part of the press of the country." With that decision, nearly every State and thousands of communities set up movie review (really movie censorship) programs.

The Court reversed itself in 1952, however. In *Burstyn* v. *Wilson,* a New York censorship case, it found that "liberty of expression by means of motion pictures is guaranteed by the 1st and 14th amendments." Still, the Court has never held that the Constitution grants the film industry the same level of protection against prior restraint that it gives to newspapers. In fact, it has upheld a requirement that films be submitted to official censors so long as those censors are required to act reasonably and their decisions are subject to speedy court review, *Freedman* v. *Maryland,* 1965.

Very few of the once-common movie review boards still exist. Most people now rely on the film industry's own rating system and on the comments of movie critics to guide their viewing choices.

Radio and Television Both radio and television broadcasting are subject to extensive federal regulation. Most of this regulation is based on the often-amended Federal Communications Act of 1934, which is administered by the Federal Communications Commission (FCC). As the Supreme Court noted in *FCC* v. *Pacifica Foundation,* 1978: "Of all forms of communication, broadcasting has the most limited 1st Amendment protection."

The Court has several times upheld this wide-ranging federal regulation as a proper exercise of the commerce power. Unlike newspapers and other print media, radio and television use the public's property—the public airwaves—to distribute their materials. They have no right to use the limited broadcast frequencies without the public's permission in the form of a proper license, said the Court in *National Broadcasting Co.* v. *United States,* 1943.

The Court has regularly rejected the argument that the 1st Amendment prohibits such regulations. Instead, it has said that regulation of this industry actually implements the constitutional guarantee. In *Red Lion Broadcasting Co.* v. *FCC,* 1969, the Court held that there is no "unabridgeable 1st Amendment

>> In *FCC* v. *Fox,* the Court said that FCC rules against "fleeting expletives" uttered by performers like U2's Bono were "unconstitutionally vague" under the Due Process Clause.

right to broadcast comparable to the right of every individual to speak, write, or publish." However, "this is not to say that the 1st Amendment is irrelevant to public broadcasting. . . . It is the right of the viewers and the listeners, not the right of the broadcasters. . . ."

The Federal Communications Act forbids prior censorship—and so the FCC cannot censor the content of programs before they are broadcast. However, the law does permit the FCC to ban the use of indecent language, and the Court has held that it can take violations of that ban into account when a station applies for the renewal of its operating license, *FCC* v. *Pacifica Foundation,* 1978.

In several decisions, the Supreme Court has given cable television somewhat broader 1st Amendment freedoms than those enjoyed by traditional network television. *United States* v. *Playboy Entertainment Group,* 2000, is fairly typical. There, the Court struck down an attempt by Congress to force many cable systems to limit sexually explicit channels to confine their programs to late night hours. The Court agreed that shielding children from such programming is a worthy goal; nevertheless, it found the 1996 law to be a violation of the 1st Amendment.

Commercial Speech Commercial speech is speech for business purposes; the term refers most often to advertising. Until the mid-1970s, it was thought that the 1st and 14th amendments did not protect such speech. In *Bigelow* v. *Virginia,* 1975, however, the Court held unconstitutional a State law that prohibited the newspaper advertising of abortion services. The following year, in *Virginia State Board of Pharmacy* v. *Virginia Citizens Consumer Council*, it struck down another Virginia law forbidding the advertisement of prescription drug prices.

Not all commercial speech is protected, however. Government can and does prohibit false and misleading advertisements, and the advertising of illegal goods or services. In fact, government can even forbid advertising that is neither false nor misleading. In 1970, Congress banned cigarette ads on radio and television. In 1986, it extended the ban to include chewing tobacco and snuff.

In most of its commercial speech cases, the Court has struck down arbitrary restrictions on advertising. In *44 Liquormart, Inc.* v. *Rhode Island,* 1996, the Court voided a State law that prohibited ads in which liquor prices were listed. In *Greater New Orleans Broadcasting Association* v. *United States,* 1999, it struck down a federal law that prohibited casino advertising on radio or television.

In 2001, the Court dealt with limits on smokeless tobacco and cigar advertising. Massachusetts had barred outdoor ads for these commodities within 1,000 feet of any school or playground. The Court held that the limit was a violation of the 1st and 14th amendments' guarantee of free speech, *P. Lorillard Co.* v. *Reilly*.

Obscene Material Both federal and State laws have made the dissemination of obscene material illegal, and the courts have generally agreed that obscenity is not protected by the 1st and 14th amendments. But what, exactly, is *obscenity*? Lawmakers and judges have wrestled with that question for decades. The Supreme Court's Justice Potter Stewart once famously said that, although he could not define the term, "I know it when I see it," *Jacobellis* v. *Ohio,* 1964.

A large part of the problem in defining *obscenity* lies in the fact that moral standards vary from time to time, place to place, and person to person. To illustrate that point: Much of what appears on television today would, in fact, have been banned as obscenity only a few decades ago.

Obscenity and the Mail In 1872, Congress passed the first in a series of laws that prevent the mailing of obscene matter. The current postal law, upheld in *Roth* v. *United States,* 1957, excludes "obscene, lewd, lascivious, or filthy" material from the mail. The Court found the law a proper exercise of the postal power (Article I, Section 8, Clause 7) and so not prohibited by the 1st Amendment. *Roth* marked the Court's first attempt to define obscenity.

Three-Part Test Today, the leading case is *Miller* v. *California,* 1973. There the Court laid down a three-part test to define obscenity. A book, film, recording, or other piece of material is legally obscene if (1) "the average person applying contemporary [local] community standards" finds that the work, taken as a whole, "appeals to the prurient interest"—that is, tends to excite lust; (2) "the work depicts or describes, in a patently offensive way," a form of sexual conduct specifically dealt with in an anti-obscenity law; and (3) "the work, taken as a whole, lacks serious literary, artistic, political, or scientific value."

In recent years, the Court has heard only a handful of cases involving questions of obscenity. Those cases have all involved the Internet.

The Internet and Free Speech The Internet has generated only a handful of Supreme Court

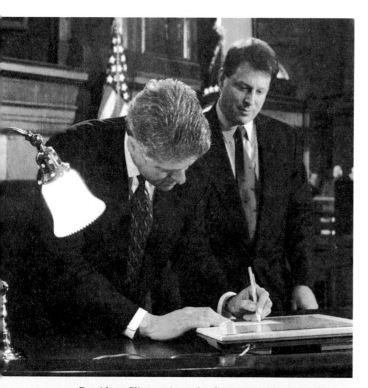

>> President Clinton signs the Communications Decency Act of 1996, part of which was later declared unconstitutional by a unanimous decision of the Supreme Court.

cases—and many of them have involved attempts by Congress to regulate access to pornographic matter. Congress first attempted to protect minors from that material in the Communications Decency Act of 1996. That law made it a crime to "knowingly" transmit any "obscene or indecent" speech or image that is "patently offensive as measured by contemporary community standards" to any person under the age of 18.

The Court promptly declared that law unconstitutional in *Reno* v. *American Civil Liberties Union, 1997.* A majority of the justices found that the words "indecent" and "patently offensive" were too vague and that the overall effect of that law was to deny to adults materials that are protected by the 1st Amendment. "Regardless of the strength of the government's interest in protecting children," said the Court, "the level of discourse reaching a mailbox cannot be limited to that which would be suitable for a sandbox."

The Supreme Court did uphold an act of Congress dealing with pornography, the Internet, and public libraries in *United States* v. *American Library Association, 2003.* There, a majority could find no constitutional fault in the Children's Internet Protection Act (CIPA) of 2002. That law provides that those public libraries that receive federal money—nearly all of them do—must use filters to block their computers' access to pornographic sites on the Internet.

The Supreme Court first ventured into the realm of free speech and video games in 2011, when it heard the case *Brown* v. *Entertainment Merchants Association.* The case involved a California law prohibiting the sale of violent video games to minors. In its 7–2 ruling, the justices declared the law in violation of the 1st Amendment. The Court ruled that video games are a form of expression and noted that the State of California had failed to show a link between playing violent video games and violent behavior.

☑ **IDENTIFY CENTRAL ISSUES** What was the basis for the Court determination in *Red Lion Broadcasting Co.* v. *FCC, 1969,* that the regulation of the radio and television industries *implements* the constitutional guarantee of free speech?

☑ ASSESSMENT

1. **Make Generalizations** How does the case of *Tinker* v. *Des Moines School District, 1969,* illustrate constitutional protection of symbolic speech?

2. **Apply Concepts** In the case *Burstyn, Inc.* v. *Wilson, 1952,* the Supreme Court voided a New York law that allowed censors to forbid the commercial showing of a motion picture that it had decided was "sacrilegious." The Court held that the law was a prior restraint on freedom of speech and of the press under the 1st Amendment. What is the meaning of the phrase "based on prior restraint on freedom of speech" in this case?

3. **Make Predictions** California is one State that is attempting to control cyber bullying by passing laws allowing school administrators to monitor student comments on social media sites. What 1st Amendment protections is the Court likely to review if asked to consider the constitutionality of these laws?

4. **Identify Central Issues** In the case *Bethel School District No. 403* v. *Fraser, 1986,* the court ruled that school officials had not violated the 1st Amendment rights of a student by suspending him for three days after he delivered a nominating speech before a student assembly whose content the administration found offensive. Why was the student's speech not protected under the 1st Amendment?

5. **Draw Conclusions** In the case *Brown* v. *Entertainment Merchants Association, 2011,* as well as other cases, the State's authority to pass laws restricting the sale or rental of violent video games to minors was challenged by the software industry. What aspects of the 1st Amendment could be argued in the software industry's favor?

8.4

The Supreme Court has outlined different rules for demonstrations, depending in part on whether they take place on public or private property.

 BOUNCE to Activate Flipped Video

Objectives

Analyze the importance of the 1st Amendment rights of petition and assembly.

Analyze Supreme Court interpretations of rights guaranteed by the Constitution, including limits on the time, place, and manner of assembly.

Compare and contrast the freedom-of-assembly issues that arise on public versus private property.

Explore how the Supreme Court has interpreted freedom of association.

Key Terms

assemble
petition
civil disobedience
content neutral
right of association

Freedom of Assembly and Petition

A crowded street demonstration by opponents of a gas pipeline; a group of anti-Obama protestors at a campaign event; a candlelight vigil by opponents of the death penalty; a march opposing unmanned aerial drones outside an air force base. . . these are all contemporary examples of citizen movements to bring about political change or to maintain continuity—and they all involve the constitutional right to freedom of assembly and petition.

Constitutional Provisions

Rights of Assembly and Petition The 1st Amendment guarantees "the right of the people peaceably to assemble, and to petition the Government for a redress of grievances." The 14th Amendment's Due Process Clause also protects those rights of assembly and petition against actions by the States or their local governments, *DeJonge* v. *Oregon,* 1937.

The Constitution protects the right of the people to **assemble** to express their views. It protects their right to organize to influence public policy, whether in political parties, interest groups, or other organizations. It also protects the people's right to **petition**—to bring their views to the attention of public officials by such varied means as written petitions, letters, or advertisements; lobbying; and parades or marches.

Notice, however, that the 1st and 14th amendments protect the rights of *peaceable* assembly and petition. The Constitution does not give to anyone the right to incite others to violence, block a public street, close a school, or otherwise endanger life, property, or public safety.

Civil Disobedience Note this important point as well: A significant part of the history of this country can be told in terms of **civil disobedience.** That is to say that much of our history has been built out of incidents in which people have purposely violated the law—nonviolently, but nonetheless deliberately, as a means of expressing their opposition to some particular law or public policy.

Do the 1st and 14th amendment guarantees of freedom of assembly and petition include a right of civil disobedience? That thorny question cannot be answered absolutely or without qualification because of the very nature of civil disobedience: those acts are expressions of opinion on some public matter.

Still, courts have consistently held that, as a general rule, civil disobedience is not a constitutionally protected right. Those who choose to take part in such activities are often aware of that fact, and they are usually willing to accept the consequences of their conduct such as the civil rights protesters of the 1950s and 1960s.

☑ **ANALYZE INFORMATION** A group of U.S. military veterans are planning to gather at a memorial to give speeches calling for an end to war. Under what circumstances would this assembly be protected by the 1st Amendment?

Time, Place, and Manner Rules

Government can make and enforce reasonable rules covering the time, place, and manner of assemblies. Thus, in *Grayned* v. *City of Rockford,* 1972, the Court upheld a city ordinance that prohibits making a noise or any other diversion near a school if that action has a disruptive effect on school activities. It has also upheld a State law that forbids parades near a courthouse when they are intended to influence court proceedings, *Cox* v. *Louisiana,* 1965.

Restrictions on Government Rules for keeping the public peace must be more than just reasonable, however. They must also be precisely drawn and fairly administered. In *Coates* v. *Cincinnati,* 1971, the Court struck down a city ordinance that made it a crime for "three or more persons to assemble" on a sidewalk or street corner "and there conduct themselves in a manner annoying to persons passing by, or occupants of adjacent buildings." The Court found the wording of the ordinance much too vague and therefore unconstitutional.

Government's rules must be **content neutral**. That is, although government can regulate assemblies on the basis of time, place, and manner, it cannot regulate gatherings on the basis of what might be said there. Thus, in *Forsyth County* v. *Nationalist Movement,* 1992, the Court threw out a Georgia county's ordinance that levied a fee of up to $1,000 for public demonstrations.

The law was contested by a white supremacist group seeking to protest the creation of a holiday to honor Martin Luther King, Jr. The Court found the ordinance not to be content neutral, particularly because county officials had unlimited power to set the exact fee to be paid by any group.

Free Speech Zones While the courts have said that governments cannot limit the content of political speech, under some circumstances it is reasonable for governments to limit the *place* and *time* of political speech by creating so-called "free speech zones." These zones are an attempt to balance the right of free speech with the right of the public to gather and move without interference from protesters.

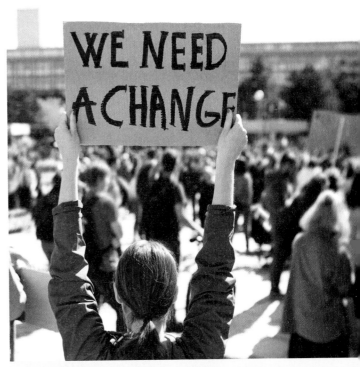

>> Peaceful protest is a right protected by the 1st Amendment. A gathering of like-minded people tells elected officials that an issue is important and should be given careful consideration. It is one way for the people's voice to be heard.

Simply stated, free speech zones are designated areas—such as a particular section of a sidewalk—to which protesters are confined. Free speech zones have stirred controversy over the years, with critics claiming that they violate the 1st Amendment guarantee of the right to free speech. Supporters maintain that the zones are necessary to protect both the public and the protesters.

☑ **IDENTIFY CENTRAL ISSUES** A college student was prevented from obtaining signatures for a petition because he was outside the "free speech zone," a designated concrete slab big enough for two people. What might make these requirements unconstitutional?

Assemblies on Public and Private Property

Over the past several years, most of the Court's freedom of assembly cases have involved organized demonstrations. Demonstrations are, of course, assemblies. Most demonstrations take place in public places—on streets and sidewalks, in parks or public buildings, and so on. This is the case because it is the *public* the demonstrators want to reach.

Demonstrations almost always involve some degree of conflict. Most often, they are held to protest something, and so there is an inherent clash of ideas. Many times there is also a conflict with the normal use of streets or other public facilities. It is hardly surprising, then, that the tension can sometimes rise to a serious level.

Given all this, the Supreme Court has often upheld laws that require advance notice and permits for demonstrations in public places. In an early leading case, *Cox* v. *New Hampshire,* 1941, it unanimously approved a State law that required a license to hold a parade or procession on a public street.

Right-to-demonstrate cases raise many difficult questions. How and to what extent can government regulate demonstrators? Does the Constitution require that police officers allow an unpopular group to continue to demonstrate even when its activities have excited others to violence? When, in the name of public peace and safety, can police order demonstrators to disband?

Gregory **v.** *Chicago* A leading and illustrative case is *Gregory* v. *Chicago,* 1969. While under police protection, comedian Dick Gregory and others marched while singing, chanting, and carrying placards, from city hall to the mayor's home some five miles away. Marching in the streets around the mayor's house, they demanded the firing of the city's school superintendent and an end to de facto segregation in the city's schools.

>> The Court has backed the government's right to place some limits on political speech. **Analyze Political Cartoons** What does this cartoon say about "free speech zones"?

A crowd of several hundred people, including many residents of the all-white neighborhood, quickly gathered. Soon, the bystanders began throwing insults and threats, as well as rocks, eggs, and other objects. The police tried to keep order, but after about an hour, they decided that serious violence was about to break out. At that point, they ordered the demonstrators to leave the area. When Gregory and others failed to do so, the police arrested them and charged them with disorderly conduct.

The convictions of the demonstrators were unanimously overturned by the Court. It noted that the marchers had exercised their constitutional rights of assembly and petition. The bystanders, not the demonstrators, had caused the disorder. As long as the demonstrators acted peacefully, they could not be punished for disorderly conduct.

Controversial Cases Many of the most controversial demonstrations have been those held by anti-abortion groups. For the most part, their efforts have been aimed at discouraging women from seeking the services of abortion clinics, and those efforts have generated many lawsuits.

In one notable case, *Madsen* v. *Women's Health Services, Inc.,* 1994, the Supreme Court upheld a Florida judge's order directing protesters not to block access to an abortion clinic. The judge's order had drawn a 36-foot buffer zone around the clinic. The High Court found that to be a reasonable limit on the demonstrators' activities.

Another major case is *Hill* v. *Colorado,* 2000. There, the Court upheld, 5–4, a State law that limits "sidewalk counseling" at clinics where abortions are performed. That statute creates an eight-foot floating buffer zone around anyone who wants to enter. No one may make an "unwanted approach" to talk, hand out a leaflet, or wave a sign. The Court found that the Colorado law does not deal with the content of abortion protestors' speech. It is aimed, instead, at *where, when,* and *how* their message is delivered.

Officials in many cities across the nation have had to reexamine their laws regarding buffer zones, based on a ruling in a 2014 case, *McCullen* v. *Coakley.* In that case, the Court struck down a Massachusetts law that established a 35-foot buffer zone around every abortion clinic in the state, including public sidewalks, saying that the zones went too far in limiting the free speech rights of abortion opponents.

Private Property What about demonstrations on private property—at shopping centers, for example? The Court has said that the 1st and 14th amendment

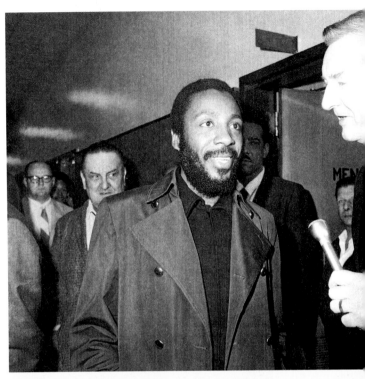

>> In *Gregory* v. *Chicago*, Justice Hugo Black said that arresting demonstrators due to bystanders' unruly behavior would be a "heckler's veto." Here, Gregory is interviewed during his 1966 trial.

rights of assembly and petition do not give people a right to trespass on private property, even to express political views.

Privately owned shopping centers are not "places of public assembly." Thus, no one has a constitutional right to do such things as hand out political leaflets or ask people to sign petitions in those places, according to the leading case on the subject, *Lloyd Corporation* v. *Tanner,* 1972.

☑ **DRAW CONCLUSIONS** In 2013, a Eugene, Oregon, judge nullified twenty-one trespassing citations issued by police to a group that had staged a protest by pitching tents in a public plaza in Eugene. What constitutional safeguards most likely guided the judge's decision?

Freedom of Association

The guarantees of freedom of assembly and petition include a **right of association**—the right to join with others to promote political, economic, and social causes. That right is not set out in so many words in the Constitution. However, in *National Association for the Advancement of Colored People* v. *Alabama,* 1958, the Supreme Court said, "it is beyond

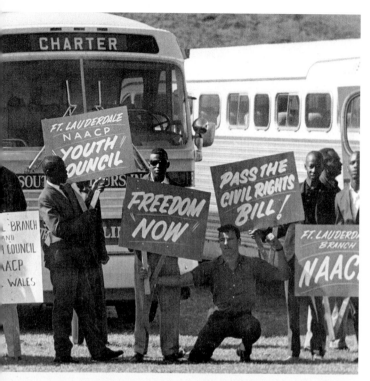

>> In 1958, the Supreme Court ruled that the NAACP did not have to disclose its membership list to the State of Alabama under the 1st Amendment's guarantee of freedom of association.

debate that freedom to engage in association for the advancement of beliefs and ideas is an inseparable aspect" of the Constitution's guarantees of free expression.

The case just cited is one of the early right-to-associate cases. There, a State law required the Alabama branch of the NAACP to disclose the names of all its members in that State. When the organization refused a court's order to do so, it was found in contempt of court and fined $100,000.

The Supreme Court overturned the contempt conviction. It said that it could find no legitimate reason why the State should have the NAACP's membership list.

In addition, a person cannot be fired from a job because of political associations—for example, membership in a political party, *Brown* v. *Socialist Workers '74 Campaign Committee*, 1982. And a person cannot be required to disclose his or her political associations in order to be licensed to practice law, *Gibson* v. *Florida*, 1966. On the other hand, the State of Washington's publication of the names of those registered voters who signed initiative petitions to put a measure on the general election ballot does not violate the Constitution's guarantee of a right of association, *Doe* v. *Reed*, 2010.

If a "compelling interest" exists, a private organization can be forced to make changes to its membership. In *Board of Directors, Rotary International* v. *Rotary Club of Duarte*, for example, the Supreme Court ruled that a law that required California's Rotary Clubs to allow women members did not violate the group's right of association. In its 1987 ruling, the Court noted that women members would not interfere with the group's goals and that ending gender-based discrimination was a compelling reason for any minor infringement on the group's rights.

☑ **SUPPORT IDEAS WITH EXAMPLES** In the case *NAACP* v. *Alabama,* 1958, what is the constitutional basis for the Supreme Court decision?

☑ ASSESSMENT

1. **Apply Concepts** A sit-in was staged on the sidewalk in front of the State Department to protest a proposed pipeline from Alaska to the Gulf Coast. Was this event protected by the Constitution? Explain your answer.

2. **Identify Central Ideas** In what way do limits on the role of government protect 1st Amendment rights of petition and assembly?

3. **Apply Concepts** In *Collin* v. *Smith*, 1978, the Court allowed a group called "followers of Nazism" to publicly and peaceably assemble to express their views in Skokie, Illinois, overturning local ordinances prohibiting this group's assembly. What does the Court's ruling say about the 1st Amendment and the States?

4. **Make Generalizations** Given its significant role in our country's history, do you think the right of civil disobedience is constitutionally protected?

5. **Analyze Information** In the case *Rutan* v. *Republican Party of Illinois*, 1990, the Supreme Court ruled that state-employee Rutan's promotion could not be denied based on her nonsupport of the Republican party. What was the likely basis for the Court's decision?

The use of scientific tests, such as DNA analysis, can help ensure due process for those accused of crime by evaluating evidence more accurately.

Due Process of Law

Did you know that DNA evidence has led to the reversal of more than 200 wrongful convictions in recent years? That the use of evidence drawn from the scientific study of body tissues has proved that all those persons were convicted, and served time in prison, for crimes they did *not* commit? Did you know that there is a strong likelihood that an untold number of innocent persons remain in prison today? As you will soon see, this point alone illustrates the importance of due process of law.

Understanding Due Process

The Constitution contains two due process clauses. The 5th Amendment declares that the Federal Government cannot deprive any person of "life, liberty, or property, without due process of law." The 14th Amendment places that same restriction on every one of the States—and, very importantly, on their local governments, as well. A thorough grasp of the meaning of these provisions is absolutely essential to an understanding of the American concept of civil rights and liberties.

It is impossible to define the two due process guarantees in exact and complete terms. The Supreme Court has consistently and purposely refused to do so. Instead, it has relied on finding the meaning of due process on a case-by-case basis. The Court first described that approach in *Davidson* v. *New Orleans,* 1878, as the "gradual process of inclusion and exclusion, as the cases presented for decision shall require."

Fundamentally, however, the Constitution's guarantee of **due process** means this: In whatever it does, government must act fairly and in accord with established rules. It may not act unfairly, arbitrarily, or unreasonably. The government can take private property for public use, for example, but it must fairly compensate the individual who loses the property—which means giving that

 BOUNCE to Activate Flipped Video

Objectives

Explain the importance of due process rights to the protection of individual rights and in limiting the powers of government.

Define the police power and understand its relationship to the subordination of personal desires and interests to the public good.

Key Terms

due process
procedural due
  process
substantive due
  process
police power
search warrant
eminent domain

person money equal to the fair market value of the land. Due process is a component of the concept of the rule of law, which holds that government is never above the law. In the words of patriot Thomas Paine, "In America THE LAW IS KING."

The concept of due process began and developed in English and then in American law as a procedural concept. That is, it first developed as a requirement that government act fairly and use fair procedures to enforce law.

Fair procedures are of little value, however, if they are used to administer unfair laws. The Supreme Court recognized this fact toward the end of the nineteenth century. It began to hold that due process requires that both the ways in which government acts and the laws under which it acts must be fair. Thus, the Court added the idea of substantive due process to the original notion of procedural due process.

In short, **procedural due process** has to do with the *how* (the procedures, the methods) of governmental action. **Substantive due process** involves the *what* (the substance, the policies) of governmental action.

Classic Due Process Cases Any number of cases may be used to illustrate these two elements of due process. Take a classic case, *Rochin* v. *California*, 1952, to exemplify procedural due process.

Rochin was a suspected narcotics dealer. Acting on a tip, three Los Angeles County deputy sheriffs went to his rooming house. They forced their way into Rochin's room, found him sitting on a bed, and spotted two capsules on a nightstand. When one of the deputies asked, "Whose stuff is this?" Rochin popped the capsules into his mouth. Although all three officers jumped him, Rochin managed to swallow the pills.

The deputies took Rochin to a hospital, where his stomach was pumped. The capsules were recovered and found to contain morphine. The State then prosecuted and convicted Rochin for violating the State's narcotics laws.

The Supreme Court unanimously held that the deputies had violated the 14th Amendment's guarantee of procedural due process. Said the Court:

> This is conduct that shocks the conscience. Illegally breaking into the privacy of the petitioner, the struggle to open his mouth and remove what was there, the forcible extraction of his stomach's contents—this course of proceeding by agents of government to obtain evidence is bound to offend

"Government cannot deprive any person of life, liberty, or property without due process of law."

 This limit is placed on the Federal Government in the **5th Amendment**.

 This limit is placed on State and local governments in the **14th Amendment**.

Due process relates to both the **procedures** and the **laws** of government.

PROCEDURAL
Due Process

The procedures, the methods, the *how* of governmental action must be fair.

SUBSTANTIVE
Due Process

The substance, the meaning, the *what* of a law or action of government must be fair.

>> Both the procedures and the laws of government must be in accord with due process. **Analyze Charts** Why are procedural and substantive due process both necessary?

even hardened sensibilities. They are methods too close to the rack and the screw. . . .

—Justice Felix Frankfurter

A second example involves 15-year-old Gerald Gault, who was confined to a State facility until the age of 21 for allegedly making an obscene phone call. In its 1967 ruling, the Court held that, like those for adults, proceedings for juveniles had to comply with the requirements of the 14th Amendment, *In re Gault.*

The case *Pierce* v. *Society of Sisters,* 1925, illustrates substantive due process. In 1922, Oregon's voters had adopted a new compulsory school-attendance law that required all persons between the ages of 8 and 16 to attend *public* schools. The law was purposely written to destroy private, especially parochial, schools in the State.

A Roman Catholic order challenged the law's constitutionality, and the Supreme Court held that its provisions violated the 14th Amendment's Due Process Clause. The Court did not find that the State had enforced the law unfairly. Rather, it held that the law itself was unconstitutional.

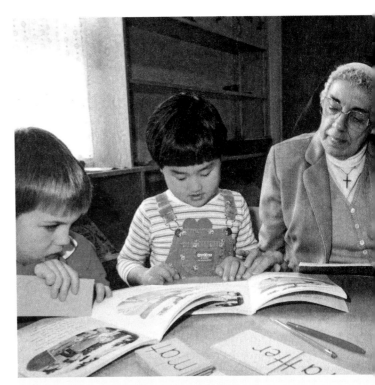

>> A nun reads to children at a parochial school. **Generate Explanations** Why is the Supreme Court ruling in *Pierce* v. *Society of Sisters* called the "Magna Carta of the parochial school system"?

The 14th Amendment and the Bill of Rights

Recall that the Supreme Court has held that the 14th Amendment's Due Process Clause includes within its meaning most of the protections set out in the Bill of Rights.

In a long series of decisions dating from 1925, the Court extended the protections of the Bill of Rights to the States through the 14th Amendment's Due Process Clause. Provisions of the Bill of Rights *incorporated* into the 14th Amendment's Due Process Clause include the 1st, 2nd, 4th, 5th, 6th, and 8th amendments. Provisions of the Bill of Rights *not incorporated* into the 14th Amendment's Due Process Clause include the 3rd, 5th, and 7th amendments.

☑ **APPLY CONCEPTS** Think of an example of a violation of the 5th Amendment right to substantive due process. Explain how the right is being violated.

Individual Rights and the Public Good

In the federal system, the reserved powers of the States include the broad and important **police power.** The police power is the authority of each State to act to protect and promote the public health, safety, morals, and general welfare. In other words, it is the power of each State to safeguard the well-being of its people.

The Police Power and Civil Liberties The use of the police power often produces conflicts with civil liberties. When it does, courts must strike a balance between the needs of society, on the one hand, and individual freedoms on the other. Any number of cases can be used to illustrate the conflict between police power and individual rights. Take as an example a matter often involved in drunk-driving cases.

Every State's laws allow the use of one or more tests to determine whether a person arrested and charged with drunk driving was in fact drunk at the time of the incident. Some of those tests are simple: walking a straight line or touching the tip of one's nose, for example. Some are more sophisticated, however, notably the breathalyzer test and the drawing of a blood sample.

Does the requirement that a person submit to such a test violate his or her rights under the 14th Amendment? Does the test involve an unconstitutional search for and seizure of evidence? Does it amount to forcing a person to testify against himself or herself? Or is that requirement a proper exercise of the police power?

Time after time, State and federal courts have come down on the side of the police power. They have supported the right of society to protect itself against drunk drivers and rejected the individual rights argument.

The leading case is *Schmerber* v. *California*, 1966. There, the Court found no objection to a situation in which a police officer had directed a doctor to draw blood from a drunk-driving suspect. The Court emphasized these points: The blood sample was drawn in accord with accepted medical practice. The officer had reasonable grounds to believe that the suspect was drunk. Further, had the officer taken the time necessary to secure a **search warrant**—a court order authorizing a search—whatever evidence was present could have disappeared from the suspect's system. In 2013, however, the Court clarified the *Schmerber* ruling, noting that, in certain instances urgent circumstances can justify a warrantless blood test of a suspected drunk driver, *Missouri* v. *McNeely*.

Protecting the Public Legislators and judges have often found the public's health, safety, morals, and/or welfare to be of overriding importance. For example:

1. To promote health, States can limit the sale of alcoholic beverages and tobacco, make laws to combat pollution, and require the vaccination of schoolchildren.

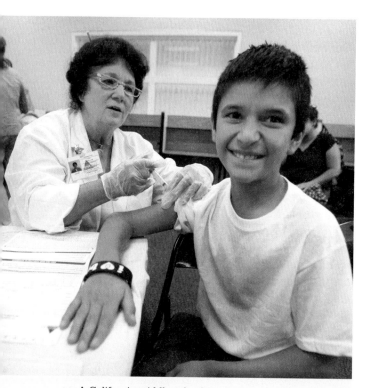

>> A California middle school student receives a free whooping cough booster shot. All 50 States require children to get certain vaccinations before entering public school.

2. To promote safety, States can regulate the carrying of concealed weapons, require the use of seat belts, and punish drunk drivers.

3. To promote morals, States can regulate gambling and outlaw the sale of obscene materials and the practice of prostitution.

4. To promote the general welfare, States can enact compulsory education laws, provide help to the medically needy, and limit the profits of public utilities.

Clearly, governments cannot use the police power in an unreasonable or unfair way, however. In short, they cannot violate the 14th Amendment's Due Process Clause.

Just Compensation Another aspect of due process relates to the right of **eminent domain**, that is, the power of the government to take private property for public use. Contrary to what many believe, this right is real. It is described in the 5th Amendment to the Constitution, also sometimes called the "Takings Clause." The property must be used by the government, or be delegated to a third party for public use. The catch—and this is where due process come into play—is that the government must provide just compensation for any property it takes. This means that the property's owners must get fair market value for the property.

When the Interstate Highway System was built in the decades following World War II, tens of thousands of land owners lost portions of their property to the new roadways. These highways would become major arteries of the nation's economy, as well as make it much easier for people to travel long distances more quickly. For those who lost their homes, family farms, or the tranquility of their back yards, the Interstate Highway Act was a bitter pill to swallow. Under the 5th Amendment, however, they were all fairly compensated for their land.

The federal courts have also ruled that, in some cases, "public use" might include economic development. In 2005, the city of New London, Connecticut, sought to create an economic development zone on the edge of the city. The idea was to set aside land for new businesses, which would lead to more jobs for city residents and more tax revenue. It made sense to find a way to bring as many as one thousand new jobs to an economically depressed area. The piece of land the city chose for the project however, was privately owned.

Can a government, this time a city, take private property for a public goal (economic development) but not necessarily public use? In *Kelo* v. *City of New London*, 2005, the Supreme Court ruled, in a controversial 5–4 decision, that the act was constitutional.

☑ **IDENTIFY CENTRAL IDEAS** Why do you think the Supreme Court held in *Kelo* v. *City of New London* that the taking of private property for the creation of an economic development zone was constitutional?

☑ ASSESSMENT

1. **Explain** Explain the importance of due process rights to the protection of individual rights.

2. **Contrast** What is the difference between substantive due process and procedural due process?

3. **Connect** What is the relationship between the police power and the subordination of personal desires and interests to the public good?

4. **Infer** What did Thomas Paine mean when he said, "THE LAW IS KING"?

5. **Identify Main Ideas** Why is due process important in relation to the government's power of eminent domain?

In re Gault, 1967

Until the 20th century, juveniles and adults in the United States were tried in the same courts and often received the same punishments. Reformers urged a separate system for juveniles, where the focus would be on rehabilitation. But juveniles did not have the same legal protections as adults. This landmark case involved 15-year-old Gerald Gault, who had been committed to the State Industrial School until the age of 21 for allegedly making a "lewd and indecent" phone call. In its ruling, the Supreme Court expanded civil rights for juveniles, ensuring that those under 18 have the same legal rights as adults in criminal court.

As you read, look for the justifications each justice gives for his opinion.

>> Associate Justice Abraham Fortas served on the Supreme Court from 1964 to 1969.

Majority Opinion, Justice Abe Fortas

. . . [W]e confront the reality . . . of the Juvenile Court process with which we deal in this case. A boy is charged with misconduct. The boy is committed to an institution where he may be restrained of liberty for years. It is of no constitutional consequence—and of limited practical meaning—that the institution to which he is committed is called an Industrial School. The fact of the matter is that, however euphemistic the title, a "receiving home" or an "industrial school" for juveniles is an institution of confinement in which the child is incarcerated for a greater or lesser time. His world becomes "a building with whitewashed walls, regimented routine and institutional hours. . . ." Instead of mother and father and sisters and brothers and friends and classmates, his world is peopled by guards, custodians, state employees, and "delinquents" confined with him for anything from waywardness to rape and homicide.

The essential difference between Gerald's case and a normal criminal case is that safeguards available to adults were discarded in Gerald's case. The summary procedure as well as the long

commitment was possible because Gerald was 15 years of age instead of over 18.

If Gerald had been over 18, he would not have been subject to Juvenile Court proceedings. For the . . . offense . . . involved, the maximum punishment would have been a fine of $5 to $50, or imprisonment in jail for not more than two months. Instead, he was committed to custody for a maximum of six years. If he had been over 18 and had committed an offense to which such a sentence might apply, he would have been entitled to substantial rights under the Constitution of the United States as well as under Arizona's laws and constitution. The United States Constitution would guarantee him rights and protections with respect to arrest, search and seizure, and pretrial interrogation. It would assure him of specific notice of the charges and adequate time . . . to prepare his defense. He would be entitled to . . . be represented by counsel, and, at least if a felony were involved, the State would be required to provide counsel if his parents were unable to afford it. If the court acted on the basis of his confession, careful procedures would be required to assure its voluntariness. If the case went to trial, confrontation and opportunity for cross-examination would be guaranteed. . . .

☑ CITE EVIDENCE What point is Justice Fortas making related to Gerald's age?

We do not mean . . . to indicate that the hearing to be held must conform with all of the requirements of a criminal trial or even of the usual administrative hearing; but we do hold that the hearing must measure up to the essentials of due process and fair treatment.

Dissenting Opinion, Justice Potter Stewart

. . . I believe the Court's decision is wholly unsound as a matter of constitutional law, and sadly unwise as a matter of judicial policy.

Juvenile proceedings are not criminal trials. They are not civil trials. They are simply not adversary proceedings. Whether treating with a delinquent child, a neglected child, . . . or a dependent child, a juvenile proceeding's whole purpose and mission is the very opposite of the mission and purpose of a prosecution in a criminal court. The object of the one is correction of a condition. The object of the other is conviction and punishment for a criminal act.

☑ COMPARE According to Justice Stewart, how does the purpose of an adult's trial differ from the purpose of a juvenile's trial?

I possess neither the specialized experience nor the expert knowledge to predict with any certainty where may lie the brightest hope for progress in dealing with the serious problems of juvenile delinquency. But I am certain that the answer does not lie in the Court's opinion in this case, which serves to convert a juvenile proceeding into a criminal prosecution.

The inflexible restrictions that the Constitution so wisely made applicable to adversary criminal trials have no . . . place in the proceedings of . . . juvenile or family courts. And to impose the Court's long catalog of requirements upon juvenile proceedings in every area of the country is to invite a long step backwards into the nineteenth century. In that era

there were no juvenile proceedings, and a child was tried in a conventional criminal court with all the trappings of a conventional criminal trial. So it was that a 12-year-old boy named James Guild was tried in New Jersey for killing Catharine Beakes. A jury found him guilty of murder, and he was sentenced to death by hanging. The sentence was executed. It was all very constitutional.

. . . The Supreme Court of Arizona found that the parents of Gerald Gault "knew of their right to counsel, to subpoena and cross examine witnesses, of the right to confront the witnesses against Gerald and the possible consequences of a finding of delinquency." It further found that "Mrs. Gault knew the exact nature of the charge against Gerald from the day he was taken to the detention home." And, as MR. JUSTICE WHITE correctly points out, . . . no issue of compulsory self-incrimination is presented by this case.

I would dismiss the appeal.

☑ DETERMINE AUTHOR'S POINT OF VIEW How did Justice Stewart feel about the sentencing of James Guild? Cite evidence to support your answer.

☑ ASSESSMENT

1. **Cite Evidence** On what constitutional principle does Justice Fortas base his opinion? Incorporate language from that part of the Constitution in your answer. Use information from the lessons and these primary sources to answer this question.

2. **Explain an Argument** According to Justice Stewart, why was granting a juvenile adult rights a step backwards for children?

3. **Compare and Contrast** Both opinions deal with protecting juveniles in the court system. How do they differ? Cite supporting evidence for each opinion.

4. **Draw Conclusions** What impact did *In re Gault* have on the civil rights of juvenile Blacks, Native Americans, and other people of color? Female juveniles? Juveniles who are immigrants?

8.6

The *Minuteman* statue was built to honor colonial militia. Militias consisted of ordinary citizens who acted to defend their nation. Colonists needed to be ready to serve "at a minute's notice."

 BOUNCE to Activate Flipped Video

Objectives

Evaluate how Supreme Court decisions regarding slavery and involuntary servitude have affected a particular racial group.

Analyze the importance of the 2nd Amendment's protection of the right to keep and bear arms.

Evaluate constitutional provisions for limiting the role of government, including those designed to guarantee the security of home and person.

Understand the Supreme Court's ongoing refinement of the exclusionary rule, including its ruling in *Mapp* v. *Ohio*.

Describe the right to privacy and its origins in constitutional law, and Supreme Court interpretations of rights guaranteed by the Constitution in selected cases, including *Roe* v. *Wade*.

Key Terms

involuntary servitude
discrimination
writs of assistance
probable cause
exclusionary rule

Freedom and Security of the Person

The Constitution of the United States is, in very large part, a statement of limited government. Many of the restrictions it puts on governmental power are intended to protect the right of every American to be free. That is, those restrictions guard the right of individuals to be free from physical restraints, to be secure in their persons, and to be secure in their homes.

Slavery and Involuntary Servitude

The 13th Amendment was added to the Constitution in 1865, ending over 200 years of legalized slavery in America. Section 1 of the amendment declares: "Neither slavery nor involuntary servitude, . . . shall exist within the United States, or any place subject to their jurisdiction." Importantly, Section 2 of this amendment gives Congress the expressed power "to enforce this article by appropriate legislation."

Until 1865, each State could decide for itself whether to allow slavery within its borders. With the 13th Amendment, that power was denied to them, and to the National Government, as well.

The 13th Amendment: Section 1 As a widespread practice, slavery disappeared in the United States more than one hundred years ago. However, there are still cases of it today. Most often, those cases have involved **involuntary servitude**—that is, forced labor. The 1867 Anti-Peonage Act makes it a crime to force someone to work for another in order to fulfill a contract or satisfy a debt. And the Supreme Court has struck down State laws making it a crime for a person to fail to work after having received money or other benefits by promising to do so.

The 13th Amendment does not forbid all forms of involuntary servitude, however. Thus, in 1918, the Supreme Court drew a distinction between "duty" and "involuntary servitude" in upholding the selective service system (the draft). Nor does imprisonment for crime violate the amendment, and those who are convicted of crime can be forced to work. Thus, in the years following the Civil War, former Confederate States passed vagrancy laws that 1) were applied only to Blacks and 2) made it a crime to "loiter" or not have a job. Once in prison, these men could legally be forced to work, whether on plantations or elsewhere. Finally, note this important point: Unlike any other provision in the Constitution, the prohibitions in the 13th Amendment cover the conduct of private individuals as well as the behavior of government.

The 13th Amendment: Section 2 Shortly after the Civil War, Congress passed several civil rights laws based on the 13th Amendment. The Supreme Court, however, sharply narrowed federal authority in several cases, especially the *Civil Rights Cases,* 1883. The Court held that racial **discrimination** (prejudice, unfairness) against African Americans by *private individuals* was allowed. Private discrimination, ruled the Court, did not place the "badge of slavery" on African Americans nor keep them in servitude.

As a result, Congress soon repealed most of the civil rights laws based on the 13th Amendment. The enforcement of the few laws that remained was at best unimpressive. For years, it was generally thought that Congress did not have the power, under either the 13th or 14th amendments, to act against those who practiced race-based discrimination.

Nearly a century later, however, in *Jones* v. *Mayer,* 1968, the Supreme Court breathed new life into the 13th Amendment. The case centered on one of the post Civil War acts Congress had not repealed. Passed in 1866, that almost-forgotten law provided in part that:

> [All] citizens of the United States; . . . of every race and color, . . . shall have the same right, in every State and Territory of the United States, . . . to inherit, purchase, lease, sell, hold, and convey real and personal property, . . . as is enjoyed by white citizens, . . .

—Civil Rights Act of 1866

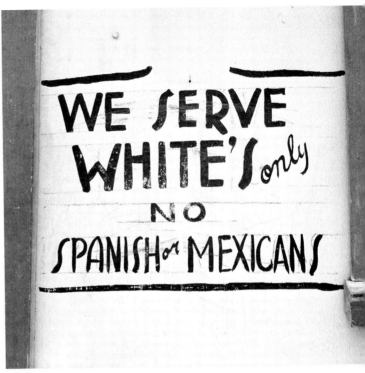

>> As this 1949 sign reveals, racial discrimination in the United States was not limited to African Americans, nor did it end with the banning of slavery in 1865.

>> Discrimination prevented Joseph and Barbara Jones from buying property in a Missouri neighborhood. Their case brought attention to the long history of race-based housing discrimination.

Jones, an African American, had sued because Mayer had refused to sell him a home, solely because of his race. Mayer contended that the 1866 law was unconstitutional, since it sought to prohibit private racial discrimination.

The Supreme Court upheld the 1866 law, declaring that the 13th Amendment abolished slavery and also gave Congress the power to abolish "the badges and incidents of slavery." Said the Court:

> At the very least, the freedom that Congress is empowered to secure under the 13th Amendment includes the freedom to buy whatever a white man can buy, the right to live wherever a white man can live.
>
> —Justice Potter Stewart

The Court affirmed that decision in several later cases. Thus, in *Runyon* v. *McCrary*, 1976, two private schools had refused to admit two African American students. By doing so, the schools had refused to enter into a contract of admission—a contract they had advertised to the general public. The Court found that the schools had violated another provision of the 1866 law, providing that: "[All] citizens of the United States, . . . of every race and color, . . . shall have the same right, . . . to make and enforce contracts . . . as is enjoyed by white citizens. . . ."

The Court has also ruled that the Civil Rights Act of 1866 protects all "identifiable classes of persons who are subjected to intentional discrimination solely because of their ancestry or ethnic characteristics"—for example Jews, *Shaare Tefila Congregation* v. *Cobb*, 1987, and Arabs, *St. Francis College* v. *Al Khazraji*, 1987.

In *Patterson* v. *McLean Credit Union*, 1989, however, the Court declared that although the 1866 law does prohibit racial discrimination in a contract of employment, any on-the-job discrimination should be handled in accord with the Civil Rights Act of 1964. Nevertheless, the Court has several times held that the 13th Amendment gives Congress significant power to attack "the badges and incidents of slavery," from whatever source they may come.

☑ **INFER** How did Supreme Court rulings on racial discrimination cases in the 1800s impact civil rights laws?

Right to Keep and Bear Arms

The 2nd Amendment was added to the Constitution to protect the concept of the citizen-soldier. It reads:

> A well-regulated Militia, being necessary to the security of a free State, the right of the people to keep and bear Arms, shall not be infringed.
>
> —Constitution of the United States

What, exactly, do these words mean? Do they protect *only* the right of each State to keep a militia, especially against encroachments by the Federal Government? Or, does the 2nd Amendment *also* give to individuals a right to keep and bear arms—just as, say, the 1st Amendment protects free speech?

For decades, the Supreme Court refused to accept the latter interpretation. In its one really important 2nd Amendment ruling, in *United States* v. *Miller*, 1939, the Court rejected the individual right argument. It upheld a section of the National Firearms Act of 1934 that made it a crime to ship sawed-off shotguns or sub-machine guns across

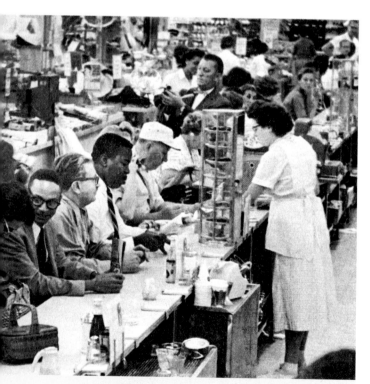

>> A sit-in at a department store in the 1960s involved a racially mixed group asking to be served at a segregated lunch counter. Actions such as this reinforced 13th Amendment rights.

State lines unless the shipper had a federal license to do so. The Court said that it could find no valid link between the shotgun involved in the case and "the preservation . . . of a well-regulated militia."

But the High Court substantially reshaped its interpretation of the 2nd Amendment in *District of Columbia* v. *Heller*, 2008. In that 5–4 decision, it struck down the District's very strict gun-control ordinance—finding that the right of law-abiding citizens to keep a handgun in their homes for self-defense is protected by the 2nd Amendment. And in *McDonald* v. *Chicago*, 2010, it went a step further, incorporating the 2nd Amendment into the 14th Amendment's Due Process Clause. Recall, the Court began that lengthy process of incorporation in 1925.

The Court also said in both *Heller* and *McDonald* that those cases do not overrule "long-standing prohibitions on the possession of firearms by felons or the mentally ill or laws forbidding the carrying of firearms in sensitive places such as schools and government buildings, or laws imposing conditions and qualifications on the commercial sale of arms."

Clearly, both federal and State courts will hear any number of cases challenging the many State and federal laws that limit an individual's right to keep and bear arms.

☑ **DRAW CONCLUSIONS** Based on the Supreme Court's striking down the strict gun control ordinance of the District of Columbia in 2008, what is one important aspect of the 2nd Amendment?

Security of Home and Person

The 3rd and 4th amendments say that government cannot violate the home or person of anyone in this country without just cause.

The 3rd and 4th Amendments The 3rd Amendment forbids the quartering (housing) of soldiers in private homes in peacetime without the owner's consent and not in wartime except "in a manner to be prescribed by law." The guarantee was added to prevent the British colonial practice of "quartering large bodies of troops among us" (Declaration of Independence). The 3rd Amendment has had little importance since 1791 and has never been the subject of a Supreme Court case.

The 4th Amendment also grew out of colonial practice. It was designed to prevent the use of **writs of assistance**—blanket search warrants with which

>> The British Quartering Act of 1765 forced American colonists to provide food and housing to British soldiers at the colonists' own personal expense.

British customs officials had invaded private homes to search for smuggled goods.

Each State constitution contains a similar provision. The guarantee also applies to the States through the 14th Amendment's Due Process Clause, *Mapp* v. *Ohio*, 1961. Unlike the 3rd Amendment, the 4th Amendment has proved a highly important guarantee.

The 4th Amendment and Probable Cause
The basic rule laid down by the 4th Amendment is this: Police officers have no general right to search for evidence or to seize either evidence or persons. Except in special circumstances, they must have a proper warrant (a court order). That warrant must be obtained with **probable cause**—that is, a reasonable suspicion of crime.

Florida v. *J.L.*, 2000, illustrates the rule. There, Miami police received a tip that a teenager was carrying a concealed weapon. Two officers went to the bus stop where the tipster said the young man could be found. The police located him, searched him, pulled a gun from his pocket, and arrested him.

The Court held that the police acted illegally because they did not have a proper warrant. All they had was an anonymous tip, unsupported by any other evidence. Their conduct amounted to just the

Of course I ate the fish. He was in "plain view". You, of all people, should understand how irresistible that is.

>> Under certain circumstances, the police can seize evidence even without a warrant. **Analyze Political Cartoons** What point is the cartoonist making about police attitudes toward such evidence?

>> Narcotics detection dogs are highly trained to work with police officers. When on duty, they are permitted to walk around a car at a traffic stop, as this takes place on public property.

sort of thing the 4th Amendment was intended to prevent.

Police do not always need a warrant, however—for example, when evidence is "in plain view." Thus, the Court upheld a search and seizure involving two men who were bagging cocaine. A policeman spotted them through an open window, entered the apartment, seized the cocaine, and arrested them. The Court upheld their conviction, rejecting a claim to 4th Amendment protection, *Minnesota* v. *Carter,* 1998.

Many 4th Amendment cases are complicated. In *Lidster* v. *Illinois,* 2004, for example, the Court upheld the use of so-called "informational roadblocks." In 1997, police had set up barriers on a busy highway near Chicago, hoping to find witnesses to a recent hit-and-run accident. When Robert Lidster was stopped, an officer smelled alcohol on him. Lidster failed several sobriety tests and was arrested on a drunk-driving charge.

Lidster's attorney filed a motion to quash (set aside) that arrest. The lawyer argued that Lidster was forced to stop by officers who, before they stopped him, had no valid reason (no probable cause) to believe that he had committed any crime.

Lidster lost that argument. The Court upheld both his conviction and the use of informational roadblocks. Lidster had simply run afoul of the long arm of coincidence.

In another significant case, *Florida* v. *Jardines,* 2013, the Court addressed circumstances in which a police officer is not in urgent pursuit of a suspect and does not have a warrant. In these cases, said the Court, the officer cannot bring a drug-sniffing dog onto the porch of home and then use the dog's indication of drugs in the house as a basis for probable cause to obtain a warrant, because the front porch of a home is protected by the 4th Amendment.

The 4th Amendment and Arrests An arrest is the seizure of a person. When officers make a lawful arrest, they do not need a warrant to search "the area from within which [the suspect] might gain possession of a weapon or destructible evidence," *Chimel* v. *California,* 1969. In fact, most arrests take place without a warrant. Police can arrest a person in a public place without one, provided they have probable cause to believe that person has committed or is about to commit a crime.

Illinois v. *Wardlow,* 2000, illustrates this point. There, the police were patrolling a high-crime area in Chicago. When William "Sam" Wardlow saw them, he ran. An officer chased him down an alley, caught him, and found that Wardlow was carrying a loaded

Supreme Court at a Glance

TITLE OF CASE	ISSUE	DECISION
Mapp v. *Ohio*, 1961	States' use of illegally obtained evidence	Evidence seized illegally cannot be used in either federal or State courts.
Minnesota v. *Carter*, 1998	Seizure of evidence "in plain view"	Police do not need a warrant for a search and seizure when evidence is in plain view.
Illinois v. *Wardlow*, 2000	Arrest of an individual without a warrant	Flight can be an important factor in determining whether police have "reasonable suspicion" to stop a suspect.
California v. *Acevedo*, 1991	Warrantless search of a container in an automobile	Whenever police lawfully stop a car, they do not need a warrant to search anything in the vehicle that they have reason to believe holds evidence of a crime.

>> Several landmark Supreme Court cases have examined the 4th Amendment's protections of a citizen's home or person. **Analyze Graphs** How is *Mapp* v. *Ohio* different from the other three cases?

pistol. The Court later held, 5–4, that Wardlow's behavior—his flight—gave the police "common sense" grounds on which to believe that he was involved in some criminal activity. (Note, however, that the Court did not hold that police have a blanket power to stop anyone who flees at the sight of a police officer.)

When, exactly, does the 4th Amendment protection come into play? The Court has several times held that this point is reached "only when the officer, by means of physical force or show of authority, has in some way restrained the liberty of a citizen," *Terry* v. *Ohio*, 1968.

Automobiles and Cell Phones An officer does not need a warrant to search an automobile, a boat, or any other vehicle when there is probable cause to believe that it is involved in illegal activities—because such a "movable scene of crime" could disappear while a warrant was being sought. *Carroll* v. *United States*, 1925, is an early leading case on the point.

Before 1991, the Court had also held that a warrant was usually needed to search a glove compartment, a paper bag, luggage, or other "closed containers" in an automobile. But, in *California* v. *Acevedo*, 1991, the Court set out what it called "one clear-cut rule to govern automobile searches." Whenever police lawfully stop a car, they do not need a warrant to search anything in that vehicle that they have reason to believe holds evidence of a crime.

Police making a routine traffic stop do not need a warrant in order to use a trained dog to sniff around the outside of a car for narcotics, *Illinois* v. *Caballes*,

2005. Unlike the front porch of a home, a vehicle in a public place is not protected against such a search.

The High Court applied the 4th Amendment to cell phones in a 2014 case, *Riley* v. *California*. There, the Court held that police must have a warrant to search the digital contents of a cell phone. In its unanimous decision, the justices noted that cell phones have a multitude of functions today and store "a cache of sensitive personal information." This fact means that searching a cell phone is a gross intrusion of privacy—one that could potentially provide police with even more information than a search of a person's home. Wrote Chief Justice Roberts: "The fact that technology now allows an individual to carry such information in his hand does not make the information any less worthy of the protection for which the Founders fought."

☑ **CITE EVIDENCE** A fugitive flees from police and is seen entering an abandoned house. Upon entering the house, the police find the fugitive, as well as several individuals using illegal drugs, and those individuals are arrested. Under the 4th Amendment, is this a lawful arrest? Cite evidence to support your answer.

The Exclusionary Rule

The heart of the guarantee against unreasonable searches and seizures lies in this question: If an unlawful search or seizure does occur, can that "tainted evidence" be used in court? If so, the

>> Police officers follow strict protocols when conducting searches. Crime scene investigators must obtain each item legally; otherwise, the evidence could be challenged in court.

>> Operating a train while under the influence of drugs can have deadly consequences. For this reason, the Court allows the drug testing of railroad workers following a train accident.

4th Amendment offers no real protection to a person accused of crime.

To meet that problem, the Supreme Court has adopted, and is still refining, the **exclusionary rule.** Essentially, the rule is this: Evidence gained as the result of an illegal act by police cannot be used at the trial of the person from whom it was seized.

The rule was first laid down in *Weeks* v. *United States,* 1914. In that narcotics case, the Court held that evidence obtained illegally by federal officers could not be used in the federal courts. For decades, however, the Court left questions of the use of such evidence in State courts for each State to decide for itself.

The Exclusionary Rule and the States

The exclusionary rule was finally extended to the States in *Mapp* v. *Ohio,* 1961. There, the Court held that the 14th Amendment forbids unreasonable searches and seizures by State and local officers just as the 4th Amendment bars such actions by federal officers. It also held that the fruits of an unlawful search or seizure cannot be used in the State courts, just as they cannot be used in the federal courts.

In *Mapp,* Cleveland police had entered Dollree Mapp's home, forcibly and without a warrant. They claimed to be searching for both a fugitive in a bombing case and evidence of gambling. Their lengthy search found nothing on either count. But they did turn up some "dirty books." Mapp was then convicted of the possession of obscene materials and sentenced to jail. The Court overturned that conviction, holding that the evidence against her had been found illegally and so could not be used at her trial.

The exclusionary rule has always been controversial. It was intended to put teeth into the 4th Amendment, and it has. It says to police: As you enforce the law, obey the law. The rule seeks to prevent, or at least deter, police misconduct.

Critics of the rule say that it means that some persons who are clearly guilty nonetheless go free. Why, they ask, should criminals be able to "beat the rap" on "a technicality"? In response, the Court has gradually narrowed the scope of the rule over the years.

Mandatory Drug Testing

Federal drug testing programs involve searches of persons, and so are covered by the 4th Amendment. To date, however, the Court has held that those programs can be conducted without warrants or even any indication of drug use by those who must take the tests. It did so in two 1989 cases. One involved the mandatory testing of those drug enforcement officers of the U.S. Customs Service (now Immigration and Customs Enforcement) who carry firearms, *National Treasury Employees Union* v. *Von Raab*.

The other had to do with the testing of railroad workers after a train accident, *Skinner* v. *Railway Labor Executives' Association*. In effect, the Court said in both cases that the violations of privacy involved were outweighed by a legitimate governmental interest—for example, in *Skinner*, discovering the cause of a train accident.

The Court has also upheld two local school districts' drug-testing programs, both covered by the 14th Amendment's Due Process Clause. It sustained an Oregon school district's program that requires all students who take part in school sports to agree to be tested for drug use, *Vernonia School District* v. *Acton*, 1995.

That ruling was extended in a case from Oklahoma, *Board of Education of Independent School District No. 92 of Pottawatomie County* v. *Earls*, 2002. There, the Court upheld the random testing of students who want to participate in *any* competitive extracurricular activity. In both of these cases, the Court said that "a warrant and finding of probable cause are unnecessary in the public school context because [they] would unduly interfere with . . . swift and informal disciplinary procedures."

The USA PATRIOT Act The USA PATRIOT Act is officially the Uniting and Strengthening America by Providing Appropriate Tools Required to Intercept and Obstruct Terrorism Act of 2001. It was passed by an overwhelming majority in both houses of Congress and signed by President George W. Bush just six weeks after the terrorist attacks of 9/11. That 342-page statute was renewed, after some contentious debate and with some modifications, in 2006.

The law provides for greatly increased governmental powers to combat domestic and international terrorist activities. Its major provisions focus on three broad areas: surveillance and investigation, immigration, and the financing of terrorist groups.

Since its enactment, the PATRIOT Act has been beset by controversy and a number of its provisions have been challenged in the federal courts. It has been the center of an ongoing debate over this question: In a democratic nation, what is the proper balance between personal liberty and national security?

Of particular 4th Amendment concern are the act's provisions that allow secret "sneak-and-peek searches." Under the statute, federal agents, acting

"Well, if you're going to wiretap your people you are going to hear things."

>> Electronic eavesdropping, or "bugging," may have wide-ranging effects on an individual's rights. **Analyze Political Cartoons** How might this king feel about 4th Amendment rights?

with a warrant, may enter a person's home or office when no one is present and conduct a search—making notes, taking photos, and so on. The agents need not notify the person who is the subject of the search for weeks or even months—and so they are able to continue their investigation without that person's knowledge.

Some aspects of the law have been upheld, including its prohibition against providing any form of material support to any known terror group. Others have been deemed an overreach by the government, such as the bulk collection of Americans' telephone records by the National Security Agency.

When the act came up for renewal in 2005, both Democrats and Republicans in Congress voiced concerns about the act's infringements on individual liberties. After a great deal of debate, lawmakers revised or eliminated several key provisions, including one that required most libraries to turn over user records to the government.

Although the act was amended and reauthorized in subsequent years, many people, including members of Congress, continued to argue that it lacked sufficient safeguards for protecting individual liberties. As a result, some parts of the act were replaced by the USA FREEDOM Act in 2015. That act both limited and made more transparent the government collection of information, and it ended the bulk collection of Americans' telephone records. It also reauthorized some parts of the USA Patriot Act.

The 4th Amendment and Wiretapping Electronic eavesdropping, such as wiretapping, videotaping, and other more sophisticated means of "bugging," is now quite widely used in the United States. These various techniques of discovery present difficult search and seizure questions that the authors of the 4th Amendment could not possibly have foreseen.

The 4th Amendment has always applied to "searches" that involve a physical intrusion—for example, a police officer entering a building or reaching inside a car. The amendment has also always applied to "seizures" that produce some tangible object—for example, a gun or a packet of methamphetamines found inside a car. Listening in on a conversation electronically, from afar, is a quite different matter.

In fact, in its first eavesdropping case, *Olmstead v. United States,* 1928, the Court held that the wiretapping there did not constitute a "search." The case arose when federal agents tapped a Seattle bootlegger's telephone calls. Their bugs produced evidence that led to Olmstead's conviction under the National Prohibition Act. The Court upheld that conviction. It found that, although the agents had not secured a warrant, there had been no "actual physical invasion" of Olmstead's home or office, and so no violation of the 4th Amendment because the agents had tapped the telephone lines *outside* those places.

Katz* v. *United States *Olmstead* stood for nearly forty years. It was finally overruled in what remains the leading case today, *Katz* v. *United States,* 1967. Katz had been convicted of transmitting gambling information across State lines. He had used a public phone booth in Los Angeles to call his contacts in Boston and Miami. Much of the evidence against him had come from an electronic tap placed on the roof—outside—of the phone booth.

The Court ruled that the bugging evidence could not be used against Katz. Despite the fact that he was in a public, glass-enclosed phone booth, he was entitled to make a *private* call, from a place where he had "a reasonable expectation of privacy." Said the Court: The 4th Amendment protects "persons, not just places." It noted, however, that the requirements of the amendment can be satisfied in such situations if police obtain a proper warrant before they install a listening device.

Congress responded to the Court's decision in *Katz* in a provision in the Omnibus Crime Control and Safe Street Act of 1968. There, Congress prohibited any wiretapping for domestic purposes

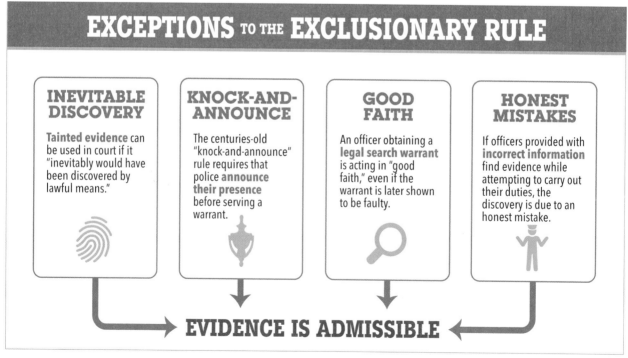

EXCEPTIONS TO THE EXCLUSIONARY RULE

INEVITABLE DISCOVERY
Tainted evidence can be used in court if it "inevitably would have been discovered by lawful means."

KNOCK-AND-ANNOUNCE
The centuries-old "knock-and-announce" rule requires that police **announce their presence** before serving a warrant.

GOOD FAITH
An officer obtaining a **legal search warrant** is acting in "good faith," even if the warrant is later shown to be faulty.

HONEST MISTAKES
If officers provided with **incorrect information** find evidence while attempting to carry out their duties, the discovery is due to an honest mistake.

EVIDENCE IS ADMISSIBLE

>> The Supreme Court has narrowed the scope of the exclusionary rule by allowing evidence to be admissible in cases that it previously had not. **Analyze Charts** What is the purpose of that rule?

except that authorized by a warrant issued by a federal judge.

Soon after September 11, President George W. Bush directed the National Security Agency (NSA), acting in secret and without court-approved warrants, to monitor the international telephone calls and e-mails of Americans with suspected ties to terrorists. The public did not become aware of that monitoring program until late 2005, and its disclosure brought a storm of protest. Many insisted that this NSA activity was illegal. Despite this, the Bush administration defended it as an appropriate exercise of the President's power as commander in chief and the practice was continued under the Obama administration.

Balancing Security and Liberty Balancing national security and American freedom remains a challenging task today and continues to be debated. Does it make sense for individual rights to be subordinated to the public good in the case of national security? Or is the Federal Government encroaching too far on Americans' constitutional rights? Caroline Fredrickson, director of the ACLU, has spoken against U.S. intelligence activities, saying, "Establishing new information collection and sharing authorities for the federal, state, and local law enforcement poses significant risks to our individual liberties, our democratic principles and, ironically, even our security."

Janet Napolitano, former Secretary of Homeland Security, voiced the opposing view: "We frequently hear about a simple inverse relationship between security and liberty. . . . If one is embraced, the other must be sacrificed. . . . The description doesn't do justice to the relationship between security and other values. . . . Security is interrelated with our core values, and among the aspects of the homeland that must be made secure are our fundamental rights and freedoms."

Public debate over the issue flared again in 2013 when a former National Security Agency (NSA) contractor and CIA employee, Edward Snowden, disclosed to several media outlets details about the agency's spying program. Many Americans, including public officials, were surprised to learn of the breadth of the program. To some, Snowden's leaks cast a necessary light on controversial government policies, but to others, including President Obama, the leak of classified documents was seen as damaging to national security, illegal, and traitorous.

☑ **INFER** How did the Supreme Court interpret the 4th Amendment in *Mapp* v. *Ohio*, 1961?

Katz. v. United States, 389 U.S. 347 (1967)

Ð 2010-2014 InTeeLocutory Apparel

>> In *Katz*, the Court ruled that calls from a public phone booth were considered private. **Analyze Political Cartoons** What does this cartoon say about this "reasonable expectation of privacy?"

© Mike Baldwin / Cornered

"Change it to, 'not guilty by reason of personal health issues.' Mentioning insanity violates my right to privacy."

>> This cartoon comments on the constitutional rights of every individual, including those accused of crimes. **Analyze Political Cartoons** What point is the cartoonist making?

The Right of Privacy

The constitutional guarantees of due process create a right of privacy—"the right to be free, except in very limited circumstances, from unwanted governmental intrusions into one's privacy," *Stanley* v. *Georgia*, 1969, and *Lawrence* v. *Texas*, 2003. It is, in the words of Justice Louis Brandeis, "the right to be let alone."

The Constitution makes no specific mention of the right of privacy, but the Supreme Court declared its existence in *Griswold* v. *Connecticut*, 1965. That case centered on a State law that outlawed birth control counseling and prohibited the use of all birth control devices. The Court held the law to be a violation of the 14th Amendment's Due Process Clause—and noted that the State had no business policing the marital bedroom.

The Supreme Court's Ruling in *Roe* v. *Wade*

The most controversial applications of the right of privacy have come in cases that raise this question: To what extent can a State limit a woman's right to an abortion? The leading case is *Roe* v. *Wade*, 1973. There, the Supreme Court struck down a Texas law that made abortion a crime except when necessary to save the life of the mother.

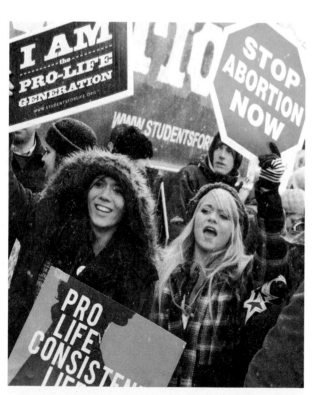

>> Students protest in Washington, D.C., in 2013. Founded in the 1970s, Students for Life of America provides resources for students interested in pro-life issues.

In *Roe*, the Court held that the 14th Amendment's right of privacy "encompass[es] a woman's decision whether or not to terminate her pregnancy." More specifically, the Court ruled that:

1. In the first trimester of pregnancy (about three months), a State must recognize a woman's right to an abortion; it cannot interfere with medical judgments in that matter during that period.

2. In the second trimester, a State, acting in the interest of women who undergo abortions, can make reasonable regulations about how, when, and where abortions can be performed but cannot prohibit the procedure.

3. In the final trimester, a State, acting to protect the unborn child, can choose to prohibit all abortions except those necessary to preserve the life or health of the mother.

Challenges to *Roe* In several later cases, the Court rejected a number of challenges to its basic holding in *Roe*. As the composition of the Court has changed, however, so has the Court's position on abortion. That shift can be seen in the Court's decisions in later cases on the matter.

In *Webster* v. *Reproductive Health Services*, 1989, the Court upheld two key parts of a Missouri law. Those provisions prohibit abortions, except those that preserve the mother's life or health, (1) in any publicly operated hospital or clinic in that State, and (2) when the mother is 20 or more weeks pregnant and tests show that the fetus is viable (capable of sustaining life outside the mother's body).

Two cases in 1990 addressed the issue of minors and abortion. In those cases, the Court said that a State may require a minor (1) to inform at least one parent before she can obtain an abortion, *Ohio* v. *Akron Center for Reproductive Health*, and (2) to tell both parents of her plans, except in cases where a judge gives permission for an abortion without parental knowledge, *Hodgson* v. *Minnesota*.

The Court's most important decision on the issue since *Roe* v. *Wade* came in *Planned Parenthood of Southeastern Pennsylvania* v. *Casey* in 1992. There, the Court announced this rule: A State may place reasonable limits on a woman's right to have an abortion, but these restrictions cannot impose an "undue burden" on her choice of that procedure.

In *Casey*, the Court applied that new standard to Pennsylvania's Abortion Control Act. It upheld several sections of the law, finding that they did not place "a substantial obstacle in the path of a woman seeking an abortion of a non-viable fetus." Those provisions, it said, do not impose an "undue burden" on a woman's choice.

The Supreme Court did strike down another key part of the Pennsylvania law in *Casey,* however. That provision required that a married woman tell her husband of her plan to have an abortion. That requirement, said the Court, did indeed amount to an "undue burden."

The issue of abortion is a polarizing one involving two sets of deeply held and overlapping beliefs— those involving religious convictions and those involving women's rights. Because of this, cases related to abortion continue to come before the Supreme Court, and those cases always prompt rallies and protests from both sides. The religious argument is that life begins at conception, which means that it should be unlawful to end a pregnancy. The women's rights argument is that a woman should be able to control her own body and the government should not be involved. Into this divide the Supreme Court occasionally must step as it attempts to remove all emotion from the issue and decides any cases that come before it based on the Constitution and existing law—in particular, *Roe* v. *Wade.*

☑ **APPLY CONCEPTS** What is the significance of the Supreme Court's ruling in *Webster* v. *Reproductive Health Services,* 1989?

>> Planned Parenthood is a pro-choice nonprofit group that provides reproductive health services in the United States and abroad.

☑ ASSESSMENT

1. **Explain** How have Supreme Court decisions regarding slavery and involuntary servitude affected Black Americans?

2. **Analyze Information** According to Supreme Court decisions, does the 2nd Amendment's protection of the right to keep and bear arms relate only to State militias, or also to the individual right to keep and bear arms? Give evidence to support your answer.

3. **Draw Conclusions** Which constitutional provisions limit the role of government in order to guarantee the security of home and person? Explain how the provisions limit the role of government.

4. **Infer** Why has the Supreme Court continued to refine the exclusionary rule?

5. **Interpret** How has the Supreme Court interpreted the Constitution in cases involving abortion?

8.7

The 6th Amendment guarantees a defendant the right to an attorney regardless of his or her ability to pay for one. A defendant may also choose to represent him- or herself in court.

BOUNCE to Activate Flipped Video

Objectives

Understand the role of limited government in the protection of individual rights, including the writ of habeas corpus, bills of attainder, and ex post facto laws.

Outline how the right to a grand jury and the guarantee against double jeopardy help safeguard the rights of the accused.

Describe issues that arise from guarantees of speedy and public trials.

Identify the rights guaranteed by the Bill of Rights, including the right to a fair trial by jury.

Examine Supreme Court interpretations of the right to an adequate defense and the guarantee against self-incrimination, including *Gideon* v. *Wainwright* and *Miranda* v. *Arizona*.

Key Terms

writ of habeas corpus	bench trial
bill of attainder	Miranda rule
ex post facto law	bail
grand jury	preventive detention
indictment	capital punishment
presentment	treason
information	Abraham Lincoln
double jeopardy	Roger B. Taney

Rights of the Accused

Think about this statement: "It is better that ten guilty persons go free than that one innocent person be punished." That maxim expresses one of the bedrock principles of the American legal system. Of course, society must punish criminals in order to preserve itself. However, the law intends that any person who is suspected or accused of a crime must be presumed innocent until proven guilty by fair and lawful means.

Article I Protections

No Imprisonment Without Just Cause The **writ of habeas corpus** is intended to prevent unjust arrests and imprisonments. The phrase *habeas corpus* comes from the Latin, meaning "you should have the body," and those are the opening words of the writ. It is a court order directed to an officer holding a prisoner. It commands that the prisoner be brought before the court and that the officer show cause—explain, with good reason—why the prisoner should not be released.

The right to seek a writ of habeas corpus is protected against the National Government in Article I, Section 9 of the Constitution. That right is guaranteed against the States in each of their own constitutions.

The Constitution says that the right to the writ cannot be suspended, "unless when in Cases of Rebellion or Invasion the public Safety may require it." President **Abraham Lincoln** suspended the writ in 1861 during the Civil War. His order covered various parts of the country, including several areas in which war was not then being waged. Chief Justice **Roger B. Taney**, sitting as a circuit judge, held Lincoln's action unconstitutional, *Ex parte Merryman,* 1861.

Taney ruled that the Constitution gives the power to suspend the writ to Congress alone. Congress then passed the Habeas Corpus Act of 1863. It gave the President the power to suspend the writ when and where, in his judgment, that action was necessary. In *Ex parte Milligan,* 1866, the Supreme Court ruled that neither Congress nor the President can suspend the writ in those locales where there is no actual fighting nor the likelihood of combat.

The right to the writ has been suspended only once since the Civil War and the Reconstruction Period that followed it. The territorial governor of Hawaii did so following the Japanese attack on Pearl Harbor in December 1941. The Supreme Court later ruled that the governor did not have the power to take that action, *Duncan* v. *Kahanamoku,* 1946.

In 2008, the Supreme Court held, for the first time, that foreign prisoners being held as enemy combatants at the U.S. naval base at Guantanamo Bay, Cuba, have a constitutional right to challenge their detention—that is, a right to seek writs of habeas corpus—in the federal courts, *Boumediene* v. *Bush* and *Al Odah* v. *United States.* Dozens of habeas corpus petitions were then filed on behalf of prisoners and the courts have dealt with them on an individual basis.

Congress–Legislators, Not Judges A **bill of attainder** is a legislative act that provides for the punishment of a person without a court trial. The Constitution prohibits Congress from passing any such measure in Article I, Section 9, and it places the same prohibition on the States in Section 10.

The Framers wrote the ban on bills of attainder into the Constitution because Parliament and several of the colonial legislatures had passed many such bills. They have been quite rare in our national history, however.

The denial of the power to pass bills of attainder is both a protection of individual freedom and one of the Constitution's several provisions for separation of powers. In effect, the ban says to members of Congress and to the States' lawmakers: Be legislators, not judges. A legislative body can pass laws that define crime and set the penalties for violations of them. But it cannot pass a law that declares a person or identifiable group of persons guilty of a crime and provides for his or their punishment.

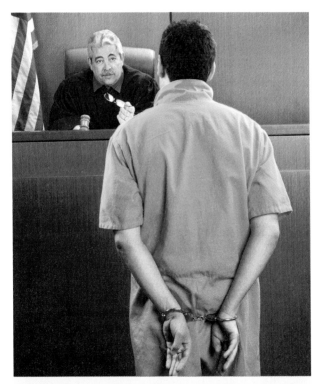

>> Alexander Hamilton wrote in support of the writ of habeas corpus, stating that "arbitrary imprisonments have been in all ages the favourite and most formidable instruments of tyranny."

>> After the attack on Pearl Harbor, the governor of Hawaii declared martial law, suspending the writ of habeas corpus and giving control of the government to the military.

United States v. *Lovett,* 1946, is one of the few attainder cases ever decided by the Supreme Court. That case involved a provision in a law appropriating funds for the army that declared that none of the monies could be used to pay the salaries of three named persons. Several members of the House thought that those three were "subversive," and they urged the President to discharge them. The Court found that provision to be a bill of attainder.

No Retroactive Criminal Laws The Constitution, in Article I, Sections 9 and 10, prohibits Congress and the States from enacting ex post facto laws. An **ex post facto law** is a law applied to an act committed before the passage of that law. The phrase *ex post facto* is from the Latin, meaning "after the fact." An ex post facto law (1) is a criminal law—one defining a crime and/or providing for its punishment; (2) applies to an act committed before its passage; and (3) works to the disadvantage of the accused.

For example, a law making it a crime to sell marijuana cannot be applied to a sale that occurred before that law was passed. Or, a law that changes the penalty for murder from life in prison to death cannot be used to sentence a person who committed a murder before the punishment was made more severe.

Retroactive civil laws are *not* forbidden. Thus, a law raising income tax rates could be passed in November and applied to income earned through the whole year.

☑ **APPLY CONCEPTS** How does the prohibition of ex post facto laws in criminal cases protect the rights of the accused?

Grand Jury and Double Jeopardy

A person suspected of a crime that could lead to death or imprisonment must be formally accused in order to be detained for prosecution. A grand jury made up of citizens holds a proceeding to decide if there is enough evidence to justify a trial. A prosecutor may also make a sworn statement that enough evidence is available for a trial.

The Right to a Grand Jury The 5th Amendment to the Constitution declares that

> No person shall be held to answer for a capital, or otherwise infamous crime, unless on a presentment or indictment of a Grand Jury. . . .
>
> —United States Constitution

The **grand jury** is the formal device by which a person can be accused of a serious crime—that is, any offense for which the punishment is death or imprisonment. In federal cases, the grand jury is a body of from 16 to 23 persons drawn from the area of the district court that it serves. The votes of at least 12 of the grand jurors are needed to return an indictment or to make a presentment.

An **indictment** is a formal complaint that the prosecutor lays before a grand jury. It charges the accused with one or more crimes. If the grand jury finds that there is enough evidence to justify a trial, it returns a "true bill of indictment." The accused person is then held for prosecution. If the grand jury does not make such a finding, the charge is dropped and the accused is set free.

A **presentment** is a formal accusation brought by the grand jury on its own motion, rather than that of the prosecutor. It is rarely used in federal courts.

A grand jury's proceedings are not a trial. Since unfair harm could come if they were public, its

>> Texas Congressman Martin Dies, Jr., (shown) led efforts to dismiss government employees, including Robert Lovett. Lovett sued, arguing that the action was an unconstitutional bill of attainder.

The Factors Lawyers Consider When Selecting a Jury

FACTORS	EXAMPLES
Demographics	What is their gender, race, age, etc.?
Personality	Are they stern, compassionate, resistant to social pressure, etc.?
Life experiences	Have they ever been the victim of a violent crime?
Value system	How do they feel about particular crimes, large corporations, etc.?
Leadership potential	Will they sway the other jurors to agree with their decision?
Nonverbal signals	Are they frowning, nodding, fidgeting, etc.?
Respect for court	Are they dressed neatly or sloppily?

>> The Constitution guarantees the right to a fair trial before an impartial jury.
Analyze Charts Why are these factors important for lawyers to consider when selecting a jury?

sessions are secret. They are also one-sided—in the law, an *ex parte* judicial proceeding. That is, only the prosecution, not the defense, is present.

The right to grand jury is intended as a protection against overzealous prosecutors. Critics say that it is too time-consuming, too expensive, and too likely to follow the dictates of the prosecutor.

The 5th Amendment's grand jury provision is the only part of the Bill of Rights relating to criminal prosecution that the Supreme Court has not brought within the coverage of the 14th Amendment's Due Process Clause. In the majority of States today, most criminal charges are not brought by grand jury indictment. They are brought, instead, by an **information,** an affidavit in which the prosecutor swears that there is enough evidence to justify a trial.

Guarantee Against Double Jeopardy The 5th Amendment's guarantee against double jeopardy is the first of several protections in the Bill of Rights especially intended to ensure fair trials in the federal courts. Fair trials are guaranteed in State courts by each State's constitution and, also, recall, by the 14th Amendment's Due Process Clause.

The 5th Amendment says in part that no person can be "twice put in jeopardy of life or limb." Today, this prohibition against **double jeopardy** means that once a person has been tried for a crime, he or she cannot be tried again for that same crime. The Constitution's ban of double jeopardy applies against the States through the 14th Amendment's Due Process Clause, *Benton* v. *Maryland,* 1969.

A person can violate both a federal *and* a State law in a single act, however—for example, by selling narcotics. That person can then be tried for the federal crime in a federal court and for the State crime in a State court. Thus, a single act can also result in several criminal charges. A person who breaks into a store, steals liquor, and sells it can be tried for illegal entry, theft, and selling liquor without a license.

In a trial in which a jury cannot agree on a verdict (a hung jury), there is no jeopardy. It is as though no trial had been held. Nor is double jeopardy involved when a case is appealed to a higher court.

Several States allow the continued confinement of violent sex predators after they have completed a prison term. The Court has twice held that that confinement is not punishment—and so does not involve double jeopardy. Rather, the practice is intended to protect the public from harm, *Kansas* v. *Hendricks,* 1997, and *Seling* v. *Young,* 2001.

☑ **GENERATE EXPLANATIONS** How does the 5th Amendment's ban on double jeopardy help to ensure a fair trial?

Going to Trial

The Constitution offers several other protections for a person accused of crime. These are found in both the 5th and 6th amendments. They cover such important areas as the right to a speedy and public trial, the right to trial by jury, the right to adequate defense, and a guarantee against self-incrimination.

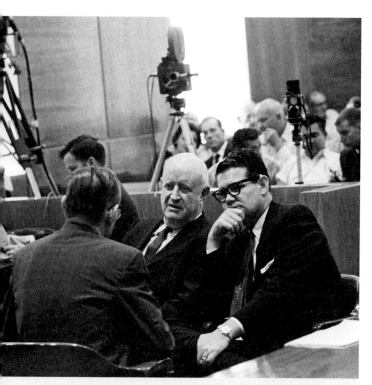

>> Billy Sol Estes (right) confers with attorneys. His pretrial hearing was broadcast live on television and radio and drew "[m]assive pretrial publicity totaling eleven volumes of press clippings."

>> During the high-profile murder and racketeering trial of James "Whitey" Bulger in 2013, photography was banned in the courtroom, and only a limited number of reporters were allowed inside.

Speedy Trial The 6th Amendment commands that:

In all criminal prosecutions, the accused shall enjoy the right to a speedy and public trial, . . .

—United States Constitution

The guarantee of a speedy trial is meant to ensure that the government will try a person accused of crime within a reasonable time and without undue delay. But how long a delay is too long? The Supreme Court has recognized that each case must be judged on its own merits.

In a leading case, *Barker* v. *Wingo,* 1972, the Court listed four criteria for determining if a delay has violated the constitutional protection. They are (1) the length of the delay, (2) the reasons for it, (3) whether the delay has in fact harmed the defendant, and (4) whether the defendant had asked for a prompt trial.

The Speedy Trial Act of 1974 says that the time between a person's arrest and the beginning of his or her federal criminal trial cannot be more than 100 days. The law does allow for some exceptions, however—for example, when the defendant must undergo extensive mental tests, or when the defendant or a key witness is ill.

The 6th Amendment guarantees a prompt trial in *federal* cases. The Supreme Court first applied this right against the States as part of the 14th Amendment's Due Process Clause in *Klopfer* v. *North Carolina,* 1967.

Public Trial The 6th Amendment says that a trial must also be public. The right to be tried in public is also part of the 14th Amendment's guarantee of procedural due process, *In re Oliver,* 1948.

A trial must not be *too* speedy or *too* public, however. The Supreme Court threw out an Arkansas murder conviction in 1923 on just those grounds. The trial had taken only 45 minutes, and it had been held in a courtroom packed by a threatening mob.

Within reason, a judge can limit both the number and the kinds of spectators who may be present at a trial. Those who seek to disrupt a courtroom can be barred from it. A judge can order a courtroom cleared when the expected testimony may be embarrassing to a witness or to someone else who is not a party to the case.

Many questions about how public a trial should be involve the media—especially newspapers and television. The guarantees of fair trial and free press often collide in the courts. On the one hand, a courtroom is a public place where the media have

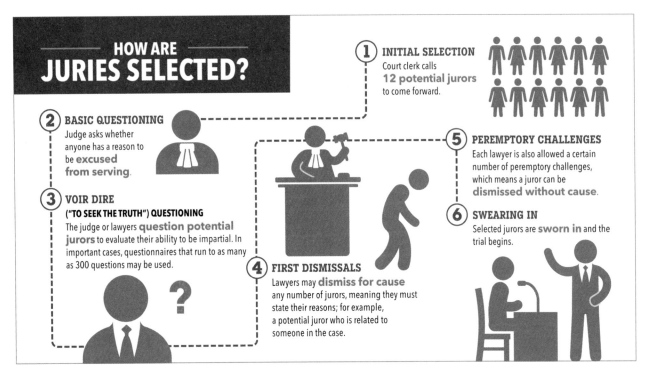

HOW ARE JURIES SELECTED?

1. INITIAL SELECTION
Court clerk calls **12 potential jurors** to come forward.

2. BASIC QUESTIONING
Judge asks whether anyone has a reason to be **excused from serving**.

3. VOIR DIRE
("TO SEEK THE TRUTH") QUESTIONING
The judge or lawyers **question potential jurors** to evaluate their ability to be impartial. In important cases, questionnaires that run to as many as 300 questions may be used.

4. FIRST DISMISSALS
Lawyers may **dismiss for cause** any number of jurors, meaning they must state their reasons; for example, a potential juror who is related to someone in the case.

5. PEREMPTORY CHALLENGES
Each lawyer is also allowed a certain number of peremptory challenges, which means a juror can be **dismissed without cause**.

6. SWEARING IN
Selected jurors are **sworn in** and the trial begins.

>> A defendant's right to a trial by jury has led courts to create a selection process for those who will serve on a jury. **Analyze Charts** How does this process help ensure an impartial jury?

a right to be present. On the other hand, media coverage can jeopardize a defendant's right to a fair trial. The Supreme Court has often held that the right to a public trial belongs to the defendant, not to the media.

What about televised trials? Television cameras are barred from all federal courtrooms. Yet most States do allow some form of in-court television reporting. Can televising a criminal trial violate a defendant's rights?

In an early major case, *Estes* v. *Texas,* 1965, the Supreme Court reversed the conviction of an oil man charged with swindling investors and others out of millions of dollars. The Court found that the media coverage of his trial had been so "circus-like" and disruptive that Estes had been denied his right to a fair trial.

Sixteen years later, the Court held in *Chandler* v. *Florida,* 1981, that nothing in the Constitution prevents a State from allowing the televising of a criminal trial. At least, televising is not prohibited as long as steps are taken to avoid too much publicity and to protect the defendant's rights.

Trial by Jury The 6th Amendment also says that a person accused of a federal crime must be tried "by an impartial jury." This guarantee reinforces an earlier one set out in the Constitution, Article III,

Section 2. The right to trial by jury is also binding on the States, but only in cases involving "serious" crimes, meaning those for which imprisonment for more than six months is possible. The trial jury is often called the petit jury. *Petit* is the French word for "small."

The 6th Amendment adds that the members of a federal court jury must be drawn from "the State and district wherein the crime shall have been committed, which district shall have been previously ascertained by law." This stipulation gives the defendant any benefit there might be in having a jury familiar with the people and problems of the area.

A defendant may ask to be tried in another place—seek a "change of venue"—on grounds that the people of the locality are so prejudiced in the case that an impartial jury cannot be drawn. The judge must decide whether a change of venue is justified.

A defendant may also waive the right to a jury trial. However, he or she can do so only if the judge is satisfied that the defendant fully understands what that action means. In fact, a judge can order a jury trial even when a defendant does not want one. If a defendant waives the right, a **bench trial** is held, which means that a judge alone hears the case. (Of course, a defendant can plead guilty and so avoid any trial.)

In federal practice, the jury that hears a criminal case must have 12 members. However, some federal civil cases are tried before juries of as few as six members. Several States now provide for smaller juries, often of six members, in both criminal and civil cases. In the federal courts, the jury that hears a criminal case can convict the accused only by a unanimous vote. Most States follow the same rule.

Composition of the Jury In a long series of cases, dating from *Strauder* v. *West Virginia,* 1880, the Supreme Court has held that a jury must be "drawn from a fair cross section of the community." *Hernandez* v. *Texas,* 1954, tested the definition of "fair cross section" when it considered whether Pete Hernandez had received a fair trial in a murder case when convicted by a jury that did not include anyone of Mexican descent. The Court ruled in Hernandez' favor, stating that the exclusion of Hispanics from jury service denied him equal protection under the law.

In a later case, *Taylor* v. *Louisiana,* 1975, the court ruled that a jury is not impartial if members of any groups "playing major roles in the community" have been excluded from it. In short, no person can be kept off a jury on such grounds as race, color, religion, national origin, or gender.

Right to Adequate Defense Every person accused of a crime has the right to the best possible defense that circumstances will allow. In a 1963 case from Florida, *Gideon* v. *Wainwright,* the Court held that an attorney must be furnished to a defendant who cannot afford one. In many places, a judge assigns a lawyer from the local community, or a private legal aid association provides counsel.

The 6th Amendment says that a defendant has the right (1) "to be informed of the nature and cause of the accusation," (2) "to be confronted with the witnesses against him" and question them in open court, (3) "to have compulsory process for obtaining witnesses in his favor" (that is, favorable witnesses can be subpoenaed), and (4) "to have the Assistance of Counsel for his defense."

These key safeguards apply in the federal courts. Still, if a State fails to honor any of them, the accused can appeal a conviction arguing that the 14th Amendment's Due Process Clause has been violated. The Supreme Court protected the right to counsel in *Gideon* v. *Wainwright,* 1963; the right of confrontation in *Pointer* v. *Texas,* 1965; and the right to call witnesses in *Washington* v. *Texas,* 1967.

These guarantees are intended to prevent the cards from being stacked in favor of the prosecution. One of the leading right-to-counsel cases, *Escobedo* v. *Illinois,* 1964, illustrates this point.

Chicago police picked up Danny Escobedo for questioning in the death of his brother-in-law. On the way to the police station, and then while he was being questioned there, he asked several times to see his lawyer. The police denied those requests.

They did so even though his lawyer was in the police station and was trying to see him, and the police knew the lawyer was there. Through a long night of questioning, Escobedo made several damaging statements. Prosecutors later used those statements in court as a major part of the evidence that led to his murder conviction.

The Supreme Court ordered Escobedo freed from prison four years later. It held that he had been improperly denied his 14th Amendment right to counsel.

>> After defending himself and being found guilty in a lower court, Clarence Gideon wrote to the Supreme Court that he had been unconstitutionally denied counsel. The Court agreed and ordered a new trial.

☑ **GENERATE EXPLANATIONS** Since the 6th Amendment requires that trials must be public, should all trials be televised? Why or why not?

MIRANDA WARNING

1. YOU HAVE THE RIGHT TO REMAIN SILENT.

2. ANYTHING YOU SAY CAN AND WILL BE USED AGAINST YOU IN A COURT OF LAW.

3. YOU HAVE THE RIGHT TO CONSULT AN ATTORNEY AND HAVE AN ATTORNEY PRESENT WHILE YOU ARE BEING QUESTIONED.

4. IF YOU CANNOT AFFORD TO HIRE A LAWYER, ONE WILL BE APPOINTED TO REPRESENT YOU BEFORE ANY QUESTIONING, IF YOU WISH.

5. YOU CAN DECIDE AT ANY TIME TO EXERCISE THESE RIGHTS AND NOT ANSWER ANY QUESTIONS OR MAKE ANY STATEMENTS.

WAIVER

DO YOU UNDERSTAND EACH OF THESE RIGHTS I HAVE EXPLAINED TO YOU? HAVING THESE RIGHTS IN MIND, DO YOU WISH TO TALK TO US NOW?

>> Many police officers carry a Miranda warning card with them, although few need to read directly from the card, since they can recite the rule from memory.

Guarantee Against Self-Incrimination

The guarantee against self-incrimination is among the several protections set out in the 5th Amendment. That provision declares that no person can be "compelled in any criminal case to be a witness against himself." This protection must be honored in both the federal and State courts, *Malloy* v. *Hogan,* 1964.

In a criminal case, the burden of proof is always on the prosecution. The defendant does not have to prove his or her innocence. The ban on self-incrimination prevents the prosecution from shifting the burden of proof to the defendant.

Applying the Guarantee The language of the 5th Amendment suggests that the constitutional guarantee against self-incrimination applies only to criminal cases. In fact, the amendment covers any governmental proceeding in which a person is legally compelled to answer any question that could lead to a criminal charge. Thus, a person may claim the right ("take the Fifth") in a variety of situations: in a divorce proceeding (which is a civil matter), before a legislative committee, at a school board's disciplinary hearing, and so on.

The courts, not the individuals who claim it, decide when the right can be properly invoked. If the plea of self-incrimination is pushed too far, a person can be held in contempt of court.

The guarantee against self-incrimination is a personal right. One can claim it only for oneself. It cannot be invoked in someone else's behalf. Thus, a person can be forced to "rat" on another, with this major exception: A husband cannot be forced to testify against his wife, or a wife against her husband.

The privilege does not protect a person from being fingerprinted or photographed or required to submit a handwriting sample or appear in a police lineup. And it does not mean that a person does not have to submit to a blood test in a drunk-driving situation, *Schmerber* v. *California,* 1966.

A person cannot, however, be forced to confess to a crime under duress—that is, as a result of torture or other physical or psychological pressure. In *Ashcraft* v. *Tennessee,* 1944, for example, the Supreme Court threw out the conviction of a man accused of hiring another person to murder his wife. The confession on which his conviction rested had been secured only after some 36 hours of continuous, threatening interrogation. The questioning was conducted by officers who worked in shifts because, they said, they became so tired that they had to rest.

Miranda **v. Arizona** In a truly historic decision, the Court refined the Escobedo holding in *Miranda* v. *Arizona*, 1966. In this case, a mentally challenged man, Ernesto Miranda, had been convicted of kidnapping and rape. Ten days after the crime, the victim picked Miranda out of a police lineup. After two hours of questioning, during which the police did not tell him of his rights, Miranda confessed.

The Supreme Court struck down Miranda's conviction. More importantly, it said that it would no longer uphold convictions in cases in which suspects had not been told of their constitutional rights before police questioning. It thus laid down the **Miranda rule**—the requirement that police must read a suspect his or her rights before any questioning occurs.

The Supreme Court is still refining the rule on a case-by-case basis. Most often the rule is closely followed. But there are exceptions. Thus, the Court has held that once police have read a suspect his rights and questioning has begun, it is up to the person in custody to very clearly assert his right to remain silent, *Berghuis* v. *Thompkins*, 2010.

The Miranda rule has always been controversial. Critics say that it "puts criminals back on the streets." Others applaud the rule, arguing that criminal law enforcement is most effective when it relies on independently secured evidence, rather than on confessions gained by questionable tactics from defendants who do not have the help of a lawyer.

☑ **ASSESS CREDIBILITY** Why do some critics claim that the Miranda rule "puts criminals back on the streets"?

Bail and Preventive Detention

Again, think about this proposition: "It is better that ten guilty persons go free than that one innocent person be punished." How do you react to that comment now, after reading about the rights of persons accused of crime? Consider those persons who are found guilty, those who do not go free but are instead punished. How should they be treated? The Constitution gives its most specific answers to that question in the 8th Amendment.

The 8th Amendment says, in part:

> Excessive bail shall not be required, nor excessive fines imposed, . . .
>
> — United States Constitution

Each State constitution sets out similar restrictions. The general rule is that the bail or fine in a case must bear a reasonable relationship to the seriousness of the crime involved.

Limits on Bail The sum of money that the accused may be required to post (deposit with the court) as a guarantee that he or she will appear in court at the proper time is called **bail**. The use of bail is justified on two bases: First, that a person should not be jailed until his or her guilt has been established; and second, that a defendant is better able to prepare for trial outside of a jail.

Note that the Constitution does not say that all persons accused of a crime are automatically entitled to bail. Rather, it guarantees that, where bail is set, the amount will not be excessive.

The leading case on bail in the federal courts is *Stack* v. *Boyle*, 1951. There, the Court ruled that "bail set at a figure higher than an amount reasonably calculated" to assure a defendant's appearance at a trial "is 'excessive' under the 8th Amendment."

In *Stack*, 12 persons had been accused of violating the Smith Act of 1940, which, recall,

>> A lawyer reviews her client's paperwork before a bail hearing. During the hearing, she will object if the bail set for her client is unreasonable.

made it a federal crime for any person to advocate the violent overthrow of government in the United States. A defendant can appeal the denial of release on bail or the amount of bail. Bail is usually set in accordance with the severity of the crime charged and with the reputation and financial resources of the accused. People with little or no income often have trouble raising bail. Therefore, the federal and most State courts release many defendants "on their own recognizance"—that is, on their honor. Failure to appear for trial, "jumping bail," is itself a punishable crime.

Preventive Detention In 1984, Congress provided for the **preventive detention** of some people accused of federal crimes. A federal judge can order that the accused be held, without bail, when there is good reason to believe that he or she will commit another serious crime before trial. Critics of the law claim that preventive detention amounts to punishment before trial. They say it undercuts the presumption of innocence to which all defendants are entitled.

The Supreme Court upheld the 1984 law, 6–3, in *United States* v. *Salerno,* 1987. The majority rejected the argument that preventive detention is punishment. Rather, it found the practice a legitimate response to a "pressing societal problem." And the Court also upheld a federal law that allows the government to keep those inmates who are deemed "sexually dangerous" behind bars even though they have served their sentenced time, *United States* v. *Comstock,* 2010.

✓ **CHECK UNDERSTANDING** The 8th Amendment prohibits the setting of "excessive bail." What is considered "excessive"?

Cruel and Unusual Punishments

The 8th Amendment also forbids "cruel and unusual punishments." The 14th Amendment extends that prohibition against the States, *Robinson* v. *California,* 1962.

The Supreme Court decided its first cruel and unusual case in 1879 in *Wilkerson* v. *Utah.* There, a territorial court had sentenced a convicted murderer to death by a firing squad. The Court held that this punishment was not forbidden by the Constitution. The kinds of penalties the Constitution intended

Incarcerated Persons in the U.S.*

YEAR	NUMBER
1980	513,800
1987	881,000
1994	1,541,200
2001	2,035,200
2008	2,393,800
2015	2,254,000

*Includes local jail inmates and prisoners held in State or federal prisons or privately operated facilities.
SOURCE: Bureau of Justice Statistics

>> The number of people in jail or prison skyrocketed between 1980 and 2007–2008. **Analyze Charts** Are overcrowded prisons "cruel and unusual punishment"? Why or why not?

to prevent, said the Court, were such barbaric tortures as burning at the stake, crucifixion, drawing and quartering, "and all others in the same line of unnecessary cruelty." The Court took the same position a few years later when, for the first time, it upheld the electrocution of a convicted murderer in a case from New York, *In re Kemmler,* 1890.

More often than not, the Court has rejected the cruel and unusual punishment argument. In *Louisiana* v. *Resweber,* 1947, the Court found that it was not unconstitutional to subject a convicted murderer to a second electrocution after the first had failed. In *Rhodes* v. *Chapman,* 1980, it held that putting two inmates in a cell that had been designed to hold only one did not violate the constitutional command.

The Court also denied the 8th Amendment claim in a 2015 case involving lethal injection. In *Glossip* v. *Gross,* the Court allowed the continued use of a lethal-injection drug that opponents criticized as unreliable and, thus, potentially resulting in needless suffering.

The Court also denied the cruel and unusual claim in a 2003 case centered on California's "three strikes" law, which says that any person convicted of three crimes must be sentenced to at least 25 years in prison. Leandro Andrade had received 50 years for stealing $153.54 worth of children's videos from two K-Mart stores. The K-Mart thefts were treated as separate offenses, and Andrade had an earlier burglary conviction on his record, as well.

8th Amendment Claims Upheld The Court has held some punishments to be cruel and unusual, but only a very few. It did so for the first time in *Weems* v. *United States* in 1910. There, the Court overturned the conviction of a Coast Guard official who had been found guilty of falsifying government pay records. He had been sentenced to 15 years at hard labor, constantly chained at wrist and ankle.

In *Robinson* v. *California*, 1962, the Court ruled that a State law that defined narcotics addiction as a crime to be punished, rather than an illness, violated the 8th and 14th Amendments, and that mandatory sentences of life in prison without the possibility of parole cannot be imposed on juvenile offenders (*Jackson* v. *Hobbs*; *Miller* v. *Alabama*, 2012). The cruel and unusual prohibition was also violated, said the Court in 2011, by California's overcrowded prison system, *Brown* v. *Plata*. In its 5–4 ruling, the Court ordered the State to reduce the size of its prison population by nearly 50,000 inmates.

☑ **GENERATE EXPLANATIONS** Explain the role of the Supreme Court in applying the 8th Amendment's ban on "cruel and unusual punishments."

Capital Punishment and Treason

Laws providing for **capital punishment**—the death penalty—date back to at least the 18th century B.C.E. and the Code of Hammurabi, which set death as the penalty for more than 25 different offenses. The punishment has been a part of American law since the colonial period, and both the Federal Government and 32 States provide for it today.

Over time, the Supreme Court was reluctant to face this highly charged question: Is capital punishment cruel and unusual and therefore prohibited by the 8th Amendment?

State Laws Struck Down The Court did meet the issue, finally, and more or less directly, in *Furman* v. *Georgia*, 1972. There, it struck down all of the then-existing State laws providing for the death penalty—but not because that punishment is cruel and unusual.

Rather, the Court voided those laws because they gave too much discretion to judges or juries in deciding whether to impose the ultimate penalty. The Court found that of all the people convicted of capital crimes, only "a random few," most of them African American or poor, or both, were "capriciously selected" for execution.

Immediately, most States and Congress began to write new capital punishment laws. Those new statutes took one of two forms. Several States made a death sentence mandatory for certain crimes—for example, the killing of a police officer or a murder committed during a rape, kidnapping, or arson. Others provided, instead, for a two-stage process in capital cases: first, a trial to settle the question of guilt or innocence; then, for those convicted, a second proceeding to decide if the circumstances involved in the crime justify a sentence of death.

In considering scores of challenges to these new laws, the Supreme Court found mandatory death penalty statutes unconstitutional. In *Woodson* v.

Capital Punishment Debate

VIEWPOINT 1	VIEWPOINT 2
"We may... assume safely that there are murderers, such as those who act in passion, for whom the threat of death has little or no deterrent effect. But for many others, the death penalty undoubtedly is a significant deterrent." —Justice Potter Stewart, *Gregg* v. *Georgia*, 1976	"The barbaric death penalty violates our Constitution. Even the most vile murderer does not release the state from its obligation to respect dignity, for the state does not honor the victim by emulating his murderer. One day the Court will outlaw the death penalty. Permanently." —William J. Brennan, former U.S. Supreme Court Justice, 1996

>> Capital punishment has had a lengthy history, and so has the controversy surrounding it. **Analyze Charts** How do these two opposing quotations summarize the debate on this issue?

Death Sentences

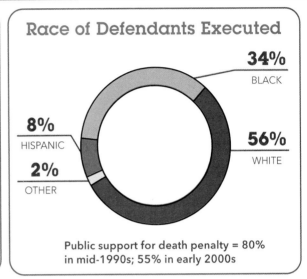

Race of Defendants Executed

Public support for death penalty = 80% in mid-1990s; 55% in early 2000s

SOURCE: Death Penalty Information Center

>> Capital punishment has been part of American law since colonial days.
Analyze Graphs What might explain the decrease in death sentences shown on the bar graph?

North Carolina, 1976, it ruled that those statutes were "unduly harsh and rigidly unworkable." They were, said the Court, simply attempts to "paper over" the decision in *Furman*.

Two-Stage Approach and Later Cases The two-stage approach was found to be constitutional in *Gregg* v. *Georgia*, 1976. There, the Court held for the first time that the "punishment of death does not invariably violate the Constitution." It declared that well-drawn two-stage laws could practically eliminate "the risk that it [the death penalty] would be inflicted in an arbitrary or capricious manner."

Opponents of the death penalty continue to appeal capital cases to the Supreme Court, but to no real avail. Most of their cases have centered on the application, not the constitutionality, of the punishment. The more important of those several cases have resulted in these rulings:

- The death penalty can be imposed only for "crimes resulting in the death of the victim," *Coker* v. *Georgia*, 1977.

- That penalty cannot be imposed on those who are mentally challenged, *Atkins* v. *Virginia*, 2002, or on those who were under the age of 18 when their crimes were committed, *Roper* v. *Simmons*, 2005.

- The question of whether the ultimate penalty is to be imposed must be decided by the jury that convicted the defendant, not the judge who presided at the trial, *Ring* v. *Arizona*, 2002.

- A delusional person who cannot understand why he has been sentenced to death cannot be executed, *Panetti* v. *Quarterman*, 2007.

- Execution by lethal injection, the method most widely used today, does not violate the 8th Amendment, *Baze* v. *Rees*, 2008.

The sum of the Court's many decisions on this issue comes down to this: The death penalty, fairly applied, is constitutional.

Continuing Controversy Even so, the death penalty remains controversial. Even among supporters there are misgivings about the fairness with which this penalty is applied.

Clearly, the application of the death penalty must be closely monitored to protect the innocent and prevent wrongful convictions. The Death Penalty Information Center reports that nearly 200 people who were sentenced to death have been exonerated and released from prison. As retired Supreme Court Justice Sandra Day O'Connor once observed: "If statistics are any indication, the system may well be allowing some innocent defendants to be executed."

That fact has also prompted many who support capital punishment to insist that the remedies for issues in the administration of the penalty should not be to abolish it. Instead, they argue, those remedies should be found in the continuing improvement of the processes by which the ultimate penalty is imposed.

Treason Treason against the United States is the only crime defined in the Constitution. The Framers provided a specific definition of the crime because they knew that the charge of treason has long been a favorite weapon in the hands of tyrants.

Treason, says Article III, Section 3, can consist of only two things: either (1) levying war against the United States or (2) "adhering to their Enemies, giving them Aid and Comfort." The Constitution adds that no person can be convicted of the crime of treason "unless on the Testimony of two Witnesses to the same overt Act, or on Confession in open Court."

The law of treason covers all citizens of the United States, at home or abroad, and all permanent resident aliens. Congress has set death as the maximum sentence for someone convicted of the federal crime but no person has ever, in fact, been executed for that offense. Indeed, the death penalty was not imposed in a federal treason case until 1942. Then, four German-born American citizens were sentenced to be hanged for aiding a group of Nazi saboteurs who had been landed on the East Coast by a German submarine. But those sentences were never carried out.

Treason can only be committed in wartime. But Congress has made it a crime, during times of either peace or war, to commit either espionage or sabotage, to attempt to overthrow the government by force, or to conspire to do any of these things.

Most State constitutions also condemn treason. The fabled abolitionist John Brown was hanged as a traitor by Virginia after his raid on Harpers Ferry in 1859. He is believed to be the only person ever executed for treason against a State.

☑ **EVALUATE ARGUMENTS** What is the two-stage process and how has it affected the Supreme Court's view of the death penalty?

☑ ASSESSMENT

1. **Identify Central Ideas** Name one way the justice system protects the rights of a person with little money who is accused of a crime.

2. **Compare and Contrast** What is the difference between a grand jury and a trial jury? How does each jury protect an individual's rights?

3. **Generate Explanations** Why is it important that a jury reflect the racial make-up of the community?

4. **Evaluate Arguments** If the right to a public trial belongs to the defendant and not the media, should reporters be denied access to the courtroom? Explain your answer.

5. **Interpret** How has the Court generally ruled when applying the 8th Amendment to the death penalty?

GO ONLINE to www.SavvasRealize.com and access your digital course

Use the following online resources to practice citizenship skills and prepare for the Topic Test.

Case Studies

Current Connections

Quest Inquiries

Quizzes

Interactivities

Texts

Flipped Videos

While online you can also check the progress you've made learning the topic and course content by viewing your grades, test scores, and assignment status.

LESSON SUMMARIES

Use these Lesson Summaries, and the longer versions available online, to review the key ideas for each lesson in this Topic.

Lesson 1: The Unalienable Rights

The Constitution guarantees civil rights and liberties to the American people. The Bill of Rights names specific civil liberties the Federal government must respect. Later constitutional amendments, along with court decisions, extended those protections to the States.

Lesson 2: Freedom of Religion

The 1st Amendment prevents the government from establishing a religion or interfering with people's free exercise of their religious beliefs. Both the Establishment and Free Exercise clauses have led to controversies that the courts have stepped in to decide.

Lesson 3: Freedom of Speech and Press

The 1st Amendment also guarantees the right to freedom of speech, including symbolic speech. However, the courts have held that some kinds of speech, such as libel and slander, are not protected. The government also has the power to regulate radio, network television, and commercial speech.

Lesson 4: Freedom of Assembly and Petition

In addition to religion and speech, the 1st Amendment protects people's right to assemble freely and petition the government. The government can make rules regulating assemblies, but these must be content-neutral. The right of association is also protected, meaning that groups can form to promote a cause.

Lesson 5: Due Process of Law

The 5th and 14th amendments say that neither the Federal Government nor the States can punish someone without due process. The government cannot treat people arbitrarily or unfairly. The courts have had to decide what this means in practice, balancing civil liberties against the government's police powers.

Lesson 6: Freedom and Security of the Person

Several constitutional amendments provide additional guarantees of freedom and security. The 2nd Amendment protects the right to bear arms. The 4th Amendment guards against unreasonable searches and seizures. The 13th Amendment bans slavery. The exclusionary rule says that evidence that is illegally obtained cannot be used in court.

Lesson 7: Rights of the Accused

The Constitution protects the rights of people accused of crimes. They cannot be imprisoned without just cause, tried twice for the same crime, forced to confess, or subjected to cruel and unusual punishment. They have the right to a speedy jury trial and must be informed of their rights by the police before questioning.

VISUAL REVIEW

Use these graphics to review some of the key terms, people, and ideas from this Topic.

First Amendment Freedoms

1st Amendment: "Congress shall make no law respecting an establishment of religion, or prohibiting the free exercise thereof; or abridging the freedom of speech, or of the press; or the right of the people peaceably to assemble, and to petition the Government for the redress of grievances."

Freedom of Religion	Freedom of Speech and Press	Freedom of Assembly and Petition
• Creates a separation of church and state (Establishment Clause) • Protects people's right to believe what they choose in matters of religion (Free Exercise Clause)	• Guarantee the right to speak, write, and otherwise communicate most ideas • Ensure the people's right to hear the ideas of others	• Protect people's right to assemble peaceably to express their views • Ensure people's right to bring their views to public attention

Protections of Freedom and Security

2nd AMENDMENT

"A well regulated Militia, being necessary to the security of a free State, the right of people to keep and bear Arms, shall not be infringed."

4th AMENDMENT

"The right of the people to be secure in their persons, houses, papers, and effects, against unreasonable searches and seizures, shall not be violated, and no Warrants shall issue, but upon probable cause, supported by Oath or affirmation, and particularly describing the place to be searched, and the persons or things to be seized."

13th AMENDMENT

"Neither slavery nor involuntary servitude,... shall exist within the United States, or any place subject to their jurisdiction."

14th AMENDMENT'S DUE PROCESS CLAUSE

"No State shall... deprive any person of life, liberty, or property, without due process of law..."

Rights of the Accused

Defendants have a right to:	Courts cannot subject defendant to:
writ of habeas corpus	double jeopardy
grand jury	forced self-incrimination
speedy, public jury trial	excessive bail
Miranda warning	cruel and unusual punishment

429

Topic 8 Assessment

KEY TERMS, PEOPLE, AND IDEAS

1. What is prior **restraint**?

2. Define civil **disobedience**.

3. What is **due process**, and why is it important?

4. Contrast **civil liberties** and **civil rights**.

5. What are the **Establishment Clause** and the **Free Exercise Clause**?

6. How do **libel** and **slander** differ?

7. What is **eminent domain**?

8. What is **probable cause**?

CRITICAL THINKING

9. **Contrast** How does the Constitution both safeguard and limit individual rights? Include examples from the topic that show how the courts balance individual rights with the common good.

10. **Evaluate** What are the time, place, and manner limits that government can put on freedom of assembly? Do you think these limits are appropriate? Why or why not?

11. **Evaluate** What general limitation is placed on individual rights? What example does *Schenck* v. *United States* cite to explain this limitation?

12. **Analyze** How has civil disobedience been used as a means of achieving political and social change?

13. **Evaluate** How does the Constitution protect due process of law?

14. **Explain** How does the Declaration of Independence reflect the principles of individual rights and natural rights?

15. **Explain** Why are rights not absolute? Why do they have limits?

16. **Interpret** This chart shows the steps of the *Lemon* test. What is the purpose of the *Lemon* test? Give examples of State laws that have failed this test and examples of laws that have passed it.

The *Lemon* Test

The courts determine whether State aid to parochial schools is constitutional by applying the *Lemon* test.		
Does the aid have a secular purpose? **AND**	Is it neutral toward religion? **AND**	Does it pose no "excessive entanglement" with religion?
If so, it is **constitutional**.		

17. **Summarize** Choose a Supreme Court case mentioned in this topic. Research the case online. Then write a simple brief (concise summary) of the case. Include the following information in your brief: the basic facts of the case, the arguments advanced by each side, the reasoning of the Court as expressed in the majority opinion, and the Court's final opinion, or holding, on the case.

18. **Assess** What are the human rights policies of the United States?

19. **Identify Central Issues** How did the Thirteenth Amendment contribute to the expansion of civil rights and liberties?

20. **Classify** Which level of government has the police power in the federal system? Provide at least four examples of ways in which exercises of the police power affect you.

21. **Writing Activity** Choose a Supreme Court case discussed in this topic or that you find online. Research the case to familiarize yourself with its basic facts. Then write an editorial for a national newspaper in which you describe the Court's ruling in the case, state your opinion on that ruling, and give evidence to support your conclusions about the decision.

DOCUMENT-BASED QUESTIONS

In two controversial cases in 2010 and 2014, the Supreme Court struck down certain limits on political spending.

DOCUMENT A

In *McCutcheon* v. *FEC*, the Court held that certain limits on individual contributions are unconstitutional.

> Many people . . . would be delighted to see fewer television commercials touting a candidate's accomplishments or disparaging an opponent's character. Money in politics may at times seem repugnant to some, but so too does much of what the 1st Amendment vigorously protects. If the 1st Amendment protects flag burning, funeral protests, and Nazi parades—despite the profound offense such spectacles cause—it surely protects political campaign speech despite popular opposition.
>
> —*Chief Justice John Roberts, Opinion of the Court,* McCutcheon *v.* FEC

DOCUMENT B

The Court's vote in *McCutcheon* was split 5–4. Justice Stephen Breyer was one of the justices who opposed the decision.

> [*McCutcheon* v. *FEC*] is a decision that substitutes judges' understandings of how the political process works for the understanding of Congress; that fails to recognize the difference between influence resting upon public opinion and influence bought by money alone; that overturns key precedent; that creates huge loopholes in the law; and that undermines, perhaps devastates, what remains of campaign finance reform.
>
> With respect, I dissent.
>
> —*Justice Stephen Breyer, Dissenting Opinion,* McCutcheon *v.* FEC

DOCUMENT C

Shaun McCutcheon, the plaintiff in *McCutcheon* v. *FEC*, weighs in on money in politics in this excerpt.

> . . . More money [in politics] means more free speech because it means more door-to-door canvassing, so people can actually talk to each other about issues and candidates. It means, not just more advertising, but better software systems to support vaster communications networks. . . .
>
> Not less money; more money in politics benefits those on both sides of the philosophical divide. Politics is always and inevitably about money, and I don't mean influence-peddling. I mean paying for the software, paying to transport canvassers from Point A to Point B, paying for broadcast access to whole voter populations at a single stroke. You can't vote for the best candidates if you never see them, hear them, or even know their names.
>
> —*Shaun McCutcheon, "The System Works—and Donald Trump Proves It," The Daily Caller, Dec. 21, 2015*

DOCUMENT D

This cartoon also voices an opinion about the effect of *McCutcheon* on campaign spending.

22. According to Document B, what is one major objection to the *McCutcheon* ruling?
    A. It goes too far in its efforts to rein in excessive campaign spending.
    B. It does not go far enough in protecting 1st Amendment rights related to campaign spending.
    C. It allows appointed judges, rather than elected lawmakers, to determine public policy.
    D. It undermines the long-established constitutional principle of judicial review.

23. What position does Document D take on the *McCutcheon* ruling?
    A. It supports the ruling.
    B. It is unhappy with the ruling.
    C. It is neutral about the ruling.
    D. It refuses to reveal an opinion about the ruling.

24. **Analyze Political Cartoons** Analyze Document D's use of symbols and emotional appeal to make its point. Then answer this question: Which groups' points of view have been omitted from this cartoon? Why do you think this was done?

25. **Writing Task** Does Document C use the same rationale for its support of the Court's decision in *McCutcheon* that Document A uses for making that decision? Explain your answer.

Citizenship and Civil Rights

ESSENTIAL QUESTION What Are the Challenges of Diversity?

New American citizens pledge allegiance at a nationalization ceremony.

Connections to Today

Sandra Day O'Connor. Sally Ride. Kamala Harris. What do these women have in common? They were the first to break the "glass ceiling" in their fields. The "glass ceiling" is an invisible barrier to career advancement faced by certain groups of people. O'Connor became the first female Supreme Court justice. Ride was the first U.S. female astronaut. Harris broke three barriers as the first female, Black, Asian American U.S. vice president. What can be done to end discrimination and unfair barriers?

NBC LEARN

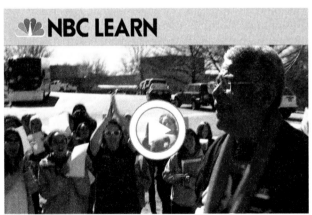

Take a tour of civil rights sites and get a firsthand account of school integration from Minnijean Trickey, one of the Little Rock 9.

 BOUNCE to Activate My Story Video

In this Topic, you will learn about the ways people can become American citizens and about government immigration policies. You will also look at the history of discrimination in this country and the steps government has taken to address that problem. Look at the lesson outline and explore the timeline. As you study this Topic, you can work on your Quest Inquiry.

LESSON OUTLINE

9.1 American Citizenship

9.2 Diversity and Discrimination

9.3 Equality Before the Law

9.4 Federal Civil Rights Laws

Citizenship and Civil Rights

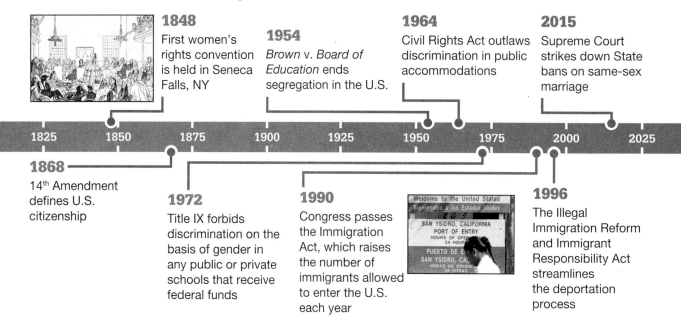

1848
First women's rights convention is held in Seneca Falls, NY

1954
Brown v. Board of Education ends segregation in the U.S.

1964
Civil Rights Act outlaws discrimination in public accommodations

2015
Supreme Court strikes down State bans on same-sex marriage

1825 1850 1875 1900 1925 1950 1975 2000 2025

1868
14th Amendment defines U.S. citizenship

1972
Title IX forbids discrimination on the basis of gender in any public or private schools that receive federal funds

1990
Congress passes the Immigration Act, which raises the number of immigrants allowed to enter the U.S. each year

1996
The Illegal Immigration Reform and Immigrant Responsibility Act streamlines the deportation process

Inquiry Center

Want to become an active and effective citizen? Make a difference in your community and beyond by using the **Inquiry Center** on the digital course.

Connect with issues you're passionate about by using the **Interest Finder**.

Investigate public policies, get involved in your community, influence public opinion, and develop leadership skills.

Synthesize the work you've done and what you've learned along the way.

Demonstrate what you've learned once you've finished your project by sharing your work.

9.1

These students recite the Pledge of Allegiance, a statement of loyalty to the United States, during their graduation ceremony. The Pledge was written in 1892 to promote American patriotism.

 BOUNCE to Activate Flipped Video

Objectives

Describe how people become American citizens by birth and by naturalization.

Explain how an American can lose his or her citizenship.

Illustrate how the United States is a nation of immigrants.

Compare and contrast the status of undocumented and legal immigrants.

Key Terms

citizen
jus soli
jus sanguinis
naturalization
immigrant
expatriation
denaturalization
deportation

American Citizenship

The concept of citizenship—of the free inhabitants of a city—was developed by the ancient Greeks and Romans. It replaced the earlier concept of kinship—of the blood relationships of the family and the tribe—as the basis for community. Today, citizenship is the badge of membership in a political society, and every state in the world has rules by which citizenship is determined. Much can be learned about the basic nature of a government by examining those rules. Who are and who may become citizens? Who are excluded from citizenship, and why?

Citizenship in the United States

An American **citizen** is one who owes allegiance to the United States and is entitled to both its protection and the privileges of its laws. As it was originally written, the Constitution referred to both "citizens of the United States" and "citizens of the States." Neither of those phrases were defined, however.

Throughout much of our earlier history, it was generally agreed that national citizenship followed that of the States. That is, a person who was a citizen of, say, Maryland, was also thought to be a citizen of the United States. Actually, the question was of little importance before the 1860s. Much of the population was the product of recent immigration, and little distinction was made between citizens and those who were not. The Civil War and the adoption of the 13th Amendment in 1865 raised the need for a constitutional definition, however. The 14th Amendment, which gave Congress the power to define citizenship, met that need in 1868.

All persons born or naturalized in the United States and subject to the jurisdiction thereof, are citizens of the United States and of the State wherein they reside.

—14th Amendment, Section 1

Thus, the Constitution declares that a person may become an American citizen in either of two ways: by birth or by naturalization.

☑ **SUMMARIZE** What benefits are citizens of the United States entitled to in return for pledging their allegiance to the United States?

Natural-Born Citizens

Most Americans are citizens simply because they were born in this country. However, even though they are deemed citizens by birth, some Americans were actually born outside the United States. Two basic rules determine citizenship at birth: jus soli and jus sanguinis.

Citizenship and the 14th Amendment According to **jus soli**—the law of the soil—citizenship is determined by place of birth, by *where* one is born. This principle is clearly stated in the 14th Amendment: "All persons born . . . in the

United States. . . ." Congress has defined the United States to include, for purposes of citizenship, the 50 States, the District of Columbia, Puerto Rico, Guam, the Virgin Islands, and the Northern Mariana Islands. Native Americans were exceptions to the "All persons" covered by the amendment until 1924, when Congress granted citizenship to all Native Americans born in the United States.

Just how broad the 14th Amendment's statement of jus soli is can be seen from a leading case on citizenship, *United States* v. *Wong Kim Ark*, 1898.

Wong Kim Ark was born in San Francisco in 1873 to parents who were citizens of China. He made a brief trip to China in 1895. Upon Wong Kim Ark's return, he was refused entry to the United States by immigration officials at San Francisco. They insisted that the 14th Amendment should not be read so literally as to mean that he had become an American citizen at birth. They declared that he was an alien and so was denied entry by the Chinese Exclusion Act of 1882. The Supreme Court held, however, that under the wording of the 14th Amendment, he was indeed a native-born citizen of this country and so not subject to the terms of the Chinese Exclusion Act.

Complicated Citizenship Situations A very small number of persons who are born *physically* in the United States do not in fact become citizens at birth. They are those few who are born not "subject to the jurisdiction of the United States"—for example, children born to foreign diplomatic officials.

Acquiring Citizenship at Birth

JUS SOLI: LAW OF SOIL	JUS SANGUINIS: LAW OF BLOOD
A child becomes an American citizen if born: • in the United States, Puerto Rico, Guam, U.S. Virgin Islands, or Northern Mariana Islands	**A child born to an American citizen on foreign soil becomes a citizen if:** • both parents are American citizens, and at least one has lived in the United States or an American territory at some time. • one parent is an American citizen who has lived in the United States for at least five years, two of those years after age 14, and the child lived in the United States continuously for at least five years between the ages of 14 and 28.

>> Citizenship can be acquired at birth either through jus soli—law of soil—or jus sanguinis—law of blood. **Analyze Charts** What is the difference between jus soli and jus sanguinis? .

According to **jus sanguinis**, the law of the blood, citizenship at birth may also be determined by parentage, to *whom* one is born. Thus, it is altogether possible for one to become a citizen at birth even when that birth occurs outside the United States. The 14th Amendment does not provide for jus sanguinis. However, Congress first recognized the doctrine in 1790 and its constitutionality has never been challenged.

☑ **COMPARE** Which is more far-reaching in terms of citizenship: jus soli or jus sanguinis?

Naturalized Citizens

Naturalization is the legal process by which a person can become a citizen of another country at some time after birth. Congress has the exclusive power to provide for naturalization (Article I, Section 8, Clause 4). No State may do so.

Individual Naturalization Naturalization is most often an individual process, conducted by a court. Generally, any person eligible to enter the United States as an immigrant may become a naturalized citizen. Hundreds of thousands of immigrants are naturalized each year. An **immigrant** is a person, born abroad, who is legally admitted as a permanent resident.

The U.S. Citizenship and Immigration Services in the Department of Homeland Security investigates each applicant, and then it reports its findings to the judge with whom a petition for naturalization has been filed. If the judge is satisfied, an oath or affirmation of citizenship is administered in open court.

Collective Naturalization At various times, entire groups have been naturalized en masse. This has most often happened when the United States has acquired new territory. Those living in the areas involved were naturalized by a treaty or by an act or a joint resolution passed by Congress.

Steps to Naturalization

1 Find out if you are eligible to be a citizen.

You must, for example:
- be 18 years old
- have been a permanent resident of the U.S. for 5 years and your State for 3 months
- be able to read, write, and speak English
- know basic U.S. history and government
- be of good moral character
- be willing to perform military or alternative service if required

2 Submit your application, which can be found online or obtained by calling U.S. Citizenship and Immigration Services (USCIS).

Documents that must be filed with the application:
- a copy of your Permanent Resident Card
- the application fee and the background check fee
- any other forms required by your circumstances

3 Complete your interview and testing.

- USCIS will interview you about your background and test 1) your ability to read, write, speak, and understand English, and 2) your knowledge of U.S. history and government.
- Your application will be granted, returned because incomplete, or denied.

4 Take the Oath of Allegiance.

- You must pledge to renounce your allegiance to any other nation and to support the United States Constitution. You may do so on the same day as your interview or attend a Naturalization Oath Ceremony on a different day.

SOURCE: U.S. Citizenship and Immigration Services

>> Each year between 500,000 and 800,000 people become U.S. citizens.
Analyze Charts Why do you think applicants must be able to read, write, and speak English?

The largest single instance of collective naturalization came with the ratification of the 14th Amendment, due in large part to the fact that it granted citizenship to formerly enslaved people. Another significant instance occurred in 1977, when Congress gave citizenship to the more than 16,000 native-born residents of the Northern Mariana Islands.

☑ **CONTRAST** What is the difference between individual naturalization and collective naturalization?

Losing One's Citizenship

Although it rarely happens, every American citizen, whether native-born or naturalized, has the right to renounce—voluntarily abandon—his or her citizenship. **Expatriation** is the legal process by which a loss of citizenship occurs.

The Supreme Court has several times held that the Constitution prohibits automatic expatriation. That is, Congress cannot take away a person's citizenship for something he or she has done. Thus, actions such as committing a crime, voting in a foreign election, or serving in the armed forces of another country are not grounds for automatic expatriation.

Naturalized citizens can lose their citizenship involuntarily. However, this **denaturalization** process can occur only by court order and only after it has been shown that the person became an American citizen by fraud or deception.

A person can neither gain nor lose American citizenship by marriage. The only significant effect that marriage has is to shorten the residency requirement for the naturalization of an immigrant who marries an American citizen.

☑ **SUMMARIZE** Under what circumstances can naturalized citizens of the United States be denaturalized?

Government Immigration Policies

We are a nation of immigrants. Except for Native Americans—and even they may be the descendants of earlier immigrants—all of us have come here from abroad or are descended from those who did.

Early Immigration Congress has the exclusive power to regulate the crossing of this nation's borders, both inward (immigration) and outward

>> In 2013, singer Tina Turner relinquished her U.S. citizenship and became a Swiss citizen. Born and raised in Tennessee, Turner has lived in Switzerland since 1994.

(emigration). It alone has the power to decide who may be admitted to the country and under what conditions. In an early leading case on the point, the Court ruled that the power of the United States to "exclude aliens from its territory is . . . not open to controversy," *Chae Chan Ping* v. *United States*, 1889. The States have no power in the field, *The Passenger Cases*, 1849.

There were only some 2.5 million people in the United States when independence was declared in 1776. Since then, the population has grown more than a hundredfold, to well over 300 million today.

That extraordinary population growth has come from two sources: births and immigration. Tens of millions of immigrants have come here since 1820, the year when such figures were first recorded.

Congress made no serious attempt to regulate immigration for more than a century after independence. As long as land was plentiful and expanding industry demanded more and still more workers, immigration was actively encouraged.

Immigration Regulation Begins By 1890, however, the open frontier was a thing of the past, and labor was no longer in short supply. Then, too, the major source of immigration had shifted. Until the 1880s, most immigrants had come from the countries of northern and western Europe.

The "new immigration" from the 1880s onward came mostly from southern and eastern Europe. All these factors combined to bring major changes in the traditional policy of encouraging immigration. Ultimately, the policy was reversed.

Congress placed the first major restrictions on immigration with the passage of the Chinese Exclusion Act in 1882. At the same time, it barred the entry of convicts, "lunatics," paupers, and others likely to become public charges. Over the next several years, a long list of "undesirables" was added to the law. Thus, contract laborers were excluded in 1885, immoral persons and anarchists in 1903, and illiterates in 1917. By 1920, more than 30 groups were denied admission on the basis of personal traits.

The tide of newcomers continued to mount, however. In the 10 years from 1905 through 1914, an average of more than a million persons, most of them from southern and eastern Europe, came to this country each year.

The Quota System Congress responded to pressure for tighter regulation by adding quantitative limits (numerical ceilings) to the qualitative restrictions (personal characteristics) already in place. The Immigration Acts of 1921 and 1924 and the National Origins Act of 1929 assigned each country in Europe a quota—a limit on the number of immigrants who could enter the United States

from that country each year. Altogether, only 150,000 quota immigrants could be admitted in any one year.

The quotas were purposely drawn to favor northern and western Europe. The quota system was not applied to the Western Hemisphere, but immigration from Asia, Africa, and elsewhere was generally prohibited.

Quota System Changes In 1952, Congress passed yet another basic law, the Immigration and Nationality Act. That statute modified the quota system, extending it to include every country outside the Western Hemisphere.

Congress finally eliminated the country-based quota system in the Immigration and Nationality Act of 1965. That law allowed as many as 270,000 immigrants to enter the United States each year, without regard to race, nationality, or country of origin. The 1965 law gave special preference to immediate relatives of American citizens or of immigrants legally residing in this country.

Current Immigration Policies Today, the admission of immigrants to the United States is governed by the Immigration Act of 1990. Like its predecessors, it was adopted only after years of intense debate, and many of its provisions are the subject of continuing controversy.

U.S. Immigration and the Immigration and Nationality Act of 1965

SOURCE: Department of Homeland Security (DHS) Immigration Statistics

SOURCE: U.S.Census Bureau; *projection

>> Immigration to the United States has grown steadily since the passage of the Immigration Acts of 1965 and 1990. **Analyze Charts** Based on the data in the pie charts, what population trends are visible?

The 1990 law provided for a substantial increase in the number of immigrants who may enter the United States each year. The annual ceiling is now set at 675,000. It also continues the family-preference policy first put in place in 1965; at least one third of those persons admitted under its terms must be the close relatives of either American citizens or resident immigrants. Those immigrants who have occupational talents that are in short supply in the United States (notably, highly skilled researchers, engineers, and scientists) also receive special preference.

People Excluded from Immigrating Only those persons who can qualify for citizenship can be admitted as immigrants. The law's list of "excludable aliens"—those barred because of some personal characteristic—is extensive. Among those excluded are: criminals (including suspected terrorists), persons with communicable diseases, drug abusers and addicts, illiterates, and mentally disturbed persons who might pose a threat to the safety of others.

On average, more than 70 million persons—non-immigrants—come here each year for temporary stays. They are mostly tourists, students, and people traveling for business reasons.

Deportation Most of the civil rights set out in the Constitution are guaranteed to "persons"—a term that covers immigrants as well as citizens. In one important respect, however, the status of immigrants is altogether unlike that of citizens: Immigrants may be subject to **deportation**, a legal process by which they are required to leave the country.

The Supreme Court has long held that the United States has the same almost-unlimited power to deport immigrants as it has to exclude them. In an early major case, the Court ruled that deportation is an inherent power, arising out of the sovereignty of the United States, and that deportation is not criminal punishment, and so does not require a criminal trial, *Fong Yue Ting* v. *United States*, 1893.

Reasons for Deportation An immigrant may be deported on any one of several grounds. The most common is illegal entry. Thousands of migrants who enter with false papers, sneak in by ship or plane, or slip across the border at night are caught each year and deported. Many of them are repeat offenders who will soon make yet another attempt to cross the border.

Conviction of any serious crime, federal or State, usually leads to a deportation order. Several thousand unauthorized immigrants have been expelled on the basis of their criminal records, especially narcotics violators. The war on terrorism has also quickened the pace of deportations.

>> This border checkpoint is one of many between the United States and Mexico. The Border Patrol is responsible for patrolling the more than 7,000 miles of Mexican and Canadian land borders.

Because deportation is a civil, not a criminal, matter, several constitutional safeguards do not apply—for example, bail and the ban on ex post facto laws.

☑ **DISTINGUISH** How do immigrants' constitutional rights differ from those granted to citizens?

Policies on Unauthorized Immigrants

No one knows just how many unauthorized people reside in the United States today. Their numbers began rising in the 1980s, and best estimates by the Department of Homeland Security and other sources put their total today in the millions. Most enter the country by slipping or being smuggled across the Mexican or Canadian borders, usually at night. Some come with forged papers.

Although varying from year to year, about half of all the people who are here illegally are from Mexico; most of the others come from other Latin American countries and from Asia. A majority of those from Mexico stay here only about four to six months a year, working on farms or in other seasonal jobs, and then they return home. Many others hope to remain here permanently.

Where Unauthorized Immigrants Live Once here, many unauthorized migrants find it easy to become "invisible," especially in larger cities, and law-enforcement agencies find it very difficult to locate them. Even so, immigration officials generally apprehend half a million or more undocumented immigrants each year. Nearly all are sent home. Most go voluntarily, but some leave only as the result of formal deportation proceedings.

Where Unauthorized Immigrants Work Consider this: Ever since 1987, it has been illegal for an employer to hire an unauthorized worker anywhere in the United States. Even so, millions of people who hold jobs in this country came here illegally. Some employers still hire these men and women, often because they are willing to work for substandard wages and in substandard conditions.

No one knows just how many unauthorized workers have taken jobs on farms or become day laborers. Or how many have become janitors or dishwashers, or seamstresses in sweatshops, or have found other menial work. However many they are, their presence has multiplied the burdens of already strained public school systems and welfare services of an increasing number of States, most notably California, Arizona, Texas, and Florida.

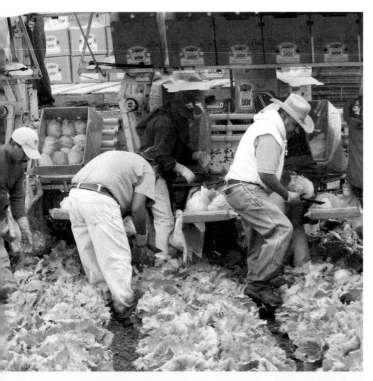

>> Migrant farmworkers are the support system behind the billion-dollar U.S. food industry. According to a 2009 survey, nearly half of the agricultural workers were undocumented.

Current Law The problems posed by unauthorized immigrants trouble and divide many different interests in American politics—chief among them labor, farm, business, religious, ethnic, and civil rights organizations. After wrestling with the matter for years, Congress was finally able to pass the Immigration Reform and Control Act of 1986.

The 1986 law established a one-year amnesty program under which many unauthorized immigrants could become legal residents. More than two million people used the process to legalize their status. Second, that law made it a crime to hire any person who is in this country illegally. Any employer who knowingly hires an unauthorized worker can be fined from $250 to as much as $10,000. Repeat offenders can be jailed for up to six months.

In 1996, Congress passed the Illegal Immigration Reform and Immigration Responsibility Act. That law streamlined the deportation process. It also toughened the penalties for smuggling unauthorized persons into this country and prevented unauthorized immigrants from claiming Social Security or public housing benefits. The statute also doubled the size of the Border Patrol—which is today the largest of the several federal law enforcement agencies.

Immigration Reform Since the passage of the 1996 law, the issue has become even more heated. Several high-profile court cases upheld the civil liberties of unauthorized immigrants. In *Zadvydas* v. *Davis*, 2001, the Supreme Court ruled that if deportation proceedings are not done quickly, the detained person must be released. In later cases, however, the pendulum swung in the opposite direction. In *Benitez* v. *Mata*, 2004, for instance, the Court said that any previously deported immigrant can be prohibited from reentering the United States. And in 2010, Arizona adopted a tough, controversial law with the goal of identifying, prosecuting, and deporting unauthorized immigrants. The law prompted protests and demonstrations from both sides.

As a result of this continuing dispute over how best to approach the matter, Congress was unable to enact any meaningful immigration reform. In 2012, President Obama, frustrated by the lack of congressional action, issued an executive order that suspended deportations of children of unauthorized immigrants for two years (Deferred Action for Childhood Arrivals, or DACA). Noting that "this is a temporary stopgap measure," the President urged Congress to pass permanent immigration reform legislation.

When Congress still had not acted by late 2014, the President issued a second executive order, known as Deferred Action for Parents of Americans and Lawful Permanent Residents (DAPA). The order was intended to allow undocumented immigrant parents of U.S. citizens to apply for work permits if they have lived in the country for five years and not committed any crimes.

DAPA was never implemented, however. Twenty-six States joined in a lawsuit against the President, charging that he had overstepped his authority. In 2017, the Department of Homeland Security officially rescinded the order.

The debate about immigration continues, and policies have seesawed back and forth during subsequent administrations. The fact remains that Americans, through their representatives in Congress, must grapple with several difficult questions: How should the nation's borders be secured? What immigration policies best serve the national interest? How should the legal status of the undocumented immigrants who currently live in the United States be addressed?

Refugees and Asylum Seekers In the wake of the atrocities committed in World War II, the United Nations passed the Refugee Convention in 1951. This treaty defined who should be recognized as a political refugee and defined the rights granted to these people. Today, nations who adhere to the Convention, including the United States, are obligated to provide protection for refugees fleeing illegal prosecutions, violence, torture, imprisonment, and possible death.

In recent years, however, there has been a flood of asylum seekers in many democracies across the globe, including the United States. As such, the issue has become increasingly complex and contentious.

People seeking asylum—a safe harbor—in the United States are afforded hearings on their cases, but with such large numbers, the wait time has grown dramatically. Where should asylees stay while awaiting their hearings—bearing in mind that tens of thousands can arrive in a short amount of time? What criteria should be used to decide who should be granted asylum and who should not? For example, should those fleeing environmental disaster be on the same footing as those escaping political violence? Should there be a cap on the number of asylees? If large groups of people are granted asylum, where should they be resettled in the United States? And if a refugee is granted asylum, should there be a pathway to full citizenship?

America has always opened its arms to immigrants and to those seeking asylum from violence and prosecution. But turbulence across the globe has added new pressures on our ability

"ANYBODY HOME?"

>> Immigration reform has been a contentious issue for years and an emotional issue for those directly affected. **Analyze Political Cartoons** What does the cartoon say about Congress?

to accept all who want to come. As a result, the debate over these issues will likely continue for the foreseeable future.

☑ **EXPRESS IDEAS CLEARLY** What did the Illegal Immigration Reform and Immigrant Responsibility Act of 1996 provide? Do you think these provisions have been successful?

☑ ASSESSMENT

1. **Evaluate Sources** Why does the definition of citizens in the 14th Amendment support jus solis rather than jus sanguinis?

2. **Analyze Information** Under what circumstances may a child born abroad become an American citizen at birth?

3. **Synthesize** What type of actions could result in an individual's involuntary expatriation?

4. **Determine Relevance** What was the significance of the Immigration and Nationality Act of 1965?

5. **Summarize** Why did the Immigration Reform and Control Act of 1986 come down so harshly on employers of unauthorized workers?

9.2

A large gathering of people can reflect the ethnic and racial diversity of the United States today.

 BOUNCE to Activate Flipped Video

Objectives

Understand what it means to live in a heterogeneous society.

Summarize the history of race-based discrimination in the United States.

Examine discrimination against women in the past and present.

Key Terms

heterogeneous
immigrants
reservations
refugee
assimilation

Diversity and Discrimination

Have you read George Orwell's classic, *Animal Farm*? Even if you have not, you may have heard its most oft-quoted line: "All animals are created equal, but some animals are more equal than others." You might keep Orwell's comment in mind as you read this material.

A Changing American Culture

A Heterogeneous Society The term **heterogeneous** is a compound of two Greek words: *hetero*, meaning "other or different," and *genos*, meaning "race, family, or kind." Something that is heterogeneous is composed of dissimilar parts, made up of elements that are unrelated to or unlike one another—in short, something composed of a mix of ingredients. "We the People of the United States" are a heterogeneous lot, and we are becoming more so, year to year.

The population of the United States is predominantly white and this has been the case throughout the nation's history. The first census in 1790 reported that there were 3,929,214 people living in this country. More than four out of five were white. African Americans made up the remaining 19 percent of the population counted in that census. As the nation's population grew over the decades, so, too, did the proportion of the American people who were white—until recently.

An Increasingly Diverse Society The ethnic composition of the American population is strikingly different from what it was only a generation ago. **Immigrants**—those people, born abroad, who are legally admitted as permanent residents—have arrived in near-record numbers every year since the mid-1960s. Over that period, the nation's Black American, Hispanic American, and Asian American populations have grown at rates several times that of the white population. Indeed, the minority population now exceeds the white population in a number of States. A look at gender balance in the population reveals that females are more numerous than males. This has been the case for more than half a century.

As a result of these changes in the American population, the United States is more heterogeneous today than ever before. That fact is certain to have a profound effect on the American social, political, and economic landscape on through the twenty-first century.

☑ **SYNTHESIZE** This section ends with the statement that the nation's increasing heterogeneity will have social, political, and economic effects. Explain how increasing diversity might affect the nation's economy.

Discrimination in America

White Americans have been historically reluctant to yield to nonwhite Americans a full and equal place in the social, economic, and political life of this nation. The white-male-dominated power structure has also been slow to recognize the claims of women to an equal place in society. Discrimination against the disabled and the LGBTQ communities have also been problematic. The efforts to address their rights are discussed in the next lesson.

Slavery Black Americans have been the victims of consistent and deliberate unjust treatment since colonial times. The ancestors of most Black Americans came to this country in chains. Over a period of some two hundred years, tens of thousands of Africans were kidnapped, forced aboard sailing ships, brought to America, and then sold as if they were property rather than human beings. As enslaved people, they were the legal property of other human beings. They could be bought and sold and forced to do their owners' bidding, however harsh the circumstances.

The badges of slavery took many forms. In 1857, for example, a Black man named Dred Scott sued for his freedom. The Supreme Court ruled, in part,

U.S. Population by Race

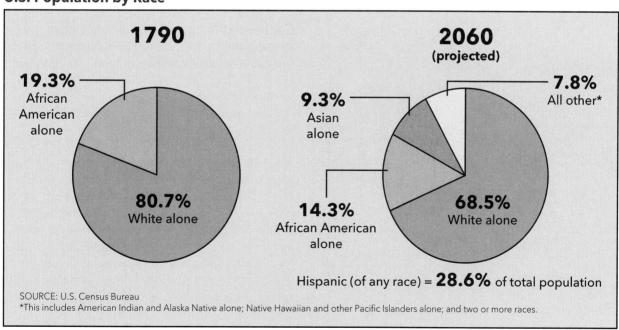

SOURCE: U.S. Census Bureau
*This includes American Indian and Alaska Native alone; Native Hawaiian and other Pacific Islanders alone; and two or more races.

>> The separation of race and Hispanic origin acknowledges that persons of Hispanic origin may be of any race. The non-Hispanic white population is expected to comprise 44 percent of the population by 2060. **Analyze Graphs** How might legislation be linked to this type of Census Bureau data?

that Scott could not sue in federal court because an enslaved person was not a citizen (*Dred Scott* v. *Sandford*).

Although members of the Abolitionist Movement made strides, it took a civil war to end more than two centuries of slavery in this country. The 13th Amendment finally abolished slavery in 1865 and the 14th resolved the citizenship rights of the formerly enslaved. Still, the Civil War and the ratification of that amendment did not end widespread racial discrimination in the United States. Instead, new forms of discrimination have taken the place of slavery over the years, such as sharecropping, disenfranchisement, segregation, legally sanctioned white privilege, low-quality schools, lending and real estate discrimination, and a 1944 GI Bill that gave huge benefits to white people but largely excluded Black Americans.

Continued Discrimination Black Americans are a large minority group in the United States, making up a significant percentage of the population. And many of the gains the nation has made toward equality for all have come out of efforts made by and on behalf of Black Americans. Recall that, for example, the struggles of Martin Luther King, Jr., and others resulted in the Civil Rights Act of 1964 and then the Voting Rights Act of 1965.

>> Cultural differences between Native Americans, such as the Piegan Blackfeet tribe, and white European immigrants created mutual mistrust, fear, and hatred, and often led to violence.

America is now a multiracial society. However, evidence suggests that some people still feel discriminated against. A 2022 Harris poll, for example, revealed that 1 in 4 people belonging to a racial or ethnic minority have reported experiencing some level of discrimination in the workplace.

Native Americans White settlers first began to arrive in America in relatively large numbers in the mid-1600s. At the time, millions of Native Americans were living in territory that was to become the United States. By 1900, however, their number had fallen drastically.

Diseases brought by white settlers decimated those first Americans. So, too, did the military campaigns that accompanied the westward expansion of the United States. One leading commentator said the following about this expansion:

'The only good Indian is a dead Indian' is not simply a hackneyed expression from cowboy movies. It was part of the strategy of westward expansion, as settlers and U.S. troops mercilessly drove the eastern Indians from their ancestral lands to the Great Plains and then took those lands too.

—Thomas E. Patterson, *The American Democracy*

Continued Discrimination Against Native Americans Several million Native Americans live in this country. About a quarter of them live on or near **reservations**, which are public lands set aside by the government for use by Native American tribes.

Like Black Americans, Native Americans have been the victims of discrimination, and the consequences of that bias remain evident today. Poverty, joblessness, and alcoholism plague many reservations. The Indian Education Act of 1972 attempted to remedy the cycle of poverty by providing financial assistance to local educational agencies for Native American children and adult programs. Still, the life expectancy of Native Americans living on reservations today is dramatically lower than the national average, and the Native American infant mortality rate is nearly twice that of white Americans.

Hispanic Americans Hispanic Americans are those in this country who have a Spanish-speaking

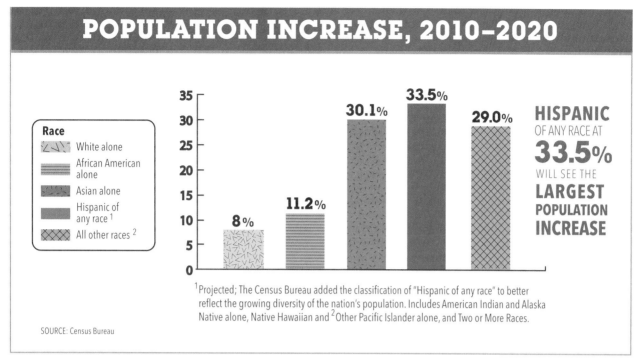

Race
- White alone
- African American alone
- Asian alone
- Hispanic of any race [1]
- All other races [2]

8%   11.2%   30.1%   33.5%   29.0%

HISPANIC OF ANY RACE AT **33.5%** WILL SEE THE **LARGEST POPULATION INCREASE**

[1] Projected; The Census Bureau added the classification of "Hispanic of any race" to better reflect the growing diversity of the nation's population. Includes American Indian and Alaska Native alone, Native Hawaiian and [2] Other Pacific Islander alone, and Two or More Races.

SOURCE: Census Bureau

>> Minority populations have grown at a faster rate than the majority population.
Analyze Data What is the rate of growth for Asian Americans? What are the benefits of diversity in a community?

background; many prefer to be called *Latinos*. Hispanic people may be of any race. The federal government considers *Hispanic* and *Latino* to be designations of ethnicity rather than race. According to a Pew survey of Hispanic Americans, there is a difference of opinion on what they believe defines a Hispanic person—race, ancestry, or culture. In addition, a large number of Hispanic Americans identify with other racial groups and, as a result, determining who make up the Hispanic American group is quite complex.

Hispanic Americans constitute the largest minority group in this country, having surpassed Black Americans sometime around the year 2000. They are also the nation's fastest-growing population group.

Mexican Americans More than 60 percent of all Hispanics in the United States were either born in Mexico or trace their ancestry there. Those born in this country of Mexican parents are often called *Chicanos*.

Most of the Mexican American population lives in the States of California, Texas, Arizona, and Illinois, but that population is spreading throughout much of the country. A majority of the residents of such large cities as El Paso and San Antonio in Texas are Hispanic, and such smaller border cities as Laredo and Brownsville in Texas are over 90 percent Latino.

Hispanic Americans from Islands *Puerto Ricans* are another large group of Hispanics that have come to the mainland from the island of Puerto Rico. Many Puerto Ricans have settled in New York, Florida, and New Jersey.

The Hispanic population also includes *Cuban Americans*. Many are people who fled the Castro dictatorship in Cuba, and their descendants. A majority of them have settled in Miami and elsewhere in Florida, as well as in California and New Jersey.

Central and South Americans The fourth major subgroup of Hispanic Americans came here from Central and South America, many as refugees. A **refugee** is one who seeks protection (refuge) from war, persecution, or some other danger. Several million persons have emigrated legally to the United States from Central and South American countries over the past several decades; they have arrived in the largest numbers from El Salvador, Guatemala, Colombia, and Honduras. Many have also come from the Dominican Republic, an island nation in the Caribbean.

Discrimination Against Hispanic Americans
Discrimination against Hispanic Americans began as soon as the United States began acquiring Mexican territory in the 1840s. Laws were passed

that hampered voter participation and taxed Spanish-speaking workers as "foreign miners," even though they were United States citizens. Labor discrimination tactics continued in the form of deportations during tough economic times when white Americans needed jobs held by Hispanic Americans and the practice of hiring undocumented workers was used for the least desirable and most unsafe jobs.

Discrimination outside the workplace has most often resulted from the segregation of many Hispanic Americans from the rest of society and the resulting ignorance about the Latino culture. In the 1940s, for example, the Zoot Suit Riots occurred because white Americans had no understanding of the fashionable dress for Hispanic Americans at the time. White Americans assumed that men dressed in "zoot suits" (high-waisted, wide-legged pants; long coats with padded shoulders; hats) were criminals, and violence broke out as a result of this mistaken assumption.

In recent times, the immigration debates have also fueled discrimination and resulted in an increased number of hate crimes against Hispanic Americans. For many Mexican Americans in particular, the U.S./Mexico border fence serves as a physical reminder of the anti-immigrant viewpoint that they feel leads to discrimination.

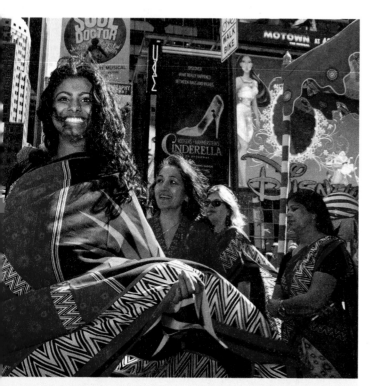

>> Women participate in a Diwali festival in New York's Times Square. The "festival of lights" has been an important Hindu celebration of the victory of light over darkness.

Discrimination Against Asian Americans The story of white America's mistreatment of Asians is a lengthy one, too. Asians have faced discrimination from the first day they arrived. As with all immigrant groups, assimilation into the white-dominated population has been difficult. **Assimilation** is the process by which people of one culture merge into and become part of another.

Chinese laborers were the first Asians to come to the United States in large numbers. They were brought here in the 1850s to 1860s as contract laborers to work in the mines and to build railroads in the West. Many white Americans, both native-born and immigrants, resented the competition of what they called "coolie labor." Their resentments were frequently expressed in acts of violence toward Asians.

Government Actions Against Asian Americans Congress brought Chinese immigration to a near halt with the Chinese Exclusion Act of 1882. Because of this and other governmental actions, only a very small number of Chinese, Japanese, and other Asians were permitted to enter the United States for more than 80 years.

Early in World War II, the Federal Government ordered the evacuation of all persons of Japanese descent from the Pacific Coast. Some 120,000 people, two thirds of them native-born American citizens, were forcibly removed to inland "war relocation camps." Years later, the government conceded that this action had been both unnecessary and unjust.

Diversity Among Asian Americans Congress made dramatic changes in American immigration policies in 1965. Since then, millions of Asian immigrants have come to this country, mostly from the Philippines, China, Korea, Vietnam, and India. The term "Asian American" encompasses an ever more diverse population. Asian Americans represent a tremendous variety of languages, religions, and cultures, and many immigrants from Asia have little in common with one another.

Asian Americans live in every part of the United States. They constitute a large percentage of the population in Hawaii and a significant percentage of the population in California and New York City.

☑ **SUPPORT IDEAS WITH EXAMPLES** How has the United States government participated in acts of discrimination? Give examples from the text you have just read to support your answer.

Discrimination Against Women

Unlike the several ethnic groups described thus far, women are not a minority in the United States. They are, in fact, a majority group. Still, traditionally in American law and public policy, women have not enjoyed the same rights as men. Their status was even lower, in many instances, than men who were themselves the target of virulent discrimination. Women have been treated as less than equal in a great many matters—including, for example, property rights, education, and employment opportunities.

Organized efforts to improve the place of women—although primarily for white women—in American society date from July 19, 1848. On that day, a convention on women's rights met in Seneca Falls, New York, and adopted a set of resolutions that deliberately echoed the words of the Declaration of Independence.

Statistical Evidence of Discrimination Those who fought and won the long struggle for women's suffrage believed that, with the vote, women would soon achieve other basic rights. That assumption proved false.

Although almost 51 percent of the population is now female, women still hold only a minor fraction of the nation's top public offices, including Congress, the 50 State legislatures, and the country's governors and judges. While women have made strides in the fields of medicine and law, they still comprise less than half of the nation's doctors and lawyers. Women are also hugely underrepresented at the upper levels of corporate management and even more so in the engineering field, where they make up only a small portion of the workforce. For women of color, the gap is even wider. At the same time, women are overrepresented in low-paying clerical and service occupations. The Bureau of Labor Statistics reports that nearly all secretaries, childcare workers,

> "When, in the course of human events, it becomes necessary for one portion of the family of man to assume among the people of the earth a position different from that which they have hitherto occupied, . . We hold these truths to be self evident: that all men and women are created equal . . ."
>
> —Declaration of Sentiments, 1848

THE CHRISTIAN SCIENCE MONITOR

'Another day, another eighty cents.'

>> Studies have shown that women earn less than 80 cents for every dollar earned by men. **Analyze Political Cartoons** What does the 80 cents refer to? What factors may a person's pay be based on?

>> The Lilly Ledbetter Fair Pay Act of 2009 was the first act signed by President Barack Obama. Once a supervisor at Goodyear, Ledbetter later became a women's equality activist.

Movement Toward Fair Pay Efforts on behalf of equal rights for women have gained significant ground in recent years. In 2009, for example, Congress amended the Civil Rights Act of 1964, which outlawed pay discrimination on the basis of gender, with the Lilly Ledbetter Fair Pay Act.

The original provision in the Civil Rights Act stipulated a 180-day "window" after the start of employment to file a discrimination law suit. But what if a woman did not know she was being discriminated against for some time, maybe years? Perhaps, as was the case with Lilly Ledbetter, she simply did not immediately realize how much her male counterparts were being paid. The Lilly Ledbetter Act instructs that the statute of limitations for filing a suit be reset with each new pay period. In other words, women can now file a lawsuit whenever they learn of discrimination, rather than being restricted to the first 180 days of a new job.

☑ **GENERATE EXPLANATIONS** Those who fought for women's suffrage thought that by gaining the right to vote, women could then achieve other basic rights. Why did this assumption proved false?

☑ ASSESSMENT

1. **Make Generalizations** The minority populations in the States of California, Hawaii, New Mexico, and Texas all exceed the State's majority population. What do these four States have in common?

2. **Connect** Why might other minority groups look to Black Americans for guidance in developing strategies for overcoming discrimination?

3. **Explain** What does it mean to live in a heterogeneous society?

4. **Compare** What do Hispanic Americans and Asian Americans have in common as minority groups in the United States?

5. **Explain** Explain why the Lilly Ledbetter Fair Pay Act was necessary and indicates an important shift toward equal pay for women.

receptionists, bookkeepers, auditing clerks, word processors, and typists are women.

Unequal Pay It is illegal to pay women less than men for the same work. The Equal Pay Act of 1963 requires employers to pay men and women the same wages if they perform the same jobs in the same establishment under the same working conditions. The Civil Rights Act of 1964 also prohibits job discrimination based on sex. Yet, decades after Congress passed those laws, white working women still earn significantly less for every dollar earned by working men, while Latinas and Black women earn even less.

Women earn less than men for a number of reasons. Some blame the so-called "Mommy track," in which women put their careers on hold to have children or work reduced hours to juggle child-care responsibilities. Others claim that a "glass ceiling" of discrimination in the corporate world and elsewhere, invisible but impenetrable, prevents women from rising to their full potential.

The Middle Passage and a Demand for Equality

Black Americans and women have been two of the largest groups in the United States to suffer discrimination. The excerpts here offer a glimpse into their struggles. In his narrative, Olaudah Equiano (c. 1745–1797) describes how he was kidnapped from his home in West Africa and imprisoned with others on a ship bound for North America. This excerpt describes part of that horrifying journey, known as the Middle Passage. The second excerpt is from the Declaration of Sentiments, written by Elizabeth Cady Stanton and four other women to outline the goals of the Seneca Falls Convention (1848). The women purposely modeled their document on the Declaration of Independence as a potent reminder of the principles of equality upon which the United States was founded.

>> Olaudah Equiano

The Interesting Narrative of the Life of Olaudah Equiano: Olaudah Equiano

At last when the ship we were in, had got in all her cargo, they made ready with many fearful noises, and we were all put under deck, so that we could not see how they managed the vessel. But this disappointment was the least of my sorrow. The stench of the hold [the cargo area of a ship, often below deck] while we were on the coast was so intolerably loathsome, that it was dangerous to remain there for any time, and some of us had been permitted to stay on the deck for the fresh air; but now that the whole ship's cargo were confined together, it became absolutely pestilential [deadly; disease-ridden]. The closeness of the place, and the heat of the climate, added to the number in the ship, which was so crowded that each had scarcely room to turn himself, almost suffocated us.

This produced copious [plentiful; abundant] perspirations, so that the air soon became unfit for respiration, from a variety of loathsome smells, and brought on a sickness among the slaves, of which many died—thus falling victims to the improvident [reckless] avarice [greediness], as I may call it, of their purchasers. This wretched [deeply distressing] situation was again aggravated by the galling [chafing] of the chains, now become insupportable, and the filth of the necessary tubs, into which the children often fell, and were almost suffocated. The shrieks of the women, and the groans of the dying, rendered the whole a scene of horror almost inconceivable. Happily perhaps, for myself, I was soon reduced so low here that it was thought necessary to keep me almost always on deck; and from my extreme youth I was not put in fetters [chains]. In this situation I expected every hour to share the fate of my companions, some of whom were almost daily brought upon deck at the point of death, which I began to hope would soon put an end to my miseries. Often did I think many of the inhabitants of the deep much more happy than myself. I envied them the freedom they enjoyed, and as often wished I could change my condition for theirs. Every circumstance I met with served only to render my state more painful, and heighten my apprehensions, and my opinion of the cruelty of the whites. One day they had taken a number of fishes; and when they had killed and satisfied themselves with as many as they thought fit, to our astonishment who were on the deck, rather than give any of them to us to eat as we expected, they tossed the remaining fish into the sea again, although we begged and prayed for some as well as we could, but in vain; . . . One day, when we had a smooth sea and moderate wind, two of my wearied countrymen who were chained together (I was near them at the time), preferring death to such a life of misery, somehow made through the nettings and jumped into the sea; . . .

☑ **ANALYZE WORD CHOICES** How does the phrase *improvident avarice* contribute to Equiano's overall description of the journey?

Declaration of Sentiments and Resolutions

When, in the course of human events, it becomes necessary for one portion of the family of man to assume among the people of the earth a position different from that which they have hitherto occupied, but one to which the laws of nature and of nature's God entitle them, a decent respect to the opinions of mankind requires that they should declare the causes that impel them to such a course.

We hold these truths to be self-evident: that all men and women are created equal; that they are endowed by their Creator with certain inalienable rights; that among these are life, liberty, and the pursuit of happiness. . . .

The history of mankind is a history of repeated injuries and usurpations [seizures] on the part of man toward woman, having in direct object the establishment of an absolute tyranny over her. To prove this, let facts be submitted to a candid [truthful] world.

He has never permitted her to exercise her inalienable right to the elective franchise.

He has compelled her to submit to law in the formation of which she had no voice. . . .

He has made her, if married, in the eye of the law, civilly dead. He has taken from her all right in property, even to the wages she earns. . . .

He has denied her the facilities for obtaining a thorough education, all colleges being closed against her. . . .

He has endeavored, in every way that he could, to destroy her confidence in her own powers, to lessen her self-respect, and to make her willing to lead a dependent and abject [miserable] life.

Now, in view of this entire disfranchisement of one-half the people of this country, their social and religious degradation, in view of the unjust laws above mentioned, and because women do feel themselves aggrieved, oppressed, and fraudulently deprived of their most sacred rights, we insist that they have immediate admission to all the rights and privileges which belong to them as citizens of the United States.

☑ **ANALYZE WORD CHOICE** What is the effect of the writers' use of words like *degradation, aggrieved, oppressed,* and *deprived*?

☑ ASSESSMENT

1. **Cite Evidence** What sensory details does Olaudah Equiano use to tell his story? Do they help or hinder the usefulness of this narrative as a piece of anti-slavery literature? Cite specific examples from the text in your answer.

2. **Examine Principles** Identify how the principles contained in the Seneca Falls Declaration might have helped lead to the expansion of civil rights and liberties in the United States.

3. **Analyze Structure** Analyze how the Seneca Falls Declaration is structured, and how that structure increases its effectiveness.

Although the statue of *Freedom* usually stands atop the Dome of the United States Capitol, it is periodically removed for restoration.

Equality Before the Law

The huge bronze statue of *Freedom* has stood atop the nation's Capitol in Washington, D.C., for over 150 years. That bold figure is meant to symbolize the basic ideas upon which the United States exists—the concepts of individual liberty, of self-government, and of equal rights for all.

Equal Protection and Individual Rights

The irony is that records unearthed by the Architect of the Capitol show that at least 400 enslaved men worked on the construction of the Capitol from 1792 to its opening in 1800; and that those enslaved men cast the huge sculpture of *Freedom,* and even hoisted it atop the new building. Those old documents also record payments to several local enslavers—for example, "To Joseph Forest, for the hire of the Negro Charles." The owners were paid $5 a month for each enslaved man who worked on the project.

The equality of all persons, proclaimed so boldly in the Declaration of Independence, is not set out in so many words in the Constitution. Still, that concept pervades the document.

The closest approach to a literal statement of equality is found in the 14th Amendment's **Equal Protection Clause.** It declares that "No State shall . . . deny to any person within its jurisdiction the equal protection of the laws."

Those words were added to the Constitution in 1868. They were originally meant to benefit those recently freed from slavery. Over time, however, they have come to

 BOUNCE to Activate Flipped Video

Objectives

Explain the importance of the Equal Protection Clause in safeguarding individual rights.

Describe the history of segregation in America.

Examine how classification by gender relates to discrimination.

Key Terms

equal protection clause
discriminate
rational basis test
strict scrutiny test
segregation
Jim Crow
separate-but-equal doctrine
integration
de jure
de facto
Earl Warren
Joseph P. Bradley
William J. Brennan

mean that the States (and their local governments) cannot draw unreasonable distinctions between any classes of persons. The Supreme Court has often held that the 5th Amendment's Due Process Clause puts the same restrictions on the Federal Government.

Government Regulation of Individual Liberty

Government must have the power to classify, to draw distinctions between persons and groups. Otherwise, it could not possibly regulate human behavior. That is to say, government must be able to **discriminate**—and it does. For example, those who rob banks fall into a special class, and they receive special treatment by government. Clearly, that sort of discrimination is reasonable.

Government may not discriminate *unreasonably*, however. Every State taxes the sale of cigarettes, and so taxes smokers but not nonsmokers. No State can tax only blonde smokers, however, or only male smokers.

Over time, the Supreme Court has rejected many equal protection challenges to a wide variety of actions by government. More often than not, however, the Supreme Court has found that what those governments have done is, in fact, constitutional.

>> The Federal Government has not banned smoking in all public buildings, but smoking is regulated in at least certain regions of 49 of the 50 States. Most courts have upheld these regulations.

The Reasoning Behind the Law

The Supreme Court most often decides equal protection cases by applying a standard known as the **rational basis test.** This test asks: Does the classification in question bear a reasonable relationship to the achievement of some proper governmental purpose?

A California case, *Michael M.* v. *Superior Court,* 1981, illustrates that test. California law says that a man who has sexual relations with a girl under 18 to whom he is not married can be prosecuted for statutory rape. However, the girl cannot be charged with that crime, even if she is a willing partner. The Court found the law to bear a reasonable relationship to a proper public policy goal: preventing teenage pregnancies.

A Compelling Governmental Interest

The Court imposes a higher standard in some equal protection cases, however. This is especially true when a case deals with (1) such "fundamental rights" as the right to vote, the right to travel between the States, or 1st Amendment rights; or (2) such "suspect classifications" as those based on race, sex, or national origin.

In these instances, the Court has said that a law must meet a higher standard than the rational basis test: the **strict scrutiny test.** A State must be able to show that some "compelling governmental interest" justifies the distinctions it has drawn between classes of people. Thus, in an alimony case, *Orr* v. *Orr*, 1979, an Alabama law that made women but not men eligible for alimony was held unconstitutional, as a denial of equal protection—because the law's distinction between men and women did not serve any compelling governmental interest.

☑ **CONTRAST** How does the rational basis test for equal protection differ from the strict scrutiny test?

A History of Segregation

Beginning in the late 1800s, nearly half the States—including some outside the South—passed racial segregation laws. Used in this context, **segregation** refers to the separation of one group from another on the basis of race. Most of those statutes were **Jim Crow** laws—laws aimed at African Americans in particular. Some were also drawn to affect Mexican Americans, Asian Americans, and Native Americans. They regularly required segregation by race in the use of both public and private facilities: schools, parks and playgrounds, hotels and restaurants, streetcars and railroads, public drinking fountains, restrooms, and cemeteries. Many also prohibited interracial marriages.

Plessy v. Ferguson The Supreme Court provided a constitutional basis for Jim Crow laws by creating the **separate-but-equal doctrine** in 1896. In *Plessy v. Ferguson*, the Court upheld a Louisiana law that required segregation in railroad coaches. It ruled that the law did not violate the Equal Protection Clause because the *separate* seating provided for African Americans was *equal* to the seating provided for whites. The doctrine was soon extended to other fields. And it stood, largely unchallenged, for nearly 60 years.

Challenges to the Separate-but-Equal Doctrine

The Supreme Court first began to chip away at the separate-but-equal doctrine in *Missouri ex rel. Gaines* v. *Canada* in 1938. Lloyd Gaines, an African American, was denied admission to the law school at the all-white University of Missouri. Gaines was fully qualified for admission—except for his race. The State did not have a separate law school for African Americans. However, it did offer to pay his tuition at a public law school in any of the four neighboring States, which did not discriminate by race.

The Court based its decision in part on an earlier case, *Yick Wo* v. *Hopkins*, 1886. In that case, a Chinese man in California sued after he was fined for failing to obtain a permit to operate a laundry in a wooden building. Yick Wo maintained that the permits were issued only to white laundry owners. The Court sided with Yick Wo, saying that the unfair application of the law violated the Equal Protection Clause.

In *Gaines*, the Court held that the separate-but-equal doctrine left Missouri with two choices: admit Gaines to the State's one law school or establish a separate-but-equal school for him. The State gave in and Gaines was admitted to the law school.

In 1950 the Court decided two major cases in line with its holding in *Gaines: Sweatt* v. *Painter* and *McLaurin* v. *Oklahoma*. Both cases involved African American university students for whom a State had provided separate educational facilities. The Court found that, in both instances, those separate facilities were, in fact, far from equal. Still, in neither of these cases did the Court re-examine the validity of the separate-but-equal doctrine.

Brown v. Board of Education Finally, in 1954, the Court reversed *Plessy* v. *Ferguson*. In the landmark case, *Brown* v. *Board of Education of Topeka,* it struck down laws that allowed or required separate public schools for white and African American students. Unanimously, the Court held segregation

>> The ruling that segregation violated the 14th Amendment eventually led to integrated classrooms.

by race in public education to be invalid. In the Court's majority opinion, Chief Justice **Earl Warren** wrote the following:

> Does segregation of children in public schools solely on the basis of race, even though the physical facilities and other 'tangible' factors may be equal, deprive the children of the minority group of equal educational opportunities? We believe that it does. . . . To separate them from others of similar age and qualifications solely because of their race generates a feeling of inferiority as to their status in the community that may affect their hearts and minds in a way unlikely ever to be undone. . . .
>
> —Majority Opinion

In 1955 the Court directed the States to make "a prompt and reasonable start" to end segregation and to accomplish that goal "with all deliberate speed."

A "reasonable start" was made in Baltimore, Louisville, St. Louis, and elsewhere. In most of the

Deep South, however, massive resistance soon developed. State legislatures passed laws, and school boards worked to block **integration**—the process of desegregation, of bringing a previously segregated group into the mainstream of society. Most of those efforts were clearly unconstitutional, but challenging them in court proved both costly and slow.

The pace of desegregation quickened after Congress passed the Civil Rights Act of 1964. That act forbids the use of federal funds to aid any State or local activity in which racial segregation is practiced. The statute also directed the Justice Department to file suits to spur desegregation efforts.

The Supreme Court hastened the process in 1969. In a case from Mississippi, *Alexander* v. *Holmes County Board of Education,* it ruled that, after 15 years, the time for "all deliberate speed" had ended. Said a unanimous Court: "[C]ontinued operation of segregated schools under a standard of allowing 'all deliberate speed' . . . is no longer constitutionally permissible."

Segregation by Neighborhood By the fall of 1970, school systems characterized by **de jure** segregation—segregation authorized by law—had been abolished. That is not to say that desegregation

had been fully accomplished, however—far from it. Some States, several school districts, and many parents and private groups sought to avoid integrated schools through established, or, often, newly created private schools.

Many integration controversies have arisen in places where the schools have never been segregated by law. They have occurred, instead, in communities in which de facto segregation has long been present, and continues. **De facto** segregation is segregation that exists in fact, even if no law requires it. Housing patterns have most often been its major cause. The concentration of Black Americans in certain sections of cities inevitably led to local school systems in which the student bodies of some schools are largely made up of Black students. That condition is quite apparent in many northern as well as southern communities today.

Efforts to desegregate those school systems have taken several forms over recent decades. Thus, for example, school district lines have been redrawn and the busing of students out of racially segregated neighborhoods has been tried. Those efforts have brought strong protests in many places and violence in some of them.

The Court first sanctioned busing in a North Carolina case, *Swann* v. *Charlotte-Mecklenburg Board of Education,* 1971. There it held that: "Desegregation plans cannot be limited to the walk-in school." Busing has been used since then to increase the racial mix in many school districts across the country—in some by court order, in others voluntarily.

Some school systems have turned to socioeconomic status—in particular, to income rather than race—in assigning students to schools within the district. That is, they have tried to promote schools with economically diverse student bodies. The results appear to be promising, both in terms of maintaining integrated schools and in improving the performance of disadvantaged students.

Other Types of Discrimination Public schools have not been fully integrated. But legally enforced racial segregation and discrimination against people based on race in all other areas of life has been eliminated. In the process, many State and local laws have either been repealed or been struck down by the courts.

The Supreme Court took a leading role in that process—holding in a number of cases that segregation by race is unconstitutional in other areas as well. Thus, it has held that the 14th Amendment's

>> Racist attitudes led some, such as these protesters in Little Rock, Arkansas, in the 1950s, to make the baseless claim that racial and school integration would lead to a classless, or communist, society.

Equal Protection Clause forbids segregation in public swimming pools and all other public recreational facilities, *Baltimore* v. *Dawson*, 1955; local transportation, *Gayle* v. *Browder*, 1956, stemming from Dr. Martin Luther King, Jr.'s bus boycott; and State prisons and local jails, *Lee* v. *Washington*, 1968. The High Court struck down all State miscegenation laws (statutes forbidding interracial marriages) in *Loving* v. *Virginia*, 1967.

In *Hernandez* v. *Texas*, 1954, the Court ruled that African Americans are not the only ethnic group to be protected by the 14th Amendment: Mexican Americans are protected, too, and must be allowed to serve on juries. This case paved the way for the Court to extend equal protection to other racial and ethnic groups that had historically been subjected to legal discrimination.

In *Morton* v. *Mancari*, 1974, for example, the Supreme Court upheld a policy of the federal Bureau of Indian Affairs that gave preference to American Indians for jobs in the bureau. Other cases have addressed the rights of Asian Americans, members of religious groups, and others.

☑ **IDENTIFY CENTRAL ISSUES** Why did it become a problem when the Supreme Court ruled that school segregation must end?

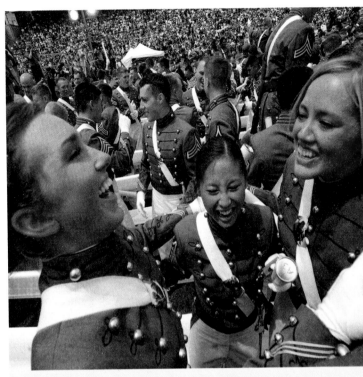

>> Cadets celebrate graduation at the U.S. Military Academy at West Point. Established in 1802, the school first admitted women in 1976. In 2012, about 15 percent of entering freshmen were women.

Gender, Sexual Orientation, and Equality

The Constitution speaks of the civil rights of "the people," "persons," and "citizens." Nowhere does it make its guarantees only to "men" or separately to "women." Its only reference to gender is in the 19th Amendment, which forbids denial of the right to vote "on account of sex." Gender has long been used as a basis of classification in the law, however. That practice reflected society's long-held view of the "proper" role of women. Most often, laws that treated men and women differently were intended to protect "the weaker sex." Over the years, the Court read that view into the 14th Amendment.

Challenging Sex Discrimination In the first case to challenge sex discrimination, *Bradwell* v. *Illinois*, 1873, the Court upheld a State law barring women from the practice of law. In that case, Justice **Joseph P. Bradley** wrote the following as part of a concurring opinion:

The civil law, as well as nature herself, has always recognized a wide

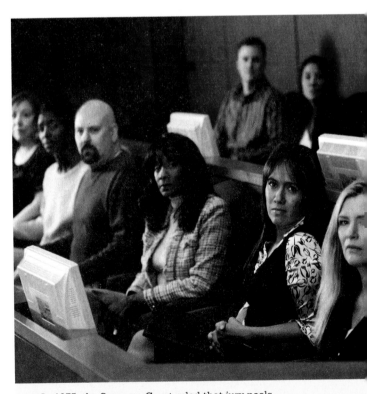

>> In 1975, the Supreme Court ruled that jury pools without women violated defendants' rights to be judged by a jury of their peers. Both men and women have served on juries since that ruling.

difference in the respective spheres and destinies of man and woman. Man is, or should be, woman's protector and defender. The natural and proper timidity and delicacy which belongs to the female sex evidently unfits it for many of the occupations of civil life.

—Concurring Opinion

Even as late as 1961, in *Hoyt* v. *Florida*, the Court could find no constitutional fault with a law that required men to serve on juries, but gave women the choice of serving or not.

A Closer Look at Sex Discrimination Matters are far different today. The Court now takes a very close look at cases involving claims of sex discrimination. It first did so in *Reed* v. *Reed*, 1971; there, it struck down an Idaho law that gave fathers preference over mothers in the administration of their children's estates.

Since then, the Supreme Court has found a number of sex-based distinctions to be unconstitutional. In *Taylor* v. *Louisiana*, 1975, it held that the 14th Amendment's Equal Protection Clause forbids the States to exclude women from jury service. Among other examples of that line

of cases, it struck down an Oklahoma law that prohibited the sale of beer to males under 21 and to females under 18, *Craig* v. *Boren*, 1976. And the Court found the practice of refusing to admit women to the rigorous citizen-soldier program offered by a public institution, the Virginia Military Institute, to be constitutionally unacceptable, *United States* v. *Virginia*, 1996.

The Court's changed attitude in cases involving sex-based discrimination was stated in the majority opinion in *Frontiero* v. *Richardson*, written by Justice **William Brennan** in 1973:

There can be no doubt that our Nation has had a long and unfortunate history of sex discrimination. Traditionally, such discrimination was rationalized by an attitude of 'romantic paternalism' which, in practical effect, put women not on a pedestal, but in a cage.

—Justice William J. Brennan, Jr.

Not all sex-based distinctions are unconstitutional, however. The Court has upheld a Florida law that gives an extra property tax exemption to widows, but not to widowers, *Kahn* v. *Shevin*, 1974; an Alabama law forbidding women to

Selected Supreme Court Decisions on Gender Discrimination

CASE	YEAR	DECISION
Hoyt v. *Florida*	1961	States may make jury service optional for women.
Reed v. *Reed*	1971	States may not choose the executor of an estate based solely on gender.
Frontiero v. *Richardson*	1973	The Federal Government may not deny benefits to the husband of a female soldier.
Kahn v. *Shevin*	1974	States may grant a property tax exemption only to widows, and not to widowers, because women as a class earn less than men.
Dothard v. *Rawlinson*	1977	States may not discriminate against women who apply for jobs in law enforcement.
United States v. *Virginia*	1996	The Virginia Military Institute must admit women as well as men. An alternate, segregated school for women would not offer the same educational opportunities.

>> Since 1971, the Supreme Court has ruled many cases based on sex-based distinctions unconstitutional. **Analyze Charts** What additional issue did the Court rule on in *United States* v. *Virginia*?

serve as prison guards in all-male penitentiaries, *Dothard* v. *Rawlinson*, 1977; and the federal selective service law that requires only men to register for the draft and excludes women from any future draft, *Rostker* v. *Goldberg*, 1981.

In effect, these cases say this: Classification by gender is not in and of itself unconstitutional. However, laws that treat men and women differently will be overturned by the courts unless (1) they are intended to serve an "important governmental objective" and (2) they are "substantially related" to achieving that goal.

Discrimination Based on Sexual Orientation

The 1970s brought change for the gay and lesbian rights movements in the United States. In 1971, a gay couple from Minnesota tried to get married. The State Supreme Court ruled that the Constitution does not protect "a fundamental right" for marriage between same-sex couples (a decision upheld by the Supreme Court), bringing the matter of gay marriage into sharper focus.

The issue continued to simmer, and by the 1990s, public policy seemed to be moving in contradictory directions. Many States passed laws and constitutional amendments defining marriage as the union of a man and a woman, and in 1996, the Federal Government implemented the Defense of Marriage Act. At the same time, a few States began making moves in the other direction. The Hawaii Supreme Court, for example, ruled that a ban on gay marriage violated the State's constitution.

During the late 1990s and early 2000s, the number of States that allowed gay marriage continued to grow. In 2003, the Supreme Court ruled, in *Lawrence* v. *Texas*, that the government had no legitimate interest "which can justify its intrusion into the personal and private life of the individual," including sexual intimacy between same-sex partners.

Ten years later, the High Court struck down a key provision of the 1996 Defense of Marriage Act (*United States* v. *Windsor*). In its sharply divided 5–4 decision, the Court held that the section of the law that denied federal benefits to legally married gay and lesbian couples was invalid, stating that it "violates basic due process and equal protection principles."

Legal challenges to State laws continued to mount, and finally, in an historic 5–4 decision in 2015, the Court struck down all State bans on same-sex marriage, *Obergefell* v. *Hodges*. The decision means that States must allow same-sex couples to marry and also must recognize same-sex marriages from other States.

☑ **INTERPRET** How is the Supreme Court's decision regarding the Defense of Marriage Act an example of checks and balances between the legislative and judicial branches of government?

☑ ASSESSMENT

1. **Check Understanding** Why did Congress add the Equal Protection Clause to the Constitution, as part of the 14th Amendment, after the Civil War? How does the Equal Protection Clause continue to affect Americans today and in the future?

2. **Interpret** In *Brown* v. *Board of Education*, why did the Court require desegregation to occur "with all deliberate speed"?

3. **Compare and Contrast** Compare and contrast *de jure* and *de facto* segregation.

4. **Apply Concepts** What type of segregation can result from differences in socioeconomic status?

5. **Make Generalizations** How might Justice Joseph Bradley's argument that a law barring women from practicing law could be upheld because of women's "timidity and delicacy" be regarded as an application of the rational basis test? How might it be regarded as unreasonable?

Brown v. Board of Education: *Majority Opinion*

Every morning, 8-year-old Linda Brown of Topeka, Kansas, had to walk through a dangerous railroad yard in order to get to the bus that took her to the "colored" school. Her parents' attempt to enroll her in a school closer to home was denied, because that school was for "whites only." Linda's parents sued and the case went all the way to the Supreme Court.

>> Linda Brown

The Opinion of the Court, Chief Justice Earl Warren

. . . The plaintiffs contend that segregated public schools are not "equal" and cannot be made "equal," and that hence they are deprived of the equal protection of the laws. . . .

☑ **ANALYZE STRUCTURE** What is the purpose of this opening statement?

. . . [T]here are findings below that the Negro and white schools involved have been equalized, or are being equalized, with respect to buildings, curricula, qualifications and salaries of teachers, and other "tangible" factors. Our decision, therefore, cannot turn on merely a comparison of these tangible factors in the Negro and white schools involved in each of the cases. We must look instead to the effect of segregation itself on public education.

☑ **EVALUATE REASONING** Why does Chief Justice Warren distinguish between "tangible" factors and "the effect of segregation itself"?

In approaching this problem, we cannot turn the clock back to 1868, when the Amendment was adopted, or even to 1896, when *Plessy* v.

Ferguson was written. We must consider public education in the light of its full development and its present place in American life throughout the Nation. Only in this way can it be determined if segregation in public schools deprives these plaintiffs of the equal protection of the laws.

Today, education is perhaps the most important function of state and local governments. Compulsory school attendance laws and the great expenditures for education both demonstrate our recognition of the importance of education to our democratic society. It is required in the performance of our most basic public responsibilities, even service in the armed forces. It is the very foundation of good citizenship. Today it is a principal instrument in awakening the child to cultural values, in preparing him for later professional training, and in helping him to adjust normally to his environment. In these days, it is doubtful that any child may reasonably be expected to succeed in life if he is denied the opportunity of an education. Such an opportunity, where the state has undertaken to provide it, is a right which must be made available to all on equal terms.

☑ **IDENTIFY KEY INFORMATION** Why is this paragraph about education in the United States critical to the point that Chief Justice Warren is making?

We come then to the question presented: Does segregation of children in public schools solely on the basis of race, even though the physical facilities and other "tangible" factors may be equal, deprive the children of the minority group of equal educational opportunities? We believe that it does.

In *Sweatt* v. *Painter*, . . . in finding that a segregated law school for Negroes could not provide them equal educational opportunities, this Court relied in large part on "those qualities which are incapable of objective measurement but which make for greatness in a law school." In *McLaurin* v. *Oklahoma State Regents*, *supra*, the Court, in requiring that a Negro admitted to a white graduate school be treated like all other students, again resorted to intangible considerations: ". . . his ability to study, to engage in discussions and exchange views with other students, and, in general, to learn his profession." Such considerations apply with added force to children in grade and high schools. To separate them from others of similar age and qualifications solely because of their race generates a feeling of inferiority as to their status in the community that may affect their hearts and minds in a way unlikely ever to be undone. The effect of this separation on their educational opportunities was well stated by a finding in the Kansas case by a court which nevertheless felt compelled to rule against the Negro plaintiffs: Segregation of white and colored children in public schools has a detrimental effect upon the colored children. The impact is greater when it has the sanction of the law, for the policy of separating the races is usually interpreted as denoting the inferiority of the negro group. A sense of inferiority affects the motivation of a child to learn. Segregation with the sanction of law, therefore, has a tendency to [retard] the educational and mental development of negro children and to deprive them of some of the benefits they would receive in a racial[ly] integrated school system. Whatever may have been the extent of psychological knowledge at the time of *Plessy* v. *Ferguson*, this finding is amply supported by modern authority. Any language in *Plessy* v. *Ferguson* contrary to this finding is rejected.

☑ **IDENTIFY CENTRAL IDEAS** Summarize the main idea of this paragraph.

We conclude that, in the field of public education, the doctrine of "separate but equal" has no place. Separate educational facilities are inherently unequal. Therefore, we hold that the plaintiffs and others similarly situated for whom the actions have been brought are, by reason of the segregation complained of, deprived of the equal protection of the laws guaranteed by the Fourteenth Amendment. This disposition makes unnecessary any discussion whether such segregation also violates the Due Process Clause of the Fourteenth Amendment.

☑ ASSESSMENT

1. **Examine Principles** What basic American principles are reflected in the majority opinion in *Brown* v. *Board of Education*? How did this ruling help lead to the expansion of civil rights and liberties in the United States?

2. **Analyze Structure** Review your answers to the questions posed throughout this excerpt. Based on those answers, how do the various portions of this document contribute to the final claim that "Separate educational facilities are inherently unequal"?

3. **Evaluate Evidence** In a brief submitted to the Court, Kenneth B. Clark and other psychologists described some of their findings related to segregation in education: "The report indicates that minority group children of all social and economic classes often react with a generally defeatist attitude and a lowering of personal ambitions." Does this statement corroborate or challenge the assertions made by Chief Justice Warren in his majority opinion? Evaluate the validity of the claims made by Warren based on this additional information.

Dr. Martin Luther King, Jr., delivered his "I Have a Dream" speech at the Lincoln Memorial in 1963, at what he called "the greatest demonstration for freedom in the history of our nation."

 BOUNCE to Activate Flipped Video

Objectives

Outline the history of civil rights legislation from Reconstruction to today.

Explore the issues surrounding affirmative action.

Key Terms

affirmative action
quota
reverse
  discrimination
Martin Luther King,
  Jr.

Federal Civil Rights Laws

Those who, for one reason or another, oppose the enactment of civil rights legislation often rely on this observation: "You can't legislate morality." That is, racism, sexism, and other forms of discrimination will not be eliminated by simply passing a law.

The History of Civil Rights Laws

The Reverend **Dr. Martin Luther King, Jr.**, responded to that contention this way: "Judicial decrees," he said, "may not change the heart, but they can restrain the heartless." Clearly, Congress has agreed with Dr. King—as it has enacted a number of civil rights laws since the 1960s.

From the 1870s to the late 1950s, Congress did not pass a single piece of meaningful civil rights legislation. Several factors contributed to that fact. For example, through that period, the nation's predominantly white population was generally unaware of or little concerned with the plight of African Americans, Native Americans, or other nonwhites in this country. Also, southern white Democrats, bolstered by such devices as the seniority system and the filibuster, held many of the most strategic posts in Congress. In addition, during much of this period, Congress was focused on economic issues. For example, in 1944 Congress passed the Servicemen's Readjustment Act (commonly known as the GI Bill of Rights), which provided educational tuition, unemployment benefits, federal assistance with home loans, and job counseling for returning veterans.

Congress' civil rights logjam was finally broken in 1957, largely as a result of the pressures brought to bear by the civil rights movement led by Dr. King. Beginning in that year, Congress passed a number of civil rights laws—notably, the Civil Rights Acts of 1957, 1960, 1964, and 1968; the Voting Rights Acts of 1965, 1970, 1975, 1982, and 2006; and Title IX in the Education Amendments of 1972.

The Civil Rights Act of 1964 The 1964 law is the most far-reaching of those statutes. It was passed after the longest debate in Senate history (83 days), and only after the Senate invoked cloture (limited debate) to kill a filibuster. Beyond its voting rights provisions, the 1964 law outlaws discrimination in a number of areas. With its several later amendments, the law had three major sections. The law

- provides that no person may be denied access to or refused service in various "public accommodations"—hotels, motels, restaurants, theaters, and the like—because of race, color, religion, national origin, or physical disability (Title II);
- prohibits discrimination against any person on grounds of race, color, religion, national origin, sex, or physical disability in any program that receives any federal funding (Title VI);
- forbids both employers and labor unions to discriminate against any person on grounds of race, color, religion, sex, physical disability, or age in job-related matters (Title VII).

The Civil Rights Act of 1968 The Civil Rights Act of 1968 is often called the Open Housing Act. With minor exceptions, it forbids anyone to refuse to sell or rent a dwelling to any person on grounds of race, color, religion, national origin, sex, or disability. It also forbids refusal to sell or rent to a family with children.

At first, the burden of enforcing the law fell on those persons who claimed to be victims of housing discrimination; they could seek damages from alleged offenders. Congress finally strengthened the law in 1988, to allow the Justice Department to bring criminal charges against those who violate its terms. Still, housing remains among the most segregated areas of American life today.

Title IX In Title IX of the Education Amendments of 1972, Congress added a key gender-based guarantee to the provisions of the Civil Rights Act of 1964. Title IX forbids discrimination on the basis of gender "in any education program or activity receiving Federal financial assistance." The statute intends to ensure that women receive equal treatment in all aspects of education. Its provisions apply to all schools, public and private, that receive federal funds, and nearly all of them do.

Since its passage, Title IX has had its most telling effect on school athletics programs, especially at the college level, by requiring roughly equal funding and opportunities for women and men. The law has been in effect for decades and it still continues to generate controversy.

☑ **COMPARE AND CONTRAST** Compare and contrast the Civil Rights Acts of 1964 and 1968. Which act provided broader protection against discrimination? Why?

Government Policies on Affirmative Action

These civil rights statutes all come down to this: Discriminatory practices based on such factors as race, color, national origin, sex, or disability are illegal. But what about the effects of *past* discrimination? Consider a Black American who,

>> Civil rights activist Rosa Parks sits in the front of a Montgomery, Alabama, bus in 1956, after the Supreme Court ruled that segregation on city buses was illegal.

for no reason of his or her own making, did not get a decent education and so today cannot get a decent job. Of what real help to that person are all of those laws that make illegal today what was done years ago?

So far, the Federal Government's chief answer to this troubling question has been a policy of **affirmative action**. That approach requires that most employers take positive steps (affirmative action) to remedy the effects of past discriminations. The policy applies to all agencies of the Federal Government, States and their local governments, and private employers who sell goods or services to any agency of the Federal Government. The Federal Government began to demand the adoption of affirmative action programs in 1965.

To illustrate the policy, take the case of a company that does business with the Federal Government. It must adopt an affirmative action plan designed to make its workforce reflect the general makeup of the population in its locale. The plan must include steps to correct or prevent inequalities in such matters as pay, promotions, and fringe benefits.

For many employers this has meant that they must hire and/or promote more workers with minority backgrounds and more females. The share of a group necessary to satisfy a particular affirmative action requirement—say, the number of females in a company's workforce or the number of Black Americans in a school's student body—is often called a **quota**.

Is Affirmative Action Reverse Discrimination?

Affirmative action policies remain highly controversial. This is principally because those policies necessarily involve race-based and/or gender-based classifications. Critics argue that affirmative action programs amount to **reverse discrimination,** or discrimination against the majority group. Affirmative action demands that preference be given to females and/or nonwhites solely on the basis of sex or race. Critics say that the Constitution requires that all public policies be "color blind."

The opponents of affirmative action have attacked the policy at the State and local levels in several States. Most often, they have relied primarily on the reverse discrimination argument.

In 1996, California's voters gave overwhelming approval to a measure that eliminated nearly all affirmative action programs conducted by public agencies in that State. Since then, several other States have adopted constitutional amendments or passed statutes banning affirmative action programs, and Florida did so through executive action by the governor.

Two Views on Affirmative Action

PRO	CON
[I]t is hard to understand the opposition [to affirmative action], often diehard, of many white liberals that has persisted since the nineteen-seventies. Did these people really imagine that passing a law against discrimination would reset race relations overnight? Do they really think that white Americans, wherever they work or go to college, do not carry a lifelong advantage because of the color of their skin? Do they really believe that there should be no sacrifice to make or price to pay for the systematic damage done to the lives of millions of American citizens and the men and women who are their ancestors? –Louis Menand, "The Changing Meaning of Affirmative Action," *The New Yorker,* 2020	Past discrimination against certain minority groups does not justify present discrimination against non-minorities. Righting a wrong with another wrong is never justified. Although past discrimination against minorities is a historical fact, contemporary Americans do not bear the responsibility for, nor should they be disadvantaged or punished because of, the deeds of past generations. Furthermore, affirmative action policies harm those they are purported to help. . . . People may view minorities at school or work as inferior and engender the notion that they are only there because of a helping hand, regardless of whether the minority benefited from an affirmative action policy or not. –Artemus Ward, "Is Affirmative Action Justified?," Bill of Rights Institute Web site

>> Since its inception, the policy of affirmative action has been divisive among Americans. **Analyze Charts** How do these views illustrate the fundamental divide on the issue of affirmative action?

The First Major Affirmative Action Case The Supreme Court decided its first major affirmative action case, *Regents of the University of California* v. *Bakke*, in 1978. Allan Bakke, a white male, had been denied admission to the university's medical school at Davis. The school had set aside 16 of the 100 seats in each year's entering class for nonwhite students. He sued the university, charging it with reverse discrimination and a violation of the Equal Protection Clause of the 14th Amendment. By a 5–4 majority, the Court held that Bakke had been denied equal protection and should be admitted to the medical school.

Nevertheless, said the Court, while the Constitution does not allow race to be used as the only factor in the making of affirmative action decisions, both the Constitution and the 1964 Civil Rights Act do allow its use as one among *several* factors in such situations. That is, race can be used as one criteria, but it cannot be the *only* criteria.

Strict Scrutiny The Supreme Court has decided several affirmative action cases since *Bakke*. In some of them it has upheld quotas, especially in such industries as construction, where longstanding discrimination was involved.

In 1995, however, the Court's decision in *Adarand Constructors* v. *Pena* marked a major departure from its previous rulings. *Adarand* arose when a white-owned Colorado company, Adarand Constructors, Inc., challenged a federal affirmative action policy. Under that policy, the government gave bonuses to highway contractors if ten percent or more of their construction work was subcontracted to "socially and economically disadvantaged" businesses, including those owned by racial minorities.

In its decision, the Court held that in the future an affirmative action program will be upheld only if it can be shown that it serves some "compelling government interest." "The Constitution protects persons, not groups," wrote Justice Sandra Day O'Connor in the majority opinion. "Whenever the government treats any person unequally because of his or her race, that person has suffered an injury" covered by "the Constitution's guarantee of equal treatment." Stated a bit differently, affirmative action programs must be "narrowly tailored" to overcome specific cases of discrimination.

Affirmative Action in the 21st Century

Controversy continued to rage over the place of affirmative action in the twenty-first century. In two

>> The Supreme Court ruling in favor of Allan Bakke (center) did not answer the question of how society can overcome the effects of discrimination and level the playing field for minorities.

key 2003 cases, *Gratz* v. *Bollinger* and *Grutter* v. *Bollinger*, a majority of the Court found that the State of Michigan (and all the States) has a compelling interest in the diversity of the student bodies of its public educational institutions. That compelling interest justifies the narrowly tailored use of race as one factor in the student admissions policies of those institutions.

The cases involved the admissions policies of the University of Michigan. Jennifer Gratz applied for admission to the University as a freshman in 1997, and Barbara Grutter sought to enter the University's law school that same year. Both women are white, and both were rejected in favor of minority applicants with lower grade point averages and lower entry test scores. Both women sued the university. After losing in the lower courts, each appealed to the Supreme Court, which ruled in favor of the university.

In *Ricci* v. *DeStefano*, 2009, a group of white and Hispanic firefighters sued the city of New Haven, Connecticut. They claimed that they had been the victims of reverse discrimination when the results of an exam were discarded after few minority firefighters qualified for a promotion. The

>> Firefighters in New Haven won their case of reverse discrimination in *Ricci* v. *DeStefano*. Justice Anthony Kennedy wrote, "No individual should face workplace discrimination based on race."

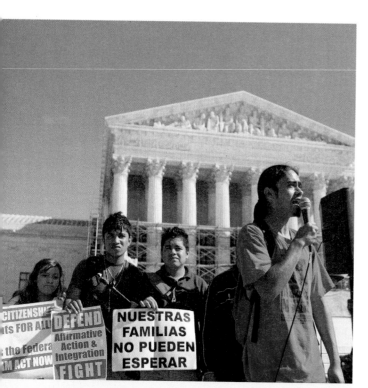

>> A number of student groups gathered to voice their support for affirmative action while awaiting the Supreme Court's ruling on *Fisher* v. *Texas*.

Court ruled, 5–4, in favor of the firefighters. It said, in effect, that race could not be used as the sole factor in promotions.

In *Fisher* v. *Texas*, 2013, the Court reaffirmed that affirmative action policies in college admissions must be "narrowly tailored" and pass strict scrutiny. In addition, the Court for the first time specified exactly how strict scrutiny should work with regard to affirmative action programs. Specifically, universities must confirm in each situation that no method other than the use of race will suffice to create a diverse student body. The Court's vote in Fisher was 7–1.

Court decisions continue to suggest that only a narrow use of affirmative action can pass constitutional muster. In *Fisher* v. *Texas*, 2016 (also called *Fisher II*), the Supreme Court ruled that using race as one of several factors in the admissions process at the University of Texas was constitutional, because the university had shown that such a policy was needed to meet its diversity goals and that no other reasonable alternative existed for achieving those goals.

Controversy continues to rage over affirmative action in hiring and college admissions. Opponents maintain that affirmative action amounts to reverse discrimination. They also contend that affirmative action can do more harm than good if it reinforces stereotypes and leads to the perception that minorities have not achieved jobs or college admissions on merit, but only due to race- or gender-based preferences.

Supporters maintain that the need for such policies remains. They point to both historical and continued discrimination against minority groups and to facts such as this: Many of those States that have banned affirmative action in college admissions have seen a significant drop in the numbers of Black Americans and Hispanic Americans who have enrolled at major public universities. Supporters also believe that diversity enhances the overall college experience and that affirmative action has a place in the admissions process as a means to achieve that diversity.

☑ **GENERATE EXPLANATIONS** What is the role of the majority group in matters of discrimination and reverse discrimination?

1. **Identify Patterns** What piece of federal legislation had the same effect on gender discrimination in education as the *Brown* v. *Board of Education* decision had on race discrimination in schools? Why?

2. **Identify Key Steps in a Process** Why was the Civil Rights Act of 1964 so effective in immediately taking away the de jure component of Jim Crow? How was the process of implementing this law different from the process of implementing the *Brown* v. *Board of Education* decision?

3. **Synthesize** How was a peaceful civil rights movement able to bring about broad changes in society, including changes in legislation passed by politicians who were elected by a majority of the voters? How did the civil rights movement manage to put pressure on politicians to change laws?

4. **Analyze Information** What is the relationship between affirmative action and quotas?

5. **Sequence Events** How, and why, are the Supreme Court's decisions about affirmative action changing over time?

Outlawing Discrimination

In 1972, Title IX of the Education Amendments was signed by President Nixon, outlawing discrimination on the basis of gender in any federally funded education program. Two of Title IX's most far-reaching effects were felt in the areas of sports and higher education. Girls' participation in high school varsity athletics jumped from 7 percent in 1971 to 41.5 percent in 2001. Then, in 1990, Congress passed the world's first civil rights law for people with disabilities. The Americans with Disabilities Act (ADA) guaranteed access to employment, public transportation, and public accommodations. As a result, the world became a more hospitable place through such aids as entrance ramps, wheelchair lifts on city buses, lowered curbs, and automatic doors.

>> Title IX led to increased opportunities for women in sports

Title IX of the 1972 Education Amendments

Prohibition against discrimination; exceptions. No person in the United States shall, on the basis of sex, be excluded from participation in, be denied the benefits of, or be subjected to discrimination under any education program or activity receiving Federal financial assistance, except that:

(1) Classes of educational institutions subject to prohibition

in regard to admissions to educational institutions, this section shall apply only to institutions of vocational education, professional education, and graduate higher education, and to public institutions of undergraduate higher education; . . .

(3) Educational institutions of religious organizations with contrary religious tenets

this section shall not apply to any educational institution which is controlled by a religious organization if the application of this subsection would not be consistent with the religious tenets of such organization;

(4) Educational institutions training individuals for military services or merchant marine

this section shall not apply to an educational institution whose primary purpose is the training of individuals for the military services of the United States, or the merchant marine;

(5) Public educational institutions with traditional and continuing admissions policy

in regard to admissions this section shall not apply to any public institution of undergraduate higher education which is an institution that traditionally and continually from its establishment has had a policy of admitting only students of one sex;

☑ **EVALUATE PREMISES** The premise behind paragraph 4 in this section of Title IX is the fact that women were not admitted to military academies when the law was passed. That changed three years later; however, military schools are still exempt from Title IX. How does this fact affect the original premise behind Section 4?

Americans with Disabilities Act

Sec. 12101. Findings and purpose

The Congress finds that

(1) physical or mental disabilities in no way diminish a person's right to fully participate in all aspects of society, yet many people with physical or mental disabilities have been precluded from doing so because of discrimination; others who have a record of a disability or are regarded as having a disability also have been subjected to discrimination;

(2) historically, society has tended to isolate and segregate individuals with disabilities, and, despite some improvements, such forms of discrimination against individuals with disabilities continue to be a serious and pervasive social problem;

(3) discrimination against individuals with disabilities persists in such critical areas as employment, housing, public accommodations, education, transportation, communication, recreation, institutionalization, health services, voting, and access to public services;

(4) unlike individuals who have experienced discrimination on the basis of race, color, sex, national origin, religion, or age, individuals who have experienced discrimination on the basis of disability have often had no legal recourse to redress such discrimination;

(5) individuals with disabilities continually encounter various forms of discrimination, including outright intentional exclusion, the discriminatory effects of architectural, transportation, and communication barriers, overprotective rules and policies, failure to make modifications to existing facilities and practices, exclusionary qualification standards and criteria, segregation, and relegation to lesser services, programs, activities, benefits, jobs, or other opportunities;

(6) census data, national polls, and other studies have documented that people with disabilities, as a group, occupy an inferior status in our society, and are severely disadvantaged socially, vocationally, economically, and educationally;

(7) the Nation's proper goals regarding individuals with disabilities are to assure equality of opportunity, full participation, independent living, and economic self-sufficiency for such individuals; . . ..

General Rule[s]:

No covered entity shall discriminate against a qualified individual on the basis of disability in regard to job application procedures, the hiring, advancement, or discharge of employees, employee compensation, job training, and other terms, conditions, and privileges of employment. . . .

It shall be considered discrimination for [any entity] which operates a fixed route system to purchase or lease a new bus, a new rapid rail vehicle, a new light rail vehicle, or any other new vehicle to be used on such system, . . . if such bus, rail vehicle, or other vehicle is not readily accessible to and usable by individuals with disabilities, including individuals who use wheelchairs. . . .

No individual shall be discriminated against on the basis of disability in the full and equal enjoyment of the goods, services, facilities, privileges, advantages, or accommodations of any place of public accommodation by any person who owns, leases (or leases to), or operates a place of public accommodation. . . .

☑ ASSESSMENT

1. **Examine Principles** Examine and identify the principles found in Title IX and the Americans with Disabilities Act. How did these laws expand civil rights and liberties in the United States?

2. **Analyze Structure** Analyze how the excerpt from the Americans with Disabilities Act is structured. In your analysis, consider the purpose of the first 7 paragraphs. How do these paragraphs and those that follow contribute to the excerpt as a whole?

3. **Determine Meaning** What do you think is meant by "fixed route systems" in the Americans with Disabilities Act?

Topic 9 Quick Study Guide

LESSON SUMMARIES

Use these Lesson Summaries, and the longer versions available online, to review the key ideas for each lesson in this Topic.

Lesson 1: American Citizenship

An American citizen owes allegiance to the United States and is entitled to its protection. All children born in the United States are citizens. Children born abroad to American citizens may also be entitled to citizenship. Others may apply for citizenship or be naturalized collectively by treaty or act of Congress.

Lesson 2: Diversity and Discrimination

Although the United States is a heterogeneous population, discrimination has long been a problem, especially against African Americans. The ancestors of most African Americans were kept in slavery until 1865. Discrimination against African Americans, Native Americans, and other minority groups continued long after. Women have also faced unequal treatment.

Lesson 3: Equality Before the Law

The Equal Protection Clause of the 14th Amendment has come to mean that the States cannot unreasonably discriminate against any group of people. In the past, courts accepted legal segregation by race, but these decisions were overturned in the 1950s and 1960s. More recent cases have held instances of discrimination against women to be unconstitutional.

Lesson 4: Federal Civil Rights Laws

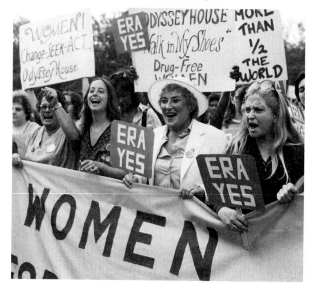

Beginning in 1957, Congress passed a number of civil rights laws. The most far-reaching, the Civil Rights Act of 1964, banned discrimination in several areas, including public accommodations such as hotels and restaurants, as well as in employment. Affirmative action programs, an attempt to remedy past discrimination, have proved controversial and several States have ended them.

VISUAL REVIEW

Use these graphics to review some of the key terms, people, and ideas from this Topic.

Affirmative Action

CAUSES
• Discriminatory practices based on such factors as race, color, national origin, or gender • Difficult for the underprivileged to obtain a quality education • Difficult for minorities to find fair opportunities in the workforce

↓

EFFECTS
• Most companies hire women and minorities • Reverse discrimination • Controversy and many court cases over the constitutionality and/or proper administration of affirmative action

American Citizenship

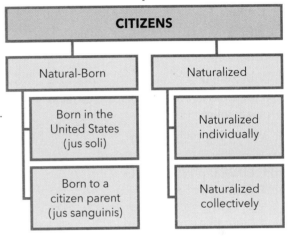

CITIZENS

Natural-Born
- Born in the United States (jus soli)
- Born to a citizen parent (jus sanguinis)

Naturalized
- Naturalized individually
- Naturalized collectively

Key Federal Civil Rights Laws

Civil Rights Act of 1964	Banned discrimination in public accommodations and employment
Civil Rights Act of 1968	Banned discrimination in selling or renting homes
Title IX of the Education Amendments of 1972	Banned gender discrimination in any education program that receives federal funding

Segregation in American Society

Late 1800s: Nearly half the States pass segregation (Jim Crow) laws.

↓

1896: The Supreme Court establishes the separate-but-equal doctrine in *Plessy* v. *Ferguson*.

↓

1954: The Supreme Court rules in *Brown* v. *Board of Education* that the separate-but-equal doctrine is unconstitutional.

↓

1955: Public schools begin to desegregate.

↓

1960s: Major civil rights legislation is passed, including the Civil Rights Act of 1964.

Topic 9 Assessment

KEY TERMS, PEOPLE, AND IDEAS

1. Compare and contrast the principles of **jus soli** and **jus sanguinis**.

2. What is **naturalization**?

3. Explain the meaning of the **separate-but-equal doctrine**.

4. What is the purpose of the **rational basis test?**

5. What is **integration**?

6. Define **refugee**.

7. How do **de jure segregation** and **de facto segregation** differ?

8. What is **affirmative action**?

CRITICAL THINKING

9. **Evaluate** What are the constitutional provisions establishing citizenship? Describe the criteria distinguishing among citizens by birth, naturalized citizens, and non-citizens.

10. **Explain** What was the intent of Jim Crow laws? What landmark Supreme Court case upheld Jim Crow laws and on what basis? Do you think facilities can truly be "separate but equal"? Why or why not?

11. **Summarize** What was the first major affirmative action case ruled on by the Supreme Court? How did the Supreme Court rule in the case? What arguments do critics use when they say that affirmative action is unconstitutional?

12. **Express Ideas Clearly** Cite two cases in which the Supreme Court found sex-based distinctions to be unconstitutional. Do you think the parameters that the Supreme Court uses when ruling on laws regarding the treatment of men and women are fair? Explain.

13. **Analyze** Why was immigration restricted in the 1880s and again in the 1920s? Outline current immigration policy. Who is excluded from entering the United States today?

14. **Support a Point of View with Evidence** Cite an example of what you consider to be reasonable discrimination by government. Explain.

15. **Contrast** How does the ethnic balance in the United States today differ from that of colonial times? Which ethnic groups are experiencing the most rapid population growth?

16. **Interpret** Immigration to the United States has changed greatly over time. What can you learn about the history of U.S. immigration from this chart? Predict how immigration may continue to change in the future.

Immigration by Region (in millions)

1910–1919		2004–2013	
E. and S. Europe	3.3	Asia	4.1
N. and W. Europe	1.7	Central America/ Caribbean	1.8
North America*	0.89	North America*	1.7
Asia	0.27	Europe	1.1
Central America/ Caribbean	0.14	Africa	1.0
South America	0.04	South America	0.95
Other	0.03	Other	0.08

*Mexico and Canada
SOURCE: Dept. of Homeland Security, 2011 *Yearbook of Immigration Statistics*

17. **Explain** What controversies have resulted over changing interpretations of civil rights in the following Supreme Court cases: *Plessy* v. *Ferguson*, *Brown* v. *Board of Education*, *Miranda* v. *Arizona*, *Regents of the University of California* v. *Bakke*, *Adarand Constructors, Inc*. v. *Pena*, and *United States* v. *Virginia*?

18. **Summarize** Today, the number of Hispanic Americans exceeds 50 million, and they constitute the largest minority group in this country. Describe the major subgroups of Hispanic Americans and the discrimination they have faced.

19. **Analyze** How has citizen participation helped achieve political and social change in the civil rights movement?

20. **Writing Activity** In this topic, you learned about the long struggle for equality and civil rights. Using reliable sources as directed by your teacher, research the lives and work of major civil rights leaders in the United States. Based on your research and the content of this topic, create a timeline about the ongoing struggles for civil rights.

DOCUMENT-BASED QUESTIONS

Congress has not been able to enact meaningful immigration reform in recent decades, in part because of a dispute over how to approach the issue.

DOCUMENT A

This excerpt argues that large-scale immigration harms American workers.

One of the reasons Congress sets limits on the number of immigrants we admit to this country is to protect job opportunities and prevent the erosion of wages for American workers. . . . While it may be in the short-term interest of some businesses to flood the labor market with foreign workers—many of whom are prepared to accept poorer wages and working conditions—doing so undermines core national interests. . . .

Between 2000 and 2014, two new immigrants were admitted to the United States for every new job that was created by our economy.

—*Federation for American Immigration Reform (FAIR), "Immigration, Labor Displacement and the American Worker"*

DOCUMENT B

This excerpt presents a different perspective on immigration's effects on the U.S. economy.

The U.S. economy does not contain a fixed number of jobs for which immigrants and native-born workers compete. For instance, if the eight million undocumented immigrant workers now in the United States were removed from the country, there would not be eight million job openings for unemployed Americans. . . . First, removing eight million undocumented workers from the economy would also remove eight million entrepreneurs, consumers, and taxpayers. This would cause the U.S. economy to lose jobs. Secondly, native-born workers and immigrant workers tend to possess different skills that often complement one another, and are therefore not interchangeable.

—*U.S. Chamber of Commerce, "Immigration Myths and Facts"*

DOCUMENT C

In 2012, President Obama issued an executive order that suspended deportations of children of illegal immigrants for two years.

The President's executive actions will give parents of American citizens or legal resident children who have lived in the U.S. for more than five years relief from deportation if they register with the government, undergo background checks, and pay taxes. It will also allow immigration enforcement officials to focus resources on deporting felons, not families.

—*Organizing for Action, "Comprehensive Immigration Reform"*

DOCUMENT D

This excerpt summarizes President Obama's immigration policies.

President Barack Obama's immigration policies have drawn ire from immigration advocates and opponents alike. Though he pledged to tackle comprehensive immigration reform in his first year in office, Obama did not make the issue a priority until his second term. His administration has deported more than two million undocumented immigrants, more than former President George W. Bush did in his two terms. . . . Through a series of executive actions in 2012 and 2014, however, Obama has tried to grant a reprieve to as many as five million undocumented immigrants in the United States.

—*Council on Foreign Relations, "The U.S. Immigration Debate"*

21. What main point is made by Document B?
    A. Removing eight million undocumented workers from the country would boost the U.S. economy.
    B. Native-born and immigrant workers tend to have interchangeable skills.
    C. Two new immigrants were admitted to the United States for every new job created between 2000 and 2014.
    D. Immigrants and native-born workers do not compete for a fixed number of jobs.

22. According to Document D, President Obama has
    A. failed to act on immigration.
    B. used executive actions to try to grant reprieve to millions of undocumented immigrants.
    C. chosen not to deport undocumented immigrations.
    D. exceeded his constitutional authority with his use of executive actions.

23. **Writing Task** Why do you think Congress has not acted on meaningful immigration reform since 1996? Using information from these documents, as well as what you learned about immigration in this topic, evaluate different perspectives on immigration reform. Be sure to note any discrepancies among the sources.

Government by the People

ESSENTIAL QUESTION What Is the Role of the People in Government?

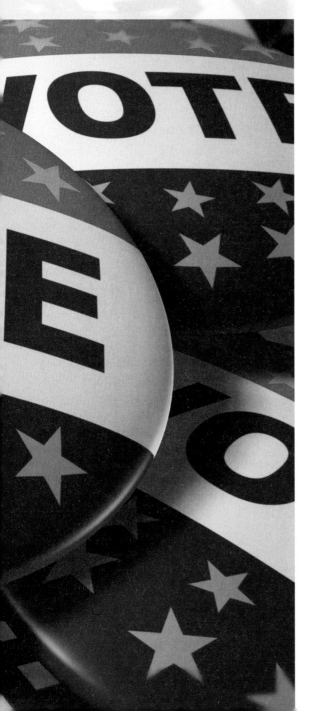

Americans consider voting to be a patriotic duty.

Connections to Today

What difference does your one vote make? Politicians spend enormous amounts of time and money to win it, so your vote must be valuable! High voter turnout can indicate that people are unhappy with how the country is being run; or it may signal the opposite—a desire to keep things the same. Campaigns use polls to figure out how to get people to vote, especially those who are likely to vote for their candidate.

In this Topic, you'll learn why people do or do not vote. What would convince you to go to the polls?

⚡ NBC LEARN
Source for Political Information

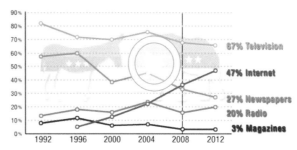

Learn about the new ways that politicans are using social media to reach voters.

 BOUNCE to Activate My Story Video

In this Topic, you will examine the many ways that the United States is a government "by the people" by considering the various mechanisms Americans use to influence public policy. Look at the lesson outline and explore the timeline. As you study this Topic, you'll complete the Quest Inquiry.

LESSON OUTLINE

10.1 The History of Voting Rights

10.2 Your Right to Vote

10.3 Voting Trends

10.4 The Voting Process

10.5 Public Opinion and Polling

10.6 Influencing Public Opinion: The Mass Media

10.7 Understanding Interest Groups

The Five Stages of Expanding Suffrage

EARLY 1800s
Religious, property, and **tax** qualifications begin to disappear in every State.

1920
19th Amendment removes voting restrictions based on **sex**.

1971
26th Amendment sets the minimum **voting age at 18**.

1870
15th Amendment prohibits voting restrictions based on **race or color**.

1965
The Voting Rights Act of 1965 enforces **racial equality** at polling places.

Timeline: EARLY 1800s — 1860 — 1890 — 1920 — 1950 — 1980

QUEST! INQUIRY

Document-Based Question: Are Special Interests Good or Bad for Democracy?

Lots of groups—some powerful, some not—are interested in every bill passed by Congress. Perhaps they stand to make or lose a lot of money. Perhaps they see a wrong that should be righted. Is the influence of these groups good or bad for democracy? In this Quest, you will consider that question.

STEP

Discuss data related to lobbyists, then generate questions you need answers to before you can formulate your opinion about special interests.

STEP

Examine the documents relating to the issue. Determine the central idea of each and evaluate the authors' differing points of view.

STEP

Write a clear, coherent essay arguing your viewpoint. Address the strengths and limitations of your position and the opposing position.

STEP

Revise your writing. Is your paper logically organized? Did you cite specific evidence from the documents to support your argument? Share your finished work with the class.

10.1

Dr. Martin Luther King, Jr., and Coretta Scott King vote in the presidential election of 1964, the same year the Civil Rights Act of 1964 outlawed discriminatory voting practices.

 BOUNCE to Activate Flipped Video

Objectives

Summarize the history of voting rights in the United States.

Identify the main intention of the 15th Amendment, and describe the results of its lack of enforcement.

Analyze the impact of political changes brought about by individuals with regard to the civil rights laws enacted in 1957, 1960, and 1964.

Analyze the provisions and effects of the Voting Rights Act of 1965.

Key Terms

suffrage
franchise
electorate
disenfranchised
poll tax
gerrymandering
injunction
preclearance
Martin Luther King, Jr.
Selma, Alabama
Lyndon B. Johnson
John Roberts

The History of Voting Rights

Soon, you will be eligible to vote—but will you exercise that right? The record suggests that while you may do so, many of your friends will not, at least not for some time. The record also suggests that some of your friends will never vote. Yet, clearly, the success of democratic government depends on popular participation and, in particular, on the regular and informed exercise of the right to vote.

Voting Rights in the United States

The Framers of the Constitution purposely left the power to set suffrage qualifications to each State. **Suffrage** means the right to vote. **Franchise** is a synonym for the right to vote.

The Size of the American Electorate When the Constitution went into effect in 1789, the right to vote was generally restricted to white male property owners. In fact, probably not one in fifteen adult white males could vote. Benjamin Franklin often made fun of this situation. He told of a man whose only property was a jackass and noted that the man would lose the right to vote if his jackass died. "Now," asked Franklin, "in whom is the right of suffrage? In the man or the jackass?"

The size of the American **electorate**—the potential voting population—is truly impressive. More than 200 million people, nearly all citizens who are at least 18 years of age, qualify to vote. That huge number is a direct result of the legal definition of suffrage. In other words, it is the result of those laws that determine who can and cannot vote. It is also the result of more than 200 years of continuing, often bitter, and sometimes violent struggle over the right to vote.

The history of American suffrage since 1789 has been marked by the gradual elimination of most restrictions on the right to vote, including religious belief, property ownership, tax payment, race, and gender. This expansion of voting rights has led to significant changes in American culture, not the least of which is the marked impact of the voices of minorities, women, and youth on American public policy. Others include a growth in the influence of the two major political parties as each has sought to win voters, an increase in the number of minority elected officials, and greater equality for women in the workplace.

The Struggle to Extend Voting Rights The growth of the American electorate has come in five identifiable stages:

1. The first stage of the struggle to extend voting rights came in the early 1800s. Religious qualifications, put in place in colonial days, quickly disappeared. No State has had a religious test for voting since 1810. Then, one by one, States began to eliminate property ownership and tax payment qualifications. By mid-century, almost all white adult males could vote in every State.

2. The second major effort to broaden the electorate followed the Civil War. The 15th Amendment, ratified in 1870, was intended to protect any citizen from being denied the right to vote because of race or color. Still, for nearly another century, African Americans were systematically barred from voting, and they remained the largest group of **disenfranchised** citizens, or citizens denied the right to vote, in the nation's population.

3. Wyoming, while still a territory, had given women the vote in 1869. By 1920, more than half of the States had followed that lead, but women were still denied the vote in federal elections. The long struggle of women to change that situation finally culminated with the ratification of the 19th Amendment in 1920. That amendment led to a host of cultural changes, including increasing attention to women's issues and growing numbers of women in public office.

4. A fourth major extension took place during the 1960s. During that time, federal legislation and court decisions focused on securing African Americans a full role in the electoral process. With the passage and vigorous enforcement of a number of civil rights acts, especially the Voting Rights Act of 1965 and its later extensions, the country took a giant step toward racial equality in polling booths throughout the nation.

The 23rd Amendment, passed in 1961, added the voters of the District of Columbia to the presidential electorate. The 24th Amendment, ratified in 1964, eliminated the poll tax (and any other tax) as a condition for voting in any federal election. A **poll tax** was a tax imposed by several States as a qualification for voting.

5. The fifth and latest expansion of the electorate came with the adoption of the 26th Amendment in 1971. It provides that no State can set the minimum age for voting at more than 18 years of age. In other words, those 18 and over were given the right to vote by this amendment.

☑ **CONNECT** What was the voting experience of African Americans after the war? What does this suggest about the legal expansion of voting rights?

The 15th Amendment

How important is the right to vote? For those who do not have it, that right can seem as important as life itself. Indeed, in the Deep South of the 1960s, civil

>> George Caleb Bingham's *The County Election* depicts an 1850 Missouri election. At the time, voting was restricted to white males, but property and tax qualifications had been eliminated.

rights workers suffered arrest, beatings, shocks with electric cattle prods, even death—all in the name of the right to vote. Their efforts inspired the nation and led to large-scale federal efforts to secure that right for Black Americans and other minority groups in the United States.

The effort to extend the franchise to Black Americans began with the 15th Amendment, which was ratified in 1870. It declares that the right to vote cannot be denied to any citizen of the United States because of "race, color, or previous condition of servitude." The amendment was plainly intended to ensure that Black American men, nearly all of them formerly enslaved and nearly all of them living in the South, could vote.

The 15th Amendment is not self-executing, however. In other words, simply stating a general principle without providing for a means of enforcement was not enough to carry out the intention of the amendment. To make it effective, Congress had to act. Yet for nearly 90 years the Federal Government paid little attention to the voting rights of Black Americans.

Lack of Enforcement During that period, Black Americans were generally and systematically

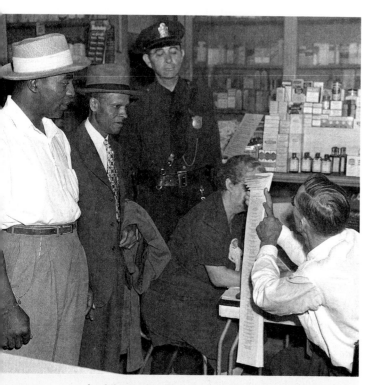

>> An Atlanta, Georgia, election official points out to World War II veteran Lewis McGuire and Dr. S. M. Lewis that the ballot states that only white people can vote in the 1945 Democratic primary.

kept from the polls in much of the South. White supremacists employed a number of tactics to that end. Their major weapon was violence. Other tactics included more subtle threats and social pressures—for example, firing a Black American man who tried to register or vote, or denying his family credit at local stores.

More formal "legal" devices were used, as well. The most effective were literacy tests. White officials regularly manipulated those tests to disenfranchise Black Americans. Registration laws served the same end. As written, they applied to all potential voters. In practice, however, they were often administered to keep Black Americans from qualifying to vote. Poll taxes, "white primaries," gerrymandering, and several other devices were also used.

Gerrymandering is the practice of drawing electoral district lines (the boundaries of the geographic area from which a candidate is elected to a public office) in order to limit the voting strength of a particular group or party.

The white primary arose out of the decades-long Democratic domination of politics in the South. It was almost a given that the Democratic candidate for an office would be elected. Therefore, only the Democrats ordinarily nominated candidates, generally in primaries. In several southern States, political parties were defined by law as "private associations" that could exclude whomever they chose, and the Democrats regularly refused to admit Black Americans. Because only party members could vote in the party's primary, Black Americans were then excluded from a critical step in the public election process.

Court Rulings Upholding Voting Rights The Supreme Court outlawed the white primary in a case from Texas, *Smith* v. *Allwright,* in 1944. The Court held that nominations are an integral part of the election process. So, when a political party holds a primary, it is performing a public function and is bound by the 15th Amendment.

The Supreme Court outlawed gerrymandering for racial discrimination in *Gomillion* v. *Lightfoot,* 1960. The Alabama legislature had redrawn the electoral districts of Tuskegee, effectively excluding Black people from the city limits. The Court ruled that the action violated the 15th Amendment, because the irregularly shaped district clearly was created to deprive Black Americans of political power.

Led by these decisions, the lower federal courts struck down many practices designed to deny the vote to Black Americans in the 1940s and 1950s.

Still, the courts could act only when individuals who claimed to be victims of discrimination sued in an effort to affect public policy. That case-by-case process was, at best, agonizingly slow.

☑ **DRAW CONCLUSIONS** How did white primaries and classifying political parties as private associations sidestep the 15th Amendment?

Civil Rights Acts of 1957, 1960, and 1964

Finally, largely in response to the civil rights movement led by Dr. **Martin Luther King, Jr.**, Congress was moved to act. In the late 1950s, it began to enact civil rights laws specifically intended to implement the 15th Amendment. These laws eventually led to many other changes in American culture, including better jobs and greater educational opportunities for African Americans.

1957 and 1960 The first of the laws Congress passed to enforce the 15th Amendment was the Civil Rights Act of 1957, which created the United States Commission on Civil Rights. One of the Commission's major duties is to inquire into claims of voter discrimination. The Commission reports its findings to Congress and the President and, through the media, to the public. The 1957 law also gave the attorney general the power to seek federal court orders to prevent interference with any person's right to vote in any federal election.

The Civil Rights Act of 1960 added an additional safeguard. It provided for the appointment of federal voting referees. Those officers were to serve anywhere a federal court found voter discrimination. They were given the power to help qualified persons to register and vote in federal elections.

The Civil Rights Act of 1964 The Civil Rights Act of 1964 is much broader and more effective than either of the two earlier measures. It outlaws discrimination in several areas, especially in job-related matters. With regard to voting rights, its most important section forbids the use of any voter registration or literacy requirement in an unfair or discriminatory manner.

The 1964 law continued a pattern set in the earlier laws. It relied on judicial action to overcome racial barriers and emphasized the use of federal court orders called injunctions. An **injunction** is a court order that either compels or restrains the performance of some act by a private individual or

>> African American students enter a school in Little Rock, Arkansas, where the governor blocked the integration of the schools in 1957, forcing President Eisenhower to intervene.

>> President Lyndon Johnson shakes hands with Martin Luther King, Jr., after signing the Civil Rights Act of 1964, which outlawed discrimination based on race, religion, or gender.

public official. The violation of an injunction amounts to contempt of court, a crime punishable by fine and/or imprisonment.

Dramatic events in **Selma, Alabama**, soon pointed out the shortcomings of this approach. In 1965, Dr. King was able to focus national attention on the issue of African American voting rights by mounting a voter registration drive in that city.

Their registration efforts were met with insults and violence by local white civilians, by city and county police, and then by State troopers. Three civil rights workers were murdered, and many were beaten when they attempted a peaceful march to the State capitol. The nation saw much of the drama on television and clamored for Congress to take action. An outraged President **Lyndon B. Johnson** urged Congress to pass new and stronger legislation to ensure the voting rights of African Americans. Congress quickly responded.

☑ **IDENTIFY CENTRAL IDEAS** How did the Civil Rights Acts of 1957 and 1960 show that the Federal Government's approach to the 15th Amendment had changed?

Voting Rights Act of 1965—Then and Now

The Voting Rights Act of 1965 made the 15th Amendment, at long last, a truly effective part of the Constitution. Unlike its predecessors, this act applied to *all* elections held anywhere in this country—State and local, as well as federal.

Originally, the Voting Rights Act was to be in effect for a period of five years. Congress has extended its life on four occasions, in the Voting Rights Act Amendments of 1970, 1975, 1982, and, most recently, 2006. The present version of the law was made effective for 25 years; its provisions will not expire until 2031.

The 1965 law directed the attorney general to challenge the constitutionality of the remaining State poll-tax laws in the federal courts. That provision led directly to *Harper* v. *Virginia Board of Elections,* 1966.

The law also suspended the use of any literacy test or similar device in any State or county where less than half of the electorate had been registered or had voted in the 1964 presidential election. The law authorized the attorney general to appoint voting examiners to serve in any of those States or counties. It also gave these federal officers the power to register voters and otherwise oversee the conduct of elections in those areas.

Preclearance Provisions The Voting Rights Act of 1965 imposed another restriction on those States where a majority of the electorate had not voted in 1964. The act declared that no new election laws, and no changes in existing election laws, could go into effect in any of those States unless first approved—given **preclearance**—by the Department of Justice. Only those new or revised

African American Elected Officials in the U.S.

YEAR	MALE	FEMALE	TOTAL
1970	1,309	160	1,469
1975	2,973	530	3,503
1980	3,936	976	4,912
1985	4,697	1,359	6,056
1990	5,420	1,950	7,370
1995	5,782	2,637	8,419
2000	5,921	3,119	9,040

SOURCE: Joint Center for Political and Economic Studies

>> The Voting Rights Act sought to equalize access to voting. **Analyze Charts** What generalization can be made about the effect of this act on the number of Black elected officials?

Why the Voting Rights Act Amendments Were Needed

DISCRIMINATORY TACTICS STILL IN USE, 1968	DISCRIMINATORY TACTICS STILL IN USE, 1975
• Extending the terms of incumbent white officials • Making certain offices appointive rather than elective • Changing the dates of elections suddenly • Changing the qualifications for office • Increasing the cost of filing fees candidates must pay to run for office • Use of gerrymandering and at-large elections to dilute the nonwhite vote	• Use of inadequate bilingual election materials • Threatening economic reprisals for voting • Locating polling places in areas where minorities are not welcomed • Use of gerrymandering and other tactics

>> The Voting Rights Act was amended in 1970, 1975, 1982, 1992, and 2006.
Analyze Charts What was the goal of the tactics shown here? Why did the tactics change over time?

laws that did not dilute the voting rights of minority groups could survive the preclearance process and take effect.

The preclearance hurdle produced a large number of court cases over the years. Those cases show that the laws most likely to run afoul of the preclearance requirement were those that dealt with (1) the location of polling places; (2) the boundaries of election districts; (3) the deadlines in the election process; (4) a shift from ward or district election to at-large elections; or (5) the qualifications candidates must meet in order to run for office.

Any State or county subject to the preclearance provisions could be removed from the law's coverage through a "bail-out" process. That is, they could be dropped from the list if they were able to demonstrate to the courts that they had not applied voting procedures in a discriminatory way for at least 10 years.

The preclearance provisions of the 1965 Voting Rights Act originally applied to six entire States: Alabama, Georgia, Louisiana, Mississippi, South Carolina, and Virginia. In addition, these provisions applied to 40 counties in North Carolina.

Through the decades, Congress extended and broadened the law. A number of States, including Alaska, Arizona, California, Idaho, New Mexico, and Oregon, were added to the law's coverage. One of the most significant adjustments was the elimination of all literacy qualifications for any aspect of the election process.

Preclearance Invalidated Since the passage of the Voting Rights Act and its extensions, significant progress has been made toward eliminating voting discrimination. Notably, the percentage of African Americans registered to vote in the South has risen, as has the number of black elected officials. In addition, white elected officials began addressing the concerns of this new segment of the electorate. At the same time, observers worry about new laws that can keep minorities away from the polls, such as shortened voter registration periods and stricter identification requirements when registering.

Over the years, the Supreme Court has faced a number of challenges to the Voting Rights Act, but it consistently sidestepped the issue of the law's constitutionality. In 2013, however, in a monumental and controversial decision, the Supreme Court invalidated the preclearance provision of the Voting Rights Act. In a split 5–4 decision, the Court declared unconstitutional the formula used to determine which States and counties must gain permission from the Justice Department before changing any law affecting voting and elections.

In his majority opinion, Chief Justice **John Roberts** said the Voting Rights Act "employed extraordinary measures to address an extraordinary

>> The controversial ruling in *Shelby County* v. *Holder* caused a storm of reaction across the country. **Analyze Political Cartoons** According to this cartoon, what might the ruling mean for voters?

problem." He went on to note, however, that in the 40 years since the Voting Rights Act had been passed,

> voting tests were abolished, disparities in voter registration and turnout due to race were erased, and African Americans attained political office in record numbers. Yet the coverage formula that Congress reauthorized in 2006 ignores these developments, keeping the focus on decades-old problems, rather than current data reflecting current needs.

The Chief Justice also injected a note of caution, however, saying:

> At the same time, voting discrimination still exists; no one doubts that. The question is whether the Act's extraordinary measures, including its disparate treatment of the States, continue to satisfy constitutional requirements. . . .
>
> —Chief Justice John Roberts, Opinion of the Court, *Shelby* v. *Holder*

The Court held that they did not. Although racial discrimination in voting is still illegal under the Voting Rights Act, "Congress must ensure that the legislation it passes to remedy the problem speaks to current conditions."

Effects of *Shelby* In the wake of the Supreme Court's decision, many States on the preclearance list moved to change their voting laws, tightening the registration process and restricting early voting opportunities. Shortly after the Shelby decision, for example, the North Carolina legislature passed a strict voter identification law, eliminated same-day voter registration, and shortened voting periods, among other changes. Many of the States previously on the preclearance list made similar moves, particularly the implementation of strict voter ID laws. Subsequent years saw comparable changes.

The elimination of preclearance and subsequent changes made by those States formerly under its jurisdiction have been controversial. Those backing the new laws argue that they are designed to protect against fraud and to safeguard the legitimacy of the

>> Chief Justice John Roberts, shown shaking hands with President Barack Obama before the 2012 State of the Union speech, based his opinion in *Shelby County* partly on the concept of States' rights.

election process. Those opposed to the measures argue that they are little more than partisan efforts to limit the participation of minority voters (who tend to vote Democratic). They also note that these restrictive laws were passed in States controlled by Republicans and that there is scant evidence to suggest any real problems with voter fraud.

Overall, the Civil Rights Acts and the Voting Rights Act have had significant effects for many groups, including all people of color, women, and immigrants. Shortly after passing the Voting Rights Act, for example, Congress passed the Immigration and Nationality Act of 1965, which abolished the existing race-based immigration quota system and replaced it with a system that prioritized refugees, people with special skills, and those with family members living in the United States. In addition, the protections of the Civil Rights Acts apply to all persons, whether citizen or immigrant.

☑ **SUMMARIZE** Give two ways that the extension of the Voting Rights Act has helped protect the right to vote.

☑ ASSESSMENT

1. **Infer** Why might various groups throughout history—including women and African Americans—have fought for the right to vote?

2. **Infer** What does the fact that it took until 1920 to pass the 19th Amendment say about American society up until that time?

3. **Identify Central Issues** What were some of the biggest barriers to the success of the 15th Amendment?

4. **Interpret** What did Chief Justice Roberts mean when he stated that the Voting Rights Act "employed extraordinary measures to address an extraordinary problem"?

5. **Check Understanding** In invalidating preclearance provisions, what larger point was the Supreme Court making about voting rights?

Civil Rights in the 1960s

On August 28, 1963, more than 200,000 people gathered in Washington, D.C., to push Congress to pass civil rights legislation. For approximately 20 minutes, Dr. Martin Luther King, Jr., mesmerized the huge crowd with one of the most powerful speeches ever delivered. Less than a year later, and partly as a result of the March on Washington and King's speech, President Lyndon Johnson signed the Civil Rights Act into law. The act had faced strong opposition in Congress, including 60 days of debate and a 14-hour filibuster in the Senate.

>> Martin Luther King, Jr., on the steps of the Lincoln Memorial in 1963

"I Have a Dream"

And so even though we face the difficulties of today and tomorrow, I still have a dream. It is a dream deeply rooted in the American dream.

I have a dream that one day this nation will rise up and live out the true meaning of its creed [set of fundamental beliefs or principles]: "We hold these truths to be self-evident; that all men are created equal."

I have a dream that one day on the red hills of Georgia, the sons of former slaves and the sons of former slave owners will be able to sit down together at the table of brotherhood.

I have a dream that one day even the state of Mississippi . . . will be transformed into an oasis of freedom and justice.

I have a dream that my four little children will one day live in a nation where they will not be judged by the color of their skin but by the content of their character.

I have a *dream* today.

I have a dream that one day, down in Alabama, . . . one day right there in Alabama little black boys and black girls will be able to join hands with little white boys and white girls as sisters and brothers.

This is our hope and this is the faith with which I return to the South.

With this faith we will be able to hew [chop, cut, shape] out of the mountain of despair a stone of hope. With this faith we will be able to transform the jangling discords of our nation into a beautiful symphony of brotherhood . . . .

–this will be the day when all of God's children will be able to sing with new meaning:

"My country 'tis of thee, sweet land of liberty, of thee I sing.

Land where my father died, land of the Pilgrims' pride, From every mountainside, let freedom ring." . . .

☑ **DETERMINE AUTHOR'S PURPOSE** Why do you think King recited a verse from the song, "America"?

When we allow freedom to ring—when we let it ring from every village and every hamlet [small village], from every state and every city, we will be able to speed up that day when all of God's children, black men and white men, Jews and Gentiles [non-Jews], Protestants and Catholics, will be able to join hands and sing in the words of the old Negro spiritual: "Free at last! Free at last!

Thank God Almighty, we are free at last!"

Civil Rights Act of 1964

An Act

To enforce the constitutional right to vote, to confer jurisdiction upon the district courts of the United States to provide injunctive relief [court action] against discrimination in public accommodations, to authorize the Attorney General to institute suits to protect constitutional rights in public facilities and public education, to extend the Commission on Civil Rights, to prevent discrimination in federally assisted programs, to establish a Commission on Equal Employment Opportunity, and for other purposes.

☑ **DETERMINE MEANING** This paragraph sets out the purpose of the Civil Rights Act, including two broad goals and several means of enforcing those goals. List the specific items from this paragraph that fall into each of these categories.

Be it enacted by the Senate and House of Representatives of the United States of America in Congress assembled, That this Act may be cited as the "Civil Rights Act of 1964."

TITLE I—Voting Rights

. . . No person acting under color of law [using authority given by a local, State, or Federal Government agency] shall–

(A) in determining whether any individual is qualified under State law or laws to vote in any Federal election, apply any standard, practice, or procedure different from the standards, practices, or procedures applied under such law or laws to other individuals within the same county, parish, or similar political subdivision who have been found by State officials to be qualified to vote;

(B) deny the right of any individual to vote in any Federal election because of an error or omission on any record or paper relating to any application, registration, or other act requisite to voting, . . .

(C) employ any literacy test as a qualification for voting in any Federal election unless (i) such test is administered to each individual and is conducted wholly in writing, and (ii) a certified copy of the test and of the answers given by the individual is furnished to him within twenty-five days of the submission of his request. . . .

TITLE II—Injunctive Relief Against Discrimination in Places of Public Accommodation

SEC. 201. (a) All persons shall be entitled to the full and equal enjoyment of the goods, services, facilities, and privileges, advantages, and accommodations of any place of public accommodation, as defined in this section, without discrimination or segregation on the ground of race, color, religion, or national origin.

(b) Each of the following establishments which serves the public is a place of public accommodation within the meaning of this title if its operations affect commerce, or if discrimination or segregation by it is supported by State action:

(1) any inn, hotel, motel, or other establishment which provides lodging to transient guests, other than an establishment located within a building which contains not more than five rooms for rent or hire and which is actually occupied by the proprietor of such establishment as his residence;

(2) any restaurant, cafeteria, lunchroom, lunch counter, soda fountain, or other facility principally engaged in selling food for consumption on the premises, including, but not limited to, any such facility located on the premises of any retail establishment; or any gasoline station;

(3) any motion picture house, theater, concert hall, sports arena, stadium or other place of exhibition or entertainment. . . .

☑ ASSESSMENT

1. **Examine Principles** Examine the excerpt from Dr. Martin Luther King, Jr.'s, speech and the Civil Rights Act of 1964. How did this speech and this law help to expand civil rights and liberties in the United States?

2. **Analyze Structure** What is the purpose of paragraph (b) of Section 201 of the Civil Rights Act? Why do you think Congress believed this paragraph was necessary?

3. **Determine Central Ideas** Title I Section C of the Civil Rights Act was expanded by the 1965 Voting Rights Act. Summarize the central idea of this section in your own words.

A U.S. soldier serving in Kosovo checks his absentee ballot before mailing. Absentee ballots allow military personnel and others who are away from home on election day to vote.

 BOUNCE to Activate Flipped Video

Objectives

Identify and explain constitutional restrictions on the States' power to set voting qualifications.

Understand the criteria for voting in elections.

Understand the voter registration process and the controversies surrounding voter registration.

Explain the other requirements that States use or have used as voting qualifications.

Key Terms

transients
registration
purging
poll books
literacy
William O. Douglas

Your Right to Vote

The history of American suffrage has been marked by two long-term trends. You've already read about the first—the gradual expansion of the electorate. Second, a significant share of what was originally the States' power over the right to vote has been gradually assumed by the Federal Government. While the Constitution reserves the power to set suffrage qualifications to the States, several constitutional provisions do limit the role of State governments in this area.

Voting Qualifications and the Federal Government

Those constitutional provisions related to the right to vote include:

1. Any person whom a State allows to vote for members of the "most numerous Branch" of its own legislature must also be allowed to vote for representatives and senators in Congress (Article 1, Section 2, Clause 1 and the 17th Amendment). This restriction is of little real meaning today. With only minor exceptions, every State allows the same voters to vote in all elections in the State.

2. No State can deprive any person of the right to vote "on account of race, color, or previous condition of servitude" (15th Amendment).

3. No State can deprive any person of the right to vote on account of sex (19th Amendment).

4. No State can require payment of any tax as a condition for taking part in the nomination or election of any federal officeholder. That is, no State can levy any tax in connection with the selection of the President, the Vice President, or members of Congress (24th Amendment).

5. No State can deprive any person who is at least 18 years of age of the right to vote because of age (26th Amendment).

Beyond these five restrictions, remember that no State can violate any other provision in the Constitution in the setting of suffrage qualifications—or in anything else that it does. A case decided by the Supreme Court in 1975, *Hill* v. *Stone,* illustrates the point.

There, the Court struck down a section of the Texas constitution that declared that only those persons who owned taxable property could vote in city bond elections. The Court found the drawing of such a distinction for voting purposes—between those who do and those who do not own taxable property—to be an unreasonable classification prohibited by the 14th Amendment's Equal Protection Clause.

☑ **EXPLAIN** Beyond the five restrictions listed in this reading, no State can violate any other provision in the Constitution when setting suffrage qualifications. Explain what this means in your own words.

>> This lithograph celebrates the passage of the 15th Amendment in 1870. **Analyze Images** What potential effects of the amendment does the lithograph portray?

Universal Criteria for Voting

Are you qualified to vote? Probably not—at least not yet. Do you know why? In this section, you will see how the States, including yours, determine who can vote. You will also see that the various qualifications they set are not very difficult to meet.

Every State requires that any person who wants to vote must be able to satisfy qualifications based on three factors: (1) citizenship, (2) residence, and (3) age. The States have some leeway in shaping the details of the first two of these factors; they have almost no discretion with regard to the third one.

Citizenship Criteria Foreign-born residents who have not become citizens are generally denied the right to vote in this country. Still, nothing in the Constitution says that these people cannot vote, and any State could allow them to do so if it chose. At one time, about a fourth of the States permitted foreign-born residents who had applied for naturalization—that is, applied for citizenship—to vote. Typically, the western States did so to help attract settlers.

States may draw a distinction between native-born and naturalized citizens with regard to suffrage. In Pennsylvania, for example, one must have become a citizen at least one month before an election in order to vote in that State.

>> In 1882 when this photograph was taken, the adults in this immigrant family could probably vote in State elections if they had applied for citizenship.

Residence Criteria To vote in this country, one must be a legal resident of the State in which he or she wishes to cast a ballot. In many States, a person must have lived in the State for at least a certain period of time before he or she can vote.

The States adopted residence requirements for two reasons: (1) to keep a candidate or political party from bringing in enough outsiders to affect the outcome of an election (a once common practice), and (2) to allow new voters at least some time in which to become familiar with the candidates and issues in an upcoming election.

For decades, every State imposed a fairly lengthy residence requirement—typically, a year in the State, 60 or 90 days in the county, and 30 days in the local precinct or ward. The requirement was longer in some southern States—for example, one year in the State, six months in the county, and three months in the precinct in Alabama, Louisiana, and South Carolina, and in Mississippi a year in the State, a year in the county, and six months in the precinct.

Residence requirements are not nearly so long today. In fact, most States now require that a voter be a legal resident but do not attach a time period to that qualification. About a third of them say that a voter must have lived in the State for at least 30 days. In a few, the period is somewhat shorter.

Laws and Court Actions These much shorter requirements are a direct result of a 1970 federal law and a 1972 Supreme Court decision. In the Voting Rights Act Amendments of 1970, Congress banned any requirement of longer than 30 days for voting in presidential elections. And in *Dunn* v. *Blumstein,* 1972, the Court found Tennessee's requirement— at the time, a year in the State and 90 days in the county—unconstitutional. The Court found such a lengthy requirement to be an unsupportable discrimination against new residents and so in conflict with the 14th Amendment's Equal Protection Clause. The Supreme Court said that "30 days appears to be an ample period of time." Election law and practice among the States quickly accepted that standard.

Nearly every State does prohibit **transients**, persons who plan to live in a State for only a short time, from gaining legal residence status there. Thus, a traveling sales agent, a member of the armed services, or a college student usually cannot vote in a State where he or she has only a temporary physical presence. In several States, however, the courts have held that college students who claim the campus community as their legal residence must be allowed to vote there.

RESIDENCE REQUIREMENTS

WHERE YOU LIVE DETERMINES WHERE YOU VOTE

In order to **VOTE** in elections today, voters must be citizens with established residence in their voting **LOCATIONS**.

- States require voters to be residents.
- A person can have only one official residence.
- Some States require voters to have lived in a place for a certain time period.
- Naturalized citizens are eligible to vote.

>> The Federal Government does not set any voting qualifications based on residence, but the States can and do set such requirements. **Analyze Charts** What is the purpose of residency requirements?

Age Criteria The 26th Amendment, added to the Constitution in 1971, declares,

> The right of citizens of the United States, who are eighteen years of age or older, to vote shall not be denied or abridged by the United States or by any State on account of age.
>
> —26th Amendment

Thus, no State can set the minimum age for voting in any election at more than 18. In other words, the amendment extends suffrage to citizens who are at least 18 years of age. Notice, however, that any State can set the age at less than 18, if it chooses to do so.

Until the 26th Amendment was adopted, the generally accepted age requirement for voting was 21. In fact, until 1970, only four States had put the age at less than 21. Georgia was the first State to allow 18-year-olds to vote; it did so in 1943, in the midst of World War II. Kentucky followed suit in 1955. Alaska entered the Union in 1959 with the voting age set at 19, and Hawaii became a State later that same year with a voting age of 20.

Both Alaska and Hawaii set the age above 18 but below 21 to avoid potential problems caused by high school students voting in local school-district elections. Whatever the fears at the time, there have been no such problems in any State since the passage of the 26th Amendment.

Efforts to lower the voting age to 18 nationwide began in the 1940s, during World War II. They included lobbying members of Congress, State-by-State grassroots campaigns, and marches and demonstrations across the country. They were finally capped by the adoption of the 26th Amendment in 1971, during the war in Vietnam. That amendment was ratified more quickly than any other amendment to the Consti tution. This fact is testament to the emotional weight of the principal argument in its favor: "Old enough to fight, old enough to vote."

The Youth Vote How have 18- to 24-year-olds responded to the 26th Amendment? Over time, young voters have been much less likely to vote than any other age group in the electorate. In 1972, 48 percent of the 18–24 age group voted, but by 1996 that figure had plummeted to 28 percent. It rose again in subsequent years, particularly in the 2020 election, but has averaged around 40 percent. Contrast that figure with the turnout of Americans 65 and older. Despite the infirmities that may accompany their age, their voting rate regularly

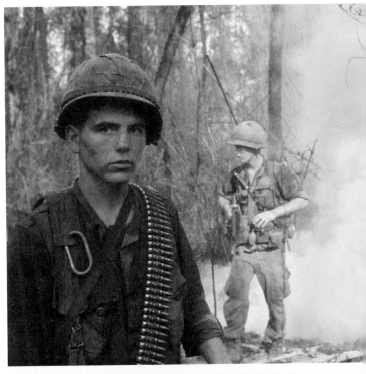

>> The service of young Americans in Vietnam helped spur passage of the 26th Amendment, which lowered the voting age to 18. Of the 58,000 soldiers killed in that war, 61 percent were 21 or under.

exceeds 60 percent, and in fact, averaged 67 percent over the same time period.

In a growing number of States, some 17-year-olds can now cast ballots in primary elections. Those States allow anyone whose 18th birthday falls after the primary but before the general election to vote in the primary election.

Several states have come very close to effectively lowering the voting age to 17 for *all* elections. In Nebraska, for example, any person who will be 18 by the Tuesday following the first Monday in November (Election Day) can qualify to vote in any election held during that calendar year.

☑ **INFER** What factors led to a general decrease in the length of residence requirements among the States?

The Voter Registration Process

One other significant qualification, registration, is nearly universal among the States today. **Registration** is a procedure of voter identification intended to prevent fraudulent voting. It gives election officials a list of those persons who are qualified to vote in an election. Several States also use voter registration to identify voters in terms of their party preference and, thus, their eligibility to take part in closed primaries.

Registration Requirements Forty-nine States—all except North Dakota—require that most, and usually all, voters be registered in order to cast ballots. Voter registration became a common feature of State election law in the early 1900s. Today, most States require all voters to register in order to vote in any election held within the State. A few, however, do not impose the requirement for all elections.

Roughly one third of the States allow voters to register at any time, up to and including election day. Elsewhere, a voter must be registered by a certain date, often 20 or 30 days before an election. That cutoff gives election officials time to prepare the poll books for an upcoming election.

Typically, a prospective voter must register his or her name, age, place of birth, present address, length of residence, and similar facts. The information is logged by a local official, usually a registrar of elections or the county clerk. A voter typically remains registered unless or until he or she moves, dies, is convicted of a serious crime, or is committed to a mental institution.

State law directs local election officials to review the lists of registered voters and to remove the names of those who are no longer eligible to vote. This process, known as **purging**, is usually done every two or four years. Unfortunately, the requirement is often ignored. When it is, the **poll books** (the official lists of qualified voters in each precinct) soon become clogged with the names of many people who, for one reason or another, are no longer eligible to vote.

Controversies Surrounding Registration There are some who think that the registration requirement should be abolished everywhere. They see the qualification as a bar to voting, especially among the poor and less educated.

Those critics buttress their case by noting that voter turnout began to decline in the early 1900s, just after most States adopted a registration requirement. They also point to the fact that voter turnout is much higher in most European democracies than in the United States. In those countries, voter registration is not a matter of individual choice but is the law. Unless a citizen "opts out," his or her name is automatically entered on registration lists. The United States is the only democratic country in which each person decides whether or not to "opt in"; that is, to register to vote.

Many people who have studied the problem favor keeping the registration requirement to defend against fraud. However, they also favor making the process more convenient. They see the problem in these terms: Where is the line between making it so easy to vote that fraud is encouraged, and making it so difficult that legitimate voting is discouraged?

Most States have eased the registration process over the last several years. In 1993, Congress passed a law that required every State (but North Dakota) to do so. That law, dubbed the "Motor Voter Act," became effective in 1995. It directs the States to (1) allow all eligible citizens to register to vote when they apply for or renew a driver's license; (2) provide for voter registration by mail; and (3) make registration forms available at the local offices of State employment, welfare, and other social service agencies. The most striking change in American culture brought about by this government policy has been a huge number of new voters added to the poll books. The Federal Election Commission reported that by the year 2000, approximately 8 million persons had registered to vote as a direct result of the Motor Voter Law.

>> Voter ID laws have mixed support and continue to be reviewed by the courts. **Analyze Political Cartoons** What is the cartoonist saying about the benefit of Voter ID laws?

The law also requires every State to mail a questionnaire to each of its registered voters every four years, so that the poll books can be purged for deaths and changes of residence. It also forbids the States to purge for any other reason, including failure to vote.

Voter ID Laws Several States now have so-called voter ID laws that require people to prove their identity when they seek to register or vote. Some government-issued photo ID—a passport or a driver's license, for example—will usually satisfy this requirement. Those who support these measures argue that they prevent people from voting under false identities and also bring greater integrity, accountability, and transparency to elections. Those opposed suggest the real intention of the laws is to limit the involvement of a particular type of voter—specifically, the elderly, disabled, poor, and minority groups. They note that these laws are generally adopted in States controlled by Republican legislatures, which suggests to them that partisan motivations might be at work.

State and federal courts have been charged with examining these contentious voter ID laws to determine whether they discriminate against any group and thus violate the Equal Protection Clause of the 14th Amendment. For the most part, the laws have been found to be constitutional, but the issue continues to generate legal challenges.

☑ **COMPARE AND CONTRAST** Compare and contrast the arguments for and against voter registration.

Historical Criteria for Voting

Suffrage qualifications based on two other factors—literacy and tax payment—were once fairly common among the States. They had a fairly long history but are no longer to be found anywhere.

Literacy Qualifications Today, no State has a suffrage qualification based on voter **literacy**—a person's ability to read and write. At one time, the literacy requirement could be, and in many places was, used to make sure that a qualified voter had the capacity to cast an informed ballot. Some States asked potential voters to prove that they could read; others asked for the ability to both read and write. And still others required those who registered to vote to show that they could read and write and also understand some piece of printed material—often, a passage from the State or Federal Constitution.

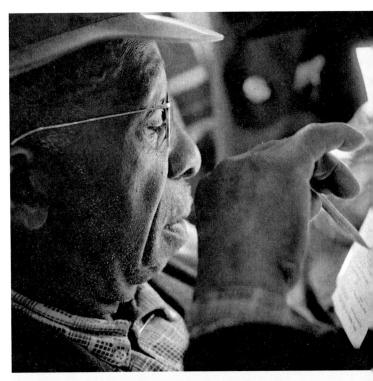

>> A man studies a practice form for a voter registration test in 1962. Until the passage of the Voting Rights Act of 1965, many States used literacy tests to disenfranchise minority voters.

Connecticut adopted the first literacy qualifications in 1855. Massachusetts followed in 1857. Both States were trying to limit voting by Irish Catholic immigrants. Mississippi adopted a literacy requirement in 1890, and soon after, most of the other southern States followed suit. The literary qualification in most southern States included an "understanding" clause. Often, whites were asked to "understand" some short, plainly worded constitutional provision; but African Americans had to interpret a long, complex passage to the satisfaction of local election officials.

Grandfather Clauses While those qualifications had been aimed at disenfranchising African Americans, they sometimes had unintended effects. Several States soon found that they needed to adjust their voting requirements by adding so-called grandfather clauses to their constitutions. These grandfather clauses were designed to enfranchise those white males who were unintentionally disqualified by their failure to meet the literacy or taxpaying requirements.

A grandfather clause was added to the Louisiana constitution in 1898; Alabama, Georgia, Maryland,

North Carolina, Oklahoma, and Virginia soon added them as well. These clauses stated that any man, or his male descendants, who had voted in the State before the adoption of the 15th Amendment (1870) could become a legal voter without regard to any literacy or taxpaying qualifications. The Supreme Court found the Oklahoma provision, the last to be adopted (in 1910), in conflict with the 15th Amendment in *Guinn* v. *United States* in 1915.

Literacy Tests Banned A number of States outside the South also adopted literacy qualifications, including Wyoming, California, Washington, New Hampshire, Arizona, New York, Oregon, and Alaska. Its unfair use finally led Congress to ban literacy qualifications in 1970. The Court agreed in *Oregon* v. *Mitchell*, 1970.

Some form of the literacy requirement was in place in 18 States when Congress finally banned its use.

Poll Taxes Property ownership, proved by the payment of property taxes, was once a very common suffrage qualification. For decades, several States also demanded the payment of a special tax, called the poll tax, as a condition for voting. Those requirements and others that called for the payment of a tax in order to vote have disappeared over the years.

>> Associate Justice of the Supreme Court Hugo Black wrote the majority opinion in *Oregon* v. *Mitchell*, affirming the unconstitutionality of voter literacy tests.

The poll tax was once found throughout the South. Beginning with Florida in 1889, each of the 11 southern States adopted the poll tax as part of the effort to discourage voting by African Americans. The device proved to be of only limited effectiveness, however. That fact, and opposition to the use of the poll tax from within the South as well as elsewhere, led most of those States to abandon it. By 1966, the tax was still in use in only Alabama, Mississippi, Texas, and Virginia.

The 24th Amendment, ratified in 1964, outlawed the poll tax, or any other tax, as a condition for voting in any federal election. The Supreme Court finally eliminated the poll tax in 1966 as a qualification for voting in all elections. In *Harper* v. *Virginia Board of Elections,* the Court held the Virginia poll tax to be in conflict with the 14th Amendment's Equal Protection Clause. The Court could find no reasonable relationship between the act of voting on one hand and the payment of a tax on the other. Justice **William O. Douglas**, writing for the majority, put the point this way:

> Once the franchise is granted to the electorate, lines may not be drawn which are inconsistent with the Equal Protection Clause. . . . Voter qualifications have no relation to wealth nor to paying this or any other tax. . . . Wealth, like race, creed, or color, is not germane to one's ability to participate intelligently in the electoral process.
>
> —Justice William O. Douglas, Opinion of the Court

Qualifications for Voting Clearly, democratic government can exist only where the right to vote is widely held, and the elimination of such practices as literacy tests and poll taxes has had profound effects on American culture as more and more Americans have been able to participate in government. Still, every State does purposely deny the vote to certain persons. For example, few of the 50 States allow people in mental institutions, or any other persons who have been legally found to be mentally incompetent, to vote.

Most States disqualify, at least temporarily, those persons who have been convicted of serious crimes. Until fairly recently, that disqualification was almost always a permanent one. Over recent years, however, most States have made it possible for the majority of convicted felons to regain the right to vote, although those guilty of such election-related offenses as bribery and ballot-box stuffing, however, are still regularly banned. A few States also do not allow anyone dishonorably discharged from the armed forces to cast a ballot.

☑ **INFER** How do the basic principles of American government demand that voting rights not be restricted to those who own property?

1. **Compare Points of View** Consider the views of those who think registration requirements should be abolished with those who favor keeping them. What are the pros and cons of each view? Explain.

2. **Infer** What was the idea behind citizens owning property in order to vote?

3. **Cause and Effect** What argument in favor of the 26th Amendment was considered crucial to its quick ratification?

4. **Infer** Why do most States, at least temporarily, bar those convicted of serious crimes from voting?

5. **Infer** Why did States with literacy requirements later create grandfather clauses? What does this say about those State's true intentions?

An enthusiastic delegate at a Democratic National Convention shows her support for the party. Citizens who identify with a political party are more likely to participate in the election process.

 BOUNCE to Activate Flipped Video

Objectives

Examine the problem of nonvoting in the United States

Identify the reasons why some people do not vote and compare these attitudes to those of voters.

Recognize the sources of information about voter behavior.

Understand the factors that influence an individual's political attitudes and actions, including voting and voter behavior.

Key Terms

off-year elections
ballot fatigue
political efficacy
political socialization
gender gap
party identification
straight-ticket voting
split-ticket voting
independents
Mitt Romney

Voting Trends

"Your vote is your voice. Use it." That's the advice of Rock the Vote, an organization that encourages young voters ages 18 to 25 to participate in the election process. In the United States, and in other democratic countries, we believe all voices should be heard. That is, we believe in voting, because it is one of the processes that individuals can use to affect public policy.

Voter Turnout in the United States

Most elections in this country are built around two-candidate contests. How many choices does a voter have in a two-candidate race? More than most people think. Not just two but, in fact, *five* options. He or she can (1) vote FOR Candidate A, (2) vote AGAINST Candidate A, (3) vote FOR Candidate B, (4) vote AGAINST Candidate B, or (5) decide not to vote for either candidate. Throughout this lesson, you will look at voter behavior in this country—at who votes and who does not, and at why those people who do vote cast their ballots as they do.

Nonvoting Consider this commentary on nonvoting from the ancient Greeks, who created the world's first democracy: In ancient Athens, idiots (*idiotes*) were those citizens who did not vote or otherwise take part in public life.

Tens of millions of Americans vote in presidential and congressional elections; in State elections; and in city, county, and other public elections. By doing so, they fulfill one of the most important responsibilities of citizenship. Elected officials make decisions every day that affect your life and voting gives you a voice in what those decisions will be. Further, elected officials tend to pay more attention to groups and communities that turn out to vote, which further increases your ability to influence public policy. Despite these facts, millions of Americans do not vote.

On any given Election Day, there are millions of people of voting age in the United States. Yet only about 60 percent of them actually vote in most presidential elections. Noncitizens are barred from the polls in every State, but they are not included in this large percentage of nonvoters. The fact is that millions of people who might vote do not.

In presidential election years, about 8 million less voters, on average, cast ballots in the elections held across the country to fill the 435 seats in the House of Representatives than vote for President. **Off-year elections**—that is, the congressional elections held in the years between presidential elections—have even lower rates of turnout, nearly always less than 50 percent. This fact demonstrates one little-known facet of the nonvoter problem: There are millions of nonvoters *among those who vote.* Thus, millions who vote in the presidential election could also vote for a congressional candidate, but they choose not to do so.

Ballot Fatigue "Nonvoting voters" are not limited to federal elections. In fact, they are much more common in State and local elections. As a general rule, the farther down the ballot an office is, the fewer the number of votes that will be cast for it. This phenomenon is sometimes called **ballot fatigue,** or drop-off. These expressions suggest that many voters exhaust their patience and/or their knowledge as they work their way down the ballot and "drop off." More votes are generally cast for the governorship than for other Statewide offices, such as lieutenant governor or secretary of state. More voters in a county usually vote in the races for Statewide offices than vote in the contests for such county offices as sheriff, county clerk, and so on.

There are other little-recognized facets of the nonvoter problem, too. Turnout in congressional elections is consistently higher in presidential years than it is in off-year elections. That same pattern holds among the States in terms of the types of elections; more people vote in general elections than in either primary or special elections.

☑ **INFER** Ballot fatigue is one reason voter turnout is far less for congressional elections for lower public offices compared to elections for President. What might be another reason?

Why People Do Not Vote

Why so many nonvoters? Why, even in a presidential election, do so many of those who could vote stay away from the polls?

Clearly, the time that it takes to vote should not be a significant part of the answer. For most people, it takes more time to choose a DVD to watch than it

Historic Events and Voter Turnout

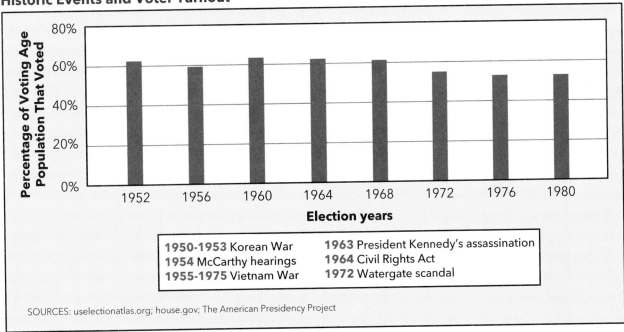

SOURCES: uselectionatlas.org; house.gov; The American Presidency Project

>> People sometimes vote based on their positions on recent events. **Analyze Graphs** How do the events listed on the graph appear to have affected voter turnout?

>> Turnout tends to be higher in places like Iran where the right to vote has been newly won. In some of those places, people turn out to vote despite the fact that doing so can be dangerous.

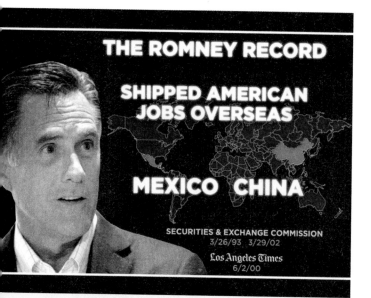

>> According to some studies, this type of negative campaigning can cause voters to react unfavorably to both the target and the sponsor of the ad.

does to go to their neighborhood polling place and cast a ballot.

Several million voters were ineligible to vote because they were in jail or prison, or on parole or probation. A few million were too ill or otherwise incapacitated to vote, or were traveling unexpectedly. Still, these numbers do not begin to explain the huge number of nonvoters in this country. So we must look elsewhere for answers.

Some Reasons for Not Voting Political scientists have discovered several reasons that people choose not to vote. As a leading example: Many who could go to the polls do not because they are convinced that it makes little real difference which candidate wins a particular election.

That fairly large group includes two quite different groups of nonvoters. On the one hand, there are many who generally approve of the way the public's business is being managed—that is, many who believe that no matter who wins an election, things will continue to go well for them and for the country.

On the other hand, that group also includes many people who feel alienated, cynical, or distrustful of political institutions and processes. These citizens deliberately refuse to vote because they don't trust political institutions and processes. They either fear or scorn "the system." To them, elections are meaningless, choiceless exercises.

Another large group of nonvoters is composed of people who have no sense of political efficacy. That is, they lack any feeling of influence or effectiveness in politics. They do not believe that they or their votes can have any real impact on what government does or does not do. Why vote when things will go on as they did before regardless of who is in office?

About 15 percent of registered voters say they are too busy to vote, and the realities of modern life have exacerbated this problem. Americans are distracted by television, new technologies, and social network sites. Many also spend hours commuting long distances or putting in extra time at work. All of these factors contribute to political disengagement.

Other Factors Other factors can also dictate whether voters show up at the polls or not. Cumbersome election procedures—for example, inconvenient registration requirements, long ballots, and long lines at polling places—discourage voters from turning out on Election Day.

Since there tend to be fewer polling places in Black and Hispanic neighborhoods, this issue generally has a larger impact on people of color. Employers who do not allow time off for voting exacerbate the nonvoting issue, as well, and some have suggested making election day a national

>> "Get Out the Vote" efforts have been around for many years. Here, a group from the Cincinnati, Ohio, chapter of the League of Women Voters stands in front of their tote board, which shows voter registration by city ward.

holiday to address this problem. Bad weather also tends to discourage voter turnout.

The nature of campaigns and the media are also cited as reasons for voter alienation. Polls show that Americans dislike negative campaigning and may become disgusted with the entire process as a result. The news media contributes to voter burnout by seizing on every controversy, with the result that candidates can seem horribly tarnished by Election Day. Perhaps voting has declined in part because our enthusiasm for candidates has waned.

Of all the reasons for nonvoting that may be cited, however, the most simple is a lack of interest. The figure varies from election to election, but generally speaking, about 20 percent of citizens say that they did not vote because they were not interested or they forgot. Those who are indifferent, who just cannot be bothered, are usually woefully misinformed. Most often, they know little or nothing about the candidates and issues in an election. Some argue that the democratic process is well served by the fact that most of these people do not go to the polls.

Comparing Voters and Nonvoters One useful way to get a handle on the problem of nonvoting is

to contrast those persons who tend to go to the polls regularly with those who do not.

The people most likely to vote display such characteristics as higher levels of income, education, and occupational status. They are usually well integrated into community life. They tend to be long-time residents who are active in, or at least comfortable with, their surroundings. They are likely to have a strong sense of *party identification* (a connection to one of the parties), and to believe that voting is an important act. They are also likely to live in those areas where laws, customs, and competition between the parties all promote turnout.

The opposite characteristics produce a profile of those less likely to vote. Nonvoters are likely to be younger than age 35, unmarried, and have lower incomes. Men are a bit less likely to vote than women—a fact that first became apparent in the 1980s.

A few of the factors that help determine whether or not a person will vote are so important that they influence turnout even when they conflict with other factors. For example, those persons with a high sense of political efficacy are likely to vote—no matter what their income, education, age, race, and so on may be. The degree of two-party competition also has an extraordinary impact on participation. Thus, the greater the competition between candidates, the more likely people will be to go to the polls, regardless of other factors.

Despite the greater weight of some of these factors, however, note this point: It is the combined presence of several factors, not one of them alone, that tends to determine whether a person will or will not vote.

☑ **CONNECT** Many reasons have been cited as to why people choose not to vote. Can you think of another logical reason that eligible voters might decide not to go to the polls that is related to political parties?

Influences on Voters and Voting Behavior

As you have read, tens of millions of potential voters do not go to the polls in this country. But many millions more do. How do those who do vote behave? What prompts many to vote most often for Republicans and many others to support the Democratic Party? Research has produced a huge amount of information about why people tend to vote as they do.

Studying Voting Behavior Most of what is known about voter behavior comes from three sources.

" The tests show it's a boy . . we can't tell whether he'll vote Republican or not. "

>> While this cartoon pokes fun at the idea, it is nonetheless true that children often vote like their parents. **Analyze Images** Which influence on voter behavior does this cartoon portray?

1. *The results of particular elections.* How individuals vote in a given election is secret in the United States. However, careful study of the returns from areas populated largely by, say, Black Americans or Catholics or high-income families will indicate how those groups voted in a given election.

2. *The field of survey research.* The polling of scientifically determined cross sections of the population is the method by which public opinion is most often identified and measured. The Gallup Organization, the Pew Research Center, and YouGov conduct perhaps the best known of these polls.

3. *Studies of political socialization.* **Political socialization** is the process by which people gain their political attitudes and opinions. That complex process begins in early childhood and continues through each person's life. Political socialization involves all of the experiences and relationships that lead people to see the political world, and to act in it, as they do.

Factors That Influence Voters Observers still have much to learn about voter behavior, but many sociological and psychological factors clearly influence the way people cast their ballots. Sociology is the study of groups and how people behave within groups. The sociological factors affecting voter behavior are really the many pieces of a voter's social and economic life. Those pieces are of two broad kinds: (1) a voter's personal characteristics—age, race, income, occupation, education, religion, and so on; and (2) a voter's group affiliations—family, co-workers, friends, and the like.

Psychology is the study of the mind and individual behavior. The psychological factors that influence voter behavior are a voter's perceptions of politics—that is, how the voter sees the parties, the candidates, and the issues in an election.

The differences between these two kinds of influences are not nearly so great as they might seem. In fact, they are closely related and they constantly interact with one another. How voters look at parties, candidates, or issues is often shaped by their own social and economic backgrounds.

☑ **DRAW CONCLUSIONS** Could the study of voter behavior help determine the outcome of upcoming elections? Why or why not?

Sociological Factors and Political Attitudes

Using data from past elections, you can draw a composite picture of the American voter in terms of a number of sociological factors. A word of caution

Voting by Income and Gender, 2004

		GEORGE W. BUSH	JOHN KERRY
INCOME	Under $50,000	42%	57%
	$50,000–$100,000	55%	44%
	$100,000–$150,000	57%	42%
	$150,000–$200,000	58%	42%
	$200,000 or more	63%	35%
GENDER	Female	48%	51%
	Male	55%	44%

SOURCE: CNN exit poll data

>> This exit poll categorizes voters based on income and gender. **Interpret Demographic Data** Which candidate did voters in the lowest income bracket support? Does this correlate to the usual trend?

here: Do not make too much of any one of these factors. Remember, each voter possesses not just one, but in fact *several* of the many characteristics involved here.

To illustrate the point: Those with a college degree are more likely to vote Democratic, while persons over age 50 tend to be Republicans. Black Americans, on the other hand, are more likely to vote for Democrats. So are members of labor unions. How, then, would a Black, 55-year-old, high-school graduate who belongs to the AFL-CIO decide to vote?

Income and Occupation For years, voters in lower income brackets were more likely to be Democrats, while voters with higher incomes tended to be Republicans. Thus, in 2004, for example, the majority of voters in the lowest income bracket favored Democrat John Kerry. Those with higher incomes voted for Republican George W. Bush. And in 2012, the majority of those with the lowest incomes chose Democrat Barack Obama, while those with incomes above $50,000 tended to vote for Republican **Mitt Romney**.

Education For many years, college graduates tended to vote for Republicans in higher percentages than those with a high school education or less. This longstanding pattern appears to have been broken, however. For most of the past several elections, college graduates and those with postgraduate degrees have tended to favor the Democratic Party, while those with a high school education or less have most often voted for the Republican candidate. At times, however, the margins have been relatively small.

Gender, Age There are often measurable differences between the partisan choices of men and women. This phenomenon is known as the **gender gap**, and it first appeared in the 1980s. Women generally tend to favor the Democrats by a margin of 5 to 10 percent, and men often give the GOP a similar edge. Thus, in 1996, for example, Bill Clinton won 54 percent of all votes cast by women, while his opponents, Bob Dole and Ross Perot, won only 38 and 7 percent of the female vote, respectively.

A number of studies show that men and women are most likely to vote differently when such issues as abortion, healthcare or other social welfare matters, or military involvements abroad are prominent in an election.

Traditionally, younger voters have been more likely to vote Democratic, while older voters are likely to find the GOP's candidates more attractive. This trend held true for every presidential election from 1960 through 1980. That long-standing pattern was broken by **Ronald Reagan's** appeal to younger voters in 1984, and by **George H.W. Bush** in 1988. However, **Bill Clinton** restored the Democrats' claim to those voters in 1992 and 1996.

Religion, Ethnic Background Historically, a majority of Protestants have preferred the GOP. Catholics and Jews generally have tended to be Democrats. Historical factors account for much of this pattern. Most of those who first came from Europe to settle in this country were of English stock and Protestant. The later tides of immigration, from southern and eastern Europe, brought many Catholics and Jews to the United States. These minority groups settled most often in the larger cities, where local Democratic Party organizations helped them to become citizens and voters.

Church attendance has also emerged as a major indicator of partisan preference. For example, 59 and 61 percent of voters who go to church at least once a week marked their ballots for George W. Bush in 2000 and 2004, 55 percent for John McCain in 2008, and 59 percent for Mitt Romney in 2012. That general pattern has held true in every election since that time.

In addition, Black Americans have supported the Democratic Party consistently and massively for decades. They form the only group that has given the Democratic candidate a clear majority in every presidential election since 1952.

In the North, Black Americans generally voted Republican until the 1930s, but, with the coming of the New Deal, they moved away from the party of Abraham Lincoln. The civil rights movement of the 1960s led to much greater Black American participation in the politics of the South. Today, Black Americans vote overwhelmingly Democratic in that region, too.

The United States is now home to tens of millions of Latinos, who are people with Spanish-speaking backgrounds. Latinos generally favor Democratic candidates. Note, however, that the label "Latino" conceals differences among Cuban Americans, who most often vote Republican, and Mexican Americans and Puerto Ricans, who are strongly Democratic.

Geography Geography—the part of the country, State, and/or locale in which a person lives—also has a measurable impact on voter behavior. After the Civil War, the States of the old Confederacy voted so consistently Democratic that the southeast quarter of the nation became known as the Solid South. For more than a century, most Southerners, regardless of any other factor, identified with the Democratic Party. Abraham Lincoln, after all, was a Republican.

The Solid South is now a thing of the past. Republican candidates are very successful throughout the region. The GOP carries most of the southern States in the presidential contest every four years, and it is now widely successful at the State

>> In this 1980 photograph, Democratic President Jimmy Carter, right, waves to supporters from a podium at the Texas-Arkansas State line. As a Democrat, the President hoped to win over voters in these traditionally Republican States.

>> Republican Mitt Romney, shown here, held this campaign rally in South Carolina in 2012. Voters in rural areas such as this tend to vote Republican.

and local levels across the region, too. Those States that have most consistently supported Republican candidates over time have been Idaho, Wyoming, and Utah in the West and Kansas, Nebraska, and the Dakotas in the Midwest.

Voter attitudes also vary in terms of the size of communities. Generally, the Democrats draw strength from the big cities of the North and East and on the Pacific Coast. Many white Democrats have moved from the central cities and taken their political preferences with them, but Republican voters are dominant in rural areas. The suburbs are generally considered "swing" areas, meaning they can swing Republican or Democratic, depending on the election.

With the move of many older Americans to the "Sunbelt" States of Florida, Arizona, and Texas during the latter part of the 20th century, as well as a growing Latino population in that region, these States gained both voters and electoral college votes. In some portions of this region, Republicans maintain an advantage. In other Sunbelt States, however, such as California, the Democrats are usually the winners.

Population Shifts Population shifts from urban to rural areas, or vice versa, also affect voting patterns. Beginning with the New Deal era of the 1930s

and 1940s, federal funds pouring into urban areas brought a migration from country to city, and with it, a move toward the Republican Party for the nation's cities. When the trend was reversed in the 1950s—from cities to suburbs—those voters took their Republican preference with them. Ronald Reagan, for example, captured the White House in 1980 without winning a single large city. In recent years, however, Americans have been moving back into urban areas in large numbers. As immigrants, minorities, and young Americans swell city populations, they have contributed to the trend toward Democratic domination in urban areas—even in States that are seen as Republican-dominated overall.

Family and Other Groups To this point, you have seen the American voter sketched in terms of several broad social and economic characteristics. The picture can also be drawn on the basis of much smaller and more personal groupings, especially such primary groups as family, friends, and co-workers.

Typically, the members of a family vote in strikingly similar ways. Most married couples share the same partisan leanings. As many as two out of every three voters follow the political attachments of their parents. Those who work together and circles of friends also tend to vote very much alike.

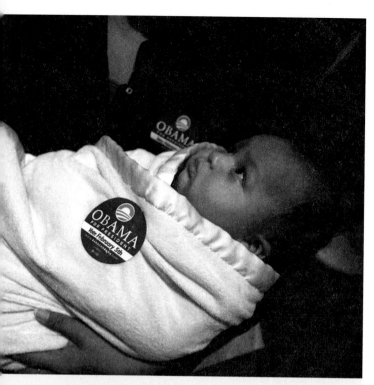

>> Family is a big factor in how a person tends to vote. Statistics show that this baby will likely vote Democratic upon turning 18.

>> A voting machine lists the 2012 presidential candidates. Those who identify themselves as independents are more likely to be young and less politically engaged than Republicans or Democrats.

This like-mindedness is hardly surprising. People of similar social and economic backgrounds tend to associate with one another. In short, a person's group associations usually reinforce the opinions he or she already holds.

☑ **MAKE PREDICTIONS** In some democratic nations, voting is not only expected, it is required. Do you think this approach would work in the United States? Why or why not?

Psychological Factors and Political Attitudes

Although they are quite important, it would be wrong to give too much weight to the sociological factors in the voting mix. For one thing, those factors are fairly static. That is, they tend to change only gradually and over time. To understand voter behavior, you must look beyond factors like occupation, education, ethnic background, and place of residence. You must also take into account voters' perceptions of politics: how they see and react to the parties, candidates, and issues.

Party Identification Many Americans have a psychological connection to one of the political parties. Indeed, one's so-called **party identification** (also called party ID)—the loyalty of people to a particular political party—is the single best predictor of how a person will vote in any given election. A person who is a Democrat or a Republican usually will vote for all or most of that party's candidates. The practice of voting for candidates of only one party in an election is called **straight-ticket voting.**

How a person establishes his or her party identification has been a topic of scholarly inquiry for decades. The social and economic factors described above can play a role, but the most important factor is political socialization. That is to say, most Americans form their party identification during their childhoods. Interestingly, that initial socialization often sticks with a person throughout his or her days.

The extent to which Americans identify with a political party has waxed and waned over the years. In the 1990s, for example, many indicators pointed to declining levels of partisanship. **Split-ticket voting**—the practice of voting for the candidates of more than one party in an election (the opposite of straight-ticket voting)—was quite common during this period. Also, the number of voters who called themselves **independents** rose. That term is used to identify those people who have no party affiliation.

In later years, however, strong party identification reemerged, with about two thirds of Americans considering themselves either Democrats or Republicans. A large portion of the others—those we might historically call independents—actually vote consistently for one party or the other. What is particularly unique about this period is the level of dislike and distrust of the "other" party. Democrats are increasingly hostile to Republicans, and vice versa. Scholars have labeled this new development "negative partisanship."

Candidates and Issues Party identification is a long-term factor. While most voters identify with one or the other of the major parties and most often support its candidates, they do not always vote that way. One or more short-term factors can cause them to switch sides in a particular election, or at least vote a split ticket. In any given election, roughly eight to ten percent of party identifiers will vote for a candidate of the other party.

The most important of these short-term factors are the candidates and the issues in an election. Clearly, the impression a candidate makes on the voters can have an impact on their choices in the voting booth. What image does a candidate project? How do the voters see that candidate in terms of personality, character, style, appearance, past record, abilities, and so on? And how do voters see the opposing candidate?

Just as clearly, issues can sometimes have a large impact on voter behavior. The role of issues varies, however, depending on such things as the emotional content of the issues themselves, the voters' awareness of them, and the ways in which the contending candidates present them to the electorate. One of the most important short-term issues is the state of the economy—both the perception of the nation's economy and how well the voter feels he or she is doing. These types of concerns are sometimes referred to as "pocketbook issues."

☑ **IDENTIFY CENTRAL IDEAS** Why could party identification be considered one of the more important factors to a political party in an election?

>> In this cartoon, both parties (symbolized by the Republican elephant and Democratic donkey), woo independent voters. **Analyze Political Cartoons** What is the reaction of the independent voter to their efforts?

☑ ASSESSMENT

1. **Analyze Information** Analyze trends in voter turnout related to the following topics: off-year elections, gender, and age.

2. **Hypothesize** What is the importance of understanding the psychological factors of voting behavior?

3. **Analyze Information** What are some of the characteristics of a likely voter?

4. **Describe** What factors can produce split-ticket voting?

5. **Infer** How can the impression a candidate gives influence voters? How do the media help to portray a candidate's impression?

10.4

A voter in Madison County, Mississippi, casts her ballot on a direct response electronic voting machine (DRE).

Objectives

Analyze how the administration of elections in the United States helps make democracy work.

Compare different methods of filling public offices at the local, state, and national levels, including the role of local precincts and polling places in the election process.

Describe the various ways in which voters can cast their ballots.

Outline the role that voting devices play in the election process.

Key Terms

ballot
absentee voting
coattail effect
precinct
polling place

The Voting Process

Most high school students are not old enough to vote. In some parts of the country, though, high school students can serve on local election boards. First in Hawaii and Oregon and now in several States, 16- and 17-year-olds can become full-fledged members of the panels that administer local elections.

Filling Elected Public Offices

We hold more elections in this country and we vote more often than most people realize. Indeed, elections are held somewhere in the United States nearly every month of the year. We also elect *far* more officeholders than most people realize—in fact, more than 500,000 of them, more than in any other country in the world.

Democratic government cannot possibly hope to succeed unless its elections are free, honest, and accurately reported. Many people see the details of the election process as much too complicated, too legalistic, too dry and boring to worry about. Those who do, miss this vital point: voting is an effective way for individuals to affect public policy. Thus, the administration of elections is of primary importance.

Extent of Federal Control Nearly all elections in the United States are held to choose the more than half a million persons who hold elective office in the more than 90,000 units of government at the State and local levels. It is quite understandable, then, that most election law in the United States is *State*—not federal—law.

Even so, a body of federal election law does exist. The Constitution gives Congress the power to fix "[t]he Times, Places, and Manner of holding Elections" of members of Congress (Article I, Section 4, Clause 1; 17th Amendment). Congress also has the power to set the time for choosing presidential electors, to set the date for casting the electoral votes, and to regulate other aspects of the presidential election process (Article II, Section 1, Clause 4; 12 Amendment).

Congress has set the date for congressional elections as the first Tuesday following the first Monday in November of every even-numbered year. It has set the same date every fourth year for the presidential election. So, in every presidential election year, elections are also held to fill seats in the House of Representatives and the Senate.

Congress also has allowed the use of voting machines and similar devices in federal elections and it has acted to protect the right to vote for certain groups of Americans. Congress has also prohibited various corrupt practices and regulates the financing of campaigns for federal office, as you will see in the pages ahead.

Help America Vote Act Congress expanded the body of federal election law with the passage of the Help America Vote Act of 2002. That law came in response to the many ballot and voter registration problems that plagued several States in the presidential election in 2000. A **ballot** is the medium by which a voter registers a choice in an election. The word comes from the Italian *ballotta*, "little ball," and reflects the practice of dropping black or white balls into a box to indicate a choice. The term *blackball* also comes from that practice. It is believed that the ancient Romans used paper ballots as early as 139 B.C.

In its major provisions, the law requires that the States:

1. replace all their lever-operated and punchcard voting devices;

2. upgrade their administration of elections, especially through the better training of local election officials and of those more than 2 million (mostly low-paid workers and volunteers) who work in precinct polling places on election day;

3. centralize and computerize their voter registration systems, to facilitate the identification of qualified voters on election day and so minimize fraudulent voting;

4. provide for provisional voting, so a person whose eligibility to vote has been challenged can nonetheless cast a ballot that will be counted if it is later found that he or she is, in fact, qualified to vote.

State law deals with all other matters relating to national elections—and with all of the details of State and local elections as well.

State Election Dates Most States hold their elections to fill State offices on the same date Congress has set for national elections: in November of every even-numbered year.

The "Tuesday-after-the-first-Monday" formula avoids holding election day on Sundays, a day of worship, and at the time it was passed in 1845, satisfied other constitutional and practical requirements.

Some States do fix other dates for some offices, however. Louisiana, Mississippi, New Jersey, and Virginia elect the governor, other executive officers, and State legislators in November of odd-numbered years. In Kentucky, the governor and other executive officers are chosen in odd-numbered years, but legislators are elected in even-numbered years. City, county, and other local election dates vary from State to State. When those elections are not held in November, they generally take place in the spring.

An Increase in Early Voting Tens of millions of Americans cast their ballots before election day.

Many of them did so by **absentee voting**—a process by which they could vote without going to their polling places on election day. Congress was responsible for the first instance of absentee voting.

>> A young Hawaiian voter signs in at the polls. In Hawaii, teens can preregister to vote at age 16, but they must be 18 by election day to actually vote.

"Callahan, get off my coattails!"

>> A campaign headquarters is the setting for this political cartoon. **Analyze Political Cartoons** Why is the gentleman in this cartoon angry?

" ...and please bless and keep safe Mommy and Daddy and Stevey and Spotty and our United States Postal Service."

CartoonStock.com

>> A prayer is offered in this pre-election cartoon for the United States Postal Service. **Analyze Political Cartoons** Why do you think this artist believes the USPS to be so important to the execution of a fair election?

In the midst of the Civil War, it provided for the casting of absentee ballots by federal troops in the elections of 1864. Over the years, every State has made at least some provision for the process.

Many States allow "no excuse" absentee voting. In these States, voters can obtain an absentee ballot some weeks before an election, without offering an excuse. They mark those ballots and return them to the local election office, usually by mail, in a sealed envelope, and before election day.

State absentee voting was originally intended to serve a relatively small group of voters, especially the ill or disabled and those who expected to be away from home on election day. Most States have broadened their laws, however—to the point where, in most of them, any qualified voter can cast an absentee ballot.

A majority of the States have also formalized early voting. They allow any voters who choose to do so to cast their ballots several days before an election—not as an absentee ballot but as though they were voting on election day itself. Indeed, in many places, election day is now just the final day on which votes can be cast. This was especially true during the COVID-19 pandemic that began during the 2020 presidential election year.

Following that election, however, many States backtracked on mail-in and early voting practices. The stated rationale for these moves was to reduce the chances of irregularities. Opponents argued they were designed to make voting harder, thus limiting access for certain groups of voters.

Election Dates and the Coattail Effect Some have long argued that all State and local elections should be held on dates other than those set for federal elections. This, they say, would help voters pay more attention to State and local candidates and issues and lessen a presidential candidate's coattail effect.

The **coattail effect** occurs when a strong candidate running for an office at the top of the ballot helps attract voters to other candidates on the party's ticket. In effect, the lesser-known office seeker "rides the coattails" of the more prestigious personality—for example, a Franklin D. Roosevelt, a Ronald Reagan, or a Barack Obama. The coattail effect is usually most apparent in presidential elections. However, a popular candidate for senator or governor can have the same kind of pulling power in State and local elections.

A reverse coattail effect can occur, too. This happens when a candidate for some major office is less than popular with many voters—for example, Barry Goldwater as the Republican presidential nominee in 1964 and George McGovern for the

Democrats in 1972. President Jimmy Carter's coattails were also of the reverse variety in 1980.

☑ **APPLY CONCEPTS** How might early voting lead to an expansion of the electorate?

Precincts, Polling Places, and Ballots

A **precinct** is a voting district. Precincts are the smallest geographic units for the conduct of elections. State law regularly restricts their size, generally to an area with no more than 500 to 1,000 or so qualified voters. A **polling place**—the place where the voters who live in a precinct actually vote—is located somewhere in or near each precinct.

A precinct election board supervises the polling place and the voting process in each precinct. Typically, the county clerk or county board of elections draws precinct lines, fixes the location of each polling place, and picks the members of the precinct boards.

On election day, the precinct board opens and closes the polls at the times set by State law. In most States, the polls are open from 7:00 or 8:00 A.M. to 7:00 or 8:00 P.M. The precinct board must also see that the ballots and ballot boxes or voting devices are available. It must make certain that only qualified voters cast ballots in the precinct. Often the board also counts the votes cast in the precinct and then sends the results to the proper place, usually to the county clerk or county board of elections.

Poll watchers, one from each party, are allowed at each polling place. They may challenge any person they believe is not qualified to vote, check to be sure that their own party's supporters do vote, and monitor the whole process, including the counting of the ballots.

Types of Ballots Whether it is for a federal, State, or local election, a ballot can take a number of different forms, ranging from a piece of paper to optical scanners and touch screens. Whatever its form, however, it is clearly an important and sensitive part of the election process.

State law requires that ballots be cast in secret, but voting was a quite public process during the nation's earlier history. Paper ballots were used in some colonial elections, but voting was more commonly *viva voce*—by voice. Voters simply stated their choices, in public, to an election board. With suffrage limited to the privileged few, many people defended oral voting as the only "manly" way in which to participate. Whatever the merits of that

>> Republican presidential candidate Barry Goldwater's landslide loss to President Lyndon B. Johnson also contributed to lost elections for dozens of Republicans running for Congress.

>> A Maryland voter casts her ballot ten days before election day. Most States allow early voting.

view, the expansion of the electorate brought with it a marked increase in intimidation, vote buying, and other corruptions of the voting process.

Paper ballots were in general use by the mid-1800s. The first ones were unofficial—slips of paper that voters prepared themselves and dropped in the ballot box. Soon candidates and parties began to prepare ballots and hand them to voters to cast, sometimes paying them to do so. Those party ballots were often printed on distinctively colored paper, and anyone watching could tell for whom voters were voting.

Political machines—local party organizations capable of mobilizing or "manufacturing" large numbers of votes on behalf of candidates for political office—flourished in many places in the late 1800s. Because these groups did not want to lose their ability to affect public policy, they fought all attempts to make voting a more dependably fair and honest process. This political corruption brought widespread demand for ballot reforms. The resulting changes were part of the so-called Progressive Movement.

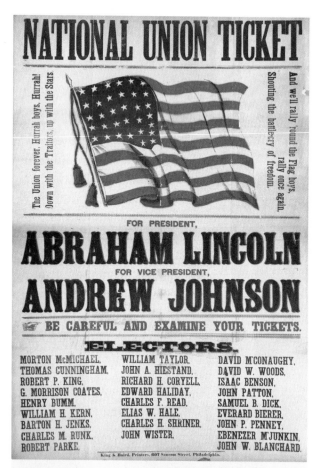

>> In the 1800s, political memorabilia, such as this advertisement for candidates Abraham Lincoln and Andrew Johnson, sometimes also served as the ballot.

The Australian Ballot A new voting arrangement was devised in Australia, where it was first used in an election in Victoria in 1856. Its successes there led to its use in other countries. By 1900, nearly all of the States were using it, and it remains the basic form of the ballot in this country for federal, State, and local elections.

As it was originally conceived, the Australian Ballot has four essential features: It (1) is provided at public expense; (2) lists the names of all candidates in an election; (3) can be marked in secret; and (4) is given out only at the polls, one to each qualified voter. The exception is mail-in and absentee ballots, which are supplied before election day.

Two basic forms of the Australian ballot have been used in this country over the past century, the office-group ballot (all candidates for an office are grouped together under the title of that office) and the party-column ballot (lists all candidates under their party's name). Most States now use the office-group ballot; only a handful of them rely on the party-column ballot.

Sample Ballots Sample ballots, clearly marked as such, are available in most States before an election. In some States they are mailed to all voters, and they appear in most newspapers and on the Internet. They cannot be cast, but they can help voters prepare for an election.

First in Oregon (1907), and now in several States, an official voter's pamphlet is mailed to voters before every election. It lists all candidates and measures that will appear on the ballot.

Bed-sheet Ballots The ballot in a typical American election is lengthy, often and aptly called a "bed-sheet" ballot. It frequently lists so many offices, candidates, and ballot measures that even the most well-informed voters have a difficult time marking it intelligently.

The long ballot came to American politics in the era of Jacksonian Democracy in the 1830s. Many held the view at the time that the greater the number of elective offices, the more democratic the governmental system. That idea remains widely accepted.

Generally, the longest ballots are found at the local level, especially among the nation's thousands of counties. The list of elected offices is likely to include several commissioners, a clerk, a sheriff, one or more judges, a prosecutor, coroner, treasurer, assessor, surveyor, school superintendent, engineer, sanitarian, and even the proverbial dogcatcher.

Critics of the bed-sheet ballot reject the notion that the more people you elect, the more democratic the system. Instead, they say, the fewer the offices voters have to fill, the better they can know the candidates and their qualifications. Those critics often point to the factor of "ballot fatigue"—that is, to the drop-off in voting that can run as high as 20 to 30 percent at or near the bottom of the typical (lengthy) ballot.

Many believe there is little reason to elect such local officials as clerks, coroners, surveyors, and engineers. Their jobs do not carry basic policy-making responsibilities. Rather, they carry out policies made by others. Many believe that to shorten the ballot and promote good government, the rule should be: Elect those who make public policies; appoint those whose basic job it is to administer those policies.

☑ **COMPARE** Compare the pro and con arguments for the "bed-sheet ballot."

Casting and Counting Ballots

Well over half the votes now cast in national elections are cast on some type of voting machine—and, increasingly, on some type of electronic voting device.

Thomas Edison received a patent for the first voting machine—the first mechanical device for the casting and counting of votes—in 1869, and the Myers Automatic Booth was first used in a public election in Lockport, New York, in 1892. The use of similar but much-improved devices soon spread to polling places across the country.

For the better part of a century, most voting machines were lever-operated, and quite cumbersome. Voters had to pull various levers in order to cast their ballots—one lever to open (unlock) the machine, others to indicate their choices of candidates, and yet another to close (lock) the machine and record their votes.

Those lever-operated machines did impact the political process by speeding up voting and reducing both fraud and counting errors. The machines were quite expensive, however, and they also posed major storage and transport problems from one election to the next.

Counting Votes Electronically Electronic data processing (EDP) techniques were first applied to the voting process in the 1960s. California and Oregon led the way and EDP is now a vital part of that process in most States.

>> Thomas Edison (shown here) invented a vote recorder in the late 1860s. When a colleague presented it to Congress, a committee chairman said, "if there is any invention on earth that we don't want down here, that is it."

For some years, the most widely used adaptations of EDP involved punch-card ballots, counted by computers. But punch-card ballots often produced problems—most frequently because voters failed to make clean punches. Their incomplete perforations left "hanging chads" that made the cards difficult or impossible for computers to read.

Punch-card ballots played a major role in the disputed presidential election vote count in Florida in 2000; and that fiasco led to the passage of the Help America Vote Act of 2002. As was noted earlier, that law required the elimination of all punch-card voting devices (and all lever-operated voting machines, as well).

Most States have turned to two other EDP-based voting systems. One of them involves the same optical-scanning technology used to grade the standardized tests students take in school. Voters mark their ballots by filling in circles, ovals, or rectangles or by completing arrows. A computer scans the marked ballots, counting and recording the votes cast.

The other system utilizes direct response electronic voting machines (DREs). Those machines are much like ATMs or cash machines. Voters make their choices on most models by touching a screen or, on some, by pushing buttons. Their votes are recorded electronically.

DREs have proved troublesome in many places and their accuracy and security have been hotly debated. Some models have malfunctioned and some do not provide a paper record of voters' choices. Many computer scientists insist that DREs can be easily compromised by hackers. Several States have abandoned them, turning instead to optical-scanning systems or even hand-counted paper ballots.

Voting by Mail One method of casting a ballot—mail-in balloting—does not require any type of voting machine. Instead, voters fill out a ballot at home and mail it back to election officials. While most States allow "no excuse" absentee balloting, a few allow all elections to be conducted by mail. Several others permit counties to decide which elections will allow mail-in voting and some allow voting by mail for small local elections or jurisdictions. During the COVID-19 pandemic that began in 2020, every State allowed some form of voting by mail.

Voting by mail has stirred controversy. Critics fear that the process threatens the secret ballot principle. They worry about fraud, especially the possibility that some voters may be subjected to undue pressures when they mark their ballots at home or any place other than a secure voting booth.

In addition, scholars have found that vote-by-mail may not actually increase turnout. They also note that vote-by-mail eliminates an important aspect of participatory government—that is, the ceremonial aspect of going to the polls, which generates energy, excitement, and a sense of community.

Supporters, on the other hand, say that many years of voting by mail in several States indicates that that process can be as fraud-proof as any other method of voting. They also make this point: The mail-in process may increase voter participation in elections and it most definitely reduces the costs of conducting them.

The Impact of the Internet Online voting—casting ballots via the Internet—has attracted considerable attention and some support. Will e-voting become widespread, even commonplace, as some predict? Only time will tell.

Online voting is not an entirely new phenomenon. The first e-vote was cast in 1997. Election officials in Harris County, Texas, allowed astronaut David Wolf to vote in Houston's city election by e-mail from the space station *Mir*.

The first public election in which some votes were cast by computer was held in 2000, in Arizona's

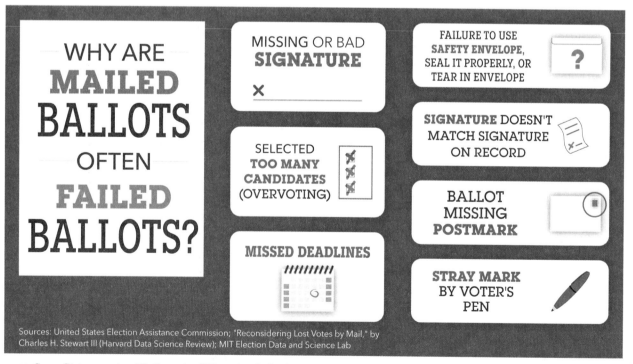

WHY ARE MAILED BALLOTS OFTEN FAILED BALLOTS?

MISSING OR BAD **SIGNATURE**

SELECTED **TOO MANY CANDIDATES** (OVERVOTING)

MISSED DEADLINES

FAILURE TO USE **SAFETY ENVELOPE,** SEAL IT PROPERLY, OR TEAR IN ENVELOPE

SIGNATURE DOESN'T MATCH SIGNATURE ON RECORD

BALLOT MISSING POSTMARK

STRAY MARK BY VOTER'S PEN

Sources: United States Election Assistance Commission; "Reconsidering Lost Votes by Mail," by Charles H. Stewart III (Harvard Data Science Review); MIT Election Data and Science Lab

>> Some States must notify the voter if his or her ballot has been rejected and provide an opportunity for the problem to be corrected. **Analyze Charts** Does the data shown support or oppose the use of mail-in ballots?

Democratic presidential primary. The Defense Department enabled 84 members of the military stationed abroad to vote electronically in the general election that year, but chose not to repeat the program because of worries about ballot security. At this point, online voting is used largely for voters living overseas or serving in the military.

A number of public officials and private companies promote online voting. They claim that it will have an impact on the political process because it will make participation much more convenient, increase voter turnout, and reduce election costs.

Many skeptics, including the Department of Homeland Security, believe that the electronic infrastructure is not ready for e-voting. Some fear digital disaster: jammed phone lines, blocked access, hackers, viruses, denial-of-service attacks, fraudulent vote counts, and violations of voter secrecy. Critics also point out that because not everyone can afford home computers, online voting could undermine the basic American principle of equality.

☑ **IDENTIFY CENTRAL IDEAS** What general concerns are voiced by critics of mail-in and online voting? On what do they base their concerns?

>> Many young people are used to being able to do many tasks using their smartphones or computers. **Analyze Political Cartoons** What point is the cartoonist making about technology and voting?

☑ ASSESSMENT

1. **Cite Evidence** Cite evidence from the text to explain why punch-card voting is no longer legal.

2. **Check Understanding** America's first elections involved public voting by voice. With the many problems plaguing existing voting systems, is it possible that voice voting might make a comeback? Why or why not?

3. **Evaluate Arguments** How might online voting be made more democratic? What are the pros and cons of this solution?

4. **Apply Concepts** What might be an advantage of holding State elections separately from federal elections?

5. **Define** Define and give an example of ballot fatigue.

An interviewer's tone of voice and intonation can influence a respondent's replies, affecting poll results. Thus, telephone pollsters undergo extensive training.

 BOUNCE to Activate Flipped Video

Objectives

Examine the term *public opinion* and understand why it is so difficult to define.

Understand the factors that influence an individual's political attitudes and actions.

Recognize how polls are used by political parties, interest groups, or the media to affect public policy and describe the challenges involved in measuring public opinion.

Identify the steps in the polling process, evaluate the role of the Internet and other electronic information on the polling process, and understand the challenges involved in evaluating polls.

Recognize the limits on the impact of public opinion in a democracy.

Key Terms

public affairs
public opinion
mass media
peer group
opinion leaders
pundit
mandate
interest groups

public opinion polls
straw vote
universe
sample
random sample
George Gallup
Elmo Roper

Public Opinion and Polling

Do you like broccoli? Blue fingernail polish? Tattoos? Hard rock music? What about sports? Old cars? You almost certainly have an opinion on each of those things. On some of them, you may hold strong opinions, and those opinions may be very important to you. Still, each of those opinions is your own view, your *private* opinion. None of them qualifies as *public* opinion.

What Is Public Opinion?

Few terms in American politics are more widely used, and less well understood, than the term *public opinion*. It appears regularly in newspapers and magazines and on blogs, and you hear it frequently on radio and television.

Quite often, the phrase is used to suggest that all or most of the American people hold the same view on some public issues, such as global warming or deficit spending. Thus, time and again, politicians say that "the people" want such and such, television commentators tell us that "the public" favors this or opposes that, and so on.

In fact, there are very few matters about which all or nearly all of "the people" think alike. "The public" holds many different and often conflicting views on nearly every public issue.

To understand what public opinion is, you must recognize this important point: Public opinion refers to a complex collection of the opinions of many different people. It is the sum of all of their views. It is *not* the single and undivided view of some mass mind.

Who Is "the Public"? Many publics exist in the United States—in fact, too many to be counted. Each public is made up of all those individuals who hold the same view on some particular public issue. Each group of people with a differing point of view is a *separate* public with regard to that issue.

For example, the people who think that Congress should concentrate on paying down the national debt belong to the public that holds that view. People who believe that the President is doing an excellent job as chief executive, or that capital punishment should be abolished, or that prayer should be permitted in public school, are members of separate publics with those particular opinions. Clearly, many people can and do belong to more than one of those publics; but almost certainly only a very few belong to all four of them.

Notice this important point: Not many issues capture the attention of all—or even nearly all—Americans. In fact, those that do are few and far between. Instead, most public issues attract the interest of *some* people (and sometimes millions of them), but those same issues are of little or no interest to many (and sometimes millions of) other people.

Public Opinion Relates Only to Public Affairs

This point is crucial, too: In its proper sense, public opinion includes only those views that relate to public affairs. **Public affairs** include politics, public issues, and the making of public policies—those events and issues that concern the people at large. To be a *public* opinion, a view must involve something of general concern and of interest to a significant portion of the people as a whole.

Of course, the American people as a whole are interested in many things—rock groups and symphony orchestras, the New York Yankees and the Dallas Cowboys, candy bars and green vegetables, and a great deal more. Many people have opinions on each of these things, views that are sometimes loosely called "public opinion." But, again, in its proper sense, public opinion involves only those views that people hold on such things as political parties and candidates, taxes, unemployment, welfare programs, national defense, foreign policy, and so on.

Expressed Group Attitudes Clearly, public opinion is so complex that it cannot be readily defined. From what has been said about it to this point, however, **public opinion** can be described this way: those attitudes held by a significant number of people on matters of government and politics.

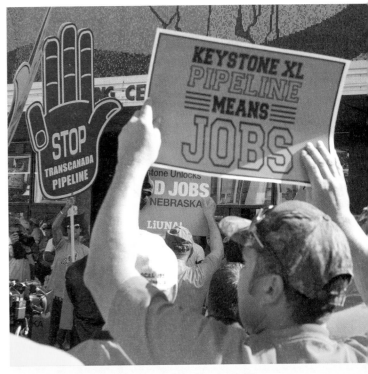

>> Supporters and opponents of the Keystone XL pipeline, which would carry crude oil from Canada down the middle of the U.S. to Nebraska, face off at a demonstration in Lincoln, Nebraska.

>> National and State politicians were featured on a Denver, Colorado, billboard during the 2012 election. **Analyze Images** Does the message on this sign qualify as public opinion? Why or why not?

As we have suggested, you can better understand the term in the plural—that is, as public opinions, the opinions of different publics. Look at it this way: public opinion is made up of expressed group attitudes.

A view must be *expressed* in order to be an opinion in the public sense. Otherwise, it cannot be identified with any public. That expression need not be oral (spoken). It can take any number of other forms, as well: a protest demonstration, a film, a billboard, a vote for or against a candidate, and so on. The point is that a person's private thoughts on an issue enter the stream of public opinion only when those thoughts are expressed publicly.

☑ **APPLY CONCEPTS** Marcia tells her boyfriend that she believes their State should offer more financial aid to college students. According to the formal definition of the term, is this an example of public opinion? Why or why not?

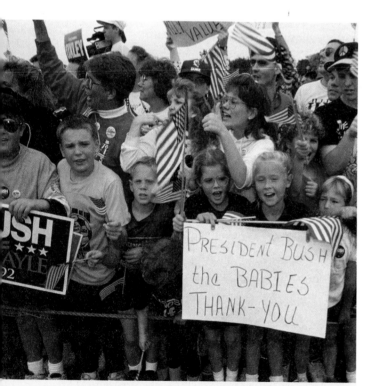

>> Young supporters cheer for President George H.W. Bush during his re-election campaign in 1988. As adults, these children are likely to support the Republican Party.

Family, School, and Political Attitudes

No one is born with a set of attitudes about government and politics. Instead, each of us learns political opinions, and we do so in a lifelong "classroom" and from many different "teachers." In other words, public opinion is formed out of a very complex process. The factors involved in it are almost infinite.

You have already considered that point when examining why people vote as they do in a previous lesson. The reasons behind voter choices provide an extensive look at how public opinion is formed. The process by which each person acquires his or her political opinions is called *political socialization*. That complex process begins in early childhood, and it continues through one's lifetime. It involves all of the many experiences and relationships that lead each of us to see the political world and to act in it as we do.

There are many different agents of political socialization at work in the opinion-shaping process. Again, you looked at these agents in a previous lesson: age, race, income, occupation, residence, group affiliations, and many others. Here, look again at two of them, the family and school. They have so large an impact that they deserve another and slightly different discussion here.

The Influence of Family Most parents do not think of themselves as agents of political socialization, nor do other members of most families. Parents and other family members do nonetheless play an important part in this process.

Children first see the political world from within the family and through the family's eyes. They begin to learn about politics much as they begin to learn about most other things in life. They learn from what their parents have to say, from the stories that their older brothers and sisters bring home from school, from watching television with the family, and so on.

Most of what smaller children learn in the family setting cannot really be described as political opinions. Clearly, toddlers are not concerned with the wisdom of spending billions of dollars on an antimissile defense system, with the causes of global warming, or the pros and cons of the monetary policies of the Federal Reserve Board.

Early Attitudes Influence Later Political Views
And yet, children do pick up some fundamental attitudes. With those attitudes, they acquire a basic slant toward such things as authority and rules of behavior, property, neighbors, people of

other racial or religious backgrounds, and the like. In short, children lay some foundations on which they will later build their political opinions.

A large number of scholarly studies report what common sense also suggests. The strong influence the family has on the development of political opinions is largely a result of the near monopoly the family has on the child in his or her earliest, most impressionable years. Those studies also show that:

> Children raised in households in which the primary caregivers are Democrats tend to become Democrats themselves, whereas children raised in homes where their caregivers are Republican tend to favor the GOP.
>
> —Benjamin Ginsberg, Theodore Lowi, and Margaret Weir, *We the People*

The Influence of School The start of formal schooling marks the initial break in the influence of the family. For the first time, children become regularly involved in activities outside the home.

From the first day, schools teach children the values of the American political system. They work to indoctrinate the young, to instill in them loyalty to a particular cause or idea. In fact, preparing students to become good citizens is an important part of our educational system.

Students may salute the flag, recite the Pledge of Allegiance, and sing patriotic songs. They learn about George Washington, Abraham Lincoln, Susan B. Anthony, Sojourner Truth, Harriet Tubman, Martin Luther King, Jr., and other great Americans. From the early grades on, they pick up growing amounts of specific political knowledge, and they begin to form political opinions. In high school, they are often required to take a course in American government and even to read books such as this one.

Influences Outside the Classroom School involves much more than books and classes, of course. It is a complex bundle of experiences and a place where a good deal of informal learning occurs—about the similarities and differences among individuals and groups, about the various ways in which decisions can be made, and about the process of compromise that must often occur in order for ideas to move forward.

Once again, the family and school are *not* the only forces at work in the process by which opinions are formed. A number of other influences are part of

>> Students say the Pledge of Allegiance at their high school graduation. Citizenship has been a major focus of American public education since the first school was founded in 1635.

the mix. These two factors are singled out here to highlight their leading roles in that process.

☑ **CONSTRUCT** Describe a situation in which informal learning in a school setting might influence a person's political opinions.

Other Factors That Influence Political Attitudes and Actions

No factor, taken by itself, shapes a person's opinion on any single issue. Some factors do play a much larger role than others in that process, however. Thus, in addition to family and school, occupation and race are usually much more significant than, say, gender or place of residence.

For example, on the question of paying down the public debt, what a person does for a living and his or her level of income will almost certainly have a much greater impact on his or her views than will gender or where he or she happens to live.

On the other hand, the relative weight of each factor that influences public opinion also depends on

>> The mass media has a larger presence in people's homes today than at any time in history. **Analyze Images** To what extent might the mass media influence this family's opinions?

>> George W. Bush chats with Oprah Winfrey during an appearance on her television show. TV personalities are opinion leaders whose ideas can greatly influence political attitudes.

the issue in question. If the issue involves, say, equal pay for women or the effects of a major oil spill in the Gulf of Mexico, then gender or where one lives will almost certainly loom larger in the opinion making mix.

Besides family, school, and such factors as occupation and race, four other factors have a major place in the opinion-making process. They are the mass media, peer groups, opinion leaders, and historic events.

The Influence of Mass Media The **mass media** include those means of communication that reach large, widely dispersed audiences (masses of people) simultaneously. No one needs to be told that the mass media, including newspapers, magazines, radio, and in particular, television and the Internet, have a huge effect on the formation of public opinion.

Take this as but one indication: The United States has well over 100 million homes with televisions, and more than 300 million people live in these homes. Viewers watch television each day, plus spend countless hours on their phones and other devices. That equates to a mind-boggling number of person-hours spent focused on a screen and a huge opportunity for shaping public opinion. You will take a longer look at the influence of the mass media later in this topic.

Influence of Peer Groups People with whom one regularly associates, including friends, classmates, neighbors, co-workers, and the like, make up one's **peer group.** When a child enters school, friends and classmates become important agents in shaping his or her attitudes and behavior. The influence of peer groups continues on through adulthood.

Belonging to a peer group usually reinforces what a person has already come to believe. One obvious reason for this is that most people trust the views of their friends. Another is that the members of a peer group have shared many of the same socializing experiences, and so tend to think along the same or similar lines.

To put this observation another way, contradictory or other unsettling opinions are not often heard within a peer group. Most people want to be liked by their friends and associates. As a result, they are usually reluctant to stray too far from what their peers think and how they behave.

Opinion Leaders and Pundits The views expressed by **opinion leaders** also bear heavily on the formation of public opinion. An opinion leader is any person who, for any reason, has an unusually strong influence on the views of others. These opinion shapers are a distinct minority in the total population, of course, but they are found everywhere.

Many opinion leaders hold public office. Some, often referred to as **pundits**, write for newspapers or magazines, or express their opinions on radio, television, or the Internet. Others are prominent in business, labor, agriculture, and civic organizations. Many are professionals—doctors, lawyers, teachers, ministers, and rabbis—and have regular contact with large numbers of people. Many others are active members of their neighborhood or church or have leadership roles in their local communities.

Whoever they may be—the President of the United States, a network television commentator, the governor, the head of a local citizens committee, or even a local talk-show host—these opinion leaders are people to whom others listen and from whom others draw ideas and convictions. Whatever their political, economic, or social standing or outlook may be, opinion leaders play a significant role in the formation of public opinion.

Historic Events and Public Policy Historic events can have a major impact on the views of large numbers of people—and so have a major impact on the content and direction of public policy. The September 11, 2001, Islamist terrorist attacks and the onset of the global war on terror constitute a leading illustration of that point. American views on national security and foreign policy have undergone dramatic shifts as a result of those events. Our history affords many other examples, as well—not the least of them the Great Depression, which began in 1929 and lasted for the better part of a decade.

The Depression was a shattering national experience. Almost overnight, need and poverty became massive national problems. Hunger and despair stalked the land. In 1929, some two million people were unemployed in the United States. By just four years later, that number had climbed to 13.5 million. In 1935, some 18 million men, women, and children were wholly dependent on public emergency relief programs. Some 10 million workers had no employment other than that provided by temporary public projects.

The Depression's Effect on Government All of this changed the place of government in the United States. The Depression persuaded many Americans to support an expanded role for government—in particular, for the National Government—in the nation's economic and social life.

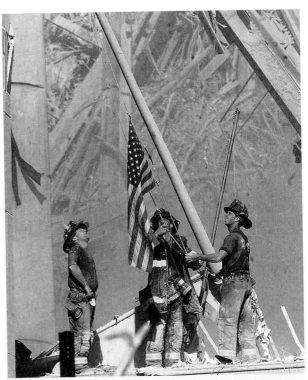

>> Firefighters raise the flag at New York's World Trade Center after the September 11, 2001, attacks by the Al Qaeda Islamist terrorist group. Events like this can affect political attitudes.

The Great Depression also prompted a majority of Americans to shift their loyalties from the Republicans to the Democrats. The Republicans had dominated the national political scene from Lincoln's election in 1860 to the onset of the Depression. That situation changed abruptly when Franklin D. Roosevelt's landslide victory in 1932 began nearly 40 years of Democratic domination.

Impact of the 1960s and 1970s on American Politics The turbulent politics of the 1960s and early 1970s furnish another example of the way in which significant occurrences can impact and shape opinions. The American people had emerged from World War II and the prosperity of the 1950s with a largely optimistic view of the future and of the United States' place in the world. That rose-colored outlook was reflected in a generally favorable, even respectful, attitude toward government in this country.

The 1960s and early 1970s changed all that. Those years were highlighted by a number of traumatic events. Of special note were the assassinations of President John Kennedy in 1963 and of the Reverend Martin Luther King, Jr., and Senator Robert Kennedy in 1968. This period also included the civil rights movement and the Vietnam War, with all of the protests, violence, and strong emotions that accompanied both of those chapters in this nation's life. The era ended with the Watergate scandal and the near-impeachment and subsequent resignation of President Richard Nixon in 1974.

Those years of turmoil and divisiveness produced a dramatic decline in the American people's estimate of their government—and most especially in their evaluation of its trustworthiness.

☑ **EXPLAIN** During a national crisis, a national television station features an interview with a well-known political correspondent. Identify the various influences on public opinion that this scenario illustrates.

Ways to Measure Public Opinion

How often have you heard this phrase: "According to a recent survey . . ."? Probably more than you can count, especially in the months leading up to an

"Get me some shares in public opinion."

>> The fortunes of business executives, politicians, and others can rise and fall based, in part, on public opinion. **Analyze Political Cartoons** How does the cartoonist make this point?

election. Polls are one of the most common means of gauging public opinion.

If public policy is to reflect public opinion, one needs to be able to find the answers to these questions: What are people's opinions on a particular issue? How many people share that view and how firmly do they hold it? In other words, there must be a way to "measure" public opinion.

The general shape of public opinion on an issue can be found through a number of key indicators. They include voting; books; pamphlets; magazine and newspaper articles; editorial comments in the press and on radio, television, and the Internet; paid advertising; letters to editors and public officials; and so on.

These and other means of expression are the devices through which the general direction of public opinion becomes known. Usually though, the means by which a view is expressed tells little—and often nothing reliable—about the size of the group that holds that opinion or how strongly it is held. In the American political system, this information is critically important. To find it, some effort must be made to measure public opinion. Elections, interest groups, the media, and personal contacts with the public all—at least to some degree—provide the means by which that measurement can be done.

Elections and Public Opinion In a democracy, the voice of the people is supposed to express itself through the ballot box. Election results are thus very often said to be indicators of public opinion. The votes cast for the various candidates are regularly taken as evidence of the people's approval or rejection of the stands taken by those candidates and their parties. As a result, a party and its victorious candidates regularly claim to have received a mandate to carry out their campaign promises. In American politics, a **mandate** refers to the instructions or commands a constituency gives to its elected officials.

In reality, however, election results are seldom an accurate measure of public opinion. Voters make choices in elections for any of several reasons, as you have seen. Very often, those choices have little or nothing to do with the candidates' stands on public questions. Then, too, candidates often disagree with some of the planks of their party's platform. As you know, candidates and parties often express their positions in broad, generalized terms. Finally, upwards of 40 percent of Americans don't vote in any given election.

In short, much of what you have read about voting behavior, and about the nature of parties, adds up to this: Elections are, at best, only useful indicators of public opinion. To call the typical election a mandate for much of anything other than a general direction in public policy is to be on very shaky ground.

How Accurately Do Interest Groups Reflect Public Opinion? Private organizations whose members share certain views and objectives, and who work to shape the making and the content of public policy are called **interest groups.** These organizations are also very aptly known as pressure groups and special interest groups.

Interest groups are a chief means by which public opinion is made known. They present their views (exert pressure) through their lobbyists, by letters, telephone calls, and e-mails, in political campaigns, and by other methods. In dealing with them, however, public officials often have difficulty determining two things: (1) How many people does an interest group really represent; and (2) How strongly do those people hold the views that an organization says they hold?

The Media: Mirrors or Molders? Earlier, you read some impressive numbers about television and the Internet that help describe the place of the media in the opinion process; you will read more of those numbers later. Here, recognize this point: The media are also a gauge for assessing public opinion.

The media are frequently said to be "mirrors" as well as "molders" of opinion. It is often claimed that the views expressed in newspaper editorials, syndicated columns, news magazines, television commentaries, and web sites are fairly good indicators of public opinion. In fact, however, the media are not very accurate mirrors of public opinion, often reflecting only the views of a vocal minority.

The Voice of the People Most public officials have frequent and wide-ranging contacts in many different forms with large numbers of people. In each of these contacts, they try to read the public's mind. Indeed, their jobs demand that they do so.

Members of Congress receive bags of mail and hundreds of phone calls and e-mails every day. Many of them make frequent trips "to keep in touch with the folks back home." Top administration figures are often on the road, too, selling the President's programs and gauging the people's reactions. Even the President does some of this, with speaking trips to different parts of the country.

Governors, State legislators, mayors, and other officials also have any number of contacts with the public. These officials encounter the public in their

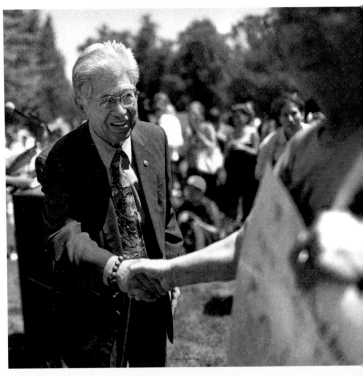

>> The late Senator Daniel Akaka (D., Hawaii) speaks with constituents in an effort to keep his finger on the pulse of public opinion.

offices, in public meetings, at social gatherings, community events, and even at ball games.

Can public officials find "the voice of the people" in all of those contacts? Many can and do, and often with surprising accuracy. But some public officials cannot. They fall into an ever-present trap: They find only what they want to find, only those views that support and agree with their own.

☑ **EXPRESS IDEAS CLEARLY** Why is it important in a democracy for elected leaders to have a mandate from the people?

Public Opinion Polls

Public opinion is best measured by **public opinion polls,** devices that attempt to collect information by asking people questions. The more accurate polls are based on scientific polling techniques.

Straw Votes Public opinion polls have existed in this country for more than a century. Until the 1930s, however, they were far from scientific. Most earlier polling efforts were of the **straw vote** variety. That is, they were polls that sought to read the public's mind simply by asking the same question of a

>> Based on straw poll results, the *Literary Digest* predicted in 1936 that Alfred Landon (shown) would be the next President. The colossal failure of that poll led to more scientific methods.

>> While he gained fame in 1936 by accurately predicting the result of the presidential election, Dr. George Gallup wrongly predicted a win for Thomas Dewey over Harry Truman in 1948.

large number of people. Straw votes are still fairly common. Many radio talk-show hosts pose questions that listeners can respond to by telephone, and television personalities regularly invite responses by e-mail.

The straw-vote technique is highly unreliable, however. It rests on the mistaken assumption that a relatively large number of responses will provide a fairly accurate picture of the public's views on a given question. The problem is this: The respondents are self-selected. Nothing in the process ensures that those who respond will represent a reasonably accurate cross section of the total population. The straw vote emphasizes the quantity rather than the quality of the sample to which its question is put.

Limitations of Straw Polls The most famous of all straw-polling mishaps took place in 1936. A widely read periodical, the *Literary Digest*, mailed postcard ballots to more than 10 million people and received answers from more than 2 million of them. Based on that huge return, the magazine confidently predicted the outcome of the presidential election that year. It said that Governor Alfred Landon, the Republican nominee, would easily defeat incumbent Franklin Roosevelt. Instead, Roosevelt won in a landslide. He captured more than 60 percent of the popular vote and carried every State but Maine and Vermont.

The *Digest* had drawn its sample on a faulty basis: from automobile registration lists and telephone directories. The *Digest* had failed to consider that in the mid-Depression year of 1936, millions of people could not afford to own cars or have private telephones.

The *Digest* poll failed to reach most of the vast pool of the poor and unemployed, millions of blue-collar workers, and most of the ethnic minorities in the country. Those were the very segments of the population from which Roosevelt and the Democrats drew their greatest support. The magazine had predicted the winner of each of the three previous presidential elections, but its failure to do so in 1936 was so colossal that it ceased publication not long thereafter.

Scientific Polling Serious efforts to take the public's pulse on a scientific basis date from the mid-1930s. They began with the work of such early pollsters as **George Gallup** and **Elmo Roper**. The techniques that they and others have developed over the decades since then have reached a highly sophisticated level.

Hundreds of national and regional polling organizations now operate in this country. Many

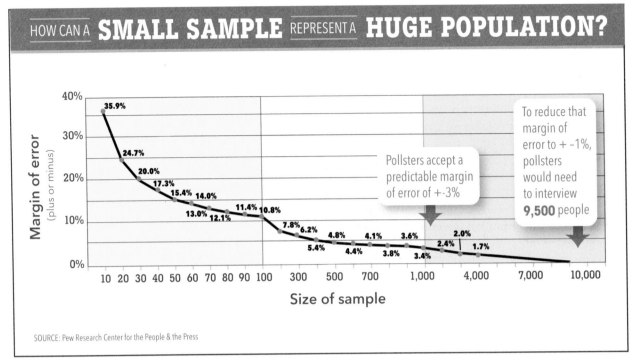

Pollsters accept a predictable margin of error of +-3%

To reduce that margin of error to + –1%, pollsters would need to interview **9,500** people

SOURCE: Pew Research Center for the People & the Press

>> Due to the law of probability, 1,500 randomly selected adults accurately reflect the views of more than 200 million Americans. **Analyze Graphs** How is the margin of error related to sample size?

of them do mostly commercial work. That is, they tap the public's preferences on everything from toothpastes and headache remedies to television shows and thousands of other things. A number of these polling organizations also poll the political preferences of the American people.

Among the best known of the national pollsters are the Gallup Organization (the Gallup Poll), the Pew Research Center, and YouGov.

The Work of National Pollsters A number of the leading national polls are joint efforts of major news-gathering and professional polling organizations. Their polls regularly report public attitudes on matters of current interest—including, for example, the level of public support of the President and/or Congress or, in election seasons, candidates running for such major offices as governor or member of the House or Senate. Those joint ventures that can most frequently be found in print and on television and the Internet. Historically, the most prominent of these collaborations have included the ABC News/*The Washington Post* poll, the CBS News/*The New York Times* poll, the NBC/*The Wall Street Journal* poll, and the CNN/*USA Today*/Gallup poll.

☑ **SUPPORT IDEAS WITH EXAMPLES** What is the MAIN drawback of straw polls?

How Polls Are Designed and Administered

Scientific poll taking is an extremely complex process that can best be described in five basic steps. In their efforts to discover and report public opinion, pollsters must: (1) define the universe to be surveyed; (2) construct a sample; (3) prepare valid questions; (4) select and control how the poll will be taken; and (5) analyze and report their findings to the public.

Defining the Universe The **universe** is a term that means the whole population that the poll aims to measure. It is the group whose opinions the poll will seek to discover. That universe can be all voters in Chicago, or every high school student in Texas, or all Republicans in New England, or all Democrats in Georgia, or all Catholic women over age 35 in the United States, and so on.

Constructing a Sample If the universe is very small—say, the 30 members of a high school class— the best way to discover what that entire universe thinks about some matter would be to question all of its members. Most polls involve much larger universes, however—for example, all of the people who live in a particular city or State or the United States. Clearly, each of those universes is so large that it would be impossible to interview all of its members. Instead, pollsters construct a much smaller **sample**—a representative slice of the total universe.

Most pollsters draw random samples (often called probability samples). A **random sample** is composed of randomly selected people, and so it is one in which all the members of its universe stand an equal chance of being interviewed. Recall, the sample used for the infamous *Literary Digest* poll in 1936 was not picked at random and so did not accurately reflect the universe it sought to measure. When this basic rule is followed, a variety of statistical laws can be applied.

Sampling and the Law of Probability Most major national polls regularly use samples composed of some 1,500 or so people to represent the nation's adult population (of more than 200 million people). How can the views of so few people possibly represent the views of so many?

The answer to that question lies in the mathematical law of probability. Flip a coin a thousand times. The law of probability says that, given an honest coin and an honest flip, heads will come up 500 times. The results of that exercise will be the same no matter how often it is repeated.

Randomized polling can be very accurate—if done well. One of the greatest challenges is finding a random pool of respondents—a sample—that accurately reflects the entire population.

Cell phones have made this even more challenging. With landlines, pollsters could randomly select numbers within a geographic area. But with cell phones, three things have changed:

1. No directories exist from which to draw a sample.
2. Even if there was a way to create a sample of cell numbers, they would not neatly represent people in one geographic area. When people move these days, they simply take their cell phones with them.
3. Most cell phones display the name of the caller, and many people simply hang up on pollsters.

And what of the Internet? Over time, there has been a move to conduct more and more polling online. This is a fast, efficient process; but here, too, there are worries about achieving a random sample. Nevertheless, most pollsters believe phone-based surveys will soon slide into the history books.

Asking Well-Drawn Questions The way in which the questions are phrased is critically important to the reliability of any poll. To illustrate that point: Most will probably say "yes" to a question put this way—"Should local taxes be reduced?" Many will also answer "yes" if asked this question: "Should a bypass be constructed to allow travelers to avoid

Questions to Ask About Polls

WHO?	WHAT?	HOW?	WHY?	WHEN?
Who conducted the poll?	What is the poll's universe?	How was the sample chosen?	Why was the poll conducted?	When was the data collected?
Polls sponsored by political campaigns may aim to mislead as much as inform.	The universe is the population the poll aims to measure. This allows you to judge whether the sample is truly representative.	Samples should be selected randomly. How were questions written and asked? The method of creating and asking questions can alter the results.	Polls meant to boost a candidate's approval ratings are not reliable.	Opinions change quickly during elections, so knowing when the data was collected is important.

>> You can ask several questions to help evaluate a poll's findings. **Analyze Charts** Why is it important to read poll results critically?

HOW DO AMERICANS FEEL ABOUT THE JUSTICE DEPARTMENT REQUIRING THE ASSOCIATED PRESS TO TURN OVER THEIR TELEPHONE RECORDS?

"Do you approve or disapprove of the Justice Department's **decision to subpoena** the phone records of AP journalists as part of an investigation into the disclosure of classified information?"

APPROVE	36%
DISAPPROVE	44%
NO OPINION	20%

"The AP reported classified information about U.S. **anti-terrorism efforts** and prosecutors have obtained AP's phone records **through a court order**. Do you think this action by federal prosecutors is or is not justified?"

JUSTIFIED	52%
NOT JUSTIFIED	33%
NO OPINION	15%

"As you may know, after the AP ran news stories that included classified information about U.S. anti-terrorism efforts, the Justice Department **secretly collected** phone records for reporters and editors who work there....Do you think that the actions of the Justice Department were acceptable or unacceptable?"

ACCEPTABLE	43%
UNACCEPTABLE	52%
NO OPINION	5%

SOURCE: Pew Research Center

>> This chart gives an example of the way the wording of a question can affect the results of a poll. **Analyze Charts** In the example shown, how did the language used influence the responses?

center city traffic?" Yet, building the bypass would almost certainly require more local tax dollars.

Responsible pollsters recognize the problem and construct their questions with great care. They try to avoid "loaded," emotionally charged words and terms that are difficult to understand. They also try to avoid questions that are worded in a way that tends to shape the answers that will be given to them.

The Interview Process How pollsters communicate with respondents can also affect accuracy. For decades, most polls were conducted door-to-door, face-to-face. That is, the interviewer questioned the respondent in person. That method was largely replaced by telephone surveys, which are less labor intensive and less expensive than door-to-door polling. And the latest development in the interview process, as mentioned earlier, is the use of online polling, which involves no actual contact with the respondent at all.

Professional pollsters see advantages and drawbacks to each approach, and some use a combination of techniques. For example, a well-run poll might boast 25 percent of its respondents from telephone calls, and another 75 percent from on-line contacts. Either way, the foremost goal is to get as random a sample as possible.

The interview itself is a very sensitive point in the process. An interviewer's tone of voice or the emphasis he or she gives to certain words can influence a respondent's replies and so affect the validity of a poll. If the questions are not carefully worded, some of the respondent's replies may be snap judgments or emotional reactions. Others may be answers that the person being interviewed thinks "ought" to be given. Thus, polling organizations try to hire and train their interviewing staff very carefully.

Analyzing Findings Polls, whether scientific or not, try to measure people's attitudes. To be of any real value, however, someone must analyze and report the results. Scientific polling organizations collect huge amounts of raw data. In order to handle these data, computers and other electronic hardware have become routine parts of the process. Pollsters use these technologies to tabulate and interpret their data, draw their conclusions, and then publish their findings.

☑ **EXPLAIN** How is it possible for a random sampling of just 1,500 people to accurately represent the opinions of all Americans?

Poll Reliability

How good are polls? On balance, the major national polls are fairly reliable. So, too, are most of the regional surveys around the country. Still, they are far from perfect. Fortunately, most responsible pollsters readily acknowledge the limits of their polls. Many of them are involved in continuing efforts to refine every aspect of the polling process.

Pollsters know that they have difficulty measuring the intensity, stability, and relevance of the opinions they report. *Intensity* is the strength of feeling with which an opinion is held. *Stability* (or fluidity) is the relative permanence or changeableness of an opinion. *Relevance* (or pertinence) is how important a particular opinion is to the person who holds it.

Polls and pollsters are sometimes said to shape the opinions they are supposed to measure. Some critics say that in an election, for example, pollsters often create a "bandwagon effect." That is, some voters, wanting to be with the winner, jump on the bandwagon of the candidate who is ahead in the polls. Another phenomenon is known as the "social desirability effect." This occurs when respondents provide answers that cast them in a positive light.

In spite of these criticisms, it is clear that scientific polls are the most useful tools there are for the difficult task of measuring public opinion. Although they may not always be precisely accurate, they do offer reasonably reliable guides to public thought. Moreover, they help to focus attention on public questions and to stimulate the discussion of them.

☑ **APPLY CONCEPTS** How might the difficulty of measuring the stability of an opinion affect the number and frequency of polls that are conducted?

☑ **ASSESSMENT**

1. **Analyze Information** If a candidate wishes to receive a mandate for his or her policies in an upcoming election, what steps might be taken before the election to formulate stands on issues that best reflect public opinion?

2. **Compare and Contrast** Compare and contrast the kind of information about public opinion that can be gathered through a poll versus the kind of information about public opinion that can be gathered through reading newspaper editorials, watching television, listening to the radio, or reading blogs on the Internet.

3. **Check Understanding** Explain why peer groups have a significant impact on individuals' political opinions.

4. **Evaluate Arguments** A national, scientifically run poll finds that 66 percent of Americans are in favor of increasing national investments in green energy. To what degree would it be fair to say that "the American public agrees that green energy is important?"

5. **Express Ideas Clearly** Name several types of factors that are MOST likely to influence an individual's political attitudes about a particular issue, such as whether or not the Social Security program should be eliminated. Explain your answer.

ABC News anchor Diane Sawyer interviews Speaker of the House John Boehner at the 2012 Republican National Convention. About 15,000 members of the media attended the convention.

Influencing Public Opinion: The Mass Media

Did you go online today using your cell phone, computer, or tablet and did you visit a social media site? If so, you joined the vast majority of teens who say they did the same thing, according to the Pew Research Center.

The Internet is a form of mass media, and its use continues to grow. Other forms, however, such as television and radio, are also part of American culture.

The Role of Mass Media

A **medium** is a means of communication; it transmits some kind of information. *Media* is the plural of medium. The *mass media* include those means of communication that can reach large, widely dispersed audiences simultaneously.

Five major elements of the mass media are especially significant in American politics: television, the Internet, newspapers, radio, and magazines. Other forms of media, including books, films, and satellite radio, play a lesser but still relevant role in the political process.

The mass media do not function as an arm of government in the United States. They are, instead, almost entirely privately owned and operated. Unlike political parties and interest groups, their prime goal is *not* to influence public affairs. They are, nonetheless, an extremely potent force in American politics.

Along with entertainment, the media provide political information. They do so directly when they report the news, in an online newspaper or a television newscast, for example.

BOUNCE to Activate Flipped Video

Objectives

Examine the role of the mass media in providing the public with political information.

Understand the role played by the mass media in the U.S. political system and give examples of the processes used by the media to affect public policy.

Analyze the impact of political changes brought about by the media, including the Internet and other electronic information, and understand the factors that limit the influence of the media on the political process.

Key Terms

medium
public agenda
sound bite
Thomas Jefferson
Theodore Roosevelt

The media also provide a large amount of political information less directly—for example, in radio and television programs, magazine articles, and blogs. These venues often deal with such public topics as crime, healthcare, climate change, or some aspect of American foreign policy. Either way, people acquire most of what they know about government and politics from the various forms of media.

Television Politics and television have gone hand in hand since the technology first appeared. The first public demonstration of television occurred at the New York World's Fair in 1939. President Franklin D. Roosevelt opened the fair on camera, and a comparative handful of local viewers watched him do so on tiny five- and seven-inch screens.

Nearly 100 years later, television is all-pervasive. As you read earlier, there are more than 100 million television households in the United States. Television replaced newspapers as the principal source of political information for a majority of Americans in the early 1960s, and it is still the principal source of news for a large segment of the population.

Three major national networks dominated television for decades: the Columbia Broadcasting System (CBS), the American Broadcasting Company (ABC), and the National Broadcasting Company (NBC). Those three giants still furnish most of the programming for more than 500 local stations. Fox Broadcasting Company, founded in 1985, is also one of the most-watched networks.

The major networks' audience share has declined drastically, however. Their main challenges have come from cable and satellite broadcasters, as well as video subscription services such as Netflix, Amazon, and Apple TV.

Newspapers, the Oldest Mass Media The world's first newspaper was almost certainly the *Acta Diurna*, a daily gazette in Rome dating from 59 B.C. Another very early forerunner of today's newspapers was *Tipao*, a court journal in Beijing first published during the Han dynasty (202 B.C. to A.D. 221).

The first regularly published newspaper in America, the *Boston News-Letter*, appeared in 1704. Other papers soon followed, in Boston and then in Philadelphia, New York, Annapolis, and elsewhere. Those first papers regularly carried political news. Several spurred the colonists to revolution, carrying the news of independence and the text of the Declaration of Independence to people throughout the colonies. **Thomas Jefferson** marked the vital role of the press in the earliest years of the nation when, in 1787, he wrote to a friend:

> . . . were it left to me to decide whether we should have a government without newspapers or newspapers without a government, I should not hesitate a moment to prefer the latter.
>
> —Thomas Jefferson, Letter to Colonel Edward Carrington, January 16, 1787

Roughly one thousand daily newspapers are published in the United States, but that number has been declining for decades. The Internet and television have been major factors in that downward trend. Nevertheless, newspapers are still an important source of information about government and politics, whether read in print or online. Most papers cover stories in greater depth than television does, and many are local papers that focus on events closer to home than most Internet news sources.

Radio Then and Now On November 2, 1920, station KDKA in Pittsburgh went on the air with presidential election returns. From that beginning, the new medium soon became immensely popular.

By the 1930s, radio had assumed much of the role in American society that television had after World War II. It was a major entertainment medium, and millions of people planned their daily schedules around their favorite programs. President Franklin Roosevelt

>> This is one of the first issues ever published of the *Boston News-Letter*. This early paper was able to avoid the censorship problems that had plagued earlier newspapers.

was the first major public figure to use radio effectively. The late author David Halberstam described the impact of FDR's famous fireside chats:

> He was the first great American radio voice. For most Americans of [that] generation, their first memory of politics would be of sitting by a radio and hearing that voice, strong, confident, totally at ease. . . . Most Americans in the previous 160 years had never even seen a President; now almost all of them were hearing him, in their own homes. It was literally and figuratively electrifying.
>
> —David Halberstam, *The Powers That Be*

Many thought that the arrival of television would bring the end of radio as a major medium. Radio has survived, however, in large part because it is so conveniently available. People can hear music, news, sports, and other radio programs in a great many places where they cannot watch television— in their cars, at work, in remote areas, and in any number of other places and situations. The arrival of satellite and Internet radio has added to radio's popularity.

Most radio stations spend little time on public affairs. Many do devote a few minutes every hour to "the news"—really, to a series of headlines. Beginning in the 1990s, talk radio became an important source of political comment. The opinions and analyses offered by a number of talk show hosts can be found on hundreds of stations across the United States.

Magazines, a Changing Media Several magazines were published in colonial America. Benjamin Franklin began one of the very first, his *General Magazine,* in Philadelphia in 1741. The progressive reform period in the early 1900s spawned several journals of opinion, including a number that featured articles by the day's leading muckrakers. The *muckrakers* were journalists who exposed wrongdoing in politics, business, and industry. The term was coined by **Theodore Roosevelt** in 1906 and is derived from the raking of muck—that is, manure and other barnyard debris. The muckrakers set the pattern for what is now called investigative reporting. Their work contributed to changes in

>> A family gathers around the radio in the mid 1920s. Radio shows of the era included "Grand Ole Opry," "Great Moments in History," "The Happiness Boys," and "The National Farm and Home Hour."

A NAUSEATING JOB, BUT IT MUST BE DONE

>> In this early 1900s image, President Roosevelt rakes through the "muck" to expose wrongdoing in the meat industry. **Analyze Political Cartoons** Who in the media might be considered muckrakers today?

the nation's laws, which had a positive impact on the lives of many Americans. For decades before radio and television, magazines constituted the only national medium.

Today's magazines include trade publications, such as *Interior Design,* and periodicals that target some special personal interest, such as *Golf Digest, Seventeen,* and *American Rifleman.* Historically, just one newsmagazine, *Time,* ranked in the top 25 periodicals in terms of circulation.

Like all other forms of media, magazine publishers have seen their circulations decline as the Internet's popularity has risen. Many now offer online versions of their publications to cater to the changing trends in media use in the United States.

The Rise of the Internet The Internet is a leading, and growing, source of political news and information for the American people. Its roots can be traced to a Defense Department research project of the cold war era. In 1969, the DoD's Advanced Research Projects Agency established a four-computer network in the Pentagon designed to protect military secrets from hostile actions. Two

>> While computer connectivity has increased dramatically with the development of the Internet, the size of computers has decreased from room-size to pocket-size.

years later, that grid (ARPANET) had grown to include some two dozen computers at 15 widely scattered locations across the country.

From those beginnings, the Internet has grown phenomenally, and it continues to do so. Ongoing advances in computer technologies allow ever faster access to information, and an ever-growing number of people are availing themselves of that technology. A vast majority of the American people report that they have access to a computer at home or elsewhere, and a rapidly growing number of adults have a smartphone they use to go online. The percentage who get news by means of online sources has grown by leaps and bounds and has easily surpassed television, radio, and newspapers.

Younger people are especially inclined to go online for political news and information. In addition, many people are adding their voices to an ongoing dialogue about public affairs, thereby increasing popular participation in government.

In addition to newspapers, magazines, and television stations, virtually all government agencies, interest groups, political parties, elected officials, and candidates' campaign organizations maintain Web sites. Also popular are blogs devoted to some specific subject. Believe it or not, these sites and blogs number in the hundreds of millions. Those devoted to public affairs typically feature links to a variety of sources. Podcasts, digital recordings that can be downloaded from the Internet, have also grown spectacularly over the years. Other electronic information, such as e-mail, texts, and various apps, have also impacted the political process by revolutionizing communications between political leaders and voters, among government officials, and among voters. Electronic voting-counting has resulted in much faster election results than hand-counting of ballots.

A Social Media Phenomenon The Internet has dramatically altered the way Americans acquire and share information, and that transformation has been taken a step further by social networking sites. Beginning in the late 1990s, a variety of social media sites were launched, some of which charged a fee. Myspace was launched in 2003, and Facebook in 2004. By 2005, about 8 percent of Americans were using social networking sites. Twitter joined the top sites in 2007, while Facebook became the largest social media network in the world.

Billions of people around the globe connect via Facebook and a large majority of them are Americans. In addition, a growing number report that they get their news from Facebook, Twitter, Reddit, and other social networking sites.

Social media networks have had a major impact on politics and government. They have become important tools for fundraising, mobilizing supporters, and uniting political activists worldwide. Humanitarian efforts have been greatly aided by these sites, as well. In 2015, for example, Syrian refugees made use of social media to find relatives from whom they had become separated and to post advice to fellow migrants about where to find affordable housing, the best tent to purchase for temporary shelter, best travel routes, pitfalls to avoid, and other valuable information.

☑ **IDENTIFY CAUSE AND EFFECT** How have modern changes in media changed politics?

How the Media Affects Politics

Clearly, the media play a significant role in American politics. Just how significant that role is, and just how much influence the media have, is the subject of a long, still unsettled debate.

Whatever its weight, the media's influence can be seen in any number of situations. It is most visible in two particular areas: (1) public policy and (2) the field of electoral politics.

The Public Agenda The **public agenda** refers to those societal issues and problems that the nation's political leaders and the public agree need government attention. Basically, the public agenda offers an answer to the question of how society should use its limited resources. But how is the public agenda set?

Private individuals, groups with an interest in a particular issue, community leaders, pundits, and many others help set the public agenda. They do so by raising public awareness about an issue, suggesting solutions, and then pushing government to take action.

The public agenda is then implemented through a variety of means, including, for example, legislative action, government regulations, and executive orders. The State legislature may pass a bill providing funding to expand adult literacy programs. The Federal Government may establish regulations to ensure quality in public water supplies, or the President may issue an executive order to create a task force on crime reduction.

Activists have often expressed frustration about the difficulty of getting important items on the public agenda. Part of the problem stems from the fact that the media often pays attention to sensational stories, rather than those that involve seemingly mundane—and yet important—public issues.

The Media and Public Policy The media, then, play a very large role in shaping the public agenda. As they report and comment on events, issues, policies, and personalities, the media determine to a very large extent what public matters the people will think and talk about—and, so, those matters about which public-policy makers will be most concerned.

Put another way, the media have the power to focus the public's attention on a specific issue. They do so by emphasizing some things and downplaying others. For example, they feature certain items on the front page or at the top of the newscast and bury others in the latter pages or segments of the program.

It is not correct to say that the media tell the people *what* to think; but it is clear that they tell the people what to think *about.* A look at any

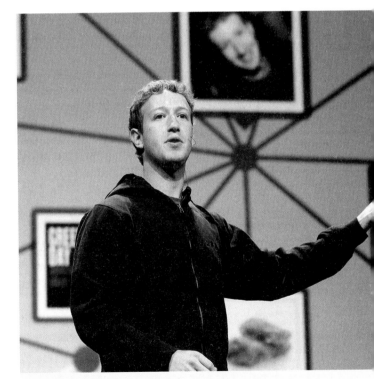

>> Mark Zuckerberg, an entrepreneur and computer programmer, co-founded the highly successful social-networking Web site Facebook while a student at Harvard.

issue of a daily newspaper or a quick review of the content of any television or Internet news story will demonstrate that point. Remember, people rely on the media for most of the information they receive on public issues.

The mass media also have a direct impact on the nation's leaders. Some years ago, Stephen Hess, a widely respected authority on the media, identified several news organizations that form the "inner ring" of influence in Washington, D.C. He cited the three major television networks, CBS, ABC, and NBC; three newspapers, *The New York Times, The Washington Post,* and *The Wall Street Journal;* the leading news wire service, the Associated Press (AP); and the three major news weeklies, *Time, Newsweek,* and *U.S. News & World Report.* CNN, MSNBC, Fox News, Reuters, and *USA Today* have since joined that select group, as have the Web sites of these top media outlets.

While the precise list of top media outlets can change, the key point remains: Leading political figures in and out of government pay close attention to the media. In fact, the President receives a daily digest of news reports, analyses, and editorial comments that are broadcasted and published. At the same time, public leaders use the Internet and, especially, social media to shape public opinion on issues.

This brings us to another vital aspect of the media's role in the United States. Throughout much of American history, the press has been considered a watchdog—the so-called "fourth branch" of government. By keeping an eye on the ruling elites, the media holds them accountable to the people. In its reports on the Vietnam War in the 1960s and 1970s, for example, the media refused to accept at face value the government's optimistic assessment of how the war was going. Instead, reporters dug into the real story and gave Americans a frank, realistic understanding of the situation, thereby helping to change attitudes and eventually end the war.

The media can also bring to light issues that public officials are neglecting. Extensive reporting on the HIV/AIDS epidemic in the 1980s and 1990s, for example, eventually led to changes in public policy and greater government action.

Reemergence of the Partisan Press In the 19th century, most communities had several newspapers, each representing a different partisan perspective. This so-called "partisan press" was based on the loyalty of large numbers of engaged citizens to their political parties—and to their papers. But as news became more nationalized in the early part of the 20th century, and as local party organizations began

WHAT IS YELLOW JOURNALISM?

FIRST USED IN THE LATE —1800s— BY COMPETING NEWSPAPER OWNERS WILLIAM RANDOLPH HEARST & JOSEPH PULITZER

CONTRIBUTED TO THE U.S. DECISION TO DECLARE WAR ON SPAIN IN 1898

USED DRAMATIC HEADLINES INFLAMMATORY PHOTOS EXAGGERATED STORIES AND FEW REAL FACTS TO INFLUENCE PUBLIC OPINION & SELL NEWSPAPERS

"YOU FURNISH THE PICTURES... I'LL FURNISH THE WAR."

–Comment made by **William Randolph Hearst** in 1897, referring to his newspaper's role in stirring up public opinion in favor of war with Spain

>> Throughout history, the press has had tremendous power to influence the public.
Analyze Charts What characteristics of "yellow journalism" can still be seen in some publications today?

Examples of the Media as Watchdog

ISSUE UNCOVERED	JOURNALIST OR NEWSPAPER	RESULT
Brutal attacks against African Americans in the South (1955)	*Jet* magazine	Traction for the growing civil rights movement
U.S. military cover up of massacre at My Lai (1969)	Seymour Hersh	Growth of antiwar sentiment
Presidential crimes (1972–1974)	*Washington Post*	President Nixon's resignation
Racial bias in the judicial system (1983)	CBS "60 Minutes"	Increased awareness of racial bias and release of wrongfully convicted man
Embezzlement of federal housing funds for low-income American Indians (1996)	*The Seattle Times*	Reform of federal housing program management
Inhumane conditions in Mexican labor camps (2014)	*Los Angeles Times*	Reviews of purchasing practices begun by U.S. companies that import from Mexico

SOURCE: News Literacy Project

>> American public opinion is divided on how well the media plays its watchdog role.
Analyze Charts What generalization can you make about the information in this chart?

to wane after the New Deal, the partisan press faded into the history books. The standard for good news reporting became fairness and objectivity.

In the last decade or so, however, many scholars have wondered whether a new partisan press has developed, made up of liberal and conservative-leaning Internet news sites, conservative talk radio, and nontraditional cable television news channels, such as Fox and MSNBC. Like the partisan press of the 19th century, these media outlets rely on loyal audiences for their success.

Has the partisan press returned? It is fair to say that a growing number of Americans think there is an ideological bias in the news. Conservatives charge that a large percentage of commentators and major news outlets have a liberal bias, while Democrats point to the huge role of Fox News and other conservative media in American politics. Others argue that although some outlets might shade to the "right" or "left," most journalists work hard to be objective.

Probably more important than the development of partisan news programs has been a perceived change in consumers' habits. With so many options available, people tend to seek out a wide range of information. Yet, it seems that most find outlets that match their preexisting ideas. This has been called the "echo chamber" phenomenon. Many worry that if citizens never listen to other perspectives, the nation will grow less tolerant and find it more difficult to reach compromises on tough policy questions.

Electoral Politics Before television, the major parties generally dominated the election process. They recruited most candidates who ran for office, and they ran those candidates' campaigns. The candidates depended on party organizations in order to reach the voters.

Now, both television and the Internet allow candidates to appeal directly to the people, without the help of a party organization. Candidates for office need not be experienced politicians who have worked their way up a party's political ladder over the course of several elections. It is not unusual for candidates to assemble their own campaign organizations and operate with only loose connections to their political parties. In addition, the Internet allows candidates to fundraise, campaign, and mobilize supporters much more easily—and more cheaply—than ever before.

Remember, too, that how voters see a candidate—the impressions they have of that candidate's personality, character, abilities, and so on—is one of the major factors that influence voting behavior. Candidates and professional campaign managers are quite aware of this fact. They know that the kind of "image" a candidate projects in the media can have a telling effect on the outcome of an election.

Candidates regularly try to manipulate media coverage to their advantage. Campaign strategists understand that, even with the Internet, most people learn almost everything they know about a candidate from television. They therefore plan campaigns that emphasize television exposure. Such technical considerations as timing, location, lighting, and camera angles loom large, often at the expense of such substantive matters as the issues involved in an election or a candidate's qualifications for public office.

Newscasts featuring candidates are usually short, sharply focused **sound bites**—snappy reports that can be aired in 30 or 45 seconds or so. Staged and carefully orchestrated visits to historic sites, factory gates, toxic-waste dumps, football games, and the like, have become a standard part of the electoral scene.

☑ **HYPOTHESIZE** What might happen to the nature of the media if the 1st Amendment guarantee of freedom of the press were to be repealed?

The Media's Limited Influence

Having said all this, it is all too easy to overstate the media's role in American politics. A number of built-in factors work to limit the media's impact on the behavior of the American voting public.

In the past, it has been commonplace for relatively few people to follow international, national, or even local political events very closely. However, this trend is changing. Due in part to the rise of social media, a growing number of Americans pay very close attention to national politics, especially

during election years. In sum, an increasing portion of the public takes in and understands much of what the media have to say about public affairs.

Among those people who do pay attention to politics, however, most are likely to be selective about it. That is, they most often watch, listen to, and read those sources that generally agree with their own viewpoints. They regularly ignore those sources with which they disagree. Thus, for example, many Democrats do not watch the televised campaign appearances or visit the Web sites of Republican candidates. Nor do many Republicans read newspaper stories about the campaign efforts of Democratic candidates.

The Media and Public Affairs Another important limit on the media's impact is the content the media carries. This is especially true of radio and television. Most television programs, for example, have little or nothing to do with public affairs, at least not directly. (A number of popular programs do relate to public affairs in an indirect way, however. Thus, many are "crime shows," and crime is certainly a matter of public concern. Many also carry a political message—for example, that the police are hard-working public servants.) Advertisers who pay the high costs of television air time want to reach the largest possible audiences. Because most people are more interested in being entertained than in being informed about public issues, a limited number of public-affairs programs air in prime time.

Pivotal Events in the Recent History of the Media

1972	Some blame **TV coverage of the Vietnam War** for breaking America's will to fight.
1974	By the time President Nixon resigns, 69% of Americans say they have a "great deal" or "fair amount" of **trust in the media**. That figure drops steadily over the next two decades.
1989	Only 25% of U.S. adults say there is a "great deal" of political **bias in the news**, but that figure nearly doubles in the coming decades.
1990s	Cable and the internet mean more competition for viewers' attention. This leads to a gradual shift **away from objectivity** and toward more subjective journalism.
2000	An ever-widening **divergence between Democrats' and Republicans'** trust in the media begins, with Democrats recording higher trust and Republicans lower trust.
2010s	"Citizen journalists" **record events on their cell phones** and share them to a mass audience via the Internet.

SOURCE: Data based on Gallup poll results

>> Trust in the media was high in the 1970s, following the uncovering of the Watergate scandal by two *Washington Post* reporters and reporting on the Vietnam War. It declined steadily after that time. **Analyze Charts** What effect do you think "citizen journalists" will have on Americans' trust in the media?

Radio and television mostly "skim" the news. They report only what their news editors determine to be the most important or the most interesting stories of the day. Even on widely watched evening news programs, most reports are presented in 60- to 90-second time slots. In short, the broadcast media seldom give the kind of in-depth coverage that a good newspaper can supply.

Newspapers are not as hampered as many other media in their ability to cover public affairs. Still, much of the content of most newspapers is nonpolitical. Like nearly all of television and radio, newspapers depend on their advertising revenues, which in turn depend on producing a product with the widest possible appeal. Newspaper readers are often more interested in the sports pages and the social, travel, advertising, and entertainment sections of a newspaper than they are in its news and editorial pages.

In-Depth News In-depth coverage of public affairs is available in the media to those who want it and will seek it out. There are a number of good newspapers around the country. In-depth coverage can also be found on the Internet, in several magazines, and on a number of radio and television stations, including public broadcast outlets. Remember, however, that there is nothing about democracy that guarantees an alert and informed public. Like voting and other forms of political participation, being an informed citizen requires some effort.

☑ **DRAW CONCLUSIONS** What does the popularity of sound bites across different media, including political ads, suggest?

>> In this cartoon, the free press and polar bears are in a case labeled "Endangered Species." **Analyze Political Cartoons** What is causing the potential extinction of the free press, according to this cartoonist?

☑ ASSESSMENT

1. **Make Predictions** How might the increasing popularity of social media, such as Facebook and Twitter, affect the popularity of radio in the future?

2. **Summarize** Describe the media's origins in the United States.

3. **Generate Explanations** What is one way in which the media influences public policy?

4. **Apply Concepts** If a man chooses to listen to his favorite candidate's podcast on immigration but skips the opposing candidate's Web meeting on the same issue, what concept does this illustrate and why?

5. **Hypothesize** If a candidate noticed too few "Likes" on her Facebook page, what might she be likely to do and why?

The Media and the Vietnam War

Since the invention of the printing press, newspapers and other media have attempted to sway public opinion and even to influence policy decisions. With the advent of television, breaking news could be reported instantaneously and graphically. Early in the Vietnam War, the media's coverage was based on government statements. Later, however, reporters went on location. As a result, the media's role in shaping public opinion grew.

As you read these two reports on the same battle, think about whose views are being expressed by each reporter.

>> Vietnamese refugees flee during the Tet Offensive, the battle that is the subject for both of the news reports featured on these pages.

Primary Source 1

"Washington Feels Vietcong Offensive Failed Maximum Objective," *The New York Times:* Hanson W. Balwin

WASHINGTON, Feb. 16 [1968]—United States officials say that the Vietcong miscalculated in the current phase of their offensive and failed to achieve their maximum objectives of overthrowing the South Vietnamese Government and establishing control in many of the major cities.

Most of these officials add, however, that the enemy did cause major damage, and governmental, administrative and military disorganization to an extent as yet unknown. . . .

They are convinced that the enemy "is about to drop the other shoe," perhaps in the form of a second attack on South Vietnamese cities, and almost certainly a major offensive against the Marine base at Khesanh, in the northwest corner of South Vietnam. . . .

A few military leaders believe that the results to date show that the enemy suffered a considerable reverse, and most believe that the enemy paid with lives for major political and psychological gains, and far more limited military gains.

☑ **DETERMINE MEANING** Who believes that "the enemy is about to drop the other shoe" and what is meant by that phrase?

Most informed observers do not view the urban offensive and the additional major impending actions as a Battle of the Bulge, a last gasp, "go for broke" offensive, before a collapse. They believe that the enemy maintains, despite heavy losses, the ability to wage a protracted war. . . .

In one respect, however, the enemy may have been disappointed. Officials point out that polls appear to show an increased support for the war in the United States, since the attacks started.

. . . [T]he "gloom and doom," as one officer described it which pervaded Washington in the first week after the offensive, has been replaced by a more pragmatic assessment of loss against gains, there is a belief that the enemy has suffered heavily but that nevertheless, he has not yet shot his bolt [closed the door on; given up]; that there will probably be a need for still more United States troops, and that there is no clear-cut end in sight.

☑ **MAKE INFERENCES** Would you describe the tone of this article as having a positive or negative outlook?

Primary Source 2

"We Are Mired in Stalemate," CBS News Broadcast: Walter Cronkite

Tonight [February 27, 1968], . . . we'd like to sum up our findings in Vietnam, an analysis that must be speculative, personal, subjective. Who won and who lost in the great Tet offensive against the cities? I'm not sure. The Vietcong did not win by a knockout, but neither did we. The referees of history may make it a draw. Another standoff may be coming in the big battles expected south of the Demilitarized Zone. Khesanh could well fall, with a terrible loss in American lives, prestige and morale. . . .

☑ **DISTINGUISH AMONG FACT, OPINION, AND REASONED JUDGMENT** How can you tell from this paragraph that the argument in this source is going to be based on fact, opinion, or reasoned judgment?

We have been too often disappointed by the optimism of the American leaders, both in Vietnam and Washington, to have faith any longer in the silver linings they find in the darkest clouds. . . . For it seems now more certain than ever that the bloody experience of Vietnam is to end in a stalemate. This summer's almost certain standoff will either end in a real give-and-take negotiations or terrible escalation; and for every means we have to escalate, the enemy can match us, and that applies to invasion of the North, the use of nuclear weapons, or the mere commitment of one hundred, or two hundred, or three hundred thousand more American troops to battle. . . .

To say that we are closer to victory today is to believe, in the face of the evidence, the optimists who have been wrong in the past. To suggest we are on the edge of defeat is to yield to unreasonable pessimism. To say that we are mired in stalemate seems the only realistic, yet unsatisfactory, conclusion. On the off chance that military and political analysts are right, in the next few months we must test the enemy's intentions, in case this is indeed his last big gasp before negotiations. But it is increasingly clear to this reporter that the only rational way out then will be to negotiate, not as victors, but as an honorable people who lived up to their pledge to defend democracy, and did the best they could.

☑ **SUMMARIZE** What solution to the Vietnam War is Cronkite promoting in the last paragraph?

☑ ASSESSMENT

1. **Cite Evidence** From where does Balwin get his information? How can you tell?

2. **Compare and Contrast** How are these excerpts similar? How are they different?

3. **Draw Conclusions** Do you believe Source 1 or Source 2 would have had more of an effect on public opinion? Why?

4. **Make Connections** What is another example in U.S. history in which the press influenced the nation's politics? How are they similar to and different from this Vietnam War example?

10.7

Members of the League of United Latin American Citizens march in support of immigration reform. LULAC focuses its efforts on education, civil rights, and employment for Hispanics.

 BOUNCE to Activate Flipped Video

Objectives

Understand the role played by interest groups in the U.S. political system.

Analyze the impact of political changes brought about by interest groups and examine the viewpoints of those who see interest groups as both good and bad for American politics.

Describe the various types of interest groups in the United States.

Give examples of the direct approach used by interest groups to affect public policy.

Examine the indirect lobbying approach and its use of grass-roots pressure, media, propaganda, and political campaigns to influence public opinion and policy.

Key Terms

interest group
public policy
public affairs
trade association
labor union
lobbying
lobbyist

amicus curiae brief
grass-roots
   pressures
Capitol Hill
James Madison
Alexis de Tocqueville

Understanding Interest Groups

An interest group is a collection of people who share certain views on public matters and work to shape public policy to their benefit. They try to persuade public officials to respond to their positions favorably. You may not think that you belong to this sort of group, but as you read this section you will likely discover that you do. You might, in fact, belong to several of them. You will probably also realize that you will become a member of many more of these groups in the years to come—because these organizations provide one of the most effective ways in which Americans can get government to react to their needs and wants.

What Are Interest Groups?

Where do you stand on the question of gun control? What about global warming? Campaign finance reform? Abortion? Prayer in public schools? What can you do to promote your views on these and other public questions? How can you increase the chance that your positions will carry the day?

Joining with others who share your opinions is both practical and democratic. Organization can provide the route to power, and organized efforts to further group interests are a fundamental part of the democratic process. Moreover, the right to do so is protected by the Constitution. Remember, the 1st Amendment guarantees "the right of the people peaceably to assemble, and to petition the Government for a redress of grievances."

Interest Groups Shape Public Policy Interest groups are sometimes called "pressure groups" and often "organized interests" or "special interests." They try to influence what government does in some specific area of special interest to them. They give themselves a variety of labels: leagues, associations, clubs, federations, unions, committees, and so on. But whatever they call themselves, every interest group seeks to influence the making and content of **public policy.**

Used in this general sense, public policy includes all of the goals that a government pursues in the many areas of human affairs in which it is involved— everything from seat belts, speed limits, zoning to flood control, old-age pensions, and the use of military force in international affairs.

Because interest groups exist to shape public policy, they can be found wherever those policies are made or can be influenced. They operate at every level of government—on **Capitol Hill** and elsewhere in Washington, D.C., in every one of the 50 State capitals, in thousands of city halls and county courthouses, and in many other places at the local level all across the country. In short, as diplomat and historian Lord Bryce put it somewhat indelicately more than a century ago: "Where the body is, there will the vultures be gathered."

Remember, our society is pluralistic. It is not dominated by any one elite. It is, instead, composed of several distinct cultures and groups. Increasingly, the members of various ethnic, racial, religious, and other groups compete for and share in the exercise of political power in the United States.

Comparing and Contrasting Political Parties and Interest Groups Interest groups are made up of people who join together for some political purpose, much like political parties. The major parties and interest groups overlap in a number of ways. They differ from each other in four significant ways, however: (1) with respect to the making of nominations, (2) in their basic focus, (3) in the scope of their interests, and (4) in the fact that they are private organizations.

First, parties nominate candidates for public office; interest groups do not. Recall, the making of nominations is a prime function of political parties. If an interest group were to nominate candidates, it would, in effect, become a political party.

Interest groups do attempt to affect the outcome of primaries and other nominating contests. They do not pick candidates who then run for office under their labels, however. It may be widely known that a particular interest group supports this or that candidate, but the candidate seeks votes as a Republican or a Democrat.

Second, parties are chiefly interested in winning elections and thereby controlling government. Interest groups are chiefly concerned with controlling or influencing the policies of government. Unlike parties, those groups do not face the problems involved in trying to appeal to the largest possible number of people. In short, political parties are

Interest Groups v. Political Parties

INTEREST GROUPS
- support specific candidates
- are interested in influencing government policies
- concentrate on those issues important to their members
- are private organizations

(overlap)
- are concerned with public policy
- unite people for a political purpose

POLITICAL PARTIES
- nominate candidates for public office
- are interested in winning elections
- concentrate on all public affairs issues
- are accountable to the public

>> Political parties and interest groups have more differences than similarities. **Analyze Charts** Based on the information shown, why do you think interest groups are sometimes criticized?

mostly interested in the *who*, and interest groups are mostly concerned with the *what*, of government. To put it another way, parties focus mostly on the candidate; interest groups focus mostly on policy questions.

Third, political parties are necessarily concerned with the whole range of public affairs, with everything of concern to voters. Interest groups almost always concentrate only on those issues that most directly affect the interests of their members.

Finally, interest groups are private organizations. Unlike political parties, they are not accountable to the public. Their members, not the voters, pass judgment on their performance.

☑ **EXPRESS IDEAS CLEARLY** In what way do interest groups raise awareness of public affairs and help shape public policy?

Origins and Viewpoints

Interest groups arose in the early days of our nation, as like-minded citizens banded together to try to influence government policies. In fact, merchants, creditors, and property owners pushed for the Constitutional Convention in 1787. In the early years of the Republic, business interests fought for and won the protective tariff on imports. The U.S. Brewers Association, the oldest organized interest group, was born in 1862 when Congress first levied a tax on beer. The association said that its purpose

was to advocate for its interests to the legislative and executive branches.

Today, no one really knows how many interest groups exist in the United States, but there are many thousands of them. Are those interest groups good or bad for the American political system?

Madison and de Tocqueville Many have long viewed interest groups with suspicion and foreboding. They have feared that some would become so powerful that they would be able to shape public policies to their own narrow and selfish ends. **James Madison** gave voice to that view in 1787. In *The Federalist* No. 10, he argued that, inevitably, people join together to pursue common interests. They form "factions," Madison's term for what we now call interest groups. He warned that those factions, left unchecked, could dominate public decision making because of size, resources, and/or leadership.

Madison believed that a society could eliminate factions only by eliminating the people's fundamental freedoms. He argued that "the mischiefs of factions" could best be controlled by a political system in which the powers of government, or the ability to make public policies, are fragmented. That is a major reason why, he said, the Constitution provides for a separation of powers and checks and balances, and for a federal system of government— to make it unlikely that one group can override the interests of other (competing) groups.

Early Interest Groups

Frederick Douglass
1818-1895
formerly enslaved,
American Anti-Slavery
Society

Mary Church Terrell
1863-1954
founder, National
Association of
Colored Women

Lewis Hine
1874-1940
photographer,
National Child
Labor Committee

Oliver Hudson Kelley
1826-1913
farmer, founder of the
National Grange

>> These early interest group founders sought a wide range of goals: equality, labor, and economic reforms. **Analyze Charts** What tactics might these leaders have used to accomplish their goals?

Nearly 50 years later, **Alexis de Tocqueville** was deeply impressed by the vast number of organizations he found in this country. Tocqueville, a Frenchman, toured much of what was the United States in the 1830s. In his work, *Democracy in America,* he wrote that

> In no country in the world has the principle of association been more successfully used, or more unsparingly applied to a multitude of different objects, than in America.

—Alexis de Tocqueville

And, in a similar vein, he also observed that

> Americans of all ages, all conditions, and all dispositions, constantly form associations . . . not only commercial and manufacturing . . . but . . . of a thousand other kinds— religious, moral, serious, futile, extensive or restricted, enormous or diminutive.

—Alexis de Tocqueville

Are those "associations" good or bad? To answer that question you must weigh the functions those groups perform in American politics against the various criticisms often leveled at them.

Positive Aspects of Interest Groups *First,* organized interests help to stimulate awareness of and interest in **public affairs.** Public affairs are those issues and events that concern the people at large. Interest groups raise awareness of public affairs mostly by developing and publicizing those policy positions they favor and by opposing those they see as threats to the interests of their members.

Second, interest groups represent their members based on what their members think as opposed to where they happen to live. Public officials are elected from districts drawn on maps. But many of the issues that concern and unite people today have less to do with where they live than with, say, how they make a living. A labor union member who lives in Chicago may have much more in common with someone who does the same kind of work in Seattle than he or she does with someone who owns a business in Chicago or runs a farm in another part of Illinois.

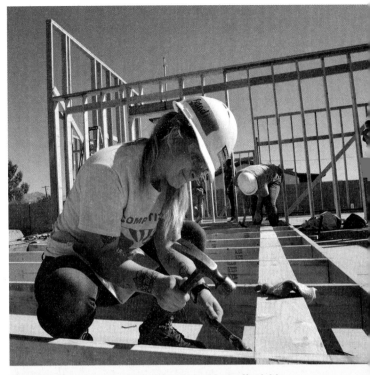

>> Habitat for Humanity volunteers build an affordable house in Tucson, Arizona. **Describe** How has your local area benefited from the work of special interest groups?

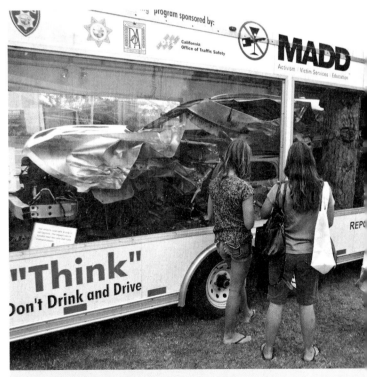

>> The interest group Mothers Against Drunk Driving seeks to focus attention on the dangers of drinking and driving. **Draw Conclusions** How might such interest groups benefit the public?

Another side to this benefit is that groups based on shared attitudes can be powerful tools to protect the interests of views not in the majority. Thus, lobbying efforts to promote a position held by a small number of people can prevent that viewpoint from being ignored or discounted by government officials, the media, and the public at large.

Third, organized interests often provide useful information to government—for example, on employment, price levels, or the sales of new and existing homes. These data are important to the making of public policy, and government officials often cannot obtain them from any other source.

Fourth, interest groups are vehicles for political participation. Most people are not inclined to run for and hold public office, or even to volunteer for a campaign. For many Americans, then, interest groups are a convenient and less time-consuming way to help shape public policy. They are a means through which like-minded citizens can pool their resources and channel their energies. One mother concerned about drunk driving cannot accomplish very much acting alone. Thousands of people united in an organization like MADD (Mothers Against Drunk Driving) certainly can.

Fifth, interest groups add another element to the checks-and-balances feature of the political process.

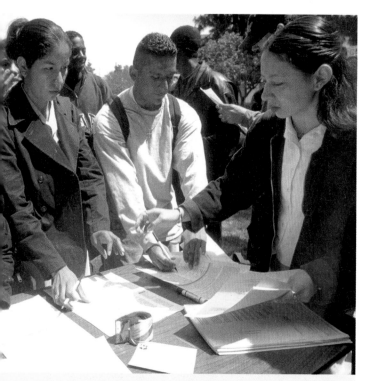

>> College students sign petitions supporting affirmative action. **Hypothesize** Why might interest groups seek support for their causes on college campuses?

Many of them keep close tabs on the work of various public agencies and officials and thus help to make sure that they perform their tasks in responsible and effective ways.

Finally, interest groups compete with one another in the public arena. That competition limits the lengths to which some groups might otherwise go as they seek to advance their own interests. For example, the automotive industry may work to weaken or postpone auto emission standards imposed under the Clean Air Act. Their efforts may be opposed—and to some extent counterbalanced—by environmental and health-related organizations.

Negative Aspects of Interest Groups All of what has just been said is not meant to suggest that interest groups are above reproach. On the contrary, they can be, and often are, criticized on several counts.

The potentially negative side of interest groups is sometimes all too apparent. Many groups push their own special interests which are not always in the best interests of other Americans. Their critics often make several more specific charges.

First, some interest groups have an influence far out of proportion to their size, or, for that matter, to their importance or contribution to the public good. Thus, the contest over "who gets what, when, and how" is not always a fair fight. The more highly organized and better-financed groups often have an advantage. Note, however, that this can also be viewed as a positive, because it protects the interests of views not in the majority.

Second, it is sometimes hard to tell just who or how many people a group really represents. Many groups have titles that suggest that they have thousands—even millions—of dedicated members. Some organizations that call themselves such things as "People United Against . . ." are, in fact, only "fronts" for a very few people with very narrow interests.

Third, many groups do not in fact represent the views of all of the people for whom they claim to speak. Very often, both in and out of politics, an organization is dominated by an active minority who conduct the group's affairs and make its policy decisions.

Finally, some groups use tactics that, if they were to become widespread, would undermine the whole political system. These practices include bribery and other heavy-handed uses of money, overt threats of revenge, and so on. Instances of that sort of behavior are not at all common, but they are not altogether unknown either. In the Abramoff scandal of the early 2000s, for example, lobbyist Jack Abramoff, several

Evaluating Interest Groups

PROS	CONS
• Raise awareness of public affairs • Represent people based on shared attitudes rather than geography • Provide useful data to government • Act as vehicles for political participation • Act as watchdogs over public officials • Compete with one another in the public arena	• Can push their own interests to the detriment of others • Can have influence exceeding their size • Can misrepresent their own size • Do not always represent the views of everyone in the group • Can use unethical tactics and exert undue influence on policy makers

>> The involvement of interest groups in politics has pros and cons. **Analyze Charts** Why might tactics such as donating money to political campaigns be considered a drawback?

associates, and a member of Congress were sent to federal prison for using bribery and other tactics to win legislative favors.

☑ **DETERMINE POINT OF VIEW** In *The Federalist* No. 10, James Madison refers to interest groups as "factions" in the following statement: "There are two methods of curing the mischiefs of faction: the one, by removing its causes; the other, by controlling its effects." To what effects might Madison be referring?

Why Do Individuals Join Interest Groups?

"Everything from A to Z." That expression can certainly be applied to the many interest groups in this country. They include, among thousands of others, AAA (the American Automobile Association), ACLU (the American Civil Liberties Union), Amnesty International, the Zionist Organization of America, the NRA (National Rifle Association), the NAACP (National Association for the Advancement of Colored People), and the Zoological Association of America. All of those thousands of organizations can be more or less readily classified and, so, usefully described as interest groups.

An American Tradition The United States has often been called "a nation of joiners." Recall Alexis

de Tocqueville's observations cited in the previous section. His comments, true when he made them, have become even more accurate over time.

No one really knows how many associations exist in the United States today. There are thousands upon thousands of them, however, and at every level in society. Each one becomes an interest group whenever it tries to influence the actions of government in order to promote its own goals.

Interest groups come in all shapes and sizes. They may have thousands or even millions of long-established members or only a handful of new or temporary members. They may be well or little known, highly structured or quite loose and informal, wealthy or with few resources. No matter what their characteristics, they are found in every field of human activity in this country.

Based on Interests and Ideas The largest number of these groups has been founded on the basis of an economic interest, and especially on the basis of business, labor, agricultural, and professional interests. Some groups are grounded in a geographic area.

Others have been born out of a cause or an idea, such as prohibition of alcohol, environmental protection, or gun control. Many groups seek to influence some aspect of the nation's foreign policy. Still others exist to promote the welfare of certain groups of people—veterans, senior citizens, a racial minority, the homeless, women, people with disabilities, and so on.

Many people belong to a number of local, regional, or national interest groups—often without realizing they do. A car dealer, for example, may belong to the local Chamber of Commerce, a car dealers' association, the American Legion, a local taxpayers' league, a garden club, a church, and the American Cancer Society. All of these are, to one degree or another, interest groups—including the church and the garden club, even though the car dealer may never think of these groups in that light.

Churches often take stands on such public issues as drinking, curfew ordinances, and legalized gambling, and they often try to influence public policy on those matters. Garden clubs frequently try to persuade cities to do such things as improve public parks and beautify downtown areas. Not every group to which people belong can properly be called an interest group, of course. However, the point is that many groups that are not considered to be interest groups are, in fact, just that.

Many people belong to groups that take conflicting stands on political issues. For example, the taxpayers' league may endorse a plan to eliminate plantings in traffic islands while the garden club wants to keep and even enlarge them.

Types of Interest Groups Most interest groups are formed on the basis of economic interests. Among those groups, the most active are those representing business, labor, agriculture, and certain professions.

Most segments of the business community also have their own interest groups, often called **trade associations**. Those that represent the pharmaceutical, oil, and natural gas industries are generally regarded as among the most powerful and effective interest groups.

A **labor union** is an organization of workers who share the same type of job or who work in the same industry. The AFL-CIO (American Federation of Labor and Congress of Industrial Organizations) is by far the largest.

Issue-oriented groups and religious organizations are other types of interest groups. Still others focus on the welfare of certain segments of the population, such as veterans, or, at the other end of the spectrum, on the common good of the overall community.

Two popular interest groups that seek to promote the interests of particular parts of the population are the National Association for the Advancement of Colored People (NAACP) and the League of United Latin American Citizens (LULAC). Founded in 1909, the NAACP is the oldest and largest civil rights interest group in the United States and is committed to the "elimination of all barriers to political, educational, social, and economic equality" of Black Americans and other minority groups. The NAACP works to put public policies into place that support its point of view on important contemporary

Labor Union Membership

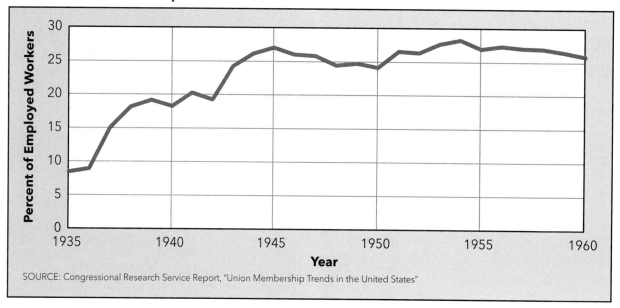

SOURCE: Congressional Research Service Report, "Union Membership Trends in the United States"

>> The 1935 Wagner Act recognized the right of workers to join unions. **Analyze Graphs** According to this graph, what effect did that law have on labor union membership?

issues, including civic engagement, education, health, legal issues, and media diversity. On the issue of participation in government, for example, the NAACP works to register minority voters and end voter suppression.

Similarly, LULAC was founded in 1929 and is the oldest civil rights organization for Hispanics in the United States. Like the NAACP, LULAC focuses on many important contemporary issues, such as civil rights, economic empowerment, housing, immigration, and technology. LULAC urges Congress to monitor the enforcement of hate-crime laws, for example, and supports comprehensive immigration reform.

The Interest Group Explosion The number of interest groups vying for political power exploded in the late 1960s. The growth was dramatic, and it occurred for several reasons.

First, many Americans began looking for different ways to shape public policy during the "counter-culture revolution." To many, political parties no longer seemed the best way to bring about change because they were "part of the problem." Interest groups, on the other hand, seemed unencumbered by the old rules and "establishment" leaders.

Second, following World War II, a host of new issues caught the public's attention, including civil rights, women's rights, the environment, and the Vietnam War. Many Americans did not have faith that traditional avenues could address these new issues. They sought different pathways for change, including interest groups.

Third, the explosion occurred because the new groups were effective, which led to the formation of opposing groups. Finally, many astute leaders, dubbed by scholars as "public interest entrepreneurs," understood the potential of group mobilization, and they employed a host of techniques to grow their organizations. Direct mail, for example, used to enlist supporters and raise money, became common in the 1970s. This led to higher membership, more powerful organizations, and ever more interest groups vying for power.

☑ **GENERATE EXPLANATIONS** The interest group Common Cause was formed in 1970, and one of the first issues its members tackled was an attempt to bring an end to the Vietnam War. How does its formation and mission relate to the interest group explosion of the late 1960s?

>> Major league baseball lobbyist Lucy Calaitti speaks with Bud Selig, major league baseball commissioner, as he prepares to testify before a House committee on steroid use in professional baseball.

>> An Environmental Defense Fund (EDF) employee collects data. The EDF grew out of a groundbreaking case in the mid-1960s in which scientists and lawyers went to court on behalf of the environment.

Processes Used By Interest Groups—The Direct Approach

Interest groups exist to influence the making and the content of public policy, and they do so in a great many ways and in a great many places. They are, in effect, an excellent illustration of political scientist Harold D. Lasswell's notion that politics is all about "who gets what, when and how."

Interest groups approach government both directly and indirectly in their attempts to influence policy. Their *direct* efforts involve immediate, face-to-face contacts with policymakers. Their *indirect* efforts entail more subtle tactics—for example, mobilizing "the folks back home" to contact their members of Congress with letters, phone calls, faxes, and e-mails for or against a particular bill.

The Direct Approach Again, the direct approach, bringing group pressures to bear directly on public policymakers, is another way of saying "lobbying." **Lobbying** is the process by which organized interests attempt to affect the decisions and actions of public officials. **Lobbyists** are those people who try to persuade public officials to do those things that interest groups want them to do.

The term *lobbying* was first used in Great Britain in the 17th century, referring to members of the public who waited in the public lobbies of the House of Commons to talk with members of Parliament. The term *lobby-agent* was reportedly being used to identify favor-seekers at sessions of New York's legislature in Albany by the late 1820s, and by the 1830s, the word *lobbyist* was well-known in Washington, D.C. Lobbying is still frequently defined in terms of legislators and legislation. However, it has a much broader application today.

Lobbying is a big business and it occurs wherever public policy is made, including Washington, D.C., every State capital, and all of the county courthouses and city halls across the country. Every important interest and many lesser ones—business groups, labor unions, farm organizations, the professions, churches, veterans, environmental groups, and many more—maintain lobbyists in Washington. Generally speaking, there are roughly 10,000 registered federal lobbyists, and they spend billions of dollars to achieve their goals.

Most lobbyists are professionals. Some are freelancers, "hired guns" who will use their contacts and talents for anyone willing to pay what they charge. Most larger companies and labor unions have their own full-time lobbyists. Many work for the hundreds of Washington law firms and public relations agencies, concentrated along K Street, that specialize in that kind of work.

Regulations The Abramoff scandal prompted Congress to tighten the statutes regulating lobbyists' behavior in 2007. As the law now stands, all persons and organizations that seek to influence members of Congress, their staffers, or any policy-making officer in the executive branch must register with the clerk of the House and the secretary of the Senate. They are required to supply such basic information as name, address, and principal place of business, plus a general description of their activities. Every lobbyist must describe his or her ongoing work in detail and account for the income from it in quarterly reports.

Former senators and top-level executive branch officials must now wait two years, but ex-House members wait only one year, before they can become lobbyists. And, since 2007, no member of Congress can receive *any* gift from lobbyists or their clients.

THE INTRICATE MECHANICS OF GOVERNMENT

PUBLIC ENTRANCE

LOBBYIST ENTRANCE

© Wiley Ink, inc./Distributed by Universal Uclick via Cartoonstock

>> **Analyze Political Cartoons** What is being suggested about the ways people can bring concerns to the government? Which is more successful according to this cartoon? Do you agree or disagree?

LOBBYING IN ACTION

① PROPOSAL IS MADE
- electric company announces plans for **wind farm**
- area is **upscale vacation homes**
- promoted as **non-polluting** form of energy

② LOBBYING BEGINS
- interest groups **in favor** build support for clean energy
- interest groups **opposed** build support for protecting natural wildlife

③ GOVERNMENT DEBATES/ LOBBYISTS PRESSURE
- project requires approval from **State** and **Federal** government agencies
- **government agencies** consider all impacts, such as to the electric power industry and the environment
- **interest groups** try to influence agencies

④ DECISION IS REACHED
- agencies issue **rulings** on project
- rulings may require **legislative action**

>> An electric company announces plans for a wind farm, and competing interests work to influence government policy on the plan. **Analyze Charts** How might interest groups exert their influence?

Lobbying Congress The benefits of maintaining close relationships with members of Congress are fairly obvious, for Congress is the prime place for the making of public policy in the Federal Government. Some lobbying efforts target individual lawmakers and their staffs, but most are aimed at the standing committees of the House and Senate. More than a century ago, Woodrow Wilson described "Congress in its committee rooms" as "Congress at work," and that remains the case today.

Lobbyists testify before congressional committees and regularly submit prepared statements that set out their organization's views on proposed legislation. What happens in a legislative body often excites the interest of several different and competing groups. For example, if the House Committee on the Judiciary is considering a bill to regulate the sale of firearms, those companies that make guns, those that sell them, and those that produce or sell ammunition and a host of other related products all have a clear stake in the bill's contents and its fate. So, too, do law enforcement agencies, hunters, wildlife conservationists, such groups as the National Rifle Association and the American Civil Liberties Union, and several others. Representatives of all of these groups are certain to be invited, or to ask for the opportunity, to present their views to the committee.

Lobbyists often provide useful information to Congress. To the point, John F. Kennedy, who served three terms in the House and was in his second term in the Senate when he won the presidency, observed:

> Competent lobbyists can present the most persuasive arguments in support of their positions. Indeed, there is no more effective manner of learning all important arguments and facts on a controversial issue than to have the opposing lobbyists present their case.
>
> —John F. Kennedy

Lobbyists are ready to do such things as make campaign contributions, provide information, write speeches, and even draft legislation. The contributions are welcome, the information is usually quite accurate, the speeches are forceful, and the bills are well drawn. Most lobbyists know that if they behaved otherwise (gave false or misleading information, for example), they would damage, if not destroy, their credibility and so their overall effectiveness.

Lobbyists work hard to influence committee action, floor debate, and then the final vote in a legislative body. If they fail in one house, they carry their fight to the other. If they lose there, too, they may turn to the executive branch, and perhaps to the courts, as well.

Lobbying and the Executive Branch A vast amount of public policy is made by those who administer the law—that is, by the executive branch. Many of the laws that Congress enacts are written in fairly broad terms. More specific details, such as the day-to-day enforcement of the measure, are left to be worked out in the executive branch. As a practical matter, Congress cannot do such things as prescribe the design specifications for military aircraft, or dictate the advice that federal extension agents are to give to farmers, or determine which of several vaccines will be most effective in the next flu season.

Because meetings with the President and Cabinet officers are difficult to arrange, most executive-branch lobbying focuses, instead, on senior aides in the White House and on the various agencies in the President's administration. The primary job of one of those White House aides, the Director of Public Engagement, is to nurture good relations with major interest groups, especially those that support the President's policies.

Organized interests regularly try to influence the President's appointment of the top officials in various agencies. If an industry group is successful in such efforts, it can improve its chances for favorable treatment by, for example, the Federal Communications Commission or the Bureau of Reclamation in the Department of the Interior.

The most successful lobbyists rely on their networks of contacts as they deal with federal agencies. Ed Rollins, sometime lobbyist and major White House aide in past Republican administrations, put that point this way:

> I've got many friends all through the agencies and equally important, I don't have many enemies. . . . I tell my clients I can get your case moved to the top of the pile.
>
> —Ed Rollins

Lobbying and the Courts Organized interests have recognized the fact that they can use the courts to realize their policy goals. You almost certainly know that in 1954, in *Brown* v. *Topeka Board of Education,* the United States Supreme Court held that segregation by race in public schools is unconstitutional. But do you know that *Brown* was taken to the Supreme Court

KEY FACTS ABOUT LOBBYISTS

— TOP 10 INDUSTRIES —
TYPICALLY REPRESENTED BY LOBBYISTS

★ Pharmaceuticals/Health Products
★ Electronics Manufacturing and Equipment
★ Insurance
★ Business Associations
★ Electric Utilities
★ Oil and Gas
★ Real Estate
★ Hospitals/Nursing Homes
★ Education
★ Securities and Investment

ONE **TECH** AND **SOCIAL**
MEDIA GIANT
moved from the top 20 spenders to the
top 10 as of 2019

Between 1998 and 2009,
LOBBYIST
SPENDING
rose almost 250%

— TOP ISSUE —
LOBBYISTS WANT TO
INFLUENCE
$$ **Federal budget** $$
and appropriations

TOP 3 FOREIGN LOBBYISTS
South Korea
Japan
China

Source: OpenSecrets.org, *The Washington Post*

>> A large amount of lobbyist spending goes to payroll, researching legislation, media campaigns, and contributions to candidates, parties, and political action committees.
Analyze Data Why might foreign countries maintain lobbyists in Washington, D.C.?

by an interest group, the National Association for the Advancement of Colored People? The massive impact that that case has had made the special-interest community realize just how useful the courts can be.

Lawsuits brought by interest groups are not at all uncommon. For some, like the American Civil Liberties Union, legal action is the primary means by which they seek to influence public policy. The ACLU regularly takes on unpopular causes—for example, those involving the free speech rights of fringe groups. Those causes usually have little chance of success in legislative bodies, but they may prevail in a courtroom.

An interest group may also file an **amicus curiae** ("friend of the court") **brief** in a case to which it is not itself a party but in which it does have a stake. An *amicus* brief consists of written arguments presented to a court in support of one side in a dispute. During each session of the Court, more than 100 different organizations submit *amicus* briefs arguing for or against the cases on the docket. In fact, just one case can elicit that many briefs.

Organized interests often try to influence the selection of federal judges, too. For example, both pro-life and pro-choice organizations have urged Republican and Democratic administrations to make nominees' stances on abortion a major condition for appointment to the federal bench.

☑ **GENERATE EXPLANATIONS** Why is it important for the government to monitor lobbyists and their behavior?

Processes Used By Interest Groups—The Indirect Approach

Organized interests also approach government in a number of indirect ways. No matter the particular tactic used, however, the goal is exactly the same as it is when they approach public officials directly—that is, to shape policies to their liking. Not infrequently, interest groups try to mask their involvement in some indirect approach, hoping to make the effort appear to be spontaneous. Their indirect approaches include what is often called "grass-roots lobbying," the molding of public opinion, and various election-related activities.

Apparently, the antelopes are lobbying for an anti-stalking law to be passed...

>> **Analyze Political Cartoons** What grass-roots lobbying tactic does this cartoon highlight?

>> AARP members honor lawmakers who passed legislation benefiting seniors. The AARP, an interest group for people age 50 and older, is one of the most powerful lobbying groups in the United States.

Grass-roots Lobbying Most lobbyists know how to bring **grass-roots pressures**—pressures from members of an interest group or from the people at large, often beginning at a very basic level—to bear on public officials. Many of the groups that the lobbyists speak for can mount campaigns using letters, postcards, phone calls, texts, and e-mails from their supporters, often on very short notice.

Some members of Congress downplay the effectiveness of such efforts, and all of them know that groups orchestrate outpourings of letters, phone calls, e-mails, and the like. Still, every congressional office monitors those communications as a way of tracking constituents' opinions.

No organization uses grass-roots lobbying more effectively than AARP, a group originally known as the American Association of Retired Persons. Founded in 1958, it now has tens of millions of members. Whenever legislation or some administrative action that affects retirees is pending, AARP swings into action. Members of Congress receive more letters, phone calls, and e-mails from members of AARP than they do from any other group.

The Internet and Interest Groups The Internet has been a real boon to interest groups, and to cause-related organizations in particular. Nearly every organized interest has a Web site, an expanding e-mail list, and a growing presence on social media. Blogging and Twitter are used by many groups and have proved quite effective in reaching people in younger age groups.

The Internet has been especially useful to those who want to organize a group but can do so only on a low budget. Some time ago, left-leaning MoveOn.org relied heavily on the Internet's capacity to organize. It was started by a pair of Silicon Valley entrepreneurs in Berkeley, California, in 1998. Eventually, they formed an Internet network linking hundreds of thousands of citizens who could be mobilized to support liberal candidates and causes. MoveOn.org raised more than $21 million for Democratic candidates in 2012, and it also conducted a massive get-out-the-vote effort.

Demonstrations and protest marches are another form of grass-roots lobbying. Most are efforts to show public officials that some group's cause does have broad public support. The massive number of Black Lives Matter demonstrations following the death of George Floyd in the spring and summer of 2020 is a good example. Some involve an element of political theater or an eye-catching gimmick to attract media (especially television) coverage. During the Vietnam War, peace groups often staged "die-ins" to protest war, and farmers might drive their tractors to Washington in "tractorcades" to dramatize their opposition to some agricultural policy.

Several groups now publish ratings of members of Congress. These rankings are based on the votes cast on measures these groups regard as crucial to their interests. Among the more prominent organizations that do so are such liberal groups as Americans for Democratic Action (ADA) and the American Civil Liberties Union (ACLU) and such conservative ones as the American Conservative

U.S. Chamber of Commerce Lifetime Scores,
Selected U.S. Representatives

NAME	PARTY	STATE	% LIFETIME "FOR" VOTES*
Kay Granger	R	Texas	93
James McGovern	D	Massachusetts	35
Nancy Pelosi	D	California	29
Donna Shalala	D	Florida	63
Michael Simpson	R	Idaho	92
Don Young	R	Alaska	79

*Based on votes cast on top Chamber issues. SOURCE: U.S. Chamber of Commerce
"For" votes are those supporting the chamber's position.

>> The Chamber of Commerce ranks members of Congress based on how often they supported top Chamber issues. **Analyze Charts** What does this data show about party support for the Chamber?

Union (ACU) and the Chamber of Commerce of the United States.

Each of these groups sees to it that the mass media publicize their ratings. They also distribute them to the group's membership. Their ultimate objective is either to persuade less-than-friendly legislators to change their voting behavior or to help bring about their defeat in future elections.

Interest Groups and Public Opinion Many organized interests spend much of their time and energy on attempts to mold public opinion. Groups that can make enough people regard them and their cause in the best possible way, and can persuade enough people to convey that feeling to public officials, have taken a major step toward achieving their policy goals.

Cell phones, televisions, newspapers, and magazines are filled with costly advertisements by oil, cell phone, drug, insurance companies, and many others—all seeking to cast the sponsor of the ad in a favorable light. Most of those ads go well beyond promoting some particular product and try also to suggest that the organizations behave as good citizens or defend family values or protect the environment, and so on.

A group's own membership can be used to shape opinions. Thus, in its decades-long opposition (since abandoned) to national health insurance proposals, the American Medical Association persuaded many doctors to put literature condemning those proposals as "socialized medicine" in their waiting rooms and to talk with patients about the issue. Using those tactics, the AMA capitalized on the tendency of most patients to respect their own physicians and regard them as experts.

Many groups use well-regarded personalities or trusted public figures to persuade people to support the group's cause. The National Rifle Association (NRA), formed in 1871, provides a good example of this strategy.

The NRA is a major political force, with millions of active members who write letters, contact their members of Congress, and raise awareness regarding important contemporary issues related to 2nd Amendment rights. The group also supports firearms education and lobbies vigorously to influence proposed gun control legislation across the nation. The NRA helps get its viewpoint out to the public through such famous personalities as the late Charlton Heston. Mr. Heston served two terms as president of the NRA and had a long

>> Actor Michael J. Fox (right) and the late former boxing champion Muhammad Ali (left) have lent their names to raising awareness and funds for Parkinson's Disease.

>> PACs and SuperPACs are two groups that lobby the government. **Analyze Political Cartoons** What is this cartoonist saying about the influence of interest groups on elections?

record of support for the 2nd Amendment. He was much better known, however, for his long career as an actor. The wide recognition of his name and the moral authority associated with many of the characters he played in movies were extremely helpful to the NRA in its efforts to protect and expand the rights of Americans to keep and bear arms.

The Mass Media and Interest Groups Almost certainly, though, the most effective vehicle for the molding of opinions and attitudes is the mass media. Interest groups know that people are more likely to regard their positions favorably if their activities are covered by the media as news rather than presented to the public in paid advertisements. With that in mind, interest groups produce a veritable flood of press releases, interviews, studies, and other materials, hoping to attract media coverage.

Propaganda Techniques Interest groups try to create the public attitudes they want by using propaganda. Propaganda is a technique of persuasion aimed at influencing individual or group behaviors. Its goal is to create a particular belief among the audience. That belief may be completely true or false, or it may lie somewhere between those extremes. Today, people tend to think of propaganda

as a form of lying and deception. As a technique, however, propaganda is neither moral nor immoral; it is, instead, amoral.

Propaganda does not use objective logic. Rather, it begins with a conclusion. Then it brings together any evidence that will support that conclusion and disregards information that will not. Propagandists are advertisers, persuaders—and occasionally even brain washers—who are interested in influencing others to agree with their point of view.

The development of the mass media in this country encouraged the use of propaganda, first in the field of commercial advertising, and then in politics. To be successful, propaganda must be presented in simple, interesting, and credible terms. Talented propagandists almost never attack the logic of a policy they oppose. Instead, they often attack it with name-calling. That is, they attach such labels as "communist" or "fascist." Other labels include "ultraliberal," "ultraconservative," "pie-in-the-sky," or "greedy." Or, they try to discredit a policy or person by card stacking—that is, presenting only one side of the issue.

Policies that propagandists support receive labels that will produce favorable reactions. They use such glittering generalities as "American," "sound," "fair," and "just." Symbols are often used

MAJOR PROPAGANDA TECHNIQUES

NAME-CALLING
ATTACHING LABELS

"The **ultraliberal** supporters say...."

GLITTERING GENERALITIES
USING POSITIVE, GENERAL TERMINOLOGY AND SYMBOLS

"I believe in **freedom** and **democracy**...."

CARD-STACKING
PRESENTING ONLY ONE — SIDE OF AN ISSUE —

"**Reduces costs** 30%...."

BANDWAGON APPROACH
FOLLOWING THE CROWD

"Join **thousands of others** by supporting...."

TESTIMONIALS
PRESENTING ENDORSEMENTS FROM CELEBRITIES OR ATHLETES

"This **famous movie star** uses our product...."

PLAIN-FOLKS APPROACH
PRETENDING TO BE COMMON PEOPLE

"**Regular folks** like you and me know that...."

>> Using a variety of persuasive techniques, propaganda seeks to create a desired belief. **Analyze Charts** How do these techniques encourage the public to "join the crowd"?

to elicit those positive reactions from people, too: Uncle Sam and the American flag are favorites. So, too, are testimonials—endorsements, or supporting statements, from such well-known personalities as television stars or professional athletes. The bandwagon approach, which urges people to follow the crowd, is another favorite technique. The plain-folks approach, in which the propagandist pretends to be one of the common people, gets heavy use, too.

Logical fallacies is another propaganda technique that may be used. In this common approach, the propagandist makes an argument that sounds logical but upon further inspection is found to lack supporting evidence or to be based on faulty reasoning. Many types of logical fallacies exist. One is the *ad hominem* approach. In this type of propaganda, the propagandist attacks the opponent, rather than the opponent's position. For example: Joe Smith proposes that we change our immigration policies, but in fact, Smith was himself arrested last year for building without a permit. Although Smith broke the law, that does not mean that his immigration proposal is poor or invalid.

Logical fallacies might also make the mistaken assumption that if A occurred after B then B must have caused A: The war was going badly and now Senator Ruiz has spoken against our involvement and so Senator Ruiz has caused the war to go badly. Other types of logical fallacies include:

- the *slippery slope,* which assumes that if A happens, eventually B, C, and D will happen (which is not necessarily true);
- the *hasty generalization,* which is a rush to a conclusion without sufficient evidence;
- the *straw man fallacy,* in which the propagandist sets up a weak version of the opponent's position and then easily disproves it;
- the *circular argument,* which attempts to make a point by using the same argument expressed in different ways: Candidate A is the best candidate for communicating with the people because she is good at speaking to voters.

Propaganda is spread through newspapers, radio, television, the Internet, movies, billboards, books, magazines, pamphlets, posters, speeches—in fact, through every form of mass communication. The more controversial or less popular a group's position, the more necessary the propaganda campaign becomes.

Interest Groups and Electioneering The most useful and the most appreciated thing that an interest group can do for a public official is to help that person win office. From the group's perspective, electing officeholders like members of Congress, State legislators, governors, and other State and local policymakers sympathetic to their interests is among the most effective things it can do. Once elected, these individuals can shape legislation and allocate money to meet the needs of the interest groups.

Groups can and do help those who run for office, and they do so in a variety of ways. Many do so through their political action committees. Recall that PACs are political arms of interest groups. They make financial contributions and hold fundraisers for candidates. They conduct voter registration and get-out-the-vote drives, supply professional campaign consultants, and provide information to be used in campaign speeches. Occasionally they even provide audiences to hear those speeches. And PACs do such other things as help staff local campaign offices, distribute campaign literature, work phone banks, and take voters to the polls on election day.

☑ **INFER** Why do interest groups continue to utilize propaganda, and why is it particularly effective?

☑ ASSESSMENT

1. **Connect** Explain the relationship between interest groups and legislation.

2. **Compare** How are political parties and interest groups similar?

3. **Draw Conclusions** How do the American people benefit MOST from public-interest groups?

4. **Classify** If a lobbyist were to organize a large-scale protest march, would this be an example of effective direct lobbying? Why or why not?

5. **Evaluate** What is the origin of interest groups in the United States? What is their role in determining and shaping public policy?

Topic 10 Quick Study Guide

LESSON SUMMARIES

Use these Lesson Summaries, and the longer versions available online, to review the key ideas for each lesson in this Topic.

Lesson 1: The History of Voting Rights

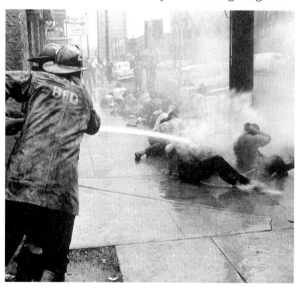

In 1789, the vote was restricted to white male property owners. Property qualifications were eliminated in the early 1800s. African American men gained the right to vote in 1870, but were largely prevented from doing so until the 1960s. Women gained the right to vote in 1920. The minimum voting age was lowered to 18 in 1971.

Lesson 2: Your Right to Vote

To qualify to vote, a person must be a citizen, a legal resident of the state where he or she will vote, and over 18. In most states, voters must be registered to cast a ballot. In the past, states used additional qualifications such as literacy tests to restrict voting, but this has been banned.

Lesson 3: Voting Trends

Millions of Americans are qualified to vote but choose not to. Many believe their votes will not make a difference or feel alienated from the political system. For those who do vote, a variety of factors influences how they will do so. These include income, occupation, racial and ethnic background, geography, and party identification.

Lesson 4: The Voting Process

Most elected officials in the United States are at the state or local level, and so most election law is written by the states. However, Congress sets the dates and rules for Federal elections. State laws require secret ballots, though the actual casting of votes may be done on paper, by machine, or electronically.

Lesson 5: Public Opinion and Polling

Public opinion refers to the attitudes held by a significant number of people on matters of government and politics. Public opinion is influenced by a huge variety of factors, including families, schools, and the mass media. Polls are a good way to measure public opinion, when done according to scientific techniques.

Lesson 6: Influencing Public Opinion: The Mass Media

The mass media has an important role in shaping public opinion. It can help set the public agenda by focusing on some issues rather than others. Its influence is limited, however, by the fact that few people follow political issues closely, and those who do generally watch or read sources that agree with views they already hold.

Lesson 7: Understanding Interest Groups

Interest groups are collections of people who share political views and work together to shape public policy. These groups vary widely in size and organization, and deal with many different kinds of issues. Interest groups may directly lobby government to advance their goals, or work indirectly to influence policymakers and public opinion.

VISUAL REVIEW

Use these graphics to review some of the key terms, people, and ideas from this Topic.

Conducting a Poll

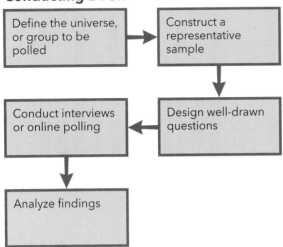

Influences on Public Opinion

Voter Qualifications

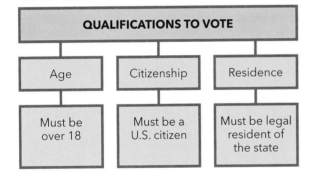

Expansion of Voting Rights in the U.S.

Topic 10 Assessment

KEY TERMS, PEOPLE, AND IDEAS

1. What is an **off-year election**, and how does it affect voter turnout?

2. What is the **gender gap**?

3. **Literacy** and a **poll tax** were once common voter requirements. What do those terms mean?

4. What is a **ballot**?

5. How is **public opinion** sometimes affected by the views expressed by **opinion leaders**?

6. What is **suffrage**?

7. What is the **public agenda**, and how does the **media** help shape it?

8. What is **propaganda**?

CRITICAL THINKING

9. **Express Ideas Clearly** How did the Civil Rights Acts and the Voting Rights Act lead to expanded civil rights?

10. **Support Ideas with Evidence** How did *South Carolina* v. *Katzenbach* (1966) and *Shelby* v. *Holder* (2013) affect the Voting Rights Act of 1965?

11. **Analyze** How was the Help America Vote Act of 2002 an attempt to resolve voting issues in the presidential election of 2000?

12. **Explain** How have the roles of television, radio, press, and the Internet in political communication changed in recent years?

13. **Evaluate** How does the mass media shape public policy today?

14. **Evaluate** How do interest groups shape public policy today?

15. **Express Ideas Clearly** In *The Federalist* No. 10, James Madison argued that factions—what we now call interest groups—could, if left unchecked, dominate public decision making because of their size, resources, and/or leadership. Do you think that Madison was correct? Do interest groups today threaten the well-being of the American political system?

16. **Analyze** The graph at the top of the next column shows voter turnout in the United States for presidential and congressional elections from 1992 to 2012. Using the data in this graph and what you read in this topic, describe recent trends in voter turnout.

Voter Turnout, 1992-2012

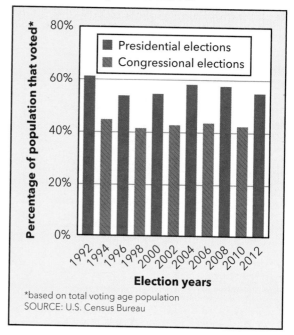

*based on total voting age population
SOURCE: U.S. Census Bureau

17. **Evaluate** Evaluate the importance of political participation and civic participation in the American democratic system. Is voting an important responsibility for American citizens?

18. **Compare and Contrast** Compare and contrast how the press influenced politics and public policy during the Vietnam War and Civil Rights movement.

19. **Explain** In what ways are interest groups both practical and democratic? Give examples of interest groups behaving in both practical and democratic ways.

20. **Interpret** What are three factors that even scientifically constructed polls have difficulty accounting for? In addition to their occasional inaccuracy, what is another common criticism of polls? Why do poll results sometimes differ from election outcomes?

21. **Writing Activity** Select a recent election at the local, State, or federal level. Using resources as guided by your teacher, research the course and outcome of this election. In an essay, evaluate the election's processes and results. Who won the election? How did the successful candidate win the support of voters? Why did the losing candidate(s) lose?

DOCUMENT-BASED QUESTIONS

The Internet has become a critical part of daily life for many Americans. Should the nation move to online voting?

DOCUMENT A

The statistics below show the percentage of American adults in various age groups who use the Internet, and how those percentages have changed over time.

- 18-29 years old: 2005: 83%; 2010: 92%; 2015: 96%
- 30-49 years old: 2005: 79%; 2010: 85%; 2015: 93%
- 50-64 years old: 2005: 66%; 2010: 74%; 2015: 81%
- 65 years or older: 2005: 28%; 2010: 43%; 2015: 58%

—*Pew Research Center, "Americans' Internet Access, 2000-2015"*

DOCUMENT B

The organization WebRoots Democracy works to encourage online voting for a number of reasons.

The potential benefits of online voting are many and include:

- Greater levels of voter participation
- A method of independently voting for those with vision-impairments
- An accessible method of voting for those with other disabilities
- Long-term savings in the cost of elections
- Accurate vote counts
- The elimination of accidentally spoilt ballots
- Greater security of the ballot
- A method of better informing the electorate about each election
- A future-proofed method of voting for an increasingly digital age

—*WebRootsDemocracy.org*

DOCUMENT C

This excerpt describes some of the complications involved in developing a secure online voting system.

Voting [online] is much trickier [than shopping or banking] for a couple of reasons. Whereas monetary transactions are based on a firm understanding of your identity, a vote is supposed to be anonymous. In case of bank trouble, investigators can trace a credit-card purchase back to you, but how can they track an anonymous vote?

And credit-card and bank fraud goes on constantly. It's just a cost of doing business. But the outcome of an election is too important; we can't simply ignore a bunch of lost or altered votes.

—*David Pogue, "When Will We Be Able to Vote Online?," Scientific American, February 1, 2016*

DOCUMENT D

President Barack Obama described his views on the importance of using technology to enhance democracy.

How do people engage and relate to their government? You know, our constitutional design is remarkable; it has lasted for many years. But it's no secret that many people feel alienated and distant from government. And I think the opportunities for us to think about how tech can empower citizens and make them feel ownership for their government is really important. . . .

How can technology enhance the experience of democracy? How can we make it easier to vote? How can we make it easier for like-minded citizens to petition their government in a way that is meaningful?

—*Barack Obama, "President Obama: The Fast Company Interview," Fast Company, June 15, 2015*

22. According to the statistics in Document A, Internet use by members of which age group increased by the most percentage points between 2005 and 2015? Which group had the smallest increase between 2005 and 2015?
   A. 30-49, 65+
   B. 18-29, 50-64
   C. 50-64, 30-49
   D. 65+, 18-29

23. What main point is made by Document C?
   A. The challenges of voting online are similar to those posed by shopping or banking online.
   B. The challenges of voting online are so great that it will likely never be a reality.
   C. Voting online must be anonymous and have a low risk of fraud.
   D. Electoral fraud is just as likely with online voting as voting with paper ballots.

24. **Writing Task** Using these documents and what you have learned in this topic, analyze the possible benefits and risks involved in online voting. Should the Federal Government and the States move to encourage online voting? In your response, defend your stand and critique the perspectives in these documents.

Elections

ESSENTIAL QUESTION Who Gets Elected?

Election campaign signs of political candidates in Boise, Idaho

Connections to Today

Clubs. Some people like them and some people don't. They can be fun because members share a common interest, such as music or community service. The more members the club has, the more impact it has. Likewise, when people want the same political outcomes—electing a President or getting a law passed—they often join a political party.

In this Topic, you'll learn how the two major political parties—Democrats and Republicans—give people the ability to shape public policy. Do political parties help unify or divide Americans?

An introduction to the methods that political operatives use to influence public opinion.

BOUNCE to Activate My Story Video

In this Topic, you will learn about political parties and about the way elections work in the United States, including the mysterious electoral college and the controversial role of money. Look at the lesson outline and explore the timeline. As you study this Topic, you'll complete the Quest Inquiry.

LESSON OUTLINE

11.1 Political Parties and What They Do

11.2 Nominations

11.3 Electing the President

11.4 Money and Elections

Elections and Political Parties

1800
Thomas Jefferson's election begins an era of Democratic Party domination.

1831
First national convention to nominate a presidential candidate is held in Baltimore.

1932
The Depression brings about a return of the Democrats to power.

1974
Federal Election Commission is established by Congress to oversee campaign finance law.

2002
Bipartisan Campaign Reform Act seeks to reduce the amount of money in elections.

1800   1850   1900   1950   2000   2050

1860
Abraham Lincoln's election begins 75 years of Republican Party supremacy.

1907
Congress passes first law regulating the use of money in federal elections.

1968
From this election on, neither party consistently holds the presidency.

2010
Supreme Court strikes down campaign spending limits as a violation of free speech.

QUEST! INQUIRY

Civic Discussion: The Electoral College

You probably already know that the electoral college is not a school. In fact, the electoral college never even meets in one place. What the electoral college does do is elect the President *and* generate a good deal of controversy. In this Quest, you will consider differing viewpoints on the electoral college and discuss whether or not this system should be abolished.

STEP 1

Read the Discussion Launch and decide with your group which are the major points in the reading.

STEP 2

Read and analyze the source documents relating to the debate. Determine the central idea of each and evaluate the authors' differing points of view.

STEP 3

Find evidence in the sources that supports your position. Prepare for the discussion, formulate arguments, consider both sides, and ask and answer clarifying questions.

STEP 4

Participate in a thoughtful, well-reasoned discussion. Present your arguments and evidence and consider and challenge those presented by others.

This aerial view of a Republican National Convention shows the festivity and crowd reaction as their nominee accepts the presidential nomination.

 BOUNCE to Activate Flipped Video

Objectives

Understand the origins of political parties in the United States and analyze their functions.

Understand multiparty and one-party systems and how they affect the functioning of a political system, and explain the two-party system of the United States.

Evaluate the role of minor parties that have been active in American politics, and understand why they are important.

Understand why the major parties have a decentralized structure.

Describe the national party machinery and party organization at the State and local levels.

Key Terms

political party
political spectrum
partisanship
single-member
  districts
plurality
bipartisan
consensus
coalition
ideological

single-issue parties
economic protest
  parties
splinter parties
ward
precinct
Thomas Jefferson
George Washington
Theodore Roosevelt

Political Parties and What They Do

"Winning isn't everything; it's the only thing." So said legendary football coach "Red" Sanders. Sanders was talking about college football teams. He might just as well have had the Republican and Democratic parties in mind. They, too, are in the business of competing and winning.

What Is a Political Party?

A **political party** is a group of persons who seek to control government through the winning of elections and the holding of public office. This definition of a political party is broad enough to cover any party, including the two major parties in American politics, the Republicans and the Democrats. Another, more specific definition can be used to describe most political parties, both here and abroad: a group of persons, joined together on the basis of certain common principles, who seek to control government in order to secure the adoption of certain public policies and programs.

This latter definition, with its emphasis on principles and policy positions, does not perfectly fit the two major parties in the United States, however. The Republican and Democratic parties care a great deal about certain issues, but they are also highly *election*-oriented. A "hybrid model" is the best way to describe parties in the United States.

You can better understand our two major parties if you recognize that each of them is an organization made up of three separate but closely related elements, three separate groups of party loyalists:

1. *The party organization.* This element of the party includes its leaders, its other activists, and its many workers—all those who give their time, money, and skills to the party. In short, these are the party "professionals," those who run the party at the national, State, and local levels.

2. *The party in government.* This component includes the party's candidates and officeholders, those thousands of persons who run for or hold elective or appointive offices in the executive, legislative, and judicial branches at the federal, State, and local levels of government.

3. *The party in the electorate.* These are the millions of people who call themselves Republicans or Democrats, and who support the party and its candidates most of the time. Many of them cast their votes on the basis of the party label, without regard to candidates or issues in an election. Observers sometimes criticize this kind of voting behavior as thoughtless. Yet knowing that a candidate is a Republican or Democrat often provides useful clues about where a candidate stands on key issues.

☑ **DRAW CONCLUSIONS** Why would voters cast their votes based solely on a candidate's party affiliation?

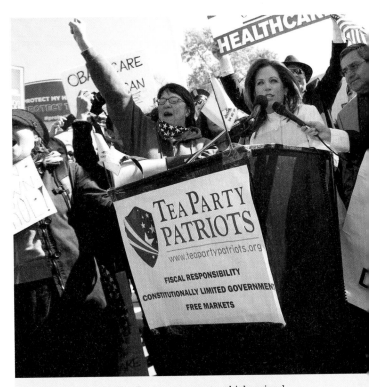

>> Party members who feel strongly about their party's candidates often volunteer to inspire others to support them by cold calling voters.

The Role of Political Parties

It is clear from our history, and from the histories of other peoples as well, that political parties are absolutely essential to democratic government. They are a vital link between the people and their government, between the governed and those who govern. Indeed, many observers argue that political parties are the principal means by which the will of the people is made known to government and by which government is held accountable to the people.

Parties serve the democratic ideal in another significant way: They work to blunt conflict; they are "power brokers." Political parties seek to modify the contending views of various interests and groups, encourage compromise, and so help to unify, rather than divide, the American people. Historically, they have been successful in their attempts to soften the impact of extremists at both ends of the **political spectrum**, the range of political views.

Again, parties are indispensable to democratic government and, so, to American government. That fact is underscored by the several significant functions they perform.

>> The grassroots Tea Party movement, which gained national attention during the 2010 election campaign, advocated lower taxes, less government, and reduction of the national debt.

Nominating Candidates The major function of a political party is to nominate— or name—candidates for public office. That is, parties select candidates and present them to the voters. Then the parties work to help those nominees win elections.

In a functioning democracy, there must be some way to find (choose and recruit) candidates for office. There must also be some mechanism to gather support for those candidates. Parties are the best device yet found to do these jobs.

The nominating function is almost exclusively a party function in the United States. It is the one activity that most clearly sets political parties apart from all of the other groups that operate in the political process. For example, interest groups do not nominate candidates for office.

Informing and Activating Supporters Parties inform the people and inspire and activate their interest and their participation in public affairs, including encouraging changes on political issues. Other groups also perform this function—in particular, the news media and interest groups.

Parties try to inform and inspire voters in several ways. Mostly, they do so by campaigning for their candidates, taking stands on current issues, and criticizing opposing candidates and their positions.

>> Former Vice President Joe Biden and his wife, Jill, wave to supporters at the end of his speech at the 2020 Democratic National Convention. The goal of such events is to create enthusiasm for the party's candidates.

How Political Parties Inform People Each party tries to inform the people as it thinks they should be informed—that is, to its own advantage. It conducts its "educational" efforts through Web sites, pamphlets, signs, buttons, and stickers; advertisements in newspapers and magazines and via radio, television, the Internet, and text messaging; at speeches, rallies, and conventions; and in many other ways.

Remember, both parties want to win elections, and that consideration has much to do with the stands they take on most issues. And so it is that both Republicans and Democrats historically have tried to shape positions that will attract as many voters as possible.

The Bonding Agent Function In the business world, a bond is an agreement that protects a person or a company against loss caused by a third party. In politics, a political party acts as a "bonding agent," to ensure the good performance of its candidates and elected officeholders.

In choosing its candidates, the party usually tries to make sure that they are both qualified and of good character—or, at the least, that they are not unqualified for the public offices they seek.

The party also prompts its successful candidates to perform well in office. The democratic process imposes this bonding agent function on a party, whether the party really wants to perform it or not. If it fails to assume the responsibility, both the party and its candidates may suffer the consequences of that failure in future elections.

Governing In several respects, government in the United States is government by party. For example, public officeholders—those who govern—are regularly chosen on the basis of party. Congress and the State legislatures are organized on party lines, and they conduct much of their business on the basis of **partisanship**—the strong support of their party and its policy stands. Most appointments to executive offices, at both the federal and State levels, are made with an eye to party.

Political parties also play a role in determining and shaping public policy. Party members and their elected officials advocate for those policies that coincide with their party's platform—and oppose those that do not. They rally support behind important legislation, which can help to get it enacted.

Parties help government function in another way as well, by helping to conquer what scholars call "constitutional obstruction." In the complicated separation of powers arrangement, the executive and legislative branches must cooperate with one another if government is to accomplish anything. It is political parties that regularly provide the channels through which these two branches are able to work together.

Political parties have also been known to play a role in the process of constitutional change. Consider this important example: The Constitution's cumbersome system for choosing a President works principally because political parties reshaped it in its earliest years, and they generally have made it work ever since.

The Watchdog Function Parties act as watchdogs over the public's business. This is particularly true of the party out of power, which criticizes the policies of the party in power. In American politics, the party in power has traditionally been the party that controls the executive branch of government.

This definition is useful under a unified government. Since the late 1960s, however, government in the United States has been more often divided, with one party controlling the White House and the other controlling one or both houses of Congress. In this situation, the term *party in power* loses some of its meaning, because it is no longer as obvious which party that is.

During President Obama's first two years in office, the government was unified under the Democrats while the Republicans attempted to convince the voters to "throw the rascals out." This scrutiny by the "out" party tends to make the "rascals" more careful of their public charge and more responsive to the people. The party out of power plays the important role of "the loyal opposition"—opposed to the party in power but loyal to the people and the nation.

During the last six years of Barack Obama's presidency, however, the Republicans controlled at least one house of Congress. While the Democrats were theoretically the party in power, their agenda was checked at every turn. So which party had more control over the direction of public policy for those six years—and which was the watchdog?

Political Parties Help Make Democracy Work Again, these functions performed by political parties and, particularly, the two major parties, testify to the important role they play in making democracy work in this country. You might well remember that point the next time a comedian on late-night television ridicules some candidate, party, or officeholder.

There was a time when the parties played an even larger role in the nation's affairs than they do today. For example, in what has been called "the golden age of parties," from roughly the late nineteenth to the mid-twentieth century,

>> A political party logo is a symbol that represents the entire party. The Republicans and Democrats have adopted the elephant and the donkey respectively to represent their parties.

party organizations operated as major welfare organizations in many places in the United States. They regularly helped newly arrived immigrants and many others among the poor to obtain food, housing, and jobs. Often they did this to win the support of these people at the polls. That once-important welfare function has long since been taken over by a number of government programs put in place in the twentieth century.

☑ **IDENTIFY CENTRAL ISSUES** How do political parties help to unify the American people?

The Two-Party System

Two major parties, the Republicans and the Democrats, dominate American politics. That is to say, this country has a two-party system. In a typical election in the United States, only the Republican or the Democratic Party's candidates have a reasonable chance of winning public office.

It is true that in some States, and in many local communities, one of the two major parties may be overwhelmingly dominant, winning election after election. And it may do so for a long time—as, for example, the Democratic Party dominated the politics of the South from the years after the Civil War into the 1960s. But, on the whole, and through most of our history, the United States has been a two-party nation.

Several factors explain why America has a two-party system. No one of these factors alone offers a satisfactory explanation, but taken together, they are quite persuasive.

The Historical Basis The two-party system in the United States is rooted in the nation's beginnings. The argument over the ratification of the Constitution caused the nation to split into two sides: the Federalists, led by Alexander Hamilton, and the Anti-Federalists, led by **Thomas Jefferson**. The Federalists were "the rich and well-born" and supported a stronger national government. The Anti-Federalists sided with the "common man" and favored a more limited national government.

Following ratification, the Framers hoped to heal the breach between the Federalists and Anti-Federalists. To them, parties were "factions" and therefore agents of divisiveness and disunity. **George Washington** expressed this view in his 1796 Farewell Address, when he warned the new nation against "the baneful effects of the spirit of party."

>> In his Farewell Address, Washington said, "The common and continual mischiefs of the spirit of party are sufficient to make it the interest and duty of a wise people to discourage and restrain it."

It is hardly surprising, then, that the Constitution does not mention political parties. What is surprising is that, despite the Framers' misgivings, parties turned out to be the main engine driving the gears of government.

Most scholars agree that parties in the United States were born during the election of 1796. In that campaign, John Adams became the presidential candidate for the Federalist Party and Thomas Jefferson carried the banner for the Democratic-Republicans. Adams won that contest, but the two candidates faced each other again in 1800, and this time Jefferson came out on top. The Federalists never returned to power. From 1800 to 1828, the United States was virtually a one-party nation, with the Democratic-Republicans—known as the Democrats by 1828—actually running unopposed in 1820.

Only rarely in American history has a party other than one of the two major parties gained any real power. This was the case in 1912, when former President **Theodore Roosevelt** formed his "Bull Moose" Progressive Party. He lost the election but came in second—ahead of the Republican Party candidate. In 1924, Robert La Follette's Progressive Party had a strong showing, and in 1968, George Wallace's American Independent Party did well in a number of southern States. In 1992, independent candidate and business executive Ross Perot netted 19 percent of the popular vote, but did not win a single electoral college vote.

Overall, the history of the American party system after 1800 can be divided into four major periods. During the first three, one or the other of the two major parties dominated, regularly holding the presidency and usually both houses of Congress. The nation is now in a new period, much of it marked by divided government. Many observers suggest that the legislative gridlock at the national level today is rooted in that divided party control.

The Force of Tradition Once established, human institutions are likely to become self-perpetuating. So it has been with the two-party system. The very fact that the nation began with a two-party system has been a leading reason for the retention of a two-party system.

The point can be made this way: Most Americans accept the idea of a two-party system simply because there has always been one. This inbred support for the arrangement is a principal reason why challenges to the system—by minor parties, for example—have made so little headway.

The Electoral System Several features of the American electoral system promote the existence of but two major parties. Many of the details of the election process work to discourage minor parties.

The prevalence of **single-member districts** is one of the most important of these features. Nearly all of the elections held in this country—from the presidential contest to those at the local levels—are single-member district elections.

That is, they are contests in which only one candidate is elected to each office on the ballot. They are winner-take-all elections. The winning candidate is the one who receives a **plurality**, or the largest number of votes cast for the office. Note that a plurality need not be a majority, which is more than half of all votes cast in any given election.

Because only one winner can come out of each contest, voters usually face only two viable choices: They can vote for the candidate of the party holding the office, or they can vote for the candidate of the party with the best chance of replacing the current officeholder. In short, the single-member district arrangement has led many voters to think of a vote for a minor party candidate as a "wasted vote."

Election Law Discourages Non-Major-Party Candidates Another important aspect of the electoral system works to the same end. Much of American election law is purposely written to discourage non-major-party candidates.

In fact, almost all of the nearly 7,400 State legislators are either Democrats or Republicans. Only a handful of minor party members or independents now sit, or have ever sat, in State legislatures. The GOP (Republican Party) and the Democrats regularly act in a **bipartisan** way in this matter. That is, the two major parties work together to shape election laws in such a way that minor party or independent candidates have a much harder time winning elective office.

Every four years, the presidential contest offers a striking illustration of this situation. In 2016, Democrat Hillary Clinton and Republican Donald Trump were listed on the ballots of all 50 States and the District of Columbia. However, only one of the other non-major party candidates—Libertarian Gary Johnson—made it to the ballot in every State. The others suffered their usual fate: making the ballot of merely one, two, or three States.

The American Ideological Consensus

Americans are, on the whole, historically an ideologically homogeneous people. That is, over time, the American people have shared many of the same ideals, basic principles, and patterns of belief.

>> Cartoonist Thomas Nast is credited with popularizing the donkey and elephant symbols. **Analyze Political Cartoons** What characteristics of each animal might appeal to its respective party?

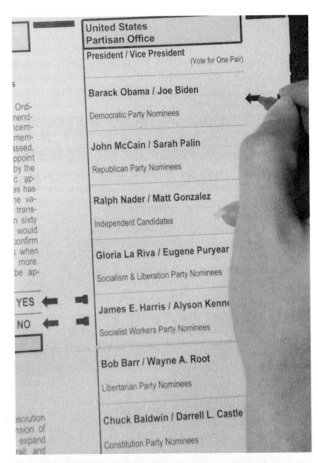

>> This absentee ballot from the 2008 presidential election lists all the candidates from the major parties and the minor parties.

This is not to say that Americans are all alike. Clearly, this is not the case. The United States is a pluralistic society—one consisting of several distinct cultures and groups. Increasingly, the members of various ethnic, racial, religious, and other social groups compete for and share in the exercise of political power in this country. Still, there is a broad **consensus**—a general agreement among various groups—on matters of fundamental importance.

Nor is it to say that Americans have always agreed with one another on important policy questions. The nation has been deeply divided at times, such as during the Civil War and the Great Depression, and over such critical issues as racial discrimination, the war in Vietnam, abortion, and immigration. Still, the United States has not been regularly plagued by sharp and unbridgeable political divisions. This country has been free of longstanding, bitter disputes based on such factors as economic class, social status, religious beliefs, or national origin.

Ideology and Political Parties Those conditions that could produce several strong rival parties simply do not exist in this country. The United States differs from most other democracies in this way. In short, the realities of American society and politics make it unlikely that a multiparty system would take hold in the United States.

Historically, this broad ideological consensus has led to parties that often look alike. Compared to other political systems, American parties tend to be moderate; both are built on compromise and usually try to occupy the "middle of the road." Both parties seek the same prize: the votes of a majority of the electorate. To capture that prize, they must win over essentially the same people. Inevitably, then, both parties stay away from extreme policy positions.

Of course there have been significant differences between the two major parties in recent decades. For example, the Democratic Party, and those who usually vote for its candidates, are more likely to support such things as social welfare programs, government regulation of business practices, and efforts to improve the status of minorities. On the other hand, the Republican Party and its supporters are more likely to favor the play of private market forces in the economy and to argue that the Federal Government should be less extensively involved in social welfare programs.

Of late, arguments between the two parties on key issues of the day have been bitter and seemingly unresolvable. One of the most important trends in recent years, in fact, has been the increasing role played by those at the extreme ends of the political spectrum. Despite this trend, the two-party model

THE AMERICAN POLITICAL SPECTRUM

LEFT		CENTER		RIGHT
PROGRESSIVE Favors major change to create an altered or entirely new social system.	**LIBERAL** Believes that government must take action on economic, political, and social issues to help citizens and the environment.	**MODERATE** Holds beliefs that fall between liberal and conservative views, usually including some of each.	**CONSERVATIVE** Seeks to keep in place the economic, political, and social structures of society.	**FAR RIGHT** Favors major change to restore society to an earlier, more conservative state of affairs.

EXAMPLES OF POSITIONS ON CLIMATE CHANGE

PROGRESSIVE Achieve net-zero greenhouse gas emissions by 2030 through strict regulations	**LIBERAL** Achieve net-zero greenhouse gas emissions by 2050, partly by taxing emissions	**MODERATE** Work toward net-zero emissions without a specific target date and through the use of a progressive emissions tax	**CONSERVATIVE** Reduce power plant carbon emissions without the federal government setting required limits or taxing emissions	**FAR RIGHT** Allow industry to decide whether and what steps it will take to address emissions

>> This graphic depicting the American political spectrum is useful for understanding the basic ideologies in the United States. In reality, however, many people cross over the lines depending on the issue. A person might be liberal on social issues but a conservative on fiscal matters, for example.

Multiparty vs. Two-Party Systems

18th German Bundestag

64 seats Left Party

63 seats Alliance '90/ Green Party

309 seats Christian Democratic Union/ Christian Social Union

193 seats Social Democratic Party

Total seats = 630*

SOURCE: German Bundestag   *1 independent member

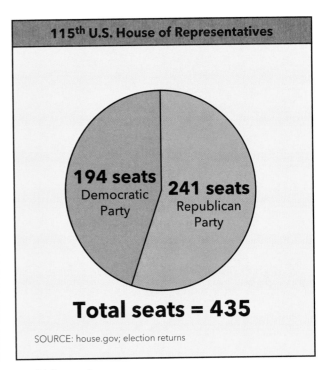

115th U.S. House of Representatives

194 seats Democratic Party

241 seats Republican Party

Total seats = 435

SOURCE: house.gov; election returns

>> In the 18th German Bundestag, no party held a majority of seats, which meant no party on its own could get bills passed. **Analyze Charts** How are majorities built in the German Bundestag?

has so far continued to push the policy agenda toward the middle.

☑ **SUMMARIZE** Describe how single-member districts discourage minor parties.

Multiparty and One-Party Politics

Some critics argue that the American two-party system should be scrapped. They would replace it with a multiparty arrangement, a system with several major and many lesser parties. Multiparty systems have long been a feature of most European democracies, and they are now found in many other democratic societies elsewhere in the world.

In a multiparty system, parties are based on a particular interest—for example, economic class, religious belief, or political ideology. Those who favor such an arrangement say it would provide for a broader representation of the electorate and be more responsive to the will of the people. They claim that a multiparty system would give voters a much more meaningful choice among candidates and policies than the present two-party system does.

Multiparty Politics Strengths and Weaknesses
Multiparty systems do tend to produce a broader, more diverse representation of the electorate. That strength, however, is also a major weakness of a multiparty system. It often leads to instability in government. One party is often unable to win the support of a majority of the voters. As a result, the power to govern must be shared by a number of parties in a **coalition**. A coalition is a temporary alliance of several groups who come together to form a working majority and so to control a government. Several of the multiparty nations of Western Europe have experienced frequent changes in party control as coalitions shift and dissolve.

Historically, the American people have shunned a multiparty approach to politics. They have refused to give substantial support to any but the two major parties and their candidates. Two of the factors mentioned here—single-member districts and the American ideological consensus—seem to make the multiparty approach impossible in the United States.

One-Party Politics In the typical dictatorship, only one political party, the party of the ruling clique, is allowed to exist. For all practical purposes, the resulting one-party system really amounts to a "no-party" system.

Many Americans are quite familiar with one-party systems of a quite different sort. What are often called "modified one-party systems" are found in roughly a fourth of the States today. That is, in those States one of the two major parties—either the Republicans or the Democrats—consistently wins most of the elections held there. Although in the remaining States there is more or less vigorous two-party competition at the Statewide level, there are also many locales in most of them where the political landscape is regularly dominated by a single party.

From the 1870s into the 1960s, the Democratic Party was so dominant throughout the southern States that a quarter of the country came to be known as the Solid South. Since the 1990s, however, the GOP has become the leading party in that part of the country.

☑ **COMPARE POINTS OF VIEW** Why might a person consider a vote for a minority candidate, even if they know that candidate is not likely to win?

Third and Minor Parties in the United States

Libertarian, Reform, Socialist, Prohibition, Natural Law, Communist, American Independent, Green, Constitution—these are only some of the many parties that have fielded presidential candidates in recent years and continue to do so. You know that none of these parties or their candidates has any real chance of winning the presidency, but this is not to say that minor parties are unimportant. The bright light created by the two major parties too often blinds us to the vital role several minor parties have played in American politics.

Their number and variety make third and minor parties difficult to describe and classify. Some have limited their efforts to a particular locale, others to a single State, and some to one region of the country. Still others have tried to woo the entire nation. Most have been short-lived, but a few have existed for decades. And, while most have lived, mothlike, around the flame of a single idea, some have had a broader, more practical base. Still, four distinct types of third and minor parties can be identified.

Ideological Parties The **ideological** parties are those based on a particular set of beliefs—a comprehensive view of social, economic, and political matters. These minor parties have seldom been able to win many votes. As a rule, however, they have been long-lived. Most of the ideological parties have been built on some shade of Marxist thought; the Socialist, Socialist Labor, Socialist Worker, and Communist parties are leading examples of that fact.

A few ideological parties have had a quite different approach, however—especially the Libertarian Party of today, which emphasizes individualism and calls for doing away with most of government's present functions and programs.

Minor Parties' Stances on the Issues

	CONSTITUTION PARTY	GREEN PARTY	LIBERTARIAN PARTY
Economy	Eliminate debt by selling federal assets	Stop wasting of taxpayer money on defense and reduce the federal debt	Repeal the income tax
Energy	Rejection of "the perceived threat of man-made global warming"	Reduce greenhouse gas emissions by 95% by 2050	Government should not subsidize any particular form of energy.
Environment	Repeal wetlands protection & Endangered Species Act	Formation of a Civilian Conservation Corps to restore damaged habitats and clean up polluted waterways	Competition and the free market will lead to necessary innovations to protect the environment.
Foreign Policy	We should withdraw from NATO	Abolish nuclear weapons; cut the defense budget in half	Abandon "attempts to act as policeman for the world"
Government Reform	Oppose National Popular Vote proposal to elect president.	Abolish the electoral college	End tax-financed subsidies to candidates or parties

SOURCES: OnTheIssues.org, party platforms

>> In recent years, these three parties have been the largest and most visible minor parties. **Analyze Charts** Would any of these stances be absorbed by one of the major parties? Why or why not?

Single-Issue Parties The **single-issue parties** focus on a single public question. Their names have usually indicated their primary concern. Thus, the Free Soil Party opposed the spread of slavery in the 1840s and 1850s; the American Party, also called the "Know Nothings," opposed Irish-Catholic immigration in the 1850s; and more recently the Right to Life Party opposes abortion.

Most of the single-issue parties have faded into history. They died away as events have passed them by, as their themes have failed to attract voters, or as one or both of the major parties have taken their key issues as their own.

Economic Protest Parties The **economic protest parties** have been rooted in periods of economic discontent. Unlike the socialist parties, these groups have not had any clear-cut ideological base. Rather, they have proclaimed their disgust with the major parties and demanded better times, and have focused their anger on such real or imagined enemies as the monetary system, "Wall Street bankers," the railroads, or foreign imports.

Often, they have been sectional parties, drawing their strength from the agricultural South and West. The Greenback Party tried to take advantage of agrarian discontent from 1876 through 1884. It appealed to struggling farmers by calling for the free coinage of silver, federal regulation of the railroads, an income tax, and labor legislation. A descendant of the Greenbacks, the Populist Party of the 1890s also demanded public ownership of railroads, telephone and telegraph companies, lower tariffs, and the adoption of the initiative and referendum.

Each of these economic protest parties has disappeared as the nation has climbed out of the difficult economic period in which that party arose.

Splinter Parties Those that have split away from one of the major parties are known as **splinter parties**. Most of the more important third and minor parties in our politics have been splinter parties. Among the leading groups that have split away from the Republicans are Theodore Roosevelt's "Bull Moose" Progressive Party of 1912 and Robert La Follette's Progressive Party of 1924. From the Democrats have come Henry Wallace's Progressive Party and the States' Rights (Dixiecrat) Party, both of 1948, and George Wallace's American Independent Party of 1968.

Most splinter parties have formed around a strong personality—most often someone who has failed to win his or her major party's presidential nomination. These parties have faded or collapsed

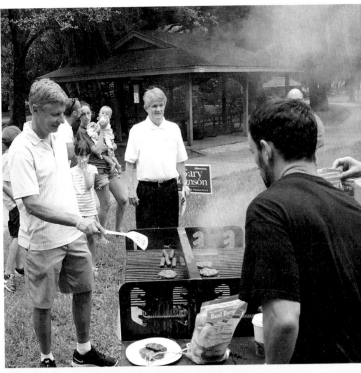

>> Libertarian Party presidential candidate Gary Johnson serves up lunch for supporters. The Libertarian Party has fielded candidates in every presidential election since its founding in 1971.

>> The Free Soil Party, whose 1848 presidential candidate was Martin Van Buren, was a single-issue party that campaigned against the spread of slavery into the western States and territories.

when that leader has stepped aside. Thus, the Bull Moose Progressive Party passed away when Theodore Roosevelt returned to the Republican fold after the election of 1912. Similarly, the American Independent Party lost nearly all of its brief strength when Governor George Wallace rejoined the Democrats after his strong showing in the presidential race in 1968.

The Green Party Like many third and minor parties in American politics, the Green Party, founded in 1996, is difficult to classify. The Green Party began as a classic single-issue party but, as the party has evolved, it simply will not fit into any of the categories set out here.

The Green Party came to prominence in 2000, with Ralph Nader as its presidential nominee. His campaign was built around a smorgasbord of issues—environmental protection, universal healthcare, campaign finance reform, curbs on corporate power, affordable housing, and much more.

Since then, the Greens have nominated presidential candidates who have continued to emphasize these same general issues. As no Green Party candidates have yet to receive more than 3 percent of the popular vote, however, the party has not been a threat to the candidacies of the major parties.

Why Third and Minor Parties Are Important
Even though most Americans do not support them, third and minor parties have still had a considerable impact on American politics. For example, it was a minor party, the Anti-Masons, that first used a national convention to nominate a presidential candidate in 1831. The National Republicans and the Democrats followed suit in 1832. Ever since, national conventions have been used by both Democrats and Republicans to pick their presidential tickets.

Third and minor parties can have a telling effect in other ways. Thus, a strong third-party candidacy can play a decisive role—often a "spoiler role"—in an election. In a presidential contest, even if a minor party ticket fails to win any electoral votes, it can still pull enough support away from one or both of the major parties to affect the outcome of the election.

Some analysts think that Ralph Nader and the Green Party did exactly that to Al Gore and the Democratic Party in 2000. Gore lost the critically important state of Florida by a little over 500 votes, a State where Ralph Nader netted more than 50,000 votes.

In 1912, a split in the Republican Party resulted in Theodore Roosevelt's third-party candidacy. Almost certainly, if Roosevelt had not quit the Republican Party, William Howard Taft would have fared much better, and Woodrow Wilson would not have become President.

2000 Presidential Election Nader's Spoiler Effect

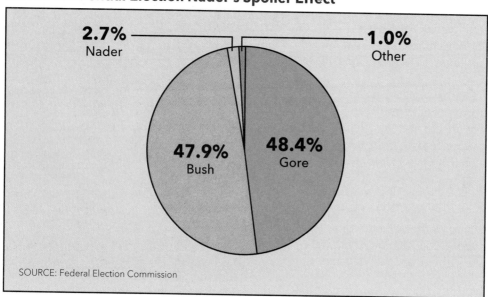

>> The possible effect of Ralph Nader's and other third-party candidacies on the 2000 election has caused a great deal of discussion and disagreement among political analysts. **Analyze Charts** If all third party votes had gone to Al Gore, how would these percentages been different?

Strong Minor Party Efforts, 1924–Present*

YEAR	PARTY	% POPULAR VOTE	ELECTORAL VOTES
1924	Progressive	16.61	13
1932	Socialist	2.22	----
1948	States' Rights (Dixiecrat)	2.41	39
1948	Progressive	2.37	----
1968	American Independent	13.53	46
1996	Reform	8.40	----
2000	Green	2.74	----
2016	Libertarian	3.28	----

* Includes all minor parties that polled at least 2% of the popular vote.
SOURCES: Census Bureau, *Historical Statistics of the U.S.*, Federal Election Commission

>> Minor parties have sometimes had a significant impact on presidential elections.
Analyze Charts Using the data in the chart, which of these minor parties may have changed election results?

The Innovator Role Played by Minor Parties

Historically, however, minor parties have been most important in their roles of critic and innovator. Unlike the major parties, they have been ready, willing, and able to take quite clear-cut stands on controversial issues.

Many of the more important issues of American politics were first brought to the public's attention by a minor party—among them, the progressive income tax, women's suffrage, and railroad and banking regulation. In 1992, Ross Perot opened many eyes to the growing federal budget deficit. Oddly enough, this very important innovator role of the minor parties has also been a major source of their frustration. When their proposals have gained any real degree of popular support, one and sometimes both of the major parties have taken over those ideas. The late Norman Thomas, who was six times the Socialist Party's candidate for President, often complained that "the major parties are stealing from my platform."

There can often be over 25 minor-party and independent presidential candidates appearing on the ballots of at least one State in a presidential election. The most visible minor-party presidential campaigns are most often those of the Libertarian, Green, and Constitution parties. More than a thousand minor-party and independent candidates also sought seats in Congress and ran for various State and local offices around the country.

☑ **DETERMINE POINT OF VIEW** Why do you think a leader or a group might seek to create a minor party even though their chances of winning are less than those of a major party?

The Decentralized Nature of the Parties

How strong, how active, and how well organized are the Republican and Democratic parties in your community? Contact the county chair or another official in one or both of the major parties. They are usually not very difficult to find. For starters, try the telephone directory or the Internet.

The two major parties are often described as though they were highly organized, close-knit, well-disciplined groups. However, neither party is anything of the kind. They are, instead, decentralized, fragmented, and often plagued by factions and internal squabbling.

Neither party has a chain of command running from the national through the State to the local level. Each of the State party organizations is only loosely tied to the party's national structure. By the same token, local party organizations are often quite independent of their parent State organizations. These various party units usually cooperate with one another, of course—but that is not always the case.

The Role of the Presidency The President's party is almost always more solidly united and better organized than the other major party. The President is automatically the party's leader, and asserts that leadership with such tools as ready access to the media, personal popularity, the power to make appointments to federal office, and the ability to dispense other favors.

The other party has no one in an even faintly comparable position. Indeed, in the American party system, there is seldom any one person who can truly be called the leader of the party out of power. Rather, a number of personalities, frequently in competition with one another, and often considering a run for the presidency, form a loosely identifiable leadership group in that party.

The Impact of Federalism Federalism is a major reason for the decentralized nature of the two major political parties. Remember, the basic goal of the major parties is to gain control of government by winning elective offices.

Today there are more than *half a million* elective offices in the United States. We elect more people to public office in this country than do the voters of any other country on the planet. In the American federal system, those offices are widely distributed over the national, State, and local levels. In short, because the governmental system is highly decentralized, so too are the major parties that serve it.

The Nominating Process The nominating process is also a major cause of party decentralization. Recall that the nominating process has a central role in the life of political parties. Consider two related aspects of the process of candidate selection.

First, candidate selection is an intraparty process. That is, nominations are made *within* the party. Second, the nominating process can be, and often is, a divisive one. Where there is a fight over a nomination, that contest pits members of the same party against one another: Republicans fight Republicans; Democrats battle Democrats. In short, the prime function of the major parties—the making of nominations—is also a prime cause of their highly fragmented character.

☑ **EXPRESS PROBLEMS CLEARLY** Why do you think the process of nominating candidates from within the party creates more conflict within parties than the other forms of the nominating process?

National Party Functions

At the national level, both major parties are composed of five basic elements. They are structured around a national convention, a national committee, a national chair, and two congressional campaign committees.

The National Convention The national convention, often described as the party's national voice, meets in the late summer of every presidential election year to pick the party's presidential and vice-presidential candidates. It also performs a few other functions, including the adoption of the party's rules and the writing of its platform.

Beyond that, however, the convention has little authority. It has no control over the party's selection of candidates for any other offices nor over the policy stands those nominees take. Often, a national convention does play a role in making peace among various factions in the party, helping them to accept a party platform that will appeal to a wide range of voters in the general election.

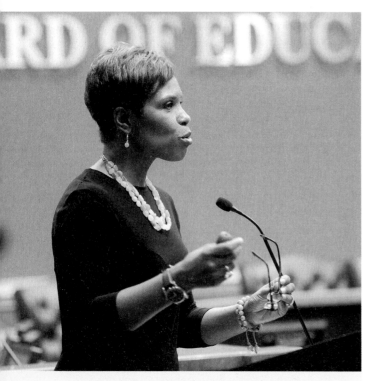

>> Valarie Wilson was elected president of the Georgia School Boards Association in 2012. She was one of the many local officials elected in this country.

The National Committee Between conventions, the party's affairs are handled, at least in theory, by the national committee and by the national chair. For years, each party's national committee was composed of a committeeman and a committeewoman from each State and several of the territories. They were chosen by the State's party organization. Over the past several years, however, both parties have expanded the committee's membership.

Make Up of the RNC and DNC Today, the Republican National Committee (RNC) also seats the party chair from each State and members from the District of Columbia, Guam, American Samoa, Puerto Rico, and the Virgin Islands. Representatives of such GOP-related groups as the National Federation of Republican Women also serve on the RNC.

The Democratic National Committee (DNC) is an even larger body. In addition to the committeeman and -woman from each State, it now includes the party's chair and vice-chair from every State and the territories. Moreover, its ranks now include a few dozen members from the party organizations of the larger States, and nearly 100 at-large members chosen by the DNC itself. Several members of Congress, as well as governors, mayors, and members of the Young Democrats, also have seats on the DNC.

On paper, the national committee appears to be a powerful organization loaded with many of the party's leading figures. In fact, it does not have a great deal of clout. Most of its work centers on the staging of the party's national convention.

The National Chair In each party, the national chair is the leader of the national committee. He or she is chosen to a four-year term by the national committee, at a meeting held right after the national convention. The choice is made by the just-nominated presidential candidate and is then ratified by the national committee.

Only a handful of women and minorities have ever held that top post. The first woman to do so was Jean Westwood of Utah, who served as the DNC chair in 1972. The first Black Americans to serve as chairs were Ron Brown (DNC, 1989–1993) and Michael Steele (RNC, 2009–2011). Tom Perez of New York, chosen to lead the DNC in 2017, was the first Latino American party chair.

Duties of the National Committee The national chair directs the work of the party's headquarters and its professional staff in

>> Mary Louise Smith, the first female RNC chair, is presented the chair's gavel by George Bush following her election to succeed him in that role.

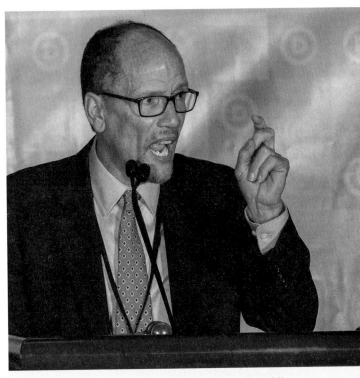

>> The child of immigrants from the Dominican Republic, Tom Perez of New York was secretary of labor under President Obama. He was elected chair of the DNC in 2017.

Washington. In presidential election years, the committee's attention is focused on the national convention and then the campaign.

In between presidential elections, the chair and the committee work to strengthen the party and its fortunes. They do so by promoting party unity, raising money, recruiting new voters, and otherwise preparing for the next presidential season. Of course, it is only with the help nationally of many citizen volunteers that they are able to complete all of these tasks.

Both parties have lately established state-of-the-art technical facilities to help their candidates and officeholders better communicate with voters. Those sophisticated facilities include such things as television studios, satellite uplinks, constantly updated Web sites and social media sites, and computerized voter registration lists.

Congressional Campaign Committees Each party also has a campaign committee in each house of Congress. These committees work to reelect incumbents and to make sure that "open seats," seats given up by retiring members, remain in the party. The committees also take a hand in carefully selected campaigns to unseat incumbents in the other party, in those races where the chances for success seem to justify those efforts.

In both parties and in both houses, the members of these congressional campaign committees are chosen by their colleagues. They serve for two-year terms—that is, for a term of Congress.

☑ **SUMMARIZE** Describe the role of the congressional campaign committees for each party.

State and Local Party Functions

National party organization is largely the product of custom and of rules adopted by the party's national conventions over time. At the State and local levels, on the other hand, party structure is largely determined by State law.

State Organization In most States, party structure is decentralized, much as it is at the national level. It is usually built around a State central committee, headed by a State chair. The chair, chosen by the committee, may be an important political figure in his or her own right. More often than not, however, he or she fronts for the governor, a U.S. senator, or some other powerful figure or group in the politics of the State.

COMMON LOCAL AND STATE PARTY ORGANIZATION

THIRD LEVEL
PRECINCT

Precincts are the smallest unit of party organization.

SECOND LEVEL
WARD

Wards are usually the next larger political unit into which municipalities are divided.

FIRST LEVEL
CONGRESSIONAL AND STATE LEGISLATIVE DISTRICTS

State party organizations are divided geographically into **congressional districts** or **counties**.

>> Local party organization can vary from State to State, but this chart shows a common example. **Analyze Charts** What is the difference between a ward and a precinct?

The party's State central committee is almost everywhere composed of members who represent major geographic subdivisions, usually counties. They are chosen in primary elections, by local caucuses, or at State conventions. Because most of these committees meet only infrequently, the chair has great independence in conducting the party's affairs.

Together, the chair and the central committee work to further the party's interests in the State. Most of the time, they attempt to do this by building an effective organization and promoting party unity, finding candidates and campaign funds, and so on. Again, much of this work is done by volunteers from the State. Remember, however, both major parties are highly decentralized, fragmented, and sometimes torn by struggles for power. This can really complicate the chair's and the committee's job.

Local Organization Local party structures vary so widely that they nearly defy even a brief description. Generally, they are found in counties and cities, and occasionally in towns, wards, and precincts. A **ward** is a unit into which cities are often divided for the election of city council members. A **precinct** is the smallest unit of election administration; the voters in each precinct cast their ballots at one polling place located within the precinct.

In some places, local party organizations are active year-round, but most often they are inactive except for those few hectic months before an election. It is especially at those times when the local party organization makes use of local citizen volunteers to help them accomplish all that needs to be done.

☑ **CHECK UNDERSTANDING** Explain the differences between party organization at the national level compared to the State and local level.

>> Bruce Clark, the Precinct 2 chair for Jackson County, Iowa, counts participants at the start of a Democratic caucus in 2012.

☑ ASSESSMENT

1. **Evaluate** Evaluate the role of political parties in shaping public policy in the United States.

2. **Express Problems Clearly** Explain the meaning of this statement: "A minor party is likely to be a victim of its own success."

3. **Categorize** Describe the place of the President in national party organization.

4. **Identify Cause and Effect** Why is party unity harder to achieve for the party out of power than it is for the party in power?

5. **Draw Conclusions** Explain the roles played by the Federalists, led by Alexander Hamilton, and the Anti-Federalists, led by Thomas Jefferson, in the formation of the two-party system in America.

11.2

The 1940 Republican National Convention was the first televised national political convention. Delegates nominated Wendell Willkie for President and Charles McNary for Vice President.

 BOUNCE to Activate Flipped Video

Objectives

Explain why the nominating process is a critical first step in the process for filling public offices.

Describe self-announcement, the caucus, and the convention as nominating methods.

Discuss the direct primary as the principle nominating method used in the United States today, and understand why some candidates use the petition as a nominating device.

Key Terms

nomination
general elections
caucus
direct primary
closed primary
open primary
blanket primary
platform
runoff primary
nonpartisan
  elections
Ross Perot
Andrew Jackson

Nominations

Nominations: A Critical First Step

Suppose your teacher stood in front of the class and said: "Here's a $100 bill. Who'd like to have it?" You, and everyone else in the room, would promptly say, or at least think: "Me!" Suppose the teacher then said: "Okay, we'll hold an election. The person who wins the most votes gets the money."

What would happen? If the election were held immediately, it is likely that each member of the class would vote for himself or herself. A few might vote for a friend. Almost certainly, however, the election would end in a tie. No one would win the money.

But suppose the teacher said: "We'll hold the election tomorrow." What do you suppose would happen then? As you think about the answer to that question, you begin to get a sense of the practical importance of the nominating process—the first step in the process of electing or appointing candidates for filling public office.

The nominating process is the process of narrowing down the list of would-be candidates. **Nomination**—the naming of those who will seek office—is a critically important step in the election and appointment process at the national, State, and local levels.

Impact of the Nominating Process You have already seen two major illustrations of the significance of the nominating process. You have read about the making of nominations (1) as a prime function of political parties in American politics, and (2) as a leading reason for the decentralized character of the two major parties in the United States.

The nominating process for filling offices also has a very real impact on the right to vote. In the typical election in this country, voters can choose between only two candidates for each office on the ballot— the Republican or the Democratic candidate. Other choices are sometimes listed, but they are not often meaningful alternatives. Most voters conclude that candidates who are not members of one of the two major parties are not likely to win, so they opt not to vote for them. This is another way of saying that we have a two-party system in the United States. It is also another way to say that the nominating stage is a critically important step in the electoral process. Those who make nominations place real, very practical limits on the choices that voters can make in the general election.

Methods of Nomination In one-party constituencies (those areas where one party regularly wins elections), the nominating process is usually the only point at which there is any real contest for public office. Once the dominant party has made its nomination, the general election is little more than a formality.

Dictatorial regimes point up the importance of the nominating process. Many of them hold **general elections**—regularly scheduled elections at which voters make the final selection of officeholders— much as democracies do. But, typically, the ballots used in those elections list only one candidate for each office—the candidate of the ruling clique; and those candidates regularly win with majorities approaching 100 percent. In a dictatorial regime, appointed offices may be filled by the leader by naming someone to the office. "Elections" are merely symbolic.

Nominations to fill elective office are made in five different ways in this country. Candidates are named to the ballot by (1) self-announcement, (2) caucus, (3) convention, (4) direct primary, and (5) petition.

Self-Announcement Self-announcement is the oldest form of the nominating process in American politics. First used in colonial times, it is still found at the small-town and rural levels in parts of the country.

The method is quite simple. A person who wants to run for office or who wishes to be appointed to an office simply announces that fact. Modesty or local custom may dictate that someone else actually

>> Lifelong Democrat Michael Bloomberg switched parties in a delayed primary in 2001 to become the Republican mayoral nominee.

>> Many dictatorships hold general elections, but there is often only one candidate on the ballot, such as when Saddam Hussein of Iraq was unanimously reelected in 2002.

> " This day learned that the Caucus Club meets, at certain times, in the garret of Tom Dawes, the Adjutant of the Boston Regiment. He has a large house, and he has a moveable partition in his garret which he takes down, and the whole club meets in one room. There they smoke tobacco till you cannot see from one end of the garret to the other. There they drink flip, I suppose, and they choose a moderator, who puts questions to the vote regularly; and selectmen, assessors, collectors, wardens, fire-wards, and representatives, are regularly chosen before they are chosen in the town.

—Charles Francis Adams (ed.) *The Works of John Adams* (1856)

>> In 1763, John Adams expressed his disapproval for Boston's Caucus Club, where influential community members met privately to decide who they would support in upcoming elections.

makes the candidate's announcement, but, still, the process amounts to the same thing.

Historical Examples Self-announcement is sometimes used by someone who failed to win a regular party nomination or by someone unhappy with the party's choice. Note that whenever a write-in candidate appears in an election, the self-announcement process has been used.

In recent history, four prominent presidential contenders have made use of the process: George Wallace, who declared himself to be the American Independent Party's nominee in 1968; and independent candidates Eugene McCarthy in 1976; John Anderson in 1980; and **Ross Perot** in 1992. And for the first time in over 50 years, a U.S. senate race was actually won by a write-in candidate when Lisa Murkowksi defeated the Republican candidate for the Alaska seat in 2010.

☑ **HYPOTHESIZE** What impact does the nominating process have on the right to vote?

The Caucus

As a nominating device, a **caucus** is a group of like-minded people who meet to select the candidates they will support in an upcoming election. The first caucus nominations were made during the later colonial period, probably in Boston in the 1720s. John Adams described the caucus this way in 1763:

> This day learned that the Caucus Club meets, at certain times, in the garret of Tom Dawes, the Adjutant of the Boston Regiment. He has a large house, and he has a moveable partition in his garret which he takes down, and the whole club meets in one room. There they smoke tobacco till you cannot see from one end of the garret to the other. There they drink flip, I suppose, and they choose a moderator, who puts questions to the vote regularly;

and selectmen, assessors, collectors, wardens, fire-wards, and representatives, are regularly chosen before they are chosen in the town.

—Charles Francis Adams (ed.) *The Works of John Adams* (1856)

The Original Caucus Originally the caucus was a private meeting of a few influential figures in the community. As political parties began to appear in the late 1700s, they took over the device and soon broadened the membership of the caucus considerably.

The coming of independence brought the need to nominate candidates for State offices: governor, lieutenant governor, and others above the local level. The legislative caucus—a meeting of a party's members in the State legislature—took on the job. At the national level, both the Federalists and the Democratic-Republicans in Congress were, by 1800, choosing their presidential and vice presidential candidates through the congressional caucus.

The legislative and congressional caucuses were quite practical in their day. Transportation and communication were difficult at best. Since legislators were already gathered regularly in a central place, it made sense for them to take on the nominating responsibility. The spread of democracy, especially in the newer States on the frontier, spurred opposition to the use of caucuses, however. They were widely condemned for their closed, unrepresentative character.

Criticisms of the Caucus Criticism of the caucus reached its peak in the early 1820s. The supporters of three of the leading contenders for the presidency in 1824—**Andrew Jackson**, Henry Clay, and John Quincy Adams—boycotted the Democratic-Republicans' congressional caucus that year. In fact, Jackson and his supporters made "King Caucus" a leading campaign issue. They argued that the process was elitist and rife with corruption. The other major contender, William H. Crawford of Georgia, became the caucus nominee at a meeting attended by fewer than one third of the Democratic-Republican Party's members in Congress.

Crawford ran a poor third in the electoral college balloting in 1824, and the reign of King Caucus at the national level was ended. With its death in presidential politics, the caucus system soon withered at the State and local levels, as well.

The caucus is still used to make local nominations in some places, especially in New England. There, a caucus is open to all members of a party, and it only faintly resembles the original closed and private

>> Residents of Harpswell, Maine, vote during a Republican town caucus. Typically, a caucus is a small representative group whose members share a specific, usually political, affiliation.

process. Also, some States rely on a caucus model to select delegates to presidential nominations conventions, a topic discussed in the next lesson.

☑ **GENERATE EXPLANATIONS** During the 1800s, why were people opposed to the use of the caucus?

The Convention

As the caucus method collapsed, the convention system took its place. It was seen as more open and fair because delegates would come from far and wide to pick party nominees. The first national convention to nominate a presidential candidate was held by a minor party, the Anti-Masons, in Baltimore in 1831. The newly formed National Republican (soon to become Whig) Party also held a convention later that same year. The Democrats picked up the practice in 1832. All major-party presidential nominees have been chosen by conventions ever since. By the 1840s, conventions were the principal means for making nominations at every level in American politics.

On paper, the convention process seems perfectly suited to representative government. A party's members meet in a local caucus to pick candidates for local offices and, at the same time, to select delegates to represent them at a county convention.

(The meeting at which delegates to local conventions are chosen are still often called caucuses.)

At the county convention, the delegates nominate candidates for county offices and select delegates to the next rung on the convention ladder, usually the State convention. There, the delegates from the county conventions pick the party's nominees for governor and other Statewide offices. State conventions also send delegates to the party's national convention, where the party selects its presidential and vice-presidential candidates.

Problems with the Convention In theory, the will of the party's rank and file membership is passed up through each of its representative levels. Practice soon pointed up the weaknesses of the theory, however, as party bosses found ways to manipulate the process. By playing with the selection of delegates, usually at the local levels, they soon dominated the entire system. Delegates simply voted as directed by the party bosses.

As a result, the caliber of most conventions declined at all levels, especially during the late 1800s. How low some of them fell can be seen in this description of a Cook County (Chicago), Illinois, convention in 1896:

Of [723] delegates, those who had been on trial for murder numbered 17; sentenced to the penitentiary for murder or manslaughter and served sentence, 7; served terms in the penitentiary for burglary, 36; served terms in the penitentiary for picking pockets, 2; served terms in the penitentiary for arson, 1; . . . jailbirds identified by detectives, 84; keepers of gambling houses, 7; keepers of houses of ill-fame, 2; convicted of mayhem, 3; ex-prize fighters, 11; poolroom proprietors, 2; saloon keepers, 265; . . . political employees, 148; no occupation, 71; . . .

—R.M. Easley "The Sine qua Non of Caucus Reform" Review of Reviews (Sept. 1897)

Replacing the Convention Many people had hailed the change from caucus to convention as a major change for the better in American politics. The abuses of the new device soon dashed their hopes. By the 1870s, the convention system was itself under attack as a major source of corruption in the nation's politics. By the 1910s, the direct primary had replaced the convention in most States as the principal nominating method in American politics.

Conventions still play a major role in the nominating process in some States—notably, Connecticut, Michigan, South Dakota, Utah, and Virginia. And, as you will see, no adequate substitute for the device has yet been found at the presidential level.

☑ **COMPARE AND CONTRAST** What are some similarities and differences between the caucus and the convention as nominating methods?

The Direct Primary

A **direct primary** is an *intra*party election. It is held within a party to pick that party's candidates for the general election. Wisconsin adopted the first Statewide direct primary law in 1903; several other States soon followed its lead. Every State now makes at least some provision for its use.

In most States, State law requires that the major parties use the primary to choose their

>> During the 1876 presidential election, charges of voter fraud were widespread and many arrests were made. **Infer** How might unscrupulous party leaders have manipulated the political system?

candidates for the United States Senate and House of Representatives, for the governorship and all other Statewide offices, and for most local offices as well. In a few States, however, different combinations of convention and primary are used to pick candidates for the top offices.

Using the Direct Primary In Michigan, for example, the major parties choose their candidates for the United States Senate and House, the governorship, and the State legislature in primaries. Nominees for lieutenant governor, secretary of state, and attorney general are picked by conventions. (In most States, minor parties are required to make their nominations by other, more difficult processes, usually in conventions or by petition. This is another of the several ways in which State election laws often, purposely, make life difficult for minor parties.)

Although the primaries are party-nominating elections, they are closely regulated by law in most States. The State usually sets the dates on which primaries are held, and it regularly conducts them, too. The State, not the parties, provides polling places and election officials, registration lists and ballots, and otherwise polices the process. Also, in 1944 the Supreme Court ruled that a State could not use a "white only" primary as a means of discriminating against Black citizens.

Forms of the Direct Primary Two basic forms of the direct primary are in use today: (1) the closed primary and (2) the open primary. The major difference between the two lies in the answer to this question: Who can vote in a party's primary—*only* those qualified voters who are party members, or *any* qualified voter?

The Closed Primary Today, more than half the States provide for the **closed primary**—a nominating election in which only declared party members can vote. The primary is closed to all but those party members. (The Supreme Court has held that a State's closed primary law cannot forbid a party to allow independent voters to participate in its primary if the party itself chooses to allow them to do so.)

In most of the closed primary States, party membership is established by registration. When voters appear at their polling places on primary election day, their names are checked against the poll books and each voter is handed the primary ballot of the party in which he or she is registered. The voter can mark only that party's ballot; he or she can vote only in that party's primary.

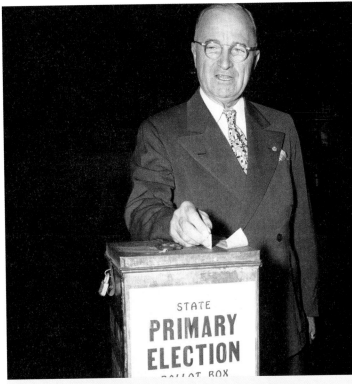

>> In his home state of Missouri, President Truman casts his ballot during the State's 1948 presidential primary.

In some of the closed primary States, however, a voter can change his or her party registration on election day. In those States, then, the primary is not as completely "closed" as it is elsewhere.

The Open Primary The **open primary**—or crossover primary—is a party's nominating election in which *any* qualified voter can cast a ballot. Although it is the form in which the direct primary first appeared, it is now found in fewer than half the States.

When voters go to the polls in some open primary States, they are handed a ballot of each party holding a primary. Usually, they receive only two ballots, those of the Republican and the Democratic parties.

Then, in the privacy of the voting booth, each voter marks the ballot of the party in whose primary he or she chooses to vote. In other open primary States, a voter must ask for the ballot of the party in whose primary he or she wants to vote. That is, each voter must make a *public* choice of party in order to vote in the primary.

The Blanket Primary Through 2000, three States used a different version of the open primary—the

blanket primary, sometimes called the "wide-open primary." Washington adopted the first blanket primary law in 1935. Alaska followed suit in 1970, and California did so in 1996. In a blanket primary, every voter received the same ballot— a long one that listed *every* candidate, regardless of party, for every nomination to be made at the primary. Voters could participate however they chose. They could confine themselves to one party's primary; or they could switch back and forth between the parties' primaries, voting to nominate a Democrat for one office, a Republican for another, and so on down the ballot.

The Supreme Court found California's version of the blanket primary unconstitutional in 2000, however. In *California Democratic Party* v. *Jones*, the High Court held that that process violated the 1st and 14th amendments' guarantees of the right of association. It ruled that a State cannot force a political party to associate with outsiders— that is, with members of other parties or with independents—when it picks its candidates for public office.

Versions of the Open Primary The Court's decision in *Jones* made the blanket primary a thing of the past. Alaska responded by adopting a more traditional version of the open primary. But California and Washington have gone quite another way.

>> A California primary ballot lists the names of all candidates for an office. The top vote-getters from each party run against the other for office.

Those two States now provide for the "top two" form of the open primary. In both States, the names of *all* those who seek nomination are listed, by office, on a single primary ballot. Then the top two vote-getters for each office, regardless of party, face one another in the general election. Thus, two Republicans, or two Democrats, may battle one another in November.

Louisiana uses yet another version of the open primary, under what is sometimes called its "open-election law." There, as in Washington, all candidates for nomination are listed on a single ballot, and the top two vote-getters, regardless of party, face off in the general election. But if a candidate wins a majority of the votes in the primary, he or she is declared the winner of the office involved—so, the primary becomes, in effect, the election. (Louisiana's "open-election" primary law applies to its State and local elections, which are held in November of the *odd*-numbered years. Since 1872, federal law has directed that congressional elections be held in November of the *even*-numbered years, and Louisiana abides by that law. It holds traditional closed primaries in the *even*-numbered years to choose candidates for seats in the United States House and Senate.)

Closed vs. Open Primaries The merits of the two basic forms of the direct primary have been argued for decades. Those who support the closed primary rely on three major arguments. They regularly claim that:

1. The closed primary prevents one party from "raiding" the other's primary in the hope of nominating weaker candidates in the opposition party.
2. It helps to make candidates more responsive to the party, its members, and its **platform**— a party's formal statement of basic principles, stands on major policy matters, and objectives for the campaign and beyond.
3. It helps make voters more thoughtful, because they must choose between the parties in order to vote in the primaries.

Those who criticize the closed primary usually contend that:

1. It compromises the secrecy of the ballot, because it forces voters to make their party preferences known in order to participate.
2. It tends to exclude independent voters from the nominating process—thereby lowering turnout rates.

The advocates of the open primary believe that that nominating arrangement addresses both of those objections to the closed primary. They say that in the typical open primary (1) voters are not forced to make their party preferences a matter of public record, and (2) independent voters are not excluded from the nominating process.

The Runoff Primary In most States, candidates need to win only a plurality of the votes cast in the primary to win their party's nomination. (Remember, a *plurality* is the greatest number of votes won by any candidate, whether a *majority* or not.) In several States, however, an absolute majority (50 percent plus one) is needed to carry a primary. If no one wins a majority in those states, a **runoff primary** is held a few weeks later. In that contest, the two top vote-getters in the first primary face one another to determine the party's nomination, and the winner of that vote becomes the party's nominee.

The Nonpartisan Primary In some States elected school and municipal offices are filled in **nonpartisan elections**. These are elections in which candidates are not identified by party labels. About half of all State judges are chosen on nonpartisan ballots, as well. The nomination of candidates for these offices takes place on a nonpartisan basis, too, and most often in nonpartisan primaries.

Typically, a contender who wins a clear majority in a nonpartisan primary then runs unopposed in the general election, subject only to write-in opposition. In many States, however, a candidate who wins a majority in the primary is declared elected at that point. If there is no majority winner, the names of the two top contenders are placed on the general election ballot.

The primary first appeared as a partisan nominating device. Many have long argued that it is not well suited for use in nonpartisan elections. Instead, they favor the petition method, as you will see in a moment.

The Presidential Primary The presidential primary developed as an offshoot of the direct primary. It is *not* a nominating device, however. Rather, the presidential primary is an election that is held as one part of the process by which presidential candidates are chosen.

The presidential primary is a very complex process. It is one or both of two things, depending on the State involved. It is a process in which a party's voters elect some or all of a State party organization's delegates to that party's national convention; and/or it is a preference election in which voters can choose

>> Sheila Abdus-Salaam being sworn in as a New York State Court of Appeals judge. In many States, judges are chosen in nonpartisan elections, in which they are not identified by party.

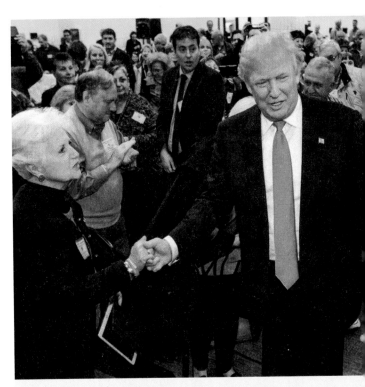

>> Businessman Donald Trump greets supporters in South Carolina during his first presidential campaign.

(vote their preference) among various contenders for the grand prize, the party's presidential nomination.

Much of what happens in presidential politics in the early months of every fourth year centers on this very complicated process.

☑ **CONTRAST** What is the major difference between the closed and the open primary?

Evaluation of the Primary

The direct primary, whether open or closed, is an *intra*party nominating election. It came to American politics as a reform of the boss-dominated convention system. It was intended to take the nominating function away from the party organization and put it in the hands of the party's rank-and-file membership.

The basic facts about the primary have never been very well understood by most voters, however. So, in closed primary States, many voters resent having to declare their party preference in order to vote in the primary. And, in both open and closed primary States, many are upset because they cannot express their support for candidates in more than one party. Many are also annoyed by the "bed-sheet ballots" they regularly see in primary elections—not realizing that the use of the direct primary almost automatically means a long ballot. And some are

concerned because the primary (and, in particular, its closed form) tends to exclude independents from the nominating process.

Problems with the Primary All of these factors, combined with a lack of appreciation of the important role that primaries play in the election process, result in this unfortunate and significant fact: Nearly everywhere, voter turnout in primary elections is less than half what it is in the general elections in November.

Primary contests can be quite expensive for the State and costly for the candidates. The fact that successful contenders must then wage—and finance—a general election campaign adds to the money problems that bedevil American politics. Unfortunately, the financial facts of political life in the United States mean that some well-qualified people refuse to seek public office simply because they cannot muster the funding absolutely necessary to finance a campaign.

Other Problems with the Primary The nominating process, whatever its form, can have a very divisive effect on a party. Remember, the process takes place *within* the party—so, when there is a contest for a nomination, that is where the contest occurs: Republicans fight with Republicans, Democrats do battle with Democrats. A bitter fight in the primaries can so wound and divide a party

1992 Presidential Primary Schedule and Results

DATE(S)	PRIMARY STATES	DEMOCRATIC CANDIDATES AND STATES WON				
		Bill Clinton (AR)	Jerry Brown (CA)	Paul Tsongas (MA)	Tom Harkin (NE)	Bob Kerry (IA)
Feb 18	NH			NH		
Feb 25	SD					SD
Mar 3	CO, GA, MD	GA	CO	MD		
Mar 7	SC	SC				
Mar 10 Super Tuesday	FL, LA, MA, MS, MO, OK, RI, TN, TX	FL, LA, MS, MO, OK, TN, TX		MA, RI		
Mar 17	IL, MI	IL, MI				
Mar 19	ND	ND				
Mar 24	CT		CT			

SOURCE: Federal Election Committee

>> Between April 5th and June 9th, the remaining 23 primaries were held. All were won by Bill Clinton. **Analyze Charts** What do the results of the Super Tuesday primaries suggest about the campaign strategies of Clinton and Tsongas?

that it cannot recover in time to present a united front for the general election. Many a primary fight has cost a party an election. Also, many speculate that when hard-fought primary campaigns are held in both parties, the voters are left feeling that all the candidates are deficient.

Finally, because many voters are not very well informed, the primary places a premium on name familiarity. That is, it often gives an edge to a contender who has a well-known name or a name that sounds like that of some well-known person. But, notice, name familiarity in and of itself usually has little or nothing to do with a candidate's qualifications for public office.

Obviously, the primary is not without its problems, nor is any other nominating device. Still, the primary does give a party's members the opportunity to participate at the very core of the political process.

☑ **SUMMARIZE** What are some of the issues voters have with the open and closed primary as a nominating method?

>> Winning nomination by petition can be a time-consuming process. Candidates may even need to go door-to-door to gather support.

Petition

One other nominating method is used fairly widely at the local level in American politics today—nomination by petition. Petitions are used for two purposes. First, they are often used to get a candidate's name on the primary election ballot. Second, in some States, candidates for public office can be nominated by means of petitions signed by a certain number of qualified voters in the election district.

Nomination by petition is found most widely at the local level, chiefly for nonpartisan school posts and municipal offices in medium-sized and smaller communities and, increasingly, for judgeships. It is also the process usually required by State law for nominating minor-party and independent candidates in many of the States. (Remember, the States often purposely make the process of getting on the ballot difficult for those candidates.) The details of the petition process vary widely from State to State, and even from one city or county to the next. Usually, however, the higher the office and/or the larger the constituency represented by the office, the greater the number of signatures needed for nomination by or to get on the primary ballot.

Filling Appointed Offices Filling appointed offices can be done with similar methods used for filling elective office. A person can be nominated for office by a local, State, or national political entity or person, such as a mayor, a State legislator, or the President. On the national level, many nominations, such as those for cabinet secretaries, ambassadors, and judges, come from the executive branch. Such nominations are subject to approval by vote of the legislative branch. On a State and local level, the process can be very similar for offices such as local advisory committees or various State boards.

☑ **INFER** Why is nomination by petition most widely found at the local level of government?

☑ ASSESSMENT

1. **Draw Conclusions** Why is the nominating process a critical first step in the process for filling elected or appointed public offices?

2. **Describe** Describe self-announcement as a nominating method and when it is used.

3. **Compare** Compare the caucus and the convention as nominating methods.

4. **Draw Conclusions** Why is the direct primary used as the principle nominating method in the United States today?

5. **Infer** Why do some candidates use the petition as a nominating device?

Campaign buttons, such as this one for the 1956 Democratic presidential candidate Adlai Stevenson, have been used by voters since the first U.S. elections as a way to promote or criticize a candidate.

 BOUNCE to Activate Flipped Video

Objectives

Describe the role of conventions in the presidential nominating process, the caucus-convention process, and the events that take place during a national convention.

Evaluate the importance of presidential primaries.

Examine the characteristics that determine who is nominated as a presidential candidate.

Describe the features of the presidential campaign.

Analyze how the electoral college provides for the election of the President.

Identify electoral college scenarios and outline the advantages and disadvantages of proposed reforms of the system.

Key Terms

presidential primary
winner-take-all
proportional
 representation
keynote address
swing voters
battleground States
district plan
proportional plan
national popular vote
 plan
Ronald Reagan
Richard M. Johnson

Electing the President

Recall, the congressional caucus was the first method the parties developed to pick their presidential candidates. The closed, unrepresentative character of that arrangement led to its downfall in the mid-1820s. For the election of 1832, both major parties turned to the national convention as their presidential nominating device, and it has continued to serve them ever since.

Presidential Primaries

Most of all the delegates to both parties' conventions come from States that hold presidential primaries. Many of those primaries are major media events. Serious contenders in both the Democratic and Republican parties must make the best possible showing in at least most of them.

Depending on the State, a **presidential primary** is an election in which a party's voters (1) choose some or all of a State party organization's delegates to their party's national convention, and/or (2) express a preference among various contenders for their party's presidential nomination.

History of the Presidential Primary The presidential primary first appeared in the early 1900s as part of the reform movement aimed at the party boss-dominated convention system. Wisconsin passed the first presidential primary law in 1905, providing for the popular election of national convention delegates. Several States soon followed that lead, and Oregon added the preference feature in 1910. By 1916 half the States had adopted presidential primary laws.

For a time, the primary system fell into disfavor so that by 1968, primaries were found in only 16 States and the District of Columbia. That same year—1968—was one of the most turbulent years in modern American history. Democrat Lyndon B. Johnson, the sitting President, decided not to seek reelection because of his weak showing in the New Hampshire primary and the growing protests against his Vietnam policies. Several Democrats jumped into the race, including Senator Robert Kennedy—the brother of the slain President, John F. Kennedy. And yet, the Democratic Party bosses backed Hubert Humphrey, the Vice President. Kennedy was drawing huge crowds and seemed wildly popular, but on the night of the California primary, which he won, Kennedy was also assassinated.

The Democratic Party was thrown into chaos and at the National Convention later that summer in Chicago there were riots in the streets. The party leaders inside the convention hall were moving to nominate Humphrey, but the masses of protestors outside wanted a more anti-war candidate. The police were called out and violence erupted. Americans watched the spectacle on television.

In the aftermath, the Democratic Party created a commission to consider reforms. The report from the panel recommended a list of changes, which lead to the system we have today. The key reforms were that average party followers, not party bosses, would select the delegates, and the delegates are bound to support the candidate they said they would support during the primary. The goal was to make the process more "open, timely, and democratic."

A System with Many Variables Recall, a presidential primary is either or both of two things: a delegate-selection process and/or a candidate preference election. Once that much has been said, however, the system becomes very hard to describe, except on a State-by-State basis.

The difficulty comes largely from two sources: (1) the fact that in each State the details of the delegate-selection process are set by State law—and those details vary from State to State, and (2) the ongoing reform efforts in the Democratic Party.

The Republican Party was not bound to these new rules pushed through by the Democrats in the aftermath of 1968, of course, but most Americans came to believe that the heavy role of party leaders was unfair. There is some modest difference, but generally speaking today States treat the two parties alike in their election laws; so, as States have responded to Democratic Party reforms, the Republicans have had to revise some of their procedures, as well.

Significance of Primary Timing Even a matter that seems as simple as the date for the primary illustrates the crazy-quilt pattern of State laws. Since 1920, New Hampshire has held the first of the presidential primaries. The State guards its first-in-the-nation title with a law that provides that its primary is to be held at least a week before the date any other State picks for its contest.

Most States grew to prefer an early date, so the primary schedule became heavily "front-loaded". In 2008, for example, the scramble for an early date meant that 16 States held their primaries on the same day—"Super Tuesday"—and three fourths of the contests had been held by mid-March.

Rule changes within the Republican Party, along with other factors, have resulted in long, drawn-out primary election seasons. For example, unlike 2008, only about 10 States hold primaries on Super Tuesday.

Name recognition and money have always been important factors in the primary process, and front-loading such as what happened in 2008 multiplied their importance. However, with the reduction in front-loaded primaries, candidates could hope to build a following

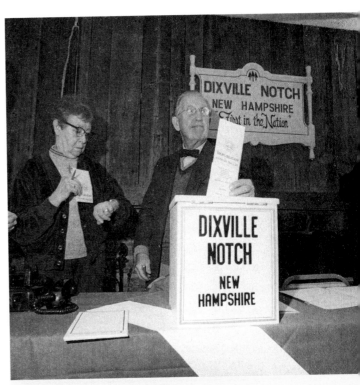

>> The town moderator of Dixville Notch prepares to cast the first primary vote in the nation. This tiny New Hampshire town casts its votes at exactly midnight each presidential election year.

over several weeks—similar to the momentum gained by Bill Clinton in 1992. In addition, voters had more time to learn about the candidates and their stands on the issues. The front-loaded process left little or no time for that strategy. Instead, contenders had to mount (and pay for) campaigns in a number of geographically separated States that held their primaries early and often within a few days of one another.

Shifting Primary Styles For decades, most presidential primaries were both delegate-selection and preference exercises. Several were also **winner-take-all** contests: The candidate who won the preference vote automatically won the support of all of the delegates chosen at that primary.

Winner-take-all primaries have now all but disappeared, however. The Democratic Party's rules actually prohibit them. Instead, the Democrats now have a complex **proportional representation** rule. Any candidate who seeks the party's presidential nomination who wins at least 15 percent of the votes cast in a primary gets the number of that State's Democratic convention delegates that corresponds to his or her share of that primary vote. Take, for example, a State that has 40 convention delegates. If a candidate wins 45 percent of the primary vote, he or she automatically gains the support of at least 18 of the delegates.

Following Republican rule changes in 2012, any State that held its primary before April 1 was prohibited from using a winner-take-all system, with the hope of discouraging the pile-up of early primaries. Still, a few States do permit winner-take-all primaries.

Preference Primary The proportional representation rule had another major impact on the shape of presidential primaries. It led several States to give up the popular selection of delegates. More than half of the presidential primary States now hold only a preference primary. The delegates themselves are actually chosen later, at party conventions. In most of these States, the delegates must be picked in line with the results of the preference primary—for example, for the Republicans in 2008, so many delegates for John McCain, so many for Mitt Romney, so many for Ron Paul, and so on. In a few States, the preference vote does not govern the choice of the delegates. In those States—Nebraska, for example—the preference primary is often called a "beauty contest."

WINNER-TAKE-ALL vs. PROPORTIONAL REPRESENTATION

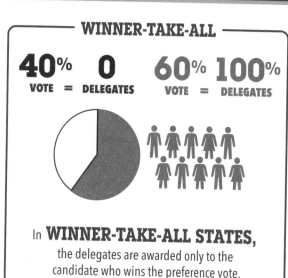

WINNER-TAKE-ALL

40% VOTE = **0** DELEGATES   **60**% VOTE = **100**% DELEGATES

In **WINNER-TAKE-ALL STATES,** the delegates are awarded only to the candidate who wins the preference vote.

PROPORTIONAL REPRESENTATION

40% VOTE = **40**% DELEGATES   **60**% VOTE = **60**% DELEGATES

In States with **PROPORTIONAL REPRESENTATION,** delegates are awarded to candidates in proportion to the number of votes each received.

>> Political party rule changes often lead to changes in how primaries are conducted. **Analyze Data** Why do you think candidates who receive less than 15% of the vote are not assigned delegates?

Most of the preference contests are also "all-candidate" primaries. These are contests in which all generally recognized contenders for a party's presidential nomination must be listed on that party's preference ballot.

☑ **MAKE GENERALIZATIONS** Based on what you have learned about the changes that were made in most State primaries by 2012, how do you think presidential candidates would feel about the effect on their candidacies?

Evaluation of the Presidential Primary

No one who has surveyed the presidential primary system needs to be told that it is complicated, or that it is filled with confusing variations. Still, these primaries are vital. For half a century now, they have played *the* major part in deciding the presidential nominating contests in both parties—and particularly in the party out of power.

Out of Power vs. In Power Presidential primaries tend to democratize the delegate-selection process. And, importantly, they force would-be nominees to test their candidacies in actual political combat.

For the party without an incumbent running for re-election, the primaries are often "knock-down, drag-out" affairs. Without the unifying force of the President as party leader, top personalities and factions in the party vie with one another, vigorously, for the presidential nomination. Here, a key function of the presidential primary can be seen: the screening out of the lesser possibilities to the point where only one or a few contenders for the nomination remain in the contest.

Such hard-fought contests do occur, but are not common, in the party in power. This tends to be true either because the President (1) is seeking reelection, or (2) is backing a personal favorite for the nomination. In either case the President regularly prevails.

A sitting President is seldom challenged for renomination, but that situation does sometimes happen. Thus, for example, **Ronald Reagan** made a stiff run at President Gerald Ford in 1976, and Senator Edward Kennedy gave President Carter a real fight in 1980.

Reform Proposals The fact that so many States now hold presidential primaries places large demands on contenders in terms of time, effort, money, scheduling, and, not least, fatigue. The

>> Voters participate in a lively debate at the start of the 2012 Iowa caucus. At caucuses, party members discuss candidates, debate the party platform, and choose convention delegates.

lengthy primary season tests the public's endurance, as well.

Some think that each of the major parties should hold a single, nationwide primary, and have both parties choose their presidential candidates in those contests. National conventions would be done away with—except perhaps to pick their vice-presidential nominees and/or write party platforms.

Most often, however, critics of the present arrangement favor one version or another of a regional primary plan. A series of primaries would be held at two- or three-week intervals across the country.

The prospects for reform are uncertain at best. Major changes would require joint action among the several States and both major parties. Neither major party has ever expressed any interest in abandoning its national convention. Both parties see the conventions as a device to promote compromise and, out of it, party unity.

Presidential Caucuses In those States that do not hold presidential primaries, delegates to the national conventions are selected in a system of local caucuses and district and/or State conventions. A caucus is a closed meeting of members of a political party who gather to select delegates to the national convention. The process works basically as it is described here, but the details do differ from State to State.

Instead of voting in a primary, a party's voters meet in local caucuses, most often at the precinct level. There they often express a preference among the contenders for the party's presidential nomination and select delegates to a local or district convention, where delegates to a State convention are elected. At the State level, and sometimes in the district conventions as well, delegates to the national convention are chosen.

Decline in Popularity The caucus-convention process dates back to the 1840s and is the oldest method for choosing national convention delegates. Its use has declined significantly over the years. As a result, only a small percentage of the delegates to either party's national convention come from States that still use this method of delegate choice.

The Iowa caucuses generally get the most attention, largely because they are now the first delegate-selection event held in every presidential election season. Iowa schedules the start of its caucus process early, and has purposely done so ever since 1972. Sometimes the event is scheduled before New Hampshire holds its first-in-the-nation presidential primary, increasing the focus on Iowa.

☑ **HYPOTHESIZE** What benefits might Iowa experience from holding the nation's first caucus?

The National Convention

Once all the primaries and caucuses have been held and all of the delegates have been chosen, another event looms large. The two major parties hold their national conventions, the quadrennial meetings at which the delegates select their presidential and vice-presidential candidates.

Convention Arrangements Not only does the Constitution say nothing about presidential nominations, but there is, as well, almost no federal or State statutory law on the matter. The convention process has been built over the years almost entirely by the two major parties.

In both parties, the national committee makes the arrangements for the party's convention. The committee picks the place and also sets the date for that meeting. Several of the nation's larger cities regularly bid for the honor (and the financial boost to local business) of hosting the quadrennial gatherings. Chicago, Baltimore, Philadelphia, New York, and St. Louis have been selected as host cities most often over the years.

Apportioning Delegates With the date and the location set, the national committee issues its "call" for the convention. That formal announcement

>> National conventions are spirited, party-building events. Here, members of the Michigan delegation at the 1948 Republican National Convention in Philadelphia, Pennsylvania, jump to their feet and cheer as Thomas Dewey's landslide victory as Republican nominee for President is announced.

names the time and place. It also tells the party's State organizations how many delegates the States may send to the national gathering.

By tradition, both parties give each State party a certain number of delegates based on that State's electoral vote. However, both parties have developed complicated formulas that also award bonus delegates to those States that have supported the party's candidates in recent elections.

The GOP's formula typically produces a convention of a couple thousand delegates. The Democrats' more complicated plan can total twice as many delegates. Given those large numbers, it should be fairly clear that neither party's national convention can be called "a deliberative body," an assembly able to give each of its decisions thoughtful consideration.

Both parties allot delegates to the District of Columbia, Puerto Rico, the Virgin Islands, Guam, and American Samoa. The Democratic convention also includes a large number of "superdelegates"— mostly party officers and Democrats who hold major elective public offices and other party activists. This amount can change from election to election and may run to over 500 superdelegates in attendance at a Democratic convention.

Convention Goals For over a century, national conventions were highly dramatic, often chaotic, and even stormy affairs at which, after days of heated bargaining, the party would finally nominate its presidential and vice-presidential candidates. Both parties' meetings have become much tamer in recent years—largely because there is now little doubt about who will win the party's grand prize. The delegates are "pledged" to a particular candidate, based on their State's primary or caucus. Regularly, the leading contender has won enough delegates in the primaries and caucuses to lock up the nomination long before the convention meets.

Each party's convention remains a major event, nonetheless. The conventions have three major goals: (1) officially naming the party's presidential and vice-presidential candidates, (2) bringing the various factions and the leading personalities in the party together in one place for a common purpose, and (3) adopting the party's platform—its formal statement of basic principles, stands on major policy matters, and objectives for the campaign and beyond.

Both parties hope that their convention will do a number of other things, as well. They want the meeting to promote party unity, capture the interest and attention of the country at large, and generate support for the party's ticket in the upcoming campaign.

>> A representative of the Republican Party defends the party's political platform. **Analyze Political Cartoons** What do you think are the characteristics of a "legitimate" party platform?

Opening the Convention Each party's convention now meets in one or two sessions per day over three or four days. Each of those sessions is tightly scheduled and closely scripted. In short, they are now made for media coverage.

The first day is dedicated to welcoming the delegates and organizing the convention, and to dozens of short speeches by an array of party figures. The second day sees a continuing parade of speakers but is highlighted by two major events: the adoption of the party's platform and the delivery of the keynote address.

Showcasing the Platform and the Party The platform comes to the convention floor as a report by the committee on platform and resolutions. In fact, it has been drawn up by the party's leadership beforehand.

Platform-writing is a fine art. Recall, the platform is a statement of party principles and stands on policy matters. But it is also an important campaign document aimed at appealing to as many people and as many groups as possible. So both parties tend to produce somewhat generalized comments on some of the hard questions facing the nation at the time. Platforms are regularly criticized for blandness. Still, the platforms are important. They do set out a number of hard-and-fast stands in many policy areas. They also reflect the compromising nature of American politics and of the two major parties. It should be noted, however, that candidates for all offices are not bound to support every plank in their party's platform.

The **keynote address** is usually a barn-burner, delivered by one of the party's most accomplished orators. The address, like nearly all the speeches given, follows a predictable pattern. It glorifies the party, its history, its leaders, and its programs, blisters the other party, and predicts a resounding victory for the party and its candidates in November.

Nominating the Vice President The convention turns to its chief task on the third day: the nomination of the party's candidates for President and Vice President. The delegates turn first to the vice-presidential choice. Historically, that task often involved some suspense and a good deal of bargaining among party factions. Nowadays, however, the soon-to-be-nominated presidential candidate announces his or her choice of a running mate before the convention meets—and the delegates ratify that choice with little or no dissent.

>> Georgia Democratic Senator Zell Miller crossed party lines at the 2004 Republican National Convention and delivered the keynote address in support of President George W. Bush.

The vice-presidential candidate then delivers his or her acceptance speech—another effort to fire up the party faithful and appeal to as many other voters as possible.

Nominating the President The third day's session culminates with the selection of the party's presidential candidate. The names of several contenders may be offered, especially in the party out of power. Once the nominating (and several seconding) speeches are made, the delegates vote. The convention secretary calls the States in alphabetical order, and the chair of each State delegation announces how that delegation's votes are cast. Each complete roll call is known as a ballot, and the balloting continues until one of the contenders wins a majority of the delegates' votes.

The first ballot almost always produces a winner, for both the Republicans and the Democrats. Indeed, the GOP has not had to take a second ballot since 1948, and the Democrats since 1952.

With its candidates named, the convention comes to the final major item on its agenda: the presidential candidate's acceptance speech. This rousing and patriotic speech caps the convention and launches the party's general election campaign.

☑ **INFER** At what time of day are most major events in the national conventions held? Why?

Who Is Nominated?

If an incumbent President wants another term, and the 22nd Amendment is not in play, the convention's choice is easily made. The sitting President is virtually certain to gain the nomination, and usually with no real opposition from within the party. The President's advantages are immense: the majesty and publicity of the office and close control of the party's machinery.

When the President is not in the field, up to a dozen or more contenders may surface in the pre-convention period. After grueling months of campaign appearances, debates, speeches, and more speeches, at most two or three of them will survive to contest the prize at the national convention. Of those two or three, who is most likely to win the nomination?

The historical record suggests that this will be the usual answer: the contender who is the most electable. Both parties usually want to pick candidates who can win, but at times some members of the party push for certain policy positions, even at the expense of electability.

Political Experience Most presidential candidates come to their nominations with substantial, well-known records in public office. This pattern has not held true in the 21st century, however. In 2012, the Republicans picked Mitt Romney, who had served just one term as governor of Massachusetts. His Democratic opponent also lacked a lengthy public service record. Barack Obama had served only four years in the Senate before being elected to the presidency in 2008.

In 2016, Donald Trump, a wealthy businessman with no prior experience in government, became another exception to this trend when he won the Republican nomination. The only other major party nominee to that point to have no experience in government or the military was Republican candidate Wendell Wilkie in 1940.

Prominence at Home Historically, governorships have produced the largest number of presidential candidacies. In fact, about half of the people who were nominated by the two major parties since 1900 were either serving or had once served as governor.

For a time, the Senate was a prime source of presidential candidates. In the four elections from 1960 through 1972, every major party nominee had served in the Senate. Viewed through a wider lens, however, senators are not as likely to be chosen to run for the presidency as are governors. Since 1900, the major parties have nominated present or former senators only about 30 percent of the time.

Although several Presidents have served in the lower chamber, neither party has ever nominated a candidate who was currently serving as a member of the House of Representatives.

Other Characteristics Most leading contenders for the nomination have been Protestants. The most notable exceptions to that statement are Democrats Alfred E. Smith (1928), John F. Kennedy (1960), and John Kerry (2004), all Catholics; and Republican Mitt Romney (2012), a Mormon.

Nominees usually have a pleasant and healthy appearance, seem to be happily married, and have an attractive (and exploitable) family. Only six have ever been divorced. One (Donald Trump) was divorced twice.

A well-developed speaking ability has always been a plus in American politics. The ability to project well over television, pioneered by John F. Kennedy in 1960, has long since become a must, as well.

>> Dwight D. Eisenhower was a soldier and war hero with no background in politics when he ran for President in 1952, but a platform of peace and prosperity won him the election by a landslide.

Shattering Barriers Since the turn of the 21st century, several longstanding barriers to the nation's highest office have been overcome. Over time, most major party first-time presidential candidates have been in their 50s or 60s when nominated. None has ever been as old as Joe Biden, who was 77 when he became the Democratic candidate in 2020. However, the largest age spread between the two major party candidates in an election (23 years) was between Bob Dole and Bill Clinton in 1996.

Until 2008, neither major party had ever nominated a member of any minority group as its presidential candidate. In that year, however, Senator Barack Obama, the child of a white mother from Kansas and a Black father from Kenya, made history by winning the Democratic Party nomination. His groundbreaking election in 2008 ended the racial barrier to the nation's highest office and moved the nation forward in its quest for racial equality.

In that same election, former secretary of state Hillary Clinton tried to become the first woman presidential candidate in the nation's history. She lost that bid to Barack Obama, but in 2016, Secretary Clinton finally shattered what she called "that highest and hardest glass ceiling." In that year, she became the first woman presidential candidate in the country's history by winning the Democratic nomination.

☑ **GENERATE EXPLANATIONS** The text states that the ability to project well over television is a must for any presidential candidate. Why do you think this is the case?

The Presidential Campaign

As you know, the Constitution calls for a presidential election to be held every four years. The first one was held in 1789, and, like clockwork, all the subsequent contests have followed along, right on schedule. That remarkable fact is unmatched in the history of any other nation in the world. Even during a civil war, two world wars, several economic depressions, and various other crises, the Constitution's command has been met.

Saturating the Country The presidential campaign is an all-out effort to win the votes of the American people. For decades, that slugfest

>> Harry Truman and his wife, Bess, arrive in Philadelphia during his 1948 "whistle stop" campaign tour. *Ferdinand Magellan,* the railroad car they rode, was custom built for U.S. Presidents.

began soon after the two parties' conventions had adjourned. But, over recent decades, it has been quite apparent some weeks, or even a month or more, before the conventions who the delegates would nominate. So those campaigns have in fact begun at some point before the candidates were formally nominated.

The campaign itself is organized chaos, and it dominates the national news scene up to election day. The candidates' campaign organizations work to show their standard bearers in the best possible light and, with negative jabs, to undercut the claims of the opposition. The voters are bombarded with radio and television interviews, speeches and advertisements, direct mail, social media messages, "whistle-stop" tours, press conferences and press releases, rallies and party dinners, stickers and buttons, pamphlets, balloons, and billboards. The candidates pose for hundreds of photographs and shake thousands of hands as each of them tries to convince the voters that he or she is the best bet for the country.

Targeting Key Voters Both campaigns focus much of their efforts on **swing voters**—the roughly one third of the electorate who have not made up their minds at the start of the campaign and are open to persuasion by either side. Campaign strategy is also driven by the electoral college, as you will see in a moment. The would-be Presidents target the **battleground States**—those States, like Florida, in which the outcome is "too close to call" and either candidate could win. Both campaigns tend to concentrate their organizational efforts, campaign funds, and candidate appearances in those States.

Debates A series of presidential debates now highlights the campaign. An incumbent President, or a candidate ahead in the polls, may not really want to debate, but both major party contenders now regularly agree to do so.

The debates are now sponsored by a nonpartisan body created by Congress in 1987, called the Commission on Presidential Debates. The participants must be party-nominated candidates who are (1) supported by at least 15 percent of the respondents in five national polls and (2) listed on the ballot of States which, taken together, will cast at least a majority (270) of the electoral votes in the upcoming election. In effect, the Commission's rules all but exclude minor party and independent candidates from the debates.

The first presidential debates, in 1960, featured then-Vice President Richard Nixon and his

Democratic opponent, Senator John F. Kennedy. Their four televised debates, which were really little more than joint appearances, generated a great deal of interest, and many analysts credit John Kennedy's strong performance in them as one of the keys to his very narrow victory in the election that year.

The next set of debates came in 1976, between President Gerald Ford and his Democratic opponent, Jimmy Carter; with another involving their vice-presidential running mates, Bob Dole and Walter Mondale. That general pattern has been followed in every campaign since then. Although the number of debates may change from year to year, Americans have come to expect to watch the candidates discuss their views in a televised debate.

Who's Watching? The first televised Kennedy-Nixon debate of 1960 was watched by 61 percent of American households, reaching over 66 million Americans. Since then, the viewership has waxed and waned depending on the candidates and the issues. The lowest viewership occurred in the Clinton-Dole debates of 1996, which averaged a mere 41 million.

Over the years, the debates have been criticized for being sound-bite opportunities rather than real discussions of the issues and their solutions. Yet a number of undecided voters have claimed that the debates helped them choose the candidate for whom they ultimately voted.

Election Day The presidential campaign finally comes to an end on election day. Millions of voters go to the polls in all 50 States and the District of Columbia. But the President, whoever that is to be, is not formally elected until the presidential electors' votes are cast and counted, several weeks later.

☑ **IDENTIFY CENTRAL IDEAS** Describe the two general approaches—and the tone of each—that campaigns take to convince voters to choose their candidates on Election Day.

The Electoral College

You have arrived at one of the least understood points in the American political process. As the people vote in the presidential election, they do not cast a vote directly for one of the presidential candidates. They vote, instead, for presidential electors. During the Constitutional Convention, two proposals were put before the Framers on how the President should be selected—by popular election or election by Congress. The Framers opted on a compromise and the electoral college was born.

>> Bill Clinton, Ross Perot, and George H.W. Bush participate in the first town hall-style debate in 1992. The format allows selected voters to pose their own questions to the candidates.

Recall, the Constitution provides for the election of the President by the electoral college, in which each State has as many electors as it has members of Congress. The Framers expected the electors to use their own judgment in selecting a President. Today the electors, once chosen, are, in fact, just "rubber stamps." They are expected to vote automatically for their party's candidates for President and Vice President. In short, the electors go through the form set out in the Constitution in order to meet the letter of the Constitution, but their behavior is far from the original intent of that document.

Choosing Electors The electors are chosen by popular vote in every State on the same day: the Tuesday after the first Monday in November of every fourth year. In every State except Maine and Nebraska, the electors are chosen at large. That is, they are chosen on a winner-take-all basis. The presidential candidate—technically, the slate of elector-candidates nominated by the party—who receives the largest number of popular votes in a State regularly wins all of that State's electoral votes.

Today, the names of the individual elector-candidates appear on the ballot in only a handful of States. In most, only the names of the presidential and vice-presidential candidates are listed. They stand as "shorthand" for the elector slates.

Counting the Electoral Votes The Constitution provides that the date Congress sets for the electors to meet "shall be the same throughout the United States." (Article II, Section 1, Clause 4) The 12th Amendment provides that "the Electors shall meet in their respective States." The electors therefore meet at their State capital on the date set by Congress, now the Monday after the second Wednesday in December. There they each cast their electoral votes, one for President and one for Vice President. The electors' ballots, signed and sealed, are sent by registered mail to the president of the Senate.

Who has won a majority of the electoral votes, and who then will be the next President of the United States, is usually known by midnight of election day, more than a month before the electors cast their ballots. But the *formal* election of the President and Vice President takes place in early January.

On that date, the president of the Senate opens the electoral votes from each State and counts them before a joint session of Congress. The candidates who win a majority of the votes for both President and Vice President are declared elected.

The official counting of electoral votes is usually a matter of form, since the winner has already been declared. In fact, one of the hallmarks of democracy involves the peaceful transfer of power from one administration to the next. At no point in American history—not after the highly contentious election of 1800 between Thomas Jefferson and John Adams, or any of the many bitter contests that have taken place since that time—has the President in power refused to honor the results of an election and step aside.

That long, illustrious record, of which Americans are justifiably proud and of which many other nations are envious, ended on January 6, 2021, when a violent mob attacked the Capitol and attempted to interfere with the certification of the election results. Members of Congress refused to allow American democracy to be thwarted, however. They had been removed from the Capitol during the rioting to undisclosed safe spaces but reconvened late that evening to complete the counting of the ballots.

Days later, the House of Representatives impeached President Trump for an unprecedented second time, charging that his actions prior to the attack had incited insurrection among his followers. Although Joseph Biden was duly inaugurated on January 20, 2021, and President Trump was later acquitted, the incident was a sobering reminder of the fragility of democracy and of the norms the American people often take for granted.

Special Cases If no candidate has won a majority—today, at least 270 of 538 electoral votes—the election is put to the House of Representatives. This

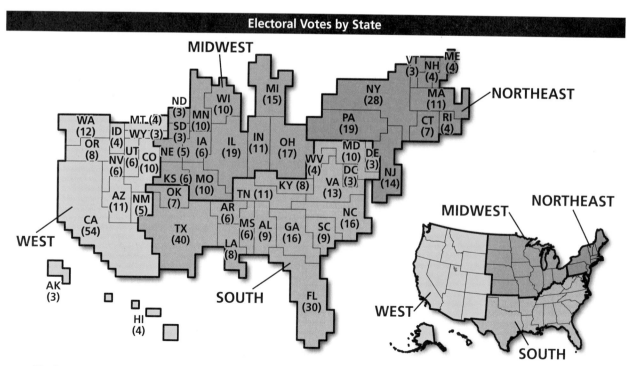

Electoral Votes by State

>> The large map shows each State sized in proportion to its number of electoral votes. **Analyze Maps** What can you surmise about the electoral vote strength of the Northeast?

1980 Presidential Election Results in Massachusetts

County	Reagan/Bush Popular Vote	Winner Reagan	Winner Carter	Carter/Mondale Popular Vote
Barnstable	41,493	✔		23,952
Berkshire	27,063		✔	29,458
Bristol	77,545		✔	83,460
Dukes	1,809		✔	2,370
Essex	130,252	✔		116,173
Franklin	12,528	✔		11,830
Hampden	72,528		✔	80,369
Hampshire	21,117		✔	27,611
Middlesex	256,999		✔	270,751
Nantucket	1,149	✔		1,040
Norfolk	136,184	✔		117,274
Plymouth	85,593	✔		58,772
Suffolk	73,271		✔	113,416
Worcester	120,100	✔		117,326
Total:	**1,057,631**			**1,053,802**
Total Electoral Votes Gained		14	0	

SOURCE: Secretary of the Commonwealth of Massachusetts, Elections Division

>> Ronald Reagan gained all of the Massachusetts electoral college votes in the presidential election of 1980. **Analyze Charts** By how many popular votes did he actually win? Does the allocation of the electoral votes in this situation seem equitable?

happened in 1800 and in 1824. The House chooses a President from among the top three candidates voted for by the electoral college. Each State delegation has one vote, and at least 26 votes are needed. If the House fails to choose a President by January 20, the 20th Amendment provides that the newly elected Vice President shall act as President until a choice is made.

The 20th Amendment also says that "the Congress may by law provide for the case wherein neither a President elect nor a Vice President elect shall have qualified" by Inauguration Day. Congress has done so, in the Presidential Succession Act of 1947. The Speaker of the House would "act as President . . . until a President or Vice President shall have qualified."

If no one receives a majority of the electoral votes for Vice President, the Senate decides between the top two candidates. It takes a majority of the whole Senate to elect. The Senate has chosen a Vice President only once: **Richard M. Johnson** in 1837.

☑ **GENERATE EXPLANATIONS** Explain why the Framers of the Constitution put the House of Representatives, rather than the Senate, in charge of choosing a President when the election process does not yield a majority winner.

Electoral College Scenarios

Under the electoral college system, at least three possible scenarios can happen in any election: (1) the winner of the popular vote is not guaranteed the presidency; (2) electors are not required to vote in accord with the popular vote; and (3) any election might have to be decided in the House of Representatives.

The First Scenario There is the ever-present possibility that the winner of the popular vote will not win the presidency. This is largely the result of two factors. The most important is the winner-take-all feature of the electoral college system. That is, the winning candidate customarily receives all of a State's electoral votes. Thus, for example, in 1992, Bill Clinton won just 46 percent of the popular vote in California. Still, he won all of that State's 54 electoral votes—despite the fact that nearly 1.5 million Californians voted for his opponent, incumbent George H.W. Bush.

The other major factor here is the way the electoral votes are distributed among the States. Remember, two of the electors in each State are allotted because of a State's two Senate seats, regardless of population. So the distribution of electoral votes among the States does not match the facts of population and voter distribution. To put it differently, States with smaller populations play a disproportionate role in the electoral college.

Consider an extreme case: California has 54 electoral votes, one for each 732,903 persons in the State, based on its 2020 population of 39,576,757 residents. Wyoming has 3 electoral votes, one for each 192,573 persons, based on its 2020 population of 577,719 residents.

Case Studies The popular vote winner has, in fact, failed to win the presidency only a few times throughout American history. In 2000, the Democratic candidate, Vice President Al Gore, won 50,999,897 popular votes—543,895 more votes than his Republican opponent, the then-governor of Texas, George W. Bush. However, Mr. Bush received 271 electoral votes—one more than the bare majority in the electoral college, and so he became the nation's 43rd President.

Florida's then 25 electoral votes were decisive in this election. The popular vote results in several Florida counties were challenged immediately after the polls closed there. The next five weeks were filled with partisan infighting, several recounts, and a number of court disputes.

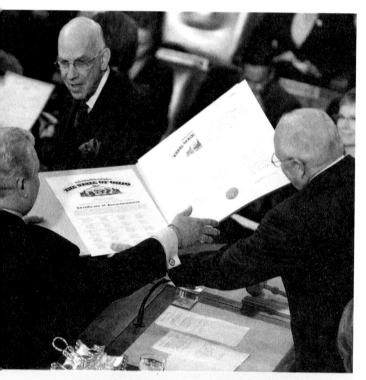

>> Members of Congress, in a joint session, count the electoral votes to certify that Barack Obama has won the 2008 presidential election.

The United States Supreme Court brought an end to the bitter contest on December 12. It ruled, in *Bush* v. *Gore,* that the differing ways in which various counties were recounting votes violated the 14th Amendment's Equal Protection Clause. The Court's controversial 5–4 decision ended those recounts. It also preserved Mr. Bush's 537 vote lead in the Statewide count, giving him Florida's 25 electoral votes.

Fewer than half of the nation's Presidents have won the White House with less than a majority (that is, less than 50 percent) of the popular votes cast in their elections. This often happens because minor party candidates get a few percentage points of the overall total. A sampling of these "minority Presidents" includes Bill Clinton in both 1992 and 1996, George W. Bush in 2000, and Donald Trump in 2016.

By now, you see the point: The winner-take-all factor produces an electoral vote that is, at best, only a distorted reflection of the popular vote.

The Second Scenario Nothing in the Constitution, nor in any federal statute, requires the electors to vote for the candidate favored by the popular vote in their States. Several States do have such laws, but they are of doubtful constitutionality, and none has ever been enforced.

To this point, however, electors have "broken their pledges," refused to vote for their party's presidential nominee, on only a handful of occasions—the most significant instance occurred in 2016. That year, an astonishing seven electors, two Republicans and five Democrats, did not cast their ballots for their party's presidential candidate. Their defections underscored the contention and bitterness that had characterized that election. To that point, no election in modern times had had more than one "faithless elector" in a single election.

In no case has the vote of a "faithless elector" had a bearing on the outcome of a presidential election. But the potential is most certainly there.

The Third Scenario In any presidential election, it is possible that the contest will be decided in the House. This has happened only twice, and not since 1824. In several other elections, however—most recently, 1968—a strong third-party bid has threatened to make it impossible for either major party candidate to win a majority in the electoral college, and so throw the election into the House of Representatives.

Three serious objections can be raised regarding election by the House. First, the voting in such cases is by States, not by individual members. A State with a small population, such as Alaska, Wyoming,

>> Shown greeting the crowds after Adlai Stevenson conceded defeat to incumbent President Eisenhower are, left to right: Mamie Eisenhower, President Eisenhower, Pat Nixon, and Vice President Richard Nixon. President Eisenhower won a huge 86 percent of the electoral votes in the 1956 election.

or Vermont, would have as much weight as the most populous State. Second, if the representatives from a State were so divided that no candidate was favored by a majority, that State would lose its vote. Third, the Constitution requires a majority of the States for election in the House—today, 26 States. If a strong third-party candidate were involved, there is a possibility that the House could not make a decision by Inauguration Day.

In such a case, Section 3 of the 20th Amendment states that "the Vice President elect shall act as President until a President shall have qualified." If no Vice President elect is available, the Presidential Succession Act would come into play. Note that it is even mathematically possible for the minority party in the House to have control of a majority of the individual State delegations. That party could then elect its candidate, even though he or she may have run second or even third in both the popular and the electoral vote contests.

☑ **DRAW CONCLUSIONS** If, in the future, third parties become more powerful, how would the electoral college system be affected?

Proposed Reforms and a Defense

These potential electoral college scenarios and their consequences have long been recognized. To that point, Thomas Jefferson once called its original version "the most dangerous blot" on the Constitution. Amendments to revise or eliminate the electoral college have been introduced in every term of Congress since 1789. Most of the proposals fall under four headings: the district plan, the proportional plan, direct popular election, and the national popular vote plan. Over the years, most advocates of change have supported proposals for the direct election of the President.

District and Proportional Plans Under the **district plan**, each State would choose its electors much as it chooses its members of Congress. That is, two electors would be chosen from the State at large, and they would be required to cast their electoral votes in line with the popular vote in their State. The State's other electors would be chosen, separately, in each of that State's congressional districts. The votes of these electors would be cast in accord with the popular vote in their districts. Remember, two States—Maine and Nebraska—now choose their electors on a district plan basis.

Under the **proportional plan**, each presidential candidate would receive a share of each State's electoral vote equal to his or her share of that State's popular vote. So a candidate who won, say, 62 percent of the votes cast in a State with 20 electors would receive 12.4 of that State's electoral votes.

Direct Popular Election Proposals for direct popular election would not reform but, instead, abolish the electoral college system. The voters in all 50 States and the District of Columbia would be given the power to actually choose the President and the Vice President. Each vote, cast anywhere in the country, would count equally in the national result. The winner would, therefore, always be the choice of a majority or at least a plurality of the nation's voters.

For several decades, a large segment of the American people has consistently supported direct popular election. Many obstacles stand in the way of this proposal, however, including the fact that it would require a constitutional amendment.

What About the Constitution? In their basic forms, neither the district nor the proportional plan would require a constitutional amendment to become effective. Remember, the Constitution leaves the manner of selecting the electors up to the State legislatures. Any of them could decide to allocate the State's electoral votes by districts or on a proportional basis.

The Constitution would have to be amended to accomplish direct popular election. Several obstacles stand in the way of that plan, however. Not the least of them is the constitutional amendment process itself. Recall, the smaller States are heavily overrepresented in the electoral college. They would lose that advantage with direct election. It is highly likely that enough senators, or representatives, from smaller States would oppose a direct election amendment to kill it.

Analyzing Proposed Reforms in Light of Goals
If the goal of reform is to ensure that the winner of the national popular vote would in fact win the presidency, only direct election would guarantee that result. Neither the district nor the proportional plan would do so.

Moreover, neither a district plan nor a proportional plan would overcome the electoral college arrangement that violates the core democratic value of equality. The district scheme prevents the weighing of all votes equally. It does, in major part, because, recall, every State has two electoral votes because it has two seats in the Senate, no matter what its population.

The proportional plan does do a better job of weighing popular votes equally. Still, because each of the smaller States is overrepresented by its two Senate-based electors, that arrangement would make it possible for the loser of the popular vote to win the White House in the electoral vote. And, again, the

Different Possible Outcomes: 1960 Presidential Election

PLANS	OUTCOME		
Electoral College (actual)	☑ John F. Kennedy	☐ Richard Nixon	
District Plan	☐ John F. Kennedy	☑ Richard Nixon	
Proportional Plan	☐ John F. Kennedy	☐ Richard Nixon	☑ Undecided, election is thrown into the House of Representatives
Direct Popular Election	☑ John F. Kennedy	☐ Richard Nixon	
National Popular Vote Plan	☑ John F. Kennedy	☐ Richard Nixon	

SOURCE: Dave Leip's Atlas of U.S. Presidential Elections, uselectionatlas.org

>> Seeing how past elections might have turned out is one way to illustrate the impact of the different plans. **Analyze Charts** Based on this information, did Kennedy win the majority of votes?

proportional plan would often throw the election into the House.

Applying the Plans to Real Scenarios If the district plan had been in place in 1960, Richard Nixon, not John F. Kennedy, would have won the presidency. And in 1976 the presidential election would almost certainly have had to be decided by the House.

Were a proportional plan in effect, in 1960, the Kennedy-Nixon election would very likely have had to go to the House. And, the House would almost certainly have had to decide who won the White House in several other elections.

States Against Direct Election Some argue that direct election would weaken the federal system because the States, as States, would lose their role in the choice of a President. Also, in several States, a Statewide election often hinges on the behavior of some particular group in the electorate. The overall result in the State depends in large part on how that group of voters cast their ballots or, often more importantly, on how heavily they do or do not turn out to vote. As but one of many examples of the point, the Black American vote in Cook County (Chicago) is regularly decisive in a presidential election in Illinois. With direct election, those key groups would not have the critical power they now enjoy, and so many of them oppose direct election of the President.

Other Arguments Against Direct Election Some believe that direct election would put too great a load on the election process. They believe this because every vote, no matter where it was cast, would count in the national result. And so candidates would have to campaign strenuously everywhere. The impact that would have on campaign time, effort, and finances would be huge and, opponents argue, probably unmanageable. Conversely, candidates might focus their campaigns and platforms on heavily populated areas, ignoring rural locales and small towns. Under the current model, small swing States get the attention of candidates, but with the popular vote model they might not.

It is also conceivable that, in a close election, a national recount would be required. Recall that a recount was ordered in Florida in the wake of the 2000 election. The possibility of such a situation on a national scale—considering that over 150 million votes have been cast in recent presidential elections—is daunting, indeed.

Others claim that, inevitably, direct election would spur various forms of voter fraud. That, they

>> Thomas Jefferson opposed the electoral college, calling it "the most dangerous blot in our Constitution, and one which some unlucky chance will someday hit and give us a pope and anti-pope."

predict, would lead to lengthy, bitter, and highly explosive post-election challenges.

Given all of this, there seems little chance that the electoral college will be abolished and direct election put in its place any time in the near future.

The National Popular Vote Plan A quite different approach to electoral college reform has surfaced: the **national popular vote plan**—in effect, a proposal to bring about the direct popular election of the President—and to do so without making any change in the words of the Constitution.

This new plan looks to the State legislatures to take the lead in electoral college reform. It calls upon each State's lawmaking body to (1) amend State election laws to provide that all of a State's electoral votes are to be awarded to the presidential candidate who wins the national popular vote and (2) enter into an interstate compact, the Agreement Among the States to Elect the President by National Popular Vote. That compact, and with it each State's election law changes, would come into force only if and when the compact has been agreed to by enough States to account for a majority (at least 270) of the 538 electoral votes.

The national popular vote plan is the only proposal to reform the electoral college that attracts any significant amount of public attention today.

A number of States, as well as the District of Columbia, have approved the plan. It is under serious consideration in several others.

The plan is sponsored by a number of prominent Republicans, Democrats, and independents. It has attracted the support of several nonpartisan groups, as well as major newspapers around the country. The plan has two main benefits: (1) it appears to satisfy the major objections that have been raised to the electoral college as it currently operates, and (2) it does so without the need for an amendment to the Constitution.

The national popular vote plan has also drawn criticism. Opponents note that its drawbacks include some of the same arguments made against direct popular election. Critics also note the possibility of diminished grassroots participation, since candidates likely would wage campaigns on a national level rather than depending on local get-out-the-vote efforts. Some also object to the plan for the simple reason that it allows the States to circumvent the Constitution.

Defending the Electoral College Defenders of the existing electoral college system react to the several proposed reforms by raising the various objections to them you have just read. Beyond that, most of these supporters argue that critics regularly exaggerate the "dangers" they see in the present system. Thus, they note that only two presidential elections have ever gone to the House of Representatives and that none has gone there since 1824.

Those who support the present electoral college system do grant the point that the candidate who lost the popular vote has in fact won the presidency five times—and as recently as 2016. But, they note, that circumstance has happened only five times in the history of presidential elections, and they add that it has happened only twice in about 200 years.

Stating the Electoral College's Strengths
Supporters also say that the present arrangement, whatever its warts, has several major strengths:

1. It is a *known* process. Each of the proposed, but untried, reforms may very well have defects that can't be known until they appear in practice.

2. In nearly every instance, the present system identifies the President-to-be quickly and certainly. Rarely does the nation have to wait very long to know the outcome of the presidential election.

3. Although it does present an enormous obstacle to minor party candidates, the present arrangement does foster stability by helping to promote the nation's two-party system.

4. Because no one region possesses enough electoral votes to elect a President, candidates must unify groups across the country and downplay regional differences. This, in turn, helps unify the nation as a whole.

5. The winner-take-all feature of the electoral college system means that minorities and other groups can have a significant impact on whether a candidate wins their State's electoral votes.

☑ **COMPARE AND CONTRAST** Explain the similarities and differences between direct election and the national popular vote plan.

☑ ASSESSMENT

1. **Identify Cause and Effect** Explain how reforms in the Democratic Party led to changes in how presidential national primaries are conducted.

2. **Explain** the process and procedures through which the President of the United States is elected.

3. **List** One general characteristic that political party leaders consider when putting forth presidential candidates is the candidates' religious beliefs. List three other characteristics, and explain why they are important.

4. **Check Understanding** Explain the pros and cons of the district and proportional plans to reform the electoral college.

5. **Evaluate Arguments** Which argument in favor of maintaining the electoral college system do you find most compelling? Why?

The Function of Presidential Debates

The presidential debates give Americans the opportunity to listen to the candidates outline their goals and strategies side-by-side. They are also often used as an opportunity for the candidates to criticize the ideas and qualifications of their opponents. The overarching topics under discussion are common, such as the economy and specific foreign policy areas. During the October 28, 1980, Carter-Reagan debate, the candidates were asked eight questions.

As you read, keep in mind the question that both candidates are answering: Can inflation in fact be controlled? If so, what measures would you pursue?

>> President Jimmy Carter (left) and Republican presidential candidate, Ronald Reagan, shake hands at the beginning of their debate.

Primary Source 1

President Jimmy Carter

[I]t's important to put the situation in perspective. In 1974, we had a so-called oil shock, wherein the price of OPEC oil was raised to an extraordinary degree. We had an even worse oil shock in 1979. In 1974, we had the worst recession, the deepest and most penetrating recession since the Second World War. The recession that resulted this time was the briefest since the Second World War. In addition, we've brought down inflation. Earlier this year, in the first quarter, we did have a very severe inflation pressure brought about by the OPEC price increase. It averaged about 18% in the first quarter of this year. In the second quarter, we had dropped it down to about 13%. The most recent figures, the last three months, on the third quarter of this year, the inflation rate is 7%—still too high, but it illustrates very vividly that in addition to providing an enormous number of jobs—nine million new jobs in the last three and a half years—that the inflationary threat is still urgent on us.

☑ **SUMMARIZE** What is Carter trying to convey about the inflation issue and his response to it?

I notice that Governor Reagan recently mentioned the Reagan-Kemp-Roth proposal. which his own running mate, George Bush, described as voodoo economics, and said that it would result in a 30% inflation rate. And *Business Week*, which is not a Democratic publication, said that this Reagan-Kemp-Roth proposal—and I quote them, I think— was completely irresponsible and would result in inflationary pressures which would destroy this nation. So our proposals are very sound and very carefully considered to stimulate jobs, to improve the industrial complex of this country, to create tools for American workers, and at the same time would be anti-inflationary in nature. So to add nine million new jobs, to control inflation, and to plan for the future with an energy policy now intact as a foundation is our plan for the years ahead.

☑ **ANALYZE WORD CHOICES** What words or phrases does Carter use to suggest the quality of Reagan's solution to inflation?

Primary Source 2

Ronald Reagan

When Mr. Carter became President, inflation was 4.8%. . . . It is now running at 12.7%. President Carter also has spoken of the new jobs created. Well, we always, with the normal growth in our country and increase in population, increase the number of jobs. But that can't hide the fact that there are eight million men and women out of work in America today, and two million of those lost their jobs in just the last few months. Mr. Carter had also promised that he would not use unemployment as a tool to fight against inflation. And yet, his 1980 economic message stated that we would reduce productivity and gross national product and increase unemployment in order to get a handle on inflation, because in January, at the beginning of the year, it was more than 18%.

☑ **ANALYZE STYLE AND RHETORIC** According to Reagan's statements, how would you characterize Carter's leadership ability?

Since then, he has blamed the people for inflation, OPEC, he has blamed the Federal Reserve system, he has blamed the lack of productivity of the American people, he has then accused the people of living too well and that we must share in scarcity, we must sacrifice and get used to doing with less. We don't have inflation because the people are living too well. We have inflation because the Government is living too well. . . . Yes, you can lick inflation by increasing productivity and by decreasing the cost of government to the place that we have balanced budgets, and are no longer grinding out printing press money, flooding the market with it because the Government is spending more than it takes in. And my economic plan calls for that. The President's economic plan calls for increasing the taxes to the point that we finally take so much money away from the people that we can balance the budget in that way. But we will have a very poor nation and a very unsound economy if we follow that path.

☑ **IDENTIFY CENTRAL IDEA** What is Reagan's solution to the problem of inflation?

☑ ASSESSMENT

1. **Make Inferences** Does the use of percentages help or hinder Carter's response?

2. **Assess an Argument** Criticisms such as Reagan's of Carter's leadership are common in debates. Should voters take a candidate's criticisms of his or her opponent at face value? Why or why not?

3. **Identify Supporting Details** What, if any, details are provided by the candidates to describe the measures they would take to deal with inflation?

4. **Draw Conclusions** When might the incumbent have the upper hand in a debate? When might his or her opponent?

5. **Evaluate** Do you think presidential debates are useful in helping voters determine for whom they will vote?

11.4

Elections are expensive. According to government data, spending on presidential election campaigns is nearing $1 billion.

Money and Elections

Running for public office costs money—and often quite a lot of it. That fact creates some very real problems. It presents the possibility that candidates will try to buy their way into office. It also makes it possible for special interests to try to buy favors from those who hold office.

The Price of an Election

Clearly, government by the people must be protected from those dangers. But how? Parties and candidates must have money. Without it, they cannot campaign or do any of the many other things they must do to win elections.

In short, dollars are absolutely necessary campaign resources. Yet, the getting and spending of campaign funds can corrupt the entire political process.

How Much Gets Spent? No one really knows how much money is spent on political campaigns in the United States. Remember, there are more than 500,000 elective offices in this country—most of them at the State and local levels.

The presidential election consumes by far the largest share of campaign dollars. As hard as it may be to believe, total spending for all of the major- and minor-party presidential efforts—for primaries and caucuses, conventions, general election campaigns, for everything—is now in the billions of dollars. That's not including outside spending by PACs, Super PACS, and other groups, which you will read about in this lesson.

 BOUNCE to Activate Flipped Video

Objectives

Analyze the impact of campaign spending on elections.

Explain how campaign contributions by individuals and organizations affect the political process.

Explain how public funding of candidates affects the political process.

Explain how campaign finance laws have changed over time.

Distinguish hard money from soft money.

Key Terms

political action
  committee (PAC)
Super PAC
subsidy
FECA
BCRA
soft money
Federal Election
  Commission (FEC)
Presidential Election
  Campaign Fund
hard money
527 organizations
John McCain
Russ Feingold

The vast sums spent on congressional campaigns also continue to climb, election after election. An average winning Senate candidate can spend tens of millions of dollars, while a House seat can cost over a million dollars. All told, over $1 billion may be spent just by the candidates—not by their parties or PACS—on congressional races.

What Does Campaign Money Pay For?

Radio and television time, professional campaign managers and consultants, newspaper and social media advertisements, pamphlets, buttons, posters and bumper stickers, office rent, polls, data processing, mass mailings, Web sites, travel—these and a host of other items make up the huge sums spent in campaigns. Television ads are far and away the largest item in most campaign budgets today, even at the local level. As humorist Will Rogers put it years ago, "You have to be loaded just to get beat."

The total amount spent in particular races varies widely, of course. How much depends on several things: the office involved, the candidate and whether he or she is the incumbent or the challenger, the nature of the opposition, and much more.

>> Born in Texas in 1930, H. Ross Perot became one of America's wealthiest executives. He is best known for being one of the most successful third-party candidates in American history.

✓ IDENTIFY What are some of the reasons campaign expenses have risen over the years?

Where the Money Comes From

Parties and their candidates draw their money from two basic sources: private contributors and the public treasury.

Individual Contributors Private donors are the major source of campaign funds in American politics. They come in various shapes and sizes:

1. Small contributors—those who give $20 or $30 or so, and only occasionally. Even in the age of Internet fundraising, less than 10 percent of people of voting age ever make a campaign contribution, so parties and candidates must look to other places for much of their funding.

2. Wealthy individuals and families—the "fat cats," who can make large donations and find it in their best interest to do so.

3. Candidates—both incumbents and challengers, their families, and, importantly, people who hold and want to keep appointive public offices. Independent Ross Perot, who ran for President in 1992, and Republican Donald Trump (2016) are tied for the all-time record in this category. Both men spent some $65 million of their own money on their bids for the presidency.

4. Various nonparty groups—especially **political action committees (PACs)** and **Super PACs**. Political action committees are the political arms of special-interest groups and other organizations with a stake in electoral politics. Super PACs are independent political action committees, unaffiliated with any political party.

5. Temporary organizations—groups formed mainly to raise campaign funds. Hundreds of these short-lived units spring up every two years at every level in American politics.

Fundraising Parties and their candidates often hold fundraisers of various sorts. The most common are $100-, $500-, and $1,000-a-plate luncheons, dinners, picnics, and similar gatherings. Some of these events now reach the $100,000-or-more level in presidential campaigns. Direct-mail requests, telethons, and Internet solicitations are also among fundraisers' oft-used tools.

As we all know, the Internet has become, by far, the most productive of those tools. Often, donations spiked immediately after an important speech or primary election victory or when the candidate challenged donors to give. Web sites including Daily Kos and Act Blue identified and profiled congressional candidates for their readers to support. Social media has greatly increased political engagement with younger voters, which could have a huge impact on elections in the future.

Government Money Public funds—subsidies from the federal and some State treasuries—are now another prime source of campaign money. A **subsidy** is a grant of money, usually from a government. Federal subsidies have so far been most important at the presidential level, as you will see shortly. Several States also provide some form of public funding of parties and/or candidacies.

Reasons for Contributing Campaign donations are a form of political participation. Those who donate do so for a number of reasons. Many small donors give simply because they believe in a party or in a candidate. Many of those who give, however, want something in return. They want access to government, and hope to get it by helping their "friends" win elections. And, notice, some contributors give to both sides in a contest: Heads they win and tails they still win.

☑ **APPLY CONCEPTS** Why do you think a candidate might prefer to have many small contributions rather than a few large ones?

Federal Finance Laws

Congress first began to regulate the use of money in federal elections in 1907. In that year, it became unlawful for any corporation or national bank to make "a money contribution in any election" to candidates for federal office. Since then, Congress has passed several laws to regulate the use of money in presidential and congressional campaigns. Today, these regulations are found in four detailed laws: **FECA,** the Federal Election Campaign Act of 1971, the FECA Amendments of 1974 and of 1976, and **BCRA,** the Bipartisan Campaign Reform Act of 2002.

The History of Campaign Finance Regulation

The earliest federal laws were loosely drawn, not often obeyed, and almost never enforced. The 1971 law replaced them. The 1974 law was the major legislative response to the Watergate scandal of the Nixon years. The 1976 law was passed in response to a landmark Supreme Court decision,

>> The first female presidential nominee Hillary Clinton (left) talks with an Iowa voter after a campaign event. Interactions such as these are one way candidates raise their visibility, which is critical to winning campaign contributions.

>> Arizona Republican Senator John McCain and Wisconsin Democratic Senator Russ Feingold coauthored the Bipartisan Campaign Reform Act of 2002.

Buckley v. *Valeo*, in 1976. This case was critically important because the Court found spending money during a campaign was akin to speech and thus protected by the 1st Amendment. The 2002 law attempted to close the **"soft money"** loophole in the 1974 and 1976 statutes; it was upheld by the High Court in *McConnell* v. *FEC* in 2003.

In 2010, the Supreme Court issued a stunning and controversial ruling that struck down part of the BCRA and called into question portions of the 1907 and 1971 laws. In *Citizens United* v. *Federal Election Commission*, a divided Court ruled, 5–4, that the government ban on political spending by corporations or labor unions violated the 1st Amendment right to free speech. Some supported the ruling. Others feared that it would, in the words of President Obama, "open the floodgates for special interests." In 2014, the High Court acted again, this time striking down limits on individual's contributions to candidates, political parties, and political action committees (*McCutcheon* v. *FEC*).

Congress cannot regulate the use of money in State and local elections. Every State now regulates at least some aspects of campaign finance, however—some of them do so more effectively than others.

☑ **IDENTIFY CAUSE AND EFFECT** Why can't Congress limit the amount of money spent on State and local elections?

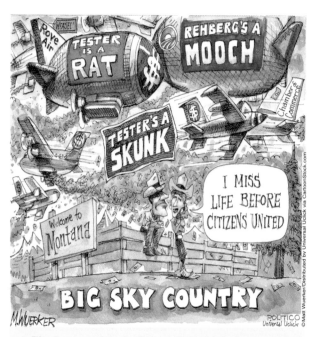

>> The Supreme Court's *Citizens United* ruling prompted cartoons depicting its effects. **Analyze Political Cartoons** What point does this cartoon make about the ruling?

FEC Requirements

The **Federal Election Commission** (FEC) administers all federal law dealing with campaign finance. Set up by Congress in 1974, the FEC is an independent agency in the executive branch. Its six members are appointed by the President, with Senate confirmation.

Federal campaign finance laws are both strongly worded and closely detailed. But they are not very well enforced. In large part this is because the FEC is both underfunded and understaffed. That is to say, members of Congress—who, remember, raise and spend campaign money—have made it practically impossible for the FEC to do an effective job. In short, the FEC finds itself in a situation much like that of the chickens who must guard the hen house.

The laws that the FEC is supposed to enforce cover four broad areas. They (1) require the timely disclosure of campaign finance data, (2) place limits on campaign contributions, (3) place limits on campaign expenditures, and (4) provide public financing for several parts of the presidential election process.

Disclosure Requirements Congress first required the reporting of certain campaign finance information in 1910. Today, the disclosure requirements are intended to spotlight the place of money in federal campaigns. Those requirements are so detailed that most candidates for federal office must now include at least one certified public accountant in their campaign organization.

Disclosing Campaign Finances to the Public No individual or group can make a contribution in the name of another. Cash gifts of more than $100 are prohibited, as are contributions and spending from foreign sources, corporations, and government contractors.

Once a candidate has raised the amount set by the FEC, usually several thousand dollars, he or she must register with the FEC and begin filing reports, which are available to the public. Any contribution or loan of more than a set amount, usually a few hundred dollars, must be identified by source and by date. Spending in any amount must be identified by the name of the person or firm to whom payment was made, by date, and by purpose. Any contribution of more than a specified amount received in the last 20 days of a campaign must be reported to the FEC no later than 48 hours after it is received.

Limits on Individual Donations Congress first began to regulate campaign contributions in 1907, when it outlawed donations by corporations and

Hard and Soft Money Raised by National Party Committees, 2000–2012 (in Millions of Dollars)

Party	2000		2002		2004	2006	2008	2010	2012
	Soft	Hard	Soft	Hard	Hard	Hard	Hard	Hard	Hard
Democratic									
National Committee	190.3	172.8	126.2	90.1	501.1	155.7	289.9	247.4	315.1
Senate	88.8	56.4	126.8	64.6	112.6	144.5	181.5	142.5	152.5
House	79.0	67.5	75.3	62.0	118.4	166.6	196.4	180.4	192.1
Total	358.2	296.7	328.3	216.6	732.1	466.8	667.8	570.4	659.7
Republican									
National Committee	231.7	296.6	152.0	226.9	498.6	289.3	476.7	216.2	444.3
Senate	62.2	71.8	88.6	78.9	100.3	105.7	105.2	126.1	122.3
House	65.9	135.6	93.0	188.1	236.0	213.7	131.9	147.3	162.8
Total	348.2	504.0	333.6	494.0	834.9	608.7	713.8	489.6	729.3

SOURCE: The Campaign Finance Institute

>> Regulating campaign finance has proven to be a difficult and controversial task.
Analyze Charts How does the data in this table reflect the 2002 campaign reform act as well as the decision in *Citizens United?*

national banks. A similar ban was first applied to labor unions in 1943. Individual contributions have been regulated since 1939.

Today, limits are set on how much a person can give per election to any one federal candidate. How much a person can contribute in any year to a political action committee (PAC) or to a national party committee has specific limits as well. The FEC adjusts these figures, to account for inflation, every two years.

Until 2014, the total of any person's contributions to all federal candidates, political parties, and committees combined was also limited by law. The Supreme Court's ruling in *McCutcheon* v. *FEC* removed those overall limits. Today, an individual can contribute to any number of candidates, PACs, or committees, as long as he or she does not exceed the individual limits explained above.

The individual limits may seem generous, but before they were imposed in 1974, some wealthy individuals gave far larger amounts. In 1972, for example, W. Clement Stone, a Chicago insurance executive, contributed more than $2 million (equal to more than $20 million in today's money) to President Richard Nixon's reelection campaign.

Contributions from Political Action Committees (PACs)
Neither corporations nor labor unions can contribute directly to any candidate

for federal office. Their political action committees, however, can and do.

Political action committees (PACs) seek to affect the making of public policy, and so they are very interested in the outcome of elections in the United States. Thousands of PACs are active today, and those organizations are of two distinct types:

1. Many PACs are the political arms of special interest groups—and especially of business associations, labor unions, and professional organizations. These groups are known in the law as "segregated fund committees." They can raise funds *only* from their members—from the executives, the employees, and the stockholders of a corporation, from the members of a labor union, and so on. They *cannot* seek contributions from the general public. Each of these PACs is a part of its parent organization. BIPAC (the Business-Industry Political Action Committee) and COPE (the AFLCIO's Committee on Political Education) are among the most active of these groups.

2. Some PACs are known as "non-connected committees." Each of them was established as an independent entity, not as a unit in some larger organization. Many are ideologically based. These PACs can raise money from the public at large. One major example is EMILY's List, which actively recruits and funds pro-choice women as Democratic

candidates. (The group takes its name from this political maxim: Early Money Is Like Yeast, it makes the dough rise.)

PACs fill their war chests with contributions from the members of the PAC's parent organization or with the dollars they raise from the public. They "bundle" the money they gather—that is, each PAC pools its many contributions into a single large fund. Then they distribute that money to those candidates who (1) are sympathetic to the PAC's policy goals, and (2) have a reasonable chance of winning their races.

3. The Court's 2010 ruling in *Citizens United* gave rise to a new type of PAC, known as the Super PAC. Super PACs are independent political action committees, unaffiliated with any political party.

Unlike traditional PACs, Super PACs are allowed to raise and spend unlimited amounts, although they must reveal their donors and cannot work directly with a candidate's campaign. Super PACs, whose major donors are corporations and unions, spend billions of dollars on elections, especially in years during which presidential elections are held.

>> Public funding is also available for candidates in presidential elections. Every federal income tax return allows taxpayers to easily donate to the Presidential Election Campaign Fund.

Limits on PAC Contributions No multi-party PAC can give more than a set amount to any one federal candidate in an election. However, there is no overall limit on PAC giving. Each political action committee can give up to a specified amount, usually several thousand dollars, per election to each of as many candidates as it chooses. A PAC may also contribute up to a specific limit per year to a political party.

Political action committees pour billions of dollars into presidential and congressional campaigns. And they funnel untold other millions into State and local contests around the country, as well.

Campaign Spending Limits Congress first began to limit federal campaign spending in 1925. Most of the limits now on the books apply only to presidential (not congressional) elections. This fact is due mostly to the Supreme Court's decision in *Buckley* v. *Valeo*, 1976. In *Buckley*, the High Court struck down all but one of the spending limits set by the FECA Amendments of 1974. It held each of the other restrictions to be contrary to the 1st Amendment's guarantees of free expression. In effect, said the Court, in politics "money is speech."

The one limit the Court did uphold is a cap on spending by those presidential contenders who accept FEC subsidies for their preconvention and/or their general election campaigns. As you will see in a moment, those who seek the presidency can either accept or reject that public money for their campaigns. In *Buckley*, the Court said that those who take the subsidies must take a spending limit along with them, as part of their deal with the FEC.

The Presidential Election Campaign Fund Congress first began to provide for the public funding of presidential campaigns in the Revenue Act of 1971. It broadened sections of that law in 1974 and again in 1976.

The 1971 law created the **Presidential Election Campaign Fund**. Every person who files a federal income tax return can "check off" (assign) three dollars of his or her tax bill (six dollars on a joint return) to the fund. The money is used to subsidize preconvention and presidential election campaigns. The FEC administers the various subsidies involved.

Preconvention Campaigns To be eligible for the public funds, a presidential contender must raise at least $100,000 in contributions from individuals (not organizations).

That amount must be gathered in $5,000 lots in each of at least 20 States, with each lot built from individual donations of no more than $250. That convoluted requirement is meant to discourage frivolous candidacies.

For each presidential hopeful who passes that test and applies for the subsidy, the FEC will match the first $250 of each individual contribution to the candidate, up to a total of half of the overall limit on preconvention spending. Presidential contenders, therefore, could receive a subsidy of tens of millions of dollars. The FEC does not match contributions from PACs or from any other political organizations.

Some presidential candidates may choose to refuse to take the public money. This is often due to the fact that they believe they will receive more money from private contributions that will more than adequately support their preconvention campaign.

Presidential Election Campaigns Each major-party nominee automatically qualifies for a public subsidy to pay for the general election campaign. This subsidy can equate to over $100 million. A candidate can refuse that funding, of course, and, in that event, be free to raise however much he or she can from private sources.

Until 2008, the nominees of both major parties took the public money each time. Because they did, each (1) could spend no more than the amount of the subsidy in the general election campaign and (2) could not accept campaign funds from any other source.

For 2008, Republican John McCain ran with the FEC money. Barack Obama, on the other hand, became the first presidential nominee in the 32-year history of the program to reject the public money. He raised and spent more than $500 million on his successful postconvention campaign.

When several presidential candidates refused the public money, many pronounced the public funding system dead, a casualty of the ever-accelerating rise in the costs of campaigning. In the words of Democratic presidential hopeful Bernie Sanders, "Nobody can become President based on that system."

The massive effect of soaring costs on the whole matter of campaign finance and its regulation can be seen in this stunning example: Just one item (direct mail), for just one candidate (Hillary Clinton), amounted to $14 million in spending during the 2016 election.

>> Political campaigns require candidates to raise a great deal of money. **Analyze Political Cartoons** How does the need for substantial funds exclude many Americans from the election process?

>> By donating their time, campaign volunteers can help reduce campaign costs for their party and its candidates.

"Some of it is soft and some of it is hard, but the main thing is that all of it is money."

>> Fundraising happens even in the shadow of the Capitol. **Analyze Political Cartoons** How can fundraising be maximized while minimizing the potential for fraud by contributors?

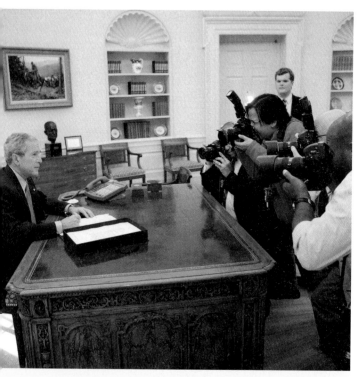

>> On the McCain-Feingold law, President Bush said, "Taken as a whole, this bill improves the current system of financing for federal campaigns, and therefore I have signed it into law."

Minor Party Candidates A minor party's candidate can also qualify for the FEC funding, but none does so automatically. For a minor party nominee to be eligible, his or her party must either (1) have won at least five percent of the popular vote in the last presidential election, or (2) win at least that much of the total vote in the current election. Since 1972, only Ross Perot in 1992 and 1996 has come even close to qualifying.

In the latter case, the public money is received *after* the election and so could not possibly help the candidate win votes in that election. (Remember, many provisions in both federal and State election law are purposely drawn to discourage the efforts of minor party and independent candidacies.)

☑ **ANALYZE INFORMATION** Why do you think that campaign finance reformers wanted to place limits on political contributions?

Loopholes in Finance Laws

President Lyndon Johnson once described the then-current body of federal campaign finance law as "more loophole than law." Over recent years, we have come dangerously close to the point where LBJ's description can be applied to the federal election money statutes.

Hard Money and Soft Money Since the 1970s, federal law has placed limits on **hard money**—that is, those contributions that are given directly to candidates for their campaigns for Congress or the White House, are limited in amount, and must be reported. That kind of campaign money is usually more difficult to raise than soft money—funds given to parties or to other political organizations, in unlimited amounts, to be used for such "party-building activities" as voter registration or get-out-the-vote drives or for campaigns for or against particular public policies.

Both major parties began to exploit the soft-money loophole in the 1980s. Officially, those funds were to be used for party-building purposes, but both parties found it easy to filter them into their presidential and congressional campaigns.

Campaign Finance Reform The torrent of money rushing through the soft-money loophole rose from about $19 million in 1980 to almost $500 million in 2000. Those huge numbers convinced many people that the nation's campaign finance laws were

Spending by Super PACs

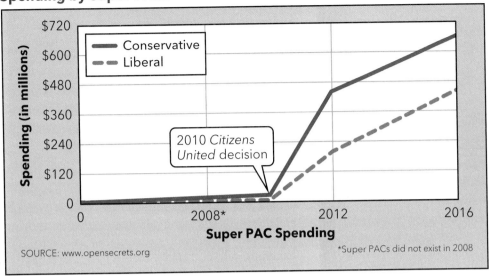

>> Super PACs did not exist in 2008, but by the end of 2010, their spending had already reached nearly $65 million. **Analyze Charts** Approximately how much did all Super PACs combined spend in the 2016 election?

in serious need of reform. With much effort from Republican Senator **John McCain** of Arizona and Democratic Senator **Russ Feingold** of Wisconsin, the Bipartisan Campaign Reform Act (BCRA) was passed and signed into law by President George W. Bush in 2002, after years of debate and delay.

The aim of this bill, also known as the McCain-Feingold Bill, was to reduce the amount of unregulated soft money in the system. In many key respects, that outcome has been achieved. The BCRA bans soft-money contributions to political parties, but the law does not say that other political organizations cannot raise and spend those dollars.

Almost immediately, creative minds in both parties found ways to skirt the ban. An important by-product of this reform has been the growing number of groups not aligned with a political party but quite interested in certain candidates and policies. These groups have been named **527 organizations** (after Section 527 of the Internal Revenue Code, which regulates their practices). They are allowed to raise unlimited sums of money. Most 527s are advocacy groups that try to influence the outcome of elections through voter mobilization efforts and television advertisements that praise or criticize a candidate's record. A great deal of the funds now flowing to 527s had previously gone to the parties in the form of soft money.

Two prominent examples of 527s have been the Swift Boat Veterans and POWs for Truth and MoveOn.org. The Swift Boat Veterans organization was set up to criticize 2004 Democratic presidential candidate John Kerry. MoveOn.org, by contrast, was run by a group of Americans who were dissatisfied with President George W. Bush. These groups and other 527s have been able to raise massive sums of money. Indeed, one estimate is that 527 groups spent more than $1 million on Web ads alone in 2016.

***Citizens United* v. FEC** An important chapter in the story of money in American elections was a decision handed down by the Supreme Court on January 21, 2010. The case was *Citizens United* v. *Federal Election Commission*, and it dealt with a provision of BCRA that outlawed explicit campaigning by nonpartisan groups within 30 days of a general election and 60 days prior to a primary election.

When the case was originally heard by the Supreme Court, the issue seemed to center on the prohibitions stipulated in BCRA. But when the justices heard arguments a second time, the topic appeared to be much broader: whether prohibitions on corporations and unions from directly spending in campaigns, established a half century before and upheld in several prior cases, were constitutional. In a 5–4 decision, the Court ruled that unions and corporations were entitled to spend money from their general treasuries (without the use of PACs)

>> Bill Burton, co-founder of Priorities USA Action Super PAC, speaks during a panel discussion. In the 2020 presidential election, Priorities USA Action spent 60 percent of its budget on television, radio, and digital advertising.

on federal elections. They could not give directly to candidates, but they were free to spend lavishly on their behalf.

The decision sent shock waves across the political system. Some suggested the ruling represented a tremendous victory for free speech; a straightforward application of basic 1st Amendment principles. However, others feared that the decision would set loose a flood of money and lead to greater corruption. One thing is for certain, the amount of "outside money" (that is, money coming from sources independent of a candidate's campaign) skyrocketed.

The Court's 2010 *Citizens United* ruling did not radically affect spending by 527s. Other independent groups, however, including Super PACs and 501(c) organizations, began spending unprecedented amounts. 501(c)s are nonprofit groups registered under the IRS tax code 501(c). 501(c)s, unlike 527s and Super PACs, do not have to disclose their donors. All three types of groups can raise and spend unlimited amounts, as long as those dollars are not given directly to a candidate or campaign.

In 2016, some $1.4 billion poured into political campaigns from these sources. This staggering sum dwarfed previous records and appeared to validate concerns about the effect of *Citizens United*. In the end, however, some of the biggest outside spenders failed in the majority of the races they sought to influence, suggesting that money may not be the deciding factor in American electoral politics. The fact remains, however, that both sides spend extraordinary sums—and that trend is unlikely to be reversed anytime soon.

☑ **COMPARE AND CONTRAST** What are the similarities and differences between hard money and soft money?

☑ **ASSESSMENT**

1. **Apply Concepts** In your own words, explain why some people are opposed to "outside money" coming into State and local campaigns.

2. **Interpret** Explain why a PAC would donate to a political campaign.

3. **Determine Relevance** In a democracy, why is it important for candidates to disclose where they get their campaign funds?

4. **Identify Central Issues** How did the *Citizens United* case affect campaign finance options?

5. **Apply Concepts** Give an example of hard money and an example of soft money.

Citizens United v. FEC, 2010

Just prior to the 2008 presidential election, a conservative nonprofit corporation called Citizens United wanted to air advertisements for a film that was highly critical of presidential candidate Hillary Clinton. The ads were deemed by a lower court to violate parts of the 2002 Bipartisan Campaign Reform Act. The case was appealed and when *Citizens United* v. *FEC* reached the Supreme Court, the Court overturned the decision on the basis that the corporation's free speech rights had been violated. In other words, corporations have as much right as American citizens to share their opinions during an election.

> As you read, compare how each source views corporations.

>> Many Americans felt deep disappointment in the Supreme Court following its decision in *Citizens United*, as illustrated by this cartoon.

Majority Opinion, Justice Anthony M. Kennedy, January 21, 2010

Speech is an essential mechanism of democracy, for it is the means to hold officials accountable to the people. . . . The right of citizens to inquire, to hear, to speak, and to use information to reach consensus is a precondition to enlightened self-government and a necessary means to protect it. The First Amendment " 'has its fullest and most urgent application' to speech uttered during a campaign for political office." . . . .

☑ **ASSESS AN ARGUMENT** Do you concur that the 1st Amendment is at "its fullest and most urgent application" during an election?

By suppressing the speech of manifold [many] corporations, both for-profit and nonprofit, the Government prevents their voices and viewpoints from reaching the public and advising voters on which persons or entities are hostile to their interests. Factions will necessarily form in our Republic, but the remedy of "destroying the liberty" of some factions is "worse than the disease." . . . Factions should be checked by permitting them all to speak . . . and by entrusting the people to judge what is true and what is false. . . .

When Government seeks to use its full power, including the criminal law, to command where a person may get his or her information or what distrusted source he or she may not hear, it uses censorship to control thought. This is unlawful. The First Amendment confirms the freedom to think for ourselves. . . .

Our Nation's speech dynamic is changing, and informative voices should not have to circumvent onerous [troublesome] restrictions to exercise their First Amendment rights. Speakers have become adept at presenting citizens with sound bites, talking points, and scripted messages that dominate the 24-hour news cycle. . . . On certain topics corporations may possess valuable expertise, leaving them the best equipped to point out errors or fallacies in speech of all sorts, including the speech of candidates and elected officials. . . .

☑ **DRAW INFERENCES** As a result of the inundation of information during elections, what is required of voters?

Dissenting Opinion, Justice John Paul Stevens, January 21, 2010

In the context of election to public office, the distinction between corporate and human speakers is significant. Although they make enormous contributions to our society, corporations are not actually members of it. They cannot vote or run for office. Because they may be managed and controlled by nonresidents, their interests may conflict in fundamental respects with the interests of eligible voters. The financial resources, legal structure, and instrumental orientation of corporations raise legitimate concerns about their role in the electoral process. Our lawmakers have a compelling constitutional basis, if not also a democratic duty, to take measures designed to guard against the potentially deleterious [damaging] effects of corporate spending in local and national races. . . .

The Court's ruling threatens to undermine the integrity of elected institutions across the Nation. The path it has taken to reach its outcome will, I fear, do damage to this institution.

☑ **EXPLAIN AN ARGUMENT** Why does Stevens believe that corporations will "undermine the integrity of elected institutions"?

It might also be added that corporations have no consciences, no beliefs, no feelings, no thoughts, no desires. . . . [T]hey are not themselves members of "We the People" by whom and for whom our Constitution was established. . . .

The Court's . . . approach to the First Amendment may well promote corporate power at the cost of the individual and collective self-expression the Amendment was meant to serve. It will undoubtedly cripple the ability of ordinary citizens, Congress, and the States to adopt even limited measures to protect against corporate domination of the electoral process. . . .

While American democracy is imperfect, few outside the majority of this Court would have thought its flaws included a dearth [shortage] of corporate money in politics.

☑ **DISTINGUISH AMONG FACT, OPINION, AND REASONED JUDGMENT** Is the statement in the last paragraph fact, opinion, or a reasoned judgment? Explain.

☑ ASSESSMENT

1. **Draw Conclusions** Justice Kennedy puts the burden of determining what is true and what is false on the voter. Is this fair?

2. **Analyze Arguments** How does Justice Stevens use the Constitution's "We the People" statement as support for his viewpoint?

3. **Compare and Contrast** Which source do you think provides the most valid argument regarding corporate free speech?

4. **Predict** What do you think happened as a result of the *Citizens* decision?

GO ONLINE to www.SavvasRealize.com
and access your digital course

Use the following online resources to practice citizenship skills and prepare for the Topic Test.

Case Studies

Current Connections

Quest Inquiries

Quizzes

Interactivities

Texts

Flipped Videos

While online you can also check the progress you've made learning the topic and course content by viewing your grades, test scores, and assignment status.

SAVVAS
realize.™

LESSON SUMMARIES

Use these Lesson Summaries, and the longer versions available online, to review the key ideas for each lesson in this Topic.

Lesson 1: Political Parties and What They Do

A political party is a group that seeks to control government by winning elections. The United States has long been dominated by a two-party system. The major parties are decentralized and often fragmented.

Lesson 2: Nominations

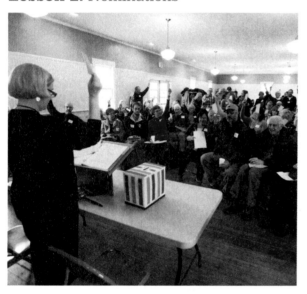

Nomination is the naming of those who will seek elected office. It is the first step in an election. Today, most candidates are chosen in direct primary elections in which party members run against one another.

Lesson 3: Electing the President

The process of electing the President begins with State primaries and caucuses and national party conventions, through which voters chose the candidates. Campaigns last for months and include the saturation of mass media with ads, publicity, and news coverage. In November, voters chose presidential electors, who later meet to formally elect a President. This complicated process has led to calls for reform.

Lesson 4: Money and Elections

Presidential campaigns are hugely expensive. Private donations are the major source of their funding. Congress regulates federal election spending, but the Supreme Court has limited its ability to do so. The Federal Election Commission attempts to enforce existing regulations. Various loopholes make controlling campaign spending difficult.

VISUAL REVIEW

Use these graphics to review some of the key terms, people, and ideas from this Topic.

Regulating Campaign Finance

- Contributions by individuals and groups are protected by 1st Amendment guarantee of free speech.
- Direct contributions by unions and corporations to campaigns are illegal.
- Federal campaigns must record donations and report regularly to Federal Election Commission.

The Electoral College

FLAWS	PROPOSALS FOR CHANGE
• Popular vote winner may not win the election. • Electors are not required to vote for popular vote winner in their State. • Elections may need to be decided in the House of Representatives.	• District plan • Proportional plan • Direct popular election • National popular vote plan

Political Parties in the United States

MAJOR PARTIES	MINOR PARTIES
• Historically, one of the two parties with a realistic chance to win elections • Currently Democratic and Republican parties • One party may dominate national elections at times • Both parties agree on some important issues and disagree on others	• Have difficulty winning elections in the American party system • May form based on an ideology or single issue, as a result of bad economic times, or from an existing party • Though rarely successful, they influence elections and the major parties

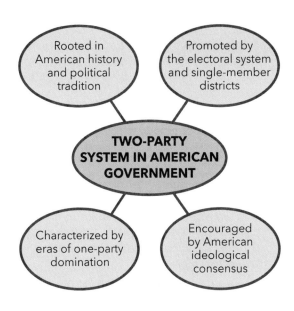

Topic 11 Assessment

KEY TERMS, PEOPLE, AND IDEAS

1. How do **minor parties** strengthen or weaken the two-party system?

2. Define **partisanship**.

3. What is a **political party**?

4. What are **political action committees**? How do **Super PACs** differ?

5. What is the role of the **Federal Election Commission**?

6. What are **527 organizations**?

7. Contrast **closed primaries** and **open primaries**.

8. What is a **nonpartisan election**?

CRITICAL THINKING

9. **Evaluate** How do political parties determine and shape public policy?

10. **Evaluate** What was the outcome of *Citizens United* v. *Federal Election Commission* (2010) and why was it a significant case?

11. **Analyze** What features of the electoral system support the existence of a two-party system? Analyze one of these features and explain its role.

12. **Summarize** What is the major purpose of a national convention? How have conventions changed over time? Do you think national conventions are useful today?

13. **Compare and Contrast** how elections are decided when using the following methods: proportional representation, popular vote, winner-take-all, and the electoral college.

14. **Draw Conclusions** What factors affect how much money is spent in a political campaign? How do campaign contributions help candidates running for public office? Does the private rather than the public financing of campaigns make elections more effective? Why or why not?

15. **Compare and Contrast** The chart in the next column contrasts the political parties in Germany's multiparty system with the U.S. Congress. Compare and contrast multiparty with two-party systems, noting the strengths and weaknesses of each.

Multiparty vs. Two-Party Systems

GERMAN BUNDESTAG, 2016	U.S. CONGRESS, 2016
• 49.2% Christian Democratic Union/ Christian Social Union • 30.6% Social Democratic Party • 10.2% Left Party • 10% Alliance '90/Green Party	• 56.2% Republican Party • 43.4% Democratic Party • 0.4% Independents

16. **Support a Point of View with Evidence** The Supreme Court has held that campaign contributions are a form of political speech. Explain why you agree or disagree.

17. **Summarize** What is the role of political parties in primary elections? Are closed primaries a fair way to nominate candidates? Explain.

18. **Analyze** What is the function of the electoral college? How well does the electoral college perform that function? What are the major benefits and drawbacks of the electoral college system?

19. **Analyze Campaign Ads** Parties, PACs, Super PACs, and other groups spend millions of dollars on advertising during every election cycle. Many of these ads attack the opposing candidate. Go to the Political Advertising Resource Center Web site and read about the things to look for when evaluating a political ad. Then choose a negative ad to analyze from this site or from the Living Room Candidate section of the Museum of the Moving Image Web site, which has ads going back to the 1950s. In your analysis, include information on the meaning of the imagery used in the ad, the way language and sound effects are used to evoke a particular response, which propaganda techniques the ad uses, and any other key points.

20. **Writing Activity** Use multiple print and electronic media to research a current issue of interest related to elections in the United States. In three paragraphs, analyze at least three different sources in terms of their factual differences, bias, point of view, and the conclusions reached in each. Then write a one-page essay in which you give your opinion on the issue, using evidence from the sources to support your viewpoint.

DOCUMENT-BASED QUESTIONS

People running for office must find ways to communicate with and appeal to all kinds of voters. Certain propaganda techniques are frequently used by candidates of all parties at all levels.

DOCUMENT A

Experts have identified a number of propaganda techniques candidates use to influence public opinion.

TECHNIQUE	DESCRIPTION
Name-Calling	Linking an opponent to negative words or images
Glittering Generalities	Linking oneself to positive words or images
Bandwagon	Appealing to the urge to "follow the crowd"
Testimonials	Presenting endorsements from celebrities
"Plain Folks"	Presenting oneself as an ordinary person like the voter
Fear	Playing on audience's anxieties about the future
Card-Stacking	Presenting only one side of an issue

DOCUMENT B

During his 1932 reelection campaign, President Herbert Hoover made this speech about his opponent Franklin Roosevelt.

Another proposal of our opponents which would wholly alter our American system of life is to reduce the protective tariff. . . . Whole towns, communities, and forms of agriculture with their homes, schools, and churches have been built up under this system of protection. The grass will grow in streets of a hundred cities, a thousand towns; the weeds will overrun the fields of millions of farms if that protection be taken away. Their churches, their hospitals, and their schoolhouses will decay.

—*Herbert Hoover, Address at Madison Square Garden, October 31, 1932*

DOCUMENT C

This poster was used by the Richard Nixon campaign in the 1972 presidential election.

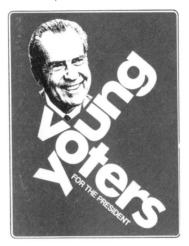

DOCUMENT D

This 2007 article quotes popular television personality Oprah Winfrey.

"I've never taken this kind of risk before nor felt compelled to stand up and speak out before because there wasn't anyone to stand up and speak up for," Winfrey told thousands of people in Cedar Rapids Saturday evening. . . . "This is very, very personal. I'm here because of my personal conviction about Barack Obama and what I know he can do for America," she said to applause.

—*CNN, "Winfrey tells Iowa crowd: 'Barack Obama is 'the one,' December 8, 2007*

21. Which of the techniques listed in Document A is used in Document B?
    A. "Plain Folks"
    C. Fear
    B. Name-Calling
    D. Glittering Generalities

22. Which of the techniques listed in Document A is used in Document C?
    A. Testimonials
    C. Glittering Generalities
    B. Bandwagon
    D. Card-Stacking

23. Which of the techniques listed in Document A is described in Document D?
    A. Testimonials
    C. Fear
    B. Card-Stacking
    D. Name-Calling

24. **Writing Task** Campaign speeches, such as Document B, are a form of political communication. Analyze this excerpt using the following questions: Does the speech show bias? Explain. Does it provide facts to back up its claims? If so, are those facts accurate? Does it use emotion to appeal to listeners?

Government and the Economy

ESSENTIAL QUESTION What is the proper role of government in the economy?

Newly printed $100 bills at the Bureau of Engraving and Printing

Connections to Today

Look at what you're wearing. Look at your phone or your iPad. The odds are that something—or part of it— was manufactured, mined, or grown outside the United States. The shirt you're wearing may have been made by workers in Cambodia. The cobalt that powers your phone probably came from a mine in Africa while app development may have been done in the U.S.—or in Israel or Sweden.

In this Topic, you'll learn about the global economy and how government policies affect what you buy.

NBC LEARN

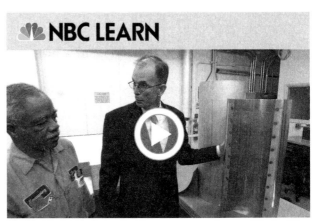

Explore the role of the Fed in monetary policy and that of the Bureau for Engraving and Printing in the creation of money.

BOUNCE to Activate My Story Video

In this Topic, you will find out why the news is always filled with stories about the economy. In particular, you will consider the role played by government in the economy of the United States and in countries around the world. Look at the lesson outline and explore the timeline. As you study this Topic, you can work on your Quest Inquiry.

LESSON OUTLINE

12.1 Types of Economic Systems

12.2 Fiscal and Monetary Policy

12.3 Financing Government

12.4 Spending and Borrowing

12.5 The U.S. in a Global Economy

Government and the Economy

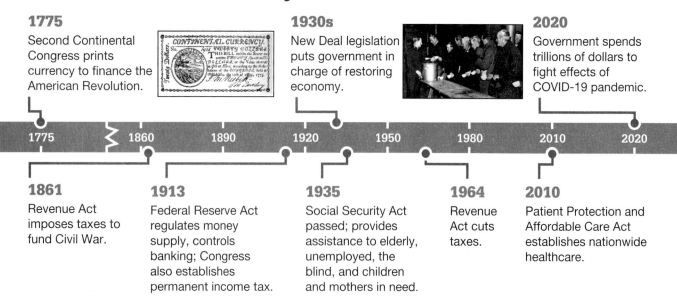

1775
Second Continental Congress prints currency to finance the American Revolution.

1930s
New Deal legislation puts government in charge of restoring economy.

2020
Government spends trillions of dollars to fight effects of COVID-19 pandemic.

1775   1860   1890   1920   1950   1980   2010   2020

1861
Revenue Act imposes taxes to fund Civil War.

1913
Federal Reserve Act regulates money supply, controls banking; Congress also establishes permanent income tax.

1935
Social Security Act passed; provides assistance to elderly, unemployed, the blind, and children and mothers in need.

1964
Revenue Act cuts taxes.

2010
Patient Protection and Affordable Care Act establishes nationwide healthcare.

Inquiry Center

Want to become an active and effective citizen? Make a difference in your community and beyond by using the **Inquiry Center** on the digital course.

Connect with issues you're passionate about by using the **Interest Finder**.

Investigate public policies, get involved in your community, influence public opinion, and develop leadership skills.

Synthesize the work you've done and what you've learned along the way.

Demonstrate what you've learned once you've finished your project by sharing your work.

12.1

Freedom of choice and competition mean that a vast variety of goods are available in a capitalist economy. Here, shoppers peruse wares at historic Charleston City Market in South Carolina.

 BOUNCE to Activate Flipped Video

Objectives

Identify the factors of production.

Understand the role played by the National Government in both the public and private sectors of the U.S. free enterprise system.

Understand the relationship between U.S. government policies and the economy.

Describe the fundamental factors in a free enterprise system and understand how the government fosters competition and entrepreneurship, as well as how government regulation can restrict private enterprise.

Key Terms

capitalism
factors of production
capital
entrepreneur
free enterprise
  system
free market
law of supply and
  demand
monopoly
laissez-faire theory
socialism
communism

collectivization
privatization
Great Leap Forward
command economy
Adam Smith
Karl Marx
Hugo Chávez
Josef Stalin
Mikhail Gorbachev
Fidel Castro
Mao Zedong
Deng Xiaoping

Types of Economic Systems

You have confronted these questions several times already: What functions should a government undertake? What should it have the power to do? What should it not be allowed to do? These questions are particularly significant in the realm of economic affairs.

Capitalism and the Factors of Production

Questions of politics and economics are inseparable. The most important economic questions faced by a nation are also political questions. For example: Who should decide what goods will be produced? How should goods and services be distributed and exchanged? What types of income or property ought to be taxed? What social services should a government provide?

Capitalism provides one response to these questions. **Capitalism** is an economic system in which individuals are free to own the means of production and maximize profits. Many aspects of capitalism will be familiar to you because the United States and most other nations in the world today have adopted this economic system.

Certain resources are necessary to any nation's economy, no matter what economic system is in place. Economists call these basic resources, used to make all goods and services, the **factors of production.**

Land Land, which in economic terms includes all natural resources, is an important factor of production. Land has a variety of economic uses, such as agriculture, mining, and forestry. Along with farms and other property, economists categorize the water in rivers and lakes and the coal, iron, and petroleum found beneath the ground as part of the land itself.

Capital A second factor of production is **capital**—all the human-made resources that are used to produce goods and services. Physical capital (also called "capital goods") includes the buildings, machines, computers, and other materials workers need to turn land and another factor, labor, into goods and services. Note that capital is a product of the economy that is then put back into the economy.

Labor Yet another factor of production is a human resource—labor. Men and women who work in mines, factories, offices, hospitals, and other places all provide labor that is an essential part of a nation's economy. In a capitalist, or free market, economy, individuals "own" their labor and can sell it to any employer. Human capital includes the knowledge

and skills that workers gain from their work experiences—an investment in themselves.

One who owns capital and puts it to productive use is called a *capitalist*. That term is applied to people who own large businesses or factories as well as investors and the owners of small businesses. The American economy is called *capitalistic* because its growth depends very largely on the energy and drive of thousands of individual capitalists, not the government.

Entrepreneurs To actually produce goods and services, someone must bring together and organize the factors of production. An **entrepreneur**—literally, an "enterpriser"—is an individual with the drive and ambition to combine land, labor, and capital resources to produce goods or offer services, and is willing to risk losses and failure. Entrepreneurs start businesses and make them grow, creating jobs and goods and services that contribute to a high standard of living.

☑ **DISTINGUISH** Are all capitalists entrepreneurs? Explain.

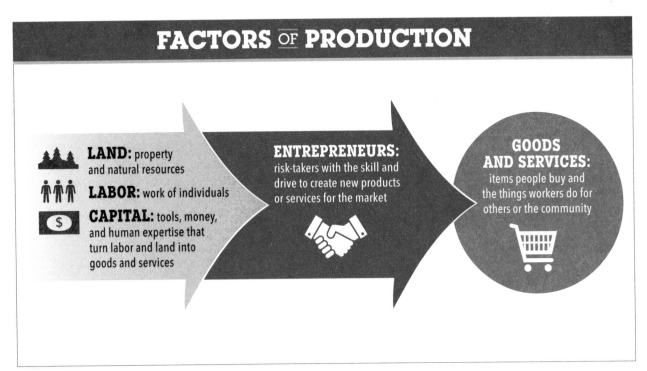

FACTORS OF PRODUCTION

LAND: property and natural resources

LABOR: work of individuals

CAPITAL: tools, money, and human expertise that turn labor and land into goods and services

ENTREPRENEURS: risk-takers with the skill and drive to create new products or services for the market

GOODS AND SERVICES: items people buy and the things workers do for others or the community

>> Land, labor, and capital are the building blocks of the economy known as the factors of production. **Analyze Information** What role do entrepreneurs play in a capitalist economy?

The American Free Enterprise System

Capitalism is often referred to as a **free enterprise system,** which is an economic system characterized by private ownership of capital and by investments that are determined by private decision, not by public authorities. This system needs a **free market,** a market in which buyers and sellers are free to buy and sell as they wish. A free market is most likely to exist in a democratic nation, such as the United States, where security and the rule of law are protected by the government.

A free enterprise system lets consumers, entrepreneurs, and workers enjoy freedom of choice. Consumers can choose from a variety of products and services. Entrepreneurs can switch from one business to another. Workers can quit their jobs and seek new ones, and they can choose to organize labor unions as a way to bargain for better working conditions or benefits.

A capitalistic system—a free enterprise system—is based on four fundamental factors: private ownership, individual initiative, profit, and competition.

>> A small business owner cuts the ribbon at the grand opening of her bakery. The 23 million small businesses in the United States account for 54 percent of national sales and 55 percent of jobs.

Private Ownership In a capitalistic system, private individuals and companies own most of the factors of production—the basic resources used to produce goods and services. They decide how this productive property will be used—for example, to build a business or invest in technology. What the property produces is theirs, as well. The owners of productive property are sometimes individuals, but more often they are groups of people who share ownership of a company.

In the American free enterprise system, the right to acquire, use, transfer, and dispose of property is one of a long list of economic rights held by the people. These rights have been secured through the 5th and 14th Amendments, which declare that no person may be deprived "of life, liberty, or property, without due process of law," as well as through court cases and legislation. The 5th Amendment also says that "just compensation" must be paid to owners when their private property is taken for some public use. These rights are vital to individuals and society because they promote equality and ensure just and favorable conditions for all.

In a free enterprise system, individuals own the right to their own labor. They sell that labor by taking a job, and the pay they receive represents the price paid for their work. Individuals also have the right to join or not join labor unions. In other economic systems, workers may have little choice as to the kinds of work they will do and little opportunity to change jobs or increase their earnings.

Individual Initiative In our economy, entrepreneurs are an essential factor in the production of goods and services. Under a free enterprise system, all individuals are free to start and run their own businesses (their own enterprises). They are also free to dissolve those businesses. Importantly, the atmosphere of a free market, as well as a free society that encourages the exchange of ideas, can and often does lead to innovation and scientific and technological discoveries. All these conditions promote growth in the economy and often improve the quality of everyday life.

The Profit Motive Just as individuals are free to choose how they will spend or invest their capital in a free enterprise system, they are also entitled to benefit from whatever their investment or enterprise earns or gains in value. The "profit motive" is the desire to gain from business dealings. It drives entrepreneurs to create goods and services people will want to buy, and is a major reason why entrepreneurs are willing to take risks.

Supply and Demand

>> A surplus occurs when supply is high and demand is low. Equilibrium occurs when supply and demand are in balance. **Analyze Graphs** What conditions are necessary for a shortage to occur?

The Role of Competition The freedom to enter or start a new business at any time leads to competition. Competition is a situation in which a number of companies offer similar products or services. They must compete against one another for customers. In a free enterprise system, competition often helps to hold down prices and keep quality high. This is usually the case because customers are likely to buy from the company with the best product at the lowest price. Competition promotes efficiency; the producer has the incentive (more sales) to keep costs low.

Under these competitive conditions, the **law of supply and demand** determines the market price for goods or services. Supply is the quantity of goods or services available for sale at a range of prices. As the price increases, more of a product will be offered for sale. Demand is buyers' desire and ability to purchase a good or service.

As the price falls, more of a product will be demanded by buyers. If supply increases and demand remains the same, prices will fall. If demand decreases and supply stays the same, prices will also fall. On the other hand, if demand increases and supply remains the same, prices will rise.

Monopolies and Trusts Competition does not always work smoothly. Sometimes a single business becomes so successful that all its rivals go out of business. A firm that is the only source of a product or service is called a **monopoly**. Monopolies can be very powerful in the marketplace.

Practically speaking, they can charge as much as they want for a product. Since there is no other supplier of that good or service, the consumer must pay the monopoly's price or do without.

In the late nineteenth century, political leaders in the United States gradually became convinced that certain monopolies were stifling competition and interfering with the free market. They were especially concerned about a type of monopoly called a *trust*. A trust exists when several corporations in the same line of business work together to eliminate competition from the market and regulate prices. By the latter part of the nineteenth century, trusts had gained tight-fisted control over the markets for petroleum, steel, coal, beef, sugar, and other commodities.

Constitutional Protections and Government Regulation In response, Congress acted under its commerce power to pass the Sherman Anti-Trust Act in 1890, which remains the basic law to curb monopolies—and thus, foster entrepreneurship—today. The Sherman Anti-Trust Act prohibits "every contract, combination in the form of a trust or otherwise, or conspiracy in restraint of trade or commerce among the several States, or with foreign nations."

Again acting under its commerce power, Congress established the Anti-Trust Division in the Department of Justice in 1933, to further promote entrepreneurship and foster competition. The Anti-Trust Division monitors business activities to determine whether competition within an industry is threatened. It can, for example, stop the sale or merger of a company if that move threatens competition in a particular market. On rare occasions, the Justice Department has acted to break up a monopoly to restore competition.

The Constitution offers several other protections that foster both competition and entrepreneurship. Thus, for example, Article I, Section 8 gives Congress the power to regulate commerce with foreign nations and among the States, to establish bankruptcy laws, to regulate the value of U.S. money, and to provide for the punishment of counterfeiting.

All of these protections together create a framework within which the free enterprise system can function. This means that entrepreneurs can start new businesses and compete in the marketplace knowing, for example, that there is a uniform national currency.

Another economic right held by Americans is found in Article I, Section 8 (Clause 8). Here, the Constitution specifies that Congress can grant inventors "the exclusive Right to their respective Writings and Discoveries." From these words evolved the U.S. patent system, created in 1790 when President Washington signed the Patent Act. Since that time, inventors and entrepreneurs have invested money and effort on innovations, secure in the knowledge that others cannot copy their ideas for a given period of time—today, generally twenty years.

Finally, the 5th and 14th amendments forbid both the Federal Government and the States (and their local governments) from acting in any unfair or arbitrary way. These amendments apply to businesses and corporations, as well as individuals. Thus, for example, the government cannot take corporate property without due process of law.

Laissez-Faire: The Theory Early capitalist philosophers believed that if only government did not interfere, the free enterprise system would work automatically. **Adam Smith** presented the classic expression of that view in his book, *The Wealth of Nations,* in 1776. Smith wrote that when all individuals are free to pursue their own private interests, an "invisible hand" works to promote the general welfare. In short, Smith introduced laissez-faire capitalism. *Laissez-faire* is a French idiom meaning "to let alone."

Laissez-faire theory holds that government should play only a very limited, hands off role in society, confined to: (1) foreign relations and national defense, (2) the maintenance of police and courts to protect private property and the health, safety, and morals of the people, and (3) those few other functions that cannot be performed by private enterprise at a profit. The proper role of government in economic affairs should be restricted to functions intended to promote and protect the free play of competition and the operation of the laws of supply and demand.

True laissez-faire capitalism has never in fact operated in this country, yet it has a profound effect on the structure of the nation's economic system, which can be described as laissez-faire capitalism with limited government involvement.

>> This engraving shows economist Adam Smith, who believed that government regulations on commerce are ill-founded and counterproductive.

☑ **ANALYZE INFORMATION** Choose one of the four factors of a free enterprise system and explain why it is essential to the success of the system.

GOVERNMENT REGULATION and PRIVATE ENTERPRISE

AREA OF REGULATION	ADVERTISING AND PRODUCT LABELING	EMPLOYMENT AND LABOR	ENVIRONMENT	PRIVACY	SAFETY AND HEALTH
HANDLED BY	Federal Trade Commission	• Labor Department • Occupational Safety and Health Administration, and others	Environmental Protection Agency	Federal Trade Commission	• Consumer Product Safety Commission • Food and Drug Administration
REGULATORY FOCUSES	Advertisements and labels must: • be truthful, not misleading • make only provable claims • be fair to competitors, customers	Ensure: • minimum wages, benefits, equal opportunity • workplace safety • citizenship or work visas for all workers	Regulate: • hazardous waste • emissions • pollution	Protect sensitive information of: • employees • customers • children	Establish standards for: • product safety • food purity • drug, cosmetic safety

>> Federal regulations can affect many areas of a business. **Analyze Information** Which government agency would a company that produces gasoline interact with regularly?

What Is a Mixed Economy?

Although the American economic system is essentially private in character, government has always played a part in it. Economists usually describe an economy in which private enterprise and governmental participation coexist as a mixed economy.

Government Regulations and the Economy

Government at every level regulates the various features of American economic life. At the national level, the government prohibits trusts, protects the environment, and ensures the quality of the food we eat, among its many other functions.

At the State level, examples of economic regulations are found in the insurance industry and in State-chartered financial institutions. Locally, regulations impacting the economy include those controlling rents, zoning, and the sale of fireworks, to name just a few.

Opponents of government regulation argue that it restricts free enterprise. For example, the high costs of obtaining licenses, keeping extensive amounts of paperwork updated, and putting products through rigorous safety testing are all viewed as

discouraging for entrepreneurs. Opponents also say that costly regulations decrease profits to the point that people are not willing to invest in starting new businesses—and that regulatory costs also drive existing companies out of business or raise prices for consumers. Those supporting government regulations, on the other hand, cite the generally accepted roles of government in areas such as ensuring the safety of citizens, protecting resources, and keeping competition healthy. Supporters believe that regulations are necessary to achieve these goals.

Government Involvement in the Economy

Government also promotes some aspects of American economic life. It constructs the roads and highways that are used to transport goods, provides such services as public health programs, the census, and weather reports, and operates Social Security and other insurance programs. It also offers a number of subsidies and various loan programs to help entrepreneurs and businesses prosper.

Federal, State, and local governments conduct some enterprises that might well be operated privately—for example, public education, the postal system, and municipal water and power systems. It has also assumed some functions that have proved unprofitable to private enterprise—for example, many local transit systems and waste disposal and recycling projects. These sorts of public efforts are sometimes called "ash-can socialism."

Mixed Economies Around the World In Europe and in most former communist countries, the concept of a mixed economy is slightly different than in the United States because the government is involved more extensively in social and economic matters. In the United Kingdom, for example, the government provides free medical care to all. The government of the People's Republic of China owns steel mills and factories. Germany's federal government requires large companies to give workers representation on managing boards. France once banned most companies from asking employees to work more than 35 hours per week. In each of these mixed economies, government intervention coexists with independent companies and market forces.

☑ **GENERATE EXPLANATIONS** Why is regulation sometimes viewed as intrusive? Write an argument against government regulation, including examples of how it might interrupt the free enterprise system.

>> German philosopher and political economist Karl Marx called capitalism the "dictatorship of the proletariat" and believed it would eventually self-destruct and be replaced by communism.

Socialism, Communism, and Karl Marx

During the Industrial Revolution that began in Great Britain in the 1700s, some workers were treated poorly, working long hours under dangerous conditions for little pay. As a result, certain political thinkers began envisioning alternatives to capitalism: economic systems known today as communism and socialism. However, some countries that adopted communism and socialism experienced significant negative consequences.

Karl Marx The father of modern socialism and communism, **Karl Marx** (1818–1883) was the most significant critic of capitalism as it developed during the early Industrial Revolution. He envisioned a society where social classes would vanish and the people would own all property in common. Exploitation of labor and unemployment would disappear.

Abundant goods would be available to all according to their needs, not necessarily how much work they contributed. Marx also expected that workers in different countries—for example, France and Germany—would share a bond far stronger than national loyalties. Thus, he theorized that communism would also end nationalism, a major cause of European wars.

Branching Out from Marxism Many European workers and thinkers of the middle and late nineteenth century accepted Marx's criticism of capitalism. His followers were deeply divided, however, by the question of how best to achieve a more equitable economy. Some argued that economic equality could be attained by peaceful, democratic means. Today, the terms **socialism** and *socialist* are usually used to identify those evolutionary ideals and the people who support them. Others argued that a fair society could come only out of a violent revolution, born out of class struggle. Over time, those who took that more strictly Marxist view came to be called communists, the advocates of **communism**.

Socialism Today Socialist governments around the world are in some ways similar to one another, but in other respects a good bit different. In most, the government places certain key industries under its control—particularly, utilities, transportation, and steel production. Many smaller companies remain in private hands, however.

These governments also aim to guarantee the public welfare by providing for the equal distribution

Marxist Economies

SOCIALISM	COMMUNISM
Goal: Change capitalism through peaceful means to bring about economic equality	**Goal:** Destroy capitalism through revolution to bring about economic equality
Some central planning	Centrally planned economy
Most property privately owned	All land and housing state owned
Large industries nationalized	No privately owned businesses
High taxes to fund healthcare, child care, education	State-provided healthcare, child care, education
Free elections	Controlled elections
Strong unions and worker protections	State-controlled unions

>> The writings of Karl Marx inspired two competing movements.
Analyze Charts How well do socialism and communism respect the rights of people as defined in a free market economy?

of such necessities and services as retirement pensions, universal healthcare, free university education, and housing. Any country that provides extensive social services at little or no direct cost to consumers is a welfare state. Because social welfare services are quite expensive, taxes in socialist countries tend to be relatively high compared to capitalist countries.

The High Price Tag of Socialism At various times in recent history, elected socialist parties have controlled governments and instituted socialist programs through democratic means. Gradually, however, most socialist parties in Europe have given up such traditional goals as nationalizing industries. And many socialist parties in Britain, France, and Germany have lost power or have abandoned some of their socialist objectives that have become too expensive and unpopular to maintain.

Socialism in Developing Countries Socialism has won a large following in developing countries in Africa and more recently in Latin America. One reason for its appeal in these nations is that large existing industries have often been owned by foreign companies. By nationalizing a foreign-owned industry and placing local people in charge, a political leader can win broad public support. He or she can also gain power by promising to provide socialist-style "cradle-to-grave" services and to redistribute land from large land owners to the poor.

After he came to power in 1999, for example, Venezuelan President **Hugo Chávez** and his nationalist-socialist party, Movement for the Fifth Republic (MVR), nationalized the oil industry, and used the profits to fund free education, healthcare, and low-cost housing. Chávez also nationalized the telecommunications and electricity industries. These moves brought Chávez enormous support, especially among the urban poor, and helped him retain power, despite broad resistance to many of his socialist, or even communist, goals.

☑ **INTERPRET** Why did Karl Marx believe that communism would end nationalism?

Communism

Marx believed that the revolution against capitalism would come first in industrialized countries with large working-class populations—in particular, France, Germany, Great Britain, and then the United States. Ironically, the revolution occurred first in Russia, then a backward, mainly agricultural nation, in 1917. Several neighboring nations were pulled under its control, and the Soviet Union was born. Its new leader, **Josef Stalin,** tightened that control and built a totalitarian dictatorship.

Stalin's Communism Stalin demanded **collectivization**, or combining, of farms, and increased production of chemicals, petroleum, and steel. The Soviet Union achieved rapid, though uneven, industrialization. Unfortunately, those advances came at a horrific cost in human lives, as well as in scarcity of consumer goods, housing, and urban services.

The Soviet Union did provide its citizens with free education, medical care, and even youth summer camps. It was far from a classless society, however. An elite class owed its privileged status to the Communist Party, which terrorized its citizens by arresting any considered disloyal and placing them in prison camps or even executing them. Private land was seized, censorship was imposed, and religious groups were persecuted.

The Decline of Communism By the late 1980s, Soviet leader **Mikhail Gorbachev** introduced a policy of *glasnost* (openness) and *perestroika* (restructuring), and the Soviet Union began to dismantle the political and economic structures of communism. In 1991, the Soviet Union dissolved into 15 independent countries. The largest and most populous of them was Russia.

Many state-owned companies in Russia were privatized. **Privatization** is the process of returning nationalized enterprises to private ownership. Today, Russia is a country with some features of free enterprise, but also extensive state intervention in the economy.

In fact, very few communist economies exist today. Most communist nations, like China and Russia, have incorporated elements of free enterprise into their economic systems.

Cuba, led by **Fidel Castro** from 1959 to 2008, developed a communist economy heavily dependent on Soviet economic aid during the cold war. As a result, the fall of the Soviet Union caused an economic crisis in Cuba. Decades later, the government approved a variety of changes, such as allowing Cubans to buy cell phones and stay in hotels. More recently, it has instituted additional reforms, such as removing its ban on many private businesses, opening up a few professional fields (previously only open to state employees) to private citizens, and permitting the private ownership of real estate. Cuba still has a centrally planned economy, however, along with a lack of basic civil rights for its citizens.

☑ **IDENTIFY CAUSE AND EFFECT** What factors account for the general failure of communism?

The Special Case of China

Mao Zedong, the founder of the People's Republic of China, was a Marxist. However, he believed the peasantry, not industrial workers, were the key to a communist revolution in agricultural China.

Dissolving the Soviet Union

>> A number of countries were formed when the Soviet Union was dissolved.
Analyze Maps What is one major reason that Russia was originally able to seize control of these areas?

U.S. Free Enterprise System and Other Economic Systems

CAPITALISM/FREE ENTERPRISE	SOCIALISM	COMMUNISM
Definition: Individuals, not government, are in charge of production and can profit from their labor. **Laissez-Faire** very limited government role **Mixed Economy** some government regulation	**Definition:** The state makes many economic decisions. Some central planning	**Definition:** The state makes all economic decisions. Centrally planned economy
Characteristics: • individual initiative essential in the production of goods and services • profit driven • competition holds down prices and keeps quality high • private ownership • supply and demand determine price	**Characteristics:** • state owns large industries • state provides social services and collects high taxes	**Characteristics:** • five-year plans by state establish economic goals • state owns and controls all aspects of economy

>> The role of the government varies in different types of economic systems.
Analyze Charts How would capitalist, socialist, and communist governments interact with businesses?

After Mao took control of the country in 1949, China developed its own version of a planned economy. Despite its huge population, the country lacked skilled workers. The government improved technical and scientific education and then assigned workers to jobs in the state sector. The government regulated the labor market, giving people little choice about where and for whom they worked.

The Great Leap Forward The **Great Leap Forward** of 1958 to 1960 was a drastic attempt to modernize China quickly. All elements of free enterprise were eliminated. Collective farms were brought together into a larger unit, the commune. Communes grew into self-sufficient bodies run by Communist Party officials.

Communist Party officials oversaw farms, industries, and government in a region, and they also managed social policy. Workers received the same rewards no matter how much they produced, so there were few incentives to work hard. The Great Leap Forward was a disastrous failure; it was followed by a severe famine during which millions of lives were lost.

The Chinese Economy Grows A new leader, **Deng Xiaoping**, came to power in 1977 and made great changes in the economy. Deng's program of the "Four Modernizations" aimed at improving agriculture, industry, science and technology, and defense. He began to move China toward a market economy and opened the country to foreign investment.

Today, China's economic system is a maze of different levels of government bodies and economic units. Although the Communist Party remains in power and directs economic growth, the state-owned sector has shrunk. The government encourages private enterprise and China has enjoyed many years of strong economic growth.

☑ **COMPARE POINTS OF VIEW** How are Stalin's and Mao's approaches to communism alike and different?

Comparing the Free Enterprise System with Other Economic Systems

Free market and **command economies**, in which government bureaucrats plan and direct most economic activity, differ in a number of significant ways. The most obvious is the level of government involvement in the economy. This main difference leads to other, less obvious distinctions.

Advantages of the Free Enterprise System Free enterprise systems tend to be more efficient and to allow for more innovation than command economies. This is because competition, which is nonexistent

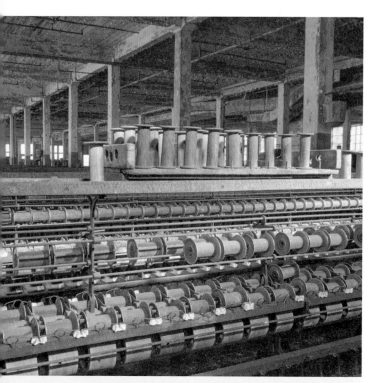

>> Although capitalism is not perfect, as evidenced by this abandoned textile mill, many countries have incorporated elements of the free enterprise system into their economies.

in a command economy, forces private companies to streamline decision-making and costs and to come up with new ideas continually.

Capitalism also leads to greater economic growth and a higher standard of living than does a command economy. As entrepreneurs work to increase profits, employees' wages often rise and the economy as a whole benefits.

Free enterprise systems also allow people to exercise basic economic freedoms, such as choosing what work they will do and deciding whether to start a new business or develop a new product. Individual initiative is rewarded and, at the same time, consumers have more choices.

Critics argue that large bureaucracies in socialist countries, on the other hand, complicate decision-making and have a depressing effect on individual initiative. Workers have little incentive to work harder and no incentive to innovate or create new products.

Comparison with Command Economies Those who defend socialism and communism, in their purest forms, argue that these systems avoid the greed and ruthlessness of capitalism. Instead, the common good replaces the profit motive, which means that everyone's basic needs are met. They criticize capitalism's drive for profits, which can lead companies to sacrifice worker safety, environmental standards, and ethics to achieve those profits.

Defenders of socialism and communism also note that these systems have much less economic inequality, and little to no unemployment. Workers theoretically have more say in management decisions. Under capitalism, there is an incentive to pay workers as little as possible and a company's management can abruptly decide to close a factory, throwing thousands out of work and disrupting an entire community. Under a command economy, on the other hand, workers on the company's board would help decide what is best for the entire workforce and community.

Despite these criticisms, perhaps the best evaluation of free enterprise versus command economies can be found in this fact: Both China and Russia, once strictly communist, have incorporated elements of the free enterprise system into their economies. So, too, have developed and developing countries in Asia, Africa, and Eastern Europe, such as Mongolia, Albania, and the Czech Republic. In fact, very few countries in the world today have purely command economies—North Korea and Cuba being two prominent examples.

☑ **EVALUATE ARGUMENTS** Using China during Mao Zedong's reign as an example, how could you debunk the argument that command economies give people more control over their daily lives than a free enterprise system allows?

☑ ASSESSMENT

1. **Identify Central Ideas** Explain how a country with little land and few natural resources could make up for such deficits—without depending on other countries—and have a healthy economy.

2. **Identify Cause and Effect** What impact does a monopoly have on consumers?

3. **Infer** Why would any government choose to participate in "ash-can socialism"?

4. **Contrast** How does government participation in the economy differ between socialist and communist countries?

5. **Identify** In a mixed economy, where can bureaucracies be found?

12.2

Crowds gather at New York City's American Union Bank during a 1931 run on the bank. The Great Depression led to New Deal legislation that greatly increased the government's role in banking.

Fiscal and Monetary Policy

For the first 120 years or so of its existence, the Federal Government played only a very limited role in the economy—whether at the local, State, or national level—and in the economic well-being of the American people. However, beginning in the early twentieth century, there were repeated economic panics and recessions. These panics and recessions culminated in the Great Depression of the 1930s, when the amount of governmental involvement began to change.

The Federal Government and the Domestic Economy

The American free enterprise system fosters competition and entrepreneurship. The Federal Government tries to support this system by attempting to ensure fairness in the market place, and, with it, the health and well-being of both consumers and workers. Because the economy functions at three levels in the United States—national, State, and local—the Federal Government's policies influence the economy at not only the national level, but at the State and local levels, as well.

In addition to fostering competition and entrepreneurship, both the executive and legislative branches help set fiscal and monetary policy. To this end, a number of independent agencies within the executive branch have an important role in the regulation of economic activities. Among the most important of them are the Federal Reserve System, the Securities and Exchange Commission (SEC), and such organizations as the Occupational Safety & Health Administration (OSHA) in the Department of Labor. Despite the prominence of some of these

BOUNCE to Activate Flipped Video

Objectives

Explain the major responsibilities of the Federal Government for domestic economic policy.

Describe the overall goals of the Federal Government's actions in the economy.

Explain how government fiscal policy influences the economy at the national level.

Explain how government monetary policy influences the economy at the national level.

Key Terms

gross domestic product
inflation
deflation
recession
fiscal policy
monetary policy
panic
open market operations
reserve requirement
discount rate
interest
Bill Clinton
George H.W. Bush
John Maynard Keynes
George W. Bush
Barack Obama

agencies, it is important to note that the government must continually balance the call for regulation with the equally critical demand for limited government involvement in the nation's economic life.

The Federal Reserve System Known as "the Fed," the Federal Reserve System is one of the most important tools the Federal Government uses to attempt to regulate the nation's economy. The Fed was established by Congress in 1913 as the central banking system for the United States. It is part of the executive branch and consists of a Board of Governors appointed by the President (one of whom is appointed to act as the chairperson), 12 regional banks, and many other member banks. The main responsibility of the Fed is to use the tools of monetary policy to promote price stability, full employment, economic growth, and other national economic goals.

Mainly, this means adjusting the federal funds rate—an interest rate at which banks lend money to other banks on a daily basis. The Fed does this to either contract or expand the amount of money in the economy in response to changes in inflation or unemployment. Raising interest rates makes money more expensive to borrow, and so, in theory, contracts the economy.

Lowering interest rates makes money less expensive to borrow, and so tends to expand the economy. The rate adjustments that the Fed makes can influence other lending rates, foreign exchange rates, and the levels of money and credit available in the economy, as well as employment and prices.

A Key Regulatory Agency The Securities and Exchange Commission (SEC) is a federal regulatory agency in the executive branch. It consists of five commissioners appointed by the President, who also selects the SEC's chairperson from among those five commissioners. Congress created the SEC in 1934 in the aftermath of the stock market crash that contributed to the Great Depression.

The commission's central responsibility is to oversee the nation's stock markets and ensure that corporations do not engage in such abuses as insider trading, which is the practice of buying or selling stock based on company information not known to other investors. The SEC also ensures that publicly traded companies truthfully disclose their finances. It brings court actions against those who violate securities laws—for example, through insider trading, fraudulent accounting practices, or providing false information to investors.

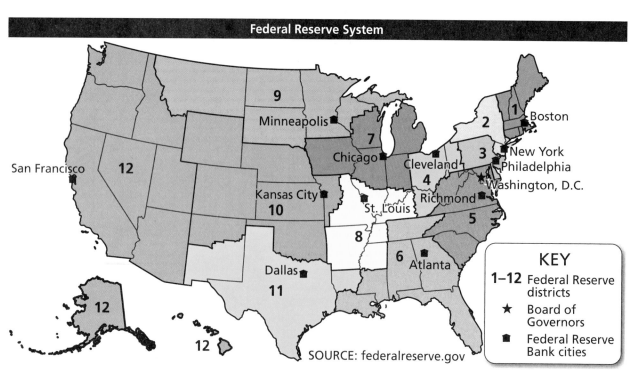

Federal Reserve System

KEY
1–12 Federal Reserve districts
★ Board of Governors
■ Federal Reserve Bank cities

SOURCE: federalreserve.gov

>> Decisions made by the Fed have great impact on both the national and global economy. **Analyze Maps** What is the benefit of having regional banks as part of the decision-making process?

The Role of the Department of Labor The Federal Government provides protections for the basic rights of workers and oversees issues of fairness and safety in the workplace. Much of this is accomplished by the Department of Labor, part of the executive branch of the government.

To meet these aims, the department works through its various agencies. For example, since the Occupational Safety & Health Administration (OSHA) was established in 1971, its inspectors have worked with employers and employees to decrease deaths in the workplace. The Employment Standards Administration (ESA) monitors fairness in contracts, benefits, and wages. The Bureau of Labor Statistics tracks major economic statistics, such as the unemployment rate and the Consumer Price Index (CPI). These data are used to evaluate the health of the nation's economy.

These various regulatory agencies have both supporters and detractors. Some feel that the rules and regulations they establish are important to the protection of American workers. Others believe that they are overly burdensome to business owners and that their influence and reach should be scaled back to better allow the free enterprise system to operate.

☑ **EXPLAIN** What is the Security and Exchange Commission's main role?

Key Goals for the Economy

"It's the economy, stupid." That slogan has become a watchword in electoral politics. It first appeared during the presidential campaign of 1992, on a sign that hung on the wall of political advisor James Carville's office in **Bill Clinton's** campaign headquarters. Mr. Clinton, the Democratic Party's nominee, faced a daunting challenge in that election: How could he possibly convince the voters that he, not incumbent **George H.W. Bush**, should sit in the White House?

Mr. Bush, the 41st President of the United States, brought a substantial record to the contest—a record highlighted by the end, at long last, of the cold war and a stunning victory in the Persian Gulf War. Mr. Clinton, and Carville and Paul Begala, his chief campaign advisor, were convinced that the key to success in November lay in the domestic, not the foreign policy realm. The nation's economy was stumbling, and, to their minds, the incumbent President was vulnerable on that score, and events proved them right.

>> James Carville was the lead strategist for Bill Clinton's 1992 presidential campaign. Carville's strategy recognized that voters were most concerned with the economy in that election year.

The successful management of the economy is vital not only to a President's political survival. It has a very direct and immediate effect on the well-being of everyone in this country. We will now explore the Federal Government's key economic goals and the principal mechanisms with which it attempts to achieve those ends.

Overall Economic Goals The American economy is both huge and complex. The nation's **gross domestic product** (GDP) is the total value of all final goods and services produced in the country each year. While private corporations and individuals have the most substantial impact on the economy's performance, the Federal Government also plays a part. In general, it seeks to achieve three key goals in the economic realm: full employment, price stability, and economic growth.

Full Employment Full employment, as you might guess, means that there are enough jobs available to employ all those who are able and willing to work. The Bureau of Labor Statistics, in the Department of Labor, compiles employment and unemployment data. Its reports are a major indicator of the nation's economic health.

Price Stability Price stability refers to the absence of significant ups and downs in the prices of goods and services. A general increase in prices throughout the economy is called **inflation**. A general decrease in prices is known as **deflation.** The Consumer Price Index, also reported by the Bureau of Labor Statistics, tracks trends in the prices of consumer goods.

Both inflation and deflation have harmful effects on the economy. Higher prices due to inflation rob consumers of purchasing power because their dollars buy less than they once did. Deflation makes it difficult for people and businesses to borrow money because the assets they use to borrow against decline in value.

Deflation also hurts farmers and other producers, who receive less for their products. This makes it difficult for them to pay off their loans, which in turns hurts banks and investors.

Economic Growth A growing economy is one in which the GDP constantly increases. That growth helps produce a higher standard of living. When there is an absence of growth and the economy shrinks, a **recession** occurs.

☑ **COMPARE AND CONTRAST** Compare and contrast the effects of inflation and deflation on the economy.

How Fiscal Policy Influences the Economy

Fiscal policy is a major tool with which both the executive and legislative branches of the Federal Government seek to achieve broad economic goals. Fiscal policy consists of the government's powers to tax and spend to influence the economy. The President, aided by agencies such as the Council of Economic Advisors, often makes specific recommendations with regard to the economy, while the legislative branch enacts laws to put fiscal policies into action. The executive branch then carries out those laws through its various executive departments and independent agencies.

In addition to deciding how to raise money through taxation and how to spend money, policymakers in both the executive and legislative branches must consider what effects their taxing and spending decisions will have on the overall economy. Federal spending represents about 20 percent of the nation's GDP. How money is taxed and spent can have a real effect throughout the domestic economy—on private enterprise, on employment, on prices, and on growth. In fact, the effects of taxing and spending may be felt well beyond the economy.

For example, the Servicemen's Readjustment Act of 1944 (GI Bill of Rights) allowed veterans to attend college, receive training, and buy houses. This increase in government spending helped lead to the prosperity and cultural changes of the late 1940s and 1950s. In particular, the GI Bill helped change the notion that a college education was only for the elite. Instead, regular Americans began to see college as a path to upward mobility. In addition, the bill began an era of government involvement in higher education and also led to an unprecedented housing boom as veterans took advantage of government-backed loans. Some scholars believe that these changes helped create a new American middle class and also contributed to the high birth rates of the time.

According to some economists, an increase in government expenditures theoretically leads to heightened economic activity; spending cuts tend to dampen that activity. Tax increases take money out

"Great news! The rate of our descent into poverty has reduced by 0.2%"

>> Inflation can affect a family's economic decisions and style of living. **Analyze Political Cartoons** What message does this cartoon convey about economic conditions?

of people's pockets and can slow economic growth. Tax cuts can boost economic activity. The economy is complex, however, and economists do not always agree on these basic effects of fiscal policy.

Historical Use of Fiscal Policy For about 150 years, Congress and the executive branch did not make vigorous use of fiscal policy. Federal income and outgo represented just a bare fraction of GDP. As recently as 1930, that fraction amounted to just over 3 percent of GDP. The ups and downs of the economy were seen by most economists as an inevitable and healthy feature of a free enterprise system.

The Great Depression of the 1930s was a particularly severe downturn. In the midst of that crisis, British economist **John Maynard Keynes** advocated an increase in governmental spending and a decrease in taxes to help end the economic misery. Over time, Keynes's ideas gained acceptance. Now, during a downturn, policymakers in Congress and the executive branch usually seek to expand the economy with greater spending and/or lower taxes. This is precisely what happened in 2008 and 2009. At that time, Congress, pressed by President **George W. Bush** and then by President **Barack Obama**, enacted a number of economic stimulus measures. One of those measures, the 2008 Troubled Asset Relief Program (TARP), was controversial. Some questioned its effectiveness and the way it was administered, while others expressed doubts about the large levels of government spending it authorized. Supporters argued that the spending was necessary to prevent the collapse of the nation's financial sector. Similarly, during the COVID-19 pandemic that began in 2020, the government took the extraordinary step of issuing stimulus payments to individuals. Once again, fiscal policy involved government spending.

Another Use for Fiscal Policy Fiscal policy can also be used to slow inflation. In theory, cuts in government spending and/or tax increases can tamp down inflation across the entire economy.

Fiscal policy does have its limits, however. For one thing, it takes time for policy changes—for example, an increase or reduction in expenditures—to have a measurable effect on the economy. Timing the delivery of hikes or cuts is a very tricky matter. Further, some types of tax cuts often have a relatively small effect on the overall economy. In addition, some Americans would prefer to allow the nation's economy to correct itself through the natural ebb and flow of the economic cycle, rather than through government involvement. So policymakers often use other means to influence economic activity.

>> British economist John Maynard Keynes advocated government intervention to ease the adverse effects of the inevitable expansion and contraction of the economy.

☑ **DRAW CONCLUSIONS** Should the Federal Government have the authority to take actions that can alter the nation's economy? Why or why not?

How Monetary Policy Influences the Economy

Monetary policy is another means by which the legislative and executive branches of the Federal Government can influence the nation's economy. **Monetary policy** involves the money supply (the amount of currency in circulation) and the availability of credit in the economy.

The Federal Reserve Board (the Fed) is responsible for the regulation of the government's monetary policy. Its Board of Governors directs the work of the Federal Reserve System as an independent agency created by Congress. It was established to function as the nation's central bank.

Congress intended the Fed to impose some order on a patchwork banking system that had become increasingly prone to **panics**. In banking, panics occur when depositors lose confidence in banks and rush to recover their funds. If enough customers do so, a bank can be overrun and driven out of business. A panic can spread to infect other banks and, conceivably, an entire banking system. The Fed was designed to avert such a calamity. It serves as a source of emergency funding to prevent panics.

The Key Function of the Fed Again, the key function of the Fed is to regulate monetary policy. By taking steps to increase the money supply, it can theoretically provide a short-term boost to the economy, leading to economic growth and an increase in employment. In theory, the Fed can produce the opposite effect by decreasing the supply of money and consequently slowing inflationary pressures.

The Fed can alter the money supply through three major mechanisms. Its tools for that purpose are open market operations, reserve requirements, and the discount rate.

Open Market Operations When the Fed seeks to alter the money supply, it does not simply send out trucks that carry bundles of cash to or from member banks. Its operations are far more sophisticated. It operates through what are called **open market operations**—a process that involves the buying or selling of government securities, such as bonds, from and to the nation's banks. By buying these government securities back from the banks, the Fed provides money to banks, which can then make loans to individuals and to businesses. If its aim is to decrease the money supply, the Fed sells government bonds through its open market operations. As it receives money from the banks that buy those securities, money is removed from circulation. Subsequently, the banks have less money to loan or invest, and so business activity slows.

Reserve Requirements The Fed can also influence or alter the amount of money in circulation by changing the reserve requirements that all banks and similar financial institutions must meet. The **reserve requirement** is the amount of money that the Federal Reserve Board determines banks must keep "in reserve" in their vaults or on deposit with one of the 12 Federal Reserve Banks. Those funds cannot be used to make loans or for any other purpose. They remain, instead, out of circulation, available for use in the event of sudden, unexpected demand.

If the Fed seeks to lower the money supply, on the other hand, it can require that banks increase the amount they have in reserve. Or the reserve requirement can be relaxed by the Fed to increase the amount of money in circulation.

Discount Rate The third mechanism available to the Fed involves the discount rate. The **discount rate** is the rate of interest a bank must pay when it borrows money from a Federal Reserve Bank.

Interest is the cost borrowers incur and must repay in order to borrow money. If the Fed raises the discount rate, banks find it more difficult to obtain money. Banks must then charge higher interest rates to their customers; borrowing decreases and less money flows into the economy. Cutting the discount rate has the opposite effect. This strategy was used in 2020 to help stimulate the economy during the COVID-19 pandemic, for example.

Main Tools Used by the Federal Government to Influence the Economy

FISCAL POLICY	MONETARY POLICY
Taxes • Decrease taxes to heighten economic activity • Increase taxes to reduce economic activity and slow inflation **Spending** • Reduce government spending to slow inflation • Increase spending to increase employment and tax revenues	**Decrease money supply** • Sell securities • Increase reserve requirement • Raise interest rates **Increase money supply** • Purchase securities • Decrease reserve requirement • Lower interest rates

>> The Fed has a variety of tools at its disposal to influence the nation's economy. **Analyze Charts** Which of these strategies might produce the quickest results?

Fiscal and Monetary Policies at the State and Local Levels While the use of fiscal policy is important at the national level, it is also critical at the State and local levels, as well. One approach sometimes used by the States during a recession, for example, is to spend more money than the government takes in through taxes. The idea behind this type of expansionary spending is to use government funds to help citizens who are struggling, to ease the tax burden, and to pump money into local economies in order to stimulate growth. At other times, States might take the opposite approach by spending less than what is collected through taxes. This use of fiscal policy is often employed to pay off government debt.

For example, a local government might impose a hotel occupancy and restaurant consumption tax to help pay for the construction of a new sports arena. Or, a State might bump up local property tax rates in order to pay for improvements in their college and university system.

The balance between taxes and spending is always a contentious matter—particularly when trying to predict long-term benefits. Will heavy State and local government investment in, for example, sports stadiums pay off because of broader economic development? Most people support the idea of good schools, but how high should local property taxes be raised in order to reach that goal? Will people move away if taxes are too high, or will they move in because the schools are excellent? Every State wants new businesses, but how far should they lower their taxes in order to attract that business?

One prominent example involves Boeing Aerospace, one of the world's largest builders of aircraft. The company announced in 2013 that it was looking for a location for a new facility. Plans for the new plant called for a massive 4.2 million-square-foot, $10 billion facility. Up for grabs were thousands of new jobs. One State after another offered tremendous tax incentives to lure the new facility.

In the end, Washington State's $9 billion in incentives was enough to keep the company in that State. Many in Washington were relieved, but others thought the legislature had gone too far. Again, fiscal policy is always controversial.

Monetary policy, on the other hand, refers to the regulation of the supply of money in an economy, springing from the manipulation of interest rates by the Federal Reserve System. One of the most serious problems with the Articles of Confederation was that each State was able to regulate its own currency—in essence, shape its own monetary policy. Because the Framers of the Constitution were adamant that the nation have a unified currency, State and local governments do not regulate monetary policy today. However, their leaders do voice their opinions regarding federal monetary policy. And why not? Even the slightest change in interest rates can have an enormous impact on the economic well-being of their governments and their citizens.

☑ **EXPLAIN** How can open market operations theoretically help to boost the economy?

☑ ASSESSMENT

1. **Identify Cause and Effect** What main event prompted the Federal Government to take a stronger role in the nation's economy?

2. **Explain** What are the three key economic goals the government aims to achieve, and why are these goals critical to a healthy economy?

3. **Generate Explanations** Why might policymakers hesitate to use fiscal policy to influence the nation's economy?

4. **Connect** How can the use of fiscal and monetary policy influence the overall domestic economy?

5. **Classify** Name three agencies within the executive branch that have important roles in the regulation of American economic activities.

An engraver works on a model of an "America the Beautiful" quarter. The Federal Government is financed largely through revenue from various types of taxes.

BOUNCE to Activate Flipped Video

Objectives

Explain how the Constitution gives Congress the power to tax and at the same time places limits on that power, as well as, how government taxation and regulation can serve as restrictions to private enterprise.

Identify the sources of revenue of the U.S. government today, including both tax and non-tax revenues.

Key Terms

fiscal policy
progressive tax
payroll tax
regressive tax
excise tax
estate tax
inheritance tax
gift tax
customs duty
interest
Benjamin Franklin
Oliver Wendell
   Holmes, Jr.
George W. Bush
Barack Obama

Financing Government

This text is mostly about fiscal policy—a subject that has a tendency to make most people's eyes glaze over. It is, nonetheless, a matter of very considerable importance to everyone in the United States.

The word *fiscal* comes from the Latin word *fiscus*, meaning originally a reed basket and later a purse or treasury. In ancient Rome, the fiscus was the public treasury, the emperor's purse.

The Power to Tax

A government's **fiscal policy** consists of the various means it uses to raise and spend money and thereby influence the nation's economy. In simplest terms, it comes to this: A cut in taxes means that citizens have more money to spend on a daily basis. That increased spending power means more jobs—which also can affect citizens on a daily basis. An increase in taxes takes money away from consumers and so can tend to slow the economy and reduce inflation. Reduced inflation means people see lower prices when they shop for groceries, eat at restaurants, and spend their money at other businesses. In short, people get more for their money.

The Treasury Department was among the first executive departments established by Congress. Since its creation in 1789, it has been the agency responsible for issuing the currency of the United States, collecting taxes and other revenues, and paying the bills of the Federal Government.

No one really likes taxes—except, perhaps, late-night television personalities who often find fodder for their monologues in that subject. They are far from the first to joke about taxes, however. More than two centuries ago, **Benjamin Franklin** famously said that "in this world nothing can be said to be certain, except death and taxes."

The Constitution underscores the central importance of the power to tax by listing it first among all of the many powers granted to Congress. The Constitution gives Congress the power

> To lay and collect Taxes, Duties, Imposts and Excises, to pay the Debts and provide for the common Defence and general Welfare of the United States. . . .
>
> —Article I, Section 8, Clause 1

First and foremost, Congress exercises its power to tax in order to raise the money needed to operate the Federal Government. However, Congress does sometimes exercise that power for purposes other than raising revenue. Usually, that other purpose is to regulate, even discourage, some activity that the government believes to be harmful to the general public.

Thus, much of the Federal Government's regulation of narcotics and other dangerous drugs is based on the power to tax. Federal law provides that only those who hold a valid license can legally manufacture, sell, or otherwise deal in those drugs—and licensing is a form of taxation. The government also regulates a number of other things by licensing—including, for example, the sale of certain firearms, prospecting on public lands, and the hunting of migratory birds.

In 1912, Congress used its taxing power to destroy a part of the domestic match industry. It did so by levying a tax of two cents per one hundred matches on those matches made with white or yellow phosphorus. Those highly poisonous substances were harmful to workers who produced the matches. Matches made from other substances sold for a penny a hundred at the time. As a result, the tax drove phosphorus matches from the market.

The Supreme Court first upheld the use of the power to tax for nonrevenue purposes in *Veazie Bank* v. *Fenno*, 1869. The Court said that Congress was acting within its powers when it levied a 10 percent tax on private bank notes. Congress had imposed that tax in 1865 to eliminate private bank notes from the economy and establish a single national currency. In 2012, the Court upheld another nonrevenue use of the power to tax. The Patient Protection and Affordable Care Act of 2010 requires citizens to buy health insurance or pay a small fine. The Court ruled that this provision was unconstitutional under the Commerce Clause, but allowable under Congress's power to tax.

Limits on the Power to Tax The power to tax is not unlimited. As with all of its other powers, Congress must exercise its power to tax in accord with every provision in the Constitution. Thus, for example, Congress cannot levy a tax on church services—clearly, such a tax would violate the 1st Amendment. In more specific terms, the Constitution puts four expressed limits—and one very significant implied limit—on the power to tax.

First, it declares that Congress is given the power to tax in order to "pay the Debts and provide for the common Defence and general Welfare of the United States." That is, taxes can be levied *only* for public purposes, not for the benefit of some private interest.

The second expressed limit is the prohibition of export taxes. Article I, Section 9, Clause 5 declares that "No Tax or Duty shall be laid on Articles exported from any State." Thus, customs duties (tariffs) can be applied only to imports—goods brought into the United States.

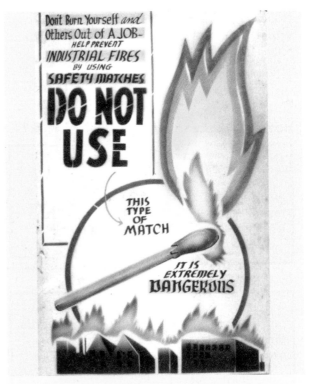

>> When the Diamond Match Company patented the first nonpoisonous match in 1910, the U.S. government distributed promotional literature to discourage the use of phosporous matches.

They may not be applied to exports, goods sent out of the country. This was part of the Commerce Compromise made by the Framers in 1787.

While Congress cannot tax exports, it can and does prohibit the export of certain items. It does so under its expressed power to regulate foreign commerce, usually for the reason of national security. For example, Congress has banned the export of computer software that allows people to encrypt files.

Third, direct taxes must be equally apportioned—that is, evenly distributed—among the States according to their populations. The Constitution originally provided that

> No Capitation, or other direct, Tax shall be laid, unless in Proportion to the Census or Enumeration herein before directed to be taken.
>
> —Article I, Section 9, Clause 4

This restriction was part of the Three-Fifths Compromise at the Constitutional Convention. In effect, delegates from the northern States insisted that enslaved people should be counted despite the fact that they had no rights. The southern delegates' goal was to gain more representatives in the House. But northern delegates countered that in that case, the enslaved would also be counted when determining how much each State owed in taxes.

The Direct Tax Restriction A direct tax is one that must be borne by the person upon whom it is levied. Examples include a tax on land, which must be paid by the owner of the property; or a capitation tax—a head or poll tax—laid on each person. Other taxes are indirect taxes, levies that may be shifted to another for payment—as, for example, the federal tax on liquor. That tax, placed initially on the distiller, is ultimately paid by the person who buys the liquor.

The direct tax restriction means, in effect, that any direct tax that Congress levies (except for the income tax) must be apportioned among the States according to their populations. Thus, a direct tax that raised, say, $1 billion would have to produce just about $120 million in California and close to $10 million in Mississippi because California has about 12 percent of the nation's population, while Mississippi has less than one percent.

Wealth is not evenly distributed among the States, of course. Therefore, a direct tax laid in proportion to population would be grossly unfair; the tax would fall more heavily on the residents of some States than it would on others. As a result, Congress has not imposed a direct tax—except for the income tax—outside the District of Columbia since 1861.

Income taxes affect businesses as well as individuals. But the effect of taxes on a business depends on how the business is structured. The most common form of business organization is a sole proprietorship—a business owned and run by

How Do Direct and Indirect Taxes Work?

| **Direct Tax** The State sets an income tax rate of 3% on earnings. **3%** | **Indirect Tax** The State sets a sales tax of 6%. **6%** | A 50" flat screen TV costs $500 + 6% sales tax = $530.00. | The **customer pays** the $30.00 sales tax **to the store** when she buys a television. |
| A worker pays the tax **directly to the government**. | The store files a tax return and **forwards** the sales tax $ it has collected from the customer **to the government**. | The **sales tax is the same** for a wealthy person and a poor person: 0.03% of a salary of $100,000/year versus 0.15% of a salary of $20,000/year = **5X the burden** | |

>> The sales tax is an example of an indirect tax because it is levied on the store, which passes it along to the customer. **Analyze Information** Why do you think the sales tax is levied as a percentage of the cost of an item, rather than as the same flat rate for all items?

The Effect of the Revenue Act of 1942

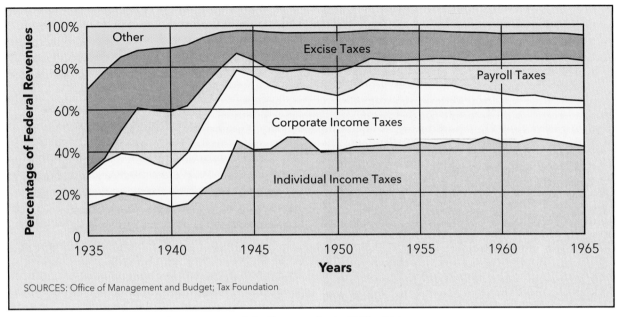

SOURCES: Office of Management and Budget; Tax Foundation

>> To help pay for World War II, Congress passed the Revenue Act in 1942, which increased the number of Americans who paid income taxes from 13 million to 50 million. **Analyze Charts** What happened to the percentage of federal revenue from the individual income tax after 1945?

one person, who pays taxes on the business income as part of his or her own income tax. Owners of an LLC—a limited liability company—also include business income on their own personal income taxes.

Corporate tax structure, however, is much more complicated. Corporations are classified as separate tax-paying entities. Payments that corporations distribute to shareholders and employees are reported by the shareholders and employees on their personal income tax returns. This means that some corporate profits can be taxed twice, once when the company earns its profits and once when each individual who has been paid by the company pays personal income tax. However, corporations can also count payroll as a tax deduction, because it is a business expense.

An income tax—whether it is for an individual or a business—is a direct tax, but it may be laid without regard to population.

> The Congress shall have power to lay and collect taxes on incomes, from whatever source derived, without apportionment among the several States, and without regard to any census or enumeration.
>
> —16th Amendment

Congress first levied an income tax in 1861, to help finance the Civil War. That tax, which expired in 1872, was later upheld by the Supreme Court in *Springer* v. *United States*, 1881. A unanimous Court found that that income tax was an indirect rather than a direct tax.

However, a later income tax law, enacted in 1894, was declared unconstitutional in *Pollock* v. *Farmers' Loan and Trust Co.*, 1895. There, the Court held that the 1894 law imposed a direct tax that Congress should have apportioned among the several States. The impossibility of taxing incomes fairly in accord with any plan of apportionment led to the adoption of the 16th Amendment, in 1913.

The fourth and final limit, in Article I, Section 8, Clause 1, declares that "all Duties, Imposts and Excises shall be uniform throughout the United States." That is, all of the indirect taxes levied by the Federal Government must be set at the same rate in all parts of the country.

Additional Limits on the Power to Tax The Federal Government cannot tax the States or any of their local governments in the exercise of their proper governmental functions. That is, federal taxes cannot be imposed on those governments when they are performing such tasks as providing public education, protecting the public health, providing police protection, or building streets and highways.

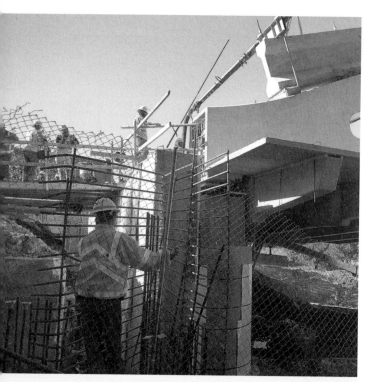

>> Because the State of Texas is performing a "proper governmental function" with the construction of this bridge in Fort Worth, the project cannot be taxed by the Federal Government.

The Supreme Court laid down that rule in *McCulloch* v. *Maryland* in 1819, when it declared that "the power to tax involves the power to destroy." If the Federal Government could tax the governmental activities of the States or their local units, it could conceivably tax them out of existence and so destroy the federal system.

The Federal Government can and does tax those State and local activities that are of a nongovernmental character, however. For example, in 1893, South Carolina created a State monopoly to sell liquor, and it claimed that each of its liquor stores was exempt from the federal saloon license tax. But in *South Carolina* v. *United States*, 1905, the Supreme Court held that the State was liable for the tax, because the sale of liquor is not a necessary or usual governmental activity. Today, most State and many local governments are engaged in a variety of businesslike enterprises.

☑ **INTERPRET** The Supreme Court declared that "the power to tax involves the power to destroy." What did the Court mean by this statement?

Federal Taxes Today

Paying taxes is a responsibility of citizenship. Without citizens' tax dollars, the Federal Government could not execute the nation's public policies or conduct the business of government. In the words of **Oliver Wendell Holmes, Jr.**, taxes are "what we pay for civilized society." This comment represents one viewpoint on taxes—the notion that tax-funded government services and programs, such as police, fire, public schools, and Social Security, have led to increased safety, reduced crime and poverty, increased levels of education, and other tangible benefits. Others, however, argue that taxes represent undue government interference with the economy and have a negative effect on both individuals and businesses. These differing viewpoints fuel the ongoing debates over which types of taxes we should have and how high or low they should be set.

Taxes on Income You will recall that the income tax was authorized by the 16th Amendment in 1913. It is the largest source of federal revenue today. It first became the major source in 1917 and 1918. And, except for a few years in the midst of the Depression of the 1930s, it has remained so.

Several features of the income tax fit its dominant role. It is a flexible tax, because its rates can be adjusted to produce whatever amount of money Congress thinks is necessary. The income tax is also

>> A pay stub shows the amount of money in federal taxes withheld from one individual's paycheck. They include personal income tax, Medicare tax, and Social Security tax.

PROGRESSIVE TAXES

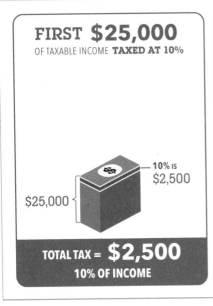

FIRST $25,000
OF TAXABLE INCOME **TAXED AT 10%**

10% IS $2,500

$25,000

TOTAL TAX = $2,500
10% OF INCOME

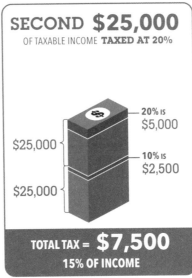

SECOND $25,000
OF TAXABLE INCOME **TAXED AT 20%**

20% IS $5,000

$25,000

10% IS $2,500

$25,000

TOTAL TAX = $7,500
15% OF INCOME

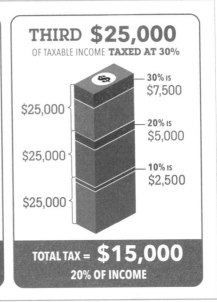

THIRD $25,000
OF TAXABLE INCOME **TAXED AT 30%**

30% IS $7,500

$25,000

20% IS $5,000

$25,000

10% IS $2,500

$25,000

TOTAL TAX = $15,000
20% OF INCOME

>> With a progressive tax, as one's income increases, so does the amount of one's income taxes. **Analyze Data** What percentage of total income would be paid on salaries of $30,000 and $95,000?

easily adapted to the principle of ability to pay. It is a **progressive tax**—a tax that takes a higher percentage from high-income groups than from low-income groups. The tax is levied on the earnings of both individuals and corporations.

Individual Income Tax The tax on individuals' incomes produces the largest amount of federal revenue, more than a trillion dollars each year.

The tax is levied on each person's taxable income—that is, one's total income in the previous year less certain exemptions and deductions. The government allows every taxpayer an exemption of several thousand dollars, plus the same amount for each of the taxpayer's dependents. The personal exemption is adjusted to account for inflation each year. Deductions are allowed for a number of things, including the cost of some medical care, most State and local taxes (except sales taxes), interest paid on home mortgages, and charitable contributions. For some people, after these exemptions and deductions, their taxable income is zero, therefore they pay no federal income tax.

By April 15 of any given year, everyone who earned taxable income in the preceding calendar year must file a tax return—a declaration of that

income and of the exemptions and deductions he or she claims. The returns are filed, by mail or online, with the Internal Revenue Service.

During World War I, tax rates were raised and new taxes introduced to help pay for the war. Afterward, those taxes were rolled back, and the nation experienced an economic boom. Then the stock market crashed and taxes were raised to help pay for President Franklin Roosevelt's New Deal programs. World War II came on the heels of the Depression, and taxes were raised still more. After the war, Congress rewrote the tax code to allow new deductions but also raised taxes on corporations. Individuals also saw their rates go up in the 1960s and 1970s, but in the 1980s, President Reagan pushed Congress to enact tax cuts. Some later Presidents did the same. Despite many increases over the years, the American tax burden is fairly low compared with that of other high-income countries, such as France and Belgium.

Most people who pay income taxes do so through withholding, a pay-as-you-go plan. Employers are required to withhold a certain amount from each employee's paycheck and send that money to the IRS. When the employee files a tax return, he or she receives a refund if the employer withheld more money than the employee owed in taxes, or must pay an additional amount if too little was withheld. Those who earn income from sources not subject to withholding (for example, rent or royalties) must estimate the tax they will owe and make quarterly payments on that amount through the year.

Corporate Income Tax Each corporation must pay a tax on its net income—that is, on all of its earnings above the costs of doing business. The corporate tax is the most complicated of all federal taxes because of the many deductions allowed. Nonprofit organizations such as churches and charitable foundations are not subject to the corporation income tax.

The share of federal revenue contributed by the corporate income tax has changed over time. In the 1940s, that share was 30 percent or more. The percentage began to decrease in the 1960s, and since the late 1970s, the corporate income tax has accounted for approximately 15 percent or less of federal revenue.

Social Insurance Taxes The Federal Government levies other taxes to finance three major social welfare programs: (1) the Old-Age, Survivors, and Disability Insurance (OASDI) program—the basic Social Security program, established by the Social Security Act of 1935; (2) Medicare—healthcare for the elderly, added to the Social Security program

in 1965; and (3) the unemployment compensation program—benefits paid to jobless workers, a program also established by the Social Security Act in 1935.

OASDI and Medicare are supported by taxes imposed on nearly all employers and their employees, and on self-employed persons. These levies are often called **payroll taxes** because the amounts owed by employees are withheld from their paychecks.

The Social Security Administration and some economists estimate that the costs of the program will outstrip Social Security tax revenues in the near future. Other economic experts, however, contend that concerns about the solvency of the Social Security program are exaggerated.

When the Social Security Act was first passed, employees paid a 1 percent tax into the fund. That figure grew slowly over the years and was set at 6.2 percent in 1990. The self-employed must pay double the tax—once to cover themselves and once to cover the employer contribution.

For Medicare, employees originally paid a 0.35 percent tax. That tax has approximately quadrupled over the years since then. In this case, too, the self-employed pay double the amount paid by those who are under someone else's employ.

The unemployment insurance program is a joint federal–State operation that makes payments

Social Security Program Revenue and Cost: Historical and Projected

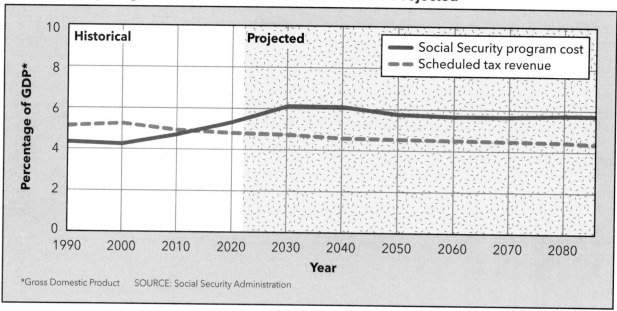

>> Social Security revenue and cost data is shown as a percentage of gross domestic product. **Analyze Graphs** What is the significance of the lines crossing between the years 2010 and 2020?

to workers who lose their jobs for reasons beyond their control. The program now covers most workers in this country. Each State and the District of Columbia, Puerto Rico, and the Virgin Islands have their own unemployment compensation laws. The amount of a worker's weekly benefits, and how many weeks these benefits last, are determined by State law.

The federal unemployment tax is about 6 percent of the first $7,000 or so that an employer pays to each employee in a year. Each employer is given a credit of up to roughly 5 percent against that tax for unemployment taxes that the employer pays to the State. So, the federal tax amounts to about 0.6 percent on taxable wages.

Notice that these social insurance taxes for OASDI, Medicare, and unemployment compensation are not progressive taxes. They are, instead, **regressive taxes**—taxes levied at a fixed rate, without regard to the level of a taxpayer's income or his or her ability to pay them. In fact, the regressive OASDI and Medicare taxes now take more money out of the paychecks of many low and middle income workers than does the progressive federal income tax.

The IRS collects these social insurance taxes. The money is then credited to trust accounts maintained by the Treasury, and Congress appropriates funds for the social insurance programs as they are needed.

Excise Taxes An **excise tax** is a tax laid on the manufacture, sale, or consumption of goods and/or the performance of services. The Federal Government has imposed and collected excise taxes since Congress acquired its taxing power in 1789.

Today, federal excise taxes are imposed on a long list of items, including gasoline, oil, tires, tobacco, alcohol, firearms, telephone services, airline tickets, and more. Many excise taxes are called "hidden taxes" because they are collected from producers who then pass them on to the customer. Some are called "luxury taxes" because they are imposed on nonessential items. And some excise taxes are known as "sin taxes," particularly those laid on tobacco, alcohol, gambling, and cannabis.

Estate and Gift Taxes An **estate tax** is a levy imposed on the assets (the estate) of someone who dies. An **inheritance tax** is another form of the so-called death tax. It is not levied on the entire net estate but, instead, on the portion inherited by each heir. Most States impose inheritance, not estate, taxes; most States also levy gift taxes. A **gift tax** is one imposed on a gift from one living person to another. Congress first provided for the estate tax in 1916. It added the gift tax in 1932 to plug a loophole

"GIBBS, I SUBTRACTED YOUR FEDERAL, STATE AND SOCIAL SECURITY TAXES AND MEDICAL FROM YOUR PAYCHECK, AND YOU OWE THE FIRM $50."

>> Taxes fund public programs and services, but some question the need for that spending and criticize the burden those taxes place on taxpayers. **Analyze Images** What comment does this cartoon make?

in the estate tax that allowed people to avoid the estate tax by giving away money or other property before death.

Most estates are not subject to the federal tax, however, because those valued below a certain threshold are exempt. The threshold varies, but suffice it to say that a person's estate must value in the millions before the tax applies. In addition, deductions are allowed for such things as State estate taxes and bequests to religious and charitable groups. Anything a husband or wife leaves to the other is taxed, if at all, only when the surviving spouse dies.

Any person may now make more than $10,000 in tax-free gifts to any other person in any one year. Gifts that spouses make to each other are not taxed, regardless of value. The estate and gift taxes are separate taxes, but they are levied at the same rate.

Customs Duties Customs duties are taxes laid on goods brought into the United States from abroad. Customs duties are also known as tariffs, import duties, or imposts. Congress decides which imports will be dutied and at what rates. Most imports are dutied, but some are not—for example, Bibles, coffee, bananas, and, with some exceptions, up to about $800 of a tourist's purchases abroad. Once the major source of income for the Federal Government, customs duties now produce just over one percent of government revenue taken in each year.

>> Container shipping is used to transport large quantities of items across the world. Each country has its own regulations regarding customs duties for items brought into that country.

Nontax Revenues Large sums of money reach the federal treasury from a multitude of nontax sources. These miscellaneous receipts now total billions of dollars a year and come from dozens of places. A large portion comes from the earnings of the Federal Reserve System, mostly in interest charges. **Interest** is a charge for borrowed money, generally a percentage of the amount borrowed. The interest on other loans, canal tolls, and fees for such items

as passports, copyrights, patents, and trademarks also generate large sums. So does the sale or lease of public lands and such other items as the fines imposed by the federal courts.

The Treasury Department maintains a "conscience fund" for the money that people pay to ease their minds over past taxpaying mistakes. Another little-known source of nontax money is *seigniorage*—the profit the United States Mint makes on the production of coins. The U.S. Postal Service sells more than $210 million in mint-condition stamps to collectors each year, and collectors spend untold millions more at local post offices.

☑ **DRAW CONCLUSIONS** How might the economy be affected when income taxes go up?

☑ ASSESSMENT

1. **Summarize** Where does the Federal Government get its revenue?

2. **Compare and Contrast** How does the way Congress regulates exports differ from the way it regulates imports?

3. **Categorize** List the different types of taxes that are paid in the United States, and explain who pays which tax.

4. **Compare and Contrast** Explain the difference between progressive taxes and regressive taxes.

5. **Draw Conclusions** How do taxes affect the economy?

Pollock v. Farmers' Loan and Trust Co., 1895

Before 1913, the U.S. Constitution granted Congress the power to levy a direct tax only if it was apportioned among the States. Instead, tariffs were the main source of government revenue. To reduce tariffs, Congress passed the Wilson-Gorman Tariff Act in 1894, which made up for the revenue loss by levying a tax on any income over $4,000. Charles Pollock, who owned stock in Farmers' Loan and Trust Company, sued the company to stop it from paying the tax on his behalf. He believed that the income tax was a direct tax and therefore violated the Constitution. In 1895, *Pollock* v. *Farmers' Loan & Trust Company* reached the Supreme Court. In a 5-4 decision, the Court agreed with Pollock that the tax was a direct tax and thus unconstitutional.

As you read, compare the arguments for and against the exemptions included by Congress in the Wilson-Gorman Tariff Act.

>> The Supreme Court's decision in *Pollock* led to a movement to change the Constitution to allow for an income tax. In this 1909 illustration, a well-dressed man is trying to get a parrot labeled *State Legislature* to repeat a phrase after him: "We don't want an Income-Tax."

Concurring Opinion, Justice Stephen J. Field

The income tax law under consideration is marked by discriminating features which affect the whole law. It discriminates between those who receive an income of $4,000 and those who do not. It thus vitiates [voids], in my judgment, by this arbitrary [random] discrimination, the whole legislation. . . . Whenever a distinction is made in the burdens a law imposes or in the benefits it confers on any citizens by reason of their birth, or wealth, or religion, it is class legislation [a law that pertains only to one group of people], and leads inevitably to oppression and abuses, and to general unrest and disturbance in society. . . .

☑ **SUMMARIZE** What is the law's discriminating feature and why is this discrimination a problem?

. . . The law. . . distinguishes . . . between corporations by exempting the property of some of them from taxation, and levying the tax on the property of others. . . . Trifling [unimportant] differences in their modes of business, but not in their results, are made the ground and occasion of the greatest possible differences in the amount of taxes levied upon their incomes, showing that the action of the legislative power upon them has been arbitrary and capricious [unpredictable], and sometimes merely fanciful. . . .

There is no safety in allowing the limitation to be adjusted except in strict compliance with the mandates of the constitution, which require its taxation, if imposed by direct taxes, to be apportioned [divided] among the states according to their representation, and, if imposed by indirect taxes, to be uniform in operation and, so far as practicable, in proportion to their property, equal upon all citizens. Unless the rule of the constitution governs, a majority may fix the limitation at such rate as will not include any of their own number.

☑ **IDENTIFY CENTRAL IDEAS** What could occur if the Constitution's tax mandates are not followed?

Dissenting Opinion, Justice Henry B. Brown, May 20, 1895 (second hearing)

I regard it as very clear that the clause requiring direct taxes to be apportioned to the population has no application to taxes which are not capable of apportionment according to population. . . . And, if the proposed tax were such that in its nature it could not be apportioned according to population, it naturally follows that it could not have been considered a direct tax. . . .

[A] tax which is wanting in uniformity among members of the same class is, or may be, invalid. But this does not deprive the legislature of the power to make exemptions, provided such exemptions rest upon some principle, and are not purely arbitrary, or created solely for the purpose of favoring some person or body of persons. Thus in every civilized country there is an exemption of small incomes, which it would be manifest cruelty to tax, and, the power to make such exemptions once granted, the amount is within the discretion of the legislature, and, so long as that power is not wantonly [without limitation] abused, the courts are bound to respect it. In this law there is an exemption of $4,000, which indicates a purpose on the part of congress that the burden of this tax should fall on the wealthy, or at least upon the well-to-do. If men who have an income or property beyond their pressing needs are

not the ones to pay taxes, it is difficult to say who are; in other words, enlightened taxation is imposed upon property, and not upon persons. . . .

☑ **SUMMARIZE** Why does Justice Brown believe tax exemptions are acceptable and how may a legislature establish them?

[A]s it implies a declaration that every income tax must be laid according to the rule of apportionment, the [Court's] decision involves nothing less than a surrender of the taxing power to the moneyed class. . . . It is certainly a strange commentary upon the constitution of the United States and upon a democratic government that congress has no power to lay a tax which is one of the main sources of revenue of nearly every civilized state.

☑ **USE CONTEXT CLUES** To whom is Justice Brown referring with the phrase "moneyed class"?

☑ ASSESSMENT

1. **Determine Author's Point of View** How would you describe the attitude of Source 1 regarding the law in question?

2. **Explain an Argument** What argument does Source 1 use to support the law's non-apportionment?

3. **Draw Conclusions** Which argument do you think is the strongest? Why? Cite the phrase(s) or sentence(s) used in the source that influenced your decision.

4. **Make Inferences** Why might this case have led to the ratification of the 16th Amendment in 1913 which allowed Congress to levy an income tax without apportionment?

The Works Progress Administration (WPA) was part of President Roosevelt's New Deal program, which ushered in a new era of government intervention in the economy.

Spending and Borrowing

The Federal Government is projected to spend trillions of dollars in the coming year. If you were to pile up a stack of, say, four trillion $1 bills, the stack would reach all the way to the moon. And even that wouldn't be enough to equal federal spending. In this lesson, you will see how the Federal Government spends that vast amount of money and how it plans for that spending through the budget process.

Federal Expenditures

The United States is a constitutional liberal democracy—or what is sometimes referred to as a western democracy. It is a system broadly defined by competitive elections, the separation of powers, and the protection of civil liberties and basic rights. To some, it means limited government action, but to others it implies an array of social welfare programs. The rubber hits the road on this issue when it comes to spending priorities. How much money should the Federal Government spend, for example, to protect and promote citizens' well-being?

Every year, the Federal Government takes trillions of dollars from some segments of the national economy. It then pumps those trillions back into other segments of the economy—all with huge effects on Americans and their wallets.

Spending Priorities The Department of Health and Human Services spends more money than any other federal agency—well over $1 trillion a year, in fact. Most of this department's spending goes for Medicare, Medicaid, and other entitlement programs.

BOUNCE to Activate Flipped Video

Objectives

Identify government expenditures and define controllable and uncontrollable spending.

Analyze the executive branch function of creating the federal budget, in conjunction with Congress.

Understand the relationship between U.S. government policies as set out in the yearly federal budget and the economy.

Analyze the impact of government taxing and spending on the U.S. economy.

Analyze the causes and effects of the public debt.

Key Terms

entitlements
controllable
  spending
uncontrollable
  spending
continuing resolution
deficit
surplus
demand-side
  economics

supply-side
  economics
public debt
Panama Canal
Herbert Hoover
Franklin D. Roosevelt
Ronald Reagan
George Washington

Entitlements are benefits that federal law says *must* be paid to all those who meet the eligibility requirements—for example, being above a certain age or below a certain income level. OASDI (the Old Age, Survivors, and Disability Insurance program)—often called "Social Security"—is the largest entitlement program today, and, is funded by the social insurance taxes withheld from the paychecks of American workers. Other major examples include Medicare, Medicaid, food stamps, unemployment insurance, and veterans' pensions. The law says that the people who receive those benefits are *entitled* (that is, have a right) to them.

OASDI is administered by an independent agency, the Social Security Administration (SSA). The department's massive outlays for OASDI make the Social Security Administration the second-largest government spender.

Defense and the Public Debt The Department of Defense (DoD) spends hundreds of billions of dollars each year. As large as this number is, it does not include the defense-related expenditures of several other federal agencies, notably the nuclear weapons development work of the Department of Energy and many of the functions of the Department of Homeland Security.

>> An elderly patient receives medical care financed by Medicare, which provides health coverage to people over 65.

Interest on the public debt is included in the Treasury Department's spending and is the fourth-largest category of federal spending. Stoked by years of deficit financing, it has consumed a larger and still larger part of the federal budget over the last several years and is also in the hundreds of billions of dollars.

Types of Spending What the Federal Government spends can be described in terms of **controllable spending** and **uncontrollable spending.** Some specific items in the federal budget are controllable. That is, Congress and the President can decide each year just how much will be spent on many of the things that the Federal Government does—for example, on national parks, highway projects, aid to education, civil service pay, and so on. Defense spending is by far the largest controllable item in the federal budget today. Economists often use the term "discretionary spending" to describe spending on those budget items about which Congress and the President can make choices.

Much federal spending is uncontrollable, however. It is because "mandatory spending" was built into many public programs when Congress created them. That level of spending cannot be changed unless Congress changes the law(s) that set the funding for those programs.

Take the interest on the public debt as a leading example of uncontrollable spending. That interest amounts to a fixed charge; once the Federal Government borrows the money, the interest on that loan must be paid when it comes due—and at the rate the government promised to pay.

Social Security benefits, food stamps, and most other entitlements are also largely uncontrollable. Once Congress has set the standards of eligibility for those programs, it really has no control over just how many people will meet those standards. Thus, Congress does not—really cannot—determine how many people covered by Social Security will become eligible for retirement benefits each year.

"Controlling" Uncontrollable Spending Those expenditures are not completely uncontrollable, however. Congress could redefine eligibility standards, or it could reduce the amount of money each beneficiary is to receive. But, clearly, those actions would be politically difficult.

In general, the percentage of federal spending that is uncontrollable has grown in recent years, while the percentage of controllable spending has decreased. In fact, the Office of Management and Budget estimates that over 60 percent of all federal

THE EXECUTIVE BRANCH AND THE BUDGET

On the first Monday in February, the President proposes a budget outlining the administration's policies and funding priorities and estimating spending, income, and borrowing for the coming fiscal year.

- Each federal agency prepares an estimate of its spending needs for the next year.

- Those spending plans are submitted to the Office of Management and Budget (OMB).

- The OMB reviews the agency proposals, often in budget hearings.

- After the OMB's review, revised spending plans for all of the agencies become part of the budget document.

- The President submits the budget document to Congress.

>> The President, Congress, and many federal agencies are involved in creating the budget. **Analyze Charts** What is the President's role in creating the budget?

spending today falls into the uncontrollable category. These trends cause concern to those officials who are responsible for maintaining control of the budget.

☑ **DRAW CONCLUSIONS** Are entitlement programs examples of controllable or uncontrollable spending? Why do you think so?

Creating the Budget

The Constitution gives to Congress the fabled "power of the purse"—the very significant power to control the financing of the Federal Government and all of its operations. This power is also sometimes called the appropriations power.

> No Money shall be drawn from the Treasury, but in Consequence of Appropriations made by Law. . . .

—Article I, Section 9, Clause 7

Congress—and only Congress—has the power to provide the enormous sums that the government consumes each year. In short, it is Congress that decides *how much* the government can spend and, just as importantly, for exactly *what* it can spend that money.

Still, despite the fact that Congress holds the power of the purse, it is the President who initiates the process by which the Federal Government spends its money. The chief executive does so by submitting (proposing) a budget to Congress soon after that body begins each of its yearly sessions. The word *budget* comes from the French *bougette*, meaning a small pouch or bag with its contents. In the eighteenth century, the budget was the bag in which the British chancellor of the exchequer (the treasurer) carried the financial documents.

The Importance of the Budget Remember, the federal budget is a hugely important document. It is, of course, a financial statement—a lengthy and detailed estimate of federal income and proposed outgo for the upcoming fiscal year. But it is also much more than that, much more than a dry listing of so many dollars from this and so many dollars for that. The budget is a major political statement, a declaration of the public policies of the United States. Put another way, the federal budget is the President's work plan for the conduct of the government and the execution of its public policies in the next fiscal year.

The annual budget-making process is a joint effort of the President and both houses of Congress. The President prepares the budget and submits it to Congress. Congress then reacts to the President's budget proposals, over a period of several months. It usually enacts most of those proposals, many of them in some altered form, in a number of appropriations measures.

The Executive Branch and the Budget

The process of building the budget is a lengthy one. In fact, it begins at least 18 months before the start of the fiscal year for which the budget is intended. First, each federal agency prepares detailed estimates of its spending needs for that 12-month period. Each agency then submits its spending plans to the President's budget-making agency, the Office of Management and Budget (OMB). The OMB reviews all of the many agency proposals, often in budget hearings at which agency officials must defend their dollar requests.

Following the OMB's review, revised and usually lowered spending plans for all of the agencies in the executive branch are fitted into the President's overall program. They become a part of the budget document—a part of the political statement—the President sends to Capitol Hill.

Congress enacts a separate budget to cover its own expenses. The federal courts' spending requests are prepared by the Administrative Office of the United States Courts and sent directly to Congress.

Congress and the Budget

Remember, Congress depends upon and works through its standing committees. The President's budget proposals, therefore, are referred to the Budget Committee in each chamber. There, in both the House and Senate committees, those money requests are studied and dissected with the help of the Congressional Budget Office (CBO).

The CBO is a staff agency created by Congress in 1974. It provides both houses of Congress and their committees with basic budget and economic data and analyses. The information that the CBO supplies is independent of the information provided by the OMB, the President's budget agency.

All tax proposals included in the President's budget are referred to the House Ways and Means Committee and, separately, to the Senate's Finance Committee. The President's budget is also sent to both the House and the Senate Appropriations Committees. Their subcommittees hold extensive hearings in which they examine agency requests, quiz agency officials, and take testimony from a wide range of interested parties.

CONGRESS AND THE BUDGET

Using the President's budget as a guide, the House and Senate work individually and then together to determine the size of the budget, estimate revenue, and set discretionary spending levels.

- House and Senate Budget committees conduct hearings on the President's budget.

- House and Senate debate and vote on their respective committee's budget resolution.

- Conference committee blends both resolutions into one final resolution.

- Each house votes on final version of the budget resolution.

>> The House and Senate spend eight months or so determining the final allocation of federal funds. **Analyze Charts** Why do you think Budget Committee hearings are usually open to the public?

FINAL STEPS TO PASSING THE BUDGET

Guided by the budget resolution, Congress sets the budget for each federal agency in detail and provides the legal authority to spend funds.

As each appropriations bill is approved by Congress, it is sent to the President to veto or sign into law.

- House and Senate Appropriations committees each develop 13 separate massive spending bills.

- Conference committee settles on one bill for each of the 13 appropriations measures.

- Each house votes on final version of each appropriations bill.

- President signs or vetoes the bills. If not approved by October 1st, Congress must pass a continuing resolution for unfunded agencies to ensure their continued operation.

>> Both the President and Congress are involved in the final steps of passing the budget. **Analyze Charts** Why are both the legislative and executive branches involved in the budget process?

Lobbyists for many interest groups are actively involved in those hearings. They testify, bring grass-roots pressures to bear on committee members, and otherwise work to promote the interests of the organizations they represent. (And campaign contributions from these groups often find their way to members of those subcommittees—in particular, to their chairmen and ranking members.)

The two Appropriations Committees shape measures that later are reported to the floor of each house. Those measures are the bills that actually appropriate the funds on which the government will operate.

Final Steps to Passing the Budget The two Budget Committees propose a concurrent resolution on the budget to their respective chambers. That measure, which must be passed by both houses by May 15, sets overall targets for federal receipts and spending in the upcoming fiscal year. The estimates are intended to guide the committees in both houses as they continue to work on the budget.

The two Budget Committees propose a second budget resolution in early September. Congress generally passes that resolution by September 15, just two weeks before the beginning of the next fiscal year. That second budget resolution sets binding expenditure limits for all federal agencies in that upcoming year. No appropriations measure can provide for any spending that exceeds those limits.

Congress passes 13 major appropriations bills each year. Recall, each of these measures must go to the White House for the President's action. Every year, Congress hopes to pass all 13 of the appropriations measures by October 1—that is, by the beginning of the Federal Government's fiscal year.

It seldom does so, however. This means that Congress must then pass emergency spending legislation to avoid a shutdown of those agencies for which appropriations have not yet been signed into law. That legislation takes the form of a **continuing resolution.** When signed by the President, the measure allows the affected agencies to continue to function on the basis of the previous year's appropriations. Should Congress and the President fail to act, many agencies of the Federal Government would, in fact, have to suspend their operations. This has, in fact, happened at various times in the nation's history.

☑ **IDENTIFY CENTRAL ISSUES** What programs do you think are considered high priorities by most Americans? How are these priorities taken into account during the creation of the federal budget?

Borrowing and the Deficit

In *Hamlet*, Shakespeare wrote, "Neither a borrower nor a lender be." That advice may make good sense in many situations. However, it most certainly has *not* been followed by the government of the United States, which has been both a borrower and a lender for more than 200 years now.

Article I, Section 8, Clause 2 of the Constitution gives Congress the power "[t]o borrow Money on the credit of the United States." Congress first exercised that power in 1790, and it has done so hundreds of times since then. For the better part of 150 years, the power to borrow was seen as a way for the government to (1) meet the costs of crisis situations, most notably wars, and/or (2) pay for large-scale projects that could not be financed out of current income— for example, the construction of the **Panama Canal** in the early 1900s.

Beginning with the 1930s Depression years, the Federal Government has borrowed, regularly and heavily, for yet another purpose: to finance budget deficits. In nearly every year since that time, it has spent more than it has collected from taxpayers. That is, the government has routinely run up a **deficit** (the shortfall between income and outgo) and it has borrowed to make up the difference.

Indeed, the government's financial books did not show a **surplus** (more income than outgo) in any fiscal year from 1970 to 1998. In fact, the government has ended only a few fiscal years "in the black"—that is, with a budget surplus. (Note that the fiscal year runs from October 1st of one year to September 30th of the next.) The deficit has grown to more than a trillion dollars and the interest that must be paid on it is a major item in the federal budget.

The Depression and Deficit Spending The collapse of the stock market in October 1929 triggered the Great Depression of the 1930s. To meet that catastrophe, deficit financing became a constant element of federal fiscal policy.

A few statistics begin to suggest the depths of that economic calamity and the miseries that accompanied it. Two million Americans were unemployed in 1929. By 1933, that number had climbed to 13.5 million. One fifth of the nation's labor force was out of work—and millions more were working for, literally, pennies a day. By 1935, 18 million people, including children and the aged, were completely dependent on emergency public relief programs.

Between 1929 and 1932, more than 5,000 banks— one of every five in the country—had failed, and their customers' deposits had vanished. By 1932, net farm income had plunged to 33 percent of its level in 1929.

Few States had made any provision for such a crisis, and those that had were overwhelmed. So, too, were churches and other private charities. Poverty and need had become national problems overnight.

>> It cost the United States $352 million (in 1914 dollars) to complete construction of the Panama Canal (shown here), which links the Atlantic and Pacific oceans.

UNDERSTANDING THE ECONOMIC CRISIS OF 2007–2008

CAUSES

- Easy availability of mortgages created an unsustainable housing boom
- Households and businesses had too much excess debt
- U.S. financial system grew too fast
- Regulatory framework was outdated
- Too many investors were insensitive to risk

EFFECTS

- **September 15, 2008:** Lehman Brothers filed for bankruptcy
- **September 16, 2008:** Stock market fell 500 points; financial sector panic ensued
- U.S. financial system at risk of collapse
- Millions of jobs lost
- Congress passed Emergency Economic Stabilization Act; the **Troubled Asset Relief Program (TARP)** was created under the act

TARP

- Initial authorization of **$700 billion**; later lowered to **$475 billion**, most of which was repaid by 2013
- Estimated total cost of the bailout at end of 2013: **$40.3 billion**

Source: Treasury Department

>> A combination of factors caused the economic crisis that led to the creation of TARP. **Analyze Charts** Which effect likely had the largest impact on the average American?

In the elections of 1932, the voters overwhelmingly rejected the tentative efforts of President **Herbert Hoover** and a Republican-controlled Congress to solve the nation's economic woes. Mr. Hoover and his advisors were committed to the traditional view of the place of government in the economy. They held that government had only a very limited power to deal with what they believed was a private economic crisis. Government, they thought, should ensure a stable money supply; beyond that, the success or failure of businesses was a matter best left to the workings of the free market.

The voters turned, instead, to the Democrats. **Franklin D. Roosevelt** won the presidency in a landslide, and his party captured huge majorities in both houses of Congress.

Keynesian Economics Almost immediately, the President and Congress launched the New Deal—a series of government spending and jobs programs designed to stimulate the economy and put Americans back to work. That response to the Depression was built largely on the theories advanced by British economist John Maynard Keynes (1883–1946), most fully developed in his work *The General Theory of Employment, Interest, and Money,* published in 1936. In particular, it was based on the Keynesian view that government should influence the economy by large increases in public spending in times of high unemployment.

Keynesians argue that even if government must borrow to support that increased spending, the higher employment that results will soon produce higher tax revenues. This notion is sometimes called **demand-side economics.**

Keynesian economic thinking continues to influence federal fiscal policy. However, President **Ronald Reagan** and several other recent Presidents have insisted that lower taxes, not greater spending, provide the best route to a stronger economy. This view, which is sometimes called **supply-side economics** or "Reaganomics," is based on the assumption that tax cuts increase the supply of money in private hands and so stimulate the economy.

An example of this approach occurred during the steep downturn in the nation's economy that began in 2007 and continued into 2009. President Bush and then President Obama persuaded Congress to enact a series of "economic stimulus" plans—pump-priming measures that could very well have been written by John Maynard Keynes himself. Those laws were variously designed to inject more than $1.5 trillion into the nation's ailing economy in order to (1) shore up the loan-making capacities of the nation's banks and other financial institutions, (2) overcome a marked decline in consumer spending, and (3) combat a rising tide of unemployment. Several years later, the Federal Government made a similar move when it spent trillions to combat the economic effects of the COVID-19 pandemic that began in late 2019.

The Borrowing Process Congress must authorize all federal borrowing. The actual borrowing is done by the Treasury Department, which issues various kinds of securities to investors. These investors are principally individuals, banks and other financial institutions, and other countries. The securities usually take the form of Treasury notes or bills, often referred to as T-bills, for short-term borrowing, and bonds for long-term purposes. They are, in effect, IOUs in which the government agrees to repay a certain sum, plus interest, on a certain date.

The Federal Government is regularly able to borrow money at lower rates of interest than the rates charged to private borrowers. This is true largely because investors can find no safer securities than those issued by the United States. If this country could not pay its debts, no one else would be able to do so, either. Federal securities are also attractive because the interest they earn cannot be taxed by any of the States or their local governments.

☑ **SUPPORT A POINT OF VIEW WITH EVIDENCE**
Do you think deficit financing is a good way to fund the Federal Government? Why or why not?

Understanding the Public Debt

Borrowing produces a debt, of course. The public debt is the result of the Federal Government's borrowing over time. More precisely, the **public debt** is the total outstanding indebtedness of the Federal Government. It includes all of the money the government has borrowed and not yet repaid, plus the accrued interest on that borrowing. The Treasury Department's Bureau of the Public Debt acts as the Federal Government's borrowing agent. It issues Treasury bills, notes, and bonds and manages the U.S. Savings Bond Program.

The Federal Government has built up a huge debt over the years. Recall, the Federal Government first went into debt during **George Washington's** administration. Still, it took 193 years—from 1789 to 1982—for the public debt to reach $1 trillion. The public debt has exploded over past decades, reaching tens of trillions of dollars.

The amounts involved here are absolutely mind-boggling. In 1981, as the debt approached

WHICH COUNTRIES OWN PART OF THE FEDERAL DEBT?

APPROXIMATELY 30% OF U.S. DEBT IS OWNED BY FOREIGN COUNTRIES

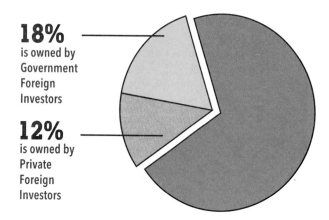

18%
is owned by Government Foreign Investors

12%
is owned by Private Foreign Investors

Source: Congressional Research Service, "Foreign Holdings of Federal Debt"

TOP 10 COUNTRIES
Japan
China
United Kingdom
Ireland
Luxembourg
Brazil
Switzerland
Belgium
Taiwan
Hong Kong

>> As a category, foreign investors make up one of the largest holders of U.S. debt.
Analyze Graphs Do government or private foreign investors own more of this portion of the debt?

$1 trillion, President Reagan said that he found "such a figure—a trillion dollars—incomprehensible." He then drew this verbal picture: "[I]f you had a stack of $1,000 bills in your hand only four inches high, you'd be a millionaire. A trillion dollars would be a stack 67 miles high."

There is no constitutional limit on the amount that may be borrowed, and so there is no constitutional limit on the public debt. Congress has put a statutory ceiling on the debt, but simply raises that ceiling whenever fiscal realities seem to call for it.

The debt has always been controversial, and its rapid rise in recent years has fueled the fire. The annual interest on the debt is the amount that must be paid each year to those from whom the government has borrowed and has grown to hundreds of billions of dollars.

Most of those who are concerned about the size of the debt are worried about its impact on future generations of Americans. They say that years of shortsightedness and failure to operate government on a pay-as-you-go basis has produced monumental debt and interest obligations that will have to be met by tomorrow's taxpayers.

☑ **COMPARE AND CONTRAST** What is the difference between an annual deficit and the public debt?

☑ **ASSESSMENT**

1. **Generate Explanations** For over 150 years, the revenue and expenditures of the Federal Government had very little impact on the economy of the United States. What were some major events that caused this situation to change?

2. **Predict Consequences** What might occur if the OMB accepted all agency funding requests without holding budget hearings? What would be the advantages and disadvantages if this were to occur?

3. **Identify Steps in a Process** Describe the basic steps involved in creating the federal budget.

4. **Analyze Information** Why do you think that for many years Congress and the President have chosen to borrow money rather than balance the federal budget?

5. **Support a Point of View with Evidence** Do you think the concern about the size of the public debt is justified? Why or why not?

12.5

As vast as the world appears, even from 22,000 miles away, globalization has brought nations closer together and greatly impacted markets and economies.

 BOUNCE to Activate Flipped Video

Objectives

Explain the causes of globalization, including recent scientific discoveries and technological innovations, and its effects on the American economy, including why certain places or regions are important to the United States.

Understand the roles of the executive and legislative branches in setting international trade and fiscal policies.

Identify international trade organizations and alliances to which the United States belongs.

Recognize the benefits and drawbacks of the global economy, including the significance to the United States of the location and key natural resources of particular countries.

Understand world economic trends today.

Key Terms

protectionism
tariff
import quota
trade embargo
North American Free
    Trade Agreement
    (NAFTA)
International
    Monetary Fund
    (IMF)
World Bank
World Trade
    Organization
Group of 7 (G7)
globalization

The U.S. in a Global Economy

There is a growing economic interdependence among nations of the world. This interdependence, often called globalization, has been both driven and enabled by many remarkable advancements in communication and transportation technologies. Everything from the enormous increase in computing power, the Internet, communications satellites, and even the building of larger ships has increased the flow of goods, and, as well, the flow of information that connects world markets. Globalization has also developed out of the drive for increased international trade promoted by the United States in the years since the Great Depression.

A Global Economy

All nations engage in trade. Trade is one of the hallmarks of civilization, and has been for thousands of years. However, improvements in transportation and communication technologies and the pressure to find new markets have spurred the growth of worldwide markets.

The United States produces a great many different goods, but it does not produce everything this country needs. No country does because of the unequal distribution of natural resources and other factors of production, such as skilled workers, among countries. The unequal distribution of factors of production means that one nation can more effectively specialize in producing certain goods—for example, petroleum or computer chips. That nation will then export petroleum or computer chips and use the profits to purchase, or import, goods from other nations who have an advantage in the production of, for example, food stuffs or automobiles.

Consider this example: the United States produces petroleum, but not enough to meet the nation's energy needs. So the

United States imports crude oil from other countries, especially Canada, Saudi Arabia, Mexico, and Venezuela, and American companies have long been banned from exporting crude oil. At the same time, the United States is able to grow many crops, such as wheat and corn, that are in demand in other countries.

In some cases, countries import and export the same products, providing greater variety to consumers in each country, as well as creating jobs in the manufacturing and transportation industries.

Today, more than just trade links America's economy to the world. Multinational corporations stretch across borders. These are companies that are headquartered in one country but do business around the world. Examples include European automakers that have opened up factories in the United States and American fast-food restaurants with locations abroad.

Multinational corporations affect relations between countries. They lobby governments for trade deals or changes in laws that will allow them to do business more easily. Governments work to promote the interests of locally headquartered companies abroad. But when relations between countries sour, multinational companies can become the target of boycotts or suffer the effects of sanctions.

The Benefits of Trade Trade allows Americans to acquire the goods they want, which this nation cannot produce as cost-effectively or efficiently as it does other goods. Equally importantly, trade provides Americans with a market for goods and services produced in the United States—and by doing so, it provides Americans with jobs.

It is the role of the Federal Government to support trade and other economic opportunities around the world, while at the same time, protecting American producers and consumers. To accomplish this, the President negotiates trade agreements with other countries, while Congress has the authority to approve or reject these agreements.

U.S. Imports and Exports For the last several years, Canada, Mexico, and China have been this nation's top trading partners, but a trade imbalance exists between the U.S. and China because the U.S. imports more goods from China than China does from the U.S.

The United States is a world leader in foreign trade. This nation is second only to China in the export of goods, and it is the world's largest exporter of services, a sizeable and quickly growing sector of world trade. Major American exports include

Winners and Losers of International Trade

WINNERS OF INTERNATIONAL TRADE	BECAUSE ...
Consumers	the variety of goods increases and price decreases
Domestic companies that export goods	they can grow and produce on a larger scale and at a lower cost.
Countries that trade	exporting leads to growth and development; new access to technology, tools, and equipment raises productivity and the standard of living.
Workers	trade creates new jobs in exporting industries.
LOSERS OF INTERNATIONAL TRADE	**BECAUSE ...**
Companies that cannot compete internationally	they must find ways to become competitive or produce other products.
Workers	they may lose jobs when companies go out of business and when imports replace domestic products; they may face poor working conditions and low wages.
Countries that trade	a crisis in another country can have economic effects on trading partners; trade agreements may affect national sovereignty.

>> Untangling the benefits and drawbacks of international trade is complex, but this chart shows some of the major winners and losers. **Analyze Charts** In addition to the reason listed on this chart, what other reason can you think of that workers benefit from international trade?

telecommunications, aerospace, medical, and military equipment.

This country also exports soybeans, corn, fruit, automobiles, and a great many other products. United States service exports include business, professional, and technical services, insurance services, financial services, and travel.

The United States is also the world's number one importer of both goods and services. Trillions of dollars worth of goods enter this country each year—more than 10 percent of all the world's imports. Consumer goods such as clothing, toys, and electronics, as well as capital goods, which include computers, electronic parts, and industrial machinery, are among this nation's major imports. Another import category is food and beverages, including animal feed. Automobiles and auto parts constitute a fourth import category.

Often, America's foreign policy concerns match those of its trade partners. For example, Canada and the United States nearly always agree on global political issues. But at times, there are conflicts. China and the United States are at odds on several matters, including the status of Taiwan and control of the South China Sea. We have grave concerns about human rights violations in many of the nations we trade with, including several in the Middle East.

>> An oil tanker enters a Texas port. In 2012, the United States imported about 57 percent of its crude oil. Canada was by far the country's top crude oil supplier, at about 2.5 million barrels a day.

Navigating our relationship with these countries can be tricky. Trade is key to America's economic well-being, but our interests spread in many directions as the world's military and democratic leader. The best way to describe the solution might be called a "dual-track" approach. Issues regarding trade and commerce continue along one track, with vigorous debates and negotiations on other topics moving down another route. At times, disputes on political issues can end the trade relationship.

Industrial Supplies The largest category of imported goods is industrial supplies and materials, including crude oil. The United States imports about 15 percent of its energy supply, and is one of the world's largest importers of crude oil in the world, along with China and India. Most of that oil comes from the countries of Canada, Saudi Arabia, Mexico, Columbia, and Iraq.

The location of U.S. trade partners matters tremendously. The United States trades with some countries, such as Canada and Mexico, because they are geographically close. It is also easier to trade with Pacific Rim countries because the Pacific Ocean can act as a shipping route. For other trade partners, such as Saudi Arabia and China, the availability of natural resources like oil and rare earth metals is more important.

☑ **DRAW CONCLUSIONS** How might economic dependence on another country affect the political relationship of the United States with that country?

U.S. Trade Policies

One goal of the Federal Government has often been to protect American producers and workers by keeping prices, and therefore profits, high, while minimizing competition from imports. The executive branch of government must do this (with congressional approval) through such agencies as the Department of Commerce and the International Trade Commission without jeopardizing relationships with its trade partners. It has employed several tools for this tricky task.

Economic Resources and Foreign Policy Most national governments try to control imports to protect native industries from foreign competition. The goals of this practice, known as **protectionism,** include safeguarding of jobs, protecting emerging or weakened industries, and enhancing national security. Governments often pursue these goals with trade barriers that hinder free trade and raise

HOW TARIFFS WORK

① **POLYSILICON** used to make solar panels sells at **$18.95**/kg.

② China adds a **57% TARIFF** to the price.

③ **PRICE** of U.S.-produced polysilicon in China is **$29.75**/kg.

④ **SOLAR PANEL** costs **$0.91**/watt.

⑤ U.S. adds a **36% TARIFF** to the price.

⑥ **PRICE** of China-produced solar panel in U.S. is **$1.24**/watt.

CHINA

UNITED STATES

Sources: *The Washington Post*; Forbes

>> Tariffs protect industries from foreign competition. **Analyze Charts** How would the cost of a China-produced solar panel be affected by a decrease in the tariff on U.S.-produced polysilicon?

the prices consumers must pay for imported goods. These trade barriers are generally of three types: tariffs, import quotas, and trade embargoes. In the United States, the decision to set up such trade barriers must ultimately be made by Congress.

A **tariff** is a tax on imported goods. A tariff increases the cost of an imported item and makes American-made products more attractive to the domestic customer. The government regularly places high tariffs on goods that are produced by important American industries. For example, the tariff on steel is relatively high because Americans produce a great deal of it and the steel industry is considered vital to national security, so the government does not wish cheaper imports to put domestic steel mills out of business.

An **import quota** is a limit put on the amount of a commodity that can be imported into a country. While recently limited by international agreements, import quotas are still in place in the United States on such items as cotton, sugar, and milk. Many European nations have put a quota on American films and television shows to encourage the production of their own features and to protect national cultures.

Trade Embargoes and Sanctions Trade embargoes and sanctions are more significant trade barriers—and are more often used to apply

diplomatic pressure or as a punishment rather than as an economic tool. A **trade embargo** is a ban on trade with a particular country. Sanctions are similar to embargoes. An embargo might be placed on all goods or only specific items. It can be placed on exports or, separately, on imports. The U.S. has used embargoes largely to promote its foreign policy positions. One example is the American embargo against communist Cuba that began in the early 1960s with the goal of pressuring the Cuban government to improve civil rights in that country.

Are embargoes effective? Proponents say they can pressure a country's leadership to improve human rights or punish a country for past behavior more effectively than a military offensive. Opponents argue that sanctions can harm the American economy as well as innocent citizens in the targeted country. In addition to Cuba, the United States maintains embargoes on North Korea and Iran and a host of other countries, either as punishment and/or as an incentive to change.

Free Trade in North America The North American Free Trade Agreement, known as **NAFTA,** became effective in 1994. NAFTA established free trade among the United States, Canada, and Mexico, and intended to eliminate, in steps, all tariffs and other barriers to trade by 2009. It created what amounts to the world's largest free trade zone.

NAFTA was approved only after a great deal of controversy and resistance, especially in the United States. Opponents of the agreement were concerned that American manufacturing operations would be moved to Mexico, where wages are lower and regulations fewer. Others worried that imports without tariffs would put American businesses at a disadvantage.

Supporters insisted that the expected increase in exports to Canada and Mexico would mean an increase in American jobs. They also argued that an improved economy in the region would be good for the U.S. economy. It also would create greater prosperity and stability in Mexico, and so reduce illegal immigration from that country.

Pros and Cons NAFTA has been replaced by a new trade agreement, but economists are still debating the effects it had on the American economy. Most agree that it was not positive for many American workers. Although the long-term results are hard to distinguish from other trends, it appears that NAFTA accelerated the loss of high-paying manufacturing jobs in the American textile and clothing sectors. However,

>> Mining equipment is one example of exports from the United States to Australia. Trade between the two countries rose 23 percent in 2005, the year after a free trade agreement (AUSFTA) was signed.

many manufacturing jobs that left the United States moved to countries other than Mexico or Canada.

NAFTA also affected the amount that industrial workers overall are paid. Wages paid for factory jobs within the United States dropped, or in some cases did not rise to meet inflation.

On the positive side, trade—in agricultural products especially—increased dramatically. Between 1993 and 2015, for example, United States merchandise exports to Mexico rose from some $40 billion to more than $230 billion.

USMCA In 2020, a new trade agreement replaced NAFTA, called the United States-Mexico-Canada Agreement (USMCA). Using NAFTA as its basis, the USMCA is designed to help American automotive and manufacturing industries, dairy farmers and other agricultural sectors, and labor unions.

Among its other provisions, the USMCA requires 40–45 percent of automobiles to be made by workers who earn at least $16 per hour. Since Mexican workers are paid much less than that amount, automobile manufacturers will have to produce more cars in the United States.

The USMCA also requires Mexico to make it easier for its workers to form unions, which will have the effect of making American unionized workers more competitive. Dairy farmers also have the potential to benefit from the USMCA, since the agreement contains a provision limiting the tariffs they must pay and giving them expanded access to Canadian markets. The agreement also includes some protections for endangered species, but nothing in it addresses climate change.

The USMCA passed with overwhelming support in Congress. Those who do oppose it offer several arguments, including that its provisions don't go far enough and that consumers will suffer if automobile prices rise due to the deal.

Other Trade Agreements While the USMCA affects only trade with Canada and Mexico, the United States has signed similar treaties, although involving much smaller trade flows, with Australia and countries in Latin America, the Middle East, Africa, and Asia. For example, in 2012 Congress ratified a free trade agreement reducing tariffs on goods imported from South Korea and making the Korean market more accessible to U.S. auto manufacturers, U.S. law firms, and U.S. suppliers of financial services.

☑ **COMPARE** What is the difference between a trade embargo and a tariff?

>> The Kajaki Dam in Afghanistan was partially funded by the World Bank. The dam provides electricity and irrigates surrounding farmland.

Trade Alliances and Organizations

The United States seeks to support industries and workers at home. It also seeks to enlarge economic opportunities, strengthen international ties, and open new markets abroad. It often accomplishes these goals through membership in free trade agreements and international alliances and organizations.

As you can imagine, no single actor or institution can do a lot to shape the world's economy. However, it is also fair to say that the United States probably plays a greater role in influencing international fiscal policy than any other nation. It does so mainly through its leadership in two important organizations: the International Monetary Fund (IMF) and the World Bank. The World Trade Organization (WTO) and the Group of 7 (G7) are also international economic organizations to which the United States belongs.

The International Monetary Fund Headquartered in Washington, D.C., the **International Monetary Fund** was created after World War II by 29 nations. Since then it has grown to some 200 countries. Some of the goals of this organization are to structure international trade, create fiscal stability, promote cross-border investment, reduce world poverty, and provide loans to developing nations.

The United States has significantly more voting power in the IMF than any other nation, based on its contribution to the fund. Both the executive and legislative branches of the Federal Government play a role in U.S. involvement in the IMF. The President, with the advice and consent of the Senate, is in charge of appointing U.S. representatives to the IMF, while Congress is responsible for authorizing and appropriating U.S. financial commitments.

The World Bank The **World Bank** is a similar institution, and it was created at the same time as the IMF. Its mission is a bit narrower, however, centering on strategies to reduce world poverty, promote global literacy, and raise the standard of living around the world. These strategies include making loans to developing nations to build bridges, dams, and to make other tangible improvements and provide advice and training.

The United States is the largest shareholder in the World Bank, which, like the IMF, is headquartered in Washington, D.C. As a result, the leader of the World Bank has traditionally been an American citizen nominated by the President. Here, too, Congress is responsible for authorizing and appropriating U.S. funds for the World Bank. Because of the various strategies used by these organizations to promote stable economic policies and reduce poverty across the globe, the IMF and the World Bank have been a source of controversy, both abroad and in the United States.

The World Trade Organization and the G7 The **World Trade Organization** was created in 1995 to help carry out and extend the goals of a 1947 treaty, the General Agreement on Tariffs and Trade (GATT), which intended to increase trade. With 164 members, the WTO provides a set of rules for international commerce, a forum for the creation of new trade agreements, and an arena in which to resolve trade issues.

Another important group to which the United States belongs is the **Group of 7**, or the "G7," an annual meeting of the leaders of seven wealthy and industrialized nations: the United States, Canada, France, Germany, Italy, Japan, and the United Kingdom. The group has no rigid structure, and leaders meet as representatives of their governments to discuss world affairs and crises.

Regional Trade Alliances The European Union (EU) is the most successful of the world's free trade organizations. It also formulates policies in other areas, such as the environment and security. The evolution of the EU began in 1957, when six European nations established the European Common Market to coordinate economic policies and trade. Over time, most Western European nations joined the group. In 1986, they created the European Economic Community (EEC) and, in an historic step, eliminated all tariffs on trade between EU members.

In 1993, the organization went even further to blur international boundaries by forming the European Union. The EU operates much like a weak Federal Government, with its own parliament, its own flag, and even an anthem. Citizens of most member nations can now travel as tourists or workers across national borders freely, without a passport. By 2011, seventeen of the member nations had given up their individual currencies and replaced them with the EU's currency, the euro.

Inspired by the EU, other nations have formed trade alliances. One of the largest is the Asian-Pacific Economic Cooperation (APEC). Its members include nations bordering the Pacific Rim, such as the United States, Japan, Canada, Chile, and China. The Southern Common Market, or MERCOSUR, is a regional trade bloc that today includes Brazil, Argentina, Paraguay, Uruguay, and Venezuela.

☑ **COMPARE** Explain the difference between the World Trade Organization and the International Monetary Fund.

>> Uruguay is a member of MERCOSUR and one of its major exports is wool. Here, a Uruguayan cowboy gathers a herd of sheep and drives them into the corral.

Manufacturing vs. Services in the U.S. Economy, 1950-2014

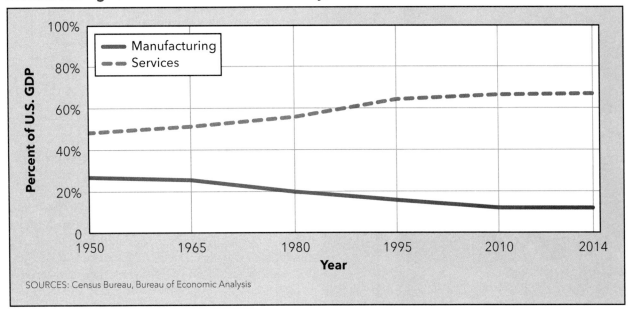

SOURCES: Census Bureau, Bureau of Economic Analysis

>> Over the last several decades, the United States has transitioned from a manufacturing to a service economy. **Analyze Charts** How does this trend affect workers in both areas?

The Consequences of the Global Economy

For the most part, a global economy seems to be a positive development. It means that more goods are available to more consumers, and that there are more markets in which producers can sell goods. Globalization and international partnerships also help developing nations expand their economies and raise their standards of living by enabling them to sell goods to more affluent countries.

And, clearly, competition in a global market lowers the price of goods. Goods made overseas, unblocked by tariffs, are less expensive and become more affordable for Americans. Increases in jobs and higher wages, in turn, allow consumers in developing nations to buy American goods and services, and this helps to increase or at least maintain American jobs.

Additionally, new, creative approaches to outsourcing may actually create new American jobs by lowering costs so that corporations are able to use the savings to grow and develop innovative products and services. Importantly, increased economic interdependence may lead to more political cooperation and so to fewer conflicts.

Risks However, with interdependence comes risk. A crisis in another nation on which Americans depend for an important commodity can have quick, profound, and direct economic effects. War and instability in major oil-producing nations, for example, can contribute to higher oil and gas prices in the United States.

Some people worry that international trade agreements may affect a nation's sovereignty if they have to get "permission" from partner nations to make decisions about such matters as civil rights, defense, or the environment. With instantaneous communications, economic downturns or market fluctuations in one part of the world now cause instability in other markets within hours.

Globalization has led to the exploitation of workers in some less developed countries. Some multinational corporations have been criticized—and some have been sued in U.S. courts—for allowing unhealthy working conditions, paying workers wages that are below poverty level, and employing children to work in factories and elsewhere.

The United States is also adversely affected by trade deficits. For example, the United States buys much more from China than China buys from the United States, and so an enormous trade deficit has developed. In addition, China has financed the budget deficit by lending the United States government money and by buying American assets. This means that China, along with Japan and many oil-exporting countries, owns a portion of the

>> Production line workers at a factory in Gimpo, South Korea, assemble mobile phones. A free trade agreement between the United States and the Republic of Korea (KORUS FTA) went into effect in 2012.

American economy, with possible implications for the economic health and future of this nation.

The United States is also moving from a manufacturing economy to a service economy, in large part because American workers cannot compete with workers in other nations who are paid much less. According to the Bureau of Economic Analysis, service industries compose a large majority of American jobs. In the ten years between 2000 and 2010, the United States lost nearly one third of its manufacturing jobs.

Tomorrow's Marketplace The trend today in the world economy is toward greater interdependence among nations—increased **globalization**. Along with the United States, most nations are joining multiple trade alliances, such as the USMCA and the EU, to open new markets and promote free trade. Developing nations are working to diversify their economies and open their markets. The United States continues to build partnerships by establishing new trade agreements with nations such as Peru, South Korea, Singapore, and Colombia and working with China to lower the U.S. trade deficit with that nation.

While it's true that trade and other economic issues lie at the heart of global connections between nations, many other issues are also creating new international communities in the 21st century. Environmental problems, for instance, often stretch beyond the borders of particular nations, and terrorism has also become a worldwide concern. Nations are also starting to work together on cybersecurity and other digital communications matters.

The good news for Americans is that the huge increase in the demand for services worldwide means that the United States will probably continue to see an increase in service exports and retain its position as the global leader in that area. Unfortunately, it also means an increase in free trade and outsourcing to emerging nations means further loss of manufacturing jobs. Although economic analysts have mixed views about the overall cost in American jobs due to outsourcing, thousands or even millions of jobs could move overseas in the coming years. Federal programs such as Trade Adjustment Assistance, which retrains workers who are laid off due to outsourcing or foreign competition, will help American workers deal with this challenge.

As the economy shifts toward services, the United States will need to rely on intellectual property as much as on exported goods.

Among other important challenges and issues the United States government must face in the future are the protection of American copyrights and patents against piracy and the need to foster stability in oil producing nations and regions.

☑ **INFER** How do trade alliances affect the United States economy as a whole?

☑ **ASSESSMENT**

1. **Identify Supporting Details** What are the advantages of NAFTA for the United States?

2. **Categorize** Is NAFTA a protectionist agreement? Why or why not?

3. **Identify Supporting Details** Give an example of a way in which U.S. foreign policy is driven by the nation's economic needs.

4. **Compare and Contrast** Distinguish between the role of the President and the role of Congress in determining U.S. economic policies.

5. **Draw Conclusions** How can economic policies affect national security?

GO ONLINE to www.SavvasRealize.com and access your digital course

Use the following online resources to practice citizenship skills and prepare for the Topic Test.

Case Studies

Current Connections

Quest Inquiries

Quizzes

Interactivities

Texts

Flipped Videos

While online you can also check the progress you've made learning the topic and course content by viewing your grades, test scores, and assignment status.

Topic 12 Quick Study Guide

LESSON SUMMARIES

Use these Lesson Summaries, and the longer versions available online, to review the key ideas for each lesson in this Topic.

Lesson 1: Types of Economic Systems

Capitalism, or the free enterprise system, is characterized by private ownership and private decision-making in a free market. This system encourages entrepreneurs. In a mixed economy, government regulation and private enterprise coexist. Socialist systems give a larger economic role to the government, and communist economies are centrally planned and government-run.

Lesson 2: Fiscal and Monetary Policy

The Federal Government works to lower unemployment, maintain price stability, and grow the economy. Fiscal policy, or taxation and government spending, directly affects the economy. So does monetary policy, changing the money supply and the availability of credit, which is managed by the Federal Reserve.

Lesson 3: Financing Government

The Constitution gives Congress the power to tax in order to finance the government, with some restrictions. Citizens pay an income tax, social insurance taxes, excise taxes on gasoline, alcohol, and other goods, and various other taxes. Taxes on corporate income are also collected.

Lesson 4: Spending and Borrowing

The Federal Government spends several trillion dollars every year. Entitlement programs and defense spending are some of the largest costs. The annual budget, set by Congress with executive branch input, controls some of this spending. When this budget leads to a deficit, Congress can borrow money. Borrowing produces a public debt, which has grown dramatically in recent decades.

Lesson 5: The U.S. in a Global Economy

Globalization has strongly affected the American economy. Americans depend on trade with foreign countries. Increased competition due to global trade has lowered the price of goods. However, it also hurt American workers who now must compete against lower paid workers in other countries.

VISUAL REVIEW

Use these graphics to review some of the key terms, people, and ideas from this Topic.

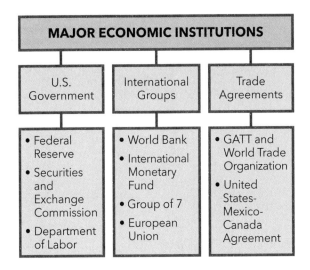

MAJOR ECONOMIC INSTITUTIONS

U.S. Government
- Federal Reserve
- Securities and Exchange Commission
- Department of Labor

International Groups
- World Bank
- International Monetary Fund
- Group of 7
- European Union

Trade Agreements
- GATT and World Trade Organization
- United States-Mexico-Canada Agreement

GOALS FOR THE ECONOMY

Full Employment
Jobs for all those able and willing to work

Price Stability
Limited inflation or deflation

Economic Growth
Increase in the GDP

FREE ENTERPRISE
- Private ownership of land, labor, and capital
- Limited government participation
- Free markets and prices
- Competition among entrepreneurs

Government Revenue and Spending

GOVERNMENT REVENUE	GOVERNMENT SPENDING
• Income taxes • Social insurance taxes • Excise, estate, and other taxes • Borrowing	• Entitlement programs • Defense • Interest on the public debt • Many other programs such as the National Parks and highway construction

Topic 12 Assessment

KEY TERMS, PEOPLE, AND IDEAS

1. What are the three **factors of production**?

2. Define the **law of supply** and **demand**.

3. How does the Federal Government use **fiscal policy** and **monetary policy** to regulate the economy?

4. Explain the difference between the government's **controllable spending** and **uncontrollable spending**.

5. What is the practice of **protectionism**?

6. What are **customs duties**?

7. What is the **public debt**?

8. How do the concepts of **supply-side economics** and **demand-side economics** differ?

CRITICAL THINKING

9. **Summarize** What are the different types of taxes? Which federal taxes raise the most revenue? Which tax are you most likely to pay on a regular basis? Why?

10. **Explain** What is the President's role in the budget-making process? The role of Congress? Is this process a joint effort between the President and Congress? Explain.

11. **Infer** What four limits on the power to tax are set out in the Constitution? Why do you think those limits were established by the Framers?

12. **Express Ideas Clearly** What are the principal economic goals of the Federal Government? What methods are used by the government to meet these goals? Do you think the government should be involved in the economy? Why or why not?

13. **Support a Point of View with Evidence** Many people believe that socialism and communism discourage individual initiative. Is this criticism valid? Why or why not?

14. **Contrast** How does capitalism differ from command economies in the treatment of the individual?

15. **Explain** Why is competition important in a free-market economy? What might happen in a market without competition?

16. **Compare and Contrast** The chart below compares the U.S. free enterprise system with socialism and communism. How do the various economic systems vary?

Economic Systems

CAPITALISM/ FREE ENTERPRISE	Individuals are in charge of production and can profit from their labor. • **Laissez-Faire** very limited government role • **Mixed Economy** some government regulation
SOCIALISM	The state makes many economic decisions; some central planning
COMMUNISM	The state makes all economic decisions; centrally planned economy

17. **Support a Point of View with Evidence** According to laissez-faire theory, what are the three major concerns of government? Do you think this amounts to too little, too much, or just the right amount of involvement by government? Why?

18. **Summarize** How does the Federal Government seek to protect American workers and producers from foreign competition?

19. **Interpret** Describe the Federal Government's power to tax, as laid out in Article I of the Constitution. How has the Supreme Court both upheld and limited the power to tax?

20. **Summarize** How does the government borrow money? Who benefits from this borrowing system, and who, if anyone, is disadvantaged by government borrowing?

21. **Writing Activity** Consider a situation in which Congress proposes legislation that would require the Federal Government to balance its budget each year. Use this textbook and outside sources to research the causes and effects of the federal deficit, evaluating sources for their reliability. Then, use the information you gathered to present oral arguments to the class in favor of or in opposition to the proposed law. Be sure to discuss the possible consequences of such a law, state your viewpoint on it, and give the reasons for your position.

DOCUMENT-BASED QUESTIONS

While trade between the United States and China provides benefits to both countries, it has also raised a host of concerns among government and business leaders.

DOCUMENT A

This chart shows the U.S. trade deficit with China.

U.S. Trade Deficit with China

YEAR	TRADE DEFICIT
1985	$6.0 million
1990	$10.4 billion
1995	$33.8 billion
2000	$83.8 billion
2005	$202.3 billion
2010	$273.0 billion
2015	$365.7 billion

SOURCE: *U.S. Census Bureau*

DOCUMENT B

U.S.–China trade is affected by a host of factors, including the one described in this excerpt.

You don't have to look far these days to find a press report about another firm, like Google, whose networks have been penetrated by Chinese cyber espionage and have lost valuable corporate intellectual property. And that's just the tip of the iceberg. . . .

When you talk to these companies behind closed doors, however, they describe attacks that originate in China, and have a level of sophistication and are clearly supported by a level of resources that can only be a nation-state entity. Attributing this espionage isn't easy, but talk to any private sector cyber analyst, and they will tell you there is little doubt that this is a massive campaign being conducted by the Chinese government.

—*House Intelligence Committee Chairman Mike Rogers, October 4, 2011*

DOCUMENT C

Senator and Democratic presidential candidate Bernie Sanders expresses his views on trade in this excerpt.

I think what the average American sees is that for many decades now, what corporate America has said is, "Hey, I'm not going to pay you 20 or 25 bucks at a factory, I don't need you anymore. We're going to shut your factory down. I'm going to move to China, pay people there a buck or two an hour. I don't have to worry about environmental regulations, I don't have to worry about trade unions, and I'm going to produce products there and I'm going to bring them back to the United States of America." Now, is that the fault of China? No. That issue has to do with the greed of corporate America who sold out American workers and essentially moved manufacturing to China and other low-wage countries.

—*Senator Bernie Sanders (I., Vermont), interview with Ezra Klein, Vox.com, July 28, 2015*

DOCUMENT D

This cartoon uses Chinese food as a symbol for concerns about U.S.-China relations.

DAVE GRANLUND© www.davegranlund.com

22. Documents B and D both express concern about which of the following?
   A. the lack of trade unions in China
   B. the high cost of U.S. environmental regulations.
   C. the need for more high tech training in the U.S.
   D. Chinese cyberattacks on U.S. companies

23. On whom does Senator Bernie Sanders place the blame for the U.S. trade deficit with China?
   A. American corporations
   B. the Chinese government
   C. American workers
   D. the U.S. government

24. **Analyze Political Cartoons** The term "takeout" has a double meaning in this cartoon. What point is the cartoonist making with this play on words?

25. **Writing Task** Use the data in Document A to draw a graph. Decide what kind of graph makes sense for this information. Be careful when specifying units of measure, and be sure to label accurately. Then, use your graph as you analyze and critique the views expressed in these documents, and take and defend a stand on whether or not Americans should try to "Buy American."

State and Local Government

ESSENTIAL QUESTION What Should Governments Do?

Former Oklahoma governor Mary Fallin, second from right, tours a tornado-damaged neighborhood.

In your final years of high school, your thoughts may be turning to what comes next. If you're thinking of continuing your studies, you may be wondering how to afford it.

In this Topic, you'll learn how and why government provides public education from kindergarten to 12th grade. Many people want community colleges funded as well. But debate swirls around public funding of higher education. Should your State pay the bill? Would this affect the taxes workers pay?

NBC LEARN

Governorship, A Stepping-Stone to the Presidency.

🅱 BOUNCE to Activate My Story Video

Much of what is done by government in this country on a daily basis is done by State and local governments. In this Topic, you will take a look at State and local governments across the nation. Look at the lesson outline and explore the graphic organizer. As you study this Topic, you can work on your Quest Inquiry.

LESSON OUTLINE

13.1 State Constitutions

13.2 State Legislatures

13.3 The Governor and State Administration

13.4 State Courts

13.5 Local Governments

13.6 State and Local Spending and Revenue

State Government Organization

EXECUTIVE BRANCH	Governor Attorney General Lieutenant Governor Secretary of State State Treasurer
LEGISLATIVE BRANCH	House of Representatives/General Assembly/ House of Delegates Senate
JUDICIAL BRANCH	Local Courts General Trial Courts Courts of Appeal State Supreme Court

Inquiry Center

Want to become an active and effective citizen? Make a difference in your community and beyond by using the **Inquiry Center** on the digital course.

Connect with issues you're passionate about by using the **Interest Finder**.

Investigate public policies, get involved in your community, influence public opinion, and develop leadership skills.

Synthesize the work you've done and what you've learned along the way.

Demonstrate what you've learned once you've finished your project by sharing your work.

A mural hanging in the Massachusetts State House depicts the drafting of that State's constitution. Massachusetts was the first State to submit its constitution to the voters for approval.

 BOUNCE to Activate Flipped Video

Objectives

Examine the history, content, and significance of the first State constitutions.

Describe the basic principles common to all State constitutions today.

Explain the procedures used to change State constitutions.

Analyze why State constitutions are in need of reform.

Key Terms

popular sovereignty
limited government
initiative
fundamental law
statutory law

State Constitutions

Not very many people have ever seen a State constitution, let alone read one. Join a rather exclusive club and look at your State's document. It is the supreme law of your State and sets out the ways in which the State government is organized. It also distributes power among the various branches of State government and authorizes the exercise of power by that government. At the same time, it limits the exercise of that power.

The constitution of every State is superior to all other forms of State and local laws within that State, but it is subordinate to the Constitution of the United States. No provision in any State's constitution may conflict with any form of federal law.

From the beginning, government in this country has been based on *written* constitutions. Every State has such a document. In fact, the United States has sometimes been described as "a land of constitutions."

The First State Constitutions

Americans' experience with such documents dates from 1606, when King James I granted a charter to the Virginia Company. That act led to the settlement at Jamestown in the following year and, with it, the first government in what would become British North America. Later, each of the other English colonies was also established and governed on the basis of a written charter.

Independence When the 13 colonies became independent, each faced the problem of establishing a new government. On May 15, 1776, the Second Continental Congress, meeting in Philadelphia, advised each of the new States to adopt such governments as shall, in the opinion of the representatives of the people, best conduce to the happiness and safety of their constituents in particular, and America in general.

—Second Continental Congress

Most of the colonial charters served as models for the first State constitutions. Indeed, in Connecticut and Rhode Island, the charters seemed so well suited to the needs of the people that they were carried over into statehood as constitutions almost without change.

The earliest State constitutions were adopted in a variety of ways. However, the people played no direct part in the process in any State. Six of the revolutionary legislatures drew up new documents and proclaimed them in force in 1776. In none of those States—Maryland, New Jersey, North Carolina, Pennsylvania, South Carolina, and Virginia—was the new constitution placed before the people for their judgment.

In Delaware and New Hampshire in 1776, and in Georgia and New York in 1777, the constitutions were prepared by conventions called by the legislature. In each case, the new document had to be approved by the legislature in order to become effective, but in none was popular approval required.

In 1780, however, Massachusetts set a new precedent when a popularly elected convention prepared a new constitution for the State, and that document was then ratified by a vote of the people. Thus, Massachusetts set the pattern of popular participation in the constitution-making process, and this example has been generally followed among the States ever since.

Assemblies representing the people drafted all of the present State constitutions; most of them became effective only after a popular vote. Only the present-day documents of Delaware (1897), Mississippi (1890), South Carolina (1895), and Vermont (1793) came into force without popular ratification.

Principles of State Constitutions The first State constitutions shared many of the same basic features. Each proclaimed the principles of **popular sovereignty** and **limited government.** That is, in each of them the people were recognized as the sole source of authority for government, and the powers given to the new government were closely limited. Seven documents began with a lengthy bill of rights. All of them made it clear that the sovereign people held "certain unalienable rights" that government must respect.

The doctrines of separation of powers and checks and balances were also built into each of the new constitutions. In practice, however, the memory of the hated royal governors was still fresh, and so, most authority was given to the legislature. For example, only New York, Massachusetts, and South Carolina allowed the governor to veto acts of the legislature.

For their time, the early State constitutions were fairly democratic. Each however, contained several provisions (and some important omissions) that were quite undemocratic by today's standards. None provided for full religious freedom. Each one set rigid qualifications for voting and officeholding, and those rules favored property owners.

☑ **EXPLAIN** How did the Revolutionary period influence the first State constitutions?

State Constitutions Today

The present-day State constitutions are the direct descendants of those earlier documents. Only 17 of the current State constitutions were written after 1900, and nearly all have been amended dozens of times.

The people of each State can create whatever kind of "Republican Form of Government" they choose,

"Look — if I'd had any idea what a constitution was, I never would have signed the darn thing, okay?"

>> **Analyze Political Cartoons** What is the cartoonist saying about the emphasis many constitutions place on popular sovereignty and limited government?

as long as they adhere to the broad limitations set out in the Federal Constitution. As a result, unique provisions can be found in each of the 50 present-day State constitutions. Still, all of them are quite similar in general outline.

Basic Principles Every State's constitution is built on the principles of popular sovereignty and limited government. Each of them recognizes that government exists only with the consent of the people, and that it must operate within certain closely defined boundaries.

In every State, the powers of government are divided among executive, legislative, and judicial branches (separation of powers). Each branch has powers with which it can restrain the actions of the other two (checks and balances). Each also provides, either expressly or by implication, for the State courts' power of judicial review.

Civil Rights Each document features a bill of rights, a listing of the freedoms and rights that the government must protect. These guarantees often mirror those set out in the first ten amendments to the national Constitution. Several of them include a number of other guarantees as well—for example, the right to self-government, to be safe from imprisonment for debt, and to organize labor unions and bargain collectively.

Governmental Structure Every State constitution deals with the structure of government at both the State and the local levels, including all three branches of State government and the organization of counties and local governments. A few follow the national pattern, providing only a broad outline. Most, however, cover the subject in considerable detail.

Governmental Powers and Processes Each document lists the powers vested in the executive branch (the governor and other executive officers), the legislature, the courts, and the units of local government. The powers to tax, spend, borrow, and provide for education are very prominent. So, too, are such processes as elections, judicial procedures, legislation, and intergovernmental (State-local) relations.

Constitutional Change Constitutions are the product of human effort. None are perfect. Thus, each State constitution sets out the means by which it may be revised or amended.

State constitutions have been amended many more times than has the United States Constitution. Every State except Delaware allows the legislature to approve amendments and refer them to the voters for final approval or rejection. Some States also allow the constitution to be amended directly by the people, through the initiative. You will learn about the initiative process in the next lesson.

Elements of State Constitutions

PRINCIPLES	CIVIL RIGHTS	STRUCTURE	POWERS	CHANGE	OTHER
• Popular sovereignty • Limited government	• Similar to U.S. Bill of Rights • May also restrict State government or enhance individual liberty	Outline of State and local government • Separation of powers • Checks and balances	• Lists powers held by State officials to govern and provide services • Empowers State to tax, spend, and borrow	• Processes for amendment	• Preambles without legal force • "Dead letter" material—provisions that no longer apply

>> State constitutions establish in detail the organization and powers of the State government. **Analyze Charts** How are State constitutions similar to the U.S. Constitution?

Miscellaneous Provisions Every State constitution contains miscellaneous provisions. Most begin with a preamble, which has no legal force but does set out the purposes of those who drafted and adopted the document. Most also contain a schedule, a series of provisions for putting a new document into effect and for avoiding conflicts with its predecessor. And most include a number of "dead letter" provisions, items that have no current force or effect but nonetheless remain a part of the constitution.

☑ **COMPARE AND CONTRAST** How are the State constitutions of today different from the U.S. Constitution?

Constitutional Change

"To amend" means "to change, modify, or improve." Governing documents can be amended over time to reflect shifting customs, shared values, collective priorities, and new legal interpretations, among other things. Constitutions may also change because a federal court strikes down a phrase or section that it determines to be unconstitutional, or the State supreme court finds a provision to be fundamentally inconsistent with the State's governing principles.

State constitutions are much less flexible, and much more detailed, than the national document. As a result, constitutional change at the State level has come about mostly through formal amendment rather than by other means.

Two kinds of formal changes have been used: amendments, which usually deal with one or a few provisions in a constitution; and revisions, the term usually used to refer to changes of a broader scope. Revisions might include, for example, an entirely new document. Most of the formal changes made in State constitutions are made by amendment.

Procedures for Change The process of formal change involves two basic steps: proposal and then ratification. Proposals for change can be made by a constitutional convention or by the legislature. In some States, they can also be made by the voters themselves. Ratification is by popular vote in every State except Delaware.

The constitutional convention is the usual device by which new constitutions have been written and older ones revised. In every State, the legislature has the power to call a convention, and that call is generally subject to voter approval. In some States, the question of calling a convention must be submitted to the voters at regular intervals. Conventions can also propose amendments. However, because they are both

>> The State of Florida has more methods by which to amend its constitution than any other State. One method involves the passage of a joint resolution by the Florida legislature.

costly and time-consuming, conventions are most often used for the broader purpose of revision.

Most amendments are proposed by the legislature. The process is comparatively simple in some States, while it is quite difficult in others. In Massachusetts, for example, an amendment must be approved by the legislature at two successive annual sessions before it goes to the voters for approval or rejection. In California, a proposal must be approved by the legislature at a single session before being sent on to the voters. Not surprisingly, more amendments are proposed (and adopted) in those States with simpler processes, such as California, than in States such as Massachusetts.

As mentioned earlier, in some States, the voters themselves can propose constitutional amendments through the **initiative,** a process by which a certain number of qualified voters sign petitions in favor of a proposal. The proposal then goes either to the State legislature or directly to the ballot, for approval or rejection by the people.

Ratification of Amendments In every State except Delaware, an amendment must be approved by a vote of the people in order to become part of the constitution. The ratification process, like the proposal process, varies among the States. Typically, the approval of a majority of those voting on an amendment adds it to the State constitution.

☑ **COMPARE AND CONTRAST** Explain how the process of amending a State constitution differs from amending the U.S. Constitution.

The Need for Reform

Almost without exception, State constitutions are in urgent need of reform. The typical document is cluttered with unnecessary details, burdensome restrictions, and obsolete sections. Many have also accumulated a great deal of repetitious, and even contradictory material.

Even the newest and most recently rewritten constitutions tend to carry over a great deal of material from earlier documents and suffer from these same faults. The need for reform can be demonstrated in several ways. Looking at the documents from two standpoints, their lengths and their ages, can produce some useful insights.

The Problem of Length Length was not a problem for the first State constitutions. They were quite short, ranging from New Jersey's 1776 document (2,500 words) to the 1780 Massachusetts constitution (12,000 words). Those early constitutions were meant simply to be statements of basic principle and organization. Purposely, they left to the legislature—and to time and practice—the task of filling in the details as they became necessary.

Through the years, however, State constitutions have grown and grown. Most today are between 15,000 and 50,000 words, and Alabama's constitution runs to more than 376,000 words.

A leading cause of this expansion is popular distrust of government, a historical and continuing fact of American political life. That distrust has often led to the insertion of detailed provisions aimed at preventing the misuse of government power.

Many restrictions on that power, which could be set out in ordinary law, have been purposely written into the State constitution, where they cannot be easily ignored or readily, and quietly, changed. Special interest groups learned long ago that public policies of particular benefit to them are much more secure in the State constitution than in a mere statute.

There has been a marked failure in every State to distinguish **fundamental law,** that which is basic and of lasting importance and should be in the constitution, from **statutory law,** that which should be enacted as ordinary law by the legislature. The line separating fundamental and statutory law may

HOW TO PROPOSE CHANGES TO A STATE CONSTITUTION

PROPOSAL BY A CONVENTION

- Constitutional conventions are used most often to **revise existing constitutions and to write new ones.**

- Every State legislature can call a constitutional convention. That call is generally **subject to voter approval.**

PROPOSAL BY A LEGISLATURE

- Most **constitutional amendments** are proposed by the legislature.

- The process varies among the States. Where the process is simpler, **more amendments are proposed and adopted.**

PROPOSAL BY INITIATIVE

Voters can propose amendments in some States:

- A specified number of voters must **sign a petition.**

- The proposal goes on **the ballot**.

- The people **approve or reject** the amendment.

>> Amendments to State constitutions are proposed in different ways, but nearly all are ratified by popular vote. **Analyze Charts** Which method of proposing changes do most States use today?

be blurry in some cases. But who can seriously argue that fundamental law includes the regulation of the length of wrestling matches or the problem of off-street parking, both of which can be found in current State constitutions?

Two other factors have contributed to the growth of State constitutions. First, the functions performed by the States, and by most of their local governments, have multiplied over recent decades, prompting many new constitutional provisions. Second, the "people" have not been stingy in the use of the initiative in those States where it is available.

The Problem of Age Most State constitutions are severely outdated. They were written for another time and are in urgent need of revision.

The Oregon constitution provides a typical example of the situation. It was written by delegates to a territorial convention in 1857 and became effective when Oregon entered the Union in 1859. It has been amended hundreds of times and, like most of the other State charters, the Oregon document is overloaded with statutory material. One of several Article XIs devotes nearly 2,000 words to a closely detailed treatment of veterans' farm and home loans. The document also contains a number of obsolete provisions, including one that bars any person who has ever engaged in a duel from holding any public office in the State.

Some States' charters have proved to be more stable than others. The oldest of all the constitutions are those in Massachusetts (1780), New Hampshire (1784), and Vermont (1793). Several States still have the constitutions with which they entered the Union and, all told, more than half have documents that are now more than 100 years old.

☑ **SUMMARIZE** Describe the reasons why most State constitutions are in need of reform.

☑ ASSESSMENT

1. **Identify Central Ideas** List the basic principles on which all State constitutions are based.

2. **Draw Conclusions** How might the two basic methods for changing State constitutions contribute to the need for reform?

3. **Compare and Contrast** Explain the differences between *fundamental law* and *statutory law*. Describe the role these two categories of law play in constitutional change and reform.

4. **Identify Central Issues** Describe the governmental structure that is established in each State constitution.

5. **Summarize** List and explain the ways changes to State constitutions may be proposed.

The Maryland State House in Annapolis, the only State capitol that has also served as the nation's Capitol, is the oldest such building still in use.

 BOUNCE to Activate Flipped Video

Objectives

Describe State legislatures.

Explain the election, terms, and compensation of legislators.

Examine the powers and organization of State legislatures.

Describe how voters may write and pass laws through direct legislation.

Key Terms

police power
constituent power
referendum

State Legislatures

In every State, the legislature is the lawmaking branch of State government. Its basic function goes to the very heart of democratic government: It is charged with translating the will of the people into the public policy of the State.

The Legislature

Every State constitution establishes a formal lawmaking body that is, in effect, the powerhouse of that State's government. If you are like many high school students, you may wonder how the work of those lawmakers affects you. To answer that question, consider just a few of the issues the State legislatures have handled over the years.

Can you drive yourself to the store? It depends. Your State legislature has created a set of laws determining when teen drivers can get their licenses. Do you have an after-school or weekend job? Some State legislatures have set a minimum hourly wage that employers must pay you. As a high school senior, you may need to meet requirements mandated by the legislature to graduate. As you can see, the work of the State legislature has a direct bearing on your life.

State Legislature Structure States call their lawmaking bodies the "legislature," the "General Assembly," the "Legislative Assembly," or the "General Court." Stemming from colonial days, all but one of the 50 State legislatures are bicameral, meaning they have two chambers. The upper house is known everywhere as "the Senate." The lower house is most commonly titled "the House of Representatives," but may also be "the Assembly," "the General Assembly," or "the House of Delegates." Nebraska, the only State with a one-house legislature, calls it "the Legislature."

Those who defend bicameralism usually claim that one house can and does act as a check on the other, and so prevents the passage of unwise legislation. Whether that widely held view is justified or not, it has proved a major barrier to the spread of one-chamber lawmaking bodies.

State Legislature Size There is no ideal size for a legislative body, but two basic considerations are important. First, a legislature should not be so large as to hamper the orderly conduct of the people's business. Second, it should not be so small that the many views and interests within the State cannot be adequately represented.

The upper house ranges in size from 20 to some 70 members. The lower house usually ranges between 100 and 150 members. However, there are only 40 seats in Alaska's lower chamber, and New Hampshire's has a whopping 400!

☑ **EXPLAIN** How can the size of a State's legislature ensure fair representation of all citizens?

State Legislators

Nearly all of the nation's thousands of State legislators are Republicans or Democrats. Only a very small percentage belong to a minor party or are independents.

To really understand your own State's legislature and its members, you have to know a good deal that you will not find in a textbook. As one widely respected authority on State government and politics tells us,

> [Y]ou need to know about all sorts of things . . . which party is in control and by how much . . . who the governor is, and how he gets along with the legislators . . . what sorts of people those legislators are: not just what they say but how long they have been there, where they come from, what they did before they ran for office and how they got elected. . . .
>
> —Alan Ehrenhalt, "Clueless in Boise," *Governing* magazine

State Legislator Qualifications Every State's constitution sets out formal requirements of age, citizenship, and/or residency for legislators. In terms of age requirements, almost everywhere, a representative

must be at least 18 or 21 years old and, in about half the States, senators must be 25 or older; in the other half, they must be 18 or 21. The realities of the politics of the State add informal qualifications far more difficult to meet, however. They have to do with a candidate's vote-getting abilities, and are based on such things as occupation, name recognition, party, race, religion, national origin, and the like.

Election of Legislators Everywhere, legislators are chosen by popular vote and, almost everywhere, candidates for the legislature are nominated at party primaries. Nominees are picked by conventions in only a few States. In Nebraska, candidates are nominated at nonpartisan primaries, and they are not identified by party in the general election.

In most States, the lawmakers are elected in November of even-numbered years. In a few States, however, they are chosen in the odd-numbered years, in the hope of separating State and local issues from national politics.

Legislative Districts Every State's constitution requires that legislators be chosen from districts within the State, and nearly all are now elected from single-member districts. Those districts are drawn by the legislature itself in most States, and they are redrawn (reapportioned) every ten years, in line with the federal census.

Most State legislatures were long dominated by the rural, less-populated areas of the State. In *Baker* v. *Carr,* 1962, however, the United States Supreme Court held that the unfair, unequal distribution of State

>> This cartoon criticizes the way State legislators have redrawn district lines. **Analyze Political Cartoons** What does "think outside the box" mean to the State legislators featured in this cartoon?

legislative seats violates the Equal Protection Clause of the 14th Amendment. That historic decision was soon followed by *Reynolds* v. *Sims* in 1964. There, the Court held that the Equal Protection Clause requires every State to draw its legislative districts on the basis of population equality. Since that time, some State legislatures have managed to adhere to these court rulings while at the same time drawing district lines to the unfair advantage of one party or group (gerrymandering).

Legislator Terms Legislators are elected to two-year terms in most States and four-year terms in a few. Several States limit the number of terms any person can serve. In most, the limit is placed on service in each chamber, separately. In a few, the restriction is applied to total legislative service in either house.

The rate of turnover in legislative seats is fairly high, although it tends to vary from State to State and time to time. In a given year, on average, about 20 percent of all lawmakers around the country are serving their first term in office. The major reasons for high turnover appear to be low pay, political instability, and term limits. Lawmakers tend to remain in office longer in those States that pay higher salaries and where one party regularly wins elections.

Legislator Compensation Far too often, capable men and women refuse to run for seats in the legislature because of the financial sacrifices that service usually entails. Legislative pay varies considerably and so the situation is more trying in some States than others. A few States pay legislators about $75,000 or more per year, but the majority pay under $40,000—and some quite a bit less than that.

Clearly, decent salaries in line with the serious responsibilities of the job will not automatically bring the most able people into State legislatures. Better pay would no doubt make public service much more appealing to qualified people, however.

Legislative Sessions Little more than a generation ago, only a handful of State legislatures met in regular sessions each year, and then usually for only a few months or so. Most met only every other year. It has long since become apparent, however, that the legislature's workload cannot be properly handled on so limited a basis.

Today, nearly all State legislatures meet for at least a short time every year; most of those sessions run for three to five months or more. Several legislatures are now in session nearly year-round.

In every State, the governor, and in three fourths of them the legislature itself, can call the body into special session. Those meetings, most common in States where legislators meet infrequently, allow the consideration of urgent matters between their regularly scheduled sessions.

☑ **PREDICT CONSEQUENCES** What would be the likely result if legislatures were not reapportioned using accurate census data?

Supreme Court Decisions

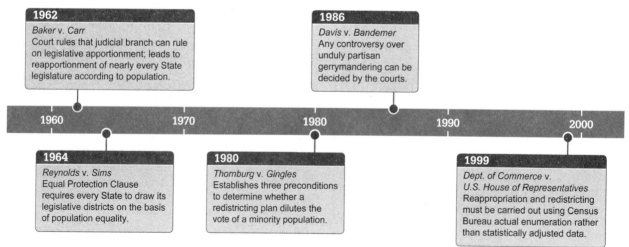

1962
Baker v. *Carr*
Court rules that judicial branch can rule on legislative apportionment; leads to reapportionment of nearly every State legislature according to population.

1986
Davis v. *Bandemer*
Any controversy over unduly partisan gerrymandering can be decided by the courts.

1964
Reynolds v. *Sims*
Equal Protection Clause requires every State to draw its legislative districts on the basis of population equality.

1980
Thornburg v. *Gingles*
Establishes three preconditions to determine whether a redistricting plan dilutes the vote of a minority population.

1999
Dept. of Commerce v. *U.S. House of Representatives*
Reappropriation and redistricting must be carried out using Census Bureau actual enumeration rather than statistically adjusted data.

1960   1970   1980   1990   2000

SOURCE: Cornell Law School Legal Information Institute; Senate.gov

>> Supreme Court decisions have affected the way congressional districts are drawn, at both the national and the State levels. **Analyze Information** What trend can you see in the decisions shown?

Powers of the Legislature

In each State, the legislature has all of those powers that (1) the State constitution does not grant exclusively to the executive or judicial branches or to local governments, and (2) neither the State constitution nor the United States Constitution denies to it. Most of the powers held by a State are vested in its legislature.

Legislative Powers The fact that the legislature can enact any law that does not conflict with any provision in federal law or in the State constitution means that there can be no all-inclusive list of the legislature's powers. Its more important powers are usually set out in the State constitution, however. Those most often mentioned include the powers to tax, spend, borrow, establish courts and fix their jurisdiction, define crimes and provide for their punishment, regulate commercial activities, and maintain public schools.

Every State's legislature possesses the **police power**—the State's hugely important power to protect and promote the public health, public safety, public morals, and the general welfare. Recall, most of what government does in this country today is done by the States (and their local governments), and most of what they do is done through the exercise of the police power. This broad power is the basis for thousands of State laws, including those that require vaccinations and set State speed limits, for example.

Nonlegislative Powers All 50 State legislatures possess certain nonlegislative powers, in addition to those they exercise when they make a law.

In the separation of powers and checks and balances scheme, the legislature exercises some *executive* powers—for example, it has the power to approve or reject the governor's appointment of a number of officials. In some States, the legislature itself appoints various executive officers.

The legislature also has certain *judicial* powers, capped by the power of impeachment. In every State except Oregon, the legislature can remove any State officer in the executive or judicial branch through that process. Each chamber also has the power to discipline and even expel one of its own members.

Recall that the legislature plays a significant role in both constitution-making and the constitutional amendment process. When, for example, it proposes an amendment to the State's constitution, it is not making law. It is, instead, exercising a nonlegislative power: the **constituent power**.

☑ **EXPLAIN** What is the purpose of the State legislature's police power?

>> In 1938, Crystal Bird Fauset of Pennsylvania (right) became the first Black woman elected to a State legislature.

>> The first Black woman to serve as speaker of a State house of representatives was Karen Bass (center) of California. She was elected to the speakership in 2008. **Analyze Information** How long did it take from the election of the first Black woman State representative before a Black woman was elected speaker?

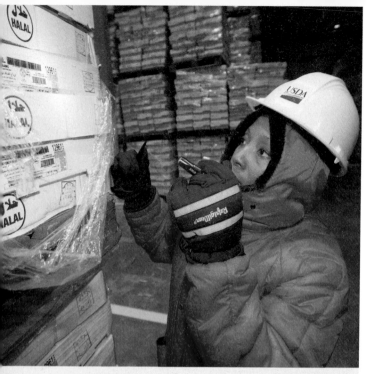

>> Each State legislature possesses the police power to protect the public's safety, health, and general welfare. One aspect of this power is authorizing State inspectors to check food deliveries for safety, as this woman is doing.

Organization of the Legislature

Both the organization and procedures of State legislatures are similar to those found in Congress. Much of their work centers around presiding officers and a committee system.

Presiding Officers Those who preside over the sessions of the States' lawmaking chambers are almost always powerful political figures, not only in the legislature itself but elsewhere in State politics.

The lower house in each of the 49 bicameral bodies elects its own presiding officer, known everywhere as the speaker. The senate chooses its own presiding officer in about half of the States; in the others, including Nebraska, the lieutenant governor has the authority to serve as president of the senate in various capacities. Where the lieutenant governor does preside, the senate selects a president *pro tempore* to serve in the lieutenant governor's absence.

Except for the lieutenant governors, each of these presiding officers is chosen by a vote on the floor of his or her chamber. In fact, the majority party's caucus usually picks those who fill the leadership posts, just before the legislature begins a new term.

The chief duties of these presiding officers revolve around the conduct of the legislature's floor business. They refer bills to committee, recognize members who seek the floor, and interpret and apply the rules of their chamber to its proceedings.

Unlike the Speaker of the House in Congress, the speaker in nearly every State appoints the chair and other members of each house committee. The senate's president or president *pro tem* has that same power in about half the States. The presiding officers regularly use this power much as they do their other powers: to reward their friends, punish their enemies, and otherwise work their influence on the legislature and its product.

The Lawmaking Process The major steps in the State lawmaking process are much the same as those in Congress. A bill must be introduced by a member of either house, be referred to and approved by a committee, receive a majority vote from all members of the chamber, and be sent to the other chamber where it moves through the same steps. The final bill is sent to the governor, who may then approve or veto the proposal.

Several hundred or, in many larger States, several thousand measures are introduced at each session of the legislature. That flood of bills makes the committee system as practical and necessary at the

>> Dennis Daugaard (left) of South Dakota was one of the few lieutenant governors in the past three decades to successfully make a bid for the governorship.

State level as it is in Congress. Much of the work of the legislature is done in committee, where members sift through that pile of proposed legislation, deciding which bills will go on to floor consideration and which will fall by the wayside.

The standing committees of each house are regularly organized on a subject-matter basis—as committees on finance, education, highways, and so on. A bill referred to one of these committees may be amended or even largely rewritten there. Or, as frequently happens, it may be ignored altogether.

"Pigeonholing" occurs in the States just as it does in Congress. In fact, in most States one of the standing committees in each house is usually the "graveyard committee." Bills are sent there to be buried. A striking illustration of a graveyard committee existed for several years in landlocked Oklahoma: the Committee on Deep Sea Navigation.

Sources of Bills Only a member may introduce a bill in either house in any State's legislature. So, in the strictest sense, legislators themselves are the source of all measures the legislature considers. In broader terms, however, the lawmakers are the authors of only a handful of bills.

A large number of measures come from public sources, from officers and agencies in the State executive branch, and from local governments. Every State governor has a legislative program, too, and it is often extensive and bold.

Many bills come from the private sector. Indeed, interest groups are the largest source of proposed legislation. Remember, those groups and the lobbyists who represent them exist for one overriding purpose: to influence public policy to the benefit of their own interests. In fact, because of the influence they wield in the form of information and campaign donations, interest groups are sometimes referred to as the "third house" of the legislature.

Of course, some measures do originate with private individuals—business owners, farmers, union members, and other citizens—who, for one reason or another, think, "There ought to be a law. . . ."

☑ **GENERATE EXPLANATIONS** Why are interest groups a major source of proposed laws?

Direct Legislation

During the Progressive Movement at the turn of the 20th century, when there was a move to strip party bosses of their powers, many States instituted processes to allow citizens to directly shape State policies. Today, in several States, voters themselves

>> Protestors crowd the Wisconsin State capitol as members of the legislature meet to discuss a proposed bill to curb the bargaining rights of public unions..

can take a direct part in the lawmaking process. The main vehicles for that participation are the initiative and the referendum.

Initiative Process Through the initiative process, voters can propose amendments to the State's constitution. In some States, they can also use that process to propose ordinary statutes. The initiative takes two quite different forms: the more common direct initiative and the little-used indirect initiative.

In both forms, a certain number of qualified voters (which varies from State to State) must sign petitions to initiate a law. Where the direct initiative is in place, a measure with sufficient signatures goes directly to the ballot, usually in the next general election. If voters approve the measure, it becomes law. If not, it dies. Where the indirect form is found, a proposed measure goes first to the legislature. If the lawmakers approve the measure, it becomes law. If the legislature fails to pass it, the measure then goes to the voters.

Referendum Process A **referendum** is a process in which the legislature refers a measure to the voters for final approval or rejection. The process takes three different forms: mandatory, optional, and popular.

A *mandatory referendum* requires the legislature to send a measure to the voters. Recall, in every State except Delaware, a proposed constitutional amendment *must* be submitted to the electorate. In

Examples of Constitutional Initiatives from Selected States

STATE	YEAR	INITIATIVE DESCRIPTION	STATUS
California	1911	To grant women the right to vote in California	Passed
Arizona	1932	To repeal the State's ban on the sale of alcoholic beverages	Passed
Ohio	1955	To provide that the compensation of any elected officer may be increased or diminished during his existing term	Defeated
Oregon	1972	To amend the Oregon Constitution to change the gubernatorial line of succession	Passed
Arkansas	1984	To instate a .00125% tax increase from which funds are to be used by the State Game & Fish Commission	Defeated
Florida	1994	To limit the use of nets for catching fish and marine animals by prohibiting the use of entangling nets in all Florida waters	Passed
Colorado	2002	To reduce the amount of campaign contributions that persons may make to candidate or political committees and political parties	Passed
Illinois	2020	To grant the State authority to impose higher income tax rates on higher income levels	Defeated

>> Each of the initiatives listed in this table made it to the ballot and was put before the State's voters. **Analyze Charts** What do the defeated constitutional initiatives have in common?

several States some other measures, such as those providing for the borrowing of funds, must also go to the voters.

An *optional referendum* involves a measure that the legislature has referred to the voters voluntarily. Such measures are rare. They usually involve "hot potato" issues: issues that lawmakers would prefer not to take direct responsibility for deciding themselves.

Under the *popular referendum*, a group of citizens may demand by petition that a measure passed by the legislature be referred to the voters for final action. Most attempts to use this form of the referendum fail because the opponents of a particular measure cannot gather the required number of signatures to force a popular vote on the target of their ire.

☑ **IDENTIFY STEPS IN A PROCESS** What are the steps that must occur in order for a proposal to become law using the direct initiative?

☑ ASSESSMENT

1. **Identify Central Issues** How is the initiative process a reflection of the principle of representative government?

2. **Compare and Contrast** How are the powers of a State legislature different from the powers of Congress?

3. **Generate Explanations** Explain the effect of the Supreme Court's decision in *Baker* v. *Carr*.

4. **Analyze Information** What would be the advantage for voters of having a nonpartisan primary compared to a partisan primary?

5. **Interpret** In what way do the nonlegislative powers of the State legislature serve as checks on the other branches of State government?

By working together, governors can deal with issues their States share. Here, Gary Locke, then governor of Washington, announces a strategy that he and the governors of California and Oregon created to help reduce global warming pollution along the West Coast.

The Governor and State Administration

The governor is the principal executive officer in each of the 50 States. He or she is always a central figure in State politics and is often a well-known national personality as well. Governors today occupy an office that is the direct descendant of the earliest public office in American politics, the colonial governorship, first established in Virginia in 1607.

The Governorship

In colonial America, the actions of the royal governors inspired much of the resentment that fueled the Revolution. That attitude was carried over into the first State constitutions. As a result, most of the powers of government were given to the legislatures; the new State governors, for the most part, had little real authority. In every State except Massachusetts and New York, the governor was chosen by the legislature, and in most of them only for a one-year term. And only in three States did the governor have a veto power.

That original separation of powers soon proved unsatisfactory. Many of the State legislatures abused their powers. Several fell prey to special interests, and the governors were unable to respond. So, as new constitutions were written, and the older ones revised, the powers of the legislatures were curbed and the powers of the governors generally increased.

Beginning with Illinois in 1917, most States have redesigned and strengthened the executive branch to make the governor the State's chief executive in more than name. Some States have gone further than others in this direction, but, overall, governors are much more powerful figures today than in decades past.

 BOUNCE to Activate Flipped Video

Objectives

Describe the main features of the office of governor.

Summarize a governor's roles, powers, duties, and the limitations of the office.

List and describe the other executive offices at the State level.

Key Terms

recall
item veto
clemency
pardon
commutation
reprieve
parole

Qualifications Anyone who wants to become the governor of a State must be able to satisfy a set of formal qualifications. Typically, he or she must be an American citizen, of at least a certain age (usually 25 or 30), have lived in the State for a given period of time (most often for between five and seven years), and be a qualified voter.

Clearly, these formal qualifications for office are not very difficult to meet. It is the informal qualifications that have real meaning. To become a governor, a person must have those characteristics that will first attract a party's nomination, and then attract the voters in the general election. Those characteristics vary from State to State, and even from election to election within a State. Race, gender, religion, name recognition, personality, party identification, experience, ideology, the ability to use the media effectively, and other factors are all part of the mix.

Most governors are attorneys. Nearly all of them were State legislators or held another elective office in the State, such as lieutenant governor, attorney general, or mayor of a large city.

The first gubernatorial elections occurred in 1775 and thousands of people have now served as governors of the various States. Very few of those governors have been women or people of color.

>> Madeleine Kunin was only the eighth woman to serve as governor when she took office in 1985, and she is the only woman governor to serve three terms (1985–1991). She was also the nation's first Jewish woman governor.

The first women governors served in 1924 when Nellie Taylor Ross of Wyoming and Miriam "Ma" Ferguson of Texas succeeded their husbands. A woman was not elected in her own right until 1974, when Ella Grasso won her race for the governorship of Connecticut. For the next 30 years or more, women governors remained few and far between. While a growing number of women have won the office in recent years, women are still dramatically underrepresented in this role.

Black Americans and other people of color are even more underrepresented in the governorship. In 1872, Louisiana's lieutenant governor, P.B.S. Pinchback, became the first to hold the office when the sitting governor faced impeachment. But it was not until 1989 that the first Black American was elected in his own right—Douglas Wilder of Virginia. Throughout the nation's history, in fact, only a handful of governorships have been filled by people of color.

Selection The governor is chosen by popular vote in every State. In nearly all of the States, only a plurality is needed for election. If no candidate wins a clear majority in Georgia or Louisiana, the two top vote-getters meet in a runoff election. If no one wins a majority in Mississippi, the lower house of the legislature picks the new governor. In Vermont, both houses make the choice.

The major parties' gubernatorial candidates are usually picked in primaries. In a few States, however, conventions choose the nominees. Just over half the States now provide for the joint election of the governor and lieutenant governor. In those States, each party's candidates for those offices run as a team, and voters cast one vote to fill both posts.

Term The one-year gubernatorial term has long since disappeared. Governors are now chosen to four-year terms nearly everywhere. About three-quarters of the States limit the number of terms a chief executive may serve, most often to two terms. Those governors who seek reelection usually do so successfully. In many States with term limits, the former governor can simply sit out one term, and then run again.

Succession Governors are mortal. Occasionally, one of them dies in office. Many of them are also politically ambitious. Every so often, one resigns in midterm to become a United States senator or accept an appointment to the President's Cabinet, for example.

When a vacancy does occur, it sets off a game of political musical chairs. The political plans and timetables of ambition of a number of public personalities are affected by the event. No matter what causes a vacancy, every State's constitution provides for a successor. In nearly every State, the lieutenant governor is first in line. In a handful of States, the office passes to the president of the senate or the secretary of state.

Removal The governor may be removed from office by impeachment in every State except Oregon. Only a few governors have been impeached and removed from office in the history of the nation.

Quite a few States allow for the governor to be recalled by the voters. The **recall** is a petition procedure by which voters may remove an elected official from office before the completion of his or her regular term.

The process generally works this way: If a certain number of qualified voters—usually a certain percentage of the number who voted in the last election held for the office—sign recall petitions, a special election must be held in which the voters decide whether to remove or retain the officeholder.

Only two governors have ever been recalled: Republican Lynn J. Frazier of North Dakota in 1921 and Democrat Gray Davis of California in 2003.

Compensation In many respects, a governor's job is not unlike that of the chief executive officer of one of the nation's larger corporations. Both administer hugely complex organizations, manage the work of thousands of employees, and oversee the spending of enormous amounts of money. Governors are not paid nearly so well as the CEOs of large companies, however. The latter make tens of millions of dollars per year in salary and benefits. A governor, on the other hand, might make less than $100,000 per year. Even if he or she is governor of a more populous State, that figure might only rise to about $200,000. Most States also provide their chief executive with an official residence, often called a governor's mansion, and money for travel and other expenses.

To the governor's salary and other material compensations must be added the intangibles of honor and prestige that go with the office. It is this factor, and a sense of public duty, that often persuades many of our better citizens to seek the post. In fact, more than a third of the nation's Presidents were governors before reaching the White House.

☑ **DRAW INFERENCES** Why do you think governors are paid significantly less than the CEOs of large corporations?

200 Years of Governors Who Became President

NAME	STATE GOVERNED	YEAR ELECTED PRESIDENT
Thomas Jefferson	Virginia	1800
James Monroe	Virginia	1816
Martin Van Buren	New York	1836
John Tyler	Virginia	1840**
James K. Polk	Tennessee	1844
Andrew Johnson	Tennessee	1865**
Rutherford B. Hayes	Ohio	1876*
Grover Cleveland	New York	1892*
William McKinley	Ohio	1896*
Theodore Roosevelt	New York	1900*
Woodrow Wilson	New Jersey	1912*
Calvin Coolidge	Massachusetts	1920*
Franklin D. Roosevelt	New York	1932*
Jimmy Carter	Georgia	1976
Ronald Reagan	California	1980
Bill Clinton	Arkansas	1992*
George W. Bush	Texas	2000*

*Sitting governor prior to assuming the vice presidency or presidency
**Elected vice president and assumed presidency upon the death of the President

>> Of the 17 individuals who served as governor before becoming President, nine were sitting governors prior to taking the highest office. **Analyze Charts** What is common among most of these governors?

>> In 2003, a record 135 candidates sought to replace California governor Gray Davis in a recall referendum. **Analyze Political Cartoons** Why did the cartoonist include a clown among the candidates?

>> As President of the United States, Bill Clinton (right) was not required to share executive authority the way Douglas Wilder (left) was as governor of Virginia (1990–1994).

>> Susana Martinez, New Mexico's first female governor and the first Hispanic female elected governor in the United States (2011–2019), promotes fire prevention in Albuquerque, New Mexico.

The Governor's Powers

Much like the President, a governor plays a number of different roles. He or she is, simultaneously, an executive, an administrator, a legislator, a party leader, an opinion leader, and a ceremonial figure. What the office amounts to depends, in no small part, on how well the governor plays these roles. And that depends on his or her personality, political muscle, and overall abilities.

Many of a governor's formal powers are hedged with constitutional and other legal restrictions. Nonetheless, the powers a governor does have, together with the prestige of the office, make it quite possible for a capable, dynamic person to be a "strong" governor, one who can accomplish much for the State and for the public good.

Executive The presidency and the governorships are similar in several ways, but the comparison can be pushed too far. Remember, the Constitution of the United States makes the President the executive in the National Government. State constitutions, on the other hand, regularly describe the governor as the chief executive in the State's government. The distinction here, between the executive and the chief executive, is a critical one. The executive authority is fragmented in most States, but not at the national level.

In nearly every State, the executive authority is shared by a number of "executive officers"—a secretary of state, an attorney general, a treasurer, and so on. Most of these executive officers are, like the governor, popularly elected, and for that reason, very largely beyond the governor's direct control. In some instances, the governor might be of one party, but other executive officers are of another.

In short, most State constitutions so divide the executive authority that the governor can best be described as a "first among equals." Yet, whatever the realities of the distribution of power, the people look to the governor for leadership in State affairs. It is also the governor whom they hold responsible for the conduct of those affairs and for the overall condition of the State.

The governor's basic legal responsibility is regularly found in a constitutional provision that directs the chief executive to "take care that the laws be faithfully executed." Though the executive power may be divided, the governor is given a number of specific powers with which to accomplish that task.

Appointment and Removal The governor can best execute the law with subordinates of his or her own choosing. Hence, the powers of appointment and removal are among the most important in the governor's arsenal.

A leading test of any administrator is his or her ability to select loyal and able assistants. Two major factors work against the governor's effectiveness here, however. First is the existence of those other elected executives; the people choose them and the governor cannot remove them. Second, the State's constitution and statutes place restrictions on the governor's power to hire and fire. Most State constitutions require that the majority of the governor's major appointees be confirmed by the State senate.

Moreover, the legislature often sets qualifications that must be met by the governor's appointees. In a vigorous two-party State, for example, the law often requires that only a certain number of the members of each board or commission can be from the same political party. Thus, a governor must appoint some members of the opposing party.

Administering the Executive Branch The governor is the State's chief administrator. Alone and unaided, he or she could not possibly "take care that the laws be faithfully executed." The day-to-day work of enforcing the State's laws, of performing its many functions, and of delivering its many services is done by the thousands of men and women in all of the agencies that make up the executive branch. The governor must supervise that work.

Here again, the constitution and statutes of the State often limit a governor's authority. Many agencies are subject to his or her direct control, but many are not. That situation puts a premium on the governor's powers of persuasion and on his or her ability to operate through such informal channels as party leadership and appeals to the public.

The Budget Always remember that a government's budget is much more than a mere bookkeeping exercise. It is a political document, a statement of public policy. Its numbers, its dollar figures, reflect the struggle over "who gets what" and who doesn't.

In most States, the governor prepares the budget that goes to the legislature. The lawmakers may then make changes in the governor's financial plan, but the governor's recommendations always carry a great deal of weight.

The governor's budget-making power can be a highly effective tool with which to control State administration. Although unable to appoint or remove the head of a particular agency, for example, the governor can use the budget-making power to affect that agency's programs and have a real impact on those who work in that agency.

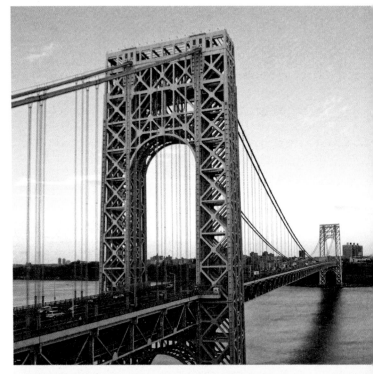

>> The governors of New York and New Jersey each appoint six board members to the Port Authority of New York and New Jersey, an interstate compact for managing harbor facilities.

Military Powers Every State's constitution makes the governor the commander in chief of the State militia—in effect, of the State's units of the National Guard. The National Guard is the organized part of the State militia. In a national emergency, the National Guard may be "called up," ordered into federal service by the President.

All of the States' National Guard units were federalized in 1940 and served as part of the nation's armed forces in World War II. Many units also saw combat duty in Korea, Vietnam, the Persian Gulf War, Bosnia, Kosovo, Afghanistan, and Iraq. Indeed, the Defense Department has relied very heavily on the Guard in the prosecution of recent wars.

When the State's Guard units are not in federal service (which is most of the time), they are commanded by the governor. On occasion, governors find it necessary to call out the Guard to deal with such emergencies as quelling prison riots, fighting dangerous forest fires, aiding in relief and evacuation after a flood, preventing looting after some other natural disaster, screening airline passengers during a pandemic, and so on.

Legislative The State's principal executive officer exercises three significant legislative powers. Those powers, together with the governor's personality, popularity, and political muscle, can make the chief executive, in fact, the State's chief legislator.

The Message Power Essentially, the message power is the power to recommend legislation. Remember, much of what lawmakers do is prompted by what the governor has urged them to do. The most effective governors push their wish lists by combining their use of the formal message power with such informal tactics as close contacts with key legislators and appeals to the public.

The media are key to getting a governor's message out to voters. The extent and nature of that coverage contribute significantly to how a governor is perceived. It is no wonder then that most governors try to foster a good working relationship with the press.

Special Sessions The governor in every State has the power to call the legislature into special session. As you know, that power is meant to permit the State to meet extraordinary situations. It can also be an important part of the governor's legislative arsenal. On many occasions, governors have persuaded reluctant lawmakers to pass a particular bill by threatening to call them back in a special session if they adjourn their regular meeting without having approved that measure.

The Veto Power Every governor can veto measures enacted by the legislature. The veto power— including the use of threats to invoke the power— can be very useful to the governor as he or she tries to influence the legislature's work.

In most States, the governor has only a few days in which to sign or veto a bill. If no action is taken within the prescribed period, the measure becomes law without his or her signature.

Only a few States give the governor a pocket veto. So, in most States, those bills a governor neither signs nor vetoes become law. On the other hand, most States give the governor the **item veto**—the power to eliminate one or more items from a bill without rejecting the entire measure. It is used most often on spending measures.

As in the Federal Government, the legislature may attempt to override a veto. In most States, a veto requires a two-thirds majority in both houses.

Judicial In every State, the chief executive has some authority of a judicial nature. First, the governor may appoint judges to fill vacancies in State courts. Second, the governor has several powers of **clemency,** which are powers of mercy that may be shown to persons convicted of crime.

With the power of **pardon**, the governor may relieve someone of the legal consequences of a crime. In most States, a pardon may be full or conditional, and usually it can be granted only after conviction. The power of **commutation** may be used to commute a sentence imposed by a court. Thus, a death sentence might be commuted to life in prison, or a sentence might be commuted to "time served," which leads to the release of a prisoner from custody.

The power to **reprieve** can be used to postpone the execution of a sentence. Reprieves are normally granted for very brief periods—for example, to allow

Examples of Special Sessions Called by Governors

GOVERNOR	STATE	SAMPLE AGENDA ITEM
Phil Bryant (R)	Mississippi	Approval of disaster aid funding after a series of tornadoes
Jay Nixon (D)	Missouri	Approval of $150 million annual economic incentive package to attract Boeing jobs to the State
John Kitzhaber (D)	Oregon	Tax protections for Nike, the sportswear company based in Oregon
Scott Walker (R)	Wisconsin	Discussion of jobs creation under his "Back to Work Wisconsin" plan
Steve Beshear (D)	Kentucky	Push to end legislative stalemate and approve State budget

>> The governor's power to call special sessions can be a persuasive tool in getting policies enacted into law. **Analyze Charts** What are the most common issues addressed in special sessions?

FEDERAL GOVERNMENT

The **voters** choose presidential electors who then elect the President and Vice President.

President

Vice President

The **President** chooses the members of the Cabinet, usually from among his or her supporters.

Cabinet Members

STATE GOVERNMENT

The **voters** elect the governor. In most States, they also elect several other executive officers.

Governor

Lieutenant Governor

Attorney General

Secretary of State

State Treasurer

>> Unlike the Federal Government, key executive officers at the State level are chosen by the voters. **Analyze Charts** How does the election of executive officers at the State level affect a governor's power?

time for an appeal or because of the late discovery of new evidence in a case. The power of **parole** permits the release of a prisoner before the completion of the original sentence.

The governor may have some or all of these powers of executive clemency. They are often shared, however. For example, the governor may share the power to pardon with an appointed board of pardons.

Governors have not often abused their clemency powers, but in her first term (1925–1927), Governor Miriam "Ma" Ferguson of Texas pardoned 3,737 convicted felons, an average of more than five per day. The pardons came so thick and fast that several Texas newspapers ran daily "pardon columns" rather than separate news stories.

Miscellaneous Duties In addition to the exercise of executive, legislative, and judicial powers, every chief executive must perform several other, often time-consuming duties. These duties are only hinted at by a listing of the powers of the office.

Among many other things, the governor receives official visitors and welcomes other distinguished personalities to the State, dedicates parks and public and private buildings, opens the State fair, and addresses countless organizations and public gatherings. Beyond those chores, he or she is often

called upon to settle labor disputes, travel elsewhere in the country and sometimes abroad to promote the State and its trade interests, and endorse any number of worthy causes. To any interested observer, the list seems nearly endless.

☑ **COMPARE** Describe how the division of power between the executive and legislative branches of State government reflects the concept of checks and balances.

Other Executive Officers

In nearly every State, the governor must share control of the administration with a number of other executive officers. Most of those other officials are, like the governor, chosen by voters. The following four positions are found in most, but not all, State governments today.

The *lieutenant governor* must be ready to succeed to the governorship should a vacancy occur, and, in half the States, presides over the senate. The office can be a stepping-stone to the governorship by succession or by future elections. It remains, in many places, not much more than a part-time job.

The *secretary of state* serves as the State's chief clerk and records-keeper. He or she has charge of a great variety of public documents, records the official acts of the governor and the legislature, and usually administers election laws.

The *treasurer* is the custodian of State funds, often the State's chief tax collector, and regularly the State's paymaster. Other names for this position include chief financial officer, director of finance, the commissioner of finance, and the comptroller of public accounts. The treasurer's major job is to make payments out of the State treasury to pay salaries and bills associated with State government.

The *attorney general* is the State's chief lawyer. He or she acts as the legal advisor to State officers and agencies as they perform their official functions, represents the State in court, and oversees the work of local prosecutors as they try cases on behalf of the State.

Much of the power of the office centers on the attorney general's formal written interpretations of constitutional and statutory law. These official interpretations, called opinions, are issued to answer questions raised by officials regarding the lawfulness of their actions or proposed actions.

☑ **CONTRAST** Describe how State executive officers vary from federal executive officers.

☑ ASSESSMENT

1. **Apply Concepts** Why are the governor's budgetary powers so important?

2. **Compare and Contrast** Explain how the U.S. Constitution gives more power to the President than State constitutions give to governors.

3. **Compare and Contrast** How is the lieutenant governor similar to and different from the Vice President of the United States?

4. **Summarize** How can a governor's legislative powers impact legislation?

5. **Summarize** Describe the governor's power to appoint and remove subordinates and explain why it is important. Describe any checks and balances that are in place.

13.4

Trial by jury is a fundamental part of the rule of law in all States.

State Courts

The Federal Government and the States have two separate court systems. Both systems are charged with making sure that the government follows the rule of law, which is one of the core principles of American democracy. This rule says that government is never above the law. To do this, the courts use their power of judicial review to restrain the other two branches of State and local government. The courts must also decide any disputes that arise related to State law.

State Courts and the Law

The law is the code of conduct by which society is governed. It is made up of several different forms, including constitutional law, statutory law, administrative law, common law, and equity.

The highest form of law in this country is **constitutional law.** It is based on the United States Constitution, the State constitutions, and judicial interpretations of those documents. **Statutory law** consists of the statutes (laws) enacted by legislative bodies, including the United States Congress, the State legislature, the people, and local governments. **Administrative law** is composed of the rules, orders, and regulations issued by federal, State, or local executive officers, acting under proper constitutional and/or statutory authority.

Common Law The common law makes up a large part of the law of each State except Louisiana. Because of an early French influence, Louisiana's legal system is largely based on French legal concepts, derived from Roman law. Nevertheless, the common law has worked its way into some aspects of Louisiana law, as well.

Common law is unwritten, judge-made law that has developed over centuries from those generally accepted ideas of right and wrong that have gained judicial recognition. It covers nearly all aspects of human conduct. State courts apply common law except when it is in conflict with written law.

BOUNCE to Activate Flipped Video

Objectives

Identify and define the kinds of law applied in State courts.

Compare and contrast criminal law and civil law.

Describe the types and purposes of juries and juror selection.

Explain how State courts are organized and describe the work that each type of court does.

Examine and evaluate the different methods by which judges are selected among the States.

Key Terms

constitutional law
statutory law
administrative law
common law
precedent
equity
criminal law
felony
misdemeanor
civil law
tort
contract
jury
information
petit jury
bench trial

justice of the peace
warrant
preliminary hearing
magistrate
appellate jurisdiction
Missouri Plan

The common law originated in England. It grew out of the decisions made by the king's judges on the basis of local customs. It developed as judges, coming upon situations similar to those found in earlier cases, applied and reapplied the rulings from those earlier cases. Thus, little by little, the law of those cases became *common* throughout England and, in time, throughout the English-speaking world.

American courts generally follow that same rule. A decision, once made, becomes a **precedent**, a guide to be followed in all later, similar cases, unless compelling reasons call for either an exception or its abandonment and the setting of a new precedent.

Most legal disputes in American courts are fought largely over the application of precedents. The opposing lawyers try to persuade the court that the precedents support their side of the case or that the precedent should not, for some reason, be followed.

Equity The **equity** branch of the law supplements common law. It developed in England to provide equity—"fairness, justice, and right"—when remedies under the common law fell short of that goal.

The common law is mostly remedial, while equity is preventative. Thus, the common law applies to or provides a remedy for matters *after* they have happened; equity, on the other hand, seeks to stop wrongs *before* they occur.

Suppose your neighbors plan to add a room to their house. You think that a part of the planned addition will be on your land and will destroy your rose garden. You can prevent the construction by getting an injunction, a court order prohibiting a specified action by the party named in the order.

A court is likely to grant the injunction for two reasons: (1) the immediacy of the threat to your property, and (2) the fact that the law can offer no fully satisfactory remedy once your garden has been destroyed. No money award can give back the pride or the pleasure your roses now give you.

At first, different courts administered equity and common law. In time, most States provided for the administration of both forms by the same courts, and the procedural differences between the two are disappearing.

Criminal Law The law as it is applied by courts in this country can also be described as either criminal or civil law. **Criminal law** is that branch of the law that regulates human conduct. It identifies and defines those actions that are crimes and provides for their punishment. A crime is a public wrong considered so damaging to society at large that it has been prohibited by law. The State, as the prosecution, is always a party to a criminal case and is represented by a district attorney.

The Use of Precedent

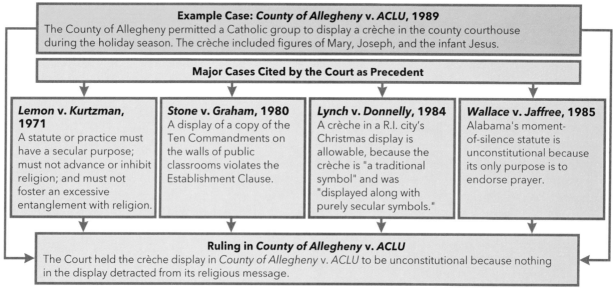

Example Case: *County of Allegheny v. ACLU*, 1989
The County of Allegheny permitted a Catholic group to display a crèche in the county courthouse during the holiday season. The crèche included figures of Mary, Joseph, and the infant Jesus.

Major Cases Cited by the Court as Precedent

***Lemon* v. *Kurtzman*, 1971**
A statute or practice must have a secular purpose; must not advance or inhibit religion; and must not foster an excessive entanglement with religion.

***Stone* v. *Graham*, 1980**
A display of a copy of the Ten Commandments on the walls of public classrooms violates the Establishment Clause.

***Lynch* v. *Donnelly*, 1984**
A crèche in a R.I. city's Christmas display is allowable, because the crèche is "a traditional symbol" and was "displayed along with purely secular symbols."

***Wallace* v. *Jaffree*, 1985**
Alabama's moment-of-silence statute is unconstitutional because its only purpose is to endorse prayer.

Ruling in *County of Allegheny* v. *ACLU*
The Court held the crèche display in *County of Allegheny* v. *ACLU* to be unconstitutional because nothing in the display detracted from its religious message.

SOURCE: *County of Allegheny et al. v. ACLU, 1989, Opinion of the Court*

>> Previous court rulings serve as the starting point during a judge's deliberations on a case. **Analyze Charts** How did previous cases inform the *Allegheny* v. *ACLU* ruling?

CRIMINAL & CIVIL LAW

A THIEF TAKES CHRIS'S WALLET.	THE POLICE ARREST THE THIEF BASED ON VIDEO EVIDENCE.	THE THIEF IS HELD IN JAIL OR IS FREE ON BAIL.	THE STATE PROSECUTES THE ACCUSED THIEF, WHO IS DEFENDED BY A LAWYER.	IF GUILTY, THE CRIMINAL IS FINED AND/OR SENTENCED TO PRISON.

CRIMINAL LAW

THE DISPUTE	THE LAW	BEFORE THE CASE	IN THE COURTS	PUNISHMENT AND RESOLUTION

CIVIL LAW

MATT DAMAGES CHRIS'S CAR.	CHRIS FILES A LAWSUIT AGAINST MATT FOR THE COST OF REPAIRS.	MATT REMAINS FREE.	BOTH MEN HIRE LAWYERS TO COLLECT EVIDENCE AND TESTIMONY ON THEIR BEHALF.	PUNISHMENTS ARE LIMITED TO MONEY, AND ANY AWARD WILL GO TO CHRIS.

>> A criminal defendant can be arrested and detained in jail even before trial, but a civil defendant is never imprisoned. **Analyze Charts** Why don't those convicted of civil crimes serve prison time?

Crimes are of two kinds. A **felony** is the greater offense, punishable by a heavy fine, imprisonment, or even death—for example, murder, robbery, assault, or kidnapping. A **misdemeanor** is a lesser wrong and may be punished by a lighter fine and/or a shorter jail term—for example, a traffic violation, underage drinking, or disorderly conduct.

Civil Law The area of law related to human conduct that is not criminal in nature is known as **civil law**. Civil law relates to those disputes between private persons and between private persons and government that are not covered by criminal law. Civil law involves a wide range of issues, such as divorce and custody disputes, torts, and contracts. People who lose civil cases pay a fine, but do not go to jail.

Both tort law and contract law are major and often-used branches of civil law. A **tort** is a wrongful act that involves injury to one's person, property, or reputation in a situation not covered by the terms of a contract—for example, an automobile accident, product liability, or libel. A **contract** is a legally binding agreement in which one party agrees to do something with or for another party—for example, an agreement covering the sale of property or the terms of employment.

☑ **COMPARE AND CONTRAST** What is the difference between common law and equity?

Understanding the Jury System

A **jury** is a body of persons selected according to law to hear evidence and decide questions of fact in a court case. There are two basic types of juries in the American legal system: (1) the grand jury and (2) the petit jury.

The major function of the grand jury is to determine whether the evidence against a person charged with a crime is sufficient to justify a trial. The grand jury is used only in criminal proceedings. The petit jury is the trial jury, and it is used in both civil and criminal matters.

The Grand Jury The grand jury has from 16 to 23 persons, depending on the State. Where larger juries are used, generally at least 12 jurors must agree that an accused person is probably guilty before a formal accusation is made. Similarly, with smaller juries, a supermajority of two thirds or three fourths is needed to indict, which means to bring the formal charge.

When a grand jury is impaneled, the judge instructs the jurors to find a true bill of indictment against any and all persons whom the prosecuting attorney brings to their attention and whom they think are probably guilty. The judge also instructs them to bring a presentment (an accusation) against any persons whom they, of their own knowledge, believe have violated the State's criminal laws.

The grand jury meets in secret. The prosecuting attorney presents witnesses and evidence against persons suspected of crime. The jurors may question those witnesses and may also summon others to testify against a suspect. After receiving the evidence and hearing witnesses, the grand jury deliberates alone and in secret. They then move to the courtroom where their report, including any indictments they may have returned, is read in their presence.

The grand jury is expensive and time-consuming. Therefore, most of the States today depend more heavily on a much simpler process of accusation: the information.

Filing Formal Charges An **information** is a formal charge filed by the prosecutor, without the action of a grand jury. It is used for most minor offenses and, in many States, for some serious cases. It is far less costly and time-consuming than a grand jury. Also,

since grand juries most often follow the prosecutor's recommendations, many argue that a grand jury is really unnecessary. Others feel that the grand jury prevents prosecutors from abusing their powers.

The Trial Jury The **petit jury**, or trial jury, hears the evidence in a case and decides the disputed facts. In very few instances, it may also have the power to interpret and apply the law. That, however, is usually the function of the judge.

The number of trial jurors may vary. As it first developed in England, the jury consisted of "12 men good and true." Although 12 is still the usual total, a lesser number, most often six, now fills jury boxes in several States.

In more than a third of the States, jury verdicts need not be unanimous in civil and minor criminal cases. Rather, some extraordinary majority is needed. If a jury cannot agree on a verdict (a so-called hung jury), either another trial with a new jury takes place or the matter is dropped.

Misdemeanor cases and civil proceedings in which only minor sums are involved are often heard without a jury, in a **bench trial**, by the judge alone. In several States, even the most serious crimes may be heard without a jury if the accused, fully informed of his or her rights, waives the right to trial by jury.

Selecting Jurors Jurors are picked in more or less the same way in most States. Periodically, a county official or special jury commissioners prepare a list of persons eligible for jury service, with names drawn from poll books, tax rolls, driver's license records, or other sources. The sheriff serves each person with a court order to appear. After eliminating those who, for good reason, cannot serve, the judge prepares a list of those who can. Persons under 18 and over 70 years of age, those who cannot read and write, the ill, and criminals are excluded in most States. Those in occupations vital to the public interest or for whom jury service would mean real hardship are often excused, too.

As with the grand jury, the States are moving away from the use of the trial jury. Leading reasons are the greater time and cost of jury trials. The competence of the average jury and the impulses that may lead it to a verdict are often questioned, as well. Much criticism of the jury system is directed not so much at the system itself as at its operation.

Several things should be said in favor of the jury system, however. It has a long and honorable place in the development of Anglo-American law. Its high purpose is to promote a fair trial, by providing an impartial body to hear the charges brought against the

>> All-male juries, such as this 1925 Tennessee jury, were the norm for many years, even after Utah in 1898 became the first State to allow women to serve.

accused. A jury tends to bring the common sense of the community to bear on the law and its application. Finally, the jury system gives citizens a chance to take part in the administration of justice, and it fosters a greater confidence in the judicial system.

☑ **APPLY CONCEPTS** What happens if a grand jury does not return an indictment?

How the State Courts Are Organized

They deal with everything from traffic tickets to murder, from disputes over nickels and dimes to settlements involving millions. They are the State and local courts and the judges who sit in them. Here, you will look at the way these courts are organized and how they conduct their business.

Each of the State constitutions creates a court system for that State. Some of these documents deal with the courts at great length, but most of them leave much of the detail of judicial organization and procedure to the legislature.

Local Trial Courts Justices of the peace—JPs—stand on the lowest rung of the State judicial ladder. They preside over what are commonly called justice courts.

JPs were once found nearly everywhere in the country. In their day, they seemed well-suited to their purpose. In justice courts, people could obtain a hearing for minor offenses quickly. JPs and their justice courts have been done away with in several States. However, they can still be found in many smaller towns and rural areas.

JPs are usually popularly elected. For the most part, they try misdemeanors—that is, cases involving such petty offenses as traffic violations, disturbing the peace, public drunkenness, and the like. JPs can almost never settle civil disputes involving more than a few hundred dollars. They do issue certain kinds of warrants, hold preliminary hearings, and often perform marriages.

A **warrant** is a court order authorizing, or making legal, some official action. Search warrants and arrest warrants are the most common of these documents. A **preliminary hearing** is generally the first step in a major criminal prosecution. There, the judge decides if the evidence is, in fact, enough to hold that person—bind that person over—for action by the grand jury or the prosecutor.

"He's big, all right, and he's definitely a wolf, but it'll be up to a jury to decide whether or not he's bad."

>> Suspects are innocent until proven guilty, which leaves jurors with a critical duty. **Analyze Political Cartoons** What does this cartoon suggest about the task of a jury? How can its effectiveness be evaluated?

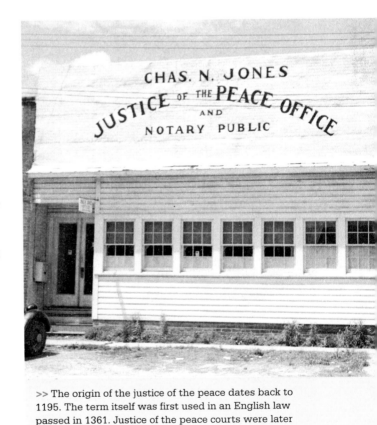

>> The origin of the justice of the peace dates back to 1195. The term itself was first used in an English law passed in 1361. Justice of the peace courts were later established across the U.S.

In some places, JPs are still paid out of the fines they take in. The more fines they impose, the higher their incomes. This "fee system" can lead to any number of abuses and raises serious questions about the fairness of the treatment a defendant can expect.

Magistrates are the city cousins of JPs. For the most part, magistrates handle those minor civil complaints and misdemeanor cases that arise in an urban setting. They preside over what often are called magistrates' courts or police courts. Magistrates, like JPs, are usually popularly elected for fairly short terms.

Municipal Courts Municipal courts were first established in Chicago in 1906. They are now found in most large cities and many smaller ones.

The jurisdiction of municipal courts is citywide. They can often hear civil cases involving several thousands of dollars as well as the usual run of misdemeanors. Many municipal courts are organized into divisions, which hear cases of a given kind—for example, civil, criminal, small claims, and probate.

Consider the small claims division, often called the small claims court. Many people cannot afford the costs of suing for the collection of a small debt. A newspaper carrier, for example, can hardly afford a lawyer to collect a month's subscription from a customer. The owner of a two-family house may have the same problem with a tenant's back rent, and many merchants are forced to forget an overdue bill or sell it to a collection agency.

Small claims courts are designed for just such situations. There, a person can bring a claim for little or no cost. The proceedings are usually informal, and the judge often handles the matter without attorneys for either side.

Juvenile Courts Individuals under 18 years of age are generally not subject to the jurisdiction of the courts in which adults are tried. Minors who are arrested for some offense, or who otherwise come to the attention of the police or other authorities, may appear in juvenile courts.

The juvenile justice system is designed to address the special needs and problems of young people. This system generally emphasizes rehabilitation more than punishment. However, under some circumstances, juvenile courts do refer certain offenders to a regular criminal court for trial.

In the 1980s and 1990s, most States responded to juvenile crime with tougher criminal laws. Often these statutes make it easier to try juveniles as adults when they are charged with serious crimes. In every State, juvenile court judges may assign certain cases involving juveniles to adult courts.

In the 2010s, new trends emerged in the approach to juvenile justice. These trends included moving more cases to the juvenile courts and out of the criminal justice system, shifting away from incarcerating youth and toward community-based solutions, providing youth with more effective public defenders, addressing racial disparities in the juvenile justice system, and responding to the mental health needs of young offenders.

At the same time, problems remain in the juvenile justice system. In some cases, for example, ordinary school disciplinary issues have become criminalized. This means that misbehaviors in school that could be resolved with counseling or school disciplinary actions are instead directed to the juvenile justice system, especially for students of color.

In the Courtroom

JUDGE	Hears the case, decides which laws apply, and sentences those convicted or awards damages
CLERK OF THE COURT	Helps the judge manage cases, keeps court records, deals with finances, and gives other administrative support
BAILIFF	Provides security in the courtroom and is chosen by the sheriff
COURT REPORTER	Records what is said during the trial, using a stenographic machine, shorthand, or a recording device; this is the "transcript" of the trial
COURT INTERPRETER	Translates the proceedings for non-English speakers or those who are deaf

>> Each government employee present during a trial has a specific role.
Analyze Charts Why is the job of a court reporter important?

General Trial Courts Most of the more important civil and criminal cases are heard in the States' general trial courts. Every State is divided into a number of judicial districts, or circuits, each generally covering one or more counties. For each district, there is a general trial court, which may be known as a district, circuit, chancery, county, or superior court, or as a court of common pleas.

These general trial courts are courts of "first instance." That is, they exercise original jurisdiction over most of the cases they hear. Most legal actions brought under State law begin in these courts. When cases do come to them on appeal from some lower court, a new trial (a trial *de novo*) is usually held.

The cases heard in trial courts are tried before a single judge. Most often a petit jury (the trial jury) hears and decides the facts at issue in a case, and the judge interprets and applies the law involved. Criminal cases are presented for trial either by a grand jury or, most often, on motion of the prosecuting attorney.

The trial court is seldom limited as to the kinds of cases it may hear. Although this court's decision on the facts in a case is usually final, disputes over questions of law may be carried to a higher court.

Courts of Appeal Most States now have one or more intermediate appellate courts. They are courts of appeal that stand between the trial courts and the State's supreme court. These appellate courts act as "gatekeepers" to ease the burden of the State's highest court.

The appellate courts have different names among the States, but they are most often called the court of appeals. Most of their work involves the review of cases decided in the trial courts. That is, these appeals courts exercise mostly **appellate jurisdiction**. Their original jurisdiction, where it exists, is limited to a few specific kinds of cases—election disputes, for example.

In exercising their appellate jurisdiction, these courts do not hold trials. Rather, they hear oral arguments from attorneys, study the briefs (written arguments) that attorneys submit, and review the record of the case in the lower court.

Ordinarily, an intermediate appellate court does not concern itself with the facts in a case. Rather, its decision turns on whether the law was correctly interpreted and applied in the lower court. Its decision occasionally may be reviewed by the State's high court, but the court of appeals' decision is final in most cases.

State Supreme Courts The State's supreme court is the highest court in its judicial system. Its major

>> The inscription on this statue of *Wisdom* at the New York supreme court building reads: "Every law not based on Wisdom is a menace to the state." To its left is a statue representing Force. It reads: "We must not use Force until just laws have been defied."

"My wife wouldn't like anything reversible. She's a judge."

>> **Analyze Political Cartoons** Which type of judge would be most likely to dislike anything "reversible"—an appellate judge or a trial court judge? Why?

function is to review the decisions of lower courts in those cases that are appealed to it.

The size of each State supreme court is fixed by that State's constitution, usually at between five and nine justices. A chief justice presides over the sessions of each State's top court.

The governor appoints the justices in many States. The voters elect them elsewhere, except in South Carolina and Virginia, where the legislature chooses.

The State supreme court is the court of last resort in the State's judicial system. It has the final say in all matters of State law. The United States Supreme Court *may* review some State supreme court decisions touching on federal law. But not very many State decisions actually go to the federal Supreme Court. Recall that an appeal from a State's highest court will be heard in the federal Supreme Court only if (1) a "federal question"—some matter of federal law—is involved in the case and (2) the Supreme Court agrees to hear that appeal. In short, most State supreme court decisions are final.

Unified Court Systems The typical State court system is organized geographically rather than by type of cases. Thus, the general trial courts are most often set up so that each hears those cases arising within its own district, circuit, or county, no matter what the subject matter may be.

In these map-based, or geographically based, court systems, a judge must hear cases in nearly all areas of the law. A backlog of cases can and often does build up in some courts, while judges sit with little to do in others. Moreover, uneven interpretations and application of the law sometimes occurs from one part of the State to another. To overcome these difficulties, a number of States have turned to a unified court system—one that is organized on a functional, or case-type, basis.

In a completely unified court system, there is technically only one court for the entire State. It is presided over (administered) by a chief judge or judicial council. The single court has a number of levels, such as supreme, intermediate, appellate, and general trial sections. Within each section, divisions are established to hear cases in certain specialized or heavy caseload areas of the law—criminal, juvenile, family, and other areas that need special attention.

In such an arrangement, a judge can be assigned to that section or division to which his or her talents and interest seem best suited. To relieve overcrowded dockets, judges may be moved from one section or division to another. In short, the unified court system is a modern response to the old common law adage: "Justice delayed is justice denied."

☑ **COMPARE AND CONTRAST** What are the pros and cons of map-based court systems versus unified court systems?

★ **VOICES** OF **GOVERNMENT** ★

New Hampshire Supreme Court Justice Joe Nadeau served nearly four decades as a judge in New Hampshire's State court system. Nadeau now dedicates his time to training new judges. During a conference in Jordan in 2006, Nadeau addressed what it means to be a judge.

❝ A black robe does not cloak a judge in wisdom, understanding or compassion. Those characteristics each person must bring to the bench and continuously work to strengthen. With the robe, however, comes the responsibility to make difficult choices without fear or favor, along with the responsibility to treat everyone fairly and impartially, and to seek justice and do justice.❞

— Retired New Hampshire Supreme Court Justice Joe Nadeau

>> Justice Nadeau believes that judges require certain personal attributes in addition to professional skills. **Analyze Information** What other characteristics do you think a judge needs?

" ...AND TEN MORE YEARS, BECAUSE I'M RUNNING FOR RE-ELECTION AND WE'RE ON TV!"

>> In many States, judges are elected by the people, either from the start or after serving one term. **Analyze Political Cartoons** What point is this cartoon making?

How Judges Are Selected

Clearly, the quality of any court system—indeed, the quality of justice itself—depends in large measure on the selection of competent, well-trained judges. Tens of thousands of judges and judicial officers (magistrates, JPs, associate judges, and so on) sit in the States' various trial and appellate courts. Nearly all of them came to office in one of three ways: (1) by popular election, (2) by appointment by the governor, or (3) by appointment by the legislature.

Selection by the legislature is used less often than other methods to choose judges, while popular election is by far the most widely used method. Midterm vacancies, caused by death or resignation, provide the only exception to that blanket rule; those vacancies are usually filled by gubernatorial appointment. Almost half of all judicial elections are nonpartisan contests today, meaning the candidate does not declare a political party affiliation.

In about half the States, governors now select most judges. In some cases, those selections must be approved by the legislature. In others, the governor must choose from a list compiled by a nominating commission, a method known as the Missouri Plan.

Election or Appointment? Most people believe that judges should be independent, that they should "stay out of politics." Whatever method of selection is used should be designed with that goal in mind.

Nearly all authorities agree that selection by the legislature is the most political of all the methods of choice. Few favor it. So, the question really becomes: Which is better, the popular election of judges or their appointment by the governor?

On the other side, those who favor popular election generally make the democratic argument. Because judges "say the law" (interpret and apply it), they should be chosen by and answer directly to the people. Some also argue that the separation of powers is undercut if the executive names the members of the judicial branch.

On the other side, those who favor appointment by the governor argue that the judicial function should be carried out only by those who are well qualified. The fact that a person has the support of a political party or is a good vote-getter does not mean that person has the capacity to be a good judge. Proponents of executive appointment insist that it is the best way to ensure that those persons who preside in courts will

>> In 2002, James Bopp (shown here) was one of the attorneys in the case *Republican Party of Minnesota* v. *White*, in which the Supreme Court ruled that judges running for election must be allowed to express their views on issues that might come before them if they are elected.

have the qualities most needed in that role: absolute honesty and integrity, fairness, and the necessary training and ability in the law.

Deciding between these two positions is difficult at best. The people have often made excellent choices, and governors have not always made wise and nonpolitical ones. Still, most authorities come down on the side of gubernatorial appointment—largely because those characteristics that make a good judge and those that make a good candidate are not too often found in the same person.

Popular election is both widely used and widely supported by citizens and party organizations. Supreme Court decisions related to campaign finance laws in the early 2000s, however, have led to ever larger amounts of spending on judicial campaigns. Concerns have been raised as to whether judges can remain impartial when their candidacies have been supported by various special interest groups.

The Missouri Plan—A Mixed Approach For most of the past century, the American Bar Association (ABA) has sponsored an approach that combines election and appointment. The method, which has been adopted by many States, is often called "the **Missouri Plan**." Some form of this system is used in about half the States.

In Missouri's version of this method, the governor appoints the seven justices of the State supreme court, the 32 judges of the court of appeals, and all judges who sit in the trial courts in the most heavily populated parts of the State. The governor must make each appointment from a panel, or list, of three candidates recommended by a judicial nominating commission. The commission is made up of a sitting judge, several members of the bar, and private citizens.

Each judge named by the governor serves until the first general election after he or she has been in office for at least a year. The judge's name then appears on the ballot without opposition. The voters decide, in a retain-reject election, whether or not that judge should be kept in office. Should the voters reject a sitting judge, the process begins again.

☑ **INTERPRET** What does it mean when people say that they believe judges should "stay out of politics"?

☑ ASSESSMENT

1. **Classify** Describe the different kinds of law applied in State courts.

2. **Compare and Contrast** What are the differences between civil law and criminal law?

3. **Draw Conclusions** What does the trend away from jury trials say about overall trends in the American justice system?

4. **Check Understanding** What is appellate jurisdiction and which State courts have this jurisdiction?

5. **Explain** How are judges selected?

Primary Sources

Commentaries on the Laws of England: William Blackstone

Sir William Blackstone's *Commentaries on the Laws of England* is based on the author's lectures at the University of Oxford. The four volumes, published from 1765 to 1769, offer an extensive examination of English law. Blackstone's masterpiece was popular in England and its fame spread across the Atlantic to the British colonies, where it had a strong influence on the development of the American legal system.

In the introduction of Section the Second (Volume Two), Blackstone describes the purpose of laws. In the introduction of Section the Third (Volume Three), he defines common law.

>> William Blackstone (1723–1780)

Section the Second. Of the Nature of Laws in general.

Municipal law, [according to Blackstone, the rule by which particular districts, communities, or nations are governed] . . . is . . . defined to be "a rule of civil conduct prescribed by the supreme power in a state, commanding what is right and prohibiting what is wrong." Let us endeavour to explain its several properties. . . .

. . . first, it is a *rule*; not a transient [short-lived] sudden order from a superior to or concerning a particular person; but something permanent, uniform, and universal. . . . It is also called a *rule*, to distinguish it from *advice* or *counsel*, which we are at liberty to follow or not, as we see proper; . . . . Counsel is only matter of persuasion, law is matter of injunction [legal requirement]; counsel acts only upon the willing, law upon the unwilling also. . . .

☑ **COMPARE AND CONTRAST** What does Blackstone write about the difference between law and advice?

Municipal law is also "a rule of *civil conduct.*" This distinguishes municipal law from the natural, ... the former of which is the rule of *moral* conduct, and the latter not only the rule of moral conduct, but also the rule of faith. These regard [man's . . .] duty to God, to himself, and to his neighbour, considered in the light of an individual. But municipal or civil law regards him also as a citizen, and bound to other duties towards his neighbour, . . .

It is likewise "a rule *prescribed.*" . . . It is requisite [required] that this resolution be notified to the people who are to obey it. . . . It may be notified by universal tradition and long practice, which supposes a previous publication, and is the case of the common law of England. It may be notified, *viva voce* [by word of mouth], by officers appointed for that purpose, as is done with regard to proclamations, and such acts of parliament as are appointed to be publicly read in . . . assemblies. It may lastly be notified by writing, printing, or the like. . . .

☑ **IDENTIFY CENTRAL IDEAS** How are people expected to know a law?

Section the Third.
Of the Laws of England.

The municipal law of England, or the rule of civil conduct prescribed to the inhabitants of this kingdom, may . . . be divided into two kinds; the *lex non scripta*, the unwritten, or common law; and the *lex scripta*, the written, or statute law.

The *lex non scripta*, or unwritten law, includes not only *general customs*, or the common law properly so called; but also the *particular customs* of certain parts of the kingdom; and likewise those *particular laws*, that are by custom observed only in certain courts and jurisdictions. . . .

. . . I therefore stile [style] these parts of our law *leges non scriptae*, because their original . . . authority are not set down in writing, as acts of parliament are, but they receive their binding power, and the force of laws, by long and immemorial usage, and by their universal reception throughout the kingdom. . . .

When a custom is actually proved to exist, the next enquiry is into the legality of it; for if it is not a good custom it ought to be no longer used. . . . To make a particular custom good, the following are necessary requisites.

1. That it have been used so long, that the memory of man runneth not to the contrary. So that if any one can shew [show] the beginning of it, it is no good custom. . . .

2. It must have been *continued*. Any interruption would cause a temporary ceasing: the revival gives it a new beginning, which will be within time of memory, and thereupon the custom will be void. . . .

3. It must have been *peaceable*, and acquiesced in; not subject to contention and dispute. . . .

4. Customs must be *reasonable*. . . .

5. Customs ought to be *certain*. . . .

6. Customs, though established by consent, must be . . . *compulsory*; and not left to the option of every man, whether he will use them or no. . . .

7. Lastly, customs must be *consistent* with each other: one custom cannot be set up in opposition to another. . . .

☑ **CITE EVIDENCE** Why does common law have authority even though it was not proclaimed by Parliament?

☑ ASSESSMENT

1. **Compare and Contrast** According to Blackstone, how are civil conduct and moral conduct the same? How do they differ?

2. **Draw Conclusions** Why is it necessary for people to be notified of a law?

3. **Summarize** What makes a custom valid as common law?

4. **Make Connections** According to Blackstone, what is the difference between statutory laws and common laws?

13.5

Services such as fire protection may be provided by a special unit of local government or by the city or county government.

Local Governments

The nation has its magnificent Capitol in Washington, D.C., and each State has its own impressive capitol. In most cities and towns, however, local government has no grand dome. Instead, government in these places is visible mainly through the day-to-day services that keep communities going.

Counties Across the United States

There are about 3,000 county governments in the United States. They come in many different shapes and sizes. Some have only a handful of employees and operate with only meager budgets. Others have tens of thousands of employees and budgets of a billion dollars or more. Many perform only a single public function, such as providing fire protection or clean, running water. Others, including nearly all cities and most urban counties, deliver a long list of essential services.

The Constitution of the United States says nothing about local governments. Instead, cities, towns, counties, and all other local governments have been created by the States. As unitary governments, the States have the reserved power to create these local governments and structure them however they choose—and also to abolish them, if they choose to do so. Local governments can only act because the State has given them the power to do so.

Counties: Some Key Facts A **county** is the major unit of local government in most States. Its main purpose is to deliver essential public services, and to do so according to the rules mandated by the State. The number of county governments in each State ranges from none in Connecticut and Rhode Island to about 250 in Texas.

[BOUNCE to Activate Flipped Video]

Objectives

Describe the typical county, its governmental structure and functions, and the need for reform in county government.

Identify the responsibilities of tribal governments.

Examine the governments of towns, townships, and special districts.

Explain the process of incorporation and compare and contrast the major forms of city government.

Evaluate the need for city planning and list some major municipal functions.

Outline the challenges that face suburbs and metropolitan areas.

Key Terms

county
township
special district
municipality
incorporation
charter
mayor-council
  government
strong-mayor
  government
weak-mayor
  government
commission
  government
council-manager
  government
zoning
metropolitan area

In Louisiana, units of government that are known elsewhere as counties are called *parishes*. In Alaska, they are known as *boroughs*. In addition to the entire States of Connecticut and Rhode Island, several other places across the country have no organized county government.

In terms of area, San Bernardino County in California is the largest in the continental United States; it spreads across about 20,000 square miles. Kalawao County in Hawaii is the smallest; it covers just 12 square miles. In fact, counties within each State often vary widely in area.

Counties also differ greatly in terms of population. About 10 million people live in Los Angeles County in Southern California, but census takers could find fewer than 100 residents of Kalawao County, Hawaii. Most counties—in fact nearly three quarters of them—have populations of fewer than 50,000.

How County Governments Are Structured

The structures of county governments differ, too, and often considerably. Even so, a county typically has four major elements: a governing body, a number of boards or commissions, appointed bureaucrats, and a variety of elected officials.

The county's governing body is frequently called the county board. It is also known as the board of commissioners, board of supervisors, legislature, police jury, assembly, and board of chosen freeholders, among other names.

The members of this governing body are almost always popularly elected. Terms of office vary, but four-year terms are the most common. Board members are usually chosen from districts within the county rather than on an at-large basis.

Generally, county boards can be grouped into two types: boards of commissioners and boards of supervisors. The board of commissioners is the smaller, more common type. It is found everywhere in the South and West, and it is also well known elsewhere. A board of commissioners most often has three or five members, but some have seven or more.

The board of supervisors is typically a much larger body and can run to 80 or more members, but usually average much fewer. The supervisors are elected from single-member districts in the county. Each supervisor may be an officer of his or her township, as well as a member of the countywide governing body.

County Government Powers

The State constitution and acts of the State legislature spell out the powers held by county governing bodies. Those powers are usually both executive and legislative, despite the American tradition of separation of powers.

TYPICAL COUNTY GOVERNMENT STRUCTURE

VOTERS

ELECT

COUNTY BOARD
Governing body

APPOINTS

OTHER COUNTY OFFICIALS
Sheriff, District attorney, Clerk, School superintendent, Assessor, Treasurer, Auditor, Coroner

PLANNING COMMISSION

BUDGET COMMISSION

COUNTY AGENT

BOARDS AND OFFICIALS
Boards and officials, Board of Health, Welfare Commission, Library Board, and others

>> A county government has a governing body, commissions, and various officials.
Analyze Charts Why do you think voters don't elect all the members of the various boards and commissions that make up county government?

Duties of County Officials

County Board	• Levies taxes and sets spending • Administers roads, county buildings and programs • Appoints boards and officials	**Clerk**	• Registers and records documents for property, birth, and death • Runs county elections
Assessor	• Sets the value of taxable property • Collects property taxes	**Sheriff**	• Runs county jail • Provides rural police protection • Carries out court orders • May collect taxes
Auditor	• Keeps financial records	**Treasurer**	• Keeps county funds
School Superintendent	• Administers public schools	**District Attorney**	• Conducts criminal investigations • Prosecutes criminal cases
Coroner	• Investigates violent deaths • Certifies causes of death		

>> Each county official has specialized duties for which he or she is responsible.
Analyze Charts Which officials are most likely to be responsible for county financial matters?

County governments' most important legislative powers deal with finance. Everywhere, county boards levy taxes, appropriate funds, and can incur limited debts. They also have a number of other legislative powers—for example, in the fields of public health and corrections.

Most boards also carry out a number of administrative functions. They supervise the county road program and manage county property, including the courthouse, jails, hospitals, and parks. They are often responsible for the administration of welfare (cash assistance) programs and the conduct of elections. They are also responsible for the hiring of most county employees—from a few dozen or so in many rural places to several thousand in most metropolitan areas. And, importantly, they determine the salaries of nearly all of the people who work for the county.

Other Elected Officials In addition to its governing body, the typical county's government regularly includes a number of other elected officials, as well as several boards and commissions whose members are also sometimes elected. Those agencies frequently include a fair board, a planning commission, a board of health, a library board, and a board of road viewers. Altogether, the nation's thousands of counties employ millions of men and women who do the day-to-day work of those local governments.

County Functions Because counties are created by the State, they are responsible for the administration of State laws. They also administer any county laws

that the State's constitution and legislature have allowed them to make.

Counties across the nation commonly undertake a dizzying number of functions. They keep the peace and maintain jails and other correctional facilities; assess property for tax purposes; collect taxes and spend county funds; build and repair roads, bridges, drains, and other public works; and maintain schools. Counties record deeds, mortgages, marriage licenses, and other documents; issue licenses for such things as hunting, fishing, and marriage; administer elections; care for the poor; and work to safeguard the health of the people who live in the county.

Many counties have taken on other functions as they have become more urban. Several of these more heavily populated counties now offer many of the public services and facilities that are usually found in cities. They provide water and sewer service; have professionally trained police, fire, and medical units; and operate airports and mass transit systems. Some also enforce zoning and other land-use regulations. Many have built and now operate auditoriums, stadiums, golf courses, swimming pools, and other recreational facilities.

In some of the New England States, towns carry out most of the functions undertaken by counties elsewhere in the country and they serve almost solely as judicial districts. In many Mid-Atlantic and Midwestern States, counties are divided into subdivisions called **townships**. In those States, counties and townships share the functions of rural local government. In the South and the West, counties are the major governing unit in rural areas.

>> Counties often provide policing services through a sheriff's office, as well as security for local courthouses and county-owned facilities and parks. Some also provide road patrol.

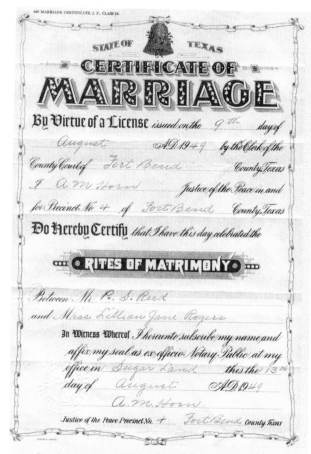

>> Issuing marriage licenses and certificates is one of the duties a county government performs.

Challenges Faced by County Governments

County organization is often chaotic. In the typical county, no single official can really be called the *chief* administrator. Rather, authority is divided among a number of elected boards and officials, each largely independent of the others. Too often, it is impossible to identify who is responsible for inefficiency or inaction (or worse) in the conduct of county affairs.

The large number of popularly elected officials adds to the chaos. Faced with the typical county's long ballot, voters are often hard-pressed to make informed choices. Also, because many of those elected officials have no basic public policy-making responsibilities, many people are convinced that popular election really is not the best way to fill those offices.

The size and number of counties in most States are another source of weakness. Nearly every county now in existence was laid out in the days of the horse and the stagecoach. Then, it made good sense to draw county lines so that no one lived more than a dozen miles or so from the county seat. Today, however, most counties are geographically ill-suited to the realities of the modern world.

One way in which many States have attempted to reform county government is through county home rule. Those States allow some or all of their counties, subject to approval by the local voters, to decide the details of their own governmental structure.

Another approach to reform seeks to deal with the fragmented authority of counties. It does so by creating the position of county manager, modeled along the lines of the council-manager form of city government. Still another approach is county-city consolidation—where a major city and the county around it join into a single unit of government. San Francisco, California, and Nashville, Tennessee, are leading examples.

☑ **EXPLAIN** Why is there a need to reform the organization of many county governments?

Tribal Governments

Tribal governments exist as a distinct form of government. Unlike State, county, or city governments, however, the governments of Native American nations have a unique "government-to-government" relationship with the United States. These Native American tribes are considered sovereign nations, with the right to govern their own people on their own territories unless otherwise specified by treaty or acts of Congress.

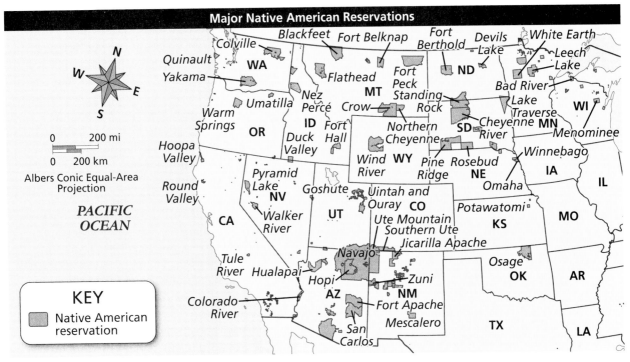

>> About 570 federally recognized tribal governments exist in this country, including more than 200 in Alaska (not shown). Various laws and treaties of the United States obligate the Federal Government to protect these tribal lands. **Analyze Maps** Why do you think most reservations are in the Midwest and West?

Sovereignty of Tribal Governments Official recognition by the Federal Government is crucial for tribal governments because it establishes their sovereignty and exempts them from State or local control. For example, some tribes have established gambling casinos on their reservations, even though the territory lies within States that do not allow that type of gambling. Because the officially recognized tribes are sovereign, they are generally not subject to State laws and regulations. Also, recognized tribes are eligible to receive federal funds that can be used to provide local services.

Traditional tribal government is organized hierarchically. At the top of the hierarchy, a tribal council serves as a link to federal and State government, provides services to the community, and makes all economic and legal decisions in the best interests of the tribe. Other than the council, tribal governments vary widely. Some, such as the Cherokee and Navajo tribes, have a written code or constitution that provides for a State-like government with executive, legislative, and judicial branches. Others are small and loosely organized.

Structure and Services of Tribal Governments
Like State and county governments, tribal governments use federal funds and tax revenue to provide services. These services depend on the size, history, and needs of the tribe. Many tribes have executive officers or departments that oversee policy and manage funds to provide healthcare, education, and welfare to tribe members. They also oversee cultural events and sites, as well as distribute information about the tribe. Even smaller tribal governments provide some services, especially important housing and health and education information and support.

☑ **EXPLAIN** Explain the main responsibilities of tribal governments.

Towns, Townships, and Special Districts

Towns and townships exist in nearly half the States. They are little known in the South or West but are commonly found from New England to the Midwest.

The term *town* is used in some States as the legal designation for smaller urban places. It is also sometimes used as another word for *township*. *Township* is also a federal public lands survey term, used to identify geographic units (often called congressional townships), each having exactly 36 square miles (36 sections).

The New England Town In New England, the town is a major unit of local government. Except for a few major cities, each of the six States in the region is divided into towns. Each town generally includes all of the rural and urban areas within its boundaries. The town delivers most of the services that are the responsibility of cities and counties elsewhere around the country.

The roots of the New England town reach back to the early colonial period. The Pilgrims landed at Plymouth Rock in 1620 as an organized congregation. At that time, the desire to be near the church, the real or perceived threat from Native Americans, the severe climate, and the fact that the land was not suited to large farms or plantations led the settlers to form tight-knit communities. Their settlements were soon known as towns, as in England. Other Puritan congregations followed the Pilgrims' pattern.

Town Meetings At least in form, much of town government today is little changed from colonial times. The main feature is a town meeting, long praised as the ideal vehicle of direct democracy. The town meeting is an assembly open to all the town's eligible voters. It meets yearly, and sometimes more often, to levy taxes, make spending and other policy decisions, and elect officers for the next year.

Between town meetings, the board of selectmen/selectwomen chosen at the annual meeting manages the town's business. Typically, the board is a three-member body and has responsibilities for such things as roads, schools, care of the poor, and sanitation. Other officers regularly selected at the annual meeting include the town clerk, a tax assessor, a tax collector, a constable, road commissioners, and school board members.

The ideal of direct democracy is still alive in many smaller New England towns. It has given way, however, to the pressures of time, population, and the complexities of public problems in many of the larger towns. There, representative government has largely replaced it. Town officers are often elected before the yearly gathering. Many of the decisions once made by the assembled voters are now made by the selectmen and selectwomen. In recent years, several towns have gone to a town manager system for the day-to-day administration of local affairs.

Townships Townships are units of local government found principally in the Northeast and the Midwest. Nowhere do townships blanket an entire State, however.

In New York, New Jersey, and Pennsylvania, townships were formed as areas were settled and the people needed the services of local government. Consequently, the township maps of those States often resemble crazy quilts. From Ohio westward, they mostly follow the regular lines drawn in federal public land surveys. Many are perfect squares.

Many of these States provide for annual township meetings, like those held in New England towns. Otherwise, the governing body is usually a board of trustees or board of supervisors. Its members are elected for fixed terms or serve because they hold other elected township offices. Township offices often include a supervisor, a clerk, a treasurer, an assessor, a constable, a justice of the peace, and a body of road commissioners.

Township functions regularly involve such matters as roads, cemeteries, drainage, and minor law enforcement. In some States, however, the township is also the basic unit of public school administration.

Many people believe that townships have outlived their usefulness. More than half the States get

>> The original concept of a town meeting is still alive in many New England towns, although some larger towns have added professional town managers to the mix.

along without them. Many rural townships have been abolished as a result of declining populations, improvements in transportation, and other factors.

Some of the more densely populated townships appear to have brighter futures than their country cousins, however. This seems especially true in the suburban areas around some larger cities. Some States, such as Pennsylvania, now allow townships to exercise many of the powers and furnish many of the services once reserved for cities.

Special Districts There are now tens of thousands of special districts across the country. A **special district** is an independent unit created to perform one or more related governmental functions at the local level. These districts are found in mind-boggling variety and in every State. School districts are by far the most common example. Tens of thousands of other special districts also blanket the country, and their numbers are growing.

Special districts are found most often, but not always, in rural and suburban areas. Many have been created to provide water, sewage, or electrical service; to furnish fire or police protection; and to build and maintain bridges, airports, swimming pools, libraries, or parks. Others have been created for such purposes as soil conservation, housing, public transportation, irrigation, or reforestation. There are even, in many places, special districts for dog or mosquito control purposes.

A leading reason for the creation of special districts has been the need to provide a particular service in a wider or a smaller area than what is covered by a county or a city. For example, a special district might be needed to handle pollution in the several counties through which a river flows. On the other hand, a special district might be set up to provide fire or police protection in some out-of-the-way locale.

In many cases, special districts have been formed because other local governments could not, or would not, provide the services desired. Others have been created to sidestep constitutional limits on the size of a city's or a county's debt; to finance a public service out of users' fees instead of from general tax revenue; or to take advantage of some federal grant program.

The governing body for a special district is almost always an elected board. It has the power to lay taxes (usually on property) or charge fees, as well as the power to spend and to carry out the function(s) for which it was created.

>> The Daytona International Speedway in Daytona Beach, Florida, is on land owned by the Daytona Beach Racing and Recreational Facilities special district.

☑ **COMPARE AND CONTRAST** What are the similarities and differences between the town meeting and the township forms of local government?

City Government

The population of the United States was once small, mostly rural, and agricultural, it is now large, mostly urban, and dominated by technology, manufacturing, and service industries. In 1790, a mere 5 percent of the population lived in the nation's few cities. In recent years, that figure is greater than 80 percent, a change that has had dramatic consequences for local governments across the country.

Urbanization The larger the number of people living in close contact with one another, the greater the strains on local governments. The larger the population, the greater the problems in providing water, police and fire protection, sewers, waste removal, streets and traffic regulation, public health services, schools, recreational facilities, and more. The larger the population, the more extensive—and expensive—all of this becomes.

Remember, each of the 50 States is a unitary government. That means that each State has complete control over all of the units of local government within its borders. All those units, including cities, were created by the State, received their powers from the State, and are subject to a variety of limitations imposed by the State.

A **municipality** is an urban governmental unit within a township that usually exists as a separate entity. Depending on local custom and State law, municipalities may be known as cities, towns, boroughs, or villages. The use and meaning of these terms vary among the States. The larger municipalities are known everywhere as cities, and the usual practice is to use that title only for those communities with significant populations.

Incorporation The procedure by which a State establishes a city as a legal body is called **incorporation**. Each State sets out in its constitution, or by statute, the conditions and the procedures under which a community may become an incorporated municipality. Typically, a State requires that a minimum number of persons live within a given area before incorporation can take place.

The fact that cities are incorporated highlights an important difference between city and county government. Cities are created largely at the request of their residents, because residents want certain public services. Counties, on the other hand, exist largely to serve the administrative needs of the State. Cities do act as agents of the State, of course—for example, in law enforcement and public health. But the principal reason for the existence of a city is for the convenience of those who live there.

City Charters A **charter** is a city's basic law, its constitution. Its contents may vary from city to city, but commonly the charter names the city, describes its boundaries, and declares it to be a municipal corporation. As a municipal corporation, a city has the right to sue and be sued in the courts; to have a corporate seal; to make contracts; and to acquire, own, manage, and dispose of property.

Generally, the charter sets out the other powers vested in the city and outlines its form of government. It also provides how and for what terms its officers are to be chosen, outlines their duties, and deals with finances and other matters.

☑ **EXPLAIN** How do States control the process of incorporation?

Forms of City Government

In general, cities across the nation use one of three basic forms of government: (1) mayor-council, (2) commission, or (3) council-manager. Over the years, the forms have become less distinct than they once were as cities have borrowed ideas from one another and modified their governments to make them work better. Some cities, however, adhere quite strictly to these original forms.

The Mayor-Council Form The **mayor-council government** is the oldest type of city government and it is used in many cities across the nation. It features an elected mayor as the chief executive and an elected council as its legislative body.

The council is almost always unicameral and typically has five, seven, or nine members. Some larger cities have more. The New York City council, for example, has about 50 members. In those cities that use the mayor-council form of government, council members are popularly elected, almost always from districts (wards) within the city. Terms of office vary, but four-year terms are the most common.

A move to nonpartisan city government began in the early 1900s. Its champions believed that (1) political parties were a major source of corruption in city government, and (2) partisan contests at the State and national levels have little to do with municipal problems and local issues. Today, less than one third of all cities still run their elections on a partisan basis.

>> The Gateway Arch in St. Louis, Missouri, commemorates the city's role in westward expansion. At the time of the 1850 census, St. Louis was the most populous city west of the Mississippi River.

VOTERS

COUNCIL
Legislative body

DEPARTMENT HEADS
Administrators of agencies, such as public safety, public works, finance, education

ELECT

MAYOR
Chief Executive

APPOINTS

>> Use of the strong-mayor form of city government often eliminates questions about who is in charge. **Analyze Charts** What can you conclude about this as a model for large cities?

Strong and Weak Mayors Generally, the voters elect the mayor. In some places, however, the council chooses one of its members to serve as mayor. The mayor presides at council meetings, usually may vote only to break a tie, and may recommend—and often veto—ordinances. In most cities, the council can override the veto.

Mayor-council governments are often described as either the strong-mayor or the weak-mayor type, depending on the powers given to the mayor. This classification is useful for purposes of description. It blurs the importance of informal power in city politics, however.

In a **strong-mayor government,** the mayor heads the city's administration, usually has the veto power, can hire and fire employees, and prepares the budget. Typically, the mayor is able to exercise strong leadership in making city policy and running the city's affairs.

In a **weak-mayor government,** the mayor has much less formal power. Executive duties are shared with other elected officials—for example, a clerk, treasurer, city engineer, police chief, and even council members.

Powers of appointment, removal, and budget are shared with the council or exercised by that body alone. The mayor seldom has a veto power.

Most mayor-council cities operate under the weak-mayor rather than the strong-mayor plan. The strong-mayor form is most often found in larger cities.

The success of the mayor-council form depends in very large measure on the power, ability, and influence of the mayor. In weak-mayor cities, responsibility for action or inaction is hard to assign. The strong-mayor plan helps to solve the problems of leadership and responsibility. Still, the mayor-council form has three large defects:

1. It depends quite heavily on the capabilities of the mayor.

2. An ongoing dispute between the mayor and the council can stall the workings of a city's government.

3. It is quite complicated and, so, is often little understood by the average citizen.

The Commission Form The **commission government** is simple in structure. Three to nine commissioners are popularly elected. Together, they form the city council, pass ordinances, and control the purse strings. Individually, they head the different departments of city government: police, fire, public works, finance, parks, and so on. Thus, both legislative and executive powers are centered in one body.

The commission form was born in Galveston, Texas, in 1901, after a tidal surge had devastated the city. When the existing mayor-council government proved unequal to the task, the Texas legislature gave Galveston a new charter, providing for five commissioners to make and enforce law in the stricken city. Intended to be temporary, the arrangement proved so effective that it soon spread to other communities across the country.

Either the voters or the commissioners themselves choose one of the commissioners to serve as the mayor. Like the other commissioners, the mayor heads one or more of the city's departments. He or she also presides at council meetings and represents the city for ceremonial purposes, but generally has no more authority than the other commissioners and rarely has a veto power.

Weaknesses of the Commission Form

Experience pointed up serious defects in the commission form. As a result, only a very few American cities use this form of government today.

The commission form suffers from three chief defects:

1. The lack of a single chief executive makes it difficult to assign responsibility and so the city often has no effective political leadership.

2. A built-in tendency toward "empire building" often surfaces. Each commissioner tries to draw as much of the city's money and influence as possible to his or her own department.

3. A lack of coordination plagues the topmost levels of policymaking and administration. Each commissioner is likely to equate the citywide public good with the particular interests and functions of his or her department.

The Council-Manager Form

The **council-manager government** is a modification of the mayor-council form. Its main features are (1) a strong council of usually five or seven members elected at-large on a nonpartisan ballot; (2) a weak mayor chosen by the voters; and (3) a manager, the city's chief administrative officer, named by the council.

The form first appeared in Ukiah, California. In 1904, that city's council appointed an "executive officer" to direct the work of city government. The first charter expressly providing for the council-manager form was granted to the city of Sumter, South Carolina, in 1912.

COMMISSION FORM OF GOVERNMENT

VOTERS

— ELECT → **BOARD OF COMMISSIONERS**
Forms the city council

— APPOINTS →

MAYOR (may be elected by voters)

PUBLIC WORKS

FINANCE

PUBLIC SAFETY

EDUCATION

Commissioners individually serve as department heads or as mayor.

>> The commission form of government is one of the simplest governing systems for a city. **Analyze Charts** Does a system of checks and balances exist in this form of government?

VOTERS

COUNCIL
Policy-making body

ELECT

APPOINTS

CITY MANAGER
Chief Administrator; hires and fires city employees, prepares budget, controls spending

APPOINTS

MAYOR

DEPARTMENT HEADS
Administrators of agencies, such as public safety, public works, finance, education

>> In the council-manager form of government, a professional manager oversees necessary services for city residents. **Analyze Charts** What are the advantages of this type of government?

City Managers The council is the city's policy-making body. The manager carries out the policies the council makes. He or she is directly responsible to that body for the efficient administration of the city. The manager serves at the council's pleasure and may be dismissed at any time and for any reason.

Today, most city managers are professionally trained career administrators. As chief administrator, the manager directs the work of all city departments and has the power to hire and fire all city employees. The manager also prepares the budget for council consideration and controls the spending of the funds the council appropriates.

The council-manager plan is backed by most experts on municipal affairs, and its use has spread widely. It is now found in many municipalities across the nation.

Pros and Cons of the Council-Manager Form

The council-manager plan has three major advantages over other forms of city government:
1. It is simple in form.
2. It is fairly clear who is responsible for policy, on the one hand, and for its application, on the other.

3. It relies on highly trained experts who are skilled in modern techniques of budgeting, planning, computerization, and other administrative tools.

In theory, the nonpolitical manager carries out the policies enacted by the council. Yet, in practice, sharp distinctions between policymaking and policy-application seldom exist. The manager is very often the chief source for new ideas and fresh approaches to the city's problems. On the other hand, the city council often finds it politically useful to share the responsibility for controversial decisions with the "expendable" city manager.

Some critics of the council-manager form hold that it is undemocratic because its chief executive is not popularly elected. Others say that it lacks strong political leadership. This is a particular shortcoming, they argue, in larger cities, where the population is often quite diverse and there can be many competing interests.

☑ **COMPARE AND CONTRAST** Compare and contrast the council-manager form of government with the mayor-council form.

City Planning and Other Municipal Functions

With few exceptions, most American cities developed haphazardly, without a plan, and with no eye to the future. The results of this shortsightedness can be seen in what is often called the core area or the inner city. These are often the older and usually overcrowded central sections of larger cities.

Industrial plants were placed anywhere their owners chose to build them. Rail lines were run through the heart of the community. Towering buildings shut out the sunlight from the narrow streets below. Main roads were laid out too close together and sometimes too far apart. Schools, police and fire stations, and other public buildings were squeezed onto cheap land or put where the dominant political organization could make a profit. The many examples of this shortsightedness are nearly endless.

Guiding Growth Fortunately, many cities have seen the need to create order out of their random growth. Most have established some sort of planning agency, supported by a trained professional staff.

A number of factors have prompted this step. The need to correct past mistakes has often been a compelling reason, of course. Also, many cities have recognized both the advantages that can result, and the pitfalls that can be avoided, through well-planned and orderly development. Importantly, the Federal Government has spurred cities on. Most federal grant and loan programs require that cities that seek aid must first have a master plan as a guide to future growth.

Zoning The practice of dividing a city into a number of districts, or zones, and regulating the uses to which property in each of them may be put is called **zoning**. Generally, a zoning ordinance places each parcel of land in the city into one of three spheres: residential, commercial, or industrial zones.

Each of these zones is then divided into subzones. For example, each of several residential zones may be broken down into several areas. One may be reserved for single-family residences, another may allow one-family and two-family dwellings, and a third, large apartment buildings.

Most zoning ordinances also prescribe limits on the height and area of buildings, determine how much of a lot may be occupied by a structure, and set out several other such restrictions on land use. They often have "setback" requirements, providing that structures must be placed at least a certain distance from the street and from other property lines.

Pros and Cons of Zoning Zoning meets opposition from many who object to this interference with their right to use their property as they choose. Even so, nearly every city of any size in the United States is zoned today.

Zoning ordinances must be reasonable. Remember that the 14th Amendment prohibits any State, and thus its cities, from depriving any person of life, liberty, or property without due process of law. Each of the 50 State constitutions contains a similar provision.

Clearly, zoning does deprive a person of the right to use his or her property for certain purposes. Thus, if an area is zoned for single-family dwellings only, one cannot build an apartment house or a service station on property in that zone. Zoning can also reduce the value of a particular piece of property. A choice corner lot, for example, may be much more valuable with a drive-through restaurant or gas station on the property rather than a house.

So, while zoning may at times deprive a person of liberty or property, the key question is this: Does it do so without due process? That is, does it do so unreasonably?

The question of reasonableness is one for the courts to decide, largely on a case-by-case basis. The

>> Without zoning laws, it is possible for an industrial plant like this one to be built in a residential neighborhood, or near a public school.

Supreme Court first upheld zoning as a proper use of the police power in *Euclid* v. *Amber Realty Co.*, 1926, a case involving an ordinance enacted by the city council of Euclid, Ohio.

For their part, city planners have tried to address the question of reasonableness in various ways. For example, nonconforming uses in existence before a zoning ordinance is passed are almost always allowed to continue. Most ordinances give the city council the right to grant exceptions, called variances, in those cases where property owners might suffer undue hardship.

City Services The services a city provides day in and day out are so extensive that it is almost impossible to catalog them. Most larger cities, and many smaller ones, issue annual reports on the city's condition. These are often book-length publications.

Consider just a few of the many things that most or all cities do. They provide police and fire protection. They build and maintain streets, sidewalks, bridges, street lights, parks and playgrounds, swimming pools, golf courses, libraries, hospitals, schools, correctional institutions, day-care centers, airports, public markets, parking facilities, auditoriums, and sports arenas. They furnish public health and sanitation services, including sewers and wastewater treatment, garbage collection and disposal, and disease prevention programs.

Cities also operate water, gas, electrical, and transportation systems. They regulate traffic, building codes, pollution, and public utilities. Many cities also build and manage public housing projects, provide summer youth camps, build and operate docks and other harbor facilities, and maintain tourist attractions.

☑ **EXPLAIN** Explain how the U.S. Constitution relates to the implementation of zoning laws.

Suburbs and Metropolitan Areas

The growth of urban areas has raised many problems for city dwellers. Urban growth also affects residents of nearby suburbs.

The Suburban Boom The nation's suburbs first began to grow rapidly in the years after World War II, and that growth has continued. As suburban populations have mushroomed, many of the nation's larger cities have actually lost residents.

>> If local officials prohibited the driving range from being built near this home, would they be infringing on the property rights of the business owner? **Analyze Political Cartoons** How does the cartoonist make the point about the fairness of zoning laws?

>> The Boston public library, shown here, is known as a "palace for the people." Public libraries are funded by cities. They loan books and other media and offer meeting space, classes, and Internet access.

These dramatic population shifts stemmed, in large part, from peoples' desire for more room, cheaper land, greater privacy, and less smoke, dirt, noise, and congestion. Many have also sought less crime, newer and better schools, safer streets and playing conditions, lower taxes, and higher social status. The car and the freeway turned millions of rooted city dwellers into mobile suburbanites.

Businesses followed customers to the suburbs, often clustering in shopping centers or malls instead of traditional downtowns. Many industries moved from the central city in search of cheaper land, lower taxes, and a more stable labor supply. Industries also sought an escape from city building codes, health inspectors, and other regulations.

This "suburbanitis" has added to city dwellers' woes. As high-income families have moved out, they have taken their civic, financial, and social resources with them. They have left behind center cities with high percentages of older people, low-income families, and minorities. Both the need for, and the stress on, city services have multiplied.

The Challenges of Metropolitan Areas

Suburbanites face their share of problems, too, including the need for water supplies, sewage disposal, police and fire protection, transportation, and traffic control. Duplication of such functions by city and suburb or by city and county can be wasteful, even dangerous. More than one fire has raged while neighboring fire departments quibbled over the responsibility for fighting it.

Attempts to meet the needs of the nation's **metropolitan areas**—cities and the areas around them—have taken several forms. Over the years, annexation has been the standard means. Outlying areas have simply been brought within a city's boundaries. Many suburbanites resist annexation, however, and many cities have been hesitant to take on the burdens involved.

Urban Special Districts

Urban Special Districts Another approach has been to create special districts designed to meet the problems of heavily populated urban areas. Their boundaries frequently cut across county and city lines to include an entire metropolitan area. They often are called metropolitan districts and can serve one purpose (for example, maintaining parks) or many.

In Oregon, a regional agency known as Metro manages several activities in an area that includes Portland, the State's largest city, and two dozen or so other municipalities. Within this region, Metro is responsible for land-use and transportation planning, solid-waste disposal programs, and the operation of the Oregon Convention Center, the Oregon Zoo, and other facilities.

>> **Analyze Political Cartoons** What does the view suggest about the potential result of allowing urban sprawl to continue?

Yet another approach to the challenges facing metropolitan areas is increasing the authority of counties. Among local governments around the country, counties are generally the largest in area and are most likely to include those places demanding new and increased services. In Miami-Dade County, Florida, a countywide metropolitan government took responsibility for areawide functions following a 1957 charter. Responsibilities include fire and police protection; an integrated water, sewer, and drainage system; zoning; and expressway construction. Miami and the county's other municipalities continue to perform strictly local functions and services.

☑ **EXPLAIN** How has the suburban boom that followed World War II affected city governments?

☑ ASSESSMENT

1. **Check Understanding** Describe one major flaw of county government.

2. **Express Ideas Clearly** Describe the various means through which metropolitan areas can gain access to basic services.

3. **Interpret** Why might zoning be used to exclude certain businesses from residential neighborhoods?

4. **Summarize** Summarize the basic organization of the mayor-council form of city government.

5. **Identify Central Issues** What are some pros and cons of having a professional manager as part of a city government?

Through bicycle police units, such as this one in Arkansas, officers can be more accessible to citizens, providing opportunities for positive interactions with the community.

 BOUNCE to Activate Flipped Video

Objectives

Explain why State and local governments have a major role in providing important services.

Identify State and local services in the fields of education, public welfare, public safety, and highways.

Describe the major federal and State limits on raising revenue.

List the four principles of sound taxation.

Identify major tax and nontax sources of State and local revenues.

Explain the State budget process.

Key Terms

Medicaid
welfare
entitlement
sales tax
regressive tax
income tax
progressive tax
property tax
assessment
inheritance tax
estate tax
budget

State and Local Spending and Revenue

Chances are you used at least one service provided by your State or local government today. Did you drive on a local road? Attend a public school? Take a walk in a park? Put the trash out? Use running water? These are just a few examples of government services that affect citizens' daily lives. The question is this: Who pays for the road crew who built the street, the school building and teachers' salaries, the park's manicured lawns, and the trash collection?

In fact, providing these and other services to State residents is a complicated business that sometimes involves all levels of government. Most spending, however, is largely the domain of State and local governments. Those are the areas we will examine in this lesson.

Education, Public Health, and Welfare

Public Education Funding Public education is among the oldest of all State responsibilities. Boston Latin School, in Massachusetts, is the oldest public school in continuous existence in the United States; it opened its doors in 1635. The State of New York created the first school districts in 1812. Today, public education is also among the most important of all State responsibilities. This is reflected in the fact that education is among the most expensive items in every State's budget.

Primary and secondary public education is largely the responsibility of local governments. Local taxes, especially property taxes, provide much of the funding for schools. Those governments can be hard-pressed to fulfill that duty because the cost of public education rises each year. At the same time, voters demand better schools. As a result, State and local governments have continually increased their education budgets, which often translates into higher taxes.

Of course, the States do provide some financial assistance to their local governments for education. The level of that aid varies, however. Some States contribute well over half the cost of primary and secondary education. Others provide only a minor fraction of the cost.

In addition, States set guidelines in order to promote quality in the schools. For example, State laws establish teacher qualifications, curricula, quality standards for educational materials, and the length of the school year.

State interest and involvement in these matters have intensified in recent years. Most States have established "curriculum frameworks" or "content standards" outlining the material that must be covered in core subjects. In addition, many States have adopted the national Common Core State Standards, a State-led effort to develop criteria for mathematics and English curriculums.

College and University Support At the college and university levels, the States also play a major role. States understand that, in order for businesses to succeed in the State, a ready supply of highly trained college graduates is key. Every State has a public higher education system, which may include universities, technical schools, and community colleges. Education at State universities and colleges is generally much less expensive than at private institutions. On average, tuition at four-year public colleges and universities is about one fourth that of private four-year schools. Nevertheless, many public institutions are ranked among the world's finest schools.

Public Health States take an active role in promoting the health and welfare of their residents. They pursue that goal through a variety of means. Most States fund ambitious public health programs. States operate public hospitals and offer direct care to millions of citizens. They immunize children against dangerous childhood diseases, such as measles and mumps. With the Federal Government, they administer such programs as **Medicaid**, which provides medical care and some other health services to low-income families. Providing all of these services has become ever more challenging as health-care costs have soared and placed a great strain on State budgets.

Education Spending Per Student*

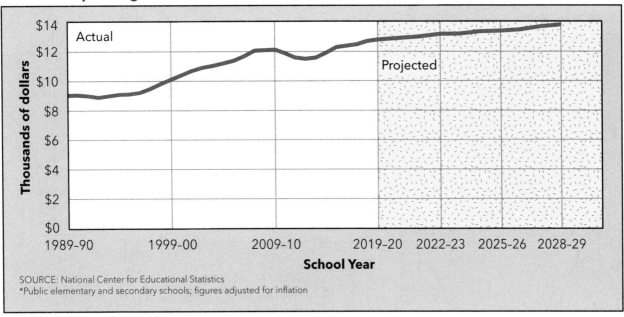

SOURCE: National Center for Educational Statistics
*Public elementary and secondary schools; figures adjusted for inflation

>> Many factors account for the steady growth in expenditures per student for education. **Analyze Graphs** What might be some categories of spending that contribute to costs per student?

Cash Assistance Another major area in which States contribute to the well-being of their citizens is cash assistance to the poor, commonly called **welfare**. States now take a leading role in this area.

Between 1936 and 1996, the Federal Government provided cash assistance to needy families through the Aid to Families with Dependent Children (AFDC) program. AFDC was an **entitlement** program, which means that anyone who met the eligibility requirements was entitled to receive benefits under the program. The Federal Government and the States shared the costs of providing AFDC benefits.

Critics of AFDC pointed to soaring costs, expanding caseloads, and the absence of time limits on benefits as serious problems with the program. Because of these issues, critics argued that the program encouraged people to depend on government assistance rather than become self-supporting.

Temporary Assistance to Needy Families (TANF)

In 1996, AFDC was replaced with a new and strikingly different program, Temporary Assistance to Needy Families (TANF). Unlike AFDC, TANF is a block grant program: The Federal Government gives States a fixed amount of money each year, regardless of whether the number of TANF recipients rises or falls. The States are then free to use the federal grant, plus the State funds they are obliged to contribute, to design and implement their own welfare programs. TANF limits recipients to a total of five years of assistance during the course of their lifetimes, and recipients must work or participate in some form of vocational training or community service.

The number of families on welfare has plunged since the mid-1990s. Many who remain on welfare must overcome a number of barriers, such as physical or mental disabilities or substance abuse, in order to obtain and hold jobs. Now that States have the primary responsibility for welfare, it is their task to find ways to help these families.

Other Efforts

States do much more to promote their citizens' health and welfare. They make and enforce antipollution laws to protect the environment, they inspect factories and other workplaces to protect worker safety, they license healthcare practitioners to ensure quality care, and so on.

The States and their local governments often go much further than the Federal Government in spelling out, through these regulations, exactly how business can be conducted, how to protect the environment, and other important matters.

☑ **IDENTIFY CAUSE AND EFFECT** How might variations in local governments' revenue sources affect public education?

AFDC and TANF, 1967-2006

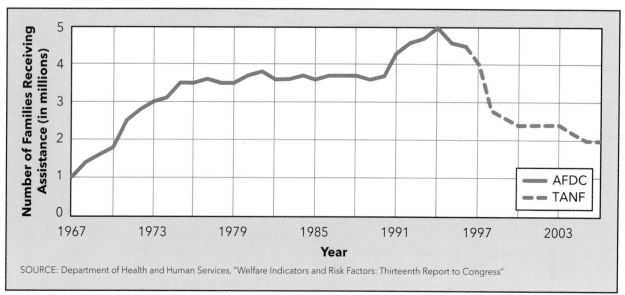

SOURCE: Department of Health and Human Services, "Welfare Indicators and Risk Factors: Thirteenth Report to Congress"

>> The number of AFDC recipients rose dramatically from 1970 to 1992, leading to the block grant program, TANF. **Analyze Graphs** How did spending change after TANF began?

Public Safety, Highways, and Other Services

One of the oldest law-enforcement groups, the legendary Texas Rangers, was established in 1835. Today, a variety of police forces, from the local sheriff to academy-trained State police, operate in every State to preserve law and order.

The State police are perhaps the most visible group, since they patrol the State's roads and highways. State law-enforcement forces perform other vital services, as well. They may function as the primary police force in rural communities, investigate crimes, provide centralized files for fingerprints and other information, and provide training and many other services to support local law enforcement agencies.

Corrections System Each State has its own corrections system for dealing with those convicted of State crimes. States operate prisons, penitentiaries, and other correctional facilities, including those for juvenile offenders.

Operating these disciplinary systems is a significant burden for States. Today, millions of people are incarcerated, and a large percentage of them are in State prisons.

Two leading causes of huge prison populations are (1) increases in the number of people sentenced for violent crimes and drug-related crimes and (2) the increased length of the average prison sentence. One result is prison overcrowding. Another is that the States spend tens of billions of dollars each year to build, staff, and maintain prisons and to house prisoners. In fact, in an effort to expand their prison capacity more affordably, many States have hired private contractors to operate some of their prisons.

Interstate Highway System Building and maintaining roads and highways is an enormous job. It regularly takes a sizeable percentage of State budgets. Again, the Federal Government is a partner with the States in funding highways. The most impressive example is the Interstate Highway System, a network of high-speed roadways that spans the length and breadth of the continental United States. Construction of the system began with the 1956 Federal-Aid Highway Act and continues to this day.

Although it continues to be expanded, the Interstate Highway System, now officially known as the Dwight D. Eisenhower System of Interstate and Defense Highways, was deemed complete in 1992. Its total length covers more than 45,000 miles. The Federal Government paid roughly 90 percent of its total cost.

>> States inspect workplaces such as this cell phone factory in order to ensure the safety of workers.

>> In 1919, a young Dwight D. Eisenhower participated in a 3,251-mile army transcontinental motor convoy. This expedition later inspired him to push Congress to fund an interstate highway system.

While the interstate system is a magnificent achievement, it constitutes only a tiny fraction of the nation's more than 4 million miles of roads. Many roadways are built with State, not federal, funds; and the States maintain those roads, as well.

Driver Safety State and local governments must also look after the physical safety of drivers on thousands of miles of roads and highways. Besides patrolling the roads, State and local governments set speed limits. The States license drivers to ensure their competence, and many States require periodic safety inspections of vehicles.

As indicated earlier, the many services the States and their local units provide are really far too numerous to be recounted here. This fact does not discount the importance of such functions as the setting aside of public lands for purposes such as conservation and recreation, the regulation of business practices, and the protection of consumers from a variety of dangers and inconveniences.

✅ **CONNECT** Why might the construction of highways and roads be considered an example of federalism at work?

Financing State and Local Government

By now, you know the answer to the question posed at the beginning of this lesson. It is the people and businesses of your State who pay for all the services the State provides. In fact, State residents have a legal obligation to pay the taxes that the State levies. For their part, State legislators must strive to make taxes fair.

The power to tax is one of the major powers of the States in the federal system. In a strictly legal sense, then, their taxing power is limited only by the restrictions imposed by the federal Constitution and those imposed by a State's own fundamental law. Of course, the power to tax is also limited by any number of practical considerations—including, especially, economic and political factors.

Federal Tax Limitations The federal Constitution does place some restrictions on the taxing abilities of State and local governments. Although few in number, those limits have a major impact.

The Constitution prohibits the States from taxing interstate and foreign trade. Remember, the Supreme Court's decision in *McCulloch* v. *Maryland*, in 1819, bars States from taxing the Federal Government or any of its agencies or functions.

>> Farmers protest high taxes and other grievances during the Great Depression. Economic conditions have a major impact on taxpayers' income, and thus on State revenues.

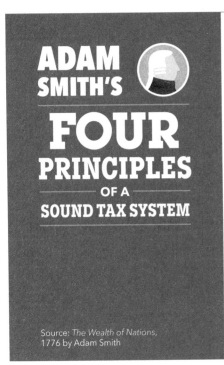

ADAM SMITH'S FOUR PRINCIPLES OF A SOUND TAX SYSTEM

① "**The subjects of every state** ought to contribute towards the support of the government as nearly as possible, in proportion to their respective abilities; that is, in proportion to the revenue which they respectively enjoy under the protection of the state."

② "**The tax which each individual** is bound to pay ought to be certain, and not arbitrary."

③ "**Every tax ought to be levied** at the time, or in the manner, in which it is most likely to be convenient for the contributor to pay it."

④ "**Every tax ought to be so contrived** as to take out and keep out of the pockets of the people as little as possible over and above what it brings into the public treasury...."

Source: *The Wealth of Nations,* 1776 by Adam Smith

>> The 18th-century economist Adam Smith attempted to establish uniform rules that would govern a sound system of taxation. **Analyze Information** Which of these principles supports the idea of the progressive tax?

The 14th Amendment's Due Process and Equal Protection clauses place important limits on the power to tax at the State and local levels. Essentially, the Due Process Clause requires that taxes be (1) imposed and administered *fairly*, (2) not so heavy as to actually confiscate property, and (3) imposed only for *public* purposes.

The Equal Protection Clause forbids the making of unreasonable classifications for the purpose of taxation. The clause thus forbids tax classifications based on race, religion, nationality, political party membership, or any other factors beyond what is reasonable.

However, most tax laws do involve some form of classification. Thus, a cigarette tax is collected only from those who buy cigarettes, a classification many people agree is a reasonable one.

State Tax Limitations Each State's constitution limits a State's taxing powers. State constitutions also limit the taxing powers of their local governments, often in great detail.

Most State constitutions create tax exemptions for religious and other nonprofit groups. State codes often set maximum rates for levies such as sales taxes or local property taxes. Some States prohibit certain taxes—for example, a general sales tax or a personal income tax.

Since local governments have no independent powers, the only taxes they can impose are those that the State allows them to levy. States have been restrictive in the matter. Even local units with home-rule charters are closely limited as to what and how they can tax.

Principles of Sound Taxation Any tax, if taken by itself, can be shown to be unfair. If a government's total revenues were to come from one tax—say, a sales, an income, or a property tax—its tax system would be very unfair. Some people would bear a much greater burden than others, and some would bear little or none. Each tax should thus be defensible as part of a tax system.

In his classic 1776 work, *The Wealth of Nations,* Scottish economist Adam Smith laid out four principles of a sound tax system. Those basic principles of equality, certainty, convenience, and economy can be seen in the graphic on this page.

Shaping a tax system that unfailingly meets these standards is just about impossible. Still, that goal should always be pursued.

☑ **DRAW CONCLUSIONS** In what ways does the 14th Amendment limit the States' power to tax?

Sources of State Revenue

Beyond the limits noted, a State can levy taxes as it chooses. The legislature decides what taxes the State will impose and at what rates. It decides, too, what taxes localities can levy. Acting under these strictures, the States and their local governments take in trillions of dollars in taxes each year.

Sales Tax Revenue The sales tax is the most productive source of State-levied income. A **sales tax** is a tax placed on the sale of various commodities; the purchaser pays it. It may be either *general* or *selective* in form. A general sales tax is one applied to the sale of most commodities. A selective sales tax is one placed on the sale of only certain commodities.

In 1932, Mississippi became the first State to levy a sales tax. Today, nearly every State does so. Some things are exempted from the tax almost everywhere—most commonly, food, medicine, and newspapers. A growing number of cities, and some urban counties, also levy sales taxes today—a "piggy-back tax," added on to and collected with the State tax.

All 50 States impose a selective sales tax on gasoline, alcoholic beverages, cigarettes, and insurance policies. Many of them also place selective sales taxes on such things as hotel and motel accommodations, restaurant meals, and theater and other amusement admissions.

Sales taxes are widely used for two major reasons: They are easy to collect, and they are dependable revenue producers. Yet a sales tax is a **regressive tax**—that is, it is not levied according to a person's ability to pay. The tax falls most heavily on those least able to pay it.

Internet sales are a confusing area with regard to the sales tax. As Internet sales continue to see explosive growth, there has been an ongoing effort by States to force Internet retailers to pay the tax. This is because otherwise the drain on their tax revenues may force them to compensate by reducing services or raising other taxes.

Income Tax Revenue The **income tax**, which is levied on the income of individuals and/or corporations, yields a significant percentage of State and local tax revenues today. Wisconsin enacted the first State income tax in 1911. Nearly all States levy an individual income tax and most also have some form of corporate income tax.

The individual income tax is usually a **progressive tax**—that is, the higher your income, the more tax you pay. Income tax rates vary among the States. Those who pay the tax receive various

State vs. Federal Government Revenues, 1930-1970

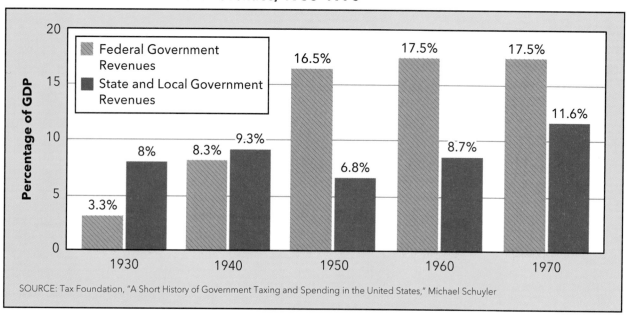

SOURCE: Tax Foundation, "A Short History of Government Taxing and Spending in the United States," Michael Schuyler

>> This graph compares federal with State and local revenues for years during and after the Great Depression and World War II. **Analyze Graphs** How did federal revenues compare to State and local revenues for the years shown?

exemptions and deductions in calculating their taxable income.

Corporate income tax rates are usually a uniform (fixed) percentage of income. Only a few States set the rates on a graduated basis.

The progressive income tax is held by many to be the fairest—or the least unfair—form of taxation, because it can be geared to a person's ability to pay. If the rates are too high, however, the tax can discourage individual enterprise.

Property Tax Revenue Property taxes have been a major source of governmental revenue since the early colonial period. Once the major source of State revenue, they are now levied almost exclusively at the local level. They provide roughly three fourths of all local government tax income today.

A **property tax** is a levy on (1) real property, such as land, buildings, and improvements that go with the property if sold; or (2) personal property, either tangible or intangible. Tangible personal property is movable wealth that is visible and the value of which can be easily assessed—for example, computers, cars, and books. Intangible personal property includes such things as stocks, bonds, mortgages, and bank accounts.

The process of determining the value of the property to be taxed is known as **assessment**. An elected county, township, or city assessor usually carries out the task.

Supporters of the property tax argue that, because government protects property and often enhances its value, property owners can logically be required to contribute to the support of government. They note that the rate at which the tax is levied can be readily adjusted to meet governmental needs.

Critics insist that the property tax is not progressive, not geared to one's ability to pay. They also argue that it is all but impossible to set the value of all property on a fair and equal basis. Finally, they say that personal property is easily hidden from assessors.

Inheritance or Estate Tax Revenue Most of the States have some form of inheritance or estate tax, sometimes called the "death tax." An **inheritance tax** is levied on the beneficiary's (heir's) share of an estate. An **estate tax** is one levied directly on the full estate itself.

Business Tax Revenue A variety of business taxes, in addition to the corporate income tax, are important sources of revenue in most States. More than half the States impose severance taxes, which are levies on

>> The amount of property tax paid by a homeowner is based on an appraisal of the property's worth. **Analyze Political Cartoons** Why did this homeowner paint a more modest dwelling on the side of his large home?

>> Boeing 787 Dreamliner jets are assembled in Everett, Washington. From 2004 to 2020, Washington State gave major tax breaks to Boeing to attract its business to the State.

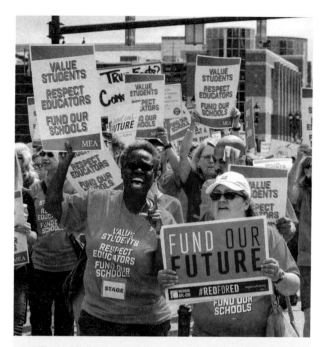

>> These Michigan teachers rallied at the State capitol to demand that the legislature increase funding for public education. **Analyze Information** How can legislators raise school funding?

>> State-run businesses, such as the Washington State ferry system, are another source of revenue for State governments.

the removal of natural resources such as timber, oil, minerals, and fish from the land or water.

Every State has various license taxes that permit people to engage in certain businesses, occupations, or activities. For example, all States require that corporations be licensed to do business in the State. Certain kinds of businesses—chain stores, amusement parks, taverns, and transportation lines—must have an additional operating license. Most States also require the licensing of doctors, lawyers, hairdressers, plumbers, electricians, insurance agents, and a host of others.

Many States have levies known as documentary and stock transfer taxes. These are charges made on the recording, registering, and transfer (sale) of such documents as mortgages, deeds, and securities. Some States also impose capital stock taxes, which are levied on the total assessed value of the shares of stock issued by a business.

Other Tax Revenues A variety of other taxes are imposed by the States and their local governments in order to raise revenues. As a leading example, payroll taxes produce huge sums; the monies generated by those taxes are held in trust funds to pay unemployment benefits, accident insurance, and retirement programs. Most States levy amusement taxes for admission to theaters, sports events, circuses, and the like. Every State imposes license taxes for various nonbusiness purposes—notably, on motor vehicles and drivers, and for such things as hunting, fishing, and marriage.

Nontax Revenues Taxes have never been very popular, and so State and local officials have long looked for nontax revenue sources. Grants from the Federal Government are one major source of nontax revenues.

Business enterprises and user fees. State and local governments also make money from a variety of publicly operated business enterprises. Toll roads and bridges are especially popular in the East. Several States, notably Washington, are in the ferry business. North Dakota markets a baking flour, sold under the brand name "Dakota Maid," and is also in the commercial banking business. Several States are in the liquor business, selling alcohol in State-operated stores.

Many cities own and operate their water, electric power, and bus transportation systems. Some cities run farmers' markets; rent space in their office buildings, warehouses, and housing projects; and operate dams and wharves. Receipts from such businesses support the local governments that own them. Other nontax sources include court fines, sales and lease of public lands, and interest from loans, investments, and late tax payments. Among the many public services for which those who use them must now pay a fee are hospitals, airports, parks, water, sewers, and garbage disposal.

Lotteries. For many years, nearly all forms of gambling were outlawed in every State except Nevada. Most States have relaxed their anti-gambling laws, hoping to attract dollars, jobs, and tourists.

State-run lotteries net tens of billions of dollars per year without raising taxes. Supporters note that they are popular, voluntary, and an alternative to illegal gambling. Opponents say that lotteries prey on the poor and encourage compulsive gambling.

Lottery proceeds are used for a number of purposes among the States. About half of the States with lotteries earmark all or most of their revenue for education. Some channel the money directly to the State's general fund, while others dedicate most of it to economic development or a wide range of other uses.

Borrowing Funds The States and many of their local governments regularly borrow money to pay for such large undertakings as the construction of schools, highways, hospitals, sports facilities, and college dormitories. Much of that borrowing is done by issuing bonds, much as the Federal Government does. Generally, State and local bonds are fairly easy to market because the interest paid on them is not subject to State or federal income taxes.

At various times in the past, many State and local governments defaulted on their debts. Thus, most State constitutions now place quite detailed limits on the power to borrow. Altogether, the debts of all State and local governments combined total trillions of dollars.

☑ **HYPOTHESIZE** Why do you think it is advantageous for States to generate revenue from a wide variety of sources?

State Budgets

A public **budget** is much more than bookkeeping entries and dollar signs. It is a financial plan, a plan for the control and use of public money, public personnel, and public property. It is also a political document, a highly significant statement of public policy. In the State budget, the State's leaders establish their State's priorities and decide who gets what, and who doesn't.

The Budget Process in the Past For more than 150 years, State budgets were the product of haphazard and uncoordinated steps centered in the legislature. Various State agencies appeared before legislative committees, each seeking its own funding, often in

State Budget Process

1. Budget Development	**2. Legislative Action, Part 1**
• Agencies request funds for the upcoming year • State budget office reviews requests and recommends a budget to the governor based on them • Governor reveals budget to the public and submits to State legislature	• Budget bill goes to committees in both houses of State legislature • House and Senate each pass their own versions • House and Senate versions are reconciled • Final budget is sent back to the governor

3. Governor's Response	**4. Legislative Action, Part 2**
• Governor reviews budget • Governor signs or vetoes the budget	• Legislature has a chance to override the governor's veto, if necessary

5. Budget Execution
• Supervised by the governor, the State budget office authorizes agencies to spend the budgeted amounts

>> Many individuals are involved in deciding how State revenues are spent.
Analyze Charts How is the State budget process similar to that of the Federal Government?

fierce competition with one another. Their chances of success depended far less on need or merit than on whatever political muscle they could bring to bear. When the legislature adjourned, no one had any real idea of how much had been appropriated or for what. Inevitably, extravagance and waste, unresolved problems, debt, favoritism, and graft were all part of the process.

State budgets are strikingly different things today. They remain highly charged political documents, but they are the end products of what is, by and large, an orderly and systematic process.

The Budget Process Today Nearly all States have adopted the executive budget, which gives the governor two vital powers: (1) to prepare the State's budget, and, after the legislature has acted upon his or her recommendations, (2) to manage the spending of the monies set aside by the legislature. In a few States, the process is somewhat different. The initial responsibility for preparing the budget is shared by the governor and the legislature.

Under the executive budget, the basic steps in the budget process are much the same at the State, local, and federal levels:

1. Each agency prepares estimates of its needs and proposed expenditures in the upcoming fiscal period.

2. Those estimates are reviewed by an executive budget agency.

3. Revised estimates, with supporting information, are brought together in a consolidated financial plan, the budget, which the governor then presents to the legislature for its consideration.

4. The legislature reacts to the proposed budget, part by part, appropriates the funds it deems necessary to pay for governmental activities, and enacts whatever revenue measures may be needed.

5. The governor supervises the execution of the budget—the actual spending of the funds provided by the legislature.

6. The execution of the budget is subject to an independent check—a post audit.

Unlike the Federal Government, every State except Vermont requires that its State's operating budget be balanced. How that is accomplished varies from State to State, however.

☑ **HYPOTHESIZE** Why is it important that a State's legislature shares budget-making responsibility with the governor?

☑ ASSESSMENT

1. **Determine Relevance** What makes Adam Smith's four principles of sound taxation important at all levels of government?

2. **Check Understanding** Why did the Constitution place limits on the power of State and local government to tax?

3. **Identify Central Issues** What is the central conflict in the relationship between taxation and government services?

4. **Identify Cause and Effect** What likely effect would the replacement of AFDC with the TANF block grant program have had on the federal budget? Explain your answer.

5. **Generate Explanations** How is a State's budget both a financial and a political statement?

GO ONLINE to www.SavvasRealize.com and access your digital course

Use the following online resources to practice citizenship skills and prepare for the Topic Test.

Case Studies

Current Connections

Quest Inquiries

Quizzes

Interactivities

Texts

Flipped Videos

While online you can also check the progress you've made learning the topic and course content by viewing your grades, test scores, and assignment status.

LESSON SUMMARIES

Use these Lesson Summaries, and the longer versions available online, to review the key ideas for each lesson in this Topic.

Lesson 1: State Constitutions

The first State constitutions were based on popular sovereignty and limited government. They also provided for a separation of powers, checks and balances, and the protection of individual rights. Today's State constitutions retain those basic principles. They also set out the structure, powers, and processes of government and detail methods of constitutional change.

Lesson 2: State Legislatures

The legislature is the lawmaking branch of State government. State legislatures are organized much like the United States Congress and their legislative process is also similar to that of Congress. Unlike Congress, some States allow voters to participate directly in the lawmaking process through the initiative and referendum.

Lesson 3: The Governor and State Administration

The governor is the chief executive officer of the State. He or she shares executive authority with other officers, but it is the governor to whom voters look for leadership. Among the powers of governors are the power to appoint and remove some officials, to prepare the budget, and to veto bills.

Lesson 4: State Courts

The law is the code of conduct by which society is governed. State courts apply constitutional, statutory, and administrative law, as well as common law and equity. The law can be classified as criminal or civil. Cases are heard by grand juries, which bring indictments, and petit juries, which decide the facts.

Lesson 5: Local Governments

Counties or their equivalent exist in all but two States. Their functions vary depending on region. A smaller unit of local government is the town or township. In addition to these, special districts also provide a wide variety of services. City governments usually take one of three forms: mayor-council, commission, or council-manager. In some areas, metropolitan districts have been established to address the issue of shrinking resources due to population shifts.

Lesson 6: State and Local Spending and Revenue

States provide services directly to citizens, including education, highways, and others. To pay for these services, State and local governments rely on a variety of methods, such as the sales tax, the income tax, and the property tax. Some States also run businesses or lotteries to raise funds. The way these revenues are used is set out in the State budget.

VISUAL REVIEW

Use these graphics to review some of the key terms, people, and ideas from this Topic.

State Government Organization

EXECUTIVE BRANCH	Governor Attorney General Lieutenant Governor Secretary of State State Treasurer
LEGISLATIVE BRANCH	House of Representatives/General Assembly/ House of Delegates Senate
JUDICIAL BRANCH	Local Courts General Trial Courts Courts of Appeal State Supreme Court

Revenues and Expenditures

REVENUES

- Federal Government
- Business taxes, licenses
- Sales tax
- Property tax
- Income tax

↓

STATE AND LOCAL GOVERNMENT

↓

EXPENDITURES

- Education
- Public welfare
- Public safety
- Health care
- Roads and transportation

Legal Terms

TERM	PURPOSE
Jury	To reach a just decision
Common Law	To guide a judge's decisions with past examples
Equity	To stop wrongs before they occur
Criminal Law	To protect the public order
Civil Law	To resolve disputes between people and between people and the government

Local Government Responsibilities

- Provide essential services, including education, public safety, road maintenance, and resource management
- Conduct elections
- Administer justice
- Plan for future growth and development
- Collect taxes for local services

KEY TERMS, PEOPLE, AND IDEAS

1. How is the **initiative** related to constitutional change?

2. What is the **police power**? The **constituent power**?

3. How does a **felony** differ from a **misdemeanor?**

4. What is the **item veto?**

5. How do the powers of **pardon** and **commutation** differ?

6. What is **fundamental law?** How does it differ from **statutory law?**

7. Describe the structure of a **council-manager government.**

8. What is the relationship between a **county** and a **township?**

CRITICAL THINKING

9. **Identify Central Ideas** How do State constitutions reflect the principles of separation of powers, popular sovereignty, limited government, and checks and balances?

10. **Compare and Contrast** How are State legislatures similar to the United States Congress? How are they different?

11. **Evaluate** Why do you think *Baker* v. *Carr*, and *Reynolds* v. *Sims* are considered to be landmark Supreme Court cases?

12. **Identify Cause and Effect** In what way might a governor's threat of a veto affect the legislature's position on a bill?

13. **Synthesize** The governor is not only the State's principle executive officer, but is also often the State's chief legislator. (a) Explain how this is so. (b) Does this arrangement violate the principle of separation of powers?

14. **Analyze** Identify the various levels of courts in most States' judicial systems. How do these State and local courts relate to the federal courts?

15. **Interpret** What is the importance of the trial jury in the State court system? How does its use affect you?

16. **Infer** Why don't State constitutions list all of the powers granted to the State legislature?

17. **Compare and Contrast** What is the major difference between local governments and tribal governments?

18. **Infer** Why do you think both the executive and legislative branches are involved in the creation of the State budget?

19. **Interpret** Why do you think State law often requires the governor to appoint some members of the opposing party to State boards and commissions?

20. **Evaluate** Think about your daily life and the powers of the federal, tribal, and State and local governments. Which level of government is most important to you? Explain why.

21. **Analyze Political Cartoons** Describe the events depicted in this cartoon. What point is the cartoonist making about the budget process and the powers of State legislatures and governors? How does this compare to what you have learned about the budget process? Which process makes more sense—the one depicted in the cartoon, or the one described in your textbook? Why?

22. **Writing Activity** In 1888, Lord Bryce wrote in *The American Commonwealth:*

"The legislature is so much the strongest force in the several States that they may almost call it government and ignore all the other authorities."

Based on what you have learned in this topic, is this still true today? Why or why not?

DOCUMENT-BASED QUESTIONS

The measures taken by States to address the COVID-19 pandemic proved controversial.

DOCUMENT A

This excerpt is from an opinion piece published by Politico, a media company that covers U.S. politics.

. . . At some point in the future, we could see a coronavirus response that has gone on too long or is too broad to justify its burdens. Or we might see instances of people who were denied civil liberties without real justification. Even now, you might feel that these measures are too little, too late, or that they are drastic, and burdensome. But if we are facing a window of opportunity that is rapidly closing, to say that the states cannot try to use their most basic authority to save lives is not only wrong—it might be deadly.

—*Elizabeth Joh, "Yes, States and Local Governments Can Close Private Businesses and Restrict Your Movement," March 18, 2020*

DOCUMENT B

This cartoon was published by the Minneapolis *Star Tribune* on March 26, 2020.

DOCUMENT C

This excerpt is from an article published by the CATO Institute, a libertarian public policy research organization.

In the early days of the COVID-19 pandemic, governors rushed to issue executive orders, mandating shutdowns and sorting people's livelihoods into "essential" or "nonessential." They issued these responses in understandable haste; governors reasonably prefer looking back and saying "we overreacted" over the alternative. Now that we are looking back, however, we see that many governors did indeed overreact—or simply pursued wrong strategies—even if their actions could be justified

by the limited information available at the time. As our gaze turns forward, state policymakers must remember that while they have broad police powers to respond to emergencies that threaten public health and safety, they are still limited by the U.S. Constitution and their states' constitutions and laws.

—*Ilya Shapiro, "State Police Powers and the Constitution," September 15, 2020*

DOCUMENT D

This excerpt is from a press release from the office of the governor of New Mexico.

Gov. Michelle Lujan Grisham and state health officials earlier in the week announced the tightened restrictions in order to stem the alarming rising tide of the virus statewide. . . . The governor reiterated her stark warning that the state's dramatically and rapidly worsening public health conditions will, if unabated, compel significant additional restrictions on day-to-day activities for all New Mexicans in order to preserve lives and protect the state's fragile health care capacity.

—*Office of the Governor, "New Emergency Public Health Order in Effect," October 16, 2020*

23. What argument does Document A use to support the restriction of civil liberties by State governments?
    A. the Federal Government's lack of leadership in response to the pandemic
    B. the States' responsibility to protect the health and well-being of their citizens
    C. the powers vested in the Federal Government by the United States Constitution
    D. the basic trust that most citizens have for their State and local governments

24. **Analyze Cartoons** Based on Document B, what idea is the cartoonist trying to convey?

25. How might the author of Document C respond to the actions described in Document D?
    A. The goal of saving lives is more important than worries about our civil liberties.
    B. The American people are tired of restrictions and have every right to ignore these new rules.
    C. Considering the failure of earlier restrictions, these tighter restrictions will be of little help.
    D. The governor must be careful not to overreact and impose overly restrictive limits on people.

26. **Writing Task** In your opinion, did State governments overstep the authority granted to them by the police power or did they not go far enough in their response to the pandemic? Use these sources as well as additional information you have learned about the pandemic in your answer.

Comparative Political Systems

ESSENTIAL QUESTION What Makes a Government Successful?

Great Hall of the People, Beijing, China

Royal crowns, palaces, ladies-in-waiting, coats of arms—these things aren't relics of the past, but the current-day trappings of the royalty that still reigns in many countries. Some monarchs have little power; others rule with absolute authority.

In this Topic, you'll learn about different forms of government around the world. Those forms of government sometimes change, depending on how their leaders handle challenges. What about monarchies? Are they still relevant today?

Explore economic development in North and South Korea.

 BOUNCE to Activate My Story Video

In this Topic, you will learn about the various types of governments in the world today. You will also take an in-depth look at the governments of three countries—the United Kingdom, China, and Russia—and compare them to the United States. Look at the lesson outline and explore the infographic. As you study this Topic, you can work on your Quest Inquiry.

LESSON OUTLINE

14.1 Democracy and the Changing World

14.2 The United Kingdom

14.3 The Russian Federation

14.4 China

WHAT MAKES DEMOCRACY SUCCEED?

FACTORS	WHY THEY MATTER
A FREE PRESS	The media reports on the government's actions and regularly communicates ideas for change
MULTIPLE PARTIES	Competition forces the government to listen to voters
CIVILIAN CONTROL OF THE MILITARY	Clear control prevents the military from taking power
ECONOMIC OPPORTUNITY FOR ALL	Education and hard work reward people for working within the law
PROFESSIONAL CIVIL SERVICE	Bureaucrats are less likely to be corrupt and keep government functioning when changes in leadership occur
COMMON TRUST AMONG CITIZENS	Everyone shares a wish for the government to thrive and settle disputes peacefully

Inquiry Center

Want to become an active and effective citizen? Make a difference in your community and beyond by using the **Inquiry Center** on the digital course.

Connect with issues you're passionate about by using the **Interest Finder**.

Investigate public policies, get involved in your community, influence public opinion, and develop leadership skills.

Synthesize the work you've done and what you've learned along the way.

Demonstrate what you've learned once you've finished your project by sharing your work.

14.1

Germans celebrate the fall of the Berlin Wall in 1989. The wall stood for 28 years, dividing communist and democratic states; its fall was a symbol of Germany's transition to democracy.

 BOUNCE to Activate Flipped Video

Objectives

Examine how regimes can make transitions to democracy.

Analyze why some countries experience setbacks or failed transitions to democracy.

Explain the factors necessary for democratic consolidation to take place.

Describe democratic change and continuity in selected countries today.

Key Terms

democratization
hard-liner
reformer
democratic
 consolidation
failed state
Lech Walesa
Nelson Mandela
Mikhail Gorbachev
Boris Yeltsin

Democracy and the Changing World

We tend to categorize countries as complete opposites: democratic or undemocratic. But such a clear distinction overlooks more subtle differences in the way the world's nations are governed. The CIA's World Factbook lists 31 different types of governments, including such entries as ecclesiastical (a government administered by a church), found in Vatican City in southern Europe, and sultanate (a government in which the supreme power is in the hands of a sultan, the head of a Muslim state), found in the Southeast Asian country of Brunei.

Transitions to Democracy

A country can be a *monarchy*, meaning it is ruled by a monarch—usually a king, queen, prince, or emperor—or a *constitutional monarchy*, meaning the monarch's powers and responsibilities are defined in written law or by custom.

All this is to say that along the route from authoritarianism to full democracy lie many varieties of government. In this topic, you will examine several of them.

Democratization refers to the change from dictatorship to democracy and is marked by the holding of free and fair elections. The digital age has allowed pro-democracy advocates to bring international pressure to bear on dictators. This internal and external pressure may pit ruling **hard-liners**, who often blame foreign enemies or internal critics for undermining the state, against ruling **reformers**, who may recognize the need to relinquish at least some power.

This is why the small step of recognizing an opposition leader or party is actually a significant step toward democracy. This may pressure governing institutions to reform without fundamentally undermining the social order. In fact, some of the most important reformers, such as **Lech Walesa** in Poland in the 1980s and **Nelson Mandela** in South Africa in the 1990s, have bargained with ruling reformers even though they had earlier been punished or imprisoned by the government. Each later won election to lead their country.

☑ **INFER** How have the Internet and globalization contributed to other countries' transition to democracy?

Examples of Transitions to Democracy

We often forget that even the American democratization process required time, reconsideration, and institutional tinkering. The Framers of the Constitution reworked our democracy after the Articles of Confederation faltered, and we have subsequently become more democratic by expanding the vote to Black Americans, women, and eighteen-year-olds. Most Americans agree that still more work needs to be done.

As political scientist Samuel Huntington argued, democratization has come in waves. The first involved North America and many northern European democracies and began in the 1800s. The second came after World War II. This time Italy, Japan, Germany, and others became strong democracies. Another wave began in the 1970s with

southern European countries like Portugal, Spain, and Greece successfully democratizing. Democracies also developed in Central and South America, in Africa and Asia, and in eastern and central Europe.

The Soviet Union and Russia The Russian Revolution in 1917 led to the creation of a communist country, the Soviet Union. The new authoritarian government used terror and other tactics to control and weaken the people. It "purged" many Communist Party members for supposed disloyalty, forcing them from the party or arresting and even executing them. It also arrested huge numbers of perceived opponents, then sent them to prison camps or killed them. It murdered those considered "class enemies," such as wealthy peasants known as *kulaks*. The government also seized private land and businesses, imposed censorship, and punished those who spoke out against its actions. It persecuted religious groups and sometimes imprisoned or killed religious leaders.

After World War II, the Soviet Union set up communist regimes in countries across Eastern Europe. They banned other parties and took total control. To hold onto power, communist governments jailed or harassed critics, spied on citizens, and set up pro-communist education and media. They banned people from leaving the Soviet Union as another way to exert power and control.

Despite the danger, citizens in these countries resisted the Soviets. Pro-freedom movements were quashed by Soviet troops in Hungary in 1956 and Czechoslovakia in 1968, and by martial law in Poland

Germany's Path to Democracy

1933
Hitler becomes chancellor.

1939–1945
Invasion of Poland triggers World War II.

1955
West Germany joins NATO; East Germany joins Warsaw Pact.

1969
Social Democrat Willy Brandt becomes chancellor and seeks better ties with East Germany.

1987
East German leader Erich Honecker pays a first official visit to West Germany.

1990
Helmut Kohl leads a reunified Germany.

1930   1950   1970   1990

1945
German army defeated.

1949
Germany is divided. Western Germany becomes the Federal Republic of Germany; Eastern Germany becomes the German Democratic Republic.

1961
Construction of the Berlin Wall.

1973
East and West Germany join the United Nations.

1989
Berlin Wall is torn down.

1991
Parliament names Berlin the new capital.

>> It took time for Germany to consolidate under one new form of government.
Analyze Charts What factors might have been most challenging for citizens during this time?

in 1981. People in communist East Germany risked their lives to flee to non-communist West Germany for freedom and opportunity.

Economic stagnation, external pressure from the West, and internal dissent eventually eroded Soviet rule. In the 1980s, reformer **Mikhail Gorbachev** became the leader of the Communist Party in the Soviet Union. He instituted new policies, including *perestroika*, a wide-ranging restructuring of political and economic life, and *glasnost*, a policy of openness and greater tolerance of dissent. When protesters in Eastern Europe demanded change, Gorbachev refused to use force to support the communist governments in these countries. As a result, the governments of East Germany, Poland, Hungary, and Czechoslovakia collapsed and democratic elections were held.

Changes occurred rapidly after **Boris Yeltsin** was elected president of Russia, a republic within the Soviet Union, in 1991. When communist officials attempted to overthrow Gorbachev, Yeltsin led massive protests and these hard-liners surrendered. Each of the Soviet republics declared their independence from the Soviet Union that autumn, and by 1992, the Soviet Union had ceased to exist.

"So, how should we play this — capitalism or socialism?"

>> Transitions in government can result in many new choices for citizens. **Analyze Political Cartoons** What is the cartoonist saying about the public's perception of options for government?

Illegitimate Power Some African, Asian, and Latin American dictators used illegitimate forms of power to gain and hold office in the 20th century. Civil war, poverty, instability, corruption, and other problems created conditions that this type of ruler exploited. These tyrants were sometimes supported by other nations, such as the United States or the Soviet Union, as pawns in the cold war struggle between democracy and communism. In other cases, they were backed by a wealthy or religious elite that sought to hold onto economic power.

In the 1960s and 1970s, for example, military governments seized power in Argentina, Brazil, Chile, and elsewhere. Claiming the need to restore order—and supported by the aristocracy and a growing middle class—these governments outlawed political parties, censored the press, and closed universities. In Argentina and Chile, the military imprisoned and executed thousands of dissidents. Others were killed by "death squads" allied to the government.

In Africa, many nations won independence following World War II, but the legacies of colonialism made progress difficult. European-drawn borders that ignored ethnic and other differences, for example, led to conflict and instability. While some new nations prospered, others struggled under military rule or corrupt dictators.

Angola, for instance, is a wealthy nation, and yet more than 40 percent of its people live below the poverty line. Meanwhile, Angola's longtime leader, Jose Eduardo dos Santos, who held the reigns through intimidation and violence for nearly 40 years, used his position to enrich himself and his family.

Many military leaders in Africa, claiming to be motivated by a sense of duty, promised to restore civilian rule once they had achieved stability. Citizens, desperate for order and peace, often welcomed these leaders. In many cases, however, the new governments gave up power only when toppled by force.

In Nigeria, General Ibrahim Babangida promised to step down but annulled the results of free elections. General Sani Abacha, who seized power in 1993, used even harsher methods, silencing critics with violence and subverting due process of law, freedom of the press, and human rights. Other dictators, such as Mobutu Sese Seko in Zaire, often seized power in the midst of turmoil and civil war. Like some other African dictators, Mobutu killed opponents and devastated the economy.

Asia, too, saw dictators seize power in the 20th century. In 1975, Pol Pot became the leader of Cambodia through a violent revolution. During his

WHAT MAKES DEMOCRACY SUCCEED?

FACTORS		WHY THEY MATTER
A FREE PRESS	→	The media reports on the government's actions and regularly communicates ideas for change
MULTIPLE PARTIES	→	Competition forces the government to listen to voters
CIVILIAN CONTROL OF THE MILITARY	→	Clear control prevents the military from taking power
ECONOMIC OPPORTUNITY FOR ALL	→	Education and hard work reward people for working within the law
PROFESSIONAL CIVIL SERVICE	→	Bureaucrats are less likely to be corrupt and keep government functioning when changes in leadership occur
COMMON TRUST AMONG CITIZENS	→	Everyone shares a wish for the government to thrive and settle disputes peacefully

>> Several factors must be in place in order for a democratic system of government to take root and flourish. **Analyze Charts** Which of these factors do you think is most important?

reign, some 1.5 million Cambodians were executed or died from starvation, disease, or forced labor as part of his plan to "restructure" society.

Following independence in the mid-twentienth century, Singapore's autocratic prime ministers limited freedom and allowed little opposition. In North Korea, communist Kim Il-Sung gained power in 1948 and ruled with an iron hand, severely restricting civil rights, limiting travel into and out of the country, and allowing no freedom of the press.

☑ **APPLY CONCEPTS** Provide an example of how a free press is an essential component of a democracy.

Outcomes of Transitions to Democracy

As the challenges of the post-Soviet era transitions demonstrate, ending authoritarian rule does not automatically lead to democracy. Certain factors are necessary for democracy to succeed.

Democratic Consolidation Democratic consolidation occurs when a country firmly establishes the necessary factors for vibrant democracy and social order. These factors include the following: a free press, free and fair elections with a competitive group of political parties, active civic participation, a civilian-controlled military and security force, the rule of law, and human rights protections. Additionally, an economic system that rewards innovation and hard work and a professional civil service implementing governing decisions are needed.

Some of these elements may not be present in the early stages of transition. As Germany and Japan demonstrated after World War II, however, and as many former Soviet bloc nations have shown, these key factors can develop over time.

Most of all, democratic consolidation occurs when a society establishes a sense of common trust among its citizens. Trust is vital because democracy requires that losers of elections accept the outcomes instead of trying to undermine the opponents' newly won democratic institutions. The British have long referred to this as "the loyal opposition."

These factors may not emerge sufficiently even if countries hold elections. Observers worry that Iraq, for example, is failing to develop the needed factors for democratic success. Iraqis have adopted a constitution and held elections. Nevertheless, the lack of trust among Sunni, Shi'ite, and Kurdish religious and ethnic groups has led to continued violence, which, in turn, has stymied progress toward democracy. The rise of the Islamist State in Iraq and Syria (ISIS) has further threatened Iraq's future.

Several countries in Asia made successful moves to democracy in the 1980s and 1990s. Taiwan and South Korea were ruled by authoritarian governments during the cold war. In both countries, members of the middle-class, workers, and students pressured the government to allow democratic reforms. Democracy has remained strong despite a host of challenges, including the transfer of power from one party to another in Taiwan and the impeachment of a president in South Korea.

Some African countries have also made the transition to democracy. South Africa was ruled for decades by its white minority under a system of segregation known as apartheid, which kept whites in power and oppressed the Black African majority. Eventually, protests and international sanctions forced the white government to concede power in the early 1990s. The country wrote a new constitution giving people of all races the right to vote. South Africa has faced serious challenges, too. Corruption, poverty, and inequality remain huge problems. Still, the democratic government has survived.

In the 1980s, several South American countries were ruled by military dictators, including Chile, Argentina, and Brazil. In Argentina, a military junta took power in 1976 and waged a "Dirty War," killing, torturing, and arresting thousands. Matters came to a head when Argentina invaded the Falkland Islands, a British island chain off the coast of South America.

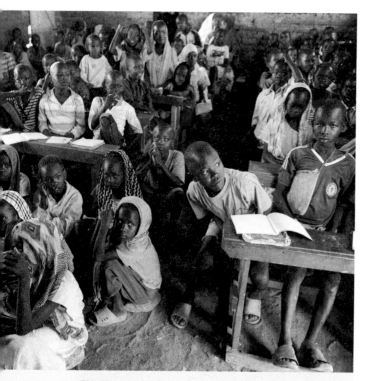

>> The Kakuma Refugee Camp in the Turkana region of Kenya serves tens of thousands of refugees from surrounding failed states.

After Great Britain defeated Argentina, a democratic system was created. In the years since, Argentina's government has weathered serious economic problems, but the country remains democratic.

Failed States Countries such as the Democratic Republic of Congo include large regions that remain outside the control of their own governments. Somalia, in East Africa, does not have a functioning government, and most of the country is ruled by warlords. These countries are known as **failed states.** In most of these areas, security is nonexistent, power is concentrated in a small group, complete disregard for basic human rights is the norm, the economy has collapsed, the healthcare and school systems are in shambles, and corruption flourishes. International terrorist groups have found refuge in these lawless lands and have used them as bases to plan and train for acts of violence.

The South Asian country of Afghanistan, for example, was occupied by the Soviet Union in the 1980s. When the Soviets withdrew in 1989, they left the country utterly devastated. The anarchy in Afghanistan allowed for the rise of the Taliban, a Sunni Islamic fundamentalist movement that gained control of much of the country. The Taliban provided a haven for Osama bin Laden and his al Qaeda terrorists to plan their September 11, 2001, attacks on the United States. In response to those attacks, a coalition of troops led by the United States moved into Afghanistan with the hope of rooting out the Taliban and creating a democratic nation. Two decades later, the United States pulled its troops out of Afghanistan, leaving behind a fragile situation largely due to a resilient Taliban in the region.

Another look at Iraq provides an additional example of the conditions that can lead to tyranny. For decades, the Kurds in Iraq were oppressed by dictator Saddam Hussein. With Hussein gone and the authority of the Iraqi government waning, the prospect of an independent Kurdish nation has grown. Many observers hope democracy will take root there, but huge disparities in wealth, stark religious and cultural differences, a lack of human rights, and growing corruption and competition between regional warlords make this possibility seem remote.

☑ **EXPRESS IDEAS CLEARLY** Why have Iraq and Russia experienced different outcomes in their respective transitions to democracy?

Democratic Change and Continuity Today

Many nations continue to struggle toward democracy and greater protection of human rights. In 2011, a fruit merchant in the North African country of Tunisia protested police bullying and the government's indifference by setting himself on fire. This sparked the Arab Spring, in which mass protests across North Africa and the Middle East unleashed civil unrest, civil war, and the overthrow of oppressive governments.

In Egypt, protestors ousted President Hosni Mubarak and some progress was made toward democracy. When dictatorial leader Mohammed Morsi refused to relinquish power, however, the military cracked down. Egypt, like its neighbors Libya and Syria, has stood up to tyrants but thus far lacks the factors necessary for democratic consolidation.

In Syria, pro-democracy rebels fought a full-scale civil war against President Bashar al-Assad, as well as against Islamist State militants. Libyan rebels ousted and then killed dictator Muammar el-Qaddafi in 2011. Since that time, however, the country has struggled to stabilize. Its government is weak and divided and unable to restrain rival armed militias.

In Southeast Asia, on the other hand, the government and people of Burma (also called Myanmar) have made progress toward democratization. Indicators of this progress in the early 2010s included the release of political prisoners, the unblocking of some Web sites, a lifting of pre-publication censorship for the press, and a move toward competitive national elections. However, accusations of human rights abuses and free speech restrictions have complicated Burma's democratization.

Two other nations that have made huge strides toward democracy are the island nation of Mauritius and the Central American country of Costa Rica. After nearly four centuries of being under the control of one European nation or another, Mauritius gained its independence from Great Britain in 1968. The nation adopted a constitution that protected individual rights, set up a representative system of government, thereby becoming one of the most democratic nations in Africa. Costa Rica was under Spanish control for nearly three centuries. In 1821, it became independent and moved toward democracy. Following a civil war in 1948, Costa Rica has remained stable, prosperous, and free. It consistently ranks high in openness and the protection of individual rights.

Human Rights Policies In all of the cases discussed, the lack of human rights policies—or the lack of enforcement of those policies—in transitioning nations is a leading cause of failed or flagging democratization. The U.S. State Department reports serious human rights abuses in Iraq, Afghanistan, Syria, Somalia, Mexico, Yemen, Burundi, and many other countries, including such violations as limits on freedom of assembly, arbitrary arrests, large numbers of refugees, discrimination against and abuse of women and minorities, trafficking in persons, child soldiers, child labor, corruption, and torture. In China, Egypt, Ethiopia, Iran, Russia, Saudi Arabia, and many other countries, the government stifles freedom of speech and press.

At the same time, progress toward greater protection of human rights has been made around the world. Free and fair elections and peaceful transitions of power took place in India, Indonesia, and Tunisia. Activists and international organizations, such as the United Nations, Amnesty International, and Human Rights Watch, report on human rights abuses and pressure governments to end them. Abuses include the oppression of minority groups and the forced removal or genocide of ethnic, religious, or other populations. The UN, for example, is pressuring the Burmese government to address the ongoing ethnic cleansing taking place in several regions within that nation. Organizations also work to protect civilian populations during wartime, such as relocating victims of the Syrian civil war.

☑ **GENERATE EXPLANATIONS** How might a country that is transitioning to democracy move farther away from democracy instead of closer to it?

☑ ASSESSMENT

1. **Identify Central Issues** For what reasons might a dictatorship change to a democracy?

2. **Hypothesize** What are some significant governmental changes that a country would experience when moving from communism to democracy?

3. **Express Ideas Clearly** Why are democratization and democratic consolidation both important when establishing a new democracy?

4. **Categorize** Was Mikhail Gorbachev a hard-liner or a reformer? Explain your reasoning.

5. **Explain** What factors make the process of forming democratic governments difficult in some Middle Eastern countries, as well as other Asian and African countries?

Queen Elizabeth II visits the maternity ward of a hospital. As the longest-reigning British monarch since Queen Victoria, she has been a steadfast figure in the United Kingdom since 1952.

 BOUNCE to Activate Flipped Video

Objectives

Explain the United Kingdom's legacy of constitutionalism.

Outline the structure of government in the United Kingdom.

Examine public policy and elections in the United Kingdom.

Compare government in the United Kingdom with that of the United States.

Key Terms

constitutionalism
parliamentary system
coalition
ministers
shadow cabinet
common law
devolution
backbenchers
party government

The United Kingdom

No other country has rivaled the democratic durability of the United Kingdom. The United Kingdom is a monarchy, but the royalty lacks any governing power. British democracy seats considerable power in the prime minister, gives political parties substantial power over public policy, and makes elections particularly influential on public policy. Like the United States, the United Kingdom is a prime example of constitutionalism, government in which power is distributed and limited by a system of laws that must be obeyed by its rulers.

A Legacy of Constitutionalism

Americans celebrate Independence Day, and the French celebrate Bastille Day. However, in the United Kingdom, instead of one democratizing moment, British democracy has risen slowly like an incoming tide. In 1215, the king signed the Magna Carta, which assured nobles that the king could not imprison them nor take their land without the support of the noble's peers. This established the idea of limited governance; Parliament would create laws that the monarchy would execute.

The United Kingdom is composed of England, Scotland, Wales, and Northern Ireland. As a set of islands geographically removed from the land wars that plagued the European continent, Britain was able to establish a global empire. Its location also allowed for internal political institutions to develop without the disruption of invasion and war. Consequently, the governing institutions have been set since the 1600s, competitive political parties have been steady since the 1800s, and full voting rights expanded to all Britons by the early 1900s.

☑ **APPLY CONCEPTS** The United States and the United Kingdom are both prime examples of constitutionalism. Explain how constitutionalism is portrayed in the United States.

Government in the United Kingdom

Political observers refer to the United Kingdom as a **parliamentary system**, where the chief executive—the prime minister—is chosen by the Parliament rather than being directly elected. The United Kingdom is a unitary system with governing sovereignty held at the national government level with the Parliament.

Parliament Britain's storied Parliament is the core institution of government. It holds both the legislative and the executive powers of the nation— powers that in the United States are divided between separate branches of the government. It is a bicameral body, made up of the House of Lords and the House of Commons, though only the House of Commons holds true legislative power.

The House of Commons The House of Commons possesses genuine legislative power. It has 650 members who are elected from single-member districts called constituencies. There are now 533 constituencies in England, 59 in Scotland, 40 in Wales, and 18 in Northern Ireland.

The party that controls the most constituencies dominates the House of Commons. On paper, the House of Commons shares similar functions with the United States Congress. It has committees that work on legislation and send it to the entire House of Commons to be voted up or down. However, the work of these committees is mostly limited to providing advice rather than actually writing legislation. Most new laws originate with the government (executive branch) but the House of Commons must debate and vote on those bills. The greatest power the majority party holds is the selection of the prime minister and his or her cabinet.

The House of Lords Until the 1800s, the House of Lords held greater governing power than the House of Commons. Its membership was based on lordships being passed down through heredity. Today, the House of Lords is largely powerless. In fact, the House of Commons eliminated the majority of the House of Lords' hereditary members in 1999. Most of its 800 or so members are appointed by the Queen, on the advice of the prime minister; members are often appointed after lifetime accomplishments in

>> Despite its size, England established the British Empire as a powerful monarchy and colonial network. **Analyze Maps** How did geographic location and a strong navy aid this expansion?

the sciences, literature, arts, politics, or business. The fact that the House of Commons could redefine membership of the House of Lords demonstrates the strengths of each chamber.

The Lords have meager lawmaking power; any measure passed by the Commons but then rejected by the Lords has only to be approved a second time by the Commons in order to become law.

The Prime Minister The prime minister's party both legislates and carries out its policy agenda, unlike the United States, where legislative and executive powers are sharply separated. The source of the prime ministers' powers are party loyalty, merged legislative and executive power, and a clear policy mandate from election results.

Most often, one party wins a majority of the House of Commons. The leader of that party usually becomes the prime minister. The prime minister's roles are many. The main ones are acting as the liaison between Parliament and the Queen, appointing and removing the cabinet and other ministers and government officials, and crafting legislation and policy.

If no single party wins a majority, then two or more parties can form a **coalition**, a temporary alliance of parties for the purpose of forming a government. Coalition government, however, has been rare. Prime Minister Winston Churchill led a coalition government during World War II, and the next such government did not occur until 2010. That year, no single party won a majority in the general election, and the Conservative Party was forced to form a coalition with the Liberal Democrats.

There are no term limits on the post of prime minister. As party leader, chief executive, and a member of the House of Commons, prime ministers dominate Parliament. However, should a prime minister lose the party's support, the party can replace the prime minister without consulting the voters. This happened in 2007, when the majority Labour Party elected Gordon Brown to replace Tony Blair. Most members of Parliament (MPs), however, know that the prime minister has the power to promote them. Thus, their own ambitions can temper any inclination to oppose the prime minister.

In extreme circumstances, the House of Commons can also move a motion of no confidence. If such a motion is agreed to, and a new government supported by a majority of MPs cannot be formed within 14 days, Parliament is dissolved and an early general election is triggered.

This occurs rarely because members of the now-unpopular prime minister's party are unlikely to want to cross the prime minister to face the voters themselves. This means that a prime minister can stay in office unless he or she becomes extremely unpopular. The last vote of no confidence occurred in 1979; the previous one in 1924.

THE GOVERNMENT OF THE UNITED KINGDOM

THE MONARCH
- King or Queen of England
- Head of state
- Performs ceremonial duties
- Lacks governing power

PARLIAMENT

House of Commons
- Elected legislature
- Stronger house
- Chooses prime minister in relation to majority leadership

House of Lords
- Appointed legislature
- Weaker house

THE COURTS

UK Supreme Courts
- Rules on appeals, highest court

Crown & County Courts
- Base decisions on common law and acts of Parliament

>> The government of the United Kingdom is made up of Parliament, the monarchy, the courts, and the regional and local governments. **Analyze Charts** What are the primary responsibilities of Parliament?

Parliamentary Leaders Parliamentary leaders influence how power is distributed, shared, and limited in a parliamentary system. The career of the nineteenth-century British politician William Gladstone provides a good example. In Gladstone's case, support for or opposition to his party and his policies—either from the electorate or within his Liberal Party—led to Gladstone's winning and losing the post of prime minister four times.

In 1874, for example, lacking support for his proposed budget cuts, Gladstone dissolved Parliament and called for an election. His party lost, however, which forced him to step down. Unlike the United States, the prime minister is always the head of the majority party in Parliament. Because his party lost the election, receiving fewer seats than the Conservative Party, Gladstone could no longer be prime minister.

In the following years, Gladstone relentlessly attacked Conservative Party policies. His criticisms were so successful that his party won the election of 1880 and Gladstone was again chosen prime minister. Opposition to Gladstone's policies on critical issues, at times from his own party, led to his loss of leadership again in 1885, 1886, and 1894.

Unlike Gladstone, Margaret Thatcher held the office of prime minister continuously, from 1979 to 1990. Thatcher was the UK's first woman prime minister. She managed to lead her party to two subsequent electoral victories—despite opposition from within the government and the electorate to some of her policies—partly as a result of a weak opposition party. In 1990, however, a faction of her Conservative Party united against her and she was ultimately forced to resign.

To become prime minister, two things must happen: Your party must win a majority of the seats in the House of Commons, and your fellow party members must select you as their leader. Afterward, as these examples show, the prime minister's power is enhanced or limited by a variety of factors. These include his or her own personality, the extent of party unity, shifting party alliances, the popularity of party policies among the voters, the size of the party's majority in the House of Commons, and the strength of the opposition party. As a result of these factors, power can sometimes shift back and forth between the prime minister, the party, and the cabinet throughout a prime minister's time in office.

The Cabinet The prime minister selects the members of the cabinet, or **ministers,** from the House of Commons, although a few may sit in the House of Lords. The prime minister is the leader of the cabinet, or "first among equals." Collectively, the

>> Known at home and abroad as the Iron Lady, Margaret Thatcher held the office of prime minister continuously from 1979 to 1990.

prime minister and the cabinet propose legislation and shape government policy. Cabinet ministers head the various executive departments, such as the Ministry of Defence, HM Treasury, or the Department of Health.

The opposition parties appoint their own teams of potential cabinet members. Each opposition member of Parliament watches, or shadows, one particular member of the cabinet. If an opposition party should win the next election, its so-called **shadow cabinet** would run the government.

The Monarchy Many formal but strictly ceremonial duties are given to the monarchy. For example, the current Queen of England, Queen Elizabeth II, "appoints" the prime minister, but in reality she simply recognizes the election outcome. The Queen opens Parliament with a speech on a yearly basis, but the speech is largely a set of policy goals written by the prime minister. However, as head of state, the Queen provides a significant point of pride. She receives foreign ambassadors, entertains visiting heads of state, and makes state visits overseas. The monarchy is considered to be a point of stability during political or social change, and it supports those who serve others both in the public and volunteer sectors.

>> Justices from the highest court in the United Kingdom, the Supreme Court, head to Westminster Abbey for an annual service marking the beginning of the legal year.

>> Prime Minister Theresa May answers questions from Parliament in the House of Commons. *Prime Minister's Questions,* held every Wednesday at noon, is broadcast live on television.

The Courts No court in the United Kingdom has the power of judicial review—the power to declare a law or its execution unconstitutional, as the Supreme Court does in the United States. There is a United Kingdom Supreme Court that acquired the House of Lords' power of judicial oversight over legislation in 2009, but the House of Commons retains supreme governing power.

The United States court system grew from the system used in the United Kingdom, which decides cases based on **common law**, meaning cases are decided based on judicial precedent. Because there is no singular constitution, weighing decisions based on previous court decisions is vital for British democratic consistency.

For criminal cases and civil suits, the United Kingdom has three separate court systems: one for England and Wales, one in Northern Ireland, and one in Scotland. In England and Wales, most civil cases are tried in county courts. The more serious criminal cases and civil disputes are tried in the Crown Court. Less serious criminal cases are tried in the magistrates' courts. The court system in Northern Ireland is similar, whereas the Scottish system is simpler, with fewer layers.

Regional and Local Government As a unitary government, ultimate sovereignty belongs to the United Kingdom Parliament. To whatever extent local governments do govern, they can do so only because the central government has created them, given them powers, and financed them.

Because of their historical and cultural differences, Parliament recognized the unique governmental needs of Scotland, Northern Ireland, and Wales in the late 1990s. It then began a process of **devolution**—the delegation of authority from the central government back to regional governments. Consequently, the legislatures of these parts of the UK can act independently in some areas. The British Parliament has reserved for itself the exclusive power to legislate on defense, foreign policy, and macroeconomic policies that affect the whole United Kingdom, as well as to govern England.

There are hundreds of local governing authorities of varying types in the United Kingdom. Much as in the United States, local governments in the United Kingdom perform a broad range of functions, from running local schools and libraries to collecting trash and maintaining roads.

☑ **COMPARE POINTS OF VIEW** In the United Kingdom, what are some of the pros and cons of having no term limit for the post of prime minister?

Public Policy and Elections

The seating in the House of Commons suggests how policy is made. The prime minister and cabinet ministers sit in the front bench on one side of the House of Commons across from the shadow cabinet of the main opposition party. Fellow party members sit on benches behind the cabinet ministers or shadow cabinet and are thus referred to as **backbenchers**, who have little or no influence over policy. Government in the United Kingdom is referred to as a **party government**, where a winning party creates and carries out policy based on the party's platform with overwhelming party loyalty. Parties command loyalty because they control nominations and will only select loyal partisans. Also, advancement from the back benches to a ministerial post requires loyal party voting.

Crafting Legislation The prime minister and cabinet craft legislation. Members of Parliament study and challenge their work by considering proposed legislation in detail in the House of Commons committees, debating it in their chambers, and questioning government ministers. One mechanism by which this is done is during Prime Minister's Questions.

These tend to be raucous weekly events with sharply worded questions for the prime minister and government, punctuated by shouts of "here-here" or "boo" as the ministers provide their answers. When policies come to a vote, party loyalty is nearly universal.

Policy gets carried out by a professional civil service. The number of government workers is large compared to the United States because of a sizable military, significant foreign service personnel, and extensive social services—especially since health care is provided by the government.

The Election Process In 2011, the Fixed Term Parliament Act established that a general election—an election in which all the seats in the Commons are at stake—be held the first Thursday in May every five years. Election campaigns last about one month.

Prior to the act, the prime minister often called an election when the political climate favored his or her party. Today, an early election can only be triggered in two ways: 1) by a vote of no confidence (rare), or 2) by a motion for a general election, agreed upon by two-thirds of the Commons.

In the United States, elections tend to be candidate-centered elections, but elections in the United Kingdom are all about parties. People vote and candidates win or lose based on party fortune. Once the results of the general election become official, the head of the winning party is appointed prime minister by the Queen and immediately moves into his or her 10 Downing Street office/home.

Two parties have dominated British politics: the Conservative Party (historically known as the Tories)

>> Seating in the House of Commons is based on how much influence each group holds. Seats surrounding the tables on the floor are for the prime minister, the leader of the opposition, and the cabinet.

and the Labour Party. The Conservatives have long drawn support from middle- and upper-class Britons. They tend to favor free market initiatives over government regulation, though British Conservatives support social welfare programs more than American parties. The working class has regularly supported the Labour Party, which favors government regulation and more social equality policies.

British parties are more highly organized and centrally directed than American political parties. High levels of party loyalty and discipline characterize the British party system. Voters regularly select candidates for the House of Commons on the basis of party membership, not their individual qualifications. Therefore, political party fortunes drive United Kingdom general election results and determine public policy.

☑ **COMPARE AND CONTRAST** Describe the differences between government elections in the United States and those in the United Kingdom.

Comparison to the United States

Given its British origins, it is no wonder that the United States has many similarities to the government of the United Kingdom. Both countries have a large international presence. Both have similar common law judicial systems that rely on precedent from earlier decisions to guide a judge's decisions. Constitutionalism, the rule of law, and recognition of citizen rights play a large part of both democracies.

The two countries differ greatly in regard to many factors, however. First, the United States is a federal system with some areas of policy reserved to States, while the United Kingdom is a unitary system with Parliament having sovereignty over the whole country. The United Kingdom is a parliamentary system where Parliament chooses the prime minister, rather than the executive being publicly elected like the American President.

This provides the prime minister with considerable legislative and executive power. The prime minister dominates Parliament. Consequently, British general elections provide the winning party with absolute policy control. The only real limits on the prime minister and the majority party's

power are a vote of no confidence by the House of Commons (which dissolves Parliament and forces the prime minister to resign) or challenges from the minority party when legislation is being crafted. If the Commons calls for an early election, voters may hand the majority to the opposing party, which they may also do in the regularly scheduled general election. In this case, the new majority party chooses a prime minister.

American Presidents, on the other hand, are elected separately from Congress, cannot directly write legislation, and are closely checked by Congress. Further, the President is both head of state and head of government. He must represent the American public, much like the British Queen. This means the President cannot be as aggressive politically as is the United Kingdom prime minister, whose only role is head of government.

Britain's government is a party government. Parties dominate by selecting House of Commons candidates and persuading them to always vote for their party's position. The U.S. Congress is not nearly as party oriented, although recently there has been polarization among American parties. Additionally, American party nomination is left up to the public; and at times, one party does not have control over the governing agenda.

☑ **COMPARE AND CONTRAST** What are the pros and cons to having a separate head of government and head of state?

☑ ASSESSMENT

1. **Explain** Describe the United Kingdom's legacy of constitutionalism.

2. **Describe** Describe the structure of the United Kingdom's Parliament.

3. **Explain** How are elections held and positions filled in the United Kingdom's Parliament?

4. **Compare** What are some of the similarities between the governments of the United States and the United Kingdom?

5. **Explain** Why did the United Kingdom decide to allow for regional governments in Scotland, Wales, and Northern Ireland?

Prime Minister Vladimir Putin (right) of Russia reversed many democratic reforms of the 1990s and effectively chose his own replacement as president, Dmitry Medvedev.

The Russian Federation

The Russian Federation is an enormous country that straddles Europe and Asia. The country is relatively young, but its history affects its contemporary form and practice. The government is considered a semi-presidential system. The president is elected separately from the legislature, the Federal Assembly. The president also appoints a prime minister to lead government. The president holds considerable power over government.

Russia and Its History

As its name suggests, Russia is a federal system with many regional governments of differing types. Russia remains an international power whose democratic development, especially the rule of law and constitutional rights, has not matched that of consolidated democracies according to critics.

The Bolshevik Revolution The Russian empire was formally established by Peter the Great in 1721. A succession of tyrannical czars ruled the empire until its collapse after heavy losses in the Russo-Japanese War (1904–1905) and World War I (1914–1918).

In the wake of World War I, a revolution in March 1917 forced the abdication of Czar Nicholas II, and the fluid situation ultimately led to the Bolshevik Revolution led by **Vladimir Lenin** on November 7, 1917. Lenin was the architect of the Communist Party and its control over what became the Soviet Union, which transformed Russia from an underdeveloped, tradition-bound country into the world's first communist state.

🅑 BOUNCE to Activate Flipped Video

Objectives
Examine Russia and its history since the Bolshevik Revolution.

Outline the structure of Russia's government.

Examine how public policy is created in Russia.

Compare government in Russia with that of the United States.

Key Terms
purge
Vladimir Lenin
Josef Stalin
Vladimir Putin

Stalin Josef Stalin became the Soviet leader after Lenin's death in 1924 and consolidated his power in a series of **purges**, "purifying" governing power by removing rivals. Stalin ruthlessly jailed millions of people in forced labor camps, and millions of others were exiled, executed, or died of famine in the 1930s and 1940s. Through an intensive and brutal program of industrialization and forced collectivization of agriculture, he built the Soviet Union into a major industrial and military power, but at a huge cost in lives and freedom.

The Soviets suffered staggering losses in World War II. But at war's end, they controlled all of Eastern Europe and emerged as one of the world's two superpowers. Rivalry with the United States and an aggressive foreign policy brought on the cold war, which lasted from the late 1940s until the early 1990s.

Soviet Government The Soviet Union—officially, the Union of Soviet Socialist Republics (USSR)—comprised 15 republics, each inhabited by a major nationality group, such as Georgians or Tajiks. The largest and most important of the republics was Russia, which comprised over 70 percent of Soviet land area and more than half of its population. Soviet government had many layers, but the real power of Soviet government stemmed from the top Communist Party leadership.

From the revolution of 1917 until 1990, the Communist Party of the Soviet Union (CPSU) was the only political party in the Soviet Union. At the top of the party was the general secretary, who held the top post in government and headed the Politburo (political bureau), whose experienced and powerful party leaders held key government posts.

The Central Committee involved broader Communist Party officials and elected the Politburo. The Supreme Soviet served as the legislative body, but it met infrequently to simply rubber-stamp the decrees of the Politburo and general secretary.

Reform Led by Gorbachev When Mikhail Gorbachev became general secretary of the party in 1985, he undertook a reform program that rested on the principles of *perestroika*, the restructuring of political and economic life, and *glasnost*, the policy of openness under which the government increased its tolerance of dissent and freedom of expression.

Gorbachev created a new legislative body, the Congress of People's Deputies, two-thirds of whom were elected by competitive elections. Gorbachev also took over the new office of president of the Soviet Union, which replaced the general secretary as governing leader. These reforms eroded the Communist Party's power. As a result, non-communist candidate Boris Yeltsin won the presidency of the Russian Republic.

Districts of the Russian Federation

>> The Russian Federation has a land area of 6,592,735 square miles and covers one-eighth of the world's land surface. **Analyze Maps** Why do you think the size of each district differs so greatly?

Throughout this time, a wave of democratization flowed across the Soviet bloc, beginning with the fall of East Germany's communist government in November 1989. By 1992, each Soviet republic claimed its independence, and the USSR ceased to exist, leaving the Russian Republic's government sovereign over Russia.

The transition to a democratic Russian Federation was not easy. President Yeltsin's market reforms were controversial and unpopular with many leaders of the Russian Parliament. Yeltsin dissolved the Parliament in 1993, despite dissolution not being a presidential power. In turn, parliamentarians impeached Yeltsin and selected their own president. The situation deteriorated; ultimately, the military intervened to attack the parliamentary building and arrest the parliamentarians in October 1993. Subsequently, the Russian Federation ratified a new constitution in December 1993.

☑ **SUMMARIZE** Describe how Russia changed between the Bolshevik Revolution and the 1980s.

Government in the Russian Federation

A new constitution was approved in a national referendum in late 1993. It proclaims the Russian Federation to be "a democratic federal legally-based state with a republican form of government." As constitutions do, it ensures an extensive list of individual rights, including guarantees of freedom of speech, press, association, and religious belief. The constitution also assures every citizen a right to freedom of movement within the federation, housing, and free medical care and education. Critics have questioned whether many of these liberties have been sufficiently protected from the state. The 1993 constitution also sets out a new government structure that provided significant power to the Russian presidency, which has grown based on the governing practices of Boris Yeltsin and **Vladimir Putin.**

The Executive Branch The Russian executive branch is similar to the French system. A presidential election determines the head of state. The executive is semi-presidential because a second key executive position is the prime minister. It is the prime minister who heads the government, the group of key executive ministers and advisors who create and execute policies passed by the Russian Parliament.

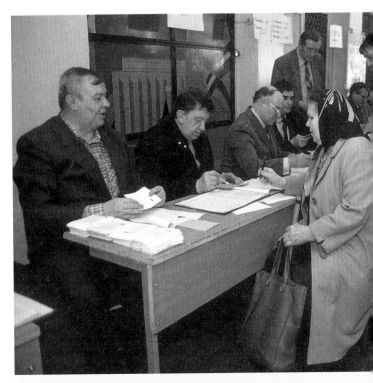

>> A woman votes on a referendum in Moscow on April 26, 1993. Later the same year, Russians voted in favor of a new constitution.

The exact power divide between the president and prime minister is not entirely clear for two reasons. First, presidents appoint prime ministers, but there are few constitutionally detailed policy powers specified for each office. Second, the practice of presidential control over the prime minister has been inconsistent. Russia's first president after the adoption of the new constitution in 1993, President Yeltsin, named and fired prime ministers frequently. Vladimir Putin then ascended to the presidency from prime minister and held tight power over the prime minister.

Complicating things further, Putin became prime minister when his two-term limit as president expired in 2008. He supported Prime Minister Dmitry Medvedev's presidential candidacy and then became prime minister. Most observers felt that Putin retained real governing power. He again won the presidency in 2012, with Medvedev returning to the prime minister post.

The Presidency The 1993 constitution created a government built on a separation of powers between executive and legislative branches, but in reality the constitution gives the president the most crucial governing role. The president has strong powers as commander in chief and is supposed to define "the basic directions of domestic and foreign policy" according to the constitution.

The president is elected by direct popular vote and may not serve more than two consecutive terms. The presidential term was changed from four to six years in 2008, under Dmitry Medvedev. He or she must be a Russian citizen, at least thirty-five years old, and a resident of Russia for 10 years.

Some argued that the ordered society that centralized leadership brought Tsarist and Soviet-era Russia meant strong presidents would be favored in Russian governance. Such observers believed that Putin was not a dedicated democrat and was bent instead on what came to be called "Putinism"—the creation of a one-party state fueled by impressive economic growth. Later events proved those concerns to be valid and in fact, restrictions on freedom of the press and the suppression of civil liberties also became characteristics of Putinism.

The Prime Minister The prime minister leads the government and carries the administration's programs to Parliament. He or she is second-in-command of the executive branch and first in line of succession. The prime minister often is the administrator of the president's policy goals; he or she does not create or implement policy alone, however. Because of the president's power, the prime minister tends to have considerable influence over the Russian legislature.

The Legislature: Federal Assembly Russia's legislature, the Federal Assembly, is a bicameral body. Its upper house, the Federation Council, is composed of 166 members, two members from each of Russia's eighty-three constituent regions. The lower house, the State Duma, has 450 members. Parties compete nationwide for Duma seats, while the Federation Council members are selected by each region.

The Duma is the more powerful chamber. Any measure passed by the Duma but rejected by the Federation Council may nonetheless become law if it is passed again by the Duma by at least a two-thirds majority. The Duma also must approve the president's choice of a prime minister. Presidential vetoes can be overridden by a two-thirds vote in each house.

Constitutional Court A nineteen-member Constitutional Court can rule on the constitutionality

ORGANIZATION OF RUSSIAN FEDERATION GOVERNMENT

PRESIDENT
- Head of state and commander-in-chief
- Drives domestic and foreign policy
- Appoints prime minister
- Appoints ministers

NOMINATES →

PRIME MINISTER
- Second in command
- First in line of succession
- Chairman of parliament
- Administrator of president's policies

NOMINATES

FEDERAL ASSEMBLY
- Must pass legislation to negate a presidential decree
- President's vetoes can be overridden by a two-thirds vote in each house

FEDERATION COUNCIL • Selected by region

STATE DUMA
- National popular election for seats
- May pass laws rejected by Federal Council

CONFIRMS

CONSTITUTIONAL COURT
- Interprets constitution
- Rules on the constitutionality of laws
- Rules on issues of civil liberties

Source: The Telegraph: Russia Now

>> Both the Russian Federation and the U.S. governments have three independent branches and a bicameral legislature. **Analyze Charts** How do the Presidents' interactions with their assemblies differ?

of federal laws, regional laws, and situations of civilian liberties. The Constitutional Court is the body to interpret the constitution, but it tends not to challenge the power of the presidency.

The criminal and commercial courts do not hold much power. Most judicial power comes from procuracy, the government bureau charged with ensuring legality, which holds considerable power over criminal investigations and ultimately controls the business before the courts.

Regional and Local Governments Regional governments in Russia are a patchwork of different organizational structures. The Russian Federation is made up of forty-six *oblasts* (provinces) and nine large, thinly populated territories, all of which are headed by elected governors. The governors of these regions have traditionally exercised great power.

The federation also includes twenty-one republics, which are home to ethnic, non-Russian minorities, and several autonomous areas. Each republic elects a president. Independence is a burning issue in some republics. In particular, the Republic of Chechnya attempted to break away from the Russian Federation in 1994, and the Russian military invaded and occupied the region. It has since battled Chechen rebels, who have launched numerous terrorist attacks.

Political Parties The one-party system of the Soviet era has given way to a multiparty system. In the 1990s, the Communist Party did rather well, as did the right-wing nationalist Liberal Democratic Party. With the emergence and popularity of Vladimir Putin, the United Russia party has become the dominant party in both elections for the Duma and presidency.

☑ **SUMMARIZE** What is the structure of the Russian executive branch, and what powers does it exert?

Public Policy Creation

The Russian presidency drives much of the Russian Federation's public policy. Further, the president holds considerable foreign policy powers and powers as commander in chief.

The constitutional powers and practice of presidents have given Russia's presidents considerable power to set policy by decree. In other words, unlike in the United States, Russian presidents can order the government to carry out a policy of the president's choice, and the legislature

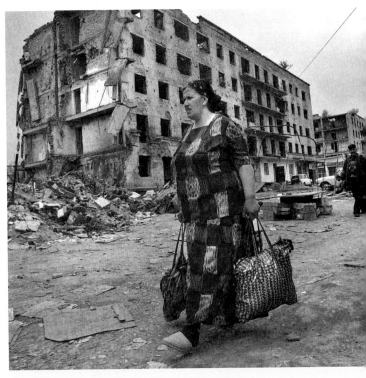

>> Residents walk through Grozny, the capital of Chechnya. While democratic principles are strong throughout the Federation, some areas, like Chechnya, continue to struggle with rebellion.

>> The Udmurtneft oil field is Russia's largest venture with China. Putin has gained support for his presidency by improving Russia's economy and, as a result, the daily lives of its people.

must pass legislation should they want to negate the decree. Further, presidents can offer amendments to legislation coming from the Federal Assembly that can become law with a simple majority of the Duma and Federation Council.

Vladimir Putin has increased presidential power based on his own popularity and his party's electoral success. Putin returned some stability to Russian life. The economy was also bolstered by rising profits from Russian oil and gas exports. Putin's United Russia party provides his policy agenda with great support in the Federal Assembly.

☑ **APPLY CONCEPTS** Describe how public policy is created in the Russian Federation. What role does the president play? The legislature?

Comparison to the United States

The United States and Russia share some distinct similarities. As a former superpower in Soviet times, Russia retains an enormous international role and has a powerful military.

Both countries are also federal democracies with far-flung and diverse regional governments. Both have separately elected presidents, though the Russian system includes a prime minister. Both the United States Congress and the Federal Assembly are bicameral institutions with the United States Senate and the Federation Council built to represent regions—or States—with equal representation, rather than being composed by population.

The similarities between the presidencies and the legislatures are offset by key differences in these institutions. Russian presidents have far more policy control than American Presidents based on institutional powers and in practice. The Russian president's control over the prime minister and government help to control the legislative agenda to a much greater extent. Also, Russian presidential decrees go further and have fewer checks than executive orders from American Presidents.

American political culture guards against centralization of power, as witnessed by America's Federal Government having considerable checks and balances. Russian political culture appreciates strong centralized leadership. This does not mean that Tsarist Russian or Soviet Russian authoritarianism is likely; rather, Russians prefer strong leaders and will vote them in with a mandate to government. Consequently, other actors like interest groups and the media that affect American politics significantly lack major influence in Russia.

☑ **COMPARE AND CONTRAST** Compare and contrast the president of the Russian Federation and the President of the United States. Which president has more power? Explain.

Comparing United States and Russian Legislatures

UNITED STATES		RUSSIA	
Senate Upper House	House of Representatives	Federation Council	State Duma
• 100 members: 2 senators from each State • 6-year terms • Popularly elected	• 435 members • Seats are distributed among the States based on their populations • 2-year terms • Popularly elected • Speaker of the House elected by the representatives • Elections held to fill vacancies	• 166 members: 2 members from each of Russia's 83 constituent regions • Selected by region • Not directly elected	• 450 members • Parties compete nationwide for seats • Popularly elected • More powerful chamber • Any measure rejected by Federal Council can become law if passed again by Duma by 2/3 majority • Duma approves president's choice of prime minister

SOURCE: The United States Senate; the United States House of Representatives; the Federal Assembly of the Russian Federation

>> While both countries' legislatures appear organizationally similar, there are notable differences. **Analyze Charts** How is popular representation different for the two legislatures?

☑ ASSESSMENT

1. **Generate Explanations** Who was Mikhail Gorbachev, and what was his contribution toward the development of the Russian Federation?

2. **Summarize** Describe Russia's transition to democracy, including the changes in Russian leadership from the 1980s to today.

3. **Apply Concepts** Describe the government in the Russian Federation, as set forth in the constitution of 1993 and in practice. Where is most of the power found?

4. **Explain** Describe the State Duma. How is it formed? What power does it have?

5. **Generate Explanations** Describe the impact Vladimir Putin has had on the Russian Federation. What does "Putinism" refer to?

14.4

Chinese children stand in uniform in front of a picture of Mao Zedong while reading from Mao's "Little Red Book," which included quotations and writings by Mao Zedong.

BOUNCE to Activate Flipped Video

Objectives

Examine China and its history starting with the birth of the People's Republic.

Outline the structure of China's government.

Examine how public policy is created in China.

Compare government in China with that of the United States.

Key Terms

Cultural Revolution
Chiang Kai-shek
Mao Zedong
Deng Xiaoping

China

China's government system is unlike the other countries profiled. China is a communist country with the world's largest population. Despite its geographic size and numerous ethnic groups, China's government is a unitary system with sovereignty held nationally. Regional governments exist but are administration units of the Chinese government rather than autonomous bodies.

China and Its History

Chinese political history is very long and its recent economic and social transformations have been massive. Nevertheless, it remains an undemocratic, single-party system that tightly controls political thought, yet permits major economic freedoms. China's socialist market economy has led to enormous economic, educational, and infrastructure development with economic autonomy, but little citizen influence on governance.

Although the political history of China can be traced back some 5,000 years, the communist People's Republic of China was born in 1949 after decades of civil war. Those years of bitter strife pitted China's Nationalist government, led by **Chiang Kai-shek**, against rebel communists led by **Mao Zedong**. The United States supported Chiang's Nationalist government.

At the same time, Mao organized a patriotic movement that appealed to the Chinese peasantry, whom the Nationalist elite had long ignored. In 1949, Mao's Red Army defeated the Nationalists, who fled to Taiwan, and renamed mainland China as the People's Republic of China.

China Under Mao Mao was determined to increase agricultural and industrial production. He turned to central planning and instituted a series of Five-Year Plans. In 1958, Mao began the Great Leap Forward, an unsuccessful campaign to develop rural China. The Great Leap Forward led to horrendous famine, during which millions of Chinese peasants died.

By the mid-1960s, Mao pursued a **Cultural Revolution,** where young dedicated Red Guards attacked and bullied teachers, intellectuals, and anyone else who seemed to lack revolutionary fervor. Artists and scholars were sent to farms to be "re-educated"; ancient books and art were destroyed. Millions were beaten, tortured, and executed.

Reform and Repression Deng Xiaoping

came into power after Mao's death in 1976. As the new leader of the Chinese Communist Party, Deng embarked on what is known as the Four Modernizations to strengthen agriculture, industry, technology, and defense. He reversed the trend of state centralization and lessened the party's focus on class struggle to allow for looser government control of the economy and to encourage some forms of private enterprise.

Although the Chinese government relaxed economic controls under Deng, it tolerated no political dissent. In May 1989, some 100,000 students and workers occupied Beijing's Tiananmen Square, demanding democratic reforms. Their demonstrations were soon crushed, however. Chinese troops and tanks moved into the square, killing hundreds of protestors and maiming thousands more. Democratic governments continue to raise concerns over China's record of human rights.

The economic growth in the quarter-century since Tiananmen Square has overshadowed the lack of democratic freedoms for Chinese citizens in the eyes of many international actors. China has grown to the world's second largest economy. As the government has permitted migration from rural to urban areas, Chinese cities have boomed while agricultural land is limited and rural poverty remains high.

Additionally, the successful reforms that Deng Xiaoping undertook became a lesson for subsequent Chinese Communist Party leaders. Each successive generation has chosen new avenues for economic reform, even if the economic freedoms that they produce have not translated into political freedoms.

☑ **IDENTIFY CAUSE AND EFFECT** Explain one reason why Mao Zedong and his rebel communists were able to defeat Chiang Kai-Shek and the Nationalist government.

Government in China

When the communists gained power, the People's Political Consultative Conference adopted a provisional constitution. That document became the basis for a new constitution adopted by the first session of the National People's Congress in 1954.

Unlike the Constitution of the United States and those of most other nations, China's constitution is not intended to be fundamental law. Instead, it is supposed to reflect current governmental policies. China has had four constitutions since its founding—in 1954, 1975, 1978, and 1982.

China's Communist Party China remains a communist state. The role of the Communist Party is not to mobilize people to vote; even though the Chinese Communist Party is the world's largest party with tens of millions of members, its membership is only about six percent of the Chinese public. Rather, the role of the Communist Party is to govern. The top-ranking members of the party hold the highest positions in the government and the military. In short, the Communist Party *is* the government of China.

>> The Forbidden City, located in Beijing, was home to twenty-four emperors over a period of 500 years, beginning with the Ming Dynasty in the early thirteenth century.

The Chinese constitution discusses the "people's democratic dictatorship," which the Communist Party leads. It is a very hierarchical party. Chinese governing institutions and the Communist Party share the same structure, which allows party leadership over those institutions. The Chinese government's main units are the National Party Congress, the Central Committee, the Politburo, and the Secretariat.

The several thousand members of the National Party Congress are chosen by party members throughout China. The Congress meets approximately every five years to elect a Central Committee that meets about once a year. The Central Committee in turn elects the Politburo, which has about 25 members. It is the Politburo that makes party policy. The Secretariat, including the General Secretary, makes the party's day-to-day decisions.

The National Government The national government of China is composed of two main bodies, the National People's Congress and the State Council.

The National People's Congress. The thousands of deputies of the National People's Congress are elected for five-year terms by local people's congresses throughout China. According to the Chinese constitution, the National People's Congress is the highest governmental authority. In reality, however, the Congress has little power. It performs its major function when it passes the policy decisions of the State Council and the Communist Party to the lower levels of government.

The National People's Congress has a Standing Committee with more than a hundred members who work on legislative issues year-round. The Standing Committee has become more influential in recent decades by regularly studying issues and even drafting legislation.

The State Council. The State Council is the main body in the executive branch of Chinese government. It is headed by the premier, who is chosen by the Central Committee of the Communist Party. The premier, several vice-premiers, several members of the state council, and the secretary-general meet regularly as a standing committee. This Standing Committee of the State Council possesses major decision-making authority, and its decisions have the force of law. As is the case with the National People's Congress, the Communist Party directly leads the actions of the State Council.

The Judicial System A nationwide system of "people's courts" deals with both criminal and civil cases. Those courts are supervised by the Supreme People's Court—in effect, the nation's Supreme Court.

GOVERNMENT IN THE PEOPLE'S REPUBLIC OF CHINA

NATIONAL PARTY CONGRESS
- Highest body of the Chinese Communist Party
- Several thousand members
- Elects the 200 Central Committee members
- Central Committee elects the 25 Politburo members
- Politburo makes party policy
- Secretariat makes party's day-to-day decisions

NATIONAL PEOPLE'S CONGRESS
- Less powerful Standing Committee handles legislative issues
- More powerful State Council possesses major decision-making authority and handles executive issues

PEOPLE'S COURTS
- Deal with criminal and civil cases
- Supervised by the higher Supreme People's Court

 >> China's main governing body is the National People's Congress led by the Chinese Communist Party. **Analyze Charts** How is power divided to reflect a hierarchy?

China's Provinces

>> China is a vast country in Asia, encompassing various groups of people and cultures. **Analyze Maps** What are the two largest groups of administrative divisions in China?

Capital punishment may be imposed for conviction of any of a long list of crimes: murder, treason, bribery, embezzlement, smuggling, drug-dealing, and many others. Most of the guarantees to a fair trial known to Western democracies are completely absent from Chinese law.

Local Political Divisions China has a unitary government, with the central government exerting direct control over local subdivisions. Local administrative regions include both provinces and autonomous (independent) regions whose people are mostly ethnic minorities. Hong Kong, which the British returned to China's control in 1997, is a special administrative region of China with its own governor and provisional legislature.

Taiwan When Mao's forces took over the mainland in 1949, Chiang Kai-shek and the Nationalists fled to the island of Formosa (Taiwan), establishing the Republic of China. In the years since, the People's Republic of China came to consider Taiwan one of its provinces, but the people of Taiwan see themselves as independent. This conflict has left the United States in an awkward position of being officially pro-Taiwan, but also recognizing the global power status of the People's Republic of China.

☑ **EXPLAIN** Describe how legislation is created and passed in the Chinese government.

Comparison to the United States

The Communist Party dominates the policy process. Any policy coming from the National People's Congress or the State Council really reflects the policy leadership of the Communist Party. In fact, the Communist Party reviews legislation and can reject it before it can be voted upon. The Communist Party has officials throughout the country. The party holds authority over regional governments, controls their policies, and determines personnel decisions.

Other political actors, such as the media or interest groups seen in constitutional republics like the United States, do not influence governing decisions. In fact, the media is controlled and regulated by the government, which also imposes tight restrictions on the Internet and cell phones. Despite the many difficulties involved in controlling information given modern technologies, China uses

>> Chinese premier Zhou Enlai and President Nixon review the troops at the airport during the arrival ceremony for President Nixon's historic 1972 visit to China.

software to block Web sites that post material the government deems unacceptable, such as those describing the Tiananmen Square demonstration and crackdown. The government also monitors citizens' activity on social media.

In comparison, China's neighbor North Korea imposes even more extreme restrictions. There, few people have any access to the Internet, and those who do can only access approved Web sites. North Korea has even banned its diplomats and other workers abroad from using the Internet, subjecting them to random inspections of their cell phones. In Cuba, an island nation in the Caribbean, people are not allowed to have Internet access in their homes. Instead, they must use government-controlled access points. Cell phone use is also restricted; for example, mobile devices that use GPS are forbidden.

Chinese economic policy has opened up in recent years, and privatization has led to great personal wealth for many Chinese. However, individuals cannot translate this wealth into political power. Further, people lack property rights that exist in constitutional republics, so the Chinese government can seize land for economic development without substantial payment. Such seizures of land have been a controversial issue,

as rural Chinese have increasingly resisted land redevelopment.

There are very few comparisons to draw between American politics and Chinese politics. American politics tends to be decentralized, full of checks and balances, and influenced by multiple actors such as interest groups, the media, and public opinion. Further, Americans tend to distrust political parties and public opinion polls show that they dislike having their political choices limited, even to two parties.

China, on the other hand, is completely governed by a single party, and more specifically by the top level of that party. There are no formal mechanisms for citizens to affect governance or policy, such as multi-party elections. Other forms of influence, such as political protests, usually are not allowed by the government. Any attempts at such gatherings have historically been shut down with force.

Ironically, both countries govern themselves differently but have become increasingly linked internationally. Many of our foreign policy interests conflict with Chinese policy and American criticism of China's human rights record is consistent. Yet both countries' business and trade interests drive them toward closer interactions, even if their relations remain difficult.

☑ **DRAW CONCLUSIONS** What is the purpose of the Chinese government controlling and regulating the media?

☑ ASSESSMENT

1. **Describe** Explain how China's current government was created.

2. **Infer** Why did the United States support Chiang Kai-Shek and the Nationalist Government during the war between the Red Army and the Nationalists?

3. **Explain** Describe the basic structure of China's government.

4. **Apply Concepts** Explain how public policy is created in China's government.

5. **Identify Central Issues** Clearly the governments of both the United States and China are quite different. However, what is one way in which they are linked?

Human Rights in China

For decades the United States, European countries, and nongovernmental organizations have raised concerns over the lack of basic freedoms and other human rights issues in China. Claims have been made about the lack of free speech, freedom of the press, and religious freedom along with accusations of forced labor, wrongful detention, and political repression. China has continually and adamantly denied these allegations. Although, sanctions have been imposed to pressure China and the United Nations has been called upon to take action to hold the Chinese accountable, but the issue remains unresolved.

As you read, look for facts backing up the arguments of each side.

>> A protester in Hong Kong expresses support for Uyghurs in Xinjiang, China.

Primary Source 1

Joint Statement on Xinjiang, U.S. Department of State, March 22, 2021

We, the Foreign Ministers of Canada and the United Kingdom, and the United States Secretary of State, are united in our deep and ongoing concern regarding China's human rights violations and abuses in Xinjiang. The evidence, including from the Chinese Government's own documents, satellite imagery, and eyewitness testimony is overwhelming. China's extensive program of repression includes severe restrictions on religious freedoms, the use of forced labour, mass detention in internment camps, forced sterilisations [sterilizations], and the concerted destruction of Uyghur heritage.

☑ **DRAW CONCLUSIONS** Why is it important that this statement provides an accounting of specific evidence of human rights violations in China?

Today, we have taken coordinated action on measures, in parallel to measures by the European Union, that send a clear message about the human rights violations and abuses in Xinjiang. We are united in calling for China to end its repressive practices against Uyghur Muslims and members of other ethnic and religious minority groups in Xinjiang, and to release those arbitrarily detained.

We underline the importance of transparency and accountability and call on China to grant the international community, including independent investigators from the United Nations, journalists, and foreign diplomats, unhindered access to Xinjiang.

We will continue to stand together to shine a spotlight on China's human rights violations. We stand united and call for justice for those suffering in Xinjiang.

☑ **ANALYZE WORD CHOICE** Why do you think the authors chose to use the phrase "shine a spotlight" in this joint statement?

Primary Source 2

Foreign Ministry Spokesperson's Remarks on the Statement by Friendly Countries in Support of China at the 47th Session of the Human Rights Council, June 22, 2021

[Today,] Belarus delivered a joint speech on behalf of 65 countries, stressing that respect for the sovereignty, independence and territorial integrity of all countries and non-interference in the internal affairs of sovereign states are basic norms governing international relations. The affairs of Hong Kong, Xinjiang and Tibet are China's internal affairs, and the outside world should not interfere. All should abide by the purposes and principles of the UN Charter, respect the right of people of all countries to independently choose the path of human rights development in light of their national conditions, oppose politicizing [making into a political issue] and double standards on human rights issues, oppose politically motivated and groundless accusations against China based on disinformation, and oppose interference in China's internal affairs under the pretext of human rights. . . .

☑ **DETERMINE MEANING** What do you think is meant by "respect the right . . . of all countries to independently choose the path of human rights development in light of their national conditions"?

Issues related to Xinjiang, Hong Kong and Tibet are not human rights issues at all. China has made clear its solemn position on many occasions and given detailed statement of the facts and truth. . . . A handful of Western countries are eager to fabricate and hype up China-related rumors and interfere in China's internal affairs in the name of human rights. . . .

These self-styled "human rights judges" are always eager to lecture others, but choose to turn a blind eye to or downplay their own serious human rights issues. The track records of Canada, the US and the UK are beyond appalling: persecution of indigenous [the earliest known inhabitants of a place] children, widespread police violence, deep-seated racism, proliferation of firearms, frequently occurrence of anti-Semitic, anti-Muslim, anti-African and anti-Asian remarks and incidents, military interventions that lead to serious humanitarian disaster and unilateral coercive measures [actions taken by one side to force its will upon others] that violate the basic human rights in other countries. With such a woeful record, what right do they have to judge the human rights situation in other countries?

☑ **PREDICT** How might the U.S. government respond to the statements made in the last paragraph of Source 2?

☑ ASSESSMENT

1. **Draw Conclusions** Why do you think the United States joined Canada and the United Kingdom in issuing Source 1?

2. **Analyze Word Choices** What words or phrases in Source 2 illustrate the attitude of the Chinese government toward the nations that are critical of them?

3. **Make Connections** Do you consider the examples mentioned in Source 2 to be human rights issues in the United States?

4. **Draw Conclusions** Do you think nations have the right to interfere in the internal affairs of another nation when it comes to dealing with human rights? Why or why not?

GO ONLINE to www.SavvasRealize.com and access your digital course

Use the following online resources to practice citizenship skills and prepare for the Topic Test.

Case Studies

Current Connections

Quest Inquiries

Quizzes

Interactivities

Texts

Flipped Videos

While online you can also check the progress you've made learning the topic and course content by viewing your grades, test scores, and assignment status.

Topic 14 Quick Study Guide

LESSON SUMMARIES

Use these Lesson Summaries, and the longer versions available online, to review the key ideas for each lesson in this Topic.

Lesson 1: Democracy and the Changing World

Democratization is the change from dictatorship to democracy. This process takes time and is not always successful. For democratic consolidation to occur, there must be a free press, free and fair elections with competitive political parties, active civic participation, a civilian-controlled military, the rule of law, human right protections, and mutual trust.

Lesson 2: The United Kingdom

The United Kingdom has a long legacy of constitutional government, like the United States. Unlike the United States, it is a unitary government and has a parliamentary system. Its head of government, the Prime Minister, is chosen by Parliament and not directly elected. It also has a monarch with a ceremonial role.

Lesson 3: The Russian Federation

In the past, tyrannical czars and communist leaders ruled Russia. In 1993, a new, democratic Russian Federation was created. Its president has enormous power, which Vladimir Putin has consolidated. He drives policy for the country. While both Russia and the United States are federal democracies, Russia's presidents have much more power and fewer checks on their authority.

Lesson 4: China

China has a communist government very different from the United States government. It is undemocratic and dominated by the Communist Party. The current government took power under Mao Zedong in 1949. Since the 1970s, China's economy has opened up, but the party retains a tight grip on government.

VISUAL REVIEW

Use these graphics to review some of the key terms, people, and ideas from this Topic.

Changes in China's Government

CHINA UNDER MAO'S RULE
• Central planning; economic chaos • Cultural Revolution

CHINA AFTER MAO
• Economic reforms and growth • Tiananmen Square protests crushed

Russia's History

Russian empire, rule by czars → Bolsheviks seize power

Bolsheviks seize power → Soviet government, rule by Lenin, Stalin and others

Soviet government, rule by Lenin, Stalin and others → *Perestroika* and *glasnost* under Gorbachev

Perestroika and *glasnost* under Gorbachev → Collapse of the Soviet Union

Collapse of the Soviet Union → Russian Federation under Yeltsin and Putin

What Makes Democracy Succeed?

FACTORS	WHY THEY MATTER
A free press	The media reports on the government's actions and regularly communicates ideas for change
Multiple parties	Competition forces the government to listen to voters
Civilian control of the military	Clear control prevents the military from taking power
Economic opportunity for all	Education and hard work reward people for working within the law
Professional civil service	Bureaucrats are less likely to be corrupt and keep government functioning when changes in leadership occur
Common trust among citizens	Everyone shares a wish for the government to thrive and settle disputes peacefully

The United States and the United Kingdom

THE UNITED STATES
• President is head of state and head of government
• President is elected by voters
• Federal system
• Less party oriented

(overlap)
• Democratic system
• Constitutional rule
• Rule of law
• Common law judicial system

THE UNITED KINGDOM
• Monarch is head of state, Prime Minister is head of government
• Prime Minister is chosen by Parliament
• Unitary system
• More party oriented

Topic 14 Assessment

KEY TERMS, PEOPLE, AND IDEAS

1. Describe the process of **democratization**.

2. What is a **parliamentary system**?

3. What is **democratic consolidation**?

4. What is **constitutionalism**?

5. Explain how the United Kingdom's court system decides cases based on **common law**.

6. What is a **failed state**?

7. How did Soviet leader Josef Stalin use **purges** to consolidate his power?

8. What was the **Cultural Revolution**?

CRITICAL THINKING

9. **Contrast** How does China's government differ from the U.S. government? Compare China's National People's Congress to the U.S. Congress.

10. **Interpret** Describe the role of the president in the Russian government. How does this role compare to that of the U.S. President?

11. **Infer** Why does the denial of human rights often accompany a violent change of government?

12. **Explain** Why do authoritarian governments engage in the following behaviors: spying on citizens, preventing citizens from emigrating, jailing or harassing critics, allowing only one political party?

13. **Make Generalizations** Describe the process of democratization in the Middle East, including Iraq and Egypt. How has the process succeeded or failed?

14. **Compare and Contrast** The governments of the United States and the United Kingdom have many similarities, but the two countries differ in a number of ways. Describe these similarities and differences.

15. **Summarize** How do human rights policies in the United States differ from those of Russia and China?

16. **Compare and Contrast** The chart at the top of the next column compares the U.S. and Russian legislatures. How are they similar? How do they differ?

17. **Express Ideas Clearly** Some of the factors that help democracy develop include a free press, a professional civil service, and equal economic opportunity. How do these factors contribute to democracy?

18. **Infer** How have the Internet and social media affected the process of democratization?

19. **Identify Central Issues** Why is having multiple political parties an important part of democracy?

Comparing United States and Russian Legislatures

UNITED STATES	
Senate Upper House	**House of Representatives**
• 100 members: 2 Senators from each State • 6-year terms • Popularly elected	• 435 members • Seats are distributed among the States based on their populations • 2-year terms • Popularly elected • Speaker of the House elected by the representatives • Elections held to fill vacancies
RUSSIA	
Federation Council	**State Duma**
• 166 members; 2 members from each of Russia's 83 constituent regions • Selected by region • Not directly elected	• 450 members • Parties compete nationwide for seats • Popularly elected • More powerful chamber • Any measure rejected by Federal Council can become law if passed again by Duma by 2/3 majority • Duma approves president's choice of prime minister

SOURCE: The United States Senate; the United States House of Representatives; the Federal Assembly of the Russian Federation

20. **Distinguish** How do political parties in China and the United States differ?

21. **Writing Activity** Think about key aspects of democracy, such as tolerance for dissent, political equality, engaged participation, majority rule, minority rights, civil society, individual freedom, the rule of law, an independent judiciary, and civilian control of the military and police. Then research the current situation in Afghanistan, China, Zimbabwe, or Argentina and write an analysis paper in which you use these criteria to evaluate the success of any moves toward democracy in that country.

DOCUMENT-BASED QUESTIONS

The issue of human rights in China has long been a point of contention between that country and the U.S.

DOCUMENT A

This excerpt is from the U.S. State Department's yearly scorecard on human rights in China.

> . . . Authorities resorted to extralegal measures such as enforced disappearance and strict house arrest, including house arrest of family members, to prevent public expression of independent opinions. Authorities continued to censor and tightly control public discourse on the internet. . . .
>
> . . . Other human rights problems during the year included alleged extrajudicial killings, including executions without due process; enforced disappearance and incommunicado detention, including prolonged illegal detentions at unofficial holding facilities known as "black jails"; torture and coerced confessions of prisoners; . . .
>
> —*Country Reports on Human Rights Practices for 2014, U.S. State Department*

DOCUMENT B

International observers note the following major areas of concern in China.

China's Human Rights Record

- Harassment, imprisonment and torture of activists
- Persecution for religious beliefs, including torture
- Discrimination against ethnic minorities
- Torture used on those accused of crimes
- Excessive use of death penalty
- Tight restrictions on Internet and media freedom
- State control of reproductive rights
- Intimidation and arrest of striking workers
- Discrimination against those with disabilities

SOURCE: BBC News, "Human Rights: What Is China Accused of?" October 21, 2015

DOCUMENT C

This excerpt from a Chinese government report cites improvements in its protection of free speech.

> In 2014 China published 46.5 billion copies of newspapers, 3.2 billion copies of periodicals, and 8.4 billion copies of books, with 6.12 copies of books per person. By the end of 2014 the population of netizens in China was 650 million, and the Internet penetration rate was 47.9 percent. Of all the netizens, 508 million were smart phone users. . . . The public can air opinions, and raise criticisms and suggestions freely through the news media, and discuss problems of this country and society. The government encourages enterprises to provide various Internet services to the public in accordance with the law so as to create a good environment for the public to acquire and exchange information.
>
> —*"Progress in China's Human Rights in 2014," Chinese State Council Information Office*

DOCUMENT D

Chinese users of social media must think twice before they post, as this chart shows.

China and Social Media

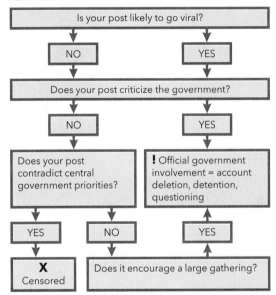

Adapted from: *Foreign Policy*

22. Which of the following does Document C NOT prove?
    A. that the Chinese government does not censor the media
    B. that a large number of books were published in 2014
    C. that nearly 50 percent of China's citizens use the Internet
    D. that there is a large market in China for smart phones

23. What is the meaning of the term *netizen*?
    A. a collection of statistics
    B. a person who uses the Internet
    C. lifetime citizens of a country
    D. a group of media users

24. **Analyze Images** How does the information in Document B relate to that in Document D?

25. **Writing Task** What discrepancies do you find among the information here? Do they all agree on the state of human rights in China? What might this mean?

Constitution Quick Study Guide

Preamble

Articles

Article I. Legislative Department

Section 1.	Legislative Power, the Congress
Section 2.	House of Representatives
Section 3.	Senate
Section 4.	Elections and Meetings
Section 5.	Legislative Proceedings
Section 6.	Compensation, Immunities, and Disabilities of Members
Section 7.	Revenue Bills; President's Veto
Section 8.	Powers of Congress
Section 9.	Powers Denied to Congress
Section 10.	Powers Denied to the States

Article II. Executive Department

Section 1.	Executive Power; The President; Term; Election; Qualifications; Compensation; Oath of Office
Section 2.	President's Powers and Duties
Section 3.	President's Powers and Duties
Section 4.	Impeachment

Article III. Judicial Department

Section 1.	Judicial Power; Courts; Terms of Office
Section 2.	Jurisdiction
Section 3.	Treason

Article IV. Relations Among the States

Section 1.	Full Faith and Credit
Section 2.	Privileges and Immunities of Citizens
Section 3.	New States, Territories
Section 4.	Protection Afforded to States by the Nation

Article V. Provisions for Amendment

Article VI. Public Debts; Supremacy of National Law; Oath

Section 1.	Validity of Debts
Section 2.	Supremacy of National Law
Section 3.	Oaths of Office

Article VII. Ratification of Constitution

Amendments

1st Amendment:	**Freedom of Religion, Speech, Press, Assembly, and Petition**
2nd Amendment:	**Right to Keep, Bear Arms**
3rd Amendment:	**Lodging Troops in Private Homes**
4th Amendment:	**Search, Seizures, Proper Warrants**
5th Amendment:	**Criminal Proceedings, Due Process, Eminent Domain**
6th Amendment:	**Criminal Proceedings**
7th Amendment:	**Jury Trials in Civil Cases**
8th Amendment:	**Bail; Cruel, Unusual Punishment**
9th Amendment:	**Unenumerated Rights**
10th Amendment:	**Powers Reserved to the States**
11th Amendment:	**Suits Against the States**
12th Amendment:	**Election of President and Vice President**
13th Amendment:	**Slavery and Involuntary Servitude**
Section 1.	Slavery and Involuntary Servitude Prohibited
Section 2.	Power of Congress
14th Amendment:	**Rights of Citizens**
Section 1.	Citizenship; Privileges and Immunities; Due Process; Equal Protection
Section 2.	Apportionment of Representation
Section 3.	Disqualification of Officers
Section 4.	Public Debt
Section 5.	Powers of Congress
15th Amendment:	**Right to Vote—Race, Color, Servitude**
Section 1.	Suffrage Not to Be Abridged
Section 2.	Power of Congress
16th Amendment:	**Income Tax**
17th Amendment:	**Popular Election of Senators**
Section 1.	Popular Election of Senators
Section 2.	Senate Vacancies
Section 3.	Inapplicable to Senators Previously Chosen
18th Amendment:	**Prohibition of Intoxicating Liquors**
Section 1.	Intoxicating Liquors Prohibited
Section 2.	Concurrent Power to Enforce
Section 3.	Time Limit on Ratification

19th Amendment:	**Equal Suffrage—Sex**
Section 1.	Suffrage Not to Be Abridged
Section 2.	Power of Congress
20th Amendment:	**Commencement of Terms; Sessions of Congress; Death or Disqualification of President-Elect**
Section 1.	Terms of President, Vice President, members of Congress
Section 2.	Sessions of Congress
Section 3.	Death or Disqualification of President-Elect
Section 4.	Congress to Provide for Certain Successors
Section 5.	Effective Date
Section 6.	Time Limit on Ratification
21st Amendment:	**Repeal of 18th Amendment**
Section 1.	Repeal of Prohibition
Section 2.	Transportation, Importation of Intoxicating Liquors
Section 3.	Time Limit on Ratification
22nd Amendment:	**Presidential Tenure**
Section 1.	Restriction on Number of Terms
Section 2.	Time Limit on Ratification
23rd Amendment:	**Inclusion of District of Columbia in Presidential Election Systems**
Section 1.	Presidential Electors for District
Section 2.	Power of Congress
24th Amendment:	**Right to Vote in Federal Elections—Tax Payment**
Section 1.	Suffrage Not to Be Abridged
Section 2.	Power of Congress
25th Amendment:	**Presidential Succession; Vice Presidential Vacancy; Presidential Inability**
Section 1.	Presidential Succession
Section 2.	Vice Presidential Vacancy
Section 3.	Presidential Inability
26th Amendment:	**Right to Vote—Age**
Section 1.	Suffrage Not to Be Abridged
Section 2.	Power of Congress
27th Amendment:	**Congressional Pay**

The Preamble states the broad purposes the Constitution is intended to serve—to establish a government that provides for greater cooperation among the States, ensures justice and peace, provides for defense against foreign enemies, promotes the general well-being of the people, and secures liberty now and in the future. The phrase We the People emphasizes the twin concepts of popular sovereignty and of representative government.

Legislative Department

Section 1. Legislative power; Congress

Congress, the nation's lawmaking body, is bicameral in form; that is, it is composed of two houses: the Senate and the House of Representatives. The Framers of the Constitution purposely separated the lawmaking power from the power to enforce the laws (Article II, the Executive Branch) and the power to interpret them (Article III, the Judicial Branch). This system of separation of powers is supplemented by a system of checks and balances; that is, in several provisions the Constitution gives to each of the three branches various powers with which it may restrain the actions of the other two branches.

Section 2. House of Representatives

▶ **Clause 1. Election** Electors means voters. Members of the House of Representatives are elected every two years. Each State must permit the same persons to vote for United States representatives as it permits to vote for the members of the larger house of its own legislature. The 17th Amendment (1913) extends this requirement to the qualification of voters for United States senators.

▶ **Clause 2. Qualifications** A member of the House of Representatives must be at least 25 years old, an American citizen for seven years, and a resident of the State he or she represents. In addition, political custom requires that a representative also reside in the district from which he or she is elected.

▶ **Clause 3. Apportionment** The number of representatives each State is entitled to is based on its population, which is counted every 10 years in the census. Congress reapportions the seats among the States after each census. In the Reapportionment Act of 1929, Congress fixed the permanent size of the House at 435 members with each State having at least one representative. Today there is one House seat for approximately every 700,000 persons in the population.

The words "three-fifths of all other persons" referred to slaves and reflected the Three-Fifths Compromise reached by the Framers at Philadelphia in 1787; the phrase was made obsolete, was in effect repealed, by the 13th Amendment in 1865.

---

* The gray words indicate portions of the Constitution altered by subsequent amendments to the document.

▶ **Clause 4. Vacancies** The executive authority refers to the governor of a State. If a member leaves office or dies before the expiration of his or her term, the governor is to call a special election to fill the vacancy.

United States Constitution

PREAMBLE

We the People of the United States, in Order to form a more perfect Union, establish Justice, insure domestic Tranquility, provide for the common defence, promote the general Welfare, and secure the Blessings of Liberty to ourselves and our Posterity, do ordain and establish this Constitution for the United States of America.

Article I

Section 1.

All legislative Powers herein granted shall be vested in a Congress of the United States, which shall consist of a Senate and House of Representatives.

Section 2.

▶ 1. The House of Representatives shall be composed of Members chosen every second Year by the People of the several States, and the Electors in each State shall have the Qualifications requisite for Electors of the most numerous Branch of the State Legislature.

▶ 2. No Person shall be a Representative who shall not have attained to the age of twenty-five Years, and been seven Years a Citizen of the United States, and who shall not, when elected, be an Inhabitant of that State in which he shall be chosen.

▶ 3. Representatives and direct Taxes* shall be apportioned among the several States which may be included within this Union, according to their respective Numbers, which shall be determined by adding to the whole Number of free Persons, including those bound to Service for a Term of Years and excluding Indians not taxed, three fifths of all other Persons. The actual Enumeration shall be made within three Years after the first Meeting of the Congress of the United States, and within every subsequent term of ten Years, in such Manner as they shall by Law direct. The Number of Representatives shall not exceed one for every thirty Thousand, but each State shall have at Least one Representative; and, until such enumeration shall be made, the State of New Hampshire shall be entitled to choose three, Massachusetts eight, Rhode Island and Providence Plantations one, Connecticut five, New York six, New Jersey four, Pennsylvania eight, Delaware one, Maryland six, Virginia ten, North Carolina five, South Carolina five, and Georgia three.

▶ 4. When vacancies happen in the Representation from any State, the Executive Authority thereof shall issue Writs of Election to fill such Vacancies.

5. The House of Representatives shall choose their Speaker and other Officers; and shall have the sole Power of Impeachment.

Section 3.

1. The Senate of the United States shall be composed of two Senators from each State chosen by the Legislature thereof for six Years; and each Senator shall have one Vote.

2. Immediately after they shall be assembled in Consequences of the first Election, they shall be divided, as equally as may be, into three Classes. The Seats of the Senators of the first Class shall be vacated at the Expiration of the second Year; of the second Class, at the Expiration of the fourth Year; and of the third Class, at the Expiration of the sixth Year; so that one-third may be chosen every second Year; and if Vacancies happen by Resignation, or otherwise, during the Recess of the Legislature of any State, the Executive thereof may make temporary Appointments until the next Meeting of the Legislature, which shall then fill such Vacancies.

3. No Person shall be a Senator who shall not have attained to the Age of thirty Years, and been nine Years a Citizen of the United States, and who shall not, when elected, be an Inhabitant of that State for which he shall be chosen.

4. The Vice President of the United States shall be President of the Senate but shall have no Vote, unless they be equally divided.

5. The Senate shall choose their other Officers, and also a President pro tempore, in the Absence of the Vice President, or when he shall exercise the Office of President of the United States.

6. The Senate shall have the sole Power to try all Impeachments. When sitting for that Purpose, they shall be on Oath or Affirmation. When the President of the United States is tried, the Chief Justice shall preside: And no Person shall be convicted without the Concurrence of two thirds of the Members present.

7. Judgment in Cases of Impeachment shall not extend further than to removal from Office, and disqualification to hold and enjoy any Office of honor, Trust, or Profit under the United States: but the Party convicted shall nevertheless be liable and subject to Indictment, Trial, Judgment and Punishment, according to Law.

▶ **Clause 5. Officers; impeachment** The House elects a Speaker, customarily chosen from the majority party in the House. Impeachment means accusation. The House has the exclusive power to impeach, or accuse, civil officers; the Senate (Article I, Section 3, Clause 6) has the exclusive power to try those impeached by the House.

Section 3. Senate

▶ **Clause 1. Composition, election, term** Each State has two senators. Each serves for six years and has one vote. Originally, senators were not elected directly by the people, but by each State's legislature. The 17th Amendment, added in 1913, provides for the popular election of senators.

▶ **Clause 2. Classification** The senators elected in 1788 were divided into three groups so that the Senate could become a "continuing body." One-third of the Senate's seats are up for election every two years.

The 17th Amendment provides that a Senate vacancy is to be filled at a special election called by the governor; State law may also permit the governor to appoint a successor to serve until that election is held.

▶ **Clause 3. Qualifications** A senator must be at least 30 years old, a citizen for at least nine years, and must live in the State from which elected.

▶ **Clause 4. Presiding officer** The Vice President presides over the Senate, but may vote only to break a tie.

▶ **Clause 5. Other officers** The Senate chooses its own officers, including a president pro tempore to preside when the Vice President is not there.

▶ **Clause 6. Impeachment trials** The Senate conducts the trials of those officials impeached by the House. The Vice President presides unless the President is on trial, in which case the Chief Justice of the United States does so. A conviction requires the votes of two-thirds of the senators present.

No President has ever been convicted. In 1868 the House voted eleven articles of impeachment against President Andrew Johnson, but the Senate fell one vote short of convicting him. In 1974 President Richard M. Nixon resigned the presidency in the face of almost certain impeachment by the House. The House brought two articles of impeachment against President Bill Clinton in late 1998. Neither charge was supported by even a simple majority vote in the Senate, on February 12, 1999.

▶ **Clause 7. Penalty on conviction** The punishment of an official convicted in an impeachment case has always been removal from office. The Senate can also bar a convicted person from ever holding any federal office, but it is not required to do so. A convicted person can also be tried and punished in a regular court for any crime involved in the impeachment case.

Section 4. Elections and Meetings

▶ **Clause 1. Election** In 1842 Congress required that representatives be elected from districts within each State with more than one seat in the House. The districts in each State are drawn by that State's legislature. Seven States now have only one seat in the House: Alaska, Delaware, Montana, North Dakota, South Dakota, Vermont, and Wyoming. The 1842 law also directed that representatives be elected in each State on the same day: the Tuesday after the first Monday in November of every even-numbered year. In 1914 Congress also set that same date for the election of senators.

▶ **Clause 2. Sessions Congress** must meet at least once a year. The 20th Amendment (1933) changed the opening date to January 3.

Section 5. Legislative Proceedings

▶ **Clause 1. Admission of members;** quorum In 1969 the Supreme Court held that the House cannot exclude any member-elect who satisfies the qualifications set out in Article I, Section 2, Clause 2.

A majority in the House (218 members) or Senate (51) constitutes a quorum. In practice, both houses often proceed with less than a quorum present. However, any member may raise a point of order (demand a "quorum call"). If a roll call then reveals less than a majority of the members present, that chamber must either adjourn or the sergeant at arms must be ordered to round up absent members.

▶ **Clause 2. Rules** Each house has adopted detailed rules to guide its proceedings. Each house may discipline members for unacceptable conduct; expulsion requires a two-thirds vote.

▶ **Clause 3. Record** Each house must keep and publish a record of its meetings. The Congressional Record is published for every day that either house of Congress is in session, and provides a written record of all that is said and done on the floor of each house each session.

▶ **Clause 4. Adjournment** Once in session, neither house may suspend (recess) its work for more than three days without the approval of the other house. Both houses must always meet in the same location.

Section 4.

▶ 1. The Times, Places and Manner of holding Elections for Senators and Representatives, shall be prescribed in each State by the Legislature thereof; but the Congress may at any time by law make or alter such Regulations, except as to the Places of choosing Senators.

▶ 2. The Congress shall assemble at least once in every Year, and such Meeting shall be on the first Monday in December, unless they shall by Law appoint a different Day.

Section 5.

▶ 1. Each House shall be the Judge of the Elections, Returns and Qualifications of its own Members, and a Majority of each shall constitute a Quorum to do Business; but a smaller Number may adjourn from day to day, and may be authorized to compel the Attendance of absent Members, in such Manner, and under such Penalties, as each House may provide.

▶ 2. Each House may determine the Rules of its Proceedings, punish its Members for disorderly Behavior, and, with the Concurrence of two thirds, expel a Member.

▶ 3. Each House shall keep a Journal of its Proceedings, and from time to time publish the same, excepting such Parts as may in their Judgment require Secrecy; and the Yeas and Nays of the Members of either House on any question shall, at the Desire of one fifth of those Present, be entered on the Journal.

▶ 4. Neither House, during the Session of Congress, shall, without the Consent of the other, adjourn for more than three days, nor to any other Place than that in which the two Houses shall be sitting.

Section 6.

▶ 1. The Senators and Representatives shall receive a Compensation for their Services, to be ascertained by Law, and paid out of the Treasury of the United States. They shall in all Cases, except Treason, Felony, and Breach of the Peace, be privileged from Arrest during their Attendance at the Session of their respective Houses, and in going to and returning from the same; and for any Speech or Debate in either House, they shall not be questioned in any other Place.

▶ 2. No Senator or Representative shall, during the Time for which he was elected, be appointed to any civil Office under the Authority of the United States, which shall have been created, or the Emoluments whereof shall have been increased during such time; and no Person holding any Office under the United States, shall be a Member of either House during his Continuance in Office.

Section 7.

▶ 1. All Bills for raising Revenue shall originate in the House of Representatives; but the Senate may propose or concur with amendments as on other Bills.

▶ 2. Every Bill which shall have passed the House of Representatives and the Senate, shall, before it become a law, be presented to the President of the United States: If he approve, he shall sign it, but if not he shall return it, with his Objections to that House in which it shall have originated, who shall enter the Objections at large on their Journal, and proceed to reconsider it. If after such Reconsideration two thirds of the House shall agree to pass the Bill, it shall be sent, together with the Objections, to the other House, by which it shall likewise be reconsidered, and if approved by two thirds of that House, it shall become a Law. But in all such Cases the Votes of both Houses shall be determined by Yeas and Nays, and the Names of the Persons voting for and against the Bill shall be entered on the Journal of each House respectively. If any Bill shall not be returned by the President within ten Days (Sunday excepted) after it shall have been presented to him, the Same shall be a law, in like Manner as if he had signed it, unless the Congress by their Adjournment, prevent its Return, in which Case it shall not be a Law.

▶ 3. Every Order, Resolution, or Vote to which the Concurrence of the Senate and House of Representatives may be necessary (except on a question of adjournment) shall be presented to the President of the United States; and before the Same shall take Effect, shall be approved by him, or, being disapproved by him, shall be repassed by two thirds of the Senate and House of Representatives, according to the Rules and Limitations prescribed in the Case of a Bill.

Section 6. Compensation, Immunities, and Disabilities of Members

▶ **Clause 1. Salaries; immunities** Each house sets its members' salaries, paid by the United States; the 27th Amendment (1992) modified this pay-setting power. This provision establishes "legislative immunity." The purpose of this immunity is to allow members to speak and debate freely in Congress itself. Treason is strictly defined in Article III, Section 3. A felony is any serious crime. A breach of the peace is any indictable offense less than treason or a felony; this exemption from arrest is of little real importance today.

▶ **Clause 2. Restrictions on office holding** No sitting member of either house may be appointed to an office in the executive or in the judicial branch if that position was created or its salary was increased during that member's current elected term. The second part of this clause—forbidding any person serving in either the executive or the judicial branch from also serving in Congress—reinforces the principle of separation of powers.

Section 7. Revenue Bills, President's Veto

▶ **Clause 1. Revenue bills** All bills that raise money must originate in the House. However, the Senate has the power to amend any revenue bill sent to it from the lower house.

▶ **Clause 2. Enactment of laws;** veto Once both houses have passed a bill, it must be sent to the President. The President may (1) sign the bill, thus making it law; (2) veto the bill, whereupon it must be returned to the house in which it originated; or (3) allow the bill to become law without signature, by not acting upon it within 10 days of its receipt from Congress, not counting Sundays. The President has a fourth option at the end of a congressional session: If he does not act on a measure within 10 days, and Congress adjourns during that period, the bill dies; the "pocket veto" has been applied to it. A presidential veto may be overridden by a two-thirds vote in each house.

▶ **Clause 3. Other measures** This clause refers to joint resolutions, measures Congress often passes to deal with unusual, temporary, or ceremonial matters. A joint resolution passed by Congress and signed by the President has the force of law, just as a bill does. As a matter of custom, a joint resolution proposing an amendment to the Constitution is not submitted to the President for signature or veto. Concurrent and simple resolutions do not have the force of law and, therefore, are not submitted to the President.

Section 8. Powers of Congress

▶ **Clause 1.** The 18 separate clauses in this section set out 27 of the many expressed powers the Constitution grants to Congress. In this clause Congress is given the power to levy and provide for the collection of various kinds of taxes, in order to finance the operations of the government. All federal taxes must be levied at the same rates throughout the country.

▶ **Clause 2.** Congress has power to borrow money to help finance the government. Federal borrowing is most often done through the sale of bonds on which interest is paid. The Constitution does not limit the amount the government may borrow.

▶ **Clause 3.** This clause, the Commerce Clause, gives Congress the power to regulate both foreign and interstate trade. Much of what Congress does, it does on the basis of its commerce power.

▶ **Clause 4.** Congress has the exclusive power to determine how aliens may become citizens of the United States. Congress may also pass laws relating to bankruptcy.

▶ **Clause 5.** has the power to establish and require the use of uniform gauges of time, distance, weight, volume, area, and the like.

▶ **Clause 6.** Congress has the power to make it a federal crime to falsify the coins, paper money, bonds, stamps, and the like of the United States.

▶ **Clause 7.** Congress has the power to provide for and regulate the transportation and delivery of mail; "post offices" are those buildings and other places where mail is deposited for dispatch; "post roads" include all routes over or upon which mail is carried.

▶ **Clause 8.** Congress has the power to provide for copyrights and patents. A copyright gives an author or composer the exclusive right to control the reproduction, publication, and sale of literary, musical, or other creative work. A patent gives a person the exclusive right to control the manufacture or sale of his or her invention.

▶ **Clause 9.** Congress has the power to create the lower federal courts, all of the several federal courts that function beneath the Supreme Court.

▶ **Clause 10.** Congress has the power to prohibit, as a federal crime: (1) certain acts committed outside the territorial jurisdiction of the United States, and (2) the commission within the United States of any wrong against any nation with which we are at peace.

Section 8.

The Congress shall have Power

▶ 1. To lay and collect Taxes, Duties, Imposts and Excises to pay the Debts and provide for the common Defence and general Welfare of the United States; but all Duties, Imposts and Excises, shall be uniform throughout the United States;

▶ 2. To borrow Money on the credit of the United States;

▶ 3. To regulate Commerce with foreign Nations, and among the several States, and with the Indian Tribes;

▶ 4. To establish an uniform Rule of Naturalization, and uniform Laws on the subject of Bankruptcies throughout the United States;

▶ 5. To coin Money, regulate the Value thereof, and of foreign Coin, and fix the Standard of Weights and Measures;

▶ 6. To provide for the Punishment of counterfeiting the Securities and current Coin of the United States;

▶ 7. To establish Post Offices and post Roads;

▶ 8. To promote the Progress of Science and useful Arts, by securing, for limited Times to Authors and Inventors the exclusive Right to their respective Writings and Discoveries;

▶ 9. To constitute Tribunals inferior to the supreme Court;

▶ 10. To define and punish Piracies and Felonies committed on the high Seas, and Offences against the Law of nations;

11. To declare War, grant Letters of Marque and Reprisal, and make Rules concerning Captures on Land and Water;

Clause 11. Only Congress can declare war. However, the President, as commander in chief of the armed forces (Article II, Section 2, Clause 1), can make war without such a formal declaration. Letters of marque and reprisal are commissions authorizing private persons to outfit vessels (privateers) to capture and destroy enemy ships in time of war; they were forbidden in international law by the Declaration of Paris of 1856, and the United States has honored the ban since the Civil War.

12. To raise and support Armies; but no Appropriation of Money to that Use shall be for a longer Term than two Years;
13. To provide and maintain a Navy;

Clauses 12 and 13. Congress has the power to provide for and maintain the nation's armed forces. It established the air force as an independent element of the armed forces in 1947, an exercise of its inherent powers in foreign relations and national defense. The two-year limit on spending for the army insures civilian control of the military.

14. To make Rules for the Government and Regulation of the land and naval Forces;

Clause 14. Today these rules are set out in three principle statutes: the Uniform Code of Military Justice, passed by Congress in 1950, and the Military Justice Acts of 1958 and 1983.

15. To provide for calling forth the Militia to execute the Laws of the Union, suppress Insurrections and repel Invasions;
16. To provide for organizing, arming, and disciplining the Militia, and for governing such Part of them as may be employed in the Service of the United States, reserving to the States respectively the Appointment of the Officers, and the Authority of training the Militia according to the discipline prescribed by Congress;

Clauses 15 and 16. In the National Defense Act of 1916, Congress made each State's militia (volunteer army) a part of the National Guard. Today, Congress and the States cooperate in its maintenance. Ordinarily, each State's National Guard is under the command of that State's governor; but Congress has given the President the power to call any or all of those units into federal service when necessary.

17. To exercise exclusive Legislation in all Cases whatsoever, over such District (not exceeding ten Miles square) as may, by Cession of Particular States, and the Acceptance of Congress, become the Seat of the Government of the United States, and to exercise like Authority over all Places purchased by the Consent of the Legislature of the State in which the Same shall be, for the Erection of Forts, Magazines, Arsenals, Dockyards and other needful Buildings;—And

Clause 17. In 1791 Congress accepted land grants from Maryland and Virginia and established the District of Columbia for the nation's capital. Assuming Virginia's grant would never be needed, Congress returned it in 1846. Today, the elected government of the District's 69 square miles operates under the authority of Congress. Congress also has the power to acquire other lands from the States for various federal purposes.

18. To make all Laws which shall be necessary and proper for carrying into Execution the foregoing Powers and all other Powers vested by this Constitution in the Government of the United States, or in any Department or Officer thereof.

Clause 18. This is the Necessary and Proper Clause, also often called the Elastic Clause. It is the constitutional basis for the many and far-reaching implied powers of the Federal Government.

Section 9.

1. The Migration or Importation of such Persons as any of the States now existing shall think proper to admit, shall not be prohibited by the Congress prior to the Year one thousand eight hundred and eight, but a Tax or duty may be imposed on such Importation, not exceeding ten dollars for each Person.

Section 9. Powers Denied to Congress

Clause 1. The phrase "such persons" referred to slaves. This provision was part of the Commerce Compromise, one of the bargains struck in the writing of the Constitution. Congress outlawed the slave trade in 1808.

Clause 2. A writ of habeas corpus, the "great writ of liberty," is a court order directing a sheriff, warden, or other public officer, or a private person, who is detaining another to "produce the body" of the one being held in order that the legality of the detention may be determined by the court.

Clause 3. A bill of attainder is a legislative act that inflicts punishment without a judicial trial. See Article I, Section 10, and Article III, Section 3, Clause 2. An ex post facto law is any criminal law that operates retroactively to the disadvantage of the accused. See Article I, Section 10.

Clause 4. A capitation tax is literally a "head tax," a tax levied on each person in the population. A direct tax is one paid directly to the government by the taxpayer—for example, an income or a property tax; an indirect tax is one paid to another private party who then pays it to the government—for example, a sales tax. This provision was modified by the 16th Amendment (1913), giving Congress the power to levy "taxes on incomes, from whatever source derived."

Clause 5. This provision was a part of the Commerce Compromise made by the Framers in 1787. Congress has the power to tax imported goods, however.

Clause 6. All ports within the United States must be treated alike by Congress as it exercises its taxing and commerce powers. Congress cannot tax goods sent by water from one State to another, nor may it give the ports of one State any legal advantage over those of another.

Clause 7. This clause gives Congress its vastly important "power of the purse," a major check on presidential power. Federal money can be spent only in those amounts and for those purposes expressly authorized by an act of Congress. All federal income and spending must be accounted for, regularly and publicly.

Clause 8. This provision, preventing the establishment of a nobility, reflects the principle that "all men are created equal." It was also intended to discourage foreign attempts to bribe or otherwise corrupt officers of the government.

Section 10. Powers Denied to the States

Clause 1. The States are not sovereign governments and so cannot make agreements or otherwise negotiate with foreign states; the power to conduct foreign relations is an exclusive power of the National Government. The power to coin money is also an exclusive power of the National Government. Several powers forbidden to the National Government are here also forbidden to the States.

Clause 2. This provision relates to foreign, not interstate, commerce. Only Congress, not the States, can tax imports; and the States are, like Congress, forbidden the power to tax exports.

▶ 2. The Privilege of the Writ of Habeas Corpus shall not be suspended, unless when in Cases of Rebellion or Invasion the public safety may require it.

▶ 3. No Bill of Attainder or ex post facto Law shall be passed.

▶ 4. No Capitation, or other direct, Tax shall be laid, unless in Proportion to the Census of Enumeration hereinbefore directed to be taken.

▶ 5. No Tax or Duty shall be laid on Articles exported from any State.

▶ 6. No Preference shall be given by any Regulation of Commerce or Revenue to the Ports of one State over those of another: nor shall Vessels bound to, or from, one State, be obliged to enter, clear or pay Duties in another.

▶ 7. No Money shall be drawn from the Treasury, but in Consequence of Appropriations made by Law; and a regular Statement and Account of the Receipts and Expenditures of all public Money shall be published from time to time.

▶ 8. No Title of Nobility shall be granted by the United States: And no Person holding any Office of Profit or Trust under them, shall, without the Consent of the Congress, accept of any present, Emolument, Office, or Title, of any kind whatever, from any King, Prince, or foreign State.

Section 10.

▶ 1. No State shall enter into any Treaty, Alliance, or Confederation; grant Letters of Marque and Reprisal; coin Money; emit Bills of Credit; make any Thing but gold and silver Coin a Tender in Payment of Debts; pass any Bill of Attainder, ex post facto Law, or Law impairing the Obligation of Contracts, or grant any Title of Nobility.

▶ 2. No State shall, without the Consent of the Congress, lay any Imposts or Duties on Imports or Exports, except what may be absolutely necessary for executing its inspection Laws; and the net Produce of all Duties and Imposts, laid by any State on Imports or Exports, shall be for the Use of the Treasury of the United States; and all such Laws shall be subject to the Revision and Control of the Congress.

3. No State shall, without the Consent of Congress, lay any Duty of Tonnage, keep Troops, or Ships of War in time of Peace, enter into any Agreement or Compact with another State, or with a foreign Power, or engage in War, unless actually invaded, or in such imminent Danger as will not admit of delay.

Article II
Section 1.

1. The executive Power shall be vested in a President of the United States of America. He shall hold his Office during the Term of four Years, and, together with the Vice President, chosen for the same Term, be elected as follows:

2. Each State shall appoint, in such Manner as the Legislature thereof may direct, a Number of Electors, equal to the whole Number of Senators and Representatives to which the State may be entitled in the Congress: but no Senator or Representative, or Person holding an Office of Trust or Profit, under the United States, shall be appointed an Elector.

3. The Electors shall meet in their respective States, and vote by Ballot for two Persons, of whom one at least shall not be an Inhabitant of the same State with themselves. And they shall make a List of all the Persons voted for, and of the Number of Votes for each; which List they shall sign and certify, and transmit sealed to the Seat of the Government of the United States, directed to the President of the Senate. The President of the Senate shall, in the Presence of the Senate and House of Representatives, open all the Certificates, and the Votes shall then be counted. The Person having the greatest Number of Votes shall be the President, if such Number be a majority of the whole Number of Electors appointed; and if there be more than one who have such Majority, and have an equal Number of Votes, then, the House of Representatives shall immediately choose by Ballot one of them for President; and if no Person have a Majority, then from the five highest on the List the said House shall in like Manner choose the President. But in choosing the President, the Votes shall be taken by States, the Representatives from each State having one Vote; a quorum for this Purpose shall consist of a Member or Members from two thirds of the States, and a Majority of all the States shall be necessary to a Choice. In every Case, after the Choice of the President, the Person having the greatest Number of Votes of the Electors shall be the Vice President. But if there should remain two or more who have equal Votes, the Senate shall choose from them by Ballot the Vice President.

Clause 3. A duty of tonnage is a tax laid on ships according to their cargo capacity. Each State has a constitutional right to provide for and maintain a militia; but no State may keep a standing army or navy. The several restrictions here prevent the States from assuming powers that the Constitution elsewhere grants to the National Government.

Executive Department
Section 1. President and Vice President

Clause 1. Executive power, term This clause gives to the President the very broad "executive power," the power to enforce the laws and otherwise administer the public policies of the United States. It also sets the length of the presidential (and vice-presidential) term of office; see the 22nd Amendment (1951), which places a limit on presidential (but not vice-presidential) tenure.

Clause 2. Electoral college This clause establishes the "electoral college," although the Constitution does not use that term. It is a body of presidential electors chosen in each State, and it selects the President and Vice President every four years. The number of electors chosen in each State equals the number of senators and representatives that State has in Congress.

Clause 3. Election of President and Vice President This clause was replaced by the 12th Amendment in 1804.

Clause 4. Date Congress has set the date for the choosing of electors as the Tuesday after the first Monday in November every fourth year, and for the casting of electoral votes as the Monday after the second Wednesday in December of that year.

Clause 5. Qualifications The President must have been born a citizen of the United States, be at least 35 years old, and have been a resident of the United States for at least 14 years.

Clause 6. Vacancy This clause was modified by the 25th Amendment (1967), which provides expressly for the succession of the Vice President, for the filling of a vacancy in the Vice Presidency, and for the determination of presidential inability.

Clause 7. Compensation The President now receives a salary of $400,000 and a taxable expense account of $50,000 a year. Those amounts cannot be changed during a presidential term; thus, Congress cannot use the President's compensation as a bargaining tool to influence executive decisions. The phrase "any other emolument" means, in effect, any valuable gift; it does not mean that the President cannot be provided with such benefits of office as the White House, extensive staff assistance, and much else.

Clause 8. Oath of office The Chief Justice of the United States regularly administers this oath or affirmation, but any judicial officer may do so. Thus, Calvin Coolidge was sworn into office in 1923 by his father, a justice of the peace in Vermont.

Section 2. President's Powers and Duties

Clause 1. Military, civil powers The President, a civilian, heads the nation's armed forces, a key element in the Constitution's insistence on civilian control of the military. The President's power to "require the opinion, in writing" provides the constitutional basis for the Cabinet. The President's power to grant reprieves and pardons, the power of clemency, extends only to federal cases.

4. The Congress may determine the Time of choosing the Electors, and the Day on which they shall give their Votes; which Day shall be the same throughout the United States.

5. No Person except a natural born Citizen, or a Citizen of the United States, at the time of the Adoption of this Constitution, shall be eligible to the Office of President; neither shall any person be eligible to that Office who shall not have attained to the Age of thirty-five Years, and been fourteen Years a Resident within the United States.

6. In Case of the Removal of the President from Office, or of his Death, Resignation, or Inability to discharge the Powers and Duties of the said Office, the Same shall devolve on the Vice President, and the Congress may by Law provide for the Case of Removal, Death, Resignation or Inability, both of the President and Vice President, declaring what Officer shall then act as President, and such Officer shall act accordingly, until the Disability be removed, or a President shall be elected.

7. The President shall, at stated Times, receive for his Services, a Compensation, which shall neither be increased nor diminished during the Period for which he shall have been elected, and he shall not receive within that Period any other Emolument from the United States, or any of them.

8. Before he enter on the Execution of his Office, he shall take the following Oath or Affirmation:
"I do solemnly swear (or affirm) that I will faithfully execute the Office of President of the United States, and will to the best of my Ability, preserve, protect and defend the Constitution of the United States."

Section 2.

1. The President shall be Commander in Chief of the Army and Navy of the United States, and of the Militia of the several States, when called into the actual Service of the United States; he may require the Opinion, in writing, of the principal Officer in each of the executive Departments, upon any Subject relating to the Duties of their respective Offices, and he shall have Power to Grant Reprieves and Pardons for Offences against the United States, except in Cases of Impeachment.

2. He shall have Power, by and with the Advice and Consent of the Senate, to make Treaties, provided two thirds of the Senators present concur; and he shall nominate, and by and with the Advice and Consent of the Senate, shall appoint Ambassadors, other public Ministers and Consuls, Judges of the supreme Court, and all other Officers of the United States, whose Appointments are not herein otherwise provided for, and which shall be established by Law: but the Congress may by Law vest the Appointment of such inferior Officers, as they think proper, in the President alone, in the Courts of Law, or in the Heads of Departments.

3. The President shall have Power to fill up all Vacancies that may happen during the Recess of the Senate, by granting Commissions which shall expire at the End of their next Session.

Section 3.

He shall from time to time give to the Congress Information of the State of the Union, and recommend to their Consideration such Measures as he shall judge necessary and expedient; he may, on extraordinary Occasions, convene both Houses, or either of them, and in Case of Disagreement between them, with Respect to the Time of Adjournment, he may adjourn them to such Time as he shall think proper; he shall receive Ambassadors and other public Ministers; he shall take Care that the Laws be faithfully executed, and shall Commission all the Officers of the United States.

Section 4.

The President, Vice President and all Civil Officers of the United States, shall be removed from Office on Impeachment for and Conviction of, Treason, Bribery, or other high Crimes and Misdemeanors.

Article III

Section 1.

The judicial Power of the United States, shall be vested in one supreme Court, and in such inferior Courts as the Congress may from time to time ordain and establish. The Judges, both of the supreme and inferior Courts, shall hold their Offices during good Behaviour, and shall, at stated Times, receive for their Services, a Compensation, which shall not be diminished during their Continuance in Office.

▶ **Clause 2. Treaties, appointments** The President has the sole power to make treaties; to become effective, a treaty must be approved by a two-thirds vote in the Senate. In practice, the President can also make executive agreements with foreign governments; these pacts, which are frequently made and usually deal with routine matters, do not require Senate consent. The President appoints the principal officers of the executive branch and all federal judges; the "inferior officers" are those who hold lesser posts.

▶ **Clause 3. Recess appointments** When the Senate is not in session, appointments that require Senate consent can be made by the President on a temporary basis, as "recess appointments." Recess appointments are valid only to the end of the congressional term in which they are made.

Section 3. President's Powers and Duties

The President delivers a State of the Union Message to Congress soon after that body convenes each year. That message is delivered to the nation's lawmakers and, importantly, to the American people, as well. It is shortly followed by the proposed federal budget and an economic report; and the President may send special messages to Congress at any time. In all of these communications, Congress is urged to take those actions the Chief Executive finds to be in the national interest. The President also has the power: to call special sessions of Congress; to adjourn Congress if its two houses cannot agree for that purpose; to receive the diplomatic representatives of other governments; to insure the proper execution of all federal laws; and to empower federal officers to hold their posts and perform their duties.

Section 4. Impeachment

The Constitution outlines the impeachment process in Article I, Section 2, Clause 5 and in Section 3, Clauses 6 and 7.

Judicial Department

Section 1. Judicial Power, Courts, Terms of Office

The judicial power conferred here is the power of federal courts to hear and decide cases, disputes between the government and individuals and between private persons (parties). The Constitution creates only the Supreme Court of the United States; it gives to Congress the power to establish other, lower federal courts (Article I, Section 8, Clause 9) and to fix the size of the Supreme Court. The words "during good behaviour" mean, in effect, for life.

Section 2. Jurisdiction

▶ **Clause 1. Cases to be heard** This clause sets out the jurisdiction of the federal courts; that is, it identifies those cases that may be tried in those courts. The federal courts can hear and decide—have jurisdiction over—a case depending on either the subject matter or the parties involved in that case. The jurisdiction of the federal courts in cases involving States was substantially restricted by the 11th Amendment in 1795.

▶ **Clause 2. Supreme Court jurisdiction** Original jurisdiction refers to the power of a court to hear a case in the first instance, not on appeal from a lower court. Appellate jurisdiction refers to a court's power to hear a case on appeal from a lower court, from the court in which the case was originally tried. This clause gives the Supreme Court both original and appellate jurisdiction. However, nearly all of the cases the High Court hears are brought to it on appeal from the lower federal courts and the highest State courts.

▶ **Clause 3. Jury trial in criminal cases** A person accused of a federal crime is guaranteed the right to trial by jury in a federal court in the State where the crime was committed; see the 5th and 6th amendments. The right to trial by jury in serious criminal cases in the State courts is guaranteed by the 6th and 14th amendments.

Section 3. Treason

▶ **Clause 1. Definition** Treason is the only crime defined in the Constitution. The Framers intended the very specific definition here to prevent the loose use of the charge of treason—for example, against persons who criticize the government. Treason can be committed only in time of war and only by a citizen or a resident alien.

▶ **Clause 2. Punishment** Congress has provided that the punishment that a federal court may impose on a convicted traitor may range from a minimum of five years in prison and/or a $10,000 fine to a maximum of death; no person convicted of treason has ever been executed by the United States. No legal punishment can be imposed on the family or descendants of a convicted traitor. Congress has also made it a crime for any person (in either peace or wartime) to commit espionage or sabotage, to attempt to overthrow the government by force, or to conspire to do any of these things.

Section 2.

▶ 1. The judicial Power shall extend to all Cases, in Law and Equity, arising under this Constitution, the Laws of the United States, and Treaties made, or which shall be made, under their Authority;— to all Cases affecting Ambassadors, other public ministers, and Consuls;— to all Cases of Admiralty and maritime Jurisdiction;— to Controversies to which the United States shall be a Party;— to Controversies between two or more States;— between a State and Citizens of another State;— between Citizens of different States;— between Citizens of the same State claiming Lands under Grants of different States, and between a State, or the Citizens thereof, and foreign States, Citizens, or Subjects.

▶ 2. In all Cases affecting Ambassadors, other public Ministers and Consuls, and those in which a State shall be a Party, the supreme Court shall have original Jurisdiction. In all the other Cases before mentioned, the supreme Court shall have appellate Jurisdiction, both as to Law and Fact, with such Exceptions, and under such Regulations as the Congress shall make.

▶ 3. The trial of all Crimes, except in Cases of Impeachment, shall be by Jury; and such Trial shall be held in the State where the said Crimes shall have been committed; but when not committed within any State, the Trial shall be at such Place or Places as the Congress may by Law have directed.

Section 3.

▶ 1. Treason against the United States shall consist only in levying War against them, or in adhering to their Enemies, giving them Aid and Comfort. No Person shall be convicted of Treason unless on the Testimony of two Witnesses to the same overt Act, or on Confession in open Court.

▶ 2. The Congress shall have Power to declare the Punishment of Treason, but no Attainder of Treason shall work Corruption of Blood, or Forfeiture except during the Life of the Person attainted.

Article IV

Section 1.

Full Faith and Credit shall be given in each State to the public Acts, Records, and judicial Proceedings of every other State. And the Congress may by general Laws prescribe the Manner in which such Acts, Records and Proceedings shall be proved, and the Effect thereof.

Section 2.

▶ 1. The Citizens of each State shall be entitled to all Privileges and Immunities of Citizens in the several States.

▶ 2. A Person charged in any State with Treason, Felony, or other Crime, who shall flee from justice, and be found in another State, shall on Demand of the executive Authority of the State from which he fled, be delivered up, to be removed to the State having Jurisdiction of the Crime.

▶ 3. No Person held to Service or Labor in one State, under the Laws thereof, escaping into another, shall, in Consequence of any Law or Regulation therein, be discharged from Service or Labor, but shall be delivered up on Claim of the Party to whom such Service or Labor may be due.

Section 3.

▶ 1. New States may be admitted by the Congress into this Union; but no new State shall be formed or erected within the Jurisdiction of any other State; nor any State be formed by the Junction of two or more States, or Parts of States, without the Consent of the Legislatures of the States concerned as well as of the Congress.

▶ 2. The Congress shall have Power to dispose of and make all needful Rules and Regulations respecting the Territory or other Property belonging to the United States; and nothing in this Constitution shall be so construed as to Prejudice any Claims of the United States, or of any particular State.

Section 4.

The United States shall guarantee to every State in this Union a Republican Form of Government, and shall protect each of them against Invasion; and on Application of the Legislature, or of the Executive (when the Legislature cannot be convened) against domestic Violence.

Relations Among States

Section 1. Full Faith and Credit

Each State must recognize the validity of the laws, public records, and court decisions of every other State.

Section 2. Privileges and Immunities of Citizens

▶ **Clause 1. Residents of other States** In effect, this clause means that no State may discriminate against the residents of other States; that is, a State's laws cannot draw unreasonable distinctions between its own residents and those of any of the other States. See Section 1 of the 14th Amendment.

▶ **Clause 2. Extradition** The process of returning a fugitive to another State is known as "interstate rendition" or, more commonly, "extradition." Usually, that process works routinely; some extradition requests are contested however—especially in cases with racial or political overtones. A governor may refuse to extradite a fugitive; but the federal courts can compel an unwilling governor to obey this constitutional command.

▶ **Clause 3. Fugitive slaves** This clause was nullified by the 13th Amendment, which abolished slavery in 1865.

Section 3. New States; Territories

▶ **Clause 1. New States** Only Congress can admit new States to the Union. A new State may not be created by taking territory from an existing State without the consent of that State's legislature. Congress has admitted 37 States since the original 13 formed the Union. Five States— Vermont, Kentucky, Tennessee, Maine, and West Virginia— were created from parts of existing States. Texas was an independent republic before admission. California was admitted after being ceded to the United States by Mexico. Each of the other 30 States entered the Union only after a period of time as an organized territory of the United States.

▶ **Clause 2. Territory, property** Congress has the power to make laws concerning the territories, other public lands, and all other property of the United States.

Section 4. Protection Afforded to States by the Nation

The Constitution does not define "a republican form of government," but the phrase is generally understood to mean a representative government. The Federal Government must also defend each State against attacks from outside its border and, at the request of a State's legislature or its governor, aid its efforts to put down internal disorders.

Provisions for Amendment

This section provides for the methods by which formal changes can be made in the Constitution. An amendment may be proposed in one of two ways: by a two-thirds vote in each house of Congress, or by a national convention called by Congress at the request of two-thirds of the State legislatures. A proposed amendment may be ratified in one of two ways: by three-fourths of the State legislatures, or by three-fourths of the States in conventions called for that purpose. Congress has the power to determine the method by which a proposed amendment may be ratified. The amendment process cannot be used to deny any State its equal representation in the United States Senate. To this point, 27 amendments have been adopted. To date, all of the amendments except the 21st Amendment were proposed by Congress and ratified by the State legislatures. Only the 21st Amendment was ratified by the convention method.

National Debts, Supremacy of National Law, Oath

Section 1. Validity of Debts

Congress had borrowed large sums of money during the Revolution and later during the Critical Period of the 1780s. This provision, a pledge that the new government would honor those debts, did much to create confidence in that government.

Section 2. Supremacy of National Law

This section sets out the Supremacy Clause, a specific declaration of the supremacy of federal law over any and all forms of State law. No State, including its local governments, may make or enforce any law that conflicts with any provision in the Constitution, an act of Congress, a treaty, or an order, rule, or regulation properly issued by the President or his subordinates in the executive branch.

Section 3. Oaths of Office

This provision reinforces the Supremacy Clause; all public officers, at every level in the United States, owe their first allegiance to the Constitution of the United States. No religious qualification can be imposed as a condition for holding any public office.

Ratification of Constitution

The proposed Constitution was signed by George Washington and 37 of his fellow Framers on September 17, 1787. (George Read of Delaware signed for himself and also for his absent colleague, John Dickinson.)

Article V

The Congress, whenever two thirds of both Houses shall deem it necessary, shall propose Amendments to this Constitution, or, on the Application of the Legislatures of two thirds of the several States, shall call a Convention for proposing Amendments, which, in either Case, shall be valid to all Intents and Purposes, as Part of this Constitution, when ratified by the Legislatures of three fourths of the several States, or by Conventions in three fourths thereof, as the one or the other Mode of Ratification may be proposed by the Congress; Provided that no Amendment which may be made prior to the Year One thousand eight hundred and eight shall in any Manner affect the first and fourth Clauses in the Ninth section of the first Article; and that no State, without its Consent, shall be deprived of its equal Suffrage in the Senate.

Article VI

Section 1.

All Debts contracted and Engagements entered into, before the Adoption of this Constitution, shall be as valid against the United States under this Constitution, as under the Confederation.

Section 2.

This Constitution, and the Laws of the United States which shall be made in Pursuance thereof; and all Treaties made, or which shall be made, under the Authority of the United States, shall be the supreme Law of the Land; and the Judges in every State shall be bound thereby, anything in the constitution or Laws of any State to the Contrary notwithstanding.

Section 3.

The Senators and Representatives before mentioned, and the Members of the several State legislatures, and all executive and judicial Officers, both of the United States and of the several States, shall be bound by Oath or Affirmation, to support this Constitution; but no religious Test shall ever be required as a Qualification to any Office or public Trust under the United States.

Article VII

The ratification of the Conventions of nine States, shall be sufficient for the Establishment of this Constitution between the States so ratifying the same.

Done in Convention by the Unanimous Consent of the States present the Seventeenth Day of September in the Year of our Lord one thousand seven hundred and Eighty-seven and of the Independence of the United States of America the twelfth. In witness whereof We have hereunto subscribed our Names.

Attest:
William Jackson,
Secretary
George Washington,
President and Deputy from Virginia

New Hampshire
John Langdon
Nicholas Gilman

Massachusetts
Nathaniel Gorham
Rufus King

Connecticut
William Samuel Johnson
Roger Sherman

New York
Alexander Hamilton

New Jersey
William Livingston
David Brearley
William Paterson
Jonathan Dayton

Pennsylvania
Benjamin Franklin
Thomas Mifflin
Robert Morris
George Clymer
Thomas Fitzsimons
Jared Ingersoll
James Wilson
Gouverneur Morris

Delaware
George Read
Gunning Bedford, Jr.
John Dickinson
Richard Bassett
Jacob Broom

Maryland
James McHenry
Daniel of St. Thomas Jenifer
Daniel Carroll

Virginia
John Blair
James Madison, Jr.

North Carolina
William Blount
Richard Dobbs Spaight
Hugh Williamson

South Carolina
John Rutledge
Charles Cotesworth Pinckney
Charles Pinckney
Pierce Butler

Georgia
William Few
Abraham Baldwin

The first 10 amendments, the Bill of Rights, were each proposed by Congress on September 25, 1789, and ratified by the necessary three-fourths of the States on December 15, 1791. These amendments were originally intended to restrict the National Government—not the States. However, the Supreme Court has several times held that most of their provisions also apply to the States, through the 14th Amendment's Due Process Clause.

1st Amendment. Freedom of Religion, Speech, Press, Assembly, and Petition

The 1st Amendment sets out five basic liberties: The guarantee of freedom of religion is both a protection of religious thought and practice and a command of separation of church and state. The guarantees of freedom of speech and press assure to all persons a right to speak, publish, and otherwise express their views. The guarantees of the rights of assembly and petition protect the right to join with others in public meetings, political parties, interest groups, and other associations to discuss public affairs and influence public policy. None of these rights is guaranteed in absolute terms, however; like all other civil rights guarantees, each of them may be exercised only with regard to the rights of all other persons.

2nd Amendment. Bearing Arms

The right of the people to keep and bear arms was insured by the 2nd Amendment.

3rd Amendment. Quartering of Troops

This amendment was intended to prevent what had been common British practice in the colonial period; see the Declaration of Independence. This provision is of virtually no importance today.

4th Amendment. Searches and Seizures

The basic rule laid down by the 4th Amendment is this: Police officers have no general right to search for or seize evidence or seize (arrest) persons. Except in particular circumstances, they must have a proper warrant (a court order) obtained with probable cause (on reasonable grounds). This guarantee is reinforced by the exclusionary rule, developed by the Supreme Court: Evidence gained as the result of an unlawful search or seizure cannot be used at the court trial of the person from whom it was seized.

5th Amendment. Criminal Proceedings; Due Process; Eminent Domain

A person can be tried for a serious federal crime only if he or she has been indicted (charged, accused of that crime) by a grand jury. No one may be subjected to double jeopardy—that is, tried twice for the same crime. All persons are protected against self-incrimination; no person can be legally compelled to answer any question in any governmental proceeding if that answer could lead to that person's prosecution. The 5th Amendment's Due Process Clause prohibits unfair, arbitrary actions by the Federal Government; a like prohibition is set out against the States in the 14th Amendment. Government may take private property for a legitimate public purpose; but when it exercises that power of eminent domain, it must pay a fair price for the property seized.

1st Amendment

Congress shall make no law respecting an establishment of religion, or prohibiting the free exercise thereof, or abridging the freedom of speech, or of the press; or the right of the people peaceably to assemble, and to petition the Government for a redress of grievances.

2nd Amendment

A well-regulated Militia being necessary to the security of a free State, the right of the people to keep and bear Arms, shall not be infringed.

3rd Amendment

No Soldier shall, in time of peace be quartered in any house, without the consent of the Owner, nor, in time of war, but in a manner to be prescribed by law.

4th Amendment

The right of the people to be secure in their persons, houses, papers, and effects, against unreasonable searches and seizures, shall not be violated, and no Warrants shall issue, but upon probable cause, supported by Oath or affirmation, and particularly describing the place to be searched, and the persons or things to be seized.

5th Amendment

No person shall be held to answer for a capital, or otherwise infamous crime, unless on a presentment or indictment of a Grand Jury, except in cases arising in the land or naval forces, or in the Militia, when in actual service in time of War, or public danger; nor shall any person be subject for the same offence to be twice put in jeopardy of life or limb; nor shall be compelled in any criminal case to be a witness against himself, nor be deprived of life, liberty, or property, without due process of law; nor shall private property be taken for public use, without just compensation.

6th Amendment

In all criminal prosecutions, the accused shall enjoy the right to a speedy and public trial, by an impartial jury of the State and district wherein the crime shall have been committed, which district shall have been previously ascertained by law, and to be informed of the nature and cause of the accusation; to be confronted with the witnesses against him; to have compulsory process for obtaining witnesses in his favor, and to have the Assistance of Counsel for his defence.

7th Amendment

In Suits at common law, where the value in controversy shall exceed twenty dollars, the right of trial by jury shall be preserved, and no fact tried by a jury, shall be otherwise re-examined in any Court of the United States, than according to the rules of the common law.

8th Amendment

Excessive bail shall not be required, nor excessive fines imposed, nor cruel and unusual punishment inflicted.

9th Amendment

The enumeration in the Constitution, of certain rights, shall not be construed to deny or disparage others retained by the people.

10th Amendment

The powers not delegated to the United States by the Constitution, nor prohibited by it to the States, are reserved to the States respectively, or to the people.

6th Amendment. Criminal Proceedings

A person accused of crime has the right to be tried in court without undue delay and by an impartial jury; see Article III, Section 2, Clause 3. The defendant must be informed of the charge upon which he or she is to be tried, has the right to cross-examine hostile witnesses, and has the right to require the testimony of favorable witnesses. The defendant also has the right to be represented by an attorney at every stage in the criminal process.

7th Amendment. Civil Trials

This amendment applies only to civil cases heard in federal courts. A civil case does not involve criminal matters; it is a dispute between private parties or between the government and a private party. The right to trial by jury is guaranteed in any civil case in a federal court if the amount of money involved in that case exceeds $20 (most cases today involve a much larger sum); that right may be waived (relinquished, put aside) if both parties agree to a bench trial (a trial by a judge, without a jury).

8th Amendment. Punishment for Crimes

Bail is the sum of money that a person accused of crime may be required to post (deposit with the court) as a guarantee that he or she will appear in court at the proper time. The amount of bail required and/or a fine imposed as punishment must bear a reasonable relationship to the seriousness of the crime involved in the case. The prohibition of cruel and unusual punishment forbids any punishment judged to be too harsh, too severe for the crime for which it is imposed.

9th Amendment. Unenumerated Rights

The fact that the Constitution sets out many civil rights guarantees, expressly provides for many protections against government, does not mean that there are not other rights also held by the people.

10th Amendment. Powers Reserved to the States

This amendment identifies the area of power that may be exercised by the States. All of those powers the Constitution does not grant to the National Government, and at the same time does not forbid to the States, belong to each of the States, or to the people of each State.

11th Amendment. Suits Against States

Proposed by Congress March 4, 1794; ratified February 7, 1795, but official announcement of the ratification was delayed until January 8, 1798. This amendment repealed part of Article III, Section 2, Clause 1. No State may be sued in a federal court by a resident of another State or of a foreign country; the Supreme Court has long held that this provision also means that a State cannot be sued in a federal court by a foreign country or, more importantly, even by one of its own residents.

12th Amendment. Election of President and Vice President

Proposed by Congress December 9, 1803; ratified June 15, 1804. This amendment replaced Article II, Section 1, Clause 3. Originally, each elector cast two ballots, each for a different person for President. The person with the largest number of electoral votes, provided that number was a majority of the electors, was to become President; the person with the second highest number was to become Vice President. This arrangement produced an electoral vote tie between Thomas Jefferson and Aaron Burr in 1800; the House finally chose Jefferson as President in 1801. The 12th Amendment separated the balloting for President and Vice President; each elector now casts one ballot for someone as President and a second ballot for another person as Vice President. Note that the 20th Amendment changed the date set here (March 4) to January 20, and that the 23rd Amendment (1961) provides for electors from the District of Columbia. This amendment also provides that the Vice President must meet the same qualifications as those set out for the President in Article II, Section 1, Clause 5.

13th Amendment. Slavery and Involuntary Servitude

Proposed by Congress January 31, 1865; ratified December 6, 1865. This amendment forbids slavery in the United States and in any area under its control. It also forbids other forms of forced labor, except punishments for crime; but some forms of compulsory service are not prohibited—for example, service on juries or in the armed forces. Section 2 gives to Congress the power to carry out the provisions of Section 1 of this amendment.

11th Amendment

The Judicial power of the United States shall not be construed to extend to any suit in law or equity, commenced or prosecuted against one of the United States by Citizens of another State, or by Citizens or Subjects of any Foreign State.

12th Amendment

The Electors shall meet in their respective States and vote by ballot for President and Vice President, one of whom, at least, shall not be an inhabitant of the same State with themselves; they shall name in their ballots the person voted for as President, and in distinct ballots the person voted for as Vice President, and they shall make distinct lists of all persons voted for as President, and of all persons voted for as Vice President, and of the number of votes for each, which lists they shall sign and certify, and transmit sealed to the seat of the government of the United States, directed to the President of the Senate;— The President of the Senate shall, in the presence of the Senate and the House of Representatives, open all the certificates and the votes shall then be counted;— the person having the greatest Number of votes for President shall be the President, if such number be a majority of the whole number of Electors appointed; and if no person have such a majority, then, from the persons having the highest numbers not exceeding three on the list of those voted for as President, the House of Representatives shall choose immediately, by ballot, the President. But in choosing the President, the votes shall be taken by States, the representation from each State having one vote; a quorum for this purpose shall consist of a member or members from two thirds of the States, and a majority of all the States shall be necessary to a choice. And if the House of Representatives shall not choose a President whenever the right of choice shall devolve upon them, before the fourth day of March next following, then the Vice President shall act as President, as in case of death or other constitutional disability of the President. The person having the greatest number of votes as Vice President, shall be the Vice President, if such number be a majority of the whole number of Electors appointed, and if no person have a majority, then from the two highest numbers on the list, the Senate shall choose the Vice President; a quorum for the purpose shall consist of two thirds of the whole number of Senators, a majority of the whole number shall be necessary to a choice. But no person constitutionally ineligible to the office of President shall be eligible to that of Vice-President of the United States.

13th Amendment

Section 1. Neither slavery nor involuntary servitude, except as a punishment for crime whereof the party shall have been duly convicted, shall exist within the United States, or any place subject to their jurisdiction.

Section 2. Congress shall have power to enforce this article by appropriate legislation.

14th Amendment

Section 1. All persons born or naturalized in the United States and subject to the jurisdiction thereof, are citizens of the United States and of the State wherein they reside. No State shall make or enforce any law which shall abridge the privileges or immunities of citizens of the United States; nor shall any State deprive any person of life, liberty, or property, without due process of law; nor deny to any person within its jurisdiction the equal protection of the laws.

Section 2. Representatives shall be apportioned among the several States according to their respective numbers, counting the whole number of persons in each State, excluding Indians not taxed. But when the right to vote at any election for the choice of electors for President and Vice President of the United States, Representatives in Congress, the Executive and Judicial officers of a State, or the members of the Legislature thereof, is denied to any of the male inhabitants of such State, being twenty-one years of age and citizens of the United States, or in any way abridged, except for participation in rebellion, or other crime, the basis of representation therein shall be reduced in the proportion which the number of such male citizens shall bear to the whole number of male citizens twenty-one years of age in such State.

Section 3. No person shall be a Senator or Representative in Congress, or elector of President and Vice President, or hold any office, civil or military, under the United States, or under any State, who, having previously taken an oath, as a member of Congress, or as an officer of the United States, or as a member of any State legislature, or as an executive or judicial officer of any State, to support the Constitution of the United States, shall have engaged in insurrection or rebellion against the same, or given aid or comfort to the enemies thereof. But Congress may, by a vote of two thirds of each House, remove such disability.

Section 4. The validity of the public debt of the United States, authorized by law, including debts incurred for payment of pensions and bounties for services in suppressing insurrection or rebellion, shall not be questioned. But neither the United States nor any State shall assume or pay any debt or obligation incurred in aid of insurrection or rebellion against the United States, or any claim for the loss or emancipation of any slave; but all such debts, obligations and claims shall be held illegal and void.

Section 5. The Congress shall have power to enforce, by appropriate legislation, the provisions of this article.

14th Amendment. Rights of Citizens

Proposed by Congress June 13, 1866; ratified July 9, 1868. Section 1 defines citizenship. It provides for the acquisition of United States citizenship by birth or by naturalization. Citizenship at birth is determined according to the principle of jus soli—"the law of the soil," where born; naturalization is the legal process by which one acquires a new citizenship at some time after birth. Under certain circumstances, citizenship can also be gained at birth abroad, according to the principle of jus sanguinis—"the law of the blood," to whom born. This section also contains two major civil rights provisions: the Due Process Clause forbids a State (and its local governments) to act in any unfair or arbitrary way; the Equal Protection Clause forbids a State (and its local governments) to discriminate against, draw unreasonable distinctions between, persons.

Most of the rights set out against the National Government in the first eight amendments have been extended against the States (and their local governments) through Supreme Court decisions involving the 14th Amendment's Due Process Clause.

The first sentence here replaced Article I, Section 2, Clause 3, the Three-Fifths Compromise provision. Essentially, all persons in the United States are counted in each decennial census, the basis for the distribution of House seats. The balance of this section has never been enforced and is generally thought to be obsolete.

This section limited the President's power to pardon those persons who had led the Confederacy during the Civil War. Congress finally removed this disability in 1898.

Section 4 also dealt with matters directly related to the Civil War. It reaffirmed the public debt of the United States; but it invalidated, prohibited payment of, any debt contracted by the Confederate States and also prohibited any compensation of former slave owners.

15th Amendment. Right to Vote— Race, Color, Servitude

Proposed by Congress February 26, 1869; ratified February 3, 1870. The phrase "previous condition of servitude" refers to slavery. Note that this amendment does not guarantee the right to vote to African Americans, or to anyone else. Instead, it forbids the States from discriminating against any person on the grounds of his "race, color, or previous condition of servitude" in the setting of suffrage qualifications.

16th Amendment. Income Tax

Proposed by Congress July 12, 1909; ratified February 3, 1913. This amendment modified two provisions in Article I, Section 2, Clause 3, and Section 9, Clause 4. It gives to Congress the power to levy an income tax, a direct tax, without regard to the populations of any of the States.

17th Amendment. Popular Election of Senators

Proposed by Congress May 13, 1912; ratified April 8, 1913. This amendment repealed those portions of Article I, Section 3, Clauses 1 and 2 relating to the election of senators. Senators are now elected by the voters in each State. If a vacancy occurs, the governor of the State involved must call an election to fill the seat; the governor may appoint a senator to serve until the next election, if the State's legislature has authorized that step.

18th Amendment. Prohibition of Intoxicating Liquors

Proposed by Congress December 18, 1917; ratified January 16, 1919. This amendment outlawed the making, selling, transporting, importing, or exporting of alcoholic beverages in the United States. It was repealed in its entirety by the 21st Amendment in 1933.

19th Amendment. Equal Suffrage—Sex

Proposed by Congress June 4, 1919; ratified August 18, 1920. No person can be denied the right to vote in any election in the United States on account of his or her sex.

15th Amendment

Section 1. The right of citizens of the United States to vote shall not be denied or abridged by the United States or by any State on account of race, color, or previous condition of servitude.

Section 2. The Congress shall have power to enforce this article by appropriate legislation.

16th Amendment

The Congress shall have power to lay and collect taxes on incomes, from whatever source derived, without apportionment among the several States, and without regard to any census or enumeration.

17th Amendment

The Senate of the United States shall be composed of two Senators from each State, elected by the people thereof, for six years; and each Senator shall have one vote. The electors in each State shall have the qualifications requisite for electors of the most numerous branch of the State legislatures.

When vacancies happen in the representation of any State in the Senate, the executive authority of such State shall issue writs of election to fill such vacancies: Provided, That the legislature of any State may empower the executive thereof to make temporary appointments until the people fill the vacancies by election as the legislature may direct.

This amendment shall not be so construed as to affect the election or term of any Senator chosen before it becomes valid as part of the Constitution.

18th Amendment.

Section 1. After one year from the ratification of this article the manufacture, sale, or transportation of intoxicating liquors within, the importation thereof into, or the exportation thereof from the United States and all territory subject to the jurisdiction thereof for beverage purposes is hereby prohibited.

Section 2. The Congress and the several States shall have concurrent power to enforce this article by appropriate legislation.

Section 3. This article shall be inoperative unless it shall have been ratified as an amendment to the Constitution by the legislatures of the several States, as provided in the Constitution, within seven years of the date of the submission hereof to the States by Congress.

19th Amendment

The right of citizens of the United States to vote shall not be denied or abridged by the United States or by any State on account of sex.

Congress shall have power to enforce this article by appropriate legislation.

20th Amendment

Section 1. The terms of the President and Vice President shall end at noon on the 20th day of January, and the terms of Senators and Representatives at noon on the 3d day of January, of the years in which such terms would have ended if this article had not been ratified; and the terms of their successors shall then begin.

Section 2. The Congress shall assemble at least once in every year, and such meeting shall begin at noon on the 3d day of January, unless they shall by law appoint a different day.

Section 3. If, at the time fixed for the beginning of the term of the President, the President elect shall have died, the Vice President elect shall become President. If a President shall not have been chosen before the time fixed for the beginning of his term, or if the President-elect shall have failed to qualify, then the Vice President elect shall act as President until a President shall have qualified; and the Congress may by law provide for the case wherein neither a President elect nor a Vice President elect shall have qualified, declaring who shall then act as President, or the manner in which one who is to act shall be selected, and such person shall act accordingly until a President or Vice President shall have qualified.

Section 4. The Congress may by law provide for the case of the death of any of the persons from whom the House of Representatives may choose a President whenever the right of choice shall have devolved upon them, and for the case of the death of any of the persons from whom the Senate may choose a Vice President whenever the right of choice shall have devolved upon them.

Section 5. Sections 1 and 2 shall take effect on the 15th day of October following the ratification of this article.

Section 6. This article shall be inoperative unless it shall have been ratified as an amendment to the Constitution by the legislatures of three fourths of the several States within seven years from the date of its submission.

21st Amendment

Section 1. The eighteenth article of amendment to the Constitution of the United States is hereby repealed.

Section 2. The transportation or importation into any State, Territory, or possession of the United States for delivery or use therein of intoxicating liquors, in violation of the laws thereof, is hereby prohibited.

Section 3. This article shall be inoperative unless it shall have been ratified as an amendment to the Constitution by conventions in the several States, as provided in the Constitution, within seven years from the date of the submission hereof to the States by the Congress.

20th Amendment. Commencement of Terms; Sessions of Congress; Death or Disqualification of President-Elect

Proposed by Congress March 2, 1932; ratified January 23, 1933. The provisions of Sections 1 and 2 relating to Congress modified Article I, Section 4, Clause 2, and those provisions relating to the President, the 12th Amendment. The date on which the President and Vice President now take office was moved from March 4 to January 20. Similarly, the members of Congress now begin their terms on January 3. The 20th Amendment is sometimes called the "Lame Duck Amendment" because it shortened the period of time a member of Congress who was defeated for reelection (a "lame duck") remains in office.

This section deals with certain possibilities that were not covered by the presidential selection provisions of either Article II or the 12th Amendment. To this point, none of these situations has occurred. Note that there is neither a President-elect nor a Vice President-elect until the electoral votes have been counted by Congress, or, if the electoral college cannot decide the matter, the House has chosen a President or the Senate has chosen a Vice President.

Congress has not in fact ever passed such a law. See Section 2 of the 25th Amendment, regarding a vacancy in the vice presidency; that provision could some day have an impact here.

Section 5 set the date on which this amendment came into force.

Section 6 placed a time limit on the ratification process; note that a similar provision was written into the 18th, 21st, and 22nd amendments.

21st Amendment. Repeal of 18th Amendment

Proposed by Congress February 20, 1933; ratified December 5, 1933. This amendment repealed all of the 18th Amendment. Section 2 modifies the scope of the Federal Government's commerce power set out in Article I, Section 8, Clause 3; it gives to each State the power to regulate the transportation or importation and the distribution or use of intoxicating liquors in ways that would be unconstitutional in the case of any other commodity. The 21st Amendment is the only amendment Congress has thus far submitted to the States for ratification by conventions.

22nd Amendment. Presidential Tenure

Proposed by Congress March 21, 1947; ratified February 27, 1951. This amendment modified Article II, Section I, Clause 1. It stipulates that no President may serve more than two elected terms. But a President who has succeeded to the office beyond the midpoint in a term to which another President was originally elected may serve for more than eight years. In any case, however, a President may not serve more than 10 years. Prior to Franklin Roosevelt, who was elected to four terms, no President had served more than two full terms in office.

23rd Amendment. Presidential Electors for the District of Columbia

Proposed by Congress June 16, 1960; ratified March 29, 1961. This amendment modified Article II, Section I, Clause 2 and the 12th Amendment. It included the voters of the District of Columbia in the presidential electorate; and provides that the District is to have the same number of electors as the least populous State—three electors—but no more than that number.

24th Amendment. Right to Vote in Federal Elections—Tax Payment

Proposed by Congress August 27, 1962; ratified January 23, 1964. This amendment outlawed the payment of any tax as a condition for taking part in the nomination or election of any federal officeholder.

25th Amendment. Presidential Succession, Vice Presidential Vacancy, Presidential Inability

Proposed by Congress July 6, 1965; ratified February 10, 1967. Section 1 revised the imprecise provision on presidential succession in Article II, Section 1, Clause 6. It affirmed the precedent set by Vice President John Tyler, who became President on the death of William Henry Harrison in 1841. Section 2 provides for the filling of a vacancy in the office of Vice President. The office had been vacant on 16 occasions and remained unfilled for the rest of each term involved. When Spiro Agnew resigned the office in 1973, President Nixon selected Gerald Ford per this provision; and, when President Nixon resigned in 1974, Gerald Ford became President and chose Nelson Rockefeller as Vice President.

22nd Amendment

Section 1. No person shall be elected to the office of the President more than twice, and no person who has held the office of President, or acted as President, for more than two years of a term to which some other person was elected President shall be elected to the office of the President more than once. But this Article shall not apply to any person holding the office of President, when this Article was proposed by the Congress, and shall not prevent any person who may be holding the office of President, or acting as President, during the term within which this Article becomes operative from holding the office of President or acting as President during the remainder of such term.

Section 2. This article shall be inoperative unless it shall have been ratified as an amendment to the Constitution by the legislatures of three fourths of the several states within seven years from the date of its submission to the States by the Congress.

23rd Amendment.

Section 1. The District constituting the seat of Government of the United States shall appoint in such manner as the Congress may direct:

A number of electors of President and Vice President equal to the whole number of Senators and Representatives in Congress to which the District would be entitled if it were a State, but in no event more than the least populous State; they shall be in addition to those appointed by the States, they shall be considered, for the purposes of the election of President and Vice President, to be electors appointed by a State; and they shall meet in the District and perform such duties as provided by the twelfth article of amendment.

24th Amendment.

Section 1. The right of citizens of the United States to vote in any primary or other election for President or Vice President, for electors for President or Vice President, or for Senator or Representative in Congress, shall not be denied or abridged by the United States or any State by reason of failure to pay any poll tax or other tax.

Section 2. The Congress shall have power to enforce this article by appropriate legislation.

25th Amendment.

Section 1. In case of the removal of the President from office or of his death or resignation, the Vice President shall become President.

Section 2. Whenever there is a vacancy in the office of the Vice President, the President shall nominate a Vice President who shall take office upon confirmation by a majority vote of both Houses of Congress.

Section 3. Whenever the President transmits to the President pro tempore of the Senate and the Speaker of the House of Representatives his written declaration that he is unable to discharge the powers and duties of his office, and until he transmits to them a written declaration to the contrary, such powers and duties shall be discharged by the Vice President as Acting President.

This section created a procedure for determining if a President is so incapacitated that he cannot perform the powers and duties of his office.

Section 4. Whenever the Vice President and a majority of either the principal officers of the executive departments or of such other body as Congress may by law provide, transmit to the President pro tempore of the Senate and the Speaker of the House of Representatives their written declaration that the President is unable to discharge the powers and duties of his office, the Vice President shall immediately assume the powers and duties of the office as Acting President.

Section 4 deals with the circumstance in which a President will not be able to determine the fact of incapacity. To this point, Congress has not established the "such other body" referred to here. This section contains the only typographical error in the Constitution; in its second paragraph, the word "department" should in fact read "departments."

Thereafter, when the President transmits to the President pro tempore of the Senate and the Speaker of the House of Representatives his written declaration that no inability exists, he shall resume the powers and duties of his office unless the Vice President and a majority of either the principal officers of the executive department or of such other body as Congress may by law provide, transmit within four days to the President pro tempore of the Senate and the Speaker of the House of Representatives their written declaration that the President is unable to discharge the powers and duties of his office. Thereupon Congress shall decide the issue, assembling within forty-eight hours for that purpose if not in session. If the Congress, within twenty-one days after receipt of the latter written declaration, or, if Congress is not in session, within twenty-one days after Congress is required to assemble, determines by two-thirds vote of both Houses that the President is unable to discharge the powers and duties of his office, the Vice President shall continue to discharge the same as Acting President; otherwise, the President shall resume the powers and duties of his office.

26th Amendment.

Section 1. The right of citizens of the United States, who are eighteen years of age or older, to vote shall not be denied or abridged by the United States or by any State on account of age.

Section 2. The Congress shall have the power to enforce this article by appropriate legislation.

26th Amendment. Right to Vote—Age

Proposed by Congress March 23, 1971; ratified July 1, 1971. This amendment provides that the minimum age for voting in any election in the United States cannot be more than 18 years. (A State may set a minimum voting age of less than 18, however.)

27th Amendment.

No law varying the compensation for the services of the Senators and Representatives, shall take effect, until an election of Representatives shall have intervened.

27th Amendment. Congressional Pay

Proposed by Congress September 25, 1789; ratified May 7, 1992. This amendment modified Article I, Section 6, Clause 1. It limits Congress's power to fix the salaries of its members—by delaying the effectiveness of any increase in that pay until after the next regular congressional election.

Declaration of Independence

Introduction

By signing the Declaration of Independence, members of the Continental Congress sent a clear message to Britain that the American colonies were free and independent states. Starting with its preamble, the document spells out all the reasons the people of the United States have the right to break away from Britain.

Primary Source

The Unanimous Declaration of the Thirteen United States of America

When in the Course of human events, it becomes necessary for one people to dissolve the political bands which have connected them with another, and to assume among the powers of the earth, the separate and equal station to which the Laws of Nature and of Nature's God entitle them, a decent respect to the opinions of mankind requires that they should declare the causes which impel [force] them to the separation. We hold these truths to be self-evident, that all men are created equal, that they are endowed [gifted] by their Creator with certain unalienable [cannot be taken away] Rights, that among these are Life, Liberty and the pursuit of Happiness. That to secure these rights, Governments are instituted among Men, deriving their just powers from the consent of the governed. That whenever any Form of Government becomes destructive of these ends, it is the Right of the People to alter or to abolish it, and to institute new Government, laying its foundation on such principles and organizing its powers in such form, as to them shall seem most likely to effect their Safety and Happiness. Prudence [cautiousness], indeed, will dictate that Governments long established should not be changed for light and transient causes; and accordingly all experience hath shown that mankind are more disposed to suffer, while evils are sufferable, than to right themselves by abolishing the forms to which they are accustomed. But when a long train of abuses and usurpations [unjust uses of power], pursuing invariably the same Object evinces a design to reduce them under absolute Despotism [rule of absolute power], it is their right, it is their duty, to throw off such Government, and to provide new Guards for their future security.

Such has been the patient sufferance of these Colonies; and such is now the necessity which constrains them to alter their former Systems of Government. The history of the present King of Great Britain is a history of repeated injuries and usurpations, all having in direct object the establishment of an absolute Tyranny over these States. To prove this, let Facts be submitted to a candid world.

He has refused his Assent to Laws, the most wholesome and necessary for the public good.

He has forbidden his Governors to pass Laws of immediate and pressing importance, unless suspended in their operation till his Assent should be obtained; and when so suspended, he has utterly neglected to attend to them.

He has refused to pass other Laws for the accommodation of large districts of people, unless those people would relinquish [give up] the right of Representation in the Legislature, a right inestimable [priceless] to them and formidable to tyrants only.

He has called together legislative bodies at places unusual, uncomfortable, and distant from the depository of their public Records, for the sole purpose of fatiguing them into compliance with his measures.

He has dissolved Representative Houses repeatedly, for opposing with manly firmness his invasions on the rights of the people.

He has refused for a long time, after such dissolutions [closing down], to cause others to be elected; whereby the Legislative powers, incapable of Annihilation, have returned to the People at large for their exercise; the State remaining in the mean time exposed to all the dangers of invasion from without, and convulsions [riots] within.

He has endeavoured to prevent the population of these States; for that purpose obstructing the Laws for Naturalization of Foreigners; refusing to pass others to encourage their migrations hither, and raising the conditions of new Appropriations of Lands.

He has obstructed the Administration of Justice by refusing his Assent to Laws for establishing Judiciary powers.

He has made Judges dependent on his Will alone, for the tenure [term] of their offices, and the amount and payment of their salaries.

He has erected a multitude of New Offices, and sent hither swarms of Officers to harass our people, and eat out their substance.

He has kept among us, in times of peace, Standing Armies without the Consent of our legislatures.

He has affected to render the Military independent of and superior to the Civil power.

He has combined with others to subject us to a jurisdiction foreign to our constitution, and unacknowledged by our laws; giving his Assent to their Acts of pretended Legislation:

For quartering [lodging] large bodies of armed troops among us:

For protecting them, by a mock Trial, from punishment for any Murders which they should commit on the Inhabitants of these States:

For cutting off our Trade with all parts of the world:

For imposing Taxes on us without our Consent:

For depriving us in many cases, of the benefits of Trial by Jury: For transporting us beyond Seas to be tried for pretended offences:

For abolishing the free System of English Laws in a neighbouring Province, establishing therein an Arbitrary government, and enlarging its Boundaries so as to render it at once an example and fit instrument for introducing the same absolute rule into these Colonies:

For taking away our Charters, abolishing our most valuable Laws, and altering fundamentally the Forms of our Governments:

For suspending our own Legislatures, and declaring themselves invested with power to legislate for us in all cases whatsoever.

He has abdicated Government here, by declaring us out of his Protection and waging War against us.

He has plundered our seas, ravaged our Coasts, burnt our towns, and destroyed the lives of our people.

He is at this time transporting large Armies of foreign Mercenaries [soldiers] to complete the works of death, desolation, and tyranny, already begun with circumstances of Cruelty and perfidy [dishonesty] scarcely paralleled in the most barbarous ages, and totally unworthy the Head of a civilized nation.

He has constrained our fellow Citizens taken Captive on the high Seas to bear Arms against their Country, to become the executioners of their friends and Brethren, or to fall themselves by their Hands.

He has excited domestic insurrections amongst us, and has endeavoured to bring on the inhabitants of our frontiers, the merciless Indian Savages whose known rule of warfare, is an undistinguished destruction of all ages, sexes and conditions.

In every stage of these Oppressions We have Petitioned for Redress [correction of wrongs] in the most humble terms: Our repeated Petitions have been answered only by repeated injury. A Prince, whose character is thus marked by every act which may define a Tyrant, is unfit to be the ruler of a free people.

Nor have We been wanting in attentions to our British brethren. We have warned them from time to time of attempts by their legislature to extend an unwarrantable jurisdiction over us. We have reminded them of the circumstances of our emigration and settlement here. We have appealed to their native justice and magnanimity [generosity], and we have conjured [begged] them by the ties of our common kindred, to disavow these usurpations, which would inevitably interrupt our connections and correspondence. They too have been deaf to the voice of justice and of consanguinity [relation by blood]. We must, therefore, acquiesce in the necessity, which denounces our Separation, and hold them, as we hold the rest of mankind, Enemies in War, in Peace Friends.

We, therefore, the Representatives of the United States of America, in General Congress, Assembled, appealing to the Supreme Judge of the world for the rectitude [justness] of our intentions, do, in the Name, and by Authority of the good People of these Colonies, solemnly publish and declare, That these United Colonies are, and of Right ought to be Free and Independent States; that they are Absolved from all Allegiance to the British Crown, and that all political connection between them and the State of Great Britain, is and ought to be totally dissolved; and that as Free and Independent States, they have full Power to levy War, conclude Peace, contract Alliances, establish Commerce, and to do all other Acts and Things which Independent States may of right do. And for the support of this Declaration, with a firm reliance on the protection of Divine Providence, we mutually pledge to each other our Lives, our Fortunes and our sacred Honor.

1. **Identify Cause and Effect** How might the ideas about equality expressed in the Declaration of Independence have influenced later historical movements, such as the abolitionist movement and the women's suffrage movement?

2. **Identify Key Steps in a Process** Why was the Declaration of Independence a necessary document for the founding of the new nation?

3. **Determine Central Ideas** Explain how the Declaration of Independence reflects the political principles of popular sovereignty, the social contract, natural rights, and individual rights.

4. **Analyze Structure** How does the Declaration organize its key points from beginning to end?

Mayflower Compact

Introduction

The Pilgrims arrived at Massachusetts in 1620. Before disembarking, they signed a covenant that established a basis for self-government derived from the consent of the governed. Forty-one men signed the compact, agreeing to abide by the laws of the government. Women, who did not enjoy equal rights, were not asked to sign.

Primary Source

In the name of God, Amen. We, whose names are underwritten, the loyal subjects of our dread Sovereign Lord King James, by the grace of God, of Great Britain, France and Ireland king, defender of the faith, etc. Having undertaken, for the glory of God, and advancement of the Christian faith, and honor of our king and country, a voyage to plant the first colony in the Northern parts of Virginia, do by these presents solemnly and mutually in the presence of God and one of another, covenant [agree] and combine ourselves together into a civil body politick, for our better ordering and preservation, and furtherance [advancement] of the ends aforesaid; and by virtue hereof to enacte, constitute [establish], and frame such just and equal laws, ordinances, acts, constitutions and offices, from time to time, as

shall be thought most meet [suitable] and convenient for the general good of the Colony unto which we promise all due submission and obedience. In witness whereof we have hereunder subscribed our names at Cape Cod the eleventh of November, in the year of the reign of our Sovereign Lord, King James, of England, France and Ireland, the eighteenth, and of Scotland the fifty-fourth. Anno Dom. 1620.

1. **Identify Cause and Effect** How do you think that having this compact might have affected the Pilgrims once they arrived in North America?

2. **Analyze Interactions** What does the Mayflower Compact say about equality, and how might this view have influenced the system of government in the United States?

3. **Analyze Interactions** How do you think the organization of the Pilgrims "together into a civil body politick" influenced later ideas about government in the United States?

Virginia Statute for Religious Freedom: Thomas Jefferson

Introduction

In 1786, the Virginia legislature adopted the Statute for Religious Freedom, written by Thomas Jefferson. The law is still part of the Virginia state constitution.

Other states followed Virginia's lead. The Statute for Religious Freedom later became the basis for the First Amendment to the United States Constitution, which guarantees freedom of religion.

Primary Source

I. *Whereas* Almighty God hath created the mind free ... that to compel a man to furnish contributions of money for the propagation [spreading] of opinions which he disbelieves and abhors [hates], is sinful and tyrannical … that our civil rights have no dependence on our religious opinions, any more than our opinions in physics or geometry….

II. *Be it … enacted by the General Assembly*, that no man shall be compelled to frequent or support any religious worship, place, or ministry whatsoever, nor shall be enforced, restrained, molested, or burdened in his body or goods, nor shall otherwise suffer, on account of his religious opinions or belief; but that all men shall be free to profess, and by argument to maintain, their opinions in matters of religion, and that the same shall in no wise diminish, enlarge, or affect their civil capacities.

III. And although we well know that this Assembly, elected by the people for the ordinary purpose of legislation only, have no power to restrain the acts of succeeding assemblies, constituted with powers equal to our own, and that therefore to declare this act to be irrevocable [impossible to invalidate or take back] would be of no effect in law; yet we are free to declare, and do declare, that the rights hereby asserted are of the natural rights of mankind, and that if any act shall hereafter be passed to repeal the present, or to narrow its operation, such an act will be infringement of natural right.

ASSESSMENT

1. **Cite Evidence** What part of this excerpt could be cited as support for the idea that government funds, which come from sources such as taxes, should not be given to religious institutions?

2. **Analyze Structure** What is the purpose of each of the three articles in the Statute?

Articles of Confederation

Introduction
The Articles of Confederation were approved on November 15, 1777, and were in effect from March 1, 1781, when they were finally ratified by all 13 states, until March 4, 1789. They established a weak central government, which led to conflicts among the states. Demand soon grew for a stronger central government, leading to the creation of the United States Constitution.

Primary Source
To all to whom these Presents shall come, we the undersigned Delegates of the States affixed to our Names send greeting. Whereas the Delegates of the United States of America in Congress assembled did on the fifteenth day of November in the Year of our Lord One Thousand Seven Hundred and Seventy seven, and in the Second Year of the Independence of America agree to certain articles of Confederation [an alliance of states, usually for the purpose of defense] and perpetual [continuing forever] Union between the States of New Hampshire, Massachusetts Bay, Rhode Island and Providence Plantations, Connecticut, New York, New Jersey, Pennsylvania, Delaware, Maryland, Virginia, North Carolina, South Carolina and Georgia in the Words following, viz. [namely] "Articles of Confederation and perpetual Union between the states of New Hampshire, Massachusetts Bay, Rhode Island and Providence Plantations, Connecticut, New York, New Jersey, Pennsylvania, Delaware, Maryland, Virginia, North Carolina, South Carolina and Georgia."

[ART. I.] The Stile [style; name] of this confederacy shall be "The United States of America."

[ART. II.] Each state retains its sovereignty [the ability to make one's own laws and govern oneself], freedom and independence, and every Power, Jurisdiction and right, which is not by this confederation expressly delegated to the United States, in Congress assembled.

[ART. III.] The said states hereby severally enter into a firm league of friendship with each other, for their common defence, the security of their Liberties, and their mutual and general welfare, binding themselves to assist each other, against all force offered to, or attacks made upon them, or any of them, on account of religion, sovereignty, trade, or any other pretence whatever.

[ART. IV.] The better to secure and perpetuate mutual friendship and intercourse [communication and actions] among the people of the different states in this union, the free inhabitants of each of these states, paupers, vagabonds and fugitives from Justice excepted, shall be entitled to all privileges and immunities of free citizens in the several states; and the people of each state shall have free ingress [entrance] and regress [return] to and from any other state, and shall enjoy therein all the privileges of trade and commerce, subject to the same duties [taxes on imports or exports], impositions [taxes] and restrictions as the inhabitants thereof respectively, provided that such restriction shall not extend so far as to prevent the removal of property imported into any state, to any other state of which the Owner is an inhabitant; provided also that no imposition, duties or restriction shall be laid by any state, on the property of the united states, or either of them.

If any Person guilty of, or charged with treason, felony, or other high misdemeanor in any state, shall flee from Justice, and be found in any of the united states, he shall upon demand of the Governor or executive power, of the state from which he fled, be delivered up and removed to the state having jurisdiction of his offence.

Full faith and credit shall be given in each of these states to the records, acts and judicial proceedings of the courts and magistrates of every other state.

[ART. V.] For the more convenient management of the general interests of the united states, delegates shall be annually appointed in such manner as the legislature of each state shall direct, to meet in Congress on the first Monday in November, in every year, with a power reserved to each state, to recall its delegates, or any of them, at any time within the year, and to send others in their stead, for the remainder of the Year.

No state shall be represented in Congress by less than two, nor by more than seven Members; and no person shall be capable of being a delegate for more than three years in any term of six years; nor shall any person, being a delegate, be capable of holding any office under the united states, for which he, or another for his benefit receives any salary, fees or emolument [payment] of any kind.

Each state shall maintain its own delegates in a meeting of the states, and while they act as members of the committee of the states.

In determining questions in the united states, in Congress assembled, each state shall have one vote.

Freedom of speech and debate in Congress shall not be impeached or questioned in any Court, or place out of Congress, and the members of congress shall be protected in their persons from arrests and imprisonments, during the time of their going to and from, and attendance on congress, except for treason, felony, or breach of the peace.

[ART. VI.] No state without the Consent of the united states in congress assembled, shall send any embassy to, or receive any embassy from, or enter into any conference, agreement, or alliance or treaty with any King, prince or state; nor shall any person holding any office of profit or trust under the united states, or any of them, accept of any present, emolument, office or title of any kind whatever from any king, prince or foreign state; nor shall the united states in congress assembled, or any of them, grant any title of nobility.

No two or more states shall enter into any treaty, confederation or alliance whatever between them, without the consent of the united states in congress assembled, specifying accurately the purposes for which the same is to be entered into, and how long it shall continue.

No state shall lay any imposts [taxes] or duties, which may interfere with any stipulations [conditions] in treaties, entered into by the united states in congress assembled, with any king, prince or state, in pursuance of any treaties already proposed by congress, to the courts of France and Spain.

No vessels of war shall be kept up in time of peace by any state, except such number only, as shall be deemed necessary by the united states in congress assembled, for the defence of such state, or its trade; nor shall any body of forces be kept up by any state, in time of peace, except such number only, as in the judgment of the united states, in congress assembled, shall be deemed requisite to garrison [assign troops to] the forts necessary for the defence of such state; but every state shall always keep up a well regulated and disciplined militia, sufficiently armed and accounted, and shall provide and constantly have ready for use, in public stores, a due number of field pieces and tents, and a proper quantity of arms, ammunition and camp equipage.

No state shall engage in any war without the consent of the united states in congress assembled, unless such state be actually invaded by enemies, or shall have received certain advice of a resolution being formed by some nation of Indians to invade such state and the danger is so imminent as not to admit of a delay, till the united states in congress assembled can be consulted: nor shall any state grant commissions to any ships or vessels of war, nor letters of marque [written permissions to cross a border] or reprisal, except it be after a declaration of war by the united states in congress assembled, and then only against the kingdom or state and the subjects thereof, against which war has been so declared, and under such regulations as shall be established by the united states in congress assembled, unless such state be infested by pirates, in which case vessels of war may be fitted out for that occasion, and kept so long as the danger shall continue, or until the united states in congress assembled shall determine otherwise.

☑ **CITE EVIDENCE** What details from Article VI show that the delegates were attempting to create a united nation, rather than just a confederation of individual states? Cite specific examples to support your answer.

[ART. VII.] When land-forces are raised by any state for the common defence, all officers of or under the rank of colonel, shall be appointed by the legislature of each state respectively by whom such forces shall be raised, or in such manner as such state shall direct, and all vacancies shall be filled up by the state which first made the appointment.

[ART. VIII.] All charges of war, and all other expences that shall be incurred for the common defence or general welfare, and allowed by the united states in congress assembled, shall be defrayed out of a common treasury, which shall be supplied by the several states, in proportion to the value of all land within each state, granted to or surveyed for any Person, as such land and the buildings and improvements thereon shall be estimated according to such mode as the united states in congress assembled, shall from time to time direct and appoint. The taxes for paying that proportion shall be laid and levied by the authority and direction of the legislatures of the several states within the time agreed upon by the united states in congress assembled.

[ART. IX.] The united states in congress assembled, shall have the sole and exclusive right and power of determining on peace and war, except in the cases mentioned in the sixth article—of sending and receiving ambassadors— entering into treaties and alliances, provided that no treaty of commerce shall be made whereby the legislative power of the respective states shall be restrained from imposing such imposts and duties

on foreigners, as their own people are subjected to, or from prohibiting the exportation or importation of any species of goods or commodities whatsoever— of establishing rules for deciding in all cases, what captures on land or water shall be legal, and in what manner prizes taken by land or naval forces in the service of the united states shall be divided or appropriated—of granting letters of marque and reprisal in times of peace—appointing courts for the trial of piracies and felonies committed on the high seas and establishing courts for receiving and determining finally appeals in all cases of captures, provided that no member of congress shall be appointed a judge of any of the said courts.

The united states in congress assembled shall also be the last resort on appeal in all disputes and differences now subsisting [existing] or that hereafter may arise between two or more states concerning boundary, jurisdiction or any other cause whatever; which authority shall always be exercised in the manner following. Whenever the legislative or executive authority or lawful agent [of any] state in controversy with another shall present a petition to congress stating the matter in question and praying for a hearing, notice thereof shall be given by order of congress to the legislative or executive authority of the other state in controversy, and a day assigned for the appearance of the parties by their lawful agents, who shall then be directed to appoint by joint consent, commissioners or judges to constitute a court for hearing and determining the matter in question; but if they cannot agree, congress shall name three persons out of each of the united states, and from the list of such persons each party shall alternately strike out one, the petitioners beginning, until the number shall be reduced to thirteen; and from that number not less than seven, nor more than nine names as congress shall direct, shall in the presence of congress be drawn out by lot, and the persons whose names shall be so drawn or any five of them, shall be commissioners or judges, to hear and finally determine the controversy, so always as a major part of the judges who shall hear the cause shall agree in the determination: and if either party shall neglect to attend at the day appointed, without shewing [showing] reasons, which congress shall judge sufficient, or being present shall refuse to strike, the congress shall proceed to nominate three persons out of each state, and the secretary of congress shall strike in behalf of such party absent or refusing; and the judgment and sentence of the court to be appointed, in the manner before prescribed, shall be final and conclusive; and if any of the parties shall refuse to submit to the authority of such court, or to appear to defend their claim or cause, the court shall nevertheless proceed to pronounce sentence, or judgment, which shall in like manner be final and decisive, the judgment or sentence and other proceedings being in either case transmitted to congress, and lodged among the acts of congress for the security of the parties concerned: provided that every commissioner, before he sits in judgment, shall take an oath to be administered by one of the judges of the supreme or superior court of the state, where the cause shall be tried, "well and truly to hear and determine the matter in question, according to the best of his judgment, without favour, affection or hope of reward;" provided also that no state shall be deprived of territory for the benefit of the united states.

All controversies concerning the private right of soil claimed under different grants of two or more states, whose jurisdictions as they may respect such lands, and the states which passed such grants are adjusted, the said grants or either of them being at the same time claimed to have originated antecedent to such settlement of jurisdiction, shall on the petition of either party to the congress of the united states, be finally determined as near as may be in the same manner as is before prescribed for deciding disputes respecting territorial jurisdiction between different states.

The united states in congress assembled shall also have the sole and exclusive right and power of regulating the alloy and value of coin struck by their own authority, or by that of the respective states—fixing the standard of weights and measures throughout the united states—regulating the trade and managing all affairs with the Indians, not members of any of the states, provided that the legislative right of any state within its own limits be not infringed or violated—establishing and regulating post-offices from one state to another, throughout all the united states, and exacting such postage on the papers passing thro' [through] the same as may be requisite to defray [pay] the expences of the said office—appointing all officers of the land forces, in the service of the united states, excepting regimental officers—appointing all the officers of the naval forces, and commissioning all officers whatever in the service of the united

states—making rules for the government and regulation of the said land and naval forces, and directing their operations.

The united states in congress assembled shall have authority to appoint a committee, to sit in the recess of congress, to be denominated "A Committee of the States," and to consist of one delegate from each state; and to appoint such other committees and civil officers as may be necessary for managing the general affairs of the united states under their direction—to appoint one of their number to preside, provided that no person be allowed to serve in the office of president more than one year in any term of three years; to ascertain the necessary sums of Money to be raised for the service of the united states, and to appropriate and apply the same for defraying the public expences—to borrow money, or emit bills on the credit of the united states, transmitting every half year to the respective states an account of the sums of money so borrowed or emitted—to build and equip a navy—to agree upon the number of land forces, and to make requisitions from each state for its quota, in proportion to the number of white inhabitants in such state; which requisition shall be binding, and thereupon the legislature of each state shall appoint the regimental officers, raise the men and clothe, arm and equip them in a soldier like manner, at the expence of the united states, and the officers and men so clothed, armed and equipped shall march to the place appointed, and within the time agreed on by the united states in congress assembled. But if the united states in congress assembled shall, on consideration of circumstances judge proper that any state should not raise men, or should raise a smaller number than its quota, and that any other state should raise a greater number of men than the quota thereof, such extra number shall be raised, officered, clothed, armed and equipped in the same manner as the quota of such state, unless the legislature of such state shall judge that such extra number cannot be safely spared out of the same, in which case they shall raise, officer, clothe, arm and equip as many of such extra number as they judge can be safely spared. And the officers and men so clothed, armed and equipped, shall march to the place appointed, and within the time agreed on by the united states in congress assembled.

The united states in congress assembled shall never engage in a war, nor grant letters of marque and reprisal in time of peace, nor enter into any treaties or alliances, nor coin money, nor regulate the value thereof, nor ascertain the sums and expences necessary for the defence and welfare of the united states, or any of them, nor emit bills, nor borrow money on the credit of the united states, nor appropriate money, nor agree upon the number of vessels of war, to be built or purchased, or the number of land or sea forces to be raised, nor appoint a commander in chief of the army or navy, unless nine states assent to the same: nor shall a question on any other point, except for adjourning from day to day be determined, unless by the votes of a majority of the united states in congress assembled.

☑ **DETERMINE CENTRAL IDEAS** How many states had to agree before an act of Congress could be enacted? Do you think this made passing laws easier or more difficult? Explain your answer.

The congress of the united states shall have power to adjourn to any time within the year, and to any place within the united states, so that no period of adjournment be for a longer duration than the space of six Months, and shall publish the Journal of their proceedings monthly, except such parts thereof relating to treaties, alliances or military operations as in their judgment require secrecy; and the yeas and nays of the delegates of each state on any question shall be entered on the Journal, when it is desired by any delegate; and the delegates of a state, or any of them, at his or their request shall be furnished with a transcript of the said Journal, except such parts as are above excepted, to lay before the legislatures of the several states.

[ART. X.] The committee of the states, or any nine of them, shall be authorised to execute, in the recess of congress, such of the powers of congress as the united states in congress assembled, by the consent of nine states, shall from time to time think expedient to vest them with; provided that no power be delegated to the said committee, for the exercise of which, by the articles of confederation, the voice of nine states in the congress of the united states assembled is requisite.

[ART. XI.] Canada acceding to this confederation, and joining in the measures of the united states, shall be admitted into, and entitled to all the advantages of this union: but no other colony shall be admitted into the same, unless such admission be agreed to by nine states.

[ART. XII.] All bills of credit emitted, monies borrowed and debts contracted by, or under the authority of congress, before the assembling of the united states, in pursuance of the present confederation, shall be deemed and considered as a charge against the united states, for payment and satisfaction whereof the said united states, and the public faith are hereby solemnly pledged.

[ART. XIII.] Every state shall abide by [conform to; agree to] the determinations of the united states in congress assembled, on all questions which by this confederation are submitted to them. And the Articles of this confederation shall be inviolably observed by every state, and the union shall be perpetual; nor shall any alteration at any time hereafter be made in any of them; unless such alteration be agreed to in a congress of the united states, and be afterwards confirmed by the legislatures of every state.

And whereas it hath pleased the Great Governor of the World to incline [bend something in a certain direction] the hearts of the legislatures we respectively represent in congress, to approve of, and to authorize us to ratify the said articles of confederation and perpetual union. Know ye that we the undersigned delegates, by virtue of the power and authority to us given for that purpose, do by these presents, in the name and in behalf of our respective constituents, fully and entirely ratify and confirm each and every of the said articles of confederation and perpetual union, and all and singular the matters and things therein contained: And we do further solemnly plight [pledge] and engage the faith of our respective constituents, that they shall abide by the determinations of the united states in congress assembled, on all questions, which by the said confederation are submitted to them. And that the articles thereof shall be inviolably [without failure] observed by the states we respectively represent, and that the union shall be perpetual. In Witness whereof we have hereunto set our hands in Congress. Done at Philadelphia in the state of Pennsylvania the ninth Day of July in the Year of our Lord one Thousand seven Hundred and Seventy-eight, and in the third year of the independence of America.

Josiah Bartlett
John Wentworth Junr
August 8th 1778
On The Part & Behalf Of The State Of New Hampshire

John Hancock
Samuel Adams
Elbridge Gerry
Francis Dana
James Lovell
Samuel Holten
On The Part And Behalf Of
The State Of Massachusetts Bay

William Ellery
Henry Marchant
John Collins
On The Part And Behalf
Of The State Of Rhode Island
And Providence Plantations

Roger Sherman
Samuel Huntington
Oliver Wolcott
Titus Hosmer
Andrew Adams
On The Part And Behalf Of
The State Of Connecticut

Jas Duane
Fras Lewis
Wm Duer.
Gouv Morris
On The Part And Behalf Of
The State Of New York

Jno Witherspoon
Nathl Scudder
On The Part And In Behalf Of
The State Of New Jersey.
Novr 26, 1778.—

Robt Morris
Daniel Roberdeau
Jona Bayard Smith.
William Clingan
Joseph Reed
22d July 1778
On The Part And Behalf Of
The State Of Pennsylvania

Tho Mckean
Feby 12 1779
John Dickinson
May 5th 1779

Nicholas Van Dyke,
On The Part & Behalf Of
The State Of Delaware

John Hanson
March 1 1781
Daniel Carroll Do
On The Part And Behalf
Of The State Of Maryland

Richard Henry Lee
John Banister
Thomas Adams
Jno Harvie
Francis Lightfoot Lee
On The Part And Behalf Of
The State Of Virginia

John Penn
July 21st 1778
Corns Harnett
Jno Williams
On The Part And Behalf
Of The State Of No Carolina

Henry Laurens
William Henry Drayton
Jno Mathews
Richd Hutson.
Thos Heyward Junr
On The Part & Behalf Of
The State Of South Carolina

Jno Walton
24th July 1778
Edwd Telfair.
Edwd Langworthy
On The Part And Behalf Of
The State Of Georgia

ASSESSMENT

1. **Draw Conclusions** As you have learned, a *confederation* is an alliance of states that typically forms for the purpose of defense. Why do you think the idea of a confederation was favored by the Framers at this point in American history? How would the idea continue to influence the Framers in subsequent years?

2. **Determine Central Ideas** Historians commonly criticize the Articles of Confederation for setting up only a "loose" confederation of states. In what way was the confederation of states "loose"? Explain your answer with evidence from the text.

3. **Explain an Argument** Explain the argument that one weakness of the Articles of Confederation was that Congress was not granted the power to levy taxes.

4. **Analyze** Explain how this document is structured and how key sections of the text contribute to the whole.

Anti-Federalist Papers

Introduction

When the Constitutional Convention of 1787 produced the new constitution, many opposed its adoption. There were numerous men who made strong arguments on behalf of the opponents, known as the Anti-Federalists. The following excerpts provide a sampling of Anti- Federalist arguments. Richard Henry Lee, a Virginian, wrote the best-known Anti-Federalist essays of the time, "Letters from the Federal Farmer to the Republican." The first selection below is from letters Lee wrote in October 1787. Luther Martin, the leading Anti-Federalist from Maryland, attended the Constitutional Convention as a delegate. The second selection is from a speech Martin gave on November 29, 1787. In it, he defends his decision to leave the Convention before its work was finished. Findley, Whitehill, and Smilie believed that they were prevented from expressing their views because of the political maneuverings of the Federalists. The third selection below is from "The Address and Reasons of Dissent of the Minority of the Convention of the State of Pennsylvania to their Constituents," which the three men published in the *Pennsylvania Packet and Daily Advertiser* on December 18, 1787.

Primary Source

"Letters from the Federal Farmer to the Republican," by Richard Henry Lee

The present moment discovers a new face in our affairs. Our object has been all along to reform our federal system and to strengthen our governments to establish peace, order, and justice in the community—but a new object now presents. The plan of government now proposed is evidently calculated totally to change, in time, our condition as a people. Instead of being thirteen republics under a federal head, it is clearly designed to make us one consolidated government. . . . This consolidation of the states has been the object of several men in this country for some time past. Whether such a change can ever be effected, in any manner; whether it can be effected without convulsions and civil wars; whether such a change will not totally destroy the liberties of this country, time only can determine. . . .

The Confederation was formed when great confidence was placed in the voluntary exertions of individuals and of the respective states; and the framers of it, to guard against usurpation [an illegal grab of power, authority, or sovereignty], so limited and checked the powers that, in many respects, they are inadequate to the exigencies [requirements; demands] of the Union. We find, therefore, members of Congress urging alterations in the federal system almost as soon as it was adopted. . . .

We expected too much from the return of peace, and, of course, we have been disappointed. Our governments have been new and unsettled; and several legislature, [by their actions] . . . have given just cause of uneasiness. . . .

The conduct of several legislatures touching paper-money and tender [method of payment] laws has prepared many honest men for changes in government, which otherwise they would not have thought of—when by the evils, on the one hand, and by the secret instigations of artful men, on the other, the minds of men were become sufficiently uneasy, a bold step was taken, which is usually followed by a revolution or a civil war. A general convention for mere commercial purposes was moved for— the authors of this measure saw that the people's attention was turned solely to the amendment of the federal system; and that, had the idea of a total change been started, probably no state would have appointed members to the Convention. The idea of destroying, ultimately, the state government and forming one consolidated system could not have been admitted. A convention, therefore, merely for vesting in Congress power to regulate trade was proposed. . . .

The plan proposed appears to be partly federal, but principally, however, calculated ultimately to make the states one consolidated government.

The first interesting question therefore suggested is how far the states can be consolidated into one entire government on free principles. In considering this question, extensive objects are to be taken into view, and important changes in the forms of government to be carefully attended to in all their consequences. The happiness of the people at large must be the great object with every honest statesman, and he will direct every movement to this point. If we are so situated as a people as not to be able to enjoy equal happiness and advantages under one government, the consolidation of the states cannot be admitted.

There are certain unalienable and fundamental rights, which in forming the social compact ought to be explicitly ascertained and fixed. A free and enlightened people, in forming this compact, will not resign all their rights to those who govern, and they will fix limits [a bill of rights] to their legislators and rulers, which will soon be plainly seen by those who are governed, as well as by those who govern; and the latter will know they cannot be passed unperceived by the former and without giving a general alarm. These rights should be made the basis of every constitution; and if a people be so situated, or have such different opinions, that they cannot agree in ascertaining and fixing them, it is a very strong argument against their attempting to form one entire society, to live under one system of laws only.

It may also be worthy our examination how far the provision for amending this plan, when it shall be adopted, is of any importance. No measures can be taken toward amendments unless two-thirds of the Congress, or two-thirds of the legislature of the several states, shall agree. While power is in the hands of the people, or democratic part of the community, more especially as at present, it is easy, according to the general course of human affairs, for the few influential men in the community to obtain conventions, alterations in government, and to persuade the common people that they may change for the better, and to get from them a part of the power. But when power is once transferred from the many to the few, all changes become extremely difficult; the government in this case being beneficial to the few, they will be exceedingly artful and adroit [skillful] in preventing any measures which may lead to a change; and nothing will produce it but great exertions and severe struggles on the part of the common people. Every man of reflection must see that the change now proposed is a transfer of power from the many to the few, and the probability is the artful and ever active aristocracy will prevent all peaceful measures for changes, unless when they shall discover some favorable moment to increase their own influence.

It is true there may be danger in delay; but there is danger in adopting the system in its present form. And I see the danger in either case will arise principally from the conduct and views of two very unprincipled parties in the United States—two fires, between which the honest and substantial people have long found themselves situated. One party is composed of little insurgents [people rising in opposition to a government], men in debt, who want no law and who want a share of the property of others—these are called levelers, Shaysites [opponents of the new Constitution], etc. The other party is composed of a few but more dangerous men, with their servile [submissive] dependents; these avariciously [greedily] grasp at all power and property. You may discover in all the actions of these men an evident dislike to free and equal government, and they will go systematically to work to change, essentially, the forms of government in this country—these are called aristocrats . . . . . .

The fact is, these aristocrats support and hasten the adoption of the proposed Constitution merely because they think it is a stepping-stone to their favorite object. I think I am well-founded in this idea; I think the general politics of these men support it, as well as the common observation among them that the proffered plan is the best that can be got at present; it will do for a few years, and lead to something better. . . .

A speech given before the Maryland State legislature, November 29, 1787, by Luther Martin

It was the states as states, by their representatives in Congress, that formed the Articles of Confederation; it was the states as states, by their legislatures, who ratified those Articles; and it was there established and provided that the states as states (that is, by their legislatures) should agree to any alterations that should hereafter be proposed in the federal government, before they should be binding; and any alterations agreed to in any other manner cannot release the states from the obligation they are under to each other by virtue of the original Articles of Confederation. The people of the different states never made any objection to the manner in which the Articles of Confederation were formed or ratified, or to the mode by which alterations were to be made in that government—with the rights of their respective states they wished not to interfere. Nor do I believe the people, in their individual capacity, would ever have expected or desired to have been appealed to on the present occasion, in violation of the rights of their respective states, if the favorers of the proposed Constitution, imagining they had a better chance of forcing it to be adopted by a hasty appeal to the people at large (who could not be so good judges of the dangerous consequence), had not insisted upon this mode . . . .

It was also my opinion that, upon principles of sound policy, the agreement or disagreement to the proposed system ought to have been by the state legislatures; in which case, let the event have been what it would, there would have been but little prospect of the public peace being disturbed thereby; whereas the attempt to force down this system, although Congress and the respective state legislatures should disapprove, by appealing to the people and to procure [acquire] its establishment in a manner totally unconstitutional, has a tendency to set the state governments and their subjects at variance with each other, to lessen the obligations of government, to weaken the bands of society, to introduce anarchy and confusion, and to light the torch of discord and civil war throughout this continent. All these considerations weighed with me most forcibly against giving my assent to the mode by which it is resolved that this system is to be ratified, and were urged by me in opposition to the measure.

. . . [A] great portion of that time which ought to have been devoted calmly and impartially to consider what alterations in our federal government would be most likely to procure and preserve the happiness of the Union was employed in a violent struggle on the one side to obtain all power and dominion in their own hands, and on the other to prevent it; and that the aggrandizement of particular states, and

particular individuals, appears to have been much more the subject sought after than the welfare of our country . . . .

When I took my seat in the Convention, I found them attempting to bring forward a system which, I was sure, never had entered into the contemplation of those I had the honor to represent, and which, upon the fullest consideration, I considered not only injurious to the interest and rights of this state but also incompatible with the political happiness and freedom of the states in general. From that time until my business compelled me to leave the Convention, I gave it every possible opposition, in every stage of its progression. I opposed the system there with the same explicit frankness with which I have here given you a history of our proceedings, an account of my own conduct, which in a particular manner I consider you as having a right to know. While there, I endeavored to act as became a free man and the delegate of a free state. Should my conduct obtain the approbation [act of approval] of those who appointed me, I will not deny it would afford me satisfaction; but to me that approbation was at most no more than a secondary consideration—my first was to deserve it. Left to myself to act according to the best of my discretion, my conduct should have been the same had I been even sure your censure would have been my only reward, since I hold it sacredly my duty to dash the cup of poison, if possible, from the hand of a state or an individual, however anxious the one or the other might be to swallow it . . . .

"The Address and Reasons of Dissent of the Minority of the Convention of the State of Pennsylvania to their Constituents," by William Findley, Robert Whitehill, and John Smilie

Our objections are comprised under three general heads of dissent, viz. [namely]:

We dissent, first, because it is the opinion of the most celebrated writers on government, and confirmed by uniform experience, that a very extensive territory cannot be governed on the principles of freedom otherwise than by a confederation of republics, possessing all the powers of internal government but united in the management of their general and foreign concerns. . . .

We dissent, secondly, because the powers vested in Congress by this Constitution must necessarily annihilate and absorb the legislative, executive, and judicial powers of the several states, and produce from their ruins one consolidated government, which from the nature of things will be an iron-handed despotism, as nothing short of the supremacy of despotic sway could connect and govern these United States under one government.

As the truth of this position is of such decisive importance, it ought to be fully investigated, and if it is founded, to be clearly ascertained; for, should it be demonstrated that the powers vested by this Constitution in Congress will have such an effect as necessarily to produce one consolidated government, the question then will be reduced to this short issue, viz.: whether satiated [satisfied] with the blessings of liberty, whether repenting [regretting] of the folly of so recently asserting their unalienable rights against foreign despots at the expense of so much blood and treasure, and such painful and arduous struggles, the people of America are now willing to resign every privilege of freemen, and submit to the dominion of an absolute government that will embrace all America in one chain of despotism; or whether they will, with virtuous indignation, spurn at the shackles prepared for them, and confirm their liberties by a conduct becoming freemen. . . .

We dissent, thirdly, because if it were practicable to govern so extensive a territory as these United States include, on the plan of a consolidated government, consistent with the principles of liberty and the happiness of the people, yet the construction of this Constitution is not calculated to attain the object; for independent of the nature of the case, it would of itself necessarily produce a despotism, and that not by the usual gradations [small steps or changes] but with the celerity [speed] that has hitherto only attended revolutions effected by the sword.

☑ **ANALYZE WORD CHOICE** Why do you think the authors use words such as *iron-handed, shackles, despotism,* and *sword*?

To establish the truth of this position, a cursory [hasty] investigation of the principles and form of this Constitution will suffice.

The first consideration that this review suggests is the omission of a Bill of Rights ascertaining and fundamentally establishing those unalienable and personal rights of men, without the full, free, and secure enjoyment of which there can be no liberty,

and over which it is not necessary for a good government to have the control—the principal of which are the rights of conscience, personal liberty by the clear and unequivocal establishment of the writ of habeas corpus, jury trial in criminal and civil cases, by an impartial jury of the vicinage [neighborhood] or county, with the common law proceedings for the safety of the accused in criminal prosecutions; and the liberty of the press, that scourge of tyrants, and the grand bulwark [safeguard] of every other liberty and privilege. The stipulations [conditions of agreement] heretofore made in favor of them in the state constitutions are entirely superseded by this Constitution. . . .

ASSESSMENT

1. **Analyze Style and Rhetoric** Rhetoric is persuasive language that is often seen to be lacking in sincerity or meaning. Do you think either of these passages qualifies as rhetoric? Why or why not?

2. **Assess an Argument** What do you think are the strongest and weakest parts of the Anti-Federalists' overall argument? Cite specific examples in the text.

3. **Analyze Interactions** How have Anti-Federalist viewpoints such as those expressed in the excerpts influenced the system of government of the United States? Consider the Bill of Rights and the final version of the U.S. Constitution as part of your answer.

4. **Analyze Structure** Analyze how the Anti-Federalist essay by Findley, Whitehill, and Smilie is structured, including how key sentences and paragraphs contribute to the whole.

Federalist No. 10: James Madison

Introduction

Of the 85 *Federalist Papers*, it is believed that 29 of them were written by James Madison. Among them was *Federalist* No. 10, which presents Madison's observations on dealing with the "mischiefs of faction" and the advantages of a republican (representative) form of government over that of a pure democracy. It was first published on November 23, 1787.

Primary Source

Among the numerous advantages promised by a well constructed Union, none deserves to be more accurately developed than its tendency to break and control the violence of faction [a group within a larger political group]. The friend of popular governments never finds himself so much alarmed for their character and fate, as when he contemplates their propensity [tendency] to this dangerous vice. He will not fail, therefore, to set a due value on any plan which, without violating the principles to which he is attached, provides a proper cure for it. The instability, injustice, and confusion introduced into the public councils, have, in truth, been the mortal diseases under which popular governments have everywhere perished; as they continue to be the favorite and fruitful topics from which the adversaries to liberty derive their most specious [seemingly true, but actually false] declamations.

The valuable improvements made by the American constitutions on the popular models, both ancient and modern, cannot certainly be too much admired; but it would be an unwarrantable partiality, to contend that they have as effectually obviated [made unnecessary] the danger on this side, as was wished and expected. Complaints are everywhere heard from our most considerate and virtuous citizens, equally the friends of public and private faith, and of public and personal liberty, that our governments are too unstable, that the public good is disregarded in the conflicts of rival parties, and that measures are too often decided, not according to the rules of justice and the rights of the minor party, but by the superior force of an interested and overbearing majority. However anxiously we may wish that these complaints had no foundation, the evidence, of known facts will not permit us to deny that they are in some degree true.

☑ **IDENTIFY POINT OF VIEW** While Madison does not define the term *faction* here, he does offer some clues as to his view of factions and what factions are. Describe that viewpoint, citing evidence from these opening paragraphs. Then list the words and phrases that tell you what a faction is.

It will be found, indeed, on a candid review of our situation, that some of the distresses under which we labor have been erroneously charged on the operation of our governments; but it will be found, at the same time, that other causes will not alone account for many of our heaviest misfortunes; and, particularly, for that prevailing and increasing distrust of public engagements, and alarm for private rights, which are echoed from one end of the continent to the other. These must be chiefly, if not wholly, effects of the unsteadiness and injustice with which a factious spirit has tainted our public administrations.

By a faction, I understand a number of citizens, whether amounting to a majority or a minority of the whole, who are united and actuated [caused to do something] by some common impulse of passion, or of interest, adversed to the rights of other citizens, or to the permanent and aggregate interests of the community.

There are two methods of curing the mischiefs of faction: the one, by removing its causes; the other, by controlling its effects.

There are again two methods of removing the causes of faction: the one, by destroying the liberty which is essential to its existence; the other, by giving to every citizen the same opinions, the same passions, and the same interests.

It could never be more truly said than of the first remedy, that it was worse than the disease. Liberty is to faction what air is to fire, an aliment without which it instantly expires. But it could not be less folly to abolish liberty, which is essential to political life, because it nourishes faction, than it would be to wish the annihilation of air, which is essential to animal life, because it imparts to fire its destructive agency.

The second expedient [a way of achieving a result] is as impracticable as the first would be unwise. As long as the reason of man continues fallible [capable of being wrong], and he is at liberty to exercise it, different opinions will be formed. As long as the connection subsists [exists] between his reason and his self- love, his opinions and his passions will have a reciprocal influence on each other; and the former will be objects to which the latter will attach themselves. The diversity in the faculties of men, from which the rights of property originate, is not less an insuperable [uncontrollable] obstacle to a uniformity of interests. The protection of these faculties is the first object of government.

From the protection of different and unequal faculties of acquiring property, the possession of different degrees and kinds of property immediately results; and from the influence of these on the sentiments and views of the respective proprietors, ensues a division of the society into different interests and parties.

The latent causes of faction are thus sown in the nature of man; and we see them everywhere brought into different degrees of activity, according to the different circumstances of civil society. A zeal for different opinions concerning religion, concerning government, and many other points, as well of speculation as of practice; an attachment to different leaders ambitiously contending for pre-eminence and power; or to persons of other descriptions whose fortunes have been interesting to the human passions, have, in turn, divided mankind into parties, inflamed them with mutual animosity, and rendered them much more disposed to vex and oppress each other than to co-operate for their common good. So strong is this propensity of mankind to fall into mutual animosities, that where no substantial occasion presents itself, the most frivolous and fanciful distinctions have been sufficient to kindle their unfriendly passions and excite their most violent conflicts. But the most common and durable source of factions has been the various and unequal distribution of property. Those who hold and those who are without property have ever formed distinct interests in society. Those who are creditors, and those who are debtors, fall under a like discrimination. A landed interest, a manufacturing interest, a mercantile interest, a moneyed interest, with many lesser interests, grow up of necessity in civilized nations, and divide them into different classes, actuated by different sentiments and views. The regulation of these various and interfering interests forms the principal task of modern legislation, and involves the spirit of party and faction in the necessary and ordinary operations of the government.

No man is allowed to be a judge in his own cause, because his interest would certainly bias his judgment, and, not improbably, corrupt his integrity. With equal, nay with greater reason, a body of men are unfit to be both judges and parties at the same time; yet what are many of the most important acts of legislation, but so many judicial determinations, not indeed concerning the rights of single persons, but concerning the rights of large bodies of citizens?

And what are the different classes of legislators but advocates and parties to the causes which they determine? Is a law proposed concerning private debts? It is a question to which the creditors are parties on one side and the debtors on the other. Justice ought to hold the balance between them. Yet the parties are, and must be, themselves the judges; and the most numerous party, or, in other words, the most powerful faction must be expected to prevail.

Shall domestic manufactures be encouraged, and in what degree, by restrictions on foreign manufactures? These are questions which would be differently decided by the landed and the manufacturing classes, and probably by neither with a sole regard to justice and the public good. The apportionment of taxes on the various descriptions of property is an act which seems to require the most exact impartiality; yet there is, perhaps, no legislative act in which greater opportunity and temptation are given to a predominant party to trample on the rules of justice. Every shilling with which they overburden the inferior number, is a shilling saved to their own pockets.

☑ **DETERMINE MEANING** Madison first defines the term *faction*, and then goes on to refine his meaning in the subsequent paragraphs. How does he do so?

It is in vain to say that enlightened statesmen will be able to adjust these clashing interests, and render them all subservient to the public good. Enlightened statesmen will not always be at the helm. Nor, in many cases, can such an adjustment be made at all without taking into view indirect and remote considerations, which will rarely prevail over the immediate interest which one party may find in disregarding the rights of another or the good of the whole.

The inference to which we are brought is, that the CAUSES of faction cannot be removed, and that relief is only to be sought in the means of controlling its EFFECTS.

If a faction consists of less than a majority, relief is supplied by the republican principle, which enables the majority to defeat its sinister views by regular vote. It may clog the administration, it may convulse the society; but it will be unable to execute and mask its violence under the forms of the Constitution. When a majority is included in a faction, the form of popular government, on the other hand, enables it to sacrifice to its ruling passion or interest both the public good and the rights of other citizens. To secure the public good and private rights against the danger of such a faction, and at the same time to preserve the spirit and the form of popular government, is then the great object to which our inquiries are directed. Let me add that it is the great desideratum [something wanted or needed] by which this form of government can be rescued from the opprobrium [disgrace; strong disapproval] under which it has so long labored, and be recommended to the esteem and adoption of mankind.

By what means is this object attainable? Evidently by one of two only. Either the existence of the same passion or interest in a majority at the same time must be prevented, or the majority, having such coexistent passion or interest, must be rendered, by their number and local situation, unable to concert and carry into effect schemes of oppression. If the impulse and the opportunity be suffered to coincide, we well know that neither moral nor religious motives can be relied on as an adequate control. They are not found to be such on the injustice and violence of individuals, and lose their efficacy in proportion to the number combined together, that is, in proportion as their efficacy becomes needful.

From this view of the subject it may be concluded that a pure democracy, by which I mean a society consisting of a small number of citizens, who assemble and administer the government in person, can admit of no cure for the mischiefs of faction. A common passion or interest will, in almost every case, be felt by a majority of the whole; a communication and concert result from the form of government itself; and there is nothing to check the inducements to sacrifice the weaker party or an obnoxious individual. Hence it is that such democracies have ever been spectacles of turbulence and contention; have ever been found incompatible with personal security or the rights of property; and have in general been as short in their lives as they have been violent in their deaths. Theoretic politicians, who have patronized this species of government, have erroneously supposed that by reducing mankind to a perfect equality in their political rights, they would, at the same time, be perfectly equalized and assimilated in their possessions, their opinions, and their passions.

A republic, by which I mean a government in which the scheme of representation takes place, opens a different prospect, and promises the cure for which we are seeking. Let us examine the points in which it varies from pure democracy, and we shall comprehend both the nature of the cure and the efficacy which it must derive from the Union.

The two great points of difference between a democracy and a republic are: first, the delegation of the government, in the latter, to a small number of citizens elected by the rest; secondly, the greater number of citizens, and greater sphere of country, over which the latter may be extended.

The effect of the first difference is, on the one hand, to refine and enlarge the public views, by passing them through the medium of a chosen body of citizens, whose wisdom may best discern the true interest of their country, and whose patriotism and love of justice will be least likely to sacrifice it to temporary or partial considerations. Under such a regulation, it may well happen that the public voice, pronounced by the representatives of the people, will be more consonant to the public good than if pronounced by the people themselves, convened for the purpose. On the other hand, the effect may be inverted. Men of factious [divisive] tempers, of local prejudices, or of sinister designs, may, by intrigue, by corruption, or by other means, first obtain the suffrages, and then betray the interests, of the people. The question resulting is, whether small or extensive republics are more favorable to the election of proper guardians of the public weal; and it is clearly decided in favor of the latter by two obvious considerations:

In the first place, it is to be remarked that, however small the republic may be, the representatives must be raised to a certain number, in order to guard against the cabals of a few; and that, however large it may be, they must be limited to a certain number, in order to guard against the confusion of a multitude. Hence, the number of representatives in the two cases not being in proportion to that of the two constituents, and being proportionally greater in the small republic, it follows that, if the proportion of fit characters be not less in the large than in the small republic, the former will present a greater option, and consequently a greater probability of a fit choice.

In the next place, as each representative will be chosen by a greater number of citizens in the large than in the small republic, it will be more difficult for unworthy candidates to practice with success the vicious arts by which elections are too often carried; and the suffrages of the people being more free, will be more likely to centre in men who possess the most attractive merit and the most diffusive and established character.

It must be confessed that in this, as in most other cases, there is a mean, on both sides of which inconveniences will be found to lie. By enlarging too much the number of electors, you render the representatives too little acquainted with all their local circumstances and lesser interests; as by reducing it too much, you render him unduly attached to these, and too little fit to comprehend and pursue great and national objects. The federal Constitution forms a happy combination in this respect; the great and aggregate interests being referred to the national, the local and particular to the State legislatures.

The other point of difference is, the greater number of citizens and extent of territory which may be brought within the compass of republican than of democratic government; and it is this circumstance principally which renders factious combinations less to be dreaded in the former than in the latter. The smaller the society, the fewer probably will be the distinct parties and interests composing it; the fewer the distinct parties and interests, the more frequently will a majority be found of the same party; and the smaller the number of individuals composing a majority, and the smaller the compass within which they are placed, the more easily will they concert and execute their plans of oppression. Extend the sphere, and you take in a greater variety of parties and interests; you make it less probable that a majority of the whole will have a common motive to invade the rights of other citizens; or if such a common motive exists, it will be more difficult for all who feel it to discover their own strength, and to act in unison with each other. Besides other impediments, it may be remarked that, where there is a consciousness of unjust or dishonorable purposes, communication is always checked by distrust in proportion to the number whose concurrence is necessary.

Hence, it clearly appears, that the same advantage which a republic has over a democracy, in controlling the effects of faction, is enjoyed by a large over a small republic,—is enjoyed by the Union over the States composing it. Does the advantage consist in the substitution of representatives whose enlightened views and virtuous sentiments render them superior to local prejudices and schemes of injustice? It will not be denied that the representation of the Union will be most likely to possess these requisite endowments. Does it consist in the greater security afforded by a greater variety of parties, against the event of any one party being able to outnumber and oppress the rest? In an equal degree does the increased variety of parties comprised within the Union, increase this security. Does it, in fine, consist in the greater obstacles opposed to the concert and accomplishment of the secret wishes of an unjust and interested majority? Here, again, the extent of the Union gives it the most palpable advantage.

The influence of factious leaders may kindle a flame within their particular States, but will be unable to spread a general conflagration [a large conflict] through the other States. A religious sect may degenerate into a political faction in a part of the Confederacy; but the variety of sects dispersed over the entire face of it must secure the national councils against any danger from that source. A rage for paper money, for an abolition of debts, for an equal division of property, or for any other improper or wicked project, will be less apt to pervade the whole body of the Union than a particular member of it; in the same proportion as such a malady is more likely to taint a particular county or district, than an entire State.

In the extent and proper structure of the Union, therefore, we behold a republican remedy for the diseases most incident to republican government. And according to the degree of pleasure and pride we feel in being republicans, ought to be our zeal in cherishing the spirit and supporting the character of Federalists.

ASSESSMENT

1. **Summarize** What is Madison's opinion of the idea that disruptive factions should simply be removed from society?

2. **Interpret** Write in your own words what Madison says in this excerpt about government and factions.

3. **Analyze Structure** How does Madison's opening paragraph contribute to his overall purpose? Following this paragraph, how does he structure his argument to persuade readers to adopt his viewpoint?

Federalist No. 39: James Madison

Introduction

In *Federalist* No. 39, James Madison takes on critics of the republican form of government favored by Madison and his allies. Those who opposed this form felt that the new government stripped individual states of their powers. They feared a federal government with too much power. Madison rebuts this argument by saying that a republic is precisely the right form of government for the young nation and that the proposed constitution will establish a strong national government and preserve some powers of the states.

Primary Source

THE last paper having concluded the observations which were meant to introduce a candid survey of the plan of government reported by the convention, we now proceed to the execution of that part of our undertaking.

The first question that offers itself is, whether the general form and aspect of the government be strictly republican. It is evident that no other form would be reconcilable with the genius of the people of America; with the fundamental principles of the Revolution; or with that honorable determination which animates every votary [devotee] of freedom, to rest all our political experiments on the capacity of mankind for self-government. If the plan of the convention, therefore, be found to depart from the republican character, its advocates must abandon it as no longer defensible.

What, then, are the distinctive characters of the republican form? Were an answer to this question to be sought, not by recurring [referring back] to

principles, but in the application of the term by political writers, to the constitution of different States, no satisfactory one would ever be found. Holland, in which no particle of the supreme authority is derived from the people, has passed almost universally under the denomination of a republic. The same title has been bestowed on Venice, where absolute power over the great body of the people is exercised, in the most absolute manner, by a small body of hereditary nobles. Poland, which is a mixture of aristocracy and of monarchy in their worst forms, has been dignified with the same appellation [designation]. The government of England, which has one republican branch only, combined with an hereditary aristocracy and monarchy, has, with equal impropriety, been frequently placed on the list of republics. These examples, which are nearly as dissimilar to each other as to a genuine republic, show the extreme inaccuracy with which the term has been used in political disquisitions.

☑ **DETERMINE THE MEANING** Why does Madison give these examples?

If we resort for a criterion to the different principles on which different forms of government are established, we may define a republic to be, or at least may bestow that name on, a government which derives all its powers directly or indirectly from the great body of the people, and is administered by persons holding their offices during pleasure, for a limited period, or during good behavior.

☑ **ANALYZE** How does Madison define a republic in this section?

It is ESSENTIAL to such a government that it be derived from the great body of the society, not from an inconsiderable proportion, or a favored class of it; otherwise a handful of tyrannical nobles, exercising their oppressions by a delegation of their powers, might aspire to the rank of republicans, and claim for their government the honorable title of republic. It is SUFFICIENT for such a government that the persons administering it be appointed, either directly or indirectly, by the people; and that they hold their appointments by either of the tenures just specified; otherwise every government in the United States, as well as every other popular government that has been or can be well organized or well executed, would be degraded from the republican character. According to the constitution of every State in the Union, some or other of the officers of government are appointed indirectly only by the people. According to most of them, the chief magistrate himself is so appointed. And according to one, this mode of appointment is extended to one of the co-ordinate branches of the legislature. According to all the constitutions, also, the tenure of the highest offices is extended to a definite period, and in many instances, both within the legislative and executive departments, to a period of years. According to the provisions of most of the constitutions, again, as well as according to the most respectable and received opinions on the subject, the members of the judiciary department are to retain their offices by the firm tenure of good behavior.

☑ **ANALYZE** How does Madison refine his definition of a republic in this section?

On comparing the Constitution planned by the convention with the standard here fixed, we perceive at once that it is, in the most rigid sense, conformable to it. The House of Representatives, like that of one branch at least of all the State legislatures, is elected immediately by the great body of the people. The Senate, like the present Congress, and the Senate of Maryland, derives its appointment indirectly from the people. The President is indirectly derived from the choice of the people, according to the example in most of the States. Even the judges, with all other officers of the Union, will, as in the several States, be the choice, though a remote choice, of the people themselves, the duration of the appointments is equally conformable to the republican standard, and to the model of State constitutions The House of Representatives is periodically elective, as in all the States; and for the period of two years, as in the State of South Carolina. The Senate is elective, for the period of six years; which is but one year more than the period of the Senate of Maryland, and but two more than that of the Senates of New York and Virginia. The President is to continue in office for the period of four years; as in New York and Delaware, the chief magistrate is elected for three years, and in South Carolina for two years. In the other States the election is annual.

In several of the States, however, no constitutional provision is made for the impeachment of the chief magistrate. And in Delaware and Virginia he is not impeachable till out of office. The President of the United States is impeachable at any time during his continuance in office. The tenure by which the judges are to hold their places, is, as it unquestionably ought to be, that of good behavior. The tenure of the ministerial offices generally, will be a subject of legal regulation, conformably to the reason of the case and the example of the State constitutions.

Could any further proof be required of the republican complexion of this system, the most decisive one might be found in its absolute prohibition of titles of nobility, both under the federal and the State governments; and in its express guaranty of the republican form to each of the latter.

☑ **ANALYZE** What is the purpose of these paragraphs? Do they help the reader further comprehend what is meant by a republic?

"But it was not sufficient," say the adversaries of the proposed Constitution, "for the convention to adhere to the republican form. They ought, with equal care, to have preserved the FEDERAL form, which regards the Union as a CONFEDERACY of sovereign states; instead of which, they have framed a NATIONAL government, which regards the Union as a CONSOLIDATION of the States." And it is asked by what authority this bold and radical innovation was undertaken? The handle which has been made of this objection requires that it should be examined with some precision.

Without inquiring into the accuracy of the distinction on which the objection is founded, it will be necessary to a just estimate of its force, first, to ascertain the real character of the government in question; secondly, to inquire how far the convention were authorized to propose such a government; and thirdly, how far the duty they owed to their country could supply any defect of regular authority.

First. In order to ascertain the real character of the government, it may be considered in relation to the foundation on which it is to be established; to the sources from which its ordinary powers are to be drawn; to the operation of those powers; to the extent of them; and to the authority by which future changes in the government are to be introduced.

On examining the first relation, it appears, on one hand, that the Constitution is to be founded on the assent and ratification of the people of America, given by deputies elected for the special purpose; but, on the other, that this assent and ratification is to be given by the people, not as individuals composing one entire nation, but as composing the distinct and independent States to which they respectively belong. It is to be the assent and ratification of the several States, derived from the supreme authority in each State, the authority of the people themselves. The act, therefore, establishing the Constitution, will not be a NATIONAL, but a FEDERAL act.

That it will be a federal and not a national act, as these terms are understood by the objectors; the act of the people, as forming so many independent States, not as forming one aggregate nation, is obvious from this single consideration, that it is to result neither from the decision of a MAJORITY of the people of the Union, nor from that of a MAJORITY of the States. It must result from the UNANIMOUS assent of the several States that are parties to it, differing no otherwise from their ordinary assent than in its being expressed, not by the legislative authority, but by that of the people themselves. Were the people regarded in this transaction as forming one nation, the will of the majority of the whole people of the United States would bind the minority, in the same manner as the majority in each State must bind the minority; and the will of the majority must be determined either by a comparison of the individual votes, or by considering the will of the majority of the States as evidence of the will of a majority of the people of the United States. Neither of these rules have been adopted. Each State, in ratifying the Constitution, is considered as a sovereign body, independent of all others, and only to be bound by its own voluntary act. In this relation, then, the new Constitution will, if established, be a FEDERAL, and not a NATIONAL constitution.

The next relation is, to the sources from which the ordinary powers of government are to be derived. The House of Representatives will derive its powers from the people of America; and the people will be represented in the same proportion, and on the same principle, as they are in the legislature of a particular State. So far the government is NATIONAL, not FEDERAL. The Senate, on the other hand, will derive its powers from the States, as political and coequal societies; and these will be represented on the principle of equality in the Senate, as they now are in the existing Congress. So far the government is FEDERAL, not NATIONAL. The executive power will be derived from a very compound source. The immediate election of the President is to be made by the States in their political characters. The votes allotted to them are in a compound ratio, which considers them partly as distinct and coequal societies, partly as unequal members of the same society. The eventual election, again, is to be made by that branch of the legislature which consists of the national representatives; but in this particular act they are to be thrown into the form of individual delegations, from so many distinct and coequal bodies politic. From this aspect of the government it appears to be of a mixed character, presenting at least as many FEDERAL as NATIONAL features.

✅ **ANALYZE** In the context of his overall argument about federal versus national, what does Madison say about where the government's powers originate?

The difference between a federal and national government, as it relates to the OPERATION OF THE GOVERNMENT, is supposed to consist in this, that in the former the powers operate on the political bodies composing the Confederacy, in their political capacities; in the latter, on the individual citizens composing the nation, in their individual capacities. On trying the Constitution by this criterion, it falls under the NATIONAL, not the FEDERAL character; though perhaps not so completely as has been understood. In several cases, and particularly in the trial of controversies to which States may be parties, they must be viewed and proceeded against in their collective and political capacities only. So far the national countenance of the government on this side seems to be disfigured by a few federal features. But this blemish is perhaps unavoidable in any plan; and the operation of the government on the people, in their individual capacities, in its ordinary and most essential proceedings, may, on the whole, designate it, in this relation, a NATIONAL government.

But if the government be national with regard to the OPERATION of its powers, it changes its aspect again when we contemplate it in relation to the EXTENT of its powers. The idea of a national government involves in it, not only an authority over the individual citizens, but an indefinite supremacy over all persons and things, so far as they are objects of lawful government. Among a people consolidated into one nation, this supremacy is completely vested in the national legislature. Among communities united for particular purposes, it is vested partly in the general and partly in the municipal legislatures. In the former case, all local authorities are subordinate to the supreme; and may be controlled, directed, or abolished by it at pleasure. In the latter, the local or municipal authorities form distinct and independent portions of the supremacy, no more subject, within their respective spheres, to the general authority, than the general authority is subject to them, within its own sphere. In this relation, then, the proposed government cannot be deemed a NATIONAL one; since its jurisdiction extends to certain enumerated objects only, and leaves to the several States a residuary [residual; left over] and inviolable sovereignty over all other objects. It is true that in controversies relating to the boundary between the two jurisdictions, the tribunal which is ultimately to decide, is to be established under the general government. But this does not change the principle of the case. The decision is to be impartially made, according to the rules of the Constitution; and all the usual and most effectual precautions are taken to secure this impartiality. Some such tribunal is clearly essential to prevent an appeal to the sword and a dissolution of the compact; and that it ought to be established under the general rather than under the local governments, or, to speak more properly, that it could be safely established under the first alone, is a position not likely to be combated.

If we try the Constitution by its last relation to the authority by which amendments are to be made, we find it neither wholly NATIONAL nor wholly FEDERAL. Were it wholly national, the supreme and ultimate authority would reside in the MAJORITY of the people of the Union; and this authority would be competent at all times, like that of a majority of every national society, to alter or abolish its established government. Were it wholly federal, on the other hand, the concurrence of each State in the Union would be essential to every alteration that would be binding on all. The mode provided by the plan of the convention is not founded on either of these principles. In requiring more than a majority, and principles. In requiring more than a majority,

and particularly in computing the proportion by STATES, not by CITIZENS, it departs from the NATIONAL and advances towards the FEDERAL character; in rendering the concurrence of less than the whole number of States sufficient, it loses again the FEDERAL and partakes of the NATIONAL character.

The proposed Constitution, therefore, is, in strictness, neither a national nor a federal Constitution, but a composition of both. In its foundation it is federal, not national; in the sources from which the ordinary powers of the government are drawn, it is partly federal and partly national; in the operation of these powers, it is national, not federal; in the extent of them, again, it is federal, not national; and, finally, in the authoritative mode of introducing amendments, it is neither wholly federal nor wholly national.

ASSESSMENT

1. **Summarize** How does Madison define a republic?

2. **Cite Evidence** What evidence does Madison offer to support his claim that the new government will be "neither wholly federal nor wholly national"?

3. **Evaluate an Argument** Evaluate Madison's claims in terms of how well he responds to the points raised by Findley, Whitehill, and Smilie in the Anti-Federalist papers. Does he offer concrete evidence to support his premises?

Federalist No. 51: James Madison

Introduction
Federalist No. 51 was first published on February 8, 1788, and was probably written by James Madison. It argues that the federal system and the separation of powers proposed in the Constitution provide a system of checks and balances that will protect the rights of the people.

Primary Source

TO WHAT expedient [resource], then, shall we finally resort, for maintaining in practice the necessary partition of power among the several departments, as laid down in the Constitution? The only answer that can be given is, that as all these exterior provisions are found to be inadequate, the defect must be supplied, by so contriving the interior structure of the government as that its several constituent parts may, by their mutual relations, be the means of keeping each other in their proper places. Without presuming to undertake a full development of this important idea, I will hazard a few general observations, which may perhaps place it in a clearer light, and enable us to form a more correct judgment of the principles and structure of the government planned by the convention.

In order to lay a due foundation for that separate and distinct exercise of the different powers of government, which to a certain extent is admitted on all hands to be essential to the preservation of liberty, it is evident that each department should have a will of its own; and consequently should be so constituted that the members of each should have as little agency as possible in the appointment of the members of the others. Were this principle rigorously adhered to, it would require that all the appointments for the supreme executive, legislative, and judiciary magistracies should be drawn from the same fountain of authority, the people, through channels having no communication whatever with one another. Perhaps such a plan of constructing the several departments would be less difficult in practice than it may in contemplation appear. Some difficulties, however, and some additional expense would attend the execution of it. Some deviations, therefore, from the principle must be admitted. In the constitution of the judiciary department in particular, it might be inexpedient to insist rigorously on the principle: first, because peculiar qualifications being essential in the members, the primary consideration ought to be to select that mode of choice which best secures these qualifications; secondly, because the permanent tenure by which the appointments are held in that department, must soon destroy all sense of dependence on the authority conferring them.

It is equally evident, that the members of each department should be as little dependent as possible on those of the others, for the emoluments [monetary payments] annexed to their offices. Were the executive magistrate, or the judges, not independent of the legislature in this particular, their independence in every other would be merely nominal.

But the great security against a gradual concentration of the several powers in the same department, consists in giving to those who administer each department the necessary constitutional means and personal motives to resist encroachments [intrusions; unwanted advances] of the others. The provision for defense must in this, as in all other cases, be made commensurate to the danger of attack. Ambition must be made to counteract ambition. The interest of the man must be connected with the constitutional rights of the place. It may be a reflection on human nature, that such devices should be necessary to control the abuses of government. But what is government itself, but the greatest of all reflections on human nature? If men were angels, no government would be necessary. If angels were to govern men, neither external nor internal controls on government would be necessary. In framing a government which is to be administered by men over men, the great difficulty lies in this: you must first enable the government to control the governed; and in the next place oblige it to control itself. A dependence on the people is, no doubt, the primary control on the government; but experience has taught mankind the necessity of auxiliary precautions.

This policy of supplying, by opposite and rival interests, the defect of better motives, might be traced through the whole system of human affairs, private as well as public. We see it particularly displayed in all the subordinate distributions of power, where the constant aim is to divide and arrange the several offices in such a manner as that each may be a check on the other—that the private interest of every individual may be a sentinel over the public rights. These inventions of prudence cannot be less requisite in the distribution of the supreme powers of the State.

But it is not possible to give to each department an equal power of self-defense. In republican government, the legislative authority necessarily predominates. The remedy for this inconveniency is to divide the legislature into different branches; and to render them, by different modes of election and different principles of action, as little connected with each other as the nature of their common functions and their common dependence on the society will admit. It may even be necessary to guard against dangerous encroachments by still further precautions. As the weight of the legislative authority requires that it should be thus divided, the weakness of the executive may require, on the other hand, that it should be fortified. An absolute negative on the legislature appears, at first view, to be the natural defense with which the executive magistrate should be armed. But perhaps it would be neither altogether safe nor alone sufficient. On ordinary occasions it might not be exerted with the requisite firmness, and on extraordinary occasions it might be perfidiously [traitorously; treacherously] abused. May not this defect of an absolute negative be supplied by some qualified connection between this weaker department and the weaker branch of the stronger department, by which the latter may be led to support the constitutional rights of the former, without being too much detached from the rights of its own department?

If the principles on which these observations are founded be just, as I persuade myself they are, and they be applied as a criterion to the several State constitutions, and to the federal Constitution it will be found that if the latter does not perfectly correspond with them, the former are infinitely less able to bear such a test.

There are, moreover, two considerations particularly applicable to the federal system of America, which place that system in a very interesting point of view.

First. In a single republic, all the power surrendered by the people is submitted to the administration of a single government; and the usurpations [illegal seizures of power] are guarded against by a division of the government into distinct and separate departments. In the compound republic of America, the power surrendered by the people is first divided between two distinct governments, and then the portion allotted to each subdivided among distinct and separate departments. Hence a double security arises to the rights of the people. The different governments will control each other, at the same time that each will be controlled by itself.

Second. It is of great importance in a republic not only to guard the society against the oppression of its rulers, but to guard one part of the society against the injustice of the other part. Different interests necessarily exist in different classes of citizens. If a majority be united by a common interest, the rights of the minority will be insecure. There are but two methods of providing against this evil: the one

by creating a will in the community independent of the majority—that is, of the society itself; the other, by comprehending in the society so many separate descriptions of citizens as will render an unjust combination of a majority of the whole very improbable, if not impracticable. The first method prevails in all governments possessing an hereditary or self-appointed authority. This, at best, is but a precarious security; because a power independent of the society may as well espouse the unjust views of the major, as the rightful interests of the minor party, and may possibly be turned against both parties. The second method will be exemplified in the federal republic of the United States. Whilst all authority in it will be derived from and dependent on the society, the society itself will be broken into so many parts, interests, and classes of citizens, that the rights of individuals, or of the minority, will be in little danger from interested combinations of the majority.

In a free government the security for civil rights must be the same as that for religious rights. It consists in the one case in the multiplicity of interests, and in the other in the multiplicity of sects. The degree of security in both cases will depend on the number of interests and sects; and this may be presumed to depend on the extent of country and number of people comprehended under the same government. This view of the subject must particularly recommend a proper federal system to all the sincere and considerate friends of republican government, since it shows that in exact proportion as the territory of the Union may be formed into more circumscribed Confederacies, or States oppressive combinations of a majority will be facilitated: the best security, under the republican forms, for the rights of every class of citizens, will be diminished: and consequently the stability and independence of some member of the government, the only other security, must be proportionately increased. Justice is the end of government. It is the end of civil society. It ever has been and ever will be pursued until it be obtained, or until liberty be lost in the pursuit. In a society under the forms of which the stronger faction can readily unite and oppress the weaker, anarchy may as truly be said to reign as in a state of nature, where the weaker individual is not secured against the violence of the stronger; and as, in the latter state, even the stronger individuals are prompted, by the uncertainty of their condition, to submit to a government which may protect the weak as well as themselves; so, in the former state, will the more powerful factions or parties be gradually induced, by a like motive, to wish for a government which will protect all parties, the weaker as well as the more powerful. It can be little doubted that if the State of Rhode Island was separated from the Confederacy and left to itself, the insecurity of rights under the popular form of government within such narrow limits would be displayed by such reiterated oppressions of factious majorities that some power altogether independent of the people would soon be called for by the voice of the very factions whose misrule had proved the necessity of it.

In the extended republic of the United States, and among the great variety of interests, parties, and sects which it embraces, a coalition of a majority of the whole society could seldom take place on any other principles than those of justice and the general good; whilst there being thus less danger to a minor from the will of a major party, there must be less pretext, also, to provide for the security of the former, by introducing into the government a will not dependent on the latter, or, in other words, a will independent of the society itself. It is no less certain than it is important, notwithstanding the contrary opinions which have been entertained, that the larger the society, provided it lie within a practical sphere, the more duly capable it will be of self-government. And happily for the REPUBLICAN CAUSE, the practicable sphere may be carried to a very great extent, by a judicious modification and mixture of the FEDERAL PRINCIPLE.

ASSESSMENT

1. **Assess an Argument** Do you agree with Madison that, "In a free government the security for civil rights must be the same as that for religious rights"? Considering the history of the United States on the issue of civil rights for both women and racial minorities, in what way is Madison's remark ironic?

2. **Analyze Interactions** What effect did *Federalist* No. 51 have on the final U.S. Constitution?

3. **Explain an Argument** Why does Madison think it is important that the new government exercise a separation of powers?

Federalist No. 78: Alexander Hamilton

Introduction

The *Federalist Papers* were the brainchild of Alexander Hamilton, who conceived them and recruited James Madison and John Jay to the project. Hamilton is usually credited as the author of 51 of the 85 essays in the collection. Here, he discusses the national judiciary to be established by Article III in the proposed constitution. He emphasizes the vital need for an independent judiciary and its role in the interpretation of laws and the determination of their constitutionality. It was first published April 11, 1788.

Primary Source

WE PROCEED now to an examination of the judiciary department of the proposed government.

In unfolding the defects of the existing Confederation, the utility and necessity of a federal judicature [system of courts] have been clearly pointed out. It is the less necessary to recapitulate the considerations there urged, as the propriety of the institution in the abstract is not disputed; the only questions which have been raised being relative to the manner of constituting it, and to its extent. To these points, therefore, our observations shall be confined.

The manner of constituting it seems to embrace these several objects: 1st. The mode of appointing the judges. 2d. The tenure by which they are to hold their places. 3d. The partition of the judiciary authority between different courts, and their relations to each other.

First. As to the mode of appointing the judges; this is the same with that of appointing the officers of the Union in general, and has been so fully discussed in the two last numbers, that nothing can be said here which would not be useless repetition.

Second. As to the tenure by which the judges are to hold their places; this chiefly concerns their duration in office; the provisions for their support; the precautions for their responsibility.

According to the plan of the convention, all judges who may be appointed by the United States are to hold their offices during good behavior;

which is conformable to the most approved of the State constitutions and among the rest, to that of this State. Its propriety having been drawn into question by the adversaries of that plan, is no light symptom of the rage for objection, which disorders their imaginations and judgments. The standard of good behavior for the continuance in office of the judicial magistracy, is certainly one of the most valuable of the modern improvements in the practice of government. In a monarchy it is an excellent barrier to the despotism of the prince; in a republic it is a no less excellent barrier to the encroachments and oppressions of the representative body. And it is the best expedient which can be devised in any government, to secure a steady, upright, and impartial administration of the laws.

Whoever attentively considers the different departments of power must perceive, that, in a government in which they are separated from each other, the judiciary, from the nature of its functions, will always be the least dangerous to the political rights of the Constitution; because it will be least in a capacity to annoy or injure them. The Executive not only dispenses the honors, but holds the sword of the community. The legislature not only commands the purse, but prescribes the rules by which the duties and rights of every citizen are to be regulated. The judiciary, on the contrary, has no influence over either the sword or the purse; no direction either of the strength or of the wealth of the society; and can take no active resolution whatever. It may truly be said to have neither FORCE nor WILL, but merely judgment; and must ultimately depend upon the aid of the executive arm even for the efficacy of its judgments.

This simple view of the matter suggests several important consequences. It proves incontestably, that the judiciary is beyond comparison the weakest of the three departments of power; that it can never attack with success either of the other two; and that all possible care is requisite to enable it to defend itself against their attacks. It equally proves, that though individual oppression may now and then proceed from the courts of justice, the general liberty of the people can never be endangered from that quarter; I mean so long as the judiciary remains truly distinct from both the legislature and the Executive. For I agree, that "there is no liberty, if the power of judging be not separated from the legislative and executive powers." And it proves, in the last place, that as liberty can have nothing to fear from the judiciary alone, but would have every thing to fear from its union with either of the other departments; that as all the effects of such a union must ensue from a dependence of the former on the latter, notwithstanding a nominal and apparent separation; that as, from the natural feebleness of the judiciary, it is in continual jeopardy of being overpowered, awed, or influenced by its co-ordinate branches; and that as nothing can contribute so much to its firmness and independence as permanency in office, this quality may therefore be justly regarded as an indispensable ingredient in its constitution, and, in a great measure, as the citadel of the public justice and the public security.

The complete independence of the courts of justice is peculiarly essential in a limited Constitution. By a limited Constitution, I understand one which contains certain specified exceptions to the legislative authority; such, for instance, as that it shall pass no bills of attainder, no ex post facto laws, and the like. Limitations of this kind can be preserved in practice no other way than through the medium of courts of justice, whose duty it must be to declare all acts contrary to the manifest tenor of the Constitution void. Without this, all the reservations of particular rights or privileges would amount to nothing.

Some perplexity respecting the rights of the courts to pronounce legislative acts void, because contrary to the Constitution, has arisen from an imagination that the doctrine would imply a superiority of the judiciary to the legislative power. It is urged that the authority which can declare the acts of another void, must necessarily be superior to the one whose acts may be declared void. As this doctrine is of great importance in all the American constitutions, a brief discussion of the ground on which it rests cannot be unacceptable.

There is no position which depends on clearer principles, than that every act of a delegated authority, contrary to the tenor of the commission under which it is exercised, is void. No legislative act, therefore, contrary to the Constitution, can be valid. To deny this, would be to affirm, that the deputy is greater than his principal; that the servant is above his master; that the representatives of the people are superior to the people themselves; that men acting by virtue of powers, may do not only what their powers do not authorize, but what they forbid.

If it be said that the legislative body are themselves the constitutional judges of their own powers, and that the construction they put upon them is conclusive upon the other departments, it may be answered, that this cannot be the natural presumption, where it is not to be collected from any particular provisions in the Constitution. It is not otherwise to be supposed, that the Constitution could intend to enable the representatives of the people to substitute their will to that of their constituents. It is far more rational to suppose, that the courts were designed to be an intermediate body between the people and the legislature, in order, among other things, to keep the latter within the limits assigned to their authority.

The interpretation of the laws is the proper and peculiar [particular] province of the courts. A constitution is, in fact, and must be regarded by the judges, as a fundamental law. It therefore belongs to them to ascertain its meaning, as well as the meaning of any particular act proceeding from the legislative body. If there should happen to be an irreconcilable variance between the two, that which has the superior obligation and validity ought, of course, to be preferred; or, in other words, the Constitution ought to be preferred to the statute, the intention of the people to the intention of their agents.

Nor does this conclusion by any means suppose a superiority of the judicial to the legislative power. It only supposes that the power of the people is superior to both; and that where the will of the legislature, declared in its statutes, stands in opposition to that of the people, declared in the Constitution, the judges ought to be governed by the latter rather than the former. They ought to regulate their decisions by the fundamental laws, rather than by those which are not fundamental.

This exercise of judicial discretion, in determining between two contradictory laws, is exemplified in a familiar instance. It not uncommonly happens, that there are two statutes existing at one time, clashing in whole or in part with each other, and neither of them containing any repealing clause or expression. In such a case, it is the province of the courts to liquidate and fix their meaning and operation. So far as they can, by any fair construction, be reconciled to each other, reason and law conspire to dictate that this should be done; where this is impracticable, it becomes a matter of necessity to give effect to one, in exclusion of the other. The rule which has obtained in the courts for determining their relative validity is, that the last in order of time shall be preferred to the first. But this is a mere rule of construction, not derived from any positive law, but from the nature and reason of the thing. It is a rule not enjoined upon the courts by legislative provision, but adopted by themselves, as consonant to truth and propriety, for the direction of their conduct as interpreters of the law. They thought it reasonable, that between the interfering acts of an EQUAL authority, that which was the last indication of its will should have the preference.

But in regard to the interfering acts of a superior and subordinate authority, of an original and derivative power, the nature and reason of the thing indicate the converse of that rule as proper to be followed. They teach us that the prior act of a superior ought to be preferred to the subsequent act of an inferior and subordinate authority; and that accordingly, whenever a particular statute contravenes the Constitution, it will be the duty of the judicial tribunals to adhere to the latter and disregard the former.

It can be of no weight to say that the courts, on the pretense of a repugnancy [something that is offensive], may substitute their own pleasure to the constitutional intentions of the legislature. This might as well happen in the case of two contradictory statutes; or it might as well happen in every adjudication [judgment] upon any single statute. The courts must declare the sense of the law; and if they should be disposed to exercise WILL instead of JUDGMENT, the consequence would equally be the substitution of their pleasure to that of the legislative body. The observation, if it prove any thing, would prove that there ought to be no judges distinct from that body.

If, then, the courts of justice are to be considered as the bulwarks [defenders] of a limited Constitution against legislative encroachments, this consideration will afford a strong argument for the permanent tenure of judicial offices, since nothing will contribute so much as this to that independent spirit in the judges which must be essential to the faithful performance of so arduous a duty.

This independence of the judges is equally requisite to guard the Constitution and the rights of individuals from the effects of those ill humors, which the arts of designing men, or the influence of particular conjunctures, sometimes disseminate among the people themselves, and which, though they speedily give place to better information, and more deliberate reflection, have a tendency, in the meantime, to occasion dangerous innovations in the government, and serious oppressions of the minor party in the community. Though I trust the friends of the proposed Constitution will never concur with its enemies, in questioning that fundamental principle of republican government, which admits the right of the people to alter or abolish the established Constitution, whenever they find it inconsistent with their happiness, yet it is not to be inferred from this principle, that the representatives of the people, whenever a momentary inclination happens to lay hold of a majority of their constituents, incompatible with the provisions in the existing Constitution, would, on that account, be justifiable in a violation of those provisions; or that the courts would be under a greater obligation to connive [secretly work to injure] at infractions in this shape, than when they had proceeded wholly from the cabals [secret political groups] of the representative body. Until the people have, by some solemn and authoritative act, annulled or changed the established form, it is binding upon themselves collectively, as well as individually; and no presumption, or even knowledge, of their sentiments, can warrant their representatives in a departure from it, prior to such an act. But it is easy to see, that it would require an uncommon portion of fortitude in the judges to do their duty as faithful guardians of the Constitution, where legislative invasions of it had been instigated by the major voice of the community.

But it is not with a view to infractions of the Constitution only, that the independence of the judges may be an essential safeguard against the effects of occasional ill humors in the society. These sometimes extend no farther than to the injury of the private rights of particular classes of citizens, by unjust and partial laws. Here also the firmness of the judicial magistracy is of vast importance in mitigating the severity and confining the operation of such laws. It not only serves to moderate the immediate mischiefs of those which may have been passed, but it operates as a check upon the legislative body in passing them; who, perceiving that obstacles to the success of iniquitous [wicked] intention are to be expected from the scruples [hesitations; doubts] of the courts, are in a manner compelled, by the very motives of the injustice they meditate, to qualify their attempts. This is a circumstance calculated to have more influence upon the character of our governments, than but few may be aware of. The benefits of the integrity and moderation of the judiciary have already been felt

in more States than one; and though they may have displeased those whose sinister expectations they may have disappointed, they must have commanded the esteem and applause of all the virtuous and disinterested. Considerate men, of every description, ought to prize whatever will tend to beget or fortify that temper in the courts: as no man can be sure that he may not be to-morrow the victim of a spirit of injustice, by which he may be a gainer to-day. And every man must now feel, that the inevitable tendency of such a spirit is to sap the foundations of public and private confidence, and to introduce in its stead universal distrust and distress.

That inflexible and uniform adherence to the rights of the Constitution, and of individuals, which we perceive to be indispensable in the courts of justice, can certainly not be expected from judges who hold their offices by a temporary commission. Periodical appointments, however regulated, or by whomsoever made, would, in some way or other, be fatal to their necessary independence. If the power of making them was committed either to the Executive or legislature, there would be danger of an improper complaisance [willingness to please] to the branch which possessed it; if to both, there would be an unwillingness to hazard the displeasure of either; if to the people, or to persons chosen by them for the special purpose, there would be too great a disposition to consult popularity, to justify a reliance that nothing would be consulted but the Constitution and the laws.

There is yet a further and a weightier reason for the permanency of the judicial offices, which is deducible from the nature of the qualifications they require. It has been frequently remarked, with great propriety, that a voluminous code of laws is one of the inconveniences necessarily connected with the advantages of a free government. To avoid an arbitrary discretion in the courts, it is indispensable that they should be bound down by strict rules and precedents, which serve to define and point out their duty in every particular case that comes before them; and it will readily be conceived from the variety of controversies which grow out of the folly and wickedness of mankind, that the records of those precedents must unavoidably swell to a very considerable bulk, and must demand long and laborious study to acquire a competent knowledge of them. Hence it is, that there can be but few men in the society who will have sufficient skill in the laws to qualify them for the stations of judges. And making the proper deductions for the ordinary depravity [moral corruption] of human nature, the number must be still smaller of those who unite the requisite integrity with the requisite knowledge. These considerations apprise us, that the government can have no great option between fit character; and that a temporary duration in office, which would naturally discourage such characters from quitting a lucrative line of practice to accept a seat on the bench, would have a tendency to throw the administration of justice into hands less able, and less well qualified, to conduct it with utility and dignity. In the present circumstances of this country, and in those in which it is likely to be for a long time to come, the disadvantages on this score would be greater than they may at first sight appear; but it must be confessed, that they are far inferior to those which present themselves under the other aspects of the subject.

Upon the whole, there can be no room to doubt that the convention acted wisely in copying from the models of those constitutions which have established good behavior as the tenure of their judicial offices, in point of duration; and that so far from being blamable on this account, their plan would have been inexcusably defective, if it had wanted this important feature of good government. The experience of Great Britain affords an illustrious comment on the excellence of the institution.

ASSESSMENT

1. **Summarize** What does Hamilton say is the role of judges?

2. **Analyze Interactions** How has *Federalist* No. 78 influenced the U.S. government?

Northwest Ordinance

Introduction
Adopted in 1787 by the Second Continental Congress, the Northwest Ordinance created a method for admitting new states to the Union. While the Articles of Confederation lacked a bill of rights, the Ordinance provided one that included many of the basic liberties that would later be included in the Constitution's Bill of Rights.

Primary Source
... **ART. 1.** No person, demeaning himself in a peaceable and orderly manner, shall ever be molested on account of his mode of worship or religious sentiments, in the said territory.

ART. 2. The inhabitants of the said territory shall always be entitled to the benefits of the writ of habeas corpus [a legal action that says an arrested person must be presented in court], and of the trial by jury. . . .

ART. 3. Religion, morality, and knowledge, being necessary to good government and the happiness of mankind, schools and the means of education shall forever be encouraged. . . .

ART. 6. There shall be neither slavery nor involuntary servitude in the said territory, otherwise than in the punishment of crimes whereof the party shall have been duly convicted: Provided, always, That any person escaping into the same, from whom labor or service is lawfully claimed in any one of the original States, such fugitive may be lawfully reclaimed and conveyed to the person claiming his or her labor or service as aforesaid.

ASSESSMENT

1. **Compare and Contrast** Which ideals expressed in this excerpt from the Northwest Ordinance became influential in other founding documents of the United States? Use specific examples in your response.

2. **Analyze Interactions** How do these excerpts from the Northwest Ordinance connect to the phrase "life, liberty, and the pursuit of happiness" from the Declaration of Independence?

Democracy in America: Alexis de Tocqueville

Introduction
Alexis de Tocqueville, a young French writer, visited the United States in 1831. During his travels, he observed firsthand the impact of Jacksonian democracy. After returning to France, Tocqueville began writing *Democracy*

in America, a detailed look at American politics, society, economics, religion, and law. The first volume was published in 1835. The book is still studied and quoted by historians and politicians today. In these excerpts from *Democracy in America,* Tocqueville discusses the role of the American people in their government and gives his view of the American character.

Primary Source

The general principles which are the groundwork of modern constitutions–principles which were imperfectly known in Europe, and not completely triumphant even in Great Britain, in the seventeenth century–were all recognized and determined by the laws of New England: the intervention of the people in public affairs, the free voting of taxes, the responsibility of authorities, personal liberty, and trial by jury, were all positively established without discussion. From these fruitful principles consequences have been derived and applications have been made such as no nation in Europe has yet ventured to attempt.

. . . it is at least true that in the United States the county and the township are always based upon the same principle, namely, that everyone is the best judge of what concerns himself alone, and the most proper person to supply his private wants.

In America the people name those who make the law and those who execute it; they themselves form the jury that punishes infractions [violations] of the law. Not only are the institutions democratic in their principle, but also in all their developments; thus the people name their representatives directly and generally choose them every year in order to keep them more completely under their dependence. It is therefore really the people who direct. . . . This majority is composed principally of peaceful citizens who, either by taste or by interest, sincerely desire the good of the country. Around them parties constantly agitate. . . .

The American taken randomly [chosen without a plan] will therefore be a man ardent [intense] in his desires, enterprising [full of energy; willing to take on new projects], adventurous—above all, an innovator [a person who creates a new way of doing something]. This spirit is in fact found in all his works; he introduces it into his political laws, his religious doctrines, his theories of social economy, his private

industry; he brings it with him everywhere, into the depths of the woods as into the heart of towns.

To evade the bondage of system and habit, of family maxims, class-opinions, and in some degree, of national prejudices; to accept tradition only as a means of information, and existing facts only as a lesson used in doing otherwise and doing better; to seek the reason of things for oneself, and in oneself alone; to tend to results without being bound to means, and to aim at the substance through the form;—such are the principle characteristics of what I shall call the philosophical method of the Americans. But if I go further, and if I seek among those characteristics the principle one which includes almost all the rest, I discover that, in most operations of the mind, each American appeals only to the individual effort of his own understanding.

ASSESSMENT

1. **Determine Central Ideas** In what way do the people "direct" the American democracy, according to Tocqueville?

2. **Summarize** What impressed Tocqueville during his time in America? Cite examples to support your answer.

3. **Draw Conclusions** In what way could Tocqueville's book be relevant today?

Emancipation Proclamation: Abraham Lincoln

Introduction

Five days after the Union victory at Antietam, Abraham Lincoln issued the Emancipation Proclamation. The presidential decree freed all enslaved persons in states under Confederate control as of January 1, 1863. One of the most important documents in American history, it changed the nature of the Union cause and paved the way for the eventual abolition of slavery by the Thirteenth Amendment in 1865.

Primary Source

Whereas on the twenty-second day of September, in the year of our Lord one thousand eight hundred and sixty-two, a proclamation was issued by the President of the United States, containing, among other things, the following, to wit [namely]:

That on the first day of January, in the year of our Lord one thousand eight hundred and sixty-three, all persons held as slaves within any State or designated part of a State, the people whereof shall then be in rebellion against the United States, shall be then, thenceforward [from then on], and forever free; and the Executive Government of the United States, including the military and naval authority thereof, will recognize and maintain the freedom of such persons, and will do no act or acts to repress such persons, or any of them, in any efforts they may make for their actual freedom. . . .

And by virtue of the power, and for the purpose aforesaid, I do order and declare that all persons held as slaves within said designated States, and parts of States, are, and henceforward shall be free; and that the Executive government of the United States, including the military and naval authorities thereof, will recognize and maintain the freedom of said persons.

And I hereby enjoin [direct; order] upon the people so declared to be free to abstain from all violence, unless in necessary self- defence; and I recommend to them that, in all cases when allowed, they labor faithfully for reasonable wages.

And I further declare and make known, that such persons of suitable condition, will be received into the armed services of the United States to garrison [occupy with troops] forts, positions, stations, and other places, and to man vessels of all sorts in said service.

And upon this act, sincerely believed to be an act of justice, warranted [authorized; justified] by the Constitution, upon military necessity, I invoke the considerate judgment of mankind, and the gracious favor of Almighty God. . . .

ASSESSMENT

1. **Draw Conclusions** The number of enslaved people who were freed because of the Emancipation Proclamation increased gradually over time. Why do you think that was?

2. **Determine Author's Purpose** Why do you think President Lincoln issued the proclamation? Explain your answer.

3. **Explain an Argument** What justification does Lincoln give for issuing the proclamation?

4. **Assess an Argument** Do you agree with the justifications you cited in the previous answer? Why or why not?

Charter of the United Nations

Introduction

After World War I, more than 50 countries joined together to form the League of Nations. The League was supposed to prevent future wars by providing a forum for the peaceful settlement of international disputes. The United States never joined the League.

The idea of an international peacekeeping organization was revisited after World War II. In 1944, representatives from the United States, the Soviet Union, China, and the United Kingdom met for several months to work out the framework for the United Nations.

In 1945, representatives of 50 countries met in San Francisco to sign the United Nations charter, bringing the organization into being.

Here are the preamble and first two articles of that charter.

Primary Source
WE THE PEOPLES OF THE UNITED NATIONS DETERMINED

- to save succeeding [later] generations from the scourge of war, which twice in our lifetime has brought untold sorrow to mankind, and
- to reaffirm faith in fundamental human rights, in the dignity and worth of the human person, in the

equal rights of men and women and of nations large and small, and

- to establish conditions under which justice and respect for the obligations arising from treaties and other sources of international law can be maintained, and
- to promote social progress and better standards of life in larger freedom,

AND FOR THESE ENDS

- to practice tolerance and live together in peace with one another as good neighbours, and
- to unite our strength to maintain international peace and security, and
- to ensure, by the acceptance of principles and the institution of methods, that armed force shall not be used, save in the common interest, and
- to employ international machinery for the promotion of the economic and social advancement of all peoples,

HAVE RESOLVED TO COMBINE OUR EFFORTS TO ACCOMPLISH THESE AIMS

Accordingly, our respective Governments, through representatives assembled in the city of San Francisco, who have exhibited their full powers found to be in good and due form, have agreed to the present Charter of the United Nations and do hereby establish an international organization to be known as the United Nations.

CHAPTER I: PURPOSES AND PRINCIPLES
Article 1
The Purposes of the United Nations are:

1. To maintain international peace and security, and to that end: to take effective collective measures for the prevention and removal of threats to the peace, and for the suppression of acts of aggression or other breaches of the peace, and to bring about by peaceful means, and in conformity with the principles of justice and international law, adjustment or settlement of international disputes or situations which might lead to a breach of the peace;

2. To develop friendly relations among nations based on respect for the principle of equal rights and self-determination of peoples, and to take other appropriate measures to strengthen universal peace;

3. To achieve international co-operation in solving international problems of an economic, social, cultural, or humanitarian character, and in promoting and encouraging respect for human rights and for fundamental freedoms for all without distinction as to race, sex, language, or religion; and

4. To be a centre for harmonizing the actions of nations in the attainment of these common ends.

Article 2
The Organization and its Members, in pursuit of the Purposes stated in Article 1, shall act in accordance with the following Principles.

1. The Organization is based on the principle of the sovereign equality of all its Members.

2. All Members, in order to ensure to all of them the rights and benefits resulting from membership, shall fulfill in good faith the obligations assumed by them in accordance with the present Charter.

3. All Members shall settle their international disputes by peaceful means in such a manner that international peace and security, and justice, are not endangered.

4. All Members shall refrain in their international relations from the threat or use of force against the territorial integrity or political independence of any state, or in any other manner inconsistent with the Purposes of the United Nations.

5. All Members shall give the United Nations every assistance in any action it takes in accordance with the present Charter, and shall refrain from giving assistance to any state against which the United Nations is taking preventive or enforcement action.

6. The Organization shall ensure that states which are not Members of the United Nations act in accordance with these Principles so far as may be necessary for the maintenance of international peace and security.

7. Nothing contained in the present Charter shall authorize the United Nations to intervene in matters which are essentially within the domestic jurisdiction of any state or shall require the Members to submit such matters to settlement under the present Charter; but this principle shall not prejudice the application of enforcement measures under Chapter VII.

ASSESSMENT

1. **Cite Evidence** The government of a country is inflicting terrible human rights abuses on members of the opposition party. Based on the excerpt, can the United Nations intervene? Cite the part(s) of the charter that support your opinion.

2. **Explain an Argument** Several years of drought in western Asia have led to widespread famine. The UN arranges to bring convoys of food to starving people. One country, a member of the UN, does not want to let relief workers come inside its borders. Does any part of the charter cited here support or rebut the country's position? Explain your answer.

3. **Draw Conclusions** Has the United Nations been successful in its mission "to save succeeding generations from the scourge of war"? Explain your answer.

Sequence

Sequence means "order," and placing things in the correct order is very important. What would happen if you tried to put toppings on a pizza before you put down the dough for the crust? When studying history and government, you need to analyze the information by sequencing significant events, individuals, and time periods in order to understand them. Practice this skill by using this reading.

> Richard Nixon was elected to the House of Representatives in 1946 and then to the Senate four years later. In 1952, with Dwight Eisenhower's election as President, Nixon became Vice President. However, Nixon lost to John F. Kennedy in the 1960 presidential election, and two years later lost an election for governor of California. However, in 1968, Nixon defeated Hubert Humphrey to win the presidency.

[1.] Identify the topic and the main events that relate to the topic. Quickly skim titles and headings to determine the topic of the passage. As you read the passage, write a list of significant events, individuals, or time periods related to the topic.

[2.] Note any dates and time words such as "before" and "after" that indicate the chronological order of events. Look through your list of events, individuals, or time periods and write down the date for each. This will give you information to apply absolute chronology by sequencing the events, individuals, or time periods. Remember that some events may have taken place over a number of months or years. Is your date the time when the event started or ended? Make sure to note enough details that you can remember the importance of the information. If no date is given, look for words such as "before" or "after" that can tell you where to place this event, time period, or individual compared to others on your list. This will allow you to apply relative chronology by sequencing the events, individuals, or time periods.

[3.] Determine the time range of the events. Place the events in chronological order on a timeline. Look for the earliest and latest events, individuals, or time periods on your list. The span of time between the first and last entries gives you the time range. To apply absolute chronology, sequence the entries by writing the date of the first event on the left side of a piece of paper and the date of the last event on the right side. Draw a line connecting the two events. This will be your timeline. Once you have drawn your timeline, put the events in order by date along the line. Label their dates. To apply relative chronology, sequence the significant individuals, events, or time periods on an undated timeline, in the order that they happened. You now have a clear image of the important events related to this topic. You can organize and interpret information from visuals by analyzing the information and applying absolute or relative chronology to the events. This will help you understand the topic better when you can see how events caused or led to other events. You will also be able to analyze information by developing connections between historical events over time.

Categorize

When you analyze information by categorizing, you create a system that helps you sort items into categories, or groups with shared characteristics, so that you can understand the information. Categorizing helps you see what groups of items have in common. Practice this skill as you study the map on this page.

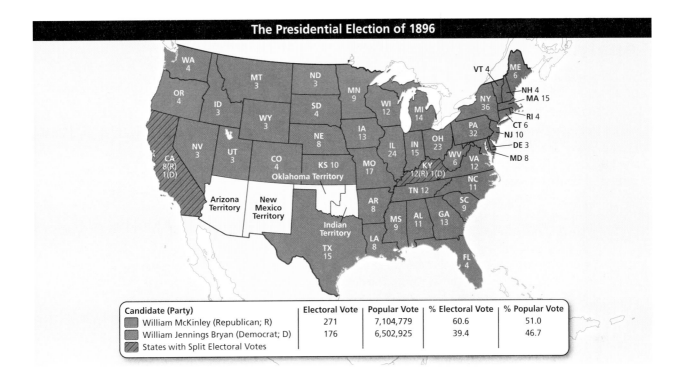

The Presidential Election of 1896

Candidate (Party)	Electoral Vote	Popular Vote	% Electoral Vote	% Popular Vote
William McKinley (Republican; R)	271	7,104,779	60.6	51.0
William Jennings Bryan (Democrat; D)	176	6,502,925	39.4	46.7
States with Split Electoral Votes				

[1.] Identify similarities and differences among items you need to understand. You need to pay careful attention and sometimes do research to find the similarities and differences among the facts, topics, or objects that you need to understand. Scientists find groups, or categories, of related animals by analyzing the details of the animals' bodies. For example, insects with similar wings, legs, and mouthparts probably belong in the same category. Gather similar information about all the things you need to understand. For example, if you know the location of one thing, try to find the locations of all the things you are studying. If you have different types of information about your topics, you will not be able to group them easily.

[2.] Create a system to group items with common characteristics. Once you have gathered similar kinds of information on the items you need to understand, look for items that share characteristics or features. Create categories based on a feature shared by all of the facts, topics, or objects you need to understand. For example, if you have gathered information on the population and political systems of several countries, you could categorize them by the size of their population or their type of political system.

[3.] Form the groupings. Put each of the items that you are studying into one of the categories that you have created. If some items do not fit, you may need to make a new category or modify your categories. Label each category for the characteristic shared by its members. Examples of labels for categories might include "Countries with more than 100 million people," "Countries with fewer than 1 million people," "Democracies," or "Dictatorships."

Analyze Cause and Effect

When you analyze information by identifying cause-and-effect relationships, you find how one event leads to the next. It is important to find evidence that one event caused another. If one event happened earlier than another, it did not necessarily cause the later event. Understanding causes and effects can help you solve problems. Practice this skill as you read the text on this page. What words in the text indicate the causes of the end of communism in the Soviet Union and the eastern bloc? Which indicate effects?

> Economic stagnation, external pressure from the West, and internal dissent eroded the Soviet bloc. In the 1980s, the reformist Soviet leader Mikhail Gorbachev pushed both *perestroika*, a wide-ranging restructuring of political and economic life, and *glasnost*, a policy of openness where the Soviet government increased its tolerance of dissent and freedom of expression. The hunger for openness spread to the central European Soviet bloc countries. In 1989, the Polish reform party Solidarity competed in parliamentary elections, Hungarians enjoyed the freedom to visit Austria, and pro-democratic protests in East Germany led Communist governments to fold throughout the region.

[1.] Choose a starting point of observation. When trying to understand a historical event, choose the time of that event. If you are trying to understand a current event, you can work backward from a starting point in the present.

[2.] Consider earlier events to try to find connections to your starting point, including any language that signals causes. Put the evidence together to identify true causes. When reading, look for events that come before your starting point. Analyze whether these earlier events caused later events. Identify words that signal cause, such as "reason," "because," and "led to." Analyze the information by developing connections between historical events. Make sure that there is evidence showing that the earlier events caused the later events and did not just happen earlier.

[3.] Consider later events to try to find connections to your starting point, including any language that signals effects. Put the evidence together to determine true effects. Look for events that come after your starting point. Analyze the information in order to determine whether these later events are effects of earlier events. Identify words that signal effect, such as "led to," "so," and "therefore." Make sure that there is evidence showing that these later events were caused by earlier events and did not just happen later.

[4.] Summarize the cause-and-effect relationship and draw conclusions. Once you have identified the cause-and-effect relationships between different events, describe these relationships. Draw a diagram that develops the connections between the two historical events. Draw conclusions about any relationships that you see.

Compare and Contrast

When you analyze information by comparing and contrasting two or more things, you look for similarities and differences between them. This skill helps you understand the things that you are comparing and contrasting. It is also a skill that you can use in making choices. Practice this skill as you read the text excerpt on this page. Compare and contrast the critics of the New Deal.

> While Roosevelt had little difficulty gaining support from Congress for his proposals, a minority of Americans expressed their opposition to the New Deal. Critics on the political right thought the changes the New Deal brought were too radical. Critics on the left thought that they were not radical enough. Several of FDR's critics attracted mass followings and made plans to challenge him for the presidency in 1936.

[1.] Look for related topics and characteristics that describe them. When you are looking for similarities and differences between two things, it can help to start by identifying relationships between them. What do the two things have in common? If two things have nothing in common, such as a dog and a piece of pie, it will be difficult to find similarities or differences. On the other hand, you can compare and contrast two countries or political systems. Look through the information you have on the things or topics you want to compare and contrast, and identify the characteristics, or features, that describe those things or topics.

[2.] Look for words that signal comparison ("both," "similar to," "also") or contrast ("unlike," "different," "instead"). Look for words that show comparison, or similarity, and those that show contrast, or difference. Take notes on these similarities and differences. This will make it possible to analyze information more quickly.

[3.] Identify similarities and differences in the topics, and draw conclusions about them. Look through your notes and analyze the ways in which your topics are similar and different. Usually, topics have both similarities and differences. Try to find patterns in these similarities and differences. For example, all the similarities between two countries might be related to climate, and all the differences might be related to economics. Draw conclusions based on these patterns. In this example, you might conclude that a country's economy does not depend on its climate. Identifying similarities and differences by comparing and contrasting two topics lets you draw conclusions that help you analyze both topics as well as other topics like them.

Identify Main Ideas and Details

You can analyze information in a selection by finding the main idea. A main idea is the most important point in a selection. Identifying the main idea will help you remember details, such as names, dates, and events, which should support the main idea. Practice this skill by reading the paragraph on this page. Find the main idea of this paragraph and the supporting details.

> During his first hundred days in office, which became known as the Hundred Days, Roosevelt proposed and Congress passed 15 major bills. These measures had three goals: relief, recovery, and reform. Roosevelt wanted to provide relief from the immediate hardships of the depression and achieve a long-term economic recovery. He also instituted reforms to prevent future depressions.

[1.] Scan titles, headings, and visuals before reading to see what the selection is about. Often, important ideas are included in titles, headings, and other special text. Special text may be primary sources, words that are highlighted, or ideas listed with bullet points. Also, take a look at visuals and captions. By analyzing these parts of the text, you should quickly get a sense of the main idea of the article.

[2.] Read the selection and then identify the main point of the selection, the point that the rest of the selection supports: this is the main idea. Read through the selection to identify the main idea. Sometimes, the main idea will be the first or second sentence of one of the first few paragraphs. Sometimes, it will be the last sentence of the first paragraph. Other times, no single sentence will tell you the main idea. You will have to come up with your own sentence answering the question, "What is the main point of this selection?"

[3.] Find details or statements within the selection that support or build on the main idea. Once you have identified the main idea, look for details that support the main idea. Many or most of the details should be related to the main idea. If you find that many of the details are not related to what you think is the main idea, you may not have identified the main idea correctly. Identify the main idea that the details in the selection support. Analyze the information in the text by finding the main idea and supporting details.

Summarize

When you analyze information by summarizing, you restate the main points of a passage in your own words. Using your own words helps you understand the information. Summarizing will help you understand a text and prepare for tests or assignments based on the text. Practice this skill by following the steps to summarize this excerpt.

> The Texas legislature carries out that responsibility as a bicameral body modeled after the Congress of the United States. Texas' upper house is called the Senate, and the lower house is called the House of Representatives. In fact, all State legislatures but one are bicameral. The exception is Nebraska, which calls its single chamber the Legislature.

Although there is no ideal size for a legislative body, two basic considerations are important. First, a legislature, and each of its houses, should not be so large as to hamper the orderly conduct of the people's business. Second, it should not be so small that the many views and interests within the State cannot be represented adequately. The Texas Senate has 31 members, representing 31 districts that are about equal in population. The Texas House of Representatives has 150 members, elected from 150 districts that are all about equal in population.

[**1.**] Identify and write down the main point of each paragraph in your own words. You may identify the main idea right at the beginning of each paragraph. In other cases, you will have to figure out the main idea. As you read each paragraph, ask yourself, "What is the point this paragraph makes?" The point the paragraph makes is the main idea. Write this idea down in your own words.

[**2.**] Use these main points to write a general statement of the overall main idea of the passage in your own words. Once you have written down the main idea for each paragraph, write down the main idea of the passage. Write the main idea in your own words. If you have trouble identifying the main idea of the passage, review the titles and headings in the passage. Often, titles and headings relate to the main idea. Also, the writer may state the main idea in the first paragraph of the passage. The main idea of a passage should answer the question, "What is the point this passage makes?"

[**3.**] Use this general statement as a topic sentence for your summary. Then, write a paragraph tying together the main points of the passage. Leave out unimportant details. Analyze the information in the passage by summarizing. Use the main idea of the passage as a topic sentence for your summary paragraph. Use the main ideas that you identified for each paragraph of the passage to write sentences supporting the main idea of the passage. Leave out details that are not needed to understand the main idea of the passage. Your summary should be in your own words, and it should be much shorter than the original passage. Once your summary is written, review it to make sure that it contains all the main points of the passage. If any are missing, revise your summary to include them. If the summary includes unimportant details, remove them.

Generalize

One good way to analyze materials about a particular subject is to make generalizations and predictions. What are the patterns and connections that link the different materials? What can you say about the different materials that is true of all them? Practice this skill by analyzing the chart, Strong Minor Party Efforts. What generalization can you make about minor political parties in the United States?

Strong Minor Party Efforts*

YEAR	PARTY	% POPULAR VOTE	ELECTORAL VOTES
1920	Socialist	3.45	---
1924	Progressive	16.61	13
1932	Socialist	2.22	---
1948	States' Rights (Dixiecrat)	2.41	39
	Progressive	2.37	---
1968	American Independent	13.53	46
1996	Reform	8.40	---
2000	Green	2.74	---

*Includes all minor parties that polled at least 2% of the popular vote.
SOURCE: U.S. Census Bureau; *Historical Statistics of the United States, Colonial Times to* 1970.

[1.] Make a list. Listing all of the specific details and facts about a subject will help you find patterns and connections.

[2.] Generate a statement. From your list of facts and specific details, decide what most of the items listed have in common. Analyze your information by making generalizations and predictions.

[3.] Ensure your generalization is logical and well supported by facts. Generalizations can be valid or invalid. A generalization that is not logical or supported by facts is invalid.

Make Predictions

You can analyze information by making generalizations and predictions. Predictions are educated guesses about the future, based on clues you find in written material and information you already have. When you analyze information by making generalizations and predictions, you are thinking critically about the material you read. Practice this skill by analyzing this graph and predicting the effect an economic downturn, with lower corporate and individual earnings, would have on government receipts.

Federal Receipts, 2014 (Estimated)

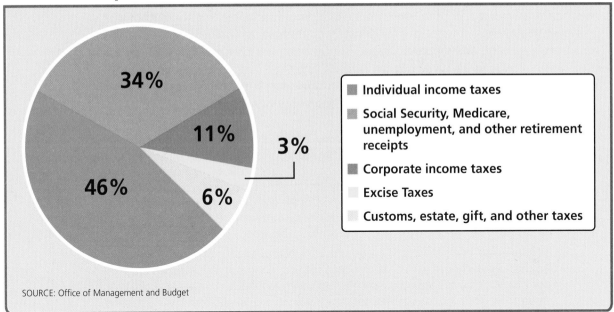

34%

11%

3%

46%

6%

- Individual income taxes
- Social Security, Medicare, unemployment, and other retirement receipts
- Corporate income taxes
- Excise Taxes
- Customs, estate, gift, and other taxes

SOURCE: Office of Management and Budget

[1.] Review the content. Read your material carefully and research any terms or concepts that are new to you. It's important to understand the material before analyzing the information to make a prediction.

[2.] Look for clues. Gathering evidence is an important part of making predictions. Look for important words, statements, and evidence that seem to support the writer's point of view. Ask questions about what you are reading, including who, what, where, when, why, and how. Look for and analyze clues to help you generalize and predict.

[3.] Consider what you already know. Use related prior knowledge and/or connect to your own experiences to help you make an informed prediction. If you have experience with the subject matter, you have a much better chance of making an accurate prediction.

[4.] Generate a list of predictions. After studying the content, list the clues you've found. Then use these clues, plus your prior knowledge, to form your predictions. List as many possible outcomes as you can based on clues in the material and the questions you have considered.

Draw Inferences

What is the author trying to tell you? To make a determination about the author's message, you analyze information by drawing inferences and conclusions. You consider details and descriptions included in the text, compare and contrast the text to prior knowledge you have about the subject, and then form a conclusion about the author's intent. Practice this skill by analyzing this document and drawing inferences about the author's view of life in the Soviet Union under communism in 1931.

> The fear of being exiled [banished, sent away] as a kulak [a landowner] has been a powerful factor in drawing workers into the collective farms. In the Stalin kolkhoz [collective farm] where I stayed, a sharp-eyed dark-haired peasant approached me in the Village Soviet hut. We were in the presence of the Communist president. He spoke to me of the successes of the kolkhoz, of the enthusiasm for the collective farm movement, and of the affection of the peasants for their young Bolshevist leader.
>
> Next morning, however, when far away from any of the Communist members of the kolkhoz, the same peasant . . . approached me and whispered, "It is terrible here in the kolkhoz. We cannot speak or we shall be sent away to Siberia. . . . We are afraid. I had three cows. They took them away and now I only get a crust of bread. It is a thousand times worse now than before the Revolution. . . . We have to keep quiet.
>
> "The Real Russia: The Peasant on the Farm," Gareth Jones, *The Times,* October 14, 1931

[1.] Study the image or text. Consider all of the details and descriptions included. What is the author trying to tell you? Look for context clues that hint at the topic and subject matter.

[2.] Make a connection. Use related prior knowledge to connect to the text or image. Analyze information by asking questions such as who, what, where, when, and how. Look for cause-and-effect relationships; compare and contrast. This strategy will help you think beyond the available surface details to understand what the author is suggesting or implying.

[3.] Form a conclusion. When you draw an inference, you combine your own ideas with evidence and details you found within the text or image to form a new conclusion. This action leads you to a new understanding of the material.

Draw Conclusions

When you analyze information by drawing inferences and conclusions, you connect the ideas in a text with what you already know in order to understand a topic better. Using this skill, you can "fill in the blanks" to see the implications or larger meaning of the information in a text. Practice this skill by reading the excerpt on this page. What conclusions can you draw based on the information in the paragraph?

Challenging Economic Times

From the Oval Office, Hoover worked hard to end the depression. But to many out-of-work Americans, the President became a symbol of failure. Some people blamed capitalism, while others questioned the responsiveness of democracy. Many believed the American system was due for an overhaul. Although some questioned the ability of America's capitalistic and democratic institutions to overcome the crisis, most Americans never lost faith in their country.

[1.] Identify the topic, main idea, and supporting details. Before reading, look at the titles and headings within a reading. This should give you a good idea of the topic, or the general subject, of a text. After reading, identify the main idea. The main idea falls within the topic and answers the question, "What is the main point of this text?" Find the details that the author presents to support the main idea.

[2.] Use what you know to make a judgment about the information. Think about what you know about this topic or a similar topic. For example, you may read that the English settlers of Jamestown suffered from starvation because many of them were not farmers and did not know how to grow food. Analyzing the information about their situation and what you know about people, you could draw the conclusion that these settlers must have had little idea, or the wrong idea, about the conditions that they would find in America.

[3.] Check and adjust your judgment until you can draw a well-supported conclusion. Look for details within the reading that support your judgment. Reading a little further, you find that these settlers thought that they would become rich after discovering gold or silver, or through trading with Native Americans for furs. You can use this information to support your conclusion that the settlers were mistaken about the conditions that they would find in America. By analyzing the information further, you might infer that the settlers had inaccurate information about America. To support your conclusions, you could look for reliable sources on what these settlers knew before they left England.

Interpret Sources

Outlines and reports are good sources of information. In order to interpret these sources, though, you'll need to identify the type of document you're reading, identify the main idea, organize the details of information, and evaluate the source for point of view and bias. Practice this skill by finding a newspaper or online report on a bill recently passed by Congress or a decision recently decided by the Supreme Court. What steps will you take to interpret this report?

[1.] Identify the type of document. Is the document a primary or secondary source? Determine when, where, and why it was written.

[2.] Examine the source to identify the main idea. After identifying the main idea, identify details or sections of text that support the main idea. If the source is an outline or report, identify the topic and subtopics; review the supporting details under each subtopic. Organize the information from the outline or report and think about how it connects back to the overall topic listed at the top of the outline or report.

[3.] Evaluate the source for point of view and bias. Primary sources often have a strong point of view or bias; it is important to analyze primary sources critically to determine their validity. Evaluating each source will help you interpret the information they contain.

Create Databases

Databases are organized collections of information which can be analyzed and interpreted. You decide on a topic, organize data, use a spreadsheet, and then pose questions which will help you to analyze and interpret your data. Practice this skill as you create a database of key facts about five counties in your state. You can find many kinds of county data in the U.S. Census. (census.gov)

[1.] Decide on a topic. Identify the information that you will convert into a table. This information may come from various sources, including textbooks, reference works, and Internet sites.

[2.] Organize the data. Study the information and decide what to include in your table. Only include data that is pertinent and available. Based on the data you choose, organize your information. Identify how many columns there will be and what the column headings will be. Decide the order in which you are going to list the data in the rows.

[3.] Use a spreadsheet. A spreadsheet is a computer software tool that allows you to organize data so that it can be analyzed. Spreadsheets allow you to make calculations as well as input data. Use a spreadsheet to help you create summaries of your data. For instance, you can compute the sum, average, minimum, and maximum values of the data. Use the graphing features of your spreadsheet program to show the data visually.

[4.] Analyze the data. Once all of your data is entered and you have made any calculations you need, you are ready to pose questions to analyze and interpret your data. Organize the information from the database and use it to form conclusions. Be sure to draw conclusions that can be supported by the data available.

Analyze Data and Models

Data and models can provide useful information about geographic distributions and patterns. To make sense of that information, though, you need to pose and answer questions about data and models. What does the data say? What does it mean? What patterns can you find? Practice this skill as you study the data in the map. What might explain the differences among states shown here?

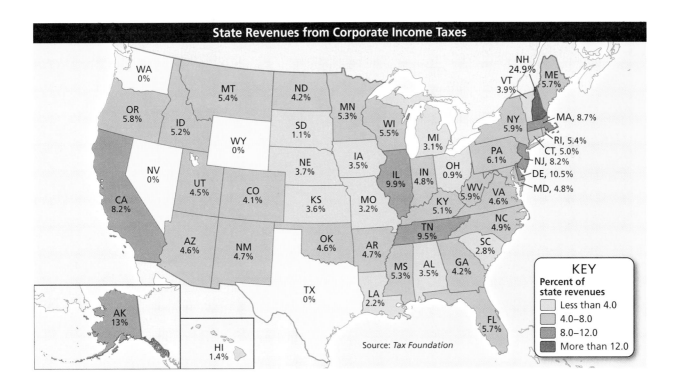

State Revenues from Corporate Income Taxes

WA 0%
MT 5.4%
ND 4.2%
MN 5.3%
NH 24.9%
VT 3.9%
ME 5.7%
OR 5.8%
ID 5.2%
WY 0%
SD 1.1%
WI 5.5%
MI 3.1%
NY 5.9%
MA, 8.7%
RI, 5.4%
CT, 5.0%
NV 0%
UT 4.5%
CO 4.1%
NE 3.7%
IA 3.5%
IL 9.9%
IN 4.8%
OH 0.9%
PA 6.1%
NJ, 8.2%
DE, 10.5%
MD, 4.8%
CA 8.2%
KS 3.6%
MO 3.2%
KY 5.1%
WV 5.9%
VA 4.6%
AZ 4.6%
NM 4.7%
OK 4.6%
AR 4.7%
TN 9.5%
NC 4.9%
SC 2.8%
MS 5.3%
AL 3.5%
GA 4.2%
TX 0%
LA 2.2%
AK 13%
HI 1.4%
FL 5.7%

Source: *Tax Foundation*

KEY
Percent of state revenues
Less than 4.0
4.0–8.0
8.0–12.0
More than 12.0

[**1.**] Read the title to learn the geographic distributions represented by the data set, graph, or model.

[**2.**] Read the data given. When reviewing a graph, read the labels and the key to help you comprehend the data provided. Pose and answer questions to further understand the material. For example, you might ask "Who could use this data?" or "How could this data be used?" or even "Why is this data presented in this particular format?" Thinking critically about the data presented will help you make predictions and comprehend the data.

[**3.**] Study the numbers, lines, and/or colors to find out what the graphs or data represent. Next, find similarities and differences between multiple models of the same data. Do any additional research to find out more about why the information in the models differs.

[**4.**] Interpret the graph, data set, or model. Look for interesting geographic distributions and patterns in the data. Look at changes over time or compare information from different categories. Draw conclusions.

Read Charts, Graphs, and Tables

If you pose and answer questions about charts, graphs, or tables you find in books or online, you can find out all sorts of information, such as how many calories are in your favorite foods or what the value of a used car is. Analyzing and interpreting the information you find in thematic charts, graphs, and tables can help you make decisions in your life. Practice this skill as you study the circle graph below. What questions does this graph raise for the future?

State and Local Spending

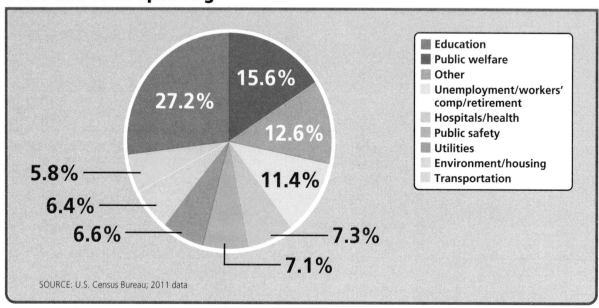

SOURCE: U.S. Census Bureau; 2011 data

[1.] Identify the title and labels of a chart, graph, or table, and read the key, if there is one, to understand the information presented. The title often tells you the topic of the chart, graph, or table, or the type of information you will find. Make sure you understand how the graph shows information. A key or legend often appears in a small box near the edge of the graph or chart. The key will tell you the meaning of lines, colors, or symbols used on the chart or graph. Notice also the column and row headings, and use your reading skills to figure out the meanings of any words you don't know.

[2.] Determine consistencies and inconsistencies, to see whether there is a trend in a graph, chart, or table. Organize information from visuals such as charts and graphs and decide whether or not there is a trend or pattern in the information that you see. Evaluate the data and determine whether the trend is consistent, or steady. Remember that there could be some inconsistencies, or exceptions to the pattern. Try not to miss the overall pattern because of a couple of exceptions.

[3.] Draw conclusions about the data in a chart, graph, or table. Once you understand the information, try to analyze and interpret the information and draw conclusions. If you see a pattern, does the pattern help you to understand the topic or predict future events?

[**4.**] Create a chart or graph to make the data more understandable or to view the data in a different way. Does the data in the chart or graph help you answer questions you have about the topic or see any causes or effects? For example, you could use your mathematical skills to create circle graphs or bar graphs that visually organize the data in a different way that allows you to interpret the data differently.

[**5.**] Use the data or information in charts and graphs to understand an issue or make decisions. Use your social studies skills to make inferences, draw conclusions, and take a stand on the issue.

Create Charts and Maps

Thematic charts, graphs, and maps are visual tools for representing information. When you create a thematic chart, graph, or map you will start by selecting the type of data you want to represent. Then you will find appropriate data to include, organize your data, and then create symbols and a key to help others understand your chart, graph, or map. Practice this skill by creating a map showing how your state's counties voted in the most recent presidential election. Research the data, then use computer software to generate the map. What patterns do you see? How might you explain them?

[**1.**] To create a chart or map, first select a region or set of data. Use a map to represent data pertaining to a specific region or location; use a chart to represent trends reflected in a set of data.

[**2.**] Research and find the data you would like to present in the chart or map. Your choice of data will be based on the theme you wish to explore. For example, a chart or map that explores the theme of changing demographics in Texas might include data about the location of different ethnic groups in Texas in the nineteenth, twentieth, and twenty-first centuries.

[**3.**] Organize the data according to the specific format of your chart or map.

[**4.**] Create symbols, a key (as needed), and a title. Create symbols to represent each piece of data you would like to highlight. Keep each symbol simple and easy to understand. After you have created the symbols, place them in a key. Add a title to your map or chart that summarizes the information presented. Your symbols and key will make it easier for others to interpret your charts and maps.

Analyze Political Cartoons

Political cartoons are visual commentaries about events or people. As you learn to analyze political cartoons, you will learn to identify bias in cartoons and interpret their meaning. You can start by carefully examining the cartoon and considering its possible meanings. Then you can draw conclusions based on your analysis. Practice this skill as you study this political cartoon.

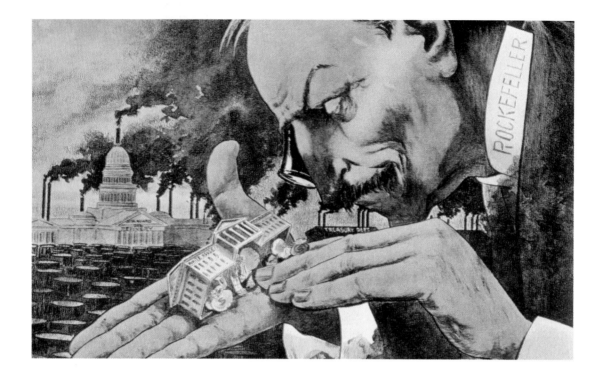

[1.] Fully examine the cartoon. Identify any symbols in the cartoon, read the text and title, and identify the main character or characters. Analyze the cartoon to identify bias and determine what each image or symbol represents. Conduct research if you need more information to decipher the cartoon.

[2.] Consider the meaning. Think about how the cartoonist uses the images and symbols in the cartoon to express his or her opinion about a subject. Try to interpret the artist's purpose in creating the image.

[3.] Draw conclusions. Use what you have gleaned from the image itself, plus any prior knowledge or research, to analyze, interpret, and form a conclusion about the artist's intentions.

Read Physical Maps

What mountain range is closest to where you live? What major rivers are closest to you? To find out, you would look at a physical map. You can use appropriate reading skills to interpret social studies information such as that found on different kinds of maps. Physical maps show physical features, such as elevation, mountains, valleys, oceans, rivers, deserts, and plains. Practice this skill as you study this map. Remember the location of your state capital. What advantages can you see to locating the state capital there? What disadvantages?

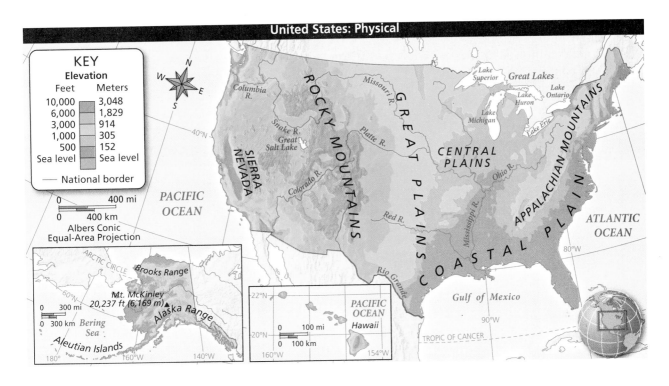

[1.] Identify the title and region shown on a map. A map's title can help you to identify the region covered by the map. The title may also tell you the type of information you will find on the map. If the map has no title, you can identify the region by reading the labels on the map.

[2.] Use the map key to interpret symbols and colors on a map. A key or legend often appears in a small box near the edge of the map. The legend will tell you the meaning of colors, symbols, or other patterns on the map. On a physical map, colors from the key often show elevation, or height above sea level, on the map.

[3.] Identify physical features, such as mountains, valleys, oceans, and rivers. Using labels on the map and colors and symbols from the key, identify the physical features on the map. The information in the key allows you to interpret the information from visuals such as a map. Rivers, oceans, lakes, and other bodies of water are usually colored blue. Colors from the key may indicate higher and lower elevation, or there may be shading on the map that shows mountains.

[4.] Draw conclusions about the region based on natural resources and physical features. Once you understand all the symbols and colors on the map, try to interpret the information from the map. Is it very mountainous or mostly flat? Does it have a coastline? Does the region have lots of lakes and rivers that suggest a good water supply? Pose and answer questions about geographic distributions and patterns shown on the map. Physical maps can give you an idea of lifestyle and economic activities of people in the region.

Read Political Maps

What is the capital of your state? What countries border China? To find out, you could look at a political map. Political maps are colorful maps that show borders, or lines dividing states or countries. Practice reading political maps by studying the map below.

America in 1783

[**1.**] Identify the title of the political map and the region shown. A map's title can help you identify the region covered by the map. The title may also tell you the type of information you will find on the map. If the map has no title, you can identify the region by reading the labels on the map.

[**2.**] Use the map key to interpret symbols and colors on the map. A key or legend often appears in a small box near the edge of the map. The key will help you interpret information from visuals, including maps, by telling you the meaning of colors, symbols, or other patterns on the visual.

[**3.**] Identify boundaries between nations or states. Evaluate government data, such as borders, using the map. It is often easy to see borders, because each state or country will be a different color. If you cannot find the borders, check the key to find the lines used to mark borders on the map.

[**4.**] Locate capital cities. Look at the key to see whether capital cities are shown on the map. They are often marked with a special symbol, such as a star.

[5.] Draw conclusions about the region based on the map. Once you understand all the symbols and colors on the map, use appropriate reading and mathematical skills to interpret social studies information, such as that shown on the map, in order to draw conclusions about the region. For example, are some countries very large with many cities? These countries are likely to be powerful and influential.

Read Special-Purpose Maps

Some maps show specific kinds of information. These special-purpose maps may show features such as climate zones, ancient trade routes, economic and government data, geographic patterns, or population. Locating and interpreting information from visuals, including special-purpose maps, is an important research skill. Practice this skill as you study the map on this page.

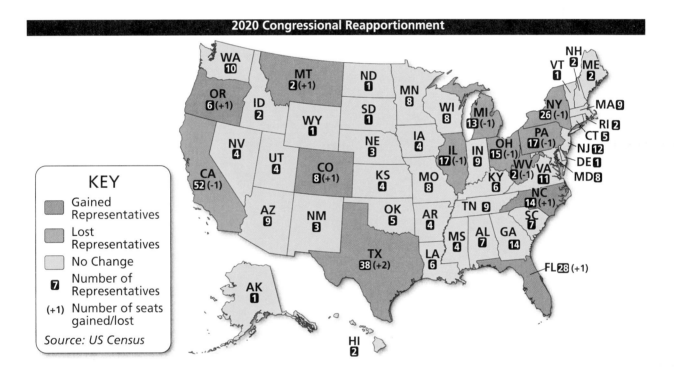

[1.] Identify the title and determine the purpose of a map. A map's title can help you identify the region covered by the map. The title may also tell you the purpose of the map. If the map has no title, see what information the map shows to determine its purpose.

[2.] Use the map key to make sense of symbols and colors on a map. A key or legend often appears in a small box near the edge of the map. The key will tell you the meaning of colors, symbols, or other patterns on the map. Special-purpose maps use these colors and symbols to present information.

[3.] Draw conclusions about the region shown on a map. Once you understand all the symbols and colors on the map, you can use appropriate skills, including reading and mathematical skills, to analyze and interpret social studies information such as maps. You can pose and answer questions about geographic patterns and distributions that are shown on maps. For example, a precipitation or climate map will show you which areas get lots of rainfall and which are very dry. You can evaluate government and economic data using maps. For example, a population map will show you which regions have lots of people and which have small, scattered populations. A historical map will show you the locations of ancient empires or trade routes. Thematic maps focus on a single theme or topic about a region. For example, you can interpret information from a thematic map representing various aspects of Texas during the nineteenth or twentieth century by studying the Great Military Map, which shows forts established in Texas during the nineteenth century, or by studying a map covering Texas during the Great Depression and World War II. By mapping this kind of detailed information, special-purpose maps can help you understand a region's history or geography.

Use Parts of a Map

If you understand how to organize and interpret information from visuals, including maps, you will be able to find the information you are looking for. Understanding how to use the parts of a map will help you find locations of specific places and estimate distances between different places. Practice this skill as you study this map.

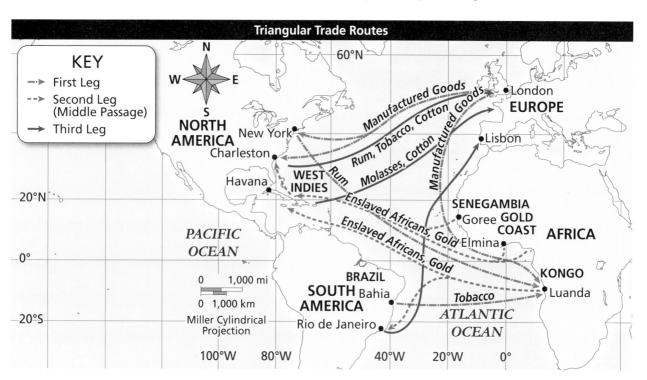

Triangular Trade Routes

[**1.**] Identify the title and region of a map. Use appropriate reading skills to interpret social studies information such as map labels. A map's title can help you to identify the region covered by the map. The title may also tell you the type of information you will find on the map. If the map has no title, you can identify the region by reading the labels on the map.

[**2.**] Use the compass rose to determine direction. Although on most maps north is at the top of the map, you should always double check the compass rose. Often, on the compass rose, the first letter of each direction represents that direction. For example, "N" represents the direction "north." Some compass roses are as simple as an arrow pointing north.

[**3.**] Use the scale to estimate the distance between places. Use appropriate mathematical skills to interpret social studies information such as a map scale. The scale on a map shows how a measurement on the map compares to the distance on the ground. For example, if one inch on the map represents a mile, the number of inches between two places on the map is the distance in miles.

[**4.**] Use the key or legend on a map to find information about colors or symbols on a map. A key or legend often appears in a small box near the edge of the map. The legend will tell you the meaning of colors, symbols, or other patterns on the map.

[**5.**] Use the latitude and longitude grid to determine absolute locations. An absolute location is an exact description of a location on Earth's surface based on latitude and longitude. You can use the latitude and longitude lines on a map to find the absolute location of a place.

Analyze Primary and Secondary Sources

Primary sources are firsthand accounts of events. By contrast, secondary sources are secondhand accounts of events. Both sources are useful, but it is important to differentiate between valid primary and secondary sources. In this lesson, you'll learn how to locate and use primary and secondary sources to acquire information about the United States. Practice this skill by analyzing two selections below arguing whether or not to ratify the Constitution and distinguishing between the primary and secondary source.

> "…[T]he great powers of the President, connected with his duration in office would lead to oppression and ruin. That he would be governed by favorites and flatterers, or that a dangerous council would be collected from the great officers of state, …that the president possessed of the power, given him by this frame of government differs but very immaterially from the establishment of monarchy in Great Britain, …that no attention has been paid to either the numbers or property in each state in forming the senate; that the mode in which they are appointed and their duration, will lead to the establishment of an aristocracy, that the senate and president are improperly connected…these are some of the many evils that will attend the adoption of this government."

—Letter V by "Cato," *The New York Journal,* November 22, 1787

Antifederalists appealed to Tom Paine's sentiment, "That government is best which governs least." They viewed with alarm the omission of annual elections and rotation in office....Elderly radicals such as General James Warren and his gifted wife Mercy, who believed that the states were the true guardians of "Republican Virtue," predicted that the new Constitution would encourage vice and speculation, and that under it America would soon go the way of imperial Rome.

—Samuel Eliot Morison, *The Oxford History of the American People,* 1965

[1.] Determine who created the source as well as when and why it was created. Determine whether it is a primary or secondary source. Identify the author of the document. Next, look for the date the document was written or the date when the document was first published. Most primary sources are written close to the date of the events described. Secondary sources are often written well after the events described. Firsthand observers or participants in an event create primary sources. People who did not witness an event create secondary sources. Primary sources record an event. Secondary sources analyze or draw conclusions about events. Secondary sources rely on both primary and secondary sources. Good research requires you to analyze and evaluate the validity of information, arguments, and counterarguments from a primary or secondary source for frame of reference.

[2.] Identify the central idea and key details, and determine whether they are facts or opinions. Read the text carefully and ask yourself, "What overall point is this text making?" This point is the main idea. Then reread the text and cite specific details that support this main idea. What insights do these details give you into the text as a whole? In a sentence or two, summarize the relationships among key details and ideas. Decide whether key details are facts or opinions. Facts can usually be confirmed in other sources. Opinions are often characterized by emotional language that shows feelings.

[3.] Decide whether the source's information is biased or if it is accurate and credible. Check statements in the text against reliable sources, such as encyclopedias or books written by experts on the topic. If reliable sources agree with the text, it is probably fairly accurate. If most of the text seems to be opinions rather than facts, it is not an accurate source of information. Still, these opinions can teach you about the author's world. A writer who observed an exciting or scary event may use emotional language to describe the event, but the source may still be a reliable account. An important part of research is analyzing and evaluating the validity of the information, arguments, and counterarguments from primary and secondary sources for bias or propaganda.

Compare Viewpoints

When people disagree about a topic, they have different viewpoints. Knowing how to analyze and evaluate the validity of information, arguments, and counterarguments from both primary and secondary sources for point of view can help you to learn more about a topic. Practice this skill by reading these quotes and comparing the viewpoints.

"Dictatorship…involves costs which the American people will never pay: The cost of having our children brought up, not as free and dignified human beings, but as pawns…

–Franklin Roosevelt, State of the Union Address, January 4, 1939

"The [Nazi Party] has laid down the directive…we must insist that all organs of education…have to [fulfill] their duty towards the community…

–Adolf Hitler, Speech delivered in German Reichstag on January 30, 1937

[1.] Identify the authors of texts presenting different points of view and identify each author's frame of reference. Frame of reference is a term that describes the experiences, values, and ideas that influence a person's opinions and actions. It can also be referred to as *point of view*. First, identify the group or individual that wrote each text. Determine if the source is primary or secondary. As you read, take note of any information about the author's experiences or background. Also, look for any signs of what the author thinks is important. These types of statements can help you analyze and evaluate the validity of information, arguments, and counterarguments from both primary and secondary sources for point of view.

[2.] Recognize any similarities and differences between the authors' frames of reference and identify the opinion of each author. Pay attention to any similarities and differences between the two authors' experiences, values, and ideas. Read carefully to identify the opinion of each author. In an article about a rock band, an author who played guitar in a band for ten years argues that Band A is the best band today because of its great guitarist. In a second article, another author who sang for many years argues that Band B is the best because of its lead singer. Notice how authors' arguments and counterarguments are shaped by their frame of reference, or point of view.

[3.] Draw conclusions about similarities and differences between authors' points of view. With some information about the point of view of each author, you can understand why they have different opinions. This helps you to analyze and evaluate the validity of the information, arguments, and counterarguments. In the example of the two authors writing about rock bands, each author stresses his or her own areas of expertise. You might decide to listen to the band recommended by the singer if you share an interest in vocals. If you are more interested in instrumentals, you might choose the band recommended by the guitarist.

Identify Bias

Being able to analyze and evaluate the validity of information, arguments, and counterarguments for bias helps you to determine whether primary or secondary sources you find online, in books, or in the media are reliable. When you are able to identify bias in written, oral, and visual material, you can see when someone is presenting only one side of an issue or basing an argument on emotion instead of facts. Practice this skill by applying the steps below whenever you read an editorial or an op-ed piece in the news media.

[1.] Identify the author of a source and the author's purpose. First, identify the author of the source. The author may be a group or an organization rather than a single person. The author may state his or her purpose very clearly in the source. If not, the type of source may give you an idea of the purpose. For example, the writer of an encyclopedia aims to summarize information about a subject. The author of a political Web site may want you to vote for a candidate.

[2.] Identify the main idea, and check whether the main idea is supported with facts or opinions. Read the document carefully and ask yourself, "What is the main point of this selection?" Your answer to this question is the main idea. Reread the document and list details that support this main idea. Decide whether these details are facts or opinions. To find out whether they are facts, check whether other reliable sources include the same information. If your source uses statements that shows feelings, those statements are probably opinions.

[3.] Look for the use of emotional language or one-sided opinions. Look for words that can show opinions such as "good" and "bad." Be aware of statements that make you feel angry, scared, or excited. Also, watch out for statements that only express one side of an issue. These are all signs of bias.

[4.] Draw conclusions about the author's bias, if any. Is the author using mostly emotional language with few facts to support his or her ideas? Are there insults or other very negative language in the source? If so, the source is probably biased. Similarly, if you notice that the author is presenting only one side of an issue, the source is probably not reliable. It is important to analyze and evaluate the information, arguments, and counterarguments in both primary and secondary sources for bias.

Evaluate Existing Arguments

When you evaluate existing arguments, you must evaluate and analyze the point of view and biases of your sources and their authors. Who is the author and what is he or she trying to accomplish? How valid are the arguments in your primary and secondary sources? If you master these skills, you will be able to analyze and interpret social studies information such as speeches. Practice this skill as you read and evaluate the excerpt on this page.

> We hold these truths to be self-evident: that all men and women are created equal; that they are endowed by their Creator with certain inalienable rights; that among these are life, liberty, and the pursuit of happiness. . . .
>
> The history of mankind is a history of repeated injuries and usurpations [seizures] on the part of man toward woman, having in direct object the establishment of an absolute tyranny over her. To prove this, let facts be submitted to a candid [fair] world.
>
> He has never permitted her to exercise her inalienable right to the elective franchise.
>
> He has compelled her to submit to law in the formation of which she had no voice. . . .

He has made her, if married, in the eye of the law, civilly dead. He has taken from her all right in property, even to the wages she earns. . . .

Now, in view of this entire disfranchisement of one-half the people of this country, their social and religious degradation, in view of the unjust laws above mentioned, and because women do feel themselves aggrieved, oppressed, and fraudulently deprived of their most sacred rights, we insist that they have immediate admission to all the rights and privileges which belong to them as citizens of the United States.

—Declaration of Sentiments and Resolutions, 1848

[1.] Identify the claim or thesis. What is the author or source claiming? The claim or thesis is usually found in the introduction and/or conclusion of a written or spoken argument.

[2.] Identify the reasons (claims to truth or facts) the author offers in support of his or her claim. What evidence does the author or source provide to support their claims? Make a list of the evidence provided to support each claim.

[3.] Evaluate the argument. Analyze and evaluate the validity of the evidence presented to support each claim. Use the appropriate skills to analyze and interpret social studies information, such as speeches. Research each claim to be sure that the author's statements are accurate. Carefully check for evidence of bias or propaganda. Be sure you understand the author's point of view and his or her frame of reference. Finally, check to be sure that the author's conclusions follow logically from the evidence presented. If the evidence is accurate, the author is free from bias, and conclusions follow logically from the evidence, the claims are probably valid.

Consider and Counter Opposing Arguments

Before you can effectively counter opposing arguments, you'll need to analyze possible counterarguments for frame of reference, bias, point of view, and propaganda. You'll plan your response ahead of time, collecting research and data. Then, you'll make a point of acknowledging the opposing view before presenting your counterarguments. To practice this skill, suppose you are preparing for a debate about raising the minimum wage in your state. Choose a side of the debate to support. What arguments will you use to support your side of the debate? What counterarguments will you anticipate the other side using? Why is it useful to anticipate the other side's arguments?

[1.] Fully understand your argument and the potential counter points. Do research as needed to find out more about other opposing views. Analyze and evaluate the validity of possible counterarguments from primary and secondary sources for frame of reference, bias, point of view, and propaganda.

[2.] Make predictions and outline a response to several of the opposing views. Continue researching as needed. Researching, analyzing, and evaluating the validity of opposing arguments will help you support and strengthen your own. Opposing arguments can consist of any reasons, conclusions, or claims that oppose yours. Outline your response to each opposing reason, conclusion, or claim.

[3.] To counter an opposing argument, first acknowledge the opposing view. This strategy shows that you have heard the opposing argument and are responding accordingly. Consider using statements such as "I understand your point, but you should also consider the following..." You can also respond by refuting facts, logic, etc. Be sure to respond to each opposing argument. Ignoring or dismissing a counterargument shows that your response is weak and unsupported.

Participate in a Discussion or Debate

When you participate in a collaborative discussion or debate, your goal is to explain, analyze, and defend a point of view. Use the steps below to hold a discussion on this question: Do you think the United States should act as a "global policeman?" Why or why not? To begin, hold a one-on-one discussion with a partner. Then work in a group to delve into the question more deeply. Finally, participate in a teacher-led discussion on this topic.

[1.] Prepare. Prepare for the discussion by reading and researching examples and opinions related to the role of the U.S. in the world. In your group, set clear goals and deadlines and establish individual roles, such as lead spokesperson and note keeper. Promote civil, democratic decision-making within your group. During the discussion, draw on your preparation by referring to evidence from texts and other research to stimulate a thoughtful, well-reasoned exchange of ideas. Build on others' ideas and express your own clearly and persuasively.

[2.] Work with peers to promote civil, democratic discussions. Propel conversations by posing and responding to questions that probe reasoning and evidence; ensure a hearing for a full range of positions on a topic or issue; clarify, verify, or challenge ideas and conclusions; and promote divergent and creative perspectives.

[3.] Respond thoughtfully to diverse perspectives. Synthesize comments, claims, and evidence made on all sides of an issue; resolve contradictions when possible; and determine what additional information or research is required to deepen the investigation or complete the task.

Give an Effective Presentation

When you create a written, visual, and oral presentation, you teach, convince, or share information with an audience. Effective presentations use both words and visuals to engage audiences. Delivery is also important. For example, you can use the way you move, speak, and look at the audience to keep people interested. Use the steps below to prepare and deliver a presentation on the history of the White House building.

[1.] Identify the purpose of your presentation and your audience. Think about the purpose of your written, visual, and oral presentation. If this is a research report, you will need facts and data to support your points. If you are trying to persuade your audience, look for powerful photos. Keep your audience in mind. Consider their interests and present your topic in a way that will engage them.

[2.] Write the text and find visual aids for your presentation. Look online and in books and magazines for information and images for your presentation. Organize the information and write it up carefully so that it is easy for your audience to understand. Diagrams can show complicated information in a clear way. Visuals also get people interested in the presentation. So choose large, colorful images that people in the back of the audience will be able to see.

[3.] Practice and work to improve your presentation. Keep practicing your oral presentation until you know the material well. Then, practice some more, focusing on improving your delivery.

[4.] Use body language, tone of voice, and eye contact to deliver an effective presentation. Answer questions if the audience has them. At the beginning of your oral presentation, take a breath, smile, and stand up tall. Speak more loudly and more clearly than you would in normal conversation. Also, try not to rush through the presentation. Glance at your notes but speak naturally, rather than reading. Look at people in the audience. If people are confused, pause to clarify. Finally, leave time for people in the audience to ask questions.

Write an Essay

An informative or explanatory essay is one in which the writer conveys or explains facts to his or her audience. The narration of a particular historical event, such as the election of 2016, is one type of informative text. To practice this skill, select an event related to the U.S. presidency that you would like to explain to your fellow classmates. Follow the steps below to write your essay.

[1.] Research. Develop the topic by selecting the most significant and relevant facts, extended definitions, concrete details, quotations, or other information and examples appropriate to your audience's knowledge of the topic.

[2.] Create an outline. Review all of the information you have gathered and decide how you want to organize your essay. You might order events chronologically, or perhaps you will organize them around an overriding theme. Keep in mind your overall purpose, as well as your audience. Organize complex ideas and information so that each new element builds on that which precedes it to create a unified whole.

[3.] Create a first draft. Use varied transitions and sentence structures to link the major sections of the text, create cohesion, and clarify the relationships among complex ideas and concepts. Use language and vocabulary appropriate for discussing the presidency. Try to incorporate techniques such as metaphor, simile, and analogy to manage the complexity of the topic. Include headings, tables, graphs, maps, and multimedia when useful to aiding comprehension. Provide a concluding statement or section that follows from and supports the information in your essay.

[4.] Revise. Develop and strengthen writing as needed by revising, editing, and rewriting. Try a new approach when necessary.

Avoid Plagiarism

When you don't attribute ideas and information to source materials and authors, you are plagiarizing. Plagiarizing–claiming others' ideas and information as your own–is considered unethical. You can avoid plagiarizing by carefully noting down which authors and sources you'll be using, citing those authors and sources in your paper, and listing them in a bibliography. To practice this skill, suppose you have been assigned to write a research paper on the impact of the Internet on the political process. Name three types of sources you might use to help you gather information. Explain how you will avoid plagiarism when you use these sources.

[1.] Keep a careful log of your notes. As you read sources to gain background information on your topic, keep track of ideas and information and the sources and authors they come from. Write down the name of each source next to your notes from that particular source so you can remember to cite it later on. Create a separate section in your notes where you keep your own thoughts and ideas so you know which ideas are your own. Using someone else's words or paraphrasing their ideas does not make them yours.

[2.] Cite sources in your paper. You must identify the source materials and authors you use to support your ideas. Whenever you use statistics, facts, direct quotations, or paraphrases of others' views, you need to attribute them to your source. Cite your sources within the body of your paper. Check your assignment to find out how they should be formatted.

[3.] List your sources in a bibliography at the end of your paper. List your source materials and authors cited in alphabetical order by author, using accepted formats. As you work, be sure to check your list of sources from your notes so that none are left out of the bibliography.

Solve Problems

Problem solving is a skill that you use every day. It is a process that requires an open mind, clear thinking, and action. Practice this skill by considering the lack of volunteers for a local project such as a food bank or park clean up and using these steps to solve the problem.

[**1.**] Understand the problem. Before trying to solve a problem, make sure that you gather as much information as possible in order to identify the problem. What are the causes and effects of the problem? Who is involved? You will want to make sure that you understand different perspectives on the problem. Try not to jump to conclusions or make assumptions. You might end up misunderstanding the problem.

[**2.**] Consider possible solutions and choose the best one. Once you have identified the problem and gathered some information, list and consider a number of possible options. Right away, one solution might seem like the right one, but try to think of other solutions. Be sure to consider carefully the advantages and disadvantages of each option. It can help to take notes listing benefits and drawbacks. Look for the solution whose benefits outweigh its drawbacks. After considering each option, choose the solution you think is best.

[**3.**] Make and implement a plan. Choose and implement a solution. Make a detailed, step-by-step plan to implement the solution that you choose. Write your plan down and assign yourself a deadline for each step. That will help you to stay on track toward completing your plan. Try to think of any problems that might come up and what you will do to address those problems. Of course, there are many things that you cannot predict. Stay flexible. Evaluate the effectiveness of the solution and adjust your plan as necessary.

Make Decisions

Everyone makes decisions. The trick is to learn how to make good decisions. How can you make good decisions? First, identify a situation that requires a decision and gather information. Then, identify possible options and predict the consequences of each option. Finally, choose the best option and take action to implement a decision. Practice this skill by considering the steps you should take when making a decision about which candidate you should vote for in a local, state, or national election.

[**1.**] Determine the options between which you must decide. In some cases, like ordering from a menu at a restaurant, your options may be clear. In other cases, you will need to identify a situation that requires a decision, gather information, and identify the options that are available to you. Spend some time thinking about the situation and brainstorm a number of options. If necessary, do a little research to find more options. Make a list of options that you might choose.

[2.] Review the costs and benefits of each option. Carefully predict the consequences of each option. You may want to make a cost-benefit list for each option. To do this, write down the option and then draw two columns underneath it. One column will be the "pro" or benefit list. The other column will be the "con" or cost list. Note the pros and cons for each of your options. Try not to rush through this process. For a very important decision, you may even want to show your list to someone you trust. This person can help you think of costs and benefits that you had not considered.

[3.] Determine the best option and act on it. Look through your cost-benefit lists. Note any especially serious costs. If an option has the possibility of an extremely negative consequence, you might want to cross it off your list right away. Look closely at the options with the most benefits and the fewest costs, and choose the one that you think is best. Once you have made a choice, take action to implement a decision. If necessary, make a detailed plan with clear steps. Set a deadline to complete the steps to keep yourself moving toward your goal.

Being an Informed Citizen

One responsibility of citizens is to stay well informed about civic affairs. This requires being involved with your community and, if necessary, being politically active. When it comes to issues they personally care about, good citizens take a stand and reach out to others.

[1.] Learn the issues. A great way to begin to understand the responsibilities of citizenship is to first find topics of interest to you. Next, become well informed about civic affairs in your town, city, or country. Read newspapers, magazines, and articles you find online about events happening in your area or around the world. Analyze the information you read to come to your own conclusions. Radio programs, podcasts, and social media are also great ways to keep up with current events and interact with others about issues.

[2.] Get involved. Attend community events to speak with others who know the issues. Become well informed about how policies are made and changed. Find out who to speak to if you would like to take part in civic affairs and policy creation. There are government websites that can help direct you to the right person. These websites will also provide his or her contact details.

[3.] Take a stand. Choose one of the issues that you learned about. Write a short essay describing the issue, your stand on it, and any actions you took related to the issue.

Political Participation

Political participation starts with an understanding of the responsibilities, duties and obligations of citizenship, such as serving the public good. When you understand your role as a political participant, you can get involved through volunteering for a political campaign, running for office, or interacting with others in person or online.

[1.] Volunteer for a political campaign. Political campaigns offer a wide variety of opportunities to help you become involved in the political process and become a responsible citizen by serving the public good. As a political campaign volunteer you may have the opportunity to attend events, make calls to voters, and explore your community while getting to know how other voters think about the responsibilities, duties, and obligations of citizenship.

[2.] Run for office in your school or community. A good way to become involved in your school or community is to run for office. Student council or community positions offer a great opportunity for you to become familiar with the campaign and election process.

[3.] Reach out to others. Start or join an interest group. Interest groups enable people to work together on common goals related to the political process. Write a letter or email to a public official. By contacting an elected official from your area, you can either support or oppose laws or policies. You can also ask for help or support regarding certain issues.

[4.] Interact online. Social networking sites and blogs offer a great way for people of all ages to interact and write about political issues. As you connect with others, you'll become more confident in your role as a citizen working for the public good.

Voting

Voting is not only a right. It is also one of the primary responsibilities, duties, and obligations of citizenship. Before you can legally vote, however, you must understand the voter registration process and the criteria for voting in elections. You should also understand the issues and know where different candidates stand on those issues.

[1.] Check eligibility and residency requirements. In order to vote in the United States, you must be a United States citizen who is 18 years or older, and you must be a resident of the place where you plan to vote.

[2.] Register to vote. You cannot vote until you understand the voter registration process. You can register at city or town election offices, or when you get a driver's license. You can also register by mail or online. You may also have the option of registering at the polls on Election Day, but this does not apply in all states. Make sure to find out what you need to do to register in your state, as well as the deadline for registering. You may have the option of declaring a political party when registering.

[**3.**] Learn the issues. As the election approaches, research the candidates and issues in order to be an informed voter. Watch televised debates, if there are any. You can also review the candidates' websites. By doing these things and thinking critically about what you learn, you will be prepared to exercise your responsibility, duty and obligation as a United States citizen.

[**4.**] Vote. Make sure to arrive at the correct polling place on Election Day to cast your ballot. Research to find out when the polls will be open. Advance voting, absentee voting, and voting by mail are also options in certain states for those who qualify.

Serving on a Jury

As an American, you need to understand the duties, obligations and responsibilities of citizenship; among these is the expectation that you may be required to serve on a jury. You will receive a written notice when you are summoned to jury duty and you'll receive instruction on the special duties and obligations of a juror. You'll follow the American code of justice which assumes that a person is innocent until proven guilty, and you'll follow instructions about keeping trial information confidential.

[**1.**] Wait to receive notification. If you are summoned to serve as a juror, you will be first notified by mail. If you are chosen to move on to the jury selection phase, lawyers from both sides will ask you questions as they select the final jury members. It is an honor to serve as a juror, as it is a responsibility offered only to American citizens.

[**2.**] Follow the law and remain impartial. Your job is to determine whether or not someone broke the law. You may also be asked to sit on the jury for civil cases (as opposed to criminal cases); these cases involve lawsuits filed against individuals or businesses for any perceived wrong doing (such as broken contracts, trespassing, discrimination, etc.). Be sure to follow the law as it is explained to you, regardless of whether you approve of the law or not. Your decision about the trial should not be influenced by any personal bias or views you may have.

[**3.**] Remember that the defendant is presumed innocent. In a criminal trial, the defendant must be proven guilty "beyond a reasonable doubt" for the verdict to be guilty. If the trial team fails to prove the defendant to be guilty beyond a reasonable doubt, the jury verdict must be "not guilty."

[**4.**] During the trial, respect the court's right to privacy. As a juror, you have specific duties, obligations, and responsibilities under the law. Do not permit anyone to talk about the case with you or in your presence, except with the court's permission. Avoid media coverage once the trial has begun so as to prevent bias. Keep an open mind and do not form or state any opinions about the case until you have heard all of the evidence, the closing arguments from the lawyers, and the judge's instructions on the applicable law.

Paying Taxes

Paying taxes is one of the responsibilities of citizenship. How do you go about figuring out how much you've already paid in taxes and how much you still owe? It's your duty and obligation to find out, by determining how much has been deducted from your pay and filing your tax return.

[**1.**] Find out how taxes are deducted from your pay. In the United States, payroll taxes are imposed on employers and employees, and they are collected and paid by the employers. Check your pay stub to find out how much money was deducted for taxes. Be sure to also save the W-2 tax form your employer sends to you. You will need this form later on when filing your tax paperwork. Also save any interest income statements. All this information will help you fulfill your obligation as an American taxpayer.

[**2.**] Check the sales taxes in your state. All but five states impose sales and use taxes on retail sale, lease, and rental of many goods, as well as some services. Sales tax is calculated as the purchase price times the appropriate tax rate. Tax rates vary widely from less than one percent to over ten percent. Sales tax is collected by the seller at the time of sale.

[**3.**] File your tax return. Filing your tax return is more than an obligation: it's also a duty and responsibility of citizenship. You may receive tax forms in the mail, or pick them up at the local Post Office or library. Fill the forms in and then mail or electronically send completed tax forms and any necessary payments to the Internal Revenue Service (IRS) and your state's department of revenue. The IRS provides free resources to help people prepare and electronically file their tax returns; go to IRS.gov to learn more. Note: certain things such as charitable donations and business expenses are tax deductible.

A

absentee voting provisions made for those unable to go to their regular polling places on election day

acquit to find not guilty of a charge

act of admission congressional act admitting a new State to the Union

Adams, John Adams (1735–1826) was a lawyer in Massachusetts, legislator, diplomat, and second U.S. President. He defended British military officers in the Boston Massacre out of a sense of fairness but became a leading advocate of American independence at the First and Second Continental Congresses. He was the principal author of the Massachusetts State constitution. Adams helped negotiate a peace treaty with Great Britain after the Revolutionary War, attained diplomatic recognition of the new United States, and structured free trade with all nations.

Adams, John Quincy (1767–1848) The sixth President of the United States from 1825 to 1829 and author of the Monroe Doctrine, John Quincy was the son of President John Adams (1797–1801). Prior to being elected President, Adams was Secretary of State. Adams served as a congressman after his presidency, from 1831 to 1848, and fought against slavery. In 1848, Adams suffered a stroke and collapsed on the floor of the House and died two days later.

Adams, Samuel A Founding Father, Adams (1722–1803) became a leader in Boston politics through his writing. He was a delegate to the First and Second Continental congresses and helped draft the Declaration of Rights.

adjourn suspend, as in a session of Congress

administration the officials in the executive branch of a government and their policies and principles

administrative law composed of the rules, orders, and regulations issued by federal, State, or local executive officers, acting under proper constitutional and/or statutory authority

affirmative action a policy of taking active steps to remedy past discrimination

Albany Plan of Union a plan proposed by Benjamin Franklin in 1754 for cooperation among the 13 colonies was never adopted

Albright, Madeleine Albright (1937–) served as U.S. ambassador to the United Nations from 1993 to 1997. Later, President Bill Clinton nominated her to became the first woman to hold the Cabinet post of U.S. secretary of state. She held that position from 1997 to 2001; thereafter she became a speaker, consultant, and author.

alien foreign-born resident, or noncitizen

Alito, Samuel (1950–) received a law degree from Yale University in 1975, where he was editor of the Yale Law Journal. Alito served in several judicial positions during the presidencies of Ronald Reagan and George H.W. Bush. In 2005, Alito was nominated by President George W. Bush and took his seat as a justice on the Supreme Court on January 31, 2006.

ambassador an official representative of the United States appointed by the President to represent the nation in matters of diplomacy

amendment a change in, or addition to a constitution or law

amicus curiae brief legal Latin term meaning "friend of the court"; a document that consists of written arguments presented to a court in support of one side in a dispute

amnesty a blanket pardon offered to a group of law violators

Anti-Federalists those persons who opposed the ratification of the Constitution in 1787–1788

appellate jurisdiction the authority of a court to review decisions of inferior (lower) courts

apportioned distributed, as in seats in a legislative body

appropriate to assign to a particular use

Aristotle (384–322 B.C.) Greek philosopher who viewed the lives of individual humans as linked in a social context. He wrote about various types of government and the obligations of the individual citizen.

Arouet, François-Marie Also known as Voltaire, Arouet (1694–1778) was an important Enlightenment thinker and writer. Voltaire's beliefs in reason, science, and religious freedom were echoed in his plays, poems, novels, essays, and historical and scientific works. Voltaire spent much of his life in exile from his home country of France, writing and speaking about his philosophy.

Arthur, Chester The 21st President of the United States, serving from 1881 to 1885, Arthur (1829–1886) took office after the assassination of President James Garfield. Arthur signed the Pendleton Act, which eliminated the spoils system and established merit as the basis for jobs in the federal workforce.

Articles of Confederation plan of government adopted by the Continental Congress after the American Revolution; established "a firm league of friendship" among the States but allowed few important powers to the Federal Government

assemble to gather with one another in order to express views on public matters

assessment the process of determining the value of property to be taxed

assimilation the process by which people of one culture merge into, and become part of, another culture

at-large election of an officeholder by the voters of an entire governmental unit (e.g. a State or country) rather than by the voters of a district or subdivision

attorney general the head of the Department of Justice

autocracy a form of government in which a single person holds unlimited power

B

backbenchers a member of the House of Commons who is not a party leader

bail sum of money that the accused may be required to post (deposit with the court) as a guarantee that he or she will appear in court at the proper time

balance the ticket when a presidential candidate chooses a running mate who can strengthen his chance of being elected by virtue of certain ideological, geographical, racial, ethnic, gender, or other characteristics

Balkans The Balkans, sometimes called Balkan Peninsula, is a geographic area in Central Europe that usually includes Slovenia, Croatia, Bosnia and Herzegovina, Serbia, Kosovo, Montenegro, Macedonia, Albania, Bulgaria, Romania, and Moldova. The term may have different interpretations of the geography, culture, and history.

ballot device that voters use to register a choice in an election

ballot fatigue phenomenon by which voters cast fewer votes for offices listed toward the bottom of the ballot

bankruptcy the legal proceeding by which a bankrupt person's assets are distributed among those to whom he or she owes debts

battleground States States in which the outcome of an election is too close to call and either candidate could win

BCRA The 2002 Bipartisan Campaign Reform Act attempted to close the soft-money loophole in earlier campaign finance laws.

bench trial trial in which the judge alone hears the case

bicameral an adjective describing a legislative body composed of two chambers

Biden, Joseph (1942–) Democratic senator from Delaware; first elected in 1972. Served as the 47th Vice President of the United States under President Barack Obama and as the 46th President of the United States.

bill a proposed law presented to a legislative body for consideration

bill of attainder legislative act that inflicts punishment without a court trial

Bill of Rights the first ten amendments to the Constitution

bipartisan supported by two parties

Blackstone, William Blackstone (1723–1780) was an English judge who wrote the *Commentaries on the Laws of England,* a series of four books that had a profound influence on the writers of America's Declaration of Independence and Constitution. Blackstone, an important Enlightenment figure, believed in protecting the rights of the innocent, and in basing judgments on common law, that is, on previous decisions about similar issues.

Blaine, James G. Blaine (1830–1893), a congressman from Maine and Speaker of the House from 1869 to 1875, was an unsuccessful candidate for President in 1876 and 1880. He served as Secretary of State in 1881 and again from 1889 to 1892.

blanket primary a voting process in which voters receive a long ballot containing the names of all contenders, regardless of party, and can vote however they choose

block grants one type of federal grants-in-aid for some particular but broadly defined area of public policy

Boehner, John (1949–) Republican Congressman from Cincinnati, Ohio, elected to the United States House of Representatives in 1990. He served as a majority leader in 2006 and a minority leader from 2007 to 2011. He became Speaker of the House in 2011.

Boston the capital and largest city of the Commonwealth of Massachusetts

Bradley, Joseph P. An Associate Justice of the Supreme Court from 1870 to 1892, Joseph P. Bradley (1813–1892) was appointed by President Ulysses S. Grant. Bradley was one of several justices to narrow the protections that the then newly passed 14th Amendment offered to African Americans.

Brennan, William J. Like Earl Warren, William J. Brennan, Jr., (1906–1997) was appointed to the Supreme Court by President Dwight D. Eisenhower, and like Warren, Brennan later proved to be one of the most liberal judges ever appointed to the Court, voting on many important equal protection cases. He served on the Court from 1956 to 1990.

brief written statement that spells out the party's legal position and cites relevant facts and legal precedents

Bryce, James Bryce (1838–1922) was a British politician who served as an ambassador to the United States from 1907 to 1913. He became especially popular upon writing *The American Commonwealth,* which is a favorable study of the U.S. government.

budget an estimate of future revenue and expenses; for a State or nation, it is a financial plan, an estimate of income and outgo for the upcoming fiscal year

bureaucracy a large, complex administrative structure that handles the everyday business of an organization

bureaucrat a person who works for a bureaucratic organization

Bush, George H.W. After graduating from Yale University, Bush (born 1924) began a career in the oil industry of Texas. He served two terms as a representative to Congress from Texas, and was later appointed ambassador to the United Nations and Director of the CIA. Bush was Vice President under Ronald Reagan and was elected the 41st President, serving from 1989 to 1993.

Bush, George W. (1946–) graduated from Yale University and Harvard Business School before returning to Texas to work in the oil industry. Serving first as governor of Texas, he was elected the 43rd President, holding office from 2001 to 2009. His election marked only the second time in American history that the son of a President (George H.W. Bush) went on to become President.

Byrd, Robert C. Byrd (1917–2010) was the U.S. representative from West Virginia from 1953 to 1959 and a senator from 1959 until 2010, serving longer than any other member in U.S. history. He considered himself a "child of the Appalachian coalfields" and spent his political career battling persistent poverty in West Virginia.

C

Cabinet an advisory body to the President

Calvert, George (Lord Baltimore) A member of Parliament who founded Maryland as a haven for Catholics, Calvert (1578 or 1579–1632) came to North America in 1628 but was not accepted due to his religion. He returned to England and requested a royal charter to establish a colony where he could practice his religion. The charter was granted in 1632, shortly after his death.

capital all the human-made resources that are used to produce goods and services

capital punishment death penalty

capitalism economic system in which individuals are free to own the means of production and maximize profits

Capitol Hill The U.S. Capitol is located inside the historic residential district called Capitol Hill in Washington, D.C. Other buildings on Capitol Hill include the U.S. Supreme Court and Library of Congress. Capitol Hill is also a figure of speech that simply means Congress.

Carter, Jimmy Carter (1924–) was the 39th President of the United States, serving from 1977 to 1981. A former naval officer and governor of Georgia, Carter was awarded the Nobel Peace prize in 2002 and is the author of 27 books. During his presidency, Carter created the Department of Education, expanded the national park system, and established a relationship with the People's Republic of China.

Castro, Fidel Castro (born 1926) was the dictatorial political leader of Cuba from 1959 to 2008. Through revolutionary tactics, he turned the island nation into the first communist state in the Western hemisphere.

categorical grants one type of federal grants-in-aid; made for some specific, closely defined purpose

caucus as a nominating device, a group of like-minded people who meet to select the candidates they will support in an upcoming election

censure to issue a formal condemnation

certificate the result of a process in which a lower court asks the Court to certify the answer to a specific question, such as a procedure or rule of law

Charles I, King Charles I (1600–1649) was king of England, Scotland, and Ireland from 1625 to 1649. He ruled with strict authority, and his quarrels with Parliament triggered a civil war. In 1649, Charles was found guilty of treason and executed.

charter a city's basic law, its constitution; a written grant of authority from the king

Chávez, Hugo Chávez (1954–2013) became president of Venezuela in 1999, sailing into office via public outrage against the traditional political elite in that country. Known as outspoken and controversial, Chávez insisted throughout his presidency that his socialist revolution would benefit everyone in Venezuela, but especially the poor.

checks and balances system of overlapping the powers of the legislative, executive, and judicial branches to permit each branch to check the actions of the others

Chiang Kai-shek Chiang Kai-shek (1887–1975) was a Chinese soldier and statesman. He was the head of the Nationalist government from 1928 until 1949.

chief administrator term for the President as head of the administration of the Federal Government

chief citizen term for the President as the representative of the people, working for the public interest

chief diplomat term for the President as the main architect of foreign policy and spokesperson to other countries

chief economist term for the President as monitor of the nation's economic condition

chief executive term for the President as vested with the executive power of the United States

chief legislator term for the President as architect of public policy and the one who sets the agenda for Congress

chief of party term for the President as the leader of his or her political party

chief of state term for the President as the ceremonial head of the United States, the symbol of all the people of the nation

Churchill, Winston Churchill (1874–1965) was a British statesman who served as prime minister of the United Kingdom from 1940 to 1945 during most of World War II and from 1951 to 1955. He was the first honorary U.S. citizen and was granted the Nobel Prize in Literature.

citizen a member of a state or nation who owes allegiance to it by birth or naturalization and is entitled to full civil rights

civil case a case involving a noncriminal matter such as a contract dispute or a claim of patent infringement

civil disobedience a form of protest in which people deliberately but non-violently violate the law as a means of expressing their opposition to some particular law or public policy

civil law the portion of the law relating to human conduct, to disputes between private parties, and to disputes between private parties and government not covered by criminal law

civil liberties guarantees of the safety of persons, opinions, and property from the arbitrary acts of government, including freedom of speech and freedom of religion

civil rights term used for positive acts of government that seek to make constitutional guarantees a reality for all people, e.g., prohibitions of discrimination

civil service those civilian employees who perform the administrative work of government

civilian nonmilitary

civilian tribunal a court operating as part of the judicial branch, entirely separate from the military establishment

clemency mercy or leniency granted to an offender by a chief executive

Clinton, Bill (1946–) William J. Clinton was elected governor of Arkansas in 1978, and was elected to be the 42nd President, serving from 1993–2001. During his administration, the United States largely enjoyed a period of peace and economic growth. In 1998, he was the second President to be impeached by the House of Representatives, but was found not guilty of the charges by the Senate and remained in office.

Clinton, Hillary Rodham Clinton (1947–) became First Lady of the United States when her husband Bill Clinton was elected to the presidency in 1993. In 2001, Clinton became a senator from New York State, during which time she made an unsuccessful bid for the presidency. In 2009, she was named secretary of state in the Obama administration, a position she held until her resignation in 2013. Clinton was nominated by the Democratic Party as its presidential candidate in 2016, but ultimately lost the election to Republican Donald Trump.

closed primary a party-nominating election in which only declared party members can vote

cloture a procedure to limit or end floor debate, especially during a filibuster

coalition a temporary alliance of several groups who come together to form a working majority and so to control a government

coattail effect effect of a strong candidate running for an office at the top of a ballot, helping to attract voters to other candidates on the party's ticket

cold war a period of more than 40 years during which relations between the two superpowers (United States and Soviet Union) were at least tense, and often hostile; a time of threats and military build-up

collective security the keeping of international peace and order

collectivization collective or state ownership of the means of production

colonialism the control of one nation over foreign lands

command economies systems in which government bureaucrats plan and direct most economic activity

commander in chief term for the President as commander of the nation's armed forces

Commerce and Slave Trade Compromise an agreement reached at the Constitutional Convention to protect slaveholders; it denied Congress the power to tax the export of goods from any State and, for twenty years, denied Congress the power to act on the slave trade

commerce power exclusive power of Congress to regulate interstate and foreign trade

commission government a form of city government in which a group of popularly elected commissioners make up the city council and are invested with all legislative and executive authority

committee chair member who heads a standing committee in a legislative body

common law an unwritten law made by a judge that has developed over centuries from those generally accepted ideas of right and wrong that have gained judicial recognition

communism ideology which calls for the collective, or state, ownership of land and other productive property

commutation the power to reduce (commute) the length of a sentence or fine for a crime

compromise an adjustment of opposing principles or systems by modifying some aspect of each in order to find the position most acceptable to the majority

concurrent jurisdiction power shared by federal and State courts to hear certain cases

concurrent powers those powers that both the National Government and the States possess and exercise

concurrent resolution a statement of position on an issue used by the House and Senate acting jointly; does not have the force of law and does not require the President's signature

concurring opinion an opinion that agrees with the decision that the Court has made but for different reasons

confederation a joining of several groups for a common purpose

conference committee temporary joint committee created to reconcile any differences between the two houses' versions of a bill

Connecticut Compromise an agreement reached during the Constitutional Convention that Congress should be composed of a Senate, in which each State would be represented equally, and a House, in which each State would be represented based on the State's population

consensus general agreement among various groups on fundamental matters; broad agreement on public questions

constituencies the people and interests that an elected official represents

constituent power the non-legislative power of Constitution-making and the constitutional amendment process

constitutional law based on the United States Constitution, the State constitutions, and judicial interpretations of those documents

constitutionalism basic principle that government and those who govern must obey the law; the rule of law

containment a policy based in the belief that if communism could be kept within its existing boundaries, it would collapse under the weight of its internal weaknesses

content neutral the government may not regulate assemblies on the basis of what might be said

continuing resolution measure that allows agencies to continue working based on the previous year's appropriations

continuous body governing unit (e.g. the United States Senate) whose seats are never all up for election at the same time

contract a legally binding agreement in which one party agrees to do something with or for another party

controllable spending amount decided upon by Congress and the President to determine how much will be spent each year on many individual government expenditures, including environment protection programs, aid to education, and so on

convene to begin a new session of Congress

copyright the exclusive, legal right of a person to reproduce, publish, and sell his or her own literary, musical, or artistic creations

council-manager government a form of city government consisting of a strong elected council, a weak elected mayor, and a manager named by the council

county a major unit of local government in most States

courts-martial courts composed of military personnel, for the trial of those accused of violating military law

criminal case a case in which a defendant is tried for committing a crime as defined by the law

criminal law the portion of the law that defines public wrongs and provides for their punishment

Cultural Revolution launched by Chinese Communist Party chairman Mao Zedong during his last decade in power (1966–1976) to renew the spirit of the Chinese Revolution. Young and dedicated Red Guards attacked and bullied intellectuals, and those that lacked revolutionary fervor. Some were sent to work farms to be re-educated.

customs duty tax laid on goods brought into the United States from abroad, also known as tariffs, import duties, or imposts

D

de facto the situation as it exists in fact

de jure in accordance with the law

defendant in a civil suit, the person against whom a court action is brought by the plaintiff; in a criminal case, the person charged with the crime

deficit yearly shortfall between revenue and spending

deficit financing the practice of funding government by borrowing to make up the difference between government spending and revenue

deflation general decrease in prices throughout the economy

delegated powers those powers, expressed, implied, or inherent, granted to the National Government by the Constitution

delegates people with authority to represent others at a conference or convention

demand-side economics theory that the higher employment that results from government borrowing will produce higher tax revenues

democracy form of government where supreme authority rests with the people

democratic consolidation the process of establishing the factors considered necessary for a democracy to succeed

democratization the change from dictatorship to democracy, marked by the holding of free and fair elections

denaturalization the process through which naturalized citizens may involuntarily lose their citizenship

Deng Xiaoping Deng Xiaoping (1904–1997) ascended to power in China in 1977, on the heels of the unpopular Cultural Revolution begun by Mao Zedong in 1966. Deng continued the authoritarian style of his predecessor, but he opened China to a market economy that lifted millions of peasants out of poverty.

deportation a legal process by which a person who is in the United States illegally is required to leave the country

détente French term meaning "a relaxation of tensions"

deterrence the policy of making America and its allies so militarily strong that their very strength will discourage, or prevent, any attack

devolution the delegation of authority from the central government to regional governments

dictatorship form of government where those who rule cannot be held responsible to the will of the people

diplomatic immunity when ambassadors are not subject to the laws of the state to which they are accredited

direct primary an election held within a party to pick that party's candidates for the general election

discharge petition enables members to force a bill that has remained in committee 30 days (7 for the Rules Committee) onto the floor for consideration

discount rate rate of interest a bank must pay when it borrows money from a Federal Reserve Bank

discriminate treat certain categories of people differently than people falling into other categories

discrimination bias, unfairness

disenfranchised denied the right to vote

dissenting opinions an opinion written by a justice who does not agree with the Court's decision, explaining the reasons why not.

District of Columbia the capital of the United States

district plan proposal for choosing presidential electors by which two electors would be selected in each State according to the Statewide popular vote and the other electors would be selected separately in each of the State's congressional districts

divine right of kings the belief that God grants authority to a government

division of powers basic principle of federalism; the constitutional provisions by which governmental powers are divided on a geographic basis (in the United States, between the National Government and the States)

docket a court's list of cases to be heard

domestic affairs all matters not directly connected to the realm of foreign affairs

double jeopardy part of the 5th Amendment stating that no person can be put in jeopardy of life or limb twice; once a person has been tried for a crime, he or she cannot be tried again for the same crime

Douglas, William O. Douglas (1898–1980) was the longest-serving justice on the United States Supreme Court. Appointed to the Court as an associate justice by President Franklin D. Roosevelt in April 1939, he served for over 36 years, until his retirement in November 1975.

draft conscription, or compulsory military service

due process doctrine that holds that the government must act fairly and in accord with established rules in all that it does

Due Process Clause part of the 14th Amendment which guarantees that no State deny basic rights to its people

duty a tax on imports

E

economic protest parties parties rooted in poor economic times, lacking a clear ideological base, dissatisfied with current economic conditions and demanding better times

Eisenhower, Dwight Elected to the presidency in 1953, Eisenhower (1890–1969) brought with him the prestige of having been commanding officer of the Allied forces in Europe during World War II, a culmination of a long military career. As the 34th President, serving from 1953 to 1961, he advocated peace and supported desegregation in schools and the military.

electoral college group of persons chosen in each State and the District of Columbia every four years who make a formal selection of the President and Vice President

electorate all of the people entitled to vote in a given election

eminent domain the power of a government to take private property for public use

enabling act a congressional act directing the people of a United States territory to frame a proposed State constitution as a step toward admission to the Union

English Bill of Rights document written by Parliament and agreed to by William and Mary of England in 1689, designed to prevent abuse of power by English monarchs; forms the basis for much in American government and politics today

engrossed a bill printed in its final form

entitlement a benefit that federal law says must be paid to all those who meet the eligibility requirements, e.g., Medicare, food stamps, and veterans' pensions

entrepreneur individual with the drive and ambition to combine land, labor, and capital resources to produce goods or offer services

Equal Protection Clause section of the U.S. Constitution that requires that the laws of a State, or of the nation, must treat any given individual in the same way as it would treat other individuals who are in similar conditions and circumstances

equity a branch of the law that supplements common law by taking a preventative approach

espionage spying

Establishment Clause part of the 1st Amendment of the Constitution that guarantees the separation of church and State

estate tax levy imposed on the assets of one who dies

ex post facto law law applied to an act committed before its passage

excise tax tax laid on the manufacture, sale, or consumption of goods and/or the performance of services

exclusionary rule ruling stating that evidence gained as the result of an illegal act by police cannot be used against the person from whom it was seized

exclusive powers those powers which can be exercised by the National Government alone

executive agreement a pact made by the President directly with the head of a foreign state; a binding international agreement with the force of law but which (unlike a treaty) does not require Senate consent

Executive Article Article II of the Constitution. Establishes the presidency and gives the executive power of the Federal Government to the President

executive departments often called the Cabinet departments, they are the traditional units of federal administration

Executive Office of the President an organization of several agencies staffed by the President's closest advisors

executive order directive, rule, or regulation issued by a chief executive or subordinates, based upon constitutional or statutory authority and having the force of law

executive power the power to execute, enforce, and administer laws

executive privilege the President's power to refuse to disclose information

expatriation the legal process by which a loss of citizenship occurs

expressed powers those delegated powers of the National Government that are spelled out, expressly, in the Constitution; also called the "enumerated powers"

extradition the legal process by which a fugitive from justice in one State is returned to that State

F

factors of production basic resources that are used to make all goods and services

failed states nations in which security is nonexistent, the economy has collapsed, healthcare and school systems are in shambles, and corruption is flourishing

FECA The Federal Election Campaign Act of 1971 was the first federal law regulating the use of money in presidential and congressional campaigns.

federal budget a detailed financial document containing estimates of federal income and spending during the coming fiscal year

Federal Election Commission (FEC) an independent agency in the executive branch that administers all federal law dealing with campaign finance

federal government a form of government in which powers are divided between a central government and several local governments

federalism a system of government in which a written constitution divides power between a central, or national, government and several regional governments like States.

Federalists those persons who supported the ratification of the Constitution in 1787–1788

Feingold, Russ A former Democratic senator from Wisconsin, Feingold (1993–2010) was co-sponsor of the Bipartisan Campaign Reform Act of 2002.

felony a serious crime which may be punished by a heavy fine and/or imprisonment or even death

feudalism a loosely organized system in which powerful lords divided their land among other, lesser lords

filibuster a stalling tactic in which senators monopolize the Senate floor with talk and other delays so a bill cannot be brought to a vote

First Lady the President's wife

fiscal policy various means the government uses to raise and spend money

fiscal year the 12-month period used by a government and the business world for its record-keeping, budgeting, revenue-collecting, and other financial management purposes

527 organizations political advocacy groups filed in accordance with Section 527 of the Internal Revenue Code, which are not aligned with a political party but try to influence political policies, and are allowed to raise unlimited sums of money

floor consideration the process by which proposed laws are considered and acted upon by the full membership of the House or Senate

floor leaders members of the House and Senate picked by their parties to carry out party decisions and steer legislative action to meet party goals

Ford, Gerald Ford (1913–2006) was the 38th President of the United States from 1974 to 1977. After the Watergate scandal forced President Nixon from office in 1974, Vice President Ford became President and served the remainder of the second Nixon term. Ford acted vigorously to maintain United States power abroad and worked to prevent a new war in the Middle East. Ford lost the presidency in 1976 due to economic problems, the effects of Watergate, and his pardon of former President Nixon.

foreign affairs a nation's relationships with other countries

foreign aid economic and military aid to other countries

foreign policy a group of policies made up of all the stands and actions that a nation takes in every aspect of its relationships with other countries; everything a nation's government says and does in world affairs

formal amendment change or addition that becomes part of the written language of the Constitution itself through one of four methods set forth in the Constitution

Framers group of delegates who drafted the United States Constitution at the Philadelphia Convention in 1787

franchise right to vote

franking privilege benefit allowing members of Congress to mail letters and other materials postage-free

Franklin, Benjamin An American author, inventor, diplomat, and legislator, Franklin (1706–1790) proposed the Albany Plan of Union that foresaw the benefits of colonial unity. He later signed the Declaration of Independence and helped frame the Constitution, urging delegates to cooperate and sign the final draft.

free enterprise system an economic system characterized by private or corporate ownership of capital goods; investments that are determined by private decision rather than by state control and determined in a free market

Free Exercise Clause the second part of the constitutional guarantee of religious freedom; guarantees to each person the right to believe whatever he or she chooses to believe in matters of religion

free market market in which buyers and sellers are free to buy and sell as they wish

full faith and credit clause requiring that each State accept the public acts, records, and judicial proceedings of every other State

Full Faith and Credit Clause Constitution's requirement that each State accept the public acts, records, and judicial proceedings of every other State

fundamental laws laws of basic and lasting importance which may not easily be changed

G

Gallup, George Gallup (1901–1984) was a pollster and statistician who founded the famous Gallup Poll. In addition to conducting polls and developing new methods to ensure polling accuracy, Gallup was a professor and an author. He also founded the American Institute of Public Opinion, the British Institute of Public Opinion, and the Audience Research Institute, Inc.

Garfield, James Garfield (1831–1881) was the 20th President of the United States, serving from March to September of 1881. He holds the record for the second-shortest time in office. A former major general in the Civil War and a member of the House Representatives from Ohio for nine consecutive terms, President Garfield was shot by Charles J. Guiteau in 1881 after refusing to appoint Guiteau to a diplomatic post.

gender gap measurable differences between the partisan choices of men and women today

general elections the regularly scheduled election at which voters make a final selection of officeholders

George II, King George II (1683–1760) was king of Great Britain from 1727 to 1760. The colony of Georgia was named in his honor after he signed a charter granting the colony to its twenty trustees in 1732. King George thought the colony would be an important buffer between the Spanish-controlled lands to the south and the other English colonies to the north.

gerrymandering the drawing of electoral district lines to the advantage of a party or group

gift tax tax on a gift by a living person

Ginsburg, Ruth Bader Ruth Bader Ginsburg (1933–2020) was the second woman appointed to the Supreme Court. President Clinton nominated her to serve as an associate justice of the Supreme Court in 1993, and she served until her death in 2020.

globalization economic interdependence among nations of the world

Glorious Revolution events that led to Parliament in 1688 inviting William and Mary of Orange to peacefully replace King James II on condition that they recognize the authority of Parliament and the rights of individuals; with the signing of the Bill of Rights, the Glorious Revolution helped calm the centuries-long struggle for supremacy between the monarchy and Parliament in England.

Gorbachev, Mikhail General Secretary of the Communist Party of the Soviet Union from 1985 to 1991, Gorbachev (born 1931) became president of the Soviet Union in 1990. Within a year, his focus on democratizing the political system and decentralizing the economy led to the collapse of the Soviet Union. Gorbachev resigned from the presidency in 1991. He received the Nobel Prize for Peace in 1990.

government the institution through which a society makes and enforces its public policies

government corporations corporations within the executive branch subject to the President's direction and control, set up by Congress to carry out certain business-like activities

grand jury formal device by which a person can be accused of a serious crime

Grant, Ulysses S. Grant (1822–1885) was the 18th President of the United States from 1869 to 1877. Grant won election after serving as the Union general who led the United States to victory over the Confederate States of America during the American Civil War. Grant supported African American rights, Native American policy, and civil service reform; additionally, he supported the creation of a transcontinental railroad. He also executed a successful foreign policy and was responsible for improving Anglo American relations.

grants-in-aid programs grants of federal money or other resources to States, cities, counties, and other local units

grass-roots pressures pressures on public officials from members of an interest group or the people at large

Great Leap Forward five-year plan for 1958 that was an attempt to modernize China quickly

gross domestic product total amount of goods and services produced in a country each year

Group of 7 (G7) forum formed in 1975 for seven of the world's most industrialized nations: the United States, Japan, Germany, France, Britain, Italy, and Canada.

Guantanamo Bay, Cuba First leased by the United States from Cuba in 1903, Guantanamo Bay houses a naval base that has been in regular use ever since. Since January 11, 2002, the base has housed individuals captured by the U.S. military during the War on Terror. This detention center has been deeply controversial since it opened, and the fate of the prisoners housed there is hotly debated from both legal and moral perspectives.

gubernatorial related to the office of governor

H

Hamilton, Alexander Hamilton (1755 or 1757–1804) immigrated to North America in 1772 from the British West Indies. He entered the Continental Army in 1776 and served under General Washington. He held a number of positions in government, including as a member of the Continental Congress and the Constitutional Convention. He studied law and practiced in New York City. Hamilton was Secretary of the Treasury in President Washington's Cabinet. He was mortally wounded in a duel with Aaron Burr in 1804.

hard money contributions that are given directly to candidates for their campaigns, are limited, and must be reported to the government

hard-liners those who fight to maintain the status quo

Harrison, William Henry Elected as the 9th President in 1841, Harrison (1773–1841) was the first President to die in office. Born into an aristocratic Virginia planter family, he spent much of his time in the Northwest, obtaining title to Indian lands and leading efforts to repel Indian attacks. He contracted pneumonia and died after only four months in office.

heterogeneous of another or different race, family or kind; composed of a mix of elements

Hobbes, Thomas (1588–1679) English philosopher who felt that people and nations were in a constant battle for power and wealth. He thought that an absolute monarchy was the best government for England. He distrusted democracy, but thought that authorized representatives as the voice of the people would prevent a monarch from being unfair or cruel.

Holmes, Jr., Oliver Wendell (1841–1935) was a justice of the U.S. Supreme Court from 1902 to 1932 who was nicknamed the Great Dissenter.

Hoover, Herbert Hoover (1874–1964) graduated from Stanford as a mining engineer and began his career in China. He later served in various humanitarian posts abroad, including head of the American Relief Administration in Europe. He was elected the 31st President in 1928, just months before the 1929 stock market crash that sent the nation into a deep depression.

Hudson River a 315-mile long waterway that flows north to south through eastern New York State

I

ideological based on a particular set of beliefs—a comprehensive view of social, economic, and political matters

immigrants those people, born abroad, who are legally admitted as permanent residents of a country

impeach to bring formal charges against a public official

implied powers those delegated powers of the National Government that are suggested by the expressed powers set out in the Constitution; those "necessary and proper" to carry out the expressed powers

import quota limit put on the amount of a commodity that can be imported into a country

income tax a tax levied on the income of individuals and/or corporations

incorporation the process by which a State establishes a city as a legal body; the term comes from the Latin words *in* (into) and *corpus* (body)

incumbent the current officeholder

independent agencies additional agencies created by Congress located outside the Cabinet departments

independent executive agencies agencies headed by a single administrator with regional subunits but lacking Cabinet status

independent regulatory commissions independent agencies created by Congress, designed to regulate important aspects of the nation's economy, largely beyond the reach of presidential control

independents a term used to describe people who have no party affiliation

indictment formal complaint before a grand jury that charges the accused with one or more crimes

inferior courts the lower federal courts, under the Supreme Court

inflation general increase in prices throughout the economy

information formal charge filed by a prosecutor without the action of a grand jury

inherent powers powers the Constitution is presumed to have delegated to the National Government because it is the government of a sovereign state within the world community

inheritance tax tax levied on the beneficiary's share of an estate

initiative a process in which a certain number of qualified voters sign petitions in favor of a proposed statute or constitutional amendment, which then goes directly to the ballot

injunction court order that forces or limits the performance of some act by a private individual or by a public official

integration incorporating people of different races equally into society without separating the races from each other

interest charge for borrowed money, generally a percentage of the amount borrowed

interest group private organizations whose members share certain views and work to shape public policy

International Monetary Fund (IMF) organization formed in 1944 to oversee the international monetary system

interstate compacts formal agreement entered into with the consent of Congress, between or among States, or between a State and a foreign state

involuntary servitude forced labor

isolationism a purposeful refusal to become generally involved in the affairs of the rest of the world

Isthmus of Panama the narrow strip of land that lies between the Caribbean Sea and the Pacific Ocean in Panama; it is the location of the Panama Canal

J

Jackson, Andrew Known as "Old Hickory" for his toughness and aggressive personality, Jackson (1767–1845) was the seventh President of the United States, serving from 1829 to 1837. His political movement is known as Jacksonian Democracy because he believed that the common man should have a say in government. He is the only President to have fought in both the Revolutionary War, as a young teenager, and in the War of 1812, where he gained military fame; he is also the first President to come from west of the Appalachian Mountains.

Jackson, Robert H. Jackson (1892–1954) was a justice of the U.S. Supreme Court from 1941 to 1954. He is best known for his opinion in *West Virginia State Board of Education* v. *Barnette,* 1943, that expanded the scope of the 1st Amendment's freedom of speech guarantee.

Jamestown first permanent English settlement in North America; founded in 1607 in Virginia and named after King James I. The founding of Jamestown gave England an entry into the competition for the Americas, which Spain had dominated since the voyages of Christopher Columbus in the late fifteenth century.

Jay, John Jay (1745–1829) was a New York lawyer, president of the Second Continental Congress, diplomat, first Chief Justice of the United States, and governor of New York. His was a voice of moderation in relations with Great Britain before the Declaration of Independence. Jay favored strong centralized government and fought for ratification of the U.S. Constitution. He also helped draft the New York State constitution and served as the State's first Chief Justice. He helped negotiate and enforce liberal terms for peace with Great Britain and served as first Secretary for Foreign Affairs before George Washington appointed him first Chief Justice of the Supreme Court.

Jefferson, Thomas Jefferson (1743–1826) was the third President of the United States, serving from 1801 to 1809. He is known as the draftsman of the Declaration of Independence and for engineering the Louisiana Purchase.

Jim Crow laws category of laws that were drafted for the purpose of discriminating against African Americans

John, King John (1167–1216) was king of England from 1199 to 1216. Soon after John became king, war broke out between England and France. After several significant losses, taxes soared, and the monarchy became ruthless in its governing. This angered the barons, who forced John to sign the Magna Carta in 1215.

Johnson, Andrew Johnson (1808–1875) was the 17th President of the United States. As Abraham Lincoln's Vice President, Johnson became President when Lincoln was assassinated. He served from 1865 to 1869.

Johnson, Lyndon (1908–1973) the 36th President of the United States from 1963 to 1969. He was elected as Vice President and took over the presidency upon the assassination of President John F. Kennedy. In 1964, he signed the Civil Rights Act into law.

Johnson, Richard M. Johnson (1780–1850) was the nation's ninth Vice President, serving from 1837 to 1841 under Martin Van Buren. Johnson was the only Vice President chosen by the Senate.

joint committee legislative committee composed of members of both houses

joint resolution a proposal for action that has the force of law when passed; usually deals with special circumstances or temporary matters

judicial activism a judicial philosophy in which supporters believe that judges should interpret and apply provisions in the Constitution and in statute law in light of ongoing changes in conditions and values

judicial power the power to interpret laws, to determine their meaning, and to settle disputes that arise within the society

judicial restraint a judicial philosophy in which supporters believe that judges should decide cases based on the original intent of the Framers or those who enacted the statute(s) involved in a case, or on precedent

judicial review the power of a court to determine the constitutionality of a governmental action

jurisdiction the authority of a court to hear a case

jury a body of persons selected according to law who hear evidence and decide questions of fact in a court case

jus sanguinis the law of blood, which determines citizenship based on the citizenship of one's parents

jus soli the law of soil, which determines citizenship based on where a person is born

justice of the peace a judge who stands on the lowest level of the State judicial system and presides over justice courts

K

Kagan, Elena Kagan (born 1960) was the fourth woman appointed to the Supreme Court. President Obama nominated her to serve as the Solicitor General of the United States in 2009. After serving as SG for a year, she was nominated by President Obama as an associate justice of the Supreme Court in 2010, where she continues to serve.

Kennedy, John F. Kennedy (1917–1963) was the youngest person ever elected President. His inaugural address in 1963 urged citizens to "Ask not what your country can do for you, ask what you can do for your country." On November 22, 1963, Kennedy was assassinated in Texas.

Keynes, John Maynard Keynes (1883–1946) was an influential British economist, known primarily for his revolutionary economic theory regarding the causes of extended unemployment. Keynes maintained that government had responsibility for stabilizing the economy through the use of fiscal policy (tax and spending programs). He believed that in periods of depression, the government should increase its spending, cut taxes, or do both to stimulate the economy.

keynote address speech given at a party convention to set the tone for the convention and the campaign to come

Khomeini, Ayatollah Khomeini (1902–1989) was an Iranian Shia (Muslim) leader and cleric. He led the revolution that overthrew the Shah (leader) of Iran in 1979. He later became the leader of Iran, dictating both political and religious law for ten years.

King, Jr., Martin Luther (1929–1968) African American clergyman, activist, and leader, King is best known for his role in the African American Civil Rights Movement where he advocated non-violent resistance to discrimination and segregation in the South.

L

labor union organization of workers who share the same type of job, or who work in the same industry, and press for government policies that will benefit its members

laissez-faire theory theory suggesting that government should play a very limited role in society

law of supply and demand law stating that when supplies of goods and services become plentiful, prices tend to drop; when supplies become scarcer, prices tend to rise

Leahy, Patrick (1940–) Democrat senator from Vermont; first elected in 1974. Elected president *pro tempore* of the Senate in 2012.

legal tender any kind of money that a creditor must, by law, accept in payment for debts

legislative power the power to make laws and to frame public policies

legitimacy the belief of the people that a government has the right to make public policy

Lenin, Vladimir Lenin (1870–1924) led the Bolshevik Revolution and was the architect of the Communist Party and its control over the Soviet Union. By the time of his death in 1924, the Soviet Union had become a one-party state in control of the country's social, political, and economic institutions.

libel false and malicious use of printed words

liberal constructionist one who argues for a broad interpretation of the Constitution's provisions, particularly those granting powers to the Federal Government

limited government basic principle of American government, which states that government is restricted in what it may do, and each individual has rights that government cannot take away; *see* constitutionalism, popular sovereignty

Lincoln, Abraham Lincoln (1809–1865) was elected 16th President of the United States, entering office in 1861 at age 52. He is known for issuing the Emancipation Proclamation, which declared that "all persons held as slaves... shall be then, thenceforward, and forever free..." He was assassinated in 1865.

line agency agency that performs the tasks for which an organization exists

line-item veto the power many governors have to reject one or more items in a bill without rejecting the entire measure; used most often on spending measures; the U.S. Congress gave this power to the President in 1996, but that law was struck down by the Supreme Court in 1998

literacy person's ability to read or write

lobbying activities by which group pressures are brought to bear on legislators, the legislative process, and all aspects of the public policymaking process

lobbyist person who tries to persuade public officials to do those things that interest groups want them to do

Locke, John (1632–1704) English philosopher who wrote about his theories concerning the natural rights of man, the social contract, the separation of Church and State, religious freedom, and liberty. Locke's theories influenced the American and French revolutions.

London capital of England; originally founded by the Romans circa a.d. 50. The time period during which many of the North American colonies were established was known as Stuart London. During this time, from 1603 to 1714, the city of London grew tremendously; also during this time London suffered two great disasters: the Plague of 1665 and the Great Fire in 1666.

Long, Huey Long (1893–1935) was the governor of Louisiana and a U.S. senator. He started a Share-the-Wealth Society for distributing housing and income to American families as an alternative to President Franklin D. Roosevelt's New Deal program. Long ran for President in 1935 but was assassinated before the election could take place.

M

Madison, James Madison (1751–1836) wrote several of the Federalist Papers and was a major figure in the movement to replace the Articles of Confederation. It is his *Notes on the Debates in the Federal Convention* that have given us a clear understanding of what occurred during those debates. During the convention, Madison was the main architect of the Virginia Plan and had a strong influence on the entire meeting. In fact, he has been referred to as the "Father of the Constitution." At that time, he favored a strong National Government but later saw the benefits of stronger State governments.

magistrate a justice who handles minor civil complaints and misdemeanor cases that arise in an urban setting

Magna Carta Great Charter forced upon King John of England by his barons in 1215; established that the power of the monarchy was not absolute and guaranteed trial by jury and due process of law to the nobility

majority leader the floor leader of the party that holds the majority of seats in each house of Congress

majority opinion the opinion on which the decision of the Court is based, which identifies the issues in the case and the reasons for the decision

majority rule the principle that the majority of the people will be right more often than they will be wrong, and will be right more often than will any one person or small group

mandate instructions or commands a constituency gives to its elected officials; the term *mandate* comes from the Latin *mandatum*, meaning "a command"

Mandela, Nelson (1918–2013) the first black president of South Africa from 1994 to 1999 in the country's first democratic election. Prior to that, he was a political prisoner in South Africa for more than 20 years. He also helped end racial segregation in his country, and he was awarded the Nobel Peace Prize in 1993.

Mao Zedong Mao Zedong (1893–1976) led the Chinese communist revolution and served as the country's chief of state from 1949 to 1959. He then served as the chairman of the Chinese Communist Party until his death. Mao is best remembered for the Great Leap Forward, his disastrous attempt to move China quickly toward improved agricultural and industrial production, and the Cultural Revolution that destroyed much of China's cultural heritage.

Marbury, William In 1803, Marbury (1762–1835) became the plaintiff in *Marbury* v. *Madison,* the Supreme Court case that established the power of judicial review. He was appointed by President John Adams to become a justice of the peace in the District of Columbia. As a result of the decision in *Marbury* v. *Madison,* Marbury lost his commission to become a judge.

Marshall, George C. Marshall (1880–1959) served as general of the Army and Army chief of staff during World War II. He later became secretary of state and then secretary of defense in the administration of Franklin Roosevelt. He was the author of a post-war European Recovery Program that became famously known as the Marshall Plan, for which he received the Nobel Prize for Peace.

Marshall, John Marshall (1755–1835) was the fourth Chief Justice of the United States Supreme Court. He had strong opinions about the power of the Supreme Court to interpret the Constitution and his rulings have had a profound impact on American law to this very day.

Marshall, Thurgood Marshall (1908–1993) was the first African American appointed to the Supreme Court (in 1967) and served as associate justice until 1991. In 1954, while an attorney, he successfully argued the case of *Brown* v. *Board of Education* (which declared racial segregation unconstitutional in American public schools) before the U.S. Supreme Court.

Marx, Karl A German philosopher best known for his multivolume work on political economics, *Das Kapital,* Marx (1818–1883) is considered the father of modern socialism and communism.

Mason, George Owner of Gunston Hall, and one of the richest planters in Virginia, Mason (1725–1792) framed Virginia's Declaration of Rights, which served as a model for Jefferson in writing the Declaration of Independence and was the basis for the U.S. Constitution's Bill of Rights. He was an influential speaker at the Constitutional Convention and worked to have the Bill of Rights and the 11th Amendment incorporated into the Constitution.

mass media means of communication that reach large audiences, especially television, radio, printed publications, and the Internet

mayor-council government the oldest, most widely used type of city government, which features an elected mayor as the chief executive and an elected council as its legislative body

McCain, John McCain (born 1936) is a Republican senator from Arizona and co-sponsor of the Bipartisan Campaign Reform Act of 2002. As the presidential nominee in 2008, he lost the presidential race to Barack Obama.

McKinley, William William McKinley (1843–1901) of Ohio served seven terms in the U.S. House of Representatives, where he championed tariffs (taxes on imported goods) as a way to protect American businesses. Elected President in 1897, he led the U.S. into the Spanish-American War, which ended with the victorious U.S. receiving territory in Guam, Puerto Rico, and the Philippines. McKinley also supported statehood for Hawaii. He was assassinated during his second term as President.

Medicaid a program administered by the States to provide medical insurance to low-income families

medium means of communication; something that transmits information

mercantilism an economic and political theory emphasizing money as the chief source of wealth to increase the absolute power of the monarchy and the nation

metropolitan area a city and the area around it

Milosevic, Slobodan Milosevic (1941–2006) was president of Serbia from 1989 to 1997. A radical nationalist, he instituted policies that led to the breakup of the socialist Yugoslav federation and instigated a series of bloody conflicts with other Balkan states, including Kosovo, Bosnia, and Croatia.

ministers cabinet members, most commonly of the House of Commons

minority leader the floor leader of the party that holds the minority of seats in each house of Congress

Miranda rule constitutional rights that police must read to a suspect before questioning can occur

misdemeanor a lesser offense, punishable by a small fine and/or a short jail term

Missouri Plan an approach to judicial selection that combines election and appointment; a nominating committee provides a list of candidates from which the governor can choose

monetary policy process through which the government can influence the nation's economy through changes in the money supply and the availability of credit

monopoly firm that is the only source of a product or service

Monroe, James Monroe (1758–1831) was President of the United States from 1817 to 1825. During his leadership, Monroe minimized partisan tensions leading to the "Era of Good Feelings." Monroe gained Florida from Spain in 1821 and declared that European action to colonize any part of the Americas would call for the intervention of the United States. Years later, this declaration formed the basis of the Monroe Doctrine, arguably the President's most significant contribution.

Montesquieu, Charles de Montesquieu (1689–1755) was a French political philosopher of the Enlightenment whose major work, *The Spirit of Laws,* was a major contribution to political theory. His theory of the separation of powers had a great impact on the Framers of the Constitution of the United States.

municipality an urban political unit within a township that usually exists as a separate governmental entity

N

national popular vote plan proposal for electing the President whereby each State's election laws would provide for all of the State's electoral votes to be awarded to the winner of the national popular vote and enter into an interstate compact agreeing to elect the President by national popular vote

NATO (North American Treaty Organization) an alliance formed to protect the freedom and security of its members through political and military action

naturalization the legal process by which citizens of one country become citizens of another

Necessary and Proper Clause the final clause of Article 1, Section 8 in the Constitution, which gives Congress the power to make all laws "necessary and proper" for executing its powers

New Jersey Plan plan that was presented as an alternative to the Virginia Plan at the Constitutional Convention; called for a unicameral legislature in which each State would be equally represented

Nixon, Richard (1913–1994) Richard Nixon was an attorney before entering politics to serve as a representative and senator from California. He was Vice President under President Eisenhower, before being elected the 37th President in 1968. He served from 1969 to 1974. As President, he ended the draft and instituted a broad environmental program. Facing impeachment due to his involvement in the Watergate scandal, Nixon resigned in August 1974.

nomination the process of candidate selection in an electoral system

nonpartisan elections elections in which candidates are not identified by party labels

North American Free Trade Agreement (NAFTA) agreement that removed trade restrictions among the United States, Canada, and Mexico, thus increasing cross-border trade

O

Obama, Barack Barack Obama (1961–) was the 44th President of the United States from 2009 to 2014. The first African American president, Obama was awarded the Nobel Peace Prize.

O'Connor, Sandra Day O'Connor (1930–) was the first woman appointed to the Supreme Court. Nominated by President Reagan in 1981, she served as associate justice of the Supreme Court until she retired in 2006. Known for her carefully researched opinions, she was considered a moderate conservative.

off-year elections congressional election that occurs between presidential election years

oligarchy a form of government in which the power to rule is held by a small, usually self-appointed elite

omnibus measure one bill that contains numerous issues and topics

open market operations processes by which the Federal Reserve buys or sells government securities from and to the nation's banks in order to alter the money supply

open primary a party-nominating election in which any qualified voter can take part

opinion leaders any person who, for any reason, has an unusually strong influence on the views of others

ordinance a law passed by a local government

ordinance power power of the President to issue executive orders; originates from the Constitution and acts of Congress

original jurisdiction the power of a court to hear a case first, before any other court

oversight function review by legislative committees of the policies and programs of the executive branch

P

Panama Canal artificial waterway that cuts across the Isthmus of Panama in Central America and links the Atlantic and Pacific oceans

panic derived from the Latin panicus, meaning "terrified"; a sudden widespread alarm about the economy that often results in a depression

pardon release from the punishment or legal consequences of a crime, by the President (in a federal case) or a governor (in a State case)

parliamentary government a form of government in which the executive branch is made up of the prime minister, or premier, and that official's cabinet; this branch is part of the legislature

parliamentary system a form of government in which the executive branch is made up of the prime minister, or premier, and that official's cabinet

parochial church-related, as in a parochial school

parole the release of a prisoner short of the complete term of the original sentence

partisans lawmakers who owe their first allegiance to their political party and vote according to the party line

partisanship the strong support of their party and its policy stands

party caucus a closed meeting of a party's house or senate members; also called a party conference

party government the direction and control of the processes of government by the party who has majority favor

party identification loyalty of people to a political party

passport a legal document issued by a state that identifies a person as a citizen of that state and permits travel to and from that state

patent a license issued to an inventor granting the exclusive right to manufacture, use, or sell his or her invention for a limited period of time

patricians rich upper class, landowning aristocrats of the Roman Republic

Patrick, Luther Luther Patrick (1894–1957) was born near Decatur, Alabama. He graduated from Purdue University and received his law degree from the University of Alabama. After serving in various judicial positions including assistant attorney general of Alabama, he served as U.S. representative from Alabama 1937 to 1943 and from 1945 to 1947.

patronage the practice of giving jobs to supporters and friends

payroll tax tax imposed on nearly all employers and their employees, and on self-employed persons, with the amounts owed by employees withheld from their paychecks

Pearl Harbor a U.S. naval base located on the island of Oahu in Hawaii

peer group people with whom one regularly associates, including friends, classmates, neighbors, and co-workers

Pelosi, Nancy Nancy Pelosi (1940–) graduated from Trinity College in Washington, D.C. As one of California's representatives beginning in 1987, Pelosi became the first female Democratic leader of the House, the first female Speaker of the House, and for the 113th Congress, served as the Minority Leader in the House.

Penn, William An English Quaker leader who advocated for religious freedom, Penn (1644–1718) came to North America in 1682 and established the colony of Pennsylvania as a haven for Quakers and other religious minorities.

perjury the act of lying under oath

Perot, Ross A two-time third party candidate for President and founder of the Reform Party in 1995, Ross Perot (1930–) used his wealth from founding Electronic Data Systems to fund his campaigns. He lost elections in 1992 and 1996.

persona non grata an unwelcome person; used to describe recalled diplomatic officials

petit jury this jury hears the evidence in a case, decides the disputed facts, and very occasionally interprets and applies the law; also known as a trial jury

petition a citizen's right to bring his or her view to the attention of public officials by such means as written petitions, letters, lobbying, and marches

Petition of Right document prepared by Parliament and signed by King Charles I of England in 1628; challenged the idea of the divine right of kings and declared that even the monarch was subject to the laws of the land

Philadelphia the largest city in the Commonwealth of Pennsylvania

picketing patrolling of a business site by workers who are on strike

pigeonholed expression describing how most bills introduced in each session of Congress are buried, put away, or never acted upon

plaintiff in civil law, the party who brings a suit or some other legal action against another (the defendant) in court

platform a political party's formal statement of basic principles, stands on major issues, and objectives

plebeians the common folk in the Roman Republic

plurality the largest number of votes cast for the office

pocket veto a type of veto a chief executive may use after a legislature has adjourned when the chief executive does not sign or reject a bill within the time allowed to do so

police power authority of each State to act to protect and promote the public health, safety, morals, and general welfare of its people

political action committees (PACs) political arms of special-interest groups and other organizations with a stake in electoral politics

political efficacy one's own influence or effectiveness on politics

political party a group of persons who seek to control government through winning elections and holding public office

political socialization process by which people gain their political attitudes and opinions

political spectrum the range of political views

politicos lawmakers who attempt to balance the basic elements of the trustee, delegate, and partisan roles

poll books list of all registered voters in each precinct

poll tax special tax, demanded by some States, as a condition of voting; outlawed by the 24th Amendment

polling place place where the voters who live in a certain precinct go to vote

Pope, Alexander Pope (1688–1744) was a famous and financially successful poet who was also a satirist and translator. He was born in London and raised in a Roman Catholic family. He is most famous for his use of the heroic couplet.

popular sovereignty a government that exists only with the consent of the governed

Powell, Colin Powell (1937–) is a four-star general who served as chairman of the Joint Chiefs of Staff from 1989 to 1993. In 2001, he became secretary of state under George W. Bush; he served in that capacity until 2005. Powell was the first African American to hold either of these Cabinet-level positions.

precedent court decision that stands as an example to be followed in future, similar cases

precinct smallest unit of election administration; a voting district

preclearance provision mandated by the Voting Rights Act of 1965 in which no new election laws and no changes in existing election laws, could go into effect in certain States unless first approved by the Department of Justice

preliminary hearing the first step in a major criminal case in which the judge decides if the evidence is enough to hold the person for action by the grand jury or prosecutor

presentment formal accusation brought by the grand jury on its own motion, rather than that of the prosecutor

president of the Senate the presiding officer of a senate; in Congress, the Vice President of the United States; in a State's legislature, either the lieutenant governor or a senator

president pro tempore the member of the United States Senate, or of the upper house of a State's legislature, chosen to preside in the absence of the president of the Senate

Presidential Election Campaign Fund money donated by taxpayers when they file their federal income tax returns, administered by the FEC, and used for the purpose of subsidizing pre-convention campaigns, national conventions, and presidential election campaigns

presidential government a form of government in which the executive and legislative branches of the government are separate, independent, and coequal

presidential primary an election in which the party's voters 1) choose State party organization's delegates to their party's national convention, and/or 2) express a preference for their party's presidential nomination

presidential succession scheme by which a presidential vacancy is filled

Presidential Succession Act of 1947 law specifying the order of presidential succession following the Vice President

preventive detention law that allows federal judges to order that an accused felon be held, without bail, when there is good reason to believe that he or she will commit yet another serious crime before the trial

prior restraint idea that government cannot curb ideas before they are expressed

privatization process of returning national enterprises to private ownership

Privileges and Immunities Clause Constitution's stipulation that all citizens are entitled to certain "privileges and immunities," regardless of their State of residence

probable cause reasonable grounds, a reasonable suspicion of crime

procedural due process concept that holds that the government must employ fair procedures and methods

process of incorporation the process of incorporating, or including, most of the guarantees in the Bill of Rights into the 14th Amendment's Due Process Clause

progressive tax type of tax that takes a higher percentage from high-income groups than from low-income groups

project grants one type of federal grants-in-aid; made for specific projects to States, localities, and private agencies who apply for them

property tax a tax levied on real and personal property

proportional plan proposal by which each presidential candidate would receive the same share of a State's electoral vote as he or she received in the State's popular vote

proportional representation rule applied in Democratic primaries whereby any candidate who wins at least fifteen percent of the votes gets the number of State Democratic convention delegates based on his or her share of that primary vote

proprietary organized by a proprietor (a person to whom the king had made a grant of land)

prorogue adjourn, as in a legislative session

protectionism practice of national governments trying to control imports to protect native industries from foreign competition

public affairs those events and issues that concern the people at large; for example, politics, public issues, and the making of public policies

public agenda public issues on which the people's attention is focused

public debt all of the money borrowed by the government and not yet repaid, plus the accrued interest on that money; also called the national debt or federal debt

public opinion complex collection of the opinions of many different people; the sum of all their views

public opinion polls device that attempts to collect information by asking people questions; poll comes from the old Teutonic word polle, meaning "the top or crown of the head," the part that shows when heads are counted

public policies all of the things a government decides to do

public policy all of the many goals that a government pursues in all of the many areas of human affairs in which it is involved

pundit expert in a particular subject or field who is frequently called on to give opinions about it to the public

purge a process of government purification by removing rivals

purging process of reviewing lists of registered voters and removing the names of those no longer eligible to vote; a purification

Putin, Vladimir (1952–) became president of the Russian Federation in 1999, taking over when Boris Yeltsin resigned at the end of that year. He won elections in 2000, 2004, and 2012. Putin was also prime minister from 2008 to 2012. During his leadership, presidential power has increased, and he has improved Russia's economy. At the same time, some argue that he is not a true democratic leader.

Q

quorum fewest number of members who must be present for a legislative body to conduct business; majority

quota percentage of a group necessary to fulfill an affirmative action requirement

quota sample sample deliberately constructed to reflect several of the major characteristics of a given population

R

random sample certain number of randomly selected people

ratification formal approval or final consent to the effectiveness of a constitution, constitutional amendment, or treaty

rational basis test test in which the Court asks whether the classification in a law has a reasonable relationship to the achievement of a proper governmental purpose

Reagan, Ronald Born in Illinois, Reagan (1911–2004) began his career as an actor, appearing in more than 50 films. Reagan later moved into politics, serving two terms as governor of California, before being elected the 40th President, serving from 1981 to 1989. Reagan was 69 when first elected President in 1980, making him the oldest candidate to win the office. During his presidency, he called for an era of national renewal and reduced reliance on government.

reapportion redistribute, as in seats in a legislative body

recall the process of removing an elected leader from office through petition and special election

recess a time when both houses of Congress temporarily suspend business

recession absence of economic growth

recognition the exclusive power of a President to legally recognize (establish formal diplomatic relations with) foreign states

record a transcript of proceedings made in trial court

redress satisfaction of a claim payment

referendum a process by which voters can challenge a statute that the legislature has recently passed or by which the legislature can refer a measure to the voters for approval or rejection

reformers those who work to change or reform government

refugee one who leaves his or her homeland to seek protection from war, persecution, or some other danger

regional security alliances treaties in which the United States and other countries involved have agreed to take collective action to meet aggression in a particular part of the world

registration procedure of voter identification intended to prevent fraudulent voting

regressive tax tax levied at a flat rate, without regard to the level of a taxpayer's income or ability to pay

representative government system of government in which public policies are made by officials selected by the voters and held accountable in periodic elections; see democracy

reprieve an official postponement of the execution of a sentence

reservations public lands set aside by a government for use by Native American tribes

reserve requirement amount of money the Federal Reserve determines banks must keep in reserve with one of the Federal Reserve Banks

reserved powers those powers that the Constitution does not grant to the National Government and does not deny to the States

resolution a measure relating to the business of either house of Congress or expressing an opinion; does not have the force of law and does not require the President's signature

reverse discrimination discrimination against a majority group

Rice, Condoleezza Rice (1954–) served as foreign policy adviser for George W. Bush's presidential campaign. Once Bush was elected, she became the first woman to head the National Security Council. In 2005, Rice became the first African American woman to serve as secretary of state. Later, Rice returned to her position as a professor at Stanford University and is the author of numerous books.

rider unpopular provision added to an important bill certain to pass so it will "ride" through the legislative process

right of association the right to associate with others to promote political, economic, and other social causes

right of legation the right to send and receive diplomatic representatives

Roberts, John Roberts (born 1955) received his J.D. from Harvard Law School in 1979. He later worked as a law clerk at the Supreme Court, Associate Counsel to President Ronald Reagan, and in the White House Counsel's office from 1982 to 1986. He was nominated to the Supreme Court by President George W. Bush and was confirmed in 2005.

Romney, Mitt Romney (born 1947) is a Republican senator from Utah. As the Republican presidential nominee in 2012, he was the first Mormon nominated by a major party to run for the office. Romney lost to the incumbent, Barack Obama.

Roosevelt, Franklin D. (1882–1945) the 32nd President of the United States from 1933 to 1945. He was the only President to be elected to the office four times. He led the country through the Great Depression and World War II and developed the system of government programs and reforms together known as the New Deal.

Roosevelt, Theodore Roosevelt (1858–1919) was the 26th President of the United States, serving from 1901 to 1909. Nicknamed Teddy, he was a hunter, soldier, naturalist, and recipient of the Nobel Peace Prize who also secured the route for and began construction on the Panama Canal.

Roper, Elmo Roper (1900–1971) developed the first scientific poll for political forecasting using small samples. While working for *Fortune* magazine, Roper accurately predicted that Franklin Roosevelt would win the presidency in 1936, 1940, and 1944; these achievements brought him significant fame. In his later years, Roper continued in the polling industry and also wrote for newspapers and the *Saturday Review* magazine.

Rousseau, Jean Jacques A Swiss-born philosopher, writer, and political theorist, Rousseau's (1712–1778) treatises and novels inspired the leaders of the French Revolution. His famous work, *The Social Contract,* expresses his idea that humans are essentially free, but the progress of civilization has substituted subservience and dependence to others for that freedom. To overcome this, people must invoke their free will to reconstruct themselves politically along democratic ideals.

rule of law concept that the government and its officers are always subject to the law

runoff primary a primary in which the top two vote-getters in the first direct primary face one another

S

sales tax a tax placed on the sale of various commodities, paid by the purchaser

sample representative slice of the public

Scalia, Antonin Born in New Jersey, Antonin Scalia (1936–2016) was appointed to the Supreme Court by President Ronald Reagan in 1986. Prior to this appointment, Scalia held a number of positions in the Federal Government, including service as a judge on the United States Court of Appeals for the District of Columbia Circuit. He died while still serving on the Supreme Court.

search warrant court order authorizing a search

secretary an official in charge of a department of government

Security Council a 15-member panel that bears the UN's major responsibility for keeping international peace

sedition crime of attempting to overthrow the government by force or to disrupt its lawful activities by violent acts

seditious speech advocating, or urging, an attempt to overthrow the government by force or to disrupt its lawful activities with violence

segregation separation of one group from another on the basis of race

select committee legislative committee created for a limited time and for some specific purpose; also known as a special committee

Selma, Alabama Southern city that came to symbolize the South's resistance to the civil rights movement during the early 1960s; the city was the scene of a large march for voting rights, led by several African American leaders, including the Rev. Martin Luther King, Jr.

senatorial courtesy an unwritten rule that is closely followed in the Senate

seniority rule unwritten rule in both houses of Congress reserving the top posts in each chamber, particularly committee chairmanships, for members with the longest records of service

separate-but-equal doctrine doctrine established by the Court in the case *Plessy* v. *Ferguson,* in which it ruled that segregation could be maintained if the separation treated separated races equally

separation of powers basic principle of American system of government that the executive, legislative, and judicial powers are divided among three independent and coequal branches of government

session period of time each year during which Congress assembles and conducts business

shadow cabinet members of opposition parties who watch, or shadow, particular cabinet members and would be ready to run the government

Shays, Daniel A young farmer with a flair for militia drill, Shays (1747–1825) became a captain in the 5th Massachusetts Regiment of the Continental Army in 1777 and gained a reputation as a courageous and competent officer. After the war, he returned to farming. Like many others, he struggled with debts in the severe post-war recession. Shays emerged as a local leader in the movement protesting high taxes and a lack of debt relief.

Shays' Rebellion a series of confrontations between debtor farmers and State government authorities in western Massachusetts in 1786–1787

Sherman, Roger Sherman (1721–1793) was a Connecticut lawyer and judge, Framer of the U.S. Constitution, and Congressman. An early supporter of American independence, he attended the First and Second Continental congresses and also helped draft the Articles of Confederation. At the Constitutional Convention, he proposed what became known as the Connecticut Compromise, which created a House of Representatives chosen by population and a Senate with the same number of representatives from each State.

shield laws laws that give reporters some protection against having to disclose their sources or reveal other confidential information in legal proceedings

single-issue parties parties that focus on a single public question

single-member district electoral district from which one person is chosen by the voters for each elected office

slander false and malicious use of spoken words

Smith, Adam Smith (1723–1790) was a Scottish philosopher whose ideas are credited with pushing forward the nineteenth-century era of free trade. His book *The Wealth of Nations* (1776) influenced many intellectual and political leaders of the time, and his theories continue to have credibility among modern economists.

socialism philosophy based on the idea that the benefits of economic activity should be fairly distributed

soft money money given to State and local party organizations, in unlimited amounts, for election-related activities

sound bite short, sharply focused report that can be aired in 30 or 45 seconds

sovereign when a state has supreme and absolute power within its own territory and can decide its own foreign and domestic policies

sovereignty utmost authority in decision making and in maintaining order of a state

Speaker of the House the presiding officer of the House of Representatives, chosen by and from the majority party in the House

special district an independent unit created to perform one or more related governmental functions at the local level

special session an extraordinary session of a legislative body, called to deal with an emergency situation

splinter parties parties that have split away from one of the major parties

split-ticket voting voting for candidates of different parties for different offices in the same election

spoils system the practice of giving offices and other favors of government to political supporters and friends

staff agency agency that supports the chief executive and other administrators by offering advice and other assistance in the management of an organization

Stalin, Josef Stalin (1878–1953) rose from poverty to become the totalitarian leader of the Soviet Union from 1929 to 1953. Under his reign, which was characterized by brutality, the former peasant society became an industrial leader and a military force to be reckoned with. Among the many sweeping reforms made by Stalin was the collectivization of farming.

standing committee permanent committee in a legislative body to which bills in a specified subject area are referred; see select committee

state a body of people, living in a defined territory, organized politically (that is, with a government), and with the power to make and enforce law without the consent of any higher authority

State budget a financial plan for the use of money, personnel, and property

statutory law a law passed by the legislature and, in some States, the voters

straight-ticket voting practice of voting for candidates of only one party in an election

straw vote poll that seeks to read the public's mind by asking the same question of a large number of people; the odd name comes from the fact that a straw, thrown up in the air, will indicate which way the wind is blowing

strict constructionist one who argues for a narrow interpretation of the Constitution's provisions, particularly those granting powers to the Federal Government

strict scrutiny test test in which the Court holds the classification in a law to a higher standard; the State or Federal Government must show that its law is not related to an ordinary governmental purpose, but to a compelling governmental interest

strong-mayor government a type of city government in which the mayor is the chief administrative officer of the city and exercises three critical powers: the budget power, the veto power, and the appointment power

subcommittee division of existing committee that is formed to address specific issues

subpoena an order for a person to appear and to produce documents or other requested materials

subsidy a grant, usually from a government, to help an organization

substantive due process concept that holds that the government must create fair policies and laws

successor a person who inherits a title or office

suffrage right to vote

Super PAC independent political action committees, unaffiliated with any political party, which are allowed to raise and spend unlimited amounts; they must reveal their donors and cannot work directly with a candidate's campaign; independent political action committees, unaffiliated with any political party

supply-side economics assumption that tax cuts increase the supply of money in private hands and stimulate the economy

Supremacy Clause a provision of the U.S. Constitution that states that the Constitution, federal law, and treaties of the United States are the "supreme Law of the Land"

surplus more income than spending

Suu Kyi, Aung San A politician and opposition leader of Myanmar, Suu Kyi (1945–) was awarded the Nobel Peace Prize in 1991. She was placed under house arrest for many years for opposing the government's military rule but was later freed and elected to public office.

swing voters members of the electorate who have not made up their minds at the start of the campaign and are open to persuasion by either side

symbolic speech expression by conduct; communicating ideas through facial expressions, with body language, or by carrying a sign or wearing an armband

T

Taft, William Howard (1857–1930) the 27th President of the United States from 1909 to 1913. He later became the tenth Chief Justice of the United States, making him the only person to have served in both offices.

Taney, Roger B. Taney (1777–1864) served as U.S. Attorney General and was appointed Chief Justice of the Supreme Court in 1836. His majority opinion in *Dred Scott* v. *Sandford*, 1857, stating that African Americans could not be considered U.S. citizens, caused much contention on the eve of the Civil War.

tariff tax on imported goods

tax a charge levied by government on persons or property to raise money to meet public needs

term two-year period of time during which Congress meets

territory a part of the United States that is not a state and has its own system of government

terrorism the use of violence to intimidate a government or society

theocracy a form of government in which a country is ruled by religious leaders

Thomas, Clarence Thomas (born 1948) was the second African American appointed to the Supreme Court. President George H.W. Bush nominated him as an associate justice of the Supreme Court in 1991 to replace Thurgood Marshall, and he continues to serve.

Three-Fifths Compromise an agreement reached at the Constitutional Convention that a slave would be counted as three-fifths of a person when counting the population of a State

Thurmond, Strom The governor of South Carolina and a U.S. senator for 48 years, Thurmond (1902–2003) was a staunch opponent of school desegregation and civil rights who ran unsuccessfully for President in 1948. He later switched party affiliation from Democratic to Republican.

Tillerson, Rex Rex Tillerson, a native of Texas, was appointed secretary of state by President Donald Trump in 2017 and confirmed by the Senate with a vote of 56–43. Prior to entering government service, Tillerson (born 1952) earned a civil engineering degree from the University of Texas at Austin, and his first job was as a production engineer. This was followed by a long career in business, culminating in his becoming chief executive officer (CEO) and chairman of Exxon/Mobil, a global energy company.

Tocqueville, Alexis de A French political scientist and historian, Tocqueville (1805–1859) is best known for writing *Democracy in America,* an analysis of the political and social system in the United States during the 1800s.

tort a wrongful act that involves injury to one's person, property, or reputation in a situation not covered by the terms of a contract

township a subdivision of a county

trade association interest group within the business community

trade embargo ban on trade with a particular country or particular countries

transients person living in a State for only a short time, without legal residence

treason betrayal of one's country; in the Constitution, by "levying war against the United States or offering comfort or aid to its enemies"

treaty a formal agreement between two or more sovereign states

Truman, Harry Harry Truman (1884–1972) was a Missouri farmer, a judge, a senator, and Vice President for a few months under President Franklin D. Roosevelt. He became the 33rd President on April 12, 1945, when Roosevelt suddenly died. During his presidency, from 1945 to 1953, Truman saw Victory in Europe Day and ordered atomic bombs dropped on Japan.

Trump, Donald J. Donald J. Trump was born in New York City in 1946. His father was a wealthy real estate developer. Upon graduation from the University of Pennsylvania in 1968, Trump joined his father's firm. By the 1990s, he owned vast real estate holdings, including the Empire State Building, various hotels, condominiums, apartment buildings, and casinos. He also starred in a reality television show, *The Apprentice* (later *The Celebrity Apprentice*). He considered a run for the presidency in 1999, but it was not until 2016 that he officially decided to run. He won the Republican nomination in the summer of 2016 and in November of that year, Donald J. Trump was elected the 45th President of the United States.

trustees lawmakers who vote based on their conscience and judgment, not the views of their constituents

Tyler, John Virginia native John Tyler (1790–1862) served in the State legislature and as Virginia governor. As a U.S. senator, his strict interpretation of the Constitution led him to resign over what he viewed as illegal actions by President Andrew Jackson regarding nullifying acts of Congress. Vice President when President William Henry Harrison died in office, he succeeded to the presidency in 1841. During his term, he approved statehood for Texas and Florida, but fought bitterly with his own Whig party over a national bank system. All but one member of his Cabinet resigned. During the Civil War, he was elected to the Confederate House of Representatives, but he died before he could serve.

U

unconstitutional contrary to constitutional provision and so illegal, null and void, of no force and effect

uncontrollable spending spending that Congress and the President have no power to change directly

unicameral an adjective describing a legislative body with one chamber; see bicameral

unitary government a centralized government in which all government powers belong to a single, central agency

United Nations an organization with 193 members that accept the obligations of the United Nations Charter, a treaty drafted in 1945

universe term used in polling that refers to the whole population that the poll aims to measure

V

veto chief executive's power to reject a bill passed by a legislature; literally (Latin) "I forbid"

Virginia Plan plan presented by the delegates from Virginia at the Constitutional Convention; called for a three-branch government with a bicameral legislature in which each State's membership would be determined by its population or its financial support for the Federal Government

visa a permit to enter another country, obtained from the country one wishes to enter

W

Walesa, Lech (1943–) a labor activist who formed Poland's first trade union. Though he was arrested for his union interactions, he was awarded the Nobel Peace Prize in 1983 and served as the president of Poland from 1990 to 1995.

ward a unit into which cities are often divided for the election of city council members

warrant a court order authorizing, or making legal, some official action, such as a search or an arrest

Warren, Earl Warren (1891–1974) was a Republican but liberal justice appointed to the Supreme Court by President Dwight D. Eisenhower. Warren was Chief Justice of the Supreme Court from 1953 to 1969 and presided over some of the Court's most important public school desegregation cases.

Washington, George Washington (1732–1799) was the first President of the United States from 1789 to 1797 and a Founding Father. Prior to his presidency, he was a general and commander in chief during the American Revolution.

weak-mayor government form of city government in which the mayor shares executive duties with other elected officials

welfare cash assistance to the poor

whips assistants to the floor leaders in the House and Senate, responsible for monitoring and marshaling votes

William and Mary of Orange King William III (1650–1702) and Queen Mary II (1662–1694) ruled jointly as king and queen of England, Scotland, and Ireland from 1689 to 1702 (Queen Mary died in 1694, but William continued to rule until 1702). Mary was the daughter of King James II, which meant that her Dutch husband could become co-ruler of England after he overthrew James's government.

Wilson, James Born and educated in Scotland, Wilson (1742–1798) emigrated to North America, arriving in the midst of the Stamp Act agitations of 1765. He studied to become an attorney, going on to specialize in land law. He entered politics just prior to the Revolutionary War and had a pivotal position of influence in the Constitutional Convention.

Wilson, Woodrow Woodrow Wilson (1856–1924) was a graduate of Princeton and the University of Virginia School of Law, and president of Princeton in 1902. He was elected to be the 28th president in 1912. Wilson served from 1913 to 1921 and advocated for a "new freedom" which stressed individualism and States' rights.

winner-take-all an almost obsolete system whereby a presidential aspirant who won the preference vote in a primary automatically won all the delegates chosen in the primary

World Bank organization formed in 1944 to provide economic assistance to developing countries to reduce global poverty levels

World Trade Organization organization created in 1995 to increase trade

writ of certiorari an order by the Court directing a lower court to send up the record in a given case for review

writ of habeas corpus court order that prevents unjust arrests and imprisonments

writs of assistance blanket search warrant with which British custom officials had invaded private homes to search for smuggled goods

Y

Yeltsin, Boris (1931–2007) a Russian politician who became president of Russia in 1990. He became the first popularly elected politician in Russia's history in 1991.

Z

zoning the practice of dividing a city into a number of districts, or zones, and regulating the uses to which property in each of them may be put

A

absentee voting > voto en ausencia Medidas para que voten, el día de las elecciones, aquellas personas que no puedan hacerlo en su lugar habitual de votación.

acquit > absolver Determinar que alguien no es culpable de un delito.

act of admission > decreto de admisión Ley del Congreso mediante la cual se admite a un nuevo estado dentro de la Unión.

Adams, John > Adams, John (1735–1826) fue abogado en Massachusetts, legislador, diplomático y segundo Presidente de los Estados Unidos. Por su sentido de la justicia, defendió a los oficiales ingleses de la Masacre de Boston, pero luego encabezó la defensa de la independencia estadounidense en el Primer y Segundo Congresos Continentales. Fue el principal autor de la Constitución del estado de Massachusetts; ayudó a negociar un tratado de paz con Gran Bretaña después de la Guerra de Independencia, consiguió el reconocimiento diplomático de los Estados Unidos y estructuró el comercio libre con todas las naciones.

Adams, John Quincy > Adams, John Quincy (1767–1848) 6° Presidente de los Estados Unidos, de 1825 a 1829, y autor de la Doctrina Monroe. John Quincy era hijo del presidente John Adams (1797–1801). Antes de ser elegido presidente, Adams fue secretario de Estado. Fungió como congresista después de su presidencia, de 1831 a 1848, y luchó contra la esclavitud. En 1848, sufrió una apoplejía y cayó en el piso de la Cámara de Representantes. Murió dos días después.

Adams, Samuel > Adams, Samuel Uno de los Padres Fundadores, Adams (1722–1803) se convirtió en líder político en Boston por medio de sus textos. Fue delegado en el Primer y el Segundo Congresos Continentales y participó en la redacción del borrador para la Declaración de Derechos.

adjourn > aplazamiento Suspender, por ejemplo, una sesión del Congreso.

administration > administración Funcionarios del poder ejecutivo de un gobierno, así como sus políticas y sus principios.

administrative law > Ley de Administración Ley compuesta por las normas, ordenamientos y reglamentos emitidos por las autoridades ejecutivas federales, estatales o locales, que actúan bajo la autoridad constitucional y o legal apropiada.

affirmative action > acción afirmativa Política que exige que la mayoría de los empleadores lleven a cabo ciertas acciones para remediar los efectos de discriminaciónes pasadas.

Albany Plan of Union > Plan de Unión de Albany Proyecto propuesto por Benjamín Franklin en 1754 cuyo objetivo era unir a las trece colonias en cuanto a asuntos comerciales, militares, así como para otros propósitos; las colonias y la Corona rechazaron el plan.

Albright, Madeleine > Albright, Madeleine (1937–) fungió como embajadora estadounidense frente a Naciones Unidas de 1993 a 1997. Posteriormente, el presidente Bill Clinton la nombró como la primera mujer que ocuparía el cargo de secretaria de Estado de los Estados Unidos dentro del gabinete presidencial, cargo que ocupó de 1997 a 2001. A partir de entonces se ha desempeñado como oradora, consultora y escritora.

alien > extranjero Persona residente nacida en otro país o que no se ha nacionalizado.

Alito, Samuel > Alito, Samuel (1950–) Obtuvo su diploma en Derecho de la Universidad de Yale en 1975, donde fue editor del *Yale Law Journal*. Alito ocupó diversos puestos judiciales durante los mandatos de Ronald Reagan y George H. W. Bush. En 2005, el presidente George W. Bush lo nombró, y Alito asumió su puesto como juez de la Corte Suprema el 31 de enero de 2006.

ambassador > embajador Representante oficial designado por el Presidente para representar a la nación en asuntos diplomáticos.

amendment > enmienda Cambio o adición a la Constitución o a una ley.

amicus curiae brief > alegato *amicus curiae* Término legal latino que significa "amigo de la corte". Es un documento conformado por alegatos escritos que se presentan ante la corte para apoyar a alguna de las partes en disputa.

amnesty > amnistía Perdón general otorgado a un grupo de personas que han violado la ley.

Anti-Federalists > antifederalistas Aquellas personas que se opusieron a la ratificación de la Constitución entre 1787 y 1788.

appellate jurisdiction > jurisdicción de apelación Autoridad de una corte para revisar decisiones de cortes inferiores; ver original jurisdiction/jurisdicción original.

apportioned > prorrateados Distribuidos como, por ejemplo, los escaños de un cuerpo legislativo.

appropriate > asignar Destinar a un uso particular.

Aristotle > Aristóteles (384–322 a.C. Filósofo griego que consideraba que las vidas humanas individuales están conectadas en un contexto social. Escribió acerca de los diversos tipos de gobierno y las obligaciones individuales del ciudadano.

Arouet, François-Marie > Arouet, François-Marie También conocido como Voltaire, Arouet (1694–1778) fue un importante pensador y escritor de la Ilustración. La creencia de Voltaire en la razón, la ciencia y la libertad religiosa hallan eco en sus obras de teatro, poemas, novelas, ensayos y en sus trabajos sobre historia y ciencia. Voltaire pasó gran parte de su vida exiliado, lejos de Francia, escribiendo y hablando sobre su filosofía.

Arthur, Chester > Arthur, Chester 21er Presidente de los Estados Unidos, ocupó el cargo de 1881 a 1885, Arthur (1829–1886) asumió la presidencia luego del asesinato del presidente James Garfield. Arthur firmó el Acta Pendleton, que elimina el sistema de botines y establece el mérito como base para la contratación de empleados federales.

Articles of Confederation > Artículos de la Confederación Plan de gobierno adoptado por el Congreso Continental, después de la Independencia de los Estados Unidos; se enunciaron como "un vínculo firme de amistad" entre los estados, pero le delegaron pocos poderes importantes al gobierno central.

assemble > congregar Reunirse con otras personas para expresar puntos de vista sobre asuntos públicos.

assessment > valuación Proceso para determinar el valor de una propiedad que será gravada.

assimilation > asimilación Proceso mediante el cual las personas de una cultura se integran en otra y se convierten en parte de ella.

at-large > elección general Elección de un funcionario público por los votantes de una unidad gubernamental completa, en vez de por los votantes de un distrito o subdivisión.

attorney general > procurador general Funcionario más alto del Departamento de Justicia.

autocracy > autocracia Forma de gobierno en la que una sola persona tiene poder político ilimitado.

B

backbenchers > diputados de segundo rango Miembro de la Cámara de los comunes de Gran Bretaña que no es líder del partido.

bail > fianza Suma de dinero que se exige que el acusado o la acusada pague como garantía de que se presentará en la corte en la fecha señalada.

balance the ticket > designar al compañero de fórmula Acción que, para reforzar sus oportunidades de ganar las elecciones, un candidato presidencial lleva a cabo cuando elige a un candidato a la vicepresidencia con base en sus características ideológicas, geográficas, raciales, étnicas, de género o de otro tipo.

Balkans > Balcanes Los Balcanes, a veces llamada península de los Balcanes, es una región geográfica en Europa central que generalmente incluye a Eslovenia, Croacia, Bosnia y Herzegovina, Serbia, Kosovo, Montenegro; Macedonia, Albania, Bulgaria, Rumania y Moldavia. El término puede tener diferentes interpretaciones geográficas, culturales e históricas.

ballot > papeleta electoral Medio que los votantes utilizan para indicar su preferencia en una elección.

ballot fatigue > fatiga al votar Fenómeno que se presenta cuando los votantes marcan menos casillas hacia el final de la papeleta electoral.

bankruptcy > bancarrota Procedimiento legal mediante el cual los bienes de una persona se distribuyen entre las personas con las que tiene deudas.

battleground States > estados reñidos Estados donde los resultados de las elecciones indican que cualquier candidato podría ser el ganador.

BCRA > BCRA (por su sigla en inglés) La Ley Bipartidista de Reforma de Campaña de 2002 intentó cerrar la brecha de los fondos no fiscalizados en las leyes de financiamiento de las campañas anteriores.

bench trial > juicio ante judicatura Proceso en el cual sólo el juez escucha el caso.

bicameral > bicameral Adjetivo que describe un cuerpo legislativo formado por dos cámaras.

Biden, Joseph > Biden, Joseph (1942–) Senador demócrata por Delaware; elegido por primera vez en 1972. Fungió como 47° vicepresidente de los Estados Unidos bajo la presidencia de Barack Obama y como el 46° presidente de los Estados Unidos.

bill > proyecto de ley Propuesta de ley que se presenta ante un cuerpo legislativo para su consideración.

bill of attainder > Escrito de proscripción y confiscación Acto legislativo que inflige un castigo sin que haya un juicio ante un jurado.

Bill of Rights > Carta de Derechos Las primeras diez enmiendas a la Constitución.

bipartisan > bipartidista Apoyado por dos partidos.

Blackstone, William > Blackstone, William (1723–1780) Juez inglés que escribió los *Comentarios acerca de las leyes de Inglaterra,* una serie de cuatro libros que tuvo una profunda influencia en los autores de la Declaración de Independencia y la Constitución de los Estados Unidos. Blackstone, importante personaje de la Ilustración, creía en la protección de los derechos de los inocentes, y en sustentar los juicios en el derecho consuetudinario, es decir, en fallos previos sobre asuntos similares.

Blaine, James G. > Blaine, James G. (1830–1893), congresista por Maine y presidente de la Cámara de representantes de 1869 a 1875, no tuvo éxito como candidato a la presidencia en 1876 y 1880. Ocupó el cargo de secretario de Estado en 1881 y, de nuevo, de 1889 a 1892.

blanket primary > elecciones primarias generales Proceso de elección en el que los votantes reciben una papeleta electoral grande que contiene los nombres de todos los candidatos, independientemente del partido, y en el cual pueden elegir libremente.

block grants > subsidios en conjunto Tipo de subsidios públicos federales que se ofrecen para un área particular pero definida en términos generales.

Boehner, John > Boehner, John (1949–) Congresista republicano de Cincinnati, Ohio, elegido para la Cámara de Representantes de los Estados Unidos en 1990. Fue líder mayoritario en 2006 y líder minoritario de 2007 a 2011. Se convirtió en presidente de la Cámara de Representantes en 2011.

Boston > Boston La ciudad más grande y capital de la mancomunidad de Massachusetts.

Bradley, Joseph P. > Bradley, Joseph P. Nombrado por el presidente Ulysses S. Grant, Joseph P. Bradley (1813–1892) sirvió como juez asociado de la Corte Suprema de 1870 a 1892. Bradley fue uno entre varios jueces que redujeron las garantías que la entonces recién aprobada Decimocuarta Enmienda otorgaba a los afroamericanos.

Brennan, William J. > Brennan, William J. (1906–1997) Al igual que Earl Warren, William J. Brennan, Jr., fue nombrado para la Corte Suprema por el presidente Dwight D. Eisenhower y, como Warren, Brennan sería uno de los jueces más liberales en la historia de la Corte, por sus votos en muchos casos de protección igualitaria. Estuvo en funciones de 1956 a 1990.

brief > alegato Reseña detallada presentada ante la Corte antes de dar un argumento oral; declaración escrita que presenta la postura legal de un partido y cita datos relevantes y precedentes legales.

Bryce, James > Bryce, James (1838–1922) Fue un político británico, embajador en los Estados Unidos de 1907 a 1913. Se hizo muy popular después de publicar *La República Norteamericana,* que constituye un estudio favorable del gobierno de los Estados Unidos

budget > presupuesto estimado de ingresos y gastos en el futuro; para un estado o nación, es un plan financiero, un estimado de los ingresos y egresos para el próximo año fiscal

bureaucracy > burocracia Estructura administrativa grande y compleja que gobierna los negocios cotidianos de una organización.

bureaucrat > burócrata Persona que trabaja en una organización burocrática.

Bush, George H.W. > Bush, George H.W. Después de graduarse de la Universidad de Yale, Bush (nacido en 1924) inició su carrera en la industria del petróleo de Texas. En dos ocasiones, fue diputado en el Congreso en representación de Texas, y luego fue nombrado embajador frente a Naciones Unidas y director de la CIA. Bush fue vicepresidente de Ronald Reagan y fue elegido como el 41er Presidente, y ocupó el cargo de 1989 a 1993.

Bush, George W. > Bush, George W. (1946–) se graduó de la Universidad de Yale y de la Escuela de Negocios de Harvard antes de regresar a Texas a trabajar en la industria petrolera. Primero ocupó la gubernatura de Texas y, más tarde, fue elegido como 43er Presidente; ocupó el cargo de 2001 a 2009. Su elección significó la segunda ocasión en la historia estadounidense en la que el hijo de un Presidente (George H. W. Bush) llegó a convertirse en Presidente.

Byrd, Robert C. > Byrd, Robert C. (1917–2010) Representante al Congreso por Virginia Occidental de 1953 a 1959, y senador de 1959 a 2010; estuvo en funciones por más tiempo que cualquier otro legislador en la historia estadounidense. Se consideraba a sí mismo "hijo de las minas de carbón de los Apalaches" y dedicó su carrera política a luchar contra la pobreza en Virginia Occidental.

C

Cabinet > gabinete Cuerpo consultivo del Presidente que tradicionalmente está formado por los funcionarios más altos de los departamentos ejecutivos y otros agentes.

Calvert, George (Lord Baltimore) > Calvert, George (Lord Baltimore) Un miembro del parlamento que fundó Maryland como un refugio para católicos. Calvert (1578 o 1579–1632) llegó a América del Norte en 1628 pero no fue aceptado a causa de su religión. Regresó a Inglaterra y solicitó una cédula real para establecer una colonia en la que pudiera practicar su religión. La cédula fue concedida en 1632, poco después de su muerte.

capital > capital Todos los recursos creados por el hombre que se utilizan para producir bienes y servicios.

capital punishment > pena capital La pena de muerte.

capitalism > capitalismo Sistema económico en el que individuos tienen la libertad de poseer los medios de producción y de aumentar sus ganancias.

Capitol Hill > Capitol Hill El Capitolio de los Estados Unidos se localiza en el distrito histórico y residencial llamado Capitol Hill, en Washington, D.C. Otros edificios en Capitol Hill son la Corte Suprema de los Estados Unidos y la Biblioteca del Congreso. *Capitol Hill* también es una figura retórica que simplemente significa "el Congreso".

Carter, Jimmy > Carter, Jimmy (1924–) fue el 39º Presidente de los Estados Unidos y ocupó el cargo de 1977 a 1981. Ex oficial de la marina y gobernador de Georgia, Carter obtuvo el Premio Nobel de la Paz en 2002 y es autor de veintisiete libros. Durante su presidencia, Carter creó el Departamento de Educación, expandió el sistema de parques nacionales y entabló relaciones diplomáticas con la República Popular China.

Castro, Fidel > Castro, Fidel (1926–) era el líder político dictatorial de Cuba de 1959 a 2008. Mediante tácticas revolucionarias, hizo de la nación isleña el primer estado comunista en el Hemisferio occidental.

categorical grants > subsidio categórico Tipo de subsidio público federal; proporcionado para un propósito específico y rigurosamente definido.

caucus > junta de dirigentes En función de instrumento nominativo, grupo de personas que comparten la misma ideología y que se reúnen para seleccionar a los candidatos que apoyarán en una elección.

censure > amonestación Pronunciamiento de una condena formal.

certificate > certificación Resultado del proceso en el que una corte inferior consulta a la Corte Suprema para que certifique una respuesta a una pregunta específica, tal como un procedimiento o una regla.

Charles I, King > Carlos I, rey (1600–1649) fue rey de Inglaterra, Escocia e Irlanda de 1625 a 1649. Gobernó con mano dura y sus disputas con el parlamento provocaron una guerra civil. En 1649, Carlos fue declarado culpable de traición fue ejecutado.

charter > carta constitucional Ley básica de una ciudad, su constitución; concesión de autoridad escrita otorgada por el rey.

Chávez, Hugo > Chávez, Hugo (1954–2013) Llegó a la presidencia de Venezuela en 1999; obtuvo el cargo mediante un atentado contra la élite política tradicional en ese país. Conocido por ser directo y controvertido, Chávez insistió durante toda su presidencia en que su revolución socialista beneficiaría a todos en Venezuela, pero en especial a los pobres

checks and balances > sistema de controles y equilibrios Sistema en el cual se traslapan las autoridades del poder legislativo, el poder ejecutivo y el poder judicial para permitir que cada poder verifique las acciones de los otros dos.

Chiang Kai-shek > Chiang Kai-shek (1887–1975) Fue un militar y hombre de estado chino. Fue líder del Gobierno Nacionalista desde 1928 hasta 1949.

chief administrator > administrador en jefe Nombre que se le da al Presidente por ser el jefe de la administración del gobierno federal.

chief citizen > primer ciudadano Nombre que se le da al Presidente por ser representante del pueblo y trabajar por el interés público.

chief diplomat > diplomático titular Nombre que se le da al Presidente por ser el arquitecto principal de la política exterior y un vocero ante otros países.

chief economist > economista en jefe Termino para referirse al Presidente en tanto supervisor la situación económica del país.

chief executive > primer mandatario Nombre que se le da al Presidente porque está investido con el poder ejecutivo de los Estados Unidos.

chief legislator > legislador en jefe Nombre que se le da al Presidente por ser arquitecto de la política pública y por ser la persona que determina la agenda del Congreso.

chief of party > jefe del partido Nombre que se le da al Presidente por ser el líder de su partido político.

chief of state > jefe de estado Nombre que se le da al Presidente por ser el funcionario ceremonial de los Estados Unidos, el símbolo de toda la gente de la nación.

Churchill, Winston > Churchill, Winston (1874–1965) Estadista británico que ocupó el cargo de primer ministro del Reino Unido, de 1940 a 1945, durante la mayor parte de la Segunda Guerra Mundial, y de 1951 a 1955. Fue el primer ciudadano honorario de los Estados Unidos y obtuvo el premio Nobel de Literatura.

citizen > ciudadano Miembro de un estado o nación por nacimiento o naturalización, que se beneficia de todos los derechos civiles y que le debe lealtad a ese estado o nación.

civil case > caso civil Caso relacionado con un asunto no criminal, como un litigio por contrato o una demanda por violación de patentes.

civil disobedience > desobediencia civil Forma de protesta en la que las personas violan la ley de forma deliberada pero no violenta para expresar su oposición a alguna ley o política pública en particular.

civil law > ley civil Área de la ley que se relaciona con la conducta humana, con litigios entre entidades privadas, así como entre partes privadas y el gobierno, que no están cubiertos bajo la ley penal.

civil liberties > libertades civiles Garantías que protegen la seguridad, las opiniones y la propiedad de las personas de actos arbitrarios del gobierno; entre ellas están la libertad de expresión y la libertad de religión.

civil rights > derechos civiles Término que designa actos positivos del gobierno con el objetivo de hacer realidad las garantías constitucionales para todo el pueblo, por ejemplo la prohibición de la discriminación.

civil service > servicio civil Grupo de empleados civiles que desempeñan el trabajo administrativo del gobierno.

civilian > civil Que no es militar.

civilian tribunal > tribunal civil Corte que actúa como parte del poder judicial y que está separada por completo de la institución militar.

clemency > clemencia Misericordia o piedad que dispensa el Presidente a un delincuente.

Clinton, Bill > Clinton, Bill (1946–) William J. Clinton fue elegido gobernador de Arkansas en 1978, y 42° Presidente para los periodos de 1993 a 2001. Durante su administración, los Estados Unidos disfrutaron en gran medida de un periodo de paz y crecimiento económico. En 1998 se convirtió en el segundo presidente impugnado por la Cámara de Representantes, pero el Senado lo declaró inocente y conservó su cargo.

Clinton, Hillary Rodham > Clinton, Hillary Rodham (1947–) se convirtió en la Primera dama de los Estados Unidos cuando su esposo, Bill Clinton, ganó la presidencia en 1993. En 2001, Clinton se hizo senadora por el estado de Nueva York y, mientras ocupaba ese cargo, intentó sin éxito ser candidata a la presidencia. En 2009, Clinton fue seleccionada para el cargo de secretaria de Estado en la administración del presidente Barack Obama, puesto que ejerció hasta su renuncia en 2013.

closed primary > elección primaria cerrada Elecciones para una nominación de un partido en la que sólo los miembros declarados del partido pueden votar.

cloture > limitación del debate Procedimiento que puede utilizarse para restringir o terminar un debate verbal de un cuerpo legislativo, especialmente en caso de una obstrucción.

coalition > coalición Alianza temporal de varios grupos que se juntan para alcanzar el poder mayoritario y controlar el gobierno.

coattail effect > efecto de refilón Efecto que produce la presencia de un candidato fuerte en la parte superior de una papeleta electoral y que ayuda a atraer votantes hacia otros candidatos de su mismo partido.

cold war > Guerra Fría Período de más de 40 años en el que las relaciones entre las dos superpotencias (Estados Unidos y la Unión Soviética) fueron por lo menos tensas, y a menudo hostiles; época de amenazas y de desarrollo armamentista.

collective security > seguridad colectiva Conservación de la paz y el orden internacionales.

collectivization > colectivización Hacer colectivos o propiedad del estado los medios de producción.

colonialism > colonialismo Control que tiene una nación sobre tierras extranjeras.

command economies > economía dirigida Sistema en el cual los burócratas del gobierno planean y dirigen la mayor parte de la actividad económica.

commander in chief > comandante en jefe Nombre que se le da al Presidente por ser el comandante de las Fuerzas Armadas de la nación.

Commerce and Slave Trade Compromise > Avenencia de Comercio y Trata de Esclavos Acuerdo durante la Convención Constitucional que protegió los intereses de los dueños de esclavos, al negarle al Congreso el poder de gravar la exportación de bienes desde cualquier estado y el poder de actuar, durante veinte años, en contra de la trata de esclavos.

commerce power > poder mercantil Poder exclusivo que tiene el Congreso para regular el comercio interestatal e internacional.

commission government > gobierno de concejo municipal forma de gobierno local en el que un grupo de concejales elegidos por voto popular conforman el concejo de gobierno de una ciudad

committee chair > presidente de comisión Miembro que encabeza una comisión permanente en un cuerpo legislativo.

common law > derecho consuetudinario Ley que no ha sido sancionada por un juez y se ha desarrollado a lo largo de los siglos, con base en ideas generalmente aceptadas de lo bueno y lo malo que se han ganado un reconocimiento judicial.

communism > comunismo Ideología que exige la propiedad colectiva, o estatal, de la tierra y de otros medios de producción.

commutation > conmutación Poder de reducir la duración de una sentencia o el monto de la multa por haber cometido un delito.

compromise > transigencia Acuerdo intermedio entre principios o sistemas opuestos, al que se llega mediante la modificación de algún aspecto de cada uno de ellos.

concurrent jurisdiction > jurisdicción coincidente Poder compartido por cortes federales y estatales para atender ciertos casos.

concurrent powers > poderes concurrentes Aquellos poderes que el gobierno nacional y los estados poseen y ejercen.

concurrent resolution > resolución conjunta Enunciado de una opinión sobre un asunto utilizado por la Cámara de Representantes y el Senado al actuar conjuntamente; no tiene el poder de la ley y no requiere la firma del Presidente.

concurring opinion > opinion coincidente Explicación escrita de los puntos de vista de uno o más jueces quienes apoyan una decisión alcanzada por una mayoría en la corte, pero desean añadir o recalcar un punto que no se remarcó en la decisión mayoritaria.

confederation > confederación Unión de diversos grupos para un propósito común.

conference committee > comité de consulta Comité conjunto temporal formado para reconciliar cualquier diferencia entre las versiones de un proyecto de ley propuesto por las dos cámaras legislativas.

Connecticut Compromise > Acuerdo de Connecticut Acuerdo alcanzado durante la Convención Constitucional que estableció que el Congreso debería estar integrado por un Senado donde cada estado estuviera representado de manera equitativa, y una Cámara de Representantes en la que la representación estuviera basada en la población de cada estado.

consensus > consenso Acuerdo general entre diversos grupos sobre temas fundamentales; acuerdo general sobre asuntos públicos.

constituencies > circunscripciones electorales Las personas e intereses que un funcionario electo representa.

constituent power > poder constituyente Poder no legislativo de la elaboración de la Constitución y del proceso de enmiendas constitucionales.

constitutional law > ley constitucional Está basada en la constitución de los Estados Unidos, las constituciones de los Estados y las interpretaciones judiciales de esos documentos.

constitutionalism > constitucionalismo Principio básico que establece que el gobierno y los gobernantes deben obedecer la ley; el gobierno de la ley.

containment > contención Política basada en la creencia de que si se pudiera evitar la expansión del régimen comunista, éste colapsaría debido a la fragilidad de su estructura interna.

content neutral > voto neutral El gobierno no regulará a las asambleas en lo concerniente a lo que se expresará en ellas.

continuing resolution > resolución ininterrumpida Medida que permite que las agencias continúen funcionando basándose en de las asignaciones del año anterior.

continuous body > cuerpo legislativo ininterrumpido Organismo del Estado (el Senado de los Estados Unidos, por ejemplo) cuya totalidad de escaños nunca se remplaza al mismo tiempo.

contract > contrato Acuerdo jurídicamente vinculante en el que una de las partes se compromete a hacer algo con o para un tercero.

controllable spending > gasto controlable Monto fijado por el Congreso y el Presidente para determinar cuánto dinero se dedicará anualmente para distintos rubros gubernamentales, como programas para la protección del ambiente y apoyos a la educación, entre otros.

convene > convene Reunir, o convocar, la sesión inaugural de la legislatura.

copyright > derechos de autor El derecho legal exclusivo de una persona para reproducir, publicar y vender sus propias creaciones literarias, musicales o artísticas.

council-manager government > gobierno de concejo–administrador consiste en un concejo fuerte y un alcalde débil, ambos elegidos por votación, y de un administrador nombrado por el concejo

county > condado Unidad importante de gobierno local en gran parte de los estados.

courts-martial > corte marcial Corte integrada por personal militar para juzgar a quienes han sido acusados de violar la ley militar.

criminal case > caso criminal Caso en el que se juzga al acusado por cometer un delito, tal y como éste se define de acuerdo a la ley.

criminal law > derecho penal Área de la ley que define los agravios públicos y que establece su castigo.

Cultural Revolution > Revolución cultural Mao Zedong, presidente del Partido Comunista chino, convocó a este proceso durante su última década en el poder (1966–1976) para renovar el espíritu de la Revolución china. Guardias rojos, jóvenes y entregados, atacaron e intimidaron a intelectuales y a aquellos que carecían de fervor revolucionario. Algunos fueron enviados a campos de trabajo para ser reeducados.

customs duty > derecho de aduana Impuesto sobre los bienes introducidos a los Estados Unidos; también se conoce como arancel, impuesto sobre importaciones o tasa sobre importaciones.

D

de facto > de facto La situación tal y como existe de hecho.

de jure > de jure De acuerdo con la ley.

defendant > acusado En un juicio civil, es la persona en contra de quien el demandante pide ejecutar una acción judicial; en un caso penal, es la persona acusada de un delito.

deficit > déficit Diferencia anual entre los ingresos y los egresos.

deficit financing > financiamiento del déficit Práctica que consiste en subvencionar al gobierno mediante préstamos, a fin de compensar la diferencia entre los gastos y los ingresos gubernamentales.

deflation > deflación Disminución general de los precios.

delegated powers > poderes delegados Poderes explícitos, implícitos o inherentes que la Constitución transfiere al gobierno nacional.

delegates > delegados Personas con autoridad para representar a otros en una conferencia o convención; representantes; miembros del Congreso que votan según los deseos de sus constituyentes.

demand-side economics > economía de demanda Teoría que establece que un alza de los empleos debido a préstamos del gobierno producirá un incremento en los ingresos tributarios.

democracy > democracia Forma de gobierno en la cual la autoridad suprema reside en el pueblo.

democratic consolidation > consolidación democrática Proceso mediante el cual se establecen los factores necesarios para el éxito de una democracia.

democratization > democratización Cambio de una dictadura a una democracia mediante elecciones libres y justas.

denaturalization > desnaturalización Proceso mediante el cual los ciudadanos naturalizados pueden perder su ciudadanía de manera involuntaria.

Deng Xiaoping > Deng Xiaoping (1904–1997) llegó al poder en China en 1977, justo después de la impopular Revolución cultural que Mao Zedong inició en 1966. Deng siguió con el estilo autoritario de su predecesor, pero abrió a China a una economía de mercado que sacó a millones de campesinos de la pobreza.

deportation > deportación proceso legal por el que una persona que se encuentra ilegalmente en los Estados Unidos es obligada a salir del país

détente > distensión Palabra francesa que significa "relajamiento de las tensiones."

deterrence > disuasión Política que consiste en convertir a los Estados Unidos y sus aliados en una fuerza militar tan poderosa que su fortaleza desaliente, o prevenga, cualquier ataque.

devolution > delegación Transferencia de la autoridad del gobierno central a los gobiernos regionales.

dictatorship > dictadura Forma de gobierno en la que los gobernantes no pueden hacerse responsables ante la voluntad del pueblo; forma de gobierno donde el líder ejerce poder y autoridad absolutos.

diplomatic immunity > inmunidad diplomática Atributo mediante el cual los embajadores no están sujetos a las leyes del estado en el que están acreditados; condición en la que un embajador no está sujeto a las leyes del estado anfitión.

direct primary > elecciones primarias Elecciones realizadas dentro de un partido para escoger a los candidatos del partido para las elecciones generales.

discharge petition > petición de exoneración Procedimiento que permite a los miembros reiniciar (después de 30 días; 7 días en el caso del comité de reglas) la discusión para considerar una propuesta de ley que se había suspendido en una comisión de debate.

discount rate > tasa de descuento Tasa de interés que debe pagar un banco que toma un préstamo del Banco de la Reserva Federal.

discriminate > discriminar Dar un trato a ciertos grupos de personas diferente del que se da a personas que forman parte de otros grupos.

discrimination > discriminación Prejuicio, injusticia.

disenfranchised > privación del derecho al voto Acción que consiste en negarle a alguien el derecho de votar.

dissenting opinions > opiniones disidentes Opinión escrita por un juez que explica por qué está en desacuerdo con la decisión de la Corte.

District of Columbia > Distrito de Columbia El Distrito de Columbia (D. C.) es la sede del gobierno de los Estados Unidos de América. Se localiza entre Maryland y Virgina, en el margen del río Potomac, y tiene una extensión de 68 millas cuadradas. La ciudad de Washignton, D. C. abarca la totalidad del Distrito de Columbia.

district plan > plan de distrito Propuesta para elegir a los electores presidenciales, mediante la cual se seleccionarían dos electores en cada estado, de acuerdo con el voto popular de todo ese estado, y los otros electores se elegirían de manera separada en cada uno de los distritos del Congreso de ese estado.

divine right of kings > derecho divino de los monarcas La creencia de que Dios otorga autoridad a los regímenes.

division of powers > división de poderes Principio básico del federalismo; estipulaciones constitucionales que establecen que los poderes gubernamentales están separados según la ubicación geográfica (en los Estados Unidos, entre el gobierno nacional y los estatales).

docket > agenda Lista de casos por atender en una corte.

domestic affairs > asuntos internos Todas las cuestiones no relacionadas con el campo de los asuntos exteriores.

double jeopardy > doble juicio Parte de la 5ª Enmienda que establece que no se puede poner en riesgo la vida de una persona o su integridad física dos veces. Una vez que se ha juzgado por un crimen a una persona, no puede volvérsele a juzgar por el mismo delito.

Douglas, William O. > Douglas, William O. (1898–1980) fue el juez que pasó el segundo mayor tiempo en funciones en la Corte Suprema. Nombrado como juez asociado de la Corte por el presidente Franklin D. Roosevelt en abril de 1939, mantuvo su cargo por 36 años, hasta su retiro en noviembre de 1975.

draft > reclutamiento Conscripción o servicio militar obligatorio.

due process > proceso legal establecido El gobierno debe actuar con justicia y de acuerdo con las reglas establecidas en todo lo que hace.

Due Process Clause > Cláusula del Debido Proceso Parte de la 14.ª enmienda que garantiza que ningún estado negará los derechos básicos a su pueblo.

duty > arancel Impuesto a las importaciones.

E

economic protest parties > partidos de protesta económica Partidos surgidos en tiempos de descontento económico, que carecen de una base ideológica bien definida, están insatisfechos por las condiciones presentes y exigen mejoras.

Eisenhower, Dwight > Eisenhower, Dwight Elegido como Presidente en 1953, Eisenhower (1890–1969) traía consigo el prestigio de haber sido comandante de las Fuerzas aliadas en Europa en la Segunda Guerra Mundial, la coronación de una larga carrera militar. Fungió como 34º Presidente de 1953 a 1961, abogó por la paz y apoyó la abolición de la segregación en la escuelas y en el ejército.

electoral college > colegio electoral Grupo de personas elegidas cada cuatro años en todos los estados y en el Distrito de Columbia a fin de elegir formalmente al Presidente y Vicepresidente.

electorate > electorado Todas las personas que tienen derecho a votar en una elección determinada.

eminent domain > dominio supremo Poder de un gobierno de expropiar la propiedad privada para uso público.

enabling act > ley de habilitación Ley del Congreso que orienta al pueblo de un territorio de los Estados Unidos para que redacte una propuesta de la constitución para el estado, como un paso hacia la admisión de dicho estado dentro de la Unión.

English Bill of Rights > Declaración Inglesa de los Derechos Documento redactado por el Parlamento y aceptado por William y Mary de Inglaterra en 1689, elaborado para evitar el abuso de poder por parte de los monarcas ingleses; constituye la base de gran parte del gobierno y la política estadounidenses actuales.

engrossed > transcrito Proyecto de ley impreso en su forma final.

entitlement > derecho Beneficio, establecido por una ley federal, que se debe pagar a todos los que cumplan los requisitos, por ejemplo: Medicare, los cupones de alimento y las pensiones para los veteranos.

entrepreneur > empresario Persona con el impulso y la ambición para combinar los recursos de la tierra, de la mano de obra y del capital para producir bienes u ofrecer servicios.

Equal Protection Clause > La Cláusula de Igualdad de Protección sección de la Constitución de los Estados Unidos que exige que las leyes de un estado o de la nación deben tratar a cualquier individuo de la misma manera que trataría a otros individuos que se encuentran en condiciones y circunstancias similares.

equity > *equity* Una rama de la ley que complementa la ley común mediante la adopción de un enfoque preventivo.

espionage > espionaje Acto de espiar.

Establishment Clause > Cláusula del Establecimiento Forma parte de la Primera Enmienda de la Constitución y garantiza la separación de la Iglesia del Estado.

estate tax > impuesto testamentario Gravamen sobre los bienes de una persona que muere.

ex post facto law > ley ex post facto Ley que se aplica a un acto cometido con anterioridad a la aprobación de la ley.

excise tax > impuesto al consumo Gravamen sobre la manufactura, la venta o el consumo de bienes y/o al suministro de servicios.

exclusionary rule > regla de exclusión Regla de acuerdo con la cual la evidencia obtenida como resultado de una acción ilegal de la policía no puede utilizarse contra la persona arrestada.

exclusive powers > poderes exclusivos Poderes que sólo el gobierno nacional puede ejercer.

executive agreement > acuerdo ejecutivo Pacto establecido de manera directa entre el Presidente y otro jefe un estado extranjero; pacto internacional obligatorio que tiene el poder de una ley pero que no requiere, a diferencia de un tratado, de la aprobación del Senado.

Executive Article > Artículo del Ejecutivo Segundo artículo de la Constitución. Define la presidencia y le otorga el poder ejecutivo del gobierno federal al Presidente.

executive departments > oficinas del poder ejecutivo A menudo llamadas Oficinas del Gabinete; son las unidades tradicionales de la administración federal.

Executive Office of the President > Oficina ejecutiva del Presidente Organización compleja, que abarca diversas oficinas separadas, cuyo personal está integrado por los consejeros y asistentes más cercanos al Presidente.

executive order > orden ejecutiva Directiva, regla o reglamento expedido por un primer mandatario o sus subordinados, con base en su autoridad estatutaria o constitucional, y que tiene el poder de una ley.

executive power > poder ejecutivo Poder para ejecutar, administrar y obligar al cumplimiento de la ley.

executive privilege > privilegio ejecutivo Poder que tiene el Presidente para rehusarse a revelar información.

expatriation > expatriación Proceso legal mediante el cual ocurre la pérdida de ciudadanía.

expressed powers > poderes explícitos Aquellos poderes delegados del gobierno nacional que se señalan explícitamente en la Constitución; también se conocen como los "poderes ennumerados".

extradition > extradición Proceso legal a través del cual un fugitivo de la justicia de un estado se retorna a ese estado.

F

factors of production > factores de producción Recursos básicos que se utilizan para elaborar todos los bienes y servicios.

failed states > estados fallidos Países con un sistema de seguridad nulo, una economía muy deteriorada, sistemas de asistencia de salud y de educación en crisis y donde prospera la corrupción.

FECA > FECA (por su sigla en inglés) La Ley Federal de las Campañas Electorales de 1971 fue la primera ley federal en regular el uso del dinero en las campañas presidenciales y del Congreso.

federal budget > presupuesto federal Documento financiero detallado que contiene las estimaciones de las recaudaciones y gastos que anticipan los ingresos y egresos federales durante el año fiscal venidero.

Federal Election Commission (FEC) > Comisión electoral federal (FEC, por su sigla en inglés) Una agencia independiente en el poder ejecutivo que administra toda la legislación federal concerniente al financiamiento de las campañas.

federal government > Gobierno Federal Forma de gobierno en la que los poderes están divididos entre un gobierno central y diversos gobiernos locales.

federalism > federalismo Sistema de gobierno en el que una constitución escrita divide los poderes del gobierno, entre un gobierno central y diversos gobiernos regionales.

Federalists > federalistas Personas que apoyaron la ratificación de la Constitución entre 1787 y 1788.

Feingold, Russ > Feingold, Russ Senador demócrata por Wisconsin de 1993 a 2010, Feingold fue uno de los patrocinadores de la Ley Bipartidista de Reforma Electoral de 2002.

felony > felonía Un crimen grave que puede castigarse con una gran multa, la prisión o incluso la muerte.

feudalism > feudalismo Sistema relativamente organizado en el cual los grandes señores les concedían sus tierras a otros señores de menor autoridad.

filibuster > obstruccionismo Tácticas de demora en las que senadores monopolizan el pleno del Senado con discursos u otras dilataciones para que se evite una votación sobre algún proyecto de ley.

First Lady > Primera dama La esposa del Presidente.

fiscal policy > política económica Métodos varios que usa el gobierno para obtener y gastar dinero.

fiscal year > año fiscal Período de 12 meses utilizado por el gobierno y el mundo de los negocios para su contabilidad, presupuesto, recaudación de ingresos y otros propósitos financieros.

527 organizations > organizaciones 527 Grupos de activistas políticos registrados de acuerdo con la Sección 527 del Código Interno de Ingresos (Internal Revenue Code), que no están asociados a ningún partido político pero tratan de influir en sus políticas y están autorizados para recaudar sumas de dinero ilimitadas.

floor consideration > consideración de la sala Proceso mediante el cual la Cámara de Representantes o el Senado consideran y reaccionan a las leyes propuestas.

floor leaders > líderes de fracciones Partidistas miembros de la Cámara de Representantes y del Senado elegidos por sus partidos con el objeto de llevar a cabo las decisiones partidistas e impulsar la acción legislativa a fin de que se cumplan los propósitos partidistas.

Ford, Gerald > Ford, Gerald (1913–2006) fue Presidente de los Estados Unidos de 1974 a 1977. Cuando el presidente Nixon se vio forzado a dejar la presidencia en 1974 por el escándalo de Watergate, el vicepresidente Ford ocupó el cargo durante el resto del periodo de Nixon. Ford se empeñó en mantener el poderío estadounidense en el extranjero y se esforzó en evitar una nueva guerra en Oriente Medio. Ford perdió la presidencia en 1976 por los problemas económicos, los efectos de Watergate y haber otorgado el perdón al ex presidente Nixon.

foreign affairs > asuntos exteriores Relaciones de una nación con otros países.

foreign aid > ayuda extranjera Auxilio militar y económico a otros países.

foreign policy > política exterior Conjunto de políticas conformado por todas las posturas y acciones que una nación asume en cada uno de los aspectos de sus relaciones con otros países; todo lo que el gobierno de una nación expresa y hace respecto a los asuntos mundiales.

formal amendment > enmienda formal Cambio o adición que se convierte en parte del lenguaje escrito de la Constitución misma, mediante uno de los cuatro métodos enunciados de la Constitución.

Framers > redactores de la Constitución Grupo de delegados que esbozaron la Constitución de los Estados Unidos en la Convención de Filadelfia en 1787.

franchise > sufragio Derecho a votar.

franking privilege > exención de franquicia Beneficio otorgado a los miembros del Congreso que les permite enviar por correo cartas y otros materiales gratis.

Franklin, Benjamin > Franklin, Benjamin Escritor, inventor, diplomático y legislador estadounidense, Franklin (1706–1790) propuso el Plan de Unión de Albany, que preveía los beneficios de la unidad entre las Colonias. Más tarde, firmó la Declaración de Independencia y ayudó a elaborar la Constitución, al insistir a los delegados que cooperaran y firmaran el borrador final.

free enterprise system > sistema de libre empresa Sistema económico caracterizado por la propiedad privada o corporativa de los bienes de capital; inversiones que están determinadas por una decisión privada, en vez del control estatal, y están sujetas a un mercado libre.

Free Exercise Clause > Cláusula de la Libertad de Cultos Segunda parte de la garantía constitucional de libertad religiosa, que garantiza a todos el derecho de creer en lo que se escoja en cuestiones de religión.

free market > mercado libre Mercado en el cual los compradores y vendedores tienen la libertad de comprar y vender como lo deseen.

full faith and credit > Cláusula de Fe y Crédito Cabal Cláusula constitucional según la cual cada estado acepta los actos públicos, documentos y procedimientos judiciales de cualquier otro estado.

Full Faith and Credit Clause > Cláusula de entera fe y crédito Requisito constitucional según el cual cada estado acepta los actos públicos, documentos y procedimientos judiciales de cualquier otro estado.

fundamental laws > leyes fundamentales Leyes de importancia primordial y duradera que no se pueden cambiar con facilidad.

G

Gallup, George > Gallup, George (1901–1984) era un encuestador y estadístico que fundó la famosa Encuesta Gallup. Además de realizar encuestas y desarrollar nuevos métodos para garantizar la precisión de los sondeos, Gallup fue profesor y escritor. También fundó el American Institute of Public Opinion, el British Institute of Public Opinion y el Audience Research Institute, Inc.

Garfield, James > Garfield, James (1831–1881) fue el 20° Presidente de los Estados Unidos; ocupó el cargo de marzo a septiembre de 1881. Tiene el récord del segundo periodo más corto en el cargo. Ex general de división de la Guerra Civil y miembro de la Cámara de Representantes por Ohio durante nueve periodos consecutivos, el presidente Garfield recibió un disparo de Charles J. Guiteau en 1881 después de negarse a nombrarlo para un cargo diplomático.

gender gap > brecha de género Diferencias medibles entre las elecciones partidistas actuales de los hombres y las mujeres.

general elections > elecciones generales Elecciones programadas regularmente en las que los votantes hacen una selección final de los funcionarios públicos.

George II, King > Jorge II, rey (1683–1760) fue rey de Gran Bretaña de 1727 a 1760. La colonia de Georgia fue nombrada en su honor después de que firmó el decreto real que concedía la colonia a sus veinte fiduciarios en 1732. El rey Jorge consideró que la colonia sería una zona de defensa importante entre los territorios controlados por España al sur y el resto de las colonias inglesas al norte.

gerrymandering > demarcación arbitraria Establecimiento de los límites de los distritos electorales de modo que den ventaja a un partido.

gift tax > impuesto a las donaciones Gravamen sobre las donaciones hechas por una persona viva.

Ginsburg, Ruth Bader > Ginsburg, Ruth Bader (1933–2020) fue la segunda mujer nombrada a la Corte Suprema. El presidente Clinton la nominó para servir como jueza asociada de la Corte Suprema en 1993, y sirvió hasta su muerte en 2020.

globalization > globalización Interdependencia económica entre naciones del mundo.

Glorious Revolution > Revolución Gloriosa Los acontecimientos que, en 1688, llevaron al parlamento a invitar a Guillermo y María de Orange a remplazar pacíficamente al rey Jacobo II a condición de que reconocieran la autoridad del parlamento y los derechos individuales. Con la firma de la Carta de Derechos, la Revolución Gloriosa ayudó a calmar la lucha centenaria por la supremacía entre el monarca y el parlamento en Inglaterra.

Gorbachev, Mikhail > Gorbachov, Mijaíl Secretario general del Partido Comunista de la Unión Soviética de 1985 a 1991, Gorbachov (nacido en 1931) asumió la presidencia de la Unión Soviética en 1990. En un solo año, su empeño en democratizar el sistema político y descentralizar la economía llevó al colapso de la Unión Soviética. Gorbachov renunció a la presidencia en 1991. Recibió el Premio Nobel de la Paz en 1990.

Gorsuch, Neil > Gorsuch, Neil Nacido en Colorado, en 1967, fue nominado para la Corte Suprema por el presidente Donald Trump en 2017. Antes de ser juez de la Corte Suprema, Gorsuch prestó servicio en el Departamento de Justicia de los Estados Unidos, luego en la Corte de Apelaciones para el 10mo. Circuito. Gorsuch obtuvo su diploma en leyes en la Universidad de Harvard.

government > gobierno Institución mediante la cual una sociedad lleva a cabo y hace cumplir sus políticas públicas.

government corporations > empresa de servicios públicos Instituciones del poder ejecutivo que están sujetas a la dirección y el control del Presidente, formadas por el Congreso para que realicen determinadas actividades de tipo empresarial.

grand jury > gran jurado Dispositivo formal a través del cual puede acusarse a una persona de un crimen serio.

Grant, Ulysses S. > Grant, Ulysses S. (1822–1885) fue Presidente de los Estados Unidos de 1869 a 1877. Ganó la elección tras haber sido el general de la Unión que llevó a los Estados Unidos a la victoria sobre los Estados Confederados de América durante la Guerra Civil estadounidense. Grant defendió los derechos de los afroestadounidenses, las políticas para los indígenas norteamericanos y la reforma al servicio civil. Además, apoyó la creación de un ferrocarril transcontinental. También puso en marcha una política exterior fructífera y consiguió mejorar las relaciones anglo–estadounidenses.

grants-in-aid programs > programa de subvención de fondos públicos Subvenciones de dinero o de otros recursos federales para los estados, sus ciudades, condados y otras unidades locales.

grass-roots pressures > presión popular Presión que los miembros de un grupo de interés o la población en general ejercen sobre funcionarios públicos.

Great Leap Forward > Gran Salto Adelante Plan quinquenal de 1958 que fue un intento de modernizar rápidamente a China.

gross domestic product > producto interno bruto Cantidad total de bienes y servicios producidos por un país cada año.

Group of 7 (G7) > Grupo de los Siete Foro conformado, en 1975, por siete de los países más industrializados del mundo: los Estados Unidos, Japón, Alemania, Francia, Gran Bretaña, Italia, and Canadá.

Guantanamo Bay, Cuba > Bahía de Guantánamo, Cuba Los Estados Unidos la rentaron a Cuba en 1903. En la bahía de Guantánamo se localiza una base naval que opera desde entonces. A partir del 11 de enero de 2002, la base retiene individuos capturados por el ejército estadounidense durante la Guerra contra el Terrorismo. Este centro de detención causa controversia desde su apertura, y la suerte de sus prisioneros se debate acaloradamente desde las perspectivas legal y moral.

gubernatorial > gubernativo relacionado con la oficina del gobernador

H

Hamilton, Alexander > Hamilton, Alexander (1755 o 1757–1804) emigró a América del Norte en 1772 desde las Indias Occidentales Británicas. Se enroló en el Ejército Continental en 1776, bajo el mando del general Washington. Ocupó diversos cargos de gobierno, como el de miembro del Congreso Constitucional y de la Convención Constitucional. Estudió derecho y ejerció esa profesión en la ciudad de Nueva York. Hamilton fue secretario del Tesoro en el gabinete del presidente Washington. Fue herido de muerte en un duelo con Aaron Burr en 1804.

hard money > fondos fiscalizados Aportaciones de campaña, realizadas directamente a los candidatos, que deben ser restringidas y enteradas al gobierno; dinero de campaña que está sujeto a las regulaciones de la FEC.

hard-liners > radicales Los que luchan por mantener el status quo.

Harrison, William Henry > Harrison, William Henry Elegido como 9° Presidente en 1841, Harrison (1773–1841) fue el primer presidente muerto en funciones. Nacido en una familia aristocrática de terratenientes de Virginia, pasó mucho tiempo en el Noroeste, ganado títulos sobre tierras indígenas y dirigiendo esfuerzos para contener los ataques indígenas. Enfermó de neumonía y murió a sólo cuatro meses de haber asumido el cargo.

heterogeneous > heterogéneo De diferente raza, familia o especie; compuesto por una mezcla de elementos.

Hobbes, Thomas > Hobbes, Thomas (1588–1679) Filósofo inglés que consideraba que las personas y las naciones estaban en pugna constante por el poder y la riqueza. Pensaba que la monarquía absoluta era la mejor forma de gobierno para Inglaterra. Desconfiaba de la democracia, pero pensaba que representantes autorizados de la voz del pueblo podrían evitar que el monarca fuera injusto o cruel.

Holmes, Jr., Oliver Wendell > Holmes, Jr., Oliver Wendell (1841–1935) Fue un juez de la Corte Suprema de justicia de los Estados Unidos de 1902 a 1932, a quien se le daba el sobrenombre de "The Great Dissenter" (El gran disidente).

Hoover, Herbert > Hoover, Herbert (1874–1964) se graduó de Stanford como ingeniero minero y comenzó su carrera en China. Luego ocupó diversos cargos humanitarios en el extranjero, incluida la jefatura de la American Relief Administration en Europa. Fue elegido como 31er presidente en 1928; unos cuantos meses antes de la crisis de los mercados de 1929 que sumió a la nación en una grave depresión.

Hudson River > río Hudson Una vía fluvial de 315 millas de largo que corre de norte a sur en el este del estado de Nueva York.

I

ideological > ideológico(a) Basado(a) en un conjunto particular de creencias; lo ideológico constituye una concepción amplia de asuntos sociales, económicos y políticos.

immigrants > inmigrantes Personas que son admitidas legalmente en calidad de residente permanente de un país.

impeach > impugnar Presentar cargos formales en contra de un funcionario público.

implied powers > poderes implícitos Aquellos poderes delegados del gobierno nacional que se sugieren o están implícitos por los poderes explícitos establecidos en la Constitución; aquellos que son "necesarios y pertinentes" para realizar los poderes explícitos.

import quota > cuota de importación Límite sobre la cantidad de un producto que se puede importar a un país.

income tax > impuesto sobre la renta Gravamen sobre el ingreso de los individuos y/o corporaciones.

incorporation > incorporación Proceso mediante el cual un estado establece a una ciudad como un cuerpo legal; el término proviene de las palabras latinas *in* (dentro) y *corpus* (cuerpo).

incumbent > titular Funcionario público actual.

independent agencies > oficinas independientes Agencias adicionales creadas por el Congreso y que se ubican fuera de los departamentos del Gabinete.

independent executive agencies > oficinas ejecutivas independientes Agencias dirigidas por un solo administrador que tienen subunidades operativas regionales pero que carecen del estatus del Gabinete.

independent regulatory commissions > comisiones regulatorias independientes Agencias independientes cuya función es regular aspectos importantes de la economía de la nación, en su mayoría fuera del control y dirección del Presidente.

independents > Independientes Término usado para describir a las personas que no están afiliadas a un partido.

indictment > denuncia Queja formal que el fiscal expone ante un gran jurado, que incluye cargos al acusado por uno o más crímenes.

inferior courts > cortes inferiores Las cortes federales menores, que están por debajo de la Corte Suprema.

inflation > inflación Incremento general de precios en la economía.

information > acusación del fiscal Acusación oficial presentada por un acusador sin acción de parte del jurado.

inherent powers > poderes inherentes Aquellos poderes que, se presume, son delegados al gobierno nacional constitucionalmente, debido a que es el gobierno de un estado soberano de la comunidad mundial.

inheritance tax > impuesto sobre la herencia Gravamen sobre lo que hereda un beneficiario.

initiative > iniciativa Proceso en el que determinado número de votantes calificados firman peticiones a favor de una propuesta que se pasa después directamente a la papeleta electoral.

injunction > mandato Orden judicial que fuerza o limita el desempeño de determinado acto, mediante la intervención de un particular o un funcionario público.

integration > integración Proceso mediante el cual se ofrece a un grupo participación igualitaria dentro de la sociedad.

interest > Interés Cargo que se hace por el dinero prestado; por lo general es un porcentaje de la cantidad prestada.

interest group > grupo de interés Organizaciones privadas cuyos miembros comparten determinados puntos de vista y trabajan para dar forma a las políticas públicas.

International Monetary Fund (IMF) > Fondo Monetario Internacional (FMI) Organismo creado en 1944 para supervisar el sistema monetario internacional.

interstate compacts > pacto interestatal Acuerdo formal suscrito con el consentimiento del Congreso, entre dos estados o entre un estado y un estado extranjero, el cual está autorizado por la Constitución.

involuntary servitude > servidumbre involuntaria Trabajo forzado.

isolationism > aislacionismo Rechazo voluntario a verse involucrado, de manera general, en los asuntos del resto del mundo.

Isthmus of Panama > Istmo de Panamá La franja estrecha de tierra que se encuentra entre el mar Caribe y el océano Pacífico, en Panamá. En él se localiza el Canal de Panamá.

J

Jackson, Andrew > Jackson, Andrew Conocido como "Old Hickory" (viejo nogal) por su dureza y su personalidad agresiva, Jackson (1767–1845) fue el séptimo Presidente de los Estados Unidos, y ocupó el cargo de 1829 a 1837. Se conoce a su movimiento político como Democracia Jacksoniana, porque creía que el hombre común debía ser tomado en cuenta por el gobierno. Es el único presidente que peleó tanto la Guerra de Independencia, en su adolescencia, como la Guerra de 1812, en la que ganó fama militar. También es el primer presidente procedente del oeste de los montes Apalaches.

Jackson, Robert H. > Jackson, Robert H. (1892–1954) fue juez de la Corte Suprema de justicia de los Estados Unidos

de 1941 a 1954. Es conocido por su opinión en el juicio de la *Junta de Educación de Virginia Occidental* contra *Barnette*, de 1943, que amplió el alcance de la garantía de libertad de expresión contenida en la 1ª Enmienda.

Jamestown > Jamestown Primer asentamiento inglés permanente en América del Norte; fundado en 1607 en Virginia y nombrado en honor del rey Jacobo (James) I. La fundación de Jamestown marcó la entrada de Inglaterra en la competencia por las Américas, que España había dominado desde los viajes de Cristóbal Colón a finales del siglo XV.

Jay, John > Jay, John (1745–1829) Fue un abogado de Nueva York, presidente del Segundo Congreso Continental, diplomático, primer presidente de la Corte Suprema estadounidense y gobernador de Nueva York. Su postura era moderada frente a Gran Bretaña antes de la Declaración de Independencia. Jay apoyaba un gobierno centralizado fuerte y luchó por la ratificación de la Constitución de los Estados Unidos. También ayudó a preparar el borrador de la Constitución del estado de Nueva York y sirvió como primer presidente de la corte de ese estado. Ayudó a negociar y a poner en práctica términos liberales para la paz con Gran Bretaña y fue el primer secretario de Asuntos exteriores, antes de que George Washington lo nombrara primer presidente de la Corte Suprema de Justicia.

Jefferson, Thomas > Jefferson, Thomas (1743–1826) fue un firme defensor de la democracia y los derechos civiles, y escribió la Declaración de la Independencia y el Estatuto de Libertad Religiosa de Virginia. Fungió como secretario de Estado en la gestión de George Washington y como vicepresidente en la de John Adams, y fue el tercer Presidente de los Estados Unidos (1801–1809). Durante su presidencia, los Estados Unidos compraron a Francia el territorio de Luisiana, expandiendo su extensión 827,000 millas cuadradas al oeste del río Mississppi.

Jim Crow laws > Leyes de Jim Crow Categoría de leyes enunciadas con el fin de discriminar principalmente a los afroestadounidenses.

John, King > Juan sin Tierra, rey (1167–1216) fue rey de Inglaterra de 1199 a 1216. Poco después de ser coronado, estalló la guerra entre Inglaterra y Francia. Después de varias derrotas importantes, se dispararon los impuestos y el monarca se convirtió en un soberano implacable. Esto enfureció a los barones que obligaron a Juan a firmar la Carta Magna en 1215.

Johnson, Andrew > Johnson, Andrew (1808–1875) Fue el 17º presidente de los Estados Unidos. Como vicepresidente de Abraham Lincoln, Johnson asumió la presidencia cuando Lincoln fue asesinado. Ocupó el cargo de 1865 a 1869.

Johnson, Lyndon > Johnson, Lyndon (1908–1973) Fue el 36º Presidente de los Estados Unidos de 1963 a 1969. Fue elegido vicepresidente y ascendió a la presidencia al momento del asesinato del presidente John F. Kennedy. En 1964, promulgó la Ley de los Derechos Civiles.

Johnson, Richard M. > Johnson, Richard M. (1780–1850) Fue el noveno vicepresidente de la nación, ocupando el cargo de 1837 a 1841, durante la presidencia de Martin Van Buren. Johnson fue el único vicepresidente escogido por el Senado.

joint committee > comité conjunto Comité legislativo compuesto por miembros de ambas cámaras.

joint resolution > resolución conjunta Propuesta de acción que tiene el poder de una ley cuando se aprueba; a menudo tiene que ver con circunstancias especiales o asuntos temporales.

judicial activism > activismo judicial Filosofía judicial que argumenta que los jueces deberían interpretar y aplicar las condiciones de la Constitución y del derecho escrito considerando los cambios progresivos de condiciones y valores.

judicial power > poder judicial Poder para interpretar las leyes, determinar su significado y resolver las disputas que surgen dentro de la sociedad.

judicial restraint > restricción judicial Filosofía judicial que argumenta que los jueces deberían tomar decisiones sobre sus casos basándose en la intención original de los creadores de la Declaración de Derechos o los que promulgan los estatutos del caso, o en el precedente.

judicial review > revisión judicial Poder de una corte para determinar la constitucionalidad de una acción gubernamental.

jurisdiction > jurisdicción Autoridad de una corte para atender un caso.

jury > jurado Conjunto de personas seleccionadas de acuerdo con la ley para que escuchen la evidencia y decidan cuestiones de hecho en un caso de la corte.

jus sanguinis > *jus sanguinis* Ley de la sangre que define la ciudadanía con base en la ciudadanía de los padres.

jus soli > *jus soli* Ley del territorio que determina la ciudadanía con base en el lugar de nacimiento de la persona.

justice of the peace > Juez de paz Juez que está en el nivel inferior del sistema judicial estatal y preside las cortes de justicia.

K

Kagan, Elena > Kagan, Elena (1960–) Fue la cuarta mujer designada para la Corte Suprema. El presidente Obama la nominó para el cargo de Procurador general de los Estados Unidos en 2009. Después de un año en el cargo, el presidente Obama la nominó como jueza asociada de la Corte Suprema en 2010, y todavía ocupa ese cargo.

Kennedy, John F. > Kennedy, John F. (1917–1963) fue la persona más joven que se haya elegido como Presidente. Su discurso de asunción de 1963 exhortaba a los ciudadanos a "No (preguntarse) lo que su país puede hacer por ustedes, pregúntense lo que ustedes pueden hacer por su país". El 22 de noviembre de 1963, Kennedy fue asesinado en Texas.

Keynes, John Maynard > Keynes, John Maynard (1883–1946) fue un influyente economista británico, conocido principalmente por su revolucionaria teoría económica que se ocupa de las causas del desempleo prolongado. Keynes pensaba que el gobierno es el responsable de estabilizar la economía mediante el uso de políticas fiscales (impuestos y programas de gastos). Creía que en los periodos de depresión, el gobierno debía incrementar sus gastos, reducir impuestos o hacer ambas cosas para estimular la economía.

keynote address > discurso de apertura Alocución dada en una convención de partido para establecer el tono de la convención y de la futura campaña.

Khomeini, Ayatollah > Jomeini, Ayatola (1902–1989) fue un líder y clérigo iraní chiita (musulmán). Encabezó la revolución que derrocó al sah (líder) de Irán, en 1979. Más tarde, él mismo se convirtió en líder de Irán, e impuso tanto leyes políticas como religiosas durante diez años.

King, Jr., Martin Luther > King, Jr., Martin Luther (1929–1968) Hombre religioso, activista y líder afroamericano, King es conocido por su papel en el Movimiento Afroestadounidense por los Derechos Civiles, en el que defendía la resistencia pacífica frente a la discriminación y la segregación en el Sur.

L

labor union > sindicato laboral Organización de trabajadores que comparten el mismo tipo de trabajo, o que laboran en la misma industria y que busca impulsar políticas gubernamentales que beneficien a sus miembros.

laissez-faire theory > laissez-faire Teoría que sugiere que el gobierno debería desempeñar un papel muy limitado dentro de la sociedad.

law of supply and demand > ley de la oferta y la demanda Ley que establece que cuando los suministros de bienes y servicios son abundantes, los precios tienden a bajar; cuando los suministros escasean, los precios tienden a subir.

Leahy, Patrick > Leahy, Patrick (1940–) Demócrata por el estado de Vermont, Leahy fue elegido senador por primera vez en 1974 y luego presidente pro tempore del Senado en 2012.

legal tender > moneda de curso legal Cualquier moneda que un acreedor debe aceptar, por ley, como pago de una deuda.

legislative power > poder legislativo Poder para hacer una ley y redactar políticas públicas.

legitimacy > legitimidad Crencia que un gobierno tiene el derecho de crear políticas públicas.

Lenin, Vladimir > Lenin, Vladimir (1870–1924) Líder de la Revolución Bolchevique y arquitecto del Partido Comunista y de su control sobre la Unión Soviética. Para el momento de su muerte, en 1924, la Unión Soviética se había transformado en un estado con un régimen de partido único que controlaba las instituciones sociales, políticas y económicas del país.

libel > libelo Utilización falsa y maliciosa de la palabra impresa.

liberal constructionist > construccionista liberal Aquel que argumenta una amplia interpretación de las estipulaciones de la Constitución, en particular las que otorgan poderes al gobierno federal.

limited government > gobierno limitado Principio básico del sistema estadounidense de gobierno que establece que el gobierno tiene restricciones en cuanto a lo que puede hacer, y en el cual cada individuo tiene ciertos derechos que el gobierno no puede enajenar; ver constitutionalism/constitucionalismo, popular sovereignty/soberanía popular.

Lincoln, Abraham > Lincoln, Abraham (1809–1865) Fue elegido 16° presidente de los Estados Unidos en 1861, y asumió su cargo a los 52 años. Se le recuerda por haber promulgado la Proclamación de Emancipación, que decretaba que "toda persona en situación de esclavitud… debe ser, de ahora en adelante, y para siempre libre…". Fue asesinado en 1865.

line agency > agencia del ramo Oficina que desempeña las tareas para las que la organización existe.

line-item veto > veto por artículos poder que tienen muchos gobernadores para rechazar uno o más artículos de un proyecto de ley sin rechazar toda la medida; usado con más frecuencia en medidas relacionadas con el gasto; el Congreso de los Estados Unidos otorgó este poder al Presidente en 1996, pero esa ley fue eliminada por la Corte Suprema en 1998

literacy > alfabetismo Capacidad de una persona para leer o escribir.

Glosario

lobbying > cabildeo Actividades mediante las cuales los grupos ejercen presión sobre los legisladores, el proceso legislativo y sobre todos los aspectos de la elaboración de políticas públicas.

lobbyist > cabildero Persona que intenta persuadir a funcionarios a realizar cosas que ciertos grupos de interés quieren que se lleven a cabo.

Locke, John > Locke, John (1632–1704) Filósofo inglés que escribió sobre sus ideas acerca de los derechos naturales del hombre, el contrato social, la separación iglesia–Estado, la libertad religiosa y la libertad. Las teorías de Locke influyeron en la Guerra de Independencia estadounidense y en la Revolución Francesa.

London > Londres Capital de Inglaterra, fundada originalmente por los romanos alrededor del año 50 d. C. El periodo durante el que muchas de las colonias norteamericanas se establecieron es conocido como Stuart London. En esta época que va de 1603 a 1714, Londres creció enormemente, pero también sufrió dos grandes desastres: la Peste de 1665 y el Gran Incendio de 1666.

Long, Huey > Long, Huey (1893–1935) Fue gobernador de Luisiana y senador estadounidense. Creó la sociedad Share-the-Wealth para dar alojamiento e ingresos a familias estadounidenses como alternativa al programa Nuevo Trato del presidente Franklin D. Roosevelt. Long se postuló a la presidencia en 1935 pero fue asesinado antes de que se llevara a cabo la elección.

M

Madison, James > Madison, James (1751–1836) fungió como el 4° Presidente de los Estados Unidos, de 1809 a 1817. Fue un estudioso de la historia, el gobierno y las leyes, formó parte del Congreso Continental e hizo importantes contribuciones a la ratificación de la Constitución, coescribiendo el Federalist. Madison escribió varios de los ensayos de los Federalist Papers y fue un personaje fundamental en el movimiento para sustituir los Artículos de la Confederación. Sus Notes on the Debates in the Federal Convention nos han permitido una comprensión clara de lo que ocurrió en esos debates. Durante la convención, Madison fue el arquitecto principal del Plan de Virginia y tuvo una gran influencia en toda la sesión. De hecho, se le ha llamado el "Padre de la Constitución". En esa época abogaba por un gobierno nacional fuerte, pero más tarde vio los beneficios de los gobiernos estatales fuertes.

magistrate > magistrado Juez que atiende demandas civiles y delitos menores que surgen en un contexto urbano.

Magna Carta > Carta Magna Constitución que los barones impusieron al rey John de Inglaterra en 1215; estableció el principio de que el poder del monarca no era absoluto y garantizó derechos fundamentales como el de un juicio con jurado y procesos establecidos legales para la nobleza.

majority leader > líder mayoritario Portavoz del partido político que posee la mayor cantidad de escaños en cada cámara del Congreso.

majority opinion > opinión mayoritaria Llamada oficialmente Opinión de la Corte; anuncia la decisión de la Corte sobre el caso y describe el razonamiento sobre el que ésta se basa.

majority rule > gobierno por mayoría En una democracia, la mayoría de personas estarán en lo correcto con más frecuencia, y estarán en lo correcto con más frecuencia que una sola persona o un grupo pequeño.

mandate > mandato Las intrucciones u órdenes que un grupo de votantes da a sus funcionarios electos. El término mandato proviene del latín mandatum, lo que significa "una orden".

Mandela, Nelson > Mandela, Nelson (1918–2013) Primer presidente negro de Sudáfrica, de 1994 a 1999, elegido en las primeras elecciones democráticas de ese país. Previamente, fue prisionero político en Sudáfrica durante más de 20 años. También ayudó a terminar con la segregación racial en su país, y obtuvo el Premio Nobel de la Paz en 1993.

Mao Zedong > Mao Zedong (1893–1976) encabezó la Revolución comunista china y fungió como jefe de Estado en China de 1949 a 1959. Posteriormente, fue presidente del Partido Comunista Chino hasta su muerte. Mao es recordado por el Gran Salto Adelante, su intento desastroso de hacer a China avanzar rápidamente hacia una mejor producción agrícola e industrial, y por la Revolución Cultural que destruyó mucho de la herencia cultural china.

Marbury, William > Marbury, William (1762–1835) Fue el demandante en el caso Marbury contra Madison, en 1803, en el que la Corte Suprema estableció el principio de la revisión judicial. Fue designado por el presidente John Adams como juez de paz en el Distrito de Columbia pero, como resultado del fallo en Marbury contra Madison, Marbury perdió su nombramiento como juez.

Marshall, George C. > Marshall, George C. (1880–1959) fue general de ejército y jefe de Estado mayor durante la Segunda Guerra Mundial. Luego se convirtió en secretario de Estado y, posteriormente, en secretario de defensa en la administración de Franklin Roosevelt. Creó un programa de recuperación europea de posguerra, conocido con el nombre de Plan Marshall, por el que recibió el Premio Nobel de la Paz.

Marshall, John > Marshall, John (1755–1835) fue el cuarto presidente de la Corte Suprema de Justicia de los Estados Unidos. Tenía opiniones muy firmes sobre el poder de la Corte Suprema para interpretar la constitución, y sus fallos han tenido un gran impacto en la legislación estadounidense hasta el día de hoy.

Marshall, Thurgood > Marshall, Thurgood (1908–1993) Fue el primer afroamericano nombrado para la Corte Suprema (en 1967); fue juez asociado hasta 1991. En 1954, cuando trabajaba como abogado, llevó con éxito el caso de Brown contra la Junta de Educación (que declaró la segregación racial inconstitucional en las escuelas públicas estadounidenses) frente a la Corte Suprema del país.

Marx, Karl > Marx, Karl Filósofo alemán conocido principalmente por su obra en varios tomos sobre política económica, Das Kapital; Marx (1818–1883) es considerado el padre del socialismo y del comunismo modernos.

Mason, George > Mason, George Propietario de Gunston Hall, y uno de los terratenientes más ricos de Virginia, Mason (1725–1792) redactó la Declaración de Derechos de Virginia, que sirvió de modelo a Jefferson al escribir la Declaración de Independencia y fue la base para la Carta de Derechos de la Constitución de los Estados Unidos. Fue un orador influyente en la Convención Constitucional y se esforzó para que la Carta de Derechos y la 11ª Enmienda fueran incorporadas a la Constitución.

mass media > medios masivos de comunicación Aquellos medios de comunicación que llegan a grandes audiencias, sobre todo la radio, televisión, publicaciones impresas e Internet.

mayor-council government > gobierno de consejo-alcalde El más antiguo y más utilizado tipo de gobierno municipal que cuenta con un alcalde que se elige como presidente ejecutivo y un consejo como su cuerpo legislativo.

McCain, John > McCain, John (1936–) Es senador republicano por Arizona y copatrocinador de la Ley Bipartidista de Reforma de Campaña de 2002. Como candidato presidencial en 2008, perdió las elecciones frente a Barack Obama.

McKinley, William > McKinley, William (1843–1901), de Ohio, cumplió siete periodos en la Cámara de Representantes federal, donde defendió con fuerza los aranceles (impuestos a los productos de importación) como una forma de proteger a los negocios estadounidenses. Elegido Presidente en 1897, llevó al país a la victoria en la Guerra Hispano–Estadounidense, por lo que recibió los territorios de Guam, Puerto Rico y Filipinas. McKinley también apoyó la estadidad de Hawái. Fue asesinado durante su segundo mandato presidencial.

Medicaid > Medicaid Programa administrado por los estados para proporcionar seguro médico a las familias de bajos ingresos.

medium > medio Un medio de comunicación; algo que transmite información.

mercantilism > mercantilismo Teoría económica y política que destaca el dinero como la fuente primaria de riqueza para incrementar el poder absoluto de la monarquía y de la nación.

metropolitan area > área metropolitana La ciudad y el área que la rodea.

Milosevic, Slobodan > Milosevic, Slobodan (1941–2006) fue presidente de Serbia de 1989 a 1997. Nacionalista radical, instituyó políticas que llevaron a la ruptura de la Federación Socialista de Yugoslavia e instigó una serie de conflictos sangrientos con otros Estados balcánicos, como Kosovo, Bosnia, y Croacia.

ministers > ministros Miembro del gabinete, y más frecuentemente de la Cámara de los Comunes.

minority leader > líder minoritario Portavoz del partido político que posee la menor cantidad de escaños en cada cámara del Congreso.

Miranda rule > Ley Miranda Derechos constitucionales que la policía debe especificar a un sospechoso antes de que se le pueda interrogar.

misdemeanor > falta leve Delito menor que se castiga mediante una pequeña multa o un breve período de encarcelamiento.

Missouri Plan > Plan Missouri Enfoque de la elección de jueces que combina la elección y el nombramiento; un comité de nominaciones ofrece una lista de candidatos de la que el gobernador puede elegir.

monetary policy > política monetaria Proceso mediante el cual el gobierno toma decisiones que afectan a la economía del país mediante cambios en la oferta monetaria y la disponibilidad de crédito.

monopoly > monopolio Empresa que es la única fuente de un producto o servicio.

Monroe, James > Monroe, James (1758–1831) Fue presidente de los Estados Unidos de 1817 a 1825. Durante su mandato, Monroe minimizó las tensiones partidistas y trajo la "Era de los buenos sentimientos". Monroe tomó Florida de manos de España en 1821 y declaró que las acciones europeas para colonizar cualquier parte de las Américas implicarían la intervención estadounidense. Años después, estas palabras formaron la base de la Doctrina Monroe, posiblemente la contribución principal de este presidente.

Montesquieu, Charles de > Montesquieu, Charles de (1689–1755) Fue un filósofo político francés de la Ilustración cuya obra principal, *El espíritu de las leyes,* fue un aporte esencial para la teoría política. Su postulado de la separación de poderes tuvo gran impacto en los redactores de la Constitución de los Estados Unidos.

municipality > municipalidad Unidad política urbana dentro de una población que por lo general existe como una entidad gubernamental independiente.

N

national popular vote plan > plan para el voto nacional popular Propuesta para elegir al Presidente de la Nación mediante la cual las leyes electorales de cada Estado decretan que los votos electorales sean otorgados al ganador del voto popular nacional y que de esta manera se llegue a un acuerdo interestatal donde se elija al presidente por voto popular.

NATO > OTAN (Organización del Tratado del Atlántico Norte) Alianza formada para proteger la libertad y seguridad de sus miembros a través de medidas políticas y militares.

naturalization > naturalización Proceso legal mediante el cual los ciudadanos de un país se convierten en ciudadanos de otro.

Necessary and Proper Clause > Cláusula de Necesidad y Conveniencia Cláusula constitucional que otorga al Congreso el poder de expedir leyes "necesarias y pertinentes" para el ejercicio de sus poderes.

New Jersey Plan > Plan Nueva Jersey Plan presentado en la Convención Constitucional como una alternativa al Plan de Virginia; proponía una legislatura unicameral en la que cada estado estuviera representado de forma equitativa.

Nixon, Richard > Nixon, Richard (1913–1994) Richard Nixon era abogado, antes de entrar en la política como diputado y senador por California. Fue vicepresidente del presidente Eisenhower antes de ser elegido como 37° Presidente en 1968. Ocupó el cargo de 1969 a 1974. Como presidente, terminó el reclutamiento militar obligatorio e instituyó un amplio programa ambiental. Frente al juicio político debido a su participación en el escándalo de Watergate, Nixon renunció en agosto de 1974.

nomination > nominación Proceso de selección de candidatos en una democracia.

nonpartisan elections > elección no partidista Elección en la que los candidatos no están identificados por afiliaciones partidarias.

North American Free Trade Agreement (NAFTA) > NAFTA (Tratado de Libre Comercio de América del Norte) Acuerdo que elimina las restricciones comerciales entre los Estados Unidos, Canadá y México, con lo cual se incrementa el comercio transfronterizo.

O

Obama, Barack > Obama, Barack (1961–) Fue el 44° presidente de los Estados Unidos, de 2009 a 2016. Obama, primer presidente afroamericano, recibió el premio Nobel de la Paz.

O'Connor, Sandra Day > O'Connor, Sandra Day (1930–) Primera mujer nombrada para la Corte Suprema. Nominada por el presidente Reagan en 1981, fue jueza asociada de la Corte Suprema hasta su retiro en 2006. Conocida por sus opiniones cuidadosamente documentadas, era considerada como una conservadora moderada.

off-year elections > elección intermedia Elección del Congreso que ocurre entre las elecciones presidenciales.

oligarchy > oligarquía Forma de gobierno en la que el poder de gobernar lo ejerce una elite pequeña y por lo general autonombrada.

omnibus measure > *omnibus measure* Proyecto de ley que contiene diversos asuntos y temas.

open market operations > operaciones de mercado abierto Proceso por el cual la Reserva Federal compra y vende valores del Estado a los bancos del país para controlar la cantidad de dinero en circulación.

open primary > elección primaria abierta Elección partidista de nominación en la que cualquier votante calificado puede tomar parte.

opinion leaders > líderes de opinión Personas que por alguna razón tienen una poderosa influencia en los puntos de vista de otras.

ordinance > ordenanza ley aprobada por un gobierno local

ordinance power > poder de decreto Poder del Presidente de emitir órdenes ejecutivas; se fundamenta en la Constitución y en los actos del Congreso.

original jurisdiction > jurisdicción original Poder de una corte de atender un caso antes que otra corte.

oversight function > función de vigilancia Revisión de las políticas y los programas de la rama ejecutiva por parte de los comités legislativos.

P

Panama Canal > Canal de Panamá Canal artificial que pasa a través del Istmo de Panamá, en Centroamérica, y conecta los océanos Atlántico y Pacífico.

panic > pánico Del latín panicus, que significa "aterrorizado"; una alarma repentina generalizada en relación con la economía, que a menudo resulta en una depresión.

pardon > perdón exoneración que lleva a cabo el Presidente o el gobernador del castigo o de las consecuencias legales de un crimen

parliamentary government > gobierno parlamentario Forma de gobierno en la que el poder ejecutivo está conformado por el primer ministro o por el jefe del gobierno, y el gabinete de dicho funcionario. Este poder es parte de la legislatura.

parliamentary system > sistema parlamentario Forma de gobierno en la que el poder ejecutivo está constituido por el primer ministro, o premier, y su gabinete.

parochial > parroquial Relacionado con la iglesia, como las escuelas parroquiales.

parole > liberación bajo palabra Libertad condicional de un prisionero poco antes de que termine el lapso de su sentencia original.

partisans > partidista Legislador que le debe fidelidad, en primer lugar, a su partido político, por lo que vota de acuerdo con la línea del partido.

partisanship > partidarismo Acción gubernamental basada en la vigorosa fidelidad a un partido político.

party caucus > junta de dirigentes de partido Reunión cerrada de los miembros de la Cámara de Representantes o del Senado; también se conoce como Conferencia de partido.

party government > gobierno de partido La dirección y el control de los procesos de gobierno por el partido que cuenta con la mayoría.

party identification > identificación con el partido Lealtad de la gente hacia un partido político.

passport > pasaporte Documento legal emitido por el estado que identifica a una persona como ciudadano de un país y le permite viajar al exterior y regresar.

patent > patente Licencia expedida a un inventor para garantizar el derecho exclusivo de manufactura, uso o venta de su invento, durante un tiempo limitado.

patricians > patricio Aristócrata propietario de tierras en la antigua Roma.

Patrick, Luther > Patrick, Luther (1894–1957) Nació cerca de Decatur, Alabama, se graduó de la Universidad de Purdue y obtuvo su título en Derecho de la Universidad de Alabama. Después de ocupar diversos cargos judiciales, incluido el de fiscal general de Alabama, sirvió como diputado federal por Alabama de 1937 a 1943 y de 1945 a 1947.

patronage > patrocinio Práctica de dar trabajo a los simpatizantes y amigos.

payroll tax > impuesto sobre la nómina Gravamen tasado a casi todos los empleadores y sus empleados, así como a las personas autoempleadas; cantidad debida por los empleados que se les descuenta de su salario.

Pearl Harbor > Pearl Harbor Base naval estadounidense que se encuentra en la isla de Oahu, en Hawái.

peer group > grupo de camaradas Gente con la que uno se asocia regularmente y que incluye a socios, amigos, compañeros de clase, vecinos y compañeros de trabajo.

Pelosi, Nancy > Pelosi, Nancy (1940–) Se graduó del Trinity College en Washington, D.C. Mientras era representante por California a principios de 1987, Pelosi se convirtió en la primera mujer en dirigir la banca demócrata en la Cámara de Representantes, la primera mujer presidenta de la Cámara y fue la líder minoritaria de la Cámara en la 113era legislatura.

Penn, William > Penn, William Líder cuáquero inglés que defendía la libertad de culto. Penn (1644–1718) llegó a América del Norte en 1682 y fundó la colonia de Pensilvania como un refugio para los cuáqueros y otras minorías religiosas.

perjury > perjurio Mentir bajo juramento.

Perot, Ross > Perot, Ross (1930–) Se anunció a sí mismo como candidato presidencial por un tercer partido, el Partido de la Reforma, que fundó en 1995. Se autoproclamó candidato presidencial y usó la fortuna que adquirió con la creación de Electronic Data Systems para financiar su campaña. Perdió las elecciones de 1992 y de 1996.

persona non grata > *persona non grata* Una persona que no es bienvenida; se utiliza para describir a los funcionarios diplomáticos destituidos.

petit jury > jurado ordinario Este jurado escucha la evidencia en un caso, decide los hechos en disputa, y muy de vez en cuando interpreta y aplica la ley; también conocido como jurado de juicio.

petition > petición Derecho de un ciudadano a presentar su opinión ante funcionarios públicos, por medio de escritos, cartas, cabildeo y marchas.

Petition of Right > Solicitud de Derecho Documento preparado por el Parlamento y firmado por el rey Charles I de Inglaterra en 1628; cuestionó la idea del derecho divino de los reyes y declaró que incluso el monarca está sujeto a las leyes de la tierra.

Philadelphia > Filadelfia La ciudad más grande en el estado de Pensilvania.

picketing > vigilancia Manifestación de los trabajadores en el sitio donde están en huelga.

pigeonholed > dar carpetazo Expresión que describe cómo proyectos de ley que se presentan ante el Congreso se olvidan, se ponen a un lado o nunca se llevan a cabo.

plaintiff > demandante En el derecho civil, la parte que entabla un juicio u otra acción legal contra otra en una corte.

platform > plataforma Un enunciado formal por parte de un partido político respecto a sus principios básicos, opiniones sobre cuestiones políticas importantes y objetivos.

plebeians > plebeyos Personas que pertenecían a la plebe en la República Romana.

plurality > mayoría En una elección, el número de votos que el candidato que va a la punta tiene de ventaja sobre su competidor más cercano.

pocket veto > veto indirecto Tipo de veto que el Presidente puede utilizar después de que una legislatura se suspende; se aplica cuando un Presidente no firma formalmente o rechaza una propuesta de ley, dentro del tiempo comprendido para eso.

police power > facultad policial Autoridad de cada Estado para proteger y promover la salud pública, la seguridad, la moral y el bienestar general de su pueblo.

political action committees (PACs) > comité de acción política Extensión política de grupos de interés especial, los cuales tienen un gran interés en la política pública.

political efficacy > eficacia política La influencia o eficacia individual en la política.

political party > partido político Grupo de personas que buscan controlar el gobierno mediante el triunfo en las elecciones y ejerciendo puestos públicos.

political socialization > socialización política Proceso mediante el que la gente obtiene sus actitudes y opiniones políticas.

political spectrum > espectro político Gama de perspectivas políticas.

politicos > políticos Legisladores que intentan equilibrar las responsabilidades de un agente, partidario político y delegado.

poll books > padrón electoral Lista de todos los votantes registrados en cada distrito.

poll tax > impuesto sobre el padrón electoral Gravamen especial, exigido por algunos estados como una condición para votar; fue derogado por la 24a Enmienda.

polling place > casilla electoral Lugar donde los votantes que viven en cierto distrito acuden a votar.

Pope, Alexander > Pope, Alexander (1688–1744) Fue un poeta famoso, escritor de sátira y traductor, que tuvo éxito económico. Nació en Londres, creció en una familia católica y se le conoce sobre todo por emplear el pareado heroico.

popular sovereignty > soberanía popular Principio básico del sistema estadounidense de gobierno que establece que el pueblo es la fuente de todos los poderes gubernamentales, y que el gobierno sólo puede existir con el consentimiento de los gobernados.

Powell, Colin > Powell, Colin (1937–) es un general de cuatro estrellas, que se desempeñó como Presidente del Estado Mayor Conjunto de 1989 a 1993. En 2001, fungió como secretario de Estado de George W. Bush y mantuvo el cargo hasta 2005. Powell fue el primer afroestadounidense en ocupar estos cargos dentro del gabinete.

precedent > precedente Decisión judicial que se toma como un ejemplo a seguir en el futuro para casos similares.

precinct > circunscripción Unidad mínima de la administración electoral; distrito de votación.

preclearance > preautorización Una de las disposiciones de la Ley de Derechos Electorales de 1965, de acuerdo con la cual ninguna ley electoral nueva ni cambio alguno a las vigentes puede entrar en vigor sin la previa aprobación del Departamento de Justicia.

preliminary hearing > audiencia preliminar El primer paso del procesamiento de un crimen mayor, en el que el juez decide si la evidencia basta para que la persona comparezca ante el gran jurado o ante el fiscal para ser sujeto de una acción.

presentment > declaración del jurado Una acusación formal hecha por el jurado de acusación en vez del fiscal.

president of the Senate > presidente del Senado Funcionario que preside un Senado; en el Congreso es el vicepresidente de los Estados Unidos; en la legislatura estatal, cualquier vicegobernador o un senador.

president pro tempore > presidente *pro tempore* Miembro del Senado de los Estados Unidos, o de la cámara superior de la legislatura estatal, elegido para ser presidente, en caso de ausencia del presidente del Senado.

Presidential Election Campaign Fund > Fondo para la campaña electoral presidencial Dinero donado por los contribuyentes al enviar declaración federal de ingresos. Administrado por la Comisión electoral federal (FEC, por su sigla en inglés), y empleado para subsidiar las campañas previas a las convenciones, las convenciones nacionales y las campañas presidenciales.

presidential government > gobierno presidencial Forma de gobierno en la que los poderes ejecutivo y legislativo del gobierno están separados, son independientes y están en la misma jerarquía.

presidential primary > elección presidencial primaria Elección en la que los votantes de un partido: eligen a varios o a todos los delegados de la organización partidista estatal para la convención nacional de su partido, y/o expresan una preferencia por alguno de los distintos contendientes para la nominación presidencial de su partido.

presidential succession > sucesión presidencial Plan mediante el cual se resuelve la vacante presidencial.

Presidential Succession Act of 1947 > Ley para la Sucesión Presidencial de 1947 Ley que especifica el orden para la sucesión presidencial, después del Vicepresidente.

preventive detention > arresto preventivo Ley que permite a los jueces federales ordenar que un acusado de felonía sea arrestado, sin derecho a fianza, cuando existen buenas razones para creer que cometerá otro crimen grave antes del juicio.

prior restraint > censura previa Concepto de acuerdo con el cual el gobierno no puede reprimir las ideas antes de que se expresen.

privatization > privatización Regresar las empresas nacionales a la iniciativa privada.

Privileges and Immunities Clause > Cláusula de Privilegios e Inmunidades Estipulación constitucional en que se conceden ciertos "privilegios e inmunidades" a los ciudadanos, sin importar su estado de residencia.

probable cause > causa probable Fundamentos razonables, sospecha razonable de un crimen.

procedural due process > procesos legales establecidos El gobierno debe emplear procedimientos y métodos justos.

process of incorporation > proceso de incorporación Proceso de integrar, o incluir, la mayor parte de las garantías de la Carta de Derechos en la Cláusula del Debido Proceso establecido de la 14ª Enmienda.

progressive tax > impuesto progresivo Tipo de impuesto que toma un porcentaje mayor de los grupos con más ingresos que de los grupos con menos ingresos

project grants > subvención de proyecto Tipo de subvención de fondos públicos; proporcionada para proyectos específicos de los estados, las localidades y las oficinas privadas que la solicitan.

property tax > impuesto a la propiedad Gravamen sobre los bienes raíces y la propiedad personal.

proportional plan > plan proporcional Propuesta para seleccionar electores presidenciales, mediante la cual cada candidato recibiría la misma cantidad de votos electorales de un estado que recibió durante la votación popular del estado.

proportional representation > regla de la representación proporcional Procedimiento aplicado en las elecciones primarias del Partido Demócrata, en el cual cualquier candidato que gane al menos el 15% de los votos emitidos en una elección primaria, obtiene el número de delegados, para la convención estatal demócrata, que le corresponda en esa proporción de las primarias.

proprietary > propiedad Organizado por un propietario (una persona a quien el rey le ha otorgado un terreno).

prorogue > prórroga Aplazamiento, por ejemplo, de una sesión legislativa.

protectionism > proteccionismo Práctica en la que gobiernos nacionales tratan de controlar las importaciones para proteger a sus industrias de la competencia extranjera.

public affairs > asuntos públicos Aquellos acontecimientos y asuntos que importan al público en general, por ejemplo: la política, los temas públicos y la determinación de las políticas públicas.

public agenda > agenda pública Asuntos públicos sobre los cuales está enfocada la atención de las personas.

public debt > deuda pública Todo el dinero que ha pedido prestado el gobierno a lo largo de los años y que todavía no paga, además del interés acumulado sobre ese capital; también se conoce como deuda nacional o deuda federal.

public opinion > opinión pública Colección compleja de opiniones de diversas personas; la suma de todos sus puntos de vista.

public opinion polls > encuestas de opinión pública Dispositivos que intentan recolectar información interrogando a las personas. El término en inglés *poll* proviene de la palabra en alemán antiguo *polle*, que significa "la coronilla", la porción visible de la cabeza que se puede contar en una multitud.

public policies > políticas públicas Todo lo que un gobierno decide llevar a cabo.

public policy > política pública Todas las metas que un gobierno se fija, en las diversas áreas de asuntos humanos en las que éste se interesa.

pundit > experto Especialista en un asunto en particular o campo del conocimiento a quien frecuentemente se pide que dé su opinión de manera pública.

purge > purga Proceso de revisión de las listas de los votantes registrados y de la eliminación de los nombres que ya no son elegibles para votar; una depuración; proceso de purificación gubernamental en el que se elimina a los rivales.

purging > purga Proceso de revisión de las listas de votantes registrados para retirar los nombres de quienes ya no pueden ejercer su derecho al voto. Una purificación.

Putin, Vladimir > Putin, Vladimir (1952–) Fue el primer presidente de la Federación Rusa en 1999, al tomar el poder después de la renuncia de Boris Yeltsin a finales de ese año. Ganó las elecciones de 2000, 2004 y 2012. También fue primer ministro de 2008 a 2012. Bajo su mando, el poder presidencial se ha acrecentado y la economía rusa se ha fortalecido. Al mismo tiempo, algunos argumentan que no es un verdadero líder democrático.

Q

quorum > quórum Mínimo número de miembros que debe estar presente para que un cuerpo legislativo funcione; mayoría.

quota > cuota Porcentaje de un grupo con el que es necesario contar para cumplir un requisito de acción afirmativa; regla que requiere que determinado número de trabajos o ascensos se den a miembros de ciertos grupos.

quota sample > muestra de cuota Muestra deliberadamente recopilada para reflejar ciertas características importantes de una determinada población.

R

random sample > muestra aleatoria Determinado número de personas seleccionadas al azar.

ratification > ratificación Aprobación formal, consentimiento definitivo de la eficacia de una constitución, de una enmienda constitucional o de un tratado.

rational basis test > prueba de razonamiento básico Examen menos intenso que el examen judicial riguroso que implementa la Corte Suprema para tomar decisiones en casos de protección equitativa; el examen pregunta si hay una relación razonable entre la clasificación en cuestión y el logro de algún propósito gubernamental.

Reagan, Ronald > Reagan, Ronald (1911–2004) fue un actor que se convirtió en político: primero como gobernador de California y después como Presidente, de 1981 a 1989. En la contienda presidencial, derrotó de manera aplastante a Jummy Carter. Durante su gestión, Reagan actualizó las leyes del impuesto sobre la renta y negoció un tratado de eliminación de misiles con la Unión Soviética.

reapportion > reasignación Redistribución, por ejemplo, de los escaños en un cuerpo legislativo.

recall > revocatorio procedimiento para remover de su cargo a un funcionario elegido, que se lleva a cabo mediante una petición y una elección especial

recess > receso Período en que ambas cámaras del Congreso suspenden actividades temporalmente.

recession > recesión Pérdida o reducción del crecimiento económico.

recognition > reconocimiento El poder exclusivo de un Presidente para reconocer legalmente estados extranjeros y consecuentemente establecer relaciones diplomáticas con ellos.

record > registro Transcripción de los procesos llevados a cabo en una corte tribunal.

redress > resarcir Satisfacer una queja, por lo general mediante un pago.

referendum > referéndum procedimiento por el que los votantes pueden cambiar un estatuto que la legislatura haya aprobado o por el que la legislatura puede someter una medida a la aprobación o rechazo de los votantes

reformers > reformistas Aquellos cuyas acciones están encaminadas a cambiar o reformar gradualmente el gobierno.

refugee > refugiado Persona que abandona su hogar para buscar protección contra la guerra, la persecución o algún otro peligro.

regional security alliances > alianzas regionales de seguridad Tratados mediante los cuales los Estados Unidos y otros países han acordado actuar colectivamente para enfrentar una agresión en una determinada parte del mundo.

registration > registro Procedimiento de identificación del votante para evitar votaciones fraudulentas.

regressive tax > impuesto regresivo Gravamen con una tasa invariable, sin considerar el nivel de ingreso de los contribuyentes o su capacidad para pagarlo.

representative government > gobierno representativo Sistema de gobierno en el que las políticas públicas están elaboradas por funcionarios elegidos por los votantes y que rinden cuentas en elecciones periódicas; ver democracy/ democracia.

reprieve > suspensión Aplazamiento oficial de la ejecución de una sentencia.

reservations > reservación Terrenos públicos que un gobierno reserva para el uso de las tribus nativas estadounidenses.

reserve requirement > reserva obligatoria Cantidad de dinero que la Reserva Federal determina que los bancos deben mantener en reserva con uno de los Bancos de la Reserva Federal.

reserved powers > poderes reservados Aquellos poderes que la Constitución no otorga al gobierno nacional y no niega a los estados.

resolution > resolución Medida relativa al funcionamiento de cualquier Cámara, o una opinión sobre un asunto; no tiene la fuerza de una ley y no requiere la firma del Presidente.

reverse discrimination > discriminación inversa Segregación en contra del grupo mayoritario.

Rice, Condoleezza > Rice, Condoleezza (1954–) fue la asesora en política exterior de la campaña presidencial de George W. Bush. Cuando Bush fue elegido, se convirtió en la primera mujer en dirigir el Consejo de Seguridad Nacional. En 2005, Rice fue la primera mujer afroestadounidense en fungir como secretaria de Estado. Más tarde, Rice regresó a su puesto como profesora en la Universidad de Stanford y es autora de numerosos libros.

rider > cláusula adicional Provisión, poco probable de ser aprobada por méritos propios, que se agrega a un proyecto de ley importante de cuya aprobación se tiene la seguridad, por tanto, se dice que dicha cláusula "cabalga" por todo ese proceso legislativo.

right of association > derecho de asociación Derecho de asociarse con otros para promover causas políticas, sociales, económicas y de otra índole.

right of legation > derecho de legación Derecho a enviar y recibir representantes diplomáticos.

Roberts, John > Roberts, John (1955–) obtuvo su posgrado en Derecho de la Escuela de Leyes de Harvard en 1979. Más tarde trabajó como asistente legal en la Corte Suprema, y Consejero legal del presidente Ronald Reagan y en la Oficina del Consejero de la Casa Blanca de 1982 a 1986. Fue propuesto para la Corte suprema por el presidente George W. Bush y confirmado en el cargo en 2005.

Romney, Mitt > Romney, Mitt (n. 1947) senador republicano de Utah. Como candidato a la presidencia en 2012, fue el primer mormón en ser nominado por uno de los principales partidos para optar por el cargo. Romney perdió ante el titular del cargo, Barack Obama.

Roosevelt, Franklin D. > Roosevelt, Franklin D. (1882–1945) El 32° Presidente de los Estados Unidos, de 1933 a 1945. Ha sido el único presidente en ser elegido para este cargo cuatro veces. Él condujo al país durante la Gran Depresión y la Segunda Guerra Mundial y desarrolló el sistema de programas gubernamentales y reformas que se conoce en conjunto como el Nuevo Trato.

Roosevelt, Theodore > Roosevelt, Theodore (1858–1919) Fue el 26° presidente de los Estados Unidos; estuvo en funciones de 1901 a 1909. Apodado Teddy, era cazador, soldado, naturalista y recibió el premio Nobel de la Paz. También logró asegurar la ruta del Canal de Panamá y comenzó su construcción.

Roper, Elmo > Roper, Elmo (1900–1971) desarrolló la primera encuesta científica que hacía predicciones políticas con muestras pequeñas. Mientras trabajaba para la revista *Fortune*, Roper predijo con precisión que Franklin Roosevelt ganaría la presidencia en 1936, 1940 y 1944; lo que le dio una fama considerable. En sus últimos años, Roper siguió dentro de la rama de los sondeos y también escribió para periódicos y para la revista *Saturday Review*.

Rousseau, Jean Jacques > Rousseau, Jean Jacques Filósofo, escritor y teórico político nacido en Suiza. Los tratados y novelas de Rousseau (1712–1778) inspiraron a los líderes de la Revolución Francesa. En su famosa obra, *El contrato social*, expone su idea de que los humanos son esencialmente libres, pero el progreso de la civilización ha reemplazado esa libertad con la servidumbre y la dependencia hacia otros. Para superar esto, la gente debe hacer uso de su libre albedrío y reconstruirse políticamente a sí mismos junto con los ideales democráticos.

rule of law > gobierno de la ley El concepto en que el gobierno y sus oficiales estan sujetos a la ley.

runoff primary > elección primaria complementaria Elección primaria en la que los dos candidatos con más votos en la elección primaria directa se enfrentan; el ganador de esa votación se convierte en el nominado.

S

sales tax > impuesto a las ventas Gravamen sobre las ventas de distintos bienes, el cual paga el comprador.

sample > muestra Una porción representativa del público.

Scalia, Antonin > Scalia, Antonin Nacido en Nueva Jersey, Antonin Scalia (1936–2016) fue nominado para la Corte Suprema por el presidente Ronald Reagan, en 1986. Antes de su nombramiento, Scalia ocupó una serie de cargos en el gobierno federal, incluyendo juez de la Corte de Apelaciones de los Estados Unidos para el Circuito del Distrito de Columbia. Murió siendo aún juez de la Corte Suprema.

search warrant > orden de allanamiento Autorización judicial para registrar algo.

secretary > secretario Funcionario a cargo de un departamento de gobierno.

Security Council > Consejo de Seguridad Panel de quince miembros de la ONU que tiene la máxima responsabilidad para la conservación de la paz internacional.

sedition > sedición Delito que consiste en intentar derrocar al gobierno mediante la fuerza, o de interrumpir las actividades legales por medio de actos violentos.

seditious speech > discurso sedicioso La convocatoria o el apoyo a un intento de derrocar al gobierno mediante la fuerza, o a la interrupción de actividades legales por medio de la violencia.

segregation > segregación Separación de un grupo respecto a otro.

select committee > comité selecto Comité legislativo creado por un tiempo limitado y para algún propósito específico; también se conoce como comité especial.

Selma, Alabama > Selma, Alabama Ciudad sureña símbolo de la reticencia del Sur frente al Movimiento de los Derechos Civiles de principios de la década de 1960. La ciudad fue escenario de una larga marcha por el derecho al voto, encabeza por varios líderes afroestadunidenses, incluido el reverendo Martin Luther King, Jr.

senatorial courtesy > cortesía senatorial Costumbre de que el Senado no aprobará una nominación presidencial, si esa designación no es aprobada por el senador del partido mayoritario de ese estado, en donde la persona designada habría de servir.

seniority rule > regla de antigüedad Regla no escrita de ambas Cámaras del Congreso, de acuerdo con la cual, los puestos más altos de cada una de ellas los ocuparán aquellos miembros que tengan un historial de servicio más antiguo; se aplica de forma más estricta a las presidencias de los comités.

separate-but-equal doctrine > doctrina de iguales pero separados Doctrina establecida por la corte en el caso Plessy contra Ferguson, en el cual se determinó que la segregación puede mantenerse siempre y cuando cada raza se trate de manera igualitaria; base constitucional para leyes que segregan a un grupo respecto a otro, con base en la raza.

separation of powers > separación de poderes Principio básico del sistema de gobierno estadounidense, según el cual los poderes ejecutivo, legislativo y judicial constituyen las tres ramas del gobierno independientes e iguales.

session > sesión Período regular durante el cual se reúne el Congreso para atender asuntos oficiales.

shadow cabinet > gabinete alterno Miembros de los partidos de oposición que vigilan, o supervisan, a un miembro particular del gabinete, y que estarían listos para ejercer el gobierno.

Shays, Daniel > Shays, Daniel Joven granjero con un don para los ejercicios paramilitares, Shays (1747–1825) se convirtió en capitán en el 5° Regimiento de Massachusetts del Ejército Continental en 1777 y se hizo una reputación de oficial valiente y capaz. Después de la guerra, regresó a la agricultura. Como muchos, tuvo problemas de deudas por la fuerte recesión de posguerra. Shays surgió como líder local en el movimiento de protesta contra los altos impuestos y la falta condonación de deudas.

Shays' Rebellion > Rebelión de Shays Una serie de enfrentamientos entre granjeros deudores y autoridades del gobierno estatal en el oeste de Massachusetts entre 1786 y 1787.

Sherman, Roger > Sherman, Roger (1721–1793) fue un abogado y juez de Connecticut, redactor de la Constitución de los Estados Unidos y legislador. Fue uno de los primeros defensores de la independencia estadounidense y asistió al Primer y Segundo Congresos Continentales. También ayudó a redactar el borrador de los Artículos de la Confederación. En la Convención Constitucional, propuso lo que se conocería como el Acuerdo de Connecticut, que creaba una Cámara de representantes conformada según la población y un Senado con el mismo número de representantes para cada estado.

shield laws > ley escudo Ley que ofrece a los periodistas cierta protección contra la revelación de sus fuentes o la publicación de otra información confidencial durante los procedimientos legales.

single-issue parties > partidos de un único asunto Partidos que se concentran en un solo aspecto de la política pública.

single-member district > distrito de un solo miembro Distrito electoral en donde los votantes eligen, en la papeleta electoral, una sola persona para cada cargo.

slander > calumnia Utilización falsa y maliciosa del discurso hablado.

Smith, Adam > Smith, Adam (1723–1790) fue un filósofo escocés a quién se atribuye el avance de la era del libre comercio en el siglo XIX. Su libro *La riqueza de las naciones* influyó a muchos líderes intelectuales y políticos de su época, y sus ideas siguen gozando de credibilidad entre los economistas modernos.

socialism > socialismo Filosofía basada en la idea de que los beneficios de la actividad económica deben distribuirse de manera equitativa entre toda la sociedad.

soft money > fondos no fiscalizados Dinero otorgado a organizaciones partidistas estatales y locales, en cantidades ilimitadas, para actividades relacionadas con las campañas electorales.

Sotomayor, Sonia > Sotomayor, Sonia (1954–) Tercera mujer nombrada para la Corte Suprema. El presidente Obama la nominó como jueza asociada de la Corte Suprema en 2009, y continúa en el cargo.

sound bite > informe sucinto Informaciones breves y concisas que pueden despacharse en 30 ó 45 segundos.

sovereign > soberano Estado que posee poder supremo y absoluto dentro de su propio territorio y puede decidir sus políticas internas y hacia el exterior; no estar subordinado ni ser responsable ante ninguna otra autoridad.

sovereignty > soberanía Autoridad suprema para tomar decisiones y mantener el orden en un estado.

Speaker of the House > Vocero de la Cámara Funcionario que preside la Cámara de Representantes y que es electo por el partido mayoritario en la Cámara, al cual pertenece.

special district > distrito especial Unidad independiente creada para llevar a cabo una o más funciones gubernamentales relacionadas a nivel local.

special session > sesión especial Sesión extraordinaria de un cuerpo legislativo, convocada para tratar una situación de emergencia.

splinter parties > partidos de escisión Partidos formados por la fractura de uno de los principales partidos; la mayor parte de los partidos pequeños importantes en el ámbito político estadounidense son partidos de escisión.

split-ticket voting > voto diferenciado Votar, en la misma elección, por candidatos de distintos partidos para puestos diferentes.

spoils system > sistema de prebendas Práctica de ofrecer cargos y otros favores gubernamentales a los simpatizantes y amigos políticos.

staff agency > oficina de apoyo Tipo de agencia cuya función es dar respaldo al Presidente y a otros administradores, ofreciendo consejos y otro tipo de asistencia en la administración de la organización.

Stalin, Josef > Stalin, José (1878–1953) emergió de la pobreza para llegar a ser el líder totalitario de la Unión Soviética de 1929 a 1953. Durante su régimen, caracterizado por su brutalidad, la antigua sociedad campesina se transformó en un líder industrial y en una potencia militar. Entre las muchas reformas radicales de Stalin se cuenta la colectivización de la agricultura.

standing committee > comisión permanente Comité permanente de un cuerpo legislativo al que se presentan las propuestas de ley sobre una materia específica; ver comité selecto.

state > estado Conjunto de personas que viven en un territorio definido y que tienen un gobierno con el poder de legislar y de hacer cumplir la ley, sin tener el consentimiento de una autoridad superior.

State budget > presupuesto estatal plan financiero para el uso de dinero, personal y propiedad

statutory law > ley estatuida ley aprobada por la legislatura de un estado, y en algunos estados, por los electores

straight-ticket voting > votación de partido único Práctica de votar en una elección por los candidatos de un solo partido.

straw vote > encuesta pre-electoral Encuesta que pretende conocer la opinión de la gente haciendo simplemente la misma pregunta a una gran cantidad de personas.

strict constructionist > construccionista estricto Persona que defiende una interpretación estrecha de las estipulaciones de la Constitución, en particular las referentes al otorgamiento de poderes al gobierno federal.

strict scrutiny test > examen judicial riguroso Estándar más alto que la prueba de fundamento razonable que una ley debe honrar en casos de protección equitativa; el Estado o el gobierno federal debe demostrar que esta ley no se relaciona con un interés ordinario del gobierno, sino con uno imperioso e inaplazable.

strong-mayor government > gobierno de alcalde fuerte tipo de gobierno de ciudad en el que el alcalde es el director administrativo de la ciudad y ejerce tres poderes críticos: el presupuesto, el veto y el poder de nombramiento

subcommittee > subcomité División de un comité existente que se forma para atender asuntos específicos.

subpoena > citación Orden para que se presente una persona o para que se presenten documentos u otros materiales solicitados.

subsidy > subsidio Una subvención en dinero, por lo general otorgada por un gobierno.

substantive due process > proceso legal duradero Concepto de acuerdo con el cual el gobierno debe crear políticas y leyes justas.

successor > sucesor Persona que hereda un título o un cargo.

suffrage > sufragio El derecho de votar.

Super PAC > Súper PAC (comités de acción política) Comités de acción política independientes, sin afiliación a partido político alguno, a los que se permite recaudar y gastar cantidades ilimitadas. Están obligados a dar a conocer a sus donadores y no pueden trabajar directamente con los comités de acción política independiente de la campaña de ningún candidato.

supply-side economics > economía de oferta Idea que supone que la reducción de impuestos aumenta el dinero de entidades privadas y estimula la economía.

Supremacy Clause > Cláusula de Supremacía Cláusula de la Constitución de los Estados Unidos que estipula que la Constitución, la ley federal y los tratados de los Estados Unidos son la "ley suprema del país".

surplus > superávit Cuando hay más ingresos que gastos.

Suu Kyi, Aung San > Suu Kyi, Aung San (1945–) Política y líder opositora de Myanmar (Birmania), que obtuvo el Premio Nobel de la Paz en 1991. Estuvo bajo arresto domiciliario durante años por oponerse al régimen militar; posteriormente fue liberada y electa para un cargo público.

swing voters > votantes indecisos Miembros del electorado que no han tomado una decisión al comienzo de una campaña y están dispuestos a inclinarse hacia cualquiera de los candidatos.

symbolic speech > discurso simbólico Expresión mediante la conducta; comunicación de ideas a través de expresiones faciales, lenguaje corporal o mediante el uso de un letrero o portando una banda en el brazo.

T

Taft, William Howard > Taft, William Howard (1857–1930) El 27° Presidente de los Estados Unidos, de 1909 a 1913. Luego se convertiría en el décimo presidente de la Corte Suprema federal, por lo que es la única persona que ha ocupado ambos cargos.

Taney, Roger B. > Taney, Roger B. (1777–1864) fungió como fiscal general federal y fue nombrado presidente de la Corte Suprema en 1836. Su opinión mayoritaria en el juicio Dred Scott contra Sandford de 1857, en la que declaró que los afroestadounidenses no podían ser considerados ciudadanos estadounidenses, causó mucha polémica en la víspera de la Guerra Civil.

tariff > arancel Impuesto que se aplica a las importaciones.

tax > impuesto Cargo gravado por el gobierno a las personas o propiedades, con el objeto de satisfacer las necesidades públicas.

term > término Lapso especificado de dos años durante el cual se desempeñará en el cargo un funcionario elegido.

territory > territorio Territorio de los Estados Unidos que no tiene calidad de estado y que tiene su propio gobierno.

terrorism > terrorismo El uso de violencia para intimidar al gobierno o a una sociedad.

theocracy > teocracia forma de gobierno en el que un país es dirigido por líderes religiosos

Thomas, Clarence > Thomas, Clarence (1948–) Fue el segundo afroamericano nombrado para la Corte Suprema. Nominado juez asociado por George H.W. Bush en 1991, sustituyó a Thurgood Marshall y aún conserva su cargo.

Three-Fifths Compromise > Avenencia de las Tres Quintas Partes Acuerdo logrado en la Convención Constitucional respecto a que un esclavo debería contarse como tres quintas partes de una persona, para propósitos de determinar la población de un estado.

Thurmond, Strom > Thurmond, Strom Gobernador de Carolina del Sur y senador de los Estados Unidos durante 48 años. Thurmond (1902–2003) fue un opositor férreo del fin de la segregación en las escuelas y de los Derechos Civiles que se postuló sin éxito para la presidencia en las elecciones de 1948. Después, cambió su afiliación del Partido Demócrata al Republicano.

Tillerson, Rex > Tillerson, Rex Nacido en Texas, en 1952, fue nominado Secretario de Estado por el presidente Donald Trump en 2017 y confirmado por el Senado con una votación de 56–43. Antes de iniciar su servicio en el gobierno, Tillerson obtuvo un diploma en ingeniería civil en la Universidad de Texas en Austin, y su primer empleo fue como ingeniero de producción. Esto fue seguido de una larga carrera empresarial, que culminó en su cargo como presidente ejecutivo y director de Exxon/Mobil, compañía mundial de energía.

Tocqueville, Alexis de > Tocqueville, Alexis de (1805–1859) Científico político e historiador francés, famoso por haber escrito *La democracia en América,* un análisis del sistema político y social de los Estados Unidos durante el siglo XIX.

tort > acto ilícito civil Hecho injusto que incluye daño a la propiedad de una persona, su reputación o a la persona en sí en una situación que no está cubierta por un contrato.

township > municipio División de un condado.

trade association > asociación comercial Grupo de interés dentro de la comunidad de negocios.

trade embargo > embargo comercial Prohibición de comerciar con un país o varios países en particular.

transients > transeúnte Persona que vive en un estado sólo por un breve tiempo, sin residencia legal.

treason > alta traición Deslealtad hacia el país propio; en la Constitución, librar una guerra en contra de los Estados Unidos, proporcionar aliento u ofrecer ayuda a sus enemigos.

treaty > tratado Acuerdo formal entre dos o más estados soberanos.

Truman, Harry > Truman, Harry (1884–1972) Fue un granjero de Missouri, juez, senador y vicepresidente de Franklin D. Roosevelt por algunos meses. Se convirtió en el 33er presidente el 12 de abril de 1945, cuando Roosevelt murió repentinamente. Durante su presidencia, de 1945 a 1953, Truman vio el Día de la Victoria en Europa y ordenó que se lanzaran las bombas atómicas sobre Japón.

Trump, Donald J. Donald J. Trump nació en la Ciudad de Nueva York en 1946. Su padre era un adinerado promotor de bienes raíces. Después de su graduación en la Universidad de Pennsylvania en 1968, Trump comenzó a trabajar para la empresa de su padre. Para la década de 1990, poseía grandes consorcios de bienes raíces, incluyendo el edificio Empire State, varios hoteles, condominios, edificios de apartamentos y casinos. También participó en el programa de televisión *The Apprentice* (llamado más tarde *The Celebrity Apprentice*). Consideró ser candidato a la presidencia en 1999, pero no fue sino hasta 2016 que decidió hacerlo oficialmente. Obtuvo la nominación por el partido republicano en el verano de 2016 y en noviembre de ese año, Donald J. Trump fue elegido como el 45to. Presidente de los Estados Unidos.

trustees > Independientes Legisladores que votan en cada asunto de acuerdo con sus conciencias y sus juicios independientes, sin considerar las opiniones de sus electores o de otros grupos.

Tyler, John > Tyler, John Oriundo de Virginia, John Tyler (1790–1862) trabajó en la legislatura del estado y fue gobernador. Como senador, su interpretación estricta de la Constitución lo hizo renunciar frente a lo que consideró acciones ilegales del presidente Andrew Jackson, sobre la anulación de acciones del Congreso. Vicepresidente a la muerte del presidente en funciones, William Henry Harrison, Tyler tomó el cargo en 1841. Como Presidente, aprobó la estadidad de Texas y Florida, pero peleó fuertemente con sus compañeros del Partido Whig sobre el sistema bancario nacional. Todos los miembros de su gabinete menos uno renunciaron. En la Guerra Civil fue elegido para la Cámara de Representantes confederada, pero murió antes de asumir el cargo.

U

unconstitutional > inconstitucional Contrario a las estipulaciones constitucionales y, por lo tanto, ilegal, nulo e inválido, que no tiene fuerza ni efecto.

uncontrollable spending > gasto incontrolable Gastos que ni el Congreso ni el Presidente tienen el poder de cambiar de manera directa.

unicameral > unicameral Adjetivo que describe un cuerpo legislativo con una sola Cámara; ver bicameral.

unitary government > gobierno unitario Gobierno centralizado en el que los poderes ejercidos por el gobierno pertenecen a una única oficina central.

United Nations > Naciones Unidas Grupo de naciones compuesto por 193 miembros, que acepta las obligaciones de la Carta de las Naciones Unidas, tratado redactado en el año 1945.

universe > universo Término que se usa en asuntos de elecciones que se refiere a la población entera que se intenta medir mediante una encuesta.

V

veto > veto Poder del Presidente para rechazar un proyecto de ley aprobado por una legislatura; literalmente "Prohíbo".

Virginia Plan > Plan de Virginia Proyecto presentado por los delegados de Virginia en la Convención Constitucional; proponía un gobierno con tres poderes y una legislatura bicameral en la que la representación de cada estado estuviera determinada por su población o por su apoyo financiero al gobierno central.

visa > visa Permiso para entrar a otro país, otorgado por el país al cual se desea entrar.

W

Walesa, Lech > Walesa, Lech (1943–) Activista laboral fundador del primer sindicato en Polonia. Aunque fue arrestado por sus actividades sindicales, obtuvo el Premio Nobel de la Paz en 1983 y fue presidente de Polonia de 1990 a 1995.

ward > barrio Unidad en la que suelen dividirse las ciudades para la elección de los miembros del consejo municipal.

warrant > mandamiento Orden judicial que autoriza o hace legal alguna acción oficial, como la orden de allanamiento o la orden de arresto.

Warren, Earl > Warren, Earl (1891–1974) Fue magistrado republicano pero liberal, nombrado para la Corte Suprema por el presidente Dwight D. Eisenhower. Warren fue presidente de la Corte Suprema de 1953 a 1969 y presidió en algunos de los casos más importantes de la corte sobre la abolición de la segregación en las escuelas.

Washington, George > Washington, George (1732–1799) Ocupó el cargo de primer presidente de los Estados Unidos de 1789 a 1797 y fue uno de los Padres Fundadores de la nueva nación. Antes de ser presidente, fue general y comandante en jefe durante la Guerra de Independencia.

weak-mayor government > gobierno de alcalde débil Forma de gobierno de una ciudad, en la que el alcalde comparte las obligaciones ejecutivas con otros funcionarios electos.

welfare > beneficencia Ayuda en efectivo a los pobres.

whips > whips Asistentes de los líderes de las fracciones partidistas en la Cámara de Representantes y el Senado que son responsables de vigilar y ordenar los votos.

William and Mary of Orange > Guillermo y María de Orange El rey Guillermo III (1650–1702) y la reina María II (1662–1694) tuvieron un reinado conjunto como soberanos de Inglaterra, Escocia e Irlanda, de 1689 a 1702 (la reina María murió en 1694, pero Guillermo siguió reinando hasta 1702). María era hija del rey Jacobo II, lo que significaba que su marido neerlandés podría convertirse en corregente de Inglaterra después de derrocado el régimen de Jacobo.

Wilson, James > Wilson, James Nacido y educado en Escocia, Wilson (1742–1798) emigró a América del Norte y llegó en medio de las revueltas por la Ley del Timbre de 1765. Estudió para convertirse en abogado, especializado en derecho inmobiliario. Entró en la política poco antes de la Guerra de Independencia y su influencia fue fundamental en la Convención Constitucional.

Wilson, Woodrow > Wilson, Woodrow (1856–1924) Graduado de Princeton y de la Escuela de Leyes de la Universidad de Virginia; fue presidente de Princeton en 1902. Fue elegido como 28° presidente en 1912. Wilson ocupó el cargo de 1913 a 1921 e impulsó la Nueva Libertad, que enfatizaba el individualismo y los derechos de cada estado.

winner-take-all > el ganador se lleva todo Sistema casi obsoleto donde un aspirante presidencial que ganaba la preferencia del voto en las elecciones primarias, automáticamente obtenía el apoyo de todos los delegados elegidos en dichas elecciones.

World Bank > Banco Mundial Organismo fundado en 1944 para proporcionar asistencia económica a los países en desarrollo y reducir la pobreza en el mundo.

World Trade Organization > Organización Mundial del Comercio Organización creada en 1995 para aumentar el comercio.

writ of certiorari > auto de avocación o *certiorari* Orden emitida por una corte superior dirigida a una corte inferior para que remita el expediente de un determinado caso para su revisión; el significado en latín de la expresión es "tener mayor certeza".

writ of habeas corpus > auto de *habeas corpus* Orden judicial que evita arrestos y encarcelamientos injustos.

writs of assistance > auto de ayuda Orden general de allanamiento con la que los funcionarios aduanales británicos invadían los hogares privados en busca de bienes de contrabando.

Y

Yeltsin, Boris > Yeltsin, Boris (1931–2007) Político ruso que ocupó la presidencia de ese país en 1990. En 1991, se convirtió en el primer político elegido por voto popular en la historia de Rusia.

Z

zoning > zonificación Práctica de dividir a una ciudad en un número de distritos, o zonas, y de regular los usos que se le puede dar a la propiedad en cada uno de ellos.

Note: Page numbers followed by *c*, chart; *g*, graph; *m*, map; *i*, illustration; *p*, photo; *f*, feature.

A

Abdus-Salaam, Sheila, 585*p*
***Abington School District* v. *Schempp* (1963),** 376
Abolitionist Movement, 446
abortion, 372, 388, 393, 412–413, 549, 571
Abramoff, Jack, 200, 542–543, 546
absentee voting, 488*p*, 507–508
absolute monarchies, 27, 30, 50
accusation, 708
acquittal, 186
Acta Diurna, 528
acts of admission, 128
acts of dissent, 384
Adams, Abigail, 235
Adams, John
  on Boston's Caucus Club, 580–581, 580*i*
  Declaration of Independence and, 61
  as envoy to England and Holland, 74
  federal judgeship appointments, 343
  at First Continental Congress, 59
  as first Vice President, 83, 223
  as last Federalist President, 566
  Massachusetts constitution, 64
  at Second Continental Congress, 60*c*, 61
  undeclared wars of, 255–256
  use of Alien and Sedition Acts, 382, 382*i*
Adams, John Quincy
  boycott of Democratic-Republican caucus, 581
  chosen by Congress, 188–189, 188*f*
  Monroe Doctrine, 295*i*
Adams, Samuel, 58, 59, 73, 80
***Adarand Constructors* v. *Pena* (1995),** 465
***ad hominem* approach,** 553
adjournment (congressional sessions), 151–152, 247–248
administration, defined, 270, 271
administrative law, 705
admiralty law, 336, 336*f*
affirmative action, 463–466, 464*f*, 465*p*, 471*f*
Affordable Care Act, 124, 647
Afghanistan
  in cold war, 299
  as a failed state, 756
  NATO and, 312
  prisoners at Guantanamo Bay, 356, 356*p*, 415
  Soviet Union and, 301, 303
  undeclared U.S. war with, 256, 293*p*, 302–303, 312, 319–320
  United Nations and, 317*p*
  World Bank and, 671*p*

Africa
  independence of nations in, 754
  in Triangular Trade, 29*m*
  See also names of specific countries
African Americans
  abolition of slavery, 108, 367, 402–404
  affirmative action, 463–466, 464*f*, 471*f*
  in the armed forces, 108*p*, 243, 258–259, 258*p*
  civil rights laws, 34, 37, 462–463, 481–482, 481*p*
  civil rights movement, 366*p*, 404*p*, 463, 463*p*, 474, 481–482, 520
  in Congress, 150–151, 150*p*
  demographics of, 444, 447*f*
  as elected officials, 482*f*, 483, 595
  15th Amendment and, 108, 158, 476*f*, 479–481, 480*p*, 482, 489*i*
  14th Amendment and, 108, 436, 455–457, 455*p*, 493–494
  gerrymandering and, 157–158, 157*i*, 480–481, 692
  as governors, 698
  influence in elections, 603
  Jim Crow laws, 454–455
  as national party chairs, 575
  as secretary of state, 307
  separate-but-equal doctrine, 455
  as speaker of a State house of representatives, 693*p*
  special interest groups for, 393–394, 394*p*, 540*f*, 544–545
  in State legislatures, 693*p*
  in the Supreme Court, 339, 354, 361*c*
  13th Amendment and, 77, 108, 126, 402–404, 446
  voting behavior of, 500, 502
  voting rights laws, 482–485, 484*p*, 485*p*
  voting rights of, 108, 158, 479–482, 480*p*, 493–494
  See also desegregation; racial discrimination; segregation; slavery/enslaved people; voting rights
agency, definition, 271
Agency for International Development (USAID), 311, 318
age requirement
  for President, 229
  for senator, 163
  for voting, 501, 503
Agnew, Spiro T., 234–235
agriculture, collectivization of, 635–636, 637, 766
Aid to Families with Dependent Children (AFDC), 117*f*, 734, 734*c*
Air Force (USAF), 321–322
Alaska, Statehood of, 128–129, 129*p*, 156
Albany Plan of Union, 46*f*, 58
Albright, Madeleine, 307, 307*p*

***Alexander* v. *Holmes County Board of Education* (1969),** 456
Alien and Sedition Acts of 1798, 382, 382*p*
aliens, civil rights for, 368–369
Alien Terrorist Removal Court, 352
Alito, Samuel, 184, 361*c*
***Al Odah* v. *United States* (2008),** 415
al-Qaeda Islamist terrorist group, 303, 322, 323*c*, 756
ambassadors, 68, 243–244, 255, 277, 308–309, 309*f*
amendment process, 104, 105–106, 105*f*
amendments to State constitutions, 687–688, 687*p*, 688*f*
amendments to U.S. Constitution, 93–94, 104–107, 105*f*, 139*c*, 188. *See also* Bill of Rights; *names of specific amendments*
American Anti-Slavery Society, 540*f*
American Association of Retired People (AARP), 549*p*, 550
American Bar Association (ABA), 714
American Battle Monuments Commission, 285
American Broadcasting Company (ABC), 528
American Civil Liberties Union (ACLU), 411, 549, 550
American Conservative Union (ACU), 550–551
American Independent Party, 566, 571–572
American Medical Association (AMA), 551
American Party, 571
American Revolution, 29, 53, 60, 61–63, 61*i*, 69
American Samoa, 155
Americans for Democratic Action (ADA), 550
Americans with Disabilities Act (ADA), 468–469
***amicus curiae* briefs,** 346, 549
Amish, religious freedoms of, 379
amnesty, 246, 442
Amtrak, 272, 284*c*, 291
Anderson, Eugenie, 309
Anderson, John, 580
Angola, 298*m*, 754
***Animal Farm* (Orwell),** 444
Antietam, 255*p*
Anti-Federalists
  Elastic Clause and, 180–182, 181*f*
  emergence of, 80–81
  on judicial review, 343–344
  in ratification of the Constitution, 80–83, 80*f*
  two-party system and, 566, 566*p*
Anti-Masons, 572, 581
anti-obscenity laws, 368, 388
Anti-Peonage Act (1867), 403

Anti-Trust Division of the Justice Department, 13, 632
apartheid, 756
appellate court judges, 353–354, 354*f*
appellate courts. *See* courts of appeals
appellate jurisdiction, 332*f*, 337, 344, 354
appointed offices, 579, 587
appointment and removal powers, 100, 185, 243–245, 244*f*, 700–701
apportionment, 155. *See also* reapportionment of Congress
appropriations, 183, 659–661, 661*f*
Appropriations Committee (House), 660–661
Arab-Israeli disputes, 302–303
Arab Spring revolutions, 302
Argentina, 754, 756
Aristotle, 7, 14–15, 14*p*, 24, 43
Arizona, statehood of, 129, 132*p*, 156
Armed Services Committee (Senate), 201
arms, right to keep and bear, 404–405, 429*f*
Army, United States, 132, 270, 318–319, 319*f*, 320–321
Army Corps of Engineers, 292*p*
Army National Guard, 179, 320
Army Reserve, 320
Arouet, François-Marie (Voltaire), 30
ARPANET, 530
arrests, 4th Amendment and, 406–407
arrest warrants, 709
Arthur, Chester, 287
Article I of the Constitution
  bicameral Congress, 94–95, 94*f*, 99, 647, 662
  courts, 97, 336, 355
  protections, 414–416, 632
Articles of Confederation
  in America's founding documents, 68*f*
  attempts to revise, 70–71, 74
  currency under, 69, 69*i*, 173
  development of, 11, 67–68
  failure of, 11, 68–70, 85*c*
  form of government in, 20*f*, 21
  inauguration of constitutional government by, 83
  influence on the Constitution, 75, 76*f*, 80*f*, 81
  number of votes per State, 67–68
  slavery/enslaved people and, 67
  State constitutions and, 63*f*
  structure of, 68, 85*c*
  taxes and, 67, 69
  trade regulation in, 69, 70
Articles of the Constitution, 93*c*
  Article I (*See* Article I of the Constitution)
  Article II, 95–96, 99, 110, 118, 338–339
  Article III, 96–97, 99, 118, 335, 336

Article IV, 93, 133, 176, 357
Article V, 93, 105–106, 127, 188
Article VI, 93, 253, 373
Article VII, 82, 93
  influence on State constitutions, 63*f*
***Ashcraft* v. *Tennessee* (1944),** 421
Asian Americans, 447*f*, 448, 457
Asian-Pacific Economic Cooperation (APEC), 672
Assad, Bashar al-, 304
assembly, freedom of, 390–393
Assembly in ancient Athens, 24
assessment for taxes, 739
Assessments, 42–43, 86–87, 140–141, 220–221, 262–263, 328–329, 360–361, 430–431, 472–473, 556–557, 622–623, 678–679, 746–747, 782–783
assessors, 719*c*
assimilation, defined, 448
Associated Press (AP), 525*f*, 532
associate justices, 342, 347, 354
asylum seekers, 443
Athenian democracy, 4*f*, 23–24, 24*i*, 28*f*
athletics programs, Title IX in, 463, 468
***Atkins* v. *Virginia* (2002),** 425
at-large congressional elections, 157, 163, 483*c*
atomic bombs, 234, 234*p*, 263, 321
Attorney General, 231*c*, 278, 280, 339
attorney general (State), 703*f*, 704
auditors, 719*c*
Australian ballots, 510
authoritarian dictatorships, 13, 18–19, 302, 753–754
authority, defined, 271
autocracy, 18, 41*c*
automobiles, searches of, 407

B

Babangida, Ibrahim, 754
Babylonian Empire, 7
backbenchers, 763
bail, 50, 341, 422–423
bail hearings, 422*p*
bailiffs, 54, 341, 710*c*
Baker, Howard, 195
***Baker* v. *Carr* (1962),** 691–692, 692*f*
Bakke, Allan, 465, 465*p*
balance of power, 101, 115–116, 241
balancing the ticket, 234
Balkans, 256, 311–312
ballot fatigue, 497, 511
ballot initiative, 134
ballots, 507–508, 509–510, 511–513, 512*f*, 583–586, 600
***Baltimore* v. *Dawson* (1955),** 457
bandwagon effect, 526, 552*f*
Bank of the United States, 123, 173, 182, 184*c*, 291
bankruptcy, 170, 173, 341
bankruptcy judges, 341

banks, 180*f*, 181, 291, 640, 640*m*, 644
***Barker* v. *Wingo* (1972),** 418
Barrett, Amy Coney, 339
***Barron* v. *Baltimore* (1833),** 369
Bass, Karen, 693*p*
battleground states, 596
***Baze* v. *Rees* (2008),** 425
***Beard* v. *Banks* (2006),** 386
bed-sheet ballots, 510–511, 586
bench trials, 419, 708
Benghazi, Libya, 184, 201
Ben-Gurion, David, 302*p*
***Benitez* v. *Mata* (2004),** 442
***Benton* v. *Maryland* (1969),** 417
Berger, Victor, 160, 160*p*
***Berghuis* v. *Thompkins* (2010),** 422
Berlin blockade, 299
Berlin Wall, 306, 752
Beshear, Steve, 702*c*
Bible readings, in public schools, 377
biblical laws, 49
bicameral legislature
  in charter colonies, 51*m*, 52–53
  in the Constitution, 77, 94–95, 99, 647, 662
  in proprietary colonies, 51*m*
  in royal colonies, 51*m*, 52
  in States, 690–691
  in the Virginia Plan, 75, 75*f*, 94
Biden, Joe, 187, 281, 564*p*, 595, 598
***Bigelow* v. *Virginia* (1975),** 388
Bill of Rights
  in the Constitution, 90*f*, 107*c*, 108, 367
  of England, 50–51, 50*i*, 54–55
  lack of, in original Constitution, 80*f*, 81
  rights guaranteed in, 99, 107*c*, 108, 334–335, 367
  in State constitutions, 64, 685, 686
  States' incorporation of, 108, 369–371, 369*i*
  summary of, 139*c*
  Virginia Declaration of Rights and, 113–114
  See also due process; *names of specific amendments*
bills in Congress
  assignment to committees, 149
  budget, 660–661, 660*f*, 661*f*
  in committees, 204–206
  conference committees, 201, 211–212, 213
  emergency legislation, 213–214
  engrossed, 209
  floor debate, 207–208, 208*p*, 209–211, 210*c*, 211*f*
  generic bills, 213–214
  introduction of, 202–203
  omnibus measures, 214
  path of, 198–200, 198*f*, 212*c*, 694–695
  public vs. private, 203–204
  readings of, 204, 209
  for revenue, 202

scheduling floor debate, 206–207, 209
sent to the President, 212–213
types of bills, 203–204, 219*f*
voting on, 207–209, 208*p*
bills of attainder, 415–416, 416*p*
bin Laden, Osama, 756
bioterrorism, 324
bipartisan actions, 567
Bipartisan Campaign Reform Act of 2002 (BCRA), 205, 560*f,* 609–610, 615, 617
Black, Hugo L., 165–166, 250, 494*p*
Black Americans. *See* African Americans
Black Lives Matter (BLM), 550
Black Plague of the 1340s, 26
Blackstone, William, 30, 72, 715–716, 715*i*
Blaine, James G., 371
Blaine Amendment, 371, 371*i*
Blair, Anthony, 760
blanket primary, 583–584
block grants, 131, 131*f,* 734
Blount, William, 164
***Board of Directors, Rotary International v. Rotary Club of Duarte* (1987),** 394
***Board of Education of Independent School District No. 92 of Pottawatomie County v. Earls* (2002),** 409
Board of Trade in London, 56, 58
boards of commissioners, 718, 718*f,* 725–726, 726*f*
boards of supervisors, 718, 718*f,* 722
boards of trustees, 722
Boeing Aerospace, 645, 739*p*
Bolshevik Revolution, 765–766
Bonaparte, Napoleon, 19, 296*c*
bonds, government, 382, 644
border checkpoints, 441*p*
border fence, 448
Border Patrol, 269*p,* 441*p,* 442
boroughs, 718
borrowing power, 172–173, 172*p,* 173*p,* 662, 741
Bosnia, 9, 311
Boston, Massachusetts
Boston Massacre, 46*f,* 58, 59
Boston public library, 729*p*
Boston Tea Party, 46*f,* 57*c,* 59, 59*i,* 87
Caucus Club in, 580–581, 580*f*
first post office in, 175
Boston Latin School, 732
Boston News-Letter, 528, 528*p*
boule, 24
***Boumediene v. Bush* (2008),** 415
Bradley, Omar, 259
Bradley, Joseph P., 457–458
***Bradwell v. Illinois* (1873),** 457
Brain Trust, 282
branches of government. *See* executive branch; judicial branch; legislative branch

Brandeis, Louis, 412
***Branzburg v. Hayes* (1972),** 386
Brazil, 756
Brennan, William J., Jr., 458
Brewers Association, U.S., 540
Brezhnev, Leonid, 301, 308*p*
briefs, 346
British colonial policies, 56–57, 57*c*
British Parliament, 94
British Quartering Act of 1765, 405, 405*i*
Brooke, Edward, *150f*
Brown, Gordon, 760
Brown, Henry B., 656
Brown, John, 426
Brown, Linda, 460
Brown, Ronald, 575
Brown, Sherrod, 190–191
***Brown v. Board of Education of Topeka* (1954),** 434*f,* 455–456, 460–461, 548–549
***Brown v. Entertainment Merchants Association* (2011),** 389
***Brown v. Plata* (2011),** 424
***Brown v. Socialist Workers '74 Campaign Committee* (1982),** 394
Brunei, 752
Bryant, Phil, 702*c*
***Buckley v. Valeo* (1976),** 384, 610, 612
budget. *See* federal budget; State budgets
budgetary power, 659, 701
budget commissions, 718*f*
Budget Committees, 660–661, 660*f*
budget deficits, 662–664, 663*f*
budget proposals, 276*f,* 660, 701
Buffalo Soldiers, 108*p,* 258*p*
bugging, 410
"Bull Moose" Progressive Party, 566–572
Bundle of Compromises, 78–79, 78*c*
Burdick, George, 246
***Burdick v. United States* (1915),** 246
bureau, defined, 271
bureaucracy, 268–270
bureaucrats, 269
Bureau of Engraving and Printing, 624*p*–625*p*
Bureau of Human Rights and Humanitarian Affairs, 367
Bureau of Indian Affairs, 457
Bureau of International Narcotics and Law Enforcement Affairs, 308
Bureau of Labor Statistics, 641
Bureau of Public Debt, 664. *See also* public debt
Burma, 757, 775*m*
Burns, James M., 147, 147*f*
***Burstyn v. Wilson* (1952),** 387
bus boycott (Montgomery, Alabama), 457
Bush, Barbara, 235*p,* 236

Bush, George H. W., 227*p,* 235*p,* 282*p*
Americans with Disabilities Act, 468–469
Cabinet nominee rejections, 184*c*
campaign of, 641
economic stimulus measures, 643
environmental legislation, 214
Operation Desert Storm, 239
as President, 147*p,* 239
recess appointments, 244*f*
sending of federal troops, 127
as Vice President, 230
voter demographic, 501
Wall Street bailout bill, 214
Bush, George W., 147*p,* 518*p*
as chief diplomat, 227*p*
economic crisis of 2007-2008, 663, 663*f*
economic stimulus measures, 643, 663
executive orders, 224*f*
executive powers, 185
military tribunals for "enemy combatants," 241, 356
Operation Iraqi Freedom, 256
presidential election, 501–502, 501*c,* 600
recess appointments, 244*f*
September 11, 2001 attacks, 256*m,* 303–304, 319, 320, 411, 519
signing statements by, 248–249
USA PATRIOT Act, 213*p,* 409–410
vetoes by, 248*f*
warrantless eavesdropping, 224*f,* 409*i,* 410–411
Bush, Laura, 233*p,* 235–236, 235*p*
***Bush v. Gore* (2000),** 600
business enterprises and user fees, 740–741
business taxes, 739–740, 739*p,* 740*p*
busing, to increase racial mix, 375, 456
Byrd, Robert C., 163

C

Cabinet
appointment of members, 185, 280–281
customs and usage, 111–112
diversity of members in, 280–281
establishment of, 279–280
executive departments, 278–279, 279*f*
in the order of succession, 231, 231*c*
in a parliamentary government, 22, 761
role of, 279–282
Senate rejections of nominees for, 184*c*
shadow cabinet, 761, 763*p*
25th Amendment and, 232
Cable News Network (CNN), 523, 532

Calhoun, John C., 234
California
    State constitutions, 684, 687
    Statehood of, 128
California Democratic Party v.
    Jones (2000), 584
California v. *Acevedo* (1991), 407*c*
Calvert, George, Lord Baltimore, 52
Cambodia, 754–755
campaign buttons, 588, 588*p*
campaigns
    contributions, 384, 608–610
    FEC requirements, 284, 610–614,
        611*c*
    federal finance laws, 609–610
    finance law reform, 614–615
    financing sources, 608–609
    PAC money, 611–612
    posters, 553, 608
    for presidency, 596–597, 596*p*,
        612–614
    public funds for, 609, 612–613
    regulating finances, 621*f*
    strategists, 533–534
Camp David Accords (1979), 302
Canada, 20, 294, 312, 667, 669–670
candidate selection, 505, 539, 574
Cantwell v. *Connecticut* (1940), 370
capital, as factor of production, 629,
    629*f*
capital goods, 629
capitalists, 629
capitalist systems, 38, 38*f*, 628–629,
    629*f*, 637*c*
capital punishment, 423, 424–426,
    424*f*, 425*f*, 775
Capitol, U.S.
    building structure and map, 2*p*–3*p*,
        142*p*–143*p*, 153
    enslaved labor in the building of, 453
    January 6, 2021 attack on, 187–188,
        598
Capitol Hill, 539
career legislators, 149
Carnley v. *Cochran* (1962), 347*f*
Carroll v. *United States* (1991), 407
Carson, Andre, 191*p*
Carter, Jimmy, 502*p*
    amnesty to draft evaders, 246
    Camp David Accords, 302
    in Carter-Ford debate, 597
    in Carter-Reagan debate, 605–606,
        605*p*
    draft registration, 288
    on human rights, 367
    recess appointments, 244*f*
    reverse coattail effect, 509
    on Soviet containment, 301
Carter, Rosalynn, 235*p*, 236
Carville, James, 641, 641*p*
casting and counting ballots, 507,
    511–513, 512*f*, 598, 600. *See also*
    voting process
Castro, Fidel, 636

categorical grants, 131, 131*f*
caucuses, 580–581, 580*i*, 591–592,
    591*p*
Cavazos, Lauro F., 281
CBS News, on the Vietnam War,
    537
ceiling to public debt, 665
cell phones
    in China, 775–776
    polls and, 524
    recording and sharing events, 534*c*
    searches of, 407
censorship, 167, 385, 386*p*, 387, 525*p*,
    617
censure, 187
Census, U.S., 156, 156*m*
Census Bureau, 132, 157, 447*c*
Centers for Disease Control and
    Prevention (CDC), 279
central banking system, the Fed
    as, 640
Central Committee (Soviet Union),
    766
Central Intelligence Agency (CIA),
    184, 266*c*, 271*c*, 322
centralized government, 19–20, 20*f*,
    27. *See also* government
certificate, appealing to the
    Supreme Court, 345
Chae Chan Ping v. *United States*
    (1889), 439
Challenger (Space Shuttle), 286
Chanakya, 10
Chandler v. *Florida* (1981), 419
change of venue, 419
chaplain of the House, 191, 191*p*
Charles I (king of England), 50
Charles II (king of England), 52*i*
charter colonies, 51*m*, 53, 684
charters, city, 724
charters, colonial, 52, 52*i*, 684
Chávez, Hugo, 635
Chechnya, Republic of, 769, 769*p*
checks and balances
    in Congress, 99*i*, 100–102, 100*f*
    interest groups and, 542
    in political process, 101
    in presidency, 99*i*, 100–102, 100*f*
    in presidential vs. parliamentary
        governments, 22
    in State constitutions, 64, 685, 686
    for treaties, 185, 185*f*, 253–254
    in the U.S. Constitution, 99–103,
        100*f*, 102*f*
Cheney, Dick, 234, 235*p*
Cherokee tribes, 721
Chiang Kai-shek, 772, 775
Chicanos, 447
chief administrative officer of the
    House, 191
chief administrator, President as,
    227, 270
chief citizen, President as, 228
chief diplomat, President as, 227*p*

chief economist, President as, 228
chief executive, President as, 227,
    270
chief financial officer (State), 704
Chief Justice
    FISA court and Alien Terrorist
        Removal court judges and, 352
    judicial philosophies of, 340
    meeting in conference, 346–347
    presiding over impeachments, 186
    recalling retired judges, 341
    selection of, 339, 339*f*
chief justice, State, 712
chief legislator, President as, 227
chief of naval operations, 319, 321
chief of party, President as, 228
chief of state, President as, 226–227
child labor, abolition of, 183
children, influences on later
    political views, 516–517
Children's Internet Protection Act
    (CIPA; 2002), 389
Chile, 754, 756
Chimel v. *California* (1969), 406
China, 772–776
    under Deng Xiaoping, 637, 773
    dictatorship in, 18
    earliest known government, 7
    government of, 637, 773–775, 774*f*,
        781*f*
    Great Leap Forward, 637
    human rights in, 777–778, 783
    local political divisions, 775, 775*m*
    under Mao Zedong, 636–637,
        772–773, 772*p*
    mixed economy in, 634
    population of, 8
    provinces and neighbors of, 775*m*
    rise and decline of communism in,
        636–637
    Taiwan, 668, 756, 775, 775*m*
    trade with U.S., 667–668, 673, 679
    U.S. compared with, 775–776
    U.S. relations with, 301, 775–776
Chinese Communist Party, 773, 774*f*
Chinese Exclusion Act of 1882, 437,
    440, 448
Chisholm, Shirley, 167*p*
Chisholm v. *Georgia* (1793), 108
Christianity, 25–26, 26*m*, 28
Christie, Chris, 228*p*
Churchill, Winston, 33, 299, 317, 760
Cicero, Marcus Tullius, 24
circuit courts, 97, 353–354, 354*f*
circular argument fallacy, 553
citizen participation, 36–37
citizenship, 436–443, 471*f*
    defined, 36, 436
    denaturalization, 439
    expatriation, 439
    for formerly enslaved people, 108,
        439, 446
    14th Amendment on, 434*f*, 436–438
    history of, 434*f*, 436–437

natural-born citizens, 437–438, 437f
naturalized citizens, 108, 176, 229, 438–439, 438f
requirements of, 108, 229
responsibilities, duties, and obligations of, 36–37, 37p
tax responsibility of, 650
of U.S. presidents, 229
voting requirement of, 489, 489p
Citizenship and Immigration Services, 242, 324, 438, 438f
Citizens' Stamp Advisory Committee, 285, 285i
***Citizens United v. FEC* (2010),** 384, 610, 612, 615–616, 615f, 617–618
city councils, 726–727, 727f
city governments, 723–729
charters, 724
city services, 729
commission governments, 725–726, 726f
council-manager governments, 726–727, 727f
incorporation, 724
mayor-council governments, 724–725, 725f
metropolitan areas, 730
planning, 728–729
suburbanitis and, 729–730
urbanization and, 723–724
urban special districts, 730–731
city managers, 727, 727f
city planning, 728–729
city services, 729
Civic Discussion: The Filibuster, 145
Civic Discussion: The Electoral College, 561
civic participation, 36–37
civic responsibilities, 36
civil cases, 352–353, 354, 370c, 420
civil disobedience, 391
civilian control of military, 281, 319, 319c
civilian tribunals, 355
civilian workforce, 278
civil law, 416, 457–458, 707, 707f
Civil Rights Act of 1866, 403–404, 471f
Civil Rights Act of 1964
affirmative action and, 464f, 465, 465p, 471f
basis in commerce power, 123, 169
courts for cases based on, 353–354
discrimination based on sex, 450
discrimination in public accommodations, 169–170, 463, 487
effects on desegregation, 123, 456
housing and, 463
passage of, 446, 463, 486
positive acts of government in, 367
Title IX, 463, 468
voting and, 478p, 481–482, 487

Civil Rights Act of 1968, 463
Civil Rights Acts of 1957 and 1960, 145, 210, 471f, 481
civil rights and liberties, 323f, 364f
affirmative action, 463–466, 464f, 465p, 471f
of aliens, 368–369
defined, 367
in employment and labor unions, 463
in federally funded programs, 463
14th Amendment and, 369–372, 370f
freedom of religion, 373–379
history of, 434f
history of federal laws on, 462–463, 463p
human rights policies, 367
individual rights, 11, 30, 366–367, 397–399, 400–401
limited government and, 368–369
for people with disabilities, 468, 469
police power and, 397–398
in public accommodations, 169–170, 463, 487
in State constitutions, 64, 686, 686c
See also desegregation
civil rights movement, 366p, 404p, 463, 463p, 474, 481–482, 520
civil service, 244, 287–288
Civil Service Act of 1883, 287
Civil Service Commission, 287. *See also* Office of Personnel Management
civil society, 37
Civil War (American)
absentee voting during, 508
commander in chief during, 255, 255p
deep divisions during, 568
ending of slavery, 108, 238, 446
expulsion of Senators during, 164
15th Amendment and, 479
French invasion of Mexico during, 295
government of the southern states after, 126
limited conscription programs, 288
taxes to finance, 626f, 649
writ of habeas corpus suspended during, 414–415
classified services, 287
Clay, Henry, 581
Clean Air Act Amendments of 1990, 214
Clean Air Act of 1970, 214
clear and present danger rule, 382–383
clemency, power of, 246, 702–703
clerk of the court, 710c
clerk of the House, 191, 204, 209p
Cleveland, Grover, 127, 159
climate change
international efforts, 294, 312, 316, 317
interstate compacts, 133

mass media and, 528
nongovernmental organizations and, 316
political spectrum and, 568f
promoting the general welfare, 12
role of government in, 12, 670
State efforts to reduce, 697p
trade agreements and, 670
Clinton, George, 83
Clinton, Hillary Rodham
as First Lady, 235p, 236, 236p, 240p
negative ads against, 617
presidential campaign of, 595–596, 609p, 613
as Secretary of State, 308
Clinton, William J., 641p, 700p
Cabinet of, 282
Communications Decency Act of 1996, 388, 388p
elections of, 590, 595
impeachment of, 100, 187–188
military force used by, 256
presidential campaign of, 641, 641p
public debt reduction by, 173, 173p
recess appointments, 244f
staff of, 240p
voter demographic, 501
***Clinton v. New York City* (1998),** 249
closed primaries, 583–584, 586
cloture, 210–211, 211c, 463
Cloture Rule (Senate), 210–211, 211c
coalition governments, 22, 569, 760
Coast Guard, U.S., 12, 12p, 177p, 324
***Coates v. Cincinnati* (1971),** 391
coattail effect in voting, 508–509, 508i
Code of Hammurabi, 424
***Coker v. Georgia* (1977),** 425
cold war, 234p, 298–299, 298m, 301, 754
collective naturalization, 438–439
collective security principle, 298
collectivization of agriculture, 635–636, 637, 766
college funding, 733
colonial America, 51–53, 51m, 56–57, 85c. *See also* Second Continental Congress
colonial assemblies, 94
colonialism, 28–29
colonial legislatures, 51m, 52, 56–57
colonial trade, 28–29, 29m
colonial unity, 57–59, 58i
Columbia Broadcasting System (CBS), 523, 528, 532, 533c, 537
command economies, 637, 638
commander in chief, President as, 95–96, 100, 110p, 227–228, 255–257
***Commentaries on the Laws of England* (Blackstone),** 715–716, 715i
Commerce and Slave Trade Compromise (1787), 77–78, 78c, 170, 648

Commerce Clause, 168–170, 182–183, 183*f*

Commerce Department, 175, 668

commerce power, 110, 168–170, 170*p*

commercial revolution, 26

commercial speech, 388

commission, defined, 271

commission governments, 725–726, 726*f*

Commission on Civil Rights, 271, 284, 481, 487

Commission on Presidential Debates, 596

committee chairs, 196–197

committee members, 148*c*, 149, 661, 694

Committee of Correspondence, 58–59

Committee of the Whole (House), 207, 207*i*

Committee on House Administration, 198

Committee on Rules and Administration (Senate), 198

committees. *See* congressional committees

Commodity Credit Corporation (CCC), 271, 292

common defense, providing for, 12, 68, 131, 171

common law, 30, 48, 705–706, 706*c*, 762

***Common Sense* (Paine),** 66

communes, in China, 637

Communications Decency Act of 1996, 388, 388*p*

communism, 634, 634*p*, 635–636, 635*c*, 636*m*, 753

communist guerrillas, 300

Communist Party (China), 773–774, 775

Communist Party of the Soviet Union (CPSU), 636, 754, 765, 766, 769

Communist Party USA, 370

communist states, 18*m*, 634–636, 634*p*, 635*c*, 636*m*, 753–754

commutation, 246, 702

compact territory, 157

competition, 631, 631*f*

compromises
    at the Constitutional Convention, 72*i*, 76–79, 78*c*
    Declaration of Independence and, 62
    First Continental Congress and, 59
    need for, 3, 33, 35, 100, 517

compulsory military service, 183, 288, 288*i*

computer hacking, 302, 512–513

computerized voting, in Congress, 208, 208*p*

concurrent jurisdiction, 337, 337*f*

concurrent powers, 121–122, 171

concurrent resolutions, 203, 219*c*, 257, 661

concurring opinions, 347–348

Confederate States of America, 11, 21, 164

confederations, 11, 19, 20*c*, 21. *See also* Articles of Confederation

conference committees, 201, 211–212, 213, 660*f*, 661*f*

Conference on International Organization, UN, 313

confidentiality of media sources, 386

Congress
    in Articles of Confederation, 68
    bicameral legislature of, 77, 94
    borrowing process, 664
    in budget creation, 659–661, 660*f*, 661*f*
    Commerce Clause, 168–170, 182–183, 183*f*
    committee chairs, 196–197
    compensation to members, 109, 152–154
    conference committees, 211–212, 213, 660*f*, 661*f*
    constitutional amendments from, 105–107, 105*f*, 188
    convening of, 96, 151, 190–191
    creation of independent agencies, 283–284
    debates, 338*f*, 547*f*
    delegated powers of, 167–168, 168*c*
    election costs, 608
    election dates for, 507
    electoral duties of, 188–189, 188*f*, 189*f*
    expressed powers of, 118, 167–178, 219*c*
    first meeting of, 83
    floor leaders, 195–196
    foreign policy, 177
    implied powers of, 118, 168, 168*c*, 179–183, 180*f*, 181*f*, 182*p*, 183*f*
    International Monetary Fund, 314, 316, 671
    joint sessions of, 192–193
    lobbyists and, 546–548, 547*f*, 548*f*
    members' roles in, 147–148, 148*c*
    Necessary and Proper Clause, 118, 179–182, 180*f*, 181*f*
    new States admitted by, 127–129, 128*m*, 129*p*
    partisan nature of, 149
    presiding officers, 193–195, 194*p*, 195*p*, 219*c*
    process of making laws, 149
    profile of members, 150–151
    ratings by interest groups, 550–551, 550*c*
    reapportionment of, 156–159, 156*m*, 157*i*, 158*p*, 165–166
    reasons for serving, 154
    representation in, 94–95, 94*f*, 148, 148*c*

    salary and nonsalary compensation, 153
    scheduling floor debate, 206–207
    select committees, 184, 186
    seniority system in, 193, 197, 199, 462
    special sessions, 152, 152*p*, 247
    subcommittees, 183, 199, 205–206, 660, 661
    terms and sessions of, 151–152, 151*f*, 155–156, 163
    trips by members, 205
    weights and measures, 176, 176*p*
    See also bills in Congress; congressional committees; congressional powers; House of Representatives; legislative branch; Senate

Congressional Budget Office (CBO), 184, 660–661

congressional campaign committees, 576

congressional committees
    actions of, 205–206
    bill pathways in, 149, 198–199, 198*f*
    budget and, 660–661, 660*f*, 661*f*
    committee chairs, 196–197
    committee members, 148*c*, 149, 193, 661, 694
    conference committees, 201, 211–212, 213, 660*f*, 661*f*
    joint committees, 191, 201, 212
    listing of, 199*f*
    lobbyists and, 547
    majority party and, 199
    select committees, 184, 186, 200–201
    seniority rule in, 193, 197, 199, 462
    standing committees, 183–185, 197–199, 198*f*, 204–206, 660
    subcommittees, 183, 199, 205–206, 660, 661

congressional districts
    for federal government, 157, 157*i*, 567
    redistricting, 157–159, 157*i*, 165–166, 165*p*
    for State governments, 691–692, 691*i*

congressional oversight, 149, 184, 241

congressional powers
    bankruptcy power, 170, 173
    borrowing power, 172–173, 172*p*, 173*p*
    commerce power, 110, 168–170, 170*p*
    copyrights and patents, 39, 118, 174–175, 174*i*, 674
    currency power, 173–174, 181, 182
    delegated powers, 167–168, 168*c*
    domestic powers, 174–176
    executive powers, 185
    expressed powers, 118, 167–178, 219*c*
    impeachment power, 100, 100*f*, 186–188, 231, 598

implied powers, 118, 168, 168c, 179–183, 180f, 181f, 182p, 183f
investigative powers, 183–184, 200
judicial powers, 176
legislative power, 148, 148c, 149
money powers, 170–174, 171f, 172p
naturalization, 176
postal powers, 153, 175, 175p
power of the purse, 659
power over territories, 128, 176, 357
power to override vetoes, 100, 213
taxing powers, 170, 171–172, 647–650
types of, 167–168, 219c
war powers, 110, 177–178, 183
weights and measures, 176, 176p
Congressional Record, 204
Congressional Research Service, 184
congressional resolutions. *See* resolutions
Congress of the Confederation, 73, 75, 80, 83, 127
Connecticut, State constitution of, 685
Connecticut colony, 51m, 53, 53i, 60c
Connecticut Compromise, 76–77, 77i, 78c
conscience fund, 654
conscription, 183, 288, 288i, 458
consensus, 181–182, 567–568
consent of the governed, 7, 30, 62–63, 64
Conservative Party (Tories), 763–764
constituencies, 163
constituent power, 693
constituent services, 149–150
constitutional amendments, 93–94, 104–107, 105f, 139c, 188. *See also* Bill of Rights; *names of specific amendments*
constitutional changes (State), 106
Constitutional Convention (1787)
basic principles of, 139c
compromises, 76–80, 78c
Framers, 73, 73f
inauguration of the new government, 83
key facts, 85c
New Jersey Plan, 75–76, 76f, 94
organizing, 70
pathway to, 85c
rules of procedure, 74
shaping of the presidency, 96
Virginia Plan, 74–75, 75f
writing and signing, 79–80
constitutional conventions, State, 687, 688f
Constitutional Court (Russian Federation), 768–769, 768f
constitutional courts, 97, 335, 340c
constitutional government, 48–49
constitutional guarantees, 37–38, 108, 126, 366–367, 378, 387

constitutionalism, 48, 98, 758
constitutional law, 705
constitutional liberal democracy, 657
constitutional monarchy, 16p, 18m, 752
constitutional obstruction, 564–565
constitutional powers. *See* concurrent powers; expressed powers; implied powers; reserved powers
constitutional republic, 17
Constitution of the United States of America
amendments to, 93–94, 104–107, 105f, 139c, 188
as an enduring document, 104–105
basic principles, 93, 97–103
checks and balances, 99–103, 100f, 102f
Commerce and Slave Trade Compromise, 77–78, 78c, 170
Contract Clause, 124
customs and usage, 111–112
debates and compromises in, 72i, 76–79, 78c
division of powers, 20, 22, 116
electoral college, 602
extradition, 135, 135p
federal bureaucracy, 270
formal amendment process, 104–107, 105f, 106p
Full Faith and Credit Clause, 68, 133–134, 133p, 134p
guarantees of rights and freedoms, 37–38, 108, 126, 366–367, 378, 387
influence on State constitutions, 63f
interpretations of, 109–112
judicial review, 101–102, 342–344
legislation and changes in, 110
limited government, 98–99, 98i, 368–369
nation's obligations in, 125–127
New Jersey Plan, 75–76, 76f, 94
outline of, 92–94, 93c
personal freedom guarantees, 366–367
popular sovereignty, 97–98, 97i
Preamble, 6, 6p, 92, 318
presidential election, 596, 597–599, 600–604
privileges and immunities, 136
ratification of, 47, 80–83, 80f, 81c, 82i, 108, 237–238
role of the government, 11–13
separation of powers, 22, 98i, 99
Supremacy Clause, 93, 122–123
Supreme Court in, 97, 335
Three-Fifths Compromise, 77, 77i, 78c
treason, 426
Virginia Plan for, 74–75, 75f, 94
See also Articles of the Constitution; Constitutional Convention; *names of specific amendments*

Constitution Party, 570c
constitutions. *See* Constitution of the United States of America; State constitutions
Consumer Financial Protection Bureau (CFPB), 291
Consumer Price Index (CPI), 641
Consumer Protection Act (2010), 290
containment policy, 299, 301, 310
contempt of Congress, 205
content-neutral requirement, 391
Continental Army, 60, 60c, 237, 320
Continental Congress. *See* First Continental Congress; Second Continental Congress
Continental Navy, 321
continuing resolutions, 661
continuous body, Senate as, 163
Contract Clause, 124
contract law, 707
Contras, 200, 200p, 300–301
controllable spending, 658
convention system, 581–582
***Cooper v. Harris* (2017),** 158
Copyright Office, 174–175
copyrights, 39, 118, 174–175, 174i, 674
coroners, 719c
corporations
defined, 271
government, 284, 284c, 291–292, 291f
incorporation process, 370
multinational, 301, 667
political spending by, 384, 610–612, 615, 617–618, 617i
private, 291
taxation of, 649, 652, 739
corrections systems, 735
corruption
Citizens United decision and, 616
in dictatorships and failed states, 7, 754, 756
of officials, 160, 164, 287, 334
prior restraint on publication and, 385
Supreme Court on, 98, 124
in voting, 510, 581, 582
Cosby, William, 334
cosponsors of bills, 203
Costa Rica, 757
council-manager governments, 726–727, 727f
Council of Economic Advisers, 277, 642
Council on Environmental Quality, 277
counterterrorism, 294, 322, 322p, 323f
counties
challenges of, 720
county governments, 71f, 717–719, 719c
county home rule, 720, 737
defined, 717
functions, 719, 720p
counting ballots, 507, 511–513, 512f, 598, 600. *See also* voting process

country, defined, 8
county agents, 718f
county boards, 718, 718f, 719c
county-city consolidation, 720
county clerks, 492, 497, 509, 719c
county conventions, 581–582
county managers, 720
County of Allegheny v. *ACLU* (1989), 706c
county treasurers, 719c
court-approved prior restraint, 385–386
court interpreters, 710c
Court of Appeals for the Armed Forces, 97, 336, 340c, 355
Court of Appeals for the Federal Circuit, 97, 340c, 352m, 353–354, 354f, 356–357
Court of Appeals for Veterans Claims, 97, 340c, 356
Court of Federal Claims, 97, 336, 340c, 357
Court of International Trade (U.S.), 97, 340c, 355
Court of Military Appeals, 355–356
court orders, 398, 405, 414, 439, 456, 481–482
court reporters, 341, 355, 710c
courts-martial, 355
courts of appeals
    appellate jurisdiction, 332f, 337, 344, 354
    appellate path, 353, 353f
    for the Armed Forces, 97, 336, 340c, 355
    Court of Military Appeals, 355–356
    for the Federal Circuit, 97, 340c, 352m, 353–354, 354f, 356–357
    State courts of appeal, 353f, 711
    for Veterans Claims, 97, 340c, 356
courts of the District of Columbia, 97, 340c, 357
court systems
    in Russian Federation, 768–769
    in United Kingdom, 760f, 762, 762p
    See also federal courts; jurisdiction; State courts
COVID-19 pandemic, 117, 626f, 664, 747
Cox v. *Louisiana* (1965), 391
Cox v. *New Hampshire* (1941), 392
Coyle v. *Smith* (1911), 129
cracking, in gerrymandering, 158
Craig v. *Boren* (1976), 458
Crawford, William H., 581
Crimea, Russian invasion of (2014), 304
criminal cases, 352–353
criminal law, 133, 416, 706–707, 707f
crisis management and peacekeeping, 311–312
Cronkite, Walter, 537
Crooker v. *California* (1958), 347f
crop-loan and farm-subsidy agency, 292

crude oil imports, 668, 668p
cruel and unusual punishments, 50, 423–424
Cuba, 776
Cuban Americans, 447
Cuban missile crisis, 224f, 247p, 299
Cultural Revolution, 773
Cunningham, Randy "Duke," 160
currency power, 173–174, 181, 182, 626f, 645
customs duties, 58, 171, 246, 647, 653
cyber threats, 302, 312
Czechoslovakia, 753–754

D

D'Amato, Alfonse, 210, 210c
Darrow, Clarence, 13, 377p
Davidson v. *New Orleans* (1878), 395
Davis v. *Bandemer* (1986), 692f
Davis, Gray, 699, 699p
Dayton, Jonathan, 73
"dead letter" provisions, 687
death penalty, 423, 424–426, 424f, 425f, 775
death squads, 754
death taxes, 653, 739
debates
    on Articles of Confederation, 67–68
    congressional, 207
    filibusters, 145, 462, 463
    on Declaration of Independence, 61–62
    presidential, 596–597, 597p, 605–606, 605p
    on ratification of the Constitution, 76–83, 76f, 78c, 237–238
debt. *See* public debt
debt imprisonment, 686
Declaration of Independence (1776)
    adoption of, 63
    Enlightenment ideas in, 30, 30p
    popular sovereignty, 63
    at the Second Continental Congress, 61
    slavery and, 62
    social contract theory in, 61–62
    State constitutions and, 63f
    writers and signers of, 56, 61, 61i
Declaration of Rights and Grievances, 58, 59–60
Declaration of Sentiments and Resolutions, 449f, 452
de facto segregation, 392–393, 456
defendants, 337
defense
    civilian control of, 281
    in colonial period, 57
    costs of national defense, 251, 279, 294
    as government responsibility, 12, 68, 177–178
    military aid and, 311
    secretary of, 281, 281p
    See also Department of Defense

Defense Intelligence Agency, 322
Defense of Marriage Act (DOMA), 134, 459
Deferred Action for Childhood Arrivals (DACA), 442
Deferred Action for Parents of Americans and Lawful Permanent Residents (DAPA), 443
deficit financing, 172–173
deficits, 173, 662
deflation, 642
DeJonge v. *Oregon* (1937), 370, 390
de jure segregation, 456
Delaware, State constitution of, 685
Delaware colony, 51m, 52–53
delegated powers, 118–119, 119c, 167–168, 168c
delegates
    in the Albany Plan of Union, 58
    Congress members as, 148–149, 148c
    to the Constitutional Convention, 72–74, 73f, 80–83, 80f
    to county conventions, 582
    to the First Continental Congress, 59–60, 60c
    to national conventions, 592–594
    to the Second Continental Congress, 60–62, 61i
    to the Stamp Act Congress, 58–59
    in writing Articles of Confederation, 67–69
delegate-selection process, 582
demand-side economics, 663–664
democracy
    ancient Rome and, 4f, 24, 25f
    Athenian, 4, 4f, 23–24, 24i, 28f
    basic principles and values, 33–37
    building on the past, 23–26, 23p, 24i, 25f
    compromise, necessity of, 3, 33, 35, 35i, 100, 517
    courts in, 96
    defined, 7, 17
    democratic consolidation, 755–756, 755f
    dictatorship vs., 7
    direct vs. indirect, 17, 17c, 24, 24i
    documents that influenced, 49–51, 54–55
    England, influence of, 30, 48
    Enlightenment ideas and, 29–30, 31–32
    equality of people, 31–32, 34, 312
    factors in success of, 750f, 755f, 781f
    failed states, 756
    forms of, 17, 17c, 24, 24i
    free enterprise system and, 37–39, 38f, 630–632, 631f, 637–638
    individual worth and, 34
    majority rule/minority rights in, 34–35
    republic vs., 17–18
    roots of, 4, 4f, 28f

transitioning to, 752–756, 753*f*, 755*f*

Democracy in America **(Tocqueville)**, 373, 541

Democratic National Committee (DNC), 575

Democratic Party
  caucus, 577*p*, 579, 591–592, 591*p*
  decentralized nature of, 573–574
  Democratic National Committee, 575
  interest groups vs., 539–540, 539*f*
  MoveOn.org, 550, 615
  national conventions, 496p, 564*p*, 574–576, 592–594
  presidential primaries, 582–587, 586*c*
  psychological factors of, 504–505
  sociological factors of, 500–502, 501*f*
  symbol of, 567*i*

Democratic Republic of Congo, 756

democratization, 752–756, 753*f*, 755*f*

demokratia, 23

demonstrations, 391–393, 550

denaturalization, 439

Deng Xiaoping, 637, 773

***Dennis* v. *United States* (1951)**, 383

***de novo* trials**, 711

Department of Agriculture, 292

Department of Commerce, 175, 668

Department of Defense (DoD), 279, 318–**320**, 319*f*, 320*p*, 658

Department of Energy (DOE), 658

Department of Health and Human Services (HHS), 279, 283, 657

Department of Homeland Security (DHS)
  establishment of, 279, 323–324
  on e-voting, 513
  immigration laws, 242, 438, 440*c*, 441–443
  naturalization, 438
  public debt and, 658
  responsibilities of, 12, 12*p*, 324
  unauthorized aliens, policies on, 441–443, 441*p*
  watching for threats, 12, 12*p*, 323
  work of, 323–324

Department of Housing and Urban Development (HUD), 237*p*, 239, 281

Department of Justice. *See* Justice Department

Department of Labor, 278, 641

Department of State, 184, 278, 307–**310**, 309*f*, 310*f*, 367

Department of Treasury. *See* Treasury Department

deportation, 441, 442, 448

***Dept. of Commerce* v. *U.S. House of Representatives* (1999)**, 692*c*

desegregation
  affirmative action and, 463–466, 464*f*
  in the armed forces, 243, 258–259, 258*p*
  busing of students, 375, 456

Civil Rights Act of 1964, 123, 456
  constitutional guarantees and, 127, 367
  de facto segregation, 392–393, 456
  de jure segregation, 456
  in education, 34*p*, 123, 127*p*, 367, 455–456, 460–461
  14th Amendment and, 455–457, 455*p*
  history of segregation, 454–457
  in housing, 456, 463
  in interstate transportation, 366*p*
  in public swimming pools, 457
  Supreme Court on, 34*p*, 339–340, 403–404, 455–457

destroyers-for-bases deal, 254

détente, 301

deterrence, 298–299

devolution, 762

Dickinson, John, 59, 61, 79

dictatorships, 7, 18–19, 18*m*, 754

***Dillon* v. *Gloss* (1921)**, 107

Dingly Tariff Act (1897), 121*i*

diplomacy, 307–317
  ambassadors, 68, 243–244, 255, 277, 308–309, 309*f*
  diplomatic immunity, 309–310, 309*f*
  North Atlantic Treaty Organization, 311–312, 312*c*
  Organization of American States, 317
  passports and visas, 310, 310*f*
  presidential powers of, 252–255, 253*p*, 254*p*
  right of legation, 308
  secretary of state, 252–253, 275*p*, 297, 307–308, 307*p*, 308*p*
  special ambassadors, 309
  United Nations, 312–317, 313*m*, 316*c*

diplomatic immunity, 309–310, 309*f*

diplomatic representatives, 96, 254–255, 295, 308

direct approach in lobbying, 546–**549**, 546*i*, 547*f*, 548*f*

direct democracy, 17, 17*c*, 24, 24*i*, 722, 722*p*

Director of National Intelligence (DNI), 322–323

Director of Public Engagement, 548

direct popular elections, 602–603, 602*c*

direct primaries, 582–587, 584*p*, 586*c*

direct response electronic voting machines (DREs), 511–512

direct taxes, 171–172, 648–649, 648*c*, 655–656

disabilities, rights of people with, 468, 469

disability of the President, 110*p*, 231–232, 231*f*

discharge petitions, 205

disclosure requirement for FEC, 610–611

discount rate, 644

discrimination
  affirmative action, 463–466, 464*f*, 465*p*, 471*f*
  against LGBTQ community, 445, 459
  against people with disabilities, 445, 468, 469
  in government regulation, 454
  reverse, 464–466
  separate-but-equal doctrine, 455
  sex discrimination, 449–450, 457–459, 458*c*
  slavery as, 445–446
  13th Amendment on, 403–404
  See also racial discrimination

disenfranchisement, 479. *See also* voting rights

dissent, acts of, 384, 384*p*, 391–393, 550

dissenting opinions, 166, 251, 348, 401, 618, 656

district attorneys, 719*c*

district courts, 97, 173, 337, 340*c*, 351–353, 352*m*

District of Columbia (D.C.)
  direct tax in, 172
  federal courts of, 97, 340*c*, 357
  federal judges of, 340
  representation of, 107, 155
  voting rights in, 479

***District of Columbia* v. *Heller* (2008)**, 405

district plan for elections, 601–603, 602*c*

distrust of government, 688

diverse citizenship, 337

diversity
  among Asian Americans, 448
  among Latino Americans, 447
  statistics on, 444–445, 445*f*, 447*f*

Divine Right of Kings theory, 10, 10*f*, 28, 41*c*

division of powers, 20, 22, 116

division of the House, 208

divorce, 133–134, 454

DNA Collection Act, 356*i*

DNA evidence, 395, 395*p*

DNA technology, 285

docket, 353

documentary and stock transfer taxes, 740

Document-based Questions, 43, 47, 87, 263, 329, 361, 431, 473, 477, 557, 623, 679, 747, 783

Dodd-Frank Wall Street Reform and Consumer Protection Act (2010), 290–291, 290*i*

***Doe* v. *Reed* (2010)**, 394

Dole, Bob, 173*p*, 595, 597

dollar diplomacy, 296

domestic affairs, 227, 277, 294

domestic economy. *See* economy

Domestic Policy Council, 277

domestic tranquility, government insurance of, 12

domestic violence, protecting
    States from, 126–127, 126p
Dos Santos, José Eduardo, 754
Dothard v. *Rawlinson* (1977), 458,
    458c
double jeopardy, 417
Douglass, Frederick, 540f
Douglas, William O., 494
draft, military, 183, 288, 288i, 458
Dred Scott v. *Sandford* (1857),
    445–446
driver licensing and safety, 736, 740
Drug Enforcement Agency (DEA),
    322
dual court system, 97, 335–336, 340c,
    352m
Dudley, Edward R., 309
due process
    classic cases on, 396–397
    constitutional amendments affected
        by, 370–371, 370f, 397
    constitutional guarantees, 395–396,
        396f
    double jeopardy and, 417
    drug-testing programs and, 409
    eminent domain and, 119, 176,
        398–399
    establishment of, 49–50
    in 14th Amendment, 370–371, 370f,
        390–391, 397
    free enterprise and, 630–631
    gun control and, 405
    individual rights and the public
        good, 397–399
    internal drug searches and, 396–397
    for juveniles, 397
    Oregon compulsory school
        attendance law, 374, 397
    personal privacy and, 412–413
    police power and, 398
    procedural and substantive, 396,
        396f
    reapportionment and, 165
    right of assembly and petition,
        390–391
    search warrants and, 405–407, 407c
    sexual orientation and, 459
    States' application of, 370
    tax limits and, 737
    trial rules and, 418–420, 421p
Duma (Russian Federation), 768,
    770c
Duncan v. *Kahanamoku* (1946), 415
Dunn v. *Blumstein* (1972), 490
Durenberger, David, 164
duties, customs, 58
Dwight D. Eisenhower System
    of Interstate and Defense
    Highways, 735–736

E

early voting, 488p, 507–508
earmarks, 203–204

Easley, R. M., 582
East Germany, 754
Eckford, Elizabeth, 34p
Economic and Social Council
    (ECOSOC), 314
economic crisis of 2007-2008, 663,
    663f
economic protest parties, 571
Economic Report, 247, 277
economic rights, 38, 630
Economic Stabilization Act of 2008,
    214
economy
    capitalist systems of, 38, 38f,
        628–629, 629f
    in China, 634, 637
    consequences of global, 673–674,
        673g
    economic goals, 641–642
    federal government role in, 39,
        631–634, 639–641, 640m
    fiscal policy and, 642–643, 644c, 645
    foreign policy and, 668–670, 669m
    free enterprise system and, 37–39,
        38f, 630–634, 631f, 631g, 637–638
    global, 668–674, 669m, 673c, 677c
    government bailout, 182p, 214, 221,
        663f
    growth of, 191, 290, 638, 640,
        641–642, 644
    history of government role in, 626f
    inequality in, 38, 634, 635c
    key goals in, 641–642, 677f
    Keynesian economics, 663–664
    major institutions in, 677f
    mixed economies, 633–634, 633f
    monetary policy and, 643–645, 644c
    protest parties, 571–573, 572c, 573c
    stagnation of, 754
    stimulus measures for, 643, 663–664
    trade alliances and organizations,
        671–672
    See also federal spending; global
        economy; international trade
Edison, Thomas, 174i, 511, 511p
education
    allotments and vouchers, 371
    under the Articles of Confederation,
        130
    busing for integration, 375, 456
    desegregation of, 34p, 123, 127p,
        455–456, 460–461
    drug testing in schools, 408–409
    evolution, teaching of, 377, 377p
    federal land grants for, 130
    Native Americans, 446
    parochial schools, 371, 371i, 374,
        375–376
    prayers in public schools, 372,
        376–377
    released time and student groups, 376
    religion and, 371–372, 371i, 374–377,
        375p

socioeconomic diversity, 456
State and local funding, 732–733,
    733c
State guidelines on curriculum, 733
Title IX, 463, 468
voting influenced by, 501, 501f
Education Amendments of 1972,
    463
Edwards v. *Aguilard* (1987), 377
Egypt, 7, 302
18th Amendment, 107, 108, 288
8th Amendment, 370c, 397, 422,
    423–424
Eisenhower, Dwight D.
    22nd Amendment, 230
    aid to South Vietnam, 300
    authorization of military force, 256
    Cabinet nominee rejections, 184c
    civil rights intervention, 127
    election of 1956, 601p
    illnesses, 231
    Interstate Highway System,
        735–736, 735p
    military experience, 595p
    residency, 229
    on role of vice-president, 234
Eisenhower, Mamie, 601p
Elastic Clause. *See* Necessary and
    Proper Clause
elected officials, number of, 506,
    511
election dates, 506, 507
election day, 498–499, 597
electioneering, 553
election of judges, 713–714, 714p
election process
    absentee voting, 488p, 507–508
    campaign posters, 553, 608
    election dates, 506–507
    electoral duties of Congress, 108,
        188–189, 188f, 189f, 598–599
    electoral politics, 533–534
    federal election law, 384, 506–507,
        609, 612–613
    hacking in, 302, 304
    for the House of Representatives, 159
    if no majority in electoral votes, 108,
        188–189, 188f, 598–599
    importance of voters, 34p
    January 6, 2021 Capitol attack and,
        187–188, 598
    non-major parties in, 567, 567p
    proposed reforms of, 601–603, 602c,
        614–616, 615c
    in Russian Federation, 768
    Russian influence in U.S. elections,
        304
    for the Senate, 162–163
    for State executive officers, 703f
    for State legislators, 691
    in United Kingdom, 763–764
    See also elections and money;
        nomination; presidential
        elections; voting process

elections and money, 607–616
    campaign spending limits, 431, 560*f*, 612
    Citizens United decision, 384, 610, 612, 615–616, 615*f*, 617–618
    election recounts, 603, 2000
    FEC requirements, 431, 610–614, 611*c*
    federal finance laws, 609–610
    loopholes in finance laws, 614–616, 615*f*
    minor party candidates, 614
    money sources in, 608–609
    money spent in, 607–608, 611*c*, 613, 616
    PAC contributions, 611–612
    See also campaigns
electoral college, 597–604
    choosing electors, 597–598
    counting the electoral votes, 598, 598*m*
    decided by the House, 188–189, 188*f*
    flaws in, 621*f*
    if no candidate wins a majority, 108, 188–189, 188*f*, 598–599
    Jefferson's opposition to, 601, 603*i*
    "minority Presidents" and, 600
    number of votes per State, 598*m*
    origin of, 111, 597
    political parties and, 566–567
    proposed reforms, 601–604, 602*c*, 621*f*
    scenarios, 599–601
    special cases, 598–599, 599*c*
    strengths of, 604
    12th Amendment and, 108
electoral duties of Congress, 108, 188–189, 188*f*, 598–599
electoral politics, 533–534
electoral votes, 188–189, 188*f*, 573*c*, 598*m*, 599*c*
electorate, size of, 478–479
electronic data processing (EDP), 511
electronic eavesdropping, 224*f*, 409*i*, 410–411
electronic media. *See* Internet
electronic voting, in Congress, 208
11th Amendment, 108
Elizabeth II (queen of the United Kingdom), 16*p*, 758*p*
Ellison, Keith, 374*p*
Ellsworth, Oliver, 76
Emancipation Proclamation, 238
embassies, 308–309, 309*f*
Emergency Economic Stabilization Act of 2008, 663*f*
emergency spending resolution, 661
EMILY's List, 611–612
eminent domain, 119, 176, 398–399
Employment Standards Administration (ESA), 641
enabling acts, 128

Engel v. *Vitale* (1962), 376
England. *See* United Kingdom
English Bill of Rights, 50–51, 50*i*, 55
engrossed bills, 209
Enlightenment ideas, 29–30, 30*p*, 31–32
Ensign, John, 164
entitlement programs, 657–658, 734
entrepreneurs, 629, 630
enumerated power. *See* expressed power
Environmental Defense Fund (EDF), 545*p*
environmental legislation, 214
environmental protection, 12, 141
Environmental Protection Agency (EPA), 272–273, 285
Equal Access Act of 1984, 376
equality of people, 31–32, 34, 312
Equal Pay Act of 1963, 450
Equal Protection Clause
    individual rights, 453–454
    redistricting and gerrymandering, 157, 691–692, 692*f*
    school desegregation, 460–461
    segregation, 455–457
    State districting, 691–692
    tax classifications, 737
    vote counting, 600
    voting requirements, 489–490, 493–495
Equal Rights Amendment (ERA), 107
Equiano, Olaudah, 451–452, 451*p*
equity law, 706
Ervin, Sam, 190*p*, 200
Escobedo, Danny, 420, 422
Escobedo v. *Illinois* (1964), 347*f*, 420
espionage, 318, 322, 426
Espionage Act of 1917, 351*f*, 382
Establishment Clause (1st Amendment), 371, 371*i*, 374–378
estate taxes, 653, 739
Estes v. *Texas* (1965), 419
ethnic background, influence on voting, 501
Euclid v. *Amber Realty Co.* (1926), 729
European colonialism, 28–29
European Economic Community (EEC), 672
European Union (EU), 21, 21*p*, 672
Evarts Act of 1891, 332*f*
Evenwel v. *Abbott* (2016), 157
Everson v. *Board of Education* (1947), 375
evolution, teaching of, 377, 377*p*
evolutionary theory of origins of states, 10, 10*f*, 41*c*
e-voting, 512–513
excise taxes, 653
excludable aliens, 441
exclusionary rule, 407–411, 410*f*
exclusive jurisdiction, 337

exclusive powers, 121
exclusive rights to inventions, 632
executive actions, 110–111, 251, 464
executive agreements, 111, 254
Executive Article, 95–96
executive branch
    Article II on, 93*c*, 95–96
    in budget creation, 659–660, 659*f*
    bureaucracy of, 270, 271*f*
    checks and balances of, 99*i*, 100–102, 100*f*
    choosing executive officers, 703*f*
    congressional oversight of, 100, 149, 184, 184*c*, 241
    defined, 22
    executive departments, 266*c*, 278–279, 279*c*
    Executive Office of the President, 266*f*, 274–278, 276*c*
    expansion of, 239–240, 242–243
    federal budget role, 659–660, 659*f*
    Federal Reserve System, 640, 640*m*
    government corporations, 284, 284*c*, 291–292, 291*f*
    independent agencies of, 175, 266*c*, 283–288, 284*c*
    independent regulatory commissions of, 288–291
    interpretation of laws by, 242
    legislative power of, 247
    line-item veto and, 213, 249
    lobbying of, 548
    in the New Jersey Plan, 76, 76*f*
    organization of, 266*f*, 325*f*
    in a parliamentary government, 22
    President in, 227–229
    in Russian Federation, 767
    Securities and Exchange Commission, 289–290, 640
    separation of powers and, 21–22, 98*i*, 99
    See also Cabinet; federal bureaucracy; President of the United States
executive departments, 266*f*, 278–279, 279*f*
Executive Office of the President (EOP), 266*f*, 274–278, 276*c*
executive officers, federal, 278
executive officers, State, 507, 703–704, 703*f*
Executive Order 9981, 258
executive orders, 242–243
executive powers
    in Article II, 95–96, 99, 111
    of Congress, 185
    congressional oversight of, 149, 184, 241
    defined, 7
    judiciary and, 245
    of the presidency, 95–96, 99, 111, 227, 238
    of the Second Continental Congress, 61

of State governors, 113, 700
of State legislatures, 693
in war, 256
See also presidential powers
executive privilege, 243, 243f
ex parte judicial proceeding, 415, 417
Ex parte Merryman **(1861)**, 415
Ex parte Milligan **(1866)**, 415
expatriation, 439
Export-Import Bank of the United States (Eximbank), 291
export taxes, 119, 647–648
ex post facto laws, 416
expressed group attitudes, 515–516
expressed powers, 167–178
    commerce power, 110, 168–170, 170p
    congressional foreign policies, 177, 261f
    congressional judicial powers, 168, 168c
    in the Constitution, 97, 118, 168
    copyrights and patents, 39, 118, 174–175, 174i, 674
    defined, 118, 219c
    money powers, 170–174, 171f, 172p, 173p
    naturalization, 176
    over territories, 176
    postal powers, 153, 175, 175p
    powers expressly denied, 119c
    to the States, 121
    war powers, 177–178
    weights and measures, 176, 176p
expression, freedom of, 380–381, 380p, 381p
extradition, 135, 135p

F

Facebook, 530, 531p
factions, 540, 566, 573, 617
factors of production, 628–629, 629f
failed states, 756
fair procedures, 396
fair trial, right to, 50, 243f, 417–419, 420
Falkland Islands, 756
Fallin, Mary, 680p–681p
false advertising, 381
family political attitudes, 503–504
family preferences and voting, 516
Farewell Address (Washington), 36, 111, 173, 294, 305–306, 566
Farmer, James, 366p
Farm Service Agency, 292
farm-subsidy agency, 258
Fascist Italy and Germany, 18, 297
Fauset, Crystal Bird, 693p
FCC v. *Fox* **(2009)**, 387p
FCC v. *Pacifica Foundation* **(1978)**, 387
federal aid, 130–132, 131f

Federal-Aid Highway Act (1956), 735
Federal Assembly (Russian Federation), 768, 768f
federal budget, 276, 659–661, 659f, 660f, 661f
federal bureaucracy, 268–270.
    See also Executive Office of the President (EOP); *specific agencies*
Federal Bureau of Investigation (FBI), 132, 184, 318, 322, 352
federal circuit courts, 97, 340c, 352m, 353–354, 354f, 356–357
Federal Communications Act of 1934, 387
Federal Communications Commission (FCC), 271, 288–289, 368, 387
Federal Communications Commission v. *Fox Television Stations* **(2009)**, 368
federal court circuits, 352m
federal courts
    appellate path in, 353, 353f
    cases heard in, 359f
    constitutional courts, 97, 335, 340f
    in dual court system, 97, 335–336, 340c, 352m
    established by Congress, 97, 351
    federal courts of appeals, 97, 340c, 352m, 353–354, 354f, 356–357
    inferior courts, 97, 335, 351–357
    judges and court officers in, 338–341, 338f, 340c, 351–352
    judicial districts, 351–352, 352m
    judicial review by, 101–103, 102f, 111, 342–344
    jurisdiction in, 336–337, 337f
    special courts, 97, 336, 340c, 357
    structure of, 359f
    for terrorism, 352
    See also judicial branch; *specific courts*
federal courts of appeals, 97, 340c, 352m, 353–354, 354f, 356–357
federal crimes, 352–353
Federal Deposit Insurance Corporation (FDIC), 271, 284c, 291
federal district courts, 97, 173, 337, 340c, 351–353, 352m
Federal Election Campaign Act 1971 (FECA), 384, 431, 609, 612–613
Federal Election Commission (FEC), 284, 431, 560f, 610–614, 611c
Federal Emergency Management Agency (FEMA), 324
federal finance laws, 609–610
federal funds rate, 640
federal government
    checks and balances, 99–103, 100f, 102f, 185, 253–254, 542
    creating budget, 659–661, 659f, 660f, 661f

    deficit of, 172–173, 662–664, 663f
    defined, 20, 20f
    delegated powers, 118–119, 119c, 167–168, 168c
    division of powers, 20, 22, 116
    domestic economy and, 639–641, 640m
    economic actions, 39, 631–634, 639–641, 640m
    federal budget, 276, 659–661, 659f, 660f, 661f
    fiscal and monetary policies, 642–645, 644c
    keeping peace within and between States, 126–127, 132–133
    limiting State taxation, 736–737
    obligations under the U.S. Constitution, 125–127
    payroll taxes, 652–653, 652c, 740
    powers denied to, 119–120, 119c
    property acquisition, 119, 176
    public debt, 68, 172–173, 658, 664–665, 664f, 673–674
    role in International Monetary Fund and World Bank, 671
    royal colonies compared with, 57
    sharing resources with State governments, 129–132, 131f
    solicitor general, 346
    State aid to, 132
    taxing power, 170–172, 647–650, 648f, 649c
    tax revenues, 170–171, 677f, 738–739, 738c
    territories, power over, 128, 176, 357
    in welfare reform, 117, 117f
    See also expressed powers; federal spending; government
federal grants-in-aid, 130–132, 131f
Federal Hall (New York City), 83
federalism, 115–124
    balancing national and State powers, 102–103, 102f, 115–116
    bicameralism and, 77, 94
    defined, 102, 116
    exclusive and concurrent powers, 121–122
    federal powers, 118–120, 119c
    impact of Bill of Rights on, 108, 369–371, 369i
    political parties and, 574
    popular sovereignty and, 106
    as principle in the Constitution, 102–103, 102f
    shared resources, 129–132, 131f
    State powers, 120–121
    strengths and disadvantages, 116–117
    Supremacy Clause, 93, 122–123
    Supreme Court and, 123–124
    welfare reform in, 117, 117f
Federalist: A Commentary on the Constitution of the United States **(the Federalist Papers)**, 81–82

Federalist **No. 1,** 80*f*
Federalist **No. 10,** 147, 540, 543
Federalist **No. 22,** 96, 335
Federalist **No. 47,** 99
Federalist **No. 51,** 12, 91, 101, 103, 247
Federalist **No. 70,** 181
Federalist **No. 71,** 230
Federalist **No. 72,** 293
Federalist **No. 76,** 278
Federalist **No. 78,** 101–102
Federalists
    Elastic Clause and, 180–182, 181*f*
    emergence of, 80–81
    on judicial review, 343–344
    in ratification of the Constitution, 80–83, 80*f*
    two-party system and, 566, 566*p*
federal jobs, 244, 287–288
federal judges
    appointment by the President, 100, 244, 335
    Constitution on, 93
    in impeachments, 186
    role and selection of, 338–339, 338*f*, 341, 549
    salary and duties of, 340–341
    terms of, 340
federal judicial districts, 341, 351–353, 352*m*
federal land grants, 130
Federal Reserve Act of 1913, 626*f*
Federal Reserve Board (Fed), 640, 640*m*, 643–645, 644*c*, 654
federal spending, 677*f*
    controllable and uncontrollable, 658–659
    defense, 251, 279, 294, 658, 664–665, 664*f*
    economic impact of, 642–643
    entitlement programs, 657–658, 734
    expanding existing programs, 276*c*
    Interstate Highway System, 398, 735–736, 735*p*
    line-item veto and, 213, 249
    public debt, 68, 172–173, 658, 664–665, 664*f*, 673–674
    public health, 733
    spending priorities, 279, 657–658
federal taxes. *See* taxes
Federal Trade Commission (FTC), 245, 354, 623*f*
federal voting referees, 481
Federation Council (Russia), 768, 768*f*, 770*c*
fee system, justices of the peace and, 710
Feingold, Russ, 216–217, 609*p*, 615
felonies, 707
felons, voting rights of, 494–495, 498
Ferguson, Miriam "Ma," 698, 793
feudalism, 4, 25, 26–27, 28*f*
Field, Stephen J., 655–656

15th Amendment, 108, 126, 158, 476*f*, 482, 489*i*
5th Amendment
    double jeopardy, 417
    Due Process Clause, 395, 396*f*, 397, 454
    eminent domain, 176, 398–399, 630
    free enterprise, 38, 630
    rights of the accused, 417–418
    right to a grand jury, 369, 416–417
    self-incrimination rights, 246, 370*c*, 421–422
    States and, 369*i*, 632
filibusters, 145, 209–211, 210*c*, 211*c*, 462, 463
Finance Committee (Senate), 198, 199, 660–661
fingerprinting, 421
firefighters discrimination case, 465–466
1st Amendment, 90*f*, 429*f*
    campaign financing, 610, 612, 616, 617–618
    Establishment Clause, 371–372, 371*i*, 374–378
    freedom of assembly and petition, 390–394, 538
    freedom of association, 393–394, 584
    freedom of media, 386–389
    freedom of religion, 373–379
    freedom of speech and press, 119, 334, 368, 370, 380–389, 610
    Free Exercise Clause, 370*c*, 374, 378–379
    Internet, 388–389
    limits on taxing power, 647–648
    obscenity, 368
    Smith Act of 1940, 383, 422–423
    symbolic speech, 383–385
    taxes and, 171, 647–648
    video games, 389
First Continental Congress, 59–60
First Lady of the United States, 235–236, 261*c*, 275
FISA court, 352
fiscal policies, 642–643, 644*c*, 645
fiscal year, 276
Fisher **v.** *Texas* **(2013),** 466
Fiske **v.** *Kansas* **(1927),** 370
501(c) groups, 616
527 organizations, 615–616
Five-Year Plans (China), 773
Fixed Term Parliament Act (2011), 763
flag burning, 384–385
Flag Protection Act of 1989, 385
Fletcher **v.** *Peck* **(1810),** 124
floor consideration, 149
floor leaders, 195–196
Florida Purchase Treaty (1819), 295
Florida **v.** *Jardines* **(2013),** 406
Florida **v.** *J.L.* **(2000),** 405
Fong Yue Ting **v.** *United States* **(1893),** 441

Food and Agriculture Organization (FAO), 314
Food and Drug Administration (FDA), 279, 285, 633*c*
food stamps, 658
Forbidden City (Beijing), 773*p*
force theory of origins of states, 10–11, 10*f*, 41*c*
Ford, Betty, 236
Ford, Gerald R.
    as Minority Leader, 195*p*
    pardon of Nixon, 246
    presidential debate, 597
    recess appointments, 244*f*
    succession to vice presidency, 189, 235
    vetoes by, 248*f*
foreign affairs
    Afghanistan war (undeclared), 256, 293*p*, 302–303, 312, 319–320
    cold war, 234*p*, 298–299, 298*m*, 301
    Congress and, 177
    cyber threats and hacking, 302, 312
    détente, 301
    international terrorism, 304
    Iraq, 19, 172*p*, 239, 303, 303*m*
    Korean War, 240, 240*p*, 250–251, 256, 299, 299*p*
    Latin America in the 1900s, 296, 296*c*
    Middle East, 302–303, 303*m*
    National Security Council and, 275–276
    Nicaragua, 300–301, 301*f*
    North Atlantic Treaty Organization, 311–312, 312*c*
    overview, 293–294
    President and, 227–228, 252–255
    Reagan's "Tear Down This Wall" speech, 306
    Russia after cold war, 303–304
    State Department and, 184, 307–310, 309*f*, 310*f*, 367
    through World War I, 294–297, 295*i*, 296*c*
    trade embargoes and sanctions, 669
    Vietnam War, 109, 178, 178*p*, 300, 300*f*
    Washington's Farewell Address on, 305–306
    World War I, 297
    World War II, 297–298, 297*i*
    See also specific countries
foreign affairs powers, 252–257, 261*c*
foreign aid, 310–311, 329
foreign commerce. *See* international trade
Foreign Intelligence Surveillance (FISA) Court, 352
foreign policies, 327*f*
    collective security, 298
    containment, 299, 301, 310
    countries transitioning to democracy, 752–756, 753*f*, 755*f*

détente, 301
deterrence, 298–299
Good Neighbor Policy, 296
human rights in China, 777–778, 783
Monroe Doctrine, 295–296, 295i
Open Door policy, 297
Roosevelt Corollary, 296, 327c
Truman Doctrine, 299
Foreign Relations Committee (Senate), 185
Forest Service, U.S., 339–340
formalized rules, 269
formal qualifications. *See* qualifications
Formosa, 668, 756, 775, 775m
***Forsyth County* v. *Nationalist Movement* (1992),** 391
Fortas, Abe, 400–401, 400p
***44 Liquormart, Inc.* v. *Rhode Island* (1996),** 388
Four Freedoms speech, 367
Four Modernizations, 773
four principles of a sound tax system, 737f
14th Amendment, 429f
Bill of Rights and, 397
citizenship defined in, 108, 436–438
civil disobedience, 391
cruel and unusual punishments, 423–424
desegregation, 455–457, 455p
Due Process Clause, 108, 370, 370f, 390–391, 395–397
Equal Protection Clause, 157–158, 453–454, 457–458, 465, 490, 493, 692–693
exclusionary rule, 408
freedom of speech and press, 376, 385–386
free enterprise, 630
impact on States, 3, 121, 369–371, 423
poll tax elimination, 494
private property, 393
ratification of, 108, 126
right to counsel, 420
sex discrimination, 457–459
voter ID laws and, 493
zoning ordinances and, 728–729
4th Amendment, 429f
arrests, 406–407
balancing security and liberty, 411
exclusionary rule, 407–411, 410f
illegal searches, 335, 405–406
mandatory drug testing, 408–409
probable cause, 405–406
USA Patriot Act, 409–410
wiretapping, 184, 410–411
Fox News, 533
Frame of Government, 53
Framers of the Constitution
balance of powers, 115–116
on bicameralism, 75, 75f, 77, 94
on the electoral college, 111, 597

meeting of, 72–74, 72i, 73f
military and, 318–319
opposition to political parties, 111
on presidential powers, 237–238
See also Anti-Federalists; compromises; Federalists
franking privilege, 153
Franklin, Benjamin
Albany Plan of Union, 58, 58i
at the Constitutional Convention, 73, 78–79
Declaration of Independence and, 56, 61
first postmaster of the U.S., 175
on liberty, 13
magazine published by, 529
political cartoon by, 58i
at Second Continental Congress, 56, 60–61, 60c
on taxes, 647
on the vice presidency, 233
on voting rights, 478
Frazier, Lynn J., 699
Fredrickson, Caroline, 411
***Freedman* v. *Maryland* (1965),** 387
freedom of the seas, 294
Freedom Ride, 366p
freedoms
of assembly and petition, 390–393, 538
of association, 393–394, 584
of expression, 380–381, 380p, 381p
individual, 35–36
to keep and bear arms, 404–405
limits to speech, 368, 368p, 381
of the press, 381, 385, 418–419
of religion, 373–379
right to privacy, 323, 410, 412–413
security of home and person, 402–403
against self-incrimination, 246, 370c, 421–422
from slavery or involuntary servitude, 108, 367, 402–404
free enterprise system, 677f
fundamental factors of, 630–632, 631g
government regulation of, 631–632, 633–634
laissez-faire theory, 632
other economic systems vs., 637–638, 637c
in the United States, 37–39, 38f, 630–632, 631f
Free Exercise Clause, 370c, 374, 378–379
free expression, right of, 380–381, 380p, 381p
free market, 630. *See also* free enterprise system
free press, guarantees of, 381, 385, 418–419
Free Soil Party, 571, 571i
free speech zones, 391–392

free trade agreements, 669–670, 670i, 674p
French and Indian War, 57
fringe benefits, for Congress members, 153
***Frontiero* v. *Richardson* (1973),** 458, 458c
full employment, 641
Full Faith and Credit Clause, 68, 133–134, 133p, 134p
fundamental law, 7, 63, 93, 96, 102, 688
fundraising, for elections, 161, 608–609
***Furman* v. *Georgia* (1972),** 424–425

G

Gaines, Lloyd, 455
Galloway, Joseph, 59
Gallup, George, 522, 522p
Galveston, Texas, 726
gambling, 398, 721, 741
Garfield, James, 231, 287
Gault, Gerald, 397, 400–401
gay and lesbian rights, 445, 459
***Gayle* v. *Browder* (1956),** 457
gender equality, 312, 449–450, 457–459, 458c
gender gap, 501
General Agreement on Tariffs and Trade (GATT), 672
general elections, in dictatorships, 579, 579p
General Services Administration (GSA), 284, 285
***General Theory of Employment, Interest, and Money* (Keynes),** 663
general trial courts, 711
general welfare. *See* public welfare
generic bills, 213–214
Geneva Convention (1949), 367
geography's influence on voting, 502–503
George II (king of England), 51
George III (king of England), 57, 61, 146
Georgia
State constitution of, 685
voting rights in, 480–481, 482, 483
Georgia colony, 51–52, 51m, 58, 59, 94
Germany
authoritarian dictatorship of, 18
Berlin Wall, 306, 752
mixed economy in, 634
Nazi dictatorship of, 18, 297
socialism in, 753f
Gerry, Elbridge, 79, 157i
gerrymandering, 157–158, 157i, 480–481, 692
"Get Out the Vote" efforts, 499p
Gettysburg Address, 17
Gibbons, Thomas, 169, 182

***Gibbons* v. *Ogden* (1824),** 169, 182,
182*i*
GI Bill (1944), 446, 642
***Gibson* v. *Florida* (1966),** 394
***Gideon* v. *Wainwright* (1963),** 420
gift taxes, 653
Ginsburg, Ruth Bader, 339
***Gitlow* v. *New York* (1925),** 370
**"Give Me Liberty or Give Me
Death" (Henry),** 65
Gladstone, William E., 73
***glasnost* policy,** 636, 754
glass ceiling, 433, 450
global economy
consequences of, 673–674, 673*c*
international trade and, 666–668,
667*c*
trade alliances and organizations,
671–672
U.S. trade policies, 668–670, 669*m*
See also international trade
globalization, 666, 674
Glorious Revolution (England), 50,
56
***Glossip* v. *Gross* (2015),** 423
Goldwater, Barry, 508, 509*p*
***Gomillion* v. *Lightfoot* (1960),** 480
good faith, 410*f*
Good Neighbor Policy, 296
Good News Club, 376
GOP. *See* Republican Party (GOP)
Gorbachev, Mikhail, 301, 306, 636,
754, 766
Gore, Al, 173*p*, 234
government
advocating violent overthrow of, 383,
422–423, 426
in ancient times, 7
authoritarian, 13, 18–19, 302,
753–754
basic concepts of, 49*c*
basic powers of, 7
bonds, 382, 644
central and local forms of, 19–20,
20*f*, 27
ceremonial head of, 226
as characteristic of a state, 9
checks and balances in (*See* checks
and balances)
China vs. United States, 775–776
classification of, 16–17
coalition government, 22, 569, 760
confederations, 11, 19, 20*f*, 21
in daily lives, 13
defined, 6, 8, 9
dictatorship vs. democracy, 7
division of powers, 20, 22, 116
domestic tranquility, 12
early theories of, 10–11, 14–15
in early times, 7–8, 17
economic regulation, 633–634, 633*f*
executive branch, 21–22
financing of, 646–654, 648*c*, 649*c*,
651*c*

formation of perfect union, 11
forms of, 16–22, 17*c*, 18*m*, 20*f*
free enterprise regulated by,
631–632, 633–634
function of, 11–13
geographic distribution of power,
19–21, 20*f*, 21*p*
as human invention, 7–8
immigration policies, 440–441, 441*p*
inauguration of the new, 33*f*, 599,
601
individual liberty and, 103, 116, 454
justice established by, 11–12
legislative branch, 21–22
legitimacy of, 28
liberty protected by, 13
limited, 11, 49, 49*c*, 54
local self-government, 116, 686
Native American systems of, 51
need for, 6–7, 9
ordered, 49, 49*c*
parliamentary, 19–20, 22, 22*p*, 759
participation as basis for
classification of, 17–19, 18*m*, 41*c*
popular sovereignty, 97–98, 97*i*, 106
presidential form of, 21
principles of, 6–9, 8*f*, 9*m*
private enterprise regulated by,
633–634, 633*f*
public debt, 68, 172–173, 658,
664–665, 664*f*, 673–674
representative, 49, 49*c*
restrictions on, 64, 98–99, 369, 391,
402
rule of law, 24, 28, 49, 98, 345, 396
Russian Federation vs. United
States, 770, 770*c*
Supreme Court, 97
theories of origins of, 10–11, 10*f*, 15,
41*c*
types of, 16–22
unauthorized aliens, policies on,
441–443, 441*p*
unitary, 20, 20*c*
in the United Kingdom, 16, 16*p*
See also federal government;
federalism
**Government Accountability Office
(GAO),** 184
government corporations, 284,
284*c*, 291–292, 291*f*
governors
appointment and removal power,
700–701, 712
in budget process, 701, 741*c*, 742
in charter colonies, 53
as chief administrators, 701
compensation, 699
executive power, 700, 700*p*
extradition power, 135
increasing power of, 697
judicial power, 702–703, 713–714
legislative power, 701–702
message power, 702

military power, 701
miscellaneous duties of, 703
National Guard and, 12*p*, 115*p*, 130,
701
in the New Jersey Plan, 76, 76*f*
presidency compared to, 700
in proprietary colonies, 53
qualifications of, 698
removal of, 699
in royal colonies, 52, 57
selection of, 698
special sessions, 692, 702, 702*c*
as stepping stone to presidency,
595, 699*c*
succession of, 698–699
terms of office for, 698
veto of, 685, 694, 702
women as, 449
governor's council, 52
**grandfather clauses for voting
rights,** 493–494
grand jury, 369, 416–417, 417*f*,
707–708
Grant, Ulysses S., 249, 249*p*
grants-in-aid programs, 130–132,
131*f*
Grasso, Ella, 698
grass-roots pressures, 549–550
***Gratz* v. *Bollinger* (2003),** 465
***Grayned* v. *City of Rockford* (1972),**
391
Great Depression
deficit spending during, 662–663
fiscal policies during, 643
government corporations in,
291–292
increased presidential role in, 238
influence on political attitudes, 519,
568
New Deal programs, 239*i*
new regulatory agencies as result of,
639*p*, 640–641
statistics on, 662
tax protests during, 736*p*
***Greater New Orleans Broadcasting
Association* v. *United States*
(1999),** 388
Great Leap Forward (China), 637
Great Society programs, 239
Greenback Party, 571
Greenbacks, 173
Green Party, 570*c*, 572, 572*f*
***Greer* v. *Spock* (1976),** 386
***Gregg* v. *Georgia* (1976),** 425
***Gregory* v. *Chicago* (1969),** 392–393,
393*p*
***Griswold* v. *Connecticut* (1965),** 413
gross domestic product (GDP),
641–642
Group of 7 (G7), 672
***Grutter* v. *Bollinger* (2003),** 465
Guam, representation of, 155
Guantanamo Bay Naval Station,
356, 356*p*, 415

Guinn v. *United States* (1915), 494
Guiteau, Charles, 287
Gulf of Tonkin Resolution (1964), 224*f*
Gulf War (1990), 239
Gun-Free School Zone Act (1990), 170

H

Habeas Corpus Act of 1863, 414–415
Habitat for Humanity, 541*p*
hacking, 302, 512–513
Halberstam, David, 529
Hamdan v. *Rumsfeld* (2006), 356
Hamilton, Alexander
    as Federalist leader, 81, 566
    Federalist No. 1, 80*f*
    Federalist No. 22, 96, 335
    Federalist No. 70, 181
    Federalist No. 71, 230
    Federalist No. 72, 293
    Federalist No. 76, 278
    Federalist No. 78, 101–102
    on federal judiciary, 96, 335, 335*i*, 415
    on foreign affairs, 293
    as Framer of the Constitution, 70, 73, 73*f*, 80, 82*i*, 83
    on judicial review, 101–102
    as liberal constructionist, 181, 181*f*
    on presidency, 230, 278
    as Secretary of Treasury, 280
    on writ of habeas corpus, 415*p*
Hammurabi's Code, 49
Hancock, John, 60–61, 60*c*, 73, 80
hard-liners, 752
hard money, in campaigns, 611*c*, 614
Harlan, John Marshall, 166
Harper v. *Virginia Board of Elections* (1966), 482
Harrington, James, 10
Harris, Kamala, 194*p*, 433
Harrison, Benjamin, 246
Harrison, William Henry, 231
hasty generalization fallacy, 553
Hatch, Orrin, 217
hate crimes, 448
Hawaii, Statehood of, 128
Hawke v. *Smith* (1920), 106
Hay, John, 297
Haynes v. *Washington* (1963), 347*f*
Hazelwood School District v. *Kuhlmeier* (1988), 386
Head Money Cases (1884), 253
Head Start, 239
Health and Human Services Department (HHS), 279, 283, 657
Heart of Atlanta Motel v. *United States* (1964), 169–170
Help America Vote Act of 2002, 507, 511
Henry, Patrick, 59, 65, 66, 73, 80–81

Hepburn v. *Griswold* (1870), 173–174
Hernandez v. *Texas* (1954), 420, 457
Hess, Stephen, 532
Heston, Charlton, 532, 551
heterogeneous society, 444–445, 445*f*
Hicklin v. *Orbeck* (1978), 136
hierarchical authority, 268–269
Hill v. *Colorado* (2000), 393
Hill v. *Stone* (1975), 489
Hine, Lewis, 540*f*
Hiroshima, Japan, bombing of, 263*p*
Hispanic Americans
    affirmative action, 465–466
    in the armed forces, 258
    capital punishment of, 425*c*
    discrimination against, 447–448, 465–466
    ethnicity of, 446–447
    first Cabinet member, 281
    as governors, 700*p*
    immigration by, 440*c*, 445
    as largest minority group, 447, 447*f*
    percentage of, in population, 440*c*, 445*c*, 447*c*
    serving on juries, 457
    as Supreme Court justice, 339
    in universities, 466
    voting and, 498, 502
historic events, political attitudes and, 519–520
Hitler, Adolf, 297
HIV/AIDS epidemic, 532
Hobbes, Thomas, 9, 10–11, 30, 60
Ho Chi Minh, 300
Hodgson v. *Minnesota* (1990), 412
Holmes, Oliver Wendell, Jr.
    on freedom of speech limits, 368, 368*p*, 381–382
    on importance of Supreme Court, 124
    on individual freedom, 35
    on sedition, 382
    on taxes, 650
Holt v. *Hobbs* (2015), 379
Homeland Security Act of 2002, 324
Homeland Security Department.
    See Department of Homeland Security
home-rule charters, 720, 737
homogeneous, defined, 8
honest mistakes, 410*f*
Hoover, Herbert, 229, 245, 623, 663
Hopkins, Stephen, 59
House Appropriations Committee, 660–661
House Committee on Agriculture, 201
House Judiciary Committee, 186–187
House of Burgesses, in Virginia, 52*i*
House of Commons (U.K.), 759–760, 763–764, 763*p*
House of Lords (U.K.), 759–760

House of Representatives
    Appropriations Committee, 660–661
    bills for revenue originating in, 202
    chaplain, 191, 191*p*
    committee list, 199*f*
    Committee of the Whole, 207, 207*i*
    compensation of members, 153, 154
    conference committees, 211–212, 660*f*, 661*f*
    congressional districts, 157, 157*i*, 567
    election process for, 159
    electoral duties of, 108, 188–189, 188*f*, 189*f*, 598–599
    establishment of, 155
    five calendars for bills, 206
    floor debate on bills, 207–208, 208*p*
    gerrymandering, 157–158, 157*i*
    growth of seats in, 161*c*
    House chamber, 144*i*
    impeachment power, 100, 100*f*, 186–188, 231, 598
    Jefferson appointed by, 188, 188*f*
    opening day of, 151
    in presidential election, 188, 188*f*
    profile of members, 150–151, 150*p*
    qualifications for office, 160–161
    ratings of members, 550–551
    reapportionment of, 156–159, 156*m*, 157*i*, 158*p*, 165–166
    redistricting, 157–159, 157*i*
    roles of members, 148–150, 148*c*
    scheduling floor debate, 206–207
    Senate compared with, 219*c*
    size of, 144*f*, 156, 156*m*, 161*f*
    Speaker of the House, 191, 193–194, 194*p*, 195*p*, 231, 231*f*
    standing committees, 183, 184, 185, 547, 660
    subcommittees, 183, 660, 661
    terms and sessions, 151–152, 151*f*, 155–156, 163
    treaty acceptance by, 185
    in Virginia Plan, 75, 75*f*
    voting on bills, 207–209, 208*p*
    See also Congress; congressional committees; congressional powers
House Rules Committee, 198, 199–200, 206–207, 212
House Select Committee on Benghazi, 201
House Select Committee to Investigate Covert Arms Transactions with Iran, 200
House-Senate Conference Committees, 211–212, 213, 660*f*, 661*f*
House Ways and Means Committee, 198, 199, 201, 202*p*, 660
housing, integration of, 456, 463
Housing and Urban Development (HUD), 237*p*, 239, 281
Hoyt v. *Florida* (1961), 458, 458*c*

Hudson River, 169
Hughes, Charles Evans, 348
human capital, 629, 629f
human rights
in China, 777–778, 783
under fascism, 297
policies for, 367
protection of, 37, 669
United Nations on, 316
human trafficking, 363, 757
Humphrey, William, 245, 589
Humphrey's Executor v. *United States* (1935), 245
Hungary, 753–754
hung jury, 417, 708
Hurricane Katrina, 117
Hussein, Saddam, 256, 579p, 756
Hutchinson, Thomas, 87
hypernationalism, 297

I

ideological consensus, 567–568
ideological parties, 570
"I Have a Dream" speech (King), 462p
illegal drugs, 177p, 236, 277, 308, 406
Illegal Immigration Reform and Immigration Responsibility Act of 1996, 434f, 442
illegitimate power, 754–755
Illinois v. *Caballes* (2005), 407
Illinois v. *Wardlow* (2000), 406–407, 407c
immigrants, 438
immigration
of children, 442, 473
current policies, 440–441, 441p
deportation, 441, 442–443
economic impact of, 473
enforcement of laws, 324, 409
excludable aliens, 441
quota system, 440, 440f, 485
reform of, 442–443, 473
refugees and asylum seekers, 443
statistics, 440f, 445
unauthorized immigrants, 441–443, 441p
in U.S. history, 439–440, 445
Immigration Act (1990), 434f, 440–441
Immigration and Customs Enforcement (ICE), 324, 409
Immigration and Nationality Act (1952), 440
Immigration and Nationality Act (1965), 440f, 485
Immigration Reform and Control Act of 1986, 442
immunizations, 733
impeachment, 100, 100f, 186–188, 231, 598, 693
implied powers, 118, 168, 168c, 179–180, 180f, 182p, 183f
import quotas, 668–669

inalienable rights, 452
income, influence on voting, 500–501, 501f
income tax, 171–172, 648–651, 651f, 655, 738–739
incorporation of cities, 724
incorporation process, 370
incumbents, 161
independent agencies, 266f
government corporations, 284c
independent executive agencies, 284–288, 284c
independent regulatory commissions, 245, 263, 284, 284c, 288–291
purpose and types of, 283–284, 284c
See also names of specific agencies
independent executive agencies, 284–288, 284c
independent regulatory commissions, 288–291
examples of, 284c, 289–290
executive, legislative, and judicial powers of, 289–290
impact of, 290–291
removal of, 245
structure of, 284c, 289
See also names of specific commissions
independent states, alliances of, 21
independent voters, defined, 505
in-depth news, 535
India, as earliest known democracy, 7
Indian Education Act of 1972, 446
indictments, 107c, 416–417, 707–708
indirect approach, in lobbying, 549–553, 550c, 552f
indirect democracy, 17, 17c, 24, 24i
indirect taxes, 172, 648–649, 648c
individual contributors of campaign money, 610–611
individual freedoms, 33, 35–36, 38, 81, 415
individual income taxes, 651–652, 651f
individual initiative, 38, 630, 637c, 638
individual liberty, 103, 116, 454
individual naturalization, 438
individual rights
government regulation of, 454
of juveniles, 400–401
public good and, 397–399
in social contract theory, 11, 30
as unalienable, 366–367
individuals, worth of, 34
industrial supplies, import of, 668
inevitable discovery rule, 410f
inferior courts, 97, 335, 351–357. *See also specific courts*
inflation, 642, 643
informal qualifications. *See* qualifications

information affidavit, 417, 708
inherent powers, 118–119, 168, 168c
inheritance taxes, 653, 739
initiatives
as means of amending State constitutions, 687, 688c
Populist Party on, 571
in State government, 394, 695, 696c
injunctions, 385, 481–482, 706
innovator role of minor parties, 573
In re Debs (1895), 127
In re Gault (1967), 397, 400–401
In re Kemmler (1890), 423
In re Oliver (1948), 418
integration. *See* desegregation
Inter-American Treaty of Reciprocal Assistance (Rio Pact), 296
interest
interest rates, 290, 640, 644–645, 644c
paid to the Fed, 654
on the public debt, 658
interest groups
campaign contributions by, 610
defined, 538–539
direct approach by, 546–549, 546i, 547f, 548f
evaluating, 543f
increase in, 545
indirect approach by, 549–553, 550c, 552f
Internet and, 550–551
mass media and, 552–553, 552f
origins and viewpoints of, 540–543, 540f, 543f
political action committees and, 611
political parties vs., 539–540, 539f
reasons for joining, 543–545, 544f
reflection of public opinion, 521
State governments and, 695, 695p
types of, 544–545, 544f
Internal Revenue Service (IRS), 268p, 652–653
International Committee of the Red Cross, 316
International Court of Justice (ICJ), 314–315
international humanitarian law, 304
internationalism, 298, 305, 312
International Monetary Fund (IMF), 314, 316, 671
international partnerships, 653. *See also* global economy
international security, 298, 314, 317
International Security Assistance Force (ISAF), 312, 312c
international terrorism, 177, 301–302, 304
international trade
Articles of Confederation on, 69, 70
benefits of, 667, 667c
climate change and, 670

Court of International Trade, 97, 340c, 355

in enslaved peoples, 77–78, 78c, 170

European colonialism and, 28–29, 29m

Federal Trade Commission, 245, 354, 623f

North American Free Trade Agreement, 669–670

protectionism and, 668–669, 669f

tax limitations on, 736

trade alliances and organizations, 544, 668, 669–670, 670i, 671–672, 674p

trade deficits, 673–674, 679

trade embargoes and sanctions, 669

Triangular Trade, 29m

winners and losers in, 666–668, 667c

International Trade Commission, 668

Internet

in China, 775–776

element of mass media, 530, 530p

free speech, 388–389

in fundraising, 608–609

impact on voting, 512–513, 530, 530p

interest groups and, 550–551

legislators use of, 148

polls and, 524

rise of, 148–149

sales taxes and, 738

internment of Japanese Americans, 369, 369p, 448

interracial marriages, 133p, 457

interstate commerce

congressional power to regulate, 110, 116, 118, 121, 168c

limits on congressional power, 170

prohibition on taxing, 736

interstate compacts, 132–133, 603, 701p

Interstate Highway System, 398, 735–736, 735p

interstate transportation, 136, 366p

Intolerable Acts (1774), 57c, 59

intraparty elections, 582

inventions, exclusive rights to, 39, 174–175, 174f, 632

investigative powers, 183–184, 200

investigative reporting, 529–530, 529i

involuntary servitude, 402–404

Iowa caucus, 591p

Iran

American hostages in, 264p–265p, 309f

Iran-Contra scandal, 200, 276, 301

as theocracy, 19

Iraq, 19, 172p, 239, 303, 303m, 755

"iron curtain," 299

Iroquois League, 51

Islamist State, 224f, 302–303, 755

isolationism, 294–295, 298, 305, 312

Israel, 255, 302, 302p, 303m, 310

issue-oriented groups, 544. *See also* interest groups

Isthmus of Panama, 296

Italy, Fascist, 18, 297

J

Jackson, Andrew

Cabinet nominee rejections, 184c

on caucuses, 581

portrayed as King Andrew the First, 238i

use of spoils system, 287

use of Cabinet, 282

use of veto, 238

Jackson, Robert H., 368

***Jackson* v. *Hobbs* (2012),** 424

***Jacobellis* v. *Ohio* (1964),** 388

Jamestown settlement, 49, 51, 684

January 6, 2021 Capitol attack, 187–188, 598

Japan, 296–297

Japanese Americans, internment of, 369, 369p, 448

Jay, John, 59, 60–61, 60c, 81

Jefferson, Thomas

Alien and Sedition Acts of 1798, 382

on amendments to the Constitution, 108

as Anti-Federalist, 180–181, 181f, 566

on bicameral legislatures, 94

on the Constitution, 73, 83, 113

on court-packing, 343

Declaration of Independence, 11, 61–62, 146, 237

on the electoral college, 601, 603i

on equality, 34

on execution of the law, 241

on justice, 11

on liberty, 13

Louisiana Purchase, 111, 128m, 295

as minister to France, 74

on Mount Rushmore, 95p

presidential election of (1801), 108, 188, 343, 598

on presidential powers, 241, 274

on the press, 528

at Second Continental Congress, 60–61, 60c

as secretary of state, 280, 307

on separation of church and state, 373, 374

staff of, 274

as strict constructionist, 180–181, 181f

Jehovah's Witnesses, 366

***Jet* magazine,** 533c

Jewish legal concepts, 49

Jim Crow laws, 454–455

job specialization, 269

John (king of England), 49, 54, 54i

Johnson, Andrew, 245, 248, 510i

Johnson, Claudia "Lady Bird," 111p, 236

Johnson, Gary, 567

Johnson, Lyndon B., 226p, 481p

on campaign finance laws, 614

decision not to seek reelection, 589

federal campaign finance laws, 614

first African American Cabinet member, 281

Great Society programs, 239

presidential election of, 509

recess appointments, 244f

succession to presidency, 111, 111p

use of federal forces to keep peace, 126–127

Vietnam War and, 178, 178p, 224f, 228, 300

Voting Rights Act of 1965, 476f, 479, 482–485, 482c, 483f

See also Civil Rights Act of 1964

Johnson, Richard M., 188–189, 189f, 599

Johnson, William Samuel, 76

Joint Chiefs of Staff, 319–320

Joint Committee on Taxation, 191, 201

Joint Committee on the Library, 201

joint committees, congressional, 191, 201, 212

joint resolutions, 107, 203, 219c, 253, 256, 438

***Jones* v. *Mayer* (1968),** 403–404, 403p

judges

in appellate courts, 353–354, 354f

appointment of, 100, 100f, 211, 243–245, 244c, 335

colonial, 52–53

in federal district courts, 351–353

removal of, 129, 186, 245

role of, 338

salaries and duties of, 340–341

selection of, 338–339, 338f, 713–714, 714p

in State courts, 710c, 713–714

terms of, 335, 340–341

judicial activism, 339–340

judicial branch, 330–357

Administrative Office, 332f

checks and balances of, 99i, 100–102, 100f

in China, 774–775, 774f

democracy and, 334–335

dual system of federal and State courts, 335–336

establishment of, 96–97, 335–336, 335i

evolution of, 332f

lobbying of, 548–549

national judiciary, 334–341, 337f, 338f, 340f

in Russian Federation, 768–769, 768f

separation of powers, 98i, 99

in United Kingdom, 762, 762p

See also federal courts; State courts; Supreme Court

judicial philosophies, 339–340
judicial powers
    Alexander Hamilton's view on, 335, 335*p*
    of Congress, 176
    defined, 7
    establishment of, 96–97, 99, 101, 118
    executive privilege vs., 243*f*
    of governors, 702–703
    judicial activism and, 339
    judicial review, 101–102, 101*i*, 111, 342–344
    in judiciary branch, 335–336
    in military justice, 355
    in Russian Federation, 769
    of State judicial branch, 96–97
    of State legislatures, 693
judicial proceedings, defined, 133
judicial restraint, 339–340
judicial review, 101–102, 101*i*, 111, 342–344
judicial systems
    in China, 774–775, 774*f*
    in Russian Federation, 768–769
    in United Kingdom, 762
    in United States, 335–336
Judiciary Act of 1789, 109*i*, 110, 332*f*, 338, 343
Judiciary Committee (House), 199
Judiciary Committee (Senate), 199
Juliard **v.** *Greenman* **(1884),** 174
jurisdiction
    of circuit-based appellate courts, 354
    of Court of Appeals for the Federal Circuit, 97, 340*c*, 352*m*, 353–354, 354*f*, 356–357
    defined, 336
    in federal court system, 97, 336–337, 337*f*
    of federal district courts, 352, 359
    of municipal courts, 710
    parties involved and, 336
    of State courts of appeal, 711
    subject matter and, 336
    of Supreme Court, 344–345
    types of, 337
jury systems
    grand jury, 369, 416–417, 417*f*, 707–708
    hung jury, 417, 708
    jury composition, 420
    jury selection, 419*f*, 708–709, 708*p*
    petit juries, 419, 708, 711
    waiving rights to jury trial, 419
jus sanguinis, 437*f*, 438
jus soli, 437, 437*f*
just compensation, 398–399
justice
    in Athenian democracy, 4*f*, 14, 24
    in the Constitution, 92, 135
    defined, 11
    in feudal and monarchical systems, 25, 26–27, 28*f*
    government and, 11–12

    in the military, 355–356, 355*p*, 356*p*
    obstruction of, 187
    symbol for, 342
justice courts, 709
Justice Department
    Anti-Trust Division of, 13
    under the attorney general, 278
    enforcement of civil rights acts, 463
    Homeland Security and, 24
    in impeachment, 186
    solicitor general, 346
    units in, 271
justices of the peace, 49, 343, 709–710, 709*p*
juvenile courts, 400–401, 710
juveniles, rights of, 400–401

K

Kagan, Elena, 339, 361, 361*c*
Kahn **v.** *Shevin* **(1974),** 458
Kansas **v.** *Hendricks* **(1997),** 417
Katz **v.** *United States* **(1967),** 410–411, 411*i*
Kelley, Oliver Hudson, 540*f*
Kelo **v.** *City of New London* **(2005),** 398–399
Kennedy, Anthony M., 617–618
Kennedy, Jacqueline, 235
Kennedy, John F.
    assassination of, 519–520
    burden of office, 252, 252*p*
    on Cabinet meetings, 281
    as Catholic, 595
    civil rights intervention, 127
    Cuban missile crisis, 224*f*
    election to presidency, 602*c*, 603
    on individual rights, 36*p*
    Khrushchev meeting, 294*p*
    on lobbyists, 547
    recess appointments, 244*f*
    South Vietnam aid, 300
    speaking ability of, 595
    in televised debates, 597
Kennedy, Robert, 520, 589
Kentucky **v.** *Dennison* **(1861),** 135
Kerry, John, 501, 501*c*, 595, 615
Keynes, John Maynard, 643, 643*p*, 663
Keynesian economics, 663–664
keynote address, at national conventions, 594, 594*p*
Khomeini, Ayatollah, 309
Khrushchev, Nikita, 294*p*, 306
Kimble **v.** *Swackhamer* **(1978),** 106
Kim Il-Sung, 755
Kim Jong-il, 18
Kim Jong-un, 18, 19*p*
King, Coretta Scott, 478*p*
King, Martin Luther, Jr.
    assassination of, 127, 135*p*, 520
    bus boycott, 457
    Civil Rights Act of 1964 and, 478*p*, 481*p*

    Civil Rights Act of 1965 and, 446
    efforts on behalf of equality, 446, 457, 481, 481*p*
    "I Have a Dream" speech, 462*p*, 486
    on justice, 12, 462
    opposition to national holiday honoring, 391
    voter registration in Selma, Alabama, 482
    on voting, 481–482, 481*p*
King, Rodney, 127
King Caucus, 581
Kissinger, Henry, 308*p*
Kitchen Cabinet, 282
Kitzhaber, John, 702*c*
Klopfer **v.** *North Carolina* **(1967),** 418
knock-and-announce rule, 410*c*
Know Nothings party, 571
Knox, Henry, 280
Korean War, 240, 240*p*, 250–251, 256, 299, 299*p*
Korematsu **v.** *United States* **(1944),** 369
Kosovo, 311, 312
kulaks, 753
Kunin, Madeleine, 698*p*
Kurds, 756
Kuwait, 239

L

labor, 629, 629*f*, 670, 673
Labor, Department of, 278, 641
labor unions, 544–545, 544*f*, 686
Labour Party (U.K.), 764
La Follette, Robert, 210*c*, 566, 571
laissez-faire theory, 632
Lamone **v.** *Benisek* **(2019),** 158–159
land, as factor of production, 629, 629*f*
land-grant colleges, 130, 130*p*
Landon, Alfred, 522
Lansing, John, 83
Lasswell, Harold D., 546
Latin America, 295, 296*c*
Latinos, 447–448, 447*f*, 502
law of probability, 524
law of supply and demand, 631, 631*f*
Lawrence **v.** *Texas* **(2003),** 412, 459
leadership characteristics, 229*c*
league of friendship, 11
League of Nations, 253, 312
League of United Latin American Citizens (LULAC), 538*p*, 545
League of Women Voters, 499*p*
Lebanon, 9
Ledbetter, Lilly, 450, 450*p*
Lee, Richard Henry
    at First Continental Congress, 59
    proposal of Declaration of Independence, 61, 62, 67
    on ratification of Constitution, 80, 82
    at Second Continental Congress, 60*c*

Lee v. *Washington* (1968), 457
Lee v. *Weisman* (1992), 377
legal entity, 8
legal tender, 173
legislative branch
    checks and balances of, 99*i*,
        100–102, 100*f*
    in China, 774–775, 774*f*
    committee system, 149
    constituent service by, 149–150
    courts in, 97
    defined, 16
    demographics of, 146*p*, 150–151,
        150*p*
    establishment of, 99
    lobbying of, 546–548, 547*f*
    in a parliamentary government, 22
    responsibilities of, 147–150, 148*c*
    role of, in democracy, 146–147
    in Russian Federation, 768, 768*f*
    separation of powers and, 21–22,
        98*i*, 99
    of States, 690–696
    See also Congress; House of
        Representatives; Senate; State
        legislatures
legislative courts, 336
legislative power
    of Congress, 99, 155, 343*c*
    defined, 7
    of executive branch, 247
    of independent agencies, 289
    of State legislatures, 701–702
    in United Kingdom, 759
legitimacy of government, 28
Lemon **Test, in education,** 375–376
Lemon v. *Kurtzman* (1971), 375, 706*c*
Lend-Lease program, 310
Lenin, Vladimir, 765
Levine, Rachel, 281
Lexington and Concord battles,
    46*f*, 60
LGBTQ rights, 445, 459
libel, 381
liberal constructionists, 180–181
Liberal Democratic Party (Russian
    Federation), 769
Libertarian Party, 570, 570*c*, 571*p*
liberty
    authority and, 36
    equality and, 34
    government and, 13, 31–32, 103
Library of Congress, 201
Libya, 302, 309, 312
licenses
    for demonstrations, 392
    for driving, 167
    for fishing and hunting, 136
    for professionals, 120*p*
    taxes on, 647, 740
    for trade, 29
Lidster v. *Illinois* (2004), 406
lieutenant governors, 581, 585, 694,
    694*p*, 698–699, 703

Lilly Ledbetter Fair Pay Act of
    2009, 450, 450*p*
limited government
    civil liberties and, 368–369
    Constitutional Convention on, 78
    defined, 49, 49*c*
    guarantees of, 49, 49*c*, 98–99,
        368–369
    in social contract theory, 11
    in State constitutions, 64, 685, 686
limited liability company (LLC),
    649
Lincoln, Abraham
    assassination of, 186
    Cabinet of, 282
    in Civil War, 255, 255*p*
    on democracy, 17
    expansion of presidential power by,
        238, 239
    on individual rights, 36
    on Mount Rushmore, 95*p*
    on object of government, 39
    political memorabilia, 510*p*
    on Reconstruction after Civil War,
        126*i*, 186
    Republican Party and, 502
    writ of habeas corpus suspension,
        414–415
line agencies, 272–273, 272*f*
line-item veto, 213, 249, 249*p*, 702
Ling v. *Northwest Indian Cemetery*
    Protective Association (1988),
    339–340
literacy tests for voting, 481, 482,
    483, 493–494, 493*p*
Literary Digest **straw poll,** 522, 524
Little Rock, Arkansas, school
    integration in, 127, 127*p*, 433,
    456*p*, 481*p*
Livingston, Philip, 59
Livingston, Robert, 61
Lloyd Corporation v. *Tanner* (1972),
    292
lobbying
    in budget creation, 661
    direct approach to, 546–549, 546*i*,
        547*f*, 548*f*
    in 18-year-old voting rights, 491
    indirect approach to, 549–550
    protection of, 390
    in State governments, 695
local governments, 717–731
    additional sales taxes for, 738
    in China, 774, 775
    counties, 717–720, 718*f*, 719*c*, 720*p*
    defined, 19
    elections in, 581–582
    federal aid to and from, 132
    government types and, 19–20, 20*f*,
        116
    local courts, 357, 709–710, 709*p*,
        710*c*
    local self-government, 116, 686
    revenue sources for, 738–741, 738*c*

    in Russian Federation, 769
    special districts, 723, 723*p*, 730–731
    State government and, 122
    towns and townships, 26–27, 719,
        721, 722–723
    tribal governments, 19, 720–721,
        721*m*
    in United Kingdom, 762
    See also city governments
local party functions, 576–577, 576*f*
local self-government, 116, 686
Locke, Gary, 697*p*
Locke, John
    in the Enlightenment, 30, 30*i*, 31–32
    influence on Declaration of
        Independence, 61–62
    influence on the Constitution, 72
    social contract theory, 10–11, 11*i*, 30
    Two Treatises of Government, 31,
        32, 46*f*
logical fallacies, 553
Long, Huey, 210
Long, Russell, 153
lords, in monarchical government,
    25
lord-vassal relationship, 26
Los Angeles Times, 533*c*
lotteries, 741
Louisiana Purchase, 111, 128*m*, 295
Louisiana v. *Resweber* (1947), 423
Loving, Richard and Mildred, 133*p*
Loving v. *Virginia* (1967), 133*p*, 457
loyal opposition, 755
LULAC (League of United Latin
    American Citizens), 538*p*, 545
luxury taxes, 653
Lynch v. *Donnelly* (1984), 364*f*, 706*c*

M
Machiavelli, Niccoló, 29
Madison, James
    on bicameralism, 95, 162
    on bureaucracy, 269–270
    checks and balances system,
        101–102, 247
    on dangers of direct democracy, 24
    Federalist No. 10, 147, 540
    Federalist No. 47, 99
    Federalist No. 51, 12, 91, 101, 103,
        247
    Federalist Papers, 80–82
    as Framer of the Constitution, 70, 73,
        73*f*, 80, 147
    insurance of domestic tranquility, 12
    on interest groups, 540
    on religious freedom, 373
    republicanism, 98
    as secretary of state, 343
    27th amendment, 109
    Virginia Plan, 74–75, 75*f*
Madsen v. *Women's Health*
    Services, Inc. (1994), 393
magazines, 529–530

magistrates, 332*f,* 710
Magna Carta, 49, 54–55, 54*i,* 758
mail-in ballots, 488*p,* 507–508, 512, 512*f*
majority leader, 196
majority-minority congressional districts, 158
majority opinion, 347
majority rule, 34–35
Malloy v. *Hogan* (1964), 421
mandates, 520
mandatory drug testing, 408–409
mandatory referendum, 695–696
Mandela, Nelson, 753
Manifest Destiny, 295
Manning, Chelsea (formerly Bradley Manning), 351*f*
Mao Zedong, 636–637, 772–773, 772*p*
Mapp, Dollree, 366, 408
Mapp v. *Ohio* (1961), 347*f,* 405, 407*c,* 408
Marbury, William, 343–344, 344*i*
Marbury v. *Madison* (1803), 102, 111, 343–344, 344*i*
March on Washington for civil rights (1963), 37
Marcy, William Learned, 287
margin of error, 523*f*
Marine Corps, 319, 321
maritime law, 336
marriage
    divorce, 133–134, 454
    5th Amendment rights, 421
    interracial, 133*p,* 457
    licenses and certificates, 719, 720*p*
    same-sex, 134, 459
Marshall, George C., 141, 281, 310
Marshall, John, 123–124, 123*i,* 169, 343–344, 344*i*
Marshall, Thomas, 233
Marshall, Thurgood, 339
Marshall Plan, 251, 310
martial law, 50
Martinez, Susana, 700*p*
Marx, Karl, 634, 634*p*
Marxist economies, 634
Maryland, State constitution of, 685
Maryland proprietary colony, 51*m,* 52–53
Mason, George, 73*f,* 79, 113–114, 113*i,* 141
Massachusetts
    Shays' Rebellion in, 69–70
    State constitution of, 63–64, 684, 687, 689
Massachusetts Bay Colony, 53
Massachusetts royal colony, 51–53, 51*m,* 57, 60*c*
mass media
    1st Amendment and, 386–389
    forms of, 527
    in-depth news, 535
    influence on political opinion, 518, 521, 531–534, 532*f,* 533*c,* 551–552

inner ring of, 532
interest groups and, 552–553, 552*f*
limited influence of, 67–68
partisan, 532–533, 532*f*
prior restraint on, 385–386, 385*p,* 387
public agenda, 531
role of, 527–531, 533*c*
Vietnam War and, 536–537, 536*p*
as watchdogs, 532
Mattis, James, 281
Maximilian, Archduke, 295
May, Theresa, 762*p*
Mayflower, 48, 48*i*
mayor-council governments, 724–725, 725*f*
McCain, John, 155*p,* 502, 609*p,* 613, 615
McCain-Feingold Law, 614*p*
McCarthy, Eugene, 580
McCarthy, Joseph, 179*p*
McConnell, Mitch, 214
McConnell v. *FEC* (2003), 610
McCullen v. *Coakley* (2014), 393
McCulloch, James, 123, 181
McCulloch v. *Maryland* (1819), 123–124, 181, 182, 650, 736
McCutcheon v. *FEC* (2014), 384, 431, 610
McDonald v. *Chicago* (2016), 98, 405
McGovern, George, 508–509
McKinley, William, 231, 253–254
McLaurin v. *Oklahoma* (1950), 455, 461
Medicaid, 658*p,* 733
Medicare, 652, 658
medium, defined, 527. See also mass media
Medvedev, Dmitry, 765*p,* 767
membership lists, 394
mental institutions, voting and, 494
mercantilism, 28–29, 29*m*
MERCOSUR. See Southern Common Market
Merit Systems Protection Board, 287–288
message power, 247, 702
metric system, 176
metropolitan areas, 730
Mexican Americans, 447, 457
Mexico, 294, 295, 296*c,* 669–670
Miami-Dade County, Florida, 731
Michael M. v. *Superior Court* (1981), 454
Middle East, 302–303, 303*m*
Middle Passage, 451
Miers, Harriet, 185
migrant workers, 442*p*
military
    branches of, 320–322
    civilian control of, 281, 319, 319*f*
    compulsory service, 183, 288, 288*i*
    congressional power over, 183, 256
    desegregation of, 243, 258–259, 258*p*
    in dictatorships, 19, 19*p*

Joint Chiefs of Staff, 319–320
military justice, 355–356, 355*p,* 356*p*
NASA and, 286
presidential power over, 95–96, 255–257
role of, 12
rule by, 50
Selective Service System and, 183, 288, 288*i*
sheltering troops in homes, 50
voting by, 508, 513
Military Commission Act of 2006, 356
military commissions, 356
military governments, 754
military justice, 355–356, 355*p,* 356*p*
Millennium Development Goals (UN), 316*c*
Miller, Clem, 197–198
Miller v. *Alabama* (2012), 424
Miller v. *California* (1973), 388
Milosevic, Slobodan, 256, 312
Mineta, Norman, 281
Minnesota v. *Carter* (1998), 406, 407*c*
minority leader, 189*f,* 196
minority rights, 34–35
minor parties, 570–573, 570*c,* 571*i,* 572*f,* 573*c,* 614
Mint, U.S., 654
Miranda rule, 421–422, 421*f*
Miranda v. *Arizona* (1966), 347*f,* 422
miscegenation laws, 457
misdemeanors, 98, 707, 709
Mississippi, State constitution of, 685
Missouri ex rel. Gaines v. *Canada* (1938), 455
Missouri Plan, for selecting judges, 713, 714
Missouri v. *Holland* (1920), 253
Missouri v. *McNeely* (2013), 398
mixed economies, 633–634, 633*f*
Mobutu Sese Seko, 754
modern state timeline, 41*c*
modified one-party system, 570
monarchical government, 27–29, 27*f,* 29*m*
monarchies, 49–50, 752, 761
monarchs, 27, 27*f,* 30
Mondale, Walter, 194, 597
monetary policies, 643–645, 644*c*
money for presidential elections. See elections and money
money powers, 170–174, 171*f,* 172*p,* 173*p*
money supply, 636*f,* 643–644. See also monetary policies
monopolies and trusts, 12–13, 39*i,* 631
Monroe, James, 295–296
Monroe Doctrine, 295–296, 295*i*
Montesquieu, Baron de, 30, 31, 31*i*
Montgomery, Alabama bus boycott, 457

Morrill Act, 130, 130p
Morris, Gouverneur, 73
Morse, Wayne, 210c
Morsi, Mohammed, 757
Morton v. *Mancari* **(1974),** 457
Mothers Against Drunk Drivers (MADD), 541p, 542
motion pictures, freedom of, 387
Motor Voter Act, 492
MoveOn.org, 550, 615
Mubarak, Hosni, 757
muckrakers, 529–530, 529i
multinational corporations, 667
multiparty politics, 569, 569f, 769
municipal courts, 710
municipality, 724
Murkowski, Lisa, 580
Murray v. *Curlett* **(1963),** 376
Muslims
  in China, 777–778, 777p
  rights of, 379
Mussolini, Benito, 297
Mutual Film Corporation v. *Ohio* **(1915),** 387
Myanmar, 757, 775m
Myers, Frank, 245
Myers, Michael, 160
Myers Automatic Booth, 511
Myers v. *United States* **(1920),** 245
Myspace, 530

N

Nadeau, Joe, 712
Nader, Ralph, 572, 572f
nanogrids, 285
Napoleon III, 295
Napolitano, Janet, 411
narcotics, 171, 406, 424, 647
nation, defined, 8
National Aeronautics and Space Administration (NASA), 283, 284–285, 285f
National Association for the Advancement of Colored People (NAACP), 544–545, 549
National Association for the Advancement of Colored People v. *Alabama* **(1958),** 393–394, 394p
National Association of Colored Women, 540f
National Broadcasting Co. v. *United States* **(1943),** 387
National Bureau of Standards, 176
national chair, of the party, 575–576
National Child Labor Committee, 540f
national committees (political parties), 575–576, 592
national conventions (political parties)
  apportioning delegates, 592–593
  establishment of, 572
  goals and functions of, 574–576, 593
  national committee and, 592

nomination of candidate, 564, 574, 592–594
party platform, 584, 593–594
proposing and ratifying amendments, 105, 188
protests at Democratic National Convention (1968), 589
National Counterterrorism Center (NCTC), 322, 322p
national debt. *See* public debt
national draft, 183, 288, 288i, 458
National Federation of Independent Business v. *Sebelius* **(2012),** 124, 346p
National Firearms Act of 1934, 404–405
National Geospatial-Intelligence Agency, 322
national government. *See* federal government
National Grange, 540f
National Guard, 12p, 115p, 130, 701
National Indian Gaming Commission, 285
National Institute of Standards and Technology, 13
nationalism, 297, 300, 368, 634–635
national judiciary, 334–341. *See also* judicial branch
National Labor Relations Board v. *Noel Canning* **(2014),** 244, 289
National Origins Act of 1929, 440
National Party Congress (China), 775, 775f
National People's Congress (China), 774, 774f
national pollsters, 523
national popular vote plan, 602c, 603–604
National Rifle Association (NRA), 543, 551–553
National Science Foundation (NSF), 285
national security, 318–324, 327f
  Department of Defense, 279, 318–320, 319f, 320p
  Department of Homeland Security, 279, 323–324
  Director of National Intelligence, 322–323
  military branches, 320–322
  National Security Agency, 322–323, 411
  National Security Council, 275–276
  See also military
National Security Act of 1947, 318–319, 321
National Security Agency (NSA), 322–323, 411
National Security Council (NSC), 275–276
National Teachers Corps, 239
National Treasury Employees Union v. *Von Raab* **(1989),** 409

National Women's Party, 362p–363p
nation-states, rise of, 26–27
Native Americans
  citizenship of, 437
  conflict with colonies, 51m, 58
  decimation of, 48, 446
  discrimination against, 446, 446p
  gambling casinos, 200
  government systems of, 51
  protected by 14th Amendment, 437
  reservations, 446
  tribal governments, 720–721, 721m
natural-born citizens, 437–438, 437f
naturalization, 176, 229, 438–439, 438f, 489
naturalized citizens, 108, 176, 229, 438–439, 438f
natural rights, principles of, 61–62
Navajo tribes, 721
Navy, U.S., 321, 321i
Navy Department, 318
Nazi Germany, 18, 297
NBC Learn
  advancements of NASA, 265
  Bureau of Engraving and Printing and the Fed, 625
  economic development in North and South Korea, 749
  governorship as stepping-stone to presidency, 681
  influencing public opinion, 559
  James Madison, 45
  John Locke, 3
  Loretta Sanchez, 143
  Minnijean Trickey, 433
  qualities of a good President, 223
  sources for political information, 475
  Supreme Court's role in civil rights, 331
  surveillance methods, 363
  women's vote, 89
Near v. *Minnesota* **(1931),** 370, 385
Nebraska Press Association v. *Stuart* **(1976),** 385
Necessary and Proper Clause, 118, 179–182, 180f, 181f
Negroponte, John, 322
New Deal legislation, 101, 626p, 657p
New England Confederation, 57, 58i
New England towns, 722, 722p
New Hampshire, State constitution of, 685, 689
New Hampshire colony, 51m, 52
New Jersey, State constitution of, 685
New Jersey colony, 51m, 52, 57
New Jersey Plan, 75–76, 76f, 94
New Jersey School Bus Case, 375
New Mexico, Statehood of, 156
newspapers
  copyrights for, 174

court proceedings and, 418–419
history of, 528
in-depth news coverage in, 535
influence on leaders, 532
partisan press, 532–533, 564
prior restraint and, 385–386, 385p, 387
in prisons, 386
propaganda in, 553
public opinion and, 514, 518, 527–528
in the ratification debate, 81–82
special interest groups and, 551
taxes on, 58
Vietnam War and, 385, 536–537, 536p
See also mass media
New York, State constitution of, 685
New York City, as first U.S. capital, 83
New York colony, 51–52, 51m, 60c, 61
New York Stock Exchange, 289p
New York Times, **on the Vietnam War,** 385, 536
New York Times **v.** *Sullivan* **(1964),** 381
New York Times **v.** *United States* **(1971),** 385
New York Weekly Journal, 34
New York World's Fair, 528
Ney, Robert, 200
Nicaragua, 300–301, 301f
Nigeria, 754
19th Amendment, 388, 457, 476f, 479
9th Amendment, 372
Nixon, Jay, 702c
Nixon, Pat, 235, 601p
Nixon, Richard
arms limitation summits, 301
China visit, 301, 776p
as congressman, 203p
first presidential debate, 596–597
presidential election results, 602c, 603
presidential pardon for, 246
resignation of, 186–187, 186p, 520
resignation of Vice President Agnew, 234–235
selection of Gerald R. Ford as Vice President, 235
Title IX, 463, 468
United States v. *Nixon* (1974), 243, 243f
as Vice President, 601p
Vietnamization of the war, 178, 300–301
Watergate scandal, 186, 228–229, 520
nobles, in monarchical government, 27, 27f
no-excuse absentee voting, 508, 512
nominations
for appointed offices, 587

convention system, 581–582, 592–594
defined, 578
direct primaries, 582–587, 584p, 586c
impact of, 578–579
methods of, 579
as party function, 564, 574
by petition, 587, 587p
for presidency, 564, 574, 594–596
by self-announcement, 579–580
winning of, 562, 567
nongovernmental organizations (NGOs), 316
nonpartisan primaries, 585
nonpartisan redistricting commissions, 158
nonprofit groups, 413p, 616, 617–618, 652
nonsalary compensation, 153
non-voters, 497–499, 497c
Norris, George, 212
North Africa uprisings, 302
North American Free Trade Agreement (NAFTA), 669–670
North Atlantic Treaty Organization (NATO), 311–312, 312c
North Carolina, State constitution of, 685
North Carolina colony, 51m, 52
Northern Mariana Islands, 439
North Korea, 18, 19p, 299–300, 302, 755, 766
Northwest Ordinance of 1787, 125, 127–128, 130
Northwest Territory, 127
no-third term tradition, 112, 230
nuclear weapons, 234, 234p, 263, 321

O

Obama, Barack, 222p–223p
Affordable Care Act, 124, 647
Afghanistan war, 110p
arms limitation agreement with Russia, 304
Cabinet nominees of, 575p
campaign financing of, 613
on child protection, in China, 367
on *Citizens United* decision, 610
as commander in chief, 110p
deportation of immigrants, 473
disrespect by House member to, 160
economic stimulus measures, 643, 663, 663f
family background, 595
as first African American president, 595
Guantanamo Bay facility closure order, 356
at hurricane damage site, 228p
inauguration, 33f
Libya and, 184, 256
Lilly Ledbetter Fair Pay Act of 2009, 450p

political experience, 595
presidential election, 595
recess appointments, 240–241, 244f
refusal of government campaign money, 613
Republicans in Congress during term of, 565
Secretary of State Clinton and, 308, 596–597
Snowden controversy and, 323, 411
State of the Union address, 484p
strikes against Islamic State, 224f
Supreme Court nominations, 349–350
suspended deportation of children (DACA), 442
suspended deportation of parents of US citizens (DAPA), 443
voter demographics, 501
wiretapping, 411
Obama, Michelle, 235p, 236
Obergefell **v.** *Hodges* **(2015),** 134, 134p, 459
oblasts **(Russia),** 769
obscene materials or wording, 368, 388
Occupational Safety and Health Administration (OSHA), 278–279, 641
occupation, influence on voting, 500–501
O'Connor, Sandra Day, 334p, 339, 349p, 361, 425, 465
office-group ballots, 510
Office of Administration, 277–278
Office of Economic Opportunity (OEO), 239
Office of Management and Budget (OMB), 276, 276c, 659f, 660
Office of National Drug Control Policy (ONDCP), 276–277, 277f
Office of Passport Services, 310
Office of Personnel Management (OPM), 286–288
Office of Science and Technology Policy, 277
Office of the Vice President, 277
Office of the United States Trade Representative, 318
off-year elections, 159, 497
Ohio **v.** *Akron Center for Reproductive Health* **(1990),** 412
Oklahoma, Statehood of, 129
Oklahoma Board of Education of Independent School District No. 92 of Pottawatomie County **v.** *Earls,* **(2002),** 409
Old-Age, Survivors, and Disability Insurance (OASDI), 652–653, 652c, 658
oligarchy, 18, 41c
Olive Branch petition, 60c, 61
Olmstead **v.** *United States* **(1928),** 410

Omnibus Crime Control and Safe Street Act (1968), 410–411
omnibus measures, 214
one-party politics, 569–570, 569f
"one person, one vote" ruling, 158, 165–166, 165p
online voting, 512–513, 557
Open Door policy in China, 297
open-election law, 584
Open Housing Act (1968), 463
opening day of the House, 190–191, 191i
open market operations, 644
open primaries, 583–584, 586
Operation Desert Storm, 239
Operation Iraqi Freedom, 256
opinion leaders and pundits, 518–519
Opinion of the Court, 347, 460
optional referendum, 698
oral arguments, 346
Ordinance of 1785, 128
ordinance power, 242
Oregon, State constitution of, 689
Oregon v. *Mitchell* (1970), 494
Organization of American States (OAS), 317
original jurisdiction, 337, 344–345
origins of states, evolutionary theory of, 10, 10f, 41c
Orr v. *Orr* (1979), 454
Orwell, George, 444
Oslo Accords, 302
Out of Order (O'Connor), 349–350
outsourcing of jobs, 673
oversight function of Congress, 149, 184, 241
overthrowing the government, advocating, 383, 423, 426

P

Pacheco, Romualdo, 149p
packing, in gerrymandering, 158
Packwood, Bob, 164, 164p
PACs. *See* political action committees (PAC)
Paine, Thomas, 65, 66
Palestinian Liberation Organization (PLO), 302
Panama Canal, 296, 662, 662p
Panetti v. *Quarterman* (2007), 425
panics, in banking, 643
paper ballots, 509–510. *See also* ballots
paper money, 173–174
pardon power, 246, 702–703
parishes, 718
Parks, Rosa, 463p
Parliament (U.K.), 16, 16p, 19–20, 54p, 759, 760f
parliamentarian of the House, 191
parliamentary leaders (U.K.), 761
parliamentary systems, 4f, 19–20, 21–22, 22p, 28f, 759

parochial schools, 371, 371i, 374, 375–376
parole, power, 424, 498, 703
parties. *See* political parties
partisan gerrymandering, 157–158, 157i
partisan press, 532–533, 532f
partisans, Congress members as, 148–149, 564
party caucuses, 195, 580–581, 580i, 591–592, 591p
party-column ballots, 510
party conferences, 195. *See also* party caucuses
party government, 763
party identification, 504–505
party officers, 598
Passenger Cases, (1849), 439
passports, 9, 310, 310f
patents, 39, 174–175, 174i, 632, 674
Paterson, William, 75
Patient Protection and Affordable Care Act (2010), 124, 626f, 647
patricians, 24
Patrick, Luther, 150
Patriot Act, USA, 213f, 409–410
patriotism, defined, 13
patronage, 287
Patterson, Thomas E., 446
Patterson v. *McLean Credit Union* (1989), 404
pay-as-you-go plan, 651–652
payroll taxes, 652–653, 652c, 740
peacekeeping, 311–312, 314–315, 315p, 319f
Pearl Harbor attack, 297–298, 297i, 369, 415, 415p
peer groups, influence of, 518
Pelosi, Nancy, 147p, 193, 209p
Pendleton Act (1883), 287
Penn, William, 52i, 53, 58
Pennsylvania, State constitution of, 685
Pennsylvania colony, 51m, 52–53, 52i, 60c, 94
Pension Benefit Guaranty Corporation, 291
Pentagon, 319
Pentagon Papers, 385, 385p
People's Republic of China. *See* China
People v. *Dorado* (1965), 347f
per curiam opinions, 347
perestroika policy, 754
Perez, Thomas, 575, 575p
perfect union, 11
Pericles, 24
perjury, 187
Perkins, Frances T. ("Ma"), 280–281
Perot, Ross, 580, 608p
Perry, Matthew, 296
Persian Gulf War (1990), 239
personal exemption, 651
personal responsibilities, 36

personal security, 402–413
persona non grata, 255
Peter the Great, 765
Petition of Right, 50
petitions
    in initiative process, 695
    in nominating, 587, 587p
    right to, 390–391
petit juries, 419, 708, 711
Philadelphia Convention. *See* Constitutional Convention
phosphorus matches, 647, 647i
picketing, 383
Piegan Blackfeet tribe, 446p
Pierce v. *Society of Sisters* (1925), 374, 397
pigeonholing, 204–205, 204p, 695
Pilgrims, 722
Pinchback, P.B.S., 698
plaintiff, 337
plain view rule, 406
Planned Parenthood, 413, 413p
Planned Parenthood of Southeastern Pennsylvania v. *Casey* (1992), 412–413
planning commissions, 718f, 728–729
platforms of political parties, 584, 593–594
Plato, 24
plebeians, 24
Pledge of Allegiance, 436p, 517p
Plessy v. *Ferguson* (1896), 455, 461
P. Lorillard Co. v. *Reilly* (2001), 388
plurality of the vote, 567
pocket veto, 213, 248
Pointer v. *Texas* (1965), 420
Poland, 753–754
police
    bicycle, 732p
    civil liberties and, 397–398
    county, 719, 720p
    federal aid to, 132
    Miranda rule, 421–422
    police power of States, 121, 397–398, 693, 694p
    warrants and, 406–409, 407c
policy committees, 195
Politburo, 766
political action committees (PACs), 552f, 608, 611–612
political campaigns, 596–597, 596p, 612–614
political divisions, 568f
political efficacy, 498
political ideals, origins of democracy, 48–53
political machines, 510
political parties, 562–577
    bonding agent function of, 564
    presidential campaigns, 596–597, 596p, 612–614
    constitutional changes and, 111
    decentralized nature of, 573–574

defined, 562–563
democracy influenced by, 563, 565
electoral system and, 566–567
elements of, 563
gerrymandering by, 157–159, 157*i*, 692
governing by, 564–565
harm from primary disputes, 586–587
identification with, 504–505
ideological parties, 570
ideology of, 568–569, 568*f*
independents and, 505
informing and activating supporters, 564
interest groups vs., 539–540, 539*f*
multiparty politics, 569, 569*f*
national chair, 574–576
national committee, 574–576
national conventions, 111, 574, 592–594
nominating candidates, 564, 574, 594–596
one-party politics, 569–570, 569*f*
origins of, 566, 566*p*
party caucuses, 195, 580–581, 580*i*, 591–592, 591*p*
party organization, 563
President's role in, 574
psychological factors of, 504–505
role of, 563–565
in Russian Federation, 769
sociological factors of, 500–502, 501*f*
State and local functions, 576–577, 576*f*
State chair, 576
symbols of, 567*i*
third and minor parties, 569, 570–573, 570*c*, 571*i*, 572*f*, 573*c*
two-party system, 565–569, 567*p*, 568*f*, 621*f*
in United Kingdom, 760, 763–764
watchdog function of, 565
See also specific parties
political platform, 584, 593–594
political socialization, 500
political spectrum, 563, 568–569, 568*f*
politicos, Congress members as, 148, 148*c*
***Politics* (Aristotle),** 14–15
politics, defined, 7–8
poll books, 492
polling places, 498–499, 509
***Pollock* v. *Farmers' Loan and Trust Co.* (1895),** 549, 655–656
poll reliability, 526
polls. *See* public opinion polls
poll taxes, 171, 479, 482, 488, 494
pollution, 117, 285, 316, 398
poll watchers, 509
Pol Pot, 754–755
polygamy, 129, 160, 246
pope, 26, 27*f*
Pope, Alexander, 16

popular referendum, 698
popular sovereignty
in the Constitution, 97–98, 97*i*
Constitutional Convention on, 78
federalism and, 106
principles of, 63, 97–98
in social contract theory, 11, 30
in State constitutions, 64, 685, 686
popular vote, 111
population
characteristic of a state, 8, 8*f*
China, 8
increase in minorities, 440–441, 440*c*, 503
San Marino, 8
Three-Fifths Compromise, 77, 77*i*, 78*c*
of the U.S., 8, 104
Populist Party (1890s), 571
Port Authority of New York and New Jersey, 132, 701*p*
postal powers, 153, 175, 175*p*
Postal Service, U.S. (USPS), 175, 284*c*, 287, 654
Powell, Colin, 307
***Powell* v. *McCormack* (1969),** 160
powers
of absolute monarchs, 27, 30, 50
of clemency, 246, 702–703
implied, 118, 168, 168*c*, 179–180, 180*f*, 182*p*, 183*f*
of law, 28
Machiavelli on, 29
over territories, 128, 176, 357
of personality, 28
of precedents, 339, 347, 347*f*
of the purse, 659
of recognition, 254–255, 254*p*
reserved, 120–121, 120*p*
to tax, 170–172, 647–650, 648*f*, 649*c*, 736
See also congressional powers; expressed powers; judicial powers; presidential powers
prayer in public schools, 372, 376–377
preambles to State constitutions, 687
Preamble to the U.S. Constitution, 6, 6*p*, 92, 318
precedents, 339, 347, 347*f*, 706, 706*c*
precinct boards, 509
precincts, 509, 577
preclearance provision of voting laws, 482–485, 483*c*
preconvention campaigns, 612–613
preference primaries, 590–591
preliminary hearings, 709
presentments, 416–417, 708
presidential Cabinet. *See* Cabinet
presidential caucuses, 580–581, 580*i*, 591–592, 591*p*
presidential debates, 596–597, 597*p*, 605–606, 605*p*

Presidential Election Campaign Fund, 612
presidential elections
campaigns, 596–597, 596*p*, 612–614
campaign spending limits, 431, 560*f*, 612
candidate qualities, 594–596
congressional funding in, 612–613
counting the votes, 507, 511–513, 512*f*, 598, 600
debates, 596–597, 597*p*, 605–606, 605*p*
donation limits, 610–611
electoral college, 108, 111
fundraising, 161, 612–613
nominations, 564, 574, 594–596
preconvention campaigns, 612–613
price of, 607
Russian interference in, 304
See also presidential primaries
presidential electors, 597–598
presidential government, 21–22
presidential nominations, 564, 574, 594–596
presidential pardons, 246
presidential powers, 237–249
of appointment and removal, 243–245, 244*f*
of clemency, 246
critics and supporters, 241
delegated powers, 118–119, 119*c*
domestic, 237–249, 261*f*
to execute the law, 241–242
executive orders and privilege, 242–243, 242*p*, 243*f*
executive powers, 95–96, 99, 111, 227, 238
foreign affairs powers, 252–255, 253*p*, 254*p*, 261*f*
Framers on, 237–238
growth of, 237–241
to recommend legislation, 247
of the veto, 75*f*, 96, 100, 213, 248–249, 248*f*, 249*p*
presidential primaries
caucuses, 580–581, 580*i*, 591–592, 591*p*
complexities of, 585–586, 586*c*
costs of, 586
defined, 588
differing State styles, 590
evaluation of, 591–592
history of, 588–589
nomination by petition, 587, 587*p*
preference primaries, 590–591
reform proposals, 591
selection of delegates, 589
of sitting presidents, 591
timing of, 589–590
presidential succession, 110, 230–232, 231*f*, 599
Presidential Succession Act (1947), 231, 599

president of the Senate, 194–195, 194*p*, 233, 598

President of the United States
bills sent from Congress to, 212–213
Cabinet appointments, 185, 280–281
campaigns for, 596–597, 596*p*, 612–614
clemency, 246
as commander in chief, 95–96, 100, 110*p*, 227–228, 255–257
congressional oversight, 149, 184, 241
congressional resolutions to balance power of, 178
date of election, 498–499, 597
executive actions, 110–111
executive agreements, 111, 254
executive privilege and orders, 243, 243*f*
federal judge nominations, 100, 244, 335
fiscal policy, 642–643, 643*c*, 645
foreign policy, 177, 252–257
growth of power of, 101, 224*f*
inauguration of, 33*f*, 599, 601
legislative power, 101
limits to power of, 240–241
nominating process for, 564, 574, 594–596
oath of office, 242
political party role, 574
power of, 101
power of recognition, 254–255, 254*p*
power to call special session of Congress, 152, 152*p*, 247
qualifications for, 229–230, 229*c*
qualities of a good President, 229*c*
roles of, 225–229
separation of powers and, 21–22, 98*i*, 99
State of the Union address, 192–193, 192*f*, 231*c*, 247, 484*p*
succession and disability, 110, 230–232, 231*f*, 599
term of office, 21, 108–109, 230, 230*p*
treaty power, 111, 185, 185*f*, 252–253
use of military force by, 95–96, 255–257
veto power of, 75*f*, 96, 100, 213, 248–249, 248*f*, 249*p*
See also presidential elections; presidential powers

president pro tempore, 153, 231, 231*c*, 694
press. *See* mass media; newspapers
pressure groups. *See* interest groups
preventive detention, 423
price stability, 642
primaries, 480, 480*p*, 582–587, 584*p*, 586*c*
primary ballots, 583–585, 586
Primary Sources
Americans with Disabilities Act, 469
Brown v. *Board of Education of Topeka* (1954; Warren), 460–461

Carter–Reagan presidential debate (1980), 605–606, 605*p*
Citizens United v. *FEC* (2010; Kennedy; Stevens), 617–618
Commentaries on the Laws of England (Blackstone), 715–716, 715*i*
Common Sense (Paine), 66
"Declaration of Sentiments and Resolutions" (Stanton), 451, 452
English Bill of Rights (1689), 54, 55
Executive Order 9981, 258
Farewell Address (Washington), 305–306
"Foreign Ministry Spokesperson's Remarks on the Statement by Friendly Countries in Support of China. . ." (2021), 778
"Give Me Liberty or Give Me Death" (Henry), 65
"I Have a Dream" speech (King), 462*p*
In re Gault (1967; Fortas; Stewart), 400–401
Interesting Narrative of the Life of Olaudah Equiano, The (Equiano), 451–452
Joint Statement on Xinjiang (U.S. Department of State), 777
Magna Carta, (1215), 54–55
Out of Order (O'Connor), 349–350
Politics (Aristotle), 14–15
Pollock v. *Farmers' Loan and Trust Co.* (1895; Field; Brown), 655–656
Social Contract, The (Rousseau), 14–15
Spirit of Laws, The (Montesquieu), 31, 31*i*
Statement by General Omar Bradley, 259
Title IX of the 1972 Education Amendments, 468
Two Treatises of Government (Locke), 31, 32, 46*f*
USA PATRIOT Act, 216–217, 216*p*
Vietnam War and the media (Balwin; Cronkite), 536–537
Virginia Declaration of Rights, 113–114, 113*p*
Wesberry v. *Sanders* (1964; Black; Harlan), 165–166
Youngstown Sheet & Tube Company v. *Sawyer* (1952; Black; Vinson), 250–251

prime ministers
in parliamentary governments, 22
in Russian Federation, 767, 768, 768*f*
in United Kingdom, 760–761, 763–764
prior restraint on publications, 385–386, 385*p*, 387
prison overcrowding, 735

prisons/imprisonment
at Guantanamo Bay Naval Station, 356, 356*p*, 415
prison guards, 458
prison labor, 403
in the Soviet Union, 636
in the U.S., 403, 423–424, 423*c*, 498
privacy, right to, 323, 410, 412–413
private bank notes, 647
private bills, 203
private corporations, 291–292, 291*c*
private enterprise, 38, 38*f*
private ownership, 37–38, 630
private prisons, 735
private property, assemblies on, 392–393
privatization of enterprises, 636
Privileges and Immunities Clause, 136, 165
Privy Council, 56
probable cause, 405–406
procedural due process, 396, 396*f*
Proclamation of 1763, 57*c*
profit motive, 630
Progressive Era, 12–13
Progressive Movement, 510
Progressive Party (1924), 566, 571
progressive taxes, 651, 651*f*, 738
Prohibition, 108
project grants, 131–132, 131*f*
propaganda techniques, 552–553, 552*f*
property ownership to vote, 478
property taxes, 132, 458, 458*c*, 494, 645, 737, 739
proportional plans for presidential elections, 602–603, 602*c*
proportional representation, 590, 590*f*
proposed amendments, 106–107, 188
proprietary colonies, 52–53, 52*i*
prorogue (Congressional sessions), 152, 247
protectionism, 369*f*, 668–669
protective tariffs, 170–171
Proxmire, William, 210*c*
psychological factors of voters, 500, 504–505
"the public," defined, 514–515
public acts, 133
public agenda, 531
publications, prior restraint on, 385–386, 385*p*, 387
public bills, 203
public debt
ceiling on, 665
Clinton and, 173, 173*p*
defaulting on, 741
defense spending and, 658, 664–665, 664*f*
deficit financing, 172–173
foreign countries and, 673–674
interest on, 658

Reagan and, 665
Second Continental Congress and, 68
Treasury Department and, 172, 664–665, 664c
Washington and, 664
public funding for campaigns, 609, 612–613
public good and personal interest, 368, 397–399
public health
Environmental Protection Agency in, 285
Food and Drug Administration, 285
Health and Human Services Department, 279, 283, 657
nongovernmental organizations and, 316
police and, 121, 397
as reserved power, 120p, 121
social welfare programs for, 297, 633
State funding of, 733
taxes levied to protect, 171, 649
Public Health Service, 318
public hearings, 205
public opinion
defined, 514–516
elections and, 520–521
influences on, 516–520, 530, 531–534, 532f, 533c, 555f
interest groups and, 561–562
Internet in, 512–513, 530, 530p
measuring of, 520–521
polls, 521–526, 523f, 524f, 525f
print media in, 528, 529–530
on public affairs, 515, 534–535, 534c, 541
radio in, 528–529
social media in, 530–531
television in, 419, 528, 528i
See also mass media
public opinion polls
design and administration, 523–525, 524c, 525f, 555f
reliability, 526
scientific polling, 522–523, 522f, 523f
straw polls, 521–522, 522p
public policies
defined, 6–7
influence on political attitudes, 519–520
interest groups' influence on, 538–539, 539f
media's effect on, 531–532, 532f
in Russian Federation, 769
public property, assemblies on, 392–393
public safety
drug control and, 277f
police and, 121
right of assembly and, 391
in workplaces, 734
writ of habeas corpus and, 414, 415p
public schools. *See* education

public trial, right to, 119, 417–419
public welfare
after World War II, 247, 297
climate change and, 12
commerce power and, 183
federal funding for, 130–131
government obligation to promote, 12–13, 68, 80f, 92
individual rights and, 34, 397–398
interest groups and, 543–544
judiciary and, 339
in laissez-faire theory, 632
police power and, 397
political parties and, 568
presidency and, 247
public opinion on, 501, 515
restrictions on State programs, 136
as role of government, 12–13
taxation and, 170–171, 171c, 647, 652–653, 652c
welfare reform, 117, 117f
Puerto Rico, 155, 447
***Puerto Rico* v. *Branstad* (1987),** 135
Pullman Strike of 1894, 127
punch-card ballots, 511
pundits, 519
pure democracy, 17, 17f
Putin, Vladimir, 765p, 767, 769–770

Q

Qaddafi, Muammar al-, 312
Qatar, 253p
qualifications
for House of Representatives, 160–161
for presidency, 229–230, 229c
for Senate, 163–164
for State governors, 698
for State legislators, 691
quarterly taxes, 652
Quayle, Dan, 194p, 282p
Quest! Inquiry
Are Special Interests Good or Bad for Democracy?, 477
Electoral College, The, 561
Filibuster, The, 145
Inquiry Center, 5, 91, 225, 267, 333, 365, 435, 627, 683, 751
Should the Constitution Be Ratified?, 47
questions on polls, 524–525, 524f, 525f
Quick Study Guide, 40–41, 84–85, 138–139, 218–219, 260–261, 326–327, 358–359, 428–429, 470–471, 554–555, 620–621, 676–677, 744–745, 780–781
quorum, 74, 83, 207–208
quorum calls, 208
quota, in affirmative action, 464
quota system, in immigration, 440, 440f, 485

R

race, U.S. population by, 445f
race-based gerrymandering, 158
racial discrimination
after abolition of slavery, 445–446
affirmative action, 463–466, 464f, 465p, 471f
apartheid, 756
against Asian Americans, 448
in capital punishment, 424, 425f
Commerce Clause and, 169–170
continuing, 446
federalism and, 117
15th Amendment, 108, 158, 479–481, 480p
free enterprise and, 38
gerrymandering, 157–158, 157i, 480, 692
in the GI Bill, 446
grandfather clauses for voting, 493–494
against Hispanic Americans, 403p, 447–448, 457
history of segregation, 454–457, 455p, 456p
in housing, 403p
in juvenile justice, 710
literacy tests, 481, 482, 483, 493–494, 493p
miscegenation laws, 133p, 457
against Native Americans, 446, 446p
poll taxes, 171, 479, 482, 488, 494
by private individuals, 403
separate-but-equal doctrine, 455
in vagrancy laws, 403
in voting rights, 480, 480p, 488, 583
white primaries, 480, 480p
See also African Americans; desegregation; slavery/enslaved people
Radical Republicans, 186
radio broadcasts, 387, 528–529
Rainey, Joseph, 150
Randolph, Edmund, 73, 74, 75f, 79, 280
random samples, 524
Rankin, Jeannette, 150, 150p
ratification of amendments, 105–106, 105f, 687–688
ratification of Articles of Confederation, 68
ratification of the Constitution, 47, 80–83, 80f, 81c, 82i, 108
rational basis test, 454
rationing, 368
Read, George, 79
Reagan, Nancy, 236
Reagan, Ronald, 227p, 301, 334p
age, 229
arms control treaty, 253p
Carter-Reagan debate, 334p, 605–606, 605p
chief of staff for, 275p

as commander in chief, 227p, 270p
disability of, 231, 232
election results of, 599c
end of the cold war and, 301, 305–306
female justice nominated by, 334p
firing striking air traffic controllers, 241p
first Hispanic Cabinet officer under, 281
Iran-Contra scandal, 200, 276, 301
Iran hostages, 310
Nicaragua, 301
presidential debate, 605p, 606
public debt, 665
recess appointments, 244f
supply-side economics, 663
tax cuts, 651, 663
"Tear Down This Wall" speech, 306
22nd Amendment, 230
25th Amendment, 232
voter demographics, 501, 503

Reaganomics, 663

Reapportionment Act of 1929, 156–157

reapportionment of Congress
federal government, 156–159, 156m, 157i, 158p, 165–166
State government, 691–692

reasonable distinctions, 136

reasonable expectation of privacy, 410, 411i

recall
of ambassadors, 255
of governors, 699
of judges, 129, 341

recess, congressional, 152

recess appointments, 240–241, 244, 244f

recessions, 159, 290, 605, 642, 645

Reconstruction policies, 150, 186, 245

records, trial, 354

record votes, 208

Red Cross, 316

redistricting, 157–159, 157i, 165–166, 165p

Red Lion Broadcasting Co. v. FCC (1969), 387

redress, 357

Reed v. Reed (1971), 458, 458c

referendum process, 571, 695–696

reformers, 446, 752

Refugee Convention (UN; 1951), 443

refugees
asylum seekers, 443, 447
foreign wars and, 294, 302, 536p
immigration and, 485
social media use by, 531
United Nations and, 316, 317p, 443

Regents of the University of California v. Bakke (1978), 465

regional governments, in Russian Federation, 769

regional security alliances, 311

regional trade alliances, 671–672

regressive taxes, 653, 738

regulatory commissions.
See independent regulatory commissions

Rehnquist Court, 340

Reich, Robert, 282

released time programs, 376

religion
early State constitutions and, 685
education and, 371–372, 371i, 374–377, 375p
freedom of, 373–379
influence on voting, 501–502, 516
presidential candidacy and, 595
seasonal displays, 377–378
tax exemptions and, 737
voting rights and, 479

religious organizations, 375, 468, 544

relocation camps, in World War II, 369, 369p, 448

removal power, 100, 186, 244–245, 700–701

Renaissance, 29

Reno v. American Civil Liberties Union (1997), 389

representative assemblies, 146

representative democracy, 17, 17c, 24

representative government, 24, 29, 49, 49c, 78

representatives
demographics of, 150–151
election process for, 159
qualifications of, 160–161
ratings of, 550–551
roles and duties of, 148–150, 148c
salary and nonsalary compensation of, 153
terms for, 151–152, 151f, 155–156, 163
See also Congress; House of Representatives

reprieve, 118, 246, 702–703

republican-form guarantee, 125–126

republicanism, 98

Republican National Committee (RNC), 575

Republican National Convention, 527p, 562p

Republican Party (GOP)
decentralized nature of, 573–574
interest groups vs., 539–540, 539f
national conventions, 527p, 562p, 574–576, 592–594
presidential primaries of, 582–587, 586c
psychological factors of, 504–505
Republican National Committee, 575
sociological factors of, 500–502
symbol of, 567i

Republican Party of Minnesota v. White (2002), 714p

Republic of Korea and U.S. (KORUS FTA), 674p

republics
defined, 17–18
Roman Republic, 4f, 7i, 24–25, 24i, 25f, 28f, 49
United States as, 17, 18m

reservations, Native American, 446

reserved powers, 120–121, 120p

reserve requirements, 644

residence
criteria for voting, 136, 490, 490f
criteria to serve as President, 229–230
moving between States, 136

resolutions, 219c
concurrent, 203, 257, 661
continuing, 661
emergency spending, 661
Gulf of Tonkin Resolution (1964), 224f
joint, 107, 203, 253, 256, 438
riders on, 203–204, 203i
simple, 203
War Powers Resolution (1973), 101, 178, 256–257

retain-reject election, 714

retirement programs, 740

retroactive criminal laws, 416

Revels, Hiram, 150

Revenue Act of 1861, 626f

Revenue Act of 1942, 649c, 649f

Revenue Act of 1964, 626f

Revenue Acts of 1971, 1974, and 1976, 612

reverse coattail effect, 508–509

reverse discrimination, 464–466

Revolutionary War, 29, 53, 60, 61–63, 61i, 69

Reynolds v. Sims (1964), 692, 692c

Reynolds v. United States (1879), 378

Rhode Island, State constitution of, 685

Rhode Island colony, 51m, 53, 685

Rhodes v. Chapman (1980), 423

Ricardo, David, 30

Ricci v. DeStefano (2009), 455p, 465–466

Rice, Condoleezza, 307

riders on resolutions, 203–204, 203i

rights
of association, 393–394, 584
to counsel, 420
to demonstrate, 391–393, 550
economic, 38, 630
of free expression, 380–381, 380p, 381p
of legation, 308
to privacy, 323, 410, 412–413
of States to self-government, 686
See also civil rights and liberties; due process; human rights; voting rights; individual rights

rights of the accused, 414–426, 429f

bail and preventive detention, 422–423
bill of attainder, 415–416, 416*p*
Bill of Rights on, 334–335
capital punishment and, 423, 424–426, 424*f*, 425*f*
cruel and unusual punishments, 50, 423–424
double jeopardy, 417
ex post facto laws, 416
right to a grand jury, 416–417, 417*f*
self-incrimination, 246, 370*c*, 421–422
treason, 426
in trials, 417–420, 419*f*
writ of habeas corpus, 81, 414–415, 415*p*
Right to Life Party, 571
Riley **v.** *California* **(2014),** 407
Ring **v.** *Arizona* **(2002),** 425
Rio Pact (Inter-American Treaty of Reciprocal Assistance), 296
road to independence, 46*f*
Roberts, Brigham H., 160
Roberts, John, 381, 407, 483–484, 484*i*
Robinson **v.** *California* **(1962),** 423, 424
Rochin **v.** *California* **(1952),** 396–397
Rockefeller, Nelson, 189
Roe **v.** *Wade* **(1973),** 412–413
Rogers, Will, 608
roll-call votes, 208–209
Rollins, Edward, 548
Roman Catholic Church, 25–26, 26*m*, 27*f*
Roman Republic
history of, 7*i*, 24, 24*i*
influence on American government, 24
influence on English laws and customs, 49
root of democracy in, 4*f*, 28*f*
structure of, 24, 25*f*
Romney, George, 127
Romney, Mitt, 501, 502, 595
Roosevelt, Eleanor, 236
Roosevelt, Franklin D.
Brain Trust, 282
as chief citizen, 228
as commander in chief, 228, 244
death of, 234
elections of, 522, 663
embargo of Bolivia, 177*p*, 669
executive agreement use, 254*p*
Executive Office of the President establishment, 275
Federal Trade Commission and, 245
Four Freedoms speech, 367
four terms of, 109, 112, 230, 230*p*
Good Neighbor Policy, 296
Great Depression and, 519
Hoover on, 623
New Deal programs, 224*f*, 238–239, 239*i*, 651, 663–664

public demonstration of television, 528
radio speeches, 529
secretary of state used by, 308
treatment of vice president, 234
United Nations, 317
use of presidential power by, 101, 238–239
use of removal power, 245
war on Japan, 152*p*
female Cabinet member, 280–281
during World War II, 152*p*, 254, 297–297*i*, 298
Yalta Conference, 299
Roosevelt, Theodore, 239*i*
age of, 231
"Bull Moose" Progressive Party of, 566, 571–572
on citizenship, 36
expansion of merit system, 287
influence on the legislative agenda, 224*f*
merit system of federal civil service, 287
on Mount Rushmore, 95*p*
muckrakers, 529–530, 529*i*
presidential qualities of, 223
recognition of Panama, 255
Roosevelt Corollary, 296
stewardship theory of, 238
succession to presidency, 231
use of power of recognition, 254*p*
Roosevelt Corollary, 296, 327*c*
Roper, Elmo, 522
Roper **v.** *Simmons* **(2005),** 425
Ross, Nellie Tayloe, 698
Rostker **v.** *Goldberg* **(1981),** 458
Roth **v.** *United States* **(1957),** 388
Rousseau, Jean Jacques, 10, 15
royal colonies, 52
Rucho **v.** *Common Cause* **(2019),** 158
rule of four, 345
rule of law, 24, 28, 98
runoff primary, 585
Runyon **v.** *McCrary,* **(1976),** 404
Russia
Communism in, 635–636, 765
constitution of, 767
history of, 781*f*
privatization in, 636
public policy creation, 769–770
regional and local governments, 769
Russian Federation formation, 766–767, 766*m*
Russian Federation government, 767–769, 768*f*
size of, 9, 9*m*
Syrian strikes, 304
transition to democracy, 735, 754, 757
Ukraine, invasion of, 304
in UN Security Council, 314
U.S. compared with, 770, 770*c*
U.S. elections, interference in, 304

U.S. relationship with, 303–304
U.S. territory purchased from, 128*m*
See also Soviet Union
Russian Revolution, 765
Rutledge, John, 59

S

sabotage, 426
Saddam Hussein, 256, 579*p*, 756
sales taxes, 648*f*, 738
saloon license tax, 650
SALT I (Strategic Arms Limitation Talks agreement), 301
same-sex marriages, 134, 434*f*, 459
sample ballots, 510
sample of a population, 524
San Bernardino county, 718
sanctions, 669
Sanders, Bernie, 613, 679
Sandinistas, 300
Sandino, Augusto, 300
San Marino, 8
Santa Fe Independent School District **v.** *Doe* **(2000),** 377
satellite radio, 527
Savannah settlement, 51
Savings Bond Program, 664
schedules, in State constitutions, 687
Schenck **v.** *United States* **(1919),** 368*p*, 382
Schmerber **v.** *California* **(1966),** 398, 421
school choice plan, 376
school newspaper censorship, 386*p*
school's influence on political attitudes, 517
school superintendents, 719*c*
school voucher programs, 376
Schwimmer **v.** *United States* **(1929),** 381
scientific polling, 522–523, 522*f*, 523*f*
Scopes trial (1925), 377*p*
Scott, Dred, 445–446
search warrants, 119, 405–409, 407*c*, 709
seasonal displays, 377–378
Seattle Times, 533*c*
2nd Amendment, 404–405, 429*f*
Second Bank of the United States, 123–124
Second Continental Congress
adoption of Declaration of Independence, 61–63, 61*i*, 62*i*
as America's first government, 61
currency of, 61, 173
debts of, 68
key delegates to, 60–61, 60*c*
Marine Corps establishment, 321
as representative assembly, 61, 146
tasks of, 56*i*, 61
Second Gulf War, 303
Secretariat (UN), 314, 315

secretaries of the executive departments, 184c, 185c, 231c, 278
secretary-general (UN), 315
secretary of defense, 184c, 185, 231c, 280–281, 319, 319c
secretary of labor, 231c, 281
secretary of state (federal)
  approval by Congress, 185f
  in the Cabinet, 280, 280p
  diplomacy, 252–253, 275p, 307–308, 307p, 308p
  in line of succession, 231f, 699
secretary of state (State), 703–704, 703f
secretary of the navy, 184c, 258, 321
secretary of war, 184c, 245, 280
secret ballots, 509
Secret Service, 324
securities, 172, 289, 290c, 640, 644, 664
Securities and Exchange Commission (SEC), 271, 284c, 289–290, 640
Security Council (UN), 314, 317
security of home and person, 402–403
sedition, 160, 382–383, 382i
Sedition Law of 1917, 382
seditious speech, 370, 382–383, 382i
segregation, 471f
  de facto, 392–393, 456
  de jure, 456
  Jim Crow laws, 454–455
  by neighborhoods, 456
  in schools, 455–456, 455p
  separate-but-equal doctrine, 455
  See also desegregation; racial discrimination
seigniorage, 654
Select Committee on Indian Affairs (Senate), 200
Select Committee on Presidential Campaign Activities (Senate Watergate Committee), 190p, 200
Select Committee on Secret Military Assistance to Iran and the Nicaraguan Opposition (Senate), 200
select committees, 184, 186, 190p, 200–201
selective sales taxes, 738
Selective Service Act of 1917, 183
Selective Service System, 288, 288i, 403
Selective Training and Service Act of 1940, 288
self-announcement, nomination by, 579–580
self-employment taxes, 652
self-incrimination, 246, 370c, 421–422
Seling v. *Young* (2001), 417
Selma, Alabama, voting rights in, 482

Senate
  in ancient Rome, 4f, 7i, 24, 25f, 28
  Appropriations Committee, 660–661
  approving judges, 338, 338f
  approving presidential appointees, 112, 185, 240–241, 243–244
  in Article I, 94–95, 94f, 343f
  in Article V, 127
  Cabinet confirmations by, 280
  in checks and balances, 100, 100f
  cloture, 463
  committee list in, 199f
  committees in, 149, 547
  conference committees, 211–212, 660f, 661f
  constituent service in, 149
  constitutional amendments, 188
  election process for, 162–163, 582–584
  electoral duties of, 188–189, 188f, 189f, 598–599
  executive powers, 185
  filibuster, 145, 209–211, 210c, 211c, 339, 462, 463, 486
  floor debates in, 206–207, 209–211, 210c, 211f
  formation of, in Constitution, 75–77, 75f, 77p, 78c
  growth of seats in, 161c
  House compared with, 219c
  impeachment power, 100, 186–188, 340
  investigations, 179p, 183–184, 190p
  lobbyists and, 547–548, 547f, 548f
  merit system in, 287–288
  opening day of, 192
  oversight, 184, 185c, 241
  president of the Senate, 194–195, 194p, 233, 598
  president pro tempore, 153, 231, 231c
  qualification for office in, 163–164
  reasons for serving in, 154
  removal power, 244–245
  salary and nonsalary compensation, 153–154
  scheduling floor debates, 206–207
  senators as presidential candidates, 595
  size of, 144f, 161–162, 161f
  special sessions, 152
  State of the Union address, 192–193, 192f, 231c, 247, 484p
  term limit proposals, 156
  terms and sessions, 149, 151–152, 155–156, 163
  treaty approval, 111, 185, 253–254
  selection of Vice President, 188–189, 189f
  voting on bills, 208–209
  See also Congress; congressional committees; congressional powers
Senate chamber, 144i

Senate Watergate Committee, 186, 190p, 200
senatorial courtesy, 112, 338
Seneca Falls Convention (1848), 434f, 449, 451
seniority rule, 197, 199
seniority system, 199, 462
separate-but-equal doctrine, 455
separation of church and state, 340, 372, 373, 374, 377. *See also* religion
separation of powers
  Aristotle on, 24
  Arouet (Voltaire) on, 30
  bills of attainder and, 415
  between branches of government, 21
  Constitutional Convention on, 72, 78, 540
  Constitution on, 97, 98i, 99
  executive privilege and executive orders, 243c, 250–251
  political parties and, 564–565
  in the Russian Federation, 767–768
  in State constitutions, 63f, 64, 99, 685, 686
September 11, 2001 attacks
  anti-terrorism efforts after, 304, 319, 320
  events of the day, 216p, 256m, 303
  public opinion after, 519, 519p
  wiretapping after, 411
serfs, 25, 26, 27f
sergeant at arms, 191
Servicemen's Readjustment Act (1944), 462, 642
sessions of Congress
  federal government, 151–152, 151f
  State government, 692
setback requirements, 728
17th Amendment, 162–163, 488, 506–507
7th Amendment, 370c, 397
sex discrimination, 312, 449–450, 457–459, 458c
sex predators, 417
sexual harassment, 164, 164p
sexual orientation discrimination, 445, 459
Shaare Tefila Congregation v. *Cobb* (1987), 404
shadow cabinet, 761, 763p
shared powers, 21, 102f, 130
Shaw v. *Reno* (1993), 158
Shays, Daniel, 69–70
Shays' Rebellion, 69–70, 69i
Shelby County v. *Holder* (2013), 483–485
sheriffs, 719c
Sherman, Roger, 59, 60c, 61, 73f, 76, 96
Sherman Anti-Trust Act of 1890, 12–13, 631–632
shield laws, 386
sidewalk counseling, 393

signing statements, 248–249
sine die, 152
single-issue parties, 571
single-member congressional districts, 157, 567, 691
Singletary, Amos, 81
sin taxes, 653
sit-ins, 404*p*
16th Amendment, 649, 650
6th Amendment, 370*c,* 418–420
Skinner v. Railway Labor Executives' Association **(1989),** 409
slander, 381
slavery/enslaved people
    abolition of slavery, 108, 367, 402–404
    in Articles of Confederation, 67
    in building the Capitol, 453
    in casting the *Freedom* statue, 67, 453, 453*p*
    citizenship for formerly enslaved people, 108, 439, 446
    Commerce and Slave Trade Compromise, 77–78, 78*c,* 170
    Declaration of Independence and, 61–62
    Emancipation Proclamation, 238
    freeing of, in Civil War, 108, 238, 406
    in the Roman Republic, 24
    slave narrative (Equiano), 450–451
    Three-Fifths Compromise, 77, 77*i,* 78*c*
    trade in enslaved Africans, 29*m,* 451–452, 451*i*
    voting rights for formerly enslaved people, 480
Slave Trade Compromise, 77–78, 78*c,* 170
slippery slope fallacy, 553
small claims courts, 710
smallpox, 316, 324
Smith, Adam, 30, 632, 632*i,* 737*f*
Smith, Alfred E., 595
Smith, Mary Louise, 575
Smith Act of 1940, 383, 422–423
Smith v. Allwright **(1944),** 480
smoking bans, 454, 454*p*
sneak-and-peek searches, 409
Snepp v. United States **(1980),** 386
Snowden, Edward, 323, 411
Snyder v. Phelps **(2011),** 381
Social Contract, The **(Rousseau),** 14, 15
social contract theory, 10–11, 10*f,* 15, 30, 61–63
social desirability effect, 526
social insurance taxes, 652–653, 652*c*
socialism, 634–635, 635*c,* 637*c*
socialist parties, 570
social media
    in campaigns, 596, 608, 609
    impact on politics, 155, 530–531, 534, 576

    refugees and, 531
    in shaping public opinion, 532
    special interest groups, 550–551
    terrorists and, 304
Social Security Act of 1935, 117*f,* 626*f,* 652
Social Security Administration (SSA), 283–284, 652, 652*c,* 658
social welfare programs
    after World War II, 297
    cash assistance, 734
    for families, 734
    federal and State sharing of, 734
    judicial activism and, 339
    political parties and, 501, 568
    for public health, 297, 633
    social insurance taxes for, 652–653
    in socialist countries, 635
    welfare reform, 117, 117*f*
    See also public welfare
sociological factors of voters, 500–502, 501*f*
soft money, in campaigns, 610, 611*c,* 614–615
sole proprietorships, 648–649
solicitor general, 346
Somalia, 9
Somoza, Anastasio, 300
Sotomayor, Sonia, 346*p,* 361
South Africa, 22*p,* 753, 756
South America
    alliances with, 317
    Monroe Doctrine and, 296
    refugees from, 447
    in Triangular Trade, 29*m*
South Carolina, State constitution of, 63, 685
South Carolina colony, 51*m,* 52
South Carolina v. United States **(1905),** 650
Southern Common Market (MERCOSUR), 672
South Korea, 224*f,* 670, 674*p,* 756
sovereign immunity, 357
sovereignty
    in absolute monarchies, 27, 50
    in Articles of Confederation, 68
    of China, 297, 772
    in the Constitution, 78, 97–98, 106
    Declaration of Independence, 63
    defined, 9
    global economy and, 673
    international trade and, 667*c,* 673
    popular, 11, 30, 41*f,* 63
    roots of democracy in, 4*f,* 28*f*
    of Russian Republic, 767
    in State constitutions, 64, 685, 686, 686*f*
    of states, 8, 9–11, 9*m*
    of tribal governments, 720–721
    of United Kingdom, 759, 762, 764
    of United States, 9, 62, 441
Soviet Union
    in Afghanistan, 301, 303

    Bolshevik Revolution, 765
    during cold war, 298–299, 298*m*
    collectivization of agriculture, 635–636, 766
    Communism in, 635–636, 765
    Cuba and, 636
    dissolving of, 306, 636, 636*m,* 754, 767
    government of, 766
    purges in, 753, 766
    reforms in, 636, 754, 766–767
    resistance within, 753–754
    Soviet government, 766–767
    Stalin, Josef, 299, 635–636, 637, 766
    totalitarianism of, 753
    in UN Security Council, 314
    U.S. relationship with, 303–304
    See also Russia
Space Shuttle Program, 286
Speaker of the House
    duties of, 193–194, 198–199, 207–209
    election and swearing in of, 191
    first woman, 147*p,* 193
    in line of succession, 110*p,* 231, 231*f,* 599
    of State House of Representatives, 693*p,* 694
special ambassadors, 309
special (select) committees, 184, 186, 190*p,* 200–201
special courts, 97, 336, 340*c,* 357
special diplomats, 309
special districts, 723, 723*p,* 730–731
special interest groups. *See* interest groups
special sessions of Congress
    federal, 152, 152*p,* 247
    State, 692, 702, 702*c*
speech, freedom of, 380–389
    freedom of expression, 380–381, 380*p,* 381*p*
    limits on, 119*c,* 368, 368*p,* 381
    media and, 386–389
    prior restraint, 385–386, 385*p,* 387
    seditious speech, 370, 382–383, 382*i*
    symbolic speech, 383–385
Speedy Trial Act of 1974, 418
spending priorities, 279, 645, 657–658
Spirit of Laws, The **(Montesquieu),** 31–32
splinter parties, 571–572
split-ticket voting, 504–505
spoils system, 287
Springer v. United States **(1881),** 649
stability in polls, 526
Stack v. Boyle **(1951),** 422–423
staff agencies, 272–273, 272*f*
Stalin, Josef, 299, 635–636, 766
Stamp Act (1765), 46*f,* 57*c,* 58, 65
Stamp Act Congress, 58–59
standing committees
    bills in, 198–199, 198*f,* 204–206
    budget and, 660

division of labor in, 197–198
investigation committees, 183–185
listing of, 199f
lobbyists and, 547
subcommittees, 183, 205–206, 660, 661
See also names of specific committees
standing votes, 208
***Stanley* v. *Georgia* (1969),** 412
Stanton, Edwin M., 245
Stanton, Elizabeth Cady, 451, 452
stare decisis, 347
State attorney general, 703f, 704
State budgets, 741–742, 741c
State central committees, of parties, 577
State chairs of political parties, 576
State constitutions, 684–689
    amendments to, 687–688, 687p, 688f
    America's founding documents and, 63f
    civil rights, 685, 686
    drafting, 63–64, 684–685
    governmental structure, 686, 686c
    length of, 688
    means for changing, 686, 686c, 687–688, 687p, 688f, 693
    need for reform in, 688–689
    for new states, 128
    powers and processes, 686, 686c
    principles in, 685, 686, 686f
    separation of powers in, 64, 99, 685
    subordinate to the U.S. Constitution, 684, 693
    written charters for colonies and, 684–685
State conventions, 577
State Council (China), 774
State courts
    in appellate path, 353f
    bail in, 422–423
    civil law and, 416, 457–458, 707, 707f
    common law and, 705–706, 706f
    courts of appeal, 353f, 711
    criminal law, 133, 416, 706–707, 707f
    in dual court system, 335–336
    equity law, 706
    on evidence illegally obtained, 407c, 408
    general trial courts, 711
    jeopardy guarantee, 417
    judge selection, 713–714, 714p
    judicial review by, 98p, 101–102
    jurisdiction of, 336, 337, 337f
    jury system in, 707–709, 708p
    juvenile courts, 710
    local trial courts, 709–710, 709p, 710c
    municipal courts, 710
    naturalization in, 132
    self-incrimination guarantee, 421
    State supreme court, 711–712
    unified court systems, 712

State Department, 184, 278, 307–310, 309f, 310f, 367. *See also* diplomacy
State governments
    barred from taxing federal government, 737
    borrowing funds, 741
    budgets, 741–742, 741c
    corrections systems, 735
    county governments, 717–719, 718f, 719c
    division of powers with federal government, 20, 22, 116
    driver safety, 736
    executive officers in, 507, 703–704, 703f
    financing, 736–737, 737f, 745f
    Interstate Highway System funding, 398, 735–736, 735p
    limits to federal taxes on, 649–650
    organization chart, 682c, 745f
    public education spending, 732–733, 733c
    public health funding, 733
    redistricting by, 157
    revenue sources, 170–171, 738–741, 738c
    social welfare, 117, 117f, 734, 734c
    special districts, 723, 723p
    State constitutions, 684–689, 686f, 688f
    as subordinate to the Constitution, 9
    towns, 721–723, 722p
    townships, 719, 721, 722–723
    See also city governments; governors; State courts; State legislatures; States
State income taxes, 738–739
State judicial system. *See* State courts
State legislatures
    in budget process, 741–742, 741c
    changes to State constitutions by, 687, 687f, 695
    committees, 694
    compensation, 692
    direct legislation of, 695–696, 696c
    initiative process, 394, 695, 696c
    judge selection by, 713
    lawmaking process, 694–695
    legislators, 691–692, 692f
    nonlegislative powers, 693
    police power, 693, 694p
    presiding officers, 694, 694p
    referendum process, 695–696
    size of, 691
    special sessions, 692, 702, 702c
    structure, 690–691, 694, 745f
State of the Union address, 192–193, 192f, 231c, 247, 484p
State party functions, 576–577, 576f
States
    absentee voting, 488p, 507–508
    admission of new, 127–129, 128m, 129p

affirmative action banned in, 464–465
amendments to the U.S. Constitution and, 105, 105f, 106–107, 402–403
Articles of Confederation, 11, 21, 67–69, 68i
Bill of Rights incorporation in, 108, 369–371, 369i
characteristics of, 8–9, 8f, 9m
confederation of, 11, 20f, 21
constitutions, 63–64, 63f, 684–689, 686c
defined, 8
delegate-selection process, 582
division of powers with federal government, 20, 22, 116
economic involvement of, 633–634
election process, 492, 691, 703f
electoral votes, 188–189, 188f, 573c, 598m, 599c
exclusionary rule, 408
federalism and, 115–116, 120–121
fiscal and monetary policies, 173, 645
Full Faith and Credit Clause and, 133–134, 133p, 134p
interstate compacts, 132–133, 603, 701p
local party functions, 576–577, 576f
modified one-party system in, 570
National Guard, 12p, 115p, 130, 701
police power, 121, 397–398, 693, 694p
political parties in, 576–577, 576f
poll taxes, 171, 479, 482, 488, 494
powers denied to, 121
powers of, 120–122
protections of, in the U.S. Constitution, 108
purpose, 14–15
ratification of U.S. Constitution, 47, 80–83, 80f, 81c, 82i
resources shared with federal government, 129–132, 131f
small vs. large, in elections, 602–603
suburban boom, 729–730
travel between, 136
voting qualifications, 488–489
in welfare reform, 117, 117f
See also federalism; governors; presidential primaries; State courts; State governments; State legislatures
States' Rights (Dixiecrat) Party, 571
State supreme courts, 711–712
State treasurer, 703f, 704
State universities, 130, 130p, 733
statutory authorization, 251
statutory law, 688–689, 705
statutory rape, 454
steamboats, 169, 169p, 182i
Steele, Michael, 575

steel mills, threatened government seizure of, 250–251
steering and policy committees, 195
Stevens, Christopher, 201
stewardship theory, 238
Stewart, Potter, 388, 401, 404, 424
St. Francis College v. *Al Khazraji* **(1987),** 404
stimulus measures, economic, 643, 663–664
Stone v. *Graham* **(1980),** 376, 706c
straight-ticket voting, 504
Strategic Arms Limitation Talks agreement (SALT I), 301
Strauder v. *West Virginia* **(1880),** 420
straw man fallacy, 553
straw polls, 521–522, 522p
straw votes, 521–522
strict constructionists, 180–181
strict scrutiny test, 454, 465
Stromberg v. *California* **(1931),** 370
strong-mayor government, 725, 725f
students, voting rights of, 490
subcommittees, 183, 205–206, 660, 661
subpoenas, 187, 205
subsidies, in federal elections, 609
substantive due process, 396, 396f
suburban boom, 729–730
succession of State governors, 698–699
succession of the President, 110, 230–231, 231f, 599
succession of the Vice President, 189, 231–232, 231f, 235
Sudan, 303m, 315p
suffrage, expansion, 476f, 478–479
Sugar Act (1764), 57c
sultanates, 752
Sumter, South Carolina, council-manager government in, 726
Sunni groups, 755, 756
superdelegates, 593
Super PACs, 608, 612, 615f, 616
superpowers, 295p, 298, 299, 766
Super Tuesday, 589
supply and demand, 631, 631f
supply-side economics, 663
Supreme Court, 342–348, 342p
 on abortion, 372, 388, 393, 412–413
 on admission of new states, 129
 on affirmative action, 465–466
 African Americans in, 354, 361c
 appealing to, 332f, 345–346, 345p
 on campaign financing, 609–610, 615–616
 on child labor, 183
 in China, 774, 774f
 civil liberties cases, 364f
 on civil rights and equality, 331
 composition of, 342
 on constitutional amendment process, 106

 on corruption by officials, 98, 124
 Court building, 23p, 330p–331p, 342, 342p, 349
 on currency, 173–174, 181, 182
 on death penalty laws, 424
 on demonstrations, 392–393
 docket, 353
 establishment of, 97, 335
 federalism and, 123–124
 on free speech, 381
 hearing cases in, 346–348, 347f, 359f
 how cases reach the court, 359
 on Japanese American internment, 369, 369p
 judicial philosophies and, 339–340
 judicial review by, 101–102, 111, 342–344
 jurisdiction of, 344–345
 justice selection, 338f
 on the line-item veto, 213, 249
 majority opinion, 347
 on military draft, 183
 nullification of acts by, 98
 opinions, 165–166, 250–251, 400–401, 460–461, 617–618, 655–656
 opinion types, 347–348
 on pardons, 246
 on prayer in schools, 374, 376–377
 precedents set by, 339, 347, 347f
 on presidential elections, 98
 on presidential removal power, 245
 on reading of rights, 422
 on redistricting, 157, 158–159
 on republican form of government, 126
 on rights of the accused, 414–415
 on same-sex marriages, 134, 459
 on segregation, 34p, 340, 403–404, 455–457
 on the seizure of property, 240
 State court decisions appealed to, 712
 State supreme courts, 711–712
 structure of, 359f
 on taxation, 649, 650, 655–656
 as third branch of government, 342–343, 343f
 as umpire of federal system, 123–124
 women in, 339, 346p, 361
 See also names of specific cases
Supreme People's Court in China, 774, 774f
Supreme Soviet, 766
surveillance, 184
surveys, 447, 520, 522, 522p, 525. *See also* public opinion polls
Swann v. *Charlotte-Mecklenburg Board of Education* **(1971),** 456
Sweatt v. *Painter* **(1950),** 455, 461
Swift Boat Veterans, 615
swing voters, 596
symbolic speech, 383–385
Syria, 302–303, 304

T

Taft, William Howard, 129, 226, 238, 239i, 245, 282
Taft-Hartley Act of 1947, 250
tainted evidence, 407–408, 410f
Taiwan, 668, 756, 775, 775m
"take care power," 242
Takings Clause, 176, 398
Taliban, 303, 312, 756
Taney, Roger B., 414–415
tariffs, 170–171, 668–669, 669f
"taxation without representation," 57, 58
Tax Court, U.S., 97, 340c, 357
tax deductions, 651
taxes
 Adam Smith's four principles of, 737, 737f
 Articles of Confederation and, 68, 69
 changes over time, 171f, 651
 corporate taxes, 649, 652, 739
 customs duties, 58, 171, 246, 647, 653
 defined, 170
 direct taxes, 171–172, 648–649, 648c, 655–656
 estate and gift taxes, 653, 739
 excise taxes, 653
 exemptions, 737
 export taxes, 119, 647–648
 federal government revenue from, 171–172, 738–739, 738c
 fiscal policy on, 642–643, 644c, 645
 income taxes, 171–172, 648–651, 651f, 655, 738–739
 indirect taxes, 172, 648–649, 648c
 inflation and, 646
 inheritance taxes, 653, 739
 licensing as, 647, 740
 limits on, 171–172, 736–737
 nontax revenues, 653–654
 power to tax, 170–172, 647–650, 648f, 649c
 progressive taxes, 651, 651f, 738
 property taxes, 132, 458, 458c, 494, 645, 737, 739
 purpose of, 170–171
 regressive taxes, 653, 738
 in royal colonies, 57, 58
 sales taxes, 648f, 738
 social insurance, 652–653, 652c
 State revenue from, 170–171, 738–741, 738c
 States' power to, 122
 tariffs, 668–669, 669f
 without representation, 57, 58
tax stamps, 58
tax withholding, 651–652
Taylor v. *Louisiana* **(1975),** 458
T-Bills (Treasury Notes), 172, 664
Tea Act (1773), 57c
Tea Party movement, 563p
"Tear Down This Wall" (Reagan), 306

Tehran hostage crisis, 309–310, 309*f*
telephone surveys, 522, 522*p*, 525, 525*f*
television
    in campaigns, 155, 498, 518, 523, 533
    freedom of speech on, 387
    influence of, 532, 533–535, 533*c*, 534*c*
    in mass media, 482, 527–528, 528*i*
    presidential debates, 597
    public opinion and, 482, 514, 516, 519, 520–521
    regulation of, 289, 290, 368, 387–388
    trials and pretrial hearings on, 418–419, 418*p*
teller votes, 208
Temporary Assistance to Needy Families (TANF), 117*f*, 734, 734*c*
Ten Commandments, display of, 376, 378
Tennessee Valley Authority (TVA), 291–292, 292*p*
10th Amendment, 108, 116, 120
Tenure of Office Act, 186, 245
term of office
    in Athenian assembly, 24
    in first State constitutions, 63–64
    in House of Representatives, 151–152, 151*f*, 155–156, 163
    of judges, 335, 340–341
    of Presidents, 21, 108–109, 230, 230*p*
    proposed term limits, 156
    in Senate, 149, 151–152, 155–156, 163
    of State governors, 698
    of State legislators, 692
    of U.K. prime ministers, 760
Terrell, Mary Church, 540*f*
territorial courts, 97, 340*c*, 357
territorial expansion, 127–129, 128*m*
territorial integrity, 127
territories, 8–9, 176
terrorism
    al Qaeda, 303, 322, 323*c*, 756
    bioterrorism, 324
    counterterrorism, 294, 322, 322*p*, 323*f*
    federal courts for, 352
    foreign policy and, 177
    social media and, 304
    United Nations and, 304
    war on, 319, 409–410
Terry v. Ohio (1968), 407
Texas, annexation of, 253
Texas Rangers, 120, 735
Texas v. Johnson (1989), 384–385
Thatcher, Margaret, 761, 761*p*
theocracy, 18*m*, 19, 41*c*
3rd Amendment, 323, 370*c*, 405
third and minor parties, 570–573, 570*c*, 571*i*, 572*f*, 573*c*
13th Amendment, 77, 108, 126, 402–404, 429*f*, 446
Thomas, Clarence, 354, 361*c*
Thomas, Norman, 573

Thornburg v. Gingles (1980), 692*c*
Thornhill v. Alabama (1940), 383
Three-Fifths Compromise, 77, 77*i*, 78*c*
three-part test for obscenity, 388
three strikes law, 423
Thurmond, Strom, 210, 210*c*, 361
Tiananmen Square protest (1989), 773
time, place, and manner rules, 391–392
Tinker v. Des Moines School District (1969), 384
Tipao, 528
Title I (Civil Rights Act of 1964), 487
Title II (Civil Rights Act of 1964), 463, 487
Title IX (Civil Rights Act Amendment, 1972), 434*f*, 439*f*, 463, 468
Tocqueville, Alexis de, 373, 541, 543
tort law, 707
totalitarian dictatorships, 18
Tower, John, 185
town caucus, 581, 581*p*
town governments, 719, 721–722, 722*p*
town hall-style debate, 597*p*
town meetings, 722, 722*p*
Town of Greece v. Galloway (2014), 377
towns, 26–27. *See also* local governments
Townshend Acts (1767), 57*c*
townships, 719, 721, 722–723
trade. *See* international trade
Trade Adjustment Assistance, 674
Trade Court, 97, 349*c*, 355
trade routes, 29*m*
Traficant, James, 160
Trans-Alaska pipeline, 136*p*, 324*p*
transients, voting rights of, 490
transition to democracy, 753, 753*f*
transit systems, 719
Transportation Security Administration (TSA), 324
transportation spending, 39, 131*f*
travel documents, 9, 310, 310*f*
treason, 426
Treasury Department
    borrowing power of, 172–173, 172*p*, 173*p*, 664, 664*c*
    conscience fund, 654
    Homeland Security and, 324
    issuing currency, 646
    power to tax, 170–172, 646–650, 648*c*, 649*c*
    public debt and, 172, 664–665, 664*c*
    spending, 658
    Tax Court and, 97, 340*c*, 357
    taxes today, 650–654, 650*p*, 651*c*, 652*c*
Treasury Notes (T-Bills), 172, 664
treaties, 111, 185, 185*f*, 252–253

Treaty of Paris (1783), 69
Treaty of Versailles (1920), 253
trial juries, 419, 708. *See also* jury systems
trials, 119, 417–420, 419*f*
Triangular Trade, 29*m*
tribal aristocracy, 19
tribal councils, 721
tribal governments, 19, 720–721, 721*m*
Trickey, Minnijean, 433
Troubled Asset Relief Program (TARP), 221, 643, 663*f*
Truman, Harry S, 583*p*
    22nd Amendment, 230
    atomic bomb and, 234, 234*p*, 263
    Cabinet, 282
    as chief administrator, 227
    desegregation of the military, 258–259, 258*p*
    election predictions, 522*p*
    foreign policy, 227, 299
    presidential campaign, 583*p*, 596*p*
    power of recognition, 255
    Presidential Succession Act, 110*p*
    recognition of Israel, 255
    seizure and operation of steel mills, 240, 240*p*, 250
    special sessions, 152, 247
    Truman Doctrine, 299
    U.S. forces in South Korea, 224*f*
    as Vice President, 234
Truman Doctrine, 299
Truman Plan, 251
Trump, Donald, 585*p*
    Cabinet, 281
    campaigns, 585*p*
    divorces, 595
    electoral vs. popular votes, 600
    foreign policy, 253*p*
    impeachments, 100, 186, 187–188, 598
    January 6, 2021 Capitol attack, 187–188, 598
    personal campaign contributions, 608
    political experience, 595
    as President, 253*p*
    Russian influence in election of, 304
trustees, Congress members as, 148
trusts, 631–632
tuition for colleges and universities, 136
TVA (Tennessee Valley Authority), 291–292, 292*p*
12th Amendment, 108, 188, 598
20th Amendment, 151, 599, 601
25th Amendment, 110, 111, 231–232, 233, 234–235
21st Amendment, 105, 121
24th Amendment, 474, 479, 488, 494
22nd Amendment, 108–109, 112, 230, 230*p*

27th Amendment, 107, 109, 153, 153*i*
26th Amendment, 104, 109, 476*f*, 479, 491
23rd Amendment, 479
Twitter, 530–531, 550
two-party system, 565–569, 566*p*, 567*p*, 568*f*, 621*f*
"two-speech rule" (Senate), 209
two-stage approach to death penalty, 425
Two Treatises of Government (Locke), 31, 32, 46*f*
Tyler, John, 184*c*, 231, 253
tyrants, 426, 754, 757

U

Ukiah, California, council-manager government in, 726
Ukraine, 205*p*, 304
unalienable rights of the people, 49, 62, 366–372
unanimous consent agreement (Senate), 209
unauthorized aliens policies, 441–443, 441*p*
unclassified services, 287
unconstitutional acts, 101, 344, 356, 371, 376–377. *See also* judicial review
uncontrollable spending, 658–659
undeclared war, 178, 255–256
unemployment compensation program, 652–653, 740
unemployment rate, 662
unequal pay, 450
unicameral legislatures, 51*m*, 53, 61, 68, 75–76, 94
UNICEF, 316
unified court systems, 712
union memberships, 670
Union of Soviet Socialist Republics (USSR). *See* Soviet Union
unitary government, 19–20, 20*f*, 99, 764. *See also* government
United Kingdom (U.K.)
    common law in, 30, 48, 706, 762
    composition of, 758, 759*m*
    constitutionalism in, 758–759
    constitutional monarchy, 16, 16*p*, 760*f*
    election process, 763–764
    Elizabeth II (queen of the United Kingdom), 16*p*, 761
    foreign policy, 303, 312, 312*c*, 777
    government system, 759–762, 759*m*, 760*f*
    in the Group of 7, 672
    Magna Carta, 49, 54–55, 54*i*, 758
    medical care, 634
    mixed economy, 634
    prime minister, 22, 760–761, 762*p*, 763–764
    public policies, 763, 763*p*

    socialism in, 635
    Supreme Court, 762
    unitary government in, 19–20, 20*f*, 99
    in the United Nations, 313, 313*m*
    U.S. compared with, 764, 781*f*
United Nations (UN)
    Charter of, 313–314, 313*m*
    Conference on International Organization, 313
    Counter-Terrorism Centre, 304
    creation of, 298, 312–313, 313*m*
    Economic and Social Council, 314
    General Assembly, 314, 314*p*
    health and, 316, 316*c*
    High Commissioner for Refugees, 317*p*
    International Court of Justice, 314–315
    Israel created by, 302
    in Korean War, 299
    Millennium Development Goals, 316*c*
    NATO and, 312
    nongovernmental organizations and, 316
    peacekeeping missions, 314, 315*p*
    Secretariat, 315
    Security Council, 314, 317
    Universal Declaration of Human Rights, 316
    U.S. relationship with, 298, 313, 317
    work of, 315–317, 316*c*
United States* v. *American Library Association (2003), 389
United States* v. *Comstock (2010), 423
United States* v. *Curtiss-Wright Export Corp. (1936), 177, 177*p*
United States* v. *Darby (1941), 183
United States* v. *Eichman (1990), 385
United States* v. *Lopez (1995), 170
United States* v. *Lovett (1946), 416
United States* v. *Miller (1939), 404
United States* v. *Nixon (1974), 243, 243*f*
United States* v. *O'Brien (1968), 383–384
United States* v. *Playboy Entertainment Group (2000), 387
United States* v. *Salerno (1987), 423
United States* v. *Virginia (1996), 458, 458*c*
United States* v. *Windsor (2013), 134, 459
United States* v. *Wong Kim Ark (1898), 437
universal criteria for voting, 489–491, 490*f*
Universal Declaration of Human Rights, 316
universe, in polling, 523, 524*f*
university funding, 733
University of Alabama, 127, 127*p*
unreasonable distinctions, 136
urbanization, 723–724

urban special districts, 730–731
Uruguay, 672*p*
USA FREEDOM Act (2015), 409–410
U.S. Agency for International Development (USAID), 311, 318
U.S. Air Force (USAF), 321–322
USA PATRIOT Act (2001), 216–217, 216*p*, 409–410
U.S. Attorney, 341
U.S. Brewers Association, 540
U.S. Census, 156, 156*m*
U.S. Chamber of Commerce, 550*c*, 551
U.S. Citizenship and Immigration Services, 242, 324, 438, 438*f*
U.S. Coast Guard, 12, 12*p*, 177*p*, 324
U.S. Commission on Civil Rights, 271, 284, 481, 487
U.S. Congress. *See* Congress
U.S. Constitution. *See* Constitution of the United States
U.S. Court of Appeals for the Armed Forces, 97, 336, 340*c*
U.S. Court of Appeals for the Federal Circuit, 97, 340*c*, 352*m*, 353–354, 354*f*, 356–357
U.S. Court of Appeals for Veterans Claims, 97, 340*c*, 356
U.S. Court of Federal Claims, 97, 336, 340*c*, 357
U.S. Court of International Trade, 97, 340*c*, 355
user fees, 740–741
U.S. Forest Service, 339–340
U.S. Immigration and Customs Enforcement (ICE), 324, 409
U.S. Marine Corps (USMC), 319, 321
U.S. Marshals, 341
U.S.-Mexico-Canada Agreement (USMCA), 670
U.S. Mint, 654
U.S. Naval Station at Guantanamo, 356, 356*p*, 415
U.S. Navy, 321, 321*i*
U.S. Postal Service (USPS), 175, 284*c*, 287, 654
U.S. Savings Bond Program, 664
USSR. *See* Soviet Union
U.S. Supreme Court building, 23*p*, 330*p*–331*p*, 342, 342*p*, 349
U.S. Tax Court, 97, 340*c*, 357
Utah, Statehood of, 129
utilities, 120, 398, 634, 729
Uyghurs, China's human rights violations against, 777–778, 777*p*

V

vaccination of schoolchildren, 378, 398
vagrancy laws, 403
Van Buren, Martin, 571*i*, 699*c*
Vandals, 19
vassals, 25, 26–27, 27*f*

Vatican City, 8–9
***Veazie Bank* v. *Fenno* (1869),** 173, 647
Venetian Republic, 19
Venezuela, 296*c*, 302, 635, 667, 672
Vermont, 128, 685, 689
***Vernonia School District* v. *Acton*
(1995),** 409
**veterans' benefits, after World
War II,** 462
**Veterans Claims, Court of Appeals
for,** 97, 340*c*, 356
veto
in the colonies, 53, 100
by the federal government, 75, 154,
186, 238
by the President, 213, 245, 248–249,
248*f*, 249*p*, 256, 661
in the Roman Republic, 25
by State governors, 107, 685, 694, 702
in the United Nations, 314
Vice President
in the Cabinet, 280, 282*p*
changing roles of, 261*c*
impeachment and, 184, 231
John Adams as first, 83
nomination of candidates for, 189*f*,
594
Office of the Vice President, 277
in presidential elections with no
majority, 599
as president of the Senate, 194–195,
194*p*, 233, 598
Senate choosing, if no majority,
188–189
structure and function of, 233–235,
235*p*, 275
succession and, 110–112, 110*p*, 189,
230–232, 231*f*, 235
25th Amendment and, 110, 111–112,
188–189, 189*f*, 231–232, 235
when the House chooses the
President, 599, 601
Vietnam War, 198*m*
amnesty for draft evaders, 246
Congressional investigation of, 241
Gulf of Tonkin Resolution (1964),
224*f*
media's influence on, 532, 534*c*,
536–537
number of troops in, 300*f*
as undeclared war, 178, 178*p*, 256,
300
unpopularity and opposition, 288,
383–384, 384*p*, 545, 550, 589
voting age and, 109, 491, 491*p*
War Powers Resolution of 1973 and,
256
Vinson, Fred, 251
Virginia
under the Articles of Confederation,
70
colony of, 51*m*, 52, 52*i*, 58–60, 60*c*,
65
company charter of, 51–52, 684

framing and ratifying of the
Constitution, 73*f*, 74–76, 81*c*,
82–83, 85*f*
Jamestown settlement, 49, 51, 684
State constitution of, 113–114, 685
Virginia Company of London, 51,
51*m*
Virginia Declaration of Rights,
113–114, 113*i*
Virginia House of Burgesses, 52*i*, 65
Virginia Military Institute, 458
Virginia Plan, 74–75, 75*f*, 94
***Virginia State Board of Pharmacy*
v. *Virginia Citizens Consumer
Council* (1976),** 388
***Virginia* v. *Black* (2003),** 384
Virgin Islands, 155, 296
visas, 310, 310*f*
voice of the people, 521
voice votes, 208
Voltaire (François-Marie Arouet),
30
**Volunteers in Service to America
(VISTA) program,** 239
vote-by-mail, 488*p*, 507–508, 512, 512*f*
vote of no confidence, 22
vote recorder, 511*p*
voter ID laws, 484, 493
voter registration, 484, 491–493
voters, 555*f*
campaign pins for, 588*p*
factors that influence, 500, 501, 505
fraud, 512
income and occupation, 500–501,
501*f*
minimum age of, 18
nonvoting, 496–499
population shifts and, 503
psychological factors of, 500,
504–505
sociological factors of, 500–502, 501*f*
studying behavior of, 500
voter's pamphlet, 510
voter turnout, 496–499, 497*f*, 508,
511–512
votes
by Congress, 148
electoral college, 188, 188*f*, 598–599,
598*m*, 599*c*
politicians' need for, 155, 162
in proportion to population, 67
voting behavior, 500, 503
voting criteria, 555*f*
age, 109, 491, 491*p*
citizenship, 489, 489*p*
constitutional provisions, 488–489
felons and, 494–495, 498
historical 493-495, 490
laws and court actions, 490
residence, 136, 490, 490*f*
youth vote, 491
voting districts, 165, 509. *See also*
reapportionment of Congress;
redistricting

voting machines, 507, 511
voting process
ballots, 507, 509–510
casting and counting ballots, 507,
511–513, 512*f*, 598, 600
in Constitutional Convention, 74
electoral college in, 108, 111,
597–599, 598*m*, 599*c*
for filling elected public offices,
506–509
Motor Voter Act, 492
online voting, 512–513, 557
popular vote vs. electoral college
vote, 600
precincts and polling places,
498–499, 509, 577
proposed automatic voting
registration, 492
voter registration process, 491–493
voting lists, purging, 492, 493
voting registration, 491–493
voting rights
after the Revolutionary War, 478
court rulings upholding, 480–481
current restricting of voter
registration, 484–485
in early State constitutions, 685
efforts to circumvent, 480, 481–483,
483*f*
electorate size, 478–479
enforcement of, 480, 481
expanding suffrage, 476*f*, 478–480,
480*p*, 555*f*
of felons, 494–495, 498
in 15th Amendment, 108, 158,
479–481, 480*p*
of formerly enslaved people, 108
gerrymandering, 157–158, 157*i*,
480–481, 692
grandfather clauses, 493–494
history of, 478–485
literacy tests, 481, 482, 483, 493–494,
493*p*
nomination process and, 579
passage of, 446
poll tax and, 171, 479, 482, 488, 494
preclearance, 482–484, 483*c*
property ownership and, 489
qualifications for, 488–489
voting age, 479
*See also names of specific voting
rights acts*
Voting Rights Act Amendments,
482, 483*f*, 490
Voting Rights Act of 1965, 476*f*, 479,
482–485, 482*c*, 483*f*
Voting Rights Acts after 1965, 463

W

Wagner Act of 1935, 544*f*
Walesa, Lech, 752
Walker, Scott, 702*c*

Wallace, George, 127, 566, 572, 580
Wallace, Henry, 571
Wallace v. Jaffree (1995), 376, 706c
"Wall Street Bailout Bill," 214
Wan v. United States (1924), 347f
War Department, 318
wards, 577
war on terrorism, 319, 409–410. *See also* terrorism
war powers, 101, 110, 177–178, 183, 255–257
War Powers Resolution (1973), 101, 178, 256–257
warrantless eavesdropping, 224f, 409i, 410–411
warrants, 119, 405–409, 407c, 709
Warren, Earl, 340, 455, 460
Warren Court, 340
Washington, D.C. *See* District of Columbia
Washington, George
　Cabinet of, 280, 280i, 307
　on citizenship, 36
　as commander in chief, 60, 60c, 67i, 69, 255, 255p
　Farewell Address, 36, 111, 173, 294, 305–306, 566
　at First Continental Congress, 59
　as first President, 44i–45i, 83, 237
　foreign policy of, 294, 305, 307
　as Framer of the Constitution, 69, 73, 73f, 74, 83
　justice appointments, 350
　on Mount Rushmore, 95p
　obligations of citizenship, 36
　on patents and copyrights, 632
　on political parties, 111, 566
　on public debt, 173, 664
　on term of office, 112, 230
　on two-chambered legislature, 94
　veto use, 248
"Washington Feels Vietcong Offensive Failed Maximum Objective" (Balwin), 536
Washington Post, 186, 533c, 534c
Washington v. Texas (1967), 420
watchdog function of political parties, 565
Watergate Committee, 186, 190p, 200
Watergate scandal, 186–187, 190p, 200, 520, 609
water resources, 117
Watts v. Indiana (1949), 347f
Waxman, Henry, 214
weak-mayor government, 725, 725f
Wealth of Nations, The (Smith), 737
"We Are Mired in Stalemate" (Cronkite), 537
Weaver, Robert C., 281
Webster v. Reproductive Health Services (1989), 412
Weeks v. United States (1914), 408
Weems v. United States (1910), 424

weights and measures, 176, 176p
welfare. *See* public welfare; social welfare programs
Welfare Reform Act, 117, 117f
Welsh v. United States (1970), 379
Wesberry v. Sanders (1964), 158, 165–166, 165p
Westwood, Jean, 575
Whig Party, 581
Whig theory, 238
whips, party, 196
Whiskey Rebellion, 255
whistle-stop campaigns, 596, 596p
White House, 264p–265p
　Executive Office of the President in, 266f, 274–278, 276c
　January 6, 2021 Capitol attack and, 187
　staff of, 275
white primaries, 480, 480p
white supremacists, 391, 480. *See also* racial discrimination
WHO (World Health Organization), 314
WikiLeaks, 351p
Wilder, Douglas, 698, 700p
Wilkerson v. Utah (1879), 423
Willkie, Wendell, 595
William and Mary of Orange, 50
Williams v. North Carolina (1945), 133–134
Wilson, Addison Graves, 160
Wilson, Edith, 235
Wilson, James, 59, 60c, 73
Wilson, Woodrow
　on arming of merchant vessels, 210
　on bicameralism, 162, 162p
　on congressional committees, 547
　election of, 572
　foreign policy, 308
　on income tax, 655
　on judicial review, 111
　on lobbyists, 547
　pardon by, 246
　removal of postmaster, 245
　State of the Union address, 192, 192f
　stroke, 231, 235
　Treaty of Versailles, 118p, 253
Wilson-Gorman Tariff Act (1894), 655
Winfrey, Oprah, 518p, 623
winner-take-all States, 590, 590f
wiretapping, 184, 410–411
Wisconsin v. Yoder (1972), 379
women
　abortion rights, 372, 388, 393, 412–413, 549, 571
　affirmative action and, 464c, 465
　as ambassadors, 309
　in Congress, 150, 150p, 190
　discrimination against, 367, 394, 449–450
　equal rights for, 107, 312, 352, 454
　First Ladies, 235–236, 261c, 275

　gender gap in voting, 501
　as governors, 698, 698p
　human trafficking of, 363, 757
　on juries, 457p, 458, 708p
　as majority group, 449
　in the military, 320–321, 320p
　National Woman's Party, 362p, 363p
　in the Roman Republic, 24
　secretary of state, 307, 308, 397p, 595
　sex discrimination, 457–459, 458c
　sexual harassment, 164
　in State legislatures, 693p
　in Supreme Court, 339
　Title IX and, 434f, 439f, 463, 468
　unequal pay, 450
　voting behavior, 501
　voting rights extended to, 362p–363p, 476f, 479
Woodson v. North Carolina (1976), 424–425
workplace safety, 734
Works Progress Administration (WPA), 239i, 657p
World Bank, 671, 671p
World Bank Group, 314, 316
World Court, 314–315
World Health Organization (WHO), 314
World Trade Center, New York City, 303
World Trade Organization (WTO), 672
World War I, 210
World War II
　aid to Great Britain in, 254
　atomic bombs in, 235, 235p
　deficit financing and, 172
　desegregation of the armed forces, 258, 258p
　foreign policy after, 298–299
　Pearl Harbor attack, 297–298, 297i, 369, 415, 415p
　sessions of Congress in, 151, 152
　Vice President and, 234
　voting age during, 109, 491
　writ of habeas corpus suspended during, 415p
WPA (Works Progress Administration), 239i, 657p
writ of certiorari, 345, 345p
writ of habeas corpus, 81, 414–415, 415p
writs of assistance, 57c, 405
WTO (World Trade Organization), 672

Y

Yalta Conference (1945), 299
Yates, Robert, 82, 83
Yates v. United States (1957), 383
yellow journalism, 532f
Yeltsin, Boris, 754, 767

Yick Wo v. *Hopkins* (1886), 455
Youngstown Sheet & Tube Company
    v. *Sawyer* (1952), 250–251, 250*p*
youth vote, 479, 491

Z
Zadvydas v. *Davis* (2001), 442
Zaire, 754
Zelensky, Volodymyr, 187
Zelman v. *Simmons-Harris* (2002),
    376
Zenger, John Peter, 96*i,* 334
zoning ordinances, 728
Zoot Suit Riots (1940s), 448

[Photography]

Front Matter

v: Goodluz/Shutterstock; **vi:** Rawpixel.com/Shutterstock; **xT:** F11photo/Shutterstock; **xB:** Library of Congress; **xiT:** Larry1235/Shutterstock; **xiB:** Vlad_g/Fotolia; **xiiT:** Asar Studios/Alamy Stock Photo; **xiiB:** Dirck Halstead/Liaison/Getty Images; **xiiiT:** Brian Jannsen/Alamy Stock Photo; **xiiiB:** Everett Collection Inc/Alamy Stock Photo; **xivT:** Paul A. Souders/Corbis; **xivB:** Lightspring/Shutterstock; **xvT:** David R.Frazier Photolibrary/Alamy Stock Photo; **xvB:** Kristoffer Tripplaar/Alamy Stock Photo; **xviT:** Sue Ogrocki/AP Images; **xviB:** Roberto Fumagalli/Alamy Stock Photo; **CF0:** Michael Flippo/Fotolia; **CF1:** Pat Benic/UPI/Newscom

Topic 1

2: F11photo/Shutterstock; **006:** Michael Flippo/Alamy Stock Photo; **7T:** Jose Luis Magana/Reuters; **7B:** Look and Learn/Bridgeman Images; **11:** GL Archive/Alamy Stock Photo; **12T:** Anam Collection/Alamy Stock Photo; **12B:** Richard Drew/AP Images; **14:** Alinari/Art Resource, NY; **16:** Jayne Fincher.Photo Int/Alamy Stock Photo; **19:** Yonhap News/YNA/Newscom; **21:** Uliana Shevchenko/Alamy Stock Photo; **22:** Obed Zilwa/AP Images; **23:** Trekandphoto/Fotolia; **24:** Bettmann/Corbis; **30:** Fine Art Images/Glow Images; **31:** Stefano Bianchetti/Corbis; **33:** Mario Tama/Staff/Getty Images; **34T:** Jim West/Alamy Stock Photo; **34B:** Bettmann/Corbis; **35:** Artley Cartoons; **36:** AF archive/Alamy Stock Photo; **37:** Visar Kryeziu/AP Images; **39:** Niday Picture Library/Alamy Stock Photo; **40T:** Hemera/Getty Images; **40B:** Jim West/Alamy Stock Photo; **43:** De Agostini Picture Library/Age Fotostock

Topic 2

44: Library of Congress; **46T:** SuperStock/Glow Images; **46B:** Everett Collection/Newscom; **47:** SuperStock; **48:** Barney Burstein/Corbis; **50:** Mary Evans Picture Library/The Image Works; **52T:** MPI/Stringer/Archive Photos/Getty Images; **52B:** Falkensteinfoto/Alamy Stock Photo; **53:** Barney Burstein/Corbis; **54:** Superstock/Glow Images; **56:** North Wind Picture Archives/Alamy Stock Photo; **58T:** North Wind Picture Archives/Alamy Stock Photo; **58B:** Everett Collection/SuperStock; **59:** Niday Picture Library/Alamy Stock Photo; **61:** Library of Congress; **62:** GL Archive/Alamy Stock Photo; **64:** North Wind Picture Archives/AP Images; **65:** The Bridgeman Art Library; **67:** John Parrot/Stocktrek Images/Alamy Stock Photo; **68:** Library of Congress; **69T:** North Wind Picture Archives/Alamy Stock Photo; **69B:** Old Paper Studios/Alamy Stock Photo; **70:** SuperStock/Glow Images; **72:** SuperStock/SuperStock; **73L:** Db Iimages/Alamy Stock Photo; **73CL:** World History Archive/Alamy Stock photo; **73C:** Stock Montage/Contributor/Getty Images; **73CR:** US Capitol Visitors Center online exhibition/wikimedia.org; **73R:** Bettmann/Corbis; **74:** Trekandphoto/Fotolia; **77T:** World History Archive/Alamy Stock Photo; **77B:** North Wind Picture Archives/Alamy Stock Photo; **79:** JT Vintage/Glasshouse Images/Alamy Stock Photo; **80L:** Stock Montage/Contributor/Getty Images; **80R:** Richmond, Virginia, USA/The Bridgeman Art Library; **82T:** Library of Congress; **82B:** North Wind Picture Archives/Alamy Stock Photo; **84T:** Barney Burstein/Corbis; **84B:** World History Archive/Alamy Stock Photo

Topic 3

88: Trekandphoto/Fotolia; **90TL:** Kevin Dietsch/UPI/Newscom; **90TR:** Al Drago/CQ Roll Call/AP Images; **90BL:** U.S. Army Photo by Spc. Anthony Jones, Oklahoma National Guard/Army.mil; **90BR:** Tim Pannell/Corbis; **92:** Kumar Sriskandan/Alamy Stock Photo; **95T:** Bettmann/Corbis; **95B:** Marcophoto81/Fotolia; **96:** Bettmann/Corbis; **97T:** Wang Ying/Xinhua/Alamy Stock Photo; **97B:** Artley Cartoons; **98T:** Artley Cartoons; **98B:** Artley Cartoons; **99:** Artley Cartoons; **101:** Artley Cartoons; **104:** Tom Barlet/Seattle Post-Intelligencer/Museum of History & Industry; **106T:** Library of Congress; **106B:** Everett Collection/Newscom; **108:** Everett Collection/Newscom; **109T:** Kevin Dietsch/UPI/Newscom; **109B:** Savvas Learning Company LLC; **110T:** AP Images; **110B:** UPPA/Photoshot/Newscom; **111:** Library of Congress; **113:** Bettmann/Corbis; **115:** Seaman Clark Lane/AB Forces News Collection/Alamy Stock Photo; **116:** SuperStock/Glow Images; **118:** Bettmann/Corbis; **120T:** Matt Detrich/AP Images; **120B:** Paul Moseley/Fort Worth Star-Telegram/Tribune News Service/Getty Images; **121T:** Library of Congress; **121B:** Anthony Dunn/Alamy Stock Photo; **122:** Scott Dorrett/Fotolia; **123:** North Wind Picture Archives/Alamy Stock Photo; **125:** AP

Images; **126T:** Library of Congress; **126B:** Master Sgt. Mark Olsen/Dvids; **127:** Steve Schapiro/Corbis; **129T:** Wilfred Osgood/National Geographic Society/Corbis; **129B:** Lee Lorenz/Cartoonbank; **130T:** Federal Highway Administration (FHWA); **130B:** Jacquelyn Martin/AP Images; **132:** Jeffrey M. Frank/Shutterstock; **133:** Bettmann/Corbis; **134:** Rudy Lawidjaja/Sipa USA/Newscom; **135T:** Bettmann/Corbis; **135B:** Randy Snyder/AP Images; **136:** Tony Waltham/Robert Harding Picture Library Ltd/Alamy Stock Photo; **138T:** Kumar Sriskandan/Alamy Stock Photo; **138B:** AP Images; **141:** Pat Bagley/Salt Lake Tribune/Cagle Cartoons, Inc.

Topic 4

142: Vlad_g/Fotolia; **145:** AP Images; **146:** Susan Walsh/AP Images; **147:** Larry Downing/Afp/Getty Images; **149:** Daniel Greene/Collection of the U.S. House of Representatives; **150T:** Bettmann/Getty Images; **150B:** Keystone Press/Alamy Stock Photo; **152T:** Reuters; **152B:** Interfoto/Alamy Stock Photo; **153:** Ed Fischer/CartoonStock; **154:** Paul M. Walsh/AP Images; **155:** Jason Reed/Reuters; **157:** North Wind/North Wind Picture Archives; **158:** NASA Earth Observatory/NOAA NGDC; **159:** Larry Downing/Reuters; **160:** Library of Congress; **162:** Library Of Congress; **163:** Chris Wildt/CartoonStock; **164:** Denis Paquin/AP Images; **165:** Charles Shaw/Getty Images; **167:** Mel Finkelstein/NY Daily News Archive/Getty Images; **170:** David Pollack/Glow Images; **172T:** Robert Weber/The New Yorker Collection/Cartoonbank; **172B:** Alexander Nemenov/Afp/Getty Images; **173:** White House/AP Images; **174:** Health, Science and Space/Alamy Stock Photo; **175:** NCJ/Mirrorpix/Newscom; **176:** Bettmann/Corbis; **177T:** PF-sdasm4/Alamy Stock Photo; **177B:** AP Images; **178:** Charles Tasnadi/AP Images; **179:** AP Images; **181L:** GL Archive/Alamy Stock Photo; **181R:** Stock Montage/Contributor/Getty Images; **182T:** Jim West/Alamy Stock Photo; **182B:** Stus.com; **186:** Bill Pierce/Time Life Pictures/Getty Images; **190:** Wally McNamee/Corbis; **191T:** Bill Clark/Roll Call Photos/Newscom; **191B:** Historical/Corbis; **192:** Harris & Ewing/Corbis; **193:** Thomas D. Mcavoy/The Life Picture Collection/Getty Images; **194T:** Hejzlar Jaroslav/CTK/Alamy Stock Photo; **194B:** Planetpix/White House Photo/Alamy Stock Photo; **195:** Francis Miller/The Life Picture Collection/Getty Images; **196:** Anna Moneymaker/Bloomberg/Getty Images; **197:** Mark Reinstein/Getty Images; **200:** Bill Gentile/Corbis; **202:** Underwood & Underwood/Corbis; **203T:** Bettmann/Corbis; **203B:** John Trever/Cagle Cartoons, Inc.; **204:** Lawrence Manning/Corbis; **205:** Raj Valley/Alamy Stock Photo; **206:** Ed Steed/CartoonStock; **207:** Alan King engraving/Alamy Stock Photo; **208T:** Brendan Hoffman/Getty Images; **208B:** Danita Delimont/Alamy Stock Photo; **209:** Chip Somodevilla/Staff/Getty Images; **213T:** Clifford Berryman/National Archives; **213B:** Ron Sachs/CNP/Corbis; **216:** Spencer Platt/Getty Images; **218:** Reuters

Topic 5

222: Asar Studios/Alamy Stock Photo; **224T:** Korean War/Alamy Stock Photo; **224B:** Ron Sachs/CNP/Corbis; **226:** Yoichi Okamoto/White House Photo Office/LBJ Library photo; **227T:** Stephen Jaffe/AFP/Newscom; **227B:** Wally McNamee/Corbis; **228:** Larry Downing/Reuters/Corbis; **230:** Everett/Glow Images; **233:** Dennis Brack/Danita Delimont/Alamy Stock Photo; **234:** Historical Premium/Corbis; **235T:** Brooks Kraft/Sygma/Corbis; **235B:** Tom Fox/Dallas Morning News/Corbis; **236:** Ron Sachs/CNP/MediaPunch/Alamy Stock Photo; **237:** Everett/Glow Images; **238:** Library of Congress; **239T:** Library of Congress; **239B:** Library of congress; **240T:** Whitehousehistory; **240B:** Ed Maloney/AP Images; **241:** Jim West/Alamy Stock Photo; **242:** Jason Vorhees/AP Images; **245:** Gradisher Martha/CartoonStock; **246:** Topical Press Agency/Stringer/Getty Images; **247:** GL Archive/Alamy Stock Photo; **249:** Niday Picture Library/Alamy Stock Photo; **250:** Allan Cash Picture Library/Alamy Stock Photo; **252:** Bettmann/Corbis; **253T:** White House Photo/Alamy Stock Photo; **253B:** World History Archive/Alamy Stock Photo; **254T:** DIZ Muenchen GmbH,Sueddeutsche Zeitung Photo/Alamy Stock Photo; **254B:** North Wind Picture Archives/Alamy Stock Photo; **255:** Library of Congress; **258:** Everett Collection Historical/Alamy Stock Photo; **260T:** J. Scott Applewhite/AP Images; **260B:** Library of Congress; **263:** Roger Viollet/Getty Images

Topic 6

264: Dirck Halstead/Liaison/Getty Images; **268:** Dan Loh/AP Images; **269T:** Al Drago/CQ Roll Call/AP Images; **269B:** Fran/Cartoon Stock;

Newscom; **574:** Zach Boyden-Holmes/Staff/Zuma Press/Newscom; **575T:** Bettmann/Getty Images; **575B:** Erik S. Lesser/EPA/Newscom; **577:** Mark Hirsch/AP Images; **578:** Everett Collection/Newscom; **579T:** Xinhua/ZUMApress/Newscom; **579B:** Keystone Pictures USA/Alamy Stock Photo; **580:** World History Archive/Alamy Stock Photo; **581:** Joel Page/Reuters/Corbis; **582:** Stock Montage/Contributor/Getty Images; **583:** Bettmann/Getty Images; **584:** Zuma Press, Inc./Alamy Stock Photo; **585T:** Hans Pennink/AP Images; **585B:** Richard Ellis/Alamy Stock Photo; **587:** Mary Beth Schneider/AP Images; **588:** Todd Strand/Independent Picture Service/Alamy Stock Photo; **589:** Bettmann/Getty Images; **591:** Glen Stubbe/Zuma Press, Inc./Alamy Stock Photo; **592:** Al Gretz/Keystone/Hulton Archive/Getty Images; **593:** Milt Priggee/Cagle Cartoons; **594:** Zuma Press,Inc./Alamy stock photo; **595:** Keystone Pictures Usa/Zumapress/Newscom; **596:** AP Images; **597:** Joe Marquette/AP Images; **600:** Chip Somodevilla/Getty Images; **601:** Bettmann/Getty Images; **603:** Stocktrek Images, Inc./Alamy Stock Photo; **605:** Arthur Grace/Zumapress/Newscom; **607:** Melpomen/Fotolia; **608:** AP Images; **609T:** Kevin E. Schmidt/Quad-City Times/ZUMA Press Inc/Alamy Stock Photo; **609B:** Lauren Victoria Burke/AP Images; **610:** Wuerker, Matt/CartoonStock; **612:** Cphoto/Fotolia; **613T:** Stahler, Jeff/CartoonStock; **613B:** Marmaduke St. John/Alamy Stock Photo; **614T:** J.B. Handelsman/The New Yorker Collection/Cartoonbank; **614B:** Brendan Smialowski/Pool/EPA/Newscom; **616:** Andrew Harrer/Bloomberg/Getty Images; **617:** Mike Flinn/CartoonStock; **620:** Joel Page/Reuters/Corbis; **623:** Kean Collection/Archive Photos/Getty Images

Topic 12

624: Kristoffer Tripplaar/Alamy Stock Photo; **626L:** Lebrecht Music and Arts Photo Library/Alamy Stock Photo; **626R:** AP Images; **628:** Richard Ellis/Alamy Stock Photo; **630:** Blend Images/Alamy Stock Photo; **632:** Old Paper Studios/Alamy Stock Photo; **634:** Adoc-photos/Corbis; **638:** Catnap/Alamy Stock Photo; **639:** World History Archive/Alamy Stock Photo; **641:** Mario Tama/Afp/Newscom; **642:** Grizelda/CartoonStock; **643:** Bettmann/Corbis; **646:** Bloomberg/Contributor/Getty Images; **647:** US National Archives and Records Administration; **650T:** Max Faulkner/AP Images; **650B:** AugustSnow/Alamy Stock Photo; **653:** Harley Schwadron/CartoonStock; **654:** Hellen Sergeyeva/Fotolia; **655:** Chronicle/Alamy Stock Photo; **657:** Minnesota Historical Society/Corbis; **658:** Najlah Feanny/Corbis; **662:** Solarisys/Shutterstock; **666:** NASA; **668:** Don Despain/Alamy Stock Photo; **670:** PRNewsFoto/Caterpillar/AP Images; **671:** PJF Military Collection/Alamy Stock Photo; **672:** Ksenia Ragozina/Shutterstock; **674:** SeongJoon Cho/Bloomberg/Getty Images; **676:** Don Despain/Alamy Stock Photo; **679:** Dave Granlund/Cagle Cartoons, Inc.

Topic 13

680: Sue Ogrocki/AP Images; **684:** Albert Herter/Malegislature/Courtesy Commonwealth of Massachusetts, State House Art Commission.; **685:** Albert Herter/Malegislature; **687:** Scott Keeler/AP Images; **690:** Ellen Isaacs/Alamy Stock Photo; **691:** Jeff Parker/Cagle Cartoons; **693T:** Roger Smith/Library of Congress Prints and Photographs Division Washington [LC-USW3-029275-C]; **693B:** Sacramento Bee/Zumapress/Newscom; **694T:** Usda Photo/Alamy Stock Photo; **694B:** Dale Wetzel/AP Images; **695:** Sylvia Buchholz/Darren Hauck/Reuters/Alamy Stock Photo; **697:** David McNew/Getty Images; **698:** Toby Talbot/AP Images; **699:** Wolverton/Cagle Cartoons; **700T:** Mark Reinstein/Alamy Stock Photo; **700B:** Susan Montoya Bryan/AP Images; **701:** Gilya3/Fotolia; **705:** Alan Klehr/Getty Images; **708:** New York Times Co./Contributor/Getty Images; **709T:** Michael Maslin The New Yorker Collection/The Cartoon Bank; **709B:** Library of Congress; **711T:** Randy Duchaine/Alamy Stock Photo; **711B:** Mike Dooley; **713:** Jack Corbett/CartoonStock; **714:** Drew Angerer/Getty Images; **715:** Art Collection 3/Alamy Stock Photo; **717:** Bill Stormont/Alamy Stock Photo; **720T:** The Bakersfield Californian/Zuma press.com/Alamy Stock Photo; **720B:** Courtesy the Fort Bend County Museum Association, Richmond, Texas.; **722:** Sandy Macys/Alamy Stock Photo; **723:** Stephen Arce/Icon Sportswire 285/Newscom; **724:** Al Mount/Fotolia; **728:** Franco Nadalin/Alamy Stock Photo; **729T:** Mark Parisi/Offthemark; **729B:** SuperStock/Glow Images; **730:** Warren Miller/Cartoon bank; **732:** Mason Vranish/Alamy Stock Photo; **735T:** Larry W. Smith/EPA/Newscom; **735B:** Eisenhower Library & Museum; **736:** Scherl/Süddeutsche Zeitung Photo/Alamy Stock Photo; **739T:** Dmitry Bandura/CartoonStock; **739B:** Jim Bryant/UPI Photo/Alamy Stock photo; **740T:** Jim West/Alamy Stock Photo; **740B:** Brian Jannsen/

Alamy Stock Photo; **744:** Bill Stormont/Alamy Stock Photo; **746:** Fischer, Ed/CartoonStock; **747:** Flat Feds by Steve Sack, The Minneapolis Star-Tribune, MN

Topic 14

748: Roberto Fumagalli/Alamy Stock Photo; **752:** Oliver Gerhard imagebroker/Newscom; **754:** Baloo -Rex May/CartoonStock; **756:** Joerg Boethling/Alamy Stock Photo; **758:** Chris Jackson/AP Images; **761:** Tim Graham/Hulton Archive/Getty Images; **762T:** Lewis Whyld/AP Images; **762B:** PA Images/Alamy Stock Photo; **763:** PA Images/Alamy Stock Photo; **765:** Al Drago/CQ Roll Call/AP Images; **767:** Frederique Lengaigne/Gamma-Rapho/Getty Images; **769T:** Maxim Marmur/AFP/Getty Images; **769B:** Sergei Karpukhin/Reuters; **772:** Hulton Archive/Stringer/Getty Images; **773:** Rafael Ben-Ari/Fotolia; **776:** Hum Historical/Alamy Stock Photo; **777:** Islemount Images/Alamy Stock Photo; **780:** HP Photo/Fotolia

End Matter

784: Stock Connection Blue/Alamy Stock Photo; **854:** Everett Collection/Newscom

[Text Acknowledgements]
Front Matter

Declaration of Independence, 1776

Topic 1

Hobbes, Thomas. (1651) The Leviathan. George Routledge and Sons.; Hobbes, Thomas. (1651) The Leviathan. George Routledge and Sons.; Thomas Jefferson; Letter from a Birmingham Jail, Martin Luther King, Jr., April 16, 1963; James Madison, Federalist Paper No. 51; Draft of Instructions to the Virginia Delegates in the Continental Congress, July 1774, Thomas Jefferson; Benjamin Franklin,Reply to the Governor, November 11, 1755; Argument of Clarence Darrow in the Case of the Communist Labor Party in the Criminal Court, Chicago (1920), p. 39; www.Monticello.org; Aristotle; Jean-Jacques Roussea,The Social Contract, 1762.; Alexander Pope, An Essay on Man epistle 3, l. 303-4 (1733); from The Gettsburg Address; Pericles Funeral Oration from History of the Peloponnesian War; Baron de Montesquieu, Complete Works, vol. 1 (The Spirit of Laws) [1748]; Two Treatises of Government, John Locke; Modern Democracies, by James Bryce, 1921; Winston Churchill speech to the House of Commons, November 11, 1947; John B. Finch, 1885; Abraham Lincoln, Message to Congress, July 4, 1861.; John F. Kennedy, Civil Rights Announcement, June 11, 1963; Theodore Roosevelt, New York State Chamber of Commerce banquet, 1902.; George Washington's Farewell Address; Abraham Lincoln, The Nature and Objects of Government, fragmentary notes, 1854; Aristotle, Politics, Book Four, Part XI, c. 350 BCE; Plato, Republic, Book VII, c. 360 BCE; Excerpt from Old Oligarch's Constitution of the Athenians by Xenophon. Published by Harvard University Press.

Topic 2

The Petition of Right, 1628., University of Groningen; English Bill of Rights, 1689, Lillian Goldman Law Library; Magna Carta, King John, 1215; English Bill of Rights, 1689, Lillian Goldman Law Library; Benjamin Franklin, 1776; member of New Jersey's Assembly; The Declaration of Rights and Grievances, 1774, Stamp Act Congress; Resolution of June 7, 1776; "Give Me Liberty or Give Me Death", 1775; Thomas Paine, Common Sense, 1776; "Articles of Confederation," transcription courtesy of the Avalon Project at Yale Law School, www.ourdocuments.gov/doc.php?flash=old&doc=3&page=transcript.; "Articles of Confederation," transcription courtesy of the Avalon Project at Yale Law School, www.ourdocuments.gov/doc.php?flash=old&doc=3&page=transcript.; George Washington Letter to James McHenry, 22 August 1785; Virginia General Assembly, January 21, 1786; The United States in Congress Assembled, February 21, 1787; William E. Gladstone, "Kin Beyond Sea," The North American Review, Sept-Oct 1878, p. 185; Edmund Randolph, Madison's Debates, May 30, 1787; from The Virginia Plan, 1787 drafted by James Madison.; from The Virginia Plan, 1787 drafted by James Madison.; from The Virginia Plan, 1787 drafted by James Madison.; Benjamin Franklin's Proposal for Prayer, June 28, 1787; Benjamin Franklin; Madison's Notes,

8 Sept 1787; Benjamin Franklin's Final Speech in the Constitutional Convention from the notes of James Madison, 1787; Alexander Hamilton The Federalist, No. 1, 1787.; Patrick Henry's Speech before the Virginia Ratifying Convention, June 5, 1788; Amos Singletary; Antifederalist No. 62, on the Organization and Powers of the Senate (Part I); Notes of Debates in the Federal Convention of 1787, James Madison; Ebenezer Stevens, The Magazine of American History with Notes and Queries, Vol. 1, p. 590, 1877; Joshua Wyeth, Tea Leaves: Being a Collection of Letters and Documents, p. LXXI, 1884, A.O. Crane.; Thomas Hutchinson, Report to the East India Company, 1773; http://www.boston-tea-party.org/account-Samuel-Cooper. html; Declaration of Sentiments, 1848

Topic 3

Omitted Chapters of History Disclosed in the Life and Papers of Edmund Randolph, p. 91, 1888, G.P. Putnam's Sons; The Federalist, No. 51; Note of the Debates in the Federal Convention of 1787; The Federalist No. 22; The Federalist No. 22; The Federalist No. 22; The Federalist No. 47; The Federalist No. 51; The Federalist No 78; The Federalist No. 51; Woodrow Wilson; George Washington's Farewell Address; Virginia Declaration of Rights; Opinion of the Court, McCulloch v. Maryland (1819); Collected Legal Papers of Oliver Wendell Holmes, pp. 295-296, 1921; Speech to the Virginia ratifying convention, 1788; Opinion of the Court, Cohens v. Virginia (1821); Why the Federal Government, Not States, Should Regulate the Environment, Mic.com, 2012

Topic 4

Murphy, Robert P. "Was TARP Good for the Taxpayers?" Mises Daily, October 07, 2010.; Benjamin, Medea and Arum Gupta. "Time for a Taxpayer Revolt" The Nation. September 29, 2008.; Government by the People; The Federalist No. 10; Representative Luther Patrick (D., Alabama), 1940; Senator Russell Long (D., Louisiana); Notes on the Debates in the Federal Convention, 1787; Congressional Government; Speech. Pittsburgh, Jan. 29, 1916; Majority Opinion, Gibbons v. Ogden, 1824; Majority Opinion, Heart of Atlanta Motel v. U.S., 1964; George Washington's Farewell Address; United States v. Curtiss-Wright Export Corp, 1936; Thomas Jefferson [refuted]; Abraham Lincoln's Second Inaugural Address, 1865; Sherrod Brown, Congress From the Inside; United States Congress; Woodrow Wilson, Congressional Government, 1885; Senate Select Committee on Presidential Campaign Activities, 1973; Woodrow Wilson, Prepared Statement, 1917; Senator George Norris (R., Nebraska), 1914; "Overview and Critique: An Overview of the Clean Air Act Amendments of 1990," Henry Waxman, 21 Environmental Law 1721 (1991); President George H.W. Bush; Staff member, Rep. Henry Waxman (D., California); Senator Mitch McConnell (R., Kentucky); President George H.W. Bush; Martin Luther King, Jr.; Thaddeus Stevens, Speech in the U.S. House of Representatives, January 3, 1867; www.treasury.gov; Time for a Taxpayer Revolt, The Nation, September 29, 2008; "TARP, the Long Goodbye," Simon Johnson, The New York Times, Sept 30, 2010; "Was TARP Good for the Taxpayers?" Robert P. Murphy, Ludwig Von Mises Institute, Oct 7, 2010; Murphy, Robert P. "Was TARP Good for the Taxpayers?" Mises Daily, October 07, 2010.; Benjamin, Medea and Arum Gupta. "Time for a Taxpayer Revolt" The Nation. September 29, 2008.; Wesberry v. Sanders, Majority Opinion, Justice Hugo Black, October 1963.; Wesberry v. Sanders, Dissenting Opinion, Justice John Marshall Harlan, October 1963; Congressional Record Vol. 147, No. 144, Senate Floor Debate, Senator Russ Feingold, October 25, 2001; Congressional Record Vol. 147, No. 144, Senate Floor Debate, Senator Orrin Hatch, October 25, 2001; From Interview with Nancy Kassebaum, April 6, 2009. Copyright © 2010 The Miller Center Foundation and the Edward M. Kennedy Institute for the United States Senate

Topic 5

William Howard Taft: Essential Writings and Addresses, edited by David H. Burton; FDR, The New York Times Magazine, September 11, 1932, p. 2; John Adams; Benjamin Franklin; Vice President Thomas Marshall; President Dwight Eisenhower, News Conference February 06, 1957; Theodore Roosevelt: An Autobiography, 1913; Theodore Roosevelt: An Autobiography, 1913; Annual Message to the Congress on the State of the Union, January 04, 1965; Letter from Thomas Jefferson to Abbé Arnoux Paris July 19. 1789.; Gerald Ford, Proclamation 4311, Sep 08, 1974; Presidential Signing

Statements: Constitutional and Institutional Implications Todd Garvey Legislative Attorney January 4, 2012; RADIO AND TELEVISION REPORT TO THE AMERICAN PEOPLE ON THE BERLIN CRISIS, JULY 25, 1961; Pres. Theodore Roosevelt; Address of Vice President Roosevelt, Minnesota State Fair, Minneapolis, Sept. 2nd, 1901; Veto of H.J.RES. 542 (War Powrs Resolution), October 24, 1973; Petition to the President of the U.S. by Leo Szilard , July 17, 1945; letter written by Harry Truman on January 12, 1953 to Prof. James L. Cate; Prompt and Utter Destruction, 1997; Youngstown Sheet & Tube Company v. Sawyer, 1952; Majority Opinion, Justice Hugo Black; Youngstown Sheet & Tube Company v. Sawyer, 1952; Dissenting Opinion, Chief Justice Fred Vinson; Executive Order 9981, July 26, 1948. President Harry Truman; Statement by General Omar Bradley before the President's Committee on Equality of Treatment and Opportunity in the Armed Forces, March 28, 1949

Topic 6

United Nations Millennium Development Goals. Copyright © United Nations Publications. Used by permission.; Federalist No. 51; Office of National Drug Control Policy; Federalist No. 76; Pres. John F. Kennedy; Abraham Lincoln; William Howard Taft, Our Chief Magistrate and His Powers, 1916; National Aeronautics and Space Act of 1958 (Pub.L. 85–568); Senator William Learned Marcy (NY) Senate Speech, 1832; Barack Obama, Statement by the President to the Press, September 17, 2010; Federalist No. 72; George Washington's Farewell Address; Speech by Pres. James Monroe to Congress, Dec. 2, 1823; April 2, 1917: Address by Woodrow Wilson to Congress Requesting a Declaration of War Against Germany; Address to the Congress Asking That a State of War Be Declared Between the United States and Japan. December 8, 1941; Radio Fireside Chat, December 29, 1940; United Nations Charter; Harry Truman's Speech to Congress, March 12, 1947; George Washington's Farewell Address, 1796; "Tear Down This Wall" speech, Ronald Reagan, 1987; The North Atlantic Treaty Washington D.C. - 4 April 1949; Charter of the United Nations; US Army Signal Corps Aeronautical Division charter, 1907; Director of National Intelligence John Negroponte; Budget of the United States Government, 2015; "Cuts to Foreign Aid Cost the U.S. Globally," US News, 2011; John Mica website

Topic 7

"Looming Large" from Out of Order: Stories from the History of the Supreme Court by Sandra Day O'Connor, copyright © 2013 by Arizona Community Foundation. Used by permission of Random House, an imprint and division of Penguin Random House LLC. All rights reserved.; Introduction from Out Of Order: Stories From The History Of The Supreme Court by Sandra Day O'Connor, copyright © 2013 by Arizona Community Foundation. Used by permission of Random House, an imprint and division of Penguin Random House LLC. All rights reserved.

Topic 8

Woodrow Wilson, Fourteen Points; Inaugural Address, Jimmy Carter; Barack Obama, Town Hall meeting in China, 2015; West Virginia Board of Education v. Barnette, 1943; Schenck v. United States, 1919; Public Law 100-383, 1988; Majority opinion, Gitlow, v. New York, 1925; Alexis de Tocqueville, Democracy in America, 1835; Majority Opinion, Lemon v. Kurtzman (1971); Prayer; Majority opinion, Engel v. Vitale (1962); Majority opinion, Epperson v. Arkansas (1968); Majority opinion, Reynolds v. United States (1879); Majority opinion, Wisconsin v. Yoder (1972); Majority opinion, West Virginia State Board of Education v. Barnette (1943); Majority opinion, Wisconsin v. Yoder (1972); Dissenting opinion, Schwimmer v. United States (1929); Majority opinion, Snyder v. Phelps (2011); Majority opinion, New York Times Company v. Sullivan (1964); public letter by Matthew Lyon, 1798; Espionage Act of 1917; Majority opinion, Schenck v. United States (1919); Majority opinion, Thornhill v. Alabama (1940); Majority Opinion, United States v. O'Brien (1968); Majority Opinion, Tinker v. Des Moines School District (1969); Majority Opinion, Texas v. Johnson (1989); Majority Opinion, Texas v. Johnson (1989); United States v. O'Brien (1968); Minnesota state law; Majority Opinion, Near v. Minnesota (1931); Majority Opinion, Nebraska Press Association v. Stuart (1976); Majority Opinion, Hazelwood School District v. Kuhlmeier (1988); Majority Opinion, Branzburg v. Hayes (1972); Ohio state law; Majority opinion, Mutual Film Corporation

v. Ohio (1915); Majority opinion, Mutual Film Corporation v. Ohio (1915); Majority Opinion, Burstyn V. Wilson (1952); Majority opinion, FCC v. Pacifica Foudnation (1978); Majority opinion, Red Lion Broadcasting Co. v. FCC (1969); Majority opinion, Red Lion Broadcasting Co. v. FCC (1969); Concurrence, Jacobellis v. Ohio (1964); U.S. postal law; Majority opinion, Miller v. California (1973); Communications Decency Act of 1996; Majority Opinion, Reno v. American Civil Liberities Union (1997); City of Cinncinnati ordinance; Colorado state law; Majority opinion, Gregory v. Chicago (1968); Majority opinion, National Association for the Advancement of Colored People v. Alabama (1958); Majority opinion, Davidson v. New Orleans (1878); Majority opinion, Rochin v. California (1952); Majority opinion, Pierce v. Society of Sisters (1925); Majority opinion, Civil Rights Cases (1883); Civil Rights Act of 1866; Majority opinion, Jones v. Mayer (1968); Majority opinion, Runyon v. McCrary (1976); Majority opinion, St. Francis College v. Al Khazraji (1987); Majority opinion, District of Columbia v. Heller (2008); Majority opinion, District of Columbia v. Heller (2008); Majority opinion, District of Columbia v. Heller (2008); Majority opinion, District of Columbia v. Heller (2008); Majority opinion, District of Columbia v. Heller (2008); Majority opinion, District of Columbia v. Heller (2008); Majority opinion, District of Columbia v. Heller (2008); Majority opinion, District of Columbia v. Heller (2008); Majority opinion, District of Columbia v. Heller (2008); Majority opinion, District of Columbia v. Heller (2008); Majority opinion, District of Columbia v. Heller (2008); Majority opinion, District of Columbia v. Heller (2008); Planned Parenthood of Southeastern Pennsylvania v. Casey (1992); Federalist Paper, #84; Majority opinion, Estes v. Texas (1965); Opinion of Berghuis v. Smith (2010,; Majority opinion, Taylor v. Louisiana (1975); Miranda Warning; Majority opinion, Stack v. Boyle (1951); Plurality, Gregg v. Georgia, 1976; "What the Constitution Requires", The New York Times, April 28, 1996; Plurality, Woodson v. North Carolina (1976); Plurality, Gregg v. Georgia, 1976; Plurality, Coker v. Georgia (1977); Speech to Minnesota Women Lawyers Association, July 2, 2001; Opinion of the Court, McCutcheon v. FEC (2014); Dissenting Opinion, McCutcheon v. FEC (2014); "The System Works—and Donald Trump Proves It," The Daily Caller, December 21, 2015; Gerald Gault, 1966; Majority Opinion, Justice Abe Fortas; Gerald Gault, 1966; Dissenting Opinion, Justice Potter Stewart

Topic 9

U.S. Citizenship and Immigration Services; Chae Chan Ping v. US, 1889; from George Orwell's Animal Farm; The American Democracy, Thomas E. Patterson; Declaration of Sentiments, 1848; Architect of the Capitol; Brown v. Board of Education, 1954; Syllabus, Alexander v. Holmes County Board of Education, 1969; Opinion of the Court, Swann v. Charlotte-Mecklenburg Board of Ed, 1971; Concurring Opinion, Bradwell v. Illinois, 1873; Syllabus, US v. Windsor, 2013; Opinion of the Court, Lawrence v. Texas, 2003; Opinion of the Court, Brown v. Board of Ed; "Martin Luther King Jr., "On Being a Good Neighbor" sermon, July 1, 1962 to March 1, 1963; Opinion of the Court, Adarand Constructors v. Pena, 1995; Opinion of the Court, Gratz v. Bollinger, Grutter v. Bollinger; Opinion of the Court, Schuette v. Coalition to Defend Affirmative Action, 2014; Opinion of the Court, Ricci v. DeStefano, 2009; Title IX of the 1972 Education Amendments; Americans With Disabilities Act; Immigration, Labor Displacement and the American Worker; Immigration Myths and Facts https://www.uschamber.com/report/immigration-myths-and-facts; Organizing for Action "Comprehensive Immigration Reform"; Council on Foreign Relations, "The U.S. Immigration Debate"; "The Changing Meaning of Affirmative Action," by Louis Menand, The New Yorker, Jan. 20, 2020.; "Is Affirmative Action Justified?," by Artemus Ward, Bill of Rights Institute website, 2021.

Topic 10

"Number on Total Lobbying Spending, Number of Lobbyists, and Top Spenders" from opensecrets.org. Copyright © Center for Responsive Politics. Used by permission.; Lobbying Data. Copyright © Center for Responsive Politics. Used by permission.; Benjamin Franklin; Opinion of the Court, Shelby v. Holder, 2013; Martin Luther King, Jr., "I Have a Dream," Aug. 28, 1963; Civil Rights Act of 1964; Syllabus, Dunn v. Blumstein, 1972; Opinion of the Court, Harper v. Virginia Board of Elections, 1966; Rock the Vote; Congressional committee chairman; Benjamin Ginsberg,

Theodore Lowi, and Margaret Weir, "We the People"; Letter to Col. Edward Carrington, Jan. 16, 1787; David Halberstam, The Powers That Be; William Randolph Hearst, 1897; American Commonwealth, Vol. I, p. 680; Alexis de Tocqueville, Democracy in America, 1835; Harold D. Lasswell; Woodrow Wilson, Congressional Government, 1885; John F. Kennedy, NY Times, Sunday magazine section, Feb. 19, 1956; Ed Rollins; Pew Research Center, "Americans' Internet Access, 2000-2015"; WebRootsDemocracy.org; David Pogue, "When Will We Be Able to Vote Online?"; "President Obama: The Fast Company Interview," Fast Company, June 15, 2015; Madison, James. 1787. The Same Subject Continued: The Union as a Safeguard Against Domestic Faction and Insurrection. In The Federalist Papers. Library of Congress.; "Washington Feels Vietcong Offensive Failed Maximum Objective" by Hanson W. Balwin, The New York Times, February 17, 1968.; Walter Cronkite's We Are Mired in Stalemate" Broadcast

Topic 11

Vince Lombardi; George Washington's Farewell Address, 1796; George Washington's Farewell Address, 1796; The Works of John Adams, 1856, Little Brown; "The Sine qua Non of Caucus Reform," Review of Reviews, by R.M. Easley. Sept. 1897; Letter From Thomas Jefferson to George Hay, Aug. 17. 23; Letter From Thomas Jefferson to George Hay, Aug. 17. 23; Remarks by the President in State of the Union Address, January 27, 2010; Sanders-Clinton debate, Feb. 2016; Statement by President George W. Bushon the signing of the Bipartisan Campaign Reform Act of 2002, March 27, 2002; Statement by the President Lyndon Johnson Upon Signing the Foreign Investors Tax Act and the Presidential Election Fund Act, November 13, 1966; Herbert Hoover, Address at Madison Square Garden, Oct. 31, 1932; "Winfrey tells Iowa crowd: 'Barack Obama is 'the one,' Dec. 8, 2007; President Jimmy Carter vs. Ronald Reagan Debate, October 28, 1980.; President Jimmy Carter vs. Ronald Reagan Debate, October 28, 1980.; Opinion of the Court, Citizens United v. Federal Election Commission. Majority Opinion, Justice Anthony M. Kennedy, January 21, 2010.; Opinion of the Court, Citizens United v. Federal Election Commission. Dissenting Opinion, Justice John Paul Stevens, January 21, 2010.

Topic 12

The Class Struggles in France 1848-1850, London magazine; James Carville Campaign slogan; November 13th, 1789, Benjamin Franklin letter to Jean-Baptiste Leroy; Majority Opinion, McCulloch v. Maryland, 1819; Oliver Wendell Holmes, Jr. Dissenting Opinion, Compañía General de Tabacos de Filipinas v. Collector of Internal Revenue, 1927; Hamlet, William Shakespeare; onald Reagan Address Before a Joint Session of the Congress on the Program for Economic Recovery, February 18, 1981; House Permanent Select Committee on Intelligence Chairman Mike Rogers Opening Statement Open Hearing: Cyber Threats and Ongoing Efforts to Protect the Nation October 4, 2011; Interview with Ezra Klein, Vox.com, July 28, 2015; Pollock v. Farmers' Loan & Trust Co., 1895; Justice Stephen Field, Concurring Opinion.; Pollock v. Farmers' Loan & Trust Co., 1895; Justice Henry B. Brown, Dissenting Opinion.

Topic 13

Elizabeth Joh; Ilya Shapiro; The Office of Governor Michelle Lujan Grisham; Resolution of the Second Continental Congress, 10 May 1776; Clueless in Boise, Governing magazine; Inscription on statue of Wisdom at the NY supreme court building; NH supreme court justice Joe Nadeau; The American Commonwealth, Lod James Bryce, 1888; from Sir William Blackstone's Commentaries on the Laws of England, 1765-1769

Topic 14

Country Reports on Human Rights Practices for 2014, US State Department; "Human Rights: What Is China Accused Of?" BBC News, Oct. 21, 2015; "Progress in China's Human Rights in 2014"; "China and Social Media" Foreign Policy Magazine; U.S. Department of State, Joint Statement on Xinjiang, March 22, 2021.; Foreign Ministry Spokesperson's Remarks on the Statement by Friendly Countries in Support of China at the 47th Session of the Human Rights Council, June 22, 2021.